core

JAVA™ 2

Volume II – Advanced Features

CAY S. HORSTMANN • GARY CORNELL

Sun Microsystems Press
A Prentice Hall Title

The publisher offers discounts on this book when ordered in bulk quantities.
For more information, contact: Corporate Sales Department, Phone: 800-382-3419;
Fax: 201-236-7141; E-mail: corpsales@prenhall.com; or write: Prentice Hall PTR,
Corp. Sales Dept., One Lake Street, Upper Saddle River, NJ 07458.

Editorial/production supervision: *Navta Associates*
Acquisitions editor: *Gregory G. Doench*
Editorial assistant: *Brandt Kenna*
Manufacturing manager: *Alexis R. Heydt-Long*
Cover design director: *Jerry Votta*
Cover designer: *Talar Agasyan-Boorujy*
Cover illustration: *Karen Strelecki*
Marketing manager: *Debby van Dijk*
Project coordinator: *Anne Garcia*
Interior designer: *Gail Cocker-Bogusz*
Sun Microsystems Press:
Marketing manager: *Michael Llwyd Alread*
Publisher: *Rachel Borden*

10 9 8 7 6 5 4 3 2 1

ISBN 0-13-092738-4

Sun Microsystems Press
A Prentice Hall Title

Contents

Chapter 2

Collections, 115

Chapter 3

Chapter 4

Chapter 5

Remote Objects, 329

Chapter 6

Advanced Swing, 409

Chapter 7

Advanced AWT, 559

Chapter 8

Chapter 9

Security, 861

Chapter 10

Chapter 11

Chapter 12

XML, 1109

List of Tables, Code Examples, and Figures

Tables

Code Examples

Figures

Preface

To the Reader

The book you have in your hands is the second volume of the fourth edition of *Core Java*. The first edition appeared in early 1996, the second in late 1996, and the third in 1997/1998. The first two editions appeared in a single volume, but the second edition was already 150 pages longer than the first, which was itself not a thin book. When we sat down to work on the third edition, it became clear that a one-volume treatment of all the features of the Java™ platform that a serious programmer needs to know was no longer possible. Hence, we decided to break up the third edition into two volumes. In the fourth edition, we again organized the material into two volumes. However, we rearranged the materials, moving streams into Volume 1 and collections into Volume 2.

The first volume covers the essential features of the language; this volume covers the advanced topics that a programmer will need to know for professional software development. Thus, as with the first volume and the previous editions of this book, we still *are targeting programmers who want to put Java technology to work on real projects.*

Please note: If you are an experienced developer who is comfortable with the new event model and advanced language features such as inner classes, *you need not have read the first volume* in order to benefit from this volume. (While we do refer to sections of the previous volume when appropriate and, of course, hope you will buy or have bought Volume 1, you can find the needed background material in any *comprehensive* introductory book about the Java platform.)

Finally, when any book is being written, errors and inaccuracies are inevitable. We would very much like to hear about them. Of course, we would prefer to hear about them only once. For this reason, we have put up a web site at `http://www.horstmann.com/corejava.html` with an FAQ, bug fixes, and workarounds. Strategically placed at the end of the bug report web page (to encourage you to read the previous reports) is a form that you can use to report bugs or problems and to send suggestions for improvements to future editions.

About This Book

The chapters in this book are, for the most part, independent of each other. You should be able to delve into whatever topic interests you the most and read the chapters in any order.

Chapter 1 covers *multithreading*, which enables you to program tasks to be done in parallel. (A *thread* is a flow of control within a program.) We show you how to set up threads and how to make sure none of them get stuck. We put this knowledge to practical use by example, showing you the techniques needed to build timers and animations.

The topic of Chapter 2 is the *collections* framework of the Java 2 platform. Whenever you want to collect multiple objects and retrieve them later, you will want to use a collection that is best suited for your circumstances, instead of just tossing the elements into a `Vector`. This chapter shows you how to take advantage of the standard collections that are prebuilt for your use.

Chapter 3 covers one of the most exciting APIs in the Java platform: the networking API. Java makes it phenomenally easy to do complex network programming. Not only do we cover this API in depth, we also discuss the important consequences of the applet security model for network programming.

Chapter 4 covers *JDBC*™, the Java database connectivity API. We show you how to write useful programs to handle realistic database chores, using a core subset of the JDBC API. Please note that this is not a complete treatment of everything you can do with the rich JDBC API. (A complete treatment of the JDBC API would require a book almost as long as this one.)

Chapter 5 covers *remote objects* and *Remote Method Invocation* (RMI). This API lets you work with Java objects that are distributed over multiple machines. We also show you where the rallying cry of "objects everywhere" can realistically be used.

Chapter 6 contains all the Swing material that didn't make it into Volume 1, especially the important but complex tree and table components. We show the basic uses of editor panes and the Java technology implementation of a "multiple document" interface. Again, we focus on the most useful constructs that you are likely to encounter in practical programming, since an encyclopedic coverage of the entire Swing library would fill several volumes and would only be of interest to dedicated taxonomists.

Chapter 7 covers the Java 2D API that you can use to create realistic drawings. The chapter also covers some advanced features of the *Abstract Windowing Toolkit* (AWT) that seemed too specialized for coverage in Volume 1 but are, nonetheless, techniques that should be part of every programmer's toolkit. These features include printing and the APIs for cut-and-paste and drag-and-drop. We actually take the cut-and-paste API one step further than Sun Microsystems itself did: We show you how to cut and paste serializable Java objects between different programs in the Java programming language via the system clipboard.

Chapter 8 shows you what you need to know about the component API for the Java platform—*JavaBeans™*. You will see how to write your own beans that other programmers can manipulate in integrated builder environments. (We do not cover the various builder environments that are designed to manipulate beans, however.) The JavaBeans™ component technology is an extraordinarily important technology for the eventual success of Java technology because it can potentially bring the same ease of use to user interface programming environments that ActiveX controls give to the millions of Visual Basic programmers. Of course, since these components are written in the Java programming language, they have the advantage over ActiveX controls in that they are immediately usable across other platforms and capable of fitting into the sophisticated security model of the Java platform.

In fact, Chapter 9 takes up that security model. The Java platform was designed from the ground up to be secure, and this chapter takes you under the hood to see how this design is implemented. We show you how to write your own class loaders and security managers for special-purpose applications. Then, we take up the new security API that allows for such important features as signed classes.

Chapter 10 discusses a specialized feature that we believe can only grow in importance: internationalization. The Java programming language is one of the few languages designed from the start to handle Unicode, but the internationalization support in the Java platform goes much further. As a result, you can internationalize Java applications so that they not only cross platforms but cross country boundaries as well. For example, we show you how to write a retirement calculator applet that uses either English, German, or Chinese—depending on the locale of the browser.

Chapter 11 takes up *native methods,* which let you call methods written for a specific machine such as the Microsoft Windows API. Obviously, this feature is controversial: Use native methods, and the cross-platform nature of the Java platform vanishes. Nonetheless, every serious programmer writing Java applications for specific platforms needs to know these techniques. There will be times when you need to turn to the operating system's API for your target platform when you are writing a serious application. We illustrate this by showing you how to access the registry functions in Windows.

Conventions

As is common in many computer books, we use `courier type` to represent computer code.

NOTE: Notes are tagged with a "notepad" icon that looks like this.

TIP: Helpful tips are tagged with this icon.

CAUTION: Notes that warn of pitfalls or dangerous situations are tagged with a "Caution" icon.

C++ NOTE: There are a number of C++ notes that explain the difference between the Java programming language and C++. You can skip them if you aren't interested in C++.

The Java platform comes with a large programming library or Application Programming Interface (API). When using an API call for the first time, we add a short summary description, tagged with an API icon. These descriptions are a bit more informal but also a little more informative than those in the official on-line API documentation.

Programs whose source code is on the CD-ROM are listed as examples, for instance, **Example 5-8: WarehouseServer.java** refers to the corresponding code on the CD-ROM. You can also download these example files from the Web.

Definitions

A *Java object* is an object that is created by a program that was written in the Java programming language.

A *Java application* is a program that was written in the Java programming language and that is launched by a Java virtual machine (that is, a virtual machine for the Java platform).

Acknowledgments

Writing a book is always a monumental effort, and rewriting doesn't seem to be much easier, especially with such a rapid rate of change in Java technology. Making a book a reality takes many dedicated people, and it is my great pleasure to acknowledge the contributions of the entire Core Java team.

Our long-suffering editor Greg Doench of Prentice Hall PTR once again did a great job, coordinating all aspects of this complex project. Julie Bettis copyedited the manuscript, with an excellent eye for consistency and always on the lookout for Teutonic constructions and violations of the Java trademark rules.

Kathi Beste, Bert Stutz, and Marilyn Stutz at Navta Associates, Inc., once again delivered an attractively typeset book. A number of other individuals at Prentice Hall PTR and Sun Microsystems Press also provided valuable assistance, but they managed to stay behind the scenes. I'd like them all to know how much I appreciate their efforts. My thanks also to my co-author of earlier editions, Gary Cornell, who has since moved on to other ventures.

I am very grateful to the excellent reviewing team who found many embarrassing errors and made lots of thoughtful suggestions for improvement. The new material for this edition was reviewed by David Geary, Bob Lynch, Paul Philion, and George Thiruvathukal.

Reviewers of earlier editions are Alec Beaton (PointBase, Inc.), Joshua Bloch (Sun Microsystems), David Brown, Dr. Nicholas J. De Lillo (Manhattan College), Rakesh Dhoopar (Oracle), Angela Gordon (Sun Microsystems), Dan Gordon (Sun Microsystems), Rob Gordon, Cameron Gregory (olabs.com), Marty Hall (The Johns Hopkins University Applied Physics Lab), Vincent Hardy (Sun Microsystems), Vladimir Ivanovic (PointBase, Inc.), Jerry Jackson (ChannelPoint Software), Tim Kimmet (Preview Systems), Chris Laffra, Charlie Lai (Sun Microsystems),

Doug Langston, Doug Lea (SUNY Oswego), Gregory Longshore, Mark Morrissey (The Oregon Graduate Institute), Mahesh Neelakanta (Florida Atlantic University), Blake Ragsdell, Stuart Reges (University of Arizona), Peter Sanders (ESSI University, Nice, France), Devang Shah (Sun Microsystems), Christopher Taylor, Luke Taylor (Valtech), Kim Topley, Janet Traub, Peter van der Linden (Sun Microsystems), and Burt Walsh.

Most importantly, my love, gratitude, and apologies go to my wife Hui-Chen and my children Tommy and Nina for their continuing support of this never-ending project.

Cay Horstmann

Cupertino, November 2001

Chapter **1**

Multithreading

You are probably familiar with *multitasking:* the ability to have more than one program working at what seems like the same time. For example, you can print while editing or sending a fax. Of course, unless you have a multiple-processor machine, what is really going on is that the operating system is doling out resources to each program, giving the impression of parallel activity. This resource distribution is possible because while you may think you are keeping the computer busy by, for example, entering data, most of the CPU's time will be idle. (A fast typist takes around $1/20$ of a second per character typed, after all, which is a huge time interval for a computer.)

Multitasking can be done in two ways, depending on whether the operating system interrupts programs without consulting with them first, or whether programs are only interrupted when they are willing to yield control. The former is called *preemptive multitasking;* the latter is called *cooperative* (or, simply, nonpreemptive) *multitasking.* Windows 3.1 and Mac OS 9 are cooperative multitasking systems, and UNIX/Linux, Windows NT (and Windows 95 for 32-bit programs),

1

and OS X are preemptive. (Although harder to implement, preemptive multitasking is much more effective. With cooperative multitasking, a badly behaved program can hog everything.)

Multithreaded programs extend the idea of multitasking by taking it one level lower: individual programs will appear to do multiple tasks at the same time. Each task is usually called a *thread*—which is short for thread of control. Programs that can run more than one thread at once are said to be *multithreaded*. Think of each thread as running in a separate context: contexts make it seem as though each thread has its own CPU—with registers, memory, and its own code.

So, what is the difference between multiple *processes* and multiple *threads*? The essential difference is that while each process has a complete set of its own variables, threads share the same data. This sounds somewhat risky, and indeed it can be, as you will see later in this chapter. But it takes much less overhead to create and destroy individual threads than it does to launch new processes, which is why all modern operating systems support multithreading. Moreover, inter-process communication is much slower and more restrictive than communication between threads.

Multithreading is extremely useful in practice. For example, a browser should be able to simultaneously download multiple images. An email program should let you read your email while it is downloading new messages. The Java programming language itself uses a thread to do garbage collection in the background—thus saving you the trouble of managing memory! Graphical user interface (GUI) programs have a separate thread for gathering user interface events from the host operating environment. This chapter shows you how to add multithreading capability to your Java applications and applets.

Fair warning: multithreading can get very complex. In this chapter, we present all of the tools that the Java programming language provides for thread programming. We explain their use and limitations and give some simple but typical examples. However, for more intricate situations, we suggest that you turn to a more advanced reference, such as *Concurrent Programming in Java* by Doug Lea [Addison-Wesley 1999].

NOTE: In many programming languages, you have to use an external thread package to do multithreaded programming. The Java programming language builds in multi-threading, which makes your job much easier.

What Are Threads?

Let us start by looking at a program that does not use multiple threads and that, as a consequence, makes it difficult for the user to perform several tasks with that program. After we dissect it, we will then show you how easy it is to have this program run separate threads. This program animates a bouncing ball by continually moving the ball, finding out if it bounces against a wall, and then redrawing it. (See Figure 1–1.)

As soon as you click on the "Start" button, the program launches a ball from the upper-left corner of the screen and the ball begins bouncing. The handler of the "Start" button calls the addBall method:

```
public void addBall()
{
   try
   {
      Ball b = new Ball(canvas);
      canvas.add(b);
      for (int i = 1; i <= 1000; i++)
      {
         b.move();
         Thread.sleep(5);
      }
   }
   catch (InterruptedException exception)
   {
   }
}
```

That method contains a loop running through 1,000 moves. Each call to move moves the ball by a small amount, adjusts the direction if it bounces against a wall, and then redraws the canvas. The static sleep method of the Thread class pauses for 5 milliseconds.

Figure 1–1: Using a thread to animate a bouncing ball

The call to `Thread.sleep` does not create a new thread—`sleep` is a static method of the `Thread` class that temporarily stops the activity of the current thread.

The `sleep` method can throw an `InterruptedException`. We will discuss this exception and its proper handling later. For now, we simply terminate the bouncing if this exception occurs.

If you run the program, the ball bounces around nicely, but it completely takes over the application. If you become tired of the bouncing ball before it has finished its 1,000 bounces and click on the "Close" button, the ball continues bouncing anyway. You cannot interact with the program until the ball has finished bouncing.

> NOTE: If you carefully look over the code at the end of this section, you will notice the call
>
> ```
> canvas.paint(canvas.getGraphics())
> ```
>
> inside the `move` method of the `Ball` class. That is pretty strange—normally, you'd call `repaint` and let the AWT worry about getting the graphics context and doing the painting. But if you try to call `canvas.repaint()` in this program, you'll find out that the canvas is never repainted since the `addBall` method has completely taken over all processing. In the next program, where we use a separate thread to compute the ball position, we'll again use the familiar `repaint`.

Obviously, the behavior of this program is rather poor. You would not want the programs that you use behaving in this way when you ask them to do a time-consuming job. After all, when you are reading data over a network connection, it is all too common to be stuck in a task that you would *really* like to interrupt. For example, suppose you download a large image and decide, after seeing a piece of it, that you do not need or want to see the rest; you certainly would like to be able to click on a "Stop" or "Back" button to interrupt the loading process. In the next section, we will show you how to keep the user in control by running crucial parts of the code in a separate *thread*.

Example 1–1 is the entire code for the program.

Example 1–1: Bounce.java

```
1. import java.awt.*;
2. import java.awt.event.*;
3. import java.awt.geom.*;
4. import java.util.*;
5. import javax.swing.*;
6.
7. /**
8.    Shows an animated bouncing ball.
9. */
```

```
10. public class Bounce
11. {
12.    public static void main(String[] args)
13.    {
14.       JFrame frame = new BounceFrame();
15.       frame.setDefaultCloseOperation(JFrame.EXIT_ON_CLOSE);
16.       frame.show();
17.    }
18. }
19.
20. /**
21.    The frame with canvas and buttons.
22. */
23. class BounceFrame extends JFrame
24. {
25.    /**
26.       Constructs the frame with the canvas for showing the
27.       bouncing ball and Start and Close buttons
28.    */
29.    public BounceFrame()
30.    {
31.       setSize(WIDTH, HEIGHT);
32.       setTitle("Bounce");
33.
34.       Container contentPane = getContentPane();
35.       canvas = new BallCanvas();
36.       contentPane.add(canvas, BorderLayout.CENTER);
37.       JPanel buttonPanel = new JPanel();
38.       addButton(buttonPanel, "Start",
39.          new ActionListener()
40.             {
41.                public void actionPerformed(ActionEvent evt)
42.                {
43.                   addBall();
44.                }
45.             });
46.
47.       addButton(buttonPanel, "Close",
48.          new ActionListener()
49.             {
50.                public void actionPerformed(ActionEvent evt)
51.                {
52.                   System.exit(0);
53.                }
54.             });
55.       contentPane.add(buttonPanel, BorderLayout.SOUTH);
56.    }
57.
58.    /**
59.       Adds a button to a container.
60.       @param c the container
```

```
61.        @param title the button title
62.        @param listener the action listener for the button
63.     */
64.    public void addButton(Container c, String title,
65.        ActionListener listener)
66.    {
67.        JButton button = new JButton(title);
68.        c.add(button);
69.        button.addActionListener(listener);
70.    }
71.
72.    /**
73.        Adds a bouncing ball to the canvas and makes
74.        it bounce 1,000 times.
75.     */
76.    public void addBall()
77.    {
78.        try
79.        {
80.            Ball b = new Ball(canvas);
81.            canvas.add(b);
82.
83.            for (int i = 1; i <= 1000; i++)
84.            {
85.                b.move();
86.                Thread.sleep(5);
87.            }
88.        }
89.        catch (InterruptedException exception)
90.        {
91.        }
92.    }
93.
94.    private BallCanvas canvas;
95.    public static final int WIDTH = 450;
96.    public static final int HEIGHT = 350;
97. }
98.
99. /**
100.    The canvas that draws the balls.
101. */
102. class BallCanvas extends JPanel
103. {
104.    /**
105.        Add a ball to the canvas.
106.        @param b the ball to add
107.     */
108.    public void add(Ball b)
109.    {
110.        balls.add(b);
111.    }
112.
```

```
113.    public void paintComponent(Graphics g)
114.    {
115.        super.paintComponent(g);
116.        Graphics2D g2 = (Graphics2D)g;
117.        for (int i = 0; i < balls.size(); i++)
118.        {
119.            Ball b = (Ball)balls.get(i);
120.            b.draw(g2);
121.        }
122.    }
123.
124.    private ArrayList balls = new ArrayList();
125. }
126.
127. /**
128.    A ball that moves and bounces off the edges of a
129.    component
130. */
131. class Ball
132. {
133.    /**
134.        Constructs a ball in the upper left corner
135.        @c the component in which the ball bounces
136.    */
137.    public Ball(Component c) { canvas = c; }
138.
139.    /**
140.        Draws the ball at its current position
141.        @param g2 the graphics context
142.    */
143.    public void draw(Graphics2D g2)
144.    {
145.        g2.fill(new Ellipse2D.Double(x, y, XSIZE, YSIZE));
146.    }
147.
148.    /**
149.        Moves the ball to the next position, reversing direction
150.        if it hits one of the edges
151.    */
152.    public void move()
153.    {
154.        x += dx;
155.        y += dy;
156.        if (x < 0)
157.        {
158.            x = 0;
159.            dx = -dx;
160.        }
161.        if (x + XSIZE >= canvas.getWidth())
162.        {
163.            x = canvas.getWidth() - XSIZE;
164.            dx = -dx;
```

```
165.        }
166.        if (y < 0)
167.        {
168.           y = 0;
169.           dy = -dy;
170.        }
171.        if (y + YSIZE >= canvas.getHeight())
172.        {
173.           y = canvas.getHeight() - YSIZE;
174.           dy = -dy;
175.        }
176.
177.        canvas.paint(canvas.getGraphics());
178.     }
179.
180.     private Component canvas;
181.     private static final int XSIZE = 15;
182.     private static final int YSIZE = 15;
183.     private int x = 0;
184.     private int y = 0;
185.     private int dx = 2;
186.     private int dy = 2;
187. }
```

java.lang.Thread

● `static void sleep(long millis)`
  sleeps for the given number of milliseconds

  Parameters: `millis`   the number of milliseconds to sleep

In the previous sections, you learned what is required to split a program into multiple concurrent tasks. Each task needs to be placed into a `run` method of a class that extends `Thread`. But what if we want to add the `run` method to a class that already extends another class? This occurs most often when we want to add multithreading to an applet. An applet class already inherits from `JApplet`, and we cannot inherit from two parent classes, so we need to use an interface. The necessary interface is built into the Java platform. It is called `Runnable`. We take up this important interface next.

Using Threads to Give Other Tasks a Chance

We will make our bouncing-ball program more responsive by running the code that moves the ball in a separate thread.

NOTE: Since most computers do not have multiple processors, the Java virtual machine (JVM) uses a mechanism in which each thread gets a chance to run for a little while, then activates another thread. The virtual machine generally relies on the host operating system to provide the thread scheduling package.

Our next program uses *two* threads: one for the bouncing ball and another for the *event dispatch thread* that takes care of user interface events. Because each thread gets a chance to run, the main thread has the opportunity to notice when you click on the "Close" button while the ball is bouncing. It can then process the "close" action.

There is a simple procedure for running code in a separate thread: place the code into the `run` method of a class derived from `Thread`.

To make our bouncing-ball program into a separate thread, we need only derive a class `BallThread` from `Thread` and place the code for the animation inside the `run` method, as in the following code:

```
class BallThread extends Thread
{
    . . .
    public void run()
    {
        try
        {
            for (int i = 1; i <= 1000; i++)
            {
                b.move();
                sleep(5);
            }
        }
        catch (InterruptedException exception)
        {
        }
    }
    . . .
}
```

You may have noticed that we are catching an exception called `Interrupted-Exception`. Methods such as `sleep` and `wait` throw this exception when your thread is interrupted because another thread has called the `interrupt` method. Interrupting a thread is a very drastic way of getting the thread's attention, even when it is not active. Typically, a thread is interrupted to terminate it. Accordingly, our `run` method exits when an `InterruptedException` occurs.

Running and Starting Threads

When you construct an object derived from `Thread`, the `run` method is not automatically called.

```
BallThread thread = new BallThread(. . .); // won't run yet
```

You must call the `start` method in your object to actually start a thread.

```
thread.start();
```

CAUTION: Do *not* call the `run` method directly—`start` will call it when the thread is set up and ready to go. Calling the `run` method directly merely executes its contents in the *same* thread—no new thread is started.

Beginners are sometimes misled into believing that every method of a `Thread` object automatically runs in a new thread. As you have seen, that is not true. The methods of any object (whether a `Thread` object or not) run in whatever thread they are called. A new thread is *only* started by the `start` method. That new thread then executes the `run` method.

In the Java programming language, a thread needs to tell the other threads when it is idle, so the other threads can grab the chance to execute the code in their `run` procedures. (See Figure 1–2.) The usual way to do this is through the static `sleep` method. The `run` method of the `BallThread` class uses the call to `sleep(5)` to indicate that the thread will be idle for the next five milliseconds. After five milliseconds, it will start up again, but in the meantime, other threads have a chance to get work done.

TIP: There are a number of static methods in the `Thread` class. They all operate on the *current thread*, that is, the thread that executes the method. For example, the static `sleep` method idles the thread that is calling `sleep`.

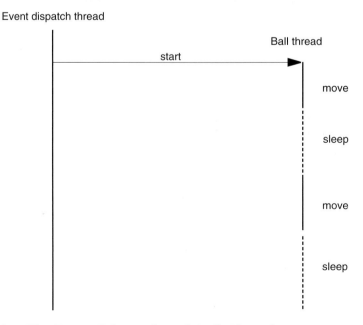

Figure 1–2: The Event Dispatch and Ball Threads

The complete code is shown in Example 1–2.

Example 1–2: BounceThread.java

```
1. import java.awt.*;
2. import java.awt.event.*;
3. import java.awt.geom.*;
4. import java.util.*;
5. import javax.swing.*;
6.
7. /**
8.    Shows an animated bouncing ball running in a separate thread
9. */
10. public class BounceThread
11. {
12.    public static void main(String[] args)
13.    {
14.       JFrame frame = new BounceFrame();
15.       frame.setDefaultCloseOperation(JFrame.EXIT_ON_CLOSE);
16.       frame.show();
17.    }
18. }
19.
20. /**
21.    The frame with canvas and buttons.
22. */
23. class BounceFrame extends JFrame
24. {
25.    /**
26.       Constructs the frame with the canvas for showing the
27.       bouncing ball and Start and Close buttons
28.    */
29.    public BounceFrame()
30.    {
31.       setSize(WIDTH, HEIGHT);
32.       setTitle("BounceThread");
33.
34.       Container contentPane = getContentPane();
35.       canvas = new BallCanvas();
36.       contentPane.add(canvas, BorderLayout.CENTER);
37.       JPanel buttonPanel = new JPanel();
38.       addButton(buttonPanel, "Start",
39.          new ActionListener()
40.             {
41.                public void actionPerformed(ActionEvent evt)
42.                {
43.                   addBall();
```

```
44.                   }
45.               });
46.
47.        addButton(buttonPanel, "Close",
48.           new ActionListener()
49.               {
50.                   public void actionPerformed(ActionEvent evt)
51.                   {
52.                       System.exit(0);
53.                   }
54.               });
55.        contentPane.add(buttonPanel, BorderLayout.SOUTH);
56.     }
57.
58.     /**
59.         Adds a button to a container.
60.         @param c the container
61.         @param title the button title
62.         @param listener the action listener for the button
63.     */
64.     public void addButton(Container c, String title,
65.         ActionListener listener)
66.     {
67.         JButton button = new JButton(title);
68.         c.add(button);
69.         button.addActionListener(listener);
70.     }
71.
72.     /**
73.         Adds a bouncing ball to the canvas and starts a thread
74.         to make it bounce
75.     */
76.     public void addBall()
77.     {
78.         Ball b = new Ball(canvas);
79.         canvas.add(b);
80.         BallThread thread = new BallThread(b);
81.         thread.start();
82.     }
83.
84.     private BallCanvas canvas;
85.     public static final int WIDTH = 450;
86.     public static final int HEIGHT = 350;
87. }
88.
89. /**
90.     A thread that animates a bouncing ball.
```

```
91.  */
92. class BallThread extends Thread
93. {
94.     /**
95.        Constructs the thread.
96.        @aBall the ball to bounce
97.     */
98.     public BallThread(Ball aBall) { b = aBall; }
99.
100.    public void run()
101.    {
102.       try
103.       {
104.          for (int i = 1; i <= 1000; i++)
105.          {
106.             b.move();
107.             sleep(5);
108.          }
109.       }
110.       catch (InterruptedException exception)
111.       {
112.       }
113.    }
114.
115.    private Ball b;
116. }
117.
118. /**
119.    The canvas that draws the balls.
120. */
121. class BallCanvas extends JPanel
122. {
123.    /**
124.       Add a ball to the canvas.
125.       @param b the ball to add
126.    */
127.    public void add(Ball b)
128.    {
129.       balls.add(b);
130.    }
131.
132.    public void paintComponent(Graphics g)
133.    {
134.       super.paintComponent(g);
135.       Graphics2D g2 = (Graphics2D)g;
136.       for (int i = 0; i < balls.size(); i++)
137.       {
```

```
138.          Ball b = (Ball)balls.get(i);
139.          b.draw(g2);
140.       }
141.    }
142.
143.    private ArrayList balls = new ArrayList();
144. }
145.
146. /**
147.    A ball that moves and bounces off the edges of a
148.    component
149. */
150. class Ball
151. {
152.    /**
153.       Constructs a ball in the upper left corner
154.       @c the component in which the ball bounces
155.    */
156.    public Ball(Component c) { canvas = c; }
157.
158.    /**
159.       Draws the ball at its current position
160.       @param g2 the graphics context
161.    */
162.    public void draw(Graphics2D g2)
163.    {
164.       g2.fill(new Ellipse2D.Double(x, y, XSIZE, YSIZE));
165.    }
166.
167.    /**
168.       Moves the ball to the next position, reversing direction
169.       if it hits one of the edges
170.    */
171.    public void move()
172.    {
173.       x += dx;
174.       y += dy;
175.       if (x < 0)
176.       {
177.          x = 0;
178.          dx = -dx;
179.       }
180.       if (x + XSIZE >= canvas.getWidth())
181.       {
182.          x = canvas.getWidth() - XSIZE;
183.          dx = -dx;
184.       }
```

```
185.        if (y < 0)
186.        {
187.           y = 0;
188.           dy = -dy;
189.        }
190.        if (y + YSIZE >= canvas.getHeight())
191.        {
192.           y = canvas.getHeight() - YSIZE;
193.           dy = -dy;
194.        }
195.
196.        canvas.repaint();
197.     }
198.
199.     private Component canvas;
200.     private static final int XSIZE = 15;
201.     private static final int YSIZE = 15;
202.     private int x = 0;
203.     private int y = 0;
204.     private int dx = 2;
205.     private int dy = 2;
206. }
207.
```

`java.lang.Thread`

- `Thread()`
  constructs a new thread. You must `start` the thread to activate its `run` method.

- `void run()`
  You must override this function and add the code that you want to have executed in the thread.

- `void start()`
  starts this thread, causing the `run()` method to be called. This method will return immediately. The new thread runs concurrently.

Running Multiple Threads

Run the program in the preceding section. Now, click on the "Start" button again while a ball is running. Click on it a few more times. You will see a whole bunch of balls bouncing away, as captured in Figure 1–3. Each ball will move 1,000 times until it comes to its final resting place.

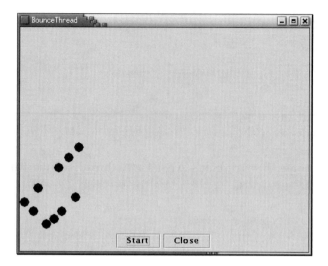

Figure 1–3: Multiple threads

This example demonstrates a great advantage of the thread architecture in the Java programming language. It is very easy to create any number of autonomous objects that appear to run in parallel.

Occasionally, you may want to enumerate the currently running threads—see the API note in the "Thread Groups" section for details.

The Runnable *Interface*

We could have saved ourselves a class by having the Ball class extend the Thread class. As an added advantage of that approach, the run method has access to the private fields of the Ball class:

```java
class Ball extends Thread
{
    public void run()
    {
        try
        {
            for (int i = 1; i <= 1000; i++)
            {
                x += dx;
                y += dy;
                . . .
                canvas.repaint();
                sleep(5);
            }
        }
        catch (InterruptedException exception)
```

```
        {
        }
    }
    . . .
    private Component canvas;
    private int x = 0;
    private int y = 0;
    private int dx = 2;
    private int dy = 2;
}
```

Conceptually, of course, this is dubious. A ball isn't a thread, so inheritance isn't really appropriate. Nevertheless, programmers sometimes follow this approach when the run method of a thread needs to access private fields of another class. In the preceding section, we've avoided that issue altogether by having the run method call only public methods of the Ball class, but it isn't always so easy to do that.

Suppose the run method needs access to private fields, but the class into which you want to put the run method already has another superclass. Then it can't extend the Thread class, but you can make the class implement the Runnable interface. As though you had derived from Thread, put the code that needs to run in the run method. For example,

```
    class Animation extends JApplet
        implements Runnable
    {
        . . .
        public void run()
        {
            // thread action goes here
        }
    }
```

You still need to make a thread object to launch the thread. Give that thread a reference to the Runnable object in its constructor. The thread then calls the run method of that object.

```
    class Animation extends JApplet
        implements Runnable
    {
        . . .
        public void start()
        {
            runner = new Thread(this);
            runner.start();
        }
        . . .
        private Thread runner;
    }
```

In this case, the `this` argument to the `Thread` constructor specifies that the object whose `run` method should be called when the thread executes is an instance of the `Animation` object.

Some people even claim that you should always follow this approach and never subclass the `Thread` class. That advice made sense for Java 1.0, before inner classes were invented, but it is now outdated. If the `run` method of a thread needs private access to another class, you can often use an inner class, like this:

```
class Animation extends JApplet
{
    . . .
    public void start()
    {
        runner = new Thread()
        {
            public void run()
            {
                // thread action goes here
            }
        };
        runner.start();
    }
    . . .
    private Thread runner;
}
```

A plausible use for the `Runnable` interface would be a thread pool in which pre-spawned threads are kept around for running. Thread pools are sometimes used in environments that execute huge numbers of threads, to reduce the cost of creating and garbage collecting thread objects.

java.lang.Thread

- `Thread(Runnable target)`
  constructs a new thread that calls the `run()` method of the specified target.

java.lang.Runnable

- `void run()`
  You must override this method and place in the thread the code that you want to have executed.

Interrupting Threads

A thread terminates when its `run` method returns. (In the first version of the Java programming environment, there also was a `stop` method that another thread could call to terminate a thread. However, that method is now deprecated. We will discuss the reason later in this chapter.)

There is no longer a way to force a thread to terminate. However, the `interrupt` method can be used to *request* termination of a thread. That means that the `run` method of a thread ought to check once in a while whether it should exit.

```
public void run()
{
   . . .
   while (no request to terminate && more work to do)
   {
      do more work
   }
   // exit run method and terminate thread
}
```

However, as you have learned, a thread should not work continuously, but it should go to sleep or wait once in a while, to give other threads a chance to do their work. But when a thread is sleeping, it can't actively check whether it should terminate. This is where the `InterruptedException` comes in. When the `interrupt` method is called on a thread object that is currently blocked, the blocking call (such as `sleep` or `wait`) is terminated by an `InterruptedException`.

There is no language requirement that a thread that is interrupted should terminate. Interrupting a thread simply grabs its attention. The interrupted thread can decide how to react to the interruption by placing appropriate actions into the `catch` clause that deals with the `InterruptedException`. Some threads are so important that they should simply ignore their interruption by catching the exception and continuing. But quite commonly, a thread will simply want to interpret an interruption as a request for termination. The `run` method of such a thread has the following form:

```
public void run()
{
   try
   {
      . . .
      while (more work to do)
      {
         do more work
      }
   }
   catch(InterruptedException exception)
   {
      // thread was interrupted during sleep or wait
   }
   finally
```

```
   {
      cleanup, if required
   }
   // exit run method and terminate thread
}
```

However, there is a problem with this code skeleton. If the `interrupt` method was called while the thread was not sleeping or waiting, then no `InterruptedException` was generated. The thread needs to call the `interrupted` method to find out if it was recently interrupted.

```
while (!interrupted() && more work to do)
{
   do more work
}
```

In particular, if a thread was blocked while waiting for input/output, the input/output operations are *not* terminated by the call to `interrupt`. When the blocking operation has returned, you need to call the `interrupted` method to find out if the current thread has been interrupted.

> NOTE: Curiously, there are two very similar methods, `interrupted` and `isInterrupted`. The `interrupted` method is a static method that checks whether the *current* thread has been interrupted. (Recall that a thread is interrupted because another thread has called its `interrupt` method.) Furthermore, calling the `interrupted` method resets the "interrupted" status of the thread. On the other hand, the `isInterrupted` method is an instance method that you can use to check whether any thread has been interrupted. Calling it does not change the "interrupted" status of its argument.

It is a bit tedious that there are two distinct ways of dealing with thread interruption—testing the "interrupted" flag and catching the `InterruptedException`.

It would have been nice if methods such as `sleep` had been defined to simply return with the "interrupted" flag set when an interruption occurs—then one wouldn't have to deal with the `InterruptedException` at all. Of course, you can manually set the "interrupted" flag when an `InterruptedException` is caught:

```
try
{
   sleep(delay);
}
catch (InterruptedException exception)
{
```

```
        Thread.currentThread().interrupt();
    }
```

You need to use this approach if the `sleep` method is called from a method that can't throw any exceptions.

NOTE: You'll find lots of published code where the `InterruptedException` is squelched, like this:

```
try { sleep(delay); }
catch (InterruptedException exception) {} // DON'T!
```

Don't do that! Either set the "interrupted" flag of the current thread, or propagate the exception to the calling method (and ultimately to the `run` method).

If you don't want to clutter up lots of nested methods with `isInterrupted` tests, you can turn the "interrupted" flag into an exception.

```
if (isInterrupted()) throw new InterruptedException();
```

Assuming that your code is already prepared to terminate the `run` method when an `InterruptedException` is thrown, this is a painless way of immediately terminating the thread when an interruption is detected. The principal disadvantage is that you have to tag your methods with

```
throws InterruptedException
```

since, alas, the `InterruptedException` is a checked exception.

java.lang.Thread

- `void interrupt()`
  sends an interrupt request to a thread. The "interrupted" status of the thread is set to `true`. If the thread is currently blocked by a call to `sleep` or `wait`, an `InterruptedException` is thrown.

- `static boolean interrupted()`
  tests whether or not the *current* thread (that is, the thread that is executing this instruction) has been interrupted. Note that this is a static method. The call has a side effect—it resets the "interrupted" status of the current thread to `false`.

- `boolean isInterrupted()`
  tests whether or not a thread has been interrupted. Unlike the `static` `interrupted` method, this call does not change the "interrupted" status of the thread.

- `static Thread currentThread()`
  returns the `Thread` object representing the currently executing thread.

Thread Properties

Thread States

Threads can be in one of four states:

- new
- runnable
- blocked
- dead

Each of these states is explained in the sections that follow.

New threads

When you create a thread with the `new` operator—for example, `new Ball()`—the thread is not yet running. This means that it is in the *new* state. When a thread is in the new state, the program has not started executing code inside of it. A certain amount of bookkeeping needs to be done before a thread can run.

Runnable threads

Once you invoke the `start` method, the thread is *runnable*. A runnable thread may not yet be running. It is up to the operating system to give the thread time to run. When the code inside the thread begins executing, the thread is *running*. (The Java platform documentation does not call this a separate state, though. A running thread is still in the runnable state.)

NOTE: The runnable state has nothing to do with the `Runnable` interface.

Once a thread is running, it doesn't necessarily keep running. In fact, it is desirable if running threads are occasionally interrupted so that other threads have a chance to run. The details of thread scheduling depend on the services that the operating system provides. If the operating system doesn't cooperate, then the Java thread implementation does the minimum to make multithreading work. An example is the so-called *green threads* package that is used by the Java 1.x platform on Solaris. It keeps a running thread active until a higher-priority thread awakes and takes control. Other thread systems (such as Windows 95 and Windows NT) give each runnable thread a slice of time to perform its task. When that slice of time is exhausted, the operating system gives another thread an opportunity to work. This approach is called *time slicing*. Time slicing has an important advantage: an uncooperative thread can't prevent other threads from running. Current releases of the Java platform on Solaris can be configured to allow use of the native Solaris threads, which also perform time-slicing.

Always keep in mind that a runnable thread may or may not be running at any given time. (This is why the state is called "runnable" and not "running.") See Figure 1–4.

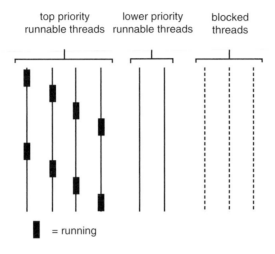

Figure 1–4: Time-slicing on a single CPU

Blocked threads

A thread enters the *blocked* state when one of the following actions occurs:

1.   Someone calls the `sleep()` method of the thread.

2.   The thread calls an operation that is *blocking on input/output*, that is, an operation that will not return to its caller until input and output operations are complete.

3.   The thread calls the `wait()` method.

4.   The thread tries to lock an object that is currently locked by another thread. We will discuss object locks later in this chapter.

5.   Someone calls the `suspend()` method of the thread. However, this method is deprecated, and you should not call it in your code. We will explain the reason later in this chapter.

Figure 1–5 shows the states that a thread can have and the possible transitions from one state to another. When a thread is blocked (or, of course, when it dies), another thread is scheduled to run. When a blocked thread is reactivated (for example, because it has slept the required number of milliseconds or because the I/O it waited for is complete), the scheduler checks to see if it has a higher priority than the currently running thread. If so, it *preempts* the current thread and picks a new thread to run. (On a machine with multiple processors, each processor can run a thread, and you can have multiple threads run in parallel. On such a machine, a thread is only preempted if a higher priority thread becomes runnable and there is no available processor to run it.)

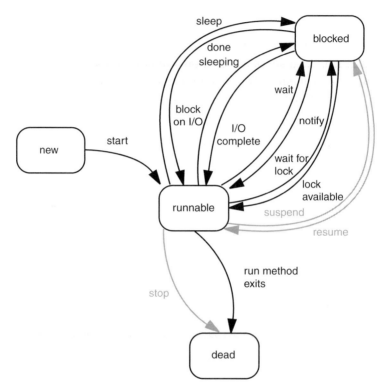

Figure 1–5: Thread states

For example, the `run` method of the `BallThread` blocks itself after it has completed a move, by calling the `sleep` method.

This gives other threads (in our case, other balls and the main thread) the chance to run.

If the computer has multiple processors, then more than one thread has a chance to run at the same time.

Moving Out of a Blocked State

The thread must move out of the blocked state and back into the runnable state, using the opposite of the route that put it into the blocked state.

1.   If a thread has been put to sleep, the specified number of milliseconds must expire.

2.   If a thread is waiting for the completion of an input or output operation, then the operation must have finished.

3.   If a thread called `wait`, then another thread must call `notifyAll` or `notify`. (We cover the `wait` and `notifyAll`/`notify` methods later in this chapter.)

4.   If a thread is waiting for an object lock that was owned by another thread, then the other thread must relinquish ownership of the lock. (You will see the details later in this chapter.)

5.   If a thread has been suspended, then someone must call its `resume` method. However, since the `suspend` method has been deprecated, the `resume` method has been deprecated as well, and you should not call it in your own code.

NOTE: A blocked thread can only reenter the runnable state through the same route that blocked it in the first place. For example, if a thread is blocked on input, you cannot call its `resume` method to unblock it.

If you invoke a method on a thread that is incompatible with its state, then the virtual machine throws an `IllegalThreadStateException`. For example, this happens when you call `sleep` on a thread that is currently blocked.

Dead Threads

A thread is dead for one of two reasons:

*   It dies a natural death because the `run` method exits normally.
*   It dies abruptly because an uncaught exception terminates the `run` method.

In particular, it is possible to kill a thread by invoking its `stop` method. That method throws a `ThreadDeath` error object which kills the thread. However, the `stop` method is deprecated, and you should not call it in your own code. We will explain later in this chapter why the `stop` method is inherently dangerous.

To find out whether a thread is currently alive (that is, either runnable or blocked), use the `isAlive` method. This method returns `true` if the thread is runnable or blocked, `false` if the thread is still new and not yet runnable or if the thread is dead.

NOTE: You cannot find out if an alive thread is runnable or blocked, or if a runnable thread is actually running. In addition, you cannot differentiate between a thread that has not yet become runnable and one that has already died.

Daemon Threads

A thread can be turned into a *daemon thread* by calling

```
t.setDaemon(true);
```

There is nothing demonic about such a thread. A daemon is simply a thread that has no other role in life than to serve others. Examples are timer threads that send regular "timer ticks" to other threads. When only daemon threads remain, then the program exits. There is no point in keeping the program running if all remaining threads are daemons.

Thread Groups

Some programs contain quite a few threads. It then becomes useful to categorize them by functionality. For example, consider an Internet browser. If many threads are trying to acquire images from a server and the user clicks on a "Stop" button to interrupt the loading of the current page, then it is handy to have a way of interrupting all of these threads simultaneously. The Java programming language lets you construct what it calls a *thread group* so you can simultaneously work with a group of threads.

You construct a thread group with the constructor:

```
String groupName = . . .;
ThreadGroup g = new ThreadGroup(groupName)
```

The string argument of the `ThreadGroup` constructor identifies the group and must be unique. You then add threads to the thread group by specifying the thread group in the thread constructor.

```
Thread t = new Thread(g, threadName);
```

To find out whether any threads of a particular group are still runnable, use the `activeCount` method.

```
if (g.activeCount() == 0)
{
    // all threads in the group g have stopped
}
```

To interrupt all threads in a thread group, simply call `interrupt` on the group object.

```
g.interrupt(); // interrupt all threads in group g
```

We'll discuss interrupting threads in greater detail in the next section.

Thread groups can have child subgroups. By default, a newly created thread group becomes a child of the current thread group. But you can also explicitly name the parent group in the constructor (see the API notes). Methods such as `activeCount` and `interrupt` refer to all threads in their group and all child groups.

One nice feature of thread groups is that you can get a notification if a thread died because of an exception. You need to subclass the `ThreadGroup` class and override the `uncaughtException` method. You can then replace the default action (which prints a stack trace to the standard error stream) with something more sophisticated, such as logging the error in a file or displaying a dialog.

`java.lang.Thread`

- `Thread(ThreadGroup g, String name)`
  creates a new `Thread` that belongs to a given `ThreadGroup`.

  Parameters: g   the thread group to which the new thread belongs

                 name   the name of the new thread

- `ThreadGroup getThreadGroup()`
  returns the thread group of this thread.

- `boolean isAlive()`
  returns `true` if the thread has started and has not yet terminated.

- `void suspend()`
  suspends this thread's execution. This method is deprecated.

- `void resume()`
  resumes this thread. This method is only valid after `suspend()` has been invoked. This method is deprecated.

- `void setDaemon(boolean on)`
  marks this thread as a daemon thread or a user thread. When there are only daemon threads left running in the system, the program exits. This method must be called before the thread is started.

- `void stop()`
  stops the thread. This method is deprecated.

`java.lang.ThreadGroup`

- `ThreadGroup(String name)`
  creates a new `ThreadGroup`. Its parent will be the thread group of the current thread.

  Parameters: name   the name of the new thread group

- `ThreadGroup(ThreadGroup parent, String name)`
  creates a new `ThreadGroup`.

  Parameters: parent   the parent thread group of the new thread group

                 name   the name of the new thread group

- `int activeCount()`
  returns an upper bound for the number of active threads in the thread group.

- `int enumerate(Thread[] list)`
  gets references to every active thread in this thread group. You can use the `activeCount` method to get an upper bound for the array; this method

returns the number of threads put into the array. If the array is too short (presumably because more threads were spawned after the call to `activeCount`), then as many threads as fit are inserted.

Parameters: `list`   an array to be filled with the thread references

- `ThreadGroup getParent()`
  gets the parent of this thread group.

- `void interrupt()`
  interrupts all threads in this thread group and all of its child groups.

- `void uncaughtException(Thread t, Throwable e)`
  Override this method to react to exceptions that terminate any threads in this thread group. The default implementation calls this method of the parent thread group if there is a parent, or otherwise prints a stack trace to the standard error stream. (However, if e is a `ThreadDeath` object, then the stack trace is suppressed. `ThreadDeath` objects are generated by the deprecated `stop` method.).

  Parameters: `t`   the thread that was terminated due to an uncaught exception

                   `e`   the uncaught exception object

Thread Priorities

In the Java programming language, every thread has a *priority*. By default, a thread inherits the priority of its parent thread. You can increase or decrease the priority of any thread with the `setPriority` method. You can set the priority to any value between `MIN_PRIORITY` (defined as 1 in the `Thread` class) and `MAX_PRIORITY` (defined as 10). `NORM_PRIORITY` is defined as 5.

Whenever the thread-scheduler has a chance to pick a new thread, it *generally* picks the *highest-priority thread that is currently runnable.*

CAUTION: We need to say right at the outset that the rules for thread priorities are highly system-dependent. When the virtual machine relies on the thread implementation of the host platform, the thread scheduling is at the mercy of that thread implementation. The virtual machine maps the thread priorities to the priority levels of the host platform (which may have more or fewer thread levels). What we describe in this section is an ideal situation that every virtual machine implementation tries to approximate to some degree.

The highest-priority runnable thread keeps running until:

- It yields by calling the `yield` method, or

- It ceases to be runnable (either by dying or by entering the blocked state), or
- A higher-priority thread has become runnable (because the higher-priority thread has slept long enough, or its I/O operation is complete, or someone unblocked it by calling the `notifyAll`/`notify` method on the object that the thread was waiting for).

Then, the scheduler selects a new thread to run. The highest-priority remaining thread is picked among those that are runnable.

What happens if there is more than one runnable thread with the same (highest) priority? One of the highest priority threads gets picked. It is completely up to the thread scheduler how to arbitrate between threads of the same priority. The Java programming language gives no guarantee that all of the threads get treated *fairly*. Of course, it would be desirable if all threads of the same priority are served in turn, to guarantee that each of them has a chance to make progress. But it is at least theoretically possible that on some platforms a thread scheduler picks a random thread or keeps picking the first available thread. This is a weakness of the Java programming language, and it is difficult to write multithreaded programs that are guaranteed to work identically on all virtual machines.

CAUTION: Some platforms (such as Windows NT) have fewer priority levels than the 10 levels that the Java platform specifies. On those platforms, no matter what mapping of priority levels is chosen, some of the 10 JVM levels will be mapped to the same platform levels. In the Sun JVM for Linux, thread priorities are ignored altogether, so you will not be able to see the "express threads" in action when you run the sample program at the end of this section.

Whenever the host platform uses fewer priority levels than the Java platform, a thread can be preempted by another thread with a seemingly lower priority. That plainly means that you cannot rely on priority levels in your multithreaded programs.

Consider, for example, a call to `yield`. It may have no effect on some implementations. The levels of all runnable threads might map to the same host thread level. The host scheduler might make no effort towards fairness and might simply keep reactivating the yielding thread, even though other threads would like to get their turn. It is a good idea to call `sleep` instead—at least you know that the current thread won't be picked again right away.

Most virtual machines have several (although not necessarily 10) priorities, and thread schedulers make some effort to rotate among equal priority threads. For example, if you watch a number of ball threads in the preceding example program, all balls progressed to the end and they appeared to get executed at approximately the same rate. Of course, that is not a guarantee. If you need to ensure a fair scheduling policy, you must implement it yourself.

Consider the following example program, which modifies the previous program to run threads of one kind of balls (displayed in red) with a higher priority than the other threads. (The bold line in the code below shows how to increase the priority of the thread.)

If you click on the "Start" button, a thread is launched at the normal priority, animating a black ball. If you click on the "Express" button, then you launch a red ball whose thread runs at a higher priority than the regular ball threads.

```java
public class BounceFrame
{
   public BounceFrame()
   {
      . . .
      addButton(buttonPanel, "Start",
         new ActionListener()
            {
               public void actionPerformed(ActionEvent evt)
               {
                  addBall(Thread.NORM_PRIORITY, Color.black);
               }
            });

      addButton(buttonPanel, "Express",
         new ActionListener()
            {
               public void actionPerformed(ActionEvent evt)
               {
                  addBall(Thread.NORM_PRIORITY + 2, Color.red);
               }
            });
   . . .
   }

   public void addBall(int priority, Color color)
   {
      Ball b = new Ball(canvas, color);
      canvas.add(b);
      BallThread thread = new BallThread(b);
      thread.setPriority(priority);
      thread.start();
   }
   . . .
}
```

Try it out. Launch a set of regular balls and a set of express balls. You will notice that the express balls seem to run faster. This is solely a result of their higher priority, *not* because the red balls run at a higher speed. The code to move the express balls is the same as that of the regular balls.

Here is why this demonstration works: five milliseconds after an express thread goes to sleep, the scheduler wakes it. Now:

- The scheduler again evaluates the priorities of all the runnable threads;
- It finds that the express threads have the highest priority.

One of the express threads gets another turn right away. This can be the one that just woke up, or perhaps it is another express thread—you have no way of knowing. The express threads take turns, and only when they are all asleep does the scheduler give the lower-priority threads a chance to run. See Figure 1–6 and Example 1–3.

Note that the lower-priority threads would have *no* chance to run if the express threads had called `yield` instead of `sleep`.

Once again, we caution you that this program works fine on Windows NT and Solaris, but the Java programming language specification gives no guarantee that it works identically on other implementations.

TIP: If you find yourself tinkering with priorities to make your code work, you are on the wrong track. Instead, read the remainder of this chapter, or delve into one of the cited references, to learn more about reliable mechanisms for controlling multithreaded programs.

Figure 1–6: Threads with different priorities

Example 1–3: BounceExpress.java

```
 1. import java.awt.*;
 2. import java.awt.event.*;
 3. import java.awt.geom.*;
 4. import java.util.*;
 5. import javax.swing.*;
 6.
 7. /**
 8.    Shows animated bouncing balls, some running in higher priority
 9.    threads
10. */
11. public class BounceExpress
12. {
13.    public static void main(String[] args)
14.    {
15.       JFrame frame = new BounceFrame();
16.       frame.setDefaultCloseOperation(JFrame.EXIT_ON_CLOSE);
17.       frame.show();
18.    }
19. }
20.
21. /**
22.    The frame with canvas and buttons.
23. */
24. class BounceFrame extends JFrame
25. {
26.    /**
27.       Constructs the frame with the canvas for showing the
28.       bouncing ball and Start and Close buttons
29.    */
30.    public BounceFrame()
31.    {
32.       setSize(WIDTH, HEIGHT);
33.       setTitle("BounceExpress");
34.
35.       Container contentPane = getContentPane();
36.       canvas = new BallCanvas();
37.       contentPane.add(canvas, BorderLayout.CENTER);
38.       JPanel buttonPanel = new JPanel();
39.       addButton(buttonPanel, "Start",
40.          new ActionListener()
41.             {
42.                public void actionPerformed(ActionEvent evt)
43.                {
44.                   addBall(Thread.NORM_PRIORITY, Color.black);
45.                }
46.             });
47.
```

```
48.        addButton(buttonPanel, "Express",
49.           new ActionListener()
50.               {
51.                   public void actionPerformed(ActionEvent evt)
52.                   {
53.                       addBall(Thread.NORM_PRIORITY + 2, Color.red);
54.                   }
55.               });
56.
57.        addButton(buttonPanel, "Close",
58.           new ActionListener()
59.               {
60.                   public void actionPerformed(ActionEvent evt)
61.                   {
62.                       System.exit(0);
63.                   }
64.               });
65.        contentPane.add(buttonPanel, BorderLayout.SOUTH);
66.    }
67.
68.    /**
69.       Adds a button to a container.
70.       @param c the container
71.       @param title the button title
72.       @param listener the action listener for the button
73.    */
74.    public void addButton(Container c, String title,
75.       ActionListener listener)
76.    {
77.       JButton button = new JButton(title);
78.       c.add(button);
79.       button.addActionListener(listener);
80.    }
81.
82.    /**
83.       Adds a bouncing ball to the canvas and starts a thread
84.       to make it bounce
85.       @param priority the priority for the threads
86.       @color the color for the balls
87.    */
88.    public void addBall(int priority, Color color)
89.    {
90.       Ball b = new Ball(canvas, color);
91.       canvas.add(b);
92.       BallThread thread = new BallThread(b);
93.       thread.setPriority(priority);
94.       thread.start();
95.    }
```

```
96.
97.     private BallCanvas canvas;
98.     public static final int WIDTH = 450;
99.     public static final int HEIGHT = 350;
100. }
101.
102. /**
103.     A thread that animates a bouncing ball.
104. */
105. class BallThread extends Thread
106. {
107.     /**
108.         Constructs the thread.
109.         @aBall the ball to bounce
110.     */
111.     public BallThread(Ball aBall) { b = aBall; }
112.
113.     public void run()
114.     {
115.         try
116.         {
117.             for (int i = 1; i <= 1000; i++)
118.             {
119.                 b.move();
120.                 sleep(5);
121.             }
122.         }
123.         catch (InterruptedException exception)
124.         {
125.         }
126.     }
127.
128.     private Ball b;
129. }
130.
131. /**
132.     The canvas that draws the balls.
133. */
134. class BallCanvas extends JPanel
135. {
136.     /**
137.         Add a ball to the canvas.
138.         @param b the ball to add
139.     */
140.     public void add(Ball b)
141.     {
142.         balls.add(b);
143.     }
```

```
144.
145.    public void paintComponent(Graphics g)
146.    {
147.       super.paintComponent(g);
148.       Graphics2D g2 = (Graphics2D)g;
149.       for (int i = 0; i < balls.size(); i++)
150.       {
151.          Ball b = (Ball)balls.get(i);
152.          b.draw(g2);
153.       }
154.    }
155.
156.    private ArrayList balls = new ArrayList();
157. }
158.
159. /**
160.    A ball that moves and bounces off the edges of a
161.    component
162. */
163. class Ball
164. {
165.    /**
166.       Constructs a ball in the upper left corner
167.       @c the component in which the ball bounces
168.       @aColor the color of the ball
169.    */
170.    public Ball(Component c, Color aColor)
171.    {
172.       canvas = c;
173.       color = aColor;
174.    }
175.
176.    /**
177.       Draws the ball at its current position
178.       @param g2 the graphics context
179.    */
180.    public void draw(Graphics2D g2)
181.    {
182.       g2.setColor(color);
183.       g2.fill(new Ellipse2D.Double(x, y, XSIZE, YSIZE));
184.    }
185.
186.    /**
187.       Moves the ball to the next position, reversing direction
188.       if it hits one of the edges
189.    */
190.    public void move()
191.    {
192.       x += dx;
```

```
193.        y += dy;
194.        if (x < 0)
195.        {
196.           x = 0;
197.           dx = -dx;
198.        }
199.        if (x + XSIZE >= canvas.getWidth())
200.        {
201.           x = canvas.getWidth() - XSIZE;
202.           dx = -dx;
203.        }
204.        if (y < 0)
205.        {
206.           y = 0;
207.           dy = -dy;
208.        }
209.        if (y + YSIZE >= canvas.getHeight())
210.        {
211.           y = canvas.getHeight() - YSIZE;
212.           dy = -dy;
213.        }
214.
215.        canvas.repaint();
216.     }
217.
218.     private Component canvas;
219.     private Color color;
220.     private static final int XSIZE = 15;
221.     private static final int YSIZE = 15;
222.     private int x = 0;
223.     private int y = 0;
224.     private int dx = 2;
225.     private int dy = 2;
226.  }
```

java.lang.Thread

- void setPriority(int newPriority)

  sets the priority of this thread. The priority must be between
  Thread.MIN_PRIORITY and Thread.MAX_PRIORITY. Use
  Thread.NORM_PRIORITY for normal priority.

- static int MIN_PRIORITY

  is the minimum priority that a Thread can have. The minimum priority
  value is 1.

- static int NORM_PRIORITY

  is the default priority of a Thread. The default priority is 5.

- `static int MAX_PRIORITY`
  is the maximum priority that a `Thread` can have. The maximum priority value is 10.

- `static void yield()`
  causes the currently executing thread to yield. If there are other runnable threads whose priority is at least as high as the priority of this thread, they will be scheduled next. Note that this is a static method.

Selfish Threads

Our ball threads were well-behaved and gave each other a chance to run. They did this by calling the `sleep` method to wait their turns. The `sleep` method blocks the thread and gives the other threads an opportunity to be scheduled. Even if a thread does not want to put itself to sleep for any amount of time, it can call `yield()` whenever it does not mind being interrupted. A thread should always call `sleep` or `yield` when it is executing a long loop, to ensure that it is not monopolizing the system. A thread that does not follow this rule is called *selfish*.

The following program shows what happens when a thread contains a *tight loop,* a loop in which it carries out a lot of work without giving other threads a chance. When you click on the "Selfish" button, a blue ball is launched whose `run` method contains a tight loop.

```
class BallThread extends Thread
{
   . . .
   public void run()
   {
      try
      {
         for (int i = 1; i <= 1000; i++)
         {
            b.move();
            if (selfish)
            {
               // busy wait for 5 milliseconds
               long t = System.currentTimeMillis();
               while (System.currentTimeMillis() < t + 5)
                  ;
            }
            else
               sleep(5);
         }
      }
      catch (InterruptedException exception)
```

```
        {
        }
    }
    . . .
    private boolean selfish;
}
```

When the `selfish` flag is set, the `run` method will last about five seconds before it returns, ending the thread. In the meantime, it never calls `sleep` or `yield`.

What actually happens when you run this program depends on your operating system and choice of thread implementation. For example, when you run this program under Solaris or Linux with the "green threads" implementation as opposed to the "native threads" implementation, you will find that the selfish ball indeed hogs the whole application. Try closing the program or launching another ball; you will have a hard time getting even a mouse-click into the application. However, when you run the same program under Windows or the native threads implementation, nothing untoward happens. The blue balls can run in parallel with other balls.

The reason for this behavioral difference is that the underlying thread package of the operating system performs *time-slicing*. It periodically interrupts threads in midstream, even if they are not cooperating. When a thread (even a selfish thread) is interrupted, the scheduler activates another thread—picked among the top-priority-level runnable threads. The green threads implementation on Solaris and Linux does not perform time-slicing, but the native thread package does. (Why doesn't everyone simply use the native threads? Until recently, X11 and Motif were not thread safe, and using native threads could lock up the window manager.) Also, as Java gets ported to new platforms, the green threads implementation tends to get implemented first because it is easier to port.

If you *know* that your program will execute on a machine whose thread system performs time-slicing, then you do not need to worry about making your threads polite. But the point of Internet computing is that you generally *do not know* the environments of the people who will use your program. You should, therefore, plan for the worst and put calls to `sleep` or `yield` in every loop.

CAUTION: When programming with threads, expect platform-dependent behavior variations. You can't assume that your threads will get pre-empted by other threads, so you must plan for the case that they run forever unless you yield control. But you can't rely on your threads running without interruption—on most platforms, they won't. You must be prepared that they can lose control at any time.

See Example 1–4 for the complete source code of the "selfish ball" program.

Example 1–4: BounceSelfish.java

```
1.  import java.awt.*;
2.  import java.awt.event.*;
3.  import java.awt.geom.*;
4.  import java.util.*;
5.  import javax.swing.*;
6.
7.  /**
8.     Shows animated bouncing balls, some running in selfish
9.     threads
10. */
11. public class BounceSelfish
12. {
13.    public static void main(String[] args)
14.    {
15.       JFrame frame = new BounceFrame();
16.       frame.setDefaultCloseOperation(JFrame.EXIT_ON_CLOSE);
17.       frame.show();
18.    }
19. }
20.
21. /**
22.    The frame with canvas and buttons.
23. */
24. class BounceFrame extends JFrame
25. {
26.    /**
27.       Constructs the frame with the canvas for showing the
28.       bouncing ball and Start and Close buttons
29.    */
30.    public BounceFrame()
31.    {
32.       setSize(WIDTH, HEIGHT);
33.       setTitle("BounceSelfish");
34.
35.       Container contentPane = getContentPane();
36.       canvas = new BallCanvas();
37.       contentPane.add(canvas, BorderLayout.CENTER);
38.       JPanel buttonPanel = new JPanel();
39.       addButton(buttonPanel, "Start",
40.          new ActionListener()
41.             {
42.                public void actionPerformed(ActionEvent evt)
43.                {
44.                   addBall(false, Color.black);
45.                }
46.             });
47.
```

```
48.         addButton(buttonPanel, "Selfish",
49.            new ActionListener()
50.               {
51.                  public void actionPerformed(ActionEvent evt)
52.                  {
53.                     addBall(true, Color.blue);
54.                  }
55.               });
56.
57.         addButton(buttonPanel, "Close",
58.            new ActionListener()
59.               {
60.                  public void actionPerformed(ActionEvent evt)
61.                  {
62.                     System.exit(0);
63.                  }
64.               });
65.         contentPane.add(buttonPanel, BorderLayout.SOUTH);
66.      }
67.
68.      /**
69.         Adds a button to a container.
70.         @param c the container
71.         @param title the button title
72.         @param listener the action listener for the button
73.      */
74.      public void addButton(Container c, String title,
75.         ActionListener listener)
76.      {
77.         JButton button = new JButton(title);
78.         c.add(button);
79.         button.addActionListener(listener);
80.      }
81.
82.      /**
83.         Adds a bouncing ball to the canvas and starts a thread
84.         to make it bounce
85.         @param priority the priority for the threads
86.         @color the color for the balls
87.      */
88.      public void addBall(boolean selfish, Color color)
89.      {
90.         Ball b = new Ball(canvas, color);
91.         canvas.add(b);
92.         BallThread thread = new BallThread(b, selfish);
93.         thread.start();
94.      }
95.
```

```
96.     private BallCanvas canvas;
97.     public static final int WIDTH = 450;
98.     public static final int HEIGHT = 350;
99.  }
100.
101. /**
102.    A thread that animates a bouncing ball.
103. */
104. class BallThread extends Thread
105. {
106.    /**
107.       Constructs the thread.
108.       @aBall the ball to bounce
109.       @boolean selfishFlag true if the thread is selfish, using
110.       a busy wait instead of calling sleep
111.    */
112.    public BallThread(Ball aBall, boolean selfishFlag)
113.    {
114.       b = aBall;
115.       selfish = selfishFlag;
116.    }
117.
118.    public void run()
119.    {
120.       try
121.       {
122.          for (int i = 1; i <= 1000; i++)
123.          {
124.             b.move();
125.             if (selfish)
126.             {
127.                // busy wait for 5 milliseconds
128.                long t = System.currentTimeMillis();
129.                while (System.currentTimeMillis() < t + 5)
130.                   ;
131.             }
132.             else
133.                sleep(5);
134.          }
135.       }
136.       catch (InterruptedException exception)
137.       {
138.       }
139.    }
140.
141.    private Ball b;
142.    boolean selfish;
143. }
```

```
144.
145. /**
146.    The canvas that draws the balls.
147. */
148. class BallCanvas extends JPanel
149. {
150.    /**
151.       Add a ball to the canvas.
152.       @param b the ball to add
153.    */
154.    public void add(Ball b)
155.    {
156.       balls.add(b);
157.    }
158.
159.    public void paintComponent(Graphics g)
160.    {
161.       super.paintComponent(g);
162.       Graphics2D g2 = (Graphics2D)g;
163.       for (int i = 0; i < balls.size(); i++)
164.       {
165.          Ball b = (Ball)balls.get(i);
166.          b.draw(g2);
167.       }
168.    }
169.
170.    private ArrayList balls = new ArrayList();
171. }
172.
173. /**
174.    A ball that moves and bounces off the edges of a
175.    component
176. */
177. class Ball
178. {
179.    /**
180.       Constructs a ball in the upper left corner
181.       @c the component in which the ball bounces
182.       @aColor the color of the ball
183.    */
184.    public Ball(Component c, Color aColor)
185.    {
186.       canvas = c;
187.       color = aColor;
188.    }
189.
190.    /**
191.       Draws the ball at its current position
192.       @param g2 the graphics context
```

```
193.    */
194.    public void draw(Graphics2D g2)
195.    {
196.       g2.setColor(color);
197.       g2.fill(new Ellipse2D.Double(x, y, XSIZE, YSIZE));
198.    }
199.
200.    /**
201.       Moves the ball to the next position, reversing direction
202.       if it hits one of the edges
203.    */
204.    public void move()
205.    {
206.       x += dx;
207.       y += dy;
208.       if (x < 0)
209.       {
210.          x = 0;
211.          dx = -dx;
212.       }
213.       if (x + XSIZE >= canvas.getWidth())
214.       {
215.          x = canvas.getWidth() - XSIZE;
216.          dx = -dx;
217.       }
218.       if (y < 0)
219.       {
220.          y = 0;
221.          dy = -dy;
222.       }
223.       if (y + YSIZE >= canvas.getHeight())
224.       {
225.          y = canvas.getHeight() - YSIZE;
226.          dy = -dy;
227.       }
228.
229.       canvas.repaint();
230.    }
231.
232.    private Component canvas;
233.    private Color color;
234.    private static final int XSIZE = 15;
235.    private static final int YSIZE = 15;
236.    private int x = 0;
237.    private int y = 0;
238.    private int dx = 2;
239.    private int dy = 2;
240. }
```

Synchronization

In most practical multithreaded applications, two or more threads need to share access to the same objects. What happens if two threads have access to the same object and each calls a method that modifies the state of the object? As you might imagine, the threads step on each other's toes. Depending on the order in which the data was accessed, corrupted objects can result. Such a situation is often called a *race condition*.

Thread Communication Without Synchronization

To avoid simultaneous access of a shared object by multiple threads, you must learn how to *synchronize* the access. In this section, you'll see what happens if you do not use synchronization. In the next section, you'll see how to synchronize object access.

In the next test program, we simulate a bank with 10 accounts. We randomly generate transactions that move money between these accounts. There are 10 threads, one for each account. Each transaction moves a random amount of money from the account serviced by the thread to another random account.

The simulation code is straightforward. We have the class `Bank` with the method `transfer`. This method transfers some amount of money from one account to another. If the source account does not have enough money in it, then the call simply returns. Here is the code for the `transfer` method of the `Bank` class.

```
public void transfer(int from, int to, double amount)
   // CAUTION: unsafe when called from multiple threads
{
   if (accounts[from] < amount) return;
   accounts[from] -= amount;
   accounts[to] += amount;
   ntransacts++;
   if (ntransacts % NTEST == 0) test();
}
```

Here is the code for the `TransferThread` class. Its `run` method keeps moving money out of a fixed bank account. In each iteration, the `run` method picks a random target account and a random amount, calls `transfer` on the bank object, and then sleeps.

```
class TransferThread extends Thread
{
   public TransferThread(Bank b, int from, int max)
   {
      bank = b;
      fromAccount = from;
      maxAmount = max;
```

```
    }

    public void run()
    {
        try
        {
            while (!interrupted())
            {
                int toAccount = (int)(bank.size() * Math.random());
                int amount = (int)(maxAmount * Math.random());
                bank.transfer(fromAccount, toAccount, amount);
                sleep(1);
            }
        }
        catch(InterruptedException e) {}
    }

    private Bank bank;
    private int fromAccount;
    private int maxAmount;
}
```

When this simulation runs, we do not know how much money is in any one bank account at any time. But we do know that the total amount of money in all the accounts should remain unchanged since all we do is move money from one account to another.

Every 10,000 transactions, the `transfer` method calls a `test` method that recomputes the total and prints it out.

This program never finishes. Just press CTRL+C to kill the program.

Here is a typical printout:

```
Transactions:10000 Sum: 100000
Transactions:20000 Sum: 100000
Transactions:30000 Sum: 100000
Transactions:40000 Sum: 100000
Transactions:50000 Sum: 100000
Transactions:60000 Sum: 100000
Transactions:70000 Sum: 100000
Transactions:80000 Sum: 100000
Transactions:90000 Sum: 100000
Transactions:100000 Sum: 100000
Transactions:110000 Sum: 100000
Transactions:120000 Sum: 100000
Transactions:130000 Sum: 94792
Transactions:140000 Sum: 94792
Transactions:150000 Sum: 94792
    . . .
```

As you can see, something is very wrong. For quite a few transactions, the bank balance remains at $100,000, which is the correct total for 10 accounts of $10,000 each. But after some time, the balance changes slightly. When you run this program, you may find that errors happen quickly, or it may take a very long time for the balance to become corrupted. This situation does not inspire confidence, and you would probably not want to deposit your hard-earned money into this bank.

Example 1–5 provides the complete source code. See if you can spot the problem with the code. We will unravel the mystery in the next section.

Example 1–5: UnsynchBankTest.java

```
1. public class UnsynchBankTest
2. {
3.    public static void main(String[] args)
4.    {
5.       Bank b = new Bank(NACCOUNTS, INITIAL_BALANCE);
6.       int i;
7.       for (i = 0; i < NACCOUNTS; i++)
8.       {
9.          TransferThread t = new TransferThread(b, i,
10.            INITIAL_BALANCE);
11.         t.setPriority(Thread.NORM_PRIORITY + i % 2);
12.         t.start();
13.      }
14.   }
15.
16.   public static final int NACCOUNTS = 10;
17.   public static final int INITIAL_BALANCE = 10000;
18. }
19.
20. /**
21.    A bank with a number of bank accounts.
22. */
23. class Bank
24. {
25.    /**
26.       Constructs the bank.
27.       @param n the number of accounts
28.       @param initialBalance the initial balance
29.       for each account
30.    */
31.    public Bank(int n, int initialBalance)
32.    {
33.       accounts = new int[n];
34.       int i;
35.       for (i = 0; i < accounts.length; i++)
```

```
36.          accounts[i] = initialBalance;
37.       ntransacts = 0;
38.    }
39.
40.    /**
41.       Transfers money from one account to another.
42.       @param from the account to transfer from
43.       @param to the account to transfer to
44.       @param amount the amount to transfer
45.    */
46.    public void transfer(int from, int to, int amount)
47.       throws InterruptedException
48.    {
49.       accounts[from] -= amount;
50.       accounts[to] += amount;
51.       ntransacts++;
52.       if (ntransacts % NTEST == 0) test();
53.    }
54.
55.    /**
56.       Prints a test message to check the integrity
57.       of this bank object.
58.    */
59.    public void test()
60.    {
61.       int sum = 0;
62.
63.       for (int i = 0; i < accounts.length; i++)
64.          sum += accounts[i];
65.
66.       System.out.println("Transactions:" + ntransacts
67.          + " Sum: " + sum);
68.    }
69.
70.    /**
71.       Gets the number of accounts in the bank.
72.       @return the number of accounts
73.    */
74.    public int size()
75.    {
76.       return accounts.length;
77.    }
78.
79.    public static final int NTEST = 10000;
80.    private final int[] accounts;
81.    private long ntransacts = 0;
82. }
83.
```

```
84. /**
85.    A thread that transfers money from an account to other
86.    accounts in a bank.
87. */
88. class TransferThread extends Thread
89. {
90.    /**
91.       Constructs a transfer thread.
92.       @param b the bank between whose account money is transferred
93.       @param from the account to transfer money from
94.       @param max the maximum amount of money in each transfer
95.    */
96.    public TransferThread(Bank b, int from, int max)
97.    {
98.       bank = b;
99.       fromAccount = from;
100.      maxAmount = max;
101.   }
102.
103.   public void run()
104.   {
105.      try
106.      {
107.         while (!interrupted())
108.         {
109.            for (int i = 0; i < REPS; i++)
110.            {
111.               int toAccount = (int)(bank.size() * Math.random());
112.               int amount = (int)(maxAmount * Math.random() / REPS);
113.               bank.transfer(fromAccount, toAccount, amount);
114.               sleep(1);
115.            }
116.         }
117.      }
118.      catch(InterruptedException e) {}
119.   }
120.
121.   private Bank bank;
122.   private int fromAccount;
123.   private int maxAmount;
124.   private static final int REPS = 1000;
125. }
```

Synchronizing Access to Shared Resources

In the previous section, we ran a program in which several threads updated bank account balances. After a while, errors crept in and some amount of money was either lost or spontaneously created. This problem occurs when two threads are simultaneously trying to update an account. Suppose two threads simultaneously carry out the instruction:

```
accounts[to] += amount;
```

The problem is that these are not *atomic* operations. The instruction might be processed as follows:

1. Load `accounts[to]` into a register.
2. Add `amount`.
3. Move the result back to `accounts[to]`.

Now, suppose the first thread executes Steps 1 and 2, and then it is interrupted. Suppose the second thread awakens and updates the same entry in the `account` array. Then, the first thread awakens and completes its Step 3.

That action wipes out the modification of the other thread. As a result, the total is no longer correct. (See Figure 1–7.)

Our test program detects this corruption. (Of course, there is a slight chance of false alarms if the thread is interrupted as it is performing the tests!)

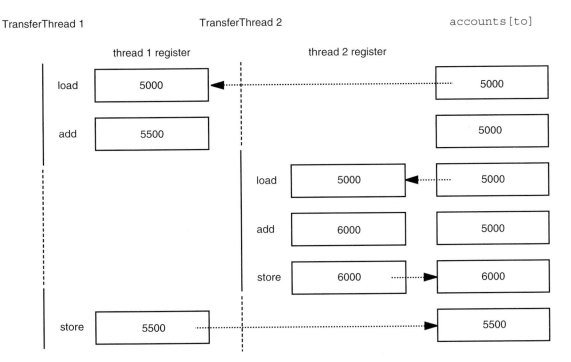

Figure 1–7: Simultaneous access by two threads

NOTE: You can actually peek at the virtual machine bytecodes that execute each statement in our class. Run the command

```
javap -c -v Bank
```

to decompile the `Bank.class` file. For example, the line

```
accounts[to] += amount;
```

is translated into the following bytecodes.

```
aload_0
getfield #16 <Field Bank.accounts [J>
iload_1
dup2
laload
iload_3
i2l
lsub
lastore
```

What these codes mean does not matter. The point is that the increment command is made up of several instructions, and the thread executing them can be interrupted at the point of any instruction.

What is the chance of this corruption occurring? It is quite low, because each thread does so little work before going to sleep again that it is unlikely that the scheduler will preempt it. We found by experimentation that we could boost the probability of corruption by various measures, depending on the target platform. On Windows 98, it helps to assign half of the transfer threads a higher priority than the other half.

```
for (i = 0; i < NACCOUNTS; i++)
{
   TransferThread t = new TransferThread(b, i,
      INITIAL_BALANCE);
   t.setPriority(Thread.NORM_PRIORITY + i % 2);
   t.start();
}
```

When a higher-priority transfer thread wakes up from its sleep, it will preempt a lower-priority transfer thread.

NOTE: This is exactly the kind of tinkering with priority levels that we tell you not to do in your own programs. We were in a bind—we wanted to show you a program that can demonstrate data corruption. In your own programs, you presumably will not want to increase the chance of corruption, so you should not imitate this approach.

On Linux, thread priorities are ignored, and instead, a slight change in the `run` method did the trick—to repeat the transfer multiple times before sleeping.

```
final int REPS = 1000;
for (int i = 0; i < REPS; i++)
{
    int toAccount = (int)(bank.size() * Math.random());
    int amount = (int)(maxAmount * Math.random() / REPS);
    bank.transfer(fromAccount, toAccount, amount);
    sleep(1);
}
```

On all platforms, it helps if you load your machine heavily, by running a few bloatware programs in parallel with the test.

The real problem is that the work of the `transfer` method can be interrupted in the middle. If we could ensure that the method runs to completion before the thread loses control, then the state of the bank account object would not be corrupted.

Many thread libraries force the programmer to fuss with so-called semaphores and critical sections to gain uninterrupted access to a resource. This is sufficient for procedural programming, but it is hardly object-oriented. The Java programming language has a nicer mechanism, inspired by the *monitors* invented by Tony Hoare.

You simply tag any operation that should not be interrupted as `synchronized`, like this:

```
public synchronized void transfer(int from, int to,
    int amount)
{
    if (accounts[from] < amount) return;
    accounts[from] -= amount;
    accounts[to] += amount;
    ntransacts++;
    if (ntransacts % NTEST == 0) test();
}
```

When one thread calls a synchronized method, it is guaranteed that the method will finish before another thread can execute any synchronized method on the same object (see Figure 1–8). When one thread calls `transfer` and then another thread also calls `transfer`, the second thread cannot continue. Instead, it is deactivated and must wait for the first thread to finish executing the `transfer` method.

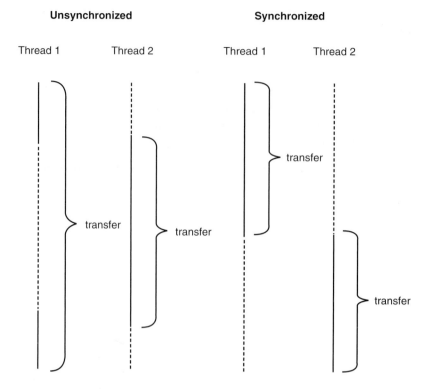

Figure 1–8: Comparison of unsynchronized and synchronized threads

Try it out. Tag the `transfer` method as `synchronized` and run the program again. You can run it forever, and the bank balance will not get corrupted.

In general, you will want to tag those methods as `synchronized` that require multiple operations to update a data structure, as well as those that retrieve a value from a data structure. You are then assured that these operations run to completion before another thread can use the same object.

Of course, the synchronization mechanism isn't free. As you'll see in the next section, some bookkeeping code is executed every time a synchronized method is called. Thus, you will not want to synchronize every method of every class. If objects are not shared among threads, then there is no need to use synchronization. If a method always returns the same value for a given object, then you don't need to synchronize that method. For example, the `size` method of our `Bank` class need not be synchronized—the size of a bank object is fixed after the object is constructed.

Because synchronization is too expensive to use for every class, it is usually a good idea to custom-build classes for thread communication. For example, suppose a browser loads multiple images in parallel and wants to know when all images are loaded. You can define a `ProgressTracker` class with synchronized methods to update and query the loading progress.

Some programmers who have experience with other threading models complain about Java synchronization, finding it cumbersome and inefficient. For system level programming, these may be valid complaints. But for application programmers, the Java model works quite nicely. Just remember to use supporting classes for thread communication—don't try to hack existing code by sprinkling a few `synchronized` keywords over it.

NOTE: In some cases, programmers try to avoid the cost of synchronization in code that performs simple independent load or store operations. However, that can be dangerous, for two reasons. First, a load or store of a 64-bit value is *not* guaranteed to be atomic. That is, if you make an assignment to a `double` or `long` field, half of the assignment could happen, then the thread might be preempted. The next thread then sees the field in an inconsistent state. Moreover, in a multiprocessor machine, each processor can work on a separate cache of data from the main memory. The `synchronized` keyword ensures that local caches are made consistent with the main memory, but unsynchronized methods have no such guarantee. It can then happen that one thread doesn't see a modification to a shared variable made by another thread.

The `volatile` keyword is designed to address these situations. Loads and stores of a 64-bit variable that is declared as `volatile` are guaranteed to be atomic. In a multiprocessor machine, loads and stores of volatile variables should work correctly even for data in processor caches.

In some situations, it might be possible to avoid synchronization and use volatile variables instead. However, not only is this issue fraught with complexity, there also have been reports of virtual machine implementations that don't handle volatile variables correctly. Our recommendation is to use synchronization, not volatile variables, to guarantee thread safety.

Object Locks

When a thread calls a synchronized method, the *object* becomes "locked." Think of each object as having a door with a lock on the inside. It is quite common among Java programmers to visualize object locks by using a "rest room" analogy. The object corresponds to a rest room stall that can hold only one person at a time. In the interest of good taste, we will use a "telephone booth" analogy instead. Imagine a traditional, enclosed telephone booth and suppose it has a latch on the inside. When a thread enters the synchronized method, it closes the door and locks it. When another thread tries to call a synchronized method on the same object, it can't open the door, so it stops running. Eventually, the first thread exits its synchronized method and unlocks the door.

Periodically, the thread scheduler activates the threads that are waiting for the lock to open, using its normal activation rules that we already discussed. Whenever one of the threads that wants to call a synchronized method on the object runs again, it checks to see if the object is still locked. If the object is now unlocked, the thread gets to be the next one to gain exclusive access to the object.

However, other threads are still free to call unsynchronized methods on a locked object. For example, the `size` method of the `Bank` class is not synchronized and it can be called on a locked object.

When a thread leaves a synchronized method by throwing an exception, it still relinquishes the object lock. That is a good thing—you wouldn't want a thread to hog the object after it has exited the synchronized method.

If a thread owns the lock of an object and it calls another synchronized method of the same object, then that method is automatically granted access. The thread only relinquishes the lock when it exits the last synchronized method.

> NOTE: Technically, each object has a *lock count* that counts how many synchronized methods the lock owner has called. Each time a new synchronized method is called, the lock count is increased. Each time a synchronized method terminates (either because of a normal return or because of an uncaught exception), the lock count is decremented. When the lock count reaches zero, the thread gives up the lock.

Note that you can have two different objects of the same class, each of which is locked by a different thread. These threads may even execute the same synchronized method. It's the object that's locked, not the method. In the telephone booth analogy, you can have two people in two separate booths. Each of them may execute the same synchronized method, or they may execute different methods—it doesn't matter.

Of course, an object's lock can only be owned by one thread at any given point in time. But a thread can own the locks of multiple objects at the same time, simply by calling a synchronized method on an object while executing a synchronized method of another object. (Here, admittedly, the telephone booth analogy breaks down.)

The `wait` and `notify` methods

Let us refine our simulation of the bank. We do not want to transfer money out of an account that does not have the funds to cover the transfer. Note that we cannot use code like:

```
if (bank.getBalance(from) >= amount)
    bank.transfer(from, to, amount);
```

It is entirely possible that the current thread will be deactivated between the successful outcome of the test and the call to `transfer`.

```
if (bank.getBalance(from) >= amount)
      // thread might be deactivated at this point
   bank.transfer(from, to, amount);
```

By the time the thread is running again, the account balance may have fallen below the withdrawal amount. You must make sure that the thread cannot be interrupted between the test and the insertion. You do so by putting both the test and the transfer action inside the same synchronized method:

```
public synchronized void transfer(int from, int to,
   int amount)
{
   while (accounts[from] < amount)
   {
      // wait
      . . .
   }
   // transfer funds
   . . .
}
```

Now, what do we do when there is not enough money in the account? We wait until some other thread has added funds. But the `transfer` method is `synchronized`. This thread has just gained exclusive access to the bank object, so no other thread has a chance to make a deposit. A second feature of synchronized methods takes care of this situation. You use the `wait` method of the `Object` class if you need to wait inside a synchronized method.

When `wait` is called inside a synchronized method, the current thread is blocked and gives up the object lock. This lets in another thread that can, we hope, increase the account balance.

The `wait` method can throw an `InterruptedException` when the thread is interrupted while it is waiting. In that case, you can either turn on the "interrupted" flag or propagate the exception—after all, the calling thread, not the bank object, should decide what to do with an interruption. In our case, we simply propagate the exception and add a `throws` specifier to the `transfer` method.

```
public synchronized void transfer(int from, int to,
   int amount) throws InterruptedException
{
   while (accounts[from] < amount)
      wait();
   // transfer funds
   . . .
}
```

Note that the `wait` method is a method of the class `Object`, not of the class `Thread`. When calling `wait`, the bank object unlocks itself and blocks the current thread. (Here, the `wait` method was called on the `this` reference.)

> **CAUTION:** If a thread holds the locks to multiple objects, then the call to `wait` unlocks *only* the object on which `wait` was called. That means that the blocked thread can hold locks to other objects, which won't get unlocked until the thread is unblocked again. That's a dangerous situation that you should avoid.

There is an essential difference between a thread that is waiting to get inside a synchronized method and a thread that has called `wait`. Once a thread calls the `wait` method, it enters a *wait list* for that object. The thread is now blocked. Until the thread is removed from the wait list, the scheduler ignores it and it does not have a chance to continue running.

To remove the thread from the wait list, some other thread must call the `notifyAll` or `notify` method on the *same object.* The `notifyAll` method removes all threads from the object's wait list. The `notify` method removes just one arbitrarily chosen thread. When the threads are removed from the wait list, then they are again runnable, and the scheduler will eventually activate them again. At that time, they will attempt to reenter the object. As soon as the object lock is available, one of them will lock the object and continue where it left off after the call to `wait`.

To understand the `wait` and `notifyAll`/`notify` calls, let's trot out the telephone booth analogy once again. Suppose a thread locks an object and then finds it can't proceed, say because the phone is broken. First of all, it would be pointless for the thread to fall asleep while locked inside the booth. Then a maintenance engineerwould be prevented from entering and fixing the equipment. By calling `wait`, the thread unlocks the object and waits outside. Eventually, a maintenance engineer enters the booth, locks it from inside, and does something. After the engineer leaves the booth, the waiting threads won't know that the situation has improved—maybe the engineer just emptied the coin reservoir. The waiting threads just keep waiting, still without hope. By calling `notifyAll`, the engineer tells all waiting threads that the object state may have changed to their advantage. By calling `notify`, the engineer picks one of the waiting threads at random and only tells that one, leaving the others in their despondent waiting state.

It is crucially important that *some* other thread calls the `notify` or `notifyAll` method periodically. When a thread calls `wait`, it has no way of unblocking itself. It puts its faith in the other threads. If none of them bother to unblock the waiting thread, it will never run again. This can lead to unpleasant *deadlock* situations. If all other threads are blocked and the last active thread calls `wait` without unblocking one of the others, then it also blocks. There is no thread left to unblock the others, and the program hangs. The waiting threads are *not* automatically reactivated when no other thread is working on the object. We will discuss deadlocks later in this chapter.

As a practical matter, it is dangerous to call `notify` because you have no control over which thread gets unblocked. If the wrong thread gets unblocked, that thread may not be able to proceed. We simply recommend that you use the `notifyAll` method and that all threads be unblocked.

When should you call `notifyAll`? The rule of thumb is to call `notifyAll` whenever the state of an object changes in a way that might be advantageous to waiting threads. For example, whenever an account balance changes, the waiting threads should be given another chance to inspect the balance. In our example, we will call `notifyAll` when we have finished with the funds transfer.

```
public synchronized void transfer(int from, int to,
    int amount)
{
    . . .
    accounts[from] -= amount;
    accounts[to] += amount;
    ntransacts++;
    notifyAll();
    . . .
}
```

This notification gives the waiting threads the chance to run again. A thread that was waiting for a higher balance then gets a chance to check the balance again. If the balance is sufficient, the thread performs the transfer. If not, it calls `wait` again.

Note that the call to `notifyAll` does not immediately activate a waiting thread. It only unblocks the waiting threads so that they can compete for entry into the object after the current thread has exited the synchronized method.

TIP: If your multithreaded program gets stuck, double-check that every `wait` is matched by a `notifyAll`.

If you run the sample program with the synchronized version of the `transfer` method, you will notice that nothing ever goes wrong. The total balance stays at $100,000 forever. (Again, you need to press CTRL+C to terminate the program.)

You will also notice that the program in Example 1–6 runs a bit slower—this is the price you pay for the added bookkeeping involved in the synchronization mechanism.

Example 1–6: SynchBankTest.java

```
1. public class SynchBankTest
2. {
3.    public static void main(String[] args)
```

```
4.     {
5.         Bank b = new Bank(NACCOUNTS, INITIAL_BALANCE);
6.         int i;
7.         for (i = 0; i < NACCOUNTS; i++)
8.         {
9.             TransferThread t = new TransferThread(b, i,
10.                INITIAL_BALANCE);
11.             t.setPriority(Thread.NORM_PRIORITY + i % 2);
12.             t.start();
13.         }
14.     }
15.
16.     public static final int NACCOUNTS = 10;
17.     public static final int INITIAL_BALANCE = 10000;
18. }
19.
20. /**
21.     A bank with a number of bank accounts.
22. */
23. class Bank
24. {
25.     /**
26.         Constructs the bank.
27.         @param n the number of accounts
28.         @param initialBalance the initial balance
29.         for each account
30.     */
31.     public Bank(int n, int initialBalance)
32.     {
33.         accounts = new int[n];
34.         int i;
35.         for (i = 0; i < accounts.length; i++)
36.             accounts[i] = initialBalance;
37.         ntransacts = 0;
38.     }
39.
40.     /**
41.         Transfers money from one account to another.
42.         @param from the account to transfer from
43.         @param to the account to transfer to
44.         @param amount the amount to transfer
45.     */
46.     public synchronized void transfer(int from, int to, int amount)
47.         throws InterruptedException
48.     {
49.         while (accounts[from] < amount)
50.             wait();
51.         accounts[from] -= amount;
52.         accounts[to] += amount;
53.         ntransacts++;
54.         notifyAll();
55.         if (ntransacts % NTEST == 0) test();
```

```
56.    }
57.
58.    /**
59.       Prints a test message to check the integrity
60.       of this bank object.
61.    */
62.    public synchronized void test()
63.    {
64.       int sum = 0;
65.
66.       for (int i = 0; i < accounts.length; i++)
67.          sum += accounts[i];
68.
69.       System.out.println("Transactions:" + ntransacts
70.          + " Sum: " + sum);
71.    }
72.
73.    /**
74.       Gets the number of accounts in the bank.
75.       @return the number of accounts
76.    */
77.    public int size()
78.    {
79.       return accounts.length;
80.    }
81.
82.    public static final int NTEST = 10000;
83.    private final int[] accounts;
84.    private long ntransacts = 0;
85. }
86.
87. /**
88.    A thread that transfers money from an account to other
89.    accounts in a bank.
90. */
91. class TransferThread extends Thread
92. {
93.    /**
94.       Constructs a transfer thread.
95.       @param b the bank between whose account money is transferred
96.       @param from the account to transfer money from
97.       @param max the maximum amount of money in each transfer
98.    */
99.    public TransferThread(Bank b, int from, int max)
100.   {
101.      bank = b;
102.      fromAccount = from;
103.      maxAmount = max;
104.   }
105.
106.   public void run()
107.   {
```

```
108.        try
109.        {
110.           while (!interrupted())
111.           {
112.               int toAccount = (int)(bank.size() * Math.random());
113.               int amount = (int)(maxAmount * Math.random());
114.               bank.transfer(fromAccount, toAccount, amount);
115.               sleep(1);
116.           }
117.        }
118.        catch(InterruptedException e) {}
119.     }
120.
121.    private Bank bank;
122.    private int fromAccount;
123.    private int maxAmount;
124. }
```

Here is a summary of how the synchronization mechanism works.

1.   To call a synchronized method, the implicit parameter must not be locked. Calling the method locks the object. Returning from the call unlocks the implicit parameter object. Thus, only one thread at a time can execute synchronized methods on a particular object.

2.   When a thread executes a call to `wait`, it surrenders the object lock and enters a wait list for that object.

3.   To remove a thread from the wait list, some other thread must make a call to `notifyAll` or `notify`, on the same object.

The scheduling rules are undeniably complex, but it is actually quite simple to put them into practice. Just follow these five rules:

1.   If two or more threads modify an object, declare the methods that carry out the modifications as synchronized. Read-only methods that are affected by object modifications must also be synchronized.

2.   If a thread must wait for the state of an object to change, it should wait inside the object, not outside, by entering a synchronized method and calling `wait`.

3.   Don't spend any significant amount of time in a synchronized method. Most operations simply update a data structure and quickly return. If you can't complete a synchronized method immediately, call `wait` so that you give up the object lock while waiting.

4.   Whenever a method changes the state of an object, it should call `notifyAll`. That gives the waiting threads a chance to see if circumstances have changed.

5.   Remember that `wait` and `notifyAll`/`notify` are methods of the
     `Object` class, not the `Thread` class. Double-check that your calls to
     `wait` are matched up by a notification *on the same object.*

Synchronized Blocks

Occasionally, it is useful to lock an object and obtain exclusive access to it for just a
few instructions without writing a new synchronized method. You use *synchronized blocks* to achieve this access. A synchronized block consists of a sequence of
statements, enclosed in { . . . } and prefixed with `synchronized (obj)`,
where `obj` is the object to be locked. Here is an example of the syntax:

```
public void run()
{
   . . .
   synchronized (bank) // lock the bank object
   {
      if (bank.getBalance(from) >= amount)
         bank.transfer(from, to, amount);
   }
   . . .
}
```

In this sample code segment, the synchronized block will run to completion
before any other thread can call a synchronized method on the `bank` object.

Application programmers tend to avoid this feature. It is usually a better idea
to take a step back, think about the mechanism on a higher level, come up
with a class that describes it, and use synchronized methods of that class.
System programmers who consider additional classes "high overhead" are
more likely to use synchronized blocks.

Synchronized Static Methods

A *singleton* is a class with just one object. Singletons are commonly used for management objects that need to be globally unique, such as print spoolers, database
connection managers, and so on.

Consider the typical implementation of a singleton.

```
public class Singleton
{
   public static Singleton getInstance()
   {
      if (instance == null)
         instance = new Singleton(. . .);
      return instance;
   }

   private Singleton(. . .) { . . . }
   . . .
```

```
    private static Singleton instance;
}
```

However, the getInstance method is not threadsafe. Suppose one thread calls getInstance and is preempted in the middle of the constructor, before the instance field has been set. Then another thread gains control and it calls getInstance. Since instance is still null, that thread constructs a second object. That's just what a singleton is supposed to prevent.

The remedy is simple: make the getInstance method synchronized:

```
public static synchronized Singleton getInstance()
{
    if (instance == null)
        instance = new Singleton(. . .);
    return instance;
}
```

Now, the method runs to completion before another thread can call it.

If you paid close attention to the preceding sections, you may wonder how this works. When a thread calls a synchronized method, it acquires the lock of an object. But this method is static—what object does a thread lock when calling Singleton.getInstance()?

Calling a static method locks the *class object* Singleton.class. (Recall from Volume 1, Chapter 5, that there is a unique object of type Class that describes each class that the virtual machine has loaded.) Therefore, if one thread calls a synchronized static method of a class, all synchronized static methods of the class are blocked until the first call returns.

 java.lang.Object

- void notifyAll()
  unblocks the threads that called wait on this object. This method can only be called from within a synchronized method or block. The method throws an IllegalMonitorStateException if the current thread is not the owner of the object's lock.

- void notify()
  unblocks one randomly selected thread among the threads that called wait on this object. This method can only be called from within a synchronized method or block. The method throws an IllegalMonitorStateException if the current thread is not the owner of the object's lock.

- void wait()
  causes a thread to wait until it is notified. This method can only be called from within a synchronized method. It throws an IllegalMonitorState-Exception if the current thread is not the owner of the object's lock.

Deadlocks

The synchronization feature in the Java programming language is convenient and powerful, but it cannot solve all problems that might arise in multithreading. Consider the following situation:

Account 1: $2,000

Account 2: $3,000

Thread 1: Transfer $3,000 from Account 1 to Account 2

Thread 2: Transfer $4,000 from Account 2 to Account 1

As Figure 1–9 indicates, Threads 1 and 2 are clearly blocked. Neither can proceed because the balances in Accounts 1 and 2 are insufficient.

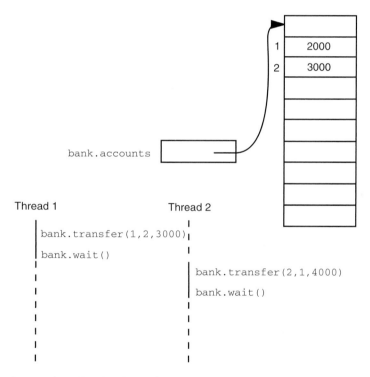

Figure 1–9: A deadlock situation

Is it possible that all 10 threads are blocked because each is waiting for more money? Such a situation is called a *deadlock*.

In our program, a deadlock cannot occur for a simple reason. Each transfer amount is for, at most, $10,000. Since there are 10 accounts and a total of $100,000 in them, at least one of the accounts must have more than $10,000 at any time. The thread moving money out of that account can therefore proceed.

But if you change the `run` method of the threads to remove the $10,000 transaction limit, deadlocks can occur quickly. Try it out. Construct each `TransferThread` with a `maxAmount` of 14000 and run the program. The program will run for a while and then hang.

Another way to create a deadlock is to make the `i`'th thread responsible for putting money into the `i`'th account, rather than for taking it out of the `i`'th account. In this case, there is a chance that all threads will gang up on one account, each trying to remove more money from it than it contains. Try it out. In the `SynchBankTest` program, turn to the `run` method of the `TransferThread` class. In the call to `transfer`, flip `fromAccount` and `toAccount`. Run the program and see how it deadlocks almost immediately.

Here is another situation in which a deadlock can occur easily: Change the `notifyAll` method to `notify` in the `SynchBankTest` program. You will find that the program hangs quickly. Unlike `notifyAll`, which notifies all threads that are waiting for added funds, the `notify` method unblocks only one thread. If that thread can't proceed, all threads can be blocked. Consider the following sample scenario of a developing deadlock.

> Account 1: $19,000
>
> All other accounts: $9,000 each
>
> Thread 1: Transfer $9,500 from Account 1 to Account 2
>
> All other threads: Transfer $9,100 from their account to another account

Clearly, all threads but Thread 1 are blocked, because there isn't enough money in their accounts.

Thread 1 proceeds. Afterward, we have the following situation:

> Account 1: $9,500
>
> Account 2: $18,500
>
> All other accounts: $9,000 each

Then, Thread 1 calls `notify`. The `notify` method picks a thread at random to unblock. Suppose it picks Thread 3. That thread is awakened, finds that there isn't enough money in its account, and calls `wait` again. But Thread 1 is still running. A new random transaction is generated, say,

> Thread 1: Transfer $9,600 to from Account 1 to Account 2

Now, Thread 1 also calls `wait`, and *all* threads are blocked. The system has deadlocked.

The culprit here is the call to `notify`. It only unblocks one thread, and it may not pick the thread that is essential to make progress. (In our scenario, Thread 2 must proceed to take money out of Account 2.) In contrast, `notifyAll` unblocks all threads.

Unfortunately, there is nothing in the Java programming language to avoid or break these deadlocks. You must design your threads to ensure that a deadlock situation cannot occur. You need to analyze your program and ensure that every blocked thread will eventually be notified, and that at least one of them can always proceed.

CAUTION: You should avoid *blocking* calls inside a synchronized method, for example a call to an I/O operation. If the thread blocks while holding the object lock, every other thread calling a synchronized method on the same object also blocks. If eventually all other threads call a synchronized method on that object, then all threads are blocked and deadlock results. This is called a "black hole." (Think of someone staying in a phone booth for a very long time, and everyone else waiting outside instead of doing useful work.)

Some programmers find Java thread synchronization overly deadlock-prone because they are accustomed to different mechanisms that don't translate well to Java. Simply trying to turn semaphores into a nested mess of synchronized blocks can indeed be a recipe for disaster. Our advice, if you get stuck with a deadlock problem, is to step back and ask yourself what communication pattern between threads you want to achieve. Then create another class for that purpose. That's the Object-Oriented way, and it often helps disentangle the logic of multithreaded programs.

Why the `stop` and `suspend` Methods Are Deprecated

The Java 1.0 platform defined a `stop` method that simply terminates a thread, and a `suspend` method that blocks a thread until another thread calls `resume`. Both of these methods have been deprecated in the Java 2 platform. The `stop` method is inherently unsafe, and experience has shown that the `suspend` method frequently leads to deadlocks. In this section, you will see why these methods are problematic and what you can do to avoid problems.

Let us turn to the `stop` method first. When a thread is stopped, it immediately gives up the locks on all objects that it has locked. This can leave objects in an inconsistent state. For example, suppose a `TransferThread` is stopped in the middle of moving money from one account to another, after the withdrawal and before the deposit. Now the bank object is *damaged*. That damage is observable from the other threads that have not been stopped.

CAUTION: Technically speaking, the `stop` method causes the thread to be stopped to throw an exception object of type `ThreadDeath`. This exception terminates all pending methods, including the `run` method.

For the same reason, *any* uncaught exception in a synchronized method can cause that method to terminate prematurely and lead to damaged objects.

When a thread wants to stop another thread, it has no way of knowing when the stop method is safe and when it leads to damaged objects. Therefore, the method has been deprecated.

> NOTE: Some authors claim that the stop method has been deprecated because it can cause objects to be permanently locked by a stopped thread. However, that is not true. A stopped thread exits all synchronized methods it has called (through the processing of the ThreadDeath exception). As a consequence, the thread relinquishes the object locks that it holds.

If you need to stop a thread safely, you can have the thread periodically check a variable that indicates whether a stop has been requested.

```
public class MyThread extends Thread
{
    public void run()
    {
        while (!stopRequested && more work to do)
        {
            do more work
        }
    }

    public void requestStop()
    {
        stopRequested = true;
    }

    private boolean stopRequested;
}
```

This code leaves the run method to control when to finish, and it is up to the run method to ensure that no objects are left in a damaged state.

Testing the stopRequested variable in the main loop of a thread work is fine, except if the thread is currently blocked. In that case, the thread will only terminate after it is unblocked. You can force a thread out of a blocked state by interrupting it. Thus, you should define the requestStop method to call interrupt:

```
public void requestStop()
{
    stopRequested = true;
    interrupt();
}
```

You can test the stopRequested variable in the catch clause for the InterruptedException. For example,

```
try
{
    wait();
}
```

```
catch (InterruptedException e)
{
    if (stopRequested)
        return; // exit the run method
}
```

Actually, many programmers take the attitude that the only reason to interrupt a thread is to stop it. Then, you don't need to test the stopRequested variable—simply exit the run method whenever you sense an interrupt.

By the way, the interrupt method does *not* generate an Interrupted-Exception when a thread is interrupted while it is working. Instead, it simply sets the "interrupted" flag. That way, interrupting a thread cannot corrupt object data. It is up to the thread to check the "interrupted" flag after all critical calculations have been completed.

Next, let us see what is wrong with the suspend method. Unlike stop, suspend won't damage objects. However, if you suspend a thread that owns a lock to an object, then the object is unavailable until the thread is resumed. If the thread that calls the suspend method tries to acquire the lock for the same object before calling resume, then the program deadlocks: the suspended thread waits to be resumed, and the suspending thread waits for the object to be unlocked.

This situation occurs frequently in graphical user interfaces. Suppose we have a graphical simulation of our bank. We have a button labeled "Pause" that suspends the transfer threads, and a button labeled "Resume" that resumes them.

```
pauseButton.addActionListener(new
    ActionListener()
    {
        public void actionPerformed(ActionEvent event)
        {
            for (int i = 0; i < threads.length; i++)
                threads[i].suspend(); // Don't do this
        }
    });
resumeButton.addActionListener(new
    ActionListener()
    {
        public void actionPerformed(ActionEvent event)
        {
            for (int i = 0; i < threads.length; i++)
                threads[i].resume(); // Don't do this
        }
    });
```

Suppose a paintComponent method paints a chart of each account, calling the bank.getBalance method, and that method is synchronized.

As you will see in the next section, both the button actions and the repainting occur in the same thread, the *event dispatch thread*.

Now consider the following scenario:

1. One of the transfer threads acquires the lock on the bank object.
2. The user clicks the "Pause" button.
3. All transfer threads are suspended; one of them still holds the lock on the bank object.
4. For some reason, the account chart needs to be repainted.
5. The paintComponent method calls the synchronized method bank.getBalance.

Now the program is frozen.

The event dispatch thread can't proceed because the bank object is locked by one of the suspended threads. Thus, the user can't click the "Resume" button, and the threads won't ever resume.

If you want to safely suspend the thread, you should introduce a variable suspendRequested and test it in a safe place of your run method—somewhere, where your thread doesn't lock objects that other threads need. When your thread finds that the suspendRequested variable has been set, keep waiting until it becomes available again.

For greater clarity, wrap the variable in a class SuspendRequestor, like this:

```
class SuspendRequestor
{
   public synchronized void set(boolean b)
   {
      suspendRequested = b;
      notifyAll();
   }

   public synchronized void waitForResume()
      throws InterruptedException
   {
      while (suspendRequested)
         wait();
   }

   private boolean suspendRequested;
}

class MyThread extends Thread
{
   public void requestSuspend()
   {
      suspender.set(true);
   }
```

```
   public void requestResume()
   {
      suspender.set(false);
   }

   public void run()
   {
      try
      {
         while (more work to do)
         {
            suspender.waitForResume();
            do more work
         }
      }
      catch (InterruptedException exception)
      {
      }
   }

   private SuspendRequestor suspender
      = new SuspendRequestor();
}
```

Now the call to `suspender.waitForResume()` blocks when suspension has been requested. To unblock, some other thread has to request resumption.

NOTE: Some programmers don't want to come up with a new class for such a simple mechanism. But they still need some object on which to synchronize, because the waiting thread needs to be added to the wait list of some object. It is possible to use a separate dummy variable, like this:

```
class MyThread extends Thread
{

   public void requestSuspend()
   {
      suspendRequested = true;
   }
   public void requestResume()
   {
      suspendRequested = false;
      synchronized (dummy)
      {
         dummy.notifyAll();
         // unblock the thread waiting on dummy
      }
   }

   private void waitForResume()
      throws InterruptedException
   {
```

```
        synchronized (dummy)
          // synchronized necessary for calling wait
        {
          while (suspendRequested)
              dummy.wait(); // block this thread
        }
      }

      . . .
      private boolean suspendRequested;
      private Integer dummy = new Integer(1);
          // any non-null object will work
    }
```

We don't like this coding style. It is just as easy to supply an additional class. Then the lock is naturally associated with that class, and you avoid the confusion that arises when you hijack an object just for its lock and wait list.

Of course, avoiding the Thread.suspend method does not automatically avoid deadlocks. If a thread calls wait, it might not wake up either. But there is an essential difference. A thread can control when it calls wait. But the Thread.suspend method can be invoked *externally* on a thread, at any time, without the thread's consent. The same is true for the Thread.stop method. For that reason, these two methods have been deprecated.

NOTE: In this section, we defined methods requestStop, requestSuspend, and requestResume. These methods provide functionality that is similar to the deprecated stop, suspend, and resume methods, while avoiding the risks of those deprecated methods. You will find that many programmers implement similar methods, but instead of giving them different names, they simply *override* the stop, suspend, and resume methods. It is entirely legal to override a deprecated method with another method that is not deprecated. If you see a call to stop, suspend, or resume in a program, you should not automatically assume that the program is wrong. First check whether the programmer overrode the deprecated methods with safer versions.

Timeouts

When you make a blocking call, such as a call to the wait method or to I/O, your thread loses control and is at the mercy of another thread or, in the case of I/O, external circumstances. You can limit that risk by using timeouts.

There are two wait methods with timeout parameters:

```
void wait(long millis)
void wait(long millis, int nanos)
```

that wait until the thread is awakened by a call to notifyAll/notify or for the given number of milliseconds, or milliseconds and nanoseconds—there are 1,000,000 nanoseconds in a millisecond.

However, when the `wait` method returns, you don't know whether the cause was a timeout or a notification. You probably want to know—there is no point in reevaluating the condition for which you were waiting if there was no notification.

You can compute the difference of the system time before and after the call:

```
long before = System.currentTimeMillis();
wait(delay);
long after = System.currentTimeMills();
if (after - before > delay)
    . . . // timeout
```

Alternatively, you can make the notifying thread set a flag.

A thread can also block indefinitely when calling an I/O operation that doesn't have a timeout. For example, as you will see in Chapter 3, to open a network socket, you need to call the socket constructor, and it doesn't have a provision for a timeout. You can always force a timeout by putting the blocking operation into a second thread, and then use the `join` method. The call

```
t.join(millis);
```

blocks the current thread until the thread `t` has completed or the given number of milliseconds has elapsed, whichever occurs first. Use this outline:

```
Thread t = new
    Thread()
    {
        public void run()
        {
            blocking operation
        }
    };
t.start();
t.join(millis);
```

The blocking operation either succeeds within the given number of milliseconds, or the `join` method returns control to the current thread. Of course, then the thread `t` is still alive. What to do about that depends on the nature of the blocking operation. If you know that the operation can be interrupted, you can call `t.interrupt()` to stop it. In the case of an I/O operation, you may know that there is an operating-system-dependent timeout. In that case, just leave `t` alive until the timeout occurs and the blocking operation returns. See the `SocketOpener` in Chapter 3 for a typical example.

java.lang.Thread

- void wait(long millis)
- void wait(long millis, int nanos)

causes a thread to wait until it is notified or until the specified amount of time has passed. This method can only be called from within a synchronized method. It throws an `IllegalMonitorStateException` if the current thread is not the owner of the object's lock.

Parameters: `millis`   the number of milliseconds

                 `nanos`   the number of nanoseconds, < 1,000,000

- `void join()`
  waits for the specified thread to cease to be alive.

- `void join(long millis)`
  waits for the specified thread to cease to be alive or for the specified number of milliseconds to pass.

Parameters: `millis`   the number of milliseconds

User Interface Programming with Threads

In the following sections, we discuss threading issues that are of particular interest to user interface programming.

Threads and Swing

As we mentioned in the introduction, one of the reasons to use threads in your programs is to make your programs more responsive. When your program needs to do something time-consuming, then you should fire up another worker thread instead of blocking the user interface.

However, you have to be careful what you do in a worker thread because, perhaps surprisingly, Swing is *not thread safe*. That is, the majority of methods of Swing classes are not synchronized. If you try to manipulate user interface elements from multiple threads, then your user interface will become corrupted.

For example, run the test program whose code you will find at the end of this section. When you click on the "Bad" button, a new thread is started that edits a combo box, randomly adding and removing values.

```java
class BadWorkerThread extends Thread
{
   public BadWorkerThread(JComboBox aCombo)
   {
      combo = aCombo;
      generator = new Random();
   }

   public void run()
   {
      try
      {
         while (!interrupted())
         {
```

```
            int i = Math.abs(generator.nextInt());
            if (i % 2 == 0)
                combo.insertItemAt(new Integer(i), 0);
            else if (combo.getItemCount() > 0)
                combo.removeItemAt(i % combo.getItemCount());

            sleep(1);
         }
      }
      catch (InterruptedException exception) {}
   }

   private JComboBox combo;
   private Random generator;
}
```

Try it out. Click on the "Bad" button. If you start the program from a console window, you will see an occasional exception report in the console (see Figure 1–10).

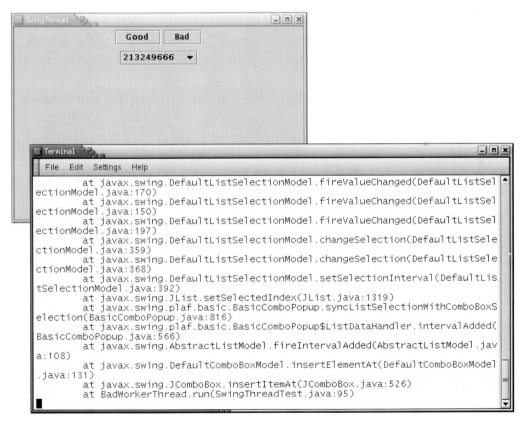

Figure 1–10: Exception reports in the console

What is going on? When an element is inserted into the combo box, the combo box fires an event to update the display. Then, the display code springs into action, reading the current size of the combo box and preparing to display the values. But the worker thread keeps on going, which can occasionally result in a reduction of the count of the values in the combo box. The display code then thinks that there are more values in the model than there actually are, asks for nonexistent values, and triggers an `ArrayIndex-OutOfBounds` exception.

This situation could have been avoided by locking the combo box object while displaying it. However, the designers of Swing decided not to expend any effort to make Swing thread safe, for two reasons. First, synchronization takes time, and nobody wanted to slow down Swing any further. More importantly, the Swing team checked out what experience other teams had with thread-safe user interface toolkits. What they found was not encouraging. When building a user interface toolkit, you want it to be extensible so that other programmers can add their own user interface components. But user interface programmers using thread-safe toolkits turned out to be confused by the demands for synchronization and tended to create components that were prone to deadlocks.

Therefore, when you use threads together with Swing, you have to follow a few simple rules. First, however, let's see what threads are present in a Swing program.

Every Java application starts with a `main` method that runs in the *main thread*. In a Swing program, the `main` method typically does the following:

- First it calls a constructor that lays out components in a frame window;

- then it invokes the `show` or `setVisible` method on the window.

When the first window is shown, a second thread is created, the *event dispatch thread*. All event notifications, such as calls to `actionPerformed` or `paintComponent`, run in the event dispatch thread. The main thread keeps running until the `main` method exits. Usually, of course, the `main` method exits immediately after displaying the frame window (see Figure 1–11). Other threads are running behind the scenes, such as the thread that posts events into the event queue, but those threads are invisible to the application programmer.

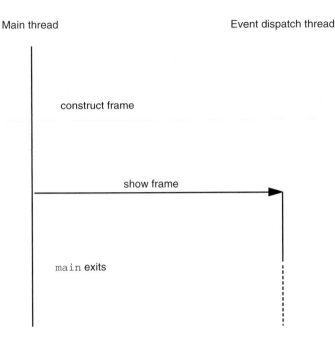

Figure 1-11: Threads in a Swing program

In a Swing application, essentially all code is contained in event handlers to respond to user interface and repaint requests. All that code runs on the event dispatch thread. Here are the rules that you need to follow.

1.   If an action takes a long time, fire up a new thread to do the work. If you take a long time in the event dispatch thread, the application seems "dead" since it cannot respond to any events.

2.   If an action can block on input or output, fire up a new thread to do the work. You don't want to freeze the user interface for the potentially indefinite time that a network connection is unresponsive.

3.   If you need to wait for a specific amount of time, don't sleep in the event dispatch thread. Instead, use a timer.

4.   The work that you do in your threads cannot touch the user interface. Read any information from the UI before you launch your threads, launch them, and then update the user interface from the event dispatching thread once the threads have completed.

The last rule is often called the *single thread rule* for Swing programming. There are a few exceptions to the single thread rule.

1. A few Swing methods are thread safe. They are specially marked in the API documentation with the sentence *"This method is thread safe, although most Swing methods are not."* The most useful among these thread-safe methods are:

   ```
   JTextComponent.setText
   JTextArea.insert
   JTextArea.append
   JTextArea.replaceRange
   ```

2. The following methods of the `JComponent` class can be called from any thread:

   ```
   repaint
   revalidate
   ```

   The `repaint` method schedules a repaint event. You use the `revalidate` method if the contents of a component have changed and the size and position of the component must be updated. The `revalidate` method marks the component's layout as invalid and schedules a layout event. (Just like paint events, layout events are *coalesced*. If there are multiple layout events in the event queue, the layout is only recomputed once.)

NOTE: We have used the `repaint` method many times in volume 1 of this book, but the `revalidate` method is less common. Its purpose is to force a layout of a component after the contents has changed. The traditional AWT has `invalidate` and `validate` methods to mark a component's layout as invalid and to force the layout of a component. For Swing components, you should simply call `revalidate` instead. (However, to force the layout of a `JFrame`, you still need to call `validate`—a `JFrame` is a `Component` but not a `JComponent`.)

3. You can safely add and remove event listeners in any thread. Of course, the `listener` methods will be invoked in the event dispatching thread.

4. You can construct components, set their properties, and add them into containers, as long as none of the components have been *realized*. A component has been realized if it can receive paint or validation events. This is the case as soon as the `show`, `setVisible(true)`, or `pack` methods have been invoked on the component, or if the component has been added to a container that has been realized. Once a component has been realized, you can no longer manipulate it from another thread.

   In particular, you can create the GUI of an application in the `main` method before calling `show`, and you can create the GUI of an applet in the applet constructor or the `init` method.

These rules look complex, but they aren't actually difficult to follow. It is an easy matter to start a new thread to start a time-consuming process. Upon a user request, gather all the necessary information from the GUI, pass them to a thread, and start the thread.

```
public void actionPerformed(ActionEvent e)
{
    // gather data needed by thread
    MyThread t = new MyThread(data);
    t.start();
}
```

The difficult part is to update the GUI to indicate progress within your thread and to present the result of the work when your thread is finished. Remember that you can't touch any Swing components from your thread. For example, if you want to update a progress bar or a label text, then you can't simply set its value from your thread.

To solve this problem, there are two convenient utility methods that you can use in any thread to add arbitrary actions to the event queue. For example, suppose you want to periodically update a label "x% complete" in a thread, to indicate progress. You can't call label.setText from your thread, but you can use the invokeLater and invokeAndWait methods of the EventQueue class to have that call executed in the event dispatching thread.

NOTE: These methods are also available in the javax.swing.SwingUtilities class. If you use Swing with Java Development Kit (JDK) 1.1, you need to use that class—the methods were added to EventQueue in JDK 1.2.

Here is what you need to do. You place the Swing code into the run method of a class that implements the Runnable interface. Then, you create an object of that class and pass it to the static invokeLater or invokeAndWait method. For example, here is how you can update a label text. First, create the class with the run method.

```
public class LabelUpdater implements Runnable
{
    public LabelUpdater(JLabel aLabel, int aPercentage)
    {
        label = aLabel;
        percentage = aPercentage;
    }

    public void run()
    {
        label.setText(percentage + "% complete");
    }
}
```

Then, create an object and pass it to the invokeLater method.

```
Runnable updater = new LabelUpdater(label, percentage);
EventQueue.invokeLater(updater);
```

The `invokeLater` method returns immediately when the event is posted to the event queue. The `run` method is executed asynchronously. The `invokeAndWait` method waits until the `run` method has actually been executed. The `EventQueue` class handles the details of the synchronization. In the situation of updating a progress label, the `invokeLater` method is more appropriate. Users would rather have the worker thread make more progress than insist on the most precise display of the completed percentage.

To invoke code in the event dispatch thread, anonymous inner classes offer a useful shortcut. For example, the sample code given above can be simplified to the following cryptic, but shorter, command:

```
EventQueue.invokeLater(new
    Runnable()
    {
        public void run()
        {
            label.setText(percentage + "% complete");
        }
    });
```

NOTE: The `invokeLater` and `invokeAndWait` methods use objects that implement the `Runnable` interface. You already saw how to construct new threads out of `Runnable` objects. However, in this case, the code of the `run` method executes in the event dispatching thread, not a new thread.

Example 1–7 demonstrates how to use the `invokeLater` method to safely modify the contents of a combo box. If you click on the "Good" button, a thread inserts and removes numbers. However, the actual modification takes place in the event dispatching thread.

Example 1–7: SwingThreadTest.java

```
 1. import java.awt.*;
 2. import java.awt.event.*;
 3. import java.util.*;
 4. import javax.swing.*;
 5.
 6. /**
 7.    This program demonstrates that a thread that
 8.    runs in parallel with the event dispatch thread
 9.    can cause errors in Swing components.
10. */
11. public class SwingThreadTest
```

```
12. {
13.    public static void main(String[] args)
14.    {
15.        SwingThreadFrame frame = new SwingThreadFrame();
16.        frame.setDefaultCloseOperation(JFrame.EXIT_ON_CLOSE);
17.        frame.show();
18.    }
19. }
20.
21. /**
22.    This frame has two buttons to fill a combo box from a
23.    separate thread. The "Good" button uses the event queue,
24.    the "Bad" button modifies the combo box directly.
25. */
26. class SwingThreadFrame extends JFrame
27. {
28.    public SwingThreadFrame()
29.    {
30.        setTitle("SwingThread");
31.        setSize(WIDTH, HEIGHT);
32.
33.        final JComboBox combo = new JComboBox();
34.
35.        JPanel p = new JPanel();
36.        p.add(combo);
37.        getContentPane().add(p, BorderLayout.CENTER);
38.
39.        JButton b = new JButton("Good");
40.        b.addActionListener(new ActionListener()
41.            {
42.                public void actionPerformed(ActionEvent event)
43.                {
44.                    combo.showPopup();
45.                    new GoodWorkerThread(combo).start();
46.                }
47.            });
48.        p = new JPanel();
49.        p.add(b);
50.        b = new JButton("Bad");
51.        b.addActionListener(new ActionListener()
52.            {
53.                public void actionPerformed(ActionEvent event)
54.                {
55.                    combo.showPopup();
56.                    new BadWorkerThread(combo).start();
57.                }
58.            });
59.        p.add(b);
```

```
60.
61.         getContentPane().add(p, BorderLayout.NORTH);
62.     }
63.
64.     public static final int WIDTH = 450;
65.     public static final int HEIGHT = 300;
66. }
67.
68. /**
69.     This thread modifies a combo box by randomly adding
70.     and removing numbers. This can result in errors because
71.     the combo box is not synchronized and the event dispatch
72.     thread accesses the combo box to repaint it.
73. */
74. class BadWorkerThread extends Thread
75. {
76.     public BadWorkerThread(JComboBox aCombo)
77.     {
78.         combo = aCombo;
79.         generator = new Random();
80.     }
81.
82.     public void run()
83.     {
84.         try
85.         {
86.             while (!interrupted())
87.             {
88.                 int i = Math.abs(generator.nextInt());
89.                 if (i % 2 == 0)
90.                     combo.insertItemAt(new Integer(i), 0);
91.                 else if (combo.getItemCount() > 0)
92.                     combo.removeItemAt(i % combo.getItemCount());
93.
94.                 sleep(1);
95.             }
96.         }
97.         catch (InterruptedException exception) {}
98.     }
99.
100.    private JComboBox combo;
101.    private Random generator;
102. }
103.
104. /**
105.     This thread modifies a combo box by randomly adding
106.     and removing numbers. In order to ensure that the
107.     combo box is not corrupted, the editing operations are
108.     forwarded to the event dispatch thread.
```

```
109. */
110. class GoodWorkerThread extends Thread
111. {
112.     public GoodWorkerThread(JComboBox aCombo)
113.     {
114.         combo = aCombo;
115.         generator = new Random();
116.     }
117.
118.     public void run()
119.     {
120.         try
121.         {
122.             while (!interrupted())
123.             {
124.                 EventQueue.invokeLater(new
125.                     Runnable()
126.                     {
127.                         public void run()
128.                         {
129.                             int i = Math.abs(generator.nextInt());
130.
131.                             if (i % 2 == 0)
132.                                 combo.insertItemAt(new Integer(i), 0);
133.                             else if (combo.getItemCount() > 0)
134.                                 combo.removeItemAt(i % combo.getItemCount());
135.                         }
136.                     });
137.                 Thread.sleep(1);
138.             }
139.         }
140.         catch (InterruptedException exception) {}
141.     }
142.
143.     private JComboBox combo;
144.     private Random generator;
145. }
```

java.awt.EventQueue

- `static void invokeLater(Runnable runnable)`
  Causes the `run` method of the `runnable` object to be executed in the event dispatch thread, after pending events have been processed.

- `static void invokeAndWait(Runnable runnable)`
  Causes the `run` method of the `runnable` object to be executed in the event dispatch thread, after pending events have been processed. This call blocks until the `run` method has terminated.

Animation

In this section, we dissect one of the most common uses for threads in applets: animation. An animation sequence displays images, giving the viewer the illusion of motion. Each of the images in the sequence is called a *frame*. If the frames are complex, they should be rendered ahead of time—the computer running the applet may not have the horsepower to compute images fast enough for real-time animation.

You can put each frame in a separate image file or put all frames into one file. We do the latter. It makes the process of loading the image much easier. In our example, we use a file with 36 images of a rotating globe, courtesy of Silviu Marghescu of the University of Maryland. Figure 1–12 shows the first few frames.

The animation applet must first acquire all the frames. Then, it shows each of them in turn for a fixed time. To draw the i'th frame, we make a method call as follows:

```
g.drawImage(image, 0, - i * imageHeight
    / imageCount, null);
```

Figure 1–13 shows the *negative* offset of the y-coordinate.

This offset causes the first frame to be well above the origin of the canvas. The top of the i'th frame becomes the top of the canvas. After a delay, we increment i and draw the next frame.

We use a MediaTracker object to load the image. Behind the scenes and transparent to the programmer, the addImage method fires up a new thread to acquire the image. Loading an image can be very slow, especially if the image has many frames or is located across the network. The waitForID call blocks until the image is fully loaded.

Figure 1–12: This file has 36 images

NOTE: Readers who are familiar with the SDK 1.4 image I/O package may wonder why we don't use ImageIO.read to read the image. That method creates a temporary file—an operation that is not legal for an applet in the sandbox.

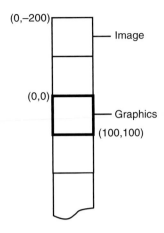

Figure 1–13: Picking a frame from a strip of frames

Once the image is loaded, we render one frame at a time. Our applet starts a single thread.

```
class Animation extends JApplet
{
    . . .
    private Thread runner = null;
}
```

You will see such a thread variable in many applets. Often, it is called `kicker`, and we once saw `killer` as the variable name. We think `runner` makes more sense, though.

First and foremost, we will use this thread to:

- Start the animation when the user is watching the applet;

- Stop the animation when the user has switched to a different page in the browser.

We do these tasks by creating the thread in the `start` method of the applet and by interrupting it in the `stop` method.

```
class Animation extends JApplet
{
    public void start()
    {
        if (runner == null)
        {
            runner = new
                Thread()
                {
                    public void run()
                    {
                        . . .
```

```
                }
            };
            runner.start();
        }
    }

    public void stop()
    {
        runner.interrupt();
        runner = null;
    }
    . . .
}
```

Here is the run method. It simply loops, painting the screen, advancing the frame counter, and sleeping when it can.

```
public void run()
{
    try
    {
        while (!Thread.interrupted())
        {
            repaint();
            current = (current + 1) % imageCount;
            Thread.sleep(200);
        }
    }
    catch(InterruptedException e) {}
}
```

Finally, we implement another mechanism for stopping and restarting the animation. When you click the mouse on the applet window, the animation stops. When you click again, it restarts. Note that we use the thread variable, runner, as an indication whether the thread is currently running or not. Whenever the thread is terminated, the variable is set to null. This is a common idiom that you will find in many multithreaded applets.

```
public void init()
{
    addMouseListener(new
        MouseAdapter()
        {
            public void mousePressed(MouseEvent evt)
            {
                if (runner == null)
                    start();
                else
```

```
                        stop();
                }
            });


        . . .

    }
```

The applet reads the name of the image and the number of frames in the strip from the `param` section in the HTML file.

```
<applet code=Animation.class width=100 height=100>
<param name=imagename value="globe.gif">
<param name=imagecount value="36">
</applet>
```

Example 1–8 is the code of the applet. Note that the `start` and `stop` methods start and stop the applet—they are *not* methods of the thread that is generated.

This animation applet is simplified to show you what goes on behind the scenes, and to help you understand other applets with a similar structure. If you are interested only in how to put a moving image on your web page, look instead at the `Animator` applet in the demo section of the JDK. That applet has many more options than ours, and it enables you to add sound.

Furthermore, as you will see in the next section, you really don't need to implement your own threads for a simple animation—you can just use a Swing timer.

Example 1–8: Animation.java

```
1. import java.awt.*;
2. import java.awt.image.*;
3. import java.awt.event.*;
4. import javax.swing.*;
5. import java.net.*;
6.
7. /**
8.    An applet that shows a rotating globe.
9. */
10. public class Animation extends JApplet
11. {
12.     public void init()
13.     {
14.         addMouseListener(new MouseAdapter()
15.             {
16.                 public void mousePressed(MouseEvent evt)
17.                 {
18.                     if (runner == null)
19.                         start();
20.                     else
```

```
21.                      stop();
22.                 }
23.             });
24.
25.         try
26.         {
27.             String imageName = getParameter("imagename");
28.             imageCount = 1;
29.             String param = getParameter("imagecount");
30.             if (param != null)
31.                 imageCount = Integer.parseInt(param);
32.             current = 0;
33.             image = null;
34.             loadImage(new URL(getDocumentBase(), imageName));
35.         }
36.         catch (Exception e)
37.         {
38.             showStatus("Error: " + e);
39.         }
40.     }
41.
42.     /**
43.         Loads an image.
44.         @param url the URL of the image file
45.     */
46.     public void loadImage(URL url)
47.         throws InterruptedException
48.             // thrown by MediaTracker.waitFor
49.     {
50.         image = getImage(url);
51.         MediaTracker tracker = new MediaTracker(this);
52.         tracker.addImage(image, 0);
53.         tracker.waitForID(0);
54.         imageWidth = image.getWidth(null);
55.         imageHeight = image.getHeight(null);
56.         resize(imageWidth, imageHeight / imageCount);
57.     }
58.
59.     public void paint(Graphics g)
60.     {
61.         if (image == null) return;
62.         g.drawImage(image, 0, - (imageHeight / imageCount)
63.             * current, null);
64.     }
65.
66.     public void start()
67.     {
```

```
68.        runner = new
69.           Thread()
70.              {
71.                 public void run()
72.                    {
73.                       try
74.                       {
75.                          while (!Thread.interrupted())
76.                          {
77.                             repaint();
78.                             current = (current + 1) % imageCount;
79.                             Thread.sleep(200);
80.                          }
81.                       }
82.                       catch(InterruptedException e) {}
83.                    }
84.              };
85.        runner.start();
86.        showStatus("Click to stop");
87.     }
88.
89.     public void stop()
90.     {
91.        runner.interrupt();
92.        runner = null;
93.        showStatus("Click to restart");
94.     }
95.
96.     private Image image;
97.     private int current;
98.     private int imageCount;
99.     private int imageWidth;
100.    private int imageHeight;
101.    private Thread runner;
102. }
```

Timers

In many programming environments, you can set up timers. A timer alerts your program elements at regular intervals. For example, to display a clock in a window, the clock object must be notified once every second.

Swing has a built-in timer class that is easy to use. You construct a timer by supplying an object of a class that implements the ActionListener interface and the delay between timer alerts, in milliseconds.

```
Timer t = new Timer(1000, listener);
```

Call

```
t.start();
```

to start the timer. Then, the `actionPerformed` method of the listener class is called whenever a timer interval has elapsed. The `actionPerformed` method is automatically called on the event dispatch thread, not the timer thread, so that you can freely invoke `Swing` methods in the callback.

To stop the timer, call

```
t.stop();
```

Then the timer stops sending action events until you restart it.

> NOTE: SDK 1.3 has an unrelated `java.util.Timer` class to schedule a `TimerTask` for later execution. The `TimerTask` class implements the `Runnable` interface and also supplies a `cancel` method to cancel the task. However, the `java.util.Timer` class has no provision for a periodic callback.

The example program at the end of this section puts the Swing timer to work. Figure 1–4 shows six different clocks.

Figure 1–14: Clock threads

Each clock is an instance of the `ClockCanvas` class. The constructor sets up the timer:

```
public ClockCanvas(String tz)
{
   calendar = new GregorianCalendar(TimeZone.getTimeZone(tz));
   Timer t = new Timer(1000, new
      ActionListener()
```

```
                {
                    public void actionPerformed(ActionEvent event)
                    {
                        calendar.setTime(new Date());
                        repaint();
                    }
                });
            t.start();
            . . .

        }
```

The `actionPerformed` method of the timer's anonymous action listener gets called approximately once per second. It calls `new Date()` to get the current time and repaints the clock.

As you can see, no thread programming is required at all in this case. The Swing timer takes care of the thread details. We could have used a timer for the animation of the preceding section as well.

You will find the complete code in Example 1–9.

Example 1–9: TimerTest.java

```
1. import java.awt.*;
2. import java.awt.event.*;
3. import javax.swing.*;
4. import java.util.*;
5. import javax.swing.Timer;
6.
7. /**
8.    This class shows a frame with several clocks that
9.    are updated by a timer thread.
10. */
11. public class TimerTest
12. {
13.    public static void main(String[] args)
14.    {
15.       TimerTestFrame frame = new TimerTestFrame();
16.       frame.setDefaultCloseOperation(JFrame.EXIT_ON_CLOSE);
17.       frame.show();
18.    }
19. }
20.
21. /**
22.    The frame holding the clocks.
23. */
24. class TimerTestFrame extends JFrame
25. {
26.    public TimerTestFrame()
```

```
27.    {
28.        setTitle("TimerTest");
29.        setSize(WIDTH, HEIGHT);
30.
31.        Container c = getContentPane();
32.        c.setLayout(new GridLayout(2, 3));
33.        c.add(new ClockCanvas("America/Los_Angeles"));
34.        c.add(new ClockCanvas("America/New_York"));
35.        c.add(new ClockCanvas("America/Caracas"));
36.        c.add(new ClockCanvas("Europe/Rome"));
37.        c.add(new ClockCanvas("Africa/Cairo"));
38.        c.add(new ClockCanvas("Asia/Taipei"));
39.    }
40.
41.    public static final int WIDTH = 450;
42.    public static final int HEIGHT = 300;
43. }
44.
45. /**
46.    The canvas to display a clock that is updated by a timer.
47. */
48. class ClockCanvas extends JPanel
49. {
50.    /**
51.        Constructs a clock canvas.
52.        @param tz the time zone string
53.    */
54.    public ClockCanvas(String tz)
55.    {
56.        zone = tz;
57.        calendar = new GregorianCalendar(TimeZone.getTimeZone(tz));
58.        Timer t = new Timer(1000, new
59.            ActionListener()
60.            {
61.                public void actionPerformed(ActionEvent event)
62.                {
63.                    calendar.setTime(new Date());
64.                    repaint();
65.                }
66.            });
67.        t.start();
68.        setSize(WIDTH, HEIGHT);
69.    }
70.
71.    public void paintComponent(Graphics g)
72.    {
73.        super.paintComponent(g);
74.        g.drawOval(0, 0, 100, 100);
```

```
75.
76.          int seconds = calendar.get(Calendar.HOUR) * 60 * 60
77.             + calendar.get(Calendar.MINUTE) * 60
78.             + calendar.get(Calendar.SECOND);
79.          double hourAngle = 2 * Math.PI
80.             * (seconds - 3 * 60 * 60) / (12 * 60 * 60);
81.          double minuteAngle = 2 * Math.PI
82.             * (seconds - 15 * 60) / (60 * 60);
83.          double secondAngle = 2 * Math.PI
84.             * (seconds - 15) / 60;
85.          g.drawLine(50, 50, 50 + (int)(30
86.             * Math.cos(hourAngle)),
87.             50 + (int)(30 * Math.sin(hourAngle)));
88.          g.drawLine(50, 50, 50 + (int)(40
89.             * Math.cos(minuteAngle)),
90.             50 + (int)(40 * Math.sin(minuteAngle)));
91.          g.drawLine(50, 50, 50 + (int)(45
92.             * Math.cos(secondAngle)),
93.             50 + (int)(45 * Math.sin(secondAngle)));
94.          g.drawString(zone, 0, 115);
95.       }
96.
97.       private String zone;
98.       private GregorianCalendar calendar;
99.
100.      public static final int WIDTH = 125;
101.      public static final int HEIGHT = 125;
102. }
```

javax.swing.Timer

- `Timer(int delay, ActionListener listener)`
  Creates a new timer that sends events to a listener.

  Parameters: `delay`   the delay, in milliseconds, between event notifications

               `listener`   the action listener to be notified when the delay has elapsed

- `void start()`
  Start the timer. After this call, the timer starts sending events to its action listener.

- `void stop()`
  Stop the timer. After this call, the timer stops sending events to its action listener.

Progress Bars

A *progress bar* is a simple component—just a rectangle that is partially filled with color to indicate the progress of an operation. By default, progress is indicated by a string *"n %"*. You can see a progress bar in the bottom right of Figure 1–15.

Figure 1–15: A progress bar

You construct a progress bar much as you construct a slider, by supplying the minimum and maximum value and an optional orientation:

```
progressBar = new JProgressBar(0, 1000);
progressBar = new JProgressBar(SwingConstants.VERTICAL, 0, 1000);
```

You can also set the minimum and maximum with the setMinimum and setMaximum methods.

Unlike a slider, the progress bar cannot be adjusted by the user. Your program needs to call setValue to update it.

If you call

```
progressBar.setStringPainted(true);
```

the progress bar computes the completion percentage and displays a string *"n %"*. If you want to show a different string, you can supply it with the setString method:

```
if (progressBar.getValue() > 900)
    progressBar.setString("Almost Done");
```

The program in Example 1–10 shows a progress bar that monitors a simulated time-consuming activity.

The SimulatedActivity class implements a thread that increments a value current ten times per second. When it reaches a target value, the thread finishes. If you want to terminate the thread before it has reached its target, you should interrupt it.

```
class SimulatedActivity extends Thread
{   . . .
    public void run()
    {
        try
```

```
      {
          while (current < target && !interrupted())
          {
              sleep(100);
              current++;
          }
      }
      catch(InterruptedException e)
      {
      }
   }

   int current;
   int target;
}
```

When you click on the "Start" button, a new `SimulatedActivity` thread is started. To update the progress bar, it would appear to be an easy matter for the simulated activity thread to make calls to the `setValue` method. But that is not thread safe. Recall that you should call Swing methods only from the event dispatch thread. In practice, it is also unrealistic. In general, a worker thread is not aware of the existence of the progress bar. Instead, the example program shows how to launch a timer that periodically polls the thread for a progress status and updates the progress bar.

CAUTION: If a worker thread is aware of a progress bar that monitors its progress, remember that it cannot set the progress bar value directly. To set the value in the event dispatch thread, the worker thread can use the `SwingUtilities.invokeLater` method.

Recall that a Swing timer calls the `actionPerformed` method of its listeners and that these calls occur in the event dispatch thread. That means it is safe to update Swing components in the timer callback. Here is the timer callback from the example program. The current value of the simulated activity is displayed both in the text area and the progress bar. If the end of the simulation has been reached, the timer is stopped and the "Start" button is reenabled.

```
public void actionPerformed(ActionEvent event)
{
    int current = activity.getCurrent();
    // show progress

    textArea.append(current + "\n");
    progressBar.setValue(current);

    // check if task is completed
    if (current == activity.getTarget())
    {
```

```
        activityMonitor.stop();
        startButton.setEnabled(true);
    }
}
```

Example 1–10 shows the full program code.

> NOTE: SDK 1.4 adds support for an *indeterminate* progress bar that shows an animation indicating some kind of progress, without giving an indication of the percentage of completion. That is the kind of progress bar that you see in your browser—it indicates that the browser is waiting for the server and has no idea how long the wait may be. To display the "indeterminate wait" animation, call the `setIndeterminate` method.

Example 1–10: ProgressBarTest.java

```
1. import java.awt.*;
2. import java.awt.event.*;
3. import java.util.*;
4. import javax.swing.*;
5. import javax.swing.event.*;
6. import javax.swing.Timer;
7.
8. /**
9.    This program demonstrates the use of a progress bar
10.    to monitor the progress of a thread.
11. */
12. public class ProgressBarTest
13. {
14.    public static void main(String[] args)
15.    {
16.       ProgressBarFrame frame = new ProgressBarFrame();
17.       frame.setDefaultCloseOperation(JFrame.EXIT_ON_CLOSE);
18.       frame.show();
19.    }
20. }
21.
22. /**
23.    A frame that contains a button to launch a simulated activity,
24.    a progress bar, and a text area for the activity output.
25. */
26. class ProgressBarFrame extends JFrame
27. {
28.    public ProgressBarFrame()
29.    {
30.       setTitle("ProgressBarTest");
31.       setSize(WIDTH, HEIGHT);
```

```
32.
33.        Container contentPane = getContentPane();
34.
35.        // this text area holds the activity output
36.        textArea = new JTextArea();
37.
38.        // set up panel with button and progress bar
39.
40.        JPanel panel = new JPanel();
41.        startButton = new JButton("Start");
42.        progressBar = new JProgressBar();
43.        progressBar.setStringPainted(true);
44.        panel.add(startButton);
45.        panel.add(progressBar);
46.        contentPane.add(new JScrollPane(textArea),
47.            BorderLayout.CENTER);
48.        contentPane.add(panel, BorderLayout.SOUTH);
49.
50.        // set up the button action
51.
52.        startButton.addActionListener(new
53.            ActionListener()
54.            {
55.                public void actionPerformed(ActionEvent event)
56.                {
57.                    progressBar.setMaximum(1000);
58.                    activity = new SimulatedActivity(1000);
59.                    activity.start();
60.                    activityMonitor.start();
61.                    startButton.setEnabled(false);
62.                }
63.            });
64.
65.
66.        // set up the timer action
67.
68.        activityMonitor = new Timer(500, new
69.            ActionListener()
70.            {
71.                public void actionPerformed(ActionEvent event)
72.                {
73.                    int current = activity.getCurrent();
74.
75.                    // show progress
76.                    textArea.append(current + "\n");
77.                    progressBar.setValue(current);
78.
79.                    // check if task is completed
```

```
80.                 if (current == activity.getTarget())
81.                 {
82.                     activityMonitor.stop();
83.                     startButton.setEnabled(true);
84.                 }
85.             }
86.         });
87.     }
88.
89.     private Timer activityMonitor;
90.     private JButton startButton;
91.     private JProgressBar progressBar;
92.     private JTextArea textArea;
93.     private SimulatedActivity activity;
94.
95.     public static final int WIDTH = 300;
96.     public static final int HEIGHT = 200;
97. }
98.
99. /**
100.    A simulated activity thread.
101. */
102. class SimulatedActivity extends Thread
103. {
104.    /**
105.       Constructs the simulated activity thread object. The
106.       thread increments a counter from 0 to a given target.
107.       @param t the target value of the counter.
108.    */
109.    public SimulatedActivity(int t)
110.    {
111.       current = 0;
112.       target = t;
113.    }
114.
115.    public int getTarget()
116.    {
117.       return target;
118.    }
119.
120.    public int getCurrent()
121.    {
122.       return current;
123.    }
124.
125.    public void run()
126.    {
127.       try
```

```
128.          {
129.              while (current < target && !interrupted())
130.              {
131.                  sleep(100);
132.                  current++;
133.              }
134.          }
135.          catch(InterruptedException e)
136.          {
137.          }
138.      }
139.
140.      private int current;
141.      private int target;
142. }
```

Progress Monitors

A progress bar is a very simple component that can be placed inside a window. In contrast, a `ProgressMonitor` is a complete dialog box that contains a progress bar (see Figure 1–16). The dialog contains "OK" and "Cancel" buttons. If you click either, the monitor dialog is closed. In addition, your program can query whether the user has canceled the dialog and terminate the monitored action. (Note that the class name does not start with a "J".)

Figure 1–16: A progress monitor dialog

You construct a progress monitor by supplying the following:

- The parent component over which the dialog should pop up;
- An object (which should be a string, icon, or component) that is displayed on the dialog;
- An optional note to display below the object;
- The minimum and maximum values.

However, the progress monitor cannot measure progress or cancel an activity by itself.

You still need to periodically set the progress value by calling the `setProgress` method. (This is the equivalent of the `setValue` method of the `JProgressBar` class.) As you update the progress value, you should also call the `isCanceled` method to see if the program user has clicked on the "Cancel" button.

When the monitored activity has concluded, you should call the `close` method to dismiss the dialog. You can reuse the same dialog by calling `start` again.

The example program looks very similar to that of the preceding section. We still need to launch a timer to watch over the progress of the simulated activity and update the progress monitor. Here is the timer callback.

```
public void actionPerformed(ActionEvent event)
{
   int current = activity.getCurrent();

   // show progress
   textArea.append(current + "\n");
   progressDialog.setProgress(current);

   // check if task is completed or canceled
   if (current == activity.getTarget()
      || progressDialog.isCanceled())
   {
      activityMonitor.stop();
      progressDialog.close();
      activity.interrupt();
      startButton.setEnabled(true);
   }
}
```

Note that there are two conditions for termination. The activity might have completed, or the user might have canceled it. In each of these cases, we close down:

- the timer that monitored the activity;
- the progress dialog;
- the activity itself (by interrupting the thread).

If you run the program in Example 1–11, you can observe an interesting feature of the progress monitor dialog. The dialog doesn't come up immediately. Instead, it waits a for a short interval to see if the activity has already been completed or is likely to complete in less time than it would take for the dialog to appear. You control the timing as follows. Use the `setMillisToDecidePopup` method to set the number of milliseconds to wait between the construction of the dialog object and the decision whether to show the pop-up at all. The default value is 500 milliseconds. The `setMillisToPopup` is the time that you estimate that the dialog needs to pop up. The Swing designers set this value to a default of 2 seconds.

Clearly they were mindful of the fact that Swing dialogs don't always come up as snappily as we all would like. You should probably not touch this value.

Example 1–11 shows the progress monitor in action, again measuring the progress of a simulated activity. As you can see, the progress monitor is convenient to use and only requires that you periodically query the thread that you want to monitor.

Example 1–11: ProgressMonitorTest.java

```
1. import java.awt.*;
2. import java.awt.event.*;
3. import java.util.*;
4. import javax.swing.*;
5. import javax.swing.event.*;
6. import javax.swing.Timer;
7.
8. /**
9.    A program to test a progress monitor dialog.
10. */
11. public class ProgressMonitorTest
12. {
13.    public static void main(String[] args)
14.    {
15.       JFrame frame = new ProgressMonitorFrame();
16.       frame.setDefaultCloseOperation(JFrame.EXIT_ON_CLOSE);
17.       frame.show();
18.    }
19. }
20.
21. /**
22.    A frame that contains a button to launch a simulated activity
23.    and a text area for the activity output.
24. */
25. class ProgressMonitorFrame extends JFrame
26. {
27.    public ProgressMonitorFrame()
28.    {
29.       setTitle("ProgressMonitorTest");
30.       setSize(WIDTH, HEIGHT);
31.
32.       Container contentPane = getContentPane();
33.
34.       // this text area holds the activity output
35.       textArea = new JTextArea();
36.
37.       // set up a button panel
38.       JPanel panel = new JPanel();
39.       startButton = new JButton("Start");
40.       panel.add(startButton);
```

```
41.
42.        contentPane.add(new JScrollPane(textArea),
43.           BorderLayout.CENTER);
44.        contentPane.add(panel, BorderLayout.SOUTH);
45.
46.        // set up the button action
47.
48.        startButton.addActionListener(new
49.           ActionListener()
50.           {
51.              public void actionPerformed(ActionEvent event)
52.              {
53.                 // start activity
54.                 activity = new SimulatedActivity(1000);
55.                 activity.start();
56.
57.                 // launch progress dialog
58.                 progressDialog = new ProgressMonitor(
59.                    ProgressMonitorFrame.this,
60.                    "Waiting for Simulated Activity",
61.                    null, 0, activity.getTarget());
62.
63.                 // start timer
64.                 activityMonitor.start();
65.
66.                 startButton.setEnabled(false);
67.              }
68.           });
69.
70.        // set up the timer action
71.
72.        activityMonitor = new Timer(500, new
73.           ActionListener()
74.           {
75.              public void actionPerformed(ActionEvent event)
76.              {
77.                 int current = activity.getCurrent();
78.
79.                 // show progress
80.                 textArea.append(current + "\n");
81.                 progressDialog.setProgress(current);
82.
83.                 // check if task is completed or canceled
84.                 if (current == activity.getTarget()
85.                    || progressDialog.isCanceled())
86.                 {
87.                    activityMonitor.stop();
88.                    progressDialog.close();
89.                    activity.interrupt();
```

```
90.                        startButton.setEnabled(true);
91.                    }
92.                }
93.            });
94.    }
95.
96.    private Timer activityMonitor;
97.    private JButton startButton;
98.    private ProgressMonitor progressDialog;
99.    private JTextArea textArea;
100.    private SimulatedActivity activity;
101.
102.    public static final int WIDTH = 300;
103.    public static final int HEIGHT = 200;
104. }
105.
106. /**
107.    A simulated activity thread.
108. */
109. class SimulatedActivity extends Thread
110. {
111.    /**
112.       Constructs the simulated activity thread object. The
113.       thread increments a counter from 0 to a given target.
114.       @param t the target value of the counter.
115.    */
116.    public SimulatedActivity(int t)
117.    {
118.        current = 0;
119.        target = t;
120.    }
121.
122.    public int getTarget()
123.    {
124.        return target;
125.    }
126.
127.    public int getCurrent()
128.    {
129.        return current;
130.    }
131.
132.    public void run()
133.    {
134.        try
135.        {
136.            while (current < target && !interrupted())
137.            {
138.                sleep(100);
139.                current++;
```

```
140.                }
141.            }
142.        catch(InterruptedException e)
143.            {
144.            }
145.        }
146.
147.     private int current;
148.     private int target;
149. }
```

Monitoring the Progress of Input Streams

The Swing package contains a useful stream filter, ProgressMonitorInput-Stream, that automatically pops up a dialog that monitors how much of the stream has been read.

This filter is extremely easy to use. You sandwich in a ProgressMonitor-InputStream between your usual sequence of filtered streams. (See Chapter 12 of Volume 1 for more information on streams.)

For example, suppose you read text from a file. You start out with a FileInputStream:

```
FileInputStream in = new FileInputStream(f);
```

Normally, you would convert fileIn to an InputStreamReader.

```
InputStreamReader reader = new InputStreamReader(in);
```

However, to monitor the stream, first turn the file input stream into a stream with a progress monitor:

```
ProgressMonitorInputStream progressIn
    = new ProgressMonitorInputStream(parent, caption, in);
```

You need to supply the parent component, a caption, and, of course, the stream to monitor. The read method of the progress monitor stream simply passes along the bytes and updates the progress dialog.

You now go on building your filter sequence:

```
InputStreamReader reader = new InputStreamReader(progressIn);
```

That's all there is to it. When the file is read, the progress monitor automatically pops up. This is a very nice application of stream filtering.

> CAUTION: The progress monitor stream uses the available method of the InputStream class to determine the total number of bytes in the stream. However, the available method only reports the number of bytes in the stream that are available *without blocking*. Progress monitors work well for files and HTTP URLs because their length is known in advance, but they don't work with all streams.

Figure 1–17: A progress monitor for an input stream

The program in Example 1–12 counts the lines in a file. If you read in a large file (such as "The Count of Monte Cristo" on the CD), then the progress dialog pops up.

Note that the program doesn't use a very efficient way of filling up the text area. It would be faster to first read in the file into a `StringBuffer` and then set the text of the text area to the string buffer contents. But in this example program, we actually like this slow approach—it gives you more time to admire the progress dialog.

To avoid flicker, the text area is not displayed while it is filled up.

Example 1–12: ProgressMonitorInputStreamTest.java

```
1. import java.awt.*;
2. import java.awt.event.*;
3. import java.io.*;
4. import java.util.*;
5. import javax.swing.*;
6. import javax.swing.event.*;
7. import javax.swing.Timer;
8.
9. /**
10.    A program to test a progress monitor input stream.
11. */
12. public class ProgressMonitorInputStreamTest
13. {
14.    public static void main(String[] args)
15.    {
16.       JFrame frame = new TextFrame();
17.       frame.setDefaultCloseOperation(JFrame.EXIT_ON_CLOSE);
18.       frame.show();
19.    }
20. }
21.
22. /**
23.    A frame with a menu to load a text file and a text area
```

```
24.     to display its contents. The text area is constructed
25.     when the file is loaded and set as the content pane of
26.     the frame when the loading is complete. That avoids flicker
27.     during loading.
28. */
29. class TextFrame extends JFrame
30. {
31.    public TextFrame()
32.    {
33.       setTitle("ProgressMonitorInputStreamTest");
34.       setSize(WIDTH, HEIGHT);
35.
36.       // set up menu
37.
38.       JMenuBar menuBar = new JMenuBar();
39.       setJMenuBar(menuBar);
40.       JMenu fileMenu = new JMenu("File");
41.       menuBar.add(fileMenu);
42.       openItem = new JMenuItem("Open");
43.       openItem.addActionListener(new
44.          ActionListener()
45.          {
46.             public void actionPerformed(ActionEvent event)
47.             {
48.                try
49.                {
50.                   openFile();
51.                }
52.                catch(IOException exception)
53.                {
54.                   exception.printStackTrace();
55.                }
56.             }
57.          });
58.
59.       fileMenu.add(openItem);
60.       exitItem = new JMenuItem("Exit");
61.       exitItem.addActionListener(new
62.          ActionListener()
63.          {
64.             public void actionPerformed(ActionEvent event)
65.             {
66.                System.exit(0);
67.             }
68.          });
69.       fileMenu.add(exitItem);
70.    }
71.
```

```
72.    /**
73.       Prompts the user to select a file, loads the file into
74.       a text area, and sets it as the content pane of the frame.
75.    */
76.    public void openFile() throws IOException
77.    {
78.       JFileChooser chooser = new JFileChooser();
79.       chooser.setCurrentDirectory(new File("."));
80.       chooser.setFileFilter(
81.          new javax.swing.filechooser.FileFilter()
82.             {
83.                public boolean accept(File f)
84.                {
85.                   String fname = f.getName().toLowerCase();
86.                   return fname.endsWith(".txt")
87.                      || f.isDirectory();
88.                }
89.                public String getDescription()
90.                {
91.                   return "Text Files";
92.                }
93.             });

95.       int r = chooser.showOpenDialog(this);
96.       if (r != JFileChooser.APPROVE_OPTION) return;
97.       final File f = chooser.getSelectedFile();

99.       // set up stream and reader filter sequence

101.      FileInputStream fileIn = new FileInputStream(f);
102.      ProgressMonitorInputStream progressIn
103.         = new ProgressMonitorInputStream(this,
104.            "Reading " + f.getName(), fileIn);
105.      InputStreamReader inReader
106.         = new InputStreamReader(progressIn);
107.      final BufferedReader in = new BufferedReader(inReader);

109.      // the monitored activity must be in a new thread.

111.      Thread readThread = new Thread()
112.      {
113.         public void run()
114.         {
115.            try
116.            {
117.               final JTextArea textArea = new JTextArea();

119.               String line;
```

```
120.            while ((line = in.readLine()) != null)
121.            {
122.                textArea.append(line);
123.                textArea.append("\n");
124.            }
125.            in.close();
126.
127.            // set content pane in the event dispatch thread
128.            EventQueue.invokeLater(new
129.                Runnable()
130.                {
131.                    public void run()
132.                    {
133.                     setContentPane(new JScrollPane(textArea));
134.                        validate();
135.                    }
136.                });
137.
138.          }
139.          catch(IOException exception)
140.          {
141.              exception.printStackTrace();
142.          }
143.        }
144.      };
145.
146.      readThread.start();
147.    }
148.
149.    private JMenuItem openItem;
150.    private JMenuItem exitItem;
151.
152.    public static final int WIDTH = 300;
153.    public static final int HEIGHT = 200;
154. }
```

 javax.swing.JProgressBar

- JProgressBar()
- JProgressBar(int direction)
- JProgressBar(int min, int max)
- JProgressBar(int direction, int min, int max)

  construct a horizontal slider with the given direction, minimum and maximum.

Parameters:	direction	one of SwingConstants.HORIZONTAL or SwingConstants.VERTICAL. The default is horizontal.
	min, max	the minimum and maximum for the progress bar values. Defaults are 0 and 100.

- `int getMinimum()`
- `int getMaximum()`
- `void setMinimum(int value)`
- `void setMaximum(int value)`

get and set the minimum and maximum values.

- `int getValue()`
- `void setValue(int value)`

get and set the current value.

- `String getString()`
- `void setString(String s)`

get and set the string to be displayed in the progress bar. If the string is `null`, then a default string "*n %*" is displayed.

- `boolean isStringPainted()`
- `void setStringPainted(boolean b)`

get and set the "string painted" property. If this property is `true`, then a string is painted on top of the progress bar. The default is `false`; no string is painted.

- `boolean isIndeterminate()`
- `void setIndeterminate(boolean b)`

get and set the "indeterminate" property (SDK 1.4). If this property is `true`, then the progress bar becomes a block that moves backwards and forwards, indicating a wait of unknown duration. The default is `false`.

javax.swing.ProgressMonitor

- `ProgressMonitor(Component parent, Object message, String note, int min, int max)`

constructs a progress monitor dialog.

Parameters:	parent	the parent component over which this dialog pops up.
	message	the message object to display in the dialog.
	note	the optional string to display under the message. If this value is `null`, then no space is set aside for the note, and a later call to `setNote` has no effect.

min, max	the minimum and maximum values of the progress bar.

- `void setNote(String note)`
  changes the note text.

- `void setProgress(int value)`
  sets the progress bar value to the given value.

- `void close()`
  closes this dialog.

- `boolean isCanceled()`
  returns `true` if the user canceled this dialog.

`javax.swing.ProgressMonitorInputStream`

- `ProgressMonitorInputStream(Component parent, Object message, InputStream in)`
  constructs an input stream filter with an associated progress monitor dialog.

Parameters:	parent	the parent component over which this dialog pops up
	message	the message object to display in the dialog
	in	the input stream that is being monitored

Using Pipes for Communication Between Threads

Sometimes, the communication pattern between threads is very simple. A *producer* thread generates a stream of bytes. A *consumer* thread reads and processes that byte stream. If no bytes are available for reading, the consumer thread blocks. If the producer generates data much more quickly than the consumer can handle it, then the write operation of the producer thread blocks. The Java programming language has a convenient set of classes, `PipedInputStream` and `PipedOutputStream`, to implement this communication pattern. (There is another pair of classes, `PipedReader` and `PipedWriter`, if the producer thread generates a stream of Unicode characters instead of bytes.)

The principal reason to use pipes is to keep each thread simple. The producer thread simply sends its results to a stream and forgets about them. The consumer simply reads the data from a stream, without having to care where it comes from. By using pipes, you can connect multiple threads with each other without worrying about thread synchronization.

Example 1–13 is a program that shows off piped streams. We have a producer thread that emits random numbers at random times, a filter thread that reads the input numbers and continuously computes the average of the data, and a consumer thread that prints out the answers. (You'll need to use CTRL+C to stop this program.) Figure 1–18 shows the threads and the pipes that connect them. UNIX users will recognize these pipe streams as the equivalent of pipes connecting processes in UNIX.

Piped streams are only appropriate if the communication between the threads is on a low level, such as a sequence of numbers as in this example. In other situations, you can use queues. The producing thread inserts objects into the queue, and the consuming thread removes them.

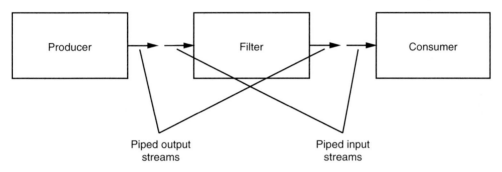

Figure 1–18: A sequence of pipes

Example 1–13: PipeTest.java

```
1. import java.util.*;
2. import java.io.*;
3.
4. /**
5.    This program demonstrates how multiple threads communicate
6.    through pipes.
7. */
8. public class PipeTest
9. {
10.    public static void main(String args[])
11.    {
12.       try
13.       {
14.          /* set up pipes */
15.          PipedOutputStream pout1 = new PipedOutputStream();
16.          PipedInputStream pin1 = new PipedInputStream(pout1);
17.
18.          PipedOutputStream pout2 = new PipedOutputStream();
19.          PipedInputStream pin2 = new PipedInputStream(pout2);
20.
21.          /* construct threads */
22.
23.          Producer prod = new Producer(pout1);
24.          Filter filt = new Filter(pin1, pout2);
```

```
25.          Consumer cons = new Consumer(pin2);
26.
27.          /* start threads */
28.
29.          prod.start();
30.          filt.start();
31.          cons.start();
32.       }
33.       catch (IOException e){}
34.    }
35. }
36.
37. /**
38.    A thread that writes random numbers to an output stream.
39. */
40. class Producer extends Thread
41. {
42.    /**
43.       Constructs a producer thread.
44.       @param os the output stream
45.    */
46.    public Producer(OutputStream os)
47.    {
48.       out = new DataOutputStream(os);
49.    }
50.
51.    public void run()
52.    {
53.       while (true)
54.       {
55.          try
56.          {
57.             double num = rand.nextDouble();
58.             out.writeDouble(num);
59.             out.flush();
60.             sleep(Math.abs(rand.nextInt() % 1000));
61.          }
62.          catch(Exception e)
63.          {
64.             System.out.println("Error: " + e);
65.          }
66.       }
67.    }
68.
69.    private DataOutputStream out;
70.    private Random rand = new Random();
71. }
72.
```

```
73. /**
74.    A thread that reads numbers from a stream and writes their
75.    average to an output stream.
76. */
77. class Filter extends Thread
78. {
79.    /**
80.       Constructs a filter thread.
81.       @param is the output stream
82.       @param os the output stream
83.    */
84.    public Filter(InputStream is, OutputStream os)
85.    {
86.       in = new DataInputStream(is);
87.       out = new DataOutputStream(os);
88.    }
89.
90.    public void run()
91.    {
92.       for (;;)
93.       {
94.          try
95.          {
96.             double x = in.readDouble();
97.             total += x;
98.             count++;
99.             if (count != 0) out.writeDouble(total / count);
100.          }
101.          catch(IOException e)
102.          {
103.             System.out.println("Error: " + e);
104.          }
105.       }
106.    }
107.
108.    private DataInputStream in;
109.    private DataOutputStream out;
110.    private double total = 0;
111.    private int count = 0;
112. }
113.
114. /**
115.    A thread that reads numbers from a stream and
116.    prints out those that deviate from previous inputs
117.    by a threshold value.
118. */
119. class Consumer extends Thread
120. {
```

```
121.    /**
122.        Constructs a consumer thread.
123.        @param is the input stream
124.    */
125.    public Consumer(InputStream is)
126.    {
127.        in = new DataInputStream(is);
128.    }
129.
130.    public void run()
131.    {
132.        for(;;)
133.        {
134.            try
135.            {
136.                double x = in.readDouble();
137.                if (Math.abs(x - oldx) > THRESHOLD)
138.                {
139.                    System.out.println(x);
140.                    oldx = x;
141.                }
142.            }
143.            catch(IOException e)
144.            {
145.                System.out.println("Error: " + e);
146.            }
147.        }
148.    }
149.
150.    private double oldx = 0;
151.    private DataInputStream in;
152.    private static final double THRESHOLD = 0.01;
153. }
```

 java.io.PipedInputStream

- `PipedInputStream()`

  creates a new piped input stream that is not yet connected to a piped output stream.

- `PipedInputStream(PipedOutputStream out)`

  creates a new piped input stream that reads its data from a piped output stream.

  Parameters: out   the source of the data

- `void connect(PipedOutputStream out)`

  attaches a piped output stream from which the data will be read.

  Parameters: out   the source of the data

java.io.PipedOutputStream

- PipedOutputStream()
  creates a new piped output stream that is not yet connected to a piped input stream.

- PipedOutputStream(PipedInputStream in)
  creates a new piped output stream that writes its data to a piped input stream.

  Parameters: in   the destination of the data

- void connect(PipedInputStream in)
  attaches a piped input stream to which the data will be written.

  Parameters: in   the destination of the data

Chapter 2

Collections

- ▼ COLLECTION INTERFACES
- ▼ CONCRETE COLLECTIONS
- ▼ THE COLLECTIONS FRAMEWORK
- ▼ ALGORITHMS
- ▼ LEGACY COLLECTIONS

Object-oriented programming (OOP) encapsulates data inside classes, but this doesn't make how you organize the data inside the classes any less important than in traditional programming languages. Of course, how you choose to structure the data depends on the problem you are trying to solve. Does your class need a way to easily search through thousands (or even millions) of items quickly? Does it need an ordered sequence of elements *and* the ability to rapidly insert and remove elements in the middle of the sequence? Does it need an array-like structure with random-access ability that can grow at run time? The way you structure your data inside your classes can make a big difference when it comes to implementing methods in a natural style, as well as for performance.

This chapter shows how Java technology can help you accomplish the traditional data structuring needed for serious programming. In college computer science programs, there is a course called *Data Structures* that usually takes a semester to complete, so there are many, many books devoted to this important topic. Exhaustively covering all the data structures that may be useful is not our goal in this chapter; instead, we cover the fundamental ones that the standard Java library supplies. We hope that, after you finish this chapter, you will find it easy to translate any of your data structures to the Java programming language.

Collection Interfaces

Before the release of the Java 2 platform, the standard library supplied only a small set of classes for the most useful data structures: `Vector`, `Stack`, `Hashtable`, `BitSet`, and the `Enumeration` interface that provides an abstract mechanism for visiting elements in an arbitrary container. That was certainly a wise choice—it takes time and skill to come up with a comprehensive collection class library.

With the advent of the Java 2 platform, the designers felt that the time had come to roll out a full-fledged set of data structures. They faced a number of conflicting design decisions. They wanted the library to be small and easy to learn. They did not want the complexity of the "Standard Template Library" (or STL) of C++, but they wanted the benefit of "generic algorithms" that STL pioneered. They wanted the legacy classes to fit into the new framework. As all designers of collection libraries do, they had to make some hard choices, and they came up with a number of idiosyncratic design decisions along the way. In this section, we will explore the basic design of the Java collections framework, show you how to put it to work, and explain the reasoning behind some of the more controversial features.

Separating Collection Interfaces and Implementation

As is common for modern data structure libraries, the Java collection library separates *interfaces* and *implementations*. Let us look at that separation with a familiar data structure, the *queue*. The Java library does not supply a queue, but it is nevertheless a good example to introduce the basic concepts.

> NOTE: If you need a queue, you can simply use the `LinkedList` class that we discuss later in this chapter.

A *queue interface* specifies that you can add elements at the tail end of the queue, remove them at the head, and find out how many elements are in the queue. You use a queue when you need to collect objects and retrieve them in a "first in, first out" fashion (see Figure 2–1).

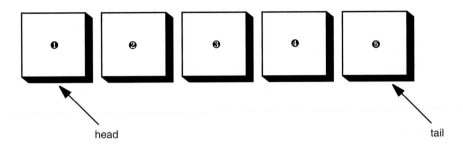

Figure 2–1: A queue

If there was a queue interface in the collections library, it might look like this:

```
interface Queue
{
    void add(Object obj);
    Object remove();
    int size();
}
```

The interface tells you nothing about how the queue is implemented. There are two common implementations of a queue, one that uses a "circular array" and one that uses a linked list (see Figure 2–2).

Circular Array

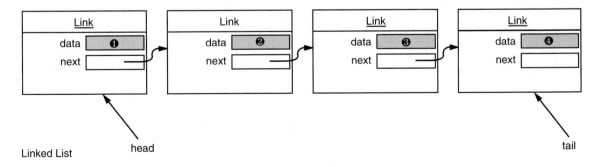

Linked List

Figure 2–2: Queue implementations

Each implementation can be expressed by a class that realizes the `Queue` interface:

```
class CircularArrayQueue implements Queue
{
   CircularArrayQueue(int capacity) { . . . }
   public void add(Object obj) { . . . }
   public Object remove() { . . . }
   public int size() { . . . }

   private Object[] elements;
   private int head;
   private int tail;
}

class LinkedListQueue implements Queue
{
   LinkedListQueue() { . . . }
   public void add(Object obj) { . . . }
   public Object remove() { . . . }
   public int size() { . . . }

   private Link head;
   private Link tail;
}
```

When you use a queue in your program, you don't need to know which implementation is actually used once the collection has been constructed. Therefore, it makes sense to use the concrete class (such as `CircularArrayQueue`) *only* when you construct the collection object. Use the *interface type* to hold the collection reference.

```
Queue expressLane = new CircularArrayQueue(100);
expressLane.add(new Customer("Harry"));
```

This approach makes it easy to change your mind and use a different implementation. You only need to change your program in one place—the constructor. If you decide that a `LinkedListQueue` is a better choice after all, your code becomes:

```
Queue expressLane = new LinkedListQueue();
expressLane.add(new Customer("Harry"));
```

Why would you choose one implementation over another? The interface says nothing about the efficiency of the implementation. A circular array is somewhat more efficient than a linked list, so it is generally preferable. However, as usual, there is a price to pay. The circular array is a *bounded* collection—it has a finite capacity. If you don't have an upper limit on the number of objects that your program will collect, you may be better off with a linked list implementation after all.

This example illustrates another issue for the designer of a collection class library. Strictly speaking, in a bounded collection, the interface of the add method should indicate that the method can fail:

```
class CircularArrayQueue
{
    public void add(Object obj)
        throws CollectionFullException
    . . .

}
```

That's a problem—now the `CircularArrayQueue` class can't implement the `Queue` interface since you can't add exception specifiers when overriding a method. Should one have two interfaces, `BoundedQueue` and `Queue`? Or should the add method throw an unchecked exception? There are advantages and disadvantages to both approaches. It is these kinds of issues that make it genuinely hard to design a logically coherent collection class library.

As we already mentioned, the Java library has no separate class for queues. We just used this example to illustrate the difference between interface and implementation since a queue has a simple interface and two well-known distinct implementations. In the next section, you will see how the Java library classifies the collections that it supports.

Collection and Iterator Interfaces in the Java Library

The fundamental interface for collection classes in the Java library is the `Collection` interface. The interface has two fundamental methods:

```
boolean add(Object obj)
Iterator iterator()
```

There are several methods in addition to these two; we will discuss them later.

The add method adds an object to the collection. The add method returns `true` if adding the object actually changed the collection, and `false` if the collection is unchanged. For example, if you try to add an object to a set and the object is already present, then the add request is rejected since sets reject duplicates.

The `iterator` method returns an object that implements the `Iterator` interface—we will describe that interface in a moment. You can use the iterator object to visit the elements in the container one by one.

The `Iterator` interface has three fundamental methods:

```
Object next()
boolean hasNext()
void remove()
```

By repeatedly calling the `next` method, you can visit the elements from the collection one by one. However, if you reach the end of the collection, the `next` method throws a `NoSuchElementException`. Therefore, you need to call the `hasNext` method before calling `next`. That method returns `true` if the iterator object still has more elements to visit. If you want to inspect all elements in a collection, you request an iterator and then keep calling the `next` method while `hasNext` returns true.

```
Iterator iter = c.iterator();
while (iter.hasNext())
{
    Object obj = iter.next();
    do something with obj
}
```

NOTE: Old-timers will notice that the `next` and `hasNext` methods of the `Iterator` interface serve the same purpose as the `nextElement` and `hasMoreElements` methods of an `Enumeration`. The designers of the Java collection library could have chosen to extend the `Enumeration` interface. But they disliked the cumbersome method names and chose to introduce a new interface with shorter method names instead.

Finally, the `remove` method removes the element that was returned by the last call to `next`.

You may well wonder why the `remove` method is a part of the `Iterator` interface. It is more efficient to remove an element if you know *where* it is. The iterator knows about *positions* in the collection. Therefore, the `remove` method is a part of the `Iterator` interface. If you visited an element that you didn't like, you can efficiently remove it.

There is an important conceptual difference between iterators in the Java collection library and iterators in other libraries. In traditional collection libraries such as the Standard Template Library of C++, iterators are modeled after array indexes. Given such an iterator, you can look up the element that is stored at that position, much like you can look up an array element `a[i]` if you have an array index `i`. Independently of the lookup, you can advance the iterator to the next position, just like you can advance an array index with the `i++` operation without performing a lookup. However, the Java iterators do not work like that. The lookup and position change are tightly coupled. The only way to look up an element is to call `next`, and that lookup advances the position.

Instead, you should think of Java iterators as being *between elements*. When you call `next`, the iterator *jumps over* the next element, and it returns a reference to the element that it just passed (see Figure 2–3).

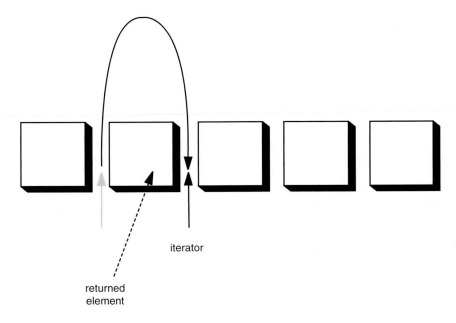

iterator

returned
element

Figure 2–3: Advancing an iterator

NOTE: Here is another useful analogy. You can think of `Iterator.next` as the equivalent of `InputStream.read`. Reading a byte from a stream automatically "consumes" the byte. The next call to `read` consumes and returns the next byte from the input. Similarly, repeated calls to `next` let you read all elements in a collection.

You must be careful when using the `remove` method. Calling `remove` removes the element that was returned by the last call to `next`. That makes sense if you want to remove a particular value—you need to see the element before you can decide that it is the one that should be removed. But if you want to remove an element by position, you first need to skip past the element. For example, here is how you remove the first element in a collection.

```
Iterator it = c.iterator();
it.next(); // skip over the first element
it.remove(); // now remove it
```

More importantly, there is a dependency between calls to the `next` and `remove` methods. It is illegal to call `remove` if it wasn't preceded by a call to `next`. If you try, an `IllegalStateException` is thrown.

If you want to remove two adjacent elements, you cannot simply call:

```
it.remove();
it.remove(); // Error!
```

Instead, you must first call `next` to jump over the element to be removed.

```
it.remove();
it.next();
it.remove();  // Ok
```

Because the collection and iterator interfaces are generic, you can write utility methods that operate on any kind of collection. For example, here is a generic `print` method that prints all elements in a collection.

```
public static void print(Collection c)
{
   System.out.print("[ ");
   Iterator iter = c.iterator();
   while (iter.hasNext())
      System.out.print(iter.next() + " ");
   System.out.println("]");
}
```

NOTE: We give this example to illustrate how to write a generic method. If you want to print the elements in a collection, you can just call `System.out.println(c)`. This works because each collection class has a `toString` method that returns a string containing all elements in the collection.

Here is a method that adds all objects from one collection to another:

```
public static boolean addAll(Collection to, Collection from)
{
   Iterator iter = from.iterator();
   boolean modified = false;
   while (iter.hasNext())
      if (to.add(iter.next()))
         modified = true;
   return modified;
}
```

Recall that the `add` method returns `true` if adding the element modified the collection. You can implement these utility methods for arbitrary collections because the `Collection` and `Iterator` interfaces supply fundamental methods such as `add` and `next`.

The designers of the Java library decided that some of these utility methods are so useful that the library should make them available. That way, users don't have to keep reinventing the wheel. The `addAll` method is one such method.

Had `Collection` been an abstract class instead of an interface, then it would have been an easy matter to supply this functionality in the class. However, you cannot supply methods in interfaces of the Java programming language. Therefore, the collection library takes a slightly different approach. The

`Collection` interface declares quite a few useful methods that all implementing classes must supply. Among them are:

```
int size()
boolean isEmpty()
boolean contains(Object obj)
boolean containsAll(Collection c)
boolean equals(Object other)
boolean addAll(Collection from)
boolean remove(Object obj)
boolean removeAll(Collection c)
void clear()
boolean retainAll(Collection c)
Object[] toArray()
```

Many of these methods are self-explanatory; you will find full documentation in the API notes at the end of this section.

Of course, it is a bother if every class that implements the `Collection` interface has to supply so many routine methods. To make life easier for implementors, the class `AbstractCollection` leaves the fundamental methods (such as add and `iterator`) abstract but implements the routine methods in terms of them. For example:

```
public class AbstractCollection
    implements Collection
{
    . . .
    public abstract boolean add(Object obj);

    public boolean addAll(Collection from)
    {
        Iterator iter = from.iterator();
        boolean modified = false;
        while (iter.hasNext())
            if (add(iter.next()))
                modified = true;
        return modified;
    }
    . . .
}
```

A concrete collection class can now extend the `AbstractCollection` class. It is now up to the concrete collection class to supply an add method, but the addAll method has been taken care of by the `AbstractCollection` superclass. However, if the subclass has a more efficient way of implementing addAll, it is free to do so.

This is a good design for a class framework. The users of the collection classes have a richer set of methods available in the generic interface, but the implementors of the actual data structures do not have the burden of implementing all the routine methods.

java.util.Collection

- `Iterator iterator()`
  returns an iterator that can be used to visit the elements in the collection.
- `int size()`
  returns the number of elements currently stored in the collection.
- `boolean isEmpty()`
  returns `true` if this collection contains no elements.
- `boolean contains(Object obj)`
  returns `true` if this collection contains an object equal to `obj`.

  Parameters: `obj`   the object to match in the collection

- `boolean containsAll(Collection other)`
  returns `true` if this collection contains all elements in the other collection.

  Parameters: `other`   the collection holding the elements to match

- `boolean add(Object element)`
  adds an element to the collection. Returns `true` if the collection changed as a result of this call.

  Parameters: `element`   the element to add

- `boolean addAll(Collection other)`
  adds all elements from the other collection to this collection. Returns `true` if the collection changed as a result of this call.

  Parameters: `other`   the collection holding the elements to add

- `boolean remove(Object obj)`
  removes an object equal to `obj` from this collection. Returns `true` if a matching object was removed.

  Parameters: `obj`   an object that equals the element to remove

- `boolean removeAll(Collection other)`
  removes all elements from the other collection from this collection. Returns `true` if the collection changed as a result of this call.

  Parameters: `other`   the collection holding the elements to add

- `void clear()`
  removes all elements from this collection.
- `boolean retainAll(Collection other)`
  removes all elements from this collection that do not equal one of the elements in the other collection. Returns `true` if the collection changed as a result of this call.

  Parameters: `other`   the collection holding the elements to be kept

- `Object[] toArray()`
  returns an array of the objects in the collection.

`java.util.Iterator`

- `boolean hasNext()`
  returns `true` if there is another element to visit.
- `Object next()`
  returns the next object to visit. Throws a `NoSuchElementException` if the end of the collection has been reached.
- `Object remove()`
  removes and returns the last visited object. This method must immediately follow an element visit. If the collection has been modified since the last element visit, then the method throws an `IllegalStateException`.

Concrete Collections

Rather than getting into more details about all the interfaces, we thought it would be helpful to first discuss the concrete data structures that the Java library supplies. Once you have a thorough understanding of what classes you will want to use, we will return to abstract considerations and see how the collections framework organizes these classes.

Linked Lists

We used arrays and their dynamic cousin, the `ArrayList` class, for many examples in Volume 1. However, arrays and array lists suffer from a major drawback. Removing an element from the middle of an array is very expensive since all array elements beyond the removed one must be moved toward the beginning of the array (see Figure 2–4). The same is true for inserting elements in the middle.

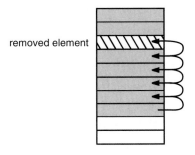

removed element

Figure 2–4: Removing an element from an array

Another well-known data structure, the *linked list,* solves this problem. Whereas an array stores object references in consecutive memory locations, a linked list stores each object in a separate *link.* Each link also stores a reference to the next link in the sequence. In the Java programming language, all linked lists are actually *doubly linked*, that is, each link also stores a reference to its predecessor (see Figure 2–5).

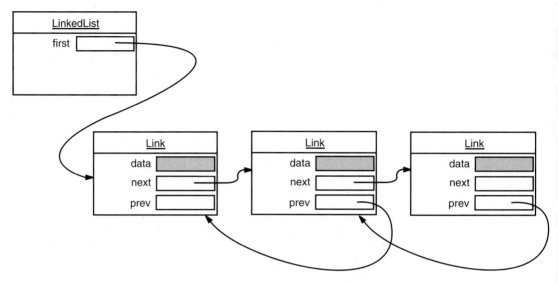

Figure 2–5: A doubly linked list

Removing an element from the middle of a linked list is an inexpensive operation—only the links around the element to be removed need to be updated (see Figure 2–6).

Figure 2–6: Removing an element from a linked list

Perhaps you once had a course in data structures where you learned how to implement linked lists. You may have bad memories of tangling up the links when removing or adding elements in the linked list. If so, you will be pleased to learn that the Java collections library supplies a class `LinkedList` ready for you to use.

The `LinkedList` class implements the `Collection` interface. You can use the familiar methods to traverse a list. The following code example prints the first three elements of a list, adds three elements, and then removes the third one.

```
LinkedList staff = new LinkedList();
staff.add("Angela");
staff.add("Bob");
staff.add("Carl");
Iterator iter = staff.iterator();
for (int i = 0; i < 3; i++)
    System.out.println(iter.next());
iter.remove(); // remove last visited element
```

However, there is an important difference between linked lists and generic collections. A linked list is an *ordered collection* where the position of the objects matters. The `LinkedList.add` method adds the object to the end of the list. But you often want to add objects somewhere in the middle of a list. This position-dependent `add` method is the responsibility of an iterator, since iterators describe positions in collections. Using iterators to add elements only makes sense for collections that have a natural ordering. For example, the *set* data type that we discuss in the next section does not impose any ordering on its elements. Therefore, there is no `add` method in the `Iterator` interface. Instead, the collections library supplies a subinterface `ListIterator` that contains an `add` method:

```
interface ListIterator extends Iterator
{
    void add(Object);
    . . .
}
```

Unlike `Collection.add`, this method does not return a `boolean`—it is assumed that the `add` operation always modifies the list.

In addition, the `ListIterator` interface has two methods that you can use for traversing a list backwards.

```
Object previous()
boolean hasPrevious()
```

Like the `next` method, the `previous` method returns the object that it skipped over.

The `listIterator` method of the `LinkedList` class returns an iterator object that implements the `ListIterator` interface.

```
ListIterator iter = staff.listIterator();
```

The add method adds the new element *before* the iterator position. For example, the code

```
ListIterator iter = staff.listIterator();
iter.next();
iter.add("Juliet");
```

skips past the first element in the linked list and adds "Juliet" before the second element (see Figure 2–7).

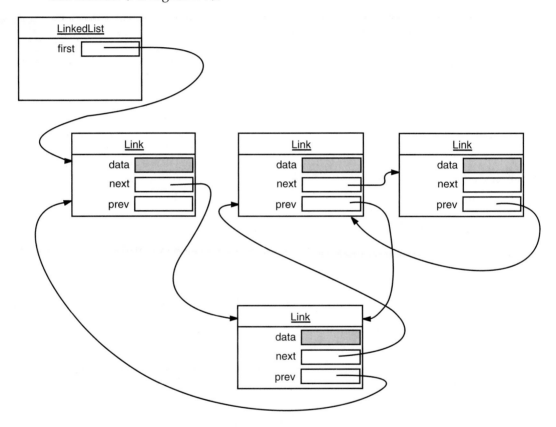

Figure 2–7: Adding an element to a linked list

If you call the add method multiple times, the elements are simply added in the order in which you supplied them. They all get added in turn before the current iterator position.

When you use the add operation with an iterator that was freshly returned from the listIterator method and that points to the beginning of the linked list, the newly added element becomes the new head of the list. When the iterator has passed the last element of the list (that is, when hasNext returns false), the added element becomes the new tail of the list. If the linked list has *n* elements, there are *n*+1 spots for adding a new element. These spots correspond to the $n+1$ possible positions of the iterator. For example, if a linked list contains three elements, A, B, and C, then the four possible positions (marked as |) for inserting a new element are:

```
|ABC
A|BC
AB|C
ABC|
```

> **NOTE:** You have to be careful with the "cursor" analogy. The `remove` operation does not quite work like the BACKSPACE key. Immediately after a call to `next`, the `remove` method indeed removes the element to the left of the iterator, just like the BACKSPACE key would. However, if you just called `previous`, the element to the right is removed. And you can't call `remove` twice in a row.
>
> Unlike the `add` method, which only depends on the iterator position, the `remove` method depends on the iterator state.

Finally, there is a `set` method that replaces the last element returned by a call to `next` or `previous` with a new element. For example, the following code replaces the first element of a list with a new value:

```
ListIterator iter = list.listIterator();
Object oldValue = iter.next(); // returns first element
iter.set(newValue); // sets first element to newValue
```

As you might imagine, if an iterator traverses a collection while another iterator is modifying it, confusing situations can occur. For example, suppose an iterator points before an element that another iterator has just removed. The iterator is now invalid and should no longer be used. The linked list iterators have been designed to detect such modifications. If an iterator finds that its collection has been modified by another iterator or by a method of the collection itself, then it throws a `ConcurrentModification-Exception`. For example, consider the following code:

```
LinkedList list = . . .;
ListIterator iter1 = list.listIterator();
ListIterator iter2 = list.listIterator();
iter1.next();
iter1.remove();
iter2.next(); // throws ConcurrentModificationException
```

The call to `iter2.next` throws a `ConcurrentModificationException` since `iter2` detects that the list was modified externally.

To avoid concurrent modification exceptions, follow this simple rule: You can attach as many iterators to a container as you like, provided that all of them are only readers. Alternatively, you can attach a single iterator that can both read and write.

Concurrent modification detection is achieved in a simple way. The container keeps track of the number of mutating operations (such as adding and removing elements). Each iterator keeps a separate count of the number of mutating operations that *it* was responsible for. At the beginning of each iterator method, the iterator simply checks whether its own mutation count equals that of the collection. If not, it throws a `ConcurrentModificationException`.

This is an excellent check and a great improvement over the fundamentally unsafe iterators in the C++ STL framework. Note, however, that it does not automatically make collections safe for multithreading. We discuss thread safety issues later in this chapter.

> NOTE: There is, however, a curious exception to the detection of concurrent modifications. The linked list only keeps track of *structural* modifications to the list, such as adding and removing links. The `set` method does *not* count as a structural modification. You can attach multiple iterators to a linked list, all of which call `set` to change the contents of existing links. This capability is required for a number of algorithms in the `Collections` class that we discuss later in this chapter.

Now you have seen the fundamental methods of the `LinkedList` class. You use a `ListIterator` to traverse the elements of the linked list in either direction, and to add and remove elements.

As you saw in the preceding section, there are many other useful methods for operating on linked lists that are declared in the `Collection` interface. These are, for the most part, implemented in the `AbstractCollection` superclass of the `LinkedList` class. For example, the `toString` method invokes `toString` on all elements and produces one long string of the format `[A, B, C]`. This is handy for debugging. Use the `contains` method to check whether an element is present in a linked list. For example, the call `staff.contains("Harry")` returns `true` if the linked list already contains a string that is equal to the String `"Harry"`. However, there is no method that returns an iterator to that position. If you want to do something with the element beyond knowing that it exists, you have to program an iteration loop by hand.

> CAUTION: The Java platform documentation points out that you should not add a reference of a collection to itself. Otherwise, it is easy to generate a stack overflow in the virtual machine. For example, the following call is fatal:
>
> ```
> LinkedList list = new LinkedList();
> list.add(list); // add list to itself
> String contents = list.toString(); // dies with infinite recursion
> ```
> Naturally, this is not a situation that comes up in everyday programming.

The library also supplies a number of methods that are, from a theoretical perspective, somewhat dubious. Linked lists do not support fast random access. If you want to see the *n*th element of a linked list, you have to start at the beginning and skip past the first *n* − 1 elements first. There is no shortcut. For that reason, programmers don't usually use linked lists in programming situations where elements need to be accessed by an integer index.

Nevertheless, the `LinkedList` class supplies a `get` method that lets you access a particular element:

```
Object obj = list.get(n);
```

Of course, this method is not very efficient. If you find yourself using it, you are probably using the wrong data structure for your problem.

You should *never* use this illusory random access method to step through a linked list. The code

```
for (int i = 0; i < list.size(); i++)
    do something with list.get(i);
```

is staggeringly inefficient. Each time you look up another element, the search starts again from the beginning of the list. The `LinkedList` object makes no effort to cache the position information.

NOTE: The `get` method has one slight optimization: if the index is at least `size() / 2`, then the search for the element starts at the end of the list.

The list iterator interface also has a method to tell you the index of the current position. In fact, because Java iterators conceptually point between elements, it has two of them: the `nextIndex` method returns the integer index of the element that would be returned by the next call to `next`; the `previousIndex` method returns the index of the element that would be returned by the next call to `previous`. Of course, that is simply one less than `nextIndex`. These methods are efficient—the iterators keep a count of the current position. Finally, if you have an integer index n, then `list.listIterator(n)` returns an iterator that points just before the element with index n. That is, calling `next` yields the same element as `list.get(n)`. Of course, obtaining that iterator is inefficient.

If you have a linked list with only a handful of elements, then you don't have to be overly paranoid about the cost of the `get` and `set` methods. But then why use a linked list in the first place? The only reason to use a linked list is to minimize the cost of insertion and removal in the middle of the list. If you only have a few elements, you can just use an array or a collection such as `ArrayList`.

We recommend that you simply stay away from all methods that use an integer index to denote a position in a linked list. If you want random access into a collection, use an array or `ArrayList`, not a linked list.

The program in Example 2–1 puts linked lists to work. It simply creates two lists, merges them, then removes every second element from the second list, and finally tests the removeAll method. We recommend that you trace the program flow and pay special attention to the iterators. You may find it helpful to draw diagrams of the iterator positions, like this:

```
|ACE      |BDFG
A|CE      |BDFG
AB|CE     B|DFG
 . . .
```

Note that the call

```
System.out.println(a);
```

prints all elements in the linked list a.

Example 2–1: LinkedListTest.java

```
1. import java.util.*;
2.
3. /**
4.    This program demonstrates operations on linked lists.
5. */
6. public class LinkedListTest
7. {
8.    public static void main(String[] args)
9.    {
10.       List a = new LinkedList();
11.       a.add("Angela");
12.       a.add("Carl");
13.       a.add("Erica");
14.
15.       List b = new LinkedList();
16.       b.add("Bob");
17.       b.add("Doug");
18.       b.add("Frances");
19.       b.add("Gloria");
20.
21.       // merge the words from b into a
22.
23.       ListIterator aIter = a.listIterator();
24.       Iterator bIter = b.iterator();
25.
26.       while (bIter.hasNext())
27.       {
28.          if (aIter.hasNext()) aIter.next();
29.          aIter.add(bIter.next());
30.       }
31.
32.       System.out.println(a);
```

```
33.
34.        // remove every second word from b
35.
36.        bIter = b.iterator();
37.        while (bIter.hasNext())
38.        {
39.           bIter.next(); // skip one element
40.           if (bIter.hasNext())
41.           {
42.              bIter.next(); // skip next element
43.              bIter.remove(); // remove that element
44.           }
45.        }
46.
47.        System.out.println(b);
48.
49.        // bulk operation: remove all words in b from a
50.
51.        a.removeAll(b);
52.
53.        System.out.println(a);
54.     }
```

java.util.List

- `ListIterator listIterator()`
  returns a list iterator for visiting the elements of the list.

- `ListIterator listIterator(int index)`
  returns a list iterator for visiting the elements of the list whose first call to next will return the element with the given index.

  Parameters: `index`   the position of the next visited element

- `void add(int i, Object element)`
  adds an element at the specified position.

  Parameters: `index`   the position of the new element

                 `element`   the element to add

- `void addAll(int i, Collection elements)`
  adds all elements from a collection to the specified position.

  Parameters: `index`   the position of the first new element

                 `elements`   the elements to add

- `Object remove(int i)`
  removes and returns an element at the specified position.

  Parameters: `index`   the position of the element to remove

- `Object set(int i, Object element)`
  replaces the element at the specified position with a new element and returns the old element.

  Parameters: `index`   the replacement position

                 `element`   the new element

- `int indexOf(Object element)`
  returns the position of the first occurrence of an element equal to the specified element, or −1 if no matching element is found.

  Parameters: `element`   the element to match

- `int lastIndexOf(Object element)`
  returns the position of the last occurrence of an element equal to the specified element, or −1 if no matching element is found.

  Parameters: `element`   the element to match

`java.util.ListIterator`

- `void add(Object element)`
  adds an element before the current position.

  Parameters: `element`   the element to add

- `void set(Object element)`
  replaces the last element visited by `next` or `previous` with a new element. Throws an `IllegalStateException` if the list structure was modified since the last call to `next` or `previous`.

  Parameters: `element`   the new element

- `boolean hasPrevious()`
  returns `true` if there is another element to visit when iterating backwards through the list.

- `Object previous()`
  returns the previous object. Throws a `NoSuchElementException` if the beginning of the list has been reached.

- `int nextIndex()`
  returns the index of the element that would be returned by the next call to `next`.

- `int previousIndex()`
  returns the index of the element that would be returned by the next call to `previous`.

java.util.LinkedList

- LinkedList()
  constructs an empty linked list.

- LinkedList(Collection elements)
  constructs a linked list and adds all elements from a collection.

  Parameters: elements   the elements to add

- void addFirst(Object element)
- void addLast(Object element)
  add an element to the beginning or the end of the list.

  Parameters: element   the element to add

- Object getFirst()
- Object getLast()
  return the element at the beginning or the end of the list.

- Object removeFirst()
- Object removeLast()
  remove and return the element at the beginning or the end of the list.

Array Lists

In the preceding section, you saw the List interface and the LinkedList class that implements it. The List interface describes an ordered collection in which the position of elements matters. There are two protocols for visiting the elements: through an iterator and by random access with methods get and set. The latter are not appropriate for linked lists, but of course they make a lot of sense for arrays. The collections library supplies the familiar ArrayList class that implements the List interface. An ArrayList encapsulates a dynamically reallocated Object[] array.

NOTE: If you are a veteran Java programmer, you will have used the Vector class whenever you needed a dynamic array. Why use an ArrayList instead of a Vector? There is one simple reason. All methods of the Vector class are *synchronized*. It is safe to access a Vector object from two threads. But if you only access a vector from a single thread—by far the more common case—your code wastes quite a bit of time with synchronization. In contrast, the ArrayList methods are not synchronized. We recommend that you use an ArrayList instead of a Vector whenever you don't need synchronization.

Hash Sets

Linked lists and arrays let you specify in which order you want to arrange the elements. However, if you are looking for a particular element and you don't remember its position, then you need to visit all elements until you find a match. That can be time-consuming if the collection contains many elements. If you don't care about the ordering of the elements, then there are data structures that let you find elements much faster. The drawback is that those data structures give you no control over the order in which the elements appear. The data structures organize the elements in an order that is convenient for their own purposes.

A well-known data structure for finding objects quickly is the *hash table*. A hash table computes an integer, called the *hash code,* for each object. You will see in the next section how these hash codes are computed. What's important for now is that hash codes can be computed quickly and that the computation only depends on the state of the object that needs to be hashed, and not on the other objects in the hash table.

A hash table is an array of linked lists. Each list is called a *bucket* (see Figure 2–8). To find the place of an object in the table, compute its hash code and reduce it modulo the total number of buckets. The resulting number is the index of the bucket that holds the element. For example, if an object has hash code 345 and there are 101 buckets, then the object is placed in bucket 42 (because the remainder of the integer division 345/101 is 42). Perhaps you are lucky and there is no other element in that bucket. Then, you simply insert the element into that bucket. Of course, it is inevitable that you sometimes hit a bucket that is already filled. This is called a *hash collision.* Then, you need to compare the new object with all objects in that bucket to see if it is already present. Provided that the hash codes are reasonably randomly distributed and the number of buckets is large enough, only a few comparisons should be necessary.

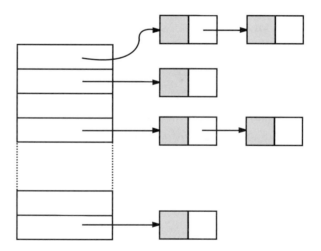

Figure 2–8: A hash table

If you want more control over the performance of the hash table, you can specify the initial bucket count. The bucket count gives the number of buckets that are used to collect objects with identical hash values. If too many elements are inserted into a hash table, the number of collisions increases and retrieval performance suffers.

If you know approximately how many elements will eventually be in the table, then you should set the initial bucket count to about 150 percent of the expected element count. Some researchers believe that it is a good idea to make the size of the hash table a prime number to prevent a clustering of keys. The evidence for this isn't conclusive, but it certainly can't hurt. For example, if you need to store about 100 entries, set the initial bucket size to 151.

Of course, you do not always know how many elements you need to store, or your initial guess may be too low. If the hash table gets too full, it needs to be *rehashed*. To rehash the table, a table with more buckets is created, all elements are inserted into the new table, and the original table is discarded. In the Java programming language, the *load factor* determines when a hash table is rehashed. For example, if the load factor is 0.75 (which is the default) and the hash table becomes more than 75 percent full, then the table is automatically rehashed, using twice as many buckets. For most applications, it is reasonable to leave the load factor at 0.75.

Hash tables can be used to implement several important data structures. The simplest among them is the *set* type. A set is a collection of elements without duplicates. The add method of a set first tries to find the object to be added, and only adds it if it is not yet present.

The Java collections library supplies a HashSet class that implements a set based on a hash table. At the time of this writing, the default constructor HashSet constructs a hash table with 101 buckets and a load factor of 0.75. These values may change in future releases. If you care at all about these values, you should specify your own, with the constructors

```
HashSet(int initialCapacity)
HashSet(int initialCapacity, float loadFactor)
```

You add elements with the add method. The contains method is redefined to make a fast lookup to find if an element is already present in the set. It only checks the elements in one bucket and not all elements in the collection.

The hash set iterator visits all buckets in turn. Since the hashing scatters the elements around in the table, they are visited in seemingly random order. You would only use a hash set if you don't care about the ordering of the elements in the collection.

The sample program at the end of this section (Example 2–2) reads words from `System.in`, adds them to a set, and finally prints out all words in the set. For example, you can feed the program the text from *Alice in Wonderland* (which you can obtain from `www.gutenberg.net`) by launching it from a command shell as

```
java SetTest < alice30.txt
```

The program reads all words from the input and adds them to the hash set. It then iterates through the unique words in the set and finally prints out a count. (*Alice in Wonderland* has 5,909 unique words, including the copyright notice at the beginning.) The words appear in random order.

NOTE: Version 1.4 of the Java Software Developer's Kit (SDK) adds a class `LinkedHashSet` that keeps track of the order in which the elements are added to the set. The iterator of a `LinkedHashSet` visits the elements in insertion order. That gives you an ordered collection with fast element lookup. Of course, there is an added implementation cost—the elements in the buckets are chained together by a doubly linked list (see Figure 2–9).

To see the difference, replace the `HashSet` with a `LinkedHashSet` in Example 2–2 below. Now the words are printed in the order in which they occurred in the input. (If a word occurs multiple times, only the first insertion matters.)

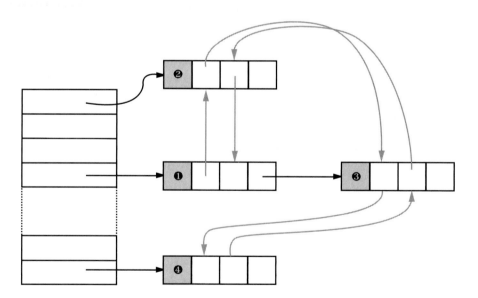

Figure 2–9: A Linked Hash Table

Example 2–2: SetTest.java

```
1. import java.util.*;
2. import java.io.*;
3.
4. /**
5.    This program uses a set to print all unique words in
6.    System.in.
7. */
8. public class SetTest
9. {
10.    public static void main(String[] args)
11.    {
12.       Set words = new HashSet(59999);
13.          // set to HashSet, LinkedHashSet or TreeSet
14.       long totalTime = 0;
15.
16.       try
17.       {
18.          BufferedReader in = new
19.             BufferedReader(new InputStreamReader(System.in));
20.          String line;
21.          while ((line = in.readLine()) != null)
22.          {
23.            StringTokenizer tokenizer = new StringTokenizer(line);
24.             while (tokenizer.hasMoreTokens())
25.             {
26.                String word = tokenizer.nextToken();
27.                long callTime = System.currentTimeMillis();
28.                words.add(word);
29.                callTime = System.currentTimeMillis() - callTime;
30.                totalTime += callTime;
31.             }
32.          }
33.       }
34.       catch (IOException e)
35.       {
36.          System.out.println("Error " + e);
37.       }
38.
39.       Iterator iter = words.iterator();
40.       while (iter.hasNext())
41.          System.out.println(iter.next());
42.       System.out.println(words.size()
43.          + " distinct words. " + totalTime + " milliseconds.");
44.    }
45. }
```

java.util.HashSet

- HashSet()

  constructs an empty hash set.

- HashSet(Collection elements)

  constructs a hash set and adds all elements from a collection.

  Parameters: elements   the elements to add

- HashSet(int initialCapacity)

  constructs an empty hash set with the specified capacity.

  Parameters: initialCapacity   the initial number of buckets

- HashSet(int initialCapacity, float loadFactor)

  constructs an empty hash set with the specified capacity and load factor.

  Parameters: initialCapacity   the initial number of buckets

  loadFactor   a number between 0.0 and 1.0 that determines at what percentage of fullness the hash table will be rehashed into a larger one

java.util.LinkedHashSet

- LinkedHashSet()

  constructs an empty linked hash set.

- LinkedHashSet(Collection elements)

  constructs a linked hash set and adds all elements from a collection.

  Parameters: elements   the elements to add

- LinkedHashSet(int initialCapacity)

  constructs an empty linked hash set with the specified capacity.

  Parameters: initialCapacity   the initial number of buckets

- HashSet(int initialCapacity, float loadFactor)

  constructs an empty linked hash set with the specified capacity and load factor.

  Parameters: initialCapacity   the initial number of buckets

  loadFactor   a number between 0.0 and 1.0 that determines at what percentage of fullness the hash table will be rehashed into a larger one

Hash functions

You can insert strings into a hash set because the String class has a hashCode method that computes a *hash code* for a string. A hash code is an integer that is somehow derived from the characters in the string. Table 2–1 lists a few examples of hash codes that result from the hashCode function of the String class.

Table 2–1: Hash codes resulting from the **hashCode** function

String	Hash code
Hello	140207504
Harry	140013338
Hacker	884756206

The hashCode method is defined in the Object class. Therefore, every object has a default hash code. That hash code is derived from the object's memory address. In general, the default hash function is not very useful because objects with identical contents may yield different hash codes. Consider this example.

```
String s = "Ok";
StringBuffer sb = new StringBuffer(s);
System.out.println(s.hashCode() + " " + sb.hashCode());
String t = new String("Ok");
StringBuffer tb = new StringBuffer(t);
System.out.println(t.hashCode() + " " + tb.hashCode());
```

Table 2–2 shows the result.

Table 2–2: Hash codes of objects with identical contents

Object	Hash code
s	3030
sb	20526976
t	3030
tb	20527144

Note that the strings s and t have the same hash value because, for strings, the hash values are derived from their *contents*. The string buffers sb and tb have different hash values because no special hash function has been defined for the StringBuffer class, and the default hash code function in the Object class derives the hash code from the object's memory address.

You should always define the hashCode method for objects that you insert into a hash table. This method should return an integer (which can be negative). The hash table code will later reduce the integer by dividing by the bucket count and taking the remainder. Just scramble up the hash codes of the data fields in some way that will give the hash codes for different objects a good chance of being widely scattered.

For example, suppose you have the class `Item` for inventory items. An item consists of a description string and a part number.

```
anItem = new Item("Toaster", 49954);
```

If you want to construct a hash set of items, you need to define a hash code. For example:

```
class Item
{
    . . .
    public int hashCode()
    {
        return 13 * description.hashCode() + 17 * partNumber;
    }
    . . .
    private String description;
    private int partNumber;
}
```

As a practical matter, if the part number uniquely identifies the item, you don't need to incorporate the hash code of the description.

Furthermore, you *also* need to make sure that the `equals` method is well defined. The `Object` class defines `equals`, but that method only tests whether or not two objects are *identical*. If you don't redefine `equals`, then every new object that you insert into the table will be considered a *different* object.

You need to redefine `equals` to check for equal contents.

```
class Item
{
    . . .
    public boolean equals(Object other)
    {
        if (other != null && getClass() == other.getClass())
        {
            Item otherItem = (Item)other;
            return description.equals(otherItem.description)
                && partNumber == otherItem.partNumber;
        }
        else
            return false;
    }
    . . .
}
```

> CAUTION: Your definitions of `equals` and `hashCode` must be *compatible:* if
> `x.equals(y)` is `true`, then `x.hashCode()` must be the same value as
> `y.hashCode()`.

`java.lang.Object`

- `boolean equals(Object obj)`

  compares two objects for equality; returns `true` if both objects are equal;
  `false` otherwise.

  Parameters: `obj`   the object to compare with the first object (may
  be `null`, in which case the method should
  return `false`)

- `int hashCode()`

  returns a hash code for this object. A hash code can be any integer, positive or
  negative. Equal objects need to return identical hash codes.

Tree Sets

The `TreeSet` class is similar to the hash set, with one added improvement. A tree
set is a *sorted collection.* You insert elements into the collection in any order. When
you iterate through the collection, the values are automatically presented in
sorted order. For example, suppose you insert three strings and then visit all elements that you added.

```
TreeSet sorter = new TreeSet();
sorter.add("Bob");
sorter.add("Angela");
sorter.add("Carl");
Iterator iter = sorter.iterator();
while (iter.hasNext()) System.out.println(iter.next());
```

Then, the values are printed in sorted order: `Angela Bob Carl`. As the name
of the class suggests, the sorting is accomplished by a tree data structure. (The
current implementation uses a *red-black tree.* For a detailed description of red-
black trees, see, for example, *Introduction to Algorithms* by Thomas Cormen,
Charles Leiserson, and Ronald Rivest [The MIT Press 1990].) Every time an
element is added to a tree, it is placed into its proper sorting position. Therefore, the iterator always visits the elements in sorted order.

Adding an element to a tree is slower than adding it to a hash table, but it is
still much faster than adding it into the right place in an array or linked list. If
the tree contains n elements, then an average of $\log_2 n$ comparisons are

required to find the correct position for the new element. For example, if the tree already contains 1,000 elements, then adding a new element requires about 10 comparisons.

Thus, adding elements into a `TreeSet` is somewhat slower than adding into a `HashSet`—see Table 2–3 for a comparison—but the `TreeSet` automatically sorts the elements.

Table 2–3: Adding elements into hash and tree sets

Document	Total number of words	Number of distinct words	Hash-Set	TreeSet
Alice in Wonderland	28195	5909	5 sec	7 sec
The Count of Monte Cristo	466300	37545	75 sec	98 sec

java.util.TreeSet

- `TreeSet()`
  constructs an empty tree set.

- `TreeSet(Collection elements)`
  constructs a tree set and adds all elements from a collection.

  Parameters: `elements` the elements to add

Object comparison

How does the `TreeSet` know how you want the elements sorted? By default, the tree set assumes that you insert elements that implement the `Comparable` interface. That interface defines a single method:

```
int compareTo(Object other)
```

The call `a.compareTo(b)` must return 0 if a and b are equal, a negative integer if a comes before b in the sort order, and a positive integer if a comes after b. The exact value does not matter; only its sign (>0, 0, or <0) matters. Several standard Java platform classes implement the `Comparable` interface. One example is the `String` class. Its `compareTo` method compares strings in dictionary order (sometimes called *lexicographic order*).

If you insert your own objects, you need to define a sort order yourself by implementing the `Comparable` interface. There is no default implementation of `compareTo` in the `Object` class.

For example, here is how you can sort `Item` objects by part number.

```
class Item implements Comparable
{
    public int compareTo(Object other)
    {
        Item otherItem = (Item)other;
        return partNumber - otherItem.partNumber;
    }
    . . .
}
```

Note that the explicit argument of the `compareTo` method has type `Object`, not `Comparable`. If the object is not of the correct type, then this `compareTo` method simply throws a `ClassCastException`. (The `compareTo` methods in the standard library behave in the same way when presented with illegal argument types.)

If you compare two *positive* integers, such as part numbers in our example, then you can simply return their difference—it will be negative if the first item should come before the second item, zero if the part numbers are identical, and positive otherwise.

CAUTION: This trick only works if the integers are from a small enough range. If `x` is a large positive integer and `y` is a large negative integer, then the difference `x - y` can overflow.

However, using the `Comparable` interface for defining the sort order has obvious limitations. You can only implement the interface once. But what can you do if you need to sort a bunch of items by part number in one collection and by description in another? Furthermore, what can you do if you need to sort objects of a class whose creator didn't bother to implement the `Comparable` interface?

In those situations, you tell the tree set to use a different comparison method, by passing a `Comparator` object into the `TreeSet` constructor. The `Comparator` interface has a single method, with two explicit parameters:

```
int compare(Object a, Object b)
```

Just like the `compareTo` method, the `compare` method returns a negative integer if a comes before b, zero if they are identical, or a positive integer otherwise.

To sort items by their description, simply define a class that implements the `Comparator` interface:

```
class ItemComparator implements Comparator
{
    public int compare(Object a, Object b)
```

```
    {
        Item itemA = (Item)a;
        Item itemB = (Item)b;
        String descrA = itemA.getDescription();
        String descrB = itemB.getDescription();
        return descrA.compareTo(descrB);
    }
}
```

You then pass an object of this class to the tree set constructor:

```
ItemComparator comp = new ItemComparator();
TreeSet sortByDescription = new TreeSet(comp);
```

If you construct a tree with a comparator, it uses this object whenever it needs to compare two elements.

Note that this item comparator has no data. It is just a holder for the comparison method. Such an object is sometimes called a *function object*.

Function objects are commonly defined "on the fly," as instances of anonymous inner classes:

```
TreeSet sortByDescription = new TreeSet(new
    Comparator()
    {
        public int compare(Object a, Object b)
        {
            Item itemA = (Item)a;
            Item itemB = (Item)b;
            String descrA = itemA.getDescription();
            String descrB = itemB.getDescription();
            return descrA.compareTo(descrB);
        }
    });
```

Using comparators, you can sort elements in any way you wish.

Sometimes, comparators do have instance fields. For example, you can have a comparator with a flag to control ascending or descending sort order.

If you look back at Table 2–3, you may well wonder if you should always use a tree set instead of a hash set. After all, adding elements does not seem to take much longer, and the elements are automatically sorted. The answer depends on the data that you are collecting. If you don't need the data sorted, there is no reason to pay for the sorting overhead. More importantly, with some data it is very difficult to come up with a sort order. Suppose you collect a bunch of rectangles. How do you sort them? By area? You can have two different rectangles with different positions but the same area. If you sort by area, the second one is not inserted into the set. The sort order for a tree must be a *total ordering:* Any two elements must be comparable, and the comparison can only be zero if the elements are equal. There is such a sort order for rectangles (the lexicographic ordering on its coordinates), but it is unnatural and cumbersome to compute. In contrast, hash functions are usually easier to define. They only need to do a reasonably good job of scrambling the objects, whereas comparison functions must tell objects apart with complete precision.

The program in Example 2–3 builds two tree sets of `Item` objects. The first one is sorted by part number, the default sort order of `Item` objects. The second set is sorted by description, using a custom comparator.

Example 2–3: TreeSetTest.java

```
1. import java.util.*;
2.
3. /**
4.    This program sorts a set of item by comparing
5.    their descriptions.
6. */
7. public class TreeSetTest
8. {
9.    public static void main(String[] args)
10.    {
11.       SortedSet parts = new TreeSet();
12.       parts.add(new Item("Toaster", 1234));
13.       parts.add(new Item("Widget", 4562));
14.       parts.add(new Item("Modem", 9912));
15.       System.out.println(parts);
16.
17.       SortedSet sortByDescription = new TreeSet(new
18.          Comparator()
19.          {
20.             public int compare(Object a, Object b)
21.             {
22.                Item itemA = (Item)a;
23.                Item itemB = (Item)b;
24.                String descrA = itemA.getDescription();
25.                String descrB = itemB.getDescription();
26.                return descrA.compareTo(descrB);
27.             }
28.          });
29.
30.       sortByDescription.addAll(parts);
31.       System.out.println(sortByDescription);
32.    }
33. }
34.
35. /**
36.    An item with a description and a part number.
```

```
37.  */
38.  class Item implements Comparable
39.  {
40.     /**
41.        Constructs an item.
42.        @param aDescription the item's description
43.        @param aPartNumber the item's part number
44.     */
45.     public Item(String aDescription, int aPartNumber)
46.     {
47.        description = aDescription;
48.        partNumber = aPartNumber;
49.     }
50.
51.     /**
52.        Gets the description of this item.
53.        @return the description
54.     */
55.     public String getDescription()
56.     {
57.        return description;
58.     }
59.
60.     public String toString()
61.     {
62.        return "[description=" + description
63.           + ", partNumber=" + partNumber + "]";
64.     }
65.
66.     public boolean equals(Object other)
67.     {
68.        if (getClass() == other.getClass())
69.        {  Item otherItem = (Item)other;
70.           return description.equals(otherItem.description)
71.              && partNumber == otherItem.partNumber;
72.        }
73.        else
74.           return false;
75.     }
76.
77.     public int hashCode()
78.     {
79.        return 13 * description.hashCode() + 17 * partNumber;
80.     }
81.
82.     public int compareTo(Object other)
83.     {
84.        Item otherItem = (Item)other;
```

```
85.        return partNumber - otherItem.partNumber;
86.    }
87.
88.    private String description;
89.    private int partNumber;
90. }
```

java.lang.Comparable

- int compareTo(Object other)

  compares this object with another object and returns a negative value if this comes before other, zero if they are considered identical in the sort order, and a positive value if this comes after other.

  Parameters: other   the object to compare

java.util.Comparator

- int compare(Object a, Object b)

  compares two objects and returns a negative value if a comes before b, zero if they are considered identical in the sort order, and a positive value if a comes after b.

  Parameters: a, b   the objects to compare

java.util.SortedSet

- Comparator comparator()

  returns the comparator used for sorting the elements, or null if the elements are compared with the compareTo method of the Comparable interface.

- Object first()
- Object last()

  return the smallest or largest element in the sorted set.

java.util.TreeSet

- TreeSet(Comparator c)

  constructs a tree set and uses the specified comparator for sorting its elements.

  Parameters: c   the comparator to use for sorting

- TreeSet(SortedSet elements)

  constructs a tree set, adds all elements from a sorted set, and uses the same element comparator as the given sorted set.

  Parameters: elements   the sorted set with the elements to add and the
                           comparator to use

Maps

A set is a collection that lets you quickly find an existing element. However, to look up an element, you need to have an exact copy of the element to find. That isn't a very common lookup—usually, you have some key information, and you want to look up the associated element. The *map* data structure serves that purpose. A map stores key/value pairs. You can find a value if you provide the key. For example, you may store a table of employee records, where the keys are the employee IDs and the values are `Employee` objects.

The Java library supplies two general purpose implementations for maps: `HashMap` and `TreeMap`. A hash map hashes the keys, and a tree map uses a total ordering on the keys to organize them in a search tree. The hash or comparison function is applied *only to the keys*. The values associated with the keys are not hashed or compared.

Should you choose a hash map or a tree map? As with sets, hashing is a bit faster, and it is the preferred choice if you don't need to visit the keys in sorted order.

Here is how you set up a hash map for storing employees.

```
HashMap staff = new HashMap();
Employee harry = new Employee("Harry Hacker");
staff.put("987-98-9996", harry);
. . .
```

Whenever you add an object to a map, you must supply a key as well. In our case, the key is a string, and the corresponding value is an `Employee` object.

To retrieve an object, you must use (and therefore, remember) the key.

```
String s = "987-98-9996";
e = (Employee)staff.get(s); // gets harry
```

If no information is stored in the map with the particular key specified, then `get` returns `null`.

Keys must be unique. You cannot store two values with the same key. If you call the `put` method twice with the same key, then the second value replaces the first one. In fact, `put` returns the previous value stored with the key parameter. (This feature is useful; if `put` returns a non-`null` value, then you know you replaced a previous entry.)

The `remove()` method removes an element from the map. The `size()` method returns the number of entries in the map.

The collections framework does not consider a map itself as a collection. (Other frameworks for data structures consider a map as a collection of *pairs,* or as a collection of values that is indexed by the keys.) However, you can obtain *views* of the map, objects that implement the `Collection` interface, or one of its subinterfaces.

There are three views: the set of keys, the collection of values (which is not a set), and the set of key/value pairs. The keys and key/value pairs form a set because there can be only one copy of a key in a map. The methods

```
Set keySet()
Collection values()
Set entrySet()
```

return these three views. (The elements of the entry set are objects of the inner class `Map.Entry`.)

Note that the `keySet` is *not* a `HashSet` or `TreeSet`, but it is an object of some other class that implements the `Set` interface. We discuss the `Set` interface and its purpose in detail in the next section. The `Set` interface extends the `Collection` interface. In fact, as you will see, it does not add any new methods. Therefore, you can use it exactly as you use the `Collection` interface.

For example, you can enumerate all keys of a map:

```
Set keys = map.keySet();
Iterator iter = keys.iterator();
while (iter.hasNext())
{
    Object key = iter.next();
    do something with  key
}
```

TIP: If you want to look at both keys and values, then you can avoid value lookups by enumerating the *entries.* Use the following code skeleton:

```
Set entries = staff.entrySet();
Iterator iter = entries.iterator();
while (iter.hasNext())
{
    Map.Entry entry = (Map.Entry)iter.next();
    Object key = entry.getKey();
    Object value = entry.getValue();
    do something with key, value
}
```

If you invoke the `remove` method of the iterator, you actually remove the key *and its associated value* from the map. However, you cannot *add* an element to the key set view. It makes no sense to add a key without also adding a value. If you try to invoke the `add` method, it throws an `UnsupportedOperationException`. The key/value set view has the same restriction, even though it would make conceptual sense to add a new key/value pair.

> **NOTE:** The legacy `Hashtable` class (which we cover later in this chapter) has methods that return enumeration objects—the classical analog to iterators—that traverse keys and values. However, having collection views is more powerful since they let you operate on all keys or values at once.

Example 2–4 illustrates a map at work. We first add key/value pairs to a map. Then, we remove one key from the map, which removes its associated value as well. Next, we change the value that is associated with a key and call the `get` method to look up a value. Finally, we iterate through the entry set.

Example 2–4: MapTest.java

```
1. import java.util.*;
2.
3. /**
4.    This program demonstrates the use of a map with key type
5.    String and value type Employee.
6. */
7. public class MapTest
8. {
9.    public static void main(String[] args)
10.    {
11.       Map staff = new LinkedHashMap(101,0.75F,true);
12.       staff.put("144-25-5464", new Employee("Angela Hung"));
13.       staff.put("567-24-2546", new Employee("Harry Hacker"));
14.       staff.put("157-62-7935", new Employee("Gary Cooper"));
15.       staff.put("456-62-5527", new Employee("Francesca Cruz"));
16.
17.       // print all entries
18.
19.       System.out.println(staff);
20.
21.       // remove an entry
22.
23.       staff.remove("567-24-2546");
24.
25.       // replace an entry
26.
27.       staff.put("456-62-5527", new Employee("Francesca Miller"));
28.
29.       // look up a value
30.
31.       System.out.println(staff.get("157-62-7935"));
```

```
32.
33.        // iterate through all entries
34.
35.        Set entries = staff.entrySet();
36.        Iterator iter = entries.iterator();
37.        while (iter.hasNext())
38.        {
39.           Map.Entry entry = (Map.Entry)iter.next();
40.           Object key = entry.getKey();
41.           Object value = entry.getValue();
42.           System.out.println("key=" + key + ", value=" + value);
43.        }
44.     }
45. }
46.
47. /**
48.    A minimalist employee class for testing purposes.
49. */
50. class Employee
51. {
52.    /**
53.       Constructs an employee with $0 salary.
54.       @param n the employee name
55.    */
56.    public Employee(String n)
57.    {
58.       name = n;
59.       salary = 0;
60.    }
61.
62.    public String toString()
63.    {
64.       return "[name=" + name + ", salary=" + salary + "]";
65.    }
66.
67.    /**
68.       Sets the employee salary to a new value.
69.       @param s the new salary.
70.    */
71.    public void setSalary(double s)
72.    {
73.       salary = s;
74.    }
75.
76.    private String name;
77.    private double salary;
78. }
```

java.util.Map

- Object get(Object key)

  gets the value associated with the key; returns the object associated with the key, or null if the key is not found in the map.

  Parameters: key the key to use for retrieval (may be null)

- Object put(Object key, Object value)

  puts the association of a key and a value into the map. If the key is already present, the new object replaces the old one previously associated with the key. This method returns the old value of the key, or null if the key was not previously present.

  Parameters: key the key to use for retrieval (may be null)

  value the associated object (may not be null)

- void putAll(Map entries)

  adds all entries from the specified map to this map.

  Parameters: entries the map with the entries to be added

- boolean containsKey(Object key)

  returns true if the key is present in the map.

  Parameters: key the key to find

- boolean containsValue(Object value)

  returns true if the value is present in the map.

  Parameters: value the value to find

- Set entrySet()

  returns a set view of Map.Entry objects, the key/value pairs in the map. You can remove elements from this set, and they are removed from the map, but you cannot add any elements.

- Set keySet()

  returns a set view of all keys in the map. You can remove elements from this set, and the keys and associated values are removed from the map, but you cannot add any elements.

- Collection values()

  returns a collection view of all values in the map. You can remove elements from this set, and the removed value and its key are removed from the map, but you cannot add any elements.

`java.util.Map.Entry`

- `Object getKey()`
- `Object getValue()`

  return the key or value of this entry.

- `Object setValue(Object value)`

  changes the value *in the associated map* to the new value and returns the old value.

  Parameters: `value`   the new value to associate with the key

`java.util.HashMap`

- `HashMap()`

  constructs an empty hash map.

- `HashMap(Map entries)`

  constructs a hash map and adds all entries from a map.

  Parameters: `entries`   the entries to add

- `HashMap(int initialCapacity)`
- `HashMap(int initialCapacity, float loadFactor)`

  construct an empty hash map with the specified capacity and load factor.

  Parameters: `initialCapacity` the initial number of buckets.

                    `loadFactor`   a number between 0.0 and 1.0 that determines at what percentage of fullness the hash table will be rehashed into a larger one. The default is 0.75.

`java.util.TreeMap`

- `TreeMap(Comparator c)`

  constructs a tree map and uses the specified comparator for sorting its keys.

  Parameters: `c`   the comparator to use for sorting

- `TreeMap(Map entries)`

  constructs a tree map and adds all entries from a map.

  Parameters: `entries`   the entries to add

- `TreeMap(SortedMap entries)`

  constructs a tree map, adds all entries from a sorted map, and uses the same element comparator as the given sorted map.

  Parameters: `entries`   the sorted set with the entries to add and the comparator to use

java.util.SortedMap

- Comparator comparator()

  returns the comparator used for sorting the keys, or null if the keys are compared with the compareTo method of the Comparable interface.

- Object firstKey()
- Object lastKey()

  return the smallest or largest key in the map.

Specialized Map Classes

The collection class library has several map classes for specialized needs that we briefly discuss in this section.

Weak hash maps

The WeakHashMap class was designed to solve an interesting problem. What happens with a value whose key is no longer used anywhere in your program? Suppose the last reference to a key has gone away. Then, there is no longer any way to refer to the value object. But since no part of the program has the key any more, the key/value pair cannot be removed from the map. Why can't the garbage collector remove it? Isn't it the job of the garbage collector to remove unused objects?

Unfortunately, it isn't quite so simple. The garbage collector traces *live* objects. As long as the map object is live, then *all* buckets in it are live and they won't be reclaimed. Thus, your program should take care to remove unused values from long-lived maps. Or, you can use a WeakHashMap instead. This data structure cooperates with the garbage collector to remove key/value pairs when the only reference to the key is the one from the hash table entry.

Here are the inner workings of this mechanism. The WeakHashMap uses *weak references* to hold keys. A WeakReference object holds a reference to another object, in our case, a hash table key. Objects of this type are treated in a special way by the garbage collector. Normally, if the garbage collector finds that a particular object has no references to it, it simply reclaims the object. However, if the object is reachable *only* by a WeakReference, the garbage collector still reclaims the object, but it places the weak reference that led to it onto a queue. The operations of the WeakHashMap periodically check that queue for newly arrived weak references. When a weak reference arrives in the queue, this is an indication that the key was no longer used by anyone and that it has been collected. The WeakHashMap then removes the associated entry.

Linked hash maps

Version 1.4 of the SDK adds a class `LinkedHashMap` that remembers in which order you inserted key/value pairs into the map. That way, you avoid the seemingly random order of keys in a `HashMap` without incurring the expense of a `TreeMap`. As entries are inserted into the table, they are joined together in a doubly linked list.

The `keySet`, `entrySet`, and `values` methods of this class yield collections whose iterators follow the links of that linked list.

For example, consider the following map insertions from Example 2–4.

```
Map staff = new LinkedHashMap();
staff.put("144-25-5464", new Employee("Angela Hung"));
staff.put("567-24-2546", new Employee("Harry Hacker"));
staff.put("157-62-7935", new Employee("Gary Cooper"));
staff.put("456-62-5527", new Employee("Francesca Cruz"));
```

Then `staff.keySet().iterator()` enumerates the keys in the order:

```
144-25-5464
567-24-2546
157-62-7935
456-62-5527
```

and `staff.values().iterator()` enumerates the values in the order:

```
Angela Hung
Harry Hacker
Gary Cooper
Francesca Cruz
```

Why would you want this behavior? Apparently, some programmers find it confusing that the order of entries in a hash table can change seemingly randomly—for example, when the hash table exceeds its load factor and is rehashed, or when values are copied from one hash table to another. The `LinkedHashMap` gives you control over the order. Also, if a hash table is sparsely filled, iteration is somewhat inefficient since the iterator must skip past all the empty buckets. Iteration in a `LinkedHashMap` is independent of the capacity of the hash table since the iterator follows the links between the entries. The drawback is, of course, that the additional links consume storage.

If you use the constructor

```
LinkedHashMap(int initialCapacity, float loadFactor,
    boolean accessOrder)
```

and set `accessOrder` to `true`, then the linked hash map uses *access order*, not insertion order, to iterate through the map entries. Every time you call `get` or `put`, the affected entry is removed from its current position and placed at the *end* of the linked list of entries. (Only the position in the linked list of entries is affected, not the hash table bucket. An entry always stays in the bucket that corresponds to the hash code of the key.)

That behavior is useful to implement a "least recently used" discipline for a cache. For example, you may want to keep frequently accessed entries in memory and read less frequently objects from a database. When you don't find an entry in the table, and the table is already pretty full, then you can get an iterator into the table and remove the first few elements that it enumerates. Those entries were the least recently used ones.

You can even automate that process. Form a subclass of `LinkedHashMap` and override the method

```
protected boolean removeEldestEntry(Map.Entry eldest)
```

Then adding a new entry causes the eldest entry to be removed whenever your method returns `true`. For example, the following cache is kept at a size of at most 100 elements.

```
Map cache = new
    LinkedHashMap(125, 0.8F, true)
    {
        protected boolean removeEldestEntry(Map.Entry eldest)
        {
            return size() > 100;
        }
    };
```

Alternatively, you can consider the `eldest` entry to decide whether to remove it. For example, you may want to check a time stamp stored with the entry.

Identity hash maps

Version 1.4 of the SDK adds another class `IdentityHashMap` for another quite specialized purpose, where the hash values for the keys should not be computed by the `hashCode` method but by the `System.identityHash-Code` method. That's the method that `Object.hashCode` uses to compute a hash code from the object's memory address. Also, for comparison of objects, the `IdentityHashMap` uses `==`, not `equals`.

In other words, different key objects are considered distinct even if they have equal contents. This class is useful for implementing object traversal algorithms (such as object serialization), in which you want to keep track of which objects have been already been traversed.

java.util.WeakHashMap

- WeakHashMap()

  constructs an empty weak hash map.

- WeakHashMap(int initialCapacity)
- WeakHashMap(int initialCapacity, float loadFactor)

  construct an empty hash map with the specified capacity and load factor.

  Parameters: initialCapacity the initial number of buckets.

  loadFactor a number between 0.0 and 1.0 that determines at what percentage of fullness the hash table will be rehashed into a larger one. The default is 0.75.

java.util.LinkedHashMap

- LinkedHashMap()

  constructs an empty hash map. (Since SDK 1.4)

- LinkedHashMap(Map entries)

  constructs a hash map and adds all entries from a map.

  Parameters: entries the entries to add

- LinkedHashMap(int initialCapacity)
- LinkedHashMap(int initialCapacity, float loadFactor)
- LinkedHashMap(int initialCapacity, float loadFactor, boolean accessOrder)

  construct an empty linked hash map with the specified capacity, load factor, and ordering.

  Parameters: initialCapacity the initial number of buckets.

  loadFactor a number between 0.0 and 1.0 that determines at what percentage of fullness the hash table will be rehashed into a larger one. The default is 0.75.

- protected boolean removeEldestEntry(Map.Entry eldest)

  Override this method to return true if you want the eldest entry to be removed. This method is called after an entry has been added to the map. The default implementation returns false—old elements are not removed by default. But you can redefine this method to selectively return true, for example if the eldest entry fits a certain condition or the map exceeds a certain size.

  Parameters: eldest the eldest entry whose removal is being contemplated

java.util.IdentityHashMap

- IdentityHashMap()
  constructs an empty identity hash map. (Since SDK 1.4)

- IdentityHashMap(Map entries)
  constructs an identity hash map and adds all entries from a map.

  Parameters: entries   the entries to add

- IdentityHashMap(int expectedMaxSize)
  constructs an empty identity hash map whose capacity is the smallest power of 2 exceeding 1.5.

  Parameters: expectedMaxSize   the expected maximum number of entries in this map

java.lang.System

- static int identityHashCode(Object obj)
  returns the same hash code (derived from the object's memory address) that Object.hashCode computes, even if the class to which obj belongs has redefined the hashCode method.

The Collections Framework

A *framework* is a set of classes that form the basis for building advanced functionality. A framework contains superclasses with useful functionality, policies, and mechanisms. The user of a framework forms subclasses to extend the functionality without having to reinvent the basic mechanisms. For example, Swing is a framework for user interfaces.

The Java collections library forms a framework for collection classes. It defines a number of interfaces and abstract classes for implementors of collections (see Figure 2–10), and it prescribes certain mechanisms, such as the iteration protocol. You can use the collection classes without having to know much about the framework—we did just that in the preceding sections. However, if you want to implement generic algorithms that work for multiple collection types, or if you want to add a new collection type, then it is helpful to understand the framework.

There are two fundamental interfaces for containers: Collection and Map. You insert elements into a collection with a method:

```
boolean add(Object element)
```

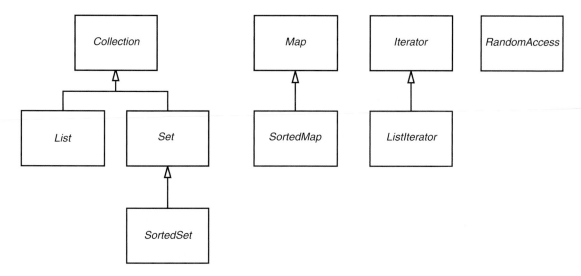

Figure 2–10: The interfaces of the collections framework

However, maps hold key/value pairs, and you use the `put` method to insert them.

```
Object put(object key, object value)
```

To read elements from a collection, you visit them with an iterator. However, you can read values from a map with the `get` method:

```
Object get(Object key)
```

A `List` is an *ordered collection.* Elements are added into a particular position in the container. An object can be placed into its position in two ways: by an integer index, and by a list iterator. The `List` interface defines methods for random access:

```
void add(int index, Object element)
Object get(int index)
void remove(int index)
```

As already discussed, the `List` interface provides these random access methods whether or not they are efficient for a particular implementation. To make it possible to avoid carrying out costly random access operations, version 1.4 of the SDK introduces a tagging interface, `RandomAccess`. That interface has no methods, but you can use it to test whether a particular collection supports efficient random access:

```
if (c instanceof RandomAccess)
{
    use random access algorithm
}
else
{
```

```
    use sequential access algorithm
}
```

The `ArrayList` and `Vector` classes implement this interface.

NOTE: From a theoretical point of view, it would have made sense to have a separate `Array` interface that extends the `List` interface and declares the random access methods. If there was a separate `Array` interface, then those algorithms that require random access would use `Array` parameters, and you could not accidentally apply them to collections with slow random access. However, the designers of the collections framework chose not to define a separate interface. They wanted to keep the number of interfaces in the library small. Also, they did not want to take a paternalistic attitude toward programmers. You are free to pass a linked list to algorithms that use random access—you just need to be aware of the performance costs.

The `ListIterator` interface defines a method for adding an element before the iterator position:

```
void add(Object element)
```

To get and remove elements at a particular position, you simply use the `next` and `remove` methods of the `Iterator` interface.

The `Set` interface is identical to the `Collection` interface, but the behavior of the methods is more tightly defined. The `add` method of a set should reject duplicates. The `equals` method of a set should be defined so that two sets are identical if they have the same elements, but not necessarily in the same order. The `hashCode` method should be defined such that two sets with the same elements yield the same hash code.

NOTE: For sets and lists, there is a well-defined notion of equality. Two sets are equal if they contain the same elements, regardless of their order. Two lists are equal if they contain the same elements in the same order. However, there is no well-defined notion of equality for collections. You should therefore not use the `equals` method on `Collection` references.

Why make a separate interface if the method signatures are the same? Conceptually, not all collections are sets. Making a `Set` interface enables programmers to write methods that only accept sets.

Finally, the `SortedSet` and `SortedMap` interfaces expose the comparison object used for sorting, and they define methods to obtain views of subsets of the containers. We discuss these views in the next section.

Now, let us turn from the interfaces to the classes that implement them. We already discussed that the collection interfaces have quite a few methods that can be trivially implemented from more fundamental methods. There are five abstract classes that supply many of these routine implementations:

```
AbstractCollection
AbstractList
AbstractSequentialList
AbstractSet
AbstractMap
```

If you implement your own collection class, then you probably want to extend one of these classes so that you can pick up the implementations of the routine operations.

The Java library supplies six concrete classes:

```
LinkedList
ArrayList
HashSet
TreeSet
HashMap
TreeMap
```

Figure 2–11 shows the relationships between these classes.

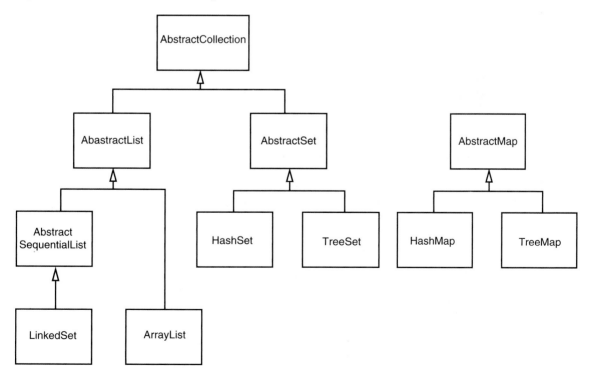

Figure 2–11: Classes in the collections framework

Core Java

Finally, there are a number of "legacy" container classes that have been present since the beginning, before there was a collections framework:

```
Vector
Stack
Hashtable
Properties
```

They have been integrated into the collections framework—see Figure 2–12. We discuss these classes later in this chapter.

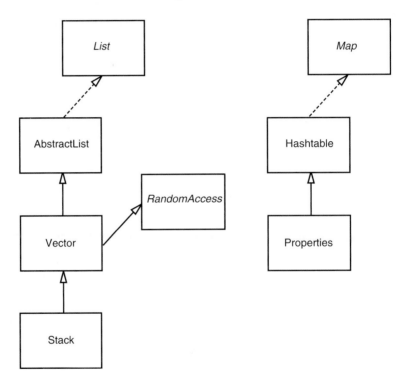

Figure 2–12: Legacy classes in the collections framework

Views and Wrappers

If you look at Figure 2–10 and Figure 2–11, you might think it is overkill to have six interfaces and five abstract classes to implement six concrete collection classes. However, these figures don't tell the whole story. By using *views*, you can obtain other objects that implement the `Collection` or `Map` interfaces. You saw one example of this with the `keySet` method of the map classes. At first glance, it appears as if the method creates a new set, fills it with all keys of the map, and returns it. However, that is not the case. Instead, the `keySet` method returns an object of a class that implements the `Set` interface and whose methods manipulate the original map. Such a collection is called a *view*. You have no way of knowing, and you need not know, exactly what class the library uses to implement the view.

The technique of views has a number of useful applications in the collections framework. Here is the most compelling one. Recall that the methods of the `Vector` class are synchronized, which is unnecessarily slow if the vector is accessed only from a single thread. For that reason, we recommended the use of the `ArrayList` instead of the `Vector` class. However, if you do access a collection from multiple threads, it is very important that the methods are synchronized. For example, it would be disastrous if one thread tried to add to a hash table while another thread is rehashing the elements. The library designers could have implemented companion classes with synchronized methods for all data structures. But they did something more useful. They supplied a mechanism that produces synchronized views for all *interfaces*. For example, the static `synchronizedMap` method in the `Collections` class can turn any map into a `Map` with synchronized access methods:

```
HashMap hashMap = new HashMap();
map = Collections.synchronizedMap(hashMap);
```

Now, you can access the `map` object from multiple threads. The methods such as `get` and `put` are synchronized—each method call must be finished completely before another thread can call another method.

NOTE: The `Collections` class contains a number of utility methods whose parameters or return values are collections. Do not confuse it with the `Collection` interface.

There are six methods to obtain synchronized collections:

```
Collections.synchronizedCollection
Collections.synchronizedList
Collections.synchronizedSet
Collections.synchronizedSortedSet
Collections.synchronizedMap
Collections.synchronizedSortedMap
```

The views that are returned by these methods are sometimes called *wrappers*.

NOTE: If a list implements the `RandomAccess` interface, then the wrapper object returned by the `synchronizedList` method belongs to a class that also implements `RandomAccess`.

You should make sure that no thread accesses the data structure through the original unsynchronized methods. The easiest way to ensure this is not to save any reference to the original object, but to simply pass the constructed collection to the wrapper method:

```
map = Collections.synchronizedMap(new HashMap());
```

There is one caveat when accessing a collection from multiple threads. Recall that you can either have multiple iterators that read from a collection, or a single thread that modifies the collection. For that reason, you will want to make sure that any iteration—

```
Iterator iter = collection.iterator();
while (iter.hasNext())
    do something with iter.next();
```

—does not occur at a time when another thread modifies the collection. If it did, then the `next` method would throw a `ConcurrentModificationException`.

If you run into problems in controlling access of the same collection in multiple threads, you may want to follow the advice of Chapter 1: figure out what higher-level purpose the collection serves, then come up with the class that expresses that purpose. Make the collection into an instance field of that class, and control access to it via synchronized methods.

Since the wrappers wrap the *interface* and not the actual collection object, you only have access to those methods that are defined in the interface. For example, the `LinkedList` class has convenience methods, `addFirst` and `addLast`, that are not part of the `List` interface. These methods are not accessible through the synchronization wrapper.

CAUTION: The `synchronizedCollection` method (as well as the `unmodifiableCollection` method discussed later in this section) returns a collection whose `equals` method does *not* invoke the `equals` method of the underlying collection. Instead, it inherits the `equals` method of the `Object` class, which just tests whether the objects are identical. If you turn a set or list into just a collection, you can no longer test for equal contents. The wrapper acts in this way because equality testing is not well defined at this level of the hierarchy.

However, the `synchronizedSet` and `synchronizedList` class do not hide the `equals` methods of the underlying collections.

The wrappers treat the `hashCode` method in the same way.

The `Collections` class has another potentially useful set of wrappers to produce unmodifiable views of collections. These wrappers add a runtime check to an existing collection. If an attempt to modify the collection is detected, then an exception is thrown and the collection remains untouched.

For example, suppose you want to let some part of your code look at, but not touch, the contents of a collection. Here is what you could do:

```
List staff = new LinkedList();
. . .
lookAt(new Collections.unmodifiableList(staff));
```

The `Collections.unmodifiableList` method returns an object of a class implementing the `List` interface. Its accessor methods retrieve values from the `staff` collection. Of course, the `lookAt` method can call all methods of the `List` interface, not just the accessors. But all mutator methods (such as `add`) have been redefined to throw an `UnsupportedOperationException` instead of forwarding the call to the underlying collection. There are similar methods to obtain unmodifiable wrappers to the other collection interfaces.

NOTE: In the API documentation, certain methods of the collection interfaces, such as `add`, are described as "optional operations." This is curious—isn't the purpose of an interface to lay out the methods that a class *must* implement? Indeed, it would have made sense to separate the read-only interfaces from the interfaces that allow full access. But that would have doubled the number of interfaces, which the designers of the library found unacceptable.

The `Arrays` class has a static `asList` method that returns a `List` wrapper around a plain Java array. This method lets you pass the array to a method that expects a list or collection argument. For example,

```
Card[] cardDeck = new Card[52];
. . .
List cardList = Arrays.asList(cardDeck);
```

The returned object is *not* an `ArrayList`. It is a view object whose `get` and `set` methods access the underlying array. All methods that would change the size of the array (such as `add` and the `remove` method of the associated iterator) throw an `UnsupportedOperationException`.

Subranges

You can form subrange views for a number of collections. For example, suppose you have a list `staff` and want to extract elements 10 to 19. You use the `subList` method to obtain a view into the subrange of the list.

```
List group2 = staff.subList(10, 20);
```

The first index is inclusive, the second exclusive—just like the parameters for the `substring` operation of the `String` class.

You can apply any operations to the subrange, and they automatically reflect the entire list. For example, you can erase the entire subrange:

```
group2.clear(); // staff reduction
```

The elements are now automatically cleared from the `staff` list.

For sorted sets and maps, you use the sort order, not the element position, to form subranges. The `SortedSet` interface declares three methods:

```
subSet(from, to)
headSet(to)
tailSet(from)
```

These return the subsets of all elements that are larger than or equal to `from` and strictly smaller than `to`. For sorted maps, there are similar methods

```
subMap(from, to)
headMap(to)
tailMap(from)
```

that return views into the maps consisting of all entries where the *keys* fall into the specified ranges.

Lightweight collection wrappers

The method call

```
Collections.nCopies(n, anObject)
```

returns an immutable object that implements the `List` interface and gives the illusion of having n elements, each of which appears as `anObject`. There is very little storage cost—the object is only stored once. This is a cute application of the wrapper technique. You can use such a list to initialize a concrete container. For example, the following call creates an `ArrayList` containing 100 strings, all set to `"DEFAULT"`:

```
ArrayList settings
    = new ArrayList(Collections.nCopies(100, "DEFAULT"));
```

The method call

```
Collections.singleton(anObject)
```

returns a wrapper object that implements the `Set` interface (unlike `ncopies` which produces a `List`). The returned object implements an immutable single-element set without the overhead of a hash table or tree. The constants `Collections.EMPTY_LIST` and `Collections.EMPTY_SET` return objects that implement the `List` and `Set` interfaces and contain no elements. The advantage is similar to that of the `singleton` method: the returned objects do not have the overhead of a data structure. Singletons and empty objects are potentially useful as parameters to methods that expect a list, set, or container.

> NOTE: JDK 1.3 added methods `singletonList` and `singletonMap` and a constant `EMPTY_MAP`.

A final note on optional operations

We'd like to end this section with a few words about the "optional" or unsupported operations in the collection and iterator interfaces. This is undoubtedly the most controversial design decision in the collections framework. The problem is caused by the undeniably powerful and convenient views. Views are good because they lead to efficient code, and their "plug and play" nature means you only need to learn a few basic concepts. A view usually has some restriction—it may be read-only, it may not be able to change the size, or it may support removal, but not insertion, as is the case for the key view of a map. The restriction is different for each view. Making a separate interface for each restricted view would lead to a bewildering tangle of interfaces that would be unusable in practice.

Should you extend the technique of "optional" methods to your own interfaces? We think not. Even though collections are used very frequently, the coding style for implementing them is not typical for other problem domains. The designers of a collection class library have to resolve a particularly brutal set of conflicting requirements. Users want the library to be easy to learn, convenient to use, completely generic, idiot-proof, and at the same time as efficient as hand-coded algorithms. It is plainly impossible to achieve all these goals simultaneously, or even to come close. Look at a few other libraries, such as the JGL library from ObjectSpace (www.objectspace.com), to see a different set of trade-offs. Or, even better, try your hand at designing your own library of collections and algorithms. You will soon run into the inevitable conflicts and feel much more sympathy with the folks from Sun. But in your own programming problems, you will rarely encounter such an extreme set of constraints. You should be able to find solutions that do not rely on the extreme measure of "optional" interface operations.

java.util.Collections

- static Collection synchronizedCollection(Collection c)
- static List synchronizedList(List c)
- static Set synchronizedSet(Set c)
- static SortedSet synchronizedSortedSet(SortedSet c)
- static Map synchronizedMap(Map c)
- static SortedMap synchronizedSortedMap(SortedMap c)

  construct a view of the collection whose methods are synchronized.

  Parameters: c   the collection to wrap

- `static Collection unmodifiableCollection(Collection c)`
- `static List unmodifiableList(List c)`
- `static Set unmodifiableSet(Set c)`
- `static SortedSet unmodifiableSortedSet(SortedSet c)`
- `static Map unmodifiableMap(Map c)`
- `static SortedMap unmodifiableSortedMap(SortedMap c)`
  construct a view of the collection whose mutator methods throw an `UnsupportedOperationException`.

  Parameters: `c`   the collection to wrap

- `static List nCopies(int n, Object value)`
- `static Set singleton(Object value)`
  construct a view of the object as either an unmodifiable list with n identical elements, or a set with a single element.

  Parameters: `n`   the number of times to repeat the value in the list

               `value`   the element value in the collection

- `static final List EMPTY_LIST`
- `static final Set EMPTY_SET`
  An unmodifiable wrapper for an empty list or set.

java.util.Arrays

- `static List asList(Object[] array)`
  returns a list view of the elements in an array that is modifiable but not resizable.

  Parameters: `array`   the array to wrap

java.util.List

- `List subList(int from, int to)`
  returns a list view of the elements within a range of positions.

  Parameters: `from`   the first position to include in the view

               `to`   the first position to exclude in the view

java.util.SortedSet

- `SortedSet subSet(Object from, Object to)`
- `SortedSet headSet(Object to)`
- `SortedSet tailSet(Object from)`
  return a view of the elements within a range.

  Parameters: `from`   the first element to include in the view

               `to`   the first element to exclude in the view

- `SortedMap subMap(Object from, Object to)`
- `SortedMap headMap(Object to)`
- `SortedMap tailMap(Object from)`

  return a map view of the entries whose keys are within a range.

  Parameters: `from`   the first key to include in the view

                    `to`   the first key to exclude in the view

Bulk Operations

So far, most of our examples used an iterator to traverse a collection, one element at a time. However, you can often avoid iteration by using one of the *bulk operations* in the library.

Suppose you want to find the *intersection* of two sets, the elements that two sets have in common. First, make a new set to hold the result.

```
Set result = new HashSet(a);
```

Here, you use the fact that every collection has a constructor whose parameter is another collection that holds the initialization values.

Now, use the `retainAll` method:

```
result.retainAll(b);
```

It retains all elements that also happen to be in b. You have formed the intersection without programming a loop.

You can carry this idea further and apply a bulk operation to a *view*. For example, suppose you have a map that maps employee IDs to employee objects, and you have a set of the IDs of all employees that are to be terminated.

```
Map staffMap = . . .;
Set terminatedIDs = . . .;
```

Simply form the key set and remove all IDs of terminated employees.

```
staffMap.keySet().removeAll(terminatedIDs);
```

Because the key set is a view into the map, the keys and associated employee names are automatically removed from the map.

By using a subrange view, you can restrict bulk operations to sublists and subsets. For example, suppose you want to add the first ten elements of a list to another container. Form a sublist to pick out the first ten:

```
relocated.addAll(staff.subList(0, 10));
```

The subrange can also be a target of a mutating operation.

```
staff.subList(0, 10).clear();
```

Interfacing with Legacy APIs

Since large portions of the Java platform API were designed before the collections framework was created, you occasionally need to translate between traditional arrays and vectors and the more modern collections.

First, consider the case where you have values in an array or vector and you want to put them into a collection. If the values are inside a `Vector`, simply construct your collection from the vector:

```
Vector values = . . .;
HashSet staff = new HashSet(values);
```

All collection classes have a constructor that can take an arbitrary collection object. Since the Java 2 platform, the `Vector` class implements the `List` interface.

If you have an array, you need to turn it into a collection. The `Arrays.asList` wrapper serves this purpose:

```
String[] values = . . .;
HashSet staff = new HashSet(Arrays.asList(values));
```

Conversely, if you need to call a method that requires a vector, you can construct a vector from any collection:

```
Vector values = new Vector(staff);
```

Obtaining an array is a bit trickier. Of course, you can use the `toArray` method:

```
Object[] values = staff.toArray();
```

But the result is an array of *objects*. Even if you know that your collection contained objects of a specific type, you cannot use a cast:

```
String[] values = (String[])staff.toArray(); // Error!
```

The array returned by the `toArray` method was created as an `Object[]` array, and you cannot change its type. Instead, you need to use a variant of the `toArray` method. Give it an array of length 0 of the type that you'd like. Then, the returned array is created as the same array type, and you can cast it:

```
String[] values = (String[])staff.toArray(new String[0]);
```

NOTE: You may wonder why you don't simply pass a `Class` object (such as `String.class`) to the `toArray` method. However, as you can see from the API notes, this method does "double duty," both to fill an existing array (provided it is long enough) and to create a new array.

---

java.util.Collection

- `Object[] toArray(Object[] array)`

  checks if the array parameter is larger than the size of the collection. If so, it adds all elements of the collection into the array, followed by a `null` terminator, and it returns the array. If the length of `array` equals the size of the collection, then the method adds all elements of the collection to the array but does not add a `null` terminator. If there isn't enough room, then the method creates a new array, *of the same type as the incoming array,* and fills it with the elements of the collection.

  Parameters: `array`   the array that holds the collection elements, or whose element type is used to create a new array to hold the collection elements

Algorithms

Generic collection interfaces have a great advantage—you only need to implement your algorithms once. For example, consider a simple algorithm to compute the maximum element in a collection. Traditionally, programmers would implement such an algorithm as a loop. Here is how you find the largest element of an array.

```
if (a.length == 0) throw new NoSuchElementException();
Comparable largest = a[0];
for (int i = 1; i < a.length; i++)
   if (largest.compareTo(a[i]) < 0)
      largest = a[i];
```

Of course, to find the maximum of an array list, the code would be slightly different.

```
if (v.size() == 0) throw new NoSuchElementException();
Comparable largest = (Comparable)v.get(0);
for (int i = 1; i < v.size(); i++)
   if (largest.compareTo(v.get(i)) < 0)
      largest = v.get(i);
```

What about a linked list? You don't have efficient random access in a linked list. But you can use an iterator.

```
if (l.isEmpty()) throw new NoSuchElementException();
Iterator iter = l.iterator();
Comparable largest = (Comparable)iter.next();
while (iter.hasNext())
{
   Object next = iter.next();
   if (largest.compareTo(next) < 0)
      largest = next;
}
```

These loops are tedious to write, and they are just a bit error-prone. Is there an off-by-one error? Do the loops work correctly for empty containers? For containers with only one element? You don't want to test and debug this code every time, but you also don't want to implement a whole slew of methods such as these:

```
Object max(Comparable[] a)
Object max(ArrayList v)
Object max(LinkedList l)
```

That's where the collection interfaces come in. Think of the *minimal* collection interface that you need to efficiently carry out the algorithm. Random access with get and set comes higher in the food chain than simple iteration. As you have seen in the computation of the maximum element in a linked list, random access is not required for this task. Computing the maximum can be done simply by iterating through the elements. Therefore, you can implement the max method to take *any* object that implements the Collection interface.

```
public static Object max(Collection c)
{
    if (c.isEmpty()) throw new NoSuchElementException();
    Iterator iter = c.iterator();
    Comparable largest = (Comparable)iter.next();
    while (iter.hasNext())
    {
        Object next = iter.next();
        if (largest.compareTo(next) < 0)
            largest = next;
    }
    return largest;
}
```

Now you can compute the maximum of a linked list, an array list, or an array, with a single method.

```
LinkedList l;
ArrayList v;
Employee[] a;
. . .
largest = max(l);
largest = max(v);
largest = max(Arrays.asList(a));
```

That's a powerful concept. In fact, the standard C++ library has dozens of useful algorithms, each of which operates on a generic collection. The Java library is not quite so rich, but it does contain the basics: sorting, binary search, and some utility algorithms.

Sorting and Shuffling

Computer old-timers will sometimes reminisce about how they had to use punched cards and how they actually had to program sorting algorithms by hand.

Nowadays, of course, sorting algorithms are part of the standard library for most programming languages, and the Java programming language is no exception.

The sort method in the `Collections` class sorts a collection that implements the `List` interface.

```
List staff = new LinkedList();
// fill collection . . .;
Collections.sort(staff);
```

This method assumes that the list elements implement the `Comparable` interface. If you want to sort the list in some other way, you can pass a `Comparator` object as a second parameter. (We discussed comparators in the section on sorted sets.) Here is how you can sort a list of employees by increasing salary.

```
Collections.sort(staff, new
    Comparator()
    {
        public int compare(Object a, Object b)
        {
            double salaryDifference = (Employee)a.getSalary()
                - (Employee)b.getSalary();
            if (salaryDifference < 0) return -1;
            if (salaryDifference > 0) return 1;
            return 0;
        }
    });
```

If you want to sort a list in *descending* order, then use the static convenience method `Collections.reverseOrder()`. It returns a comparator that returns `b.compareTo(a)`. (The objects must implement the `Comparable` interface.) For example:

```
Collections.sort(staff, Collections.reverseOrder())
```

sorts the elements in the list `staff` in reverse order, according to the ordering given by the `compareTo` method of the element type.

You may wonder how the `sort` method sorts a list. Typically, when you look at a sorting algorithm in a book on algorithms, it is presented for arrays and uses random element access. But random access in a list can be inefficient. You can actually sort lists efficiently by using a form of merge sort (see, for example, *Algorithms in C++*, by Robert Sedgewick [Addison-Wesley 1998, p. 366–369]). However, the implementation in the Java programming language does not do that. It simply dumps all elements into an array, sorts the array, using a different variant of merge sort, and then copies the sorted sequence back into the list.

The merge sort algorithm used in the collections library is a bit slower than *quick sort*, the traditional choice for a general-purpose sorting algorithm. However, it has one major advantage: it is *stable*, that is, it doesn't switch equal elements. Why do you care about the order of equal elements? Here is a common scenario. Suppose you have an employee list that you already sorted by name. Now you sort by salary. What happens to employees with equal salary? With a stable sort, the ordering by name is preserved. In other words, the outcome is a list that is sorted first by salary, then by name.

Because collections need not implement all of their "optional" methods, all methods that receive collection parameters need to describe when it is safe to pass a collection to an algorithm. For example, you clearly cannot pass an unmodifiableList list to the sort algorithm. What kind of list *can* you pass? According to the documentation, the list must be modifiable but need not be resizable.

These terms are defined as follows:

- A list is *modifiable* if it supports the set method.

- A list is *resizable* if it supports the add and remove operations.

The Collections class has an algorithm shuffle that does the opposite of sorting—it randomly permutes the order of the elements in a list. You supply the list to be shuffled and a random number generator. For example,

```
ArrayList cards = . . .;
Collections.shuffle(cards);
```

If you supply a list that does not implement the RandomAccess interface, then the shuffle method copies the elements into an array, shuffles the array, and copies the shuffled elements back into the list.

The program in Example 2–5 fills an array list with 49 Integer objects containing the numbers 1 through 49. It then randomly shuffles the list and selects the first 6 values from the shuffled list. Finally, it sorts the selected values and prints them out.

Example 2–5: ShuffleTest.java

```
1. import java.util.*;
2.
3. /**
4.    This program demonstrates the random shuffle and sort
5.    algorithms.
6. */
7. public class ShuffleTest
8. {
9.    public static void main(String[] args)
10.   {
11.      List numbers = new ArrayList(49);
12.      for (int i = 1; i <= 49; i++)
13.         numbers.add(new Integer(i));
14.      Collections.shuffle(numbers);
15.      List winningCombination = numbers.subList(0, 6);
```

```
16.        Collections.sort(winningCombination);
17.        System.out.println(winningCombination);
18.    }
19. }
```

java.util.Collections

- `static void sort(List elements)`
- `static void sort(List elements, Comparator c)`

    sort the elements in the list, using a stable sort algorithm. The algorithm is guaranteed to run in O(n log n) time, where n is the length of the list.

    Parameters: elements   the list to sort

    c   the comparator to use for sorting

- `static void shuffle(List elements)`
- `static void shuffle(List elements, Random r)`

    randomly shuffle the elements in the list. This algorithm runs in O($n \cdot a(n)$) time, where n is the length of the list and $a(n)$ is the average time to access an element.

    Parameters: elements   the list to shuffle

    r   the source of randomness for shuffling

- `static Comparator reverseOrder()`

    returns a comparator that sorts elements in the reverse order of the one given by the `compareTo` method of the `Comparable` interface.

Binary Search

To find an object in an array, you normally need to visit all elements until you find a match. However, if the array is sorted, then you can look at the middle element and check if it is larger than the element that you are trying to find. If so, you keep looking in the first half of the array; otherwise, you look in the second half. That cuts the problem in half. You keep going in the same way. For example, if the array has 1024 elements, you will locate the match (or confirm that there is none) after 10 steps, whereas a linear search would have taken you an average of 512 steps if the element is present, and 1024 steps to confirm that it is not.

The `binarySearch` of the `Collections` class implements this algorithm. Note that the collection must already be sorted or the algorithm will return the wrong answer. To find an element, supply the collection (which must implement the `List` interface—more on that in the note below) and the element to be located. If the collection is not sorted by the `compareTo` element of the `Comparable` interface, then you need to supply a comparator object as well.

```
i = Collections.binarySearch(c, element);
i = Collections.binarySearch(c, element, comparator);
```

If the return value of the `binarySearch` method is ≥ 0, it denotes the index of the matching object. That is, `c.get(i)` is equal to `element` under the comparison order. If the value is negative, then there is no matching element. However, you can use the return value to compute the location where you *should* insert `element` into the collection to keep it sorted. The insertion location is

```
insertionPoint = -i - 1;
```

It isn't simply `-i` because then the value of 0 would be ambiguous. In other words, the operation

```
if (i < 0)
    c.add(-i - 1, element);
```

adds the element in the correct place.

To be worthwhile, binary search requires random access. If you have to iterate one by one through half of a linked list to find the middle element, you have lost all advantage of the binary search. Therefore, the `binarySearch` algorithm reverts to a linear search if you give it a linked list.

> NOTE: In SDK version 1.3, there was no separate interface for an ordered collection with efficient random access, and the `binarySearch` method employed a very crude device, checking whether the list parameter extends the `AbstractSequentialList` class. This has been fixed in version 1.4. Now the `binarySearch` method checks if the list parameter implements the `RandomAccess` interface. If it does, then the method carries out a binary search. Otherwise, it uses a linear search.

java.util.Collections

- `static int binarySearch(List elements, Object key)`
- `static int binarySearch(List elements, Object key, Comparator c)`

  search for a key in a sorted list, using a linear search if `elements` extends the `AbstractSequentialList` class, and a binary search in all other cases. The methods are guaranteed to run in $O(a(n) \log n)$ time, where n is the length of the list and $a(n)$ is the average time to access an element. The methods return either the index of the key in the list, or a negative value i if the key is not present in the list. In that case, the key should be inserted at index `-i - 1` for the list to stay sorted.

Parameters:	elements	the list to search
	key	the object to find
	c	the comparator used for sorting the list elements

Simple Algorithms

The Collections class contains several simple but useful algorithms. Among them is the example from the beginning of this section, finding the maximum value of a collection. Others include copying elements from one list to another, filling a container with a constant value, and reversing a list. Why supply such simple algorithms in the standard library? Surely most programmers could easily implement them with simple loops. We like the algorithms because they make life easier for the programmer *reading* the code. When you read a loop that was implemented by someone else, you have to decipher the original programmer's intentions. When you see a call to a method such as Collections.max, you know right away what the code does.

The following API notes describe the simple algorithms in the Collections class.

java.util.Collections

- static Object min(Collection elements)
- static Object max(Collection elements)
- static Object min(Collection elements, Comparator c)
- static Object max(Collection elements, Comparator c)

  return the smallest or largest element in the collection.

  Parameters: elements   the collection to search

                  c   the comparator used for sorting the elements

- static void copy(List to, List from)

  copies all elements from a source list to the same positions in the target list. The target list must be at least as long as the source list.

  Parameters: to   the target list

                  from   the source list

- static void fill(List l, Object value)

  sets all positions of a list to the same value.

  Parameters: l   the list to fill

                  value   the value with which to fill the list

- static void replaceAll(List l, Object oldValue, Object newValue)

  replaces all elements equal to oldValue with newValue. This method was added in SDK 1.4.

  Parameters: l   the list whose elements are replaced

                  oldValue   the value to be replaced

                  newValue   the replacement value

- `static int indexOfSubList(List l, List s)`
- `static int lastIndexOfSubList(List l, List s)`

return the index of the first or last sublist of `l` equalling `s`, or -1 if no sublist of `l` equals `s`. For example, if `l` is `[s, t, a, r]` and `s` is `[t, a, r]`, then both methods return the index 1. These methods were added in SDK 1.4.

Parameters:	`l`	the list to search
	`s`	the sublist to match

- `static void reverse(List l)`

reverses the order of the elements in a list. For example, reversing the list `[t, a, r]` yields the list `[r, a, t]`. This method runs in O(*n*) time, where *n* is the length of the list.

Parameters:	`l`	the list to reverse

- `static void rotate(List l, int d)`

rotates the elements in the list, moving the entry with index `i` to position `(i + d) % l.size()`. For example, rotating the list `[t, a, r]` by 2 yields the list `[a, r, t]`. This method runs in O(*n*) time, where *n* is the length of the list. This method was added in SDK 1.4.

Parameters:	`l`	the list to reverse

Writing Your Own Algorithms

If you write your own algorithm (or in fact, any method that has a collection as a parameter), you should work with *interfaces*, not concrete implementations, whenever possible. For example, suppose you want to fill a JComboBox with a set of strings. Traditionally, such a method might have been implemented like this:

```
void fillComboBox(JComboBox comboBox, Vector choices)
{
   for (int i = 0; i < choices.size(); i++)
      comboBox.addItem(choices.get(i));
}
```

However, you now constrained the caller of your method—the caller must supply the choices in a vector. If the choices happened to be in another container, they first need to be repackaged. It is much better to accept a more general collection.

You should ask yourself what is the most general collection interface that can do the job. In this case, you just need to visit all elements, a capability of the basic `Collection` interface. Here is how you can rewrite the `fillComboBox` method to accept collections of any kind.

```
void fillComboBox(JComboBox comboBox, Collection choices)
{
   Iterator iter = choices.iterator();
```

```
    while (iter.hasNext())
        comboBox.addItem(iter.next());
}
```

Now, anyone can call this method with a vector or even with an array, wrapped with the `Arrays.asList` wrapper.

NOTE: If it is such a good idea to use collection interfaces as method parameters, why doesn't the Java library follow this rule more often? For example, the `JComboBox` class has two constructors:

```
JComboBox(Object[] items)
JComboBox(Vector items)
```

The reason is simply timing. The Swing library was created before the collections library. You should expect future APIs to rely more heavily on the collections library. In particular, vectors should be "on their way out" because of the synchronization overhead.

If you write a method that *returns* a collection, you don't have to change the return type to a collection interface. The user of your method might in fact have a slight preference to receive the most concrete class possible. However, for your own convenience, you may want to return an interface instead of a class, because you can then change your mind and reimplement the method later with a different collection.

For example, let's write a method `getAllItems` that returns all items of a combo box. You could simply return the collection that you used to gather the items, say, an `ArrayList`.

```
ArrayList getAllItems(JComboBox comboBox)
{
    ArrayList items = new ArrayList(comboBox.getItemCount());
    for (int i = 0; i < comboBox.getItemCount(); i++)
        items.set(i, comboBox.getItemAt(i));
    return items;
}
```

But a better approach is to change the return type to `List`.

```
List getAllItems(JComboBox comboBox)
```

Then, you are free to change the implementation later. For example, you may decide that you don't want to *copy* the elements of the combo box but simply provide a view into them. You achieve this by returning an anonymous subclass of `AbstractList`.

```
List getAllItems(final JComboBox comboBox)
{
    return new
        AbstractList()
```

```
        {
            public Object get(int i)
            {
                return comboBox.getItemAt(i);
            }
            public int size()
            {
                return comboBox.getItemCount();
            }
        };
    }
```

Of course, this is an advanced technique. If you employ it, be careful to document exactly which "optional" operations are supported. In this case, you must advise the caller that the returned object is an unmodifiable list.

Legacy Collections

In this section, we discuss the collection classes that existed in the Java programming language since the beginning: the `Hashtable` class and its useful `Properties` subclass, the `Stack` subclass of `Vector`, and the `BitSet` class.

The `Hashtable` Class

The classic `Hashtable` class serves the same purpose as the `HashMap` and has essentially the same interface. Just like methods of the `Vector` class, the `Hashtable` methods are synchronized. If you do not require synchronization or compatibility with legacy code, you should use the `HashMap` instead.

> NOTE: The name of the class is `Hashtable`, with a lowercase `t`. Under Windows, you'll get strange error messages if you use `HashTable`, because the Windows file system is not case-sensitive but the Java compiler is.

Enumerations

The legacy collections use the `Enumeration` interface for traversing sequences of elements. The `Enumeration` interface has two methods, `hasMoreElements` and `nextElement`. These are entirely analogous to the `hasNext` and `next` methods of the `Iterator` interface.

For example, the `elements` method of the `Hashtable` class yields an object for enumerating the values in the table:

```
Enumeration e = staff.elements();
while (e.hasMoreElements())
{
    Employee e = (Employee)e.nextElement();
    . . .
}
```

You will occasionally encounter a legacy method that expects an enumeration parameter. The static method `Collections.enumeration` yields an enumeration object that enumerates the elements in the collection. For example,

```
ArrayList streams = . . .; // a sequence of input streams
SequenceInputStream in
    = new SequenceInputStream(Collections.enumeration(streams)   );
        // the SequenceInputStream constructor expects an enumeration
```

> NOTE: In C++, it is quite common to use iterators as parameters. Fortunately, in programming for the Java platform, very few programmers use this idiom. It is much smarter to pass around the collection than to pass an iterator. The collection object is more useful. The recipients can always obtain the iterator from it when they need it, plus they have all the collection methods at their disposal. However, you will find enumerations in some legacy code since they were the only available mechanism for generic collections until the collections framework appeared in the Java 2 platform.

java.util.Enumeration

- `boolean hasMoreElements()`
  returns `true` if there are more elements yet to be inspected.
- `Object nextElement()`
  returns the next element to be inspected. Do not call this method if `hasMoreElements()` returned `false`.

java.util.Hashtable

- `Enumeration keys()`
  returns an enumeration object that traverses the keys of the hash table.
- `Enumeration elements()`
  returns an enumeration object that traverses the elements of the hash table.

java.util.Vector

- `Enumeration elements()`
  returns an enumeration object that traverses the elements of the vector.

Property Sets

A *property set* is a map structure of a very special type. It has three particular characteristics.

- The keys and values are strings.
- The table can be saved to a file and loaded from a file.
- There is a secondary table for defaults.

The Java platform class that implements a property set is called `Properties`.

Property sets are useful in specifying configuration options for programs. The environment variables in UNIX and DOS are good examples. On a PC, your AUTOEXEC.BAT file might contain the settings:

```
SET PROMPT=$p$g
SET TEMP=C:\Windows\Temp
SET CLASSPATH=c:\jdk\lib;.
```

Here is how you would model those settings as a property set in the Java programming language.

```
Properties settings = new Properties();
settings.put("PROMPT", "$p$g");
settings.put("TEMP", "C:\\Windows\\Temp");
settings.put("CLASSPATH", "c:\\jdk\\lib;.");
```

Use the `store` method to save this list of properties to a file. Here, we just print the property set to the standard output. The second argument is a comment that is included in the file.

```
settings.store(System.out, "Environment settings");
```

The sample table gives the following output.

```
#Environment settings
#Sun Jan 21 07:22:52  1996
CLASSPATH=c:\\jdk\\lib;.
TEMP=C:\\Windows\\Temp
PROMPT=$p$g
```

System information

Here's another example of the ubiquity of the `Properties` set: information about your system is stored in a `Properties` object that is returned by a method of the `System` class. Applications have complete access to this information, but applets that are loaded from a web page do not—a security exception is thrown if they try to access certain keys. The code at the end of this section prints out the key/value pairs in the `Properties` object that stores the system properties.

Here is an example of what you would see when you run the program. You can see all the values stored in this `Properties` object. (What you would get will, of course, reflect your machine's settings.)

```
java.runtime.name=Java(TM) 2 Runtime Environment, Standard Edition
sun.boot.library.path=/usr/local/j2sdk1.4.0/jre/lib/i386
java.vm.version=1.4.0-beta-b65
java.vm.vendor=Sun Microsystems Inc.
java.vendor.url=http://java.sun.com/
path.separator=:
java.vm.name=Java HotSpot(TM) Client VM
file.encoding.pkg=sun.io
```

```
sun.os.patch.level=unknown
java.vm.specification.name=Java Virtual Machine Specification
user.dir=/home/cay
java.runtime.version=1.4.0-beta-b65
java.awt.graphicsenv=sun.awt.X11GraphicsEnvironment
os.arch=i386
java.io.tmpdir=/tmp
line.separator=

java.vm.specification.vendor=Sun Microsystems Inc.
java.awt.fonts=
os.name=Linux
java.library.path=/usr/local/j2sdk1.4.0/jre/lib/i386:/usr/local/
j2sdk1.4.0/jre/lib/i386/native_threads/:/usr/local/j2sdk1.4.0/
jre/lib/i386/client:/usr/local/j2sdk1.4.0/jre/../lib/i386
java.specification.name=Java Platform API Specification
java.class.version=48.0
java.util.prefs.PreferencesFactory=java.util.prefs.FileSystem-
PreferencesFactory
os.version=2.4.3-20mdk
user.home=/home/cay
user.timezone=
java.awt.printerjob=sun.print.PSPrinterJob
file.encoding=ISO-8859-1
java.specification.version=1.4
user.name=cay
java.class.path=.
java.vm.specification.version=1.0
sun.arch.data.model=32
java.home=/usr/local/j2sdk1.4.0/jre
java.specification.vendor=Sun Microsystems Inc.
user.language=en
java.vm.info=mixed mode
java.version=1.4.0-beta
java.ext.dirs=/usr/local/j2sdk1.4.0/jre/lib/ext
sun.boot.class.path=/usr/local/j2sdk1.4.0/jre/lib/rt.jar:/usr/
local/j2sdk1.4.0/jre/lib/i18n.jar:/usr/local/j2sdk1.4.0/jre/lib/
sunrsasign.jar:/usr/local/j2sdk1.4.0/jre/lib/jsse.jar:/usr/local/
j2sdk1.4.0/jre/lib/jce.jar:/usr/local/j2sdk1.4.0/jre/lib/char-
sets.jar:/usr/local/j2sdk1.4.0/jre/classes
java.vendor=Sun Microsystems Inc.
file.separator=/
java.vendor.url.bug=http://java.sun.com/cgi-bin/bugreport.cgi
sun.cpu.endian=little
sun.io.unicode.encoding=UnicodeLittle
user.region=US
sun.cpu.isalist=
```

NOTE: For security reasons, applets can only access a small subset of these properties.

NOTE: The list of system properties shows a disadvantage of the `Properties` format. There is no hierarchy to the property keys, and it is cumbersome to use an artificial hierarchy, such as dot-separated tokens. There are two solutions. You can use XML to store properties in a hierarchical format—see chapter 12. Alternatively, SDK 1.4 introduces a `Preferences` class that can attach properties to individual classes.

Example 2–6: SystemInfo.java

```
1. import java.util.*;
2.
3. /**
4.    This program prints out all system properties.
5. */
6. public class SystemInfo
7. {
8.    public static void main(String args[])
9.    {
10.       Properties systemProperties = System.getProperties();
11.       Enumeration enum = systemProperties.propertyNames();
12.       while (enum.hasMoreElements())
13.       {
14.          String key = (String)enum.nextElement();
15.          System.out.println(key + "=" +
16.             systemProperties.getProperty(key));
17.       }
18.    }
19. }
```

Property defaults

A property set is also a useful gadget whenever you want to allow the user to customize an application. Here is how your users can customize the `NotHelloWorld` program to their hearts' content. We'll allow them to specify the following in the configuration file `CustomWorld.ini`:

- Window size
- Font
- Point size
- Background color
- Message string

If the user doesn't specify some of the settings, we will provide defaults.

The `Properties` class has two mechanisms for providing defaults. First, whenever you look up the value of a string, you can specify a default that should be used automatically when the key is not present.

```
String font = settings.getProperty("FONT", "Courier");
```

If there is a `"FONT"` property in the property table, then `font` is set to that string. Otherwise, `font` is set to `"Courier"`.

If you find it too tedious to specify the default in every call to `getProperty`, then you can pack all the defaults into a secondary property set and supply that in the constructor of your lookup table.

```
Properties defaultSettings = new Properties();
defaultSettings.put("FONT", "Courier");
defaultSettings.put("SIZE", "10");
defaultSettings.put("MESSAGE", "Hello, World");
. . .
Properties settings = new Properties(defaultSettings);
FileInputStream sf = new FileInputStream("CustomWorld.ini");
settings.load(sf);
. . .
```

Yes, you can even specify defaults to defaults if you give another property set parameter to the `defaultSettings` constructor, but it is not something one would normally do.

Figure 2–13 is the customizable `"Hello World"` program. Just edit the `.ini` file to change the program's appearance to the way *you* want (see Figure 2–13).

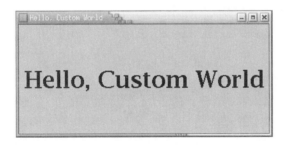

Figure 2–13: The customized Hello World program

Here are the current property settings.

```
#Environment settings
#Sun Jan 21 07:22:52  1996
FONT=Serif
SIZE=400 200
MESSAGE=Hello, Custom World
COLOR=0 50 100
PTSIZE=36
```

NOTE: The `Properties` class *extends* the `Hashtable` class. That means that all methods of `Hashtable` are available to `Properties` objects. Some methods are useful. For example, `size` returns the number of possible properties (well, it isn't *that* nice—it doesn't count the defaults). Similarly, `keys` returns an enumeration of all keys, except for the defaults. There is also a second function, called `propertyNames`, that returns all keys. The `put` function is downright dangerous. It doesn't check that you put strings into the table.

Does the *is-a* rule for using inheritance apply here? Is every property set a hash table? Not really. That these are true is really just an implementation detail. Maybe it is better to think of a property set as having a hash table. But then the hash table should be a private instance variable. Actually, in this case, a property set uses two hash tables, one for the defaults and one for the nondefault values.

We think a better design would be the following:

```
class Properties
{
    public String getProperty(String) { . . . }
    public void put(String, String) { . . . }
    . . .
    private Hashtable nonDefaults;
    private Hashtable defaults;
}
```

We don't want to tell you to avoid the `Properties` class in the Java library. Provided you are careful to put nothing but strings in it, it works just fine. But think twice before using "quick and dirty" inheritance in your own programs.

Example 2–7: CustomWorld.java

```
1. import java.awt.*;
2. import java.awt.event.*;
3. import java.util.*;
4. import java.io.*;
5. import javax.swing.*;
6.
7. /**
8.    This program demonstrates how to customize a "Hello, World"
9.    program with a properties file.
10. */
11. public class CustomWorld
12. {
13.    public static void main(String[] args)
14.    {
15.       CustomWorldFrame frame = new CustomWorldFrame();
16.       frame.setDefaultCloseOperation(JFrame.EXIT_ON_CLOSE);
17.       frame.show();
18.    }
19. }
```

```
20.
21. /**
22.    This frame displays a message. The frame size, message text,
23.    font, and color are set in a properties file.
24. */
25. class CustomWorldFrame extends JFrame
26. {
27.    public CustomWorldFrame()
28.    {
29.       Properties defaultSettings = new Properties();
30.       defaultSettings.put("FONT", "Monospaced");
31.       defaultSettings.put("SIZE", "300 200");
32.       defaultSettings.put("MESSAGE", "Hello, World");
33.       defaultSettings.put("COLOR", "0 50 50");
34.       defaultSettings.put("PTSIZE", "12");
35.
36.       Properties settings = new Properties(defaultSettings);
37.       try
38.       {
39.          FileInputStream sf
40.             = new FileInputStream("CustomWorld.ini");
41.          settings.load(sf);
42.       }
43.       catch (FileNotFoundException e) {}
44.       catch (IOException e) {}
45.
46.       StringTokenizer st = new StringTokenizer
47.          (settings.getProperty("COLOR"));
48.       int red = Integer.parseInt(st.nextToken());
49.       int green = Integer.parseInt(st.nextToken());
50.       int blue = Integer.parseInt(st.nextToken());
51.
52.       Color foreground = new Color(red, green, blue);
53.
54.       String name = settings.getProperty("FONT");
55.       int size = Integer.parseInt(settings.getProperty("PTSIZE"));
56.       Font f = new Font(name, Font.BOLD, size);
57.
58.       st = new StringTokenizer(settings.getProperty("SIZE"));
59.       int hsize = Integer.parseInt(st.nextToken());
60.       int vsize = Integer.parseInt(st.nextToken());
61.       setSize(hsize, vsize);
62.       setTitle(settings.getProperty("MESSAGE"));
63.
64.
65.       JLabel label = new JLabel(settings.getProperty("MESSAGE"),
66.          SwingConstants.CENTER);
67.       label.setFont(f);
```

```
68.        label.setForeground(foreground);
69.        getContentPane().add(label);
70.    }
71. }
```

 java.util.Properties

- `Properties()`
  creates an empty property list.

- `Properties(Properties defaults)`
  creates an empty property list with a set of defaults.

  Parameters: defaults   the defaults to use for lookups

- `String getProperty(String key)`
  gets a property association; returns the string associated with the key, or the string associated with the key in the default table if it wasn't present in the table.

  Parameters: key   the key whose associated string to get

- `String getProperty(String key, String defaultValue)`
  gets a property with a default value if the key is not found; returns the string associated with the key, or the default string if it wasn't present in the table.

  Parameters: key   the key whose associated string to get

  defaultValue   the string to return if the key is not present

- `void load(InputStream in) throws IOException`
  loads a property set from an `InputStream`.

  Parameters: in   the input stream

Stacks

Since version 1.0, the standard library had a `Stack` class with the familiar `push` and `pop` methods. However, the `Stack` class extends the `Vector` class, which is not satisfactory from a theoretical perspective—you can apply such un-stack-like operations as `insert` and `remove` to insert and remove values anywhere, not just the top of the stack.

 java.util.Stack

- `void push(Object item)`
  pushes an item onto the stack.

  Parameters: item   the item to be added

- `Object pop()`
  pops and returns the top item of the stack. Don't call this method if the stack is empty.

- `Object peek()`
  returns the top of the stack without popping it. Don't call this method if the stack is empty.

Bit Sets

The Java platform `BitSet` class stores a sequence of bits. (It is not a *set* in the mathematical sense—bit *vector* or bit *array* would have been more appropriate terms.) Use a bit set if you need to store a sequence of bits (for example, flags) efficiently. Because a bit set packs the bits into bytes, it is far more efficient to use a bit set than to use an `ArrayList` of `Boolean` objects.

The `BitSet` class gives you a convenient interface for reading, setting, or resetting individual bits. Use of this interface avoids the masking and other bit-fiddling operations that would be necessary if you stored bits in `int` or `long` variables.

For example, for a `BitSet` named `bucketOfBits`,

    bucketOfBits.get(i)

returns `true` if the i'th bit is on, and `false` otherwise. Similarly,

    bucketOfBits.set(i)

turns the i'th bit on. Finally,

    bucketOfBits.clear(i)

turns the i'th bit off.

C++ NOTE: The C++ `bitset` template has the same functionality as the Java platform `BitSet`.

---

java.util.BitSet

- `BitSet(int nbits)`
  constructs a bit set.

  Parameters: nbits   the initial number of bits

- `int length()`
  returns the "logical length" of the bit set: one plus the index of the highest set bit.

- `boolean get(int bit)`
  gets a bit.

| *Parameters:* | bit | the position of the requested bit |

- `void set(int bit)`
  sets a bit.

| *Parameters:* | bit | the position of the bit to be set |

- `void clear(int bit)`
  clears a bit.

| *Parameters:* | bit | the position of the bit to be cleared |

- `void and(BitSet set)`
  logically ANDs this bit set with another.

| *Parameters:* | set | the bit set to be combined with this bit set |

- `void or(BitSet set)`
  logically ORs this bit set with another.

| *Parameters:* | set | the bit set to be combined with this bit set |

- `void xor(BitSet set)`
  logically XORs this bit set with another.

| *Parameters:* | set | the bit set to be combined with this bit set |

- `void andNot(BitSet set)`
  clears all bits in this bitset that are set in the other bit set.

| *Parameters:* | set | the bit set to be combined with this bit set |

The "sieve of Eratosthenes" benchmark

As an example of using bit sets, we want to show you an implementation of the "sieve of Eratosthenes" algorithm for finding prime numbers. (A prime number is a number like 2, 3, or 5 that is divisible only by itself and 1, and the sieve of Eratosthenes was one of the first methods discovered to enumerate these fundamental building blocks.) This isn't a terribly good algorithm for finding the number of primes, but for some reason it has become a popular benchmark for compiler performance. (It isn't a good benchmark either, since it mainly tests bit operations.)

Oh well, we bow to tradition and include an implementation. This program counts all prime numbers between 2 and 1,000,000. (There are 78,498 primes, so you probably don't want to print them all out.) You will find that the program takes a little while to get going, but eventually it picks up speed.

Without going into too many details of this program, the key is to march through a bit set with one million bits. We first turn on all the bits. After that, we turn off the bits that are multiples of numbers known to be prime. The positions of the bits that remain after this process are, themselves, the prime numbers. Example 2–8 illustrates this program in the Java programming language, and Example 2–9 is the C++ code.

NOTE: Even though the sieve isn't a good benchmark, we couldn't resist timing the two implementations of the algorithm. Here are the timing results on a 233 MHz IBM Thinkpad with 224 megabytes of RAM, running Linux Mandrake 8.

    g++ 2.96: 1740 milliseconds

    JDK 1.4: 1133 milliseconds

We have run this test for five editions of *Core Java*, and in the last two editions the Java programming language beat C++. However, in all fairness, we should point out that the culprit for the bad C++ result is the lousy implementation of the standard `bitset` template in the g++ compiler. When we reimplemented `bitset`, the time for C++ went down to 630 milliseconds.

Of course, these are perfect benchmark results because they allow you to put on any spin that you like. If you want to "prove" that the Java programming language is twice as slow as C++, make use of the latter results. Or you can "prove" that it has now over-taken C++. Point out that it is only fair to compare the language implementation as a whole, including standard class libraries, and quote the first set of numbers.

Example 2–8: Sieve.java

```
1. import java.util.*;
2.
3. /**
4.      This program runs the Sieve of Erathostenes benchmark.
5.      It computes all primes up to 1,000,000.
6. */
7. public class Sieve
8. {
9.     public static final boolean PRINT = false;
10.
11.    public static void main(String[] s)
12.    {
13.        int n = 1000000;
14.        long start = System.currentTimeMillis();
15.        BitSet b = new BitSet(n);
16.        int count = 0;
17.        int i;
18.        for (i = 2; i <= n; i++)
19.            b.set(i);
20.        i = 2;
21.        while (i * i <= n)
```

```
22.        {
23.            if (b.get(i))
24.            {
25.                if (PRINT) System.out.println(i);
26.                count++;
27.                int k = 2 * i;
28.                while (k <= n)
29.                {
30.                    b.clear(k);
31.                    k += i;
32.                }
33.            }
34.            i++;
35.        }
36.        while (i <= n)
37.        {
38.            if (b.get(i))
39.            {
40.                if (PRINT) System.out.println(i);
41.                count++;
42.            }
43.            i++;
44.        }
45.        long end =  System.currentTimeMillis();
46.        System.out.println(count + " primes");
47.        System.out.println((end - start) + " milliseconds");
48.    }
49. }
```

Example 2-9: Sieve.cpp

```
1. #ifndef AVOID_STANDARD_BITSET
2.
3. #include <bitset>
4.
5. #else
6.
7. template<int N>
8. class bitset
9. {
10. public:
11.    bitset() : bits(new char[(N - 1) / 8 + 1]) {}
12.
13.    bool test(int n)
14.    {
15.        return (bits[n >> 3] & (1 << (n & 7))) != 0;
16.    }
17.
18.    void set(int n)
```

```
19.     {
20.         bits[n >> 3] |= 1 << (n & 7);
21.     }
22.
23.     void reset(int n)
24.     {
25.         bits[n >> 3] &= ~(1 << (n & 7));
26.     }
27.
28. private:
29.     char* bits;
30. };
31.
32. #endif
33.
34. #include <iostream>
35. #include <ctime>
36.
37. using namespace std;
38.
39. int main()
40. {
41.     const int N = 1000000;
42.     clock_t cstart = clock();
43.
44.     bitset<N + 1> b;
45.     int count = 0;
46.     int i;
47.     for (i = 2; i <= N; i++)
48.         b.set(i);
49.     i = 2;
50.     while (i * i <= N)
51.     {
52.         if (b.test(i))
53.         {
54.             int k = 2 * i;
55.             while (k <= N)
56.             {   b.reset(k);
57.                 k += i;
58.             }
59.         }
60.         i++;
61.     }
62.     for (i = 2; i <= N; i++)
63.     {
64.         if (b.test(i))
65.         {
66. #ifdef PRINT
```

```
67.           cout << i << "\n";
68. #endif
69.           count++;
70.      }
71.    }
72.
73.    clock_t cend = clock();
74.    double millis = 1000.0
75.       * (cend - cstart) / CLOCKS_PER_SEC;
76.
77.    cout << count << " primes\n"
78.       << millis << " milliseconds\n";
79.
80.    return 0;
81. }
```

Chapter *3*

Networking

▼ CONNECTING TO A SERVER

▼ IMPLEMENTING SERVERS

▼ SENDING E-MAIL

▼ ADVANCED SOCKET PROGRAMMING

▼ URL CONNECTIONS

▼ POSTING FORM DATA

▼ HARVESTING INFORMATION FROM THE WEB

The Java programming language is supposed to become the premier tool for connecting computers over the Internet and corporate intranets and, in this realm, Java mostly lives up to the hype. If you are accustomed to programming network connections in C or C++, you will be pleasantly surprised at how easy it is to program them in the Java programming language. For example, as you saw in the applet chapter in Volume 1, it is easy to open a URL (uniform resource locator) on the Net: simply pass the URL to the `showDocument` method in the `AppletContext` class.

We begin this chapter by talking a little bit about basic networking. Then, we move on to reviewing and extending the information that was briefly presented in the applet chapter in Volume 1. The rest of the chapter moves on to the intricacies of doing sophisticated work on the Net with the Java programming language. For example, we give you a glimpse into server-side programming with Java. In particular, we show you how to use a combination of an applet and a servlet to harvest information on the Internet.

In the first part of this chapter, we assume that you have no network programming experience. If you have written TCP/IP programs before and ports and sockets are no mystery to you, you should breeze through the sample code. Toward the end of this chapter, the code becomes complex and is geared more toward those with some experience in network programming.

Connecting to a Server

Before writing our first network program, let's learn about a great debugging tool for network programming that you already have, namely, telnet. Most systems (both UNIX and Windows) always come with telnet. However, it is optional with some installations, and you may not have requested it when you installed the operating system. If you can't run telnet from a command shell, then you need to add it from your operating system installation disk.

You may have used telnet to connect to a remote computer and to check your e-mail, but you can use it to communicate with other services provided by Internet hosts as well. Here is an example of what you can do. Type

```
telnet time-A.timefreq.bldrdoc.gov 13
```

As Figure 3–1 shows, you should get back a line like this:

```
52088 01-06-28 14:35:13 50 0 0 644.8 UTC(NIST) *
```

```
Terminal                                                    _ □ ×
 File   Edit   Settings   Help
~$ telnet time-A.timefreq.bldrdoc.gov 13
Trying 132.163.4.102...
Connected to time-A.timefreq.bldrdoc.gov.
Escape character is '^]'.

52088 01-06-28 14:35:13 50 0 0 644.8 UTC(NIST) *
Connection closed by foreign host.
~$ []
```

Figure 3–1: Output of the "time of day" service

What is going on? You have connected to the "time of day" service that most UNIX machines constantly run. The particular server that you connected to is operated by the National Institute of Standards and Technology in Boulder, Colorado, and gives the measurement of a Cesium atomic clock. (Of course, the reported time is not completely accurate due to network delays.) By convention, the "time of day" service is always attached to "port" number 13.

NOTE: In network parlance, a port is not a physical device, but an abstraction to facilitate communication between a server and a client (see Figure 3–2).

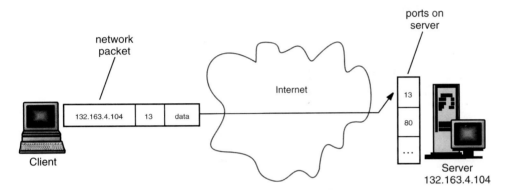

Figure 3–2: A client connecting to a server port

What is happening is that the server software is continuously running on the remote machine, waiting for any network traffic that wants to chat with port 13. When the operating system on the remote computer gets a network package that contains a request to connect to port number 13, it wakes up the listening server process and establishes the connection. The connection stays up until it is terminated by one of the parties.

When you began the telnet session with `time-A.timefreq.bldrdoc.gov` at port 13, an unrelated piece of network software knew enough to convert the string `"time-A.timefreq.bldrdoc.gov"` to its correct Internet Protocol address, 132.163.4.102. The software then sent a connection request to that computer, asking for a connection to port 13. Once the connection was established, the remote program sent back a line of data and then closed the connection. In general, of course, clients and servers engage in a more extensive dialog before one or the other closes the connection.

Here is another experiment, along the same lines, that is a bit more interesting. Do the following:

1. On Windows, turn on the local key echo in the Terminal Preferences dialog box.
2. Connect to `java.sun.com` on port 80.
3. Type the following, *exactly as it appears, without pressing backspace.*
4. `GET / HTTP/1.0`
5. Now, press the ENTER key *two times.*

Figure 3–3 shows the response. It should look eerily familiar—you got a page of HTML-formatted text, namely, the main web page for Java technology.

This is *exactly* the same process that your web browser goes through to get a web page.

```
height="30" border="0" ALT="Sun Microsystems, Inc."></A><BR>
                    <FONT SIZE="-2">
                    Copyright &copy; 1995-2001
                    <A HREF="http://www.sun.com">Sun Microsystems, Inc.</A><BR>
                    All Rights Reserved. <a
                    href="http://www.sun.com/share/text/termsofuse.html">Terms
                    of Use</a>. <A HREF="http://www.sun.com/privacy">Privacy Po
licy</A>.
                    </FONT>
                    </TD></TR>
                    </TABLE>
            </TD>
    </TR>
</TABLE>

<!-- End Footer Segment -->

<!-- end server side include for footer -->

</BODY>
</HTML>
Connection closed by foreign host.
~$ 
```

Figure 3–3: Using telnet to access an HTTP port

Our first network program in Example 3–1 will do the same thing we did using telnet—connect to a port and print out what it finds.

Example 3–1: SocketTest.java

```
1. import java.io.*;
2. import java.net.*;
3.
4. /**
5.    This program makes a socket connection to the atomic clock
6.    in Boulder, Colorado, and prints the time that the
```

```
7.      server sends.
8.  */
9.  public class SocketTest
10. {
11.     public static void main(String[] args)
12.     {
13.         try
14.         {
15.             Socket s = new Socket("time-A.timefreq.bldrdoc.gov",
16.                 13);
17.
18.             BufferedReader in = new BufferedReader
19.                 (new InputStreamReader(s.getInputStream()));
20.             boolean more = true;
21.             while (more)
22.             {
23.                 String line = in.readLine();
24.                 if (line == null)
25.                     more = false;
26.                 else
27.                     System.out.println(line);
28.             }
29.
30.         }
31.         catch (IOException e)
32.         {
33.             e.printStackTrace();
34.         }
35.     }
36. }
```

This program is extremely simple, but before we analyze the two key lines, note that we are importing the `java.net` package and catching any input/output errors because the code is encased in a `try`/`catch` block. (Since many things can go wrong with a network connection, most of the network-related methods threaten to throw I/O errors. You must catch them for the code to compile.)

As for the code itself, the key lines are as follows:

```
Socket s = new Socket("time-A.timefreq.bldrdoc.gov", 13);
BufferedReader in = new BufferedReader
    (new InputStreamReader(s.getInputStream()));
```

The first line opens a *socket*, which is an abstraction for the network software that enables communication out of and into this program. We pass the remote address and the port number to the socket constructor. If the connection fails, then an `UnknownHostException` is thrown. If there is another problem, then an IOException occurs. Since UnknownHostException is a subclass of IOException and this is a sample program, we just catch the superclass.

Once the socket is open, the getInputStream method in java.net.Socket returns an InputStream object that you can use just like any other stream. (See Chapter 12 of Volume 1.) Once you have grabbed the stream, this program simply

1.   Reads all characters sent by the server using readLine;
2.   Prints each line out to standard output.

This process continues until the stream is finished and the server disconnects. You know this happens when the readLine method returns a null string.

> NOTE: This program works only with very simple servers, such as a "time of day" service. In more complex networking programs, the client sends request data to the server, and the server may not immediately disconnect at the end of a response. You will see how to implement that behavior in several examples throughout this chapter.

Plainly, the Socket class is pleasant and easy to use because Java technology hides the complexities of establishing a networking connection and sending data across. The java.net package essentially gives you the same programming interface you would use to work with a file.

Implementing Servers

Now that we have implemented a basic network client that receives data from the Net, let's implement a simple server that can send information out to the Net. Once you start the server program, it waits for some client to attach to its port. We chose port number 8189, which is not used by any of the standard services. The ServerSocket class is used to establish a socket. In our case, the command

```
ServerSocket s = new ServerSocket(8189);
```

establishes a server that monitors port 8189. The command

```
Socket incoming = s.accept();
```

tells the program to wait indefinitely until a client connects to that port. Once someone connects to this port by sending the correct request over the network, this method returns a Socket object that represents the connection that was made. You can use this object to get an input reader and an output writer from that socket, as is shown in the following code:

```
BufferedReader in = new BufferedReader
    (new InputStreamReader(incoming.getInputStream()));
PrintWriter out = new PrintWriter
    (incoming.getOutputStream(), true /* autoFlush */);
```

Everything that the server sends to the server output stream becomes the input of the client program, and all the output from the client program ends up in the server input stream.

In all of the examples in this chapter, we will transmit text through sockets. We, therefore, turn the streams into readers and writers. Then, we can use the `readLine` method (defined in `BufferedReader`, but not in `Input-Stream`) and the `print` method (defined in `PrintWriter`, but not in `OutputStream`). If we wanted to transmit *binary data,* we would turn the streams into `DataInputStream` and `DataOutputStreams`. To transmit *serialized objects,* we would use `ObjectInputStream` and `ObjectOutput-Streams` instead.

Let's send the client a greeting:

```
out.println("Hello! Enter BYE to exit.");
```

When you use telnet to connect to this server program at port 8189, you will see the above greeting on the terminal screen.

In this simple server, we just read the client input, a line at a time, and echo it. This demonstrates that the program gets the client's input. An actual server would obviously compute and return an answer that depended on the input.

```
String line = in.readLine();
if (line != null)
{
   out.println("Echo: " + line);
   if (line.trim().equals("BYE")) done = true;
}
else done = true;
```

In the end, we close the incoming socket.

```
incoming.close();
```

That is all there is to it. Every server program, such as an HTTP web server, continues performing this loop:

1. It gets a command from the client ("get me this information") through an incoming data stream.
2. It somehow fetches the information.
3. It sends the information to the client through the outgoing data stream.

Example 3–2 is the complete program.

Example 3–2: EchoServer.java

```
1. import java.io.*;
2. import java.net.*;
3.
```

```
4. /**
5.    This program implements a simple server that listens to
6.    port 8189 and echoes back all client input.
7. */
8. public class EchoServer
9. {
10.    public static void main(String[] args )
11.    {
12.       try
13.       {
14.          // establish server socket
15.          ServerSocket s = new ServerSocket(8189);
16.
17.          // wait for client connection
18.          Socket incoming = s.accept( );
19.          BufferedReader in = new BufferedReader
20.             (new InputStreamReader(incoming.getInputStream()));
21.          PrintWriter out = new PrintWriter
22.             (incoming.getOutputStream(), true /* autoFlush */);
23.
24.          out.println( "Hello! Enter BYE to exit." );
25.
26.          // echo client input
27.          boolean done = false;
28.          while (!done)
29.          {
30.             String line = in.readLine();
31.             if (line == null) done = true;
32.             else
33.             {
34.                out.println("Echo: " + line);
35.
36.                if (line.trim().equals("BYE"))
37.                   done = true;
38.             }
39.          }
40.          incoming.close();
41.       }
42.       catch (Exception e)
43.       {
44.          e.printStackTrace();
45.       }
46.    }
47. }
```

To try it out, you need to compile and run the program. Then, use telnet to connect to the following server and port:

Server: 127.0.0.1
Port: 8189

The IP address 127.0.0.1 is a special address, called the *local loopback address,* that denotes the local machine. Since you are running the echo server locally, that is where you want to connect.

NOTE: If you are using a dial-up connection, you need to have it running for this experiment. Even though you are only talking to your local machine, the network software must be loaded.

Actually, anyone in the world can access your echo server, provided it is running and they know your IP address and the magic port number.

When you connect to the port, you will get the message shown in Figure 3–4:

```
Hello! Enter BYE to exit.
```

Type anything and watch the input echo on your screen. Type BYE (all uppercase letters) to disconnect. The server program will terminate as well.

```
~$ telnet localhost 8189
Trying 127.0.0.1...
Connected to localhost.localdomain.
Escape character is '^]'.
Hello! Enter BYE to exit.
Hello there! How are you today?
Echo: Hello there! How are you today?
I am fine, thanks. And you?
Echo: I am fine, thanks. And you?
BYE
Echo: BYE
Connection closed by foreign host.
~$
```

Figure 3–4: Accessing an echo server

Serving Multiple Clients

There is one problem with the simple server in the preceding example. Suppose we want to allow multiple clients to connect to our server at the same time. Typically, a server runs constantly on a server computer, and clients from all over the Internet may want to use the server at the same time. Rejecting multiple connections allows any one client to monopolize the service by connecting to it for a long time. We can do much better through the magic of threads.

Every time we know the program has established a new socket connection, that is, when the call to accept was successful, we will launch a new thread to take care of the connection between the server and *that* client. The main program will just go back and wait for the next connection. For this to happen, the main loop of the server should look like this:

```
while (true)
{
    Socket incoming = s.accept();
    Thread t = new ThreadedEchoHandler(incoming);
    t.start();
}
```

The ThreadedEchoHandler class derives from Thread and contains the communication loop with the client in its run method.

```
class ThreadedEchoHandler extends Thread
{   . . .
    public void run()
    {
        try
        {
            BufferedReader in = new BufferedReader
                (new InputStreamReader(incoming.getInputStream()));
            PrintWriter out = new PrintWriter
                (incoming.getOutputStream(), true /* autoFlush */);

            String line;
            while ((line = in.readLine()) != null)
            {
                process line
            }
            incoming.close();
        }
        catch(Exception e)
        {
            handle exception
        }
    }
}
```

Because each connection starts a new thread, multiple clients can connect to the server at the same time. You can easily check out this fact. Compile and run the server program (Example 3–3). Open several telnet windows as we have in Figure 3–5. You can communicate through all of them simultaneously. The server program never dies. Use CTRL+C to kill it.

Figure 3–5: Simultaneous access to the threaded echo server

Example 3–3: ThreadedEchoServer.java

```
1. import java.io.*;
2. import java.net.*;
3.
4. /**
```

```
5.    This program implements a multithreaded server that listens to
6.    port 8189 and echoes back all client input.
7. */
8. public class ThreadedEchoServer
9. {
10.    public static void main(String[] args )
11.    {
12.       try
13.       {
14.          int i = 1;
15.          ServerSocket s = new ServerSocket(8189);
16.
17.          for (;;)
18.          {
19.             Socket incoming = s.accept( );
20.             System.out.println("Spawning " + i);
21.             Thread t = new ThreadedEchoHandler(incoming, i);
22.             t.start();
23.             i++;
24.          }
25.       }
26.       catch (Exception e)
27.       {
28.          e.printStackTrace();
29.       }
30.    }
31. }
32.
33. /**
34.    This class handles the client input for one server socket
35.    connection.
36. */
37. class ThreadedEchoHandler extends Thread
38. {
39.    /**
40.       Constructs a handler.
41.       @param i the incoming socket
42.       @param c the counter for the handlers (used in prompts)
43.    */
44.    public ThreadedEchoHandler(Socket i, int c)
45.    {
46.       incoming = i; counter = c;
47.    }
48.
49.    public void run()
50.    {
51.       try
52.       {
```

```
53.         BufferedReader in = new BufferedReader
54.             (new InputStreamReader(incoming.getInputStream()));
55.         PrintWriter out = new PrintWriter
56.             (incoming.getOutputStream(), true /* autoFlush */);
57.
58.         out.println( "Hello! Enter BYE to exit." );
59.
60.         boolean done = false;
61.         while (!done)
62.         {
63.             String str = in.readLine();
64.             if (str == null) done = true;
65.             else
66.             {
67.                 out.println("Echo (" + counter + "): " + str);
68.
69.                 if (str.trim().equals("BYE"))
70.                     done = true;
71.             }
72.         }
73.         incoming.close();
74.     }
75.     catch (Exception e)
76.     {
77.         e.printStackTrace();
78.     }
79.   }
80.
81.   private Socket incoming;
82.   private int counter;
83. }
```

java.net.ServerSocket

- `ServerSocket(int port) throws IOException`
  creates a server socket that monitors a port.

  Parameters: port   the port number

- `Socket accept() throws IOException`
  waits for a connection. This method will block (that is, idle) the current thread
  until the connection is made. The method returns a `Socket` object through
  which the program can communicate with the connecting client.

- `void close() throws IOException`
  closes the server socket.

Sending E-Mail

In this section, we show you a practical example of socket programming: a program that sends e-mail to a remote site.

To send e-mail, you make a socket connection to port 25, the SMTP port. SMTP is the Simple Mail Transport Protocol that describes the format for e-mail messages. You can connect to any server that runs an SMTP service. On UNIX machines, that service is typically implemented by the `sendmail` daemon. However, the server must be willing to accept your request. It used to be that sendmail servers were routinely willing to route e-mail from anyone, but in these days of spam floods, most servers now have built-in checks and only accept requests from users, domains, or IP address ranges that they trust.

Once you are connected to the server, send a mail header (in the SMTP format, which is easy to generate), followed by the mail message.

Here are the details:

1. Open a socket to your host.

   ```
   Socket s = new Socket("mail.yourserver.com", 25); // 25 is SMTP
   PrintWriter out = new PrintWriter(s.getOutputStream());
   ```

2. Send the following information to the print stream:

   ```
   HELO sending host
   MAIL FROM: <sender email address>
   RCPT TO: <recipient email address>
   DATA
   mail message
   (any number of lines)
   .
   QUIT
   ```

The SMTP specification (RFC 821) states that lines must be terminated with `\r` followed by `\n`.

Most SMTP servers do not check the veracity of the information—you may be able to supply any sender you like. (Keep this in mind the next time you get an e-mail message from `president@whitehouse.gov` inviting you to a black-tie affair on the front lawn. Anyone could have connected to an SMTP server and created a fake message.)

The program in Example 3–4 is a very simple e-mail program. As you can see in Figure 3–6, you type in the sender, recipient, mail message, and SMTP server. Then, click on the "Send" button, and your message is sent.

The program simply sends the sequence of commands that we just discussed. It displays the commands that it sends to the SMTP server and the responses that it receives. Note that the communication with the mail server occurs in a separate thread so that the user interface thread is not blocked when the program tries to connect to the mail server. (See Chapter 1 for more details on threads in Swing applications.)

Figure 3–6: The `MailTest` program

Example 3–4: MailTest.java

```
1. import java.awt.*;
2. import java.awt.event.*;
3. import java.util.*;
4. import java.net.*;
5. import java.io.*;
6. import javax.swing.*;
7.
8. /**
9.    This program shows how to use sockets to send plain text
10.    mail messages.
11. */
12. public class MailTest
13. {
14.    public static void main(String[] args)
15.    {
16.       JFrame frame = new MailTestFrame();
17.       frame.setDefaultCloseOperation(JFrame.EXIT_ON_CLOSE);
18.       frame.show();
19.    }
20. }
21.
22. /**
23.    The frame for the mail GUI.
24. */
25. class MailTestFrame extends JFrame
26. {
27.    public MailTestFrame()
```

```
28.        {
29.            setSize(WIDTH, HEIGHT);
30.            setTitle("MailTest");
31.
32.            getContentPane().setLayout(new GridBagLayout());
33.
34.            GridBagConstraints gbc = new GridBagConstraints();
35.            gbc.fill = GridBagConstraints.HORIZONTAL;
36.            gbc.weightx = 0;
37.            gbc.weighty = 0;
38.
39.            gbc.weightx = 0;
40.            add(new JLabel("From:"), gbc, 0, 0, 1, 1);
41.            gbc.weightx = 100;
42.            from = new JTextField(20);
43.            add(from, gbc, 1, 0, 1, 1);
44.
45.            gbc.weightx = 0;
46.            add(new JLabel("To:"), gbc, 0, 1, 1, 1);
47.            gbc.weightx = 100;
48.            to = new JTextField(20);
49.            add(to, gbc, 1, 1, 1, 1);
50.
51.            gbc.weightx = 0;
52.            add(new JLabel("SMTP server:"), gbc, 0, 2, 1, 1);
53.            gbc.weightx = 100;
54.            smtpServer = new JTextField(20);
55.            add(smtpServer, gbc, 1, 2, 1, 1);
56.
57.            gbc.fill = GridBagConstraints.BOTH;
58.            gbc.weighty = 100;
59.            message = new JTextArea();
60.            add(new JScrollPane(message), gbc, 0, 3, 2, 1);
61.
62.            communication = new JTextArea();
63.            add(new JScrollPane(communication), gbc, 0, 4, 2, 1);
64.
65.            gbc.weighty = 0;
66.            JButton sendButton = new JButton("Send");
67.            sendButton.addActionListener(new
68.                ActionListener()
69.                {
70.                    public void actionPerformed(ActionEvent evt)
71.                    {
72.                        new
73.                            Thread()
74.                            {
75.                                public void run()
```

```
76.                         {
77.                             sendMail();
78.                         }
79.                     }.start();
80.                 }
81.             });
82.         JPanel buttonPanel = new JPanel();
83.         buttonPanel.add(sendButton);
84.         add(buttonPanel, gbc, 0, 5, 2, 1);
85.     }
86.
87.     /**
88.         Add a component to this frame.
89.         @param c the component to add
90.         @param gbc the grid bag constraints
91.         @param x the grid bax column
92.         @param y the grid bag row
93.         @param w the number of grid bag columns spanned
94.         @param h the number of grid bag rows spanned
95.     */
96.     private void add(Component c, GridBagConstraints gbc,
97.         int x, int y, int w, int h)
98.     {
99.         gbc.gridx = x;
100.         gbc.gridy = y;
101.         gbc.gridwidth = w;
102.         gbc.gridheight = h;
103.         getContentPane().add(c, gbc);
104.     }
105.
106.     /**
107.         Sends the mail message that has been authored in the GUI.
108.     */
109.     public void sendMail()
110.     {
111.         try
112.         {
113.             Socket s = new Socket(smtpServer.getText(), 25);
114.
115.             out = new PrintWriter(s.getOutputStream());
116.             in = new BufferedReader(new
117.                 InputStreamReader(s.getInputStream()));
118.
119.             String hostName
120.                 = InetAddress.getLocalHost().getHostName();
121.
122.             receive();
123.             send("HELO " + hostName);
```

```
124.          receive();
125.          send("MAIL FROM: <" + from.getText() + ">");
126.          receive();
127.          send("RCPT TO: <" + to.getText() + ">");
128.          receive();
129.          send("DATA");
130.          receive();
131.          StringTokenizer tokenizer = new StringTokenizer(
132.             message.getText(), "\n");
133.          while (tokenizer.hasMoreTokens())
134.             send(tokenizer.nextToken());
135.          send(".");
136.          receive();
137.          s.close();
138.       }
139.       catch (IOException exception)
140.       {
141.          communication.append("Error: " + exception);
142.       }
143.    }
144.
145.    /**
146.       Sends a string to the socket and echoes it in the
147.       communication text area.
148.       @param s the string to send.
149.    */
150.    public void send(String s) throws IOException
151.    {
152.       communication.append(s);
153.       communication.append("\n");
154.       out.print(s);
155.       out.print("\r\n");
156.       out.flush();
157.    }
158.
159.    /**
160.       Receives a string from the socket and displays it
161.       in the communication text area.
162.    */
163.    public void receive() throws IOException
164.    {
165.       String line = in.readLine();
166.       if (line != null)
167.       {
168.          communication.append(line);
169.          communication.append("\n");
170.       }
171.    }
```

```
172.
173.    private BufferedReader in;
174.    private PrintWriter out;
175.    private JTextField from;
176.    private JTextField to;
177.    private JTextField smtpServer;
178.    private JTextArea message;
179.    private JTextArea communication;
180.
181.    public static final int WIDTH = 300;
182.    public static final int HEIGHT = 300;
183. }
```

Advanced Socket Programming

Socket timeouts

In real-life programs, you don't just want to read from a socket, because the read methods will block until data is available. If the host is unreachable, then your application waits for a long time, and you are at the mercy of the underlying operating system to time out eventually.

Instead, you should decide what timeout value is reasonable for your particular application. Then, call the setSoTimeout method to set a timeout value (in milliseconds).

```
Socket s = new Socket(. . .);
s.setSoTimeout(10000); // time out after 10 seconds
```

If the timeout value has been set for a socket, then all subsequent read operations throw an InterruptedIOException when the timeout has been reached before input is available. You can catch that exception and react to the timeout.

```
try
{
   String line
   while ((String line = in.readLine()) != null)
   {
      process line
   }
}
catch (InterruptedIOException exception)
{
   react to timeout
}
```

There is one additional timeout issue that you need to address. The constructor

```
Socket(String host, int port)
```

can block indefinitely until an initial connection to the host is established.

As of SDK 1.4, you can overcome this problem by first constructing an unconnected socket and then connecting it with a timeout:

```
Socket s = new Socket();
s.connect(new InetSocketAddress(host, port), timeout);
```

> **TIP:** If you use an older version of the SDK, you need to construct the socket in a separate thread and wait for that thread to either complete or time out.
>
> ```
> Socket socket = null;
> Thread t = new Thread()
>     {
>         public void run()
>         {
>             try
>             {
>                 socket = new Socket(host, port);
>             }
>             catch (IOException exception)
>             {
>             }
>         }
>     };
>
> t.start();
> try
> {
>     t.join(timeout);
> }
> catch (InterruptedException exception)
> {
> }
> ```
>
> The `join` method returns when the thread has completed or when the timeout has expired, whichever happens first. If the `socket` variable is not `null`, then the socket has been successfully opened within the allotted time.

Half-Close

When a client program sends a request to the server, the server needs to be able to determine when the end of the request occurs. For that reason, many Internet protocols (such as SMTP) are line-oriented. Other protocols contain a header that specifies the size of the request data. Otherwise, indicating the end of the request data is harder than writing data to a file. With a file, you'd just close the file at the end of the data. But if you close a socket, then you immediately disconnect from the server.

The *half-close* overcomes this problem. You can close the output stream of a socket, thereby indicating to the server the end of the request data, but keep the input stream open so that you can read the response.

The client side looks like this:

```
Socket socket = new Socket(host, port);
BufferedReader reader = new BufferedReader(
   new InputStreamReader(socket.getInputStream()));
PrintWriter writer = new PrintWriter(
   socket.getOutputStream());
// send request data
writer.print(. . .);
writer.flush();
socket.shutdownOutput();
// now socket is half closed
// read response data
String line;
while ((line = reader.readLine()) != null)
   . . .
socket.close();
```

The server side simply reads input until the end of the input stream is reached.

Of course, this protocol is only useful for one-shot services such as HTTP where the client connects, issues a request, catches the response, and then disconnects.

Internet addresses

Usually, you don't have to worry too much about Internet addresses—the numerical host addresses that consist of four bytes (or, with IPv6, six bytes) such as 132.163.4.102. However, you can use the InetAddress class if you need to convert between host names and Internet addresses.

As of SDK 1.4, the java.net package supports IPv6 Internet addresses, *provided the host operating system does*. For example, you'll be able to make use of IPv6 addresses on Solaris but, at the time of this writing, not on Windows.

The static getByName method returns an InetAddress object of a host. For example,

```
InetAddress address
   = InetAddress.getByName("time-A.timefreq.bldrdoc.gov");
```

returns an InetAddress object that encapsulates the sequence of four bytes 132.163.4.102. You can access the bytes with the getAddress method.

```
byte[] addressBytes = address.getAddress();
```

Some host names with a lot of traffic correspond to multiple Internet addresses, to facilitate load balancing. For example, at the time of this writing, the host name java.sun.com corresponds to three different Internet addresses. One of them is picked at random when the host is accessed. You can get all hosts with the getAllByName method.

```
InetAddress[] addresses = InetAddress.getAllByName(host);
```

Finally, you sometimes need the address of the local host. If you simply ask for the address of localhost, you always get the address 127.0.0.1, which isn't very useful. Instead, use the static getLocalHost method to get the address of your local host.

```
InetAddress address
    = InetAddress.getLocalHost();
```

Example 3–5 is a simple program that prints the Internet address of your local host if you do not specify any command-line parameters, or all Internet addresses of another host if you specify the host name on the command line, such as

```
java InetAddressTest java.sun.com
```

Example 3–5: InetAddressTest.java

```
1. import java.net.*;
2.
3. /**
4.    This program demonstrates the InetAddress class.
5.    Supply a host name as command line argument, or run
6.    without command line arguments to see the address of the
7.    local host.
8. */
9. public class InetAddressTest
10. {
11.    public static void main(String[] args)
12.    {
13.        try
14.        {
15.            if (args.length > 0)
16.            {
17.                String host = args[0];
18.                InetAddress[] addresses
19.                    = InetAddress.getAllByName(host);
20.                for (int i = 0; i < addresses.length; i++)
21.                    System.out.println(addresses[i]);
22.            }
23.            else
24.            {
25.                InetAddress localHostAddress
26.                    = InetAddress.getLocalHost();
27.                System.out.println(localHostAddress);
28.            }
29.        }
30.        catch (Exception e)
```

```
31.          {
32.                e.printStackTrace();
33.          }
34.      }
35. }
```

> **NOTE:** In this book, we cover only the TCP (Transmission Control Protocol) networking protocol. TCP establishes a reliable connection between two computers. The Java platform also supports the so-called UDP (User Datagram Protocol) protocol, which can be used to send packets (also called *datagrams*) with much less overhead than that for TCP. The drawback is that the packets can be delivered in random order, or even dropped altogether. It is up to the recipient to put the packets in order and to request retransmission of missing packets. UDP is most suited for applications where missing packets can be tolerated, for example, in audio or video streams, or for continuous measurements.

`java.net.Socket`

- `Socket(String host, int port)`
  creates a socket and connects it to a port on a remote host.

Parameters:	`host`	the host name
	`port`	the port number

- `Socket()`
  creates a socket that has not yet been connected.

- `void connect(SocketAddress address)`
  connects this socket to the given address. (Since SDK 1.4)

- `void connect(SocketAddress address, int timeout)`
  connects this socket to the given address or returns if the time interval expired. (Since SDK 1.4)

Parameters:	`address`	the remote address
	`timeout`	the timeout in milliseconds

- `boolean isConnected()`
  returns `true` if the socket is connected. (Since SDK 1.4)

- `void close()`
  closes the socket.

- `boolean isClosed()`
  returns `true` if the socket is closed. (Since SDK 1.4)

- `InputStream getInputStream()`
  gets the input stream to read from the socket.

- `OutputStream getOutputStream()`
  gets an output stream to write to this socket.

- `void setSoTimeout(int timeout)`
  sets the blocking time for read requests on this `Socket`. If the timeout is reached, then an `InterruptedIOException` is raised.

  Parameters: `timeout`   the timeout in milliseconds (0 for infinite timeout)

- `void shutdownOutput()`
  sets the output stream to "end of stream."

- `void shutdownInput()`
  sets the input stream to "end of stream."

- `boolean isOutputShutdown`
  returns `true` if output has been shut down. (Since SDK 1.4)

- `boolean isInputShutdown`
  returns `true` if input has been shut down. (Since SDK 1.4)

java.net.InetAddress

- `static InetAddress getByName(String host)`
- `static InetAddress[] getAllByName(String host)`
  These methods construct an `InetAddress`, or an array of all Internet addresses, for the given host name.

- `static InetAddress getLocalHost()`
  constructs an `InetAddress` for the local host.

- `byte[] getAddress()`
  returns an array of bytes that contains the numerical address.

- `String getHostAddress()`
  returns a string with decimal numbers, separated by periods, for example `"132.163.4.102"`.

- `String getHostName()`
  returns the host name.

java.net.InetSocketAddress

Since SDK 1.4:

- `InetSocketAddress(String hostname, int port)`
  constructs an address object with the given host and port, resolving the host name during construction. If the host name cannot be resolved, then the address object's `unresolved` property is set to `true`.

- `boolean isUnresolved()`
  returns `true` if this address object could not be resolved.

URL Connections

In the last section, you saw how to use socket-level programming to connect to an SMTP server and send an e-mail message. It is nice to know that this can be done, and to get a glimpse of what goes on "under the hood" of an Internet service such as e-mail. However, if you are planning an application that incorporates e-mail, you will probably want to work at a higher level and use a library that encapsulates the protocol details. For example, Sun Microsystems has developed the Java-Mail API as a standard extension of the Java platform. In the JavaMail API, you simply issue a call such as

```
Transport.send(message);
```

to send a message. The library takes care of message protocols, multiple recipients, handling attachments, and so on.

For the remainder of this chapter, we will concentrate on higher-level services that the standard edition of the Java platform provides. Of course, the runtime library uses sockets to implement these services. But you don't have to worry about the protocol details when you use the higher-level services.

URLs and URIs

The `URL` and `URLConnection` classes encapsulate much of the complexity of retrieving information from a remote site. Here is how you specify a URL.

```
URL url = new URL(urlString);
```

The Java 2 platform supports both HTTP and FTP resources.

If you simply want to fetch the contents of the resource, then you can use the `openStream` method of the `URL` class. This method yields an `InputStream` object. Using this stream object, you can easily read the contents of the resource.

```
InputStream uin = url.openStream();
BufferedReader in
   = new BufferedReader(new InputStreamReader(uin));
String line;
while ((line = in.readLine()) != null)
{
   process line;
}
```

As of SDK 1.4, the `java.net` package makes a useful distinction between URLs (uniform resource *locators*) and URIs (uniform resource *identifiers*).

A URI is a purely syntactical construct that specifies the various parts of the string specifying a web resource. A URL is a special kind of URI, namely one with sufficient information to *locate* a resource. Other URIs, such as

```
mailto:cay@horstmann.com
```

are not locators—there is no data to locate from this identifier. Such a URI is called a URN (uniform resource *name*).

In the Java library, the URI class has no methods for accessing the resource that the identifier specifies—its sole purpose is parsing. In contrast, the URL class can open a stream to the resource. For that reason, the URL class only works with identifiers of a kind that the Java library knows how to handle, such as an HTTP or FTP URL.

To see why a URI class is necessary, consider how complex URLs can be. For example,

```
http://maps.yahoo.com/py/maps.py?csz=Cupertino+CA
ftp://username:password@ftp.yourserver.com/pub/file.txt
```

The URI specification gives rules for the makeup of these identifiers. A URI has the syntax

```
[scheme:]schemeSpecificPart[#fragment]
```

Here, the [. . .] denotes an optional part, and the : and # are included literally in the identifier.

If the scheme: part is present, the URI is called *absolute*. Otherwise, it is called *relative*.

An absolute URI is *opaque* if the schemeSpecificPart does not begin with a / such as

```
mailto:cay@horstmann.com
```

All absolute non-opaque URIs and all relative URIs are *hierarchical*. Examples are:

```
http://java.sun.com/index.html
../../java/net/Socket.html#Socket()
```

The schemeSpecificPart of a hierarchical URI has the structure

```
[//authority][path][?query]
```

where again [. . .] denotes optional parts.

For server-based URIs, the authority part has the form

```
[user-info@]host[:port]
```

The port must be an integer.

RFC 2396, which standardizes URIs, also supports a registry-based mechanism where the authority has a different format, but they are not in common use.

One of the purposes of the `URI` class is to parse an identifier and break it up into its various components. You can retrieve them with the methods

```
getScheme
getSchemeSpecificPart
getAuthority
getUserInfo
getHost
getPort
getPath
getQuery
getFragment
```

The other purpose of the `URI` class is the handling of absolute and relative identifiers. If you have an absolute URI such as

```
http://docs.mycompany.com/api/java/net/ServerSocket.html
```

and a relative URI such as

```
../../java/net/Socket.html#Socket()
```

then you can combine the two into an absolute URI.

```
http://docs.mycompany.com/api/java/net/Socket.html#Socket()
```

This process is called *resolving* a relative URL.

The opposite process is called *relativization*. For example, suppose you have a *base* URI

```
http://docs.mycompany.com/api
```

and a URI

```
http://docs.mycompany.com/api/java/lang/String.html
```

then the relativized URI is

```
java/lang/String.html
```

The URI class supports both of these operations:

```
relative = base.relativize(combined);
combined = base.resolve(relative);
```

Using a URLConnection to Retrieve Information

If you want additional information about a web resource, then you should use the `URLConnection` class, which gives you much more control than the basic `URL` class.

When working with a `URLConnection` object, you must carefully schedule your steps, as follows:

1. Call the `openConnection` method of the `URL` class to obtain the `URLConnection` object:

```
URLConnection connection = url.openConnection();
```

2. Set any request properties, using the methods

```
setDoInput
setDoOutput
setIfModifiedSince
setUseCaches
setAllowUserInteraction
setRequestProperty
```

We discuss these methods later in this section and in the API notes.

3. Connect to the remote resource by calling the `connect` method.

```
connection.connect();
```

Besides making a socket connection to the server, this method also queries the server for *header information.*

4. After connecting to the server, you can query the header information. There are two methods, `getHeaderFieldKey` and `getHeaderField`, to enumerate all fields of the header. As of SDK 1.4, there is also a method `getHeaderFields` that gets a standard `Map` object containing the header fields. For your convenience, the following methods query standard fields.

```
getContentType
getContentLength
getContentEncoding
getDate
getExpiration
getLastModified
```

5. Finally, you can access the resource data. Use the `getInputStream` method to obtain an input stream for reading the information. (This is the same input stream that the `openStream` method of the `URL` class returns.) There is also a method `getObject`; however, in practice, it isn't very useful. The objects that are returned by standard content types such as `text/plain` and `image/gif` require classes in the `com.sun` hierarchy for processing. It is possible to register your own content handlers, but we will not discuss that technique in this book.

CAUTION: Some programmers form the wrong mental image when using the URL-Connection class and think that the `getInputStream` and `getOutputStream` methods are similar to those of the `Socket` class. But that isn't quite true. The URL-Connection class does quite a bit of magic behind the scenes, in particular the handling of request and response headers. For that reason, it is important that you follow the setup steps for the connection.

Let us now look at some of the `URLConnection` methods in detail. There are several methods to set properties of the connection before connecting to the server. The most important ones are `setDoInput` and `setDoOutput`. By default, the connection yields an input stream for reading from the server but no output stream for writing. If you want an output stream (for example, for posting data to a web server—see the next section), then you need to call

```
connection.setDoOutput(true);
```

Next, you may want to set some of the request headers. The request headers are sent together with the request command to the server. Here is an example:

```
GET www.server.com/index.html HTTP/1.0
Referer: http://www.somewhere.com/links.html
Proxy-Connection: Keep-Alive
User-Agent: Mozilla/4.76 (Windows ME; U) Opera 5.11   [en]
Host: www.server.com
Accept: text/html, image/gif, image/jpeg, image/png, */*
Accept-Language: en
Accept-Charset: iso-8859-1,*,utf-8
Cookie: orangemilano=192218887821987
```

The `setIfModifiedSince` method tells the connection that you are only interested in data that has been modified since a certain date. The `setUseCaches` and `setAllowUserInteraction` are only used inside applets. The `setUseCaches` method directs the ambient browser to first check the browser cache. The `setAllowUserInteraction` method allows an application to pop up a dialog for querying the user name and password for password-protected resources (see Figure 3–7). These settings have no effect outside of applets.

Figure 3–7: A network password dialog

Finally, there is a catch-all `setRequestProperty` method that you can use to set any name/value pair that is meaningful for the particular protocol. For the format of the HTTP request headers, see RFC 2616. Some of these parameters are not well documented and are passed around by word of mouth from one programmer to the next. For example, if you want to access a password-protected web page, you must do the following:

1. Concatenate the user name, a colon, and the password.

   ```
   String input = username + ":" + password;
   ```

2. Compute the Base 64 encoding of the resulting string. (The Base64 encoding encodes a sequence of bytes into a sequence of printable ASCII characters.)

   ```
   String encoding = base64Encode(input);
   ```

3. Call the `setRequestProperty` method with a name of `"Authoriza-tion"` and value `"Basic " + encoding`:

   ```
   connection.setRequestProperty("Authorization",
      "Basic " + encoding);
   ```

> TIP: You just saw how to access a password-protected web page. To access a pass-word-protected file by FTP, you use an entirely different method. You simply construct a URL of the form
>
> ```
> ftp://username:password@ftp.yourserver.com/pub/file.txt
> ```
>
> This, too, does not seem to be well documented. We found out by looking inside `rt.jar`, locating the promising-looking class `sun.net.www.proto-col.ftp.FtpURLConnection`, and decompiling that class with `javap`.

Once you call the `connect` method, you can query the response header information. First, let us see how to enumerate all response header fields. The implementors of this class felt a need to express their individuality by introducing yet another iteration protocol. The call

```
String key = connection.getHeaderFieldKey(n);
```

gets the nth key from the response header, where n starts from 1! It returns `null` if n is zero or larger than the total number of header fields. There is no method to return the number of fields; you simply keep calling `getHeaderFieldKey` until you get `null`. Similarly, the call

```
String value = connection.getHeaderField(n);
```

returns the nth value.

Mercifully, as of SDK 1.4, there is a method `getHeaderFields` that returns a `Map` of response header fields that you can access as explained in Chapter 2.

```
Map headerFields = connection.getHeaderFields();
```

Here is a set of response header fields from a typical HTTP request.

```
Date: Wed, 29 Aug 2001 00:15:48 GMT
Server: Apache/1.3.3 (Unix)
Last-Modified: Sun, 24 Jun 2001 20:53:38 GMT
```

```
ETag: "28094e-12cd-37729ad2"
Accept-Ranges: bytes
Content-Length: 4813
Connection: close
Content-Type: text/html
```

As a convenience, six methods query the values of the most common header types and convert them to numeric types when appropriate. Table 3–1 shows these convenience methods. The methods with return type `long` return the number of seconds since January 1, 1970 GMT.

Table 3–1: Convenience methods for response header values

Key name	Method name	Return type
Date	getDate	long
Expires	getExpiration	long
Last-Modified	getLastModified	long
Content-Length	getContentLength	int
Content-Type	getContentType	String
Content-Encoding	getContentEncoding	String

The program in Example 3–6 lets you experiment with URL connections. Supply a URL and an optional user name and password on the command line when running the program, for example:

```
java URLConnectionTest http://www.yourserver.com user pw
```

The program prints out

- All keys and values of the header;
- The return values of the six convenience methods in Table 3–1;
- The first ten lines of the requested resource.

The program is straightforward, except for the computation of the Base 64 encoding. There is an undocumented class, `sun.misc.Base64Encoder`, that you can use instead of the one that we provide in the example program. Simply replace the call to `base64Encode` with

```
String encoding
    = new sun.misc.BASE64Encoder().encode(input.getBytes());
```

However, we supplied our own class because we do not like to rely on the classes in the `sun` or `com.sun` packages.

NOTE: The `javax.mail.internet.MimeUtility` class in the JavaMail standard extension package also has a method for Base64 encoding. SDK 1.4 includes a package containing the visible (non-`public`) class `java.util.prefs.Base64`.

Example 3–6: URLConnectionTest.java

```
1. import java.io.*;
2. import java.net.*;
3. import java.util.*;
4.
5. /**
6.    This program connects to an URL and displays the
7.    response header data and the first 10 lines of the
8.    requested data.
9.
10.   Supply the URL and an optional username and password (for
11.   HTTP basic authentication) on the command line.
12. */
13. public class URLConnectionTest
14. {
15.    public static void main(String[] args)
16.    {
17.       try
18.       {
19.          String urlName;
20.          if (args.length > 0)
21.             urlName = args[0];
22.          else
23.             urlName = "http://java.sun.com";
24.
25.          URL url = new URL(urlName);
26.          URLConnection connection = url.openConnection();
27.
28.          // set username, password if specified on command line
29.
30.          if (args.length > 2)
31.          {
32.             String username = args[1];
33.             String password = args[2];
34.             String input = username + ":" + password;
35.             String encoding = base64Encode(input);
36.             connection.setRequestProperty("Authorization",
37.                "Basic " + encoding);
38.          }
39.
40.          connection.connect();
41.
42.          // print header fields
43.
44.          int n = 1;
45.          String key;
46.          while ((key = connection.getHeaderFieldKey(n)) != null)
47.          {
48.             String value = connection.getHeaderField(n);
49.             System.out.println(key + ": " + value);
```

```
50.            n++;
51.        }
52.
53.        // print convenience functions
54.
55.        System.out.println("----------");
56.        System.out.println("getContentType: "
57.            + connection.getContentType());
58.        System.out.println("getContentLength: "
59.            + connection.getContentLength());
60.        System.out.println("getContentEncoding: "
61.            + connection.getContentEncoding());
62.        System.out.println("getDate: "
63.            + connection.getDate());
64.        System.out.println("getExpiration: "
65.            + connection.getExpiration());
66.        System.out.println("getLastModifed: "
67.            + connection.getLastModified());
68.        System.out.println("----------");
69.
70.
71.        BufferedReader in = new BufferedReader(new
72.            InputStreamReader(connection.getInputStream()));
73.
74.        // print first ten lines of contents
75.
76.        String line;
77.        n = 1;
78.        while ((line = in.readLine()) != null && n <= 10)
79.        {
80.            System.out.println(line);
81.            n++;
82.        }
83.        if (line != null) System.out.println(". . .");
84.     }
85.     catch (IOException exception)
86.     {
87.         exception.printStackTrace();
88.     }
89.  }
90.
91.  /**
92.     Computes the Base64 encoding of a string
93.     @param s a string
94.     @return the Base 64 encoding of s
95.  */
96.  public static String base64Encode(String s)
97.  {
98.     ByteArrayOutputStream bOut
99.         = new ByteArrayOutputStream();
100.    Base64OutputStream out = new Base64OutputStream(bOut);
```

```
101.        try
102.        {
103.            out.write(s.getBytes());
104.            out.flush();
105.        }
106.        catch (IOException exception)
107.        {
108.        }
109.        return bOut.toString();
110.    }
111. }
112.
113. /**
114.    This stream filter converts a stream of bytes to their
115.    Base64 encoding.
116.
117.    Base64 encoding encodes 3 bytes into 4 characters.
118.    |11111122|22223333|33444444|
119.    Each set of 6 bits is encoded according to the
120.    toBase64 map. If the number of input bytes is not
121.    a multiple of 3, then the last group of 4 characters
122.    is padded with one or two = signs. Each output line
123.    is at most 76 characters.
124. */
125. class Base64OutputStream extends FilterOutputStream
126. {
127.    /**
128.        Constructs the stream filter
129.        @param out the stream to filter
130.    */
131.    public Base64OutputStream(OutputStream out)
132.    {
133.        super(out);
134.    }
135.
136.    public void write(int c) throws IOException
137.    {
138.        inbuf[i] = c;
139.        i++;
140.        if (i == 3)
141.        {
142.            super.write(toBase64[(inbuf[0] & 0xFC) >> 2]);
143.            super.write(toBase64[((inbuf[0] & 0x03) << 4) |
144.                ((inbuf[1] & 0xF0) >> 4)]);
145.            super.write(toBase64[((inbuf[1] & 0x0F) << 2) |
146.                ((inbuf[2] & 0xC0) >> 6)]);
147.            super.write(toBase64[inbuf[2] & 0x3F]);
148.            col += 4;
149.            i = 0;
150.            if (col >= 76)
151.            {
```

```
152.                super.write('\n');
153.                col = 0;
154.             }
155.          }
156.       }
157.
158.    public void flush() throws IOException
159.    {
160.       if (i == 1)
161.       {
162.          super.write(toBase64[(inbuf[0] & 0xFC) >> 2]);
163.          super.write(toBase64[(inbuf[0] & 0x03) << 4]);
164.          super.write('=');
165.          super.write('=');
166.       }
167.       else if (i == 2)
168.       {
169.          super.write(toBase64[(inbuf[0] & 0xFC) >> 2]);
170.          super.write(toBase64[((inbuf[0] & 0x03) << 4) |
171.             ((inbuf[1] & 0xF0) >> 4)]);
172.          super.write(toBase64[(inbuf[1] & 0x0F) << 2]);
173.          super.write('=');
174.       }
175.    }
176.
177.    private static char[] toBase64 =
178.    {
179.       'A', 'B', 'C', 'D', 'E', 'F', 'G', 'H',
180.       'I', 'J', 'K', 'L', 'M', 'N', 'O', 'P',
181.       'Q', 'R', 'S', 'T', 'U', 'V', 'W', 'X',
182.       'Y', 'Z', 'a', 'b', 'c', 'd', 'e', 'f',
183.       'g', 'h', 'i', 'j', 'k', 'l', 'm', 'n',
184.       'o', 'p', 'q', 'r', 's', 't', 'u', 'v',
185.       'w', 'x', 'y', 'z', '0', '1', '2', '3',
186.       '4', '5', '6', '7', '8', '9', '+', '/'
187.    };
188.
189.    private int col = 0;
190.    private int i = 0;
191.    private int[] inbuf = new int[3];
192. }
```

NOTE: A commonly asked question is whether the Java platform supports access of secure web pages. If you open a connection to an `https` URL inside an applet, then the applet will indeed access the page, by taking advantage of the SSL implementation of the browser. However, before SDK 1.4, there was no support for `https` URLs. For patent and export restrictions, you need to install a separate extension library and a cryptographic service provider for the RSA algorithm. As of SDK 1.4, SSL support is a part of the standard library.

java.net.URL

- InputStream openStream()

  opens an input stream for reading the resource data.

- URLConnection openConnection();

  returns a URLConnection object that manages the connection to the resource.

java.net.URLConnection

- void setDoInput(boolean doInput)

  If doInput is true, then the user can receive input from this URLConnection.

- void setDoOutput(boolean doOutput)

  If doOutput is true, then the user can send output to this URLConnection.

- void setIfModifiedSince(long time)

  configures this URLConnection to fetch only data that has been modified since a given time. The time is given in seconds from midnight, GMT, January 1, 1970.

- void setUseCaches(boolean useCaches)

  If useCaches is true, then data can be retrieved from a local cache. Note that the URLConnection itself does not maintain such a cache. The cache must be supplied by an external program such as a browser.

- void setAllowUserInteraction(boolean allowUserInteraction)

  If allowUserInteraction is true, then the user can be queried for passwords. Note that the URLConnection itself has no facilities for executing such a query. The query must be carried out by an external program such as a browser or browser plug-in.

- void setRequestProperty(String key, String value)

  sets a request header field.

- Map getRequestProperties()

  returns a map of request header key/value pairs. This method was added in SDK 1.4.

- void connect()

  connects to the remote resource and retrieves response header information.

- Map getHeaderFields()

  returns a map of response header field name/value pairs. This method was added in SDK 1.4.

- `String getHeaderFieldKey(int n)`

  gets the nth response header field key, or `null` if n is ≤ 0 or larger than the number of response header fields.

- `String getHeaderField(int n)`

  gets the nth response header field value, or `null` if n is ≤ 0 or larger than the number of response header fields.

- `int getContentLength()`

  gets the content length, if available, or `-1` if unknown.

- `String getContentType`

  gets the content type, such as `text/plain` or `image/gif`.

- `String getContentEncoding()`

  gets the content encoding, such as `gzip`. This value is not commonly used, as the default `identity` encoding is not supposed to be specified with a `Content-Encoding` header.

- `long getDate()`
- `long getExpiration()`
- `long getLastModifed()`

  These methods get the date of creation, expiration, and last modification of the resource. The dates are specified as seconds from midnight, GMT, January 1, 1970.

- `InputStream openInputStream()`
- `OutputStream openOutputStream()`

  These methods return a stream for reading from the resource or writing to the resource.

- `Object getObject()`

  selects the appropriate content handler to read the resource data and convert it into an object. This method is not useful for reading standard types such as `text/plain` or `image/gif` unless you install your own content handler.

Posting Form Data

In the preceding section, you saw how to read data from a web server. Now we will show you how your programs can send data back to a web server and to programs that the web server invokes, using the CGI and servlet mechanisms.

CGI Scripts and Servlets

Even before Java technology came along, there was a mechanism for writing interactive web applications. To send information from a web browser to the web server, a user would fill out a *form*, like the one in Figure 3–8.

Figure 3–8: An HTML form

When the user clicks on the "Submit" button, the text in the text fields and the settings of the check boxes and radio buttons are sent back to the server to be processed by a *CGI script*. (CGI stands for *Common Gateway Interface*.) The CGI script to use is specified in the ACTION attribute of the FORM tag.

The CGI script is a program that resides on the server computer. There are usually many CGI scripts on a server, conventionally residing in the cgi-bin directory. The web server launches the CGI script and feeds it the form data.

The CGI script processes the form data and produces another HTML page that the web server sends back to the browser. This sequence is illustrated in Figure 3–9. The response page can contain new information (for example, in an information-search program) or just an acknowledgment. The web browser then displays the response page.

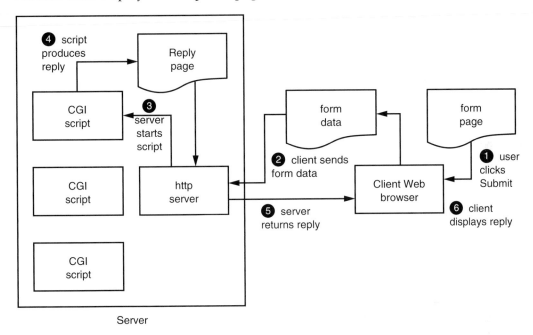

Figure 3–9: Data flow during execution of a CGI script

CGI programs are commonly written in Perl, but they can be written in any language that can read from standard input and write to standard output.

NOTE: We will not discuss how to design HTML forms that interact with CGI. A good reference for that topic is *HTML & XHTML: The Definitive Guide* (4th edition) by Chuck Musciano and Bill Kennedy [O'Reilly, 2000]. Our interest lies in the interface between CGI and Java programs, not in HTML forms.

CGI is often a good mechanism to use because it is well established and system administrators are familiar with it. It does have a major disadvantage. Each request forks a new process and not just a new thread. Furthermore, it is difficult to control the security of those scripts. The newer *servlet* technology overcomes both of these disadvantages. Servlet engines use Java technology to start each servlet in a separate thread and to control the security privileges of servlets. You will see an example servlet later in this chapter. For more informa-tion on servlets, we recommend the book *Core Java Web Server* by Chris Taylor and Tim Kimmet [Prentice-Hall, 1998].

Sending Data to a Web Server

When data is sent to a web server, it does not matter whether the data is inter-preted by a CGI script or a servlet. The client sends the data to the web server in a standard format, and the web server takes care of passing it on to the program that generates the response.

There are two methods with which to send information to a web server: the `GET` method and the `POST` method.

In the `GET` method, you simply attach parameters to the end of the URL. The URL has the form

```
http://host/script?parameters
```

For example, at the time of this writing, the Yahoo web site has a script `py/maps.py` at the host `maps.yahoo.com`. The script requires two parameters, `addr` and `csz`. You need to separate the parameters by an `&` and encode the parameters, using the following scheme.

Replace all spaces with a `+`. Replace all nonalphanumeric characters by a `%`, followed by a two-digit hexadecimal number. For example, to transmit the street name *S. Main*, you use `S%2e+Main`, since the hexadecimal number `2e` (or decimal 46) is the ASCII code of the "." character.
This encoding keeps any intermediate programs from messing with spaces and interpreting other special characters. This encoding scheme is called URL *encoding*.

For example, to get a map of 1 Infinite Loop, Cupertino, CA, simply request the following URL:

```
http://maps.yahoo.com/py/maps.py?addr=1+Infinite+Loop&csz=
    Cupertino+CA
```

The `GET` method is simple, but it has a major limitation that makes it relatively unpopular. Most browsers have a limit on the number of characters that you can include in a `GET` request.

In the `POST` method, you do not attach parameters to a URL. Instead, you get an output stream from the `URLConnection` and write name/value pairs to the output stream. You still have to URL-encode the values and separate them with `&` characters.

Let us look at this process in more detail. To post data to a script, you first establish a `URLConnection`.

```
URL url = new URL("http://host/script");
URLConnection connection = url.openConnection();
```

Then, you call the `setDoOutput` method to set up the connection for output.

```
connection.setDoOutput(true);
```

Next, you call `getOutputStream` to get a stream through which you can send data to the server. If you are sending text to the server, it is convenient to wrap that stream into a `PrintWriter`.

```
PrintWriter out
    = new PrintWriter(connection.getOutputStream());
```

Now you are ready to send data to the server:

```
out.print(name1 + "=" + URLEncoder.encode(value1) + "&");
out.print(name2 + "=" + URLEncoder.encode(value2));
```

Finally, close the output stream.

```
out.close();
```

You read the server response in the usual way.

```
BufferedReader in = new BufferedReader(new
    InputStreamReader(connection.getInputStream()));
String line;
while ((line = in.readLine()) != null)
{
    process line
}
```

Let us run through a practical example. The web site at `http://www.census.gov/ipc/www/idbprint.html` contains a form to request population data (see Figure 3–10). If you look at the HTML source, you will see the following HTML tag:

```
<FORM METHOD=POST ACTION="/cgi-bin/ipc/idbsprd">
```

This tag indicates that the name of the script that is executed when the user clicks the "Submit" button is `/cgi-bin/ipc/idbsprd`, and that you need to use the `POST` method to send data to the script.

Next, you need to find out the field names that the script expects. Look at the user interface components. Each of them has a `NAME` attribute, for example,

```
<SELECT NAME="tbl" SIZE=8>
<OPTION VALUE="001">001 Total Midyear Population
more options . . .
</SELECT>
```

This tells you that the name of the field is `tbl`. This field specifies the population table type. If you specify the table type `001`, you will get a table of the total midyear population. If you look further, you will also find a country field name `cty` with values such as `US` for the United States and `CH` (!) for China. (Sadly, the Census Bureau seems to be unaware of the ISO-3166 standard for country codes.)

Finally, there is a field named `optyr` for the year range selection. For this example, we will just set it to `latest checked`. Then, the remaining fields will not be filled and the latest available data will be displayed.

For example, to get the latest data for the total midyear population of China, you construct this string:

```
tbl=1&cty=CH&optyr=latest+checked
```

Send the string to the URL

```
http://www.census.gov/cgi-bin/ipc/idbsprd:
```

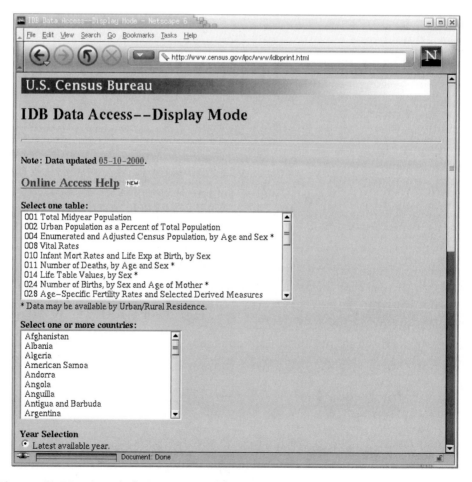

Figure 3–10: A web form to request census data

The script sends back the following reply:

```
<PRE>
U.S. Bureau of the Census, International Data Base

Table 001. Total Midyear Population
-------------------------
CtYear          Population
-------------------------


CH1999          1246871951
-------------------------
Source: U.S. Bureau of the Census, International
        Data Base.
</PRE>
```

As you can see, the script formats the reply as a minimally acceptable HTML page, by placing `<PRE>` and `</PRE>` tags around the data. This particular script doesn't bother with constructing a pretty table, though. That is the reason we picked it as an example—it is easy to see what happens with this script, whereas it can be confusing to decipher a complex set of HTML tags that other scripts produce.

The program in Example 3–7 sends POST data to an arbitrary URL. You can use it to send data to the Census Bureau script that we just discussed or to any other URL. You specify the data in a properties file (by default `PostTest.properties`), for example,

```
URL=http://www.census.gov/cgi-bin/ipc/idbsprd
tbl=001
cty=CH
optyr=latest checked
```

Here is how the program works. First, we check if the user supplied a command-line argument to override the default property file. Then, we read the property file.

```
Properties props = new Properties();
FileInputStream in = new FileInputStream(fileName);
props.load(in);
```

Next, we use the URL property to construct the URL object, and we remove that property so that it isn't sent to the web server.

```
URL url = new URL(props.getProperty("URL"));
props.remove("URL");
```

In the `doPost` method, we first open the connection, call `doOutput(true)`, and open the output stream. Then, we enumerate the names and values in the `Properties` object. For each of them, we send the name, = character, `value`, and & separator character:

```
out.print(name);
out.print('=');
out.print(URLEncoder.encode(value));
if (more pairs) out.print('&');
```

Finally, we read the response from the server.

There is one twist with reading the response. If a script error occurs, then the call to `connection.getInputStream()` throws a `FileNotFoundException`. However, the server still sends an error page back to the browser (such as the ubiquitous "Error 404 -page not found"). To capture this error page, you cast the `URLConnection` object to the `HttpURLConnection` class and call its `getErrorStream` method:

```
InputStream err
    = ((HttpURLConnection)connection).getErrorStream();
```

Then, you can read the error page from the stream `err`.

If you run the program with the supplied properties file, then you will see the result from the Census Bureau script. We supply a second file, `Zip.properties`, that performs a zip code lookup, using a script provided by the United States Postal Service. The query result contains a list of city names for a given zip code.

The technique that this program displays is useful whenever you need to query information from an existing web site. Simply find out the parameters that you need to send (usually by inspecting the HTML source of a web page that carries out the same query), and then strip out the HTML tags and other unnecessary information from the reply.

Example 3–7: PostTest.java

```
1. import java.io.*;
2. import java.net.*;
3. import java.util.*;
4.
5. /**
6.    This program demonstrates how to use the URLConnection class
7.    for a POST request. The URL and form data are in a .properties
8.    file whose name should be supplied on the command line.
9. */
10. public class PostTest
11. {
12.    public static void main(String[] args)
13.    {
14.        try
15.        {
16.            String fileName;
17.            if (args.length > 0)
```

```
18.            fileName = args[0];
19.        else
20.            fileName = "PostTest.properties";
21.        Properties props = new Properties();
22.        FileInputStream in = new FileInputStream(fileName);
23.        props.load(in);
24.
25.        URL url = new URL(props.getProperty("URL"));
26.        props.remove("URL");
27.        String r = doPost(url, props);
28.        System.out.println(r);
29.     }
30.     catch (IOException exception)
31.     {
32.        exception.printStackTrace();
33.     }
34.   }
35.
36.   /**
37.      Makes a POST request and returns the server response.
38.      @param url the URL to post to
39.      @param nameValuePairs a table of name/value pairs to
40.      supply in the request.
41.      @return the server reply (either from the input stream
42.      or the error stream)
43.   */
44.   public static String doPost(URL url,
45.      Properties nameValuePairs) throws IOException
46.   {
47.      URLConnection connection = url.openConnection();
48.      connection.setDoOutput(true);
49.
50.      PrintWriter out
51.         = new PrintWriter(connection.getOutputStream());
52.
53.      Enumeration enum = nameValuePairs.keys();
54.
55.      while (enum.hasMoreElements())
56.      {
57.         String name = (String)enum.nextElement();
58.         String value = nameValuePairs.getProperty(name);
59.         out.print(name);
60.         out.print('=');
61.         out.print(URLEncoder.encode(value));
62.         if (enum.hasMoreElements()) out.print('&');
63.      }
64.
65.      out.close();
66.
```

```
67.      BufferedReader in;
68.      StringBuffer response = new StringBuffer();
69.      try
70.      {
71.          in = new BufferedReader(new
72.              InputStreamReader(connection.getInputStream()));
73.      }
74.      catch (IOException e)
75.      {
76.          if (!(connection instanceof HttpURLConnection)) throw e;
77.          InputStream err
78.              = ((HttpURLConnection)connection).getErrorStream();
79.          if (err == null) throw e;
80.          in = new BufferedReader(new InputStreamReader(err));
81.      }
82.      String line;
83.
84.      while ((line = in.readLine()) != null)
85.          response.append(line + "\n");
86.
87.      in.close();
88.      return response.toString();
89.   }
90. }
```

Our example program uses the URLConnection class to post data to a web site. More for curiosity's sake than for practical usage, you may like to know exactly what information the URLConnection sends to the server in addition to the data that you supply.

The URLConnection object first sends a request header to the server. The first line of the header must be

```
Content-Type: type
```

where *type* is usually one of the following:

```
text/plain
text/html
application/octet-stream
application/x-www-form-urlencoded
```

The content type must be followed by the line

```
Content-Length: length
```

for example,

```
Content-Length: 1024
```

The end of the header is indicated by a blank line. Then, the data portion follows. The web server strips off the header and routes the data portion to the server script.

Note that the URLConnection object buffers all data that you send to the output stream since it must first determine the total content length.

java.net.HttpURLConnection

- InputStream getErrorStream()
  returns a stream from which you can read web server error messages.

java.net.URLEncoder

- static String encode(String s)
  returns the URL-encoded form of the string s. In URL encoding, the characters 'A' – 'Z', 'a' – 'z', '0' – '9', '-', '_', '.' and '*' are left unchanged. Space is encoded into '+', and all other characters are encoded into "%UV", where $0x UV$ is the lower order byte of the character.

java.net.URLDecoder

- static string decode(String s)
  returns the decoding of the URL encoded string s.

Harvesting Information from the Web

The last example showed you how to read data from a web server. The Internet contains a wealth of information both interesting and not: it is the lack of guidance through this mass of information that is the major complaint of most web users. One promise of the Java technology is that it may help to bring order to this chaos: you can use Java applets to retrieve information and present it to the user in an appealing format.

There are many possible uses. Here are a few that come to mind:

- An applet can look at all the web pages the user has specified as interesting and find which have recently changed.
- An applet can visit the web pages of all scheduled airlines to find out which is running a special.
- Applets can gather and display recent stock quotes, monetary exchange rates, and other financial information.
- Applets can search FAQs, press releases, articles, and so on, and return text that contains certain keywords.

We give a simple example of such an applet. The National Weather Service stores weather reports in various files on the server http://iwin.nws.noaa.gov. For example, an hourly forecast for California is stored at

    http://iwin.nws.noaa.gov/iwin/ca/hourly.html

Other directories contain similar reports.

Our applet presents the user with two lists, one with states and another with report types. If you click on Get report, the applet fetches the report and places it into a text area (see Figure 3–11). You will find the code for the applet in Example 3–8.

The applet code itself is straightforward. The only interesting action occurs in the `getWeather` method. That method first builds up the query string. It obtains the base URL (`http://iwin.nws.noaa.gov/iwin/`) from the `queryBase` parameter of the applet tag. Then, it adds the state and report name and the extension `.html`:

```
String queryBase = getParameter("queryBase");
String query = queryBase + state + "/" + report + ".html";
```

Next, we create an URL object and call `openStream`.

```
URL url = new URL(query);
BufferedReader in = new BufferedReader(new
    InputStreamReader(url.openStream()));
```

The remainder of the method simply reads the file, removes HTML tags, and places the file in the text area.

```
String line;
while ((line = in.readLine()) != null)
    weather.append(removeTags(line) + "\n");
```

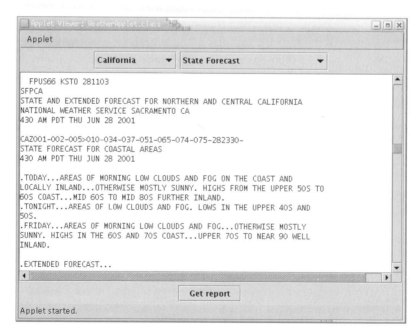

Figure 3–11: The WeatherReport applet

Example 3–8: WeatherApplet.java

```
1. import java.net.*;
2. import java.io.*;
3. import java.util.*;
4. import java.awt.*;
5. import java.awt.event.*;
6. import java.applet.*;
7. import javax.swing.*;
8.
9. /**
10.    This applet displays weather data from a NOAA server.
11.    The data is mostly in text format, so it can be displayed
12.    in a text area.
13. */
14. public class WeatherApplet extends JApplet
15. {
16.    public void init()
17.    {
18.       Container contentPane = getContentPane();
19.       contentPane.setLayout(new BorderLayout());
20.
21.       // Set up the lists of choices for states and reports
22.       JPanel comboPanel = new JPanel();
23.       state = makeCombo(states, comboPanel);
24.       report = makeCombo(reports, comboPanel);
25.       contentPane.add(comboPanel, BorderLayout.NORTH);
26.
27.       // Add the text area
28.       weather = new JTextArea(20, 80);
29.       weather.setFont(new Font("Courier", Font.PLAIN, 12));
30.
31.       // Add the report button
32.       contentPane.add(new JScrollPane(weather),
33.          BorderLayout.CENTER);
34.       JPanel buttonPanel = new JPanel();
35.       JButton reportButton = new JButton("Get report");
36.       reportButton.addActionListener(new
37.          ActionListener()
38.          {
39.             public void actionPerformed(ActionEvent evt)
40.             {
41.                weather.setText("");
42.                new
43.                   Thread()
44.                   {
45.                      public void run()
46.                      {
47.                         getWeather(getItem(state, states),
48.                            getItem(report, reports));
```

```
49.                             }
50.                         }.start();
51.                     }
52.              });
53.
54.          buttonPanel.add(reportButton);
55.          contentPane.add(buttonPanel, BorderLayout.SOUTH);
56.      }
57.
58.      /**
59.         Makes a combo box.
60.         @param items the array of strings whose first column
61.         contains the combo box display entries
62.         @param parent the parent to add the combo box to
63.      */
64.      public JComboBox makeCombo(String[][] items, Container parent)
65.      {
66.          JComboBox combo = new JComboBox();
67.          for (int i = 0; i < items.length; i++)
68.             combo.addItem(items[i][0]);
69.          parent.add(combo);
70.          return combo;
71.      }
72.
73.      /**
74.         Gets the query string for a combo box display entry.
75.         @param box the combo box
76.         @param items the array of strings whose first column
77.         contains the combo box display entries and whose second
78.         column contains the corresponding query strings
79.         @return the query string
80.      */
81.      public String getItem(JComboBox box, String[][] items)
82.      {
83.          return items[box.getSelectedIndex()][1];
84.      }
85.
86.      /**
87.         Puts together the URL query and fills the text area with
88.         the data.
89.         @param state the state part of the query
90.         @param report the report part of the query
91.      */
92.      public void getWeather(String state, String report)
93.      {
94.          String r = new String();
95.          try
96.          {
```

```
 97.          String queryBase = getParameter("queryBase");
 98.          String query
 99.             = queryBase + state + "/" + report + ".html";
100.          URL url = new URL(query);
101.          BufferedReader in = new BufferedReader(new
102.             InputStreamReader(url.openStream()));
103.
104.          String line;
105.          while ((line = in.readLine()) != null)
106.             weather.append(removeTags(line) + "\n");
107.       }
108.       catch(IOException e)
109.       {
110.          showStatus("Error " + e);
111.       }
112.    }
113.
114.    /**
115.       Removes HTML tags from a string.
116.       @param s a string
117.       @return s with <...> tags removed.
118.    */
119.    public static String removeTags(String s)
120.    {
121.       while (true)
122.       {
123.          int lb = s.indexOf('<');
124.          if (lb < 0) return s;
125.          int rb = s.indexOf('>', lb);
126.          if (rb < 0) return s;
127.          s = s.substring(0, lb) + " " + s.substring(rb + 1);
128.       }
129.    }
130.
131.    private JTextArea weather;
132.    private JComboBox state;
133.    private JComboBox report;
134.
135.    private String[][] states =
136.       {
137.          { "Alabama", "al" },
138.          { "Alaska", "ak" },
139.          { "Arizona", "az" },
140.          { "Arkansas", "ar" },
141.          { "California", "ca" },
142.          { "Colorado", "co" },
143.          { "Connecticut", "ct" },
144.          { "Delaware", "de" },
145.          { "Florida", "fl" },
```

```
146.            { "Georgia", "ga" },
147.            { "Hawaii", "hi" },
148.            { "Idaho", "id" },
149.            { "Illinois", "il" },
150.            { "Indiana", "in" },
151.            { "Iowa", "ia" },
152.            { "Kansas", "ks" },
153.            { "Kentucky", "ky" },
154.            { "Louisiana", "la" },
155.            { "Maine", "me" },
156.            { "Maryland", "md" },
157.            { "Massachusetts", "ma" },
158.            { "Michigan", "mi" },
159.            { "Minnesota", "mn" },
160.            { "Mississippi", "ms" },
161.            { "Missouri", "mo" },
162.            { "Montana", "mt" },
163.            { "Nebraska", "ne" },
164.            { "Nevada", "nv" },
165.            { "New Hampshire", "nh" },
166.            { "New Jersey", "nj" },
167.            { "New Mexico", "nm" },
168.            { "New York", "ny" },
169.            { "North Carolina", "nc" },
170.            { "North Dakota", "nd" },
171.            { "Ohio", "oh" },
172.            { "Oklahoma", "ok" },
173.            { "Oregon", "or" },
174.            { "Pennsylvania", "pa" },
175.            { "Rhode Island", "ri" },
176.            { "South Carolina", "sc" },
177.            { "South Dakota", "sd" },
178.            { "Tennessee", "tn" },
179.            { "Texas", "tx" },
180.            { "Utah", "ut" },
181.            { "Vermont", "vt" },
182.            { "Virginia", "va" },
183.            { "Washington", "wa" },
184.            { "West Virginia", "wv" },
185.            { "Wisconsin", "wi" },
186.            { "Wyoming", "wy" }
187.         };
188.
189.    private String[][] reports =
190.         {
191.            { "Hourly (State Weather Roundup)", "hourly" },
192.            { "State Forecast", "state" },
193.            { "Zone Forecast", "zone" },
```

```
194.              { "Short Term (NOWCASTS)", "shortterm" },
195.              { "Forecast Discussion", "discussion" },
196.              { "Weather Summary", "summary" },
197.              { "Public Information", "public" },
198.              { "Climate Data", "climate" },
199.              { "Hydrological Data", "hydro" },
200.              { "Watches", "watches" },
201.              { "Special Weather Statements", "special" },
202.              { "Warnings and Advisories", "allwarnings" }
203.         };
204. }
```

Unfortunately, when you try running this applet, you will be disappointed. Both the applet viewer and the browser refuse to run it. Whenever you click on Get report, a security violation is generated. We discuss the reason for this violation, and how to overcome this problem, in the next section. Right now, we'll just show you how to force the applet viewer to run the applet anyway.

First, create a text file with the following contents:

```
grant
{
    permission java.net.SocketPermission
        "iwin.nws.noaa.gov:80", "connect";
};
```

Call it `WeatherApplet.policy`. We will discuss policy files in detail in Chapter 9. However, this particular policy file is easy to understand. It simply grants the applet the permission to connect to the host `iwin.nws.noaa.gov` on port 80, the HTTP port. Why the applet needs such a permission is the topic of the next section.

Now start the applet viewer with the following command line:

```
appletviewer -J-Djava.security.policy=WeatherApplet.policy
    WeatherApplet.html
```

The `-J` option of the applet viewer passes command-line arguments to the Java bytecode interpreter. The `-D` option of the Java bytecode interpreter sets the value of a system property. Here, we set the system property `java.security.policy` to the name of a policy file that contains the security permissions for this program.

If you want to run the applet in a browser, you first have to sign it. Then, you and, more importantly, anyone else who wants to run it, must tell the browser:

- To verify the signature (unless it was guaranteed by a trusted certificate authority);
- To agree with the requested privileges.

We discuss applet signing in detail in Chapter 9.

Applet Security

As you just saw, your applet was forbidden from doing a very simple operation, namely, connecting to port 80 of a web server. In this section, we discuss the reason for this prohibition and describe how to deploy the applet without making your users fuss with certificates.

Web browsers allow an applet to read and write data only on the host that serves the applet. Applets can connect only to sockets on the computer from which the applet came. This rule is often described as "applets can only phone home."

At first, this restriction seems to make no sense. Why should the applet be denied an operation that the ambient browser carries out all the time, namely, to get data from a web host? To understand the rationale, it helps to visualize the three hosts involved, as shown in Figure 3–12:

- The originating host — your computer that delivers the web page and Java applet to clients;

- The local host — the user's machine that runs your applet;

- The third-party data repository that your applet would like to see.

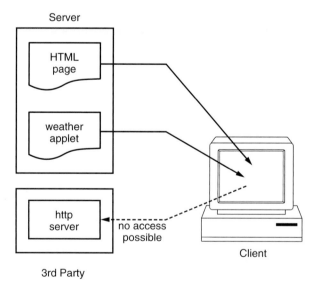

Figure 3–12: Applet security disallows connection to a third party

The applet security rule says that the applet can read and write data only on the originating host. Certainly it makes sense that the applet cannot write to the local host. If it could, it might be able to plant viruses or alter important files. After all, the applet starts running immediately when the user stumbles upon our web page, and the user must be protected from damage by malicious or incompetent applets.

It also makes sense that the applet cannot read from the local host. Otherwise, it might browse the files on the local computer for sensitive information, such as credit card numbers, open a socket connection to the applet host, and write the information back. You might open a great-looking web page, interact with an applet that does something fun or useful, and be completely unaware of what that applet does in other threads. The browser denies your applet all access to the files on your computer.

DILBERT reprinted by permission of United Feature Syndicate, Inc.

But why can't the applet read other files from the Web? Isn't the Web a wealth of publicly available information, made available for everyone to read? If you browse the Web from home, through a service provider, this is indeed the situation. But it is quite different when you do your Web surfing in your office (searching only for work-relevant information, of course). Many companies have their computer sitting behind a firewall.

A firewall is a computer that filters traffic going into and out of the corporate network. This computer will deny attempts to access services with less than stellar security histories. For example, there are known security holes in many FTP implementations. The firewall might simply disallow anonymous FTP requests or shunt them off to an isolated FTP server. It might also deny a request to access the mail port on all machines except the mail server. Depending on the security philosophy, the firewall (shown in Figure 3–13) can also apply filtering rules to the traffic between the corporate network and the Internet.

(If you are interested in this topic, turn to *Firewalls and Internet Security: Repelling the Wily Hacker* by William R. Cheswick and Steven M. Bellovin [Addison-Wesley, 1994].)

Having a firewall allows a company to use the Web to distribute internal information that is of interest to employees but should not be accessible outside the company. The company simply sets up a web server, tells the address only to its employees, and programs the firewall to deny any access requests to that server from the outside. The employees can then browse the internal information with the same web tools they already know and use.

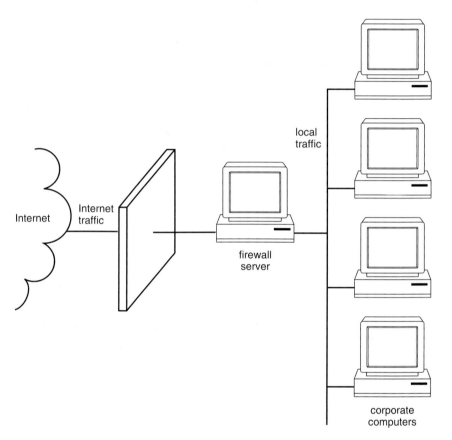

Figure 3–13: A firewall provides security

If an employee visits your web page, the applet is downloaded into the computer behind the firewall and starts running there. If it were able to read all the web pages that the ambient browser can read, it would have access to the corporate information. Then, it could open a connection to the host from which it came and send all that private information back. That is obviously insecure. Since the browser has no idea which web pages are public and which are confidential, it disallows access to all of them.

That is too bad—you simply cannot write an applet that goes out on the Web, grabs information, processes and formats it, and presents it to the applet user. For example, our weather report applet does not want to write any information back to its host. Why doesn't the browser let the applet strike a deal? If the applet promises not to write anywhere, it ought to be able to read from everywhere. That way, it would just be a harvester and processor, showing an ephemeral result on the user's screen.

The trouble is that a browser cannot distinguish *read* from *write* requests. When you ask to open a stream on a URL, this is obviously a read request. Well, maybe not. The URL might be of the form

```
http://www.rogue.com/cgi-bin/cracker.pl?Garys+password+is+Sicily
```

Here, the culprit is the CGI mechanism. It is designed to take arbitrary arguments and process them. The script that handles the CGI request can, and often does, store the request data. It is easy to hide information in a CGI query text. (A data stream that contains hidden information is called a *covert channel* in security circles.)

So, should the browser disallow all CGI queries and allow access only to plain web pages? The solution is not that simple. The browser has no way of knowing that the server to which it connects on port 80 (the HTTP port) is actually a standard HTTP server. It might be just a shell that saves all requests to a file and returns an HTML page: "Sorry, the information you requested is not available." Then, the applet could transmit information by pretending to read from the URL

```
http://www.rogue.com/Garys/password/is/Sicily
```

Since the browser cannot distinguish read from write requests, it must disallow them both.

To summarize: Applets run on the computer browsing your web page, but they can connect *only* to the computer serving the web page. That is the "applets can only phone home" rule.

Proxy Servers

How, then, can you distribute an applet that harvests information for your users? You could make a web page that shows the applet in action with fake data, stored on your server. (This is exactly the approach that Sun takes with their stock-ticker sample applet.) You could then provide a button with which the user downloads the applet and a policy file. Users could then run it from the applet viewer.

That approach will probably greatly limit the attractiveness of your applet. Many people will be too lazy to download and install the applet locally if they did not first get to use it a few times with real data on your web page.

Fortunately, there is a way to feed the applet real data: install a proxy server on your HTML server. That proxy server is a service that grabs requested information from the Web and sends it to whoever requested it. For example, suppose your applet makes a GET request

```
http://www.yourserver.com/proxysvr?URL=http://iwin.nws.noaa.gov
    /iwin/CA/hourly.html
```

to the proxy server that resides on the same host as the applet code. Then the proxy server fetches the web page for the applet and sends it as the result of the GET request (see Figure 3–14).

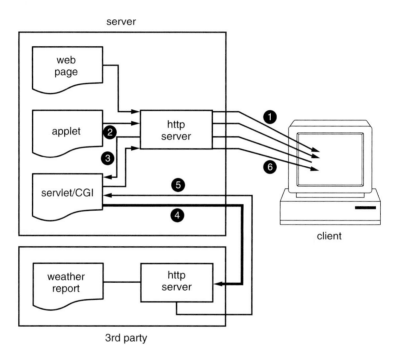

Figure 3–14: Data flow in the weather report applet

Proxy servers for this purpose must exist, but we could not find one, so we wrote our own. You can see the code in Example 3–9. We implemented the proxy as a *servlet*, a program that is started by a servlet engine. Most web servers can either run servlets directly or can be extended to do so.

Servlets are not a part of the standard edition of the Java platform, and a detailed discussion of servlets is beyond the scope of this book. For details, please turn to *Core Java Web Server* by Chris Taylor and Tim Kimmet [Prentice-Hall 1998]. However, the servlet in Example 3–9 is quite simple. Here is a brief explanation of how it works.

When the web server receives a GET request for the servlet, it calls its doGet method. The HttpServletRequest parameter contains the request parameters. The servlet uses the `getParameter` method to get the value of the `URL` parameter. In any servlet, you send your response to the `PrintStream` that the `getWriter` method of the `HttpServletResponse` class returns. This servlet simply connects to the resource given in the `URL` parameter, reads the data a line at a time, and sends it to the response stream. Finally, you can see how the `sendError` method is used for error reporting.

The next section tells you how to configure the servlet if you use the Apache Tomcat Servlet Container. That software contains a small web server that you can run locally to test the weather report applet.

You don't have to use servlets to implement a proxy server. The sidebar tells you how you can implement the proxy server in C or Perl.

Example 3–9: ProxySvr.java

```
1. import java.io.*;
2. import java.net.*;
3. import javax.servlet.*;
4. import javax.servlet.http.*;
5.
6. /**
7.    A very simple proxy servlet. The URL request parameter
8.    specifies the resource to get. The servlet gets the
9.    requested information and returns it to the caller.
10. */
11. public class ProxySvr extends HttpServlet
12. {
13.    public void doGet(HttpServletRequest request,
14.       HttpServletResponse response)
15.       throws ServletException, IOException
16.    {
17.       String query = null;
18.
19.       response.setContentType("text/html");
20.       PrintWriter out = response.getWriter();
21.
22.       query = request.getParameter("URL");
23.       if (query == null)
24.       {
25.          response.sendError(HttpServletResponse.SC_BAD_REQUEST,
26.             "Missing URL parameter");
27.          return;
28.       }
29.
30.       try
31.       {
32.          query = URLDecoder.decode(query);
```

```
33.        }
34.        catch(Exception exception)
35.        {
36.            response.sendError(HttpServletResponse.SC_BAD_REQUEST,
37.                "URL decode error " + exception);
38.             return;
39.        }
40.
41.        try
42.        {
43.            URL url = new URL(query);
44.            BufferedReader in = new BufferedReader(new
45.                InputStreamReader(url.openStream()));
46.
47.            String line;
48.            while ((line = in.readLine()) != null)
49.                out.println(line);
50.            out.flush();
51.        }
52.        catch(IOException exception)
53.        {
54.            response.sendError(HttpServletResponse.SC_NOT_FOUND,
55.                "Exception: " + exception);
56.        }
57.    }
58. }
```

Example 3–10: proxysvr.c

```
 1. #include <netdb.h>
 2. #include <sys/types.h>
 3. #include <sys/socket.h>
 4. #include <netinet/in.h>
 5. #include <arpa/inet.h>
 6. #include <stdio.h>
 7. #include <string.h>
 8. #include <stdlib.h>
 9.
10. #define MAXLINE 512
11. #define MAXNAME 128
12. #define HTTP 80
13.
14. unsigned writen(fd, vptr, n)
15. int fd;
16. char* vptr;
17. unsigned n;
18. {
19.     unsigned nleft;
20.     unsigned nwritten;
21.     char* ptr;
```

```
22.
23.     ptr = (char*)vptr;
24.     nleft = n;
25.     while (nleft > 0)
26.     {
27.         if ((nwritten = write(fd, ptr, nleft)) <= 0)
28.             return nwritten;
29.         nleft -= nwritten;
30.         ptr += nwritten;
31.     }
32.     return n - nleft;
33. }
34.
35. unsigned readline(fd, vptr, maxlen)
36. int fd;
37. char* vptr;
38. int maxlen;
39. {
40.     unsigned n;
41.     unsigned rc;
42.     char* ptr;
43.     char c;
44.
45.     ptr = vptr;
46.     for (n = 1; n < maxlen; n++)
47.     {
48.         if ((rc = read(fd, &c, 1)) == 1)
49.         {
50.             *ptr++ = c;
51.             if (c == '\n')
52.             {
53.                 *ptr = 0;
54.                 return n;
55.             }
56.         }
57.         else if (rc == 0)
58.         {
59.             if (n == 1) return 0;
60.             else
61.             {
62.                 *ptr = 0;
63.                 return n;
64.             }
65.         }
66.         else
67.             return -1;
68.     }
69.     *ptr = 0;
70.     return n;
71. }
72.
```

```
73. void error(msg)
74. char* msg;
75. {
76.     fputs(msg, stderr);
77.     fputc('\n', stderr);
78.     exit(1);
79. }
80.
81. void url_decode(in, out, outlen)
82. char* in;
83. char* out;
84. int outlen;
85. {
86.     int i = 0;
87.     int j = 0;
88.     while (in[i] != '\0' && j < outlen - 1)
89.     {
90.         if (in[i] == '+') out[j] = ' ';
91.         else if (in[i] == '%')
92.         {
93.             int ch;
94.             sscanf(in + i + 1, "%x", &ch);
95.             out[j] = ch;
96.             i += 2;
97.         }
98.         else out[j] = in[i];
99.         i++;
100.        j++;
101.    }
102.    out[j] = 0;
103. }
104.
105. int main(argc, argv)
106. int argc;
107. char** argv;
108. {
109.     int sockfd;
110.     struct sockaddr_in serv_addr;
111.     int n;
112.     char* name;
113.     struct hostent* hostptr;
114.     char url[MAXLINE + 1];
115.     char sendline[MAXLINE + 1];
116.     char recvline[MAXLINE + 1];
117.     char server_name[MAXNAME];
118.     char file_name[MAXLINE];
119.     int port;
120.     int service = 0;
121.     char* p;
122.     char* q;
123.
```

```
124.    url_decode(argv[1], url, sizeof(url));
125.
126.    p = strstr(url, "URL=http://");
127.    if (p != url)
128.        error("Sorry--can only recognize URL=service://server/file");
129.    service = HTTP;
130.    p += strlen("URL=http://");
131.    q = strchr(p, '/');
132.    if (q == NULL)
133.        error("Sorry--can only recognize //server/file");
134.    strncpy(server_name, p, q - p);
135.    server_name[q - p] = '\0';
136.    strncpy(file_name, q, sizeof(file_name) - 1);
137.    file_name[sizeof(file_name) - 1] = '\0';
138.    port = service;
139.
140.    if ((sockfd = socket(PF_INET, SOCK_STREAM, 0)) < 0)
141.        error("Can't open stream socket");
142.
143.    bzero((char*)&serv_addr, sizeof(serv_addr));
144.    serv_addr.sin_family = AF_INET;
145.    hostptr = gethostbyname(server_name);
146.    if (hostptr == 0) error("Can't find host");
147.    name = inet_ntoa(*(struct in_addr*)*hostptr->h_addr_list);
148.    serv_addr.sin_addr.s_addr = inet_addr(name);
149.    serv_addr.sin_port = htons(port);
150.
151.    if (connect(sockfd, (struct sockaddr*)&serv_addr,
152.        sizeof(serv_addr)) < 0)
153.        error("Can't connect to server");
154.
155.    sendline[sizeof(sendline) - 1] = 0;
156.    if (service == HTTP)
157.    {
158.        strcpy(sendline, "GET ");
159.        strncat(sendline, file_name, sizeof(sendline) - 1
160.            - strlen(sendline));
161.    }
162.    strncat(sendline, "\r\n", sizeof(sendline) - 1
163.        - strlen(sendline));
164.
165.    n = strlen(sendline);
166.    if (writen(sockfd, sendline, n) != n)
167.        error("Write error on socket");
168.
169.    fputs("Content-type: text/html\n\n", stdout);
170.
171.    do
172.    {
173.        n = readline(sockfd, recvline, MAXLINE);
174.        if (n < 0)
175.            error("Read error on socket");
```

```
176.        else if (n > 0)
177.        {
178.            recvline[n] = 0;
179.            fputs(recvline, stdout);
180.        }
181.    }
182.    while (n > 0);
183.
184.    return 0;
185. }
```

Example 3–11: proxysvr.pl

```perl
1. ($url) = @ARGV;
2.
3. $url =~ tr/+/ /;
4. $url =~ s/%([a-fA-F0-9][a-fA-F0-9])/pack("C", hex($1))/eg;
5.
6. $pos = index($url, "URL=http://");
7.
8. if ($pos != 0)
9. {
10.    die "Sorry--can only recognize URL=http://server/file";
11. }
12.
13. $port = 80;
14.
15. $pos = 11;
16. $pos2 = index($url, "/", $pos);
17. if ($pos2 < 0)
18. {
19.    die "Sorry--can only recognize //server/file";
20. }
21.
22. $server_name = substr($url, $pos, $pos2 - $pos);
23. $file_name = substr($url, $pos2);
24. $AF_INET = 2;
25. $SOCK_STREAM =1;
26.
27. $sockaddr = 'S n a4 x8';
28.
29. ($name, $aliases, $proto) = getprotobyname ('tcp');
30. ($name,$aliases,$type,$len,$thataddr)
31.    = gethostbyname($server_name);
32. $that = pack($sockaddr, $AF_INET, $port, $thataddr);
33.
34. if (!socket (S, $AF_INET, $SOCK_STREAM, $proto))
35. {
36.    die $!;
37. }
```

```
38.
39. if (!connect (S, $that))
40. {
41.    die $!;
42. }
43.
44. select(S); $|=1; select(STDOUT);
45.
46. $command = "GET ".$file_name;
47.
48. print S $command."\r\n";
49.
50. print "Content-type: text/html\n\n";
51. while (<S>)
52. {
53.    print;
54. }
```

Comparing Servlets, Perl, and C for Server-side Processing

CGI scripts can be written in any language that can read from standard input and write to standard output. The "traditional" choice for CGI scripts is Perl. However, we actually wrote our first proxy server script in C because we did not realize that Perl can connect to sockets.

The Perl and C codes are listed in Example 3–10 and 3–11. As you can see, the C code is quite long. Even the most elementary operations (for example, reading a line of input) must be programmed in gory detail in C. Networking code is even worse. We didn't come up with the networking code ourselves. We modified a sample program from *UNIX Network Programming*, by W. Richard Stevens (Prentice-Hall, 1990). Have a look at the code, and you will really appreciate the simplicity and elegance of the `java.net` package.

The Perl code is much shorter but, as you can see by glancing at it, is completely unreadable to the uninitiated. There are charming variable names like `$!` and `$|` and inscrutable statements such as

```
$url =~ s/%([a-fA-F0-9][a-fA-F0-9])/pack("C", hex($1))/eg;
```

This means "replace all strings of the form '% followed by two hex digits' by the corresponding hex value." (No, we didn't figure that out ourselves. Like everybody else, we copied it from another script.) The remainder of the program is a modification of an example from *Programming Perl*, (3rd edition) by Larry Wall, Tom Christiansen, and Jon Orwant (O'Reilly, 2000). We don't pretend to understand the details, but it works.

As a result of this experiment, we can heartily recommend servlets as a great mechanism for server-side processing. The network programming and string handling in the Java platform beat the daylights out of C, and the Java programming language code is far more readable and maintainable than the Perl equivalent.

Testing the `WeatherReport` *Applet*

In this section, we show you how to test the weather report applet. You need a web server that can execute either servlets or CGI scripts. We give you detailed instructions for the Apache Tomcat servlet container. If you use another web server, you will need to make the appropriate adjustments.

Here are the steps.

1. Download Tomcat from `http://jakarta.apache.org/tomcat/index.html`.

2. Install Tomcat. To keep the instructions uncluttered, let's assume you installed it in the `/tomcat` directory. If you use another directory, modify the instructions accordingly.

3. Compile the servlet code:

    ```
    javac -classpath /tomcat/lib/servlet.jar:. ProxySvr.java
    ```

4. Copy the class file `ProxySvr.class` to the `/tomcat/webapps/examples/WEB-INF/classes` directory.

5. Edit the `/tomcat/webapps/examples/WEB-INF/web.xml` file by adding the lines

    ```
    <servlet>
        <servlet-name>
            ProxySvr
        </servlet-name>
        <servlet-class>
            ProxySvr
        </servlet-class>
    </servlet>
    ```

    and

    ```
    <servlet-mapping>
        <servlet-name>
            ProxySvr
        </servlet-name>
        <url-pattern>
            /ProxySvr
        </url-pattern>
    </servlet-mapping>
    ```

    in the appropriate places. (Just follow the syntax of the other examples.)

6. Copy the files

    ```
    WeatherApplet.html
    WeatherApplet*.class
    ```

    to the `/tomcat/webapps/examples` directory. Note that there are several inner class files that you need to copy.

7. Edit the `WeatherApplet.html` file and change the `PARAM` tag to

   ```
   <PARAM NAME="queryBase" VALUE=
   "http://localhost:8080/examples/ProxySvr?URL=http://
   iwin.nws.noaa.gov/iwin/">
   ```

8. Start Tomcat.

9. Start the applet by running

   ```
   appletviewer http://localhost:8080/examples/WeatherApplet.html
   ```

   Alternatively, use your browser to view that URL. Your browser needs to be able to handle Java 2 applets (such as Netscape 6 or Opera). Note that no security policy file is required

Now that you have seen the applet in action, let us review why the proxy server solves the applet security problem. When the user selects a state and report type, the weather applet requests the information from the proxy server on its local host. The proxy server then goes out to the National Weather Service, gets the data, and feeds it back to the applet.

This looks like a lot of trouble, but we have avoided the security risk. The applet only talks to the proxy server. The proxy server cannot peek at documents that may be accessible from the machine that is running the applet.

You can use this technique whenever you want to deploy an applet that harvests information from other web sites. In effect, you have offloaded the harvesting to the server, and you use the applet for presenting the results.

Now the security monkey is on *your* back. By installing the proxy server on your web server, you enable anyone to access it and download any files that are visible from your server. It is then up to you to configure your network so that the proxy server cannot pick up any of your confidential files. Alternatively, you can implement the proxy server so that it retrieves only URLs of a certain form. In our case, a useful restriction would be to reject any requests other than for URLs starting with `http://iwin.nws.noaa.gov`.

Does it make sense to have the server merely grab the information and reflect it to the applet? In this case, it does, but in general, it often makes sense for the server to cache it, thus improving performance when there are multiple requests, or to preprocess the information. In this example, we used server-side processing to avoid a security issue. In many other situations, it is best to process as much information as possible on the server because the server software is easier to control and maintain. Applets still have their place—interacting with the user and presenting results. In a typical 3-tier (or *n*-tier) application, the applet is paired with a servlet or other server-side programming mechanism that does the "heavy lifting."

Chapter 4

Database Connectivity: JDBC

- ▼ THE DESIGN OF JDBC
- ▼ THE STRUCTURED QUERY LANGUAGE
- ▼ INSTALLING JDBC
- ▼ BASIC JDBC PROGRAMMING CONCEPTS
- ▼ EXECUTING QUERIES
- ▼ SCROLLABLE AND UPDATABLE RESULT SETS
- ▼ METADATA
- ▼ TRANSACTIONS
- ▼ ADVANCED CONNECTION MANAGEMENT

In the summer of 1996, Sun released the first version of the Java Database Connectivity (JDBC) kit. This package lets programmers connect to a database, query it, or update it, using the Structured Query Language or SQL. (SQL, usually pronounced like "sequel," is an industry standard for database access.) When JDBC was first announced, we considered this one of the most important developments in programming for the Java platform. It is not just that databases are among the most common use of hardware and software today. After all, there are a lot of products running after this market, so why did we think the Java programming language had the potential to make a big splash? The reason that Java and JDBC have an essential advantage over other database programming environments is this:

- Programs developed with the Java programming language and JDBC are platform independent and vendor independent.

The same database program written in the Java programming language can run on an NT box, a Solaris server, or a database appliance powered by the Java platform. You can move your data from one database to another, for example, from Microsoft SQL Server to Oracle, or even to a tiny database embedded in a device, and the same program can still read your data. This is in sharp contrast to traditional database programming. It is all too common that one writes database applications in a proprietary database language, using a database management system that is available only from a single vendor. The result is that you can run the resulting application only on one or two platforms. We believe that *because of their universality,* the Java programming language and JDBC will eventually replace proprietary database languages and call level interfaces used by vendors such as Oracle, Informix, and Microsoft for accessing databases.

NOTE: Some database vendors now build a Java Virtual Machine into the database itself so that you can write stored procedures in Java. This technology is part of the SQLJ specification. For more information on SQLJ, see `http://www.sqlj.org`.

As part of the release of Java 2 in 1998, a second version of JDBC was issued as well. At the time of this writing, support for JDBC 2 is still not universal, but many JDBC 2 drivers are available. JDBC 2 introduces several major features such as scrollable cursors and support for advanced SQL types. The JDBC 3 specification was in its final review phase as this chapter was finished. JDBC 3 enhancements are more technical in nature. In this chapter, we alert you when you need to be aware of the version differences.

We still must caution you that the JDK offers no tools for database programming with the Java programming language. For form designers, query builders, and report generators, you need to turn to third-party packages. "Corporate" or "professional" versions of development environments for the Java platform, such as Visual Café and JBuilder, ship with database integration tools.

In this chapter:

- We explain some of the ideas behind JDBC—the "Java Database Connectivity" API.
- We give you an introduction (or a refresher) in SQL, the industry-standard Structured Query Language for databases.
- We provide enough details and examples so that you can get started in using JDBC for common programming situations.

NOTE: Over the years, many technologies were invented to make database access more efficient and fail-safe. Standard databases support indexes, triggers, stored procedures, and transaction management. JDBC supports all these features, but we do not discuss them in detail in this chapter. One could write an entire book on advanced database programming for the Java platform, and many such books have been written. The material in this chapter will give you enough information to effectively use JDBC with a departmental database. To go further with JDBC, we suggest *JDBC API Tutorial and Reference* by Seth White, Maydene Fisher, Rick Cattell, Graham Hamilton, and Mark Hapner [Addison-Wesley 1999].

The Design of JDBC

From the start, the developers of the Java technology at Sun were aware of the potential that Java showed for working with databases. Starting in 1995, they began working on extending the standard Java library to deal with SQL access to databases. What they first hoped to do was to extend Java so that it could talk to any random database, using only "pure" Java. It didn't take them very long to realize that this is an impossible task: there are simply too many databases out there, using too many protocols. Moreover, while database vendors were all in favor of Sun providing a standard network protocol for database access, they were only in favor of it if Sun decided to use *their* network protocol.

What all the database vendors and tool vendors *did* agree on was that it would be useful if Sun provided a pure Java API for SQL access *along* with a driver manager to allow third-party drivers to connect to specific databases. Database vendors could provide their own drivers to plug into the driver manager. There would then be a simple mechanism for registering third-party drivers with the driver manager—the point being that all the drivers needed to do was follow the requirements laid out in the driver manager API.

After a fairly long period of public discussion, the API for database access became the JDBC API, and the rules for writing drivers were encapsulated in the JDBC service provider interface, or SPI. (The SPI is of interest only to database vendors and database tool providers; we don't cover it here.)

This protocol follows the very successful model of Microsoft's ODBC, which provided a C programming language interface for database access. Both JDBC and ODBC are based on the same idea: Programs written according to the JDBC API would talk to the JDBC driver manager, which, in turn, would use the drivers that were plugged into it at that moment to talk to the actual database.

NOTE: A list of JDBC drivers currently available can be found at the web site `http://industry.java.sun.com/products/jdbc/drivers`

More precisely, the JDBC consists of two layers. The top layer is the JDBC API. This API communicates with the JDBC manager driver API, sending it the various SQL statements. The manager should (transparently to the programmer) communicate with the various third-party drivers that actually connect to the database and return the information from the query or perform the action specified by the query.

> NOTE: The JDBC specification will actually allow you to pass any string to the under-lying driver. The driver can pass this string to the database. This feature allows you to use specialized versions of SQL that may be supported by the driver and its associated database.

All this means the Java/JDBC layer is all that most programmers will ever have to deal with. Figure 4–1 illustrates what happens.

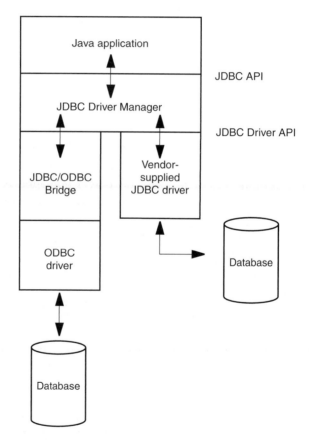

Figure 4–1: JDBC-to-database communication path

JDBC drivers are classified into the following *types:*

- A *type 1 driver* translates JDBC to ODBC and relies on an ODBC driver to com-municate with the database. Sun includes one such driver, the *JDBC/ODBC bridge,* with the JDK. However, the bridge requires deployment and proper configuration of an ODBC driver. When JDBC was first released, the bridge was handy for testing, but it was never intended for production use. At this point, there are plenty of better drivers available, and we advise against using the JDBC/ODBC bridge.

- A *type 2 driver* is a driver, written partly in the Java programming language and partly in native code, that communicates with the client API of a database. When you use such a driver, you must install some platform-specific code in addition to a Java library.

- A *type 3 driver* is a pure Java client library that uses a database-independent protocol to communicate database requests to a server component, which then translates the requests into a database-specific protocol. The client library is independent of the actual database, thus simplifying deployment.

- A *type 4 driver* is a pure Java library that translates JDBC requests directly to a database-specific protocol.

Most database vendors supply either a type 3 or type 4 driver with their database. Furthermore, a number of third-party companies specialize in producing drivers with better standards conformance, support for more platforms, better performance, or, in some cases, simply better reliability than the drivers that are provided by the database vendors.

In summary, the ultimate goal of the JDBC is to make possible the following:

- Programmers can write applications in the Java programming language to access any database, using standard SQL statements—or even specialized extensions of SQL—while still following Java language conventions. (All JDBC drivers must support at least the entry-level version of SQL 92.)

- Database vendors and database tool vendors can supply the low-level drivers. Thus, they can optimize their drivers for their specific products.

NOTE: If you are curious as to why Sun just didn't adopt the ODBC model, their response, as given at the JavaOne conference in May 1996, was:

- ODBC is hard to learn.
- ODBC has a few commands with lots of complex options. The preferred style in the Java programming language is to have simple and intuitive methods, but to have lots of them.
- ODBC relies on the use of `void*` pointers and other C features that are not natural in the Java programming language.
- An ODBC-based solution is inherently less safe and harder to deploy than a pure Java solution.

Typical Uses of JDBC

You can use JDBC in both applications and applets. In an applet, all the normal security restrictions apply. By default, the security manager assumes that all applets written in the Java programming language are untrusted.

In particular, applets that use JDBC are only able to open a database connection to the server from which they are downloaded. That means the Web server and the database server must be the same machine, which is not a typical setup. Of course, the Web server can have a proxy service that routes database traffic to another machine. With signed applets, this restriction can be loosened.

Applications, on the other hand, have complete freedom to access remote database servers. If you implement a traditional client/server program (see Figure 4–2), it probably makes more sense to use an application, not an applet, for database access.

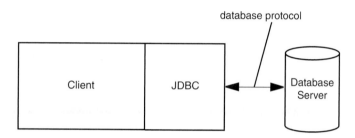

Figure 4–2: A client/server application

However, the world is moving away from client/server and toward a "three-tier model" or even more advanced "*n*-tier models." In the three-tier model, the client does not make database calls. Instead, it calls on a middleware layer on the server that in turn makes the database queries. The three-tier model has a couple of advantages. It separates *visual presentation* (on the client) from the *business logic* (in the middle tier) and the raw data (in the database). Therefore, it becomes possible to access the same data and the same business rules from multiple clients, such as a Java application or applet or a web form.

Communication between the client and middle tier can occur through HTTP (when you use a web browser as the client), RMI (when you use an application or applet—see Chapter 5), or another mechanism. JDBC is used to manage the communication between the middle tier and the back-end database. Figure 4–3 shows the basic architecture. There are, of course, many variations of this model. In particular, the Java 2 Enterprise Edition defines a structure for *application servers* that manage code modules called *Enterprise JavaBeans,* and provide valuable services such as load balancing, request caching, security, and simple database access. In that architecture, JDBC still plays an important role for issuing complex database queries. (For more information on the Enterprise Edition, see `http://java.sun.com/j2ee`.)

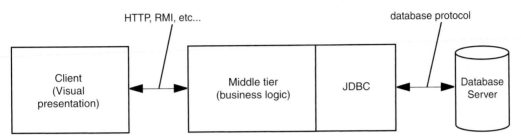

Figure 4–3: A three-tier application

The Structured Query Language

JDBC is an interface to SQL, which is the interface to essentially all modern relational databases. Desktop databases usually have a graphical user interfaces that lets users manipulate the data directly, but server-based databases are accessed purely through SQL. Most desktop databases have a SQL interface as well, but it often does not support the full range of ANSI SQL92 features, the current standard for SQL.

The JDBC package can be thought of as nothing more than an application programming interface (API) for communicating SQL statements to databases. We will give a short introduction to SQL in this section. If you have never seen SQL before, you may not find this material sufficient. If so, you should turn to one of the many books on the topic. We recommend *Client/Server Databases* by James Martin and Joe Leben [Prentice-Hall 1998] or the venerable and opinionated book *A Guide to the SQL Standard* by Chris. J. Date [Addison-Wesley 1997].

You can think of a database as a bunch of named tables with rows and columns. Each column has a *column name*. The rows contain the actual data. These are sometimes called *records*.

As the example database for this book, we use a set of tables that describe a collection of books on HTML. (Thanks to Cye H. Waldman at `http://wwwiz.com/books` for supplying the sample data.)

Table 4–1: The **Authors** table

Author_ID	Name	URL
ARON	Aronson, Larry	http://...
ARPA	Arpajian, Scott	http://...
...	...	...

Table 4–2: The **Books** table

Title	ISBN	Publisher_ID	URL	Price
Beyond HTML	0-07-882198-3	**00788**	http://...	27.95
10 Minute Guide to HTML	0-78970541-9	**07897**	http://...	15.00
...	...	...	...	...

Table 4–3: The **BooksAuthors** table

ISBN	Author_ID	Seq_No
1-56-884454-9	TAYL	1
1-56884645-2	SMIT	1
1-56884645-2	BEBA	2
...	...	...

Table 4–4: The **Publishers** table

Publisher_ID	Name	URL
01262	Academic Press	www.apnet.com/
18835	Coriolis	www.coriolis.com/
...	...	...

Figure 4–4 shows a view of the Books table. Figure 4–5 shows the result of *joining* this table with a table of publishers. Both the Books and the Publishers table contain a numerical code for the publisher. When we join both tables on the publisher code, we obtain a *query result* made up of values from the joined tables. Each row in the result contains the information about a book, together with the publisher name and Web page URL. Note that the publisher names and URLs are duplicated across several rows since we have several rows with the same publisher.

The benefit of joining tables is to avoid unnecessary duplication of data in the database tables. For example, a naive database design might have had columns for the publisher name and URL right in the Books table. But then the database itself, and not just the query result, would have many duplicates of these entries. If a publisher's Web address changed, *all* entries would need to be updated. Clearly, this is somewhat error prone. In the relational model, we distribute data into multiple tables such that no information is ever unnecessarily duplicated. For example, each publisher URL is contained only once in the publisher table. If the information needs to be combined, then the tables are joined.

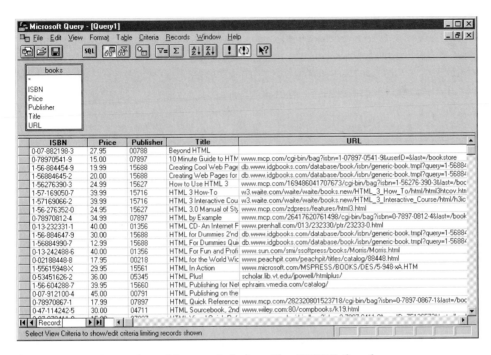

Figure 4–4: Sample table containing the HTML books

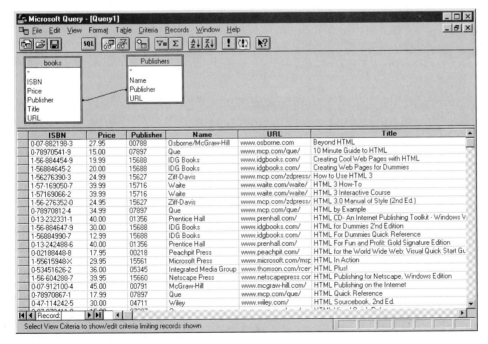

Figure 4–5: Two tables joined together

In the figures, you can see a graphical tool to inspect and link the tables. Many vendors have tools to express queries in a simple form by connecting column names and filling information into forms. Such tools are often called *query by example* (QBE) tools. In contrast, a query that uses SQL is written out in text, using the SQL syntax. For example:

```
SELECT Books.ISBN, Books.Price, Books.Title,
    Books.Publisher_Id, Publishers.Name, Publishers.URL
FROM Books, Publishers
WHERE Books.Publisher_Id = Publishers.Publisher_Id
```

In the remainder of this section, you will learn how to write such queries. If you are already familiar with SQL, just skip this section.

By convention, SQL keywords are written in all caps, although this is not necessary.

The SELECT operation is quite flexible. You can simply select all elements in the Books table with the following query:

```
SELECT * FROM Books
```

The FROM statement is required in every SQL SELECT statement. The FROM clause tells the database which tables to examine to find the data.

You can choose the columns that you want.

```
SELECT ISBN, Price, Title
FROM Books
```

You can restrict the rows in the answer with the WHERE clause.

```
SELECT ISBN, Price, Title
FROM Books
WHERE Price <= 29.95
```

Be careful with the "equals" comparison. SQL uses = and <>, not == or != =, as in the Java programming language, for equality testing.

NOTE: Some database vendors support the use of != for inequality testing. This is not standard SQL, so we recommend against using it.

The WHERE clause can also use pattern matching, using the LIKE operator. The wildcard characters are not the usual * and ?, however. Use a % for zero or more characters and an underscore for a single character. For example:

```
SELECT ISBN, Price, Title
FROM Books
WHERE Title NOT LIKE '%H_M%'
```

Note that strings are enclosed in single quotes, not double quotes. A single quote inside a string is denoted as a pair of single quotes. For example,

```
SELECT Title
FROM Books
WHERE Books.Title LIKE '%''%'
```

reports all titles that contain a single quote.

You can select data from multiple tables.

```
SELECT * FROM Books, Publishers
```

Without a `WHERE` clause, this query is not very interesting. It lists *all combinations* of rows from both tables. In our case, where `Books` has 37 rows and `Publishers` has 18 rows, the result is a table with 37 × 18 entries and lots of duplications. We really want to constrain the query to say that we are only interested in *matching* books with their publishers.

```
SELECT * FROM Books, Publishers
WHERE Books.Publisher_Id = Publishers.Publisher_Id
```

This query result has 37 rows, one for each book, since each book has a publisher in the `Publisher` table.

Whenever you have multiple tables in a query, the same column name can occur in two different places. That happened in our example. There is a publisher code column called `Publisher_Id` in both the `Books` and the `Publishers` table. When an ambiguity would otherwise result, you must prefix each column name with the name of the table to which it belongs, such as `Books.Publisher_Id`.

Now you have seen all SQL constructs that were used in the query at the beginning of this section:

```
SELECT Books.ISBN, Books.Price, Books.Title,
   Books.Publisher_Id,  Publishers.Name, Publishers.URL
FROM Books, Publishers
WHERE Books.Publisher_Id = Publishers.Publisher_Id
```

You can use SQL to change the data inside a database as well, by using so-called *action queries* (i.e., queries that move or change data). For example, suppose you want to reduce by $5.00 the current price of all books that do not have "HTML 3" in their title.

```
UPDATE Books
SET Price = Price - 5.00
WHERE Title NOT LIKE '%HTML 3%'
```

Similarly, you can change several fields at the same time by separating the `SET` clauses with commas. There are many other SQL keywords you can use in an action query. Probably the most important besides `UPDATE` is `DELETE`, which allows the query to delete those records that satisfy certain criteria. Finally,

SQL comes with built-in functions for taking averages, finding maximums and minimums in a column, and a lot more. Consult a book on SQL for more information.

Typically, to insert values into a table, you use the INSERT statement:

```
INSERT INTO Books
VALUES ('Beyond HTML', '0-07-882198-3', '00788', '', 27.95)
```

You need a separate INSERT statement for every row being inserted in the table.

Of course, before you can query, modify, and insert data, you must have a place to store data. Use the CREATE TABLE command to make a new table. You specify the name and data type for each column. For example,

```
CREATE TABLE Books
(
    Title CHAR(60),
    ISBN CHAR(13),
    Publisher_Id CHAR(5),
    URL CHAR(80),
    Price DECIMAL(6,2)
)
```

Table 4–5 shows the most common SQL data types.

Table 4–5: SQL Data Types

Data Types	Description
INTEGER or INT	Typically, a 32-bit integer
SMALLINT	Typically, a 16-bit integer
NUMERIC(m,n), DECIMAL(m,n) or DEC(m,n)	Fixed-point decimal number with m total digits and n digits after the decimal point
FLOAT(n)	A floating-point number with n binary digits of precision
REAL	Typically, a 32-bit floating-point number
DOUBLE	Typically, a 64-bit floating-point number
CHARACTER(n) or CHAR(n)	Fixed-length string of length n
VARCHAR(n)	Variable-length strings of maximum length n
BOOLEAN	A boolean value
DATE	Calendar date, implementation dependent
TIME	Time of day, implementation dependent
TIMESTAMP	Date and time of day, implementation dependent
BLOB	A binary large object
CLOB	A character large object

In this book, we are not discussing the additional clauses, such as keys and constraints, that you can use with the CREATE TABLE command.

Installing JDBC

First, you need a database program that is compatible with JDBC. You will also need to create a database for your experimental use. We assume you will call this database COREJAVA. Create a new database, or have your database administrator create one with the appropriate permissions. You need to be able to create, update, and drop tables.

If you have never installed a client/server database before, you may find that setting up the database is somewhat complex and that it can be difficult to diagnose the cause for failure. It may be best to seek expert help if your setup is not working correctly.

One alternative is to install a pure Java database such as Cloudscape (http://www.cloudscape.com), PointBase (http://www.pointbase.com), or InstantDB (http://www.lutris.com/products/instantDB). These databases are less powerful but simple to set up. The most complex part is setting up the class path, which should not pose a challenge for a seasoned Java programmer.

Essentially all database vendors already have JDBC drivers. You need to locate the vendor's instructions to load the driver into your program and to connect to the database. In the next section, we will explain the setups for two typical databases that are available on a variety of platforms:

- IBM DB2
- Cloudscape

Instructions for other databases are similar, although, of course, the details will vary.

We recommend against using the JDBC/ODBC bridge driver that comes with the Java 2 SDK. We recommend even more strongly against using that driver with a desktop database such as Microsoft Access. Not only are the installation and configuration somewhat cumbersome, but both the bridge driver and desktop databases have restrictions that can easily lead to confusion. Ultimately, one learns very little about real databases from this setup.

NOTE: Some desktop databases support SQL through a proprietary mechanism, not JDBC or ODBC. For example, Borland has a BDE engine and Microsoft has a Jet engine that give somewhat better performance than ODBC for local database access. These mechanisms are not compatible with the Java platform.

Basic JDBC Programming Concepts

Programming with the JDBC classes is, by design, not very different from programming with the usual Java platform classes: you build objects from the JDBC core classes, extending them by inheritance if need be. This section takes you through the details.

 NOTE: The classes that you use for JDBC programming are contained in the `java.sql` and `javax.sql` packages.

Database URLs

When connecting to a database, you must specify the data source and you may need to specify additional parameters. For example, network protocol drivers may need a port, and ODBC drivers may need various attributes.

As you might expect, JDBC uses a syntax similar to ordinary URLs to describe data sources. Here are examples of the syntax:

```
jdbc:db2:COREJAVA
jdbc:cloudscape:COREJAVA;create=true
```

These JDBC URLs specify a DB2 or Cloudscape database named COREJAVA. The general syntax is

```
jdbc:subprotocol name:other stuff
```

where a subprotocol is used to select the specific driver for connecting to the database.

The format for the `other stuff` parameter depends on the subprotocol used. You need to look up your vendor's documentation for the specific format.

Making the Connection

You need to find out the names of the JDBC driver classes used by your vendor. Typical driver names are

```
COM.ibm.db2.jdbc.app.DB2Driver
COM.cloudscape.core.JDBCDriver
```

Next, you must find the library in which the driver is located, such as `db2java.zip` or `cloudscape.jar`. You must place the full path name to that driver onto the class path. Use one of the following three mechanisms:

*   Launch your database programs with the `-classpath` command-line argument.
*   Modify the CLASSPATH environment variable.
*   Copy the database library into the `jre/lib/ext` directory.

The `DriverManager` is the class responsible for selecting database drivers and creating a new database connection. However, before the driver manager can activate a driver, the driver must be registered.

There are two methods for registering drivers. The `jdbc.drivers` property contains a list of class names for the drivers that the driver manager will register at startup. The names are separated by colons.

You can specify the property with a command-line argument, such as

```
java -Djdbc.drivers=COM.ibm.db2.jdbc.app.DB2Driver MyProg
```

Or your application can add read a properties file with the line

```
jdbc.drivers=COM.ibm.db2.jdbc.app.DB2Driver
```

and add that setting to the system properties. (See Chapter 2 for more information on properties.)

You can also supply multiple drivers; separate them with colons, such as

```
COM.ibm.db2.jdbc.app.DB2Driver:COM.cloudscape.core.JDBCDriver
```

This approach allows users of your application to install appropriate drivers simply by modifying a property file.

Our sample programs read all database parameters from a properties file `database.properties`. Make sure to edit that file to match your database.

Alternatively, you can manually register a driver by loading its class. For example,

```
Class.forName("COM.ibm.db2.jdbc.app.DB2Driver");
    // force registration of driver
```

After registering drivers, you open a database connection with code that is similar to the following example:

```
String url = "jdbc:db2:COREJAVA";
String username = "db2inst1";
String password = "wombat";
Connection conn = DriverManager.getConnection(url,
    username, password);
```

The driver manager will try to find a driver that can use the protocol specified in the database URL by iterating through the available drivers currently registered with the driver manager.

For our example programs, we find it convenient to use a properties file to specify the URL, user name, and password in addition to the database driver. A typical properties file has the following contents:

```
jdbc.drivers=COM.ibm.db2.jdbc.app.DB2Driver
jdbc.url=jdbc:db2:COREJAVA
```

```
jdbc.username=db2inst1
jdbc.password=wombat
```

Here is the code for reading a properties file and opening the database connection.

```
Properties props = new Properties();
FileInputStream in
    = new FileInputStream("database.properties");
props.load(in);
in.close();

String drivers = props.getProperty("jdbc.drivers");
if (drivers != null)
    System.setProperty("jdbc.drivers", drivers);
String url = props.getProperty("jdbc.url");
String username = props.getProperty("jdbc.username");
String password = props.getProperty("jdbc.password");
return DriverManager.getConnection(url, username, password);
```

The getConnection method returns a Connection object. In the following sections, you will see how to use the connection object to execute SQL statements.

TIP: A good way to debug JDBC-related problems is to enable JDBC tracing. Call the DriverManager.setLogWriter method to send trace messages to a PrintWriter. The trace output contains a detailed listing of the JDBC activity.

Testing Your Database Installation

Setting up JDBC for the first time can be a bit tricky. You need several pieces of vendor-specific information, and the slightest configuration error can lead to very bewildering error messages.

You should first test your database setup without JDBC. Find out how you can connect to your database and enter SQL commands. Unless a database administrator tells you to use another database, create a database called COREJAVA.

Enter the following commands:

```
CREATE TABLE Greetings (Name CHAR(20))
INSERT INTO Greetings VALUES ('Hello, World!')
SELECT * FROM Greetings
```

At this point, you should see a display of the "Hello, World!" entry.

Now clean up:

```
DROP TABLE Greetings
```

Once you know that your database installation is working, and that you can log onto the database, you need to gather five pieces of information:

- The database user name and password
- The name of the database to use (such as COREJAVA)

•The JDBC URL format

•The JDBC driver name

•The location of the library files with the driver code

The first two depend on your database setup. The other three are supplied in the JDBC specific documentation from your database vendor. For example, for IBM DB2, you may have

•Database user name = `db2inst1` (the installation default), password = the password supplied during installation

•Database name = `COREJAVA`

•JDBC URL format = `jdbc:db2:`*databaseName*

•JDBC driver = `COM.ibm.db2.jdbc.app.DB2Driver`

•Library file = `/usr/IBMdb2/V7.1/java/db2java.zip`

For Cloudscape, you may have

•Database user name and password are empty

•Database name = `COREJAVA`

•JDBC URL format = `jdbc:cloudscape:`*databaseName*`;create=true`

•JDBC driver = `COM.cloudscape.core.JDBCDriver`

•Library file = `/usr/local/cloudscape/lib/cloudscape.jar`

Example 4–1 is a small test program that you can use to test your JDBC setup. Prepare the `database.properties` file with the information that you collected. Then start the test program with the driver library on the class path, such as

```
java -classpath .:/usr/IBMdb2/V7.1/java/db2java.zip TestDB
```

(Remember to use a semicolon instead of a colon as the path separator on Windows.)

This program executes the same SQL instructions as the manual test. If you get a SQL error message, then you need to keep working on your setup. It is extremely common to make one or more small errors with capitalization, path names, the JDBC URL format, or the database configuration. Once the test program displays "Hello, World!", then everything is fine, and you can move on to the next section.

Example 4–1: TestDB.java

```
1. import java.sql.*;
2. import java.io.*;
3. import java.util.*;
4.
5. /**
6.    This program tests that the database and the JDBC
7.    driver are correctly configured.
8. */
```

```
 9.  class TestDB
10.  {
11.     public static void main (String args[])
12.     {
13.        try
14.        {
15.           Connection conn = getConnection();
16.           Statement stat = conn.createStatement();
17.
18.           stat.execute("CREATE TABLE Greetings (Name CHAR(20))");
19.           stat.execute(
20.              "INSERT INTO Greetings VALUES ('Hello, World!')");
21.
22.           ResultSet result
23.              = stat.executeQuery("SELECT * FROM Greetings");
24.           result.next();
25.           System.out.println(result.getString(1));
26.           result.close();
27.
28.           stat.execute("DROP TABLE Greetings");
29.
30.           stat.close();
31.           conn.close();
32.        }
33.        catch (SQLException ex)
34.        {
35.           while (ex != null)
36.           {
37.              ex.printStackTrace();
38.              ex = ex.getNextException();
39.           }
40.        }
41.        catch (IOException ex)
42.        {
43.           ex.printStackTrace();
44.        }
45.     }
46.
47.     /**
48.        Gets a connection from the properties specified
49.        in the file database.properties
50.        @return the database connection
51.     */
52.     public static Connection getConnection()
53.        throws SQLException, IOException
54.     {
55.        Properties props = new Properties();
56.        FileInputStream in
57.           = new FileInputStream("database.properties");
```

```
58.        props.load(in);
59.        in.close();
60.
61.        String drivers = props.getProperty("jdbc.drivers");
62.        if (drivers != null)
63.            System.setProperty("jdbc.drivers", drivers);
64.        String url = props.getProperty("jdbc.url");
65.        String username = props.getProperty("jdbc.username");
66.        String password = props.getProperty("jdbc.password");
67.
68.        return
69.            DriverManager.getConnection(url, username, password);
70.    }
71. }
```

Executing SQL Commands

To execute a SQL command, you first create a `Statement` object. The `Connection` object that you obtained from the call to `DriverManager.getConnection` can be used to create statement objects.

```
Statement stat = conn.createStatement();
```

Next, you place the statement that you want to execute into a string, for example,

```
String command = "UPDATE Books"
    + " SET Price = Price - 5.00"
    + " WHERE Title NOT LIKE '%HTML 3%'";
```

Then you call the `executeUpdate` method of the `Statement` class:

```
stat.executeUpdate(command);
```

The `executeUpdate` method returns a count of the rows that were affected by the SQL command. For example, the call to `executeUpdate` in the preceding example returns the number of book records whose price was lowered by $5.00.

The `executeUpdate` method can execute actions such as `INSERT`, `UPDATE`, and `DELETE` as well as data definition commands such as `CREATE TABLE`, and `DROP TABLE`. However, you need to use the `executeQuery` method to execute `SELECT` queries. There is also a catch-all `execute` statement to execute arbitrary SQL statements. It's not as commonly used, except for queries that a user supplies interactively.

When you execute a query, you are interested in the result. The `executeQuery` object returns an object of type `ResultSet` that you use to walk through the result a row at a time.

```
ResultSet rs = stat.executeQuery("SELECT * FROM Books")
```

NOTE: You can use the same `Statement` object for multiple, unrelated commands. However, a statement has a single open result set. If you issue multiple queries whose results you analyze concurrently, then you need multiple `Statement` objects.

Be forewarned, though, that at least one commonly used database (Microsoft SQL Server) has a JDBC driver that allows only one active statement at a time. Use the `getMaxStatements` method of the `DatabaseMetaData` class to find out the number of concurrently open statements that your JDBC driver supports.

This sounds restrictive, but in practice, you should probably not fuss with multiple concurrent result sets. If the result sets are related, then you should be able to issue a combined query and analyze a single result. It is much more efficient to let the database combine queries than it is for a Java program to iterate through multiple result sets.

The basic loop for analyzing a result set looks like this:

```
while (rs.next())
{
    look at a row of the result set
}
```

CAUTION: The iteration protocol of the `ResultSet` class is slightly different from the protocol of the `Iterator` and `Enumeration` interfaces that we discussed in Chapter 2. Here, the iterator is initialized to a position *before* the first row. You must call the `next` method once to move it to the first row.

When inspecting an individual row, you will want to know the contents of each column. A large number of accessor methods give you this information.

```
String isbn = rs.getString(1);
float price = rs.getDouble("Price");
```

There are accessors for every Java programming language *type,* such as `getString` and `getDouble`. Each accessor has two forms, one that takes a numeric argument and one that takes a string argument. When you supply a numeric argument, you refer to the column with that number. For example, `rs.getString(1)` returns the value of the first column in the current row.

CAUTION: Unlike array indexes, database column numbers start at 1.

When you supply a string argument, you refer to the column in the result set with that name. For example, `rs.getDouble("Price")` returns the value of the column with name `Price`. Using the numeric argument is a bit more efficient, but the string arguments make the code easier to read and maintain.

Each `get` method will make reasonable type conversions when the type of the method doesn't match the type of the column. For example, the call `rs.getString("Price")` converts the floating-point value of the `Price` column to a string.

> NOTE: SQL data types and Java data types are not exactly the same. See Table 4–6 for a listing of the basic SQL data types and their equivalents in the Java programming language.

Table 4–6: SQL data types and their corresponding Java language types

SQL data type	Java data type
INTEGER or INT	int
SMALLINT	short
NUMERIC (m, n), DECIMAL (m, n) or DEC (m, n)	java.sql.Numeric
FLOAT (n)	double
REAL	float
DOUBLE	double
CHARACTER (n) or CHAR (n)	String
VARCHAR (n)	String
BOOLEAN	boolean
DATE	java.sql.Date
TIME	java.sql.Time
TIMESTAMP	java.sql.Timestamp
BLOB	java.sql.Blob
CLOB	java.sql.Clob
ARRAY	java.sql.Array

Advanced SQL Types (JDBC 2)

In addition to numbers, strings, and dates, many databases can store *large objects* such as images or other data. In SQL, binary large objects are called BLOBs, and character large objects are called CLOBs. The `getBlob` and `getClob` methods return objects of type `BLOB` and `CLOB`. These classes have methods to fetch the bytes or characters in the large objects.

A SQL ARRAY is a sequence of values. For example, in a Student table, you can have a Scores column that is an ARRAY OF INTEGER. The getArray method returns an object of type java.sql.Array (which is different from the java.lang.reflect.Array class that we discussed in Volume 1). The java.sql.Array interface has methods to fetch the array values.

> NOTE: The BLOB, CLOB, and ARRAY types are features of SQL3. Java platform support for BLOB and CLOB has been greatly enhanced in JDBC 2, and support for ARRAY is a new feature in JDBC 2.

When you get a BLOB or an array from a database, the actual contents are only fetched from the database when you request individual values. This is a useful performance enhancement, since the data can be quite voluminous.

Some databases are able to store user-defined structured types. JDBC 2 supports a mechanism for automatically mapping structured SQL types to Java objects.

However, in this introductory chapter, we do not discuss BLOBs, arrays, and user-defined types any further.

java.sql.DriverManager

- static Connection getConnection(String url, String user, String password)

  establishes a connection to the given database and returns a Connection object.

Parameters:	url	the URL for the database
	user	the database logon ID
	password	the database logon password

java.sql.Connection

- Statement createStatement()

  creates a statement object that can be used to execute SQL queries and updates without parameters.

- void close()

  immediately closes the current connection.

`java.sql.Statement`

- ResultSet executeQuery(String sql)

  executes the SQL statement given in the string and returns a ResultSet to view the query result.

  Parameters: sql   the SQL query

- int executeUpdate(String sql)

  executes the SQL INSERT, UPDATE, or DELETE statement specified by the string. Also used to execute Data Definition Language (DDL) statements such as CREATE TABLE. Returns the number of records affected, or -1 for a statement without an update count.

  Parameters: sql   the SQL statement

- boolean execute(String sql)

  executes the SQL statement specified by the string. Returns true if the statement returns a result set, false otherwise. Use the getResultSet or getUpdateCount method to obtain the statement outcome.

  Parameters: sql   the SQL statement

- int getUpdateCount()

  Returns the number of records affected by the preceding update statement, or -1 if the preceding statement was a statement without an update count. Call this method only once per executed statement.

- ResultSet getResultSet()

  Returns the result set of the preceding query statement, or null if the preceding statement did not have a result set. Call this method only once per executed statement.

`java.sql.ResultSet`

- boolean next()

  makes the current row in the result set move forward by one. Returns false after the last row. Note that you must call this method to advance to the first row.

- *Xxx* get*Xxx*(int columnNumber)
- *Xxx* get*Xxx*(String columnName)

  (*Xxx* is a type such as int, double, String, Date, etc.)
  return the value of the column with column index columnNumber or with column names, converted to the specified type. Not all type conversions are legal. See documentation for details.

- int findColumn(String columnName)

  gives the column index associated with a column name.

- `void close()`
  immediately closes the current result set.

java.sql.SQLException

Most JDBC methods throw this exception, and you must be prepared to catch it. The following methods give more information about the exceptions.

- `String getSQLState()`
  gets the SQLState formatted, using the X/Open standard.

- `int getErrorCode()`
  gets the vendor-specific exception code.

- `SQLException getNextException()`
  gets the exception chained to this one. It may contain more information about the error.

Populating a Database

We now want to write our first, real, JDBC program. Of course, it would be nice if we could execute some of the fancy queries that we discussed earlier. Unfortunately, we have a problem: right now, there is no data in the database. And you won't find a database file on the CD-ROM that you can simply copy onto your hard disk for the database program to read, because no database file format lets you interchange SQL relational databases from one vendor to another. SQL does not have anything to do with files. It is a language to issue queries and updates to a database. How the database executes these statements most efficiently and what file formats it uses toward that goal are entirely up to the *implementation* of the database. Database vendors try very hard to come up with clever strategies for query optimization and data storage, and different vendors arrive at different mechanisms. Thus, while SQL statements are portable, the underlying data representation is not.

To get around our problem, we provide you with a small set of data in a series of text files that contain the raw SQL instructions to create the tables and insert the values. We also give you a program that reads a file with SQL instructions, one instruction per line, and executes them.

Specifically, the program reads data from a text file in a format such as

```
CREATE TABLE Publisher (Publisher_Id char(5), Name char(30), URL char(80))
INSERT INTO Publisher VALUES ('01262', 'Academic Press', 'www.apnet.com')
INSERT INTO Publisher VALUES ('18835', 'Coriolis', 'www.coriolis.com/')
. . .
```

At the end of this section, you can see the code for the program that reads the SQL statement file and executes the statements. Even if you are not interested in looking at the implementation, you must run this program if you want to execute the more interesting examples in the remainder of this chapter. Run the program as follows:

```
java ExecSQL Books.sql
java ExecSQL Authors.sql
java ExecSQL Publishers.sql
java ExecSQL BooksAuthors.sql
```

Before running the program, check the file `database.properties`. It looks like this:

```
jdbc.drivers=COM.cloudscape.core.JDBCDriver
jdbc.url=jdbc:cloudscape:COREJAVA;create=true
jdbc.username=
jdbc.password=
```

These values work for the Cloudscape database; change them if you use another database.

CAUTION: Make sure that both the database driver and the current directory are on the class path. Alternatively, start up the program as

```
java -classpath driverPath:. ExecSQL SQLfile
```

The following steps provide an overview of the `ExecSQL` program.

1. Connect to the database. The `getConnection` method reads the properties in the file `database.properties` and adds the `jdbc.drivers` property to the system properties. The driver manager uses the `jdbc.drivers` property to load the appropriate database driver. The `getConnection` method uses the `jdbc.url`, `jdbc.username`, and `jdbc.password` properties to open the database connection.

2. Open the file with the SQL commands. If no file was supplied, then prompt the user to enter the commands on the console. In that way, you can use the `ExecSQL` program to interactively issue simple queries.

3. Execute each command with the generic `execute` method. If it returns `true`, the command had a result set. The four SQL files that we provide for the book database all end in a `SELECT *` statement so that you can see that the data was successfully inserted.

4. If there was a result set, print out the result. Because this is a generic result set, we need to use *meta data* to find out how many columns the result has. You will learn more about meta data later in this chapter.

5. If there is any SQL exception, we print the exception and any chained exceptions that may be contained in it.

Example 4–2 provides the code for the program.

Example 4–2: ExecSQL.java

```
1. import java.io.*;
2. import java.util.*;
3. import java.sql.*;
4.
5. /**
6.    Executes all SQL statements in a file.
7.    Call this program as
8.    java -classpath driverPath:. ExecSQL commandFile
9. */
10. class ExecSQL
11. {
12.    public static void main (String args[])
13.    {
14.       try
15.       {
16.
17.          Reader reader;
18.          if (args.length == 0)
19.             reader = new InputStreamReader(System.in);
20.          else
21.             reader = new FileReader(args[0]);
22.
23.          Connection conn = getConnection();
24.          Statement stat = conn.createStatement();
25.
26.          BufferedReader in = new BufferedReader(reader);
27.
28.          boolean done = false;
29.          while (!done)
30.          {
31.             if (args.length == 0)
32.                System.out.println(
33.                   "Enter command or a blank line to exit:");
34.
35.             String line = in.readLine();
36.             if (line == null || line.length() == 0)
37.                done = true;
38.             else
39.             {
40.                try
41.                {
42.                   boolean hasResultSet = stat.execute(line);
43.                   if (hasResultSet)
44.                      showResultSet(stat);
45.                }
46.                catch (SQLException ex)
47.                {
48.                   while (ex != null)
```

```
49.                        {
50.                            ex.printStackTrace();
51.                            ex = ex.getNextException();
52.                        }
53.                    }
54.                }
55.            }
56.
57.            in.close();
58.            stat.close();
59.            conn.close();
60.        }
61.        catch (Exception ex)
62.        {
63.            ex.printStackTrace();
64.        }
65.    }
66.
67.    /**
68.        Gets a connection from the properties specified
69.        in the file database.properties
70.        @return the database connection
71.    */
72.    public static Connection getConnection()
73.        throws SQLException, IOException
74.    {
75.        Properties props = new Properties();
76.        FileInputStream in
77.            = new FileInputStream("database.properties");
78.        props.load(in);
79.        in.close();
80.
81.        String drivers = props.getProperty("jdbc.drivers");
82.        if (drivers != null)
83.            System.setProperty("jdbc.drivers", drivers);
84.        String url = props.getProperty("jdbc.url");
85.        String username = props.getProperty("jdbc.username");
86.        String password = props.getProperty("jdbc.password");
87.
88.        return
89.            DriverManager.getConnection(url, username, password);
90.    }
91.
92.    /**
93.        Prints a result set.
94.        @param stat the statement whose result set should be
95.        printed
96.    */
97.    public static void showResultSet(Statement stat)
98.        throws SQLException
99.    {
```

```
100.        ResultSet result = stat.getResultSet();
101.        ResultSetMetaData metaData = result.getMetaData();
102.        int columnCount = metaData.getColumnCount();
103.
104.        for (int i = 1; i <= columnCount; i++)
105.        {
106.            if (i > 1) System.out.print(", ");
107.            System.out.print(metaData.getColumnLabel(i));
108.        }
109.        System.out.println();
110.
111.        while (result.next())
112.        {
113.            for (int i = 1; i <= columnCount; i++)
114.            {
115.                if (i > 1) System.out.print(", ");
116.                System.out.print(result.getString(i));
117.            }
118.            System.out.println();
119.        }
120.        result.close();
121.    }
122. }
```

Executing Queries

In this section, we will write a program that executes queries against the
COREJAVA database. For this program to work, you must have populated
the COREJAVA database with tables, as described in the preceding section.
Figure 4–6 shows the query application.

Figure 4–6: The QueryDB application

You can select the author and the publisher or leave either of them as "Any." Click on "Query"; all books matching your selection will be displayed in the text box.

You can also change the data in the database. Select a publisher and type an amount into the text box next to the "Change prices" button. When you click on the button, all prices of that publisher are adjusted by the amount you entered, and the text area contains a message indicating how many records were changed. However, to minimize unintended changes to the database, you can't change all prices at once. The author field is ignored when you change prices. After a price change, you may want to run a query to verify the new prices.

In this program, we use one new feature, *prepared statements*. Consider the query for all books by a particular publisher, independent of the author. The SQL query is

```
SELECT Books.Price, Books.Title
FROM Books, Publishers
WHERE Books.Publisher_Id = Publishers.Publisher_Id
AND Publishers.Name = the name from the list box
```

Rather than build a separate query command every time the user launches such a query, we can *prepare* a query with a host variable and use it many times, each time filling in a different string for the variable. That technique gives us a performance benefit. Whenever the database executes a query, it first computes a strategy of how to efficiently execute the query. By preparing the query and reusing it, you ensure that the planning step is done only once. (The reason you do not *always* want to prepare a query is that the optimal strategy may change as your data changes. You have to balance the expense of optimization versus the expense of querying your data less efficiently.)

Each host variable in a prepared query is indicated with a ?. If there is more than one variable, then you must keep track of the positions of the ? when setting the values. For example, our prepared query becomes

```
String publisherQuery =
    "SELECT Books.Price, Books.Title " +
    "FROM Books, Publishers " +
    "WHERE Books.Publisher_Id = Publishers.Publisher_Id " +
    "AND Publishers.Name = ?";
PreparedStatement publisherQueryStat
    = conn.prepareStatement(publisherQuery);
```

Before executing the prepared statement, you must bind the host variables to actual values with a `set` method. As with the `ResultSet get` methods, there are different `set` methods for the various types. Here, we want to set a string to a publisher name.

```
publisherQueryStat.setString(1, publisher);
```

The first argument is the host variable that we want to set. The position 1 denotes the first ?. The second argument is the value that we want to assign to the host variable.

If you reuse a prepared query that you have already executed and the query has more than one host variable, all host variables stay bound as you set them unless you change them with a `set` method. That means you only need to call `set` on those host variables that change from one query to the next.

Once all variables have been bound to values, you can execute the query

```
ResultSet rs = publisherQueryStat.executeQuery();
```

You process the result set in the usual way. Here, we add the information to the text area `result`.

```
result.setText("");
while (rs.next())
    result.appendText(rs.getString(1) + ", " +
        rs.getString(2y) + "\n");
rs.close();
```

There are a total of four prepared queries in this program, one each for the cases shown in Table 4–7.

Table 4–7: Selected queries

Author	Publisher
any	any
any	specified
specified	any
specified	specified

The price update feature is implemented as a simple UPDATE statement. For variety, we did not choose to make a prepared statement in this case. Note that we call `executeUpdate`, not `executeQuery`, since the UPDATE statement does not return a result set and we don't need one. The return value of `executeUpdate` is the count of changed rows. We display the count in the text area.

```
String updateStatement = "UPDATE Books ...";
int r = stat.executeUpdate(updateStatement);
result.setText(r + " records updated");
```

The following steps provide an overview of the program.

1. Arrange the components in the frame, using a grid bag layout (see Chapter 9 in Volume 1).

2. Populate the author and publisher text boxes by running two queries that return all author and publisher names in the database.

3.   When the user selects "Query," find which of the four query types needs to be executed. If this is the first time this query type is executed, then the prepared statement variable is `null`, and the prepared statement is constructed. Then, the values are bound to the query and the query is executed.

The queries involving authors are more complex. Because a book can have multiple authors, the `BooksAuthors` table gives the correspondence between authors and books. For example, the book with ISBN number 1-56-604288-7 has two authors with codes `HARR` and `KIDD`. The `BooksAuthors` table has the rows

```
1-56-604288-7, HARR, 1
1-56-604288-7, KIDD, 2
```

to indicate this fact. The third column lists the order of the authors. (We can't just use the position of the records in the table. There is no fixed row ordering in a relational table.) Thus, the query has to snake (join) itself from the `Books` table to the `BooksAuthors` table, then to the `Authors` table to compare the author name with the one selected by the user.

```
SELECT Books.Price, Books.Title
FROM Books, Publishers, BooksAuthors, Authors
WHERE Books.Publisher_Id = Publishers.Publisher_Id
AND Publishers.Name = ?
AND Books.ISBN = BooksAuthors.ISBN
AND BooksAuthors.Author = Authors.Author
AND Authors.Name = ?
```

TIP: Some Java programmers avoid complex SQL statements such as this one. A surprisingly common, but very inefficient, workaround is to write lots of Java code that iterates through multiple result sets. But the database is *a lot* better at executing query code than a Java program—that's the core competency of a database. As a rule of thumb: If you can do it in SQL, don't do it in Java.

4.   The results of the query are displayed in the results text box.

5.   When the user selects "Change prices," then the update query is constructed and executed. The query is quite complex because the WHERE clause of the UPDATE statement needs the publisher *code* and we know only the publisher *name*. This problem is solved with a nested subquery.

```
UPDATE Books
SET Price = Price + price change
WHERE Books.Publisher_Id =
    (SELECT Publisher_Id
    FROM Publishers
    WHERE Name = publisher name)
```

6.   We initialize the connection and statement objects in the constructor. We hang on to them for the life of the program. Just before the program exits, we trap the "window closing" event, and these objects are closed.

```java
class QueryDB extends Frame
{
   QueryDB()
   {
      conn = getConnection();
      stat = conn.createStatement();
      . . .
      add(new
         WindowAdapter()
         {
            public void windowClosing(WindowEvent event)
            {
               try
               {
                  stat.close();
                  conn.close();
               }
               catch(SQLException ex)
               {
                  while (ex != null)
                  {
                     ex.printStackTrace();
                     ex = ex.getNextException();
                  }
               }
            }
         });
   }
   . . .
   Connection conn;
   Statement stat;
}
```

Example 4–3 is the complete program code.

Example 4–3: QueryDB.java

```java
1. import java.net.*;
2. import java.sql.*;
3. import java.awt.*;
4. import java.awt.event.*;
5. import java.io.*;
6. import java.util.*;
7. import javax.swing.*;
8.
9. /**
```

```
10.     This program demonstrates several complex database queries.
11. */
12. public class QueryDB
13. {
14.    public static void main(String[] args)
15.    {
16.       JFrame frame = new QueryDBFrame();
17.       frame.setDefaultCloseOperation(JFrame.EXIT_ON_CLOSE);
18.       frame.show();
19.    }
20. }
21.
22. /**
23.    This frame displays combo boxes for query parameters,
24.    a text area for command results, and buttons to launch
25.    a query and an update.
26. */
27. class QueryDBFrame extends JFrame
28. {
29.    public QueryDBFrame()
30.    {
31.       setTitle("QueryDB");
32.       setSize(WIDTH, HEIGHT);
33.       getContentPane().setLayout(new GridBagLayout());
34.       GridBagConstraints gbc = new GridBagConstraints();
35.
36.       authors = new JComboBox();
37.       authors.setEditable(false);
38.       authors.addItem("Any");
39.
40.       publishers = new JComboBox();
41.       publishers.setEditable(false);
42.       publishers.addItem("Any");
43.
44.       result = new JTextArea(4, 50);
45.       result.setEditable(false);
46.
47.       priceChange = new JTextField(8);
48.       priceChange.setText("-5.00");
49.
50.       try
51.       {
52.          conn = getConnection();
53.          stat = conn.createStatement();
54.
55.          String query = "SELECT Name FROM Authors";
56.          ResultSet rs = stat.executeQuery(query);
57.          while (rs.next())
58.             authors.addItem(rs.getString(1));
59.          rs.close();
```

```
60.
61.            query = "SELECT Name FROM Publishers";
62.            rs = stat.executeQuery(query);
63.            while (rs.next())
64.                publishers.addItem(rs.getString(1));
65.            rs.close();
66.        }
67.        catch(SQLException ex)
68.        {
69.            result.setText("");
70.            while (ex != null)
71.            {
72.                result.append("" + ex);
73.                ex = ex.getNextException();
74.            }
75.        }
76.        catch (IOException ex)
77.        {
78.            result.setText("" + ex);
79.        }
80.
81.        gbc.fill = GridBagConstraints.NONE;
82.        gbc.weightx = 100;
83.        gbc.weighty = 100;
84.        add(authors, gbc, 0, 0, 2, 1);
85.
86.        add(publishers, gbc, 2, 0, 2, 1);
87.
88.        gbc.fill = GridBagConstraints.NONE;
89.        JButton queryButton = new JButton("Query");
90.        queryButton.addActionListener(new
91.            ActionListener()
92.            {
93.                public void actionPerformed(ActionEvent event)
94.                {
95.                    executeQuery();
96.                }
97.            });
98.        add(queryButton, gbc, 0, 1, 1, 1);
99.
100.       JButton changeButton = new JButton("Change prices");
101.       changeButton.addActionListener(new
102.           ActionListener()
103.           {
104.               public void actionPerformed(ActionEvent event)
105.               {
106.                   changePrices();
107.               }
108.           });
109.       add(changeButton, gbc, 2, 1, 1, 1);
```

```
110.
111.        gbc.fill = GridBagConstraints.HORIZONTAL;
112.        add(priceChange, gbc, 3, 1, 1, 1);
113.
114.        gbc.fill = GridBagConstraints.BOTH;
115.        add(new JScrollPane(result), gbc, 0, 2, 4, 1);
116.
117.        add(new
118.           WindowAdapter()
119.           {
120.              public void windowClosing(WindowEvent event)
121.              {
122.                 try
123.                 {
124.                    stat.close();
125.                    conn.close();
126.                 }
127.                 catch(SQLException ex)
128.                 {
129.                    while (ex != null)
130.                    {
131.                       ex.printStackTrace();
132.                       ex = ex.getNextException();
133.                    }
134.                 }
135.              }
136.           });
137.     }
138.
139.     /**
140.        Add a component to this frame.
141.        @param c the component to add
142.        @param gbc the grid bag constraints
143.        @param x the grid bax column
144.        @param y the grid bag row
145.        @param w the number of grid bag columns spanned
146.        @param h the number of grid bag rows spanned
147.     */
148.     private void add(Component c, GridBagConstraints gbc,
149.        int x, int y, int w, int h)
150.     {
151.        gbc.gridx = x;
152.        gbc.gridy = y;
153.        gbc.gridwidth = w;
154.        gbc.gridheight = h;
155.        getContentPane().add(c, gbc);
156.     }
157.
158.     /**
159.        Executes the selected query.
```

```
160.      */
161.      private void executeQuery()
162.      {
163.         ResultSet rs = null;
164.         try
165.         {
166.            String author
167.                = (String)authors.getSelectedItem();
168.            String publisher
169.                = (String)publishers.getSelectedItem();
170.            if (!author.equals("Any")
171.                && !publisher.equals("Any"))
172.            {
173.                if (authorPublisherQueryStmt == null)
174.                {
175.                    String authorPublisherQuery =
176. "SELECT Books.Price, Books.Title " +
177. "FROM Books, BooksAuthors, Authors, Publishers " +
178. "WHERE Authors.Author_Id = BooksAuthors.Author_Id AND " +
179. "BooksAuthors.ISBN = Books.ISBN AND " +
180. "Books.Publisher_Id = Publishers.Publisher_Id AND " +
181. "Authors.Name = ? AND " +
182. "Publishers.Name = ?";
183.                    authorPublisherQueryStmt
184.                        = conn.prepareStatement(authorPublisherQuery);
185.                }
186.                authorPublisherQueryStmt.setString(1, author);
187.                authorPublisherQueryStmt.setString(2,
188.                    publisher);
189.                rs = authorPublisherQueryStmt.executeQuery();
190.            }
191.            else if (!author.equals("Any")
192.                && publisher.equals("Any"))
193.            {
194.                if (authorQueryStmt == null)
195.                {
196.                    String authorQuery =
197. "SELECT Books.Price, Books.Title " +
198. "FROM Books, BooksAuthors, Authors " +
199. "WHERE Authors.Author_Id = BooksAuthors.Author_Id AND " +
200. "BooksAuthors.ISBN = Books.ISBN AND " +
201. "Authors.Name = ?";
202.                    authorQueryStmt
203.                        = conn.prepareStatement(authorQuery);
204.                }
205.                authorQueryStmt.setString(1, author);
206.                rs = authorQueryStmt.executeQuery();
207.            }
208.            else if (author.equals("Any")
209.                && !publisher.equals("Any"))
```

```
210.            {
211.                if (publisherQueryStmt == null)
212.                {
213.                    String publisherQuery =
214. "SELECT Books.Price, Books.Title " +
215. "FROM Books, Publishers " +
216. "WHERE Books.Publisher_Id = Publishers.Publisher_Id AND " +
217. "Publishers.Name = ?";
218.                    publisherQueryStmt
219.                        = conn.prepareStatement(publisherQuery);
220.                }
221.                publisherQueryStmt.setString(1, publisher);
222.                rs = publisherQueryStmt.executeQuery();
223.            }
224.            else
225.            {
226.                if (allQueryStmt == null)
227.                {
228.                    String allQuery =
229. "SELECT Books.Price, Books.Title FROM Books";
230.                    allQueryStmt
231.                        = conn.prepareStatement(allQuery);
232.                }
233.                rs = allQueryStmt.executeQuery();
234.            }
235.
236.            result.setText("");
237.            while (rs.next())
238.            {
239.                result.append(rs.getString(1));
240.                result.append(", ");
241.                result.append(rs.getString(2));
242.                result.append("\n");
243.            }
244.            rs.close();
245.        }
246.        catch(SQLException ex)
247.        {
248.            result.setText("");
249.            while (ex != null)
250.            {
251.                result.append("" + ex);
252.                ex = ex.getNextException();
253.            }
254.        }
255.    }
256.
257.    /**
258.        Executes an update statement to change prices.
259.    */
```

```
260.    public void changePrices()
261.    {
262.       String publisher
263.          = (String)publishers.getSelectedItem();
264.       if (publisher.equals("Any"))
265.       {
266.          result.setText
267.             ("I am sorry, but I cannot do that.");
268.          return;
269.       }
270.       try
271.       {
272.          String updateStatement =
273. "UPDATE Books " +
274. "SET Price = Price + " + priceChange.getText() +
275. " WHERE Books.Publisher_Id = " +
276. "(SELECT Publisher_Id FROM Publishers WHERE Name = '" +
277.             publisher + "')";
278.          int r = stat.executeUpdate(updateStatement);
279.          result.setText(r + " records updated.");
280.       }
281.       catch(SQLException ex)
282.       {
283.          result.setText("");
284.          while (ex != null)
285.          {
286.             result.append("" + ex);
287.             ex = ex.getNextException();
288.          }
289.       }
290.    }
291.
292.    /**
293.       Gets a connection from the properties specified
294.       in the file database.properties
295.       @return the database connection
296.    */
297.    public static Connection getConnection()
298.       throws SQLException, IOException
299.    {
300.       Properties props = new Properties();
301.       FileInputStream in
302.          = new FileInputStream("database.properties");
303.       props.load(in);
304.       in.close();
305.
306.       String drivers = props.getProperty("jdbc.drivers");
307.       if (drivers != null)
308.          System.setProperty("jdbc.drivers", drivers);
309.       String url = props.getProperty("jdbc.url");
```

```
310.        String username = props.getProperty("jdbc.username");
311.        String password = props.getProperty("jdbc.password");
312.
313.        return
314.           DriverManager.getConnection(url, username, password);
315.     }
316.
317.     public static final int WIDTH = 400;
318.     public static final int HEIGHT = 400;
319.
320.     private JComboBox authors;
321.     private JComboBox publishers;
322.     private JTextField priceChange;
323.     private JTextArea result;
324.     private Connection conn;
325.     private Statement stat;
326.     private PreparedStatement authorQueryStmt;
327.     private PreparedStatement authorPublisherQueryStmt;
328.     private PreparedStatement publisherQueryStmt;
329.     private PreparedStatement allQueryStmt;
330. }
```

`java.sql.Connection`

- `PreparedStatement prepareStatement(String sql)`
  returns a `PreparedStatement` object containing the precompiled statement. The string `sql` contains a SQL statement that can contain one or more
  parameter placeholders denoted by `?` characters.

`java.sql.PreparedStatement`

- `void setXxx(int n, Xxx x)`
  (*Xxx* is a type such as `int`, `double`, `String`, `Date`, etc.)
  sets the value of the nth parameter to x.
- `void clearParameters()`
  clears all current parameters in the prepared statement.
- `ResultSet executeQuery()`
  executes a prepared SQL query and returns a `ResultSet` object.
- `int executeUpdate()`
  executes the prepared SQL `INSERT`, `UPDATE`, or `DELETE` statement represented
  by the `PreparedStatement` object. Returns the number of rows affected, or 0
  for DDL statements.

Scrollable and Updatable Result Sets

The most useful improvements in JDBC 2 are in the `ResultSet` class. As you have
seen, the `next` method of the `ResultSet` class iterates over the rows in a result set.

That is certainly adequate for a program that needs to analyze the data. However, consider a visual data display that shows a table or query result (see Figure 4–7). You usually want the user to be able to move both forward and backward in the result set. But in JDBC 1, there was no `previous` method. Programmers who wanted to implement backwards iteration had to manually cache the result set data. The *scrolling* result set in JDBC 2 lets you move forward and backward through a result set and jump to any position in the result set.

	TITLE	ISBN	PUBLISHER_ID	URL	PRICE	
8	HTML 3 Interacti	1-57169066-	15716	w3.waite.com /w	39.99	
9	HTML 3.0 Manua	1-56-276352	15627	www.mcp.com/z	24.95	
10	HTML by Exampl	0-78970812-	07897	www.mcp.com/z	34.99	
11	HTML CD- An In	0-13-232331	01356	www.prenhall.co	40	
12	HTML for Dumm	1-56-884647	15688	db.www.idgbook	30	
13	HTML For Dumm	1-56884990-	15688	db.www.idgbook	12.99	
14	HTML For Fun ar	0-13-242488	01356	www.sun.com/si	40	
15	HTML for the Wo	0-02188448-	00218	www.peachpit.cc	17.95	
16	HTML In Action	1-55615948-	15561	www.microsoft.c	29.95	
17	HTML Plus!	0-53451626-	05345	scholar.lib.vt.ed	36	
18	HTML Publishing	1-56-604288	15660	ephraim.vmedia.	39.95	
19	HTML Publishing	0-07-912100	00791		45	
20	HTML Quick Refe	0-78970867-	07897	www.mcp.com/z	17.99	

Figure 4–7: A GUI view of a query result

Furthermore, once you display the contents of a result set to users, they may be tempted to edit it. If you supply an editable view to your users, you have to make sure that the user edits are posted back to the database. In JDBC 1, you had to program UPDATE statements. In JDBC 2, you can simply update the result set entries, and the database is automatically updated.

JDBC 2 delivers additional enhancements to result sets, such as the capability of updating a result set with the most recent data if the data has been modified by another concurrent database connection. JDBC 3 adds another refinement, specifying the behavior of result sets when a transaction is committed. One form of the getStatement method of the Connection class lets you specify the *holdability* of the result sets. You can choose to have result sets automatically close when a transaction is committed, or to keep them open. However, these advanced features are outside the scope of this introductory chapter. We refer you to the *JDBC API Tutorial and Reference* by Seth White, et al. [Addison-Wesley 1999], and the JDBC specification documents at http://java.sun.com/products/jdbc for more information.

Scrollable Result Sets (JDBC 2)

To obtain scrolling result sets from your queries, you must obtain a different `Statement` object with the method

```
Statement stat = conn.createStatement(type, concurrency);
```

For a prepared statement, use the call

```
PreparedStatement stat = conn.prepareStatement(command,
    type, concurrency);
```

The possible values of `type` and `concurrency` are listed in Table 4–8 and Table 4–9. You have the following choices:

- Do you want the result set to be scrollable or not? If not, use `Result-Set.TYPE_FORWARD_ONLY`.

- If the result set is scrollable, do you want it to be able to reflect changes in the database that occurred after the query that yielded it? (In our discussion, we will assume the `ResultSet.TYPE_SCROLL_INSENSITIVE` setting for scrolling result sets. This assumes that the result set does not "sense" database changes that occurred after the query.)

- Do you want to be able to update the database by editing the result set? (See the next section for details.)

For example, if you simply want to be able to scroll through a result set but you don't want to edit its data, you use:

```
Statement stat
    = conn.createStatement(ResultSet.TYPE_SCROLL_INSENSITIVE,
        ResultSet.CONCUR_READ_ONLY);
```

Table 4–8: `ResultSet` type values

TYPE_FORWARD_ONLY	The result set is not scrollable.
TYPE_SCROLL_INSENSITIVE	The result set is scrollable but not sensitive to database changes.
TYPE_SCROLL_SENSITIVE	The result set is scrollable and sensitive to database changes.

Table 4–9: `ResultSet` concurrency values

CONCUR_READ_ONLY	The result set cannot be used to update the database.
CONCUR_UPDATABLE	The result set can be used to update the database.

All result sets that are returned by method calls

```
ResultSet rs = stat.executeQuery(query)
```

are now scrollable. A scrolling result set has a *cursor* that indicates the current position.

NOTE: Actually, a database driver might not be able to honor your request for a scrolling or updatable cursor. (The `supportsResultSetType` and `supportsResultSet Concurrency` methods of the `DatabaseMetaData` class tell you which types and concurrency modes are supported by a particular database.) But even if a database supports all result set modes, a particular query might not be able to yield a result set with all the properties that you requested. (For example, the result set of a complex query may not be updatable.) In that case, the `executeQuery` method returns a `ResultSet` of lesser capabilities and adds a *warning* to the connection object. You can retrieve warnings with the `getWarnings` method of the `Connection` class. Alternatively, you can use the `getType` and `getConcurrency` methods of the `ResultSet` class to find out what mode a result set actually has. If you do not check the result set capabilities and issue an unsupported operation, such as `previous` on a result set that is not scrollable, then the operation throws a `SQLException`.

CAUTION: In JDBC 1 drivers, the `Connection` class does not have a method

```
Statement createStatement(int type, int concurrency);
```

If a program that you compiled for JDBC 2 inadvertently loads a JDBC 1 driver and then calls this nonexistent method, the program will crash. Unfortunately, there is no JDBC 2 mechanism for querying a driver as to whether it is JDBC 2 compliant. In JDBC 3, you can use the `getJDBCMajorVersion` and `getJDBCMinor-Version` methods of the `DatabaseMetaData` class to find the JDBC version number of the driver.

Scrolling is very simple. You use

```
if (rs.previous()) . . .
```

to scroll backward. The method returns `true` if the cursor is positioned on an actual row; `false` if it now is positioned before the first row.

You can move the cursor backward or forward by a number of rows with the command

```
rs.relative(n);
```

If *n* is positive, the cursor moves forward. If *n* is negative, it moves backwards. If *n* is zero, the call has no effect. If you attempt to move the cursor outside the current set of rows, it is set to point either after the last row or before the first row, depending on the sign of *n*. Then, the method returns `false` and the cursor does not move. The method returns `true` if the cursor landed on an actual row.

Alternatively, you can set the cursor to a particular row number:

```
rs.absolute(n);
```

You get the current row number with the call

```
int n = rs.getRow();
```

The first row in the result set has number 1. If the return value is 0, the cursor is not currently on a row—it is either before the first or after the last row.

NOTE: The order of the rows in a result set is completely arbitrary. You should never attach any significance to the row numbers.

There are convenience methods

```
first
last
beforeFirst
afterLast
```

to move the cursor to the first, to the last, before the first, or after the last position.

Finally, the methods

```
isFirst
isLast
isBeforeFirst
isAfterLast
```

test whether the cursor is at one of these special positions.

Using a scrollable result set is very simple. The hard work of caching the query data is carried out behind the scenes by the database driver.

TIP: If you want to implement a scrollable view in a web application, then the scrollable result set has a major drawback. It requires you to keep the connection to the database open between page requests. However, users can walk away from their computer for a long time, or simply abandon your site, leaving the connection occupied. That is not good—database connections are scarce resources. In such a situation, use a *row set*. The RowSet interface extends the ResultSet interface, but row sets aren't tied to a database connection. They can be cached, or they can present data from a source other than a database. The article http://developer.java.sun.com/developer/technicalArticles/javaserverpages/cachedrowset shows how to use row sets in a web application.

Updatable Result Sets (JDBC 2)

If you want to be able to edit result set data and have the changes automatically reflected in the database, you need to create an updatable result set. Updatable result sets don't have to be scrollable, but if you present data to a user for editing, you usually want to allow scrolling as well.

To obtain updatable result sets, you create a statement as follows.

```
Statement stat
    = conn.createStatement(ResultSet.TYPE_SCROLL_INSENSITIVE,
        ResultSet.CONCUR_UPDATABLE);
```

Then, the result sets returned by a call to `executeQuery` are updatable.

NOTE: Not all queries return updatable result sets. If your query is a join that involves multiple tables, the result may not be updatable. If your query involves only a single table or if it joins multiple tables by their primary keys, you should expect the result set to be updatable. Call the `getConcurrency` method of the `ResultSet` class to find out for sure.

For example, suppose you want to raise the prices of some books, but you don't have a simple criterion for issuing an UPDATE command. Then, you can iterate through all books and update prices, based on arbitrary conditions.

```
String query = "SELECT * FROM Books";
ResultSet rs = stat.executeQuery(query);
while (rs.next())
{
    if (. . .)
    {
        double increase = . . .
        double price = rs.getDouble("Price");
        rs.updateDouble("Price", price + increase);
        rs.updateRow();
    }
}
```

There are update*Xxx* methods for all data types that correspond to SQL types, such as `updateDouble`, `updateString`, and so on. As with the get*Xxx* methods, you specify the name or the number of the column. Then, you specify the new value for the field.

NOTE: If you use the update*Xxx* method whose first parameter is the column number, be aware that this is the column number in the *result set*. It may well be different from the column number in the database.

The update*Xxx* method only changes the row values, not the database. When you are done with the field updates in a row, you must call the updateRow method. That method sends all updates in the current row to the database. If you move the cursor to another row without calling updateRow, all updates are discarded from the row set and they are never communicated to the database. You can also call the cancelRowUpdates method to cancel the updates to the current row.

The preceding example shows how you modify an existing row. If you want to add a new row to the database, you first use the moveToInsertRow method to move the cursor to a special position, called the *insert row*. You build up a new row in the insert row position by issuing update*Xxx* instructions. Finally, when you are done, call the insertRow method to deliver the new row to the database. When you are done inserting, call moveToCurrentRow to move the cursor back to the position before the call to moveToInsertRow. Here is an example.

```
rs.moveToInsertRow();
rs.updateString("Title", title);
rs.updateString("ISBN", isbn);
rs.updateString("Publisher_Id", pubid);
rs.updateString("URL", url);
rs.updateDouble("Price", price);
rs.insertRow();
rs.moveToCurrentRow();
```

Note that you have no influence *where* the new data is added in the result set or the database.

Finally, you can delete the row under the cursor.

```
rs.deleteRow();
```

The deleteRow method immediately removes the row from both the result set and the database.

The updateRow, insertRow, and deleteRow methods of the ResultSet class give you the same power as executing UPDATE, INSERT, and DELETE SQL commands. However, programmers who are used to the Java programming language will find it more natural to manipulate the database contents through result sets than by constructing SQL statements. Once JDBC 2 drivers are widely available, this programming style is likely to become quite popular.

CAUTION: If you are not careful, you can write staggeringly inefficient code with updatable result sets. It is *much* more efficient to execute an UPDATE statement than it is to make a query and iterate through the result, changing data along the way. Updatable result sets make sense for interactive programs in which a user can make arbitrary changes, but for most programmatic changes, a SQL UPDATE is more appropriate.

---

javax.sql.Connection

- Statement createStatement(int type, int concurrency)
- PreparedStatement prepareStatement(String command, int type, int concurrency)

  (JDBC 2) create a statement or prepared statement that yields result sets with the given type and concurrency.

Parameters:	command	the command to prepare
	type	one of the constants TYPE_FORWARD_ONLY, TYPE_SCROLL_INSENSITIVE, or TYPE_SCROLL_SENSITIVE of the ResultSet interface
	concurrency	one of the constants CONCUR_READ_ONLY or CONCUR_UPDATABLE of the ResultSet interface

- SQLWarning getWarnings()

  returns the first of the pending warnings on this connection, or null if no warnings are pending. The warnings are chained together—keep calling getNextWarning on the returned SQLWarning object until that method returns null. This call does not consume the warnings. The SQLWarning class extends SQLException. Use the inherited getErrorCode and getSQLState to analyze the warnings.

- void clearWarnings()

  clears all warnings that have been reported on this connection.

java.sql.ResultSet

- int getType()

  (JDBC 2) returns the type of this result set, one of TYPE_FORWARD_ONLY, TYPE_SCROLL_INSENSITIVE, or TYPE_SCROLL_SENSITIVE.

- int getConcurrency()

  (JDBC 2) returns the concurrency setting of this result set, one of CONCUR_READ_ONLY or CONCUR_UPDATABLE.

- boolean previous()

  (JDBC 2) moves the cursor to the preceding row. Returns true if the cursor is positioned on a row.

- int getRow()

  (JDBC 2) gets the number of the current row. Rows are numbered starting with 1.

- boolean absolute(int r)

  (JDBC 2) moves the cursor to row r. Returns true if the cursor is positioned on a row.

- `boolean relative(int d)`
  (JDBC 2) moves the cursor by d rows. If d is negative, the cursor is moved backward. Returns `true` if the cursor is positioned on a row.
- `boolean first()`
- `boolean last()`
  (JDBC 2) move the cursor to the first or last row. Return `true` if the cursor is positioned on a row.
- `void beforeFirst()`
- `void afterLast()`
  (JDBC 2) move the cursor before the first or after the last row.
- `boolean isFirst()`
- `boolean isLast()`
  (JDBC 2) test if the cursor is at the first or last row.
- `boolean isBeforeFirst()`
- `boolean isAfterLast()`
  (JDBC 2) test if the cursor is before the first or after the last row.
- `void moveToInsertRow()`
  (JDBC 2) moves the cursor to the *insert row*. The insert row is a special row that is used for inserting new data with the update*Xxx* and `insertRow` methods.
- `void moveToCurrentRow()`
  (JDBC 2) moves the cursor back from the insert row to the row that it occupied when the `moveToInsertRow` method was called.
- `void insertRow()`
  (JDBC 2) inserts the contents of the insert row into the database and the result set.
- `void deleteRow()`
  (JDBC 2) deletes the current row from the database and the result set.
- `void update`*Xxx*`(int column, `*Xxx*` data)`
- `void update`*Xxx*`(String columnName, `*Xxx*` data)`
  (*Xxx* is a type such as `int`, `double`, `String`, `Date`, etc.)
  (JDBC 2) update a field in the current row of the result set.
- `void updateRow()`
  (JDBC 2) sends the current row updates to the database.
- `void cancelRowUpdates()`
  (JDBC 2) cancels the current row updates.

java.sql.DatabaseMetaData

- `boolean supportsResultSetType(int type)`
  (JDBC 2) returns `true` if the database can support result sets of the given type.

  Parameters: command   the command to prepare

	type	one of the constants `TYPE_FORWARD_ONLY`, `TYPE_SCROLL_INSENSITIVE`, or `TYPE_SCROLL_SENSITIVE` of the `ResultSet` interface

- `boolean supportsResultSetConcurrency(int type, int concurrency)` (JDBC 2) Returns `true` if the database can support result sets of the given combination of type and concurrency.

Parameters:	command	the command to prepare
	type	one of the constants `TYPE_FORWARD_ONLY`, `TYPE_SCROLL_INSENSITIVE`, or `TYPE_SCROLL_SENSITIVE` of the `Result-Set` interface
	concurrency	one of the constants `CONCUR_READ_ONLY` or `CONCUR_UPDATABLE` of the `ResultSet` interface

Metadata

In the preceding sections, you saw how to populate, query, and update database tables. However, JDBC can give you additional information about the *structure* of a database and its tables. For example, you can get a list of the tables in a particular database or the column names and types of a table. This information is not useful when you are implementing a particular database application. After all, if you design the tables, you know the tables and their structure. Structural information is, however, extremely useful for programmers who write tools that work with any database.

In this section, we will show you how to write such a simple tool. This tool lets you browse all tables in a database.

The combo box on top displays all tables in the database. Select one of them, and the center of the frame is filled with the field names of that table and the values of the first record, as shown in Figure 4–8. Click on "Next" to scroll through the records in the table.

Figure 4–8: The ViewDB application

We fully expect tool vendors to develop much more sophisticated versions of programs like this one. For example, it would be possible to let the user edit the values or add new ones, and then update the database. We developed this program mostly to show you how such tools can be built.

In SQL, data that describes the database or one of its parts is called *metadata* (to distinguish it from the actual data that is stored in the database). You can get two kinds of metadata: about a database and about a result set.

To find out more about the database, you need to request an object of type `DatabaseMetaData` from the database connection.

```
DatabaseMetaData meta = conn.getMetaData();
```

Now you are ready to get some metadata. For example, the call

```
ResultSet rs = meta.getTables(null, null, null, new String[]
    { "TABLE" });
```

returns a result set that contains information about all tables in the database. (See the API note for other parameters to this method.)

Each row in the result set contains information about the table. We only care about the third entry, the name of the table. (Again, see the API note for the other columns.) Thus, `rs.getString(3)` is the table name. Here is the code that populates the combo box.

```
while (rs.next())
    tableNames.addItem(rs.getString(3));
rs.close();
```

The `DatabaseMetaData` class gives data about the database. There is a second metadata class, `ResultSetMetaData`, that reports information about a result set. Whenever you have a result set from a query, you can inquire about the number of columns and each column's name, type, and field width.

We will make use of this information to make a label for each name and a text field of sufficient size for each value.

```
ResultSet rs = stat.executeQuery("SELECT * FROM " + tableName);
ResultSetMetaData meta = rs.getMetaData();
for (int i = 1; i <= meta.getColumnCount(); i++)
{
    String columnName = meta.getColumnLabel(i);
    int columnWidth = meta.getColumnDisplaySize(i);
    Label l = new Label(columnName);
    TextField tf = new TextField(columnWidth);
    . . .
}
```

There is a second important use for database meta data. Databases are complex, and the SQL standard leaves plenty of room for variability. There are well over a hundred methods in the `DatabaseMetaData` class to inquire about the database, including calls with exotic names such as

```
md.supportsCatalogsInPrivilegeDefinitions()
```

and

```
md.nullPlusNonNullIsNull()
```

Clearly, these are geared toward advanced users with special needs, in particular, those who need to write highly portable code that works with multiple databases. In our sample program, we only give one example of this technique. We ask the database metadata whether the JDBC driver supports scrolling result sets. If so, we open a scrolling result set and add a "Previous" button for scrolling backwards.

```
if (meta.supportsResultSetType(
    ResultSet.TYPE_SCROLL_INSENSITIVE)) . . .
```

The following steps provide a brief overview of the sample program.

1. Have the border layout put the table name combo box on the top and the table values in the center.

2. Connect to the database. Find out if it supports scrolling result sets. If so, create the `Statement` object to yield scrolling result sets. Otherwise, just create a default `Statement`.

3. Get the table names and fill them into the choice component.

4. If scrolling is supported, add the "Previous" button. Always add the "Next" button.

5. When the user selects a table, make a query to see all its values. Get the result set metadata. Throw out the old scroll pane from the center panel. Create a panel containing a gridbag layout of labels and text fields. Add it to the frame and call the `validate` method to recompute the frame layout. Then, call `showNextRow` to show the first row.

6. The `showNextRow` method is called to show the first record and is also called whenever the "Next" button is clicked. It gets the next row from the table and fills the column values into the text boxes.

7. There is a slight subtlety in detecting the end of the result set. When the result set is scrolling, we can simply use the `isLast` method. But when it isn't scrolling, that method call will cause an exception (or even a JVM error if the driver is a JDBC 1 driver). Therefore, we use a different strategy for non-scrolling result sets. When `rs.next()` returns `false`, we close the result set and set `rs` to `null`.

8. The "Previous" button calls `showPreviousRow`, which moves the result set backwards. Since this button is only installed when the result set is scrollable, we know that the `previous` and `isFirst` method are supported.

9. The showRow method simply fills in all the result set fields into the text fields of the data panel.

Example 4–4 is the program.

Example 4–4: ViewDB.java

```
1. import java.net.*;
2. import java.sql.*;
3. import java.awt.*;
4. import java.awt.event.*;
5. import java.io.*;
6. import java.util.*;
7. import javax.swing.*;
8.
9. /**
10.    This program uses metadata to display arbitrary tables
11.    in a database.
12. */
13. public class ViewDB
14. {
15.    public static void main(String[] args)
16.    {
17.       JFrame frame = new ViewDBFrame();
18.       frame.setDefaultCloseOperation(JFrame.EXIT_ON_CLOSE);
19.       frame.show();
20.    }
21. }
22.
23. /**
24.    The frame that holds the data panel and the navigation
25.    buttons.
26. */
27. class ViewDBFrame extends JFrame
28. {
29.    public ViewDBFrame()
30.    {
31.       setTitle("ViewDB");
32.       setSize(WIDTH, HEIGHT);
33.
34.       Container contentPane = getContentPane();
35.
36.       tableNames = new JComboBox();
37.       tableNames.addActionListener(new
38.          ActionListener()
39.          {
40.             public void actionPerformed(ActionEvent event)
41.             {
42.                showTable((String)tableNames.getSelectedItem());
43.             }
```

```
44.                 });
45.             contentPane.add(tableNames, BorderLayout.NORTH);
46.
47.             try
48.             {
49.                 conn = getConnection();
50.                 meta = conn.getMetaData();
51.                 createStatement();
52.                 getTableNames();
53.             }
54.             catch(Exception ex)
55.             {
56.                 JOptionPane.showMessageDialog(this, ex);
57.             }
58.
59.             JPanel buttonPanel = new JPanel();
60.             contentPane.add(buttonPanel, BorderLayout.SOUTH);
61.
62.             if (scrolling)
63.             {
64.                 previousButton = new JButton("Previous");
65.                 previousButton.addActionListener(new
66.                     ActionListener()
67.                     {
68.                         public void actionPerformed(ActionEvent event)
69.                         {
70.                             showPreviousRow();
71.                         }
72.                     });
73.                 buttonPanel.add(previousButton);
74.             }
75.
76.             nextButton = new JButton("Next");
77.             nextButton.addActionListener(new
78.                 ActionListener()
79.                 {
80.                     public void actionPerformed(ActionEvent event)
81.                     {
82.                         showNextRow();
83.                     }
84.                 });
85.             buttonPanel.add(nextButton);
86.
87.             add(new
88.                 WindowAdapter()
89.                 {
90.                     public void windowClosing(WindowEvent event)
91.                     {
92.                         try
93.                         {
```

```
94.                   stat.close();
95.                   conn.close();
96.               }
97.               catch(SQLException ex)
98.               {
99.                   while (ex != null)
100.                  {
101.                      ex.printStackTrace();
102.                      ex = ex.getNextException();
103.                  }
104.              }
105.          }
106.      });
107.   }
108. }
109.
110.   /**
111.      Creates the statement object used for executing queries.
112.      If the database supports scrolling cursors, the statement
113.      is created to yield them.
114.   */
115.   public void createStatement() throws SQLException
116.   {
117.      if (meta.supportsResultSetType(
118.         ResultSet.TYPE_SCROLL_INSENSITIVE))
119.      {
120.         stat = conn.createStatement(
121.            ResultSet.TYPE_SCROLL_INSENSITIVE,
122.            ResultSet.CONCUR_READ_ONLY);
123.         scrolling = true;
124.      }
125.      else
126.      {
127.         stat = conn.createStatement();
128.         scrolling = false;
129.      }
130.   }
131.
132.   /**
133.      Gets all table names of this database and adds them
134.      to the combo box.
135.   */
136.   public void getTableNames() throws SQLException
137.   {
138.      ResultSet mrs = meta.getTables(null, null, null,
139.         new String[] { "TABLE" });
140.      while (mrs.next())
141.         tableNames.addItem(mrs.getString(3));
142.      mrs.close();
143.   }
```

```
144.
145.    /**
146.       Prepares the text fields for showing a new table, and
147.       shows the first row.
148.       @param tableName the name of the table to display
149.    */
150.    public void showTable(String tableName)
151.    {
152.       try
153.       {
154.          if (rs != null) rs.close();
155.          rs = stat.executeQuery("SELECT * FROM " + tableName);
156.          if (scrollPane != null)
157.             getContentPane().remove(scrollPane);
158.          dataPanel = new DataPanel(rs);
159.          scrollPane = new JScrollPane(dataPanel);
160.          getContentPane().add(scrollPane, BorderLayout.CENTER);
161.          validate();
162.          showNextRow();
163.       }
164.       catch(Exception ex)
165.       {
166.          JOptionPane.showMessageDialog(this, ex);
167.       }
168.    }
169.
170.    /**
171.       Moves to the previous table row.
172.    */
173.    public void showPreviousRow()
174.    {
175.       try
176.       {
177.          if (rs == null || rs.isFirst()) return;
178.          rs.previous();
179.          dataPanel.showRow(rs);
180.       }
181.       catch(Exception ex)
182.       {
183.          System.out.println("Error " + ex);
184.       }
185.    }
186.
187.    /**
188.       Moves to the next table row.
189.    */
190.    public void showNextRow()
191.    {
192.       try
193.       {
```

```
194.            if (rs == null || scrolling && rs.isLast()) return;
195.
196.            if (!rs.next() && !scrolling)
197.            {
198.               rs.close();
199.               rs = null;
200.               return;
201.            }
202.
203.            dataPanel.showRow(rs);
204.         }
205.      catch(Exception ex)
206.      {
207.            System.out.println("Error " + ex);
208.      }
209.   }
210.
211.   /**
212.      Gets a connection from the properties specified
213.      in the file database.properties
214.      @return the database connection
215.   */
216.   public static Connection getConnection()
217.      throws SQLException, IOException
218.   {
219.      Properties props = new Properties();
220.      FileInputStream in
221.         = new FileInputStream("database.properties");
222.      props.load(in);
223.      in.close();
224.
225.      String drivers = props.getProperty("jdbc.drivers");
226.      if (drivers != null)
227.         System.setProperty("jdbc.drivers", drivers);
228.      String url = props.getProperty("jdbc.url");
229.      String username = props.getProperty("jdbc.username");
230.      String password = props.getProperty("jdbc.password");
231.
232.      return
233.         DriverManager.getConnection(url, username, password);
234.   }
235.
236.   public static final int WIDTH = 300;
237.   public static final int HEIGHT = 200;
238.
239.   private JButton previousButton;
240.   private JButton nextButton;
241.   private DataPanel dataPanel;
242.   private JScrollPane scrollPane;
243.   private JComboBox tableNames;
```

```
244.
245.     private Connection conn;
246.     private Statement stat;
247.     private DatabaseMetaData meta;
248.     private ResultSet rs;
249.     private boolean scrolling;
250. }
251.
252. /**
253.    This panel displays the contents of a result set.
254. */
255. class DataPanel extends JPanel
256. {
257.    /**
258.       Constructs the data panel.
259.       @param rs the result set whose contents this panel displays
260.    */
261.    public DataPanel(ResultSet rs) throws SQLException
262.    {
263.       fields = new ArrayList();
264.       setLayout(new GridBagLayout());
265.       GridBagConstraints gbc = new GridBagConstraints();
266.       gbc.weighty = 100;
267.
268.       ResultSetMetaData rsmd = rs.getMetaData();
269.       for (int i = 1; i <= rsmd.getColumnCount(); i++)
270.       {
271.          String columnName = rsmd.getColumnLabel(i);
272.          int columnWidth = rsmd.getColumnDisplaySize(i);
273.          JTextField tb = new JTextField(columnWidth);
274.          fields.add(tb);
275.
276.          gbc.weightx = 0;
277.          gbc.anchor = GridBagConstraints.EAST;
278.          gbc.fill = GridBagConstraints.NONE;
279.          add(new JLabel(columnName), gbc, 0, i - 1, 1, 1);
280.
281.          gbc.weightx = 100;
282.          gbc.anchor = GridBagConstraints.WEST;
283.          gbc.fill = GridBagConstraints.HORIZONTAL;
284.          add(tb, gbc, 1, i - 1, 1, 1);
285.       }
286.    }
287.
288.    /**
289.       Shows a database row by populating all text fields
290.       with the column values.
291.    */
292.    public void showRow(ResultSet rs) throws SQLException
```

```
293.    {
294.        for (int i = 1; i <= fields.size(); i++)
295.        {
296.            String field = rs.getString(i);
297.            JTextField tb
298.                = (JTextField)fields.get(i - 1);
299.            tb.setText(field);
300.        }
301.    }
302.
303.    /**
304.        Adds a component to this panel.
305.        @param c the component to add
306.        @param gbc the grid bag constraints
307.        @param x the grid bax column
308.        @param y the grid bag row
309.        @param w the number of grid bag columns spanned
310.        @param h the number of grid bag rows spanned
311.    */
312.    private void add(Component c,
313.        GridBagConstraints gbc, int x, int y, int w, int h)
314.    {
315.        gbc.gridx = x;
316.        gbc.gridy = y;
317.        gbc.gridwidth = w;
318.        gbc.gridheight = h;
319.        add(c, gbc);
320.    }
321.
322.    private ArrayList fields;
323. }
```

`java.sql.Connection`

- DatabaseMetaData getMetaData()
  returns the metadata for the connection as a `DataBaseMetaData` object.

`java.sql.DatabaseMetaData`

- ResultSet getTables(String catalog, String schemaPattern,
  String tableNamePattern, String types[])

  gets a description of all tables in a catalog that match the schema and table name patterns and the type criteria. (A *schema* describes a group of related tables and access permissions. A *catalog* describes a related group of schemas. These concepts are important for structuring large databases.)

  The `catalog` and `schema` parameters can be " " to retrieve those tables without a catalog or schema, or `null` to return tables regardless of catalog or schema.

The `types` array contains the names of the table types to include. Typical types are `TABLE`, `VIEW`, `SYSTEM TABLE`, `GLOBAL TEMPORARY`, `LOCAL TEMPORARY`, `ALIAS`, and `SYNONYM`. If `types` is `null`, then tables of all types are returned.

The result set has five columns, all of which are of type `String`, as shown in Table 4–10.

Table 4–10: Five columns of the result set

1	TABLE_CAT	Table catalog (may be `null`)
2	TABLE_SCHEM	Table schema (may be `null`)
3	TABLE_NAME	Table name
4	TABLE_TYPE	Table type
5	REMARKS	Comment on the table

- `int getJDBCMajorVersion()`
- `int getJDBCMinorVersion()`
  (JDBC 3) Return the major and minor JDBC version numbers of the driver that established the database connection. For example, a JDBC 3.0 driver has major version number 3 and minor version number 0.

- `int getMaxStatements()`
  Returns the maximum number of concurrently open statements per database connection, or 0 if the number is unlimited or unknown.

`java.sql.ResultSet`

- `ResultSetMetaData getMetaData()`
  gives you the metadata associated with the current `ResultSet` columns.

`java.sql.ResultSetMetaData`

- `int getColumnCount()`
  returns the number of columns in the current `ResultSet` object.
- `int getColumnDisplaySize(int column)`
  tells you the maximum width of the column specified by the index parameter.

  Parameters: column   the column number

- `String getColumnLabel(int column)`
  gives you the suggested title for the column.

  Parameters: column   the column number

- `String getColumnName(int column)`
  gives the column name associated with the column index specified.

  Parameters: column   the column number

Transactions

While we do not want to go deep into transaction support, we do want to show you how to group a set of statements to form a transaction that can be committed when all has gone well, or rolled back as if none of the commands had been issued if an error has occurred in one of them.

The major reason for grouping commands into transactions is *database integrity.* For example, suppose we want to add a new book to our book database. Then, it is important that we simultaneously update the `Books`, `Authors`, and `BooksAuthors` table. If the update were to add new rows into the first two tables but not into the third, then the books and authors would not be properly matched up.

If you group updates to a transaction, then the transaction either succeeds in its entirety and it can be *committed,* or it fails somewhere in the middle. In that case, you can carry out a *rollback* and the database automatically undoes the effect of all updates that occurred since the last committed transaction. Furthermore, queries are guaranteed to report only on the committed state of the database.

By default, a database connection is in *autocommit mode,* and each SQL command is committed to the database as soon as it is executed. Once a command is committed, you cannot roll it back.

To check the current autocommit mode setting, call the `getAutoCommit` method of the `Connection` class.

You turn off autocommit mode with the command

```
conn.setAutoCommit(false);
```

Now you create a statement object in the normal way:

```
Statement stat = conn.createStatement();
```

Call `executeUpdate` any number of times:

```
stat.executeUpdate(command1);
stat.executeUpdate(command2);
stat.executeUpdate(command3);
    . . .
```

When all commands have been executed, call the `commit` method:

```
conn.commit();
```

However, if an error occurred, call

```
conn.rollback();
```

Then, all commands until the last commit are automatically reversed. You typically issue a rollback when your transaction was interrupted by a `SQLException`.

Batch Updates (JDBC 2)

Suppose a program needs to execute many INSERT statements to populate a database table. In JDBC 2, you can improve the performance of the program by using a *batch update*. In a batch update, a sequence of commands is collected and submitted as a batch.

> NOTE: Use the supportsBatchUpdates method of the DatabaseMetaData class to find out if your database supports this feature.

The commands in a batch can be actions such as INSERT, UPDATE, and DELETE as well as data definition commands such as CREATE TABLE and DROP TABLE. However, you cannot add SELECT commands to a batch since executing a SELECT statement returns a result set.

To execute a batch, you first create a Statement object in the usual way:

```
Statement stat = conn.createStatement();
```

Now, instead of calling executeUpdate, you call the addBatch method:

```
String command = "CREATE TABLE . . ."
stat.addBatch(command);

while (. . .)
{
   command = "INSERT INTO . . . VALUES (" + . . . + ")";
   stat.addBatch(command);
}
```

Finally, you submit the entire batch.

```
int[] counts = stat.executeBatch();
```

The call to executeBatch returns an array of the row counts for all submitted commands. (Recall that an individual call to executeUpdate returns an integer, namely, the count of the rows that are affected by the command.) In our example, the executeBatch method returns an array with first element equal to 0 (because the CREATE TABLE command yields a row count of 0) and all other elements equal to 1 (because each INSERT command affects one row).

For proper error handling in batch mode, you want to treat the batch execution as a single transaction. If a batch fails in the middle, you want to roll back to the state before the beginning of the batch.

First, turn autocommit mode off, then collect the batch, execute it, commit it, and finally restore the original autocommit mode:

```
boolean autoCommit = conn.getAutoCommit();
conn.setAutoCommit(false);
Statement stat = conn.getStatement();
```

```
. . .
// keep calling stat.addBatch(. . .);
. . .
stat.executeBatch();
conn.commit();
conn.setAutoCommit(autoCommit);
```

java.sql.Connection

- void setAutoCommit(boolean b)

  sets the autocommit mode of this connection to b. If autocommit is true, all statements are committed as soon as their execution is completed.

- boolean getAutoCommit()

  gets the autocommit mode of this connection.

- void commit()

  commits all statements that were issued since the last commit.

- void rollback()

  undoes the effect of all statements that were issued since the last commit.

java.sql.Statement

- void addBatch(String command)

  (JDBC 2) adds the command to the current batch of commands for this statement.

- int[] executeBatch()

  (JDBC 2) executes all commands in the current batch. Returns an array of row counts, containing an element for each command in the batch that denotes the number of rows affected by that command.

java.sql.DatabaseMetaData

- boolean supportsBatchUpdates()

  (JDBC 2) returns true if the driver supports batch updates.

Advanced Connection Management

The simplistic database connection setup of the preceding sections, with a database.properties file, is suitable for small test programs, but it won't scale for larger applications.

When deploying a JDBC 2 application in an enterprise environment, the management of database connections is integrated with the Java Naming and Directory Interface (JNDI). A directory manages the location of data sources across the enterprise. Using a directory allows for centralized management of user names, passwords, database names, and JDBC URLs.

In such an environment, you use the following code to establish a database connection:

```
Context jndiContext = . . .;
DataSource source
    = (DataSource)jndiContext.lookup("jdbc/corejava");
Connection conn = source.getConnection(username, password);
```

Note that the `DriverManager` is no longer involved. Instead, the JNDI service locates a *data source*. A data source is an interface that allows for simple JDBC connections as well as more advanced services, such as executing distributed transactions that involve multiple databases. The `DataSource` interface is defined in the `javax.sql` standard extension package.

Management of user names and logins is just one of the issues that require special attention. A second issue involves the cost of establishing database connections.

Our simple database programs established a single database connection at the start of the program and closed it at the end of the program. However, in many programming situations, this approach won't work. Consider a typical web application. Such an application serves multiple page requests in parallel. Multiple requests may need simultaneous access the database. With many databases, a connection is not intended to be shared by multiple threads. Thus, each request needs its own connection. A simplistic approach would be to establish a connection for each page request and close it afterwards. But that would be very costly. Establishing a database connection can be quite time-consuming. Connections are intended to be used for multiple queries, not to be closed after one or two queries.

The solution is to *pool* the connections. This means that database connections are not physically closed but are kept in a queue and reused. Connection pooling is an important service, and the JDBC specification provides hooks for implementors to supply it. However, the Java SDK itself does not provide any implementation, and database vendors don't usually include one with their JDBC driver either. Instead, vendors of application servers such as BEA WebLogic or IBM WebSphere supply connection pool implementations as part of the application server package.

Using a connection pool is completely transparent to the programmer. You acquire a connection from a source of pooled connections, by obtaining a data source and calling `getConnection`. When you are done using the connection, call `close`. That doesn't close the physical connection but tells the pool that you are done using it.

TIP: If you deploy a simple Web application, using just a servlet container such as Apache Tomcat, you need to supply your own connection pool. Implementations of varying quality are available on the Internet. If you only need support for a single database login, and you don't use transactions, then the implementation at `http://developer.java.sun.com/developer/onlineTraining/Programming/JDCBook/conpool.html` should get you started.

CAUTION: In Web applications, you need to be particularly careful about recycling connections when an error occurs. Suppose an exception is thrown and the call to `close` is skipped. Then a user can drain the connection pool quickly simply by hitting the browser's "Reload" button in frustration, executing the same faulty service request over and over. Be sure to close the connections in `finally` clauses, like this:

```
public void myService() throws SQLException
{
    Connection conn = null;
    try
    {
        conn = ds.getConnection();
        . . .
    }
    finally
    {
        if (conn != null) conn.close();
    }
}
```

This code has one flaw—if the `conn.close()` call throws an exception, it masks the original exception. That's an unfortunate consequence of the Java exception handling mechanism. However, saving and rethrowing the original exception would be fiendishly complex—we leave it as the proverbial exercise for the reader.

You have now learned about the JDBC fundamentals and know enough to implement simple database applications. However, as we mentioned at the beginning of this chapter, databases are complex and there are quite a few advanced topics that are beyond the scope of an introductory chapter. For an overview of advanced JDBC capabilities, you can read the JDBC specifications at `http://java.sun.com/products/jdbc`.

Chapter 5

Remote Objects

▼ REMOTE METHOD INVOCATIONS

▼ SETTING UP REMOTE METHOD INVOCATION

▼ PARAMETER PASSING IN REMOTE METHODS

▼ USING RMI WITH APPLETS

▼ SERVER OBJECT ACTIVATION

▼ JAVA IDL AND CORBA

Periodically, the programming community starts thinking of "objects everywhere" as the solution to all its problems. The idea is to have a happy family of collaborating objects that can be located anywhere. These objects are, of course, supposed to communicate through standard protocols across a network. For example, you'll have an object on the client where the user can fill in a request for data. The client object sends a message to an object on the server that contains the details of the request. The server object gathers the requested information, perhaps by accessing a database or by communicating with additional objects. Once the server object has the answer to the client request, it sends the answer back to the client. Like most bandwagons in programming, this plan contains a fair amount of hype that can obscure the utility of the concept. This chapter:

- Explains the models that make interobject communication possible;
- Explains situations where distributed objects can be useful;

- Shows you how to use remote objects and the associated *remote method invocation* (RMI) for communicating between two Java virtual machines (which may run on different computers);

- Introduces you to CORBA, the Common Object Request Broker Architecture that allows communication between objects that are written in different programming languages (such as the Java programming language, C++, and so on).

Introduction to Remote Objects: The Roles of Client and Server

Let's go back to that idea of locally collecting information on a client computer and sending the information across the Net to a server. We are supposing that a user on a local machine will fill out an information request form. The form data gets sent to the vendor's server, and the server processes the request and will, in turn, want to send back product information the client can view, as shown in Figure 5–1.

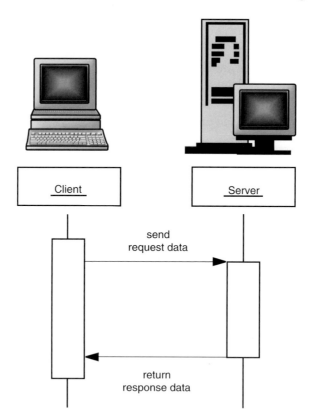

Figure 5–1: Transmitting objects between client and server

In the traditional client/server model, the request is translated to an intermediary format (such as name/value pairs or XML data). The server parses the request format, computes the response, and formats the response for transmission to the client. The client then parses the response and displays it to the user.

But if your data is structured, then there is a significant coding hassle: you have to come up with appropriate ways of translating the data to and from the transmission format.

> NOTE: Another method for sending a request for data to a server is with HTML forms. Then, the client is simply the browser, and the server needs to gather the requested information and format it as HTML. Even in that model, it makes sense to separate the form processing from the data gathering. Typically, the form processing happens on the web server, and the data gathering happens on a different server, called an *application server.* You again have two communicating objects, the client object on the web server and the server object on the application server. This is a very common model in practice. In this chapter, we stick to a more traditional client/server example because it makes the roles of the client and server more intuitive.

What would go into a possible solution? Well, keeping in mind that objects sending requests to one another is the central tenet of OOP, we could put objects on different machines and have them send messages *directly* to each other. Let's assume that the client object was written in the Java programming language so that it can theoretically run anywhere. For the server objects, there are two obvious possibilities:

- The server object was *not* written in the Java programming language (either because it is a legacy object or because somebody hasn't jumped on the appropriate bandwagon).

- The server object *was* written in the Java programming language.

The first situation requires us to have a way for objects to talk to each other *regardless* of what language they were originally written in. If you think about it, you will agree with us that even the theoretical possibility of this is an amazing achievement. How can what is ultimately a sequence of bytes written in an arbitrary language, that we may have no knowledge of, tell us what services it offers, what messages it responds to? Of course, getting this to work in practice isn't easy, but the idea is elegant. The "common object request broker architecture," or CORBA standard, by the Object Management Group or OMG (www.omg.org) defines a common mechanism for interchanging data and discovering services.

The fundamental idea is that we delegate the task of finding out this information and activating any requested services to a so-called *Object Request Broker* (or ORB). You can think of an ORB as a kind of universal translator for interobject communication. Objects don't talk directly to each other. They always use an object broker to bargain between them. ORBs are located across the network, and it is important that they can communicate with each other. Most ORBs follow the specification set up by the OMG for inter-ORB communication. This specification is called the Internet Inter-ORB Protocol or IIOP.

NOTE: Microsoft uses COM, a different, lower-level protocol for interobject communication. ORB-like services are bundled into the Windows operating system. As recently as 1999, Microsoft positioned COM as a competitor to CORBA. However, at the time of this writing, Microsoft is deemphasizing COM in favor of its .NET model for XML-based communication between software components.

CORBA is completely language neutral. Client and server programs can be written in C++, the Java programming language, or any other language with a CORBA binding. You use an *Interface Definition Language* (or IDL) to specify the signatures of the messages and the types of the data your objects can send and understand. (IDL specifications look a lot like interfaces in the Java programming language; in fact, you can think of them as defining interfaces that the communicating objects must support. One nice feature of this model is that you can supply an IDL specification for an existing legacy object and then access its services through the ORB even if it was written long before the first ORB arrived.)

There are quite a few people who believe that CORBA is the object model of the future, and that the Java programming language is an excellent choice for implementing CORBA clients and servers. However, frankly speaking, CORBA has had a reputation—sometimes deserved—for slow performance, complex implementations, and interoperability problems. After running into quite a few CORBA problems while writing this chapter, and encountering many of the same issues when updating it two years later, our sentiments about CORBA are similar to those expressed by French president Charles De Gaulle's about Brazil: It has a great future . . . and always will.

If both communicating objects are written in the Java programming language, then the full generality and complexity of CORBA is not required. Sun developed a simpler mechanism, called Remote Method Invocation (RMI), specifically for communication between Java applications.

NOTE: CORBA supporters initially did not like RMI because it completely ignored the CORBA standard. However, starting with SDK 1.3, CORBA and RMI have become more interoperable. In particular, you can use RMI with the IIOP protocol instead of the proprietary Java Remote Method Protocol. For more information on RMI over IIOP, see the introductory article at `http://www.javaworld.com/javaworld/jw-12-1999/jw-12-iiop.html` and the tutorial at `http://java.sun.com/j2se/1.4/docs/guide/rmi-iiop/rmiiiopexample.html`.

While CORBA may be interesting tomorrow, RMI is easier to understand and more convenient to use. For that reason, we will start out this chapter with RMI. Of course, RMI is useful only for communication between Java objects. In the last section of this chapter, we briefly introduce CORBA programming and show you how to hook up a C++ client with a server implemented in the Java programming language and a client implemented in the Java programming language with a C++ server.

Remote Method Invocations

The Remote Method Invocation mechanism lets you do something that sounds simple. If you have access to an object on a different machine, you can call methods of the remote object. Of course, the method parameters must somehow be shipped to the other machine, the object must be informed to execute the method, and the return value must be shipped back. RMI handles these details.

For example, the client seeking product information can query a `Warehouse` object on the server. It calls a remote method, `find`, which has one parameter: a `Customer` object. The `find` method returns an object to the client: the product information object. (See Figure 5–2.)

Figure 5–2: Invoking a remote method on a server object

In RMI terminology, the object whose method makes the remote call is called the *client object*. The remote object is called the *server object*. It is important to remember that the client/server terminology applies only to a single method call. The computer running the code in the Java programming language that calls the remote method is the client for *that* call, and the computer hosting the object that processes the call is the server for *that* call. It is entirely possible that the roles are reversed somewhere down the road. The server of a previous call can itself become the client when it invokes a remote method on an object residing on another computer.

Stubs and Parameter Marshalling

When client code wants to invoke a remote method on a remote object, it actually calls an ordinary method of the Java programming language that is encapsulated in a surrogate object called a *stub*. The stub resides on the client machine, not on the server. The stub packages the parameters used in the remote method into a block of bytes. This packaging uses a device-independent encoding for each parameter. For example, numbers are always sent in big-endian byte ordering. Objects are encoded with the serialization mechanism that is described in Chapter 12 of Volume 1. The process of encoding the parameters is called *parameter marshalling*. The purpose of parameter marshalling is to convert the parameters into a format suitable for transport from one virtual machine to another.

To sum up: the stub method on the client builds an information block that consists of:

- An identifier of the remote object to be used;
- A description of the method to be called;
- The marshalled parameters.

The stub then sends this information to the server. On the server side, a receiver object performs the following actions for every remote method call:

- It unmarshals the parameters.
- It locates the object to be called.
- It calls the desired method.
- It captures and marshals the return value or exception of the call.
- It sends a package consisting of the marshalled return data back to the stub on the client.

The client stub unmarshals the return value or exception from the server. This value becomes the return value of the stub call. Or, if the remote method threw an exception, the stub rethrows it in the process space of the caller. Figure 5–3 shows the information flow of a remote method invocation.

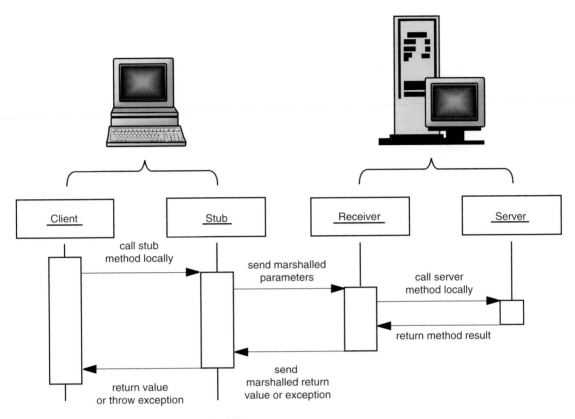

Figure 5–3: Parameter marshalling

This process is obviously complex, but the good news is that it is completely automatic and, to a large extent, transparent for the programmer. Moreover, the designers of the remote Java object tried hard to give remote objects the same "look and feel" as local objects.

The syntax for a remote method call is the same as for a local call. If centralWarehouse is a stub object for a central warehouse object on a remote machine and getQuantity is the method you want to invoke on it, then a typical call looks like this:

```
centralWarehouse.getQuantity("SuperSucker 100 Vacuum Cleaner");
```

The client code always uses object variables whose type is an interface to access remote objects. For example, associated to this call would be an interface:

```
interface Warehouse
{
    int getQuantity(String description)
        throws RemoteException;
    . . .
}
```

An object declaration for a variable that will implement the interface is:

```
Warehouse centralWarehouse = . . .;
```

Of course, interfaces are abstract entities that only spell out what methods can be called along with their signatures. Variables whose type is an interface must always be bound to an actual object of some type. When calling remote methods, the object variable refers to a *stub object*. The client program does not actually know the type of those objects. The stub classes and the associated objects are created automatically.

While the designers did a good job of hiding many details of remote method invocation from the programmer, a number of techniques and caveats still must be mastered. Those programming tasks are the topic of the rest of this chapter.

NOTE: Remote objects are garbage collected automatically, just as local objects are. However, the current distributed collector uses reference counting and cannot detect cycles of objects that refer to each other but have no external reference into the cycle. Cycles must be explicitly broken by the programmer before they can be reclaimed.

Dynamic Class Loading

When you pass a remote object to another program, either as a parameter or return value of a remote method, then that program must be able to deal with the associated stub object. That is, it must have the code for the stub class. The stub methods don't do a lot of interesting work. They just marshal and unmarshal the parameters and then contact the server for method calls. Of course, they do all this work transparently to the programmer.

Furthermore, the classes for parameters, return values, and exception objects may need to be loaded as well. This loading can be more complex than you might think. For example, you may declare a remote method with a certain return type that is known to the client, but the method actually returns an object of a subclass that is not known to the client. The class loader will then load that derived class.

While unglamorous, the stub classes must be available to the running client program. One obvious way to make these classes available is to put them on the local file system. However, if the server program is extended and new classes for return types and exceptions are added, then it would be a hassle to keep updating the client.

For that reason, RMI clients can automatically load stub classes from another place. The process is similar to the class loading process of applets that run in a browser.

Whenever a program loads new code from another network location, there is a security issue. For that reason, you need to use a *security manager* in RMI client applications. This is a safety mechanism that protects the program from viruses in stub code. For specialized applications, programmers can substitute their own class loaders and security managers, but those provided by the RMI system suffice for normal usage. (See Chapter 9 for more information on class loaders and security managers.)

Setting Up Remote Method Invocation

Running even the simplest remote object example requires quite a bit more setup than does running a standalone program or applet. You must run programs on both the server and client computers. The necessary object information must be separated into client-side interfaces and server-side implementations. There is also a special lookup mechanism that allows the client to locate objects on the server.

To get started with the actual coding, we walk through each of these requirements, using a simple example. In our first example, we generate a couple of objects of a type `Product` on the server computer. We then run a program on a client computer that locates and queries these objects.

NOTE: You can try out this example on a single computer or on a pair of networked computers. We give you instructions for both scenarios.

Even if you run this code on a single computer, you must have network services available. In particular, be sure that you have TCP/IP running. If your computer doesn't have a network card, then you can activate TCP/IP by establishing a dialup networking connection.

Interfaces and Implementations

Your client program needs to manipulate server objects, but it doesn't actually have copies of them. The objects themselves reside on the server. The client code must still know what it can do with those objects. Their capabilities are expressed in an interface that is shared between the client and server and so resides simultaneously on both machines.

```
interface Product // shared by client and server
   extends Remote
{
   String getDescription() throws RemoteException;
}
```

Just as in this example, *all* interfaces for remote objects must extend the `Remote` interface defined in the `java.rmi` package. All the methods in those interfaces must also declare that they will throw a `RemoteException`. The reason for the declaration is that remote method calls are inherently less reliable than local calls—it is always possible that a remote call will fail. For example, the server or the network connection may be temporarily unavailable, or there may be a network problem. Your client code must be prepared to deal with these possibilities. For these reasons, the Java programming language forces you to catch the `RemoteException` with *every* remote method call and to specify the appropriate action to take when the call does not succeed.

The client accesses the server object through a stub that implements this interface.

```
Product p = ...;
   // see below how the client gets a stub
   // reference to a remote object
String d = p.getDescription();
System.out.println(d);
```

In the next section, you will see how the client can obtain a reference to this kind of remote object.

Next, on the server side, you must implement the class that actually carries out the methods advertised in the remote interface.

```
public class ProductImpl // server
   extends UnicastRemoteObject
   implements Product
{
   public ProductImpl(String d)
      throws RemoteException
   {
      descr = d;
   }

   public String getDescription()
      throws RemoteException
   {
      return "I am a " + descr + ". Buy me!";
   }

   private String descr;
}
```

NOTE: The `ProductImpl` constructor is declared to throw a `RemoteException` because the `UnicastRemoteObject` might throw that exception if it can't connect to the network service that keeps track of server objects.

This class has a single method, `getDescription`, that can be called from the remote client.

You can tell that the class is a server for remote methods because it extends `UnicastRemoteObject`, which is a concrete Java platform class that makes objects remotely accessible.

NOTE: The `ProductImpl` class is *not* a typical server class because it does so little work. Normally, you only want to have server classes that do some heavy-duty work that a client could not carry out locally. We just use the `Product` example to walk you through the mechanics of calling remote methods.

Server classes generally extend the class `RemoteServer` from the `java.rmi.server` package, but `RemoteServer` is an abstract class that defines only the basic mechanisms for the communication between server objects and their remote stubs. The `UnicastRemoteObject` class that comes with RMI extends the `RemoteServer` abstract class and is concrete—so you can use it without writing any code. The "path of least resistance" for a server class is to derive from `UnicastRemoteObject`, and all server classes in this chapter will do so. Figure 5–4 shows the inheritance relationship between these classes.

Figure 5–4: Inheritance diagram

A `UnicastRemoteObject` object resides on a server. It must be alive when a service is requested and must be reachable through the TCP/IP protocol. This is the class that we will be extending for all the server classes in this book and is the only server class available in the current version of the RMI package. Sun or third-party vendors may, in the future, design other classes for use by servers for RMI. For example, Sun is talking about a `MulticastRemoteObject` class for objects that are replicated over multiple servers. Other possibilities are for objects that are activated on demand or ones that can use other communications protocols, such as UDP.

> NOTE: Occasionally, you may not want a server class that extends the `Unicast-RemoteServer` class, perhaps because it already extends another class. In that situation, you need to manually instantiate the server objects and pass them to the static `exportObject` method. Note that the server class must still implement a remote interface.
>
> ```
> Remote server = new MyServer();
> UnicastRemoteObject.exportObject(server, 0);
> ```
>
> Alternatively, you can call
>
> ```
> UnicastRemoteObject.exportObject(this, 0);
> ```
>
> in the constructor. The second parameter is 0 to indicate that any suitable port can be used to listen to client connections.

When you use RMI (or any distributed object mechanism, for that matter), there is a somewhat bewildering set of classes to master. In this chapter, we use a uniform naming convention for all of our examples that, hopefully, makes it easier to recognize the purpose of each class. (See Table 5–1.)

Table 5–1: Naming conventions for RMI classes

No suffix (e.g., `Product`)	A remote interface
`Impl` suffix (e.g., `ProductImpl`)	A server class implementing that interface
`Server` suffix (e.g., `ProductServer`)	A server program that creates server objects
`Client` suffix (e.g., `ProductClient`)	A client program that calls remote methods
`_Stub` suffix (e.g., `ProductImpl_Stub`)	A stub class that is automatically generated by the `rmic` program
`_Skel` suffix (e.g., `ProductImpl_Skel`)	A skeleton class that is automatically generated by the `rmic` program; needed for SDK 1.1.

You need to generate stubs for the `ProductImpl` class. Recall that stubs are the classes that marshal (encode and send) the parameters and marshal the results of method calls across the network. The programmer never uses those classes directly. Moreover, they need *not* be written by hand. The `rmic` tool generates them automatically, as in the following example.

```
rmic -v1.2 ProductImpl
```

This call to the `rmic` tool generates a class file `ProductImpl_Stub.class`. If your class is in a package, you must call `rmic` with the full package name.

If your client uses SDK 1.1, you should instead call

```
rmic ProductImpl
```

Then, two files are generated: the stub file and a second class file named `ProductImpl_Skel.class`. This "skeleton" file is no longer necessary with the Java 2 platform.

NOTE: Remember to first compile the source file with `javac` before running `rmic`. If you are generating stubs for a class in a package, you must give `rmic` the full package name.

Locating Server Objects

To access a remote object that exists on the server, the client needs a local stub object. How can the client request such a stub? The most common method is to call a remote method of another server object and to get a stub object as a return value. There is, however, a chicken-and-egg problem here. The *first* server object needs to be located some other way. The Sun RMI library provides a *bootstrap registry service* to locate the first server object.

A server program registers objects with the bootstrap registry service, and the client retrieves stubs to those objects. You register a server object by giving the bootstrap registry service a reference to the object and a *name*. The name is a string that is (hopefully) unique.

```
// server
ProductImpl p1 = new ProductImpl("Blackwell Toaster");
Naming.bind("toaster", p1);
```

The client code gets a stub to access that server object by specifying the server name and the object name in the following way:

```
// client
Product p
   = (Product)Naming.lookup("rmi://yourserver.com/toaster");
```

RMI URLs start with `rmi://` and are followed by a server, an optional port number, another slash, and the name of the remote object. Another example is:

```
rmi://localhost:99/central_warehouse
```

By default, the port number is 1099.

> NOTE: Because it is notoriously difficult to keep names unique in a global registry, you should not use this technique as the general method for locating objects on the server. Instead, there should be relatively few named server objects registered with the bootstrap service. These should be objects that can locate other objects for you. In our example, we temporarily violate this rule and register relatively trivial objects to show you the mechanics for registering and locating objects.

For security reasons, an application can bind, unbind, or rebind registry objects references only if it runs on the same host as the registry. This prevents hostile clients from changing the registry information. However, any client can look up objects.

The code in Example 5–1 through Example 5–3 shows a complete server program that registers two `Product` objects under the names `toaster` and `microwave`.

> TIP: If you compare our server with the server examples in the tutorial documentation, you will note that we do not install a security manager in the server. Contrary to the statements in the tutorial, a security manager is neither necessary nor particularly beneficial for RMI servers. Since adding a security manager yields yet another fertile source for configuration errors, we suggest that you only install a security manager if you want to constrain the actions in the server implementation or if the server is itself an RMI client of another server.

Example 5–1: ProductServer.java

```
1. import java.rmi.*;
2. import java.rmi.server.*;
3.
4. /**
5.    This server program instantiates two remote objects,
6.    registers them with the naming service, and waits for
7.    clients to invoke methods on the remote objects.
8. */
9. public class ProductServer
10. {
11.    public static void main(String args[])
12.    {
13.       try
14.       {
15.          System.out.println
16.             ("Constructing server implementations...");
17.
18.          ProductImpl p1
```

```
19.                = new ProductImpl("Blackwell Toaster");
20.          ProductImpl p2
21.                = new ProductImpl("ZapXpress Microwave Oven");
22.
23.          System.out.println
24.             ("Binding server implementations to registry...");
25.
26.          Naming.rebind("toaster", p1);
27.          Naming.rebind("microwave", p2);
28.
29.          System.out.println
30.             ("Waiting for invocations from clients...");
31.       }
32.       catch(Exception e)
33.       {
34.          e.printStackTrace();
35.       }
36.    }
37. }
```

Example 5–2: ProductImpl.java

```
1. import java.rmi.*;
2. import java.rmi.server.*;
3.
4. /**
5.    This is the implementation class for the remote product
6.    objects.
7. */
8. public class ProductImpl
9.    extends UnicastRemoteObject
10.    implements Product
11. {
12.    /**
13.       Constructs a product implementation
14.       @param n the product name
15.    */
16.    public ProductImpl(String n) throws RemoteException
17.    {
18.       name = n;
19.    }
20.
21.    public String getDescription() throws RemoteException
22.    {
23.       return "I am a " + name + ". Buy me!";
24.    }
25.
26.    private String name;
27. }
```

Example 5–3: Product.java

```
1. import java.rmi.*;
2.
3. /**
4.    The interface for remote product objects.
5. */
6. public interface Product extends Remote
7. {
8.    /**
9.       Gets the description of this product.
10.      @return the product description
11.   */
12.   String getDescription() throws RemoteException;
13. }
```

Starting the server

Our server program isn't quite ready to run, yet. Because it uses the bootstrap RMI registry, that service must be available. To start the RMI registry under UNIX, you execute the statement

```
rmiregistry &
```

Under Windows, call

```
start rmiregistry
```

at a DOS prompt or from the Run dialog box. (The `start` command is a Windows command that starts a program in a new window.)

Now you are ready to start the server. Under UNIX, use the command:

```
java ProductServer &
```

Under Windows, use the command:

```
start java ProductServer
```

If you run the server program as

```
java ProductServer
```

then the program will never exit normally. This seems strange—after all, the program just creates two objects and registers them. Actually, the `main` function does exit immediately after registration, as you would expect. But, when you create an object of a class that extends `UnicastRemoteObject`, a separate thread is started that keeps the program alive indefinitely. Thus, the program stays around in order to allow clients to connect to it.

TIP: The Windows version of the SDK contains a command, `javaw`, that starts the bytecode interpreter as a separate Windows process and keeps it running. Some sources recommend that you use `javaw`, not `start java`, to run a Java session in the background in Windows for RMI. Doing so is not a good idea, for two reasons.

Windows has no tool to kill a `javaw` background process—it does not show up in the task list. It turns out that you need to kill and restart the bootstrap registry service when you change the stub of a registered class. To kill a process that you started with the `start` command, all you have to do is click on the window and press CTRL+C.

There is another important reason to use the `start` command. When you run a server process by using `javaw`, messages sent to the output or error streams are discarded. In particular, they *are not* displayed *anywhere.* If you want to see output or error messages, use `start` instead. Then, error messages at least show up on the console. And trust us, you will want to see these messages. There are lots of things that can go wrong when you experiment with RMI. The most common error is probably that you forget to run `rmic`. Then, the server complains about missing stubs. If you use `javaw`, you won't see that error message, and you'll scratch your head wondering why the client can't find the server objects.

Before writing the client program, let's verify that we succeeded in registering the remote objects. The `Naming` class has a method `list` that returns a list of all currently registered names. Example 5–4 shows a simple program that lists the names in the registry.

In our case, its output is

```
rmi:/toaster
rmi:/microwave
```

Example 5–4: ShowBindings.java

```
1. import java.rmi.*;
2. import java.rmi.server.*;
3.
4. /**
5.    This programs shows all bindings in the naming service.
6. */
7. public class ShowBindings
8. {
9.    public static void main(String[] args)
10.   {
11.       try
12.       {
13.           String[] bindings = Naming.list("");
14.           for (int i = 0; i < bindings.length; i++)
15.               System.out.println(bindings[i]);
16.       }
17.       catch(Exception e)
18.       {
19.           e.printStackTrace();
20.       }
21.   }
22. }
```

The Client Side

Now, we can write the client program that asks each newly registered product object to print its description.

Client programs that use RMI should install a security manager to control the activities of the dynamically loaded stubs. The `RMISecurityManager` is such a security manager. You install it with the instruction

```
System.setSecurityManager(new RMISecurityManager());
```

> **NOTE:** If all classes (including stubs) are available locally, then you do not actually need a security manager. If you know all class files of your program at deployment time, you can deploy them all locally. However, it often happens that the server program evolves and new classes are added over time. Then you benefit from dynamic class loading. Any time you load code from another source, you need a security manager.
>
> Applets already have a security manager which is able to control the stub classes. When using RMI from an applet, you do not install another security manager. However, for applications that are RMI clients, you should use the `RMISecurityManager`.

Example 5–5 shows the complete client program. The client simply obtains references to two `Product` objects in the RMI registry and invokes the `getDescription` method on both objects.

Example 5–5: ProductClient.java

```
1. import java.rmi.*;
2. import java.rmi.server.*;
3.
4. /**
5.    This program demonstrates how to call a remote method
6.    on two objects that are located through the naming service.
7. */
8. public class ProductClient
9. {
10.    public static void main(String[] args)
11.    {
12.       System.setProperty("java.security.policy", "client.policy");
13.       System.setSecurityManager(new RMISecurityManager());
14.       String url = "rmi://localhost/";
15.          // change to "rmi://yourserver.com/"
16.          // when server runs on remote machine
17.          // yourserver.com
18.       try
19.       {
20.          Product c1 = (Product)Naming.lookup(url + "toaster");
21.          Product c2 = (Product)Naming.lookup(url + "microwave");
```

```
22.                System.out.println(c1.getDescription());
23.                System.out.println(c2.getDescription());
24.          }
25.          catch(Exception e)
26.          {
27.                e.printStackTrace();
28.          }
29.      }
30. }
```

Running the client

By default, the `RMISecurityManager` restricts all code in the program from establishing network connections. But the program needs to make network connections

- To reach the RMI registry;
- To contact the server objects.

NOTE: Once the client program is deployed, it also needs permission to load its stub classes. We address this issue later when we discuss deployment.

To allow the client to connect to the RMI registry and the server object, you need to supply a *policy file*. We discuss policy files in greater detail in Chapter 9. For now, just use and modify the samples that we supply. Here is a policy file that allows an application to make any network connection to a port with port number at least 1024. (The RMI port is 1099 by default, and the server objects also use ports ≥ 1024.)

```
grant
{
    permission java.net.SocketPermission
        "*:1024-65535", "connect";
};
```

NOTE: Multiple server objects on the same server can share a port. However, if a remote call is made and the port is busy, another port is opened automatically. Thus, you should expect somewhat fewer ports to be used than the remote objects on the server.

In the client program, we instruct the security manager to read the policy file, by setting the `java.security.policy` property to the file name.

```
System.setProperty("java.security.policy", "client.policy");
```

Alternatively, you can specify the system property setting on the command line:

```
java -Djava.security.policy=client.policy ProductClient
```

NOTE: In SDK 1.1, a policy file was not required for RMI clients.

If the RMI registry and server are still running, you can proceed to run the client. Or, if you want to start from scratch, kill the RMI registry and the server. Then follow these steps:

1. Compile the source files for the interface, implementation, client, and server classes.

   ```
   javac Product*.java
   ```

2. Run `rmic` on the implementation class.

   ```
   rmic -v1.2 ProductImpl
   ```

3. Start the RMI registry:

   ```
   rmiregistry &
   ```

   or

   ```
   start rmiregistry
   ```

4. Start the server:

   ```
   java ProductServer &
   ```

   or

   ```
   start java ProductServer
   ```

5. Run the client:

   ```
   java ProductClient
   ```

   (Make sure the `client.policy` file is in the current directory.)

The program simply prints

```
I am a Blackwell Toaster. Buy me!
I am a ZapXpress Microwave Oven. Buy me!
```

This output doesn't seem all that impressive, but consider what goes on behind the scenes when the client program executes the call to the getDescription method. The client program has a reference to a stub object that it obtained from the lookup method. It calls the getDescription method, which sends a network message to a receiver object on the server side. The receiver object invokes the getDescription method on the ProductImpl object located on the server. That method computes a string. The receiver sends that string across the network. The stub receives it and returns it as the result. See Figure 5–5.

Figure 5–5: Calling the remote getDescription method

`java.rmi.Naming`

- `static Remote lookup(String url)`
  returns the remote object for the URL. Throws the `NotBound` exception if the name is not currently bound.
- `static void bind(String name, Remote obj)`
  binds `name` to the remote object `obj`. Throws an `AlreadyBoundException` if the object is already bound.
- `static void unbind(String name)`
  unbinds the name. Throws the `NotBound` exception if the name is not currently bound.
- `static void rebind(String name, Remote obj)`
  binds `name` to the remote object `obj`. Replaces any existing binding.
- `static String[] list(String url)`
  returns an array of strings of the URLs in the registry located at the given URL. The array contains a snapshot of the names present in the registry.

Preparing for Deployment

Deploying an application that uses RMI can be tricky because so many things can go wrong, and because the error messages that you get when something does go wrong are so poor. We have found that it really pays off to stage the deployment locally. In this preparatory step, separate the class files into three subdirectories:

```
server
download
client
```

The `server` directory contains all files that are needed to *run the server*. You will later move these files to the machine running the server process. In our example, the `server` directory contains the following files:

```
server:
    ProductServer.class
    ProductImpl.class
    Product.class
    ProductImpl_Stub.class
```

CAUTION: Add the stub classes to the `server` directory. They are needed when the server registers the implementation object. Contrary to popular belief, the server will not locate them in the download directory, even if you set the codebase.

The `download` directory contains those class files that will be loaded into the client, *as well as the classes they depend on.* In our example, you must add the following classes to the download directory:

```
download:
    ProductImpl_Stub.class
    Product.class
```

If your program was written with SDK 1.1, then you also need to supply the skeleton classes (such as `ProductImpl_Skel.class`). You will later place these files on a web server.

CAUTION: In addition to the interface stubs, your download directory must include the class files on which the stub files depend. This includes the remote interfaces (such as `Product`) and any classes or interfaces that occur as method parameter or return types. If you don't include those class files, then the server will mysteriously die when trying to register the server class.

Finally, the `client` directory contains the files that are needed to *start the client.* These are:

```
client:
   ProductClient.class
   Product.class
   client.policy
```

You will deploy these files on the client computer.

> CAUTION: You must deploy the class files for the remote interfaces (such as
> Product) to the client. You must also deploy all class files on which these inter-
> faces depend. If you don't, then the client will not load. It does not download
> these classes.

Now you have all class files partitioned correctly, and you can test that they can all be loaded.

We assume that you can start a web server on your computer. If you installed Tomcat to try out the servlet in Chapter 3, then simply use Tomcat and make the download directory a subdirectory of the webapps directory. Alternatively, you can get a lightweight server from ftp://java.sun.com/pub/jdk1.1/rmi/ class-server.zip. That server is not a full-blown web server, but it is easier to install and has enough functionality to serve class files.

First, move the download directory into the web documents directory of the web server (or establish a symbolic link).

Next, edit the client.policy file. It must give the client these permissions:

- To connect to ports 1024 and above to reach the RMI registry and the server implementations;

- To connect to the HTTP port (usually 80 or 8080) to load the stub class files.

Change the file to look like this:

```
grant
{
   permission java.net.SocketPermission
      "*:1024-65535", "connect";
   permission java.net.SocketPermission
      "*:80", "connect";
};
```

Finally, you are ready to test your setup.

1. Start the web server.

2. Start a new shell. Make sure that the *class path is not set* to anything. Change to a directory that contains *no class files*. Then start the RMI registry.

CAUTION: If you just want to test out your program and have client, server, and stub class files in a single directory, then you can start the RMI registry in that directory. However, for deployment, make sure to start the registry in a shell with *no class path* and in a directory with *no class files.* Otherwise, the RMI registry may find spurious class files which will confuse it when it should download additional classes from a different source. There is a reason for this behavior; see http://java.sun.com/products/jdk/1.2/docs/guide/rmi/codebase.html. In a nutshell, each stub object is annotated with the code base from which supporting classes can be downloaded. If the RMI registry finds the class on its class path, that codebase annotation is empty, and supporting classes will not be located from another source.

RMI registry confusion is a major source of grief for RMI deployment. The easiest way of protecting yourself is to make sure that the RMI registry cannot find any classes.

3. Start a new shell. Change to the `server` directory. Start the server, giving a URL to the download directory as the value of the `java.rmi.server.codebase` property:

```
java
    -Djava.rmi.server.codebase=http://localhost/download/
    ProductServer &
```

If you use Tomcat, you need to use the URL

```
http://localhost:8080/download/
```

CAUTION: It is very important that you make sure that *the URL ends with a slash (/).*

4. Change to the `client` directory. Make sure the `client.policy` file is in that directory. Start the client.

```
java -Djava.security.policy=client.policy ProductClient
```

If both the server and the client started up without a hitch, then you are ready to go to the next step and deploy the classes on a separate client and server. If not, you need to do some more tweaking.

TIP: If you do not want to install a web server locally, you can use a file URL to test class loading. However, the setup is a bit trickier. Add the line

```
permission java.io.FilePermission
    "downloadDirectory", "read";
```

to your client policy file. Here, the download directory is the full path name to the download directory, enclosed in quotes, and ending in a minus sign (to denote all files in that directory and its subdirectories). In Windows file names, you have to double each backslash. For example,

```
permission java.io.FilePermission
    "/home/test/download/-", "read";
```

or (under Windows)

```
permission java.io. FilePermission
  "c:\\home\\test\\download\\-", "read";
```

Start the RMI registry, then the server with

```
java -Djava.rmi.server.codebase=file://home/test/download/
   ProductServer &
```

or

```
start java
   -Djava.rmi.server.codebase=file:/c:\home\test\download/
   ProductServer
```

(Remember to add a slash at the end of the URL.) Then start the client.

Deploying the Program

Now that you have tested the deployment of your program, you are ready to distribute it onto the actual clients and servers.

Move the classes in the download directory to the web server. Make sure to use that URL when starting the server. Move the classes in the server directory onto your server and start the RMI registry and the server.

Your server setup is now finalized. But you need to make two changes in the client. First, edit the policy file and replace * with your server name:

```
grant
{
    permission java.net.SocketPermission
        "yourserver.com:1024-65535", "connect";
    permission java.net.SocketPermission
        "yourserver.com:80", "connect";
};
```

Finally, replace localhost in the RMI URL of the client program with the actual server.

```
String url = "rmi://yourserver.com/";
Product c1 = (Product)Naming.lookup(url + "toaster");
. . .
```

Then, recompile the client and try it. If everything works, then congratulations are in order. If not, you may find the following sidebar helpful. It contains a checklist of a number of problems that can commonly arise when trying to get RMI to work.

TIP: In practice, you would not want to hard code the RMI URLs into your program. Instead, you can store them in a property file. We will use that technique in Example 5–13.

RMI Deployment Checklist

Deploying RMI is tough because it either works, or it fails with a very cryptic error message. Judging from the traffic on the RMI discussion list at `http://archives.java.sun.com/archives/rmi-users.html`, many programmers initially run into grief. If you do too, you may find it helpful to check out the following issues. We managed to get every one of them wrong at least once during testing.

- Did you put the stub class files into the server directory?
- Did you put the interface class files into the download and client directory?
- Did you include the dependent classes for each class? For example, in the next section, you will see an interface `Warehouse` that has a method with a parameter of type `Customer`. Be sure to include `Customer.class` whenever you deploy `Warehouse.class`.
- When starting `rmiregistry`, was the `CLASSPATH` unset? Was the current directory free from class files?
- Do you use a policy file when starting the client? Does the policy file contain the correct server names (or * to connect to any host)?
- If you use a `file:` URL for testing, do you specify the correct file name in the policy file? Does it end in a `/-` or `\\-` ? Did you remember to use `\\` for Windows file names?
- Does your codebase URL end in a slash?

Finally, note that the RMI registry remembers the class files that it found as well as those that it failed to find. If you keep adding or removing various class files to test which files are really necessary, make sure to restart `rmiregistry` each time.

Parameter Passing in Remote Methods

You often want to pass parameters to remote objects. This section explains some of the techniques for doing so—along with some of the pitfalls.

Passing Nonremote Objects

When a remote object is passed from the server to the client, the client receives a stub. Using the stub, it can manipulate the server object by invoking remote methods. The object, however, stays on the server. It is also possible to pass and return *any* objects via a remote method call, not just those that implement the `Remote` interface. For example, the `getDescription` method of the preceding section returned a `String` object. That string was created on the server and had to be transported to the client. Since `String` does not implement the `Remote` interface, the client cannot return a string stub object. Instead, the client gets a *copy* of the string. Then, after the call, the client has its own `String` object to work with. This means that there is no need for any further connection to any object on the server to deal with that string.

Whenever an object that is not a remote object needs to be transported from one Java virtual machine to another, the Java virtual machine makes a copy and sends that copy across the network connection. This technique is very different from parameter passing in a local method. When you pass objects into a local method or return them as method results, only object *references* are passed. However, object references are memory addresses of objects in the local Java virtual machine. This information is meaningless to a different Java virtual machine.

It is not difficult to imagine how a copy of a string can be transported across a network. The RMI mechanism can also make copies of more complex objects, provided they are *serializable*. RMI uses the serialization mechanism described in Chapter 12 of Volume 1 to send objects across a network connection. This means that only the information in any classes that implement the `Serializable` interface can be copied. The following program shows the copying of parameters and return values in action. This program is a simple application that lets a user shop for a gift. On the client, the user runs a program that gathers information about the gift recipient, in this case, age, sex, and hobbies (see Figure 5–6).

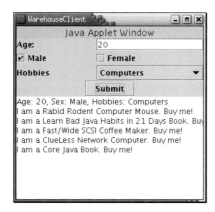

Figure 5–6: Obtaining product suggestions from the server

An object of type `Customer` is then sent to the server. Since `Customer` is not a remote object, a copy of the object is made on the server. The server program sends back an array list of products. The array list contains those products that match the customer profile, and it always contains that one item that will delight anyone, namely, a copy of the book *Core Java*. Again, `ArrayList` is not a remote class, so the array list is copied from the server back to its client. As described in Chapter 12 of volume 1, the serialization mechanism makes copies of all objects that are referenced inside a copied object. In our case, it makes a copy of all array list entries as well. We added an extra complexity: the entries are actually remote `Product` objects. Thus, the recipient gets a copy of the array list, filled with stub objects to the products on the server (see Figure 5–7).

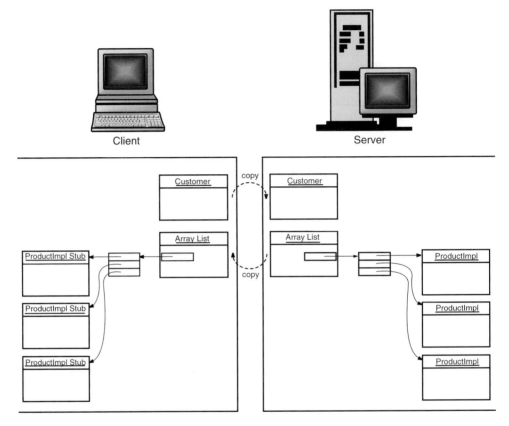

Figure 5–7: Copying local parameter and result objects

To summarize, remote objects are passed across the network as stubs. Non-remote objects are copied. All of this is automatic and requires no programmer intervention.

Whenever code calls a remote method, the stub makes a package that contains copies of all parameter values and sends it to the server, using the object serialization mechanism to marshal the parameters. The server unmarshals them. Naturally, the process can be quite slow—especially when the parameter objects are large.

Let's look at the complete program. First, we have the interfaces for the product and warehouse services, as shown in Example 5–6 and Example 5–7.

Example 5–6: Product.java

```
1. import java.rmi.*;
2.
3. /**
4.    The interface for remote product objects.
```

```
5. */
6. public interface Product extends Remote
7. {
8.      /**
9.          Gets the description of this product.
10.         @return the product description
11.     */
12.     String getDescription() throws RemoteException;
13.
14.     final int MALE = 1;
15.     final int FEMALE = 2;
16.     final int BOTH = MALE + FEMALE;
17. }
```

Example 5–7: Warehouse.java

```
1. import java.rmi.*;
2. import java.util.*;
3.
4. /**
5.     The remote interface for a warehouse with products.
6. */
7. public interface Warehouse extends Remote
8. {
9.      /**
10.         Gets products that are good matches for a customer.
11.         @param c the customer to match
12.         @return an array list of matching products
13.     */
14.     ArrayList find(Customer c) throws RemoteException;
15. }
```

Example 5–8 shows the implementation for the product service. Products store a description, an age range, the gender targeted (male, female, or both), and the matching hobby. Note that this class implements the getDescription method advertised in the Product interface, and it also implements another method, match, which is not a part of that interface. The match method is an example of a *local method,* a method that can be called only from the local program, not remotely. Since the match method is local, it need not be prepared to throw a RemoteException.

Example 5–9 contains the code for the Customer class. Note once again that Customer is not a remote class—none of its methods can be executed remotely. However, the class is serializable. Therefore, objects of this class can be transported from one virtual machine to another.

Examples 5–10 and 5–11 shows the interface and implementation for the warehouse service. Like the ProductImpl class, the WarehouseImpl class has local and remote methods. The add and read methods are local; they are used by the server to add products to the warehouse. The `find` method is remote; it is used to find items in the warehouse.

To illustrate that the `Customer` object is actually copied, the `find` method of the `WarehouseImpl` class clears the customer object it receives. When the remote method returns, the `WarehouseClient` displays the customer object that it sent to the server. As you will see, that object has not changed. The server cleared only *its copy*. In this case, the `reset` operation serves no useful purpose except to demonstrate that local objects are copied when they are passed as parameters.

In general, the methods of server classes such as `ProductImpl` and `WarehouseImpl` should be synchronized. Then, it is possible for multiple client stubs to make simultaneous calls to a server object, even if some of the methods change the state of the server. (See Chapter 2 for more details on synchronized methods.) In Example 5–11, we synchronize the methods of the `WarehouseImpl` class because it is conceivable that the local `add` and the remote `find` methods are called simultaneously. We don't synchronize the methods of the `ProductImpl` class because the product server objects don't change their state. Example 5–12 shows the server program that creates a warehouse object and registers it with the bootstrap registry service.

NOTE: Remember that you must start the registry and the server program and keep both running before you start the client.

Example 5–13 shows the code for the client. When the user clicks on the "Submit" button, a new customer object is generated and passed to the remote `find` method. Then, the customer record is displayed in the text area (to prove that the `clear` call in the server did not affect it). Finally, the product descriptions of the returned products in the array list are added to the text area. Note that each `getDescription` call is again a remote method invocation. That would not be a good design in practice—you would normally pass small objects such as product descriptions by value. But we want to demonstrate that a remote object is automatically replaced by a stub during marshalling.

TIP: If you start the server with

```
java -Djava.rmi.server.logCalls=true WarehouseServer &
```

then the server logs all remote method calls on its console. Try it—you'll get a good impression of the RMI traffic.

Example 5–8: ProductImpl.java

```
1. import java.rmi.*;
2. import java.rmi.server.*;
```

```
3.
4. /**
5.    This is the implementation class for the remote product
6.    objects.
7. */
8. public class ProductImpl
9.    extends UnicastRemoteObject
10.   implements Product
11. {
12.    /**
13.       Constructs a product implementation
14.       @param n the product name
15.       @param s the suggested sex (MALE, FEMALE, or BOTH)
16.       @param age1 the lower bound for the suggested age
17.       @param age2 the upper bound for the suggested age
18.       @param h the hobby matching this product
19.    */
20.    public ProductImpl(String n, int s, int age1, int age2,
21.       String h) throws RemoteException
22.    {
23.       name = n;
24.       ageLow = age1;
25.       ageHigh = age2;
26.       sex = s;
27.       hobby = h;
28.    }
29.
30.    /**
31.       Checks whether this product is a good match for a
32.       customer. Note that this method is a local method since
33.       it is not part of the Product interface.
34.       @param c the customer to match against this product
35.       @return true if this product is appropriate for the
36.       customer
37.    */
38.    public boolean match(Customer c)
39.    {
40.       if (c.getAge() < ageLow || c.getAge() > ageHigh)
41.          return false;
42.       if (!c.hasHobby(hobby)) return false;
43.       if ((sex & c.getSex()) == 0) return false;
44.       return true;
45.    }
46.
47.    public String getDescription() throws RemoteException
48.    {
49.       return "I am a " + name + ". Buy me!";
50.    }
51.
52.    private String name;
53.    private int ageLow;
54.    private int ageHigh;
```

```
55.    private int sex;
56.    private String hobby;
57. }
```

Example 5–9: Customer.java

```
1. import java.io.*;
2.
3. /**
4.    Description of a customer. Note that customer objects are not
5.    remote--the class does not implement a remote interface.
6. */
7. public class Customer implements Serializable
8. {
9.    /**
10.       Constructs a customer.
11.       @param theAge the customer's age
12.       @param theSex the customer's sex (MALE or FEMALE)
13.       @param theHobbies the customer's hobbies
14.    */
15.    public Customer(int theAge, int theSex, String[] theHobbies)
16.    {
17.       age = theAge;
18.       sex = theSex;
19.       hobbies = theHobbies;
20.    }
21.
22.    /**
23.       Gets the customer's age.
24.       @return the age
25.    */
26.    public int getAge() { return age; }
27.
28.    /**
29.       Gets the customer's sex
30.       @return MALE or FEMALE
31.    */
32.    public int getSex() { return sex; }
33.
34.    /**
35.       Tests whether this customer has a particular hobby.
36.       @param aHobby the hobby to test
37.       @return true if this customer has the hobby
38.    */
39.    public boolean hasHobby(String aHobby)
40.    {
41.       if (aHobby == "") return true;
42.       for (int i = 0; i < hobbies.length; i++)
43.          if (hobbies[i].equals(aHobby)) return true;
44.
45.       return false;
46.    }
```

```
47.
48.    /**
49.       Resets this customer record to default values.
50.    */
51.    public void reset()
52.    {
53.       age = 0;
54.       sex = 0;
55.       hobbies = null;
56.    }
57.
58.    public String toString()
59.    {
60.       String result = "Age: " + age + ", Sex: ";
61.       if (sex == Product.MALE) result += "Male";
62.       else if (sex == Product.FEMALE) result += "Female";
63.       else result += "Male or Female";
64.       result += ", Hobbies:";
65.       for (int i = 0; i < hobbies.length; i++)
66.          result += " " + hobbies[i];
67.       return result;
68.    }
69.
70.    private int age;
71.    private int sex;
72.    private String[] hobbies;
73. }
```

Example 5–10: Warehouse.java

```
1. import java.rmi.*;
2. import java.util.*;
3.
4. /**
5.    The remote interface for a warehouse with products.
6. */
7. public interface Warehouse extends Remote
8. {
9.    /**
10.       Gets products that are good matches for a customer.
11.       @param c the customer to match
12.       @return an array list of matching products
13.    */
14.    ArrayList find(Customer c) throws RemoteException;
15. }
```

Example 5–11: WarehouseImpl.java

```
1. import java.io.*;
2. import java.rmi.*;
3. import java.util.*;
4. import java.rmi.server.*;
5. import java.util.*;
```

```
6.
7. /**
8.    This class is the implementation for the remote
9.    Warehouse interface.
10. */
11. public class WarehouseImpl
12.    extends UnicastRemoteObject
13.    implements Warehouse
14. {
15.    /**
16.       Constructs a warehouse implementation.
17.    */
18.    public WarehouseImpl()
19.       throws RemoteException
20.    {
21.       products = new ArrayList();
22.       coreJavaBook = new ProductImpl("Core Java Book",
23.          0, 200, Product.BOTH, "Computers");
24.    }
25.
26.    /**
27.       Reads in a set of product descriptions. Each line has t
28.       the format
29.       name|sex|age1|age2|hobby, e.g.
30.       Blackwell Toaster|BOTH|18|200|Household
31.       @param reader the reader to read from
32.    */
33.    public void read(BufferedReader reader) throws IOException
34.    {
35.       String line;
36.       while ((line = reader.readLine()) != null)
37.       {
38.          StringTokenizer tokenizer = new StringTokenizer(line,
39.             "|");
40.          String name = tokenizer.nextToken();
41.          String s = tokenizer.nextToken();
42.          int sex = 0;
43.          if (s.equals("MALE")) sex = Product.MALE;
44.          else if (s.equals("FEMALE")) sex = Product.FEMALE;
45.          else if (s.equals("BOTH")) sex = Product.BOTH;
46.          int age1 = Integer.parseInt(tokenizer.nextToken());
47.          int age2 = Integer.parseInt(tokenizer.nextToken());
48.          String hobby = tokenizer.nextToken();
49.          add(new ProductImpl(name, sex, age1, age2, hobby));
50.       }
51.    }
52.
53.    /**
54.       Add a product to the warehouse. Note that this is a local
55.       method.
56.       @param p the product to add
57.    */
```

```
58.   public synchronized void add(ProductImpl p)
59.   {
60.       products.add(p);
61.   }
62.
63.   public synchronized ArrayList find(Customer c)
64.       throws RemoteException
65.   {
66.       ArrayList result = new ArrayList();
67.       // add all matching products
68.       for (int i = 0; i < products.size(); i++)
69.       {
70.           ProductImpl p = (ProductImpl)products.get(i);
71.           if (p.match(c)) result.add(p);
72.       }
73.       // add the product that is a good match for everyone
74.       result.add(coreJavaBook);
75.
76.       // we reset c just to show that c is a copy of the
77.       // client object
78.       c.reset();
79.       return result;
80.   }
81.
82.   private ArrayList products;
83.   private ProductImpl coreJavaBook;
84. }
```

Example 5–12: WarehouseServer.java

```
1. import java.io.*;
2. import java.rmi.*;
3. import java.rmi.server.*;
4.
5. /**
6.    This server program instantiates a remote warehouse
7.    objects, registers it with the naming service, and waits
8.    for clients to invoke methods.
9. */
10. public class WarehouseServer
11. {
12.    public static void main(String[] args)
13.    {
14.       try
15.       {
16.          System.out.println
17.             ("Constructing server implementations...");
18.
19.          WarehouseImpl w = new WarehouseImpl();
20.          w.read(new BufferedReader(new
21.             FileReader("products.dat")));
22.
```

```
23.          System.out.println
24.             ("Binding server implementations to registry...");
25.
26.          Naming.rebind("central_warehouse", w);
27.
28.          System.out.println
29.             ("Waiting for invocations from clients...");
30.       }
31.       catch(Exception e)
32.       {
33.          e.printStackTrace();
34.       }
35.    }
36. }
```

Example 5–13: WarehouseClient.java

```
1. import java.awt.*;
2. import java.awt.event.*;
3. import java.io.*;
4. import java.rmi.*;
5. import java.rmi.server.*;
6. import java.util.*;
7. import javax.swing.*;
8.
9. /**
10.    The client for the warehouse program.
11. */
12. public class WarehouseClient
13. {
14.    public static void main(String[] args)
15.    {
16.       System.setProperty("java.security.policy", "client.policy");
17.       System.setSecurityManager(new RMISecurityManager());
18.       JFrame frame = new WarehouseClientFrame();
19.       frame.setDefaultCloseOperation(JFrame.EXIT_ON_CLOSE);
20.       frame.show();
21.    }
22. }
23.
24. /**
25.    A frame to select the customer's age, sex, and hobbies, and to
26.    show the matching products resulting from a remote call to the
27.    warehouse.
28. */
29. class WarehouseClientFrame extends JFrame
30. {
31.    public WarehouseClientFrame()
32.    {
33.       setTitle("WarehouseClient");
34.       setSize(WIDTH, HEIGHT);
35.       initUI();
36.
```

```
37.        try
38.        {
39.            Properties props = new Properties();
40.            String fileName = "WarehouseClient.properties";
41.            FileInputStream in = new FileInputStream(fileName);
42.            props.load(in);
43.            String url = props.getProperty("warehouse.url");
44.            if (url == null)
45.                url = "rmi://localhost/central_warehouse";
46.
47.            centralWarehouse = (Warehouse)Naming.lookup(url);
48.        }
49.        catch(Exception e)
50.        {
51.            System.out.println("Error: Can't connect to warehouse. " + e);
52.        }
53.    }
54.
55.    /**
56.        Initializes the user interface.
57.    */
58.    private void initUI()
59.    {
60.        getContentPane().setLayout(new GridBagLayout());
61.
62.        GridBagConstraints gbc = new GridBagConstraints();
63.        gbc.fill = GridBagConstraints.HORIZONTAL;
64.        gbc.weightx = 100;
65.        gbc.weighty = 0;
66.
67.        add(new JLabel("Age:"), gbc, 0, 0, 1, 1);
68.        age = new JTextField(4);
69.        age.setText("20");
70.        add(age, gbc, 1, 0, 1, 1);
71.
72.        male = new JCheckBox("Male", true);
73.        female = new JCheckBox("Female", true);
74.        add(male, gbc, 0, 1, 1, 1);
75.        add(female, gbc, 1, 1, 1, 1);
76.
77.        add(new JLabel("Hobbies"), gbc, 0, 2, 1, 1);
78.        String[] choices = { "Gardening", "Beauty",
79.            "Computers", "Household", "Sports" };
80.        gbc.fill = GridBagConstraints.BOTH;
81.        hobbies = new JComboBox(choices);
82.        add(hobbies, gbc, 1, 2, 1, 1);
83.
84.        gbc.fill = GridBagConstraints.NONE;
85.        JButton submitButton = new JButton("Submit");
86.        add(submitButton, gbc, 0, 3, 2, 1);
87.        submitButton.addActionListener(new
88.            ActionListener()
```

```
89.              {
90.                 public void actionPerformed(ActionEvent evt)
91.                 {
92.                    callWarehouse();
93.                 }
94.              });
95.
96.         gbc.weighty = 100;
97.         gbc.fill = GridBagConstraints.BOTH;
98.         result = new JTextArea(4, 40);
99.         result.setEditable(false);
100.        add(result, gbc, 0, 4, 2, 1);
101.     }
102.
103.     /**
104.        Add a component to this frame.
105.        @param c the component to add
106.        @param gbc the grid bag constraints
107.        @param x the grid bax column
108.        @param y the grid bag row
109.        @param w the number of grid bag columns spanned
110.        @param h the number of grid bag rows spanned
111.     */
112.     private void add(Component c, GridBagConstraints gbc,
113.        int x, int y, int w, int h)
114.     {  gbc.gridx = x;
115.        gbc.gridy = y;
116.        gbc.gridwidth = w;
117.        gbc.gridheight = h;
118.        getContentPane().add(c, gbc);
119.     }
120.
121.     /**
122.        Call the remote warehouse to find matching products.
123.     */
124.     private void callWarehouse()
125.     {
126.        try
127.        {
128.          Customer c = new Customer(Integer.parseInt(age.getText()),
129.               (male.isSelected() ? Product.MALE : 0)
130.               + (female.isSelected() ? Product.FEMALE : 0),
131.               new String[] { (String)hobbies.getSelectedItem() });
132.          ArrayList recommendations = centralWarehouse.find(c);
133.          result.setText(c + "\n");
134.          for (int i = 0; i < recommendations.size(); i++)
135.          {
136.             Product p = (Product)recommendations.get(i);
137.             String t = p.getDescription() + "\n";
138.             result.append(t);
139.          }
140.       }
```

```
141.        catch(Exception e)
142.        {
143.            result.setText("Exception: " + e);
144.        }
145.    }
146.
147.    private static final int WIDTH = 300;
148.    private static final int HEIGHT = 300;
149.
150.    private Warehouse centralWarehouse;
151.    private JTextField age;
152.    private JCheckBox male;
153.    private JCheckBox female;
154.    private JComboBox hobbies;
155.    private JTextArea result;
156. }
```

Passing Remote Objects

Passing remote objects from the server to the client is simple. The client receives a stub object, then saves it in an object variable whose type is the same as the remote interface. The client can now access the actual object on the server through the variable. The client can copy this variable in its own local machine—all those copies are simply references to the same stub. It is important to note that only the *remote interfaces* can be accessed through the stub. A remote interface is any interface extending Remote. All local methods are inaccessible through the stub. (A local method is any method that is not defined in a remote interface.) Local methods can run only on the virtual machine containing the actual object.

Next, stubs are generated only from classes that implement a remote interface, and only the methods specified in the interfaces are provided in the stub classes. If a subclass doesn't implement a remote interface but a superclass does, and an object of the subclass is passed to a remote method, only the superclass methods are accessible. To understand this better, consider the following example. We derive a class BookImpl from ProductImpl.

```
class BookImpl extends ProductImpl
{
    public BookImpl(String title, String theISBN,
        int sex, int age1, int age2, String hobby)
    {
        super(title + " Book", sex, age1, age2, hobby);
        ISBN = theISBN;
    }
    public String getStockCode() { return ISBN; }
    private String ISBN;
}
```

Now, suppose we pass a book object to a remote method, either as a parameter or as a return value. The recipient obtains a stub object. But that stub is not a book stub. Instead, it is a stub to the superclass `ProductImpl` since only that class implements a remote interface (see Figure 5–8). Thus, in this case, the `getStock-Code` method isn't available remotely.

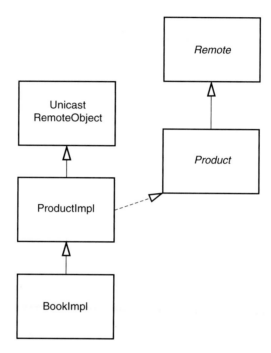

Figure 5–8: Only the `ProductImpl` methods are remote

A remote class can implement multiple interfaces. For example, the `BookImpl` class can implement a second interface in addition to `Product`. Here, we define a remote interface `StockUnit` and have the `BookImpl` class implement it.

```
interface StockUnit extends Remote
{
   public String getStockCode() throws RemoteException;
}

class BookImpl extends ProductImpl implements StockUnit
{
   public BookImpl(String title, String theISBN,
      int sex, int age1, int age2, String hobby)
      throws RemoteException
   {
      super(title + " Book", sex, age1, age2, hobby);
         ISBN = theISBN;
   }

   public String getStockCode() throws RemoteException
   {
```

```
        return ISBN;
   }

   private String ISBN;
}
```

Figure 5–9 shows the inheritance diagram.

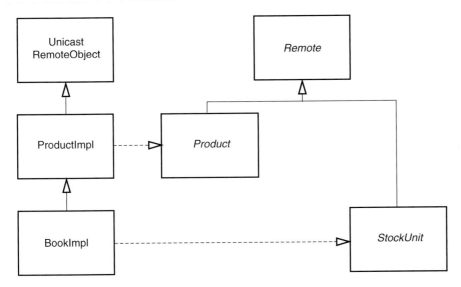

Figure 5–9: `BookImpl` has additional remote methods

Now, when a book object is passed to a remote method, the recipient obtains a stub that has access to the remote methods in both the `Product` and the `Stock-Unit` class. In fact, you can use the `instanceof` operator to find out whether a particular remote object implements an interface. Here is a typical situation where you will use this feature. Suppose you receive a remote object through a variable of type `Product`.

```
ArrayList result = centralWarehouse.find(c);
for (int i = 0; i < result.size(); i++)
{
    Product p = (Product)result.elementAt(i);
    . . .
}
```

Now, the remote object may or may not be a book. We'd like to use `instanceof` to find out whether it is or not. But we can't test

```
if (p instanceof BookImpl) // wrong
{
    BookImpl b = (BookImpl)p;
    . . .
}
```

The object p refers to a stub object, and `BookImpl` is the class of the server object. We could cast the stub object to a `BookImpl_Stub`,

```
if (p instanceof BookImpl_Stub)
{
   BookImpl_Stub b = (BookImpl_Stub)p; // not useful
   . . .
}
```

but that would not do us much good. The stubs are generated mechanically by the `rmic` program for internal use by the RMI mechanism, and clients should not have to think about them. Instead, we cast to the second interface:

```
if (p instanceof StockUnit)
{
   StockUnit s = (StockUnit)p;
   String c = s.getStockCode();
   . . .
}
```

This code tests whether the stub object to which p refers implements the `StockUnit` interface. If so, it calls the `getStockCode` remote method of that interface.

To summarize:

- If an object belonging to a class that implements a remote interface is passed to a remote method, the remote method receives a stub object.

- You can cast that stub object to any of the remote interfaces that the implementation class implements.

- You can call all remote methods defined in those interfaces, but you cannot call any local methods through the stub.

Using Remote Objects in Sets

As we saw in Chapter 2, objects inserted in sets must override the `equals` method. In the case of a hash set or hash table, the `hashCode` method must be defined as well. However, there is a problem when trying to compare remote objects. To find out if two remote objects have the same contents, the call to `equals` would need to contact the servers containing the objects and compare their contents. And that call could fail. But the `equals` method in the class `Object` is not declared to throw a `RemoteException`, whereas all methods in a remote interface must throw that exception. Since a subclass method cannot throw more exceptions than the superclass method it replaces, you cannot define an `equals` method in a remote interface. The same holds for `hashCode`.

Instead, you must rely on the redefinitions of the `equals` and `hashCode` methods in the `RemoteObject` class that is the superclass for all stub and server objects. These methods do not look at the object contents, just at the location of the server objects. The `equals` method of the `RemoteObject` class deems two stubs equal if they refer to the same server object. Two stubs that refer to different server objects are never equal, even if those objects have identical contents. Similarly, the hash code is computed only from the object identifier. Stubs that refer to different server objects will likely have different hash codes, even if the server objects have identical contents.

This limitation refers only to stubs. You can redefine `equals` or `hashCode` for the server object classes. Those methods are called when you are inserting server objects in a collection on the server, but they are never called when you are comparing or hashing stubs. To clarify the difference between client and server behavior, look at the inheritance diagram in Figure 5–10.

The `RemoteObject` class is the base for *both* stub and server classes. On the stub side, you cannot override the `equals` and `hashCode` methods because the stubs are mechanically generated. On the server side, you can override the methods for the implementation classes, but they are only used locally on the server. If you do override these methods, implementation and stub objects are no longer considered identical.

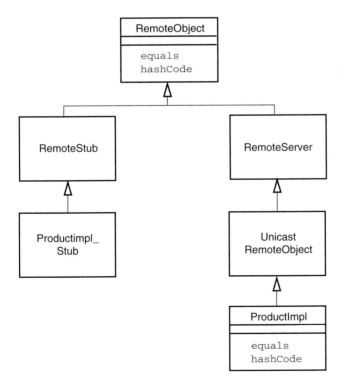

Figure 5–10: Inheritance of `equals` and `hashCode` methods

To summarize: You can use stub objects in hash tables, but you must remember that equality testing and hashing do not take the contents of the remote objects into account.

Cloning Remote Objects

Stubs do not have a `clone` method, so you cannot clone a remote object by invoking `clone` on the stub. The reason is again somewhat technical. If `clone` were to make a remote call to tell the server to clone the implementation object, then the `clone` method would need to throw a `RemoteException`. But the `clone` method in the `Object` superclass promised never to throw any exception except `CloneNotSupportedException`. That is the same limitation that you encountered in the previous section, when you saw that `equals` and `hashCode` don't look up the remote object value at all but just compare stub references. But it makes no sense for `clone` to make another clone of a stub—if you wanted to have another reference to the remote object, you could just copy the stub variable. Therefore, `clone` is simply not defined for stubs.

If you want to clone a remote object, you must write another method, say, `remoteClone`. Place it into the interface that defines the remote object services. Of course, that method may throw a `RemoteException`. In the implementation class, simply define `remoteClone` to call `clone` and return the cloned implementation object.

```
interface Product extends Remote
{
   public Object remoteClone()
      throws RemoteException, CloneNotSupportedException;
   . . .
}

class ProductImpl extends UnicastRemoteObject
   implements Product
{
   public Object remoteClone()
      throws CloneNotSupportedException
   { return clone(); }
   . . .
}
```

Inappropriate Remote Parameters

Suppose we enhance our shopping application by having the application show a picture of each gift. Can we simply add the remote method

```
void paint(Graphics g) throws RemoteException
```

to the `Product` interface? Unfortunately, this code cannot work, and it is important to understand why. The problem is that the `Graphics` class does not implement remote interfaces. Therefore, a copy of an object of type `Graphics` would need to be passed to the remote object, and you can't do this. Why? Well, `Graphics` is an abstract class, and `Graphics` objects are returned via a call to the `getGraphics` method of the `Component` class. This call, in turn, can happen only when you have some subclass that implements a graphics context on a particular platform. Those objects, in turn, need to interact with the native graphics code, and to do so, they must store pointers to the memory blocks that are needed by the native graphics methods. The Java programming language, of course, has no pointers, so this information is stored as integers in the graphics object and is only cast back to pointers in the native peer methods. Now, first of all, the target machine may be a different platform. For example, if the client runs Windows and the server runs X11, then the server does not have the native methods available to render Windows graphics. But even if the server and the client have the same graphics system, the pointer values would not be valid on the server. Therefore, it makes no sense to copy a graphics object. For that reason, the `Graphics` class is not serializable and so cannot be sent via RMI.

Instead, if the server wants to send an image to the client, it has to come up with some other mechanism for transporting the data across the network. As it turns out, this data transport is actually difficult to do for images. The `Image` class is just as device-dependent as the `Graphics` class. We could send the image data as a sequence of bytes in JPEG format. Another alternative is to send an array of integers representing the pixels. In the next section, we show how to solve this problem in a more mundane way: by sending a URL to the client and using a method of the `Applet` class that can read an image from a URL.

Using RMI with Applets

There are a number of special concerns when running RMI with applets. Applets have their own security manager since they run inside a browser. Thus, we do not use the `RMISecurityManager` on the client side.

We must take care where to place the stub and server files. Consider a browser that opens a web page with an `applet` tag. The browser loads the class file referenced in that tag and all other class files as they are needed during execution. The class files are loaded from the same host that contains the web page. Because of applet security restrictions, the applet can make network connections only to its originating host. Therefore, the server objects must reside on the same host as the web page. That is, the same server must store

- Web pages;
- Applet code;
- Stub classes;

- Server objects;
- The RMI registry.

Here is a sample applet that further extends our shopping program. Just like the preceding application, the applet gets the customer information and then selects matching products. However, this applet sends images of the recommended items. As we mentioned previously, it is not easy to send an image from the server to the client because images are stored in a format that depends on the local graphics system. Instead, the server simply sends the client a string with the image file name, and we use the `getImage` method of the `Applet` class to obtain the image (see Figure 5–11).

Figure 5–11: The warehouse applet

Here is how you must distribute the code for this kind of situation:

- `java.rmi.registry.RegistryImpl`—Anywhere on the host; the registry must be running before the applet starts
- `WarehouseServer`—Anywhere on the host; must be running before the applet starts
- `WarehouseImpl`—Can be anywhere on the host as long as `WarehouseServer` can find it
- `WarehouseApplet`—Directory referenced in `APPLET` tag

- Stubs—Must be in the same directory as `WarehouseApplet`

The applet looks for the RMI registry on the same host that contains the applet. To find out its host, it uses the `getCodeBase` and `getHost` methods:

```
String url = "rmi://" + getCodeBase().getHost()
    + "/central_warehouse";
centralWarehouse = (Warehouse)Naming.lookup(url);
```

Example 5–14 shows the code for the applet. Note that the applet does not install a security manager. Example 5–15 shows the applet HTML page. The product and warehouse implementations have been changed slightly to add the image file name field. See the companion code for these straightforward modifications.

Example 5–14: WarehouseApplet.java

```java
1. import java.awt.*;
2. import java.awt.event.*;
3. import java.io.*;
4. import java.rmi.*;
5. import java.rmi.server.*;
6. import java.util.*;
7. import javax.swing.*;
8.
9. /**
10.    The warehouse client applet.
11. */
12. public class WarehouseApplet extends JApplet
13. {
14.    public void init()
15.    {
16.       initUI();
17.
18.       try
19.       {
20.          String warehouseName = getParameter("warehouse.name");
21.          if (warehouseName == null)
22.             warehouseName = "central_warehouse";
23.          String url = "rmi://" + getCodeBase().getHost()
24.             + "/" + warehouseName;
25.          centralWarehouse = (Warehouse)Naming.lookup(url);
26.       }
27.       catch(Exception e)
28.       {
29.          showStatus("Error: Can't connect to warehouse. " + e);
30.       }
31.    }
32.
33.    /**
34.       Initializes the user interface.
35.    */
36.    private void initUI()
37.    {
```

```
38.          getContentPane().setLayout(new GridBagLayout());
39.
40.          GridBagConstraints gbc = new GridBagConstraints();
41.          gbc.fill = GridBagConstraints.HORIZONTAL;
42.          gbc.weightx = 100;
43.          gbc.weighty = 0;
44.
45.          add(new JLabel("Age:"), gbc, 0, 0, 1, 1);
46.          age = new JTextField(4);
47.          age.setText("20");
48.          add(age, gbc, 1, 0, 1, 1);
49.
50.          male = new JCheckBox("Male", true);
51.          female = new JCheckBox("Female", true);
52.          add(male, gbc, 0, 1, 1, 1);
53.          add(female, gbc, 1, 1, 1, 1);
54.
55.          add(new JLabel("Hobbies"), gbc, 0, 2, 1, 1);
56.          String[] choices = { "Gardening", "Beauty",
57.             "Computers", "Household", "Sports" };
58.          gbc.fill = GridBagConstraints.BOTH;
59.          hobbies = new JComboBox(choices);
60.          add(hobbies, gbc, 1, 2, 1, 1);
61.
62.          gbc.fill = GridBagConstraints.NONE;
63.          JButton submitButton = new JButton("Submit");
64.          add(submitButton, gbc, 0, 3, 2, 1);
65.          submitButton.addActionListener(new
66.             ActionListener()
67.             {
68.                public void actionPerformed(ActionEvent evt)
69.                {
70.                   callWarehouse();
71.                }
72.             });
73.
74.          gbc.weighty = 100;
75.          gbc.fill = GridBagConstraints.BOTH;
76.          result = new JTextArea(4, 40);
77.          result.setEditable(false);
78.          add(result, gbc, 0, 4, 2, 1);
79.
80.          imagePanel = new JPanel();
81.          imagePanel.setMinimumSize(new Dimension(0, 60));
82.          add(imagePanel, gbc, 0, 5, 2, 1);
83.       }
84.
85.       /**
86.          Add a component to this frame.
87.          @param c the component to add
88.          @param gbc the grid bag constraints
89.          @param x the grid bax column
90.          @param y the grid bag row
```

```
91.          @param w the number of grid bag columns spanned
92.          @param h the number of grid bag rows spanned
93.       */
94.      private void add(Component c, GridBagConstraints gbc,
95.         int x, int y, int w, int h)
96.      {  gbc.gridx = x;
97.         gbc.gridy = y;
98.         gbc.gridwidth = w;
99.         gbc.gridheight = h;
100.        getContentPane().add(c, gbc);
101.     }
102.
103.     /**
104.         Call the remote warehouse to find matching products.
105.      */
106.     private void callWarehouse()
107.     {
108.        try
109.        {
110.           Customer c = new Customer(Integer.parseInt(age.getText()),
111.              (male.isSelected() ? Product.MALE : 0)
112.              + (female.isSelected() ? Product.FEMALE : 0),
113.              new String[] { (String)hobbies.getSelectedItem() });
114.           ArrayList recommendations = centralWarehouse.find(c);
115.           result.setText(c + "\n");
116.           imagePanel.removeAll();
117.           for (int i = 0; i < recommendations.size(); i++)
118.           {
119.              Product p = (Product)recommendations.get(i);
120.              String t = p.getDescription() + "\n";
121.              result.append(t);
122.              Image productImage
123.                 = getImage(getCodeBase(), p.getImageFile());
124.             imagePanel.add(new JLabel(new ImageIcon(productImage)));
125.           }
126.        }
127.        catch(Exception e)
128.        {
129.           result.setText("Exception: " + e);
130.        }
131.     }
132.
133.     private static final int WIDTH = 300;
134.     private static final int HEIGHT = 300;
135.
136.     private Warehouse centralWarehouse;
137.     private JTextField age;
138.     private JCheckBox male;
139.     private JCheckBox female;
140.     private JComboBox hobbies;
141.     private JTextArea result;
142.     private JPanel imagePanel;
143. }
```

Example 5–15: WarehouseApplet.html

```
1. <applet code="WarehouseApplet.class" width="600" height="400">
2.    <param name="warehouse.name" value="central_warehouse"/>
3. </applet>
```

Server Object Activation

In the preceding sample programs, we used a server program to instantiate and register objects so that clients could make remote calls on them. However, in some cases, it may be wasteful to instantiate lots of server objects and have them wait for connections, whether or not client objects use them. The *activation* mechanism lets you delay the object construction, so that a server object is only constructed when at least one client invokes a remote method on it.

To take advantage of activation, the client code is completely unchanged. The client simply requests a remote reference and makes calls through it.

However, the server program is replaced by an activation program that constructs *activation descriptors* of the objects that are to be constructed at a later time, and binds receivers for remote method calls with the naming service. When a call is made for the first time, the information in the activation descriptor is used to construct the object.

A server object that is used in this way should extend the `Activatable` class and, of course, implement one or more remote interfaces. For example,

```
class ProductImpl
   extends Activatable
   implements Product
{
   . . .
}
```

Because the object construction is delayed until a later point in time, it must happen in a standardized form. Therefore, you must provide a constructor that takes two parameters:

- An activation ID (which you simply pass to the superclass constructor);
- A single object containing all construction information, wrapped in a `MarshalledObject`.

If you need multiple construction parameters, you must package them up in a single object. You can always use an `Object[]` array or an `ArrayList`. As you will see momentarily, you will place a serialized (or marshalled) copy of the construction information inside the activation descriptor. Your server object constructor should use the `get` method of the `MarshalledObject` class to deserialize the construction information.

In the case of the `ProductImpl` class, this is quite simple—there is only one piece of information necessary for construction, namely the product name.

That information can be wrapped into a `MarshalledObject` and unwrapped in the constructor:

```
public ProductImpl(ActivationID id, MarshalledObject data)
{
    super(id, 0);
    String n = (String)data.get();
    name = n;
    System.out.println("Constructed " + name);
}
```

By passing 0 as the second parameter of the superclass constructor, we indicate that the RMI library should assign a suitable port number to the listener port.

This constructor prints a message so that you can see that the product objects are activated on demand.

NOTE: Your server objects don't actually have to extend the `Activatable` class. If they don't, then place the static method call

```
Activatable.exportObject(this, id, 0)
```

in the constructor of the server class.

Now let us turn to the activation program. First, you need to define an activation group. An activation group describes common parameters for launching the virtual machine that contains the server objects. The most important parameter is the security policy.

As with our other server objects, we will not do security checks. (Presumably they come from a trusted source.) However, the virtual machine in which the activated objects run has a security manager installed. To enable all permissions, supply a file `server.policy` with the following contents:

```
grant
{
    permission java.security.AllPermission;
};
```

Construct an activation group descriptor as follows:

```
Properties props = new Properties();
props.put("java.security.policy", "/server/server.policy");
ActivationGroupDesc group = new ActivationGroupDesc(prop, null);
```

The second parameter is used to describe special command options; we will not need any for this example, so we pass a `null` reference.

Next, you create a group ID with the call

```
ActivationGroupID id
    = ActivationGroup.getSystem().registerGroup(group);
```

Now you are ready to construct the activation descriptors. For each object that should be constructed on demand, you need

- The activation group ID for the virtual machine in which the object should be constructed;

- The name of the class (such as `"ProductImpl"` or `"com.mycompany.MyClassImpl"`);

- The URL string from which to load the class files. This should be the base URL, not including package paths;

- The marshalled construction information.

For example,

```
MarshalledObject param
    = new MarshalledObject("Blackwell Toaster");
ActivationDesc desc = new ActivationDesc(id, "ProductImpl",
    "http://myserver.com/download/", param);
```

Pass the descriptor to the static `Activatable.register` method. It returns an object of some class that implements the remote interfaces of the implementation class. You can bind that object with the naming service:

```
Product p = (Product)Activatable.register(desc);
Naming.rebind("toaster", p);
```

Unlike the server programs of the preceding examples, the activation program exits after registering and binding the activation receivers. The server objects are only constructed when the first remote method call occurs.

Examples 5–16 and 5–17 show the code for the activatable product implementation and the activation program. The product interface and the client program are unchanged.

To launch this program, follow these steps:

1. Compile all source files.
2. Run `rmic` to generate a stub for the `ProductImpl` class:
    ```
    rmic -v1.2 ProductImpl
    ```
3. Start the RMI registry.
4. Start the RMI activation daemon.
    ```
    rmid -J-Djava.security.policy=rmid.policy &
    ```
    or
    ```
    start rmid -J-Djava.security.policy=rmid.policy
    ```
    The `rmid` program listens to activation requests and activates objects in a separate virtual machine. To launch a virtual machine, the `rmid` program needs certain permissions. These are specified in a policy file

(see Example 5–18). The -J option is used to pass an option to the virtual machine running the activation daemon.

5. Run the activation program. In this setup, we assume that you start the program in the directory that contains the class files and the server policy file.

```
java ProductActivator
```

The program will exit after the activation receivers have been registered with the naming service.

6. Run the client program

```
java -Djava.security.policy=client.policy ProductClient
```

The client will print the familiar product descriptions. When you run the client for the first time, you will also see the constructor messages in the server shell window.

Example 5–16: ProductImpl.java

```java
1. import java.io.*;
2. import java.rmi.*;
3. import java.rmi.activation.*;
4.
5. /**
6.    This is the implementation class for the remote product
7.    objects.
8. */
9. public class ProductImpl
10.    extends Activatable
11.    implements Product
12. {
13.    /**
14.       Constructs a product implementation
15.       @param id the activation id
16.       @param data the marshalled construction parameter (containing the
17.       product name)
18.    */
19.    public ProductImpl(ActivationID id, MarshalledObject data)
20.       throws RemoteException, IOException, ClassNotFoundException
21.    {
22.       super(id, 0);
23.       String n = (String)data.get();
24.       name = n;
25.       System.out.println("Constructed " + name);
26.    }
27.
28.    public String getDescription() throws RemoteException
29.    {
30.       return "I am a " + name + ". Buy me!";
31.    }
32.
```

```
33.    private String name;
34. }
```

Example 5–17: ProductActivator.java

```
1. import java.io.*;
2. import java.net.*;
3. import java.rmi.*;
4. //import java.rmi.server.*;
5. import java.rmi.activation.*;
6. import java.util.*;
7.
8. /**
9.    This server program activates two remote objects and
10.   registers them with the naming service.
11. */
12. public class ProductActivator
13. {
14.    public static void main(String args[])
15.    {
16.       try
17.       {
18.          System.out.println
19.             ("Constructing activation descriptors...");
20.
21.          Properties props = new Properties();
22.          // use the server.policy file in the current directory
23.          props.put("java.security.policy",
24.             new File("server.policy").getCanonicalPath());
25.        ActivationGroupDesc group = new ActivationGroupDesc(props, null);
26.          ActivationGroupID id
27.             = ActivationGroup.getSystem().registerGroup(group);
28.          MarshalledObject p1param
29.             = new MarshalledObject("Blackwell Toaster");
30.          MarshalledObject p2param
31.             = new MarshalledObject("ZapXpress Microwave Oven");
32.
33.          String classDir = ".";
34.          // turn the class directory into a file URL
35.        // for this demo we assume that the classes are in the current dir
36.          String classURL
37.            = new File(classDir).getCanonicalFile().toURL().toString();
38.
39.          ActivationDesc desc1 = new ActivationDesc
40.             (id, "ProductImpl", classURL, p1param);
41.          ActivationDesc desc2 = new ActivationDesc
42.             (id, "ProductImpl", classURL, p2param);
43.
44.          Product p1 = (Product)Activatable.register(desc1);
45.          Product p2 = (Product)Activatable.register(desc2);
46.
```

```
47.        System.out.println
48.           ("Binding activable implementations to registry...");
49.
50.        Naming.rebind("toaster", p1);
51.        Naming.rebind("microwave", p2);
52.
53.        System.out.println
54.           ("Exiting...");
55.     }
56.     catch(Exception e)
57.     {
58.        e.printStackTrace();
59.     }
60.  }
61. }
```

Example 5–18: rmid.policy

```
1. grant
2. {
3.    permission com.sun.rmi.rmid.ExecPermission
4.       "${java.home}${/}bin${/}java";
5.    permission com.sun.rmi.rmid.ExecOptionPermission
6.       "-Djava.security.policy=*";
7. };
```

Example 5–19: server.policy

```
1. grant
2. {
3.    permission java.security.AllPermission;
4. };
```

Example 5–20: client.policy

```
1. grant
2. {
3.    permission java.net.SocketPermission
4.       "*:1024-65535", "connect,accept";
5.    permission java.net.SocketPermission
6.       "localhost:80", "connect";
7. };
```

`java.rmi.activation.Activatable`

- `protected Activatable(ActivationID id, int port)`
  Constructs the activatable object and establishes a listener on the given port.

Parameters:	`id`	the activation ID
	`port`	the port number, or 0 to have a suitable port number assigned

- `static Remote exportObject(Remote obj, ActivationID id, int port)`
  Makes a remote object activatable. Returns the activation receiver that should be made available to remote callers.

Parameters:	obj	the server object that belongs to a class implementing one or more remote interfaces
	id	the activation ID
	port	the port number, or 0 to have a suitable port number assigned

- `Remote register(ActivationDescriptor desc)`
  Registers the descriptor for an activatable object and prepares it for receiving remote calls. Returns the activation receiver that should be made available to remote callers.

Parameters:	desc	the activation descriptor

java.rmi.MarshalledObject

- `MarshalledObject(Object obj)`
  Constructs an object containing the serialized data of a given object.

Parameters:	obj	the object to be serialized

- `Object get()`
  Deserializes the stored object data and returns the object.

java.rmi.activation.ActivationGroupDesc

- `ActivationGroupDesc(Properties props, ActivationGroupDesc.CommandEnvironment env)`
  Constructs an activation group descriptor that specifies virtual machine properties for a virtual machine that hosts activated objects.

Parameters:	props	system properties of the virtual machine
	env	command environment (including the path to the virtual machine executable, and command-line options), or `null` if no special settings are required

java.rmi.activation.ActivatationGroup

- `static ActivationSystem getSystem()`
  Returns a reference to the activation system.

- `ActivationGroupID registerGroup(ActivationGroupDesc group)`

`java.rmi.activation.ActivationSystem`

Registers an activation group and returns the group ID.

Parameters: group   the activation group descriptor

`java.rmi.activation.ActivatationDesc`

- `ActivationDesc(ActivationGroupID id, String className, String location, MarshalledObject data)`
  Constructs an activation descriptor.

  Parameters: id   the activation group ID

  className   the fully qualified name of the server class

  location   the URL from which to load class files

  data   the marshalled construction information

Java IDL and CORBA

Unlike RMI, CORBA lets you make calls between Java objects and objects written in other languages. CORBA depends on having an Object Request Broker (ORB) available on both client and server. You can think of an ORB as a kind of universal translator for interobject CORBA communication. The CORBA 2 specification defines more than a dozen "services" that the ORB can use for various kinds of housekeeping tasks. These range from a "startup service" to get the process going, to a "life cycle service" that you use to create, copy, move, or destroy objects to a "naming service" that allows you to search for objects if you know their name.

The Java 2 platform contains an implementation of a CORBA 2 compliant ORB. Thus, all applications and applets that you deploy for the Java 2 platform have the ability to connect to remote CORBA objects.

NOTE: Sun refers to the CORBA support in the Java 2 platform as "Java IDL." That term is really a misnomer. IDL refers to the interface definition language, a language for describing class interfaces. The important aspect of the technology is connectivity with CORBA, not just support for IDL.

Here are the steps for implementing CORBA objects:

1. Write the interface that specifies how the object works, using IDL, the *interface definition language* for defining CORBA interfaces. IDL is a special language to specify interfaces in a language-neutral form.

2. Using the IDL compiler(s) for the target language(s), generate the needed stub and helper classes.

3. Add the implementation code for the server objects, using the language of your choice. (The skeleton created by the IDL compiler is only glue code. You still need to provide the actual implementation code for the server methods.) Compile the implementation code.

4. Write a server program that creates and registers the server objects. The most convenient method for registration is to use the CORBA *naming service,* a service that is similar to the `rmiregistry`.

5. Write a client program that locates the server objects and invokes services on them.

6. Start the naming service and the server program on the server and the client program on the client.

These steps are quite similar to the steps that you use to build distributed applications with RMI. There are two important differences:

- You can use any language with a CORBA binding to implement clients and servers.

- You use IDL to specify interfaces.

In the following sections, you will see how to use IDL to define CORBA interfaces, and how to connect clients implemented in the Java programming language with C++ servers and C++ clients with servers implemented in the Java programming language.

However, CORBA is a complex subject, and we only give you a couple of basic examples to show you how to get started. For more information, we recommend *Client/Server Programming with Java and CORBA* by Robert Orfali and Dan Harkey [John Wiley & Sons 1998]. More advanced, and definitely not for the faint of heart, is *Advanced CORBA Programming with C++* by Michi Henning and Steve Vinoski [Addison-Wesley 1999].

The Interface Definition Language

To introduce the IDL syntax, let us quickly run through the same example that we used for RMI. In RMI, you started out with an interface in the Java programming language. With CORBA, the starting point is an interface in IDL syntax:

```
interface Product
{
    string getDescription();
};
```

There are a few subtle differences between IDL and the Java programming language. In IDL, the interface definition ends with a semicolon. Note that `string` is written in lower case. In fact, the `string` class refers to the CORBA notion of a string, which is different from a Java string. In the Java programming language, strings contain 16-bit Unicode characters. In CORBA, strings only contain 8-bit characters. If you send the 16-bit string through the ORB and the string has characters with nonzero high byte, an exception is thrown. This kind of type mismatch problem is the price you pay for interoperability between programming languages.

NOTE: CORBA also has `wchar` and `wstring` types for "wide" characters. However, there is no guarantee that wide character strings use the Unicode encoding.

The "IDL to Java" compiler (Java IDL compiler) translates IDL definitions to definitions for interfaces in the Java programming language. For example, suppose you place the IDL `Product` definition into a file `Product.idl` and run

```
idlj Product.idl
```

The result is a file `ProductOperations.java` with the following contents

```
interface ProductOperations
{
    String getDescription();
}
```

and a file `Product.java` that defines an interface

```
public interface Product extends
    ProductOperations,
    org.omg.CORBA.Object,
    org.omg.CORBA.portable.IDLEntity
{
}
```

NOTE: In SDK1.2, the `idltojava` program is used to translate IDL files.

The IDL compiler also generates a number of other source files—the stub class for communicating with the ORB and three helper classes that you will encounter later in this section and the next.

NOTE: You cannot do any programming in IDL. IDL can only express interfaces. The CORBA objects that IDL describes must still be implemented, for example, in C++ or the Java programming language.

The rules that govern the translation from IDL to the Java programming language are collectively called the *Java programming language binding*. Language bindings are standardized by the OMG; all CORBA vendors are required to use the same rules for mapping IDL constructs to a particular programming language.

We will not discuss all aspects of IDL or the Java programming language binding—see the CORBA documentation at the web site of the Object Management Group (www.omg.org) for a full description. However, there are a number of important concepts that every IDL user needs to know.

When defining a method, you have more choices for parameter passing than the Java programming language offers. Every parameter can be declared as in, out, or inout. An in parameter is simply passed to the method—this is the same parameter-passing mechanism as in the Java programming language. However, the Java programming language has no analog to an out parameter. A method stores a value in each out parameter before it returns. The caller can retrieve the values stored in out parameters.

For example, a find method might store the product object that it has found:

```
interface Warehouse
{
   boolean locate(in String descr, out Product p);
   . . .
};
```

If the parameter is declared as out only, then the method should not expect the parameter to be initialized. However, if it is declared as inout, then the caller needs to supply a value for the method, and the method can change that value so that the caller can retrieve the changed value. In the Java programming language, these parameters are simulated with special *holder classes* that are generated by the Java IDL compiler.

The IDL compiler generates a class with suffix Holder for every interface. For example, when compiling the Product interface, it automatically generates a ProductHolder class. Every holder class has a public instance variable called value.

When a method has an out parameter, the IDL compiler changes the method signature to use a holder, for example

```
interface Warehouse
{
   boolean locate(String descr, ProductHolder p);
   . . .
};
```

When calling the method, you need to pass in a holder object. After the method returns, you retrieve the value of the out parameter from the holder object. Here is how you call the locate method.

```
Warehouse w = . . .;
String descr = . . .;
Product p;
ProductHolder pHolder = new ProductHolder();
```

```
if (w.locate(descr, pHolder))
    p = pHolder.value;
```

There are predefined holder classes for fundamental types (such as `IntHolder`, `DoubleHolder` and so on).

NOTE: IDL does not support overloaded methods. You need to come up with a different name for each method.

In IDL, you use the `sequence` construct to define arrays of variable size. You must first define a type before you can declare sequence parameters or return values. For example, here is the definition of a "sequence of products" type.

```
typedef sequence<Product> ProductSeq;
```

Then you can use that type in method declarations:

```
interface Warehouse
{
    ProductSeq find(in Customer c);
    . . .
};
```

In the Java programming language, sequences correspond to arrays. For example, the `find` method is mapped to

```
Product[] find(Customer c)
```

If a method can throw an exception, you first define the exception type and then use a `raises` declaration. In the following example, the `find` method can raise a `BadCustomer` exception.

```
interface Warehouse
{
    exception BadCustomer { string reason; };
    ProductSeq find(in Customer c) raises BadCustomer;
    . . .
};
```

The IDL compiler translates the exception type into a class.

```
final public class BadCustomer
    extends org.omg.CORBA.UserException
{
    public BadCustomer() {}
    public BadCustomer(String __reason) { reason = __reason; }
    public String reason;
}
```

If you catch such an exception, you can look into its public instance variables.

The `raises` specifier becomes a `throws` specifier of the Java method

```
ProductSeq find(Customer c) throws BadCustomer
```

Interfaces can contain constants, for example,

```
interface Warehouse
{
    const int SOLD_OUT = 404;
    . . .
};
```

Interfaces can also contain attributes. Attributes look like instance variables, but they are actually shorthand for a pair of accessor and mutator methods. For example, here is a `Book` interface with an `isbn` attribute:

```
interface Book
{
    attribute string isbn;
    . . .
};
```

The equivalent in the Java programming language is a pair of methods, both with the name `isbn`:

```
String isbn() // accessor
void isbn(String __isbn) // mutator
```

If the attribute is declared as `readonly`, then no mutator method is generated.

You cannot specify variables in CORBA interfaces—the data representation for objects is part of the implementation strategy, and IDL does not address implementation at all.

CORBA supports interface inheritance, for example,

```
interface Book : Product { /* . . . */ };
```

You use the colon (`:`) to denote inheritance. An interface can inherit multiple interfaces.

In IDL, you can group definitions of interfaces, types, constants, and exceptions into *modules*.

```
module corejava
{
    interface Product
    {
        . . .
    };

    interface Warehouse
    {
        . . .
    };
};
```

Modules are translated to packages in the Java programming language.

Once you have the IDL file, you run the IDL compiler that your ORB vendor supplies to get stubs and helper classes for your target language (such as the Java programming language or the C++ language).

For example, to convert IDL files to the Java programming language, you run the `idltojava` program. Supply the name of the IDL file on the command line:

```
idlj Product.idl
```

The program creates five source files:

- `Product.java`, the interface definition;

- `ProductOperations.java`, the interface that contains the actual operations. (`Product` extends `ProductOperations` as well as a couple of CORBA-specific interfaces.);

- `ProductHolder.java`, the holder class for `out` parameters;

- `ProductHelper.java`, a helper class, which you will see used in the next section;

- `_ProductStub.java`, the stub class for communicating with the ORB.

The same IDL file can be compiled to C++. We will use a freely available ORB called omniORB for our examples. The omniORB package contains an IDL-to-C++ compiler called `omniidl`. To generate C++ stubs, invoke it as

```
omniidl -bcxx Product.idl
```

You get two C++ files:

- `Product.hh`, a header file that defines classes `Product`, `Product_Helper`, and `POA_Product` (the superclass for the server implementation class);

- `ProductSK.cc`, a C++ file that contains the source code for these classes.

NOTE: While the language binding is standardized, it is up to each vendor to decide how to generate and package the code that realizes the binding. IDL-to-C++ compilers of other vendors will generate a different set of files.

A CORBA Example

In our first example, we show you how to call a C++ server object from a client implemented in the Java programming language, using the CORBA support that is built into the Java 2 platform. On the server side, we will use omniORB, a freely available ORB that works with the Java 2 platform. You can download omniORB from `http://www.uk.research.att.com/omniORB/index.html`.

NOTE: The omniORB product is free, but on Windows, it requires the Microsoft C++ compiler. On Linux, you can use omniORB with the GNU C++ compiler.

NOTE: In principle, of course, you can use any CORBA 2 compliant ORB on the server. However, you will need to make some changes to the C++ code if you use a different ORB. Also, if our experience is any guide, you may run into bootstrapping issues. At the end of this section, we give you a couple of tips on connecting to other ORBs.

Our example C++ server object simply reports the value of an environment variable on the server. The interface is

```
interface Env
{
    string getenv(in string name);
};
```

For example, the following program fragment in the Java programming language obtains the value of the PATH environment variable of the process in which the server object runs.

```
Env env = . . .;
String value = env.getenv("PATH")
```

The C++ implementation code for this interface is straightforward. We simply call the getenv method in the standard C library.

```
class EnvImpl
    : public POA_Env, public PortableServer::RefCountServantBase
{
public:
    virtual char* getenv(const char *name)
    {
        char* value = std::getenv(name);
        return CORBA::string_dup(value);
    }
};
```

You don't need to understand the C++ code to follow this section—just treat it as a bit of legacy code that you want to encapsulate in a CORBA object so that you can call it from programs written in the Java programming language.

On the server side, you now need to write a C++ program that does the following:

1.   Starts the ORB;
2.   Creates an object of the EnvImpl class and registers it with the ORB;
3.   Uses the name server to bind the object to a name;
4.   Waits for invocations from a client.

You can find that program in Example 5–22 at the end of this section. We will not discuss the C++ code in detail. If you are interested, consult the omniORB documentation for more information. The documentation contains a good tutorial that explains each step in detail.

Let us now turn to the client code. You already saw how to invoke a method on the server object once you have a reference to the remote object. However, to get to that reference, you have to go through a different set of mumbo-jumbo than in RMI.

First, you initialize the ORB. The ORB is simply a code library that knows how to talk to other ORBs and how to marshal and unmarshal parameters.

```
ORB orb = ORB.init(args, null);
```

Next, you need to locate the naming service that helps you locate other objects. However, in CORBA, the naming service is just another CORBA object. To call the naming service, you first need to locate it. In the days of CORBA 1, this was a major problem, since there was no standard way of getting a reference to it. However, a CORBA 2 ORB lets you locate certain standard services by name. The call

```
String[] services = orb.list_initial_services();
```

lists the names of the standard services that the ORB can connect to. The naming service has the standard name `NameService`. Most ORBs have additional initial services, such as the `RootPOA` service that is used to access the root Portable Object Adaptor.

To obtain an object reference to the service, you use the `resolve_initial_references` method. It returns a generic CORBA object, an instance of the class `org.omg.corba.Object`. You need to use the full package prefix; if you just use `Object`, then the compiler assumes that you mean `java.lang.Object`.

```
org.omg.CORBA.Object object
    = orb.resolve_initial_references("NameService");
```

Next, you need to convert this reference into a `NamingContext` reference so that you can invoke the methods of the `NamingContext` interface. In RMI, you would simply cast the reference to a different type. However, in CORBA, you cannot simply cast references.

```
NamingContext namingContext
    = (NamingContext)object; // ERROR
```

Instead, you have to use the `narrow` method of the helper class of the target interface.

```
NamingContext namingContext
    = NamingContextHelper.narrow(object);
```

Now that you have the naming context, you can use it to locate the object that the server placed into it. The naming context associates names with server objects. Names are nested sequences of *name components*. You can use the nesting levels to organize hierarchies of names, much like you use directories in a file system.

A name component consists of an *ID* and a *kind*. The ID is a name for the component that is unique among all names with the same parent component. The kind is some indication of the type of the component. These kinds are not standardized; we use `"Context"` for name components that have nested names, and `"Object"` for object names.

In our example, the server program has placed the `EnvImpl` object into the name expressed by the sequence

```
(id="corejava", kind="Context"), (id="Env", kind="Object")
```

We retrieve a remote reference to it by building up an array of name components and passing it to the `resolve` method of the `NamingContext` interface.

```
NameComponent[] path =
    {
        new NameComponent("corejava", "Context"),
        new NameComponent("Env", "Object")
    };
org.omg.CORBA.Object envObj = namingContext.resolve(path);
```

Once again, we must narrow the resulting object reference:

```
Env env = EnvHelper.narrow(envObj);
```

Now we are ready to call the remote method:

```
String value = env.getenv("PATH");
```

You will find the complete code in Example 5–21.

This example shows the steps to follow in a typical client program:

1. Start the ORB.
2. Locate the naming service by retrieving an initial reference to `"NameService"` and narrowing it to a `NamingContext` reference.
3. Locate the object whose methods you want to call by assembling its name and calling the `resolve` method of the `NamingContext`.
4. Narrow the returned object to the correct type and invoke your methods.

To actually test this program, do the following.

1. Compile the IDL file, using both the C++ and Java IDL compilers.
2. Compile the C++ server program. The compilation instructions depend on the ORB. For example, with OmniORB on Linux, you use

```
g++
    -o EnvServer
    -D__x86__  -D__linux__  -D__OSVERSION__=2
    -I/usr/local/omni/include
    -L/usr/local/omni/lib/i586_linux_2.0_glibc2.1/
    EnvServer.cpp EnvSK.cc
    -lomniORB3 -ltcpwrapGK -lomnithread -lpthread
```

To find out what you need with your particular ORB, compile one of the example programs that are supplied with your installation and make the appropriate modifications to compile your own programs.

3. Compile the Java client program.
4. Start the naming service on the server (for example, `omniNames` if you use omniORB). The naming service runs until you kill it.
5. Start the server:

    ```
    ./EnvServer &
    ```

    The server also runs until you kill it.
6. Run the client, for example

    ```
    java EnvClient -ORBInitialPort 2809
    ```

    The client program should report the PATH of the server process.

TIP: There are a couple of OmniORB configuration issues that you need to follow carefully. Be sure to set the `LD_LIBRARY_PATH` (on Unix/Linux) or the `PATH` (on Windows) to include the directory containing the OmniORB libraries. You also need to make a configuration file and set the `OMNIORB_CONFIG` environment variable. The configuration file contains the IOR (Interoperable Object Reference) of the name service. See the sidebar at the end of this section for more details on IORs, and precisely follow the steps in the OmniORB documentation.

If the server is on a remote machine, or if the initial port of the server ORB is not the same as the Java IDL default of 900, then you need to set the `ORBInitial-Host` and `ORBInitialPort` properties. For example, OmniORB uses port 2809, so you need to set the initial port.

There are two methods for setting these properties. You can set the system properties

```
org.omg.CORBA.ORBInitialHost
org.omg.CORBA.ORBInitialPort
```

for example, by starting the `java` interpreter with the `-D` option. Or, you can specify the values on the command line:

```
java EnvClient -ORBInitialHost warthog -ORBInitialPort 2809
```

The command line parameters are passed to the ORB by the call

```
ORB orb = ORB.init(args, null);
```

In principle, your ORB vendor should tell you with great clarity how its bootstrap process works. In practice, we have found that vendors blithely assume that you would never dream of mixing their precious ORB with another, and they tend to be less than forthcoming with this information. If your client won't find the naming service, try forcing the initial ports for both the server and the client to the same value.

TIP: If you have trouble connecting to the naming service, print out a list of initial services that your ORB can locate.

```
public class ListServices
{
    public static void main(String args[]) throws Exception
    {
        ORB orb = ORB.init(args, null);
        String[] services = orb.list_initial_services();
        for (int i = 0; i < services.length; i++)
            System.out.println(services[i]);
    }
}
```

With some ORBs, `NameService` isn't among the listed services, no matter how much you tweak the configuration. Then, you should switch to Plan B and locate the server object by its Interoperable Object Reference, or IOR. See the sidebar for more information.

In this section, you saw how to connect to a server that was implemented in C++. We believe that is a particularly useful scenario. You can wrap legacy services into CORBA objects and access them from any program for the Java 2 platform, without having to deploy additional system software on the client. In the next section, you will see the opposite scenario, where the server is implemented in the Java programming language and the client in C++.

Example 5–21: EnvClient.java

```
1. import org.omg.CosNaming.*;
2. import org.omg.CORBA.*;
3.
4. public class EnvClient
5. {
```

```
6.    public static void main(String args[])
7.    {
8.        try
9.        {
10.           ORB orb = ORB.init(args, null);
11.           org.omg.CORBA.Object namingContextObj
12.               = orb.resolve_initial_references("NameService");
13.           NamingContext namingContext
14.               = NamingContextHelper.narrow(namingContextObj);
15.
16.           NameComponent[] path =
17.               {
18.                   new NameComponent("corejava", "Context"),
19.                   new NameComponent("Env", "Object")
20.               };
21.           org.omg.CORBA.Object envObj
22.               = namingContext.resolve(path);
23.           Env env = EnvHelper.narrow(envObj);
24.           System.out.println(env.getenv("PATH"));
25.        }
26.        catch(Exception e)
27.        {
28.            e.printStackTrace();
29.        }
30.    }
31. }
```

Example 5–22: EnvServer.cpp

```
1. #include <iostream>
2. #include <cstdlib>
3.
4. #include "Env.hh"
5.
6. using namespace std;
7.
8. class EnvImpl :
9.    public POA_Env,
10.    public PortableServer::RefCountServantBase
11. {
12. public:
13.    virtual char* getenv(const char *name);
14. };
15.
16. char* EnvImpl::getenv(const char *name)
17. {
18.    char* value = std::getenv(name);
19.    return CORBA::string_dup(value);
20. }
21.
22. static void bindObjectToName(CORBA::ORB_ptr orb,
```

```
23.     const char name[], CORBA::Object_ptr objref)
24. {
25.     CosNaming::NamingContext_var rootContext;
26.
27.     try
28.     {
29.        // Obtain a reference to the root context of the
30.        // name service:
31.        CORBA::Object_var obj;
32.        obj = orb->resolve_initial_references("NameService");
33.
34.        // Narrow the reference returned.
35.        rootContext = CosNaming::NamingContext::_narrow(obj);
36.        if( CORBA::is_nil(rootContext) )
37.        {
38.           cerr << "Failed to narrow the root naming context."
39.              << endl;
40.           return;
41.        }
42.     }
43.     catch(CORBA::ORB::InvalidName& ex)
44.     {
45.        // This should not happen!
46.        cerr << "Service required is invalid [does not exist]."
47.           << endl;
48.        return;
49.     }
50.
51.     try
52.     {
53.        // Bind a context called "test" to the root context:
54.
55.        CosNaming::Name contextName;
56.        contextName.length(1);
57.        contextName[0].id   = (const char*) "corejava";
58.        contextName[0].kind = (const char*) "Context";
59.
60.        CosNaming::NamingContext_var corejavaContext;
61.        try
62.        {
63.           // Bind the context to root.
64.           corejavaContext
65.              = rootContext->bind_new_context(contextName);
66.        }
67.        catch(CosNaming::NamingContext::AlreadyBound& ex)
68.        {
69.           // If the context already exists, this exception will
70.           // be raised. In this case, just resolve the name and
71.           // assign the context to the object returned:
72.           CORBA::Object_var obj;
73.           obj = rootContext->resolve(contextName);
74.           corejavaContext
75.              = CosNaming::NamingContext::_narrow(obj);
```

```
76.            if( CORBA::is_nil(corejavaContext) )
77.            {
78.                cerr << "Failed to narrow naming context." << endl;
79.                return;
80.            }
81.        }
82.
83.        // Bind objref with given name to the context:
84.        CosNaming::Name objectName;
85.        objectName.length(1);
86.        objectName[0].id   = name;
87.        objectName[0].kind = (const char*) "Object";
88.
89.        try
90.        {
91.            corejavaContext->bind(objectName, objref);
92.        }
93.        catch(CosNaming::NamingContext::AlreadyBound& ex)
94.        {
95.            corejavaContext->rebind(objectName, objref);
96.        }
97.    }
98.    catch(CORBA::COMM_FAILURE& ex)
99.    {
100.        cerr
101.            << "Caught system exception COMM_FAILURE -- unable to "
102.            << "contact the naming service." << endl;
103.    }
104.    catch(CORBA::SystemException&)
105.    {
106.        cerr << "Caught a CORBA::SystemException while using the "
107.            << "naming service." << endl;
108.    }
109. }
110.
111. int main(int argc, char *argv[])
112. {
113.    cout << "Creating and initializing the ORB..." << endl;
114.
115.    CORBA::ORB_var orb = CORBA::ORB_init(argc, argv, "omniORB3");
116.
117.    CORBA::Object_var obj
118.        = orb->resolve_initial_references("RootPOA");
119.    PortableServer::POA_var poa
120.        = PortableServer::POA::_narrow(obj);
121.    poa->the_POAManager()->activate();
122.
123.    EnvImpl* envImpl = new EnvImpl();
124.    poa->activate_object(envImpl);
125.
126.    // Obtain a reference to the object, and register it in
127.    // the naming service.
128.    obj = envImpl->_this();
```

```
129.
130.     cout << orb->object_to_string(obj) << endl;
131.     cout << "Binding server implementations to registry..."
132.        << endl;
133.     bindObjectToName(orb, "Env", obj);
134.     envImpl->_remove_ref();
135.
136.     cout << "Waiting for invocations from clients..." << endl;
137.     orb->run();
138.
139.     return 0;
140. }
```

Locating Objects Through IORs

If you can't configure your server ORB and name service so that your client can invoke it, you can still locate CORBA objects by using an *Interoperable Object Reference,* or IOR. An IOR is a long string starting with `IOR:` and followed by many hexadecimal digits, for example:

```
IOR:012020201000000049444c3a4163636f756e743a312e3000010000000
00000004e000000010100200f0000003231362e31352e3131322e31373900
20350420202e00000001504d43000000000010000000049444c3a4163636f756
e743a312e30000e0000004a61636b20422e20517569636b00
```

An IOR describes an object uniquely. By convention, many server classes print out the IORs of all objects they register, to enable clients to locate them. You can then paste the server IOR into the client program. Specifically, use the following code:

```
String ref = "IOR:012020201000000049444c3a4163636f...";
   // paste IOR from server
org.omg.CORBA.Object object = orb.string_to_object(ref);
```

Then, narrow the returned object to the appropriate type, for example:

```
Env env = EnvHelper.narrow(object);
```

or

```
NamingContext context = NamingContextHelper.narrow(object);
```

When testing the code for this book, we successfully used this method to connect clients with Visibroker and OmniORB. (Some Java releases have bugs that prevent them from recognizing the OmniORB name service.)

`org.omg.CORBA.ORB`

- `static ORB init(String[] args, Properties props)`
  creates a new ORB and initializes it.

Parameters:	`args`	command-line arguments for configuring the ORB
	`props`	a table with properties for configuring the ORB

- `String[] list_initial_services()`
  returns a list of the initially available services such as `"NameService"`.
- `org.omg.CORBA.Object resolve_initial_references(String name)`
  returns an object that carries out one of the initial services.

  Parameters: `name`   the name of the initial service
- `org.omg.CORBA.Object string_to_object(String ior)`
  locates the object with a given IOR.

`org.omg.CosNaming.NamingContext`

- `org.omg.CORBA.Object resolve(NameComponent[] name)`
  returns the object that is bound to the given name.

`org.omg.CosNaming.NameComponent`

- `NameComponent(String id, String kind)`
  constructs a new name component.

  Parameters: `id`   A string describing the identity of this component

                 `kind`   A string describing the type of this component

Implementing CORBA Servers

If you are deploying a CORBA infrastructure, you will find that the Java programming language is a good implementation language for CORBA server objects. The language binding is natural, and it is easier to build robust server software than with C++. This section describes how to implement a CORBA server in the Java programming language.

The example program in this section is similar to that of the preceding section. We supply a service to look up a system property of a Java virtual machine. Here is the IDL description:

```
interface SysProp
{
    string getProperty(in string name);
};
```

For example, our client test program calls the server as follows:

```
CORBA::String_var key = "java.vendor";
CORBA::String_var value = sysProp->getProperty(key);
```

The result is a string describing the vendor of the Java virtual machine that is executing the server program. We won't look into the details of the C++ client program. You will find the code in Example 5–24.

To implement the server, you run the `idlj` compiler with the `-fall` option. (By default, `idlj` only creates client-side stubs.)

```
idlj -fall SysProp.java
```

Then you extend the `SysPropPOA` class that the `idlj` compiler generated from the IDL file. Here is the implementation:

```
class SysPropImpl extends SysPropPOA
{
    public String getProperty(String key)
    {
        return System.getProperty(key);
    }
}
```

> NOTE: You can choose any name you like for the implementation class. In this book, we follow the RMI convention and use the suffix `Impl` for the implementation class name. Other programmers use a suffix `Servant` or `_i`.

> NOTE: If your implementation class already extends another class, you cannot simultaneously extend the implementation base class. In that case, you can instruct the `idlj` compiler to create a *tie* class. Your server class then implements the operations interface instead of extending the implementation base class. However, any server objects must be created by means of the tie class. For details, check out the `idlj` documentation at `http://java.sun.com/j2se/1.4/docs/guide/idl/index.html`.

Next, you need to write a server program that carries out the following tasks:

1. Start the ORB.
2. Locate and activate the root Portable Object Adaptor (POA).
3. Create the server implementation.
4. Use the POA to convert the servant reference to a CORBA object reference. (The server implementation class extends `SysPropPOA` which itself extends `org.omg.PortableServer.Servant`.)
5. Print out its IOR (for name-service-challenged clients—see the Sidebar on page 400).
6. Bind the server implementation to the naming service.
7. Wait for invocations from clients.

You will find the complete code in Example 5–23. Here are the highlights.

You start the ORB as you would for a client program:

```
ORB orb = ORB.init(args, null);
```

Next, activate the root POA:

```
POA rootpoa
    = (POA)orb.resolve_initial_references("RootPOA");
rootpoa.the_POAManager().activate();
```

Construct the server object and convert it to a CORBA object:

```
SysPropImpl impl = new SysPropImpl();
org.omg.CORBA.Object ref
    = rootpoa.servant_to_reference(impl);
```

Next, obtain the IOR with the `object_to_string` method and print it out:

```
System.out.println(orb.object_to_string(impl));
```

You obtain a reference to the naming service in exactly the same way as with a client program:

```
org.omg.CORBA.Object namingContextObj =
    orb.resolve_initial_references("NameService");
NamingContext namingContext
    = NamingContextHelper.narrow(namingContextObj);
```

You then build up the desired name for the object. Here, we call the object `SysProp`:

```
NameComponent[] path =
    {
        new NameComponent("SysProp", "Object")
    };
```

CAUTION: We don't use a nested name because at the time of this writing, the `orbd` name service that is included in the Java SDK does not support nested names.

You use the `rebind` method to bind the object to the name:

```
namingContext.rebind(path, impl);
```

Finally, you wait for client invocations:

```
orb.run();
```

To test this program, do the following.

1.   Compile the IDL file, using both the C++ and Java IDL compilers.

2.   Compile the server program.

3.   Compile the C++ client program.

4.   Start the `orbd` naming service on the server. This program is a part of the Java SDK.

      ```
      orbd -ORBInitialPort 2809
      ```

5.   Start the server:

      ```
      java SysPropServer -ORBInitialPort 2809
      ```

      The server also runs until you kill it.

6. Run the client.

```
./SysPropClient
```

It should print out the JVM vendor of the server.

> NOTE: In this example, we use the *transient* name service. The `orbd` tool also includes a persistent name service that remembers names and object references even if the name service has been shut down and restarted. See the Java IDL documentation for more information on the persistent name service.

You have now seen how to use CORBA to connect clients and servers that were written in different programming languages. This concludes our discussion of CORBA. CORBA has a number of other interesting features, such as dynamic method invocation and a number of standard services such as transaction handling and persistence. We refer you to *Client/Server Programming with Java and CORBA* by Robert Orfali and Dan Harkey [John Wiley & Sons 1998] for an in-depth discussion of advanced CORBA issues.

Example 5–23: SysPropServer.java

```java
1.  import org.omg.CosNaming.*;
2.  import org.omg.CORBA.*;
3.  import org.omg.PortableServer.*;
4.
5.  class SysPropImpl extends SysPropPOA
6.  {
7.     public String getProperty(String key)
8.     {
9.        return System.getProperty(key);
10.    }
11. }
12.
13. public class SysPropServer
14. {
15.    public static void main(String args[])
16.    {
17.       try
18.       {
19.          System.out.println(
20.             "Creating and initializing the ORB...");
21.
22.          ORB orb = ORB.init(args, null);
23.
24.          System.out.println(
25.             "Registering server implementation with the ORB...");
26.
```

```
27.          POA rootpoa
28.              = (POA)orb.resolve_initial_references("RootPOA");
29.          rootpoa.the_POAManager().activate();
30.
31.          SysPropImpl impl = new SysPropImpl();
32.          org.omg.CORBA.Object ref
33.              = rootpoa.servant_to_reference(impl);
34.
35.          System.out.println(orb.object_to_string(ref));
36.
37.          org.omg.CORBA.Object namingContextObj =
38.               orb.resolve_initial_references("NameService");
39.          NamingContext namingContext
40.              = NamingContextHelper.narrow(namingContextObj);
41.
42.          NameComponent[] path =
43.              {
44.                  // new NameComponent("corejava", "Context"),
45.                  new NameComponent("SysProp", "Object")
46.              };
47.
48.          System.out.println(
49.              "Binding server implementation to name service...");
50.
51.          namingContext.rebind(path, ref);
52.
53.          System.out.println(
54.              "Waiting for invocations from clients...");
55.          orb.run();
56.      }
57.      catch (Exception e)
58.      {
59.          e.printStackTrace(System.out);
60.      }
61.   }
62. }
```

Example 5–24: SysPropClient.cpp

```cpp
1. #include <iostream>
2. #include "SysProp.hh"
3.
4. CORBA::Object_ptr getObjectReference(CORBA::ORB_ptr orb,
5.    const char serviceName[])
6. {
7.    CosNaming::NamingContext_var rootContext;
8.
9.    try
10.   {
11.       // Obtain a reference to the root context of the
```

```
12.        // name service:
13.        CORBA::Object_var initServ;
14.        initServ = orb->resolve_initial_references("NameService");
15.
16.        // Narrow the object returned by
17.        // resolve_initial_references()
18.        // to a CosNaming::NamingContext object
19.        rootContext = CosNaming::NamingContext::_narrow(initServ);
20.        if (CORBA::is_nil(rootContext))
21.        {
22.            cerr << "Failed to narrow naming context." << endl;
23.            return CORBA::Object::_nil();
24.        }
25.    }
26.    catch(CORBA::ORB::InvalidName&)
27.    {
28.        cerr << "Name service does not exist." << endl;
29.        return CORBA::Object::_nil();
30.    }
31.
32.    // Create a name object, containing the name corejava/SysProp:
33.    CosNaming::Name name;
34.    name.length(1);
35.
36.    name[0].id   = serviceName;
37.    name[0].kind = "Object";
38.
39.    CORBA::Object_ptr obj;
40.    try
41.    {
42.        // Resolve the name to an object reference, and assign
43.        // the returned reference to a CORBA::Object:
44.        obj = rootContext->resolve(name);
45.    }
46.    catch(CosNaming::NamingContext::NotFound&)
47.    {
48.        // This exception is thrown if any of the components of the
49.        // path [contexts or the object] aren't found:
50.        cerr << "Context not found." << endl;
51.        return CORBA::Object::_nil();
52.    }
53.    return obj;
54. }
55.
56. int main (int argc, char *argv[])
57. {
58.    CORBA::ORB_ptr orb = CORBA::ORB_init(argc, argv, "omniORB3");
59.
60.    CORBA::Object_var obj = getObjectReference(orb, "SysProp");
```

```
61.    SysProp_var sysProp = SysProp::_narrow(obj);
62.
63.    if (CORBA::is_nil(sysProp))
64.    {
65.       cerr << "hello: cannot invoke on a nil object reference."
66.          << endl;
67.       return 1;
68.    }
69.
70.    CORBA::String_var key = "java.vendor";
71.    CORBA::String_var value = sysProp->getProperty(key);
72.
73.    cerr << key << "=" << value << endl;
74.
75.    return 0;
76. }
```

org.omg.CORBA.ORB

- `void connect(org.omg.CORBA.Object obj)`
  connects the given implementation object to this ORB, enabling the ORB to forward calls to the object's methods.

- `String object_to_string(org.omg.CORBA.Object obj)`
  returns the IOR string of the given object.

org.omg.CosNaming.NamingContext

- `void bind(NameComponent[] name, org.omg.CORBA.Object obj)`
- `void rebind(NameComponent[] name, org.omg.CORBA.Object obj)`
  bind an object to a name. The `bind` method throws an `AlreadyBound` exception if the object has been previously bound. The `rebind` method replaces any previously bound objects.

  Parameters: name   the name to which the object is bound

                       obj   the object to store in the naming context

Chapter 6

Advanced Swing

▼ LISTS

▼ TREES

▼ TABLES

▼ STYLED TEXT COMPONENTS

▼ COMPONENT ORGANIZERS

In this chapter, we continue our discussion of the Swing user interface tool-kit from Volume 1. Swing is a very rich toolkit, and Volume 1 only covered basic and commonly used components. That leaves us with three significantly more complex components for lists, trees, and tables, whose exploration will occupy the bulk of this chapter. Components for styled text, in particular HTML, are inter-nally even more complex, and we show you how to put them to practical use. We finish the chapter by covering component organizers such as tabbed panes and desktop panes with internal frames.

Lists

If you want to present a set of choices to a user, and a radio button or checkbox set consumes too much space, you can use a combo box or a list. Combo boxes were covered in Volume 1 because they are relatively simple. The `JList` component has many more features, and its design is similar to that of the tree and table components. For that reason, it is our starting point for the discussion of complex Swing components.

409

Of course, you can have lists of strings, but you can also have lists of arbitrary objects, with full control of how they appear. The internal architecture of the list component that makes this generality possible is rather elegant. Unfortunately, the designers at Sun felt that they needed to show off that elegance, rather than hiding it from the programmer who just wants to use the component. You will find that the list control is somewhat awkward to use for common cases because you need to manipulate some of the machinery that makes the general cases possible. We'll walk you through the simple and most common case, a list box of strings, and then give a more complex example that shows off the flexibility of the list component.

The JList Component

The JList component is similar to a set of check boxes or radio buttons, except that the items are placed inside a single box and are selected by clicking on the items themselves, not on buttons. If you permit multiple selection for a list box, the user can select any combination of the items in the box.

Figure 6–1 shows an admittedly silly example. The user can select the attributes for the fox, such as "quick," "brown," "hungry," "wild," and, because we ran out of attributes, "static," "private," and "final." You can, thus, have the *static, final* fox jump over the lazy dog.

To construct this list component, you first start out with an array of strings, then pass the array to the JList constructor:

```
String[] words= { "quick", "brown", "hungry", "wild", ... };
JList wordList = new JList(words);
```

Alternatively, you can use an anonymous array:

```
JList wordList = new JList(new String[]
    {"quick", "brown", "hungry", "wild", ... });
```

Figure 6–1: A list box

List boxes do not scroll automatically. To make a list box scroll, you must insert it into a scroll pane:

```
JScrollPane scrollPane = new JScrollPane(wordList);
```

Then, you need to add the scroll pane, not the list, into the surrounding panel.

We must admit that the separation of the list display and the scrolling mechanism is elegant in theory, but it is a pain in practice. Essentially all lists that we ever encountered needed scrolling. It seems cruel to force programmers to go through hoops in the default case, just so they can appreciate that elegance.

By default, the list component displays eight items; use the `setVisibleRow-Count` method to change that value:

```
wordList.setVisibleRowCount(10); // display 10 items
```

By default, a user can select multiple items. This requires some knowledge of mouse technique: To add more items to a selection, press the CTRL key while clicking on each item. To select a contiguous range of items, click on the first one, then hold down the SHIFT key and click on the last one.

You can also restrict the user to a more limited selection mode with the `setSelectionMode` method:

```
wordList.setSelectionMode
    (ListSelectionModel.SINGLE_SELECTION);
    // select one item at a time
wordList.setSelectionMode
    (ListSelectionModel.SINGLE_INTERVAL_SELECTION);
    // select one item or one range of items
```

You may recall from Volume 1 that the basic user interface components send out action events when the user activates them. List boxes use a different notification mechanism. Rather than listening to action events, you need to listen to list selection events. Add a list selection listener to the list component, and implement the method

```
public void valueChanged(ListSelectionEvent evt)
```

in the listener.

When the user selects items, a flurry of list selection events is generated. For example, suppose the user clicks on a new item. When the mouse button goes down, there is an event that reports a change in selection. This is a transitional event—the call

```
event.isAdjusting()
```

returns `true` if the selection is not yet final. Then, when the mouse button goes up, there is another event, this time with `isAdjusting` returning `false`. If you are not interested in the transitional events, then you can wait for the event for which `isAdjusting` is `false`. However, if you want to give the user instant feedback as soon as the mouse button is clicked, then you need to process all events.

Once you are notified that an event has happened, you will want to find out what items are currently selected. The getSelectedValues method returns an *array of objects* containing all selected items.

You need to cast *each* array element to a string.

```
Object[] values = list.getSelectedValues();
for (int i = 0; i < values.length; i++)
    do something with (String)values[i];
```

CAUTION: You cannot cast the return value of getSelectedValues from an Object[] array to a String[] array. The return value was not created as an array of strings, but as an array of objects, each of which happens to be a string. If you want to process the return value as an array of strings, you can use the following code:

```
int length = values.length;
String[] words = new String[length];
System.arrayCopy(values, 0, words, 0, length);
```

If your list does not allow multiple selections, you can call the convenience method getSelectedValue. It returns the first selected value (which you know to be the only value if multiple selections are disallowed).

```
String selection = (String)source.getSelectedValue();
```

NOTE: List components do not react to double clicks from a mouse. As envisioned by the designers of Swing, you use a list to select an item, and then you need to click a button to make something happen. However, some user interfaces allow a user to double-click on a list to indicate selection of a list item and acceptance of an action. We don't think this is a good user interface style because it is difficult for users to discover that they are supposed to double-click. But if you do want to implement this behavior, you have to add a mouse listener to the list box, then trap the mouse event as follows:

```
public void mouseClicked(MouseEvent evt)
{
    if (evt.getClickCount() == 2)
    {
        JList source = (JList)evt.getSource();
        Object[] selection = source.getSelectedValues();
        doAction(selection);
    }
}
```

Example 6–1 is the listing of the program that demonstrates a list box filled with strings. Notice how the `valueChanged` method builds up the message string from the selected items.

Example 6–1: ListTest.java

```
 1. import java.awt.*;
 2. import java.awt.event.*;
 3. import javax.swing.*;
 4. import javax.swing.event.*;
 5.
 6. /**
 7.    This program demonstrates a simple fixed list of strings.
 8. */
 9. public class ListTest
10. {
11.    public static void main(String[] args)
12.    {
13.       JFrame frame = new ListFrame();
14.       frame.setDefaultCloseOperation(JFrame.EXIT_ON_CLOSE);
15.       frame.show();
16.    }
17. }
18.
19. /**
20.    This frame contains a word list and a label that shows a
21.    sentence made up from the chosen words. Note that you can
22.    select multiple words with Ctrl+click and Shift+click.
23. */
24. class ListFrame extends JFrame
25. {
26.    public ListFrame()
27.    {
28.       setTitle("ListTest");
29.       setSize(WIDTH, HEIGHT);
30.
31.       String[] words =
32.       {
33.          "quick","brown","hungry","wild","silent",
34.          "huge","private","abstract","static","final"
35.       };
36.
37.       wordList = new JList(words);
38.       JScrollPane scrollPane = new JScrollPane(wordList);
39.
40.       JPanel p = new JPanel();
41.       p.add(scrollPane);
42.       wordList.addListSelectionListener(new
43.          ListSelectionListener()
44.          {
45.             public void valueChanged(ListSelectionEvent event)
46.             {
```

```
47.              Object[] values = wordList.getSelectedValues();
48.
49.              StringBuffer text = new StringBuffer(prefix);
50.              for (int i = 0; i < values.length; i++)
51.              {
52.                 String word = (String)values[i];
53.                 text.append(word);
54.                 text.append(" ");
55.              }
56.              text.append(suffix);
57.
58.              label.setText(text.toString());
59.           }
60.        });
61.
62.     Container contentPane = getContentPane();
63.     contentPane.add(p, BorderLayout.SOUTH);
64.     label = new JLabel(prefix + suffix);
65.     contentPane.add(label, BorderLayout.CENTER);
66.   }
67.
68.   private static final int WIDTH = 400;
69.   private static final int HEIGHT = 300;
70.   private JList wordList;
71.   private JLabel label;
72.   private String prefix = "The ";
73.   private String suffix = "fox jumps over the lazy dog.";
74. }
```

 javax.swing.JList

- JList(Object[] items)

  constructs a list that displays these items.

- void setVisibleRowCount(int c)

  sets the preferred number of rows in the list that can be displayed without a scroll bar.

- void setSelectionMode(int mode)

  determines whether single-item or multiple-item selections are allowed.

  Parameters: mode   one of SINGLE_SELECTION, SINGLE_INTERVAL_SELECTION, MULTIPLE_INTERVAL_SELECTION

- void addListSelectionListener(ListSelectionListener listener)

  adds to the list a listener that's notified each time a change to the selection occurs.

- Object[] getSelectedValues()

  returns the selected values or an empty array if the selection is empty.

- `Object getSelectedValue()`
  returns the first selected value or `null` if the selection is empty.

`javax.swing.event.ListSelectionListener`

- `void valueChanged(ListSelectionEvent e)`
  is called whenever the list selection changes.

List Models

In the preceding section, you have seen the most common method for using a list component:

- Specify a fixed set of strings for display in the list,
- Add a scrollbar,
- Trap the list selection events.

In the remainder of the section on lists, we will cover more complex situations that require a bit more finesse:

- Very long lists
- Lists with changing contents
- Lists that don't contain strings

In the first example, we constructed a `JList` component that held a fixed collection of strings. However, the collection of choices in a list box is not always fixed. How do we add or remove items in the list box? Somewhat surprisingly, there are no methods in the `JList` class to achieve this. Instead, you have to understand a little more about the internal design of the list component. As with text components, the list component uses the model-view-controller design pattern to separate the visual appearance (a column of items that are rendered in some way) from the underlying data (a collection of objects).

The `JList` class is responsible for the visual appearance of the data. It actually knows very little about how the data is stored—all it knows is that it can retrieve the data through some object that implements the `ListModel` interface:

```
public interface ListModel
{
    public int getSize();
    public Object getElementAt(int i);
    public void addListDataListener(ListDataListener l);
    public void removeListDataListener(ListDataListener l);
}
```

Through this interface, the `JList` can get a count of elements and retrieve each one of the elements. Also, the `JList` object can add itself as a *list data listener*. It then gets notified if the collection of elements changes, so that it can repaint the list.

Why is this generality useful? Why doesn't the JList object simply store a vector of objects?

Note that the interface doesn't specify how the objects are stored. In particular, it doesn't force them to be stored at all! The getElementAt method is free to recompute each value whenever it is called. This is potentially useful if you want to show a very large collection without having to store the values.

Here is a somewhat silly example: we let the user choose among *all three-letter words* in a list box (see Figure 6–2).

Figure 6–2: Choosing from a very long list of selections

There are 26 · 26 · 26 = 17,576 three-letter combinations. Rather than storing all these combinations, we recompute them as requested when the user scrolls through them.

This turns out to be easy to implement. The tedious part, adding and removing listeners, has been done for us in the AbstractListModel class which we extend. We only need to supply the getSize and getElementAt methods:

```
class WordListModel extends AbstractListModel
{
    public WordListModel(int n) { length = n; }
    public int getSize() { return (int)Math.pow(26, length); }
    public Object getElementAt(int n)
    {
        // compute nth string
        . . .
    }
    . . .
}
```

The computation of the *n*th string is a bit technical—you'll find the details in the code listing in Example 6–2.

Now that we supplied a model, we can simply build a list that lets the user scroll through the elements supplied by the model:

```
JList wordList = new JList(new WordListModel(3));
wordList.setSelectionMode(ListSelectionModel.SINGLE_SELECTION);
JScrollPane scrollPane = new JScrollPane(wordList);
```

The point is that the strings are never *stored*. Only those strings that the user actually requests to see are generated.

There is one other setting that we must make. We must tell the list component that all items have a fixed width and height:

```
wordList.setFixedCellWidth(50);
wordList.setFixedCellHeight(15);
```

Otherwise, the list component would compute each item to measure its width and height. That would take a long time.

As a practical matter, such very long lists are rarely useful. It is extremely cumbersome for a user to scroll through a huge selection. For that reason, we believe that the list control has been completely over-engineered. A selection that a user can comfortably manage on the screen is certainly small enough to be stored directly in the list component. That arrangement would have saved programmers from the pain of having to deal with the list model as a separate entity. On the other hand, the `JList` class is consistent with the `JTree` and `JTable` class where this generality is useful.

Example 6–2: LongListTest.java

```
1. import java.awt.*;
2. import java.awt.event.*;
3. import javax.swing.*;
4. import javax.swing.event.*;
5.
6.
7. /**
8.    This program demonstrates a list that dynamically computes
9.    list entries.
10. */
11. public class LongListTest
12. {
13.    public static void main(String[] args)
14.    {
15.       JFrame frame = new LongListFrame();
16.       frame.setDefaultCloseOperation(JFrame.EXIT_ON_CLOSE);
17.       frame.show();
18.    }
19. }
20.
21. /**
```

```
22.    This frame contains a long word list and a label that shows a
23.    sentence made up from the chosen word.
24. */
25. class LongListFrame extends JFrame
26. {
27.    public LongListFrame()
28.    {
29.       setTitle("LongListTest");
30.       setSize(WIDTH, HEIGHT);
31.
32.       wordList = new JList(new WordListModel(3));
33.       wordList.setSelectionMode
34.          (ListSelectionModel.SINGLE_SELECTION);
35.
36.       wordList.setFixedCellWidth(50);
37.       wordList.setFixedCellHeight(15);
38.
39.       JScrollPane scrollPane = new JScrollPane(wordList);
40.
41.       JPanel p = new JPanel();
42.       p.add(scrollPane);
43.       wordList.addListSelectionListener(new
44.          ListSelectionListener()
45.          {
46.             public void valueChanged(ListSelectionEvent evt)
47.             {
48.                StringBuffer word
49.                   = (StringBuffer)wordList.getSelectedValue();
50.                setSubject(word.toString());
51.             }
52.
53.          });
54.
55.       Container contentPane = getContentPane();
56.       contentPane.add(p, BorderLayout.SOUTH);
57.       label = new JLabel(prefix + suffix);
58.       contentPane.add(label, BorderLayout.CENTER);
59.       setSubject("fox");
60.    }
61.
62.    /**
63.       Sets the subject in the label.
64.       @param word the new subject that jumps over the lazy dog
65.    */
66.    public void setSubject(String word)
67.    {
68.       StringBuffer text = new StringBuffer(prefix);
```

```
69.         text.append(word);
70.         text.append(suffix);
71.         label.setText(text.toString());
72.      }
73.
74.      private static final int WIDTH = 400;
75.      private static final int HEIGHT = 300;
76.      private JList wordList;
77.      private JLabel label;
78.      private String prefix = "The quick brown ";
79.      private String suffix = " jumps over the lazy dog.";
80. }
81.
82. /**
83.     A model that dynamically generates n-letter words.
84. */
85. class WordListModel extends AbstractListModel
86. {
87.     /**
88.         Constructs the model.
89.         @param n the word length
90.     */
91.     public WordListModel(int n) { length = n; }
92.
93.     public int getSize()
94.     {
95.         return (int)Math.pow(LAST - FIRST + 1, length);
96.     }
97.
98.     public Object getElementAt(int n)
99.     {
100.        StringBuffer r = new StringBuffer();;
101.        for (int i = 0; i < length; i++)
102.        {
103.           char c = (char)(FIRST + n % (LAST - FIRST + 1));
104.           r.insert(0, c);
105.           n = n / (LAST - FIRST + 1);
106.        }
107.        return r;
108.     }
109.
110.     private int length;
111.     public static final char FIRST = 'a';
112.     public static final char LAST = 'z';
113. }
```

javax.swing.JList

- JList(ListModel dataModel)
  constructs a list that displays the elements in the specified model.

- void setFixedCellWidth(int width)
  if the width is greater than zero, specifies the width of every cell in the list. The default value is –1, which forces the size of each cell to be measured.

- void setFixedCellHeight(int height)
  if the height is greater than zero, specifies the height of every cell in the list. The default value is –1, which forces the size of each cell to be measured.

javax.swing.ListModel

- int getSize()
  returns the number of elements of the model.

- Object getElementAt(int index)
  returns an element of the model.

Inserting and Removing Values

You cannot directly edit the collection of list values. Instead, you must access the *model* and then add or remove elements. That, too, is easier said than done. Suppose you want to add more values to a list. You can obtain a reference to the model:

```
ListModel model = list.getModel();
```

But that does you no good—as you saw in the preceding section, the ListModel interface has no methods to insert or remove elements since, after all, the whole point of having a list model is that it need not *store* the elements.

Let's try it the other way around. One of the constructors of JList takes a vector of objects:

```
Vector values = new Vector();
values.addElement("quick");
values.addElement("brown");
. . .
JList list = new JList(values);
```

Of course, you can now edit the vector and add or remove elements, but the list does not know that this is happening, so it cannot react to the changes. In particular, the list cannot update its view when you add the values.

NOTE: There is no JList constructor that takes an ArrayList parameter. But, since construction from a Vector isn't all that useful, that's not a real limitation.

Instead, you have to construct a particular model, the `DefaultListModel`, fill it with the initial values, and associate it with the list.

```
DefaultListModel model = new DefaultListModel();
model.addElement("quick");
model.addElement("brown");
. . .
JList list = new JList(model);
```

Now you can add or remove values from the `model` object. The `model` object then notifies the list of the changes, and the list repaints itself.

```
model.removeElement("quick");
model.addElement("slow");
```

As you can see, the `DefaultListModel` class doesn't uses the same method names as the collection classes.

The default list model uses a vector internally to store the values. It inherits the list notification mechanism from `AbstractListModel`, just as the example model class of the preceding section.

CAUTION: There are `JList` constructors that construct a list from an array or vector of objects or strings. You might think that these constructors use a `DefaultListModel` to store these values. That is not the case—the constructors build a trivial model that can access the values without any provisions for notification if the contents changes. For example, here is the code for the constructor that constructs a `JList` from a `Vector`:

```
public JList(final Vector listData)
{
    this (new AbstractListModel()
    {
        public int getSize() { return listData.size(); }
        public Object getElementAt(int i)
        { return listData.elementAt(i); }
    });
}
```

That means, if you change the contents of the vector after the list is constructed, then the list may show a confusing mix of old and new values until it is completely repainted. (The keyword `final` in the constructor above does not prevent you from changing the vector elsewhere—it only means that the constructor itself won't modify the value of the `listData` reference; the keyword is required because the `listData` object is used in the inner class.)

- `ListModel getModel()`
  gets the model of this list.

javax.swing.DefaultListModel

- void addElement(Object obj)

  adds the object to the end of the model.

- boolean removeElement(Object obj)

  removes the first occurrence of the object from the model. Returns true if the object was contained in the model, false otherwise.

Rendering Values

So far, all lists that you saw in this chapter contained only strings. It is actually just as easy to show a list of icons—simply pass an array or vector filled with Icon objects. More interestingly, you can easily represent your list values with any drawing whatsoever.

While the JList class can display strings and icons automatically, you need to install a *list cell renderer* into the JList object for all custom drawing. A list cell renderer is any class that implements the following interface:

```
interface ListCellRenderer
{
    Component getListCellRendererComponent(JList list,
        Object value, int index,
        boolean isSelected, boolean cellHasFocus);
}
```

If you install a list cell renderer into a list, it gets called for each list value: first, if you did not select fixed-sized cells, to measure the size of the graphical representation of the value; then, to draw it. You must provide a class that returns an object of type Component, such that the getPreferredSize and paint methods of the returned object carry out these tasks as appropriate for your list values.

A simple way to do this is to create an inner class with these two methods:

```
class MyCellRenderer implements ListCellRenderer
{
    public Component getListCellRendererComponent(final JList list,
        final Object value, final int index,
        final boolean isSelected, final boolean cellHasFocus)
    {
        return new
            JPanel()
            {
                public void paintComponent(Graphics g)
                {
                    // paint code goes here
                }
                public Dimension getPreferredSize()
                {
```

```
                    // size measurement code goes here
            }
        };
    }
}
```

In Example 6–3, we display the font choices graphically by showing the actual appearance of each font (see Figure 6–3). In the `paintComponent` method, we display each name in its own font. We also need to make sure to match the usual colors of the look and feel of the `JList` class. We obtain these colors by calling the `getForeground`/`getBackground` and `getSelectionForeground`/ `getSelectionBackground` methods of the `JList` class. In the `getPreferredSize` method, we need to measure the size of the string, using the techniques that you saw in Chapter 7 of Volume 1.

Figure 6–3: A list box with rendered cells

To install the cell renderer, simply call the `setCellRenderer` method:

```
fontList.setCellRenderer(new FontCellRenderer());
```

Now all list cells are drawn with the custom renderer.

There is actually a simpler method for writing custom renderers that works in many cases. If the rendered image just contains text, an icon, and possibly a change of color, then you can get by with configuring a `JLabel`. For example, to show the font name in its own font, we can use the following renderer:

```
class FontCellRenderer implements ListCellRenderer
{
    public Component getListCellRendererComponent(JList list,
        Object value, int index, boolean isSelected,
            boolean cellHasFocus)
    {
        JLabel label = new JLabel();
        Font font = (Font)value;
```

```
            label.setText(font.getFamily());
            label.setFont(font);
            label.setOpaque(true);
            label.setBackground(isSelected
                ? list.getSelectionBackground()
                : list.getBackground());
            label.setForeground(isSelected
                ? list.getSelectionForeground()
                : list.getForeground());
            return label;
        }
    }
```

Note that here we don't write any `paintComponent` or `getPreferredSize` methods; the `JLabel` class already implements these methods to our satisfaction. All we need to do is to configure the label appropriately by setting its text, font, and color.

For added conciseness, the `FontCellRenderer` can even extend `JLabel`, configure *itself* with every call to `getListCellRendererComponent`, and then return `this`:

```
    class FontCellRenderer extends JLabel implements ListCellRenderer
    {
        public Component getListCellRendererComponent(JList list,
            Object value, int index, boolean isSelected,
                boolean cellHasFocus)
        {
            Font font = (Font)value;
            setText(font.getFamily());
            setFont(font);
            setOpaque(true);
            setBackground(isSelected
                ? list.getSelectionBackground()
                : list.getBackground());
            setForeground(isSelected
                ? list.getSelectionForeground()
                : list.getForeground());
            return this;
        }
    }
```

This code is a convenient shortcut for those cases where an existing component—in this case, `JLabel`—already provides all functionality that is needed to render a cell value.

Example 6–3: ListRenderingTest.java

```
1. import java.util.*;
2. import java.awt.*;
3. import java.awt.event.*;
4. import javax.swing.*;
```

```
5.  import javax.swing.event.*;
6.
7.  /**
8.     This program demonstrates the use of cell renderers in
9.     a list box.
10. */
11. public class ListRenderingTest
12. {
13.    public static void main(String[] args)
14.    {
15.       JFrame frame = new ListRenderingFrame();
16.       frame.setDefaultCloseOperation(JFrame.EXIT_ON_CLOSE);
17.       frame.show();
18.    }
19. }
20.
21. /**
22.    This frame contains a list with a set of fonts and a text
23.    area that is set to the selected font.
24. */
25. class ListRenderingFrame extends JFrame
26. {
27.    public ListRenderingFrame()
28.    {
29.       setTitle("ListRenderingTest");
30.       setSize(WIDTH, HEIGHT);
31.
32.       ArrayList fonts = new ArrayList();
33.       final int SIZE = 24;
34.       fonts.add(new Font("Serif", Font.PLAIN, SIZE));
35.       fonts.add(new Font("SansSerif", Font.PLAIN, SIZE));
36.       fonts.add(new Font("Monospaced", Font.PLAIN, SIZE));
37.       fonts.add(new Font("Dialog", Font.PLAIN, SIZE));
38.       fonts.add(new Font("DialogInput", Font.PLAIN, SIZE));
39.       fontList = new JList(fonts.toArray());
40.       fontList.setVisibleRowCount(4);
41.       fontList.setSelectionMode
42.          (ListSelectionModel.SINGLE_SELECTION);
43.       fontList.setCellRenderer(new FontCellRenderer());
44.       JScrollPane scrollPane = new JScrollPane(fontList);
45.
46.       JPanel p = new JPanel();
47.       p.add(scrollPane);
48.       fontList.addListSelectionListener(new
49.          ListSelectionListener()
50.          {
51.             public void valueChanged(ListSelectionEvent evt)
52.             {
53.                Font font = (Font)fontList.getSelectedValue();
54.                text.setFont(font);
```

```
55.              }
56.
57.          });
58.
59.      Container contentPane = getContentPane();
60.      contentPane.add(p, BorderLayout.SOUTH);
61.      text = new JTextArea(
62.          "The quick brown fox jumps over the lazy dog");
63.      text.setFont((Font)fonts.get(0));
64.      text.setLineWrap(true);
65.      text.setWrapStyleWord(true);
66.      contentPane.add(text, BorderLayout.CENTER);
67.   }
68.
69.   private JTextArea text;
70.   private JList fontList;
71.   private static final int WIDTH = 400;
72.   private static final int HEIGHT = 300;
73. }
74.
75. /**
76.    A cell renderer for Font objects that renders the font name
77.    in its own font.
78. */
79. class FontCellRenderer implements ListCellRenderer
80. {
81.   public Component getListCellRendererComponent
82.       (final JList list, final Object value,
83.       final int index, final boolean isSelected,
84.       final boolean cellHasFocus)
85.   {
86.       return new
87.          JPanel()
88.          {
89.              public void paintComponent(Graphics g)
90.              {
91.                  Font font = (Font)value;
92.                  String text = font.getFamily();
93.                  FontMetrics fm = g.getFontMetrics(font);
94.                  g.setColor(isSelected
95.                      ? list.getSelectionBackground()
96.                      : list.getBackground());
97.                  g.fillRect(0, 0, getWidth(), getHeight());
98.                  g.setColor(isSelected
99.                      ? list.getSelectionForeground()
100.                     : list.getForeground());
101.                 g.setFont(font);
102.                 g.drawString(text, 0, fm.getAscent());
103.             }
```

```
104.
105.            public Dimension getPreferredSize()
106.            {
107.                Font font = (Font)value;
108.                String text = font.getFamily();
109.                Graphics g = getGraphics();
110.                FontMetrics fm = g.getFontMetrics(font);
111.                return new Dimension(fm.stringWidth(text),
112.                    fm.getHeight());
113.            }
114.        };
115.    }
116. }
```

javax.swing.JList

- `Color getBackground()`
  returns the background color for unselected cells.

- `Color getSelectionBackground()`
  returns the background color for selected cells.

- `void setCellRenderer(ListCellRenderer cellRenderer)`
  sets the renderer that is used to paint the cells in the list.

javax.swing.ListCellRenderer

- `Component getListCellRendererComponent(JList list, Object item, int index, boolean isSelected, boolean hasFocus)`
  returns a component whose `paint` method will draw the cell contents. If the list cells do not have fixed size, that component must also implement `getPreferredSize`.

Parameters:	`list`	the list whose cell is being drawn
	`item`	the item to be drawn
	`index`	the index where the item is stored in the model
	`isSelected`	`true` if the specified cell was selected
	`hasFocus`	`true` if the specified cell has the focus

Trees

Every computer user who uses a hierarchical file system has encountered *tree* displays such as the one in Figure 6–4. Of course, directories and files form only one of the many examples of treelike organizations. Programmers are familiar with inheritance trees for classes. There are many tree structures that arise in everyday life, such as the hierarchy of countries, states, and cities shown in Figure 6–5.

As programmers, we often have to display these tree structures. Fortunately, the Swing library has a JTree class for this purpose. The JTree class (together with its helper classes) takes care of laying out the tree and of processing user requests for expanding and collapsing nodes. In this section, you will learn how to put the

Figure 6–4: A directory tree

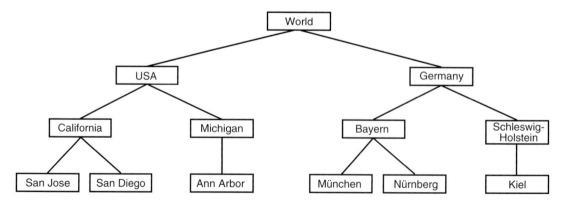

Figure 6–5: A hierarchy of countries, states, and cities

JTree class to use. As with the other complex Swing components, we must focus on the common and useful cases and cannot cover every nuance—we recommend that you consult *Core Java Foundation Classes* by Kim Topley [Prentice-Hall 1998] or *Graphic Java 2* by David M. Geary [Prentice-Hall 1999] if you want to achieve an unusual effect.

Before going any further, let's settle on some terminology (see Figure 6–6). A tree is composed of *nodes*. Every node is either a *leaf*, or it has *child nodes*. Every node, with the exception of the root node, has exactly one *parent*. A tree has exactly one root node. Sometimes you have a collection of trees, each of which has its own root node. Such a collection is called a *forest*.

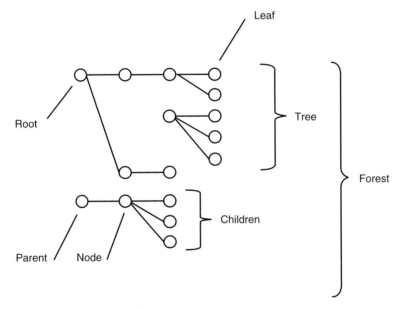

Figure 6–6: Tree terminology

Simple Trees

In our first example program, we simply display a tree with a few nodes (see Figure 6–8 on page 431). As with most other Swing components, the JTree component follows the model/view/controller pattern. You provide a model of the hierarchical data, and the component displays it for you. To construct a JTree, you supply the tree model in the constructor:

```
TreeModel model = . . .;
JTree tree = new JTree(model);
```

NOTE: There are also constructors that construct trees out of a collection of elements:

```
JTree(Object[] nodes)
JTree(Vector nodes)
JTree(Hashtable nodes) // the values become the nodes
```

These constructors are not very useful. They merely build a forest of trees, each with a single node. The third constructor seems particularly useless since the nodes appear in the essentially random order given by the hash codes of the keys.

How do you obtain a tree model? You can construct your own model by creating a class that implements the `TreeModel` interface. You will see later in this chapter how to do that. For now, we'll stick with the `DefaultTreeModel` that the Swing library supplies.

To construct a default tree model, you must supply a root node.

```
TreeNode root = . . .;
DefaultTreeModel model = new DefaultTreeModel(root);
```

`TreeNode` is another interface. You populate the default tree model with objects of any class that implements the interface. For now, we will use the concrete node class that Swing supplies, namely `DefaultMutableTreeNode`. This class implements the `MutableTreeNode` interface, a subinterface of `TreeNode` (see Figure 6–7).

Figure 6–7: Tree classes

A default mutable tree node holds an object, the *user object.* The tree renders the user objects for all nodes. Unless you specify a renderer, the tree simply displays the string that is the result of the `toString` method.

In our first example, we use strings as user objects. In practice, you would usually populate a tree with more expressive user objects. For example, when displaying a directory tree, it makes sense to use `File` objects for the nodes.

You can specify the user object in the constructor, or you can set it later with the `setUserObject` method.

```
DefaultMutableTreeNode node
    = new DefaultMutableTreeNode("Texas");
node.setUserObject("California");
```

Next, you establish the parent/child relationships between the nodes. Start with the root node, and use the `add` method to add the children:

```
DefaultMutableTreeNode root
    = new DefaultMutableTreeNode("World");
DefaultMutableTreeNode country
    = new DefaultMutableTreeNode("USA");
root.add(country);
DefaultMutableTreeNode state
    = new DefaultMutableTreeNode("California");
country.add(state);
```

Figure 6–8 illustrates how the tree will look.

Figure 6–8: A simple tree

Link up all nodes in this fashion. Then, construct a `DefaultTreeModel` with the root node. Finally, construct a `JTree` with the tree model.

```
DefaultTreeModel treeModel = new DefaultTreeModel(root);
JTree tree = new JTree(treeModel);
```

Or, as a shortcut, you can simply pass the root node to the `JTree` constructor. Then the tree automatically constructs a default tree model:

```
JTree tree = new JTree(root);
```

Example 6–4 contains the complete code.

Example 6–4: SimpleTree.java

```
1. import java.awt.*;
2. import java.awt.event.*;
3. import javax.swing.*;
4. import javax.swing.tree.*;
5.
6. /**
7.    This program shows a simple tree.
8. */
9. public class SimpleTree
10. {
11.    public static void main(String[] args)
12.    {
13.       JFrame frame = new SimpleTreeFrame();
14.       frame.setDefaultCloseOperation(JFrame.EXIT_ON_CLOSE);
15.       frame.show();
16.    }
17. }
18.
19. /**
20.    This frame contains a simple tree that displays a
21.    manually constructed tree model.
22. */
23. class SimpleTreeFrame extends JFrame
24. {
25.    public SimpleTreeFrame()
26.    {
27.       setTitle("SimpleTree");
28.       setSize(WIDTH, HEIGHT);
29.
30.       // set up tree model data
31.
32.       DefaultMutableTreeNode root
33.          = new DefaultMutableTreeNode("World");
34.       DefaultMutableTreeNode country
35.          = new DefaultMutableTreeNode("USA");
36.       root.add(country);
37.       DefaultMutableTreeNode state
38.          = new DefaultMutableTreeNode("California");
39.       country.add(state);
40.       DefaultMutableTreeNode city
41.          = new DefaultMutableTreeNode("San Jose");
42.       state.add(city);
43.       city = new DefaultMutableTreeNode("Cupertino");
44.       state.add(city);
45.       state = new DefaultMutableTreeNode("Michigan");
```

```
46.        country.add(state);
47.        city = new DefaultMutableTreeNode("Ann Arbor");
48.        state.add(city);
49.        country = new DefaultMutableTreeNode("Germany");
50.        root.add(country);
51.        state = new DefaultMutableTreeNode("Schleswig-Holstein");
52.        country.add(state);
53.        city = new DefaultMutableTreeNode("Kiel");
54.        state.add(city);
55.
56.        // construct tree and put it in a scroll pane
57.
58.        JTree tree = new JTree(root);
59.        Container contentPane = getContentPane();
60.        contentPane.add(new JScrollPane(tree));
61.    }
62.
63.    private static final int WIDTH = 300;
64.    private static final int HEIGHT = 200;
65. }
```

When you run the program, the tree first looks as in Figure 6–9. Only the root node and its children are visible. Click on the circle icons (the *handles*) to open up the subtrees. The line sticking out from the handle icon points to the right when the subtree is collapsed, and it points down when the subtree is expanded (see Figure 6–10). We don't know what the designers of the Metal look and feel had in mind, but we think of the icon as a door handle. You push down on the handle to open the subtree.

NOTE: Of course, the display of the tree depends on the selected look and feel. We just described the Java look and feel (a.k.a. "Metal"). In the Windows and Motif look and feel, the handles have the more familiar look—a "+" or "−" in a box (see Figure 6–11).

Figure 6–9: The initial tree display

Figure 6–10: Collapsed and expanded subtrees

Figure 6–11: A tree with the Windows look and feel

Up to SDK 1.3, the Java look and feel does not display the tree outline by default (see Figure 6–12). As of SDK 1.4, the default line style is "angled."

In SDK 1.4, use the following magic incantation to turn off the lines joining parents and children:

```
tree.putClientProperty("JTree.lineStyle", "None");
```

Conversely, to make sure that the angled lines are shown, use

```
tree.putClientProperty("JTree.lineStyle", "Angled");
```

Figure 6–12: A tree with no connecting lines

There is also another line style, `"Horizontal"`, that is shown in Figure 6–13. The tree is displayed with horizontal lines separating only the children of the root. We aren't quite sure what it is good for.

Figure 6–13: A tree with the horizontal line style

By default, there is no handle for collapsing the root of the tree. If you like, you can add one with the call

```
tree.setShowsRootHandles(true);
```

Figure 6–14 shows the result. Now you can collapse the entire tree into the root node.

Figure 6–14: A tree with a root handle

Conversely, you can hide the root altogether. You do that to display a *forest*, a set of trees, each of which has its own root. You still must join all trees in the forest to a common root. Then, you hide the root with the instruction

```
tree.setRootVisible(false);
```

Look at Figure 6–15. There appear to be two roots, labeled "USA" and "Germany." The actual root that joins the two is made invisible.

Figure 6–15: A forest

Let's turn from the root to the leaves of the tree. Note that the leaves have a different icon than the other nodes (see Figure 6–16).

When displaying the tree, each node is drawn with an icon. There are actually three kinds of icons: a leaf icon, an opened non-leaf icon, and a closed non-leaf icon. For simplicity, we'll refer to the last two as folder icons.

The node renderer needs to know which icon to use for each node. By default, the decision process works like this: If the `isLeaf` method of a node returns `true`, then the leaf icon is used. Otherwise, a folder icon is used.

Figure 6–16: Leaf icons

The `isLeaf` method of the `DefaultMutableTreeNode` class returns `true` if the node has no children. Thus, nodes with children get folder icons, and nodes without children get leaf icons.

Sometimes, that behavior is not appropriate. Suppose we added a node "Montana" to our sample tree, but we're at a loss as to what cities to add. We would not want the state node to get a leaf icon since conceptually only the cities are leaves.

The `JTree` class has no idea which nodes should be leaves. It asks the tree model. If a childless node isn't automatically a conceptual leaf, you can ask the tree model to use a different criterion for leafiness, namely to query the "allows children" node property.

For those nodes that should not have children, call

```
node.setAllowsChildren(false);
```

Then, tell the tree model to ask the value of the "allows children" property to determine whether a node should be displayed with a leaf icon. You use the `setAsksAllowsChildren` method of the `DefaultTreeModel` class to set this behavior:

```
model.setAsksAllowsChildren(true);
```

With this decision criterion, nodes that allow children get folder icons, and nodes that don't allow children get leaf icons.

Alternatively, if you construct the tree by supplying the root node, supply the setting for the "asks allows children" property in the constructor.

```
JTree tree = new JTree(root, true);
   // nodes that don't allow children get leaf icons
```

javax.swing.JTree

- `JTree(TreeModel model)`
  constructs a tree from a tree model.

- `JTree(TreeNode root)`
- `JTree(TreeNode root, boolean asksAllowChildren)`
  construct a tree with a default tree model that displays the root and its children.

Parameters:	`root`	The root node
	`asksAllowsChildren`	true to use the "allows children" node property for determining whether a node is a leaf

- `void setShowsRootHandles(boolean b)`
  If b is `true`, then the root node has a handle for collapsing or expanding its children.

- `void setRootVisible(boolean b)`
  If b is true, then the root node is displayed. Otherwise, it is hidden.

javax.swing.tree.TreeNode

- `boolean isLeaf()`
  returns `true` if this node is conceptually a leaf.

- `boolean getAllowsChildren()`
  returns `true` if this node can have child nodes.

javax.swing.tree.MutableTreeNode

- `void setUserObject(Object userObject)`
  sets the "user object" that the tree node uses for rendering.

javax.swing.tree.TreeModel

- `boolean isLeaf(Object node)`
  returns `true` if node should be displayed as a leaf node.

javax.swing.tree.DefaultTreeModel

- `void setAsksAllowsChildren(boolean b)`
  If b is true, then nodes are displayed as leaves when their `getAllowsChildren` method returns `false`. Otherwise, they are displayed as leaves when their `isLeaf` method returns `true`.

javax.swing.tree.DefaultMutableTreeNode

- DefaultMutableTreeNode(Object userObject)
  constructs a mutable tree node with the given user object.
- void add(MutableTreeNode child)
  adds a node as the last child of this node.
- void setAllowsChildren(boolean b)
  If b is true, then children can be added to this node.

javax.swing.JComponent

- void putClientProperty(Object key, Object value)
  adds a key/value pair to a small table that each component manages. This is an "escape hatch" mechanism that some Swing components use for storing look-and-feel specific properties.

Editing trees and tree paths

In the next example program, you will see how to edit a tree. Figure 6–17 shows the user interface. If you click on the "Add Sibling" or "Add Child" button, the program adds a new node (with title New) to the tree. If you click on the "Delete" button, the program deletes the currently selected node.

Figure 6–17: Editing a tree

To implement this behavior, you need to find out which tree node is currently selected. The JTree class has a surprising way of identifying nodes in a tree. It does not deal with tree nodes, but with *paths of objects,* called *tree paths*. A tree path starts at the root and consists of a sequence of child nodes—see Figure 6–18.

Figure 6–18: A tree path

You may wonder why the `JTree` class needs the whole path. Couldn't it just get a `TreeNode` and keep calling the `getParent` method? In fact, the `JTree` class knows nothing about the `TreeNode` interface. That interface is never used by the `TreeModel` interface; it is only used by the `DefaultTreeModel` implementation. You can have other tree models in which the nodes do not implement the `TreeNode` interface at all. If you use a tree model that manages other types of objects, then those objects may not have `getParent` and `getChild` methods. They would of course need to have some other connection to each other. It is the job of the tree model to link nodes together. The `JTree` class itself has no clue about the nature of their linkage. For that reason, the `JTree` class always needs to work with complete paths.

The `TreePath` class manages a sequence of `Object` (not `TreeNode`!) references. A number of `JTree` methods return `TreePath` objects. When you have a tree path, you usually just need to know the terminal node, which you get with the `getLastPathComponent` method. For example, to find out the currently selected node in a tree, you use the `getSelectionPath` method of the `JTree` class. You get a `TreePath` object back, from which you can retrieve the actual node.

```
TreePath selectionPath = tree.getSelectionPath();
DefaultMutableTreeNode selectedNode = (DefaultMutableTreeNode)
    selectionPath.getLastPathComponent();
```

Actually, because this particular query is so common, there is a convenience method that gives the selected node immediately.

```
DefaultMutableTreeNode selectedNode = (DefaultMutableTreeNode)
    tree.getLastSelectedPathComponent();
```

This method is not called `getSelectedNode` because the tree does not know that it contains nodes—its tree model only deals with paths of objects.

> NOTE: Tree paths are one of two ways that the `JTree` class uses to describe nodes. There are also quite a few `JTree` methods that take or return an integer index, the *row position*. A row position is simply the row number (starting with 0) of the node in the tree display. Only visible nodes have row numbers, and the row number of a node changes if other nodes before it are expanded, collapsed, or modified. For that reason, you should avoid row positions. All `JTree` methods that use rows have equivalents that use tree paths instead.

Once you have the selected node, you can edit it. However, do not simply add children to a tree node:

```
selectedNode.add(newNode); // NO!
```

If you change the structure of the nodes, you change the model but the associated view is not notified. You could send out a notification yourself, but if you use the insertNodeInto method of the DefaultTreeModel class, the model class takes care of that. For example, the following call appends a new node as the last child of the selected node and notifies the tree view.

```
model.insertNodeInto(newNode, selectedNode,
    selectedNode.getChildCount());
```

The analogous call removeNodeFromParent removes a node and notifies the view:

```
model.removeNodeFromParent(selectedNode);
```

If you keep the node structure in place but you changed the user object, you should call the following method:

```
model.nodeChanged(changedNode);
```

The automatic notification is a major advantage of using the DefaultTree-Model. If you supply your own tree model, you have to implement it by hand. (See *Core Java Foundation Classes* by Kim Topley for details.)

> CAUTION: The DefaultTreeModel class has a reload method that reloads the entire model. However, don't call reload simply to update the tree after making a few changes. When the tree is regenerated, all nodes beyond the root's children are collapsed again. It is quite disconcerting to your users if they have to keep expanding the tree after every change.

When the view is notified of a change in the node structure, it updates the display but it does not automatically expand a node to show newly added children. In particular, if a user in our sample program adds a new child node to a node whose children are currently collapsed, then the new node is silently added to the collapsed subtree. This gives the user no feedback that the command was actually carried out. In such a case, you should make a special effort to expand all parent nodes so that the newly added node becomes visible. You use the makeVisible method of the JTree class for this purpose. The makeVisible method expects a tree path leading to the node that should become visible.

Thus, you need to construct a tree path from the root to the newly inserted node. To get a tree path, you first call the getPathToRoot method of the DefaultTreeModel class. It returns a TreeNode[] array of all nodes from a node to the root node. You pass that array to a TreePath constructor.

For example, here is how you make the new node visible:

```
TreeNode[] nodes = model.getPathToRoot(newNode);
TreePath path = new TreePath(nodes);
tree.makeVisible(path);
```

> **NOTE:** It is curious that the `DefaultTreeModel` class feigns almost complete igno-
> rance about the `TreePath` class, even though its job is to communicate with a `JTree`.
> The `JTree` class uses tree paths a lot, and it never uses arrays of node objects.

But now suppose your tree is contained inside a scroll pane. After the tree node
expansion, the new node may still not be visible because it falls outside the viewport. To overcome that problem, call

```
tree.scrollPathToVisible(path);
```

instead of calling `makeVisible`. This call expands all nodes along the path, and
it tells the ambient scroll pane to scroll the node at the end of the path into view
(see Figure 6–19).

Figure 6–19: The scroll pane scrolls to display a new node

By default, tree nodes cannot be edited. However, if you call

```
tree.setEditable(true);
```

then the user can edit a node simply by double-clicking, editing the string, and
pressing the ENTER key. Double-clicking invokes the *default cell editor,* which is
implemented by the `DefaultCellEditor` class (see Figure 6–20). It is possible
to install other cell editors, but we will defer our discussion of cell editors until
the section on tables, where cell editors are more commonly used.

Figure 6–20: The Default Cell Editor

Example 6–5 shows the complete source code of the tree editing program. Run the program, add a few nodes, and edit them by double-clicking them. Observe how collapsed nodes expand to show added children and how the scroll pane keeps added nodes in the viewport.

Example 6–5: TreeEditTest.java

```
1. import java.awt.*;
2. import java.awt.event.*;
3. import javax.swing.*;
4. import javax.swing.tree.*;
5.
6. /**
7.    This program demonstrates tree editing.
8. */
9. public class TreeEditTest
10. {
11.    public static void main(String[] args)
12.    {
13.       JFrame frame = new TreeEditFrame();
14.       frame.setDefaultCloseOperation(JFrame.EXIT_ON_CLOSE);
15.       frame.show();
16.    }
17. }
18.
19. /**
20.    A frame with a tree and buttons to edit the tree.
21. */
22. class TreeEditFrame extends JFrame
23. {
24.    public TreeEditFrame()
25.    {
26.       setTitle("TreeEditTest");
27.       setSize(WIDTH, HEIGHT);
28.
29.       // construct tree
30.
31.       TreeNode root = makeSampleTree();
32.       model = new DefaultTreeModel(root);
33.       tree = new JTree(model);
34.       tree.setEditable(true);
35.
36.       // add scroll pane with tree to content pane
37.
38.       JScrollPane scrollPane = new JScrollPane(tree);
39.       getContentPane().add(scrollPane, BorderLayout.CENTER);
40.
41.       makeButtons();
42.       // make button panel
43.
44.    }
```

```
45.
46.    public TreeNode makeSampleTree()
47.    {
48.       DefaultMutableTreeNode root
49.          = new DefaultMutableTreeNode("World");
50.       DefaultMutableTreeNode country
51.          = new DefaultMutableTreeNode("USA");
52.       root.add(country);
53.       DefaultMutableTreeNode state
54.          = new DefaultMutableTreeNode("California");
55.       country.add(state);
56.       DefaultMutableTreeNode city
57.          = new DefaultMutableTreeNode("San Jose");
58.       state.add(city);
59.       city = new DefaultMutableTreeNode("Cupertino");
60.       state.add(city);
61.       state = new DefaultMutableTreeNode("Michigan");
62.       country.add(state);
63.       city = new DefaultMutableTreeNode("Ann Arbor");
64.       state.add(city);
65.       country = new DefaultMutableTreeNode("Germany");
66.       root.add(country);
67.       state = new DefaultMutableTreeNode("Schleswig-Holstein");
68.       country.add(state);
69.       city = new DefaultMutableTreeNode("Kiel");
70.       state.add(city);
71.       return root;
72.    }
73.
74.    /**
75.       Makes the buttons to add a sibling, add a child, and
76.       delete a node.
77.    */
78.    public void makeButtons()
79.    {
80.       JPanel panel = new JPanel();
81.       JButton addSiblingButton = new JButton("Add Sibling");
82.       addSiblingButton.addActionListener(new
83.          ActionListener()
84.          {
85.             public void actionPerformed(ActionEvent event)
86.             {
87.                DefaultMutableTreeNode selectedNode
88.                   = (DefaultMutableTreeNode)
89.                   tree.getLastSelectedPathComponent();
90.
91.                if (selectedNode == null) return;
92.
93.                DefaultMutableTreeNode parent
94.                   = (DefaultMutableTreeNode)
95.                   selectedNode.getParent();
96.
```

```
97.             if (parent == null) return;
98.
99.             DefaultMutableTreeNode newNode
100.               = new DefaultMutableTreeNode("New");
101.
102.          int selectedIndex = parent.getIndex(selectedNode);
103.          model.insertNodeInto(newNode, parent,
104.             selectedIndex + 1);
105.
106.          // now display new node
107.
108.          TreeNode[] nodes = model.getPathToRoot(newNode);
109.          TreePath path = new TreePath(nodes);
110.          tree.scrollPathToVisible(path);
111.        }
112.     });
113.   panel.add(addSiblingButton);
114.
115.   JButton addChildButton = new JButton("Add Child");
116.   addChildButton.addActionListener(new
117.       ActionListener()
118.       {
119.          public void actionPerformed(ActionEvent event)
120.          {
121.             DefaultMutableTreeNode selectedNode
122.               = (DefaultMutableTreeNode)
123.               tree.getLastSelectedPathComponent();
124.
125.             if (selectedNode == null) return;
126.
127.             DefaultMutableTreeNode newNode
128.               = new DefaultMutableTreeNode("New");
129.             model.insertNodeInto(newNode, selectedNode,
130.               selectedNode.getChildCount());
131.
132.             // now display new node
133.
134.             TreeNode[] nodes = model.getPathToRoot(newNode);
135.             TreePath path = new TreePath(nodes);
136.             tree.scrollPathToVisible(path);
137.          }
138.     });
139.   panel.add(addChildButton);
140.
141.   JButton deleteButton = new JButton("Delete");
142.   deleteButton.addActionListener(new
143.       ActionListener()
144.       {
145.          public void actionPerformed(ActionEvent event)
146.          {
147.             DefaultMutableTreeNode selectedNode
```

```
148.                    = (DefaultMutableTreeNode)
149.                    tree.getLastSelectedPathComponent();
150.
151.               if (selectedNode != null &&
152.                    selectedNode.getParent() != null)
153.                    model.removeNodeFromParent(selectedNode);
154.            }
155.         });
156.      panel.add(deleteButton);
157.      getContentPane().add(panel, BorderLayout.SOUTH);
158.   }
159.
160.   private DefaultTreeModel model;
161.   private JTree tree;
162.   private static final int WIDTH = 400;
163.   private static final int HEIGHT = 200;
164. }
```

javax.swing.JTree

- `TreePath getSelectionPath()`
  gets the path to the currently selected node (or the path to the first selected node if multiple nodes are selected). Returns `null` if no node is selected.

- `Object getLastSelectedPathComponent()`
  gets the node object that represents the currently selected node (or the first node if multiple nodes are selected). Returns `null` if no node is selected.

- `void makeVisible(TreePath path)`
  expands all nodes along the path.

- `void scrollPathToVisible(TreePath path)`
  expands all nodes along the path and, if the tree is contained in a scroll pane, scrolls to ensure that the last node on the path is visible.

javax.swing.tree.TreePath

- `Object getLastPathComponent()`
  gets the last object on this path, i.e., the node object that the path represents.

javax.swing.tree.TreeNode

- `TreeNode getParent()`
  returns the parent node of this node.

- `TreeNode getChildAt(int index)`
  looks up the child node at the given index. The index must be between 0 and `getChildCount() - 1`.

- `int getChildCount()`
  returns the number of children of this node.

- `Enumeration children()`
  returns an enumeration object that iterates through all children of this node.

`javax.swing.DefaultTreeModel`

- `void insertNodeInto(MutableTreeNode newChild, MutableTreeNode parent, int index)`
  inserts `newChild` as a new child node of `parent` at the given index.

- `void removeNodeFromParent(MutableTreeNode node)`
  removes `node` from this model.

- `void nodeChanged(TreeNode node)`
  notifies the tree model listeners that `node` has changed.

- `void nodesChanged(TreeNode parent, int[] changedChildIndexes)`
  notifies the tree model listeners that all child nodes of `parent` with the given indexes have changed.

- `void reload()`
  reloads all nodes into the model. This is a drastic operation that you should only use if the nodes have changed completely due to some outside influence.

Node Enumeration

Sometimes you need to find a node in a tree by starting at the root and visiting all children until you have found a match. The `DefaultMutableTreeNode` class has several convenience methods for iterating through nodes.

The `breadthFirstEnumeration` and `depthFirstEnumeration` methods return enumeration objects whose `nextElement` method visits all children of the current node, using either a breadth-first or depth-first traversal. Figure 6–21 shows the traversals for a sample tree—the node labels indicate the order in which the nodes are traversed.

Breadth-first enumeration is the easiest to visualize. The tree is traversed in layers. The root is visited first, followed by all of its children, then followed by the grandchildren, and so on.

To visualize depth-first enumeration, imagine a rat trapped in a tree-shaped maze. It rushes along the first path until it comes to a leaf. Then, it backtracks and turns around to the next path, and so on.

Computer science types also call this *postorder traversal,* because the search process first visits the children before visiting the parents. The `postOrderTraversal` method is a synonym for `depthFirstTraversal`. For completeness, there is also a `preOrderTraversal`, a depth-first search that enumerates parents before the children.

Here is the typical usage pattern:

```
Enumeration breadthFirst = node.breadthFirstEnumeration();
while (breadthFirst.hasMoreElements())
    do something with breadthFirst.nextElement();
```

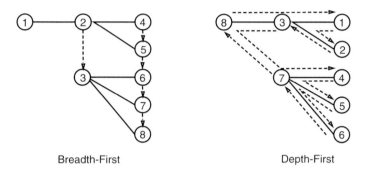

Breadth-First   Depth-First

Figure 6–21: Tree traversal orders

Finally, there is a related method `pathFromAncestorEnumeration` that finds a path from an ancestor to a given node and then enumerates the nodes along that path. That's no big deal—it just keeps calling `getParent` until the ancestor is found and then presents the path in reverse order.

In our next example program, we put node enumeration to work. The program displays inheritance trees of classes. Type the name of a class into the text field on the bottom of the frame. The class and all of its superclasses are added to the tree (see Figure 6–22).

Figure 6–22: An inheritance tree

In this example, we take advantage of the fact that the user objects of the tree nodes can be objects of any type. Since our nodes describe classes, we will store Class objects in the nodes.

Of course, we don't want to add the same class object twice, so we need to check whether a class already exists in the tree. The following method finds the node with a given user object if it exists in the tree.

```
public DefaultMutableTreeNode findUserObject(Object obj)
{
    Enumeration e = root.breadthFirstEnumeration();
    while (e.hasMoreElements())
    {
        DefaultMutableTreeNode node
            = (DefaultMutableTreeNode)e.nextElement();
        if (node.getUserObject().equals(obj))
            return node;
    }
    return null;
}
```

Rendering Nodes

In your applications, you will often need to change the way in which a tree component draws the nodes. The most common change is, of course, to choose different icons for nodes and leaves. Other changes might involve changing the font of the node labels or drawing images at the nodes. All these changes are made possible by installing a new *tree cell renderer* into the tree. By default, the JTree class uses DefaultTreeCellRenderer objects to draw each node. The Default-TreeCellRenderer class extends the JLabel class. The label contains the node icon and the node label.

NOTE: The cell renderer does not draw the "handles" for expanding and collapsing subtrees. The handles are part of the look and feel, and it is recommended that you not change them.

You can customize the display in three ways.

1. You can change the icons, font, and background color used by a Default-TreeCellRenderer. These settings are used for all nodes in the tree.

2. You can install a renderer that extends the DefaultTreeCellRenderer class and vary the icons, fonts, and background color for each node.

3. You can install a renderer that implements the TreeCellRenderer interface, to draw a custom image for each node.

Let us look at these possibilities one by one. The easiest customization is to construct a `DefaultTreeCellRenderer` object, change the icons, and install it into the tree:

```
DefaultTreeCellRenderer renderer
   = new DefaultTreeCellRenderer();
renderer.setLeafIcon(new ImageIcon("blue-ball.gif"));
   // used for leaf nodes
renderer.setClosedIcon(new ImageIcon("red-ball.gif"));
   // used for collapsed nodes
renderer.setOpenIcon(new ImageIcon("yellow-ball.gif"));
   // used for expanded nodes
tree.setCellRenderer(renderer);
```

You can see the effect in Figure 6–22. We just use the "ball" icons as placeholders—presumably your user interface designer would supply you with appropriate icons to use for your applications.

We don't recommend that you change the font or background color for an entire tree—that is really the job of the look and feel.

However, it can be useful to change the font for individual nodes in a tree to highlight some of them. If you look carefully at Figure 6–22, you will notice that the *abstract* classes are set in italics.

To change the appearance of individual nodes, you install a tree cell renderer. Tree cell renderers are very similar to the list cell renderers we discussed in Chapter 9 of Volume 1. The `TreeCellRenderer` interface has a single method

```
Component getTreeCellRendererComponent(JTree tree,
    Object value, boolean selected, boolean expanded,
    boolean leaf, int row, boolean hasFocus)
```

This method is called for each node. It returns a *component* whose `paint` method renders the node in the tree display. The `paint` method is invoked with an appropriate `Graphics` object, with coordinates and clip rectangle set so that the drawing appears at the correct location.

NOTE: You may wonder why you don't simply get to place a `paint` method into the class that implements the tree cell renderer interface. There is a very good reason. It is usually easier for you to tweak existing components than to program the actual drawing code. For example, the default tree cell renderer simply extends `JLabel` and lets the label worry about the correct spacing between the icon and the label text.

The `getTreeCellRendererComponent` method of the `DefaultTree-CellRenderer` class returns `this`—in other words, a label. (Recall that the `DefaultTreeCellRenderer` class extends the `JLabel` class.) To customize the component, extend the `DefaultTreeCellRenderer` class. Override the getTreeCellRendererComponent method as follows: call the superclass method, so that it can prepare the label data. Customize the label properties, and finally return this.

```
class MyTreeCellRenderer extends DefaultTreeCellRenderer
{
    public Component getTreeCellRendererComponent(JTree tree,
        Object value, boolean selected, boolean expanded,
        boolean leaf, int row, boolean hasFocus)
    {
        super.getTreeCellRendererComponent(tree, value,
            selected, expanded, leaf, row, hasFocus);
        DefaultMutableTreeNode node
            = (DefaultMutableTreeNode)value;
        look at node.getUserObject();
        Font font = appropriate font;
        setFont(font);
        return this;
    }
};
```

CAUTION: The value parameter of the getTreeCellRendererComponent method is the *node* object, *not* the user object! Recall that the user object is a feature of the DefaultMutableTreeNode, and that a JTree can contain nodes of an arbitrary type. If your tree uses DefaultMutableTreeNode nodes, then you must retrieve the user object in a second step, as we did in the preceding code sample.

CAUTION: The DefaultTreeCellRenderer uses the *same* label object for all nodes, only changing the label text for each node. If you change the font for a particular node, you must set it back to its default value when the method is called again. Otherwise, all subsequent nodes will be drawn in the changed font! Look at the code in Example 6–6 to see how to restore the font to the default.

We will not show an example for a tree cell renderer that draws arbitrary graphics. You can look at the list cell renderer at the beginning of this chapter—the technique is entirely analogous.

Let's put tree cell renderers to work. Example 6–6 shows the complete source code for the class tree program. The program displays inheritance hierarchies, and it customizes the display to show abstract classes in italics. You can type the name of any class into the text field at the bottom of the frame. Press the ENTER key or click the "Add" button to add the class and its superclasses to the tree. You must enter the full package name, such as java.util.ArrayList.

This program is a bit tricky because it uses reflection to construct the class tree. This work is contained inside the addClass method. (The details are not that important. We use the class tree in this example because inheritance trees yield a nice supply of trees without laborious coding. If you display trees in your own applications, you will have your own source of hierarchical data.) The method uses the breadth-first search algorithm to find whether the current class is already in the tree by calling the `findUserObject` method that we implemented in the preceding section. If the class is not already in the tree, we add the superclass to the tree, then make the new class node a child and make that node visible.

The `ClassNameTreeCellRenderer` sets the class name in either the normal or italic font, depending on the `ABSTRACT` modifier of the `Class` object. We don't want to set a particular font since we don't want to change whatever font the look and feel normally uses for labels. For that reason, we use the font from the label and *derive* an italic font from it. Recall that there is only a single shared `JLabel` object that is returned by all calls. We need to hang on to the original font and restore it in the next call to the `getTreeCellRendererComponent` method.

Finally, note how we change the node icons in the `ClassTreeFrame` constructor.

Example 6–6: ClassTree.java

```
 1. import java.awt.*;
 2. import java.awt.event.*;
 3. import java.lang.reflect.*;
 4. import java.util.*;
 5. import javax.swing.*;
 6. import javax.swing.event.*;
 7. import javax.swing.tree.*;
 8.
 9. /**
10.    This program demonstrates cell rendering by showing
11.    a tree of classes and their superclasses.
12. */
13. public class ClassTree
14. {
15.    public static void main(String[] args)
16.    {
17.       JFrame frame = new ClassTreeFrame();
18.       frame.setDefaultCloseOperation(JFrame.EXIT_ON_CLOSE);
19.       frame.show();
20.    }
21. }
22.
23. /**
24.    This frame displays the class tree and a text field and
25.    add button to add more classes into the tree.
26. */
27. class ClassTreeFrame extends JFrame
28. {
29.    public ClassTreeFrame()
30.    {
```

```
31.       setTitle("ClassTree");
32.       setSize(WIDTH, HEIGHT);
33.
34.       // the root of the class tree is Object
35.       root = new DefaultMutableTreeNode(java.lang.Object.class);
36.       model = new DefaultTreeModel(root);
37.       tree = new JTree(model);
38.
39.       // add this class to populate the tree with some data
40.       addClass(getClass());
41.
42.       // set up node icons
43.       ClassNameTreeCellRenderer renderer
44.           = new ClassNameTreeCellRenderer();
45.       renderer.setClosedIcon(new ImageIcon("red-ball.gif"));
46.       renderer.setOpenIcon(new ImageIcon("yellow-ball.gif"));
47.       renderer.setLeafIcon(new ImageIcon("blue-ball.gif"));
48.       tree.setCellRenderer(renderer);
49.
50.       getContentPane().add(new JScrollPane(tree),
51.           BorderLayout.CENTER);
52.
53.       addTextField();
54.   }
55.
56.   /**
57.      Add the text field and "Add" button to add a new class.
58.   */
59.   public void addTextField()
60.   {
61.       JPanel panel = new JPanel();
62.
63.       ActionListener addListener = new
64.           ActionListener()
65.           {
66.               public void actionPerformed(ActionEvent event)
67.               {
68.                   // add the class whose name is in the text field
69.                   try
70.                   {
71.                       String text = textField.getText();
72.                       addClass(Class.forName(text));
73.                       // clear text field to indicate success
74.                       textField.setText("");
75.                   }
76.                   catch (ClassNotFoundException e)
77.                   {
78.                       JOptionPane.showMessageDialog(null,
79.                           "Class not found");
80.                   }
81.               }
82.           };
83.
```

```
84.        // new class names are typed into this text field
85.        textField = new JTextField(20);
86.        textField.addActionListener(addListener);
87.        panel.add(textField);
88.
89.        JButton addButton = new JButton("Add");
90.        addButton.addActionListener(addListener);
91.        panel.add(addButton);
92.
93.        getContentPane().add(panel, BorderLayout.SOUTH);
94.     }
95.
96.     /**
97.        Finds an object in the tree.
98.        @param obj the object to find
99.        @return the node containing the object or null
100.       if the object is not present in the tree
101.    */
102.    public DefaultMutableTreeNode findUserObject(Object obj)
103.    {
104.       // find the node containing a user object
105.       Enumeration e = root.breadthFirstEnumeration();
106.       while (e.hasMoreElements())
107.       {
108.          DefaultMutableTreeNode node
109.             = (DefaultMutableTreeNode)e.nextElement();
110.          if (node.getUserObject().equals(obj))
111.             return node;
112.       }
113.       return null;
114.    }
115.
116.    /**
117.       Adds a new class and any parent classes that aren't
118.       yet part of the tree
119.       @param c the class to add
120.       @return the newly added node.
121.    */
122.    public DefaultMutableTreeNode addClass(Class c)
123.    {
124.       // add a new class to the tree
125.
126.       // skip non-class types
127.       if (c.isInterface() || c.isPrimitive()) return null;
128.
129.       // if the class is already in the tree, return its node
130.       DefaultMutableTreeNode node = findUserObject(c);
131.       if (node != null) return node;
132.
133.       // class isn't present--first add class parent recursively
134.
135.       Class s = c.getSuperclass();
136.
```

```
137.        DefaultMutableTreeNode parent;
138.        if (s == null)
139.           parent = root;
140.        else
141.           parent = addClass(s);
142.
143.        // add the class as a child to the parent
144.        DefaultMutableTreeNode newNode
145.           = new DefaultMutableTreeNode(c);
146.        model.insertNodeInto(newNode, parent,
147.           parent.getChildCount());
148.
149.        // make node visible
150.        TreePath path = new TreePath(model.getPathToRoot(newNode));
151.        tree.makeVisible(path);
152.
153.        return newNode;
154.     }
155.
156.     private DefaultMutableTreeNode root;
157.     private DefaultTreeModel model;
158.     private JTree tree;
159.     private JTextField textField;
160.     private static final int WIDTH = 400;
161.     private static final int HEIGHT = 300;
162. }
163.
164. /**
165.    This class renders a class name either in plain or italic.
166.    Abstract classes are italic.
167. */
168. class ClassNameTreeCellRenderer extends DefaultTreeCellRenderer
169. {
170.     public Component getTreeCellRendererComponent(JTree tree,
171.        Object value, boolean selected, boolean expanded,
172.        boolean leaf, int row, boolean hasFocus)
173.     {
174.        super.getTreeCellRendererComponent(tree, value,
175.           selected, expanded, leaf, row, hasFocus);
176.        // get the user object
177.        DefaultMutableTreeNode node
178.           = (DefaultMutableTreeNode)value;
179.        Class c = (Class)node.getUserObject();
180.
181.        // the first time, derive italic font from plain font
182.        if (plainFont == null)
183.        {
184.           plainFont = getFont();
185.           /*
186.              the tree cell renderer is sometimes called with a
187.              label that has a null font
188.           */
```

```
189.        if (plainFont != null)
190.            italicFont = plainFont.deriveFont(Font.ITALIC);
191.        }
192.
193.        // set font to italic if the class is abstract
194.        if ((c.getModifiers() & Modifier.ABSTRACT) == 0)
195.            setFont(plainFont);
196.        else
197.            setFont(italicFont);
198.        return this;
199.    }
200.
201.    private Font plainFont = null;
202.    private Font italicFont = null;
203. }
```

javax.swing.tree.DefaultMutableTreeNode

- Enumeration breadthFirstEnumeration()
- Enumeration depthFirstEnumeration()
- Enumeration preOrderEnumeration()
- Enumeration postOrderEnumeration()

  return enumeration objects for visiting all nodes of the tree model in a
  particular order. In breadth-first traversal, children that are closer to the root
  are visited before those that are farther away. In depth-first traversal,
  all children of a node are completely enumerated before its siblings
  are visited. The postOrderEnumeration method is a synonym for
  depthFirstEnumeration. The preorder traversal is identical to the
  postorder traversal except that parents are enumerated before their children.

javax.swing.tree.TreeCellRenderer

- Component getTreeCellRendererComponent(JTree tree,
  Object value, boolean selected, boolean expanded,
  boolean leaf, int row, boolean hasFocus)

  returns a component whose paint method is invoked to render a tree cell.

Parameters:	tree	the tree containing the node to be rendered
	value	the node to be rendered
	selected	true if the node is currently selected
	expanded	true if the children of the node are visible
	leaf	true if the node needs to be displayed as a tree
	row	the display row containing the node
	hasFocus	true if the node currently has input focus

javax.swing.tree.DefaultTreeCellRenderer

- void setLeafIcon(Icon icon)
- void setOpenIcon(Icon icon)
- void setClosedIcon(Icon icon)

set the icon to show for a leaf node, an expanded node, and a collapsed node.

Listening to Tree Events

Most commonly, a tree component is paired with some other component. When the user selects tree nodes, some information shows up in another window. Look at Figure 6–23 for an example. When the user selects a class, the instance and static variables of that class are displayed in the text area to the right.

Figure 6–23: A class browser

To obtain this behavior, you install a *tree selection listener.* The listener must implement the TreeSelectionListener interface, an interface with a single method

```
void valueChanged(TreeSelectionEvent event)
```

That method is called whenever the user selects or deselects tree nodes.

You add the listener to the tree in the normal way:

```
tree.addTreeSelectionListener(listener);
```

You can specify whether the user is allowed to select a single node, a contiguous range of nodes, or an arbitrary, potentially discontiguous, set of nodes. The JTree class uses a TreeSelectionModel to manage node selection. You need to retrieve the model to set the selection state to one of SINGLE_TREE_SELECTION, CONTIGUOUS_TREE_SELECTION, or DISCONTIGUOUS_TREE_SELECTION. (Discontiguous selection mode is the default.) For example, in our class browser, we only want to allow selection of a single class:

```
int mode = TreeSelectionModel.SINGLE_TREE_SELECTION;
tree.getSelectionModel().setSelectionMode(mode);
```

Apart from setting the selection mode, you need not worry about the tree selection model.

NOTE: How the user selects multiple items depends on the look and feel. In the Metal look and feel, hold down the CTRL key while clicking on an item to add the item to the selection, or to remove it if it was currently selected. Hold down the SHIFT key while clicking on an item to select a *range* of items, extending from the previously selected item to the new item.

To find out the current selection, you query the tree with the `getSelection-Paths` method:

```
TreePath[] selectedPaths = tree.getSelectionPaths();
```

If you restricted the user to a single selection, you can use the convenience method `getSelectionPath`, which returns the first selected path, or `null` if no path was selected.

CAUTION: The `TreeSelectionEvent` class has a `getPaths` method that returns an array of `TreePath` objects, but that array describes *selection changes*, not the current selection.

Example 6–7 puts tree selection to work. This program builds upon Example 6–6; however, to keep the program short, we did not use a custom tree cell renderer. In the frame constructor, we restrict the user to single item selection and add a tree selection listener. When the `valueChanged` method is called, we ignore its event parameter and simply ask the tree for the current selection path. As always, we need to get the last node of the path and look up its user object. We then call the `getFieldDescription` method, which uses reflection to assemble a string with all fields of the selected class. Finally, that string is displayed in the text area.

Example 6–7: ClassBrowserTest.java

```
1. import java.awt.*;
2. import java.awt.event.*;
3. import java.lang.reflect.*;
4. import java.util.*;
5. import javax.swing.*;
6. import javax.swing.event.*;
7. import javax.swing.tree.*;
8.
```

```
 9.  /**
10.     This program demonstrates tree selection events.
11.  */
12.  public class ClassBrowserTest
13.  {
14.     public static void main(String[] args)
15.     {
16.        JFrame frame = new ClassBrowserTestFrame();
17.        frame.setDefaultCloseOperation(JFrame.EXIT_ON_CLOSE);
18.        frame.show();
19.     }
20.  }
21.
22.  /**
23.     A frame with a class tree, a text area to show the properties
24.     of the selected class, and a text field to add new classes.
25.  */
26.  class ClassBrowserTestFrame extends JFrame
27.  {
28.     public ClassBrowserTestFrame()
29.     {
30.        setTitle("ClassBrowserTest");
31.        setSize(WIDTH, HEIGHT);
32.
33.        // the root of the class tree is Object
34.        root = new DefaultMutableTreeNode(java.lang.Object.class);
35.        model = new DefaultTreeModel(root);
36.        tree = new JTree(model);
37.
38.        // add this class to populate the tree with some data
39.        addClass(getClass());
40.
41.        // set up selection mode
42.        tree.addTreeSelectionListener(new
43.           TreeSelectionListener()
44.           {
45.              public void valueChanged(TreeSelectionEvent event)
46.              {
47.                 // the user selected a different node
48.                 // --update description
49.                 TreePath path = tree.getSelectionPath();
50.                 if (path == null) return;
51.                 DefaultMutableTreeNode selectedNode
52.                    = (DefaultMutableTreeNode)
53.                    path.getLastPathComponent();
54.                 Class c = (Class)selectedNode.getUserObject();
55.                 String description = getFieldDescription(c);
56.                 textArea.setText(description);
57.              }
58.           });
59.        int mode = TreeSelectionModel.SINGLE_TREE_SELECTION;
60.        tree.getSelectionModel().setSelectionMode(mode);
61.
```

```
62.         // this text area holds the class description
63.         textArea = new JTextArea();
64.
65.         // add tree and text area to the content pane
66.         JPanel panel = new JPanel();
67.         panel.setLayout(new GridLayout(1, 2));
68.         panel.add(new JScrollPane(tree));
69.         panel.add(new JScrollPane(textArea));
70.
71.         getContentPane().add(panel, BorderLayout.CENTER);
72.
73.         addTextField();
74.      }
75.
76.      /**
77.         Add the text field and "Add" button to add a new class.
78.      */
79.      public void addTextField()
80.      {
81.         JPanel panel = new JPanel();
82.
83.         ActionListener addListener = new
84.            ActionListener()
85.            {
86.               public void actionPerformed(ActionEvent event)
87.               {
88.                  // add the class whose name is in the text field
89.                  try
90.                  {
91.                     String text = textField.getText();
92.                     addClass(Class.forName(text));
93.                     // clear text field to indicate success
94.                     textField.setText("");
95.                  }
96.                  catch (ClassNotFoundException e)
97.                  {
98.                     JOptionPane.showMessageDialog(null,
99.                        "Class not found");
100.                 }
101.              }
102.           };
103.
104.        // new class names are typed into this text field
105.        textField = new JTextField(20);
106.        textField.addActionListener(addListener);
107.        panel.add(textField);
108.
109.        JButton addButton = new JButton("Add");
110.        addButton.addActionListener(addListener);
111.        panel.add(addButton);
112.
113.        getContentPane().add(panel, BorderLayout.SOUTH);
114.     }
```

```
115.
116.    /**
117.       Finds an object in the tree.
118.       @param obj the object to find
119.       @return the node containing the object or null
120.       if the object is not present in the tree
121.    */
122.    public DefaultMutableTreeNode findUserObject(Object obj)
123.    {
124.       // find the node containing a user object
125.       Enumeration e = root.breadthFirstEnumeration();
126.       while (e.hasMoreElements())
127.       {
128.          DefaultMutableTreeNode node
129.             = (DefaultMutableTreeNode)e.nextElement();
130.          if (node.getUserObject().equals(obj))
131.             return node;
132.       }
133.       return null;
134.    }
135.
136.    /**
137.       Adds a new class and any parent classes that aren't
138.       yet part of the tree
139.       @param c the class to add
140.       @return the newly added node.
141.    */
142.    public DefaultMutableTreeNode addClass(Class c)
143.    {
144.       // add a new class to the tree
145.
146.       // skip non-class types
147.       if (c.isInterface() || c.isPrimitive()) return null;
148.
149.       // if the class is already in the tree, return its node
150.       DefaultMutableTreeNode node = findUserObject(c);
151.       if (node != null) return node;
152.
153.       // class isn't present--first add class parent recursively
154.
155.       Class s = c.getSuperclass();
156.
157.       DefaultMutableTreeNode parent;
158.       if (s == null)
159.          parent = root;
160.       else
161.          parent = addClass(s);
162.
163.       // add the class as a child to the parent
164.       DefaultMutableTreeNode newNode
165.          = new DefaultMutableTreeNode(c);
166.       model.insertNodeInto(newNode, parent,
```

```
167.        parent.getChildCount());
168.
169.     // make node visible
170.     TreePath path = new TreePath(model.getPathToRoot(newNode));
171.     tree.makeVisible(path);
172.
173.     return newNode;
174.   }
175.
176.   /**
177.      Returns a description of the fields of a class.
178.      @param the class to be described
179.      @return a string containing all field types and names
180.   */
181.   public static String getFieldDescription(Class c)
182.   {
183.     // use reflection to find types and names of fields
184.     StringBuffer r = new StringBuffer();
185.     Field[] fields = c.getDeclaredFields();
186.     for (int i = 0; i < fields.length; i++)
187.     {
188.       Field f = fields[i];
189.       if ((f.getModifiers() & Modifier.STATIC) != 0)
190.           r.append("static ");
191.       r.append(f.getType().getName());
192.       r.append(" ");
193.       r.append(f.getName());
194.       r.append("\n");
195.     }
196.     return r.toString();
197.   }
198.
199.   private DefaultMutableTreeNode root;
200.   private DefaultTreeModel model;
201.   private JTree tree;
202.   private JTextField textField;
203.   private JTextArea textArea;
204.   private static final int WIDTH = 400;
205.   private static final int HEIGHT = 300;
206. }
```

`javax.swing.JTree`

- `TreePath getSelectionPath()`
- `TreePath[] getSelectionPaths()`

  returns the first selected path, or an array of paths to all selected nodes. If no paths are selected, both methods return `null`.

`javax.swing.event.TreeSelectionListener`

- `void valueChanged(TreeSelectionEvent event)`

  is called whenever nodes are selected or deselected.

javax.swing.event.TreeSelectionEvent

- TreePath getPath()
- TreePath[] getPaths()

get the first path, or all paths, that have *changed* in this selection event. If you want to know the current selection, not the selection change, you should call JTree.getSelectionPaths instead.

Custom Tree Models

In the final example, we implement a program that inspects the contents of a variable, just like a debugger does (see Figure 6–24).

Figure 6–24: An object inspection tree

Before going further, compile and run the example program! Each node corresponds to an instance variable. If the variable is an object, expand it to see *its* instance variables. The program inspects the contents of the frame window. If you poke around a few of the instance variables, you should be able to find some familiar classes. You'll also gain some respect for how complex the Swing user interface components are under the hood.

What's remarkable about the program is that the tree does not use the DefaultTreeModel. If you already have data that is hierarchically organized, you may not want to build a duplicate tree and worry about keeping both trees synchronized. That is the situation in our case—the inspected objects are already linked to each other through the object references, so there is no need to replicate the linking structure.

The TreeModel interface has only a handful of methods. The first group of methods enables the JTree to find the tree nodes by first getting the root, then the children. The JTree class only calls these methods when the user actually expands a node.

```
Object getRoot()
int getChildCount(Object parent)
Object getChild(Object parent, int index)
```

This example shows why the `TreeModel` interface, like the `JTree` class itself, does not need an explicit notion of nodes. The root and its children can be any objects. The `TreeModel` is responsible for telling the `JTree` how they are connected.

The next method of the `TreeModel` interface is the reverse of `getChild`:

```
int getIndexOfChild(Object parent, Object child)
```

Actually, this method can be implemented in terms of the first three—see the code in Example 6–8.

The tree model tells the `JTree` which nodes should be displayed as leaves:

```
boolean isLeaf(Object node)
```

If your code changes the tree model, then the tree needs to be notified so that it can redraw itself. The tree adds itself as a `TreeModelListener` to the model. Thus, the model must support the usual listener management methods:

```
void addTreeModelListener(TreeModelListener l)
void removeTreeModelListener(TreeModelListener l)
```

You can see implementations for these methods in Example 6–8.

When the model modifies the tree contents, it calls one of the four methods of the `TreeModelListener` interface:

```
void treeNodesChanged(TreeModelEvent e)
void treeNodesInserted(TreeModelEvent e)
void treeNodesRemoved(TreeModelEvent e)
void treeStructureChanged(TreeModelEvent e)
```

The `TreeModelEvent` object describes the location of the change. The details of assembling a tree model event that describes an insertion or removal event are quite technical. You only need to worry about firing these events if your tree can actually have nodes added and removed. In Example 6–8, we show you how to fire one event: replacing the root with a new object.

TIP: The Swing programmers evidently got tired enough of event firing that they provide a convenience class `javax.swing.EventListenerList` that collects listeners. See Chapter 8 in Volume 1 for more information on this class.

Finally, if the user edits a tree node, your model gets called with the change:

```
void valueForPathChanged(TreePath path, Object newValue)
```

If you don't allow editing, this method is never called.

If you don't need to support editing, then it is very easy to construct a tree model. Implement the three methods

```
Object getRoot()
int getChildCount(Object parent)
Object getChild(Object parent, int index)
```

These methods describe the structure of the tree. Supply routine implementations of the other five methods, as in Example 6–8. Then, you are ready to display your tree.

Now let's turn to the implementation of the example program. Our tree will contain objects of type `Variable`.

NOTE: Had we used the `DefaultTreeModel`, our nodes would have been objects of type `DefaultMutableTreeNode` with *user objects* of type `Variable`.

For example, suppose you inspect the variable

```
Employee joe;
```

That variable has a *type* `Employee.class`, a *name* `"joe"`, and a *value*, the value of the object reference `joe`. We define a class `Variable` that describes a variable in a program:

```
Variable v = new Variable(Employee.class, "joe", joe);
```

If the type of the variable is a primitive type, you must use an object wrapper for the value.

```
new Variable(double.class, "salary", new Double(salary));
```

If the type of the variable is a class, then the variable has *fields*. Using reflection, we enumerate all fields and collect them in an `ArrayList`. Since the `getFields` method of the `Class` class does not return fields of the superclass, we need to call `getFields` on all superclasses as well. You will find the code in the `Variable` constructor. The `getFields` method of our `Variable` class returns the array of fields. Finally, the `toString` method of the `Variable` class formats the node label. The label always contains the variable type and name. If the variable is not a class, the label also contains the value.

NOTE: If the type is an array, then we do not display the elements of the array. This would not be difficult to do; we leave it as the proverbial "exercise for the reader."

Let's move on to the tree model. The first two methods are very simple.

```
public Object getRoot()
{
```

```
        return root;
    }

    public int getChildCount(Object parent)
    {
        return ((Variable)parent).getFields().size();
    }
```

The getChild method returns a new Variable object that describes a particular field. The getType and getName method of the Field class yield the field type and name. By using reflection, you can read the field value as f.get(parentValue). That method can throw an IllegalAccessException. However, we made all fields accessible in the Variable constructor, so this won't happen in practice.

Here is the complete code of the getChild method.

```
    public Object getChild(Object parent, int index)
    {
        ArrayList fields = ((Variable)parent).getFields();
        Field f = (Field)fields.get(index);
        Object parentValue = ((Variable)parent).getValue();
        try
        {
            return new Variable(f.getType(), f.getName(),
                f.get(parentValue));
        }
        catch(IllegalAccessException e)
        {
            return null;
        }
    }
```

These three methods reveal the structure of the object tree to the JTree component. The remaining methods are routine—see the source code in Example 6–8.

There is one remarkable fact about this tree model: it actually describes an *infinite* tree. You can verify this by following one of the WeakReference objects. Click on the variable named referent. It leads you right back to the original object. You get an identical subtree, and you can open its WeakReference object again, ad infinitum. Of course, you cannot *store* an infinite set of nodes. The tree model simply generates the nodes on demand, as the user expands the parents.

This example concludes our discussion on trees. We move on to the table component, another complex Swing component. Superficially, trees and tables don't seem to have much in common, but you will find that they both use the same concepts for data models and cell rendering.

Example 6–8: ObjectInspectorTest.java

```
1. import java.awt.*;
2. import java.awt.event.*;
```

```
 3. import java.lang.reflect.*;
 4. import java.util.*;
 5. import javax.swing.*;
 6. import javax.swing.event.*;
 7. import javax.swing.tree.*;
 8.
 9. /**
10.    This program demonstrates how to use a custom tree
11.    model. It displays the fields of an object.
12. */
13. public class ObjectInspectorTest
14. {
15.    public static void main(String[] args)
16.    {
17.       JFrame frame = new ObjectInspectorFrame();
18.       frame.setDefaultCloseOperation(JFrame.EXIT_ON_CLOSE);
19.       frame.show();
20.    }
21. }
22.
23. /**
24.    This frame holds the object tree.
25. */
26. class ObjectInspectorFrame extends JFrame
27. {
28.    public ObjectInspectorFrame()
29.    {
30.       setTitle("ObjectInspectorTest");
31.       setSize(WIDTH, HEIGHT);
32.
33.       // we inspect this frame object
34.
35.       Variable v = new Variable(getClass(), "this", this);
36.       ObjectTreeModel model = new ObjectTreeModel();
37.       model.setRoot(v);
38.
39.       // construct and show tree
40.
41.       tree = new JTree(model);
42.       getContentPane().add(new JScrollPane(tree),
43.          BorderLayout.CENTER);
44.    }
45.
46.    private JTree tree;
47.    private static final int WIDTH = 400;
48.    private static final int HEIGHT = 300;
49. }
50.
51. /**
52.    This tree model describes the tree structure of a Java
53.    object. Children are the objects that are stored in instance
54.    variables.
```

```
55.  */
56.  class ObjectTreeModel implements TreeModel
57.  {
58.     /**
59.        Constructs an empty tree.
60.     */
61.     public ObjectTreeModel()
62.     {
63.        root = null;
64.     }
65.
66.     /**
67.        Sets the root to a given variable.
68.        @param v the variable that is being described by this tree
69.     */
70.     public void setRoot(Variable v)
71.     {
72.        Variable oldRoot = v;
73.        root = v;
74.        fireTreeStructureChanged(oldRoot);
75.     }
76.
77.     public Object getRoot()
78.     {
79.        return root;
80.     }
81.
82.     public int getChildCount(Object parent)
83.     {
84.        return ((Variable)parent).getFields().size();
85.     }
86.
87.     public Object getChild(Object parent, int index)
88.     {
89.        ArrayList fields = ((Variable)parent).getFields();
90.        Field f = (Field)fields.get(index);
91.        Object parentValue = ((Variable)parent).getValue();
92.        try
93.        {
94.           return new Variable(f.getType(), f.getName(),
95.              f.get(parentValue));
96.        }
97.        catch(IllegalAccessException e)
98.        {
99.           return null;
100.       }
101.    }
102.
103.    public int getIndexOfChild(Object parent, Object child)
104.    {
105.       int n = getChildCount(parent);
106.       for (int i = 0; i < n; i++)
```

```
107.            if (getChild(parent, i).equals(child))
108.                return i;
109.        return -1;
110.    }
111.
112.    public boolean isLeaf(Object node)
113.    {
114.        return getChildCount(node) == 0;
115.    }
116.
117.    public void valueForPathChanged(TreePath path,
118.        Object newValue)
119.    {}
120.
121.    public void addTreeModelListener(TreeModelListener l)
122.    {
123.        listenerList.add(TreeModelListener.class, l);
124.    }
125.
126.    public void removeTreeModelListener(TreeModelListener l)
127.    {
128.        listenerList.remove(TreeModelListener.class, l);
129.    }
130.
131.    protected void fireTreeStructureChanged(Object oldRoot)
132.    {
133.        TreeModelEvent event
134.            = new TreeModelEvent(this, new Object[] {oldRoot});
135.        EventListener[] listeners = listenerList.getListeners(
136.            TreeModelListener.class);
137.        for (int i = 0; i < listeners.length; i++)
138.            ((TreeModelListener)listeners[i]).treeStructureChanged(
139.                event);
140.    }
141.
142.    private Variable root;
143.    private EventListenerList listenerList
144.        = new EventListenerList();
145. }
146.
147. /**
148.    A variable with a type, name, and value.
149. */
150. class Variable
151. {
152.    /**
153.        Construct a variable
154.        @param aType the type
155.        @param aName the name
156.        @param aValue the value
157.    */
158.    public Variable(Class aType, String aName, Object aValue)
```

```
159.    {
160.        type = aType;
161.        name = aName;
162.        value = aValue;
163.        fields = new ArrayList();
164.
165.        /*
166.            find all fields if we have a class type
167.            except we don't expand strings and null values
168.        */
169.
170.        if (!type.isPrimitive() && !type.isArray() &&
171.            !type.equals(String.class) && value != null)
172.        {
173.            // get fields from the class and all superclasses
174.            for (Class c = value.getClass(); c != null;
175.                c = c.getSuperclass())
176.            {
177.                Field[] f = c.getDeclaredFields();
178.                AccessibleObject.setAccessible(f, true);
179.
180.                // get all nonstatic fields
181.                for (int i = 0; i < f.length; i++)
182.                    if ((f[i].getModifiers() & Modifier.STATIC) == 0)
183.                        fields.add(f[i]);
184.            }
185.        }
186.    }
187.
188.    /**
189.        Gets the value of this variable.
190.        @return the value
191.    */
192.    public Object getValue()
193.    {
194.        return value;
195.    }
196.
197.    /**
198.        Gets all nonstatic fields of this variable.
199.        @return an array list of variables describing the fields
200.    */
201.    public ArrayList getFields()
202.    {
203.        return fields;
204.    }
205.
206.    public String toString()
207.    {
208.        String r = type + " " + name;
209.        if (type.isPrimitive())
```

```
210.          r += "=" + value;
211.      else if (type.equals(String.class))
212.          r += "=" + value;
213.      else if (value == null)
214.          r += "=null";
215.      return r;
216.  }
217.
218.  private Class type;
219.  private String name;
220.  private Object value;
221.  private ArrayList fields;
222. }
```

javax.swing.tree.TreeModel

- Object getRoot()

  returns the root node.

- int getChildCount(Object parent)

  gets the number of children of the parent node.

- Object getChild(Object parent, int index)

  gets the child node of the parent node at the given index.

- int getIndexOfChild(Object parent, Object child)

  gets the index of the child node. It must be a child of the parent node.

- boolean isLeaf(Object node)

  returns true if node is conceptually a leaf of the tree.

- void addTreeModelListener(TreeModelListener l)
- void removeTreeModelListener(TreeModelListener l)

  add and remove listeners that are notified when the information in the tree model changes.

- void valueForPathChanged(TreePath path, Object newValue)

  is called when a cell editor has modified the value of a node.

  Parameters: path   the path to the node that has been edited

  newValue   the replacement value returned by the editor

javax.swing.event.TreeModelListener

- void treeNodesChanged(TreeModelEvent e)
- void treeNodesInserted(TreeModelEvent e)
- void treeNodesRemoved(TreeModelEvent e)
- void treeStructureChanged(TreeModelEvent e)

  are called by the tree model when the tree has been modified.

• `TreeModelEvent(Object eventSource, TreePath node)`
  constructs a tree model event.

     Parameters: `eventSource`   the tree model generating this event

                         `node`   the path to the node that is being changed

Tables

The `JTable` component displays a two-dimensional grid of objects. Of course, tables are very common in user interfaces. The Swing team has put a lot of effort into the table control. Tables are inherently complex, but—perhaps more successfully than with other Swing classes—the `JTable` component hides much of that complexity. You can produce fully functional tables with rich behavior by writing a few lines of code. Of course, you can write more code and customize the display and behavior for your specific applications.

In this section, we explain how to make simple tables, how the user interacts with them, and how to make some of the most common adjustments. As with the other complex Swing controls, it is impossible to cover all aspects in complete detail. If you need more information, you can find it in *Core Java Foundation Classes* by Kim Topley or *Graphic Java 2* by David Geary.

A Simple Table

As with the tree control, a `JTable` does not store its own data, but obtains its data from a *table model*. The `JTable` class has a constructor that wraps a two-dimensional array of objects into a default model. That is the strategy that we will use in our first example. Later in this chapter, we will turn to table models.

Figure 6–25 shows a typical table, describing properties of the planets of the solar system. (A planet is *gaseous* if it consists mostly of hydrogen and helium. You should take the "Color" entries with a grain of salt—that column was added because it will be useful in a later code example.)

Planet	Radius	Moons	Gaseous	Color
Mercury	2440.0	0	false	java.awt.Color[r=255...
Venus	6052.0	0	false	java.awt.Color[r=255...
Earth	6378.0	1	false	java.awt.Color[r=0,g...
Mars	3397.0	2	false	java.awt.Color[r=255...
Jupiter	71492.0	16	true	java.awt.Color[r=255...
Saturn	60268.0	18	true	java.awt.Color[r=255...
Uranus	25559.0	17	true	java.awt.Color[r=0,g...
Neptune	24766.0	8	true	java.awt.Color[r=0,g...
Pluto	1137.0	1	false	java.awt.Color[r=0,g...

Figure 6–25: A simple table

As you can see from the code in Example 6–9, the data of the table is stored as a two-dimensional array of `Object` values:

```
Object[][] cells =
{
    {
        "Mercury", new Double(2440),  new Integer(0),
        Boolean.FALSE, Color.yellow
    },
    {
        "Venus", new Double(6052), new Integer(0),
        Boolean.FALSE, Color.yellow
    },
    . . .
}
```

The table simply invokes the `toString` method on each object to display it. That's why the colors show up as `java.awt.Color[r=...,g=...,b=...]`.

You supply the column names in a separate array of strings:

```
String[] columnNames =
    {
        "Planet", "Radius", "Moons", "Gaseous", "Color"
    };
```

Then, you construct a table from the cell and column name arrays. Finally, add scroll bars in the usual way, by wrapping the table in a `JScrollPane`.

```
JTable table = new JTable(cells, columnNames);
JScrollPane pane = new JScrollPane(table);
```

The resulting table already has surprisingly rich behavior. Resize the table vertically until the scroll bar shows up. Then, scroll the table. Note that the column headers don't scroll out of view!

Next, click on one of the column headers and drag it to the left or right. See how the entire column becomes detached (see Figure 6–26). You can drop it to a different location. This rearranges the columns *in the view only.* The data model is not affected.

Figure 6–26: Moving a column

To *resize* columns, simply place the cursor between two columns until the cursor shape changes to an arrow. Then, drag the column boundary to the desired place (see Figure 6–27).

Planet	Moons	adius	Gaseous ◄───►	Color
Mercury	0	0	false	java.awt.Color...
Venus	0	0	false	java.awt.Color...
Earth	1	0	false	java.awt.Color...
Mars	2	0	false	java.awt.Color...
Jupiter	16	.0	true	java.awt.Color...
Saturn	18	.0	true	java.awt.Color...
Uranus	17	.0	true	java.awt.Color...
Neptune	8	.0	true	java.awt.Color...
Pluto	1	0	false	java.awt.Color...

Figure 6–27: Resizing columns

Users can select rows by clicking anywhere in a row. The selected rows are highlighted; you will see later how to get selection events. Users can also edit the table entries by clicking on a cell and typing into it. However, in this code example, the edits do not change the underlying data. In your programs, you should either make cells uneditable or handle cell editing events and update your model. We will discuss those topics later in this section.

Example 6–9: PlanetTable.java

```
1. import java.awt.*;
2. import java.awt.event.*;
3. import javax.swing.*;
4. import javax.swing.table.*;
5.
6. /**
7.    This program demonstrates how to show a simple table
8. */
9. public class PlanetTable
10. {
11.    public static void main(String[] args)
12.    {
13.       JFrame frame = new PlanetTableFrame();
14.       frame.setDefaultCloseOperation(JFrame.EXIT_ON_CLOSE);
15.       frame.show();
16.    }
17. }
18.
19. /**
20.    This frame contains a table of planet data.
21. */
22. class PlanetTableFrame extends JFrame
23. {
24.    public PlanetTableFrame()
25.    {
26.       setTitle("PlanetTable");
```

```
27.        setSize(WIDTH, HEIGHT);
28.
29.        JTable table = new JTable(cells, columnNames);
30.
31.        getContentPane().add(new JScrollPane(table),
32.            BorderLayout.CENTER);
33.    }
34.
35.    private Object[][] cells =
36.    {
37.        {
38.            "Mercury", new Double(2440),  new Integer(0),
39.            Boolean.FALSE, Color.yellow
40.        },
41.        {
42.            "Venus", new Double(6052), new Integer(0),
43.            Boolean.FALSE, Color.yellow
44.        },
45.        {
46.            "Earth", new Double(6378), new Integer(1),
47.            Boolean.FALSE, Color.blue
48.        },
49.        {
50.            "Mars", new Double(3397), new Integer(2),
51.            Boolean.FALSE, Color.red
52.        },
53.        {
54.            "Jupiter", new Double(71492), new Integer(16),
55.            Boolean.TRUE, Color.orange
56.        },
57.        {
58.            "Saturn", new Double(60268), new Integer(18),
59.            Boolean.TRUE, Color.orange
60.        },
61.        {
62.            "Uranus", new Double(25559), new Integer(17),
63.            Boolean.TRUE, Color.blue
64.        },
65.        {
66.            "Neptune", new Double(24766), new Integer(8),
67.            Boolean.TRUE, Color.blue
68.        },
69.        {
70.            "Pluto", new Double(1137), new Integer(1),
71.            Boolean.FALSE, Color.black
72.        }
73.    };
74.
75.    private String[] columnNames =
76.    {
77.        "Planet", "Radius", "Moons", "Gaseous", "Color"
78.    };
```

```
79.
80.     private static final int WIDTH = 400;
81.     private static final int HEIGHT = 200;
82. }
```

javax.swing.JTable

API

- JTable(Object[][] entries, Object[] columnNames)

  constructs a table with a default table model.

  Parameters: entries   the cells in the table

                 colummNames   the titles for the columns

Table Models

In the preceding example, the table-rendered objects were stored in a two-dimensional array. However, you should generally not use that strategy in your own code. If you find yourself dumping data into an array to display it as a table, you should instead think about implementing your own table model.

Table models are particularly simple to implement because you can take advantage of the AbstractTableModel class that implements most of the required methods. You only need to supply three methods:

```
public int getRowCount();
public int getColumnCount();
public Object getValueAt(int row, int column);
```

There are many ways for implementing the getValueAt method. You can simply compute the answer. Or you can look up the value from a database or from some other repository. Let us look at a couple of examples.

In the first example, we construct a table that simply shows some computed values, namely, the growth of an investment under different interest rate scenarios (see Figure 6–28).

5%	6%	7%	8%	9%	10%
$100,000.00	$100,000.00	$100,000.00	$100,000.00	$100,000.00	$100,000.00
$105,000.00	$106,000.00	$107,000.00	$108,000.00	$109,000.00	$110,000.00
$110,250.00	$112,360.00	$114,490.00	$116,640.00	$118,810.00	$121,000.00
$115,762.50	$119,101.60	$122,504.30	$125,971.20	$129,502.90	$133,100.00
$121,550.63	$126,247.70	$131,079.60	$136,048.90	$141,158.16	$146,410.00
$127,628.16	$133,822.56	$140,255.17	$146,932.81	$153,862.40	$161,051.00
$134,009.56	$141,851.91	$150,073.04	$158,687.43	$167,710.01	$177,156.10
$140,710.04	$150,363.03	$160,578.15	$171,382.43	$182,803.91	$194,871.71
$147,745.54	$159,384.81	$171,818.62	$185,093.02	$199,256.26	$214,358.88
$155,132.82	$168,947.90	$183,845.92	$199,900.46	$217,189.33	$235,794.77
$162,889.46	$179,084.77	$196,715.14	$215,892.50	$236,736.37	$259,374.25
$171,033.94	$189,829.86	$210,485.20	$233,163.90	$258,042.64	$285,311.67
$179,585.63	$201,219.65	$225,219.16	$251,817.01	$281,266.48	$313,842.84
$188,564.91	$213,292.83	$240,984.50	$271,962.37	$306,580.46	$345,227.12
$197,993.16	$226,090.40	$257,853.42	$293,719.36	$334,172.70	$379,749.83
$207,892.82	$239,655.82	$275,903.15	$317,216.91	$364,248.25	$417,724.82

Figure 6–28: Growth of an investment

The `getValueAt` method computes the appropriate value and formats it:

```
public Object getValueAt(int r, int c)
{
   double rate = (c + minRate) / 100.0;
   int nperiods = r;

   double futureBalance = INITIAL_BALANCE
      * Math.pow(1 + rate, nperiods);

   return
      NumberFormat.getCurrencyInstance().format(futureBalance);
}
```

The `getRowCount` and `getColumnCount` methods simply return the number of rows and columns.

```
public int getRowCount()
{
   return years;
}

public int getColumnCount()
{
   return maxRate - minRate + 1;
}
```

If you don't supply column names, the `getColumnName` method of the `Abstract-TableModel` names the columns A, B, C, and so on. To change column names, override the `getColumnName` method. You will usually want to override that default behavior. In this example, we simply label each column with the interest rate.

```
public String getColumnName(int c)
{
   double rate = (c + minRate) / 100.0;
   return
      NumberFormat.getPercentInstance().format(rate);
}
```

You can find the complete source code in Example 6–10.

Example 6–10: InvestmentTable.java

```
1. import java.awt.*;
2. import java.awt.event.*;
3. import java.text.*;
4. import javax.swing.*;
5. import javax.swing.table.*;
6.
7. /**
8.    This program shows how to build a table from a table model.
9. */
```

```
10. public class InvestmentTable
11. {
12.    public static void main(String[] args)
13.    {
14.       JFrame frame = new InvestmentTableFrame();
15.       frame.setDefaultCloseOperation(JFrame.EXIT_ON_CLOSE);
16.       frame.show();
17.    }
18. }
19.
20. /**
21.    This frame contains the investment table.
22. */
23. class InvestmentTableFrame extends JFrame
24. {
25.    public InvestmentTableFrame()
26.    {
27.       setTitle("InvestmentTable");
28.       setSize(WIDTH, HEIGHT);
29.
30.       TableModel model = new InvestmentTableModel(30, 5, 10);
31.       JTable table = new JTable(model);
32.       getContentPane().add(new JScrollPane(table), "Center");
33.    }
34.
35.    private static final int WIDTH = 600;
36.    private static final int HEIGHT = 300;
37. }
38.
39. /**
40.    This table model computes the cell entries each time they
41.    are requested. The table contents shows the growth of
42.    an investment for a number of years under different interest
43.    rates.
44. */
45. class InvestmentTableModel extends AbstractTableModel
46. {
47.    /**
48.       Constructs an investment table model.
49.       @param y the number of years
50.       @param r1 the lowest interest rate to tabulate
51.       @param r2 the highest interest rate to tabulate
52.    */
53.    public InvestmentTableModel(int y, int r1, int r2)
54.    {
55.       years = y;
56.       minRate = r1;
57.       maxRate = r2;
```

```
58.      }
59.
60.      public int getRowCount()
61.      {
62.         return years;
63.      }
64.
65.      public int getColumnCount()
66.      {
67.         return maxRate - minRate + 1;
68.      }
69.
70.      public Object getValueAt(int r, int c)
71.      {
72.         double rate = (c + minRate) / 100.0;
73.         int nperiods = r;
74.
75.         double futureBalance = INITIAL_BALANCE
76.            * Math.pow(1 + rate, nperiods);
77.
78.         return
79.            NumberFormat.getCurrencyInstance().format(futureBalance);
80.      }
81.
82.      public String getColumnName(int c)
83.      {
84.         double rate = (c + minRate) / 100.0;
85.         return
86.            NumberFormat.getPercentInstance().format(rate);
87.      }
88.
89.      private int years;
90.      private int minRate;
91.      private int maxRate;
92.
93.      private static double INITIAL_BALANCE = 100000.0;
94. }
```

Displaying database records

Probably the most common information to be displayed in a table is a set of
records from a database. If you use a professional development environment, it
almost certainly includes convenient JavaBeans for accessing database information. However, if you don't have database beans or if you are simply curious what
goes on under the hood, you will find the next example interesting. Figure 6–29
shows the output—the result of a query for all rows in a database table.

Figure 6–29: Displaying a query result in a table

In the example program, we define a ResultSetTableModel that fetches data from the result set of a database query. (See Chapter 4 for more information on Java database access and result sets.)

You can obtain the column count and the column names from the *result set metadata* object rsmd:

```
public String getColumnName(int c)
{
   try
   {
      return rsmd.getColumnName(c + 1);
   }
   catch(SQLException e)
   {
      . . .
   }
}

public int getColumnCount()
{
   try
   {
      return rsmd.getColumnCount();
   }
   catch(SQLException e)
```

```
        {
            . . .
        }
    }
```

If the database supports scrolling cursors, then it is particularly easy to get a cell value: just move the cursor to the requested row and fetch the column value.

```
public Object getValueAt(int r, int c)
{
    try
    {
        ResultSet rs = getResultSet();
        rs.absolute(r + 1);
        return rs.getObject(c + 1);
    }
    catch(SQLException e)
    {
        e.printStackTrace();
        return null;
    }
}
```

It makes a lot of sense to use this data model instead of the `DefaultTableModel`. If you created an array of values, then you would duplicate the cache that the database driver is already managing.

If the database does not support scrolling cursors or if you are using a JDBC 1 driver, then the query data must be cached manually. The example program contains such a manual cache. We factored out the common behavior in a base class `ResultSetTableModel`. The subclass `ScrollingResultSetTableModel` uses a scrolling cursor, and the subclass `CachingResultSetTableModel` caches the result set.

Example 6–11: ResultSetTable.java

```
1.  import java.awt.*;
2.  import java.awt.event.*;
3.  import java.io.*;
4.  import java.sql.*;
5.  import java.util.*;
6.  import javax.swing.*;
7.  import javax.swing.table.*;
8.
9.  /**
10.     This program shows how to display the result of a
11.     database query in a table.
12.  */
13. public class ResultSetTable
14. {
15.     public static void main(String[] args)
16.     {
```

```
17.         JFrame frame = new ResultSetFrame();
18.         frame.setDefaultCloseOperation(JFrame.EXIT_ON_CLOSE);
19.         frame.show();
20.     }
21. }
22.
23. /**
24.    This frame contains a combo box to select a database table
25.    and a table to show the data stored in the table
26. */
27. class ResultSetFrame extends JFrame
28. {
29.    public ResultSetFrame()
30.    {
31.       setTitle("ResultSet");
32.       setSize(WIDTH, HEIGHT);
33.
34.       /* find all tables in the database and add them to
35.          a combo box
36.       */
37.
38.       Container contentPane = getContentPane();
39.       tableNames = new JComboBox();
40.       tableNames.addActionListener(new
41.          ActionListener()
42.          {
43.             public void actionPerformed(ActionEvent evt)
44.             {
45.                try
46.                {
47.                   if (scrollPane != null)
48.                      getContentPane().remove(scrollPane);
49.                   String tableName
50.                      = (String)tableNames.getSelectedItem();
51.                   if (rs != null) rs.close();
52.                   String query = "SELECT * FROM " + tableName;
53.                   rs = stat.executeQuery(query);
54.                   if (scrolling)
55.                      model
56.                         = new ScrollingResultSetTableModel(rs);
57.                   else
58.                      model = new CachingResultSetTableModel(rs);
59.
60.                   JTable table = new JTable(model);
61.                   scrollPane = new JScrollPane(table);
62.                   getContentPane().add(scrollPane,
63.                      BorderLayout.CENTER);
64.                   pack();
65.                   doLayout();
66.                }
67.                catch(SQLException e)
68.                {
69.                   e.printStackTrace();
```

```
70.                 }
71.             }
72.         });
73.         JPanel p = new JPanel();
74.         p.add(tableNames);
75.         contentPane.add(p, BorderLayout.NORTH);
76.
77.         try
78.         {
79.             conn = getConnection();
80.             DatabaseMetaData meta = conn.getMetaData();
81.             if (meta.supportsResultSetType(
82.                 ResultSet.TYPE_SCROLL_INSENSITIVE))
83.             {
84.                 scrolling = true;
85.                 stat = conn.createStatement(
86.                     ResultSet.TYPE_SCROLL_INSENSITIVE,
87.                     ResultSet.CONCUR_READ_ONLY);
88.             }
89.             else
90.             {
91.                 stat = conn.createStatement();
92.                 scrolling = false;
93.             }
94.             ResultSet tables = meta.getTables(null, null, null,
95.                 new String[] { "TABLE" });
96.             while (tables.next())
97.                 tableNames.addItem(tables.getString(3));
98.             tables.close();
99.         }
100.        catch(IOException e)
101.        {
102.            e.printStackTrace();
103.        }
104.        catch(SQLException e)
105.        {
106.            e.printStackTrace();
107.        }
108.
109.        addWindowListener(new
110.            WindowAdapter()
111.            {
112.                public void windowClosing(WindowEvent event)
113.                {
114.                    try
115.                    {
116.                        conn.close();
117.                    }
118.                    catch (SQLException e)
119.                    {
120.                        e.printStackTrace();
121.                    }
122.                }


123.            });
124.     }
125.
126.     /**
127.        Gets a connection from the properties specified in
128.        the file database.properties.
129.        @return the database connection
130.     */
131.     public static Connection getConnection()
132.        throws SQLException, IOException
133.     {
134.        Properties props = new Properties();
135.        FileInputStream in
136.           = new FileInputStream("database.properties");
137.        props.load(in);
138.        in.close();
139.
140.        String drivers = props.getProperty("jdbc.drivers");
141.        if (drivers != null)
142.           System.setProperty("jdbc.drivers", drivers);
143.        String url = props.getProperty("jdbc.url");
144.        String username = props.getProperty("jdbc.username");
145.        String password = props.getProperty("jdbc.password");
146.
147.        return
148.           DriverManager.getConnection(url, username, password);
149.     }
150.
151.     private JScrollPane scrollPane;
152.     private ResultSetTableModel model;
153.     private JComboBox tableNames;
154.     private ResultSet rs;
155.     private Connection conn;
156.     private Statement stat;
157.     private boolean scrolling;
158.
159.     private static final int WIDTH = 400;
160.     private static final int HEIGHT = 300;
161. }
162.
163. /**
164.     This class is the superclass for the scrolling and the
165.     caching result set table model. It stores the result set
166.     and its metadata.
167. */
168. abstract class ResultSetTableModel extends AbstractTableModel
169. {
170.     /**
171.        Constructs the table model.
172.        @param aResultSet the result set to display.
173.     */
174.     public ResultSetTableModel(ResultSet aResultSet)
175.     {
```

```
176.        rs = aResultSet;
177.        try
178.        {
179.            rsmd = rs.getMetaData();
180.        }
181.        catch(SQLException e)
182.        {
183.            e.printStackTrace();
184.        }
185.    }
186.
187.    public String getColumnName(int c)
188.    {
189.        try
190.        {
191.            return rsmd.getColumnName(c + 1);
192.        }
193.        catch(SQLException e)
194.        {
195.            e.printStackTrace();
196.            return "";
197.        }
198.    }
199.
200.    public int getColumnCount()
201.    {
202.        try
203.        {
204.            return rsmd.getColumnCount();
205.        }
206.        catch(SQLException e)
207.        {
208.            e.printStackTrace();
209.            return 0;
210.        }
211.    }
212.
213.    /**
214.        Gets the result set that this model exposes.
215.        @return the result set
216.    */
217.    protected ResultSet getResultSet()
218.    {
219.        return rs;
220.    }
221.
222.    private ResultSet rs;
223.    private ResultSetMetaData rsmd;
224. }
225.
226. /**
227.    This class uses a scrolling cursor, a JDBC 2 feature,
228.    to locate result set elements.
```

```
229.  */
230. class ScrollingResultSetTableModel extends ResultSetTableModel
231. {
232.     /**
233.         Constructs the table model.
234.         @param aResultSet the result set to display.
235.     */
236.     public ScrollingResultSetTableModel(ResultSet aResultSet)
237.     {
238.         super(aResultSet);
239.     }
240.
241.     public Object getValueAt(int r, int c)
242.     {
243.         try
244.         {
245.             ResultSet rs = getResultSet();
246.             rs.absolute(r + 1);
247.             return rs.getObject(c + 1);
248.         }
249.         catch(SQLException e)
250.         {
251.             e.printStackTrace();
252.             return null;
253.         }
254.     }
255.
256.     public int getRowCount()
257.     {
258.         try
259.         {
260.             ResultSet rs = getResultSet();
261.             rs.last();
262.             return rs.getRow();
263.         }
264.         catch(SQLException e)
265.         {
266.             e.printStackTrace();
267.             return 0;
268.         }
269.     }
270. }
271.
272. /*
273.     This class caches the result set data; it can be used
274.     if scrolling cursors are not supported
275. */
276. class CachingResultSetTableModel extends ResultSetTableModel
277. {
278.     public CachingResultSetTableModel(ResultSet aResultSet)
279.     {
280.         super(aResultSet);
281.         try
```

```
282.          {
283.              cache = new ArrayList();
284.              int cols = getColumnCount();
285.              ResultSet rs = getResultSet();
286.
287.              /* place all data in an array list of Object[] arrays
288.                 We don't use an Object[][] because we don't know
289.                 how many rows are in the result set
290.              */
291.
292.              while (rs.next())
293.              {
294.                  Object[] row = new Object[cols];
295.                  for (int j = 0; j < row.length; j++)
296.                      row[j] = rs.getObject(j + 1);
297.                  cache.add(row);
298.              }
299.          }
300.          catch(SQLException e)
301.          {
302.              System.out.println("Error " + e);
303.          }
304.      }
305.
306.      public Object getValueAt(int r, int c)
307.      {
308.          if (r < cache.size())
309.              return ((Object[])cache.get(r))[c];
310.          else
311.              return null;
312.      }
313.
314.      public int getRowCount()
315.      {
316.          return cache.size();
317.      }
318.
319.      private ArrayList cache;
320. }
```

A Sort Filter

The last two examples drove home the point that tables don't store the cell data; they get them from a model. The model need not store the data either. It can compute the cell values or fetch them from somewhere else.

In this section, we introduce another useful technique, a *filter model* that presents information from another table in a different form. In our example, we will *sort* the rows in a table. Run the program in Example 6–12 and *double-click* on one of the column headers. You will see how the rows are rearranged so that the column entries are sorted (See Figure 6–30).

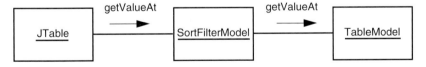

Figure 6–30: Sorting the rows of a table

However, we won't physically rearrange the rows in the data model. Instead, we will use a *filter model* that keeps an array with the permuted row indexes.

The filter model stores a reference to the actual table model. When the `JTable` needs to look up a value, the filter model computes the actual row index and gets the value from the model. For example,

```
public Object getValueAt(int r, int c)
{
    return model.getValueAt(actual row index, c);
}
```

All other methods are simply passed on to the original model.

```
public String getColumnName(int c)
{
    return model.getColumnName(c);
}
```

Figure 6–31 shows how the filter sits between the `JTable` object and the actual table model.

```
  ┌──────────┐  getValueAt  ┌─────────────────┐  getValueAt  ┌──────────────┐
  │          │   ───────▶   │                 │   ───────▶   │              │
  │  JTable  │              │ SortFilterModel │              │  TableModel  │
  │          │              │                 │              │              │
  └──────────┘              └─────────────────┘              └──────────────┘
```

Figure 6–31: A table model filter

There are two complexities when you implement such a sort filter. First, you need to be notified when the user double-clicks on one of the column headers. We don't want to go into too much detail on this technical point. You can find the code in the `addMouseListener` method of the `SortFilterModel` in Example 6–12. Here is the idea behind the code. First, get the table header component and attach a mouse listener. When a double click is detected, you need to find out in which table column the mouse click fell. Then, you need to translate the table column to the model column—they can be different if the user moved the table columns around. Once you know the model column, you can start sorting the table rows.

There is a problem with sorting the table rows. We don't want to physically rearrange the rows. What we want is a sequence of row indexes that tell us how we would rearrange them if they were being sorted. However, the sort algorithms in the `Arrays` and `Collections` classes don't tell us how they rearrange the elements. Of course, you could reimplement a sorting algorithm and keep track of the object rearrangements. But there is a much smarter way. The trick is to come up with custom objects and a custom comparison method so that the library sorting algorithm can be pressed into service.

We will sort objects of a type `Row`. A `Row` object contains the index r of a row in the model. Compare two such objects as follows: find the elements in the model and compare them. In other words, the `compareTo` method for `Row` objects computes

```
model.getValueAt(r_1, c).compareTo(model.getValueAt(r_2, c))
```

Here r1 and r2 are the row indexes of the `Row` objects, and c is the column whose elements should be sorted.

If the entries of a particular column aren't comparable, we simply compare their string representations. That way, the columns with `Boolean` and `Color` values can still be sorted. (Neither of those two classes implement the `Comparable` interface.)

We make the `Row` class into an inner class of the `SortFilterModel` because the `compareTo` method needs to access the current model and column. Here is the code:

```
class SortFilterModel extends AbstractTableModel
{   . . .
    private class Row implements Comparable
    {
        public int index;
        public int compareTo(Object other)
        {
            Row otherRow = (Row)other;
            Object a = model.getValueAt(index, sortColumn);
            Object b = model.getValueAt(otherRow.index, sortColumn);
            if (a instanceof Comparable)
                return ((Comparable)a).compareTo(b);
            else
                return a.toString().compareTo(b.toString());
        }
    }

    private TableModel model;
    private int sortColumn;
    private Row[] rows;
}
```

In the constructor, we build an array `rows`, initialized such that `rows[i]` is set to `i`:

```
public SortFilterModel(TableModel m)
{
   model = m;
   rows = new Row[model.getRowCount()];
   for (int i = 0; i < rows.length; i++)
   {
      rows[i] = new Row();
      rows[i].index = i;
   }
}
```

In the `sort` method, we invoke the `Arrays.sort` algorithm. It sorts the `Row` objects. Because the comparison criterion looks at the model elements in the appropriate column, the elements are arranged so that afterwards `row[0]` contains the index of the smallest element in the column, `row[1]` contains the index of the next-smallest element, and so on.

When the array is sorted, we notify all table model listeners (in particular, the `JTable`) that the table contents have changed and must be redrawn.

```
public void sort(int c)
{
   sortColumn = c;
   Arrays.sort(rows);
   fireTableDataChanged();
}
```

Finally, we can show you the exact computation of the `getValueAt` method of the filter class. It simply translates a row index `r` to the model row index `rows[r].index`:

```
public Object getValueAt(int r, int c)
{
   return model.getValueAt(rows[r].index, c);
}
```

The sort model filter shows again the power of the model-view pattern. Because the data and the display are separated, we are able to change the mapping between the two.

Example 6–12: TableSortTest.java

```
1. import java.awt.*;
2. import java.awt.event.*;
3. import java.util.*;
4. import javax.swing.*;
5. import javax.swing.event.*;
6. import javax.swing.table.*;
7.
8. /**
```

```
9.    This program demonstrates how to sort a table column.
10.   Double-click on a table column to sort it.
11. */
12. public class TableSortTest
13. {
14.    public static void main(String[] args)
15.    {
16.       JFrame frame = new TableSortFrame();
17.       frame.setDefaultCloseOperation(JFrame.EXIT_ON_CLOSE);
18.       frame.show();
19.    }
20. }
21.
22. /**
23.    This frame contains a table of planet data.
24. */
25. class TableSortFrame extends JFrame
26. {
27.    public TableSortFrame()
28.    {
29.       setTitle("TableSortTest");
30.       setSize(WIDTH, HEIGHT);
31.
32.       // set up table model and interpose sorter
33.
34.       DefaultTableModel model
35.          = new DefaultTableModel(cells, columnNames);
36.       final SortFilterModel sorter = new SortFilterModel(model);
37.
38.       // show table
39.
40.       final JTable table = new JTable(sorter);
41.       getContentPane().add(new JScrollPane(table),
42.          BorderLayout.CENTER);
43.
44.       // set up double click handler for column headers
45.
46.       table.getTableHeader().addMouseListener(new
47.          MouseAdapter()
48.          {
49.             public void mouseClicked(MouseEvent event)
50.             {
51.                // check for double click
52.                if (event.getClickCount() < 2) return;
53.
54.                // find column of click and
55.                int tableColumn
56.                   = table.columnAtPoint(event.getPoint());
57.
58.                // translate to table model index and sort
59.                int modelColumn
```

```
60.              = table.convertColumnIndexToModel(tableColumn);
61.            sorter.sort(modelColumn);
62.          }
63.        });
64.    }
65.
66.    private Object[][] cells =
67.    {
68.      {
69.        "Mercury", new Double(2440),  new Integer(0),
70.        Boolean.FALSE, Color.yellow
71.      },
72.
73.      {
74.        "Venus", new Double(6052), new Integer(0),
75.        Boolean.FALSE, Color.yellow
76.      },
77.      {
78.        "Earth", new Double(6378), new Integer(1),
79.        Boolean.FALSE, Color.blue
80.      },
81.      {
82.        "Mars", new Double(3397), new Integer(2),
83.        Boolean.FALSE, Color.red
84.      },
85.      {
86.        "Jupiter", new Double(71492), new Integer(16),
87.        Boolean.TRUE, Color.orange
88.      },
89.      {
90.        "Saturn", new Double(60268), new Integer(18),
91.        Boolean.TRUE, Color.orange
92.      },
93.      {
94.        "Uranus", new Double(25559), new Integer(17),
95.        Boolean.TRUE, Color.blue
96.      },
97.      {
98.        "Neptune", new Double(24766), new Integer(8),
99.        Boolean.TRUE, Color.blue
100.      },
101.      {
102.        "Pluto", new Double(1137), new Integer(1),
103.        Boolean.FALSE, Color.black
104.      }
105.    };
106.
107.    private String[] columnNames =
108.    {
109.      "Planet", "Radius", "Moons", "Gaseous", "Color"
110.    };
111.
```

```
112.    private static final int WIDTH = 400;
113.    private static final int HEIGHT = 200;
114. }
115.
116. /**
117.    This table model takes an existing table model and produces
118.    a new model that sorts the rows so that the entries in
119.    a particular column are sorted.
120. */
121. class SortFilterModel extends AbstractTableModel
122. {
123.    /**
124.        Constructs a sort filter model.
125.        @param m the table model to filter
126.    */
127.    public SortFilterModel(TableModel m)
128.    {
129.        model = m;
130.        rows = new Row[model.getRowCount()];
131.        for (int i = 0; i < rows.length; i++)
132.        {
133.            rows[i] = new Row();
134.            rows[i].index = i;
135.        }
136.    }
137.
138.    /**
139.        Sorts the rows.
140.        @param c the column that should become sorted
141.    */
142.    public void sort(int c)
143.    {
144.        sortColumn = c;
145.        Arrays.sort(rows);
146.        fireTableDataChanged();
147.    }
148.
149.    // Compute the moved row for the three methods that access
150.    // model elements
151.
152.    public Object getValueAt(int r, int c)
153.    {
154.        return model.getValueAt(rows[r].index, c);
155.    }
156.
157.    public boolean isCellEditable(int r, int c)
158.    {
159.        return model.isCellEditable(rows[r].index, c);
160.    }
161.
162.    public void setValueAt(Object aValue, int r, int c)
163.    {
```

```
164.        model.setValueAt(aValue, rows[r].index, c);
165.    }
166.
167.    // delegate all remaining methods to the model
168.
169.    public int getRowCount()
170.    {
171.        return model.getRowCount();
172.    }
173.
174.    public int getColumnCount()
175.    {
176.        return model.getColumnCount();
177.    }
178.
179.    public String getColumnName(int c)
180.    {
181.        return model.getColumnName(c);
182.    }
183.
184.    public Class getColumnClass(int c)
185.    {
186.        return model.getColumnClass(c);
187.    }
188.
189.    /**
190.        This inner class holds the index of the model row
191.        Rows are compared by looking at the model row entries
192.        in the sort column.
193.    */
194.    private class Row implements Comparable
195.    {
196.        public int index;
197.        public int compareTo(Object other)
198.        {
199.          Row otherRow = (Row)other;
200.          Object a = model.getValueAt(index, sortColumn);
201.         Object b = model.getValueAt(otherRow.index, sortColumn);
202.          if (a instanceof Comparable)
203.              return ((Comparable)a).compareTo(b);
204.          else
205.              return a.toString().compareTo(b.toString());
206.
207.            //              return index - otherRow.index;
208.        }
209.    }
210.
211.    private TableModel model;
212.    private int sortColumn;
213.    private Row[] rows;
214. }
```

`javax.swing.table.TableModel`

- `int getRowCount()`
- `int getColumnCount()`

  get the number of rows and columns in the table model.

- `Object getValueAt(int row, int column)`

  gets the value at the given row and column.

- `void setValueAt(Object newValue, int row, int column)`

  sets a new value at the given row and column.

- `boolean isCellEditable(int row, int column)`

  returns `true` if the cell at the given row and column is editable.

- `String getColumnName(int column)`

  gets the column title.

`javax.swing.table.AbstractTableModel`

- `void fireTableDataChanged()`

  notifies all table model listeners that the table data has changed.

`javax.swing.JTable`

- `JTableHeader getTableHeader()`

  returns the table header component of this table.

- `int columnAtPoint(Point p)`

  returns the number of the table column that falls under the pixel position p.

- `int convertColumnIndexToModel(int tableColumn)`

  returns the model index of the column with the given index. This value is different from `tableColumn` if some of the table columns are moved or hidden.

Cell Rendering and Editing

In the next example, we again display our planet data, but this time, we want to give the table more information about the *column types*. If you define the method

```
Class getColumnClass(int columnIndex)
```

of your table model to return the class that describes the column type, then the `JTable` class picks an appropriate *renderer* for the class. Table 6–1 shows the renderers that the `JTable` class provides by default.

You can see the check boxes and images in Figure 6–32. (Thanks to Jim Evins, `http://www.snaught.com/JimsCoolIcons/Planets`, for providing the planet images!)

Table 6–1: Default renderers

Type	Rendered as
ImageIcon	image
Boolean	check box
Object	string

Figure 6–32: A table with cell renderers

For other types, you can supply your own cell renderers. Table cell renderers are similar to the tree cell renderers that you saw earlier. They implement the TableCellRenderer interface, which has a single method

```
Component getTableCellRendererComponent(JTable table,
    Object value, boolean isSelected, boolean hasFocus,
    int row, int column)
```

That method is called when the table needs to draw a cell. You return a component whose paint method is then invoked to fill the cell area.

To display a cell of type Color, you can simply return a panel whose background color you set to the color object stored in the cell. The color is passed as the value parameter.

```
class ColorTableCellRenderer implements TableCellRenderer
{
    public Component getTableCellRendererComponent(JTable table,
        Object value, boolean isSelected, boolean hasFocus,
        int row, int column)
    {
        panel.setBackground((Color)value);
        return panel;
```

```
    }

    private JPanel panel = new JPanel();
}
```

You need to tell the table to use this renderer with all objects of type `Color`. The `setDefaultRenderer` method of the `JTable` class lets you establish this association. You supply a `Class` object and the renderer:

```
table.setDefaultRenderer(Color.class,
    new ColorTableCellRenderer());
```

That renderer is now used for all objects of the given type.

> NOTE: For a more realistic cell renderer, you would want to give visual clues when the cell is *selected* and when it has *editing focus.* To do that, you need the cell dimensions and the color schemes for selection and focus. In the Java look and feel, selection is indicated by a pale blue background.
>
> To get the cell dimensions, call the `getCellRect` method of the `JTable` class. For the selection colors, call `getSelectionBackground` and `getSelectionForeground`.

> TIP: If your renderer simply draws a text string or an icon, you can extend the `DefaultTableCellRenderer` class. It takes care of selection handling and focus for you.

Cell editing

To enable cell editing, the table model must indicate which cells are editable by defining the `isCellEditable` method. Most commonly, you will want to make certain columns editable. In the example program, we allow editing in four columns.

```
public boolean isCellEditable(int r, int c)
{
    return c == NAME_COLUMN
        || c == MOON_COLUMN
        || c == GASEOUS_COLUMN
        || c == COLOR_COLUMN;
}

private static final int NAME_COLUMN = 0;
private static final int MOON_COLUMN = 2;
private static final int GASEOUS_COLUMN = 3;
private static final int COLOR_COLUMN = 4;
```

> NOTE: The `AbstractTableModel` defines the `isCellEditable` method to always return `false`. The `DefaultTableModel` overrides the method to always return `true`.

If you run the program in Example 6–13, note that you can click on the check boxes in the Gaseous column and turn the check marks on and off. If you click on the Moons column, a combo box appears (see Figure 6–33). You will see in a minute how to install such a combo box as cell editor.

Finally, click on a cell in the first column. The cell gains focus. You can start typing and the cell contents change.

![TableCellRenderTest window showing a table with columns Planet, Radius, Moons, Gaseous, Color, Image for Mercury, Venus, Earth, Mars with an open combo box showing numbers 0-7]

Figure 6–33: A cell editor

What you just saw in action are the three variations of the `DefaultCellEditor` class. A `DefaultCellEditor` can be constructed with a `JTextField`, a `JCheckBox`, or a `JComboBox`. The `JTable` class automatically installs a check box editor for Boolean cells and a text field editor for all editable cells that don't supply their own renderer. The text fields let the user edit the strings that result from applying `toString` to the return value of the `getValueAt` method of the table model.

When the edit is complete, the cell editor passes the result back to the model by calling its `setValueAt` method. It is up to you to define the `setValueAt` method of your model to turn the edited result back into an appropriate value.

> **CAUTION:** It is easy for the default text field editor to turn your cell value into a string, simply by calling `getValueAt` and applying `toString`. However, for the reverse conversion, the monkey is on your back. When the editing is finished, the cell editor calls `setValueAt` with the resulting `String` object. Your `setValueAt` method needs to know how to parse that string. For example, if your cell stores integers, you need to call `Integer.parseInt`.

To get a combo box editor, you set a cell editor manually—the `JTable` component has no idea what values might be appropriate for a particular type. For the Moons column, we wanted to enable the user to pick any value between 0 and 20. Here is the code for initializing the combo box.

```
JComboBox moonCombo = new JComboBox();
for (int i = 0; i <= 20; i++)
    moonCombo.addItem(new Integer(i));
```

To construct a `DefaultCellEditor`, supply the combo box in the constructor:

```
TableCellEditor moonEditor = new DefaultCellEditor(moonCombo);
```

Next, we need to install the editor. Unlike the color cell renderer, this editor does not depend on the object *type*—we don't necessarily want to use it for all objects of type `Integer`. Instead, we need to install it into a particular column.

The `JTable` class stores information about table columns in objects of type `TableColumn`. A `TableColumnModel` class manages the columns. (Figure 6–34 shows the relationships among the most important table classes.) If you don't want to insert or remove columns dynamically, you won't use the table column model much. However, to get a particular `TableColumn` object, you need to get the column model to ask it for the column object:

```
TableColumnModel columnModel = table.getColumnModel()
TableColumn moonColumn
    = columnModel.getColumn(PlanetTableModel.MOON_COLUMN);
```

Finally, you can install the cell editor:

```
moonColumn.setCellEditor(moonEditor);
```

If your cells are taller than the default, you also want to set the row height.

```
table.setRowHeight(height);
```

By default, all rows of the table have the same height. You can set the heights of individual rows with the call

```
table.setRowHeight(row, height);
```

The actual row height equals the row height that has been set with these methods, reduced by the row margin. The default row margin is 1, but you can change it with the call

```
table.setRowMargin(margin);
```

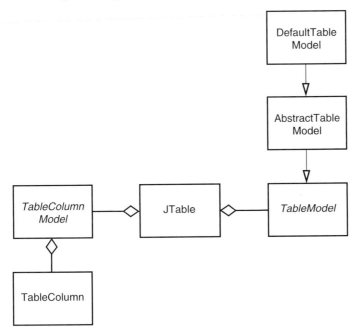

Figure 6–34: Relationship between Table classes

Custom editors

Run the example program again and click on a color. A *color chooser* pops up to let you pick a new color for the planet. Select a color and click OK. The cell color is updated (See Figure 6–35).

The color cell editor is not a standard table cell editor but a custom implementation. To create a custom cell editor, you implement the `TableCellEditor` interface. That interface is a bit tedious, and as of SDK 1.3, an `AbstractCellEditor` class is provided to take care of the event handling details.

The `getTableCellEditorComponent` method of the `TableCellEditor` interface requests a component to render the cell. It is exactly the same as the `get-TableCellRenderer` method of the `TableCellRenderer` interface, except that there is no `focus` parameter. Since the cell is being edited, it is presumed to have focus. The editor component temporarily *replaces* the renderer when the editing is in progress. In our example, we return a blank panel that is not colored. This is an indication to the user that the cell is currently being edited.

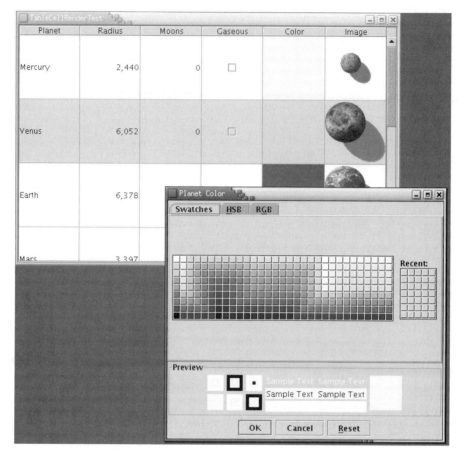

Figure 6–35: Editing the cell color with a color chooser

Next, you want to have your editor pop up when the user clicks on the cell.

The JTable class calls your editor with an event (such as a mouse click) to find out if that event is acceptable to initiate the editing process. The Abstract-CellEditor class defines the method to accept all events.

```
public boolean isCellEditable(EventObject anEvent)
{
    return true;
}
```

However, if you override this method to false, then the table would not go through the trouble of inserting the editor component.

Once the editor component is installed, the shouldSelectCell method is called, presumably with the same event. You should initiate editing in this method, for example, by popping up an external edit dialog.

```
public boolean shouldSelectCell(EventObject anEvent)
{
    colorDialog.setVisible(true);
    return true;
}
```

If the table wants to cancel or stop the edit (because the user has clicked on another table cell), it calls the `cancelCellEditing` or `stopCellEditing` method. You should then hide the dialog. When your `stopCellEditing` method is called, the table would like to use the partially edited value. You should return `true` if the current value is valid. In the color chooser, any value is valid. But if you edit other data, you can ensure that only valid data is retrieved from the editor.

Also, you should call the superclass methods that take care of event firing—otherwise, the editing won't be properly canceled.

```
public void cancelCellEditing()
{
    colorDialog.setVisible(false);
    super.cancelCellEditing();
}
```

Finally, you need to supply a method that yields the value that the user supplied in the editing process:

```
public Object getCellEditorValue()
{
    return colorChooser.getColor();
}
```

To summarize, your custom editor should do the following:

1. Extend the `AbstractCellEditor` class and implement the `Table-CellEditor` interface.

2. Define the `getTableCellEditorComponent` method to supply a component. This can either be a dummy component (if you pop up a dialog) or a component for in-place editing such as a combo box or text field.

3. Define the `shouldSelectCell`, `stopCellEditing` and `cancel-CellEditing` methods to handle the start, completion, and cancellation of the editing process. The `stopCellEditing` and `cancelCellEditing` should call the superclass methods to ensure that listeners are notified.

4. Define the `getCellEditorValue` method to return the value that is the result of the editing process.

Finally, you need to indicate when the user is finished editing by calling the `stopCellEditing` and `cancelCellEditing` methods. When constructing the color dialog, we install accept and cancel callbacks that fire these events.

```
colorDialog = JColorChooser.createDialog(null,
    "Planet Color", false, colorChooser,
    new
        ActionListener() // OK button listener
```

```
    {
       public void actionPerformed(ActionEvent event)
       {
          stopCellEditing();
       }
    },
new
    ActionListener() // Cancel button listener
    {
       public void actionPerformed(ActionEvent event)
       {
          cancelCellEditing();
       }
    });
```

Also, when the user closes the dialog, editing should be canceled. This is achieved by installing a window listener:

```
colorDialog.addWindowListener(new
    WindowAdapter()
    {
       public void windowClosing(WindowEvent event)
       {
          cancelCellEditing();
       }
    });
```

This completes the implementation of the custom editor.

You now know how to make a cell editable and how to install an editor. There is one remaining issue—how to update the model with the value that the user edited. When editing is complete, the JTable class calls the following method of the table model:

```
void setValueAt(Object value, int r, int c)
```

You need to override the method to store the new value. The value parameter is the object that was returned by the cell editor. If you implemented the cell editor, then you know the type of the object that you return from the getCellEditorValue method. In the case of the DefaultCellEditor, there are three possibilities for that value. It is a Boolean if the cell editor is a check box, a string if it is a text field. If the value comes from a combo box, then it is the object that the user selected.

If the value object does not have the appropriate type, then you need to convert it. That happens most commonly when a number is edited in a text field. In our example, we populated the combo box with Integer objects so that no conversion is necessary.

Example 6–13: TableCellRenderTest.java

```
1. import java.awt.*;
2. import java.awt.event.*;
3. import java.util.*;
```

```
4. import javax.swing.*;
5. import javax.swing.event.*;
6. import javax.swing.table.*;
7.
8. /**
9.    This program demonstrates cell rendering and editing
10.   in a table.
11. */
12. public class TableCellRenderTest
13. {
14.    public static void main(String[] args)
15.    {
16.       JFrame frame = new TableCellRenderFrame();
17.       frame.setDefaultCloseOperation(JFrame.EXIT_ON_CLOSE);
18.       frame.show();
19.    }
20. }
21.
22. /**
23.    This frame contains a table of planet data.
24. */
25. class TableCellRenderFrame extends JFrame
26. {
27.    public TableCellRenderFrame()
28.    {
29.       setTitle("TableCellRenderTest");
30.       setSize(WIDTH, HEIGHT);
31.
32.       TableModel model = new PlanetTableModel();
33.       JTable table = new JTable(model);
34.
35.       // set up renderers and editors
36.
37.       table.setDefaultRenderer(Color.class,
38.          new ColorTableCellRenderer());
39.       table.setDefaultEditor(Color.class,
40.          new ColorTableCellEditor());
41.
42.       JComboBox moonCombo = new JComboBox();
43.       for (int i = 0; i <= 20; i++)
44.          moonCombo.addItem(new Integer(i));
45.       TableColumnModel columnModel = table.getColumnModel();
46.       TableColumn moonColumn
47.          = columnModel.getColumn(PlanetTableModel.MOON_COLUMN);
48.       moonColumn.setCellEditor(new DefaultCellEditor(moonCombo));
49.
50.       // show table
51.
52.       table.setRowHeight(100);
```

```
53.        getContentPane().add(new JScrollPane(table),
54.            BorderLayout.CENTER);
55.     }
56.
57.     private static final int WIDTH = 600;
58.     private static final int HEIGHT = 400;
59. }
60.
61. /**
62.    The planet table model specifies the values, rendering
63.    and editing properties for the planet data.
64. */
65. class PlanetTableModel extends AbstractTableModel
66. {
67.     public String getColumnName(int c)
68.     {
69.        return columnNames[c];
70.     }
71.
72.     public Class getColumnClass(int c)
73.     {
74.        return cells[0][c].getClass();
75.     }
76.
77.     public int getColumnCount()
78.     {
79.        return cells[0].length;
80.     }
81.
82.     public int getRowCount()
83.     {
84.        return cells.length;
85.     }
86.
87.     public Object getValueAt(int r, int c)
88.     {
89.        return cells[r][c];
90.     }
91.
92.     public void setValueAt(Object obj, int r, int c)
93.     {
94.        cells[r][c] = obj;
95.     }
96.
97.     public boolean isCellEditable(int r, int c)
98.     {
99.        return c == NAME_COLUMN
100.            || c == MOON_COLUMN
101.            || c == GASEOUS_COLUMN
102.            || c == COLOR_COLUMN;
```

```
103.      }
104.
105.      public static final int NAME_COLUMN = 0;
106.      public static final int MOON_COLUMN = 2;
107.      public static final int GASEOUS_COLUMN = 3;
108.      public static final int COLOR_COLUMN = 4;
109.
110.      private Object[][] cells =
111.      {
112.          {
113.              "Mercury", new Double(2440),  new Integer(0),
114.              Boolean.FALSE, Color.yellow,
115.              new ImageIcon("Mercury.gif")
116.          },
117.          {
118.              "Venus", new Double(6052), new Integer(0),
119.              Boolean.FALSE, Color.yellow,
120.              new ImageIcon("Venus.gif")
121.          },
122.          {
123.              "Earth", new Double(6378), new Integer(1),
124.              Boolean.FALSE, Color.blue,
125.              new ImageIcon("Earth.gif")
126.          },
127.          {
128.              "Mars", new Double(3397), new Integer(2),
129.              Boolean.FALSE, Color.red,
130.              new ImageIcon("Mars.gif")
131.          },
132.          {
133.              "Jupiter", new Double(71492), new Integer(16),
134.              Boolean.TRUE, Color.orange,
135.              new ImageIcon("Jupiter.gif")
136.          },
137.          {
138.              "Saturn", new Double(60268), new Integer(18),
139.              Boolean.TRUE, Color.orange,
140.              new ImageIcon("Saturn.gif")
141.          },
142.          {
143.              "Uranus", new Double(25559), new Integer(17),
144.              Boolean.TRUE, Color.blue,
145.              new ImageIcon("Uranus.gif")
146.          },
147.          {
148.              "Neptune", new Double(24766), new Integer(8),
149.              Boolean.TRUE, Color.blue,
150.              new ImageIcon("Neptune.gif")
151.          },
```

```
152.        {
153.            "Pluto", new Double(1137), new Integer(1),
154.            Boolean.FALSE, Color.black,
155.            new ImageIcon("Pluto.gif")
156.        }
157.    };
158.
159.    private String[] columnNames =
160.    {
161.        "Planet", "Radius", "Moons", "Gaseous", "Color", "Image"
162.    };
163. }
164.
165. /**
166.    This renderer renders a color value as a panel with the
167.    given color.
168. */
169. class ColorTableCellRenderer implements TableCellRenderer
170. {
171.    public Component getTableCellRendererComponent(JTable table,
172.        Object value, boolean isSelected, boolean hasFocus,
173.        int row, int column)
174.    {
175.        panel.setBackground((Color)value);
176.        return panel;
177.    }
178.
179.    // the following panel is returned for all cells, with
180.    // the background color set to the Color value of the cell
181.
182.    private JPanel panel = new JPanel();
183. }
184.
185. /**
186.    This editor pops up a color dialog to edit a cell value
187. */
188. class ColorTableCellEditor extends AbstractCellEditor
189.    implements TableCellEditor
190. {
191.    ColorTableCellEditor()
192.    {
193.        panel = new JPanel();
194.        // prepare color dialog
195.
196.        colorChooser = new JColorChooser();
197.        colorDialog = JColorChooser.createDialog(null,
198.            "Planet Color", false, colorChooser,
199.            new
200.                ActionListener() // OK button listener
```

```
201.              {
202.                   public void actionPerformed(ActionEvent event)
203.                   {
204.                       stopCellEditing();
205.                   }
206.              },
207.          new
208.              ActionListener() // Cancel button listener
209.              {
210.                   public void actionPerformed(ActionEvent event)
211.                   {
212.                       cancelCellEditing();
213.                   }
214.              });
215.      colorDialog.addWindowListener(new
216.          WindowAdapter()
217.          {
218.              public void windowClosing(WindowEvent event)
219.              {
220.                  cancelCellEditing();
221.              }
222.          });
223.  }
224.
225.  public Component getTableCellEditorComponent(JTable table,
226.      Object value, boolean isSelected, int row, int column)
227.  {
228.      // this is where we get the current Color value. We
229.      // store it in the dialog in case the user starts editing
230.      colorChooser.setColor((Color)value);
231.      return panel;
232.  }
233.
234.  public boolean shouldSelectCell(EventObject anEvent)
235.  {
236.      // start editing
237.      colorDialog.setVisible(true);
238.
239.      // tell caller it is ok to select this cell
240.      return true;
241.  }
242.
243.  public void cancelCellEditing()
244.  {
245.      // editing is canceled--hide dialog
246.      colorDialog.setVisible(false);
247.      super.cancelCellEditing();
248.  }
249.
```

```
250.    public boolean stopCellEditing()
251.    {
252.       // editing is complete--hide dialog
253.       colorDialog.setVisible(false);
254.       super.stopCellEditing();
255.
256.       // tell caller is is ok to use color value
257.       return true;
258.    }
259.
260.    public Object getCellEditorValue()
261.    {
262.       return colorChooser.getColor();
263.    }
264.
265.    private Color color;
266.    private JColorChooser colorChooser;
267.    private JDialog colorDialog;
268.    private JPanel panel;
269. }
```

javax.swing.JTable

- void setRowHeight(int height)

  sets the height of all rows of the table to height pixels.

- void setRowHeight(int row, int height)

  sets the height of the given row of the table to height pixels.

- void setRowMargin(int margin)

  sets the amount of empty space between cells in adjacent rows.

- int getRowHeight()

  gets the default height of all rows of the table.

- int getRowHeight(int row)

  gets the height of the given row of the table.

- int getRowMargin()

  gets the amount of empty space between cells in adjacent rows.

- Rectangle getCellRect(int row, int column, boolean includeSpacing)

  returns the bounding rectangle of a table cell.

Parameters:	row, column	the row and column of the cell
	includeSpacing	true if the space around the cell should be included

- Color getSelectionBackground()
- Color getSelectionForeground()

  return the background and foreground colors to use for selected cells.

`javax.swing.table.TableModel`

- Class getColumnClass(int columnIndex)

  gets the class for the values in this column. This information is used by the cell renderer and editor.

`javax.swing.table.TableCellRenderer`

- Component getTableCellRendererComponent(JTable table,
  Object value, boolean selected, boolean hasFocus,
  int row, int column)

  returns a component whose paint method is invoked to render a table cell.

Parameters:	table	the table containing the cell to be rendered
	value	the cell to be rendered
	selected	true if the cell is currently selected
	hasFocus	true if the cell currently has focus
	row, column	the row and column of the cell

`javax.swing.table.TableColumnModel`

- TableColumn getColumn(int index)

  gets the table column object that describes the column with the given index.

`javax.swing.table.TableColumn`

- void setCellEditor(TableCellEditor editor)
- void setCellRenderer(TableCellRenderer renderer)

  set the cell editor or renderer for all cells in this column.

`javax.swing.DefaultCellEditor`

- DefaultCellEditor(JComboBox comboBox)

  constructs a cell editor that presents the combo box for selecting cell values.

`javax.swing.CellEditor`

- boolean isCellEditable(EventObject event)

  returns true if the event is suitable for initiating the editing process for this cell.

- boolean shouldSelectCell(EventObject anEvent)

  starts the editing process. Returns true if the edited cell should be *selected*. Normally, you want to return true, but you can return false if you don't want the editing process to change the cell selection.

- void cancelCellEditing()

  cancels the editing process. You can abandon partial edits.

- boolean stopCellEditing()

  stops the editing process, with the intent of using the result. Returns `true` if the edited value is in a proper state for retrieval.

- Object getCellEditorValue()

  returns the edited result.

- void addCellEditorListener(CellEditorListener l)
- void removeCellEditorListener(CellEditorListener l)

  add and remove the obligatory cell editor listener.

javax.swing.table.TableCellEditor

- Component getTableCellEditorComponent(JTable table,
  Object value, boolean selected, int row, int column)

  returns a component whose `paint` method renders a table cell.

Parameters:	table	the table containing the cell to be rendered
	value	the cell to be rendered
	selected	`true` if the cell is currently selected
	row, column	the row and column of the cell

javax.swing.JColorChooser

- JColorChooser()

  constructs a color chooser with an initial color of white.

- Color getColor()
- void setColor(Color c)

  get and set the current color of this color chooser.

- static JDialog createDialog(Component parent, String title,
  boolean modal, JColorChooser chooser, ActionListener okLis-
  tener, ActionListener cancelListener)

  creates a dialog box that contains a color chooser.

Parameters:	parent	the component over which to pop up the dialog
	title	the title for the dialog box frame
	modal	`true` if this call should block until the dialog is closed
	chooser	the color chooser to add to the dialog
	okListener, cancelListener	the listeners of the OK and Cancel buttons

- `static Color showDialog(Component component, String title, Color initialColor)`

  creates and shows a modal dialog box that contains a color chooser.

Parameters:	`component`	the component over which to pop up the dialog
	`title`	the title for the dialog box frame
	`initialColor`	the initial selected color

Working with Rows and Columns

In this subsection, you will see how to manipulate the rows and columns in a table. As you read through this material, you should keep in mind that a Swing table is quite asymmetric—there are different operations that you can carry out on rows and columns. The table component was optimized to display rows of information with the same structure, such as the result of a database query, not an arbitrary two-dimensional grid of objects. You will see this asymmetry throughout this subsection.

Resizing columns

The `TableColumn` class gives you control over the resizing behavior of columns. You can set the preferred, minimum, and maximum width with the methods

```
void setPreferredWidth(int width)
void setMinWidth(int width)
void setMaxWidth(int width)
```

This information is used by the table component to lay out the columns.

Use the method

```
void setResizable(boolean resizable)
```

to control whether the user is allowed to resize the column.

You can programmatically resize a column with the method

```
void setWidth(int width)
```

When a column is resized, the default is to leave the total size of the table unchanged. Of course, the width increase or decrease of the resized column must then be distributed over other columns. The default behavior is to change the size of all columns to the right of the resized column. That's a good default because it allows a user to adjust all columns to a desired width, moving from left to right.

You can set another behavior from Table 6–2 by using the method

```
void setAutoResizeMode(int mode)
```

of the `JTable` class.

Table 6–2: Resize modes

Mode	Behavior
AUTO_RESIZE_OFF	Don't resize other columns; change the table size
AUTO_RESIZE_NEXT_COLUMN	Resize the next column only
AUTO_RESIZE_SUBSEQUENT_ COLUMNS	Resize all subsequent columns equally; this is the default behavior
AUTO_RESIZE_LAST_COLUMN	Resize the last column only
AUTO_RESIZE_ALL_COLUMNS	Resize all columns in the table; this is not a good choice because it makes it challenging for the user to adjust multiple columns to a desired size

Selecting Rows, Columns, and Cells

Depending on the selection mode, the user can select rows, columns, or individual cells in the table. By default, row selection is enabled. Clicking inside a cell selects the entire row (see Figure 6–36). Call

```
table.setRowSelectionAllowed(false)
```

to disable row selection.

Figure 6–36: Selecting a row

When row selection is enabled, you can control whether the user is allowed to select a single row, a contiguous set of rows, or any set of rows. You need to retrieve the *selection model* and use its `setSelectionMode` method:

```
table.getSelectionModel().setSelectionMode(mode);
```

Here, `mode` is one of the three values:

```
ListSelectionModel.SINGLE_SELECTION
ListSelectionModel.SINGLE_INTERVAL_SELECTION
ListSelectionModel.MULTIPLE_INTERVAL_SELECTION
```

Column selection is disabled by default. You turn it on with the call

```
table.setColumnSelectionAllowed(true)
```

Enabling both row and column selection is equivalent to enabling cell selection. Then the user selects ranges of cells (see Figure 6–37). You can also enable that setting with the call

```
table.setCellSelectionEnabled(true)
```

A	B	C	D	E	F	G	H	I	J
1	2	3	4	5	6	7	8	9	10
2	4	6	8	10	12	14	16	18	20
3	6	9	12	15	18	21	24	27	30
4	8	12	16	20	24	28	32	36	40
5	10	15	20	25	30	35	40	45	50
6	12	18	24	30	36	42	48	54	60
7	14	21	28	35	42	49	56	63	70
8	16	24	32	40	48	56	64	72	80
9	18	27	36	45	54	63	72	81	90
10	20	30	40	50	60	70	80	90	100

Figure 6–37: Selecting a range of cells

NOTE: In early versions of the Swing toolkit, when setting both row and column selections, every mouse click selects a "+" shaped area consisting of both the row and the column containing the cursor.

You can find out which rows and columns are selected by calling the `getSelectedRows` and `getSelectedColumns` methods. Both return an `int[]` array of the indexes of the selected items.

You can run the program in Example 6–14 to watch cell selection in action. Enable row, column, or cell selection in the Selection menu and watch how the selection behavior changes.

Hiding and displaying columns

The `removeColumn` method of the `JTable` class removes a column from the table view. The column data is not actually removed from the model—it is just hidden from view. The `removeColumn` method takes a `TableColumn` argument. If you have the column number (for example, from a call to `getSelectedColumns`), you need to ask the table model for the actual table column object:

```
TableColumnModel columnModel = table.getColumnModel();
TableColumn column = columnModel.getColumn(i);
table.removeColumn(column);
```

If you remember the column, you can later add it back in:

```
table.addColumn(column);
```

This method adds the column to the end. If you want it to appear elsewhere, you have to call the `moveColumn` method.

You can also add a new column that corresponds to a column index in the table model, by adding a new `TableColumn` object:

```
table.addColumn(new TableColumn(modelColumnIndex));
```

You can have multiple table columns that view the same column of the model.

However, there is no `JTable` method to actually insert a new column into the model or to remove a column from the model. There are also no `JTable` methods for hiding or showing rows. If you want to hide rows, you can create a filter model similar to the sort filter that you saw earlier.

Adding and removing rows in the default table model

The `DefaultTableModel` class is a concrete class that implements the `TableModel` interface. It stores a two-dimensional grid of objects. If you already have your data in a tabular arrangement, then there is no point in copying all the data into a default table model, but it is handy if you quickly need to make a table from a small data set. The `DefaultTableModel` class has methods for adding rows and columns, and for removing rows.

The `addRow` and `addColumn` methods add a row or column of new data. You supply an `Object[]` array or a vector that holds the new data. With the `addColumn` method, you also need to supply a name for the new column. These methods add the new data to the end of the grid. To insert a row in the middle, use the `insertRow` method. There is no method for inserting a column in the middle of the grid.

Conversely, the `removeRow` method removes a row from the model. There is no method for removing a column.

Since the `JTable` object registers itself as a table model listener, the model notifies the table when data is inserted or removed. At that time, the table refreshes the display.

The program in Example 6–14 shows both selection and editing at work. A default table model contains a simple data set (a multiplication table). The Edit menu contains these commands:

- Hide all selected columns.
- Show all columns that you've ever hidden.
- Remove selected rows from the model.
- Add a row of data to the end of the model.

This example concludes the discussion of Swing tables. Tables are conceptually a bit easier to grasp than trees because the underlying data model—a grid of objects—is easy to visualize. However, under the hood, the table component is actually quite a bit more complex than the tree component. Column headers, resizable columns, and column-specific renderers and editors all add to the complexity. In this section, we focused on those topics that you are most likely to encounter in practice: displaying database information, sorting, and custom cell rendering and editing. If you have special advanced needs, we once again refer you to *Core Java Foundation Classes* by Kim Topley and *Graphic Java 2* by David Geary.

Example 6–14: TableSelectionTest.java

```java
1. import java.awt.*;
2. import java.awt.event.*;
3. import java.util.*;
4. import java.text.*;
5. import javax.swing.*;
6. import javax.swing.table.*;
7.
8. /**
9.    This program demonstrates selection, addition, and removal
10.   of rows and columns.
11. */
12. public class TableSelectionTest
13. {
14.    public static void main(String[] args)
15.    {
16.       JFrame frame = new TableSelectionFrame();
17.       frame.setDefaultCloseOperation(JFrame.EXIT_ON_CLOSE);
18.       frame.show();
19.    }
20. }
21.
22. /**
23.    This frame shows a multiplication table and has menus for
24.    setting the row/column/cell selection modes, and for
25.    adding and removing rows and columns.
26. */
27. class TableSelectionFrame extends JFrame
28. {
29.    public TableSelectionFrame()
30.    {
31.       setTitle("TableSelectionTest");
32.       setSize(WIDTH, HEIGHT);
33.
34.       // set up multiplication table
35.
36.       model = new DefaultTableModel(10, 10);
37.
38.       for (int i = 0; i < model.getRowCount(); i++)
39.          for (int j = 0; j < model.getColumnCount(); j++)
```

```
40.          model.setValueAt(
41.             new Integer((i + 1) * (j + 1)), i, j);
42.
43.       table = new JTable(model);
44.       Container contentPane = getContentPane();
45.       contentPane.add(new JScrollPane(table), "Center");
46.
47.       removedColumns = new ArrayList();
48.
49.       // create menu
50.
51.       JMenuBar menuBar = new JMenuBar();
52.       setJMenuBar(menuBar);
53.
54.       JMenu selectionMenu = new JMenu("Selection");
55.       menuBar.add(selectionMenu);
56.
57.       final JCheckBoxMenuItem rowsItem
58.          = new JCheckBoxMenuItem("Rows");
59.       final JCheckBoxMenuItem columnsItem
60.          = new JCheckBoxMenuItem("Columns");
61.       final JCheckBoxMenuItem cellsItem
62.          = new JCheckBoxMenuItem("Cells");
63.
64.       rowsItem.setSelected(table.getRowSelectionAllowed());
65.       columnsItem.setSelected(table.getColumnSelectionAllowed());
66.       cellsItem.setSelected(table.getCellSelectionEnabled());
67.
68.       rowsItem.addActionListener(new
69.          ActionListener()
70.          {
71.             public void actionPerformed(ActionEvent event)
72.             {
73.                table.clearSelection();
74.                table.setRowSelectionAllowed(
75.                   rowsItem.isSelected());
76.                cellsItem.setSelected(
77.                   table.getCellSelectionEnabled());
78.             }
79.          });
80.       selectionMenu.add(rowsItem);
81.
82.       columnsItem.addActionListener(new
83.          ActionListener()
84.          {
85.             public void actionPerformed(ActionEvent event)
86.             {
87.                table.clearSelection();
88.                table.setColumnSelectionAllowed(
```

```
89.                         columnsItem.isSelected());
90.                 cellsItem.setSelected(
91.                     table.getCellSelectionEnabled());
92.             }
93.         });
94.     selectionMenu.add(columnsItem);
95.
96.     cellsItem.addActionListener(new
97.         ActionListener()
98.         {
99.             public void actionPerformed(ActionEvent event)
100.            {
101.                table.clearSelection();
102.                table.setCellSelectionEnabled(
103.                    cellsItem.isSelected());
104.                rowsItem.setSelected(
105.                    table.getRowSelectionAllowed());
106.                columnsItem.setSelected(
107.                    table.getColumnSelectionAllowed());
108.            }
109.        });
110.    selectionMenu.add(cellsItem);
111.
112.    JMenu tableMenu = new JMenu("Edit");
113.    menuBar.add(tableMenu);
114.
115.    JMenuItem hideColumnsItem = new JMenuItem("Hide Columns");
116.    hideColumnsItem.addActionListener(new
117.        ActionListener()
118.        {
119.            public void actionPerformed(ActionEvent event)
120.            {
121.                int[] selected = table.getSelectedColumns();
122.                TableColumnModel columnModel
123.                    = table.getColumnModel();
124.
125.                // remove columns from view, starting at the last
126.                // index so that column numbers aren't affected
127.
128.
129.                for (int i = selected.length - 1; i >= 0; i--)
130.                {
131.                    TableColumn column
132.                        = columnModel.getColumn(selected[i]);
133.                    table.removeColumn(column);
134.
135.                    // store removed columns for "show columns"
136.                    // command
137.
```

```
138.                 removedColumns.add(column);
139.             }
140.         }
141.     });
142.     tableMenu.add(hideColumnsItem);
143.
144.     JMenuItem showColumnsItem = new JMenuItem("Show Columns");
145.     showColumnsItem.addActionListener(new
146.         ActionListener()
147.         {
148.             public void actionPerformed(ActionEvent event)
149.             {
150.                 // restore all removed columns
151.                 for (int i = 0; i < removedColumns.size(); i++)
152.                     table.addColumn(
153.                         (TableColumn)removedColumns.get(i));
154.                 removedColumns.clear();
155.             }
156.         });
157.     tableMenu.add(showColumnsItem);
158.
159.     JMenuItem addRowItem = new JMenuItem("Add Row");
160.     addRowItem.addActionListener(new
161.         ActionListener()
162.         {
163.             public void actionPerformed(ActionEvent event)
164.             {
165.                 // add a new row to the multiplication table in
166.                 // the model
167.
168.                 Integer[] newCells
169.                     = new Integer[model.getColumnCount()];
170.                 for (int i = 0; i < newCells.length; i++)
171.                     newCells[i] = new Integer((i + 1)
172.                         * (model.getRowCount() + 1));
173.                 model.addRow(newCells);
174.             }
175.         });
176.     tableMenu.add(addRowItem);
177.
178.     JMenuItem removeRowsItem = new  JMenuItem("Remove Rows");
179.     removeRowsItem.addActionListener(new
180.         ActionListener()
181.         {
182.             public void actionPerformed(ActionEvent event)
183.             {
184.                 int[] selected = table.getSelectedRows();
185.
186.                 // remove rows from model, starting at the last
187.                 // index so that the row numbers aren't affected
188.
```

```
189.
190.             for (int i = selected.length - 1; i >= 0; i--)
191.                 model.removeRow(selected[i]);
192.          }
193.       });
194.    tableMenu.add(removeRowsItem);
195.
196.    JMenuItem clearCellsItem = new  JMenuItem("Clear Cells");
197.    clearCellsItem.addActionListener(new
198.       ActionListener()
199.       {
200.          public void actionPerformed(ActionEvent event)
201.          {
202.             // set all selected cells to 0
203.
204.             for (int i = 0; i < table.getRowCount(); i++)
205.               for (int j = 0; j < table.getColumnCount(); j++)
206.                  if (table.isCellSelected(i, j))
207.                     table.setValueAt(new Integer(0), i, j);
208.          }
209.       });
210.    tableMenu.add(clearCellsItem);
211. }
212.
213.    private DefaultTableModel model;
214.    private JTable table;
215.    private ArrayList removedColumns;
216.
217.    private static final int WIDTH = 400;
218.    private static final int HEIGHT = 300;
219. }
```

javax.swing.JTable

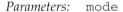

- void setAutoResizeMode(int mode)

  sets the mode for automatic resizing of table columns.

  Parameters: mode   one of AUTO_RESIZE_OFF,
                                 AUTO_RESIZE_NEXT_COLUMN,
                                 AUTO_RESIZE_SUBSEQUENT_COLUMNS,
                                 AUTO_RESIZE_LAST_COLUMN,
                                 AUTO_RESIZE_ALL_COLUMNS

- ListSelectionModel getSelectionModel()

  returns the list selection model. You need that model to choose between row, column, and cell selection.

- void setRowSelectionAllowed(boolean b)

  If b is true, then rows can be selected when the user clicks on cells.

- void setColumnSelectionAllowed(boolean b)
  If b is true, then columns can be selected when the user clicks on cells.
- void setCellSelectionEnabled(boolean b)
  If b is true, then individual cells are selected. This is equivalent to calling both setRowSelectionAllowed(b) and setColumnSelectionAllowed(b).
- boolean getRowSelectionAllowed()
  Returns true if row selection is allowed.
- boolean getColumnSelectionAllowed()
  Returns true if column selection is allowed.
- boolean getCellSelectionEnabled()
  Returns true if both row and column selection are allowed.
- void addColumn(TableColumn column)
  adds a column to the table view.
- void moveColumn(int from, int to)
  moves the column at table index from so that its index becomes to. Only the view is affected.
- void removeColumn(TableColumn column)
  removes the given column from the view.

javax.swing.table.TableColumn

- TableColumn(int modelColumnIndex)
  constructs a table column for viewing the model column with the given index.
- void setPreferredWidth(int width)
- void setMinWidth(int width)
- void setMaxWidth(int width)
  set the preferred, minimum, and maximum width of this table column to width.
- void setWidth(int width)
  sets the actual width of this column to width.
- void setResizable(boolean b)
  If b is true, this column is resizable.

javax.swing.ListSelectionModel

- void setSelectionMode(int mode)

Parameters:	mode	one of SINGLE_SELECTION, SINGLE_INTERVAL_SELECTION, and MULTIPLE_INTERVAL_SELECTION

`javax.swing.table.DefaultTableModel`

- `void addRow(Object[] rowData)`
- `void addColumn(Object columnName, Object[] columnData)`
  add a row or column of data to the end of the table model.

- `void insertRow(int row, Object[] rowData)`
  adds a row of data at index `row`.

- `void removeRow(int row)`
  removes the given row from the model.

- `void moveRow(int start, int end, int to)`
  moves all rows with indexes between `start` and `end` to a new location starting at `to`.

Styled Text Components

In Volume 1, we discussed the basic text component classes `JTextField` and `JTextArea`. Of course, these classes are very useful for obtaining text input from the user. There is another useful class, `JEditorPane`, that displays and edits text in HTML and RTF format. (RTF is the "rich text format" that is used by a number of Microsoft applications for document interchange. It is a poorly documented format that doesn't work well even between Microsoft's own applications. We do not cover the RTF capabilities in this book; Sun claims only "limited" support for it. We wouldn't be surprised to see this feature dropped in the future since it would make more sense for Sun to spend its resources on improving the HTML support.)

Frankly, at this point, the `JEditorPane` is pretty limited. The HTML renderer can display simple files, but it chokes at many complex pages that you typically find on the Web. The HTML editor is limited and unstable. Of course, except for HTML editors, few applications require users to edit HTML text, so this is not a major restriction.

We think that the perfect application for the `JEditorPane` is to display program help in HTML format. Since you have control over the help files that you provide, you can stay away from features that the `JEditorPane` does not display well.

NOTE: For more information on an industrial-strength help system, check out Java-Help at `http://java.sun.com/products/javahelp/index.html`.

NOTE: The subclass `JTextPane` of `JEditorPane` can hold styled text with special fonts and text formats, as well as embedded components. We will not cover that component in this book. If you need to implement a component that allows users of your program to enter styled text, have a look at the implementation of the StylePad demo that is included in the SDK.

The program in Example 6–15 contains an editor pane that shows the contents of an HTML page. Type a URL into the text field. The URL must start with `http:` or `file:`. Then, click the Load button. The selected HTML page is displayed in the editor pane (see Figure 6–38).

Figure 6–38: The editor pane displaying an HTML page

The hyperlinks are active: if you click on a link, the application loads it. The Back button returns to the previous page.

This program is in fact a very simple browser. Of course, it does not have any of the comfort features, such as page caching or bookmark lists, that you expect from a commercial browser. Also, the editor pane does not yet display applets.

If you click on the Editable check box, then the editor pane becomes editable. You can type in text and use the BACKSPACE key to delete text. The component also understands the CTRL+X, CTRL+C, and CTRL+V shortcuts for cut, copy, and paste.

However, you would have to do quite a bit of programming to add support for fonts and formatting.

When the component is editable, then hyperlinks are not active. Also, with some web pages you can see JavaScript commands, comments, and other tags when edit mode is turned on (see Figure 6–39). The example program lets you investigate the editing feature, but we recommend that you omit that feature in your programs.

TIP: By default, the `JEditorPane` is in edit mode. You should call `editorPane.setEditable(false)` to turn it off.

Figure 6–39: The editor pane in edit mode

The features of the editor pane that you saw in the example program are very easy to use. You use the `setPage` method to load a new document. The parameter is either a string or a `URL` object. The `JEditorPane` class extends the `JTextComponent` class. Therefore, you can call the `setText` method as well—it simply displays plain text.

To listen to hyperlink clicks, you add a `HyperlinkListener`. The `Hyperlink-Listener` interface has a single method, `hyperlinkUpdate`, that is called when the user moves over or clicks on a link. The method has a parameter of type `HyperlinkEvent`.

You need to call the `getEventType` method to find out what kind of event occurred. There are three possible return values:

```
HyperlinkEvent.EventType.ACTIVATED
HyperlinkEvent.EventType.ENTERED
HyperlinkEvent.EventType.EXITED
```

The first value indicates that the user clicked on the hyperlink. In that case, you typically want to open the new link. You can use the second and third values to give some visual feedback, such as a tooltip, when the mouse hovers over the link.

NOTE: It is a complete mystery why there aren't three separate methods to handle activation, entry, and exit in the `HyperlinkListener` interface.

The `getURL` method of the `HyperlinkEvent` class returns the URL of the hyperlink. For example, here is how you can install a hyperlink listener that follows the links that a user activates:

```
editorPane.addHyperlinkListener(new
    HyperlinkListener()
    {
        public void hyperlinkUpdate(HyperlinkEvent event)
        {
            if (event.getEventType()
                == HyperlinkEvent.EventType.ACTIVATED)
            {
                try
                {
                    editorPane.setPage(event.getURL());
                }
                catch(IOException e)
                {
                    editorPane.setText("Exception: " + e);
                }
            }
        }
    });
```

The event handler simply gets the URL and updates the editor pane. The `setPage` method can throw an `IOException`. In that case, we display an error message as plain text.

The program in Example 6–15 shows all the features that you need to put together an HTML help system. Under the hood, the `JEditorPane` is even more complex than the tree and table components. However, if you don't need to write a text editor or a renderer of a custom text format, that complexity is hidden from you.

Example 6–15 EditorPaneTest.java

```
1. import java.awt.*;
2. import java.awt.event.*;
3. import java.io.*;
4. import java.util.*;
5. import javax.swing.*;
6. import javax.swing.event.*;
7.
8. /**
9.    This program demonstrates how to display HTML documents
10.   in an editor pane.
11. */
12. public class EditorPaneTest
13. {
14.    public static void main(String[] args)
15.    {
16.       JFrame frame = new EditorPaneFrame();
17.       frame.setDefaultCloseOperation(JFrame.EXIT_ON_CLOSE);
18.       frame.show();
19.    }
20. }
21.
22. /**
23.    This frame contains an editor pane, a text field and button
24.    to enter a URL and load a document, and a Back button to
25.    return to a previously loaded document.
26. */
27. class EditorPaneFrame extends JFrame
28. {
29.    public EditorPaneFrame()
30.    {
31.       setTitle("EditorPaneTest");
32.       setSize(WIDTH, HEIGHT);
33.
34.       final Stack urlStack = new Stack();
35.       final JEditorPane editorPane = new JEditorPane();
36.       final JTextField url = new JTextField(30);
37.
38.       // set up hyperlink listener
39.
40.       editorPane.setEditable(false);
41.       editorPane.addHyperlinkListener(new
42.          HyperlinkListener()
43.          {
44.             public void hyperlinkUpdate(HyperlinkEvent event)
45.             {
46.                if (event.getEventType()
47.                   == HyperlinkEvent.EventType.ACTIVATED)
48.                {
49.                   try
50.                   {
```

```
51.                         // remember URL for back button
52.                         urlStack.push(event.getURL().toString());
53.                         // show URL in text field
54.                         url.setText(event.getURL().toString());
55.
56.                         editorPane.setPage(event.getURL());
57.                      }
58.                      catch(IOException e)
59.                      {
60.                         editorPane.setText("Exception: " + e);
61.                      }
62.                   }
63.                }
64.             });
65.
66.          // set up checkbox for toggling edit mode
67.
68.          final JCheckBox editable = new JCheckBox();
69.          editable.addActionListener(new
70.             ActionListener()
71.             {
72.                public void actionPerformed(ActionEvent event)
73.                {
74.                   editorPane.setEditable(editable.isSelected());
75.                }
76.             });
77.
78.          // set up load button for loading URL
79.
80.          ActionListener listener = new
81.             ActionListener()
82.             {
83.                public void actionPerformed(ActionEvent event)
84.                {
85.                   try
86.                   {
87.                      // remember URL for back button
88.                      urlStack.push(url.getText());
89.
90.                      editorPane.setPage(url.getText());
91.                   }
92.                   catch(IOException e)
93.                   {
94.                      editorPane.setText("Exception: " + e);
95.                   }
96.                }
97.             };
98.
99.          JButton loadButton = new JButton("Load");
100.         loadButton.addActionListener(listener);
101.         url.addActionListener(listener);
102.
103.         // set up back button and button action
```

```
104.
105.        JButton backButton = new JButton("Back");
106.        backButton.addActionListener(new
107.           ActionListener()
108.           {
109.              public void actionPerformed(ActionEvent event)
110.              {
111.                 if (urlStack.size() <= 1) return;
112.                 try
113.                 {
114.                    // get URL from back button
115.                    urlStack.pop();
116.                    // show URL in text field
117.                    String urlString = (String)urlStack.peek();
118.                    url.setText(urlString);
119.
120.                    editorPane.setPage(urlString);
121.                 }
122.                 catch(IOException e)
123.                 {
124.                    editorPane.setText("Exception: " + e);
125.                 }
126.              }
127.           });
128.
129.        Container contentPane = getContentPane();
130.        contentPane.add(new JScrollPane(editorPane),
131.           BorderLayout.CENTER);
132.
133.        // put all control components in a panel
134.
135.        JPanel panel = new JPanel();
136.        panel.add(new JLabel("URL"));
137.        panel.add(url);
138.        panel.add(loadButton);
139.        panel.add(backButton);
140.        panel.add(new JLabel("Editable"));
141.        panel.add(editable);
142.
143.        contentPane.add(panel, BorderLayout.SOUTH);
144.     }
145.
146.     private static final int WIDTH = 600;
147.     private static final int HEIGHT = 400;
148. }
```

javax.swing.JEditorPane

- void setPage(URL url)

  loads the page from url into the editor pane.

- void addHyperlinkListener(HyperLinkListener listener)

  adds a hyperlink listener to this editor pane.

`javax.swing.event.HyperlinkListener`

- `void hyperlinkUpdate(HyperlinkEvent event)`
  is called whenever a hyperlink was selected.

`javax.swing.HyperlinkEvent`

- `URL getURL()`
  returns the URL of the selected hyperlink.

Component Organizers

We conclude the discussion of advanced Swing features with a presentation of components that help organize other components. These include the *split pane,* a mechanism for splitting an area into multiple parts whose boundaries can be adjusted, the *tabbed pane,* which uses tab dividers to allow a user to flip through multiple panels, and the *desktop pane,* which can be used to implement applications that display multiple *internal frames.*

Split Panes

Split panes are used to split a component into two parts, with an adjustable boundary in between. Figure 6–40 shows a frame with two split panes. The outer pane is split horizontally, with a text area on the bottom and another split pane on the top. That pane is split vertically, with a list on the left and a label containing an image on the right.

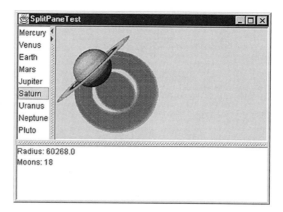

Figure 6–40: A frame with two nested split panes

You construct a split pane by specifying the orientation, one of `JSplitPane.HORIZONTAL_SPLIT` or `JSplitPane.VERTICAL_SPLIT`, followed by the two components. For example,

```
JSplitPane innerPane
    = new JSplitPane(JSplitPane.HORIZONTAL_SPLIT,
        planetList, planetImage);
```

That's all you have to do. If you like, you can add "one touch expand" icons to the splitter bar. You see those icons in the top pane in Figure 6–40. In the Metal look and feel, they are small triangles. If you click on one of them, the splitter moves all the way in the direction of the tip of the triangle, expanding one of the panes completely.

To add this capability, call

```
innerPane.setOneTouchExpandable(true);
```

The "continuous layout" feature continuously repaints the contents of both components as the user adjusts the splitter. That looks classier, but it can be slow. You turn on that feature with the call

```
innerPane.setContinuousLayout(true);
```

In the example program, we left the bottom splitter at the default (no continuous layout). When you drag it, you only move a black outline. When you are done, the components are repainted.

The program in Example 6–16 is very straightforward. It populates a list box with planets. When the user makes a selection, the planet image is displayed to the right and a description is placed in the text area on the bottom. When you run the program, adjust the splitters and try out the "one touch expansion" and "continuous layout" features.

Example 6–16: SplitPaneTest.java

```
1. import java.awt.*;
2. import java.awt.event.*;
3. import java.util.*;
4. import javax.swing.*;
5. import javax.swing.event.*;
6.
7. /**
8.     This program demonstrates the split pane component
9.     organizer.
10. */
11. public class SplitPaneTest
12. {
13.     public static void main(String[] args)
14.     {
15.         JFrame frame = new SplitPaneFrame();
16.         frame.setDefaultCloseOperation(JFrame.EXIT_ON_CLOSE);
17.         frame.show();
18.     }
19. }
20.
21. /**
22.     This frame consists of two nested split panes to demonstrate
```

```
23.     planet images and data.
24. */
25. class SplitPaneFrame extends JFrame
26. {
27.    public SplitPaneFrame()
28.    {
29.       setTitle("SplitPaneTest");
30.       setSize(WIDTH, HEIGHT);
31.
32.       // set up components for planet names, images, descriptions
33.
34.       final JList planetList = new JList(planets);
35.       final JLabel planetImage = new JLabel();
36.       final JTextArea description = new JTextArea();
37.
38.       planetList.addListSelectionListener(new
39.          ListSelectionListener()
40.          {
41.             public void valueChanged(ListSelectionEvent event)
42.             {
43.                Planet value
44.                   = (Planet)planetList.getSelectedValue();
45.
46.                // update image and description
47.
48.                planetImage.setIcon(value.getImage());
49.                description.setText(value.getDescription());
50.             }
51.          });
52.
53.       // set up split panes
54.
55.       JSplitPane innerPane
56.          = new JSplitPane(JSplitPane.HORIZONTAL_SPLIT,
57.             planetList, planetImage);
58.
59.       innerPane.setContinuousLayout(true);
60.       innerPane.setOneTouchExpandable(true);
61.
62.       JSplitPane outerPane
63.          = new JSplitPane(JSplitPane.VERTICAL_SPLIT,
64.             innerPane, description);
65.
66.       getContentPane().add(outerPane, "Center");
67.    }
68.
69.    private Planet[] planets =
70.       {
71.          new Planet("Mercury", 2440, 0),
72.          new Planet("Venus", 6052, 0),
73.          new Planet("Earth", 6378, 1),
74.          new Planet("Mars", 3397, 2),
```

```
75.              new Planet("Jupiter", 71492, 16),
76.              new Planet("Saturn", 60268, 18),
77.              new Planet("Uranus", 25559, 17),
78.              new Planet("Neptune", 24766, 8),
79.              new Planet("Pluto", 1137, 1),
80.           };
81.      private static final int WIDTH = 300;
82.      private static final int HEIGHT = 200;
83.  }
84.
85.  /**
86.      Describes a planet.
87.  */
88.  class Planet
89.  {
90.      /**
91.          Constructs a planet.
92.          @param n the planet name
93.          @param r the planet radius
94.          @param m the number of moons
95.      */
96.      public Planet(String n, double r, int m)
97.      {   name = n;
98.          radius = r;
99.          moons = m;
100.         image = new ImageIcon(name + ".gif");
101.     }
102.
103.     public String toString()
104.     {
105.         return name;
106.     }
107.
108.     /**
109.         Gets a description of the planet.
110.         @return the description
111.     */
112.     public String getDescription()
113.     {
114.         return "Radius: " + radius + "\nMoons: " + moons + "\n";
115.     }
116.
117.     /**
118.         Gets an image of the planet.
119.         @return the image
120.     */
121.     public ImageIcon getImage()
122.     {
123.         return image;
124.     }
125.
126.     private String name;
```

```
127.    private double radius;
128.    private int moons;
129.    private ImageIcon image;
130. }
```

javax.swing.JSplitPane

- JSplitPane()
- JSplitPane(int direction)
- JSplitPane(int direction, boolean continuousLayout)
- JSplitPane(int direction, Component first, Component second)
- JSplitPane(int direction, boolean continuousLayout, Component first, Component second)

  construct a new split pane.

Parameters:	direction	one of HORIZONTAL_SPLIT or VERTICAL_SPLIT
	continousLayout	true if the components are continuously updated when the splitter is moved
	first, second	the components to add

- boolean isOneTouchExpandable()
- void setOneTouchExpandable(boolean b)

  get and set the "one-touch expandable" property. When this property is set, the splitter has two icons to completely expand one or the other component.

- boolean isContinuousLayout()
- void setContinuousLayout(boolean b)

  get and set the "continuous layout" property. When this property is set, then the components are continuously updated when the splitter is moved.

- void setLeftComponent(Component c)
- void setTopComponent(Component c)

  These operations have the same effect, to set c as the first component in the split pane.

- void setRightComponent(Component c)
- void setBottomComponent(Component c)

  These operations have the same effect, to set c as the second component in the split pane.

Tabbed Panes

Tabbed panes are a familiar user interface device to break up a complex dialog into subsets of related options. You can also use tabs to let a user flip through a set of documents or images (see Figure 6–41). That is what we will do in our sample program.

Figure 6–41: A tabbed pane

To create a tabbed pane, you first construct a `JTabbedPane` object, then you add tabs to it.

```
JTabbedPane tabbedPane = new JTabbedPane();
tabbedPane.addTab(title, icon, component);
```

The last parameter of the `addTab` method has type `Component`. If you want to add multiple components into the same tab, you first pack them up in a container, such as a `JPanel`.

The icon is optional; there is an `addTab` method that does not require an icon:

```
tabbedPane.addTab(title, component);
```

You can also add a tab in the middle of the tab collection with the `insertTab` method:

```
tabbedPane.insertTab(title, icon, component, index);
```

To remove a tab from the tab collection, use

```
tabPane.removeTabAt(index);
```

When you add a new tab to the tab collection, it is not automatically displayed. You must select it with the `setSelectedIndex` method. For example, here is how you show a tab that you just added to the end:

```
tabbedPane.setSelectedIndex(tabbedPane.getTabCount() - 1);
```

If you have a lot of tabs, then they can take up quite a bit of space. Starting with SDK 1.4, you can display the tabs in scrolling mode, where only one row of tabs is displayed, together with a set of arrow buttons that allow the user to scroll through the tab set (see Figure 6–42).

You set the tab layout to wrapped or scrolling mode by calling

```
tabbedPane.setTabLayoutPolicy(JTabbedPane.WRAP_TAB_LAYOUT);
```

or

```
tabbedPane.setTabLayoutPolicy(JTabbedPane.SCROLL_TAB_LAYOUT);
```

Figure 6–42: A tabbed pane with scrolling tabs

The example program shows a useful technique with tabbed panes. Sometimes, you want to update a component just before it is displayed. In our example program, we will load the planet image only when the user actually clicks on a tab.

To be notified whenever the user clicks on a new tab, you install a `Change-Listener` with the tabbed pane. Note that you must install the listener with the tabbed pane itself, not with any of the components.

```
tabbedPane.addChangeListener(listener);
```

When the user selects a tab, the `stateChanged` method of the change listener is called. You retrieve the tabbed pane as the source of the event. Call the `getSelectedIndex` method to find out which pane is about to be selected.

```
public void stateChanged(ChangeEvent event)
{
    int n = tabbedPane.getSelectedIndex();
    . . .
}
```

In Example 6–17, we first set all tab components to `null`. When a new tab is selected, we test if its component is still `null`. If so, we replace it with the image. (This happens instantaneously when you click on the tab. You will not see an empty pane.) Just for fun, we also change the icon from a yellow ball to a red ball to indicate which panes have been visited.

Example 6–17: TabbedPaneTest.java

```
1. import java.awt.*;
2. import java.awt.event.*;
3. import java.util.*;
4. import javax.swing.*;
5. import javax.swing.event.*;
6.
```

```
7.  /**
8.     This program demonstrates the tabbed pane component organizer.
9.  */
10. public class TabbedPaneTest
11. {
12.    public static void main(String[] args)
13.    {
14.       JFrame frame = new TabbedPaneFrame();
15.       frame.setDefaultCloseOperation(JFrame.EXIT_ON_CLOSE);
16.       frame.show();
17.    }
18. }
19.
20. /**
21.    This frame shows a tabbed pane and radio buttons to
22.    switch between wrapped and scrolling tab layout.
23. */
24. class TabbedPaneFrame extends JFrame
25. {
26.    public TabbedPaneFrame()
27.    {
28.       setTitle("TabbedPaneTest");
29.       setSize(WIDTH, HEIGHT);
30.
31.       final JTabbedPane tabbedPane = new JTabbedPane();
32.       // we set the components to null and delay their
33.       // loading until the tab is shown for the first time
34.
35.       ImageIcon icon = new ImageIcon("yellow-ball.gif");
36.
37.       tabbedPane.addTab("Mercury", icon, null);
38.       tabbedPane.addTab("Venus", icon, null);
39.       tabbedPane.addTab("Earth", icon, null);
40.       tabbedPane.addTab("Mars", icon, null);
41.       tabbedPane.addTab("Jupiter", icon, null);
42.       tabbedPane.addTab("Saturn", icon, null);
43.       tabbedPane.addTab("Uranus", icon, null);
44.       tabbedPane.addTab("Neptune", icon, null);
45.       tabbedPane.addTab("Pluto", icon, null);
46.
47.       getContentPane().add(tabbedPane, "Center");
48.
49.       tabbedPane.addChangeListener(new
50.          ChangeListener()
51.          {
52.             public void stateChanged(ChangeEvent event)
53.             {
54.
55.                // check if this tab still has a null component
56.
```

```
57.              if (tabbedPane.getSelectedComponent() == null)
58.              {
59.                 // set the component to the image icon
60.
61.                 int n = tabbedPane.getSelectedIndex();
62.                 String title = tabbedPane.getTitleAt(n);
63.                 ImageIcon planetIcon
64.                    = new ImageIcon(title + ".gif");
65.                 tabbedPane.setComponentAt(n,
66.                    new JLabel(planetIcon));
67.
68.                 // indicate that this tab has been
69.                 // visited--just for fun
70.
71.                 tabbedPane.setIconAt(n,
72.                    new ImageIcon("red-ball.gif"));
73.              }
74.           }
75.        });
76.
77.     JPanel buttonPanel = new JPanel();
78.     ButtonGroup buttonGroup = new ButtonGroup();
79.     JRadioButton wrapButton = new JRadioButton("Wrap tabs");
80.     wrapButton.addActionListener(new
81.        ActionListener()
82.        {
83.           public void actionPerformed(ActionEvent event)
84.           {
85.              tabbedPane.setTabLayoutPolicy(
86.                 JTabbedPane.WRAP_TAB_LAYOUT);
87.           }
88.        });
89.     buttonPanel.add(wrapButton);
90.     buttonGroup.add(wrapButton);
91.     wrapButton.setSelected(true);
92.     JRadioButton scrollButton
93.        = new JRadioButton("Scroll tabs");
94.     scrollButton.addActionListener(new
95.        ActionListener()
96.        {
97.           public void actionPerformed(ActionEvent event)
98.           {
99.              tabbedPane.setTabLayoutPolicy(
100.                 JTabbedPane.SCROLL_TAB_LAYOUT);
101.           }
102.        });
103.     buttonPanel.add(scrollButton);
104.     buttonGroup.add(scrollButton);
105.     getContentPane().add(buttonPanel, BorderLayout.SOUTH);
```

```
106.     }
107.
108.     private static final int WIDTH = 400;
109.     private static final int HEIGHT = 300;
110. }
111.
```

`javax.swing.JTabbedPane`

- `JTabbedPane()`
- `JTabbedPane(int placement)`
  construct a tabbed pane.

  Parameters: placement   one of SwingConstants.TOP, SwingCon-
  stants.LEFT, SwingConstants.RIGHT,
  or SwingConstants.BOTTOM

- `void addTab(String title, Component component)`
- `void addTab(String title, Icon icon, Component c)`
- `void addTab(String title, Icon icon, Component c, String tooltip)`
  add a tab to the end of the tabbed pane.

- `void insertTab(String title, Icon icon, Component c, String tool-
  tip, int index)`
  inserts a tab to the tabbed pane at the given index.

- `void removeTabAt(int index)`
  removes the tab at the given index.

- `void setSelectedIndex(int index)`
  selects the tab at the given index.

- `int getSelectedIndex()`
  returns the index of the selected tab.

- `Component getSelectedComponent()`
  returns the component.

- `String getTitleAt(int index)`
- `void setTitleAt(int index, String title)`
- `Icon getIconAt(int index)`
- `void setIconAt(int index, Icon icon)`
- `Component getComponentAt(int index)`
- `void setComponentAt(int index, Component c)`
  get or set the title, icon, or component at the given index.

- `int indexOfTab(Icon icon)`
- `int indexOfTab(String title)`
- `int indexOfComponent(Component c)`
  return the index of the tab with the given title, icon, or component.

- `int getTabCount()`
  returns the total number of tabs in this tabbed pane.

- `void setTabLayoutPolicy(int policy)`
  sets the tab layout policy. Tabs can be wrapped or scrolling.

  Parameters: `policy`   one of `JTabbedPane.WRAP_TAB_LAYOUT`
                                 or `JTabbedPane.SCROLL_TAB_LAYOUT`

- `void addChangeListener(ChangeListener listener)`
  adds a change listener that is notified when the user selects a different tab.

Desktop Panes and Internal Frames

Many applications present information in multiple windows that are all contained inside a large frame. If you minimize the application frame, all of its windows are hidden at the same time. In the Windows environment, this user interface is sometimes called the *multiple document interface* or MDI. Figure 6–43 shows a typical application that utilizes this interface.

Figure 6–43: A multiple document interface application

For some time, this user interface style was very popular, but it has become less prevalent in recent years. In particular, most browsers display a separate top-level frame for each web page. (A conspicuous exception is the Opera browser, shown in Figure 6–43). Which is better? There are advantages and disadvantages to both approaches. MDI reduces window clutter. But having separate top-level windows means that you can use the buttons and hotkeys of the host windowing system to flip through your windows.

In the world of Java, where you can't rely on a rich host windowing system, it makes a lot of sense to have your application manage its frames.

Figure 6–44 shows a Java application with three internal frames. Two of them have decorations on the border to maximize and iconify them. The third is in its iconified state.

In the Metal look and feel, the internal frames have distinctive "grabber" areas that you use to move the frames around. You can resize the windows by dragging the resize corners.

Figure 6–44: A Java application with three internal frames

To achieve this capability, follow these steps:

1. Use a regular `JFrame` window for the application.

2. Set the content pane of the `JFrame` to a `JDesktopPane`.

   ```
   desktop = new JDesktopPane();
   setContentPane(desktop);
   ```

3. Construct `JInternalFrame` windows. You can specify whether you want the icons for resizing or closing the frame. Normally, you want all icons.

   ```
   JInternalFrame iframe = new JInternalFrame(title,
       true, // resizable
   ```

```
true, // closable
true, // maximizable
true); // iconifiable
```

4. Add components to the content pane of the frame.

```
iframe.getContentPane().add(c);
```

5. Set a frame icon. The icon is shown in the top-left corner of the frame.

```
iframe.setFrameIcon(icon);
```

NOTE: In the current version of the Metal look and feel, the frame icon is not displayed in iconized frames.

6. Set the size of the internal frame. As with regular frames, internal frames initially have a size of 0 by 0 pixels. Since you don't want to have all internal frames display on top of each other, you should use a variable position for the next frame. Use the `reshape` method to set both the position and size of the frame:

```
iframe.reshape(nextFrameX, nextFrameY, width, height);
```

7. As with `JFrames`, you need to make the frame visible.

```
iframe.setVisible(true);
```

NOTE: In earlier versions of Swing, internal frames were automatically visible and this call was not necessary.

8. Add the frame to the `JDesktopPane`:

```
desktop.add(iframe);
```

9. You probably want to make the new frame the *selected frame*. Of the internal frames on the desktop, only the selected frame receives keyboard focus. In the Metal look and feel, the selected frame has a blue title bar, whereas the other frames have a gray title bar. You use the `setSelected` method to select a frame. However, the "selected" property can be *vetoed*—the currently selected frame can refuse to give up focus. In that case, the `setSelected` method throws a `PropertyVetoException` that you need to handle.

```
try
{
    iframe.setSelected(true);
}
catch(PropertyVetoException e)
{
    // attempt was vetoed
}
```

10. You probably want to move the position for the next internal frame down so that it won't overlay the existing frame. A good distance between frames is the height of the title bar, which you can obtain as

```
int frameDistance =
    iframe.getHeight() - iframe.getContentPane().getHeight()
```

11. Use that distance to determine the next internal frame position.

```
nextFrameX += frameDistance;
nextFrameY += frameDistance;
if (nextFrameX + width > desktop.getWidth())
    nextFrameX = 0;
if (nextFrameY + height > desktop.getHeight())
    nextFrameY = 0;
```

Cascading and Tiling

In Windows, there are standard commands for *cascading* and *tiling* windows (see Figures 6–45 and 6–46). The Java `JDesktopPane` and `JInternalFrame` classes have no built-in support for these operations. In Example 6–18, we show you how you can implement these operations yourself.

To cascade all windows, you reshape windows to the same size and stagger their positions. The `getAllFrames` method of the `JDesktopPane` class returns an array of all internal frames.

```
JInternalFrame[] frames = desktop.getAllFrames();
```

However, you need to pay attention to the frame state. An internal frame can be in one of three states:

- Icon
- Resizable
- Maximum

You use the `isIcon` method to find out which internal frames are currently icons and should be skipped. However, if a frame is in the maximum state, you have to first set it to be resizable by calling `setMaximum(false)`. This is another property that can be vetoed. Therefore, you have to catch the `PropertyVetoException`.

The following loop cascades all internal frames on the desktop:

```
for (int i = 0; i < frames.length; i++)
{
   if (!frames[i].isIcon())
   {
      try
      {
         // try to make maximized frames resizable
         // this might be vetoed
```

```
        frames[i].setMaximum(false);
        frames[i].reshape(x, y, width, height);

        x += frameDistance;
        y += frameDistance;
        // wrap around at the desktop edge
        if (x + width > desktop.getWidth()) x = 0;
        if (y + height > desktop.getHeight()) y = 0;
     }
     catch(PropertyVetoException e)
     {}
  }
}
```

Figure 6–45: Cascaded internal frames

Tiling frames is trickier, particularly if the number of frames is not a perfect square. First, count the number of frames that are not icons. Then, compute the number of columns as

```
int cols = (int)Math.sqrt(frameCount);
```

Then the number of rows is

```
int rows = frameCount / cols;
```

except that the last

```
extra = frameCount % cols
```

columns have `rows + 1` rows.

Figure 6–46: Tiled internal frames

Here is the loop for tiling all frames on the desktop.

```
int width = desktop.getWidth() / cols;
int height = desktop.getHeight() / rows;
int r = 0;
int c = 0;
for (int i = 0; i < frames.length; i++)
{
   if (!frames[i].isIcon())
   {
      try
      {
         frames[i].setMaximum(false);
         frames[i].reshape(c * width,
            r * height, width, height);
         r++;
         if (r == rows)
         {
            r = 0;
            c++;
            if (c == cols - extra)
            {
               // start adding an extra row
               rows++;
```

```
                    height = desktop.getHeight() / rows;
                }
            }
        }
        catch(PropertyVetoException e)
        {}
    }
}
```

The example program shows another common frame operation: to move
the selection from the current frame to the next frame that isn't an icon. The
JDesktopPane class has no method to return the selected frame. Instead, you
must traverse all frames and call isSelected until you find the currently
selected frame. Then, look for the next frame in the sequence that isn't an icon,
and try to select it by calling

```
frames[next].setSelected(true);
```

As before, that method can throw a PropertyVetoException, in which case
you keep looking. If you come back to the original frame, then no other frame was
selectable, and you give up. Here is the complete loop:

```
for (int i = 0; i < frames.length; i++)
{
    if (frames[i].isSelected())
    {
        // find next frame that isn't an icon and can be
        // selected
        try
        {
            int next = (i + 1) % frames.length;
            while (next != i && frames[next].isIcon())
                next = (next + 1) % frames.length;
            if (next == i) return;
                // all other frames are icons
            frames[next].setSelected(true);
            frames[next].toFront();
            return;
        }
        catch(PropertyVetoException e)
        {}
    }
}
```

Vetoing Property Settings

Now that you have seen all these veto exceptions, you may wonder how your
frames can issue a veto. The JInternalFrame class uses a general *JavaBeans*
mechanism for monitoring the setting of properties. We discuss this mechanism in
full detail in Chapter 8. For now, we just want to show you how your frames can

veto requests for property changes.

Frames don't usually want to use a veto to protest iconization or loss of focus. But it is very common for frames to check whether it is okay to *close* them. You close a frame with the setClosed method of the JInternal-Frame class. Because the method is vetoable, it calls all registered *vetoable change listeners* before proceeding to make the change. That gives each of the listeners the opportunity to throw a PropertyVetoException and thereby terminate the call to setClosed before it changed any settings.

In our example program, we put up a dialog to ask the user whether it is okay to close the window (see Figure 6–47). If the user doesn't agree, the window stays open.

Figure 6–47: The user can veto the close property

Here is how you achieve such a notification.

1. Add a listener object to each frame. The object must belong to some class that implements the VetoableChangeListener interface. It is best to do that right after constructing the frame. In our example, we use the frame class that constructs the internal frames. Another option would be to use an anonymous inner class.

    ```
    iframe.addVetoableChangeListener(listener);
    ```

2. Implement the vetoableChange method, the only method required by the VetoableChangeListener interface. The method receives a Property-ChangeEvent object. Use the getName method to find the name of the property that is about to be changed (such as "closed" if the method call to

veto is `setClosed(true)`. As you will see in Chapter 8, the property name
is obtained by removing the `"set"` prefix from the method name and
changing the next letter to lowercase.

Use the `getNewValue` method to get the proposed new value.

```
String name = event.getPropertyName();
Object value = event.getNewValue();
if (name.equals("closed") && value.equals(Boolean.TRUE))
{
    ask user for confirmation
}
```

3. Simply throw a `PropertyVetoException` to block the property change.
    Return normally if you don't want to veto the change.

```
class DesktopFrame extends JFrame
    implements VetoableChangeListener
{
    . . .
    public void vetoableChange(PropertyChangeEvent event)
        throws PropertyVetoException
    {
        . . .
        if (not ok)
            throw new PropertyVetoException("reason", event);
        // return normally if ok
    }
}
```

Dialogs in internal frames

If you use internal frames, you should not use the `JDialog` class for dialogs.
Those dialogs have two disadvantages:

- They are heavyweight since they create a new frame in the windowing system.
- The windowing system does not know how to position them relative to the
  internal frame that spawned them.

Instead, for simple dialogs, use the `showInternalXxxDialog` methods of the
`JOptionPane` class. They work exactly like the `showXxxDialog` methods,
except they position a lightweight window over an internal frame.

As for more complex dialogs, construct them with a `JInternalFrame`. Unfortunately, then you have no built-in support for modal dialogs.

In our sample program, we use an internal dialog to ask the user whether it is
okay to close a frame.

```
int result
   = JOptionPane.showInternalConfirmDialog(iframe,
       "OK to close?");
```

NOTE: If you simply want to be *notified* when a frame is closed, then you should not use the veto mechanism. Instead, install an `InternalFrameListener`. An internal frame listener works just like a `WindowListener`. When the internal frame is closing, the `internalFrameClosing` method is called instead of the familiar `window-Closing` method. The other six internal frame notifications (opened/closed, iconified/deiconified, activated/deactivated) also correspond to the window listener methods.

Outline dragging

One criticism that developers have leveled against internal frames is that performance has not been great. By far the slowest operation is to drag a frame with complex content across the desktop. The desktop manager keeps asking the frame to repaint itself as it is being dragged, which is quite slow.

Actually, if you use Windows or X Windows with a poorly written video driver, you'll experience the same problem. Window dragging appears fast on most systems because the video hardware supports the dragging operation by mapping the image inside the frame to different screen location during the dragging process.

To improve performance without greatly degrading the user experience, you can set "outline dragging" on. When the user drags the frame, only the outline of the frame is continuously updated. The inside is repainted only when the user drops the frame to its final resting place.

To turn on outline dragging, call

```
desktop.setDragMode(JDesktopPane.OUTLINE_DRAG_MODE);
```

This setting is the equivalent of "continuous layout" in the `JSplitPane` class.

NOTE: In early versions of Swing, you had to use the magic incantation

```
desktop.putClientProperty(
    "JDesktopPane.dragMode", "outline");
```

to turn on outline dragging.

In the sample program, you can use the Window -> Drag Outline check box menu selection to toggle outline dragging on or off.

NOTE: The internal frames on the desktop are managed by a `DesktopManager` class. You don't need to know about this class for normal programming. It is possible to implement different desktop behavior by installing a new desktop manager, but we won't cover that.

Example 6–18 populates a desktop with internal frames that show HTML pages. The File -> Open menu option pops up a file dialog for reading a local HTML file into a new internal frame. If you click on any link, the linked document is displayed in another internal frame. Try out the Window -> Cascade and Window -> Tile commands. This example concludes our discussion of advanced Swing features.

Example 6–18: InternalFrameTest.java

```
1. import java.awt.*;
2. import java.awt.event.*;
3. import java.beans.*;
4. import java.io.*;
5. import java.net.*;
6. import java.util.*;
7. import javax.swing.*;
8. import javax.swing.event.*;
9.
10. /**
11.    This program demonstrates the use of internal frames.
12. */
13. public class InternalFrameTest
14. {
15.    public static void main(String[] args)
16.    {
17.       JFrame frame = new DesktopFrame();
18.       frame.setDefaultCloseOperation(JFrame.EXIT_ON_CLOSE);
19.       frame.show();
20.    }
21. }
22.
23. /**
24.    This desktop frames contains editor panes that show HTML
25.    documents.
26. */
27. class DesktopFrame extends JFrame
28. {
29.    public DesktopFrame()
30.    {
31.       setTitle("InternalFrameTest");
32.       setSize(WIDTH, HEIGHT);
33.
34.       desktop = new JDesktopPane();
35.       setContentPane(desktop);
36.
37.
38.       // set up menus
39.
40.       JMenuBar menuBar = new JMenuBar();
41.       setJMenuBar(menuBar);
42.       JMenu fileMenu = new JMenu("File");
43.       menuBar.add(fileMenu);
```

```
44.        JMenuItem openItem = new JMenuItem("Open");
45.        openItem.addActionListener(new
46.            ActionListener()
47.            {
48.                public void actionPerformed(ActionEvent event)
49.                {
50.                    openFile();
51.                }
52.            });
53.        fileMenu.add(openItem);
54.        JMenuItem exitItem = new JMenuItem("Exit");
55.        exitItem.addActionListener(new
56.            ActionListener()
57.            {
58.                public void actionPerformed(ActionEvent event)
59.                {
60.                    System.exit(0);
61.                }
62.            });
63.        fileMenu.add(exitItem);
64.        JMenu windowMenu = new JMenu("Window");
65.        menuBar.add(windowMenu);
66.        JMenuItem nextItem = new JMenuItem("Next");
67.        nextItem.addActionListener(new
68.            ActionListener()
69.            {
70.                public void actionPerformed(ActionEvent event)
71.                {
72.                    selectNextWindow();
73.                }
74.            });
75.        windowMenu.add(nextItem);
76.        JMenuItem cascadeItem = new JMenuItem("Cascade");
77.        cascadeItem.addActionListener(new
78.            ActionListener()
79.            {
80.                public void actionPerformed(ActionEvent event)
81.                {
82.                    cascadeWindows();
83.                }
84.            });
85.        windowMenu.add(cascadeItem);
86.        JMenuItem tileItem = new JMenuItem("Tile");
87.        tileItem.addActionListener(new
88.            ActionListener()
89.            {
90.                public void actionPerformed(ActionEvent event)
91.                {
92.                    tileWindows();
93.                }
94.            });
```

```
95.        windowMenu.add(tileItem);
96.        final JCheckBoxMenuItem dragOutlineItem
97.           = new JCheckBoxMenuItem("Drag Outline");
98.        dragOutlineItem.addActionListener(new
99.           ActionListener()
100.          {
101.             public void actionPerformed(ActionEvent event)
102.             {
103.                desktop.setDragMode(dragOutlineItem.isSelected()
104.                   ? JDesktopPane.OUTLINE_DRAG_MODE
105.                   : JDesktopPane.LIVE_DRAG_MODE);
106.             }
107.          });
108.       windowMenu.add(dragOutlineItem);
109.    }
110.
111.    /**
112.       Creates an internal frame on the desktop.
113.       @param c the component to display in the internal frame
114.       @param t the title of the internal frame.
115.    */
116.    public void createInternalFrame(Component c, String t)
117.    {
118.       final JInternalFrame iframe = new JInternalFrame(t,
119.          true, // resizable
120.          true, // closable
121.          true, // maximizable
122.          true); // iconifiable
123.
124.       iframe.getContentPane().add(c);
125.       desktop.add(iframe);
126.
127.       iframe.setFrameIcon(new ImageIcon("document.gif"));
128.
129.       // add listener to confirm frame closing
130.       iframe.addVetoableChangeListener(new
131.          VetoableChangeListener()
132.          {
133.             public void vetoableChange(PropertyChangeEvent event)
134.                throws PropertyVetoException
135.             {
136.                String name = event.getPropertyName();
137.                Object value = event.getNewValue();
138.
139.                // we only want to check attempts to close a frame
140.                if (name.equals("closed")
141.                   && value.equals(Boolean.TRUE))
142.                {
143.                   // ask user if it is ok to close
144.                   int result
145.                      = JOptionPane.showInternalConfirmDialog(
146.                         iframe, "OK to close?");
```

```
147.
148.                          // if the user doesn't agree, veto the close
149.                          if (result != JOptionPane.YES_OPTION)
150.                              throw new PropertyVetoException(
151.                                  "User canceled close", event);
152.                      }
153.                  }
154.              });
155.
156.          // position frame
157.          int width = desktop.getWidth() / 2;
158.          int height = desktop.getHeight() / 2;
159.          iframe.reshape(nextFrameX, nextFrameY, width, height);
160.
161.          iframe.show();
162.
163.          // select the frame--might be vetoed
164.          try
165.          {
166.              iframe.setSelected(true);
167.          }
168.          catch(PropertyVetoException e)
169.          {}
170.
171.          /* if this is the first time, compute distance between
172.              cascaded frames
173.          */
174.
175.          if (frameDistance == 0)
176.              frameDistance = iframe.getHeight()
177.                  - iframe.getContentPane().getHeight();
178.
179.          // compute placement for next frame
180.
181.          nextFrameX += frameDistance;
182.          nextFrameY += frameDistance;
183.          if (nextFrameX + width > desktop.getWidth())
184.              nextFrameX = 0;
185.          if (nextFrameY + height > desktop.getHeight())
186.              nextFrameY = 0;
187.      }
188.
189.      /**
190.          Cascades the non-iconified internal frames of the desktop.
191.      */
192.      public void cascadeWindows()
193.      {
194.          JInternalFrame[] frames = desktop.getAllFrames();
195.          int x = 0;
196.          int y = 0;
197.          int width = desktop.getWidth() / 2;
198.          int height = desktop.getHeight() / 2;
```

```
199.
200.        for (int i = 0; i < frames.length; i++)
201.        {
202.           if (!frames[i].isIcon())
203.           {
204.              try
205.              {
206.                 // try to make maximized frames resizable
207.                 // this might be vetoed
208.                 frames[i].setMaximum(false);
209.                 frames[i].reshape(x, y, width, height);
210.
211.                 x += frameDistance;
212.                 y += frameDistance;
213.                 // wrap around at the desktop edge
214.                 if (x + width > desktop.getWidth()) x = 0;
215.                 if (y + height > desktop.getHeight()) y = 0;
216.              }
217.              catch(PropertyVetoException e)
218.              {}
219.           }
220.        }
221.     }
222.
223.     /**
224.        Tiles the non-iconified internal frames of the desktop.
225.     */
226.     public void tileWindows()
227.     {
228.        JInternalFrame[] frames = desktop.getAllFrames();
229.
230.        // count frames that aren't iconized
231.        int frameCount = 0;
232.        for (int i = 0; i < frames.length; i++)
233.        {
234.           if (!frames[i].isIcon())
235.              frameCount++;
236.        }
237.
238.        int rows = (int)Math.sqrt(frameCount);
239.        int cols = frameCount / rows;
240.        int extra = frameCount % rows;
241.           // number of columns with an extra row
242.
243.        int width = desktop.getWidth() / cols;
244.        int height = desktop.getHeight() / rows;
245.        int r = 0;
246.        int c = 0;
247.        for (int i = 0; i < frames.length; i++)
248.        {
249.           if (!frames[i].isIcon())
250.           {
```

```
251.          try
252.          {
253.              frames[i].setMaximum(false);
254.              frames[i].reshape(c * width,
255.                  r * height, width, height);
256.              r++;
257.              if (r == rows)
258.              {
259.                  r = 0;
260.                  c++;
261.                  if (c == cols - extra)
262.                  {
263.                      // start adding an extra row
264.                      rows++;
265.                      height = desktop.getHeight() / rows;
266.                  }
267.              }
268.          }
269.          catch(PropertyVetoException e)
270.          {}
271.      }
272.  }
273.  }
274.
275.  /**
276.     Brings the next non-iconified internal frame to the front.
277.  */
278.  public void selectNextWindow()
279.  {
280.      JInternalFrame[] frames = desktop.getAllFrames();
281.      for (int i = 0; i < frames.length; i++)
282.      {
283.          if (frames[i].isSelected())
284.          {
285.              // find next frame that isn't an icon and can be
286.              // selected
287.              try
288.              {
289.                  int next = (i + 1) % frames.length;
290.                  while (next != i && frames[next].isIcon())
291.                      next = (next + 1) % frames.length;
292.                  if (next == i) return;
293.                      // all other frames are icons or veto selection
294.                  frames[next].setSelected(true);
295.                  frames[next].toFront();
296.                  return;
297.              }
298.              catch(PropertyVetoException e)
299.              {}
300.          }
301.      }
302.  }
```

```
303.
304.    /**
305.       Asks the user to open an HTML file.
306.    */
307.    public void openFile()
308.    {
309.       // let user select file
310.
311.       JFileChooser chooser = new JFileChooser();
312.       chooser.setCurrentDirectory(new File("."));
313.       chooser.setFileFilter(new
314.          javax.swing.filechooser.FileFilter()
315.          {
316.             public boolean accept(File f)
317.             {
318.                String fname = f.getName().toLowerCase();
319.                return fname.endsWith(".html")
320.                   || fname.endsWith(".htm")
321.                   || f.isDirectory();
322.             }
323.             public String getDescription()
324.             {
325.                return "HTML Files";
326.             }
327.          });
328.       int r = chooser.showOpenDialog(this);
329.
330.       if (r == JFileChooser.APPROVE_OPTION)
331.       {
332.          // open the file that the user selected
333.
334.          String filename = chooser.getSelectedFile().getPath();
335.          try
336.          {
337.             URL fileUrl = new URL("file:" + filename);
338.             createInternalFrame(createEditorPane(fileUrl),
339.                filename);
340.          }
341.          catch(MalformedURLException e)
342.          {
343.          }
344.       }
345.    }
346.
347.    /**
348.       Creates an editor pane.
349.       @param u the URL of the HTML document
350.    */
351.    public Component createEditorPane(URL u)
352.    {
353.       // create an editor pane that follows hyperlink clicks
354.
```

```
355.       JEditorPane editorPane = new JEditorPane();
356.       editorPane.setEditable(false);
357.       editorPane.addHyperlinkListener(new
358.           HyperlinkListener()
359.           {
360.               public void hyperlinkUpdate(HyperlinkEvent event)
361.               {
362.                   if (event.getEventType()
363.                       == HyperlinkEvent.EventType.ACTIVATED)
364.                       createInternalFrame(createEditorPane(
365.                           event.getURL()), event.getURL().toString());
366.               }
367.           });
368.       try
369.       {
370.           editorPane.setPage(u);
371.       }
372.       catch(IOException e)
373.       {
374.           editorPane.setText("Exception: " + e);
375.       }
376.       return new JScrollPane(editorPane);
377.   }
378.
379.   private JDesktopPane desktop;
380.   private int nextFrameX;
381.   private int nextFrameY;
382.   private int frameDistance;
383.
384.   private static final int WIDTH = 600;
385.   private static final int HEIGHT = 400;
386. }
```

javax.swing.JDesktopPane

- `JInternalFrame[] getAllFrames()`
  gets all internal frames in this desktop pane.
- `void setDragMode(int mode)`
  sets the drag mode to live or outline drag mode.

  Parameters: mode one of JDesktopPane.LIVE_DRAG_MODE
  or JDesktopPane.OUTLINE_DRAG_MODE

javax.swing.JInternalFrame

- `JInternalFrame()`
- `JInternalFrame(String title)`
- `JInternalFrame(String title, boolean resizable)`
- `JInternalFrame(String title, boolean resizable, boolean closable)`
- `JInternalFrame(String title, boolean resizable, boolean closable,
  boolean maximizable)`

- `JInternalFrame(String title, boolean resizable, boolean closable, boolean maximizable, boolean iconifiable)`
  construct a new internal frame.

Parameters:	`title`	the string to display in the title bar
	`resizable`	true if the frame can be resized
	`closable`	true if the frame can be closed
	`maximizable`	true if the frame can be maximized
	`iconifiable`	true if the frame can be iconified

- `boolean isResizable()`
- `boolean isClosable()`
- `boolean isMaximizable()`
- `boolean isIconifiable()`

  get and set the `resizable`, `closable`, `maximizable`, and `iconifiable` properties. When the property is `true`, an icon appears in the frame title to resize, close, maximize, or iconify the internal frame.

- `boolean isIcon()`
- `void setIcon(boolean b)`
- `boolean isMaximum()`
- `void setMaximum(boolean b)`
- `boolean isClosed()`
- `void setClosed(boolean b)`

  get or set the `icon`, `maximum`, or `closed` property. When this property is `true`, the internal frame is iconified, maximized, or closed.

- `boolean isSelected()`
- `void setSelected(boolean b)`

  get or set the `selected` property. When this property is `true`, the current internal frame becomes the selected frame on the desktop.

- `void moveToFront()`
- `void moveToBack()`

  move this internal frame to the front or the back of the desktop.

- `void reshape(int x, int y, int width, int height)`
  moves and resizes this internal frame.

Parameters:	`x, y`	the top-left corner of the frame
	`width, height`	the width and height of the frame

- `Container getContentPane()`
- `void setContentPane(Container c)`

  get and set the content pane of this internal frame.

- `JDesktopPane getDesktopPane()`
  gets the desktop pane of this internal frame.
- `Icon getFrameIcon()`
- `void setFrameIcon(Icon anIcon)`
  get and set the frame icon that is displayed in the title bar.
- `boolean isVisible()`
- `void setVisible(boolean b)`
  get and set the "visible" property.
- `void show()`
  makes this internal frame visible and brings it to the front.

`javax.swing.JComponent`

- `void addVetoableChangeListener(VetoableChangeListener listener)`
  adds a vetoable change listener that is notified when an attempt is made to
  change a constrained property.

`java.beans.VetoableChangeListener`

- `void vetoableChange(PropertyChangeEvent event)`
  is called when the `set` method of a constrained property notifies the vetoable
  change listeners.

`java.beans.PropertyChangeEvent`

- `String getPropertyName()`
  returns the name of the property that is about to be changed.
- `Object getNewValue()`
  returns the proposed new value for the property.

`java.beans.PropertyVetoException`

- `PropertyVetoException(String reason, PropertyChangeEvent event)`
  constructs a property veto exception.

  Parameters: reason   the reason for the veto

        event   the vetoed event

Chapter 7

Advanced AWT

In Volume 1, you have seen how to use the methods of the `Graphics` class to create simple drawings. Those methods are sufficient for simple applets and applications, but they fall short for complex shapes or when you require complete control over the appearance of the graphics. The Java 2D API is a more recent class library that you can use to produce high-quality drawings. In this chapter, we give you an overview of that API.

We then turn to the topic of printing and show how you can implement printing capabilities into your programs.

Finally, we cover two techniques for transferring data between programs: the system clipboard and the drag-and-drop mechanism. You can use these techniques to transfer data between two Java applications, or between a Java application and a native program.

The Rendering Pipeline

The original JDK 1.0 had a very simple mechanism for drawing shapes. You select color and paint mode, and call methods of the `Graphics` class such as `drawRect` or `fillOval`. The Java 2D API supports many more options.

- You can easily produce a wide variety of *shapes*.
- You have control over the *stroke*, the pen that traces shape boundaries.
- You can *fill* shapes with solid colors, varying hues, and repeating patterns.
- You can use *transformations* to move, scale, rotate, or stretch shapes.
- You can *clip* shapes to restrict them to arbitrary areas.
- You can select *composition rules* to describe how to combine the pixels of a new shape with existing pixels.
- You can give *rendering hints* to make trade-offs between speed and drawing quality.

To draw a shape, you go through the following steps:

1. Obtain an object of the `Graphics2D` class. This class is a subclass of the `Graphics` class. If you use a version of the JDK that is enabled for Java 2D technology, methods such as `paint` and `paintComponent` automatically receive an object of the `Graphics2D` class. Simply use a cast, as follows:

   ```
   public void paintComponent(Graphics g)
   {
       Graphics2D g2 = (Graphics2D)g;
       . . .
   }
   ```

2. Use the `setRenderingHints` method to set rendering hints: trade-offs between speed and drawing quality.

   ```
   RenderingHints hints = . . .;
   g2.setRenderingHints(hints);
   ```

3. Use the `setStroke` method to set the *stroke*. The stroke is used to draw the outline of the shape. You can select the thickness and choose among solid and dotted lines.

   ```
   Stroke stroke = . . .;
   g2.setStroke(stroke);
   ```

4. Use the `setPaint` method to set the *paint*. The paint is used to fill areas such as the stroke path or the interior of a shape. You can create solid color paint, paint with changing hues, or tiled fill patterns.

```
Paint paint = . . .;
g2.setPaint(paint);
```

5. Use the `setClip` method to set the clipping region.

```
Shape clip = . . .;
g2.clip(clip);
```

6. Use the `setTransform` method to set a *transformation* from user space to device space. You use transformations if it is easier for you to define your shapes in a custom coordinate system than by using pixel coordinates.

```
AffineTransform transform = . . .;
g2.transform(transform);
```

7. Use the `setComposite` method to set a *composition rule* that describes how to combine the new pixels with the existing pixels.

```
Composite composite = . . .;
g2.setComposite(composite);
```

8. Create a shape. The Java 2D API supplies many shape objects and methods to combine shapes.

```
Shape shape = . . .;
```

9. Draw or fill the shape. If you draw the shape, its outline is stroked. If you fill the shape, the interior is painted.

```
g2.draw(shape);
g2.fill(shape);
```

Of course, in many practical circumstances, you don't need all these steps. There are reasonable defaults for the settings of the 2D graphics context. You only need to change the settings if you want to change the defaults.

In the following sections, you will see how to describe shapes, strokes, paints, transformations, and composition rules.

The various `set` methods simply set the state of the 2D graphics context. They don't cause any drawing. Similarly, when you construct `Shape` objects, no drawing takes place. A shape is only rendered when you call `draw` or `fill`. At that time, the new shape is computed in a *rendering pipeline* (see Figure 7–1).

stroke   transform   clip   fill   compose

Figure 7–1: The rendering pipeline

In the rendering pipeline, the following steps take place to render a shape.

1. The path of the shape is stroked.
2. The shape is transformed.
3. The shape is clipped. If there is no intersection between the shape and the clipping area, then the process stops.
4. The remainder of the shape after clipping is filled.
5. The pixels of the filled shape are composed with the existing pixels. (In Figure 7–1, the circle is part of the existing pixels, and the cup shape is superimposed over it.)

In the next section, you will see how to define shapes. Then, we turn to the 2D graphics context settings.

`java.awt.Graphics2D`

- `void draw(Shape s)`

  draws the outline of the given shape with the current stroke.
- `void fill(Shape s)`

  fills the interior of the given shape with the current paint.

Shapes

Here are some of the methods in the `Graphics` class to draw shapes:

```
drawLine
drawRectangle
drawRoundRect
draw3DRect
drawPolygon
drawPolyline
drawOval
drawArc
```

There are also corresponding `fill` methods. These methods have been in the `Graphics` class ever since JDK 1.0. The Java 2D API uses a completely different, object-oriented approach. Instead of methods, there are classes:

```
Line2D
Rectangle2D
RoundRectangle2D
Ellipse2D
Arc2D
QuadCurve2D
CubicCurve2D
GeneralPath
```

These classes all implement the `Shape` interface.

Finally, there is a `Point2D` class that describes a point with an x- and a y-coordinate. Points are useful to define shapes, but they aren't themselves shapes.

To draw a shape, you first create an object of a class that implements the `Shape` interface and then call the `draw` method of the `Graphics2D` class.

The `Line2D`, `Rectangle2D`, `RoundRectangle2D`, `Ellipse2D`, and `Arc2D` classes correspond to the `drawLine`, `drawRectangle`, `drawRoundRect`, `drawOval`, and `drawArc` methods. (The concept of a "3D rectangle" has died the death that it so richly deserved—there is no analog to the `draw3DRect` method.) The Java 2D API supplies two additional classes: quadratic and cubic curves. We discuss these shapes later in this section. There is no `Polygon2D` class. Instead, the `GeneralPath` class describes paths that are made up from lines, quadratic and cubic curves. You can use a `GeneralPath` to describe a polygon; we show you how later in this section.

The classes

```
Rectangle2D
RoundRectangle2D
Ellipse2D
Arc2D
```

all inherit from a common superclass `RectangularShape`. Admittedly, ellipses and arcs are not rectangular, but they have a *bounding rectangle* (see Figure 7–2).

Figure 7–2: The bounding rectangle of an ellipse and an arc

Each of the classes whose name ends in "2D" has two subclasses for specifying coordinates as `float` or `double` quantities. In Volume 1, you already encountered

```
Rectangle2D.Float
Rectangle2D.Double
```

The same scheme is used for the other classes, such as

```
Arc2D.Float
Arc2D.Double
```

Internally, all graphics classes use `float` coordinates since `float` numbers use less storage space, and they have sufficient precision for geometric computations. However, the Java programming language makes it a bit more tedious to manipulate `float` numbers. For that reason, most methods of the graphics classes use `double` parameters and return values. Only when constructing a 2D object, you need to choose between a constructor with `float` or `double` coordinates. For example,

```
Rectangle2D floatRect
   = new Rectangle2D.Float(5F, 10F, 7.5F, 15F);
Rectangle2D doubleRect
   = new Rectangle2D.Double(5, 10, 7.5, 15);
```

The *Xxx*2D.Float and *Xxx*2D.Double classes are subclasses of the *Xxx*2D classes. After object construction, there is essentially no benefit in remembering the subclass, and you can just store the constructed object in a superclass variable, just like in the code example.

As you can see from the curious names, the *Xxx*2D.Float and *Xxx*2D.Double classes are also inner classes of the *Xxx*2D classes. That is just a minor syntactical convenience, to avoid an inflation of outer class names.

Figure 7–3 shows the relationships between the shape classes. However, the Double and Float subclasses are omitted. Legacy classes from the pre-2D library are marked with a gray fill.

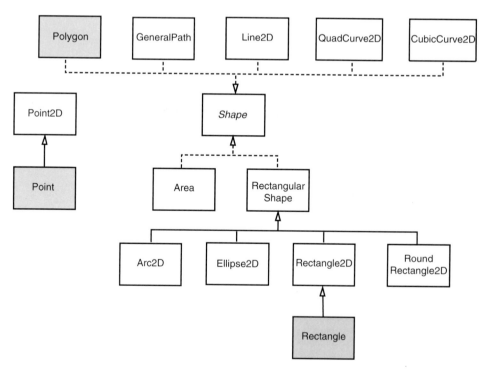

Figure 7–3: Relationships between the shape classes

Using the Shape Classes

You already saw how to use the Rectangle2D, Ellipse2D, and Line2D classes in Chapter 7 of Volume 1. In this section, you will learn how to work with the remaining 2D shapes.

For the `RoundRectangle2D` shape, you specify the top left corner, width and height, and the x- and y-dimension of the corner area that should be rounded (see Figure 7–4). For example, the call

```
RoundRectangle2D r = new RoundRectangle2D.Double(150, 200,
    100, 50, 20, 20);
```

produces a rounded rectangle with circles of radius 20 at each of the corners.

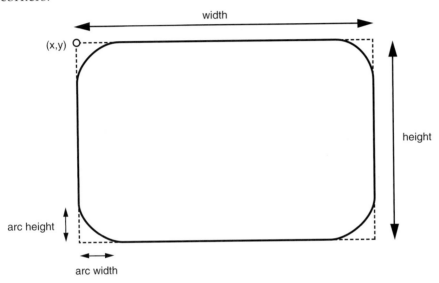

Figure 7–4: Constructing a `RoundRectangle2D`

To construct an arc, you specify the bounding box, followed by the start angle and the angle swept out by the arc (see Figure 7–5) and the closure type, one of `Arc2D.OPEN`, `Arc2D.PIE`, or `Arc2D.CHORD`.

```
Arc2D a = new Arc2D(x, y, width, height,
    startAngle, arcAngle, closureType);
```

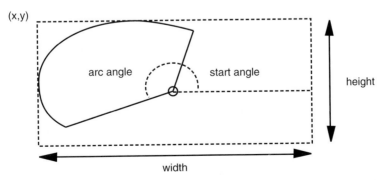

Figure 7–5: Constructing an elliptical arc

Figure 7–6 illustrates the arc types.

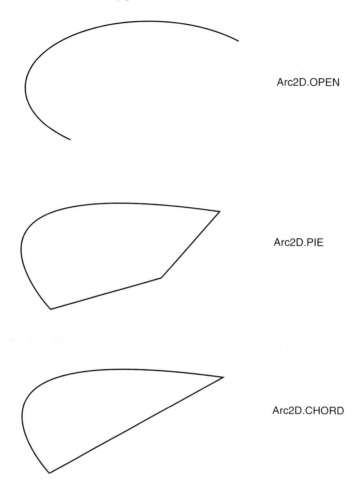

Figure 7–6: Arc types

However, the angles are not simply given in degrees, but they are distorted such that a 45-degree angle denotes the diagonal position, *even if width and height are not the same*. If you draw circular arcs (for example in a pie chart), then you don't need to worry about this. However, for elliptical arcs, be prepared for an adventure in trigonometry—see the sidebar for details.

The Java 2D package supplies *quadratic* and *cubic* curves. In this chapter, we do not want to get into the mathematics of these curves. We suggest you get a feel for how the curves look by running the program in Example 7–1. As you can see in Figures 7–7 and 7–8, quadratic and cubic curves are specified by two *end points* and one or two *control points*. Moving the control points changes the shape of the curves.

Specifying Angles for Elliptical Arcs

The algorithm for drawing elliptical arcs uses distorted angles, which the caller must precompute. This sidebar tells you how. If you belong to the large majority of programmers who never draw elliptical arcs, just skip the sidebar. However, since the official documentation completely glosses over this topic, we thought it is worth recording it to save those who need this information a few hours of trigonometric agony.

You convert actual angles to distorted angles with the following formula.

```
distortedAngle = Math.atan2(Math.sin(angle) * width,
    Math.cos(angle) * height);
```

Sometimes (such as in the example program at the end of this section), you know an end point of the arc, or another point on the line joining the center of the ellipse and that end point. In that case, first compute

```
dx = p.getX() - center.getX();
dy = p.getY() - center.getY();
```

Then, the distorted angle is

```
distortedAngle = Math.atan2(-dy * width, dx * height);
```

(The minus sign in front of dy is necessary because in the pixel coordinate system, the y-axis points downwards, which leads to angle measurements that are clockwise, but you need to supply an angle that is measured counterclockwise.)

Convert the result from radians to degrees:

```
distortedAngle = Math.toDegrees(distortedAngle);
```

The result is a value between −180 and 180.

Compute both the distorted start and end angles in this way. Then, compute the difference between the two distorted angles.

If either the start angle or the difference is negative, add 360. Then, supply the start angle and the angle difference to the arc constructor.

```
Arc2D a = new Arc2D(x, y, width, height,
    distortedStartAngle, distortedAngleDifference,
    closureType);
```

Not only is the documentation vague on the exact nature of the distortion, it is also quite misleading in calling the distorted angle difference value the "arc angle." Except for the case of a circular arc, that value is neither the actual arc angle nor its distortion.

If you run the example program at the end of this section, then you can visually check that this calculation yields the correct values for the arc constructor (see Figure 7–9).

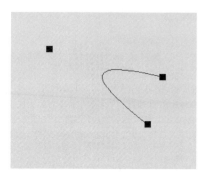

Figure 7–7: A quadratic curve

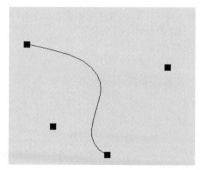

Figure 7–8: A cubic curve

To construct quadratic and cubic curves, you give the coordinates of the end points and the control points. For example,

```
QuadCurve2D q = new QuadCurve2D.Double(startX, startY,
    controlX, controlY, endX, endY);
CubicCurve2D c = new CubicCurve2D.Double(startX, startY,
    control1X, control1Y, control2X, control2Y, endX, endY);
```

Quadratic curves are not very flexible, and they are not commonly used in practice. Cubic curves (such as the Bezier curves drawn by the `CubicCurve3D` class) are, however, very common. By combining many cubic curves so that the slopes at the connection points match, you can create complex smooth-looking curved shapes. For more information, we refer you to *Computer Graphics: Principles and Practice, Second Edition in C* by James D. Foley, Andries van Dam, Steven K. Feiner, et al. [Addison Wesley 1995].

You can build arbitrary sequences of line segments, quadratic curves, and cubic curves, and store them in a `GeneralPath` object. You specify the first coordinate of the path with the `moveTo` method. For example,

```
GeneralPath path = new GeneralPath();
path.moveTo(10, 20);
```

Then, you extend the path by calling one of the methods `lineTo`, `quadTo`, or `curveTo`. These methods extend the path by a line, a quadratic curve, or a cubic curve. To call `lineTo`, supply the end point. For the two curve methods, supply the control points, then the end point. For example,

```
path.lineTo(20, 30);
path.curveTo(control1X, control1Y, control2X, control2Y, endX, endY);
```

You can close the path by calling the `closePath` method. It draws a line back to the last `moveTo`.

To make a polygon, simply call `moveTo` to go to the first corner point, followed by repeated calls to `lineTo` to visit the other corner points. Finally, call `closePath` to close the polygon. The program in Example 7–1 shows this in more detail.

A general path does not have to be connected. You can call `moveTo` at any time to start a new path segment.

Finally, you can use the `append` method to add arbitrary `Shape` objects to a general path. The outline of the shape is added to the end to the path. The second parameter of the `append` method is `true` if the new shape should be connected to the last point on the path, `false` if it should not be connected. For example, the call

```
Rectangle2D r = . . .;
path.append(r, false);
```

appends the outline of a rectangle to the path without connecting it to the existing path. But

```
path.append(r, true);
```

adds a straight line from the end point of the path to the starting point of the rectangle, and then adds the rectangle outline to the path.

The program in Example 7–1 lets you create sample paths. Figures 7–7 and 7–8 show sample runs of the program. You pick a shape maker from the combo box. The program contains shape makers for

- Straight lines
- Rectangles, round rectangles, and ellipses
- Arcs (showing lines for the bounding rectangle and the start and end angles, in addition to the arc itself)
- Polygons (using a `GeneralPath`)
- Quadratic and cubic curves

Use the mouse to adjust the control points. As you move them, the shape continuously repaints itself.

The program is a bit complex because it handles a multiplicity of shapes and it supports dragging of the control points.

An abstract superclass `ShapeMaker` encapsulates the commonality of the shape maker classes. Each shape has a fixed number of control points that the user can move around. The `getPointCount` method returns that value. The abstract method

```
Shape makeShape(Point2D[] points)
```

computes the actual shape, given the current positions of the control points. The `toString` method returns the class name so that the `ShapeMaker` objects can simply be dumped into a `JComboBox`.

To enable dragging of the control points, the `ShapePanel` class handles both mouse and mouse motion events. If the mouse is pressed on top of a rectangle, subsequent mouse drags move the rectangle.

The majority of the shape maker classes are simple—their `makeShape` methods just construct and return the requested shape. However, the `ArcMaker` class needs to compute the distorted start and end angles. Furthermore, to demonstrate that the computation is indeed correct, the returned shape is a `GeneralPath` containing the arc itself, the bounding rectangle, and the lines from the center of the arc to the angle control points (see Figure 7–9).

Figure 7–9: The ShapeTest program

Example 7–1: ShapeTest.java

```
1. import java.awt.*;
2. import java.awt.event.*;
3. import java.awt.geom.*;
4. import java.util.*;
5. import javax.swing.*;
6.
7. /**
8.    This program demonstrates the various 2D shapes.
```

```
 9. */
10. public class ShapeTest
11. {
12.    public static void main(String[] args)
13.    {
14.       JFrame frame = new ShapeTestFrame();
15.       frame.setDefaultCloseOperation(JFrame.EXIT_ON_CLOSE);
16.       frame.show();
17.    }
18. }
19.
20. /**
21.    This frame contains a combo box to select a shape
22.    and a panel to draw it.
23. */
24. class ShapeTestFrame extends JFrame
25. {
26.    public ShapeTestFrame()
27.    {
28.       setTitle("ShapeTest");
29.       setSize(WIDTH, HEIGHT);
30.
31.       Container contentPane = getContentPane();
32.
33.       final ShapePanel panel = new ShapePanel();
34.       contentPane.add(panel, BorderLayout.CENTER);
35.       final JComboBox comboBox = new JComboBox();
36.       comboBox.addItem(new LineMaker());
37.       comboBox.addItem(new RectangleMaker());
38.       comboBox.addItem(new RoundRectangleMaker());
39.       comboBox.addItem(new EllipseMaker());
40.       comboBox.addItem(new ArcMaker());
41.       comboBox.addItem(new PolygonMaker());
42.       comboBox.addItem(new QuadCurveMaker());
43.       comboBox.addItem(new CubicCurveMaker());
44.       comboBox.addActionListener(new
45.          ActionListener()
46.          {
47.             public void actionPerformed(ActionEvent event)
48.             {
49.                ShapeMaker shapeMaker =
50.                   (ShapeMaker)comboBox.getSelectedItem();
51.                panel.setShapeMaker(shapeMaker);
52.             }
53.          });
54.       contentPane.add(comboBox, BorderLayout.NORTH);
55.    }
56.
57.    private static final int WIDTH = 300;
58.    private static final int HEIGHT = 300;
```

```
59.  }
60.
61.  /**
62.     This panel draws a shape and allows the user to
63.     move the points that define it.
64.  */
65.  class ShapePanel extends JPanel
66.  {
67.     public ShapePanel()
68.     {
69.        addMouseListener(new
70.           MouseAdapter()
71.           {
72.              public void mousePressed(MouseEvent event)
73.              {
74.                 Point p = event.getPoint();
75.                 for (int i = 0; i < points.length; i++)
76.                 {
77.                    double x = points[i].getX() - SIZE / 2;
78.                    double y = points[i].getY() - SIZE / 2;
79.                    Rectangle2D r
80.                       = new Rectangle2D.Double(x, y, SIZE, SIZE);
81.                    if (r.contains(p))
82.                    {
83.                       current = i;
84.                       return;
85.                    }
86.                 }
87.              }
88.
89.              public void mouseReleased(MouseEvent event)
90.              {
91.                 current = -1;
92.              }
93.           });
94.        addMouseMotionListener(new
95.           MouseMotionAdapter()
96.           {
97.              public void mouseDragged(MouseEvent event)
98.              {
99.                 if (current == -1) return;
100.                points[current] = event.getPoint();
101.                repaint();
102.             }
103.          });
104.       current = -1;
105.    }
106.
107.    /**
108.       Set a shape maker and initialize it with a random
```

```
109.        point set.
110.        @param aShapeMaker a shape maker that defines a shape
111.        from a point set
112.    */
113.    public void setShapeMaker(ShapeMaker aShapeMaker)
114.    {
115.        shapeMaker = aShapeMaker;
116.        int n = shapeMaker.getPointCount();
117.        points = new Point2D[n];
118.        for (int i = 0; i < n; i++)
119.        {
120.            double x = generator.nextDouble() * getWidth();
121.            double y = generator.nextDouble() * getHeight();
122.            points[i] = new Point2D.Double(x, y);
123.        }
124.        repaint();
125.    }
126.
127.    public void paintComponent(Graphics g)
128.    {
129.        super.paintComponent(g);
130.        if (points == null) return;
131.        Graphics2D g2 = (Graphics2D)g;
132.        for (int i = 0; i < points.length; i++)
133.        {   double x = points[i].getX() - SIZE / 2;
134.            double y = points[i].getY() - SIZE / 2;
135.            g2.fill(new Rectangle2D.Double(x, y, SIZE, SIZE));
136.        }
137.
138.        g2.draw(shapeMaker.makeShape(points));
139.    }
140.
141.    private Point2D[] points;
142.    private static Random generator = new Random();
143.    private static int SIZE = 10;
144.    private int current;
145.    private ShapeMaker shapeMaker;
146. }
147.
148. /**
149.    A shape maker can make a shape from a point set.
150.    Concrete subclasses must return a shape in the makeShape
151.    method.
152. */
153. abstract class ShapeMaker
154. {
155.    /**
156.        Constructs a shape maker.
157.        @param aPointCount the number of points needed to define
158.        this shape.
```

```
159.      */
160.     public ShapeMaker(int aPointCount)
161.     {
162.        pointCount = aPointCount;
163.     }
164.
165.     /**
166.        Gets the number of points needed to define this shape.
167.        @return the point count
168.     */
169.     public int getPointCount()
170.     {
171.        return pointCount;
172.     }
173.
174.     /**
175.        Makes a shape out of the given point set.
176.        @param p the points that define the shape
177.        @return the shape defined by the points
178.     */
179.     public abstract Shape makeShape(Point2D[] p);
180.
181.     public String toString()
182.     {
183.        return getClass().getName();
184.     }
185.
186.     private int pointCount;
187. }
188.
189. /**
190.     Makes a line that joins two given points.
191. */
192. class LineMaker extends ShapeMaker
193. {
194.     public LineMaker() { super(2); }
195.
196.     public Shape makeShape(Point2D[] p)
197.     {
198.        return new Line2D.Double(p[0], p[1]);
199.     }
200. }
201.
202. /**
203.     Makes a line that joins two given corner points.
204. */
205. class RectangleMaker extends ShapeMaker
206. {
207.     public RectangleMaker() { super(2); }
208.
```

```
209.   public Shape makeShape(Point2D[] p)
210.   {
211.      Rectangle2D s = new Rectangle2D.Double();
212.      s.setFrameFromDiagonal(p[0], p[1]);
213.      return s;
214.   }
215. }
216.
217. /**
218.    Makes a round rectangle that joins two given corner points.
219. */
220. class RoundRectangleMaker extends ShapeMaker
221. {
222.    public RoundRectangleMaker() { super(2); }
223.
224.    public Shape makeShape(Point2D[] p)
225.    {
226.       RoundRectangle2D s
227.          = new RoundRectangle2D.Double(0, 0, 0, 0, 20, 20);
228.       s.setFrameFromDiagonal(p[0], p[1]);
229.       return s;
230.    }
231. }
232.
233. /**
234.    Makes an ellipse contained in a bounding box with two given
235.    corner points.
236. */
237. class EllipseMaker extends ShapeMaker
238. {
239.    public EllipseMaker() { super(2); }
240.
241.    public Shape makeShape(Point2D[] p)
242.    {
243.       Ellipse2D s = new Ellipse2D.Double();
244.       s.setFrameFromDiagonal(p[0], p[1]);
245.       return s;
246.    }
247. }
248.
249. /**
250.    Makes an arc contained in a bounding box with two given
251.    corner points, and with starting and ending angles given
252.    by lines emanating from the center of the bounding box and
253.    ending in two given points. To show the correctness of
254.    the angle computation, the returned shape contains the arc,
255.    the bounding box, and the lines.
256. */
257. class ArcMaker extends ShapeMaker
258. {
259.    public ArcMaker() { super(4); }
```

```
260.
261.    public Shape makeShape(Point2D[] p)
262.    {
263.       double centerX = (p[0].getX() + p[1].getX()) / 2;
264.       double centerY = (p[0].getY() + p[1].getY()) / 2;
265.       double width = Math.abs(p[1].getX() - p[0].getX());
266.       double height = Math.abs(p[1].getY() - p[0].getY());
267.
268.       double distortedStartAngle
269.          = Math.toDegrees(Math.atan2(-(p[2].getY() - centerY)
270.             * width, (p[2].getX() - centerX) * height));
271.       double distortedEndAngle
272.          = Math.toDegrees(Math.atan2(-(p[3].getY() - centerY)
273.             * width, (p[3].getX() - centerX) * height));
274.       double distortedAngleDifference
275.          = distortedEndAngle - distortedStartAngle;
276.       if (distortedStartAngle < 0)
277.          distortedStartAngle += 360;
278.       if (distortedAngleDifference < 0)
279.          distortedAngleDifference += 360;
280.
281.       Arc2D s = new Arc2D.Double(0, 0, 0, 0,
282.          distortedStartAngle, distortedAngleDifference,
283.          Arc2D.OPEN);
284.       s.setFrameFromDiagonal(p[0], p[1]);
285.
286.       GeneralPath g = new GeneralPath();
287.       g.append(s, false);
288.       Rectangle2D r = new Rectangle2D.Double();
289.       r.setFrameFromDiagonal(p[0], p[1]);
290.       g.append(r, false);
291.       Point2D center = new Point2D.Double(centerX, centerY);
292.       g.append(new Line2D.Double(center, p[2]), false);
293.       g.append(new Line2D.Double(center, p[3]), false);
294.       return g;
295.    }
296. }
297.
298. /**
299.    Makes a polygon defined by six corner points.
300. */
301. class PolygonMaker extends ShapeMaker
302. {
303.    public PolygonMaker() { super(6); }
304.
305.    public Shape makeShape(Point2D[] p)
306.    {
307.       GeneralPath s = new GeneralPath();
308.       s.moveTo((float)p[0].getX(), (float)p[0].getY());
309.       for (int i = 1; i < p.length; i++)
310.          s.lineTo((float)p[i].getX(), (float)p[i].getY());
```

```
311.        s.closePath();
312.        return s;
313.    }
314. }
315.
316. /**
317.    Makes a quad curve defined by two end points and a control
318.    point.
319. */
320. class QuadCurveMaker extends ShapeMaker
321. {
322.    public QuadCurveMaker() { super(3); }
323.
324.    public Shape makeShape(Point2D[] p)
325.    {
326.        return new QuadCurve2D.Double(p[0].getX(), p[0].getY(),
327.            p[1].getX(), p[1].getY(), p[2].getX(), p[2].getY());
328.    }
329. }
330.
331. /**
332.    Makes a cubic curve defined by two end points and two control
333.    points.
334. */
335. class CubicCurveMaker extends ShapeMaker
336. {
337.    public CubicCurveMaker() { super(4); }
338.
339.    public Shape makeShape(Point2D[] p)
340.    {
341.        return new CubicCurve2D.Double(p[0].getX(), p[0].getY(),
342.            p[1].getX(), p[1].getY(), p[2].getX(), p[2].getY(),
343.            p[3].getX(), p[3].getY());
344.    }
```

---

java.awt.geom.RoundRectangle2D.Double

• RoundRectangle2D.Double(double x, double y, double w, double h,
  double arcWidth, double arcHeight)

constructs a round rectangle with the given bounding rectangle and arc dimensions.

Parameters:	x, y	top-left corner of bounding rectangle
	w, h	width and height of bounding rectangle
	arcWidth	the horizontal distance from the center to the end of the elliptical boundary arc
	arcHeight	the vertical distance from the center to the end of the elliptical boundary arc

java.awt.geom.Arc2D.Double

- Arc2D.Double(double x, double y, double w, double h,
  double startAngle, double arcAngle, int type)

  constructs an arc with the given bounding rectangle, start, and arc angle
  and arc type.

Parameters:	x, y	top-left corner of bounding rectangle
	w, h	width and height of bounding rectangle
	startAngle	the angular measurement between the x-axis and the line joining the center of the bounding rectangle with the starting point of the arc, in radians, and distorted so that an "angle" of $\pi/4$ corresponds to the angle between the x-axis and the line joining the center and top-right corner of the bounding rectangle
	arcAngle	the difference between the distorted end and start angles—see the sidebar on page 567. For a circular arc, this value equals the angle swept out by the arc.
	type	one of Arc2D.OPEN, Arc2D.PIE, and Arc2D.CHORD

 java.awt.geom.QuadCurve2D.Double

- QuadCurve2D.Double(double x1, double y1, double ctrlx, double
  ctrly, double x2, double y2)

  constructs a quadratic curve from a start point, a control point, and an
  end point.

Parameters:	x1, y1	the start point
	ctrlx, ctrly	the control point
	x2, y2	the end points

 java.awt.geom.CubicCurve2D.Double

- CubicCurve2D.Double(double x1, double y1, double ctrlx1, double
  ctrly1, double ctrlx2, double ctrly2, double x2, double y2)

  constructs a cubic curve from a start point, two control points, and an
  end point.

Parameters: x1, y1   the start point

ctrlx1, ctrly1   the first control point

ctrlx2, ctrly2   the second control point

x2, y2   the end points

---

java.awt.geom.GeneralPath

- `GeneralPath()`

  constructs an empty general path.

- `void moveTo(float x, float y)`

  makes `(x, y)` the *current point*, i.e., the starting point of the next segment.

- `void lineTo(float x, float y)`
- `void quadTo(float ctrlx, float ctrly, float x, float y)`
- `void curveTo(float ctrl1x, float ctrl1y, float ctrl2x, float ctrl2y, float x, float y)`

  draw a line, quadratic curve, or cubic curve from the current point to the end point `(x, y)`, and make that end point the current point.

- `void append(Shape s, boolean connect)`

  adds the outline of the given shape to the general path. If `connect` is `true`, the current point of the general path is connected to the starting point of the added shape by a straight line.

- `void closePath()`

  closes the path by drawing a straight line from the current point to the first point in the path.

Areas

In the preceding section, you saw how you can specify complex shapes by constructing general paths that are composed of lines and curves. By using a sufficient number of lines and curves, you can draw essentially any shape. For example, the shapes of characters in the fonts that you see on the screen and on your printouts are all made up of lines and cubic curves.

However, occasionally, it is easier to describe a shape by composing it from *areas,* such as rectangles, polygons, or ellipses. The Java 2D API supports four *constructive area geometry* operations that combine two areas to a new area:

- add—The combined area contains all points that are in the first or the second area.

- `subtract`—The combined area contains all points that are in the first but not the second area.

- `intersect`—The combined area contains all points that are in the first and the second area.

- `exclusiveOr`—The combined area contains all points that are in either the first or the second area, but not in both.

Figure 7–10 shows these operations.

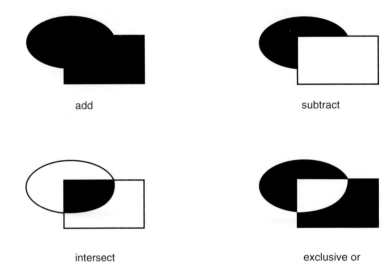

Figure 7–10: Constructive Area Geometry Operations

To construct a complex area, you start out with a default area object.

```
Area a = new Area();
```

Then, you combine the area with any shape:

```
a.add(new Rectangle2D.Double(. . .));
a.subtract(path);
. . .
```

The `Area` class implements the `Shape` interface. You can stroke the boundary of the area with the `draw` method or paint the interior with the `fill` method of the `Graphics2D` class.

The program in Example 7–2 shows the constructive area geometry operations. Select one of the four operations, and see the result of combining an ellipse and a rectangle with the operation that you selected (see Figure 7–11).

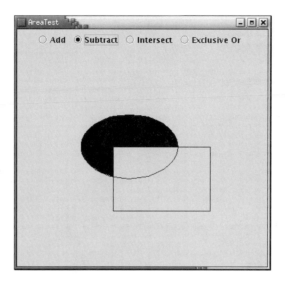

Figure 7–11: The AreaTest Program

Example 7–2: AreaTest.java

```
1. import java.awt.*;
2. import java.awt.event.*;
3. import java.awt.geom.*;
4. import java.util.*;
5. import javax.swing.*;
6.
7. /**
8.    This program demonstrates constructive area geometry
9.    operations.
10. */
11. public class AreaTest
12. {
13.    public static void main(String[] args)
14.    {
15.       JFrame frame = new AreaTestFrame();
16.       frame.setDefaultCloseOperation(JFrame.EXIT_ON_CLOSE);
17.       frame.show();
18.    }
19. }
20.
21. /**
22.    This frame contains a set of radio buttons to define
23.    area operations and a panel to show their result.
24. */
25. class AreaTestFrame extends JFrame
26. {
27.    public AreaTestFrame()
```

```
28.     {
29.         setTitle("AreaTest");
30.         setSize(WIDTH, HEIGHT);
31.
32.         area1
33.             = new Area(new Ellipse2D.Double(100, 100, 150, 100));
34.         area2
35.             = new Area(new Rectangle2D.Double(150, 150, 150, 100));
36.
37.         Container contentPane = getContentPane();
38.         panel = new
39.             JPanel()
40.             {
41.                 public void paintComponent(Graphics g)
42.                 {
43.                     super.paintComponent(g);
44.                     Graphics2D g2 = (Graphics2D)g;
45.                     g2.draw(area1);
46.                     g2.draw(area2);
47.                     if (area != null) g2.fill(area);
48.                 }
49.             };
50.
51.         contentPane.add(panel, BorderLayout.CENTER);
52.
53.         JPanel buttonPanel = new JPanel();
54.         ButtonGroup group = new ButtonGroup();
55.
56.         JRadioButton addButton = new JRadioButton("Add", false);
57.         buttonPanel.add(addButton);
58.         group.add(addButton);
59.         addButton.addActionListener(new
60.             ActionListener()
61.             {
62.                 public void actionPerformed(ActionEvent event)
63.                 {
64.                     area = new Area();
65.                     area.add(area1);
66.                     area.add(area2);
67.                     panel.repaint();
68.                 }
69.             });
70.
71.         JRadioButton subtractButton
72.             = new JRadioButton("Subtract", false);
73.         buttonPanel.add(subtractButton);
74.         group.add(subtractButton);
75.         subtractButton.addActionListener(new
76.             ActionListener()
77.             {
78.                 public void actionPerformed(ActionEvent event)
79.                 {
```

```
80.              area = new Area();
81.              area.add(area1);
82.              area.subtract(area2);
83.              panel.repaint();
84.          }
85.      });
86.
87.      JRadioButton intersectButton
88.          = new JRadioButton("Intersect", false);
89.      buttonPanel.add(intersectButton);
90.      group.add(intersectButton);
91.      intersectButton.addActionListener(new
92.          ActionListener()
93.          {
94.              public void actionPerformed(ActionEvent event)
95.              {
96.                  area = new Area();
97.                  area.add(area1);
98.                  area.intersect(area2);
99.                  panel.repaint();
100.             }
101.         });
102.
103.     JRadioButton exclusiveOrButton
104.         = new JRadioButton("Exclusive Or", false);
105.     buttonPanel.add(exclusiveOrButton);
106.     group.add(exclusiveOrButton);
107.     exclusiveOrButton.addActionListener(new
108.         ActionListener()
109.         {
110.             public void actionPerformed(ActionEvent event)
111.             {
112.                 area = new Area();
113.                 area.add(area1);
114.                 area.exclusiveOr(area2);
115.                 panel.repaint();
116.             }
117.         });
118.
119.     contentPane.add(buttonPanel, BorderLayout.NORTH);
120.  }
121.
122.  private JPanel panel;
123.  private Area area;
124.  private Area area1;
125.  private Area area2;
126.
127.  private static final int WIDTH = 400;
128.  private static final int HEIGHT = 400;
129. }
```

java.awt.geom.Area

- void add(Area other)
- void subtract(Area other)
- void intersect(Area other)
- void exclusiveOr(Area other)

carry out the constructive area geometry operation with this area and the other area and set this area to the result.

Strokes

The draw operation of the Graphics2D class draws the boundary of a shape by using the currently selected *stroke*. By default, the stroke is a solid line that is one pixel wide. You can select a different stroke by calling the setStroke method. You supply an object of a class that implements the Stroke interface. The Java 2D API defines only one such class, called BasicStroke. In this section, we look at the capabilities of the BasicStroke class.

You can construct strokes of arbitrary thickness. For example, here is how you draw lines that are 10 pixels wide.

```
g2.setStroke(new BasicStroke(10.0F));
g2.draw(new Line2D.Double(. . .));
```

When a stroke is more than a pixel thick, then the *end* of the stroke can have different styles. Figure 7–12 shows these so-called *end cap styles.* There are three choices:

- A *butt cap* simply ends the stroke at its end point.
- A *round cap* adds a half-circle to the end of the stroke.
- A *square cap* adds a half-square to the end of the stroke.

Butt
Cap

Round
Cap

Square
Cap

Figure 7–12: End Cap Styles

When two thick strokes meet, there are three choices for the *join style* (see Figure 7–13).

- A *bevel join* joins the strokes with a straight line that is perpendicular to the bisector of the angle between the two strokes.
- A *round join* extends each stroke to have a round cap.
- A `miter join` extends both strokes by adding a "spike."

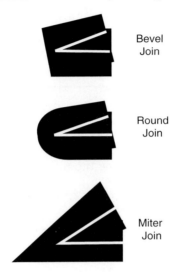

Bevel
Join

Round
Join

Miter
Join

Figure 7–13: Join Styles

The miter join is not suitable for lines that meet at small angles. If two lines join with an angle that is less than the *miter limit*, then a bevel join is used instead. That usage prevents extremely long spikes. By default, the miter limit is ten degrees.

You specify these choices in the `BasicStroke` constructor, for example:

```
g2.setStroke(new BasicStroke(10.0F, BasicStroke.CAP_ROUND,
    BasicStroke.JOIN_ROUND));
g2.setStroke(new BasicStroke(10.0F, BasicStroke.CAP_BUTT,
    BasicStroke.JOIN_MITER, 15.0F /* miter limit */));
```

Finally, you can specify dashed lines by setting a *dash pattern*. In the program in Example 7–3, you can select a dash pattern that spells out SOS in Morse code. The dash pattern is a `float[]` array of numbers that contains the lengths of the "on" and "off" strokes (see Figure 7–14).

10   10   10   10   10   10   30   10   30   . . .

Figure 7–14: A dash pattern

You specify the dash pattern and a *dash phase* when constructing the `BasicStroke`. The dash phase indicates where in the dash pattern each line should start. Normally, you set this value to 0.

```
float[] dashPattern
   = { 10, 10, 10, 10, 10, 10, 30, 10, 30, ... };
g2.setStroke(new BasicStroke(10.0F, BasicStroke.CAP_BUTT,
   BasicStroke.JOIN_MITER, 10.0F /* miter limit */,
   dashPattern, 0 /* dash phase */));
```

NOTE: End cap styles are applied to the ends of *each dash* in a dash pattern.

The program in Example 7–3 lets you specify end cap styles, join styles, and dashed lines (see Figure 7–15). You can move the ends of the line segments to test out the miter limit: select the miter join, then move the line segment to form a very acute angle. You will see the miter join turn into a bevel join.

Figure 7–15: The StrokeTest program

The program is similar to the program in Example 7–1. The mouse listener remembers if you click on the end point of a line segment, and the mouse motion listener monitors the dragging of the end point. A set of radio buttons signal the user choices for the end cap style, join style, and solid or dashed line. The `paintComponent` method of the `StrokePanel` class constructs a `GeneralPath` consisting of the two line segments that join the three points that the user can move with the mouse. It then constructs a `BasicStroke`, according to the selections that the user made, and finally draws the path.

Example 7-3: StrokeTest.java

```
1. import java.awt.*;
2. import java.awt.event.*;
3. import java.awt.geom.*;
4. import java.util.*;
5. import javax.swing.*;
6.
7. /**
8.    This program demonstrates different stroke types.
9. */
10. public class StrokeTest
11. {
12.    public static void main(String[] args)
13.    {
14.       JFrame frame = new StrokeTestFrame();
15.       frame.setDefaultCloseOperation(JFrame.EXIT_ON_CLOSE);
16.       frame.show();
17.    }
18. }
19.
20. /**
21.    This frame lets the user choose the cap, join, and
22.    line style, and shows the resulting stroke.
23. */
24. class StrokeTestFrame extends JFrame
25. {
26.    public StrokeTestFrame()
27.    {
28.       setTitle("StrokeTest");
29.       setSize(WIDTH, HEIGHT);
30.
31.       Container contentPane = getContentPane();
32.       canvas = new StrokePanel();
33.       contentPane.add(canvas, BorderLayout.CENTER);
34.
35.       buttonPanel = new JPanel();
36.       buttonPanel.setLayout(new GridLayout(3, 3));
37.       contentPane.add(buttonPanel, BorderLayout.NORTH);
38.
39.       ButtonGroup group1 = new ButtonGroup();
40.       makeCapButton("Butt Cap", BasicStroke.CAP_BUTT, group1);
41.       makeCapButton("Round Cap", BasicStroke.CAP_ROUND, group1);
42.       makeCapButton("Square Cap", BasicStroke.CAP_SQUARE,
43.          group1);
44.
45.       ButtonGroup group2 = new ButtonGroup();
46.       makeJoinButton("Bevel Join", BasicStroke.JOIN_BEVEL,
47.          group2);
```

```
48.        makeJoinButton("Miter Join", BasicStroke.JOIN_MITER,
49.           group2);
50.        makeJoinButton("Round Join", BasicStroke.JOIN_ROUND,
51.           group2);
52.
53.        ButtonGroup group3 = new ButtonGroup();
54.        makeDashButton("Solid Line", false, group3);
55.        makeDashButton("Dashed Line", true, group3);
56.     }
57.
58.     /**
59.        Makes a radio button to change the cap style.
60.        @param label the button label
61.        @param style the cap style
62.        @param group the radio button group
63.     */
64.     private void makeCapButton(String label, final int style,
65.        ButtonGroup group)
66.     {
67.        // select first button in group
68.        boolean selected = group.getButtonCount() == 0;
69.        JRadioButton button = new JRadioButton(label, selected);
70.        buttonPanel.add(button);
71.        group.add(button);
72.        button.addActionListener(new
73.           ActionListener()
74.           {
75.              public void actionPerformed(ActionEvent event)
76.              {
77.                 canvas.setCap(style);
78.              }
79.           });
80.     }
81.
82.     /**
83.        Makes a radio button to change the join style.
84.        @param label the button label
85.        @param style the join style
86.        @param group the radio button group
87.     */
88.     private void makeJoinButton(String label, final int style,
89.        ButtonGroup group)
90.     {
91.        // select first button in group
92.        boolean selected = group.getButtonCount() == 0;
93.        JRadioButton button = new JRadioButton(label, selected);
94.        buttonPanel.add(button);
95.        group.add(button);
96.        button.addActionListener(new
97.           ActionListener()
98.           {
99.              public void actionPerformed(ActionEvent event)
```

```
100.                {
101.                    canvas.setJoin(style);
102.                }
103.            });
104.    }
105.
106.    /**
107.        Makes a radio button to set solid or dashed lines
108.        @param label the button label
109.        @param style false for solid, true for dashed lines
110.        @param group the radio button group
111.    */
112.    private void makeDashButton(String label, final boolean style,
113.        ButtonGroup group)
114.    {
115.        // select first button in group
116.        boolean selected = group.getButtonCount() == 0;
117.        JRadioButton button = new JRadioButton(label, selected);
118.        buttonPanel.add(button);
119.        group.add(button);
120.        button.addActionListener(new
121.            ActionListener()
122.            {
123.                public void actionPerformed(ActionEvent event)
124.                {
125.                    canvas.setDash(style);
126.                }
127.            });
128.    }
129.
130.    private StrokePanel canvas;
131.    private JPanel buttonPanel;
132.
133.    private static final int WIDTH = 400;
134.    private static final int HEIGHT = 400;
135. }
136.
137. /**
138.    This panel draws two joined lines, using different
139.    stroke objects, and allows the user to drag the three
140.    points defining the lines.
141. */
142. class StrokePanel extends JPanel
143. {
144.    public StrokePanel()
145.    {
146.        addMouseListener(new
147.            MouseAdapter()
148.            {
149.                public void mousePressed(MouseEvent event)
150.                {
151.                    Point p = event.getPoint();
```

```
152.                    for (int i = 0; i < points.length; i++)
153.                    {
154.                        double x = points[i].getX() - SIZE / 2;
155.                        double y = points[i].getY() - SIZE / 2;
156.                        Rectangle2D r
157.                            = new Rectangle2D.Double(x, y, SIZE, SIZE);
158.                        if (r.contains(p))
159.                        {
160.                            current = i;
161.                            return;
162.                        }
163.                    }
164.               }

165.
166.               public void mouseReleased(MouseEvent event)
167.               {
168.                   current = -1;
169.               }
170.            });
171.
172.         addMouseMotionListener(new
173.            MouseMotionAdapter()
174.            {
175.                public void mouseDragged(MouseEvent event)
176.                {
177.                    if (current == -1) return;
178.                    points[current] = event.getPoint();
179.                    repaint();
180.                }
181.            });
182.
183.         points = new Point2D[3];
184.         points[0] = new Point2D.Double(200, 100);
185.         points[1] = new Point2D.Double(100, 200);
186.         points[2] = new Point2D.Double(200, 200);
187.         current = -1;
188.         width = 10.0F;
189.      }
190.
191.      public void paintComponent(Graphics g)
192.      {
193.         super.paintComponent(g);
194.         Graphics2D g2 = (Graphics2D)g;
195.         GeneralPath path = new GeneralPath();
196.         path.moveTo((float)points[0].getX(),
197.             (float)points[0].getY());
198.         for (int i = 1; i < points.length; i++)
199.            path.lineTo((float)points[i].getX(),
200.                (float)points[i].getY());
201.         BasicStroke stroke;
202.         if (dash)
203.         {
204.            float miterLimit = 10.0F;
```

```
205.          float[] dashPattern = { 10F, 10F, 10F, 10F, 10F, 10F,
206.              30F, 10F, 30F, 10F, 30F, 10F,
207.              10F, 10F, 10F, 10F, 10F, 30F };
208.          float dashPhase = 0;
209.          stroke = new BasicStroke(width, cap, join,
210.              miterLimit, dashPattern, dashPhase);
211.       }
212.       else
213.          stroke = new BasicStroke(width, cap, join);
214.       g2.setStroke(stroke);
215.       g2.draw(path);
216.    }
217.
218.    /**
219.       Sets the join style.
220.       @param j the join style
221.    */
222.    public void setJoin(int j)
223.    {
224.       join = j;
225.       repaint();
226.    }
227.
228.    /**
229.       Sets the cap style.
230.       @param c the cap style
231.    */
232.    public void setCap(int c)
233.    {
234.       cap = c;
235.       repaint();
236.    }
237.
238.    /**
239.       Sets solid or dashed lines
240.       @param d false for solid, true for dashed lines
241.    */
242.    public void setDash(boolean d)
243.    {
244.       dash = d;
245.       repaint();
246.    }
247.
248.    private Point2D[] points;
249.    private static int SIZE = 10;
250.    private int current;
251.    private float width;
252.    private int cap;
253.    private int join;
254.    private boolean dash;
255. }
```

java.awt.Graphics2D

- void setStroke(Stroke s)

  sets the stroke of this graphics context to the given object that implements the Stroke interface.

java.awt.BasicStroke

- BasicStroke(float width)
- BasicStroke(float width, int cap, int join)
- BasicStroke(float width, int cap, int join, float miterlimit)
- BasicStroke(float width, int cap, int join, float miterlimit, float[] dash, float dashPhase)

  construct a stroke object with the given attributes.

Parameters:	width	the width of the pen
	cap	the end cap style, one of CAP_BUTT, CAP_ROUND, and CAP_SQUARE
	join	the join style, one of JOIN_BEVEL, JOIN_MITER, and JOIN_ROUND
	miterlimit	the angle, in degrees, below which a miter join is rendered as a bevel join
	dash	an array of the lengths of the alternating filled and blank portions of a dashed stroke
	dashPhase	the "phase" of the dash pattern. A segment of this length, preceding the starting point of the stroke, is assumed to have the dash pattern already applied.

Paint

When you fill a shape, its inside is covered with *paint*. You use the setPaint method to set the paint style to an object whose class implements the Paint interface. In the Java 2D API, there are three such classes:

- The Color class implements the Paint interface. To fill shapes with a solid color, simply call setPaint with a Color object, such as

  g2.setPaint(Color.red);

- The GradientPaint class varies colors by interpolating between two given color values (see Figure 7–16).

- The TexturePaint class fills an area with repetitions of an image (see Figure 7–17).

Figure 7–16: Gradient paint

Figure 7–17: Texture paint

You construct a GradientPaint object by giving two points and the colors that you want at these two points.

```
g2.setPaint(new GradientPaint(p1, Color.red, p2, Color.blue));
```

Colors are interpolated along the line joining the two points. Colors are constant along lines that are perpendicular to that joining line. Points beyond an end point of the line are given the color at the end point.

Alternatively, if you call the GradientPaint constructor with true for the cyclic parameter,

```
g2.setPaint(new GradientPaint(p1, Color.red, p2, Color.blue, true));
```

then the color variation *cycles* and keeps varying beyond the end points.

To construct a TexturePaint object, you need to specify a BufferedImage and an *anchor* rectangle. The anchor rectangle is extended indefinitely in x- and y-directions to tile the entire coordinate plane. The image is scaled to fit into the anchor and then replicated into each tile.

We will introduce the BufferedImage class later in this chapter when we discuss images in detail. You create a BufferedImage object by giving the image size and the *image type*. The most common image type is TYPE_INT_ARGB, in which each pixel is specified by an integer that describes the *alpha* or transparency, red, green, and blue values. For example,

```
BufferedImage bufferedImage = new BufferedImage(width, height,
    TYPE_INT_ARGB);
```

Then, you obtain a graphics context to draw into the buffered image.

```
Graphics2D g2 = bufferedImage.createGraphics();
```

Any drawing operations on g2 now fill the buffered image with pixels. When you are done, then you can create your TexturePaint object:

```
g2.setPaint(new TexturePaint(bufferedImage, anchorRectangle));
```

The program in Example 7–4 lets the user choose between a solid color paint, a gradient paint, and a texture paint. Then, an ellipse is filled with the specified paint.

The texture paint uses an image that is read from a GIF file. As you will see later in this chapter, the ImageIO class makes it simple to read a graphics file into a buffered image, by calling

```
bufferedImage = ImageIO.read(new File("blue-ball.gif"));
```

NOTE: The ImageIO class was added in SDK version 1.4. If you have an older version of the SDK, you need to use the following code instead:

```
Image image = Toolkit.getDefaultToolkit().getImage
    ("blue-ball.gif");
MediaTracker tracker = new MediaTracker(this);
tracker.addImage(image, 0);
try { tracker.waitForID(0); }
catch (InterruptedException e) {}
bufferedImage = new BufferedImage(image.getWidth(null),
    image.getHeight(null), BufferedImage.TYPE_INT_ARGB);
Graphics2D g2 = bufferedImage.createGraphics();
g2.drawImage(image, 0, 0, null);
```

To show the significance of the anchor rectangle, we specify the anchor to have twice the size of the image:

```
Rectangle2D anchor = new Rectangle2D.Double(0, 0,
   2 * bufferedImage.getWidth(),
   2 * bufferedImage.getHeight());
paint = new TexturePaint(bufferedImage, anchor);
```

As you can see when you select Texture Paint, the image is scaled to fit the anchor, and it is then replicated to fill the shape. Tiles that meet the boundary of the shape are clipped.

Example 7–4: PaintTest.java

```
1. import java.awt.*;
2. import java.awt.event.*;
3. import java.awt.geom.*;
4. import java.awt.image.*;
5. import java.io.*;
6. import java.util.*;
7. import javax.imageio.*;
8. import javax.swing.*;
9.
10. /**
11.    This program demonstrates the various paint modes.
12. */
13. public class PaintTest
14. {
15.    public static void main(String[] args)
16.    {
17.       JFrame frame = new PaintTestFrame();
18.       frame.setDefaultCloseOperation(JFrame.EXIT_ON_CLOSE);
19.       frame.show();
20.    }
21. }
22.
23. /**
24.    This frame contains radio buttons to choose the paint mode
25.    and a panel that draws a circle in the selected paint mode.
26. */
27. class PaintTestFrame extends JFrame
28. {
29.    public PaintTestFrame()
30.    {
31.       setTitle("PaintTest");
32.       setSize(WIDTH, HEIGHT);
33.
34.       Container contentPane = getContentPane();
35.       canvas = new PaintPanel();
36.       contentPane.add(canvas, BorderLayout.CENTER);
37.
```

```
38.        JPanel buttonPanel = new JPanel();
39.        ButtonGroup group = new ButtonGroup();
40.
41.        JRadioButton colorButton = new JRadioButton("Color", true);
42.        buttonPanel.add(colorButton);
43.        group.add(colorButton);
44.        colorButton.addActionListener(new
45.           ActionListener()
46.           {
47.              public void actionPerformed(ActionEvent event)
48.              {
49.                 canvas.setColor();
50.              }
51.           });
52.
53.        JRadioButton gradientPaintButton
54.           = new JRadioButton("Gradient Paint", false);
55.        buttonPanel.add(gradientPaintButton);
56.        group.add(gradientPaintButton);
57.        gradientPaintButton.addActionListener(new
58.           ActionListener()
59.           {
60.              public void actionPerformed(ActionEvent event)
61.              {
62.                 canvas.setGradientPaint();
63.              }
64.           });
65.
66.        JRadioButton texturePaintButton
67.           = new JRadioButton("Texture Paint", false);
68.        buttonPanel.add(texturePaintButton);
69.        group.add(texturePaintButton);
70.        texturePaintButton.addActionListener(new
71.           ActionListener()
72.           {
73.              public void actionPerformed(ActionEvent event)
74.              {
75.                 canvas.setTexturePaint();
76.              }
77.           });
78.
79.        contentPane.add(buttonPanel, BorderLayout.NORTH);
80.     }
81.
82.     private PaintPanel canvas;
83.     private static final int WIDTH = 400;
84.     private static final int HEIGHT = 400;
85. }
86.
87. /**
```

```
88.     This panel paints a circle in various paint modes.
89.  */
90.  class PaintPanel extends JPanel
91.  {
92.     public PaintPanel()
93.     {
94.        try
95.        {
96.           bufferedImage = ImageIO.read(new File("blue-ball.gif"));
97.        }
98.        catch (IOException exception)
99.        {
100.          exception.printStackTrace();
101.       }
102.       setColor();
103.    }
104.
105.    public void paintComponent(Graphics g)
106.    {
107.       super.paintComponent(g);
108.       Graphics2D g2 = (Graphics2D)g;
109.       g2.setPaint(paint);
110.       Ellipse2D circle
111.          = new Ellipse2D.Double(0, 0, getWidth(), getHeight());
112.       g2.fill(circle);
113.    }
114.
115.    /**
116.       Paints in a plain color.
117.    */
118.    public void setColor()
119.    {
120.       paint = Color.red; // Color implements Paint
121.       repaint();
122.    }
123.
124.    /**
125.       Sets the paint mode to gradient paint.
126.    */
127.    public void setGradientPaint()
128.    {
129.       paint = new GradientPaint(0, 0, Color.red,
130.          (float)getWidth(), (float)getHeight(), Color.blue);
131.       repaint();
132.    }
133.
134.    /**
135.       Sets the paint mode to texture paint.
136.    */
137.    public void setTexturePaint()
```

```
138.    {
139.        Rectangle2D anchor = new Rectangle2D.Double(0, 0,
140.            2 * bufferedImage.getWidth(),
141.            2 * bufferedImage.getHeight());
142.        paint = new TexturePaint(bufferedImage, anchor);
143.        repaint();
144.    }
145.
146.    private Paint paint;
147.    private BufferedImage bufferedImage;
148. }
```

java.awt.Graphics2D

- void setPaint(Paint s)

  sets the paint of this graphics context to the given object that implements the Paint interface.

java.awt.GradientPaint

- GradientPaint(float x1, float y1, Color color1, float x2, float y2, Color color2)
- GradientPaint(float x1, float y1, Color color1, float x2, float y2, Color color2, boolean cyclic)
- GradientPaint(Point2D p1, Color color1, Point2D p2, Color color2)
- GradientPaint(Point2D p1, Color color1, Point2D p2, Color color2, boolean cyclic)

  construct a gradient paint object that fills shapes with color such that the start point is colored with color1, the end point is colored with color2, and the colors in between are linearly interpolated. Colors are constant along lines that are perpendicular to the line joining the start and the end point. By default, the gradient paint is not cyclic, that is, points beyond the start and end points are colored with the same color as the start and end point. If the gradient paint is *cyclic,* then colors continue to be interpolated, first returning to the starting point color and then repeating indefinitely in both directions.

Parameters:	x1, y1, or p1	the start point
	color1	the color to use for the start point
	x2, y2, or p2	the end point
	color2	the color to use for the end point
	cyclic	true if the color change pattern repeats, false if the colors beyond the start and end point are constant

---

`java.awt.TexturePaint`

A P I

- `TexturePaint(BufferedImage texture, Rectangle2D anchor)`
  creates a texture paint object.

  Parameters: `texture`   the texture to use for filling shapes

                        `anchor`   the anchor rectangle that defines the tiling of the space to be painted. The rectangle is repeated indefinitely in x- and y-directions, and the texture image is scaled to fill each tile.

Coordinate Transformations

Suppose you need to draw an object such as an automobile. You know, from the manufacturer's specifications, the height, wheelbase, and total length. You could, of course, figure out all pixel positions, assuming some number of pixels per meter. However, there is an easier way. You can ask the graphics context to carry out the conversion for you.

```
g2.scale(pixelsPerMeter, pixelsPerMeter);
g2.draw(new Line2D.Double(coordinates in meters));
   // converts to pixels and draws scaled line
```

The `scale` method of the `Graphics2D` class sets the *coordinate transformation* of the graphics context to a scaling transformation. That transformation changes *user coordinates* (the units that the user specifies) to *device coordinates* (pixels). Figure 7–18 shows how the transformation works.

Coordinate transformations are very useful in practice. They allow you to work with convenient coordinate values. The graphics context takes care of the dirty work of transforming them to pixels.

User coordinates

Device coordinates

Figure 7–18: User and device coordinates

There are four fundamental transformations:

- Scaling: blowing up, or shrinking, all distances from a fixed point;
- Rotation: rotating all points around a fixed center;
- Translation: moving all points by a fixed amount;
- Shear: leaving one line fixed and "sliding" the lines parallel to it by an amount that is proportional to the distance from the fixed line.

Figure 7–19 shows how these four fundamental transformations act on a unit square.

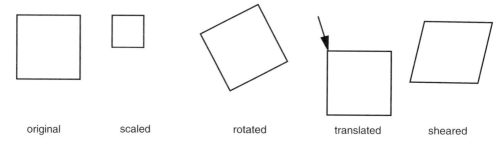

| original | scaled | rotated | translated | sheared |

Figure 7–19: The fundamental transformations

The `scale`, `rotate`, `translate`, and `shear` methods of the `Graphics2D` class set the coordinate transformation of the graphics context to one of these fundamental transformations.

You can *compose* the transformations. For example, you may want to rotate shapes *and* double their size. Then, you need to supply both a rotation and a scaling transformation.

```
g2.rotate(angle);
g2.scale(2, 2);
g2.draw(. . .);
```

In this case, it does not matter in which order you supply the transformations. However, with most transformations, order does matter. For example, if you want to rotate and shear, then it makes a difference which of the transformations you supply first. You need to figure out what your intention is. The graphics context will apply the transformations in the opposite order in which you supplied them. That is, the last transformation that you supply is applied first.

You can supply as many transformations as you like. For example, consider the following sequence of transformations:

```
g2.translate(x, y);
g2.rotate(a);
g2.translate(-x, -y);
```

The last transformation (which is applied first) moves the point (x, y) to the origin. The second transformation rotates with an angle a around the origin. The final transformation moves the origin back to (x, y). The overall effect is a rotation with center point (x, y)—see Figure 7–20. Because rotating about a point other than the origin is such a common operation, there is a shortcut:

```
g2.rotate(a, x, y);
```

If you know some matrix theory, you are probably aware that all rotations, translations, scalings, shears, and their compositions can be expressed by matrix transformations of the form:

$$\begin{bmatrix} x_{new} \\ y_{new} \\ 1 \end{bmatrix} = \begin{bmatrix} a & c & e \\ b & d & f \\ 0 & 0 & 1 \end{bmatrix} \cdot \begin{bmatrix} x \\ y \\ 1 \end{bmatrix}$$

Figure 7–20: Composing transformations

Such a transformation is called an *affine transformation.* In the Java 2D API, the AffineTransform class describes such a transformation. If you know the components of a particular transformation matrix, you can construct it directly as

```
AffineTransform t = new AffineTransform(a, b, c, d, e, f);
```

There are also factory methods getRotateInstance, getScaleInstance, getTranslateInstance, and getShearInstance that construct the matrices that represent these transformation types. For example, the call

```
t = AffineTransform.getScaleInstance(2.0F, 0.5F);
```

returns a transformation that corresponds to the matrix

$$
\begin{bmatrix}
2 & 0 & 0 \\
0 & 0.5 & 0 \\
0 & 0 & 1
\end{bmatrix}
$$

Finally, there are instance methods setToRotation, setToScale, setToTranslation, and setToShear that set a transformation object to a new type. Here is an example.

```
t.setToRotation(angle); // sets t to a rotation
```

You can set the coordinate transformation of the graphics context to an AffineTransform object.

```
g2.setTransform(t); // replaces current transformation
```

However, in practice, you don't want to call the setTransform operation since it replaces any existing clipping shape that the graphics context may have. For example, a graphics context for printing in landscape mode already contains a 90-degree rotation transformation. If you call setTransform, you obliterate that rotation. Instead, call the transform method.

```
g2.transform(t); // composes current transformation with t
```

It composes the existing transformation with the new AffineTransform object.

If you just want to apply a transformation temporarily, then you should first get the old transformation, then compose with your new transformation, and finally restore the old transformation when you are done.

```
AffineTransform oldTransform = g2.getTransform();
   // save old transform
g2.transform(t); // apply temporary transform
   // now draw on g2
g2.setTransform(oldTransform); // restore old transform
```

The program in Example 7–5 lets the user choose among the four fundamental transformations. The paintComponent method draws a square, then applies the selected transformation and redraws the square. However, for a good visual appearance, we want to have the square and its transform appear on the *center* of the display panel. For that reason, the paintComponent method first sets the coordinate transformation to a translation.

```
g2.translate(getWidth() / 2, getHeight() / 2);
```

This translation moves the origin to the center of the component.

Then, the paintComponent method draws a square that is centered around the origin.

```
square = new Rectangle2D.Double(-50, -50, 100, 100);
. . .
g2.setPaint(Color.gray);
g2.draw(square);
```

However, because the graphics context applies the translation to the shape, the square is actually drawn with its center lying at the center of the component.

Next, the transformation that the user selected is composed with the current transformation, and the square is drawn once again.

```
g2.transform(t);
g2.setPaint(Color.black);
g2.draw(square);
```

The original square is drawn in gray, and the transformed one in black (see Figure 7–21).

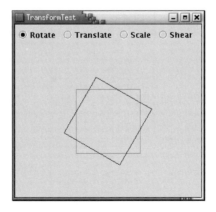

Figure 7–21: The TransformTest program

Example 7–5: TransformTest.java

```
1. import java.awt.*;
2. import java.awt.event.*;
3. import java.awt.geom.*;
4. import java.util.*;
5. import javax.swing.*;
6.
7. /**
8.    This program displays the effects of various transformations.
9. */
10. public class TransformTest
11. {
12.    public static void main(String[] args)
13.    {
14.       JFrame frame = new TransformTestFrame();
15.       frame.setDefaultCloseOperation(JFrame.EXIT_ON_CLOSE);
16.       frame.show();
17.    }
18. }
19.
20. /**
21.    This frame contains radio buttons to choose a transformations
22.    and a panel to display the effect of the chosen
23.    transformation.
24. */
25. class TransformTestFrame extends JFrame
26. {
27.    public TransformTestFrame()
28.    {
29.       setTitle("TransformTest");
30.       setSize(WIDTH, HEIGHT);
31.
32.       Container contentPane = getContentPane();
33.       canvas = new TransformPanel();
34.       contentPane.add(canvas, BorderLayout.CENTER);
35.
36.       JPanel buttonPanel = new JPanel();
37.       ButtonGroup group = new ButtonGroup();
38.
39.       JRadioButton rotateButton
40.          = new JRadioButton("Rotate", true);
41.       buttonPanel.add(rotateButton);
42.       group.add(rotateButton);
43.       rotateButton.addActionListener(new
44.          ActionListener()
45.          {
46.             public void actionPerformed(ActionEvent event)
47.             {
48.                canvas.setRotate();
```

```
49.               }
50.           });
51.
52.       JRadioButton translateButton
53.           = new JRadioButton("Translate", false);
54.       buttonPanel.add(translateButton);
55.       group.add(translateButton);
56.       translateButton.addActionListener(new
57.           ActionListener()
58.           {
59.              public void actionPerformed(ActionEvent event)
60.              {
61.                 canvas.setTranslate();
62.              }
63.           });
64.
65.       JRadioButton scaleButton
66.           = new JRadioButton("Scale", false);
67.       buttonPanel.add(scaleButton);
68.       group.add(scaleButton);
69.       scaleButton.addActionListener(new
70.           ActionListener()
71.           {
72.              public void actionPerformed(ActionEvent event)
73.              {
74.                 canvas.setScale();
75.              }
76.           });
77.
78.       JRadioButton shearButton
79.           = new JRadioButton("Shear", false);
80.       buttonPanel.add(shearButton);
81.       group.add(shearButton);
82.       shearButton.addActionListener(new
83.           ActionListener()
84.           {
85.              public void actionPerformed(ActionEvent event)
86.              {
87.                 canvas.setShear();
88.              }
89.           });
90.
91.       contentPane.add(buttonPanel, BorderLayout.NORTH);
92.    }
93.
94.    private TransformPanel canvas;
95.    private static final int WIDTH = 300;
96.    private static final int HEIGHT = 300;
97. }
98.
99. /**
```

```
100.    This panel displays a square and its transformed image
101.    under a transformation.
102. */
103. class TransformPanel extends JPanel
104. {
105.    public TransformPanel()
106.    {
107.       square = new Rectangle2D.Double(-50, -50, 100, 100);
108.       t = new AffineTransform();
109.       setRotate();
110.    }
111.
112.    public void paintComponent(Graphics g)
113.    {
114.       super.paintComponent(g);
115.       Graphics2D g2 = (Graphics2D)g;
116.       g2.translate(getWidth() / 2, getHeight() / 2);
117.       g2.setPaint(Color.gray);
118.       g2.draw(square);
119.       g2.transform(t);
120.          /* we don't use setTransform because we want
121.             to compose with the current translation
122.          */
123.       g2.setPaint(Color.black);
124.       g2.draw(square);
125.    }
126.
127.    /**
128.       Set the transformation to a rotation.
129.    */
130.    public void setRotate()
131.    {
132.       t.setToRotation(Math.toRadians(30));
133.       repaint();
134.    }
135.
136.    /**
137.       Set the transformation to a translation.
138.    */
139.    public void setTranslate()
140.    {
141.       t.setToTranslation(20, 15);
142.       repaint();
143.    }
144.
145.    /**
146.       Set the transformation to a scale transformation.
147.    */
148.    public void setScale()
149.    {
150.       t.setToScale(2.0, 1.5);
```

```
151.        repaint();
152.    }
153.
154.    /**
155.        Set the transformation to a shear transformation.
156.    */
157.    public void setShear()
158.    {
159.        t.setToShear(-0.2, 0);
160.        repaint();
161.    }
162.
163.    private Rectangle2D square;
164.    private AffineTransform t;
165. }
```

java.awt.geom.AffineTransform

- AffineTransform(double a, double b, double c, double d, double e, double f)
- AffineTransform(float a, float b, float c, float d, float e, float f)

  construct the affine transform with matrix

$$
\begin{bmatrix}
a & c & e \\
b & d & f \\
0 & 0 & 1
\end{bmatrix}
$$

- AffineTransform(double[] m)
- AffineTransform(float[] m)

  construct the affine transform with matrix

$$
\begin{bmatrix}
m[0] & m[2] & m[4] \\
m[1] & m[3] & m[5] \\
0 & 0 & 1
\end{bmatrix}
$$

- static AffineTransform getRotateInstance(double a)

  creates a counterclockwise rotation around the origin by the angle a (in radians). The transformation matrix is

$$
\begin{bmatrix}
\cos(a) & -\sin(a) & 0 \\
\sin(a) & \cos(a) & 0 \\
0 & 0 & 1
\end{bmatrix}
$$

- `static AffineTransform getRotateInstance(double a, double x, double y)`

  creates a counterclockwise rotation around the point (x, y) by the angle a (in radians).

- `static AffineTransform getScaleInstance(double sx, double sy)`

  creates a scaling transformation that scales the x-axis by `sx` and the y-axis by `sy`. The transformation matrix is

$$\begin{bmatrix} sx & 0 & 0 \\ 0 & sy & 0 \\ 0 & 0 & 1 \end{bmatrix}$$

- `static AffineTransform getShearInstance(double shx, double shy)`

  creates a shear transformation that shears the x-axis by `shx` and the y-axis by `shy`. The transformation matrix is

$$\begin{bmatrix} 1 & shx & 0 \\ shy & 1 & 0 \\ 0 & 0 & 1 \end{bmatrix}$$

- `static AffineTransform getTranslateInstance(double tx, double ty)`

  creates a translation that moves the x-axis by `tx` and the y-axis by `ty`. The transformation matrix is

$$\begin{bmatrix} 1 & 0 & tx \\ 0 & 1 & ty \\ 0 & 0 & 1 \end{bmatrix}$$

- `void setToRotation(double a)`
- `void setToRotation(double a, double x, double y)`
- `void setToScale(double sx, double sy)`
- `void setToShear(double sx, double sy)`
- `void setToTranslation(double tx, double ty)`

  set this affine transformation to a basic transformation with the given parameters. See the get*Xxx*Instance method for an explanation of the basic transformations and their parameters.

java.awt.Graphics2D

- void setTransform(AffineTransform t)

  replaces the existing coordinate transformation of this graphics context with t.

- void transform(AffineTransform t)

  composes the existing coordinate transformation of this graphics context with t.

- void rotate(double a)
- void rotate(double a, double x, double y)
- void scale(double sx, double sy)
- void shear(double sx, double sy)
- void translate(double tx, double ty)

  compose the existing coordinate transformation of this graphics context with a basic transformation with the given parameters. See the AffineTransform.get*Xxx*Instance method for an explanation of the basic transformations and their parameters.

Clipping

By setting a *clipping shape* in the graphics context, you constrain all drawing operations the interior of that clipping shape.

```
g2.setClip(clipShape); // but see below
g2.draw(shape);
    // draws only the part that falls inside the clipping shape
```

However, in practice, you don't want to call the setClip operation since it replaces any existing clipping shape that the graphics context may have. For example, as you will see later in this chapter, a graphics context for printing comes with a clip rectangle that ensures that you don't draw on the margins. Instead, call the clip method.

```
g2.clip(clipShape); // better
```

The clip method intersects the existing clipping shape with the new one that you supply.

If you just want to apply a clipping area temporarily, then you should first get the old clip, then add your new clip, and finally restore the old clip when you are done:

```
Shape oldClip = g2.getClip(); // save old clip
g2.clip(clipShape); // apply temporary clip
// now draw on g2
g2.setClip(oldClip); // restore old clip
```

In Example 7–6, we show off the clipping capability with a rather dramatic drawing of a line pattern that is clipped by a complex shape, namely, the outline of a set of characters (see Figure 7–22).

Figure 7–22: The ClipTest program

To obtain character outlines, you need a *font render context.* Use the `getFont-RenderContext` method of the `Graphics2D` class.

```
FontRenderContext context = g2.getFontRenderContext();
```

Next, using

- a string
- a font
- the font render context

create a `TextLayout` object:

```
TextLayout layout = new TextLayout("Hello", font, context);
```

This text layout object describes the layout of a sequence of characters, as rendered by a particular font render context. The layout depends on the font render context—the same characters will appear differently on a screen or a printer.

More importantly for our current application, the `getOutline` method returns a `Shape` object that describes the shape of the outline of the characters in the text layout. The outline shape starts at the origin (0, 0), which is not suitable for most drawing operations. Therefore, you need to supply an affine transform to the `getOutline` operation that specifies where you would like the outline to appear. We simply supply a translation that moves the base point to the point (0, 100).

```
AffineTransform transform
   = AffineTransform.getTranslateInstance(0, 100);
Shape outline = layout.getOutline(transform);
```

Then, we append the outline to the clipping shape.

```
GeneralPath clipShape = new GeneralPath();
clipShape.append(outline, false);
```

Finally, we set the clipping shape and draw a set of lines. The lines appear only inside the character boundaries.

```
g2.setClip(clipShape);
Point2D p = new Point2D.Double(0, 0);
for (int i = 0; i < NLINES; i++)
{
    double x = . . .;
    double y = . . .;
    Point2D q = new Point2D.Double(x, y);
    g2.draw(new Line2D.Double(p, q)); // lines are clipped
}
```

Here is the complete program.

Example 7–6: ClipTest.java

```
1. import java.awt.*;
2. import java.awt.event.*;
3. import java.awt.font.*;
4. import java.awt.geom.*;
5. import java.util.*;
6. import javax.swing.*;
7.
8. /**
9.    This program demonstrates the use of a clip shape.
10. */
11. public class ClipTest
12. {
13.    public static void main(String[] args)
14.    {
15.       JFrame frame = new ClipTestFrame();
16.       frame.setDefaultCloseOperation(JFrame.EXIT_ON_CLOSE);
17.       frame.show();
18.    }
19. }
20.
21. /**
22.    This frame contains radio buttons to turn a clip off
23.    and on, and a panel to draw a set of lines with or without
24.    clipping.
25. */
26. class ClipTestFrame extends JFrame
27. {
28.    public ClipTestFrame()
29.    {
```

```
30.        setTitle("ClipTest");
31.        setSize(WIDTH, HEIGHT);
32.
33.        Container contentPane = getContentPane();
34.
35.        final JCheckBox checkBox = new JCheckBox("Clip");
36.        checkBox.addActionListener(new
37.            ActionListener()
38.            {
39.                public void actionPerformed(ActionEvent event)
40.                {
41.                    panel.repaint();
42.                }
43.            });
44.        contentPane.add(checkBox, BorderLayout.NORTH);
45.
46.        panel = new
47.            JPanel()
48.            {
49.                public void paintComponent(Graphics g)
50.                {
51.                    super.paintComponent(g);
52.                    Graphics2D g2 = (Graphics2D)g;
53.
54.                    if (clipShape == null)
55.                        clipShape = makeClipShape(g2);
56.
57.                    g2.draw(clipShape);
58.
59.                    if (checkBox.isSelected())
60.                        g2.clip(clipShape);
61.
62.                    // draw line pattern
63.                    final int NLINES =50;
64.                    Point2D p = new Point2D.Double(0, 0);
65.                    for (int i = 0; i < NLINES; i++)
66.                    {
67.                        double x = (2 * getWidth() * i) / NLINES;
68.                        double y = (2 * getHeight() * (NLINES - 1 - i))
69.                            / NLINES;
70.                        Point2D q = new Point2D.Double(x, y);
71.                        g2.draw(new Line2D.Double(p, q));
72.                    }
73.                }
74.            };
75.        contentPane.add(panel, BorderLayout.CENTER);
76.    }
77.
```

```
78.    /**
79.       Makes the clip shape.
80.       @param g2 the graphics context
81.       @return the clip shape
82.    */
83.    Shape makeClipShape(Graphics2D g2)
84.    {
85.       FontRenderContext context = g2.getFontRenderContext();
86.       Font f = new Font("Serif", Font.PLAIN, 100);
87.       GeneralPath clipShape = new GeneralPath();
88.
89.       TextLayout layout = new TextLayout("Hello", f, context);
90.       AffineTransform transform
91.          = AffineTransform.getTranslateInstance(0, 100);
92.       Shape outline = layout.getOutline(transform);
93.       clipShape.append(outline, false);
94.
95.       layout = new TextLayout("World", f, context);
96.       transform
97.          = AffineTransform.getTranslateInstance(0, 200);
98.       outline = layout.getOutline(transform);
99.       clipShape.append(outline, false);
100.      return clipShape;
101.   }
102.
103.   private JPanel panel;
104.   private Shape clipShape;
105.   private static final int WIDTH = 300;
106.   private static final int HEIGHT = 300;
107. }
```

java.awt.Graphics

- void setClip(Shape s)

  sets the current clipping shape to the shape s.

- Shape getClip()

  returns the current clipping shape.

java.awt.Graphics2D

- void clip(Shape s)

  intersects the current clipping shape with the shape s.

- FontRenderContext getFontRenderContext()

  returns a font render context that is necessary for constructing
  TextLayout objects.

java.awt.font.TextLayout

- `TextLayout(String s, Font f, FontRenderContext context)`
  constructs a text layout object from a given string and font, using the font render context to obtain font properties for a particular device.
- `float getAdvance()`
  returns the width of this text layout.
- `float getAscent()`
- `float getDescent()`
  return the height of this text layout above and below the baseline.
- `float getLeading()`
  returns the distance between successive lines in the font used by this text layout.

Transparency and Composition

In the standard RGB color model, every color is described by its red, green, and blue components. However, it is also convenient to be able to describe areas of an image that are *transparent* or partially transparent. When you superimpose an image onto an existing drawing, the transparent pixels do not obscure the pixels under them at all, whereas partially transparent pixels are mixed with the pixels under them. Figure 7–23 shows the effect of overlaying a partially transparent rectangle on an image. You can still see the details of the image shine through from under the rectangle.

In the Java 2D API, transparency is described by an *alpha channel*. Each pixel has, in addition to its red, green, and blue color components, an alpha value between 0 (fully transparent) and 1 (fully opaque). For example, the rectangle in Figure 7–23 was filled with a pale yellow color with 50% transparency:

```
new Color(0.7F, 0.7F, 0.0F, 0.5F);
```

Figure 7–23: Overlaying a partially transparent rectangle on an image

Now let us look at what happens if you superimpose two shapes. You need to blend or *compose* the colors and alpha values of the source and destination pixels. Porter and Duff, two researchers in the field of computer graphics, have formulated twelve possible *composition rules* for this blending process. The Java 2D API implements eight of these rules. Before we go any further, we'd like to point out that only two of these rules have practical significance. If you find the rules arcane or confusing, just use the SRC_OVER rule. It is the default rule for a Graphics2D object, and it gives the most intuitive results.

Here is the theory behind the rules. Suppose you have a *source pixel* with alpha value a_S. In the image, there is already a *destination pixel* with alpha value a_D. You want to compose the two. The diagram in Figure 7–24 shows how to design a composition rule.

Porter and Duff consider the alpha value as the probability that the pixel color should be used. From the perspective of the source, there is a probability a_S that it wants to use the source color and a probability of $1 - a_S$ that it doesn't care. The same holds for the destination. When composing the colors, let us assume that the probabilities are independent. Then there are four cases, as shown in Figure 7–24. If the source wants to use the source color, and the destination doesn't care, then it seems reasonable to let the source have its way. That's why the upper-right corner of the diagram is labeled "S." The probability for that event is $a_S \cdot (1 - a_D)$. Similarly, the lower-left corner is labeled "D." What should one do if both destination and source would like to select their color? That's where the Porter-Duff rules come in. If we decide that the source is more important, then we label the lower-right corner with an "S" as well. That rule is called SRC_OVER. In that rule, you combine the source colors with a weight of a_S and the destination colors with a weight of $(1 - a_S) \cdot a_D$.

The visual effect is a blending of the source and destination, with preference given to the source. In particular, if a_S is 1, then the destination color is not taken into account at all. If a_S is zero, then the source pixel is completely transparent and the destination color is unchanged.

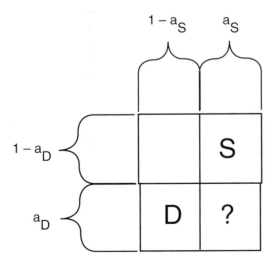

Figure 7–24: Designing a Composition Rule

There are other rules, depending on what letters you put in the boxes of the probability diagram. Table 7–1 and Figure 7–25 show all rules that are supported by the Java 2D API. The images in the figure show the results of the rules when a rectangular source region with an alpha of 0.75 is combined with an elliptical destination region with an alpha of 1.0.

Table 7–1 : The Porter-Duff Composition Rules

`CLEAR`	Source clears destination.
`SRC`	Source overwrites destination and empty pixels.
`DST`	Source does not affect destination.
`SRC_OVER`	Source blends with destination and overwrites empty pixels.
`DST_OVER`	Source does not affect destination and overwrites empty pixels.
`SRC_IN`	Source overwrites destination.
`SRC_OUT`	Source clears destination and overwrites empty pixels.
`DST_IN`	Source alpha modifies destination.
`DST_OUT`	Source alpha complement modifies destination.
`SRC_ATOP`	Source blends with destination.
`DST_ATOP`	Source alpha modifies destination. Source overwrites empty pixels.
`XOR`	Source alpha complement modifies destination. Source overwrites empty pixels.

As you can see, most of the rules aren't very useful. Consider, as an extreme case, the `DST_IN` rule. It doesn't take the source color into account at all, but it uses the alpha of the source to affect the destination. The `SRC` rule is potentially useful—it forces the source color to be used, turning off blending with the destination.

The `DST`, `SRC_ATOP`, `DST_ATOP`, and `XOR` rules have been added in SDK 1.4.

For more information on the Porter-Duff rules, see, for example, Foley, van Dam, Feiner, et al., Section 17.6.1.

You use the `setComposite` method of the `Graphics2D` class to install an object of a class that implements the `Composite` interface. The Java 2D API supplies one such class, `AlphaComposite`, that implements the eight Porter-Duff rules in Figure 7–25.

The factory method `getInstance` of the `AlphaComposite` class yields an `AlphaComposite` object. You need to supply the rule and the alpha value to be used for source pixels. For example, consider the following code.

```
int rule = AlphaComposite.SRC_OVER;
float alpha = 0.5;
g2.setComposite(AlphaComposite.getInstance(rule, alpha));
g2.setPaint(Color.blue);
g2.fill(rectangle);
```

CLEAR

SRC

DST

SRC_OVER

DST_OVER

SRC_IN

SRC_OUT

DST_IN

DST_OUT

SRC_ATOP

DST_ATOP

XOR

Figure 7–25: Porter-Duff Composition Rules

Then, the rectangle is painted with blue color and an alpha value of 0.5.
Because the composition rule is SRC_OVER, it is transparently overlaid on the
existing image.

The program in Example 7–7 lets you explore these composition rules. Pick
a rule from the combo box and use the slider to set the alpha value of the
AlphaComposite object.

Furthermore, the program displays a verbal description of each rule. Note that the
descriptions are computed from the composition rule diagrams. For example, a
"DS" in the second row stands for "blends with destination."

The program has one important twist. There is no guarantee that the graphics
context that corresponds to the screen has an alpha channel. (In fact, it generally

does not.) When pixels are deposited to a destination without an alpha channel, then the pixel colors are multiplied with the alpha value and the alpha value is discarded. Since several of the Porter-Duff rules use the alpha values of the destination, a destination alpha channel is important. For that reason, we use a buffered image with the ARGB color model to compose the shapes. After the images have been composed, we draw the resulting image to the screen.

```
BufferedImage image = new BufferedImage(getWidth(),
    getHeight(), BufferedImage.TYPE_INT_ARGB);
Graphics2D gImage = image.createGraphics();
// now draw to gImage
g2.drawImage(image, null, 0, 0);
```

Here is the complete code for the program. Figure 7–26 shows the screen display. As you run the program, move the alpha slider from left to right to see the effect on the composed shapes. In particular, note that the only difference between the DST_IN and DST_OUT rules is how the destination (!) color changes when you change the source alpha.

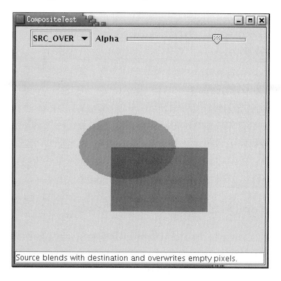

Figure 7–26: The CompositeTest program

Example 7–7: CompositeTest.java

```
1. import java.awt.*;
2. import java.awt.event.*;
3. import java.awt.image.*;
4. import java.awt.geom.*;
5. import java.util.*;
6. import javax.swing.*;
7. import javax.swing.event.*;
```

```
8.
9.  /**
10.    This program demonstrates the Porter-Duff composition rules.
11.  */
12. public class CompositeTest
13. {
14.    public static void main(String[] args)
15.    {
16.       JFrame frame = new CompositeTestFrame();
17.       frame.setDefaultCloseOperation(JFrame.EXIT_ON_CLOSE);
18.       frame.show();
19.    }
20. }
21.
22. /**
23.    This frame contains a combo box to choose a composition
24.    rule, a slider to change the source alpha channel,
25.    and a panel that shows the composition.
26. */
27. class CompositeTestFrame extends JFrame
28. {
29.    public CompositeTestFrame()
30.    {
31.       setTitle("CompositeTest");
32.       setSize(WIDTH, HEIGHT);
33.
34.       Container contentPane = getContentPane();
35.       canvas = new CompositePanel();
36.       contentPane.add(canvas, BorderLayout.CENTER);
37.
38.       ruleCombo = new JComboBox(new
39.          Object[]
40.          {
41.             new Rule("CLEAR", "   ", "   "),
42.             new Rule("SRC", " S", " S"),
43.             new Rule("DST", "   ", "DD"),
44.             new Rule("SRC_OVER", " S", "DS"),
45.             new Rule("DST_OVER", " S", "DD"),
46.             new Rule("SRC_IN", "   ", " S"),
47.             new Rule("SRC_OUT", " S", "   "),
48.             new Rule("DST_IN", "   ", " D"),
49.             new Rule("DST_OUT", "   ", "D "),
50.             new Rule("SRC_ATOP", "   ", "DS"),
51.             new Rule("DST_ATOP", " S", " D"),
52.             new Rule("XOR", " S", "D "),
53.          });
54.       ruleCombo.addActionListener(new
55.          ActionListener()
56.          {
57.             public void actionPerformed(ActionEvent event)
58.             {
```

```
59.                    Rule r = (Rule)ruleCombo.getSelectedItem();
60.                    canvas.setRule(r.getValue());
61.                    explanation.setText(r.getExplanation());
62.                 }
63.            });
64.
65.        alphaSlider = new JSlider(0, 100, 75);
66.        alphaSlider.addChangeListener(new
67.            ChangeListener()
68.            {
69.                public void stateChanged(ChangeEvent event)
70.                {
71.                    canvas.setAlpha(alphaSlider.getValue());
72.                }
73.            });
74.        JPanel panel = new JPanel();
75.        panel.add(ruleCombo);
76.        panel.add(new JLabel("Alpha"));
77.        panel.add(alphaSlider);
78.        contentPane.add(panel, BorderLayout.NORTH);
79.
80.        explanation = new JTextField();
81.        contentPane.add(explanation, BorderLayout.SOUTH);
82.
83.        canvas.setAlpha(alphaSlider.getValue());
84.        Rule r = (Rule)ruleCombo.getSelectedItem();
85.        canvas.setRule(r.getValue());
86.        explanation.setText(r.getExplanation());
87.    }
88.
89.    private CompositePanel canvas;
90.    private JComboBox ruleCombo;
91.    private JSlider alphaSlider;
92.    private JTextField explanation;
93.    private static final int WIDTH = 400;
94.    private static final int HEIGHT = 400;
95. }
96.
97. /**
98.    This class describes a Porter-Duff rule.
99. */
100. class Rule
101. {
102.    /**
103.        Constructs a Porter-Duff rule
104.        @param n the rule name
105.        @param pd1 the first row of the Porter-Duff square
106.        @param pd2 the second row of the Porter-Duff square
107.    */
108.    public Rule(String n, String pd1, String pd2)
109.    {
```

```
110.        name = n;
111.        porterDuff1 = pd1;
112.        porterDuff2 = pd2;
113.     }
114.
115.     /**
116.        Gets an explanation of the behavior of this rule.
117.        @return the explanation
118.     */
119.     public String getExplanation()
120.     {
121.        StringBuffer r = new StringBuffer("Source ");
122.        if (porterDuff2.equals("  "))
123.           r.append("clears");
124.        if (porterDuff2.equals(" S"))
125.           r.append("overwrites");
126.        if (porterDuff2.equals("DS"))
127.           r.append("blends with");
128.        if (porterDuff2.equals(" D"))
129.           r.append("alpha modifies");
130.        if (porterDuff2.equals("D "))
131.           r.append("alpha complement modifies");
132.        if (porterDuff2.equals("DD"))
133.           r.append("does not affect");
134.        r.append(" destination");
135.        if (porterDuff1.equals(" S"))
136.           r.append(" and overwrites empty pixels");
137.        r.append(".");
138.        return r.toString();
139.     }
140.
141.     public String toString()
142.     {
143.        return name;
144.     }
145.
146.     /**
147.        Gets the value of this rule in the AlphaComposite class
148.        @return the AlphaComposite constant value, or -1 if
149.        there is no matching constant.
150.     */
151.     public int getValue()
152.     {
153.        try
154.        {
155.           Integer i = (Integer)
156.              AlphaComposite.class.getField(name).get(null);
157.           return i.intValue();
158.        }
159.        catch (Exception ex)
160.        {
```

```
161.          return -1;
162.       }
163.    }
164.
165.    private String name;
166.    private String porterDuff1;
167.    private String porterDuff2;
168. }
169.
170. /**
171.    This panel draws two shapes, composed with a
172.    composition rule.
173. */
174. class CompositePanel extends JPanel
175. {
176.    public CompositePanel()
177.    {
178.       shape1 = new Ellipse2D.Double(100, 100, 150, 100);
179.       shape2 = new Rectangle2D.Double(150, 150, 150, 100);
180.    }
181.
182.    public void paintComponent(Graphics g)
183.    {
184.       super.paintComponent(g);
185.       Graphics2D g2 = (Graphics2D)g;
186.
187.       BufferedImage image = new BufferedImage(getWidth(),
188.          getHeight(), BufferedImage.TYPE_INT_ARGB);
189.       Graphics2D gImage = image.createGraphics();
190.       gImage.setPaint(Color.red);
191.       gImage.fill(shape1);
192.       AlphaComposite composite
193.          = AlphaComposite.getInstance(rule, alpha);
194.       gImage.setComposite(composite);
195.       gImage.setPaint(Color.blue);
196.       gImage.fill(shape2);
197.       g2.drawImage(image, null, 0, 0);
198.    }
199.
200.    /**
201.       Sets the composition rule.
202.       @param r the rule (as an AlphaComposite constant)
203.    */
204.    public void setRule(int r)
205.    {
206.       rule = r;
207.       repaint();
208.    }
209.
210.    /**
211.       Sets the alpha of the source
```

```
212.         @param a the alpha value between 0 and 100
213.     */
214.     public void setAlpha(int a)
215.     {
216.         alpha = (float)a / 100.0F;
217.         repaint();
218.     }
219.
220.     private int rule;
221.     private Shape shape1;
222.     private Shape shape2;
223.     private float alpha;
224. }
```

java.awt.Graphics2D

- `void setComposite(Composite s)`
  sets the composite of this graphics context to the given object that implements the `Composite` interface.

java.awt.AlphaComposite

- `static AlphaComposite getInstance(int rule)`
- `static AlphaComposite getInstance(int rule, float alpha)`
  construct an alpha composite object.

  Parameters: rule   One of CLEAR, SRC, SRC_OVER, DST_OVER, SRC_IN, SRC_OUT, DST_IN, DST_OUT

  alpha   the alpha value for the source pixels

Rendering Hints

In the preceding sections you have seen that the rendering process is quite complex. While the Java 2D API is surprisingly fast in most cases, there are cases when you would like to have control over trade-offs between speed and quality. You achieve this by setting *rendering hints*. The setRenderingHint method of the Graphics2D class lets you set a single hint. The hint keys and values are declared in the RenderingHints class. Table 7–2 summarizes the choices.

The most useful of these settings involves *antialiasing*. This is a technique to remove the "jaggies" from slanted lines and curves. As you can see in Figure 7–27, a slanted line must be drawn as a "staircase" of pixels. Especially on low-resolution screens, this can look ugly. But if, rather than drawing each pixel completely on or off, you color in the pixels that are partially covered, with the color value proportional to the area of the pixel that the line covers, then the result looks much smoother. This technique is called antialiasing. Of course, antialiasing takes a bit longer because it takes time to compute all those color values.

Table 7–2: Rendering Hints

Key	Values	Explanation
KEY_ANTIALIASING	VALUE_ANTIALIAS_ON VALUE_ANTIALIAS_OFF VALUE_ANTIALIAS_ DEFAULT	Turn antialiasing for shapes on or off.
KEY_RENDERING	VALUE_RENDER_QUALITY VALUE_RENDER_SPEED VALUE_RENDER_DEFAULT	When available, select rendering algorithms for greater quality or speed.
KEY_DITHERING	VALUE_DITHER_ENABLE VALUE_DITHER_DISABLE VALUE_DITHER_DEFAULT	Turn dithering for colors on or off. Dithering approximates color values by drawing groups of pixels of similar colors.
KEY_TEXT_ ANTIALIASING	VALUE_TEXT_ANTIALIAS_ON VALUE_TEXT_ANTIALIAS_OFF VALUE_TEXT_ANTIALIAS_ DEFAULT	Turn antialiasing for fonts on or off.

KEY_FRACTIONAL-
  METRICS
	VALUE_FRACTIONALMETRICS_ON
	VALUE_FRACTIONALMETRICS_OFF
	VALUE_FRACTIONALMETRICS_
	  DEFAULT
		Turn the computation of fractional character dimensions on or off. Fractional character dimensions lead to better placement of characters.

KEY_ALPHA_
  INTERPOLATION
	VALUE_ALPHA_INTERPOLATION_
	  QUALITY
	VALUE_ALPHA_INTERPOLATION_
	  SPEED
	VALUE_ALPHA_INTERPOLATION_
	  DEFAULT
		Turn precise computation of alpha composites on or off.

KEY_COLOR_
  RENDERING
	VALUE_COLOR_RENDER_
	  QUALITY
	VALUE_COLOR_RENDER_
	  SPEED
	VALUE_COLOR_RENDER_
	  DEFAULT
		Select quality or speed for color rendering.

KEY_INTERPOLATION	VALUE_INTERPOLATION_
	  NEAREST_NEIGHBOR
	VALUE_INTERPOLATION_
	  BILINEAR
	VALUE_INTERPOLATION_
	  BICUBIC
		Select a rule for interpolating pixels when scaling images.

KEY_STROKE_CONTROL	VALUE_STROKE_NORMALIZE VALUE_STROKE_PURE VALUE_STROKE_DEFAULT	Select a rule for combining strokes.

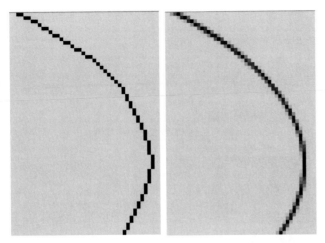

Figure 7–27: Antialiasing

For example, here is how you can request the use of antialiasing.

```
g2.setRenderingHint(RenderingHints.KEY_ANTIALIASING,
    RenderingHints.VALUE_ANTIALIAS_ON);
```

It also makes sense to use antialiasing for fonts.

```
g2.setRenderingHint(RenderingHints.KEY_TEXT_ANTIALIASING,
    RenderingHints.VALUE_TEXT_ANTIALIAS_ON);
```

The other rendering hints are not as commonly used.

You can also put a bunch of key/value hint pairs into a map and set them all at once by calling the setRenderingHints method. Any collection class implementing the map interface will do, but you may as well use the Rendering-Hints class itself. It implements the Map interface and supplies a default map implementation if you pass null to the constructor. For example,

```
RenderingHints hints = new RenderingHints(null);
hints.put(RenderingHints.KEY_ANTIALIASING,
    RenderingHints.VALUE_ANTIALIAS_ON);
hints.put(RenderingHints.KEY_TEXT_ANTIALIASING,
    RenderingHints.VALUE_TEXT_ANTIALIAS_ON);
g2.setRenderingHints(hints);
```

That is the technique that we use in Example 7–8. The program draws an image that we thought might benefit from some of the hints. You can turn various rendering hints on or off. Not all platforms support all the hints, so you should not expect every one of the settings to have an effect. On Windows 98, antialiasing smooths out the ellipse, and text antialiasing improves the look of the italic font. The other hints seemed to have no effect, but they might with other platforms or with more complex images.

Figure 7–28 shows a screen capture of the program.

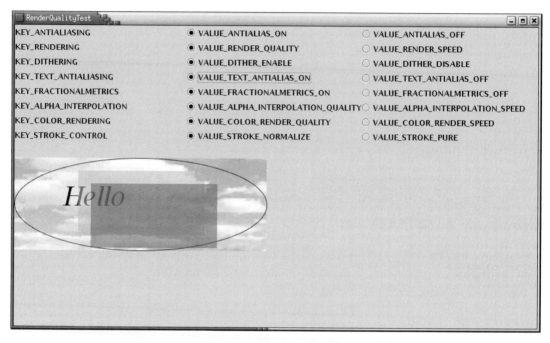

Figure 7–28: The RenderingHints program

Example 7–8: RenderQualityTest.java

```
1. import java.awt.*;
2. import java.awt.event.*;
3. import java.awt.geom.*;
4. import java.io.*;
5. import java.util.*;
6. import javax.imageio.*;
7. import javax.swing.*;
8.
9. /**
10.    This program demonstrates the effect of the various
11.    rendering hints.
12. */
13. public class RenderQualityTest
14. {
15.    public static void main(String[] args)
16.    {
17.       JFrame frame = new RenderQualityTestFrame();
18.       frame.setDefaultCloseOperation(JFrame.EXIT_ON_CLOSE);
19.       frame.show();
20.    }
21. }
22.
```

```
23. /**
24.    This frame contains buttons to set rendering hints
25.    and an image that is drawn with the selected hints.
26. */
27. class RenderQualityTestFrame extends JFrame
28. {
29.    public RenderQualityTestFrame()
30.    {
31.       setTitle("RenderQualityTest");
32.       setSize(WIDTH, HEIGHT);
33.
34.       buttonBox = new JPanel();
35.       buttonBox.setLayout(new GridLayout(9, 3));
36.       hints = new RenderingHints(null);
37.
38.       makeButtons("KEY_ANTIALIASING",
39.          "VALUE_ANTIALIAS_ON",
40.          "VALUE_ANTIALIAS_OFF");
41.       makeButtons("KEY_RENDERING",
42.          "VALUE_RENDER_QUALITY",
43.          "VALUE_RENDER_SPEED");
44.       makeButtons("KEY_DITHERING",
45.          "VALUE_DITHER_ENABLE",
46.          "VALUE_DITHER_DISABLE");
47.       makeButtons("KEY_TEXT_ANTIALIASING",
48.          "VALUE_TEXT_ANTIALIAS_ON",
49.          "VALUE_TEXT_ANTIALIAS_OFF");
50.       makeButtons("KEY_FRACTIONALMETRICS",
51.          "VALUE_FRACTIONALMETRICS_ON",
52.          "VALUE_FRACTIONALMETRICS_OFF");
53.       makeButtons("KEY_ALPHA_INTERPOLATION",
54.          "VALUE_ALPHA_INTERPOLATION_QUALITY",
55.          "VALUE_ALPHA_INTERPOLATION_SPEED");
56.       makeButtons("KEY_COLOR_RENDERING",
57.          "VALUE_COLOR_RENDER_QUALITY",
58.          "VALUE_COLOR_RENDER_SPEED");
59.       makeButtons("KEY_INTERPOLATION",
60.          "VALUE_INTERPOLATION_NEAREST NEIGHBOR",
61.          "VALUE_INTERPOLATION_BILINEAR");
62.       makeButtons("KEY_STROKE_CONTROL",
63.          "VALUE_STROKE_NORMALIZE",
64.          "VALUE_STROKE_PURE");
65.
66.       Container contentPane = getContentPane();
67.       canvas = new RenderQualityPanel();
68.       contentPane.add(canvas, BorderLayout.CENTER);
69.       contentPane.add(buttonBox, BorderLayout.NORTH);
70.    }
71.
72.    /**
73.       Makes a set of buttons for a rendering hint key and values
74.       @param key the key name
```

```
75.        @param value1 the name of the first value for the key
76.        @param value2 the name of the second value for the key
77.     */
78.    void makeButtons(String key, String value1, String value2)
79.    {
80.       try
81.       {
82.          final RenderingHints.Key k = (RenderingHints.Key)
83.             RenderingHints.class.getField(key).get(null);
84.          final Object v1
85.             = RenderingHints.class.getField(value1).get(null);
86.          final Object v2
87.             = RenderingHints.class.getField(value2).get(null);
88.          JLabel label = new JLabel(key);
89.          buttonBox.add(label);
90.          ButtonGroup group = new ButtonGroup();
91.          JRadioButton b1 = new JRadioButton(value1, true);
92.          buttonBox.add(b1);
93.          group.add(b1);
94.          b1.addActionListener(new
95.             ActionListener()
96.             {
97.                public void actionPerformed(ActionEvent event)
98.                {
99.                   hints.put(k, v1);
100.                   canvas.setRenderingHints(hints);
101.                }
102.          });
103.          JRadioButton b2 = new JRadioButton(value2, false);
104.          buttonBox.add(b2);
105.          group.add(b2);
106.          b2.addActionListener(new
107.             ActionListener()
108.             {
109.                public void actionPerformed(ActionEvent event)
110.                {
111.                   hints.put(k, v2);
112.                   canvas.setRenderingHints(hints);
113.                }
114.          });
115.          hints.put(k, v1);
116.       }
117.       catch (Exception ex)
118.       {
119.       }
120.    }
121.
122.    private RenderQualityPanel canvas;
123.    private JPanel buttonBox;
124.    private RenderingHints hints;
125.    private static final int WIDTH = 600;
126.    private static final int HEIGHT = 500;
```

```
127. }
128.
129. /**
130.    This panel produces a drawing that hopefully shows some
131.    of the difference caused by rendering hints.
132. */
133. class RenderQualityPanel extends JPanel
134. {
135.    public RenderQualityPanel()
136.    {
137.       color1 = new Color(0.7F, 0.7F, 0.0F, 0.5F);
138.       color2 = new Color(0.0F, 0.3F, 0.3F, 0.5F);
139.       try
140.       {
141.          image = ImageIO.read(new File("clouds.jpg"));
142.       }
143.       catch (IOException exception)
144.       {
145.          exception.printStackTrace();
146.       }
147.    }
148.
149.    public void paintComponent(Graphics g)
150.    {
151.       super.paintComponent(g);
152.       Graphics2D g2 = (Graphics2D)g;
153.       g2.setRenderingHints(hints);
154.
155.       g2.drawImage(image, 0, 0, null);
156.       g2.draw(new Ellipse2D.Double(0, 0,
157.          image.getWidth(null), image.getHeight(null)));
158.       g2.setFont(new Font("Serif", Font.ITALIC, 40));
159.       g2.drawString("Hello", 75, 75);
160.       g2.setPaint(color1);
161.       g2.translate(0,-80);
162.       g2.fill(new Rectangle2D.Double(100, 100, 200, 100));
163.       g2.setPaint(color2);
164.       g2.fill(new Rectangle2D.Double(120, 120, 200, 100));
165.    }
166.
167.    /**
168.       Sets the hints and repaints.
169.       @param h the rendering hints
170.    */
171.    public void setRenderingHints(RenderingHints h)
172.    {
173.       hints = h;
174.       repaint();
175.    }
176.
177.    private RenderingHints hints = new RenderingHints(null);
178.    private Color color1;
```

```
179.     private Color color2;
180.     private Image image;
181. }
```

java.awt.Graphics2D

- void setRenderingHint(RenderingHints.Key key, Object value)
  sets a rendering hint for this graphics context.
- void setRenderingHints(Map m)
  sets all rendering hints whose key/value pairs are stored in the map.

java.awt.RenderingHints

- RenderingHints(Map m)
  constructs a rendering hints map for storing rendering hints. If m is null, a default map implementation is provided.

Reading and Writing Images

Prior to version 1.4, the Java SDK had very limited capabilities for reading and writing image files. It was possible to read GIF and JPEG images, but there was no official support for writing images at all.

This situation is now much improved. SDK 1.4 introduces the javax.imageio package that contains "out of the box" support for reading and writing several common file formats, as well as a framework that enables third parties to add readers and writers for other formats. Specifically, the SDK contains readers for the GIF, JPEG, and PNG formats and writers for JPEG and PNG. (We suspect that writing GIF files is not supported due to patent issues.)

NOTE: If you use an older version of the SDK, you need to look elsewhere to write GIF and JPEG files. You can find a GIF encoder at www.acme.com/java. There is a package, com.sun.image.codec.jpeg, that is part of the SDK from Sun Microsystems and that supports saving images in JPEG format. You can find more information about this package at http://java.sun.com/products/jdk/1.2/docs/guide/2d/api-jpeg/overview-summary.html.

The basics of the library are extremely straightforward. To load an image, use the static read method of the ImageIO class:

```
File f = . . .;
BufferedImage image = ImageIO.read(f);
```

The ImageIO class picks an appropriate reader, based on the file type. It may consult the file extension and the "magic number" at the beginning of the file for that purpose. If no suitable reader can be found or the reader can't decode the file contents, then the read method returns null.

Writing an image to a file is just as simple:

```
File f = . . .;
String format = . . .;
ImageIO.write(image, format, f);
```

Here the format string is a string identifying the image format, such as "JPEG" or "PNG". The ImageIO class picks an appropriate writer and saves the file.

Obtaining Readers and Writers for Image File Types

For more advanced image reading and writing operations that go beyond the static read and write methods of the ImageIO class, you first need to get the appropriate ImageReader and ImageWriter objects. The ImageIO class enumerates readers and writers that match one of the following:

- an image format (such as "JPEG")
- a file suffix (such as "jpg")
- a MIME type (such as "image/jpeg")

NOTE: MIME is the Multipurpose Internet Mail Extensions standard. The MIME standard defines common data formats such as "image/jpeg" and "application/pdf". For an HTML version of the RFC (Request for Comments) that defines the MIME format, see http://www.oac.uci.edu/indiv/ehood/MIME.

For example, you can obtain a reader that reads JPEG files as follows:

```
ImageReader reader = null;
Iterator iter = ImageIO.getImageReadersByFormatName("JPEG");
if (iter.hasNext) reader = (ImageReader)iter.next();
```

The getImageReadersBySuffix and getImageReadersByMIMEType method enumerate readers that match a file extension or MIME type.

It is possible that the ImageIO class can locate multiple readers that can all read a particular image type. In that case, you have to pick one of them, but it isn't clear how you can decide which one is the best. To find out more information about a reader, obtain its *service provider interface*:

```
ImageReaderSpi spi = reader.getOriginatingProvider();
```

Then you can get the vendor name and version number:

```
String vendor = spi.getVendor();
String version = spi.getVersion();
```

Perhaps that information can help you to decide among the choices, or you may just present a list of readers to your program users and make them choose.

However, for now, we will assume that the first enumerated reader is at least adequate.

In the sample program at the end of this section, we have a couple of problems that the API doesn't address well. First, we want to find all file suffixes of all available readers, so that we can use them in a file filter. The `IOImage` class is willing to tell us the names of all reader formats and the names of all supported MIME types. But we can't enumerate all supported file suffixes, nor can we get all readers. So, we first enumerate all format names, then we get all readers for a given format name. An `ImageReader` won't reveal the supported file suffixes, but the associated service provider interface object does. With a couple of nested loops and the handy `addAll` method of the `Set` interface, we manage to collect all file suffixes. You can find the full code in the `getReaderSuffixes` method in Example 7–9.

For saving files, we have a similar problem. We'd like to present the user a menu of all supported image types. Unfortunately, the `getWriterFormat-Names` of the `IOImage` class returns a rather curious list with redundant names, such as

```
JPG

jpeg

jpg

PNG

JPEG

png
```

That's not something one would want to present in a menu. It would be nice if there was some notion of a "preferred" format name. To pare down the list, we pick the first format name and look up the first writer associated with it. Then we ask it what its format names are, in the hope that it will list the most popular one first. Indeed, for the JPEG writer, this works fine: It lists `"JPEG"` before the other options. The PNG writer, on the other hand, lists `"png"` in lowercase before `"PNG"`. Hopefully, that will be addressed at some time in the future. (We don't want to force the format name into uppercase—that wouldn't work for a format such as "PostScript".)

Once we pick a writer, we add the first format name to the format name set and remove all of its format names from the original set. We keep going until all format names are handled. The details are in the `getWriterFormats` method of Example 7–9. Note that this method would break down if someone would provide a single writer that can write multiple image formats.

As a practical matter, most programmers won't be bothered by these issues. If you have a fixed number of file formats that your application supports, then you can simply find the appropriate readers, writers, and file suffixes for them.

Reading and Writing Files with Multiple Images

Some files, in particular, animated GIF files, contain multiple images. The `read` method of the `ImageIO` class reads a single image. To read multiple images, turn the input source (for example, an input stream or file) into an `ImageInputStream`.

```
InputStream in = . . .;
ImageInputStream imageIn = ImageIO.createImageInputStream(in);
```

Then attach the image input stream to the reader:

```
reader.setInput(imageIn, true);
```

The second parameter indicates that the input is in "seek forward only" mode. Otherwise, random access is used, either by buffering stream input as it is read, or by using random file access. Random access is required for certain operations. For example, to find out the number of images in a GIF file, you need to read the entire file. If you then want to fetch an image, the input must be read again.

This consideration is only important if you read from a stream, and if the input contains multiple images, and the image format doesn't have the information that you request (such as the image count) in the header. If you read from a file, simply use

```
File f = . . .;
ImageInputStream imageIn = ImageIO.createImageInputStream(f);
reader.setInput(imageIn);
```

Once you have a reader, you can read the images in the input by calling

```
BufferedImage image = reader.read(index);
```

where `index` is the image index, starting with 0.

If the input is in "seek forward only" mode, you need to keep reading images until the `read` method throws an `IndexOutOfBoundsException`. Otherwise, you can call the `getNumImages` method:

```
int n = reader.getNumImages(true);
```

Here, the parameter indicates that you allow a search of the input to determine the number of images. That method throws an `IllegalStateException` if the input is in "seek forward only" mode. Alternatively, you can set the "allow search" parameter to `false`. Then the `getNumImages` method returns –1 if it can't determine the number of images without a search. In that case, you'll have to switch to Plan B and keep reading images until you get an `IndexOutOfBoundsException`.

Some files contain thumbnails, smaller versions of an image for preview purposes. You can get the number of thumbnails of an image with the call

```
int count = reader.getNumThumbnails(index);
```

Then you get a particular index as

```
BufferedImage thumbnail = reader.getThumbnail(index,
    thumbnailIndex);
```

Another consideration is that you sometimes want to get the image size before actually getting the image, in particular, if the image comes from a slow network connection. Use the calls

```
int width = reader.getWidth(index);
int height = reader.getHeight(index);
```

to get the dimensions of an image with a given index. The image dimensions should be available before the actual image data. If there is no image with the given index, the methods throw an `IndexOutOfBoundsException`.

To write a file with multiple images, you first need an `ImageWriter`. The `IOImage` class can enumerate the writers that are capable of writing a particular image format:

```
String format = . . .;
ImageWriter writer = null;
Iterator iter = IOImage.getImageWritersByFormatName(format);
if (iter.hasNext()) writer = (ImageWriter)iter.next();
```

Next, turn an output stream or file into an `ImageOutputStream` and attach it to the writer. For example,

```
File f = . . .;
ImageOutputStream imageOut = ImageIO.createImageOutputStream(f);
writer.setOutput(imageOut);
```

You need to wrap each image into an `IIOImage` object. You can optionally supply a list of thumbnails and image metadata (such as compression algorithms and color information). In this example, we just use `null` for both; see the SDK documentation for additional information.

```
IIOImage iioImage = new IIOImage(images[i], null, null);
```

Write out the *first* image using the `write` method:

```
writer.write(new IIOImage(images[0], null, null));
```

For subsequent images, use

```
if (writer.canInsertImage(i))
    writer.writeInsert(i, iioImage, null);
```

The third parameter can contain an `ImageWriteParam` object to set image writing details such as tiling and compression; use `null` for default values.

Not all file formats can handle multiple images. In that case, the `canInsert-Image` method returns `false` for `i > 0`, and only a single image is saved.

The program in Example 7–9 lets you load and save files in the formats for which the SDK supplies readers and writers. The program displays multiple images (see Figure 7–29), but not thumbnails.

Figure 7–29: An Animated GIF Image

Example 7–9: ImageIOTest.java

```
1. import java.awt.*;
2. import java.awt.event.*;
3. import java.awt.image.*;
4. import java.io.*;
5. import java.util.*;
6. import java.util.List;
7. import javax.imageio.*;
8. import javax.imageio.stream.*;
9. import javax.swing.*;
10.
11. /**
12.    This program lets you read and write image files in the
13.    formats that the SDK supports. Multi-file images are
14.    supported.
15. */
16. public class ImageIOTest
17. {
18.    public static void main(String[] args)
19.    {
```

```
20.       JFrame frame = new ImageIOFrame();
21.       frame.setDefaultCloseOperation(JFrame.EXIT_ON_CLOSE);
22.       frame.show();
23.    }
24. }
25.
26. /**
27.    This frame displays the loaded images. The menu has items
28.    for loading and saving files.
29. */
30. class ImageIOFrame extends JFrame
31. {
32.    public ImageIOFrame()
33.    {
34.       setTitle("ImageIOTest");
35.       setSize(WIDTH, HEIGHT);
36.
37.       JMenu fileMenu = new JMenu("File");
38.       JMenuItem openItem = new JMenuItem("Open");
39.       openItem.addActionListener(new
40.          ActionListener()
41.          {
42.             public void actionPerformed(ActionEvent event)
43.             {
44.                openFile();
45.             }
46.          });
47.       fileMenu.add(openItem);
48.
49.       JMenu saveMenu = new JMenu("Save");
50.       fileMenu.add(saveMenu);
51.       Iterator iter = writerFormats.iterator();
52.       while (iter.hasNext())
53.       {
54.          final String formatName = (String)iter.next();
55.          JMenuItem formatItem = new JMenuItem(formatName);
56.          saveMenu.add(formatItem);
57.          formatItem.addActionListener(new
58.             ActionListener()
59.             {
60.                public void actionPerformed(ActionEvent event)
61.                {
62.                   saveFile(formatName);
63.                }
64.             });
65.       }
66.
```

```
67.    JMenuItem exitItem = new JMenuItem("Exit");
68.    exitItem.addActionListener(new
69.       ActionListener()
70.       {
71.          public void actionPerformed(ActionEvent event)
72.          {
73.             System.exit(0);
74.          }
75.       });
76.    fileMenu.add(exitItem);
77.
78.
79.    JMenuBar menuBar = new JMenuBar();
80.    menuBar.add(fileMenu);
81.    setJMenuBar(menuBar);
82. }
83.
84. /**
85.    Open a file and load the images.
86. */
87. public void openFile()
88. {
89.    JFileChooser chooser = new JFileChooser();
90.    chooser.setCurrentDirectory(new File("."));
91.
92.    chooser.setFileFilter(new
93.       javax.swing.filechooser.FileFilter()
94.       {
95.          public boolean accept(File f)
96.          {
97.             if (f.isDirectory()) return true;
98.             String name = f.getName();
99.             int p = name.lastIndexOf('.');
100.            if (p == -1) return false;
101.            String suffix
102.               = name.substring(p + 1).toLowerCase();
103.            return readerSuffixes.contains(suffix);
104.         }
105.         public String getDescription()
106.         {
107.            return "Image files";
108.         }
109.      });
110.   int r = chooser.showOpenDialog(this);
111.   if (r != JFileChooser.APPROVE_OPTION) return;
112.   File f = chooser.getSelectedFile();
113.   Box box = Box.createVerticalBox();
```

```
114.        try
115.        {
116.            String name = f.getName();
117.            String suffix
118.                = name.substring(name.lastIndexOf('.') + 1);
119.            Iterator iter
120.                = ImageIO.getImageReadersByFormatName(suffix);
121.            ImageReader reader = (ImageReader)iter.next();
122.            ImageInputStream imageIn
123.                = ImageIO.createImageInputStream(f);
124.            reader.setInput(imageIn);
125.            int count = reader.getNumImages(true);
126.            images = new BufferedImage[count];
127.            for (int i = 0; i < count; i++)
128.            {
129.                images[i] = reader.read(i);
130.                box.add(new JLabel(new ImageIcon(images[i])));
131.            }
132.        }
133.        catch (IOException exception)
134.        {
135.            JOptionPane.showMessageDialog(this, exception);
136.        }
137.        setContentPane(new JScrollPane(box));
138.        validate();
139.    }
140.
141.    /**
142.        Save the current image in a file
143.        @param formatName the file format
144.    */
145.    public void saveFile(final String formatName)
146.    {
147.        if (images == null) return;
148.        Iterator iter = ImageIO.getImageWritersByFormatName(
149.            formatName);
150.        ImageWriter writer = (ImageWriter)iter.next();
151.        final List writerSuffixes = Arrays.asList(
152.            writer.getOriginatingProvider().getFileSuffixes());
153.        JFileChooser chooser = new JFileChooser();
154.        chooser.setCurrentDirectory(new File("."));
155.
156.        chooser.setFileFilter(new
157.            javax.swing.filechooser.FileFilter()
158.            {
159.                public boolean accept(File f)
160.                {
```

```
161.            if (f.isDirectory()) return true;
162.            String name = f.getName();
163.            int p = name.lastIndexOf('.');
164.            if (p == -1) return false;
165.            String suffix
166.               = name.substring(p + 1).toLowerCase();
167.            return writerSuffixes.contains(suffix);
168.         }
169.         public String getDescription()
170.         {
171.            return formatName + " files";
172.         }
173.      });

175.      int r = chooser.showSaveDialog(this);
176.      if (r != JFileChooser.APPROVE_OPTION) return;
177.      File f = chooser.getSelectedFile();
178.      try
179.      {
180.         ImageOutputStream imageOut
181.            = ImageIO.createImageOutputStream(f);
182.         writer.setOutput(imageOut);

184.         writer.write(new IIOImage(images[0], null, null));
185.         for (int i = 1; i < images.length; i++)
186.         {
187.            IIOImage iioImage
188.               = new IIOImage(images[i], null, null);
189.            if (writer.canInsertImage(i))
190.               writer.writeInsert(i, iioImage, null);
191.         }
192.      }
193.      catch (IOException exception)
194.      {
195.         JOptionPane.showMessageDialog(this, exception);
196.      }
197.   }

199.   /**
200.      Gets a set of all file suffixes that are recognized
201.      by image readers.
202.      @return the file suffix set
203.   */
204.   public static Set getReaderSuffixes()
205.   {
206.      TreeSet readerSuffixes = new TreeSet();
207.      String[] informalNames = ImageIO.getReaderFormatNames();
```

```
208.       for (int i = 0; i < informalNames.length; i++)
209.       {
210.          Iterator iter = ImageIO.getImageReadersByFormatName(
211.             informalNames[i]);
212.          while (iter.hasNext())
213.          {
214.             ImageReader reader = (ImageReader)iter.next();
215.             String[] s = reader.getOriginatingProvider()
216.                .getFileSuffixes();
217.             readerSuffixes.addAll(Arrays.asList(s));
218.          }
219.       }
220.       return readerSuffixes;
221.    }
222.
223.    /**
224.       Gets a set of "preferred" format names of all
225.       image writers. The preferred format name is the first
226.       format name that a writer specifies.
227.       @return the format name set
228.    */
229.    public static Set getWriterFormats()
230.    {
231.       TreeSet writerFormats = new TreeSet();
232.       TreeSet formatNames = new TreeSet(Arrays.asList(
233.          ImageIO.getWriterFormatNames()));
234.       while (formatNames.size() > 0)
235.       {
236.          String name = (String)formatNames.iterator().next();
237.          Iterator iter = ImageIO.getImageWritersByFormatName(
238.             name);
239.          ImageWriter writer = (ImageWriter)iter.next();
240.          String[] names = writer.getOriginatingProvider()
241.             .getFormatNames();
242.          writerFormats.add(names[0]);
243.          formatNames.removeAll(Arrays.asList(names));
244.       }
245.       return writerFormats;
246.    }
247.
248.    private BufferedImage[] images;
249.    private static Set readerSuffixes = getReaderSuffixes();
250.    private static Set writerFormats = getWriterFormats();
251.    private static final int WIDTH = 400;
252.    private static final int HEIGHT = 400;
253. }
```

javax.imageio.ImageIO

- `static BufferedImage read(File input)`
- `static BufferedImage read(InputStream input)`
- `static BufferedImage read(URL input)`

  read an image from `input`.

- `static boolean write(RenderedImage image, String formatName, File output)`
- `static boolean write(RenderedImage image, String formatName, OutputStream output)`

  write an image in the given format to `output`. Returns `false` if no appropriate writer was found.

- `static Iterator getImageReadersByFormatName(String formatName)`
- `static Iterator getImageReadersBySuffix(String fileSuffix)`
- `static Iterator getImageReadersByMIMEType(String mimeType)`
- `static Iterator getImageWritersByFormatName(String formatName)`
- `static Iterator getImageWritersBySuffix(String fileSuffix)`
- `static Iterator getImageWritersByMIMEType(String mimeType)`

  get all readers and writers that are able to handle the given format (e.g. "JPEG", file suffix (e.g. "jpg"), or MIME type (e.g. "image/jpeg").

- `static String[] getReaderFormatNames()`
- `static String[] getReaderMIMETypes()`
- `static String[] getWriterFormatNames()`
- `static String[] getWriterMIMETypes()`

  get all format names and MIME type names supported by readers and writers.

- `ImageInputStream createImageInputStream(Object input)`
- `ImageOutputStream createImageOutputStream(Object output)`

  create an image input or image output stream from the given object. The object can be a file, a stream, a `RandomAccessFile`, or another object for which a service provider exists. Return `null` if no registered service provider can handle the object.

javax.imageio.ImageReader

- `void setInput(Object input)`
- `void setInput(Object input, boolean seekForwardOnly)`

  set the input source of the reader.

<table>
<tr><td>*Parameters:*</td><td>input</td><td>an <code>ImageInputStream</code> object, or another object that this reader can accept.</td></tr>
<tr><td></td><td>seekForwardOnly</td><td>true if the reader should read forward only. By default, the reader uses random access and, if necessary, buffers image data.</td></tr>
</table>

- <code>BufferedImage read(int index)</code>

  reads the image with the given image index (starting at 0). Throws an <code>IndexOutOfBoundsException</code> if no such image is available.

- <code>int getNumImages(boolean allowSearch)</code>

  gets the number of images in this reader. If <code>allowSearch</code> is <code>false</code>, and the number of images cannot be determined without reading forward, then <code>-1</code> is returned. If <code>allowSearch</code> is <code>true</code> and the reader is in "seek forward only" mode, an <code>IllegalStateException</code> is thrown.

- <code>int getNumThumbnails(int index)</code>

  gets the number of thumbnails of the image with the given index.

- <code>BufferedImage readThumbnail(int index, int thumbnailIndex)</code>

  gets the thumbnail with index <code>thumbnailIndex</code> of the image with the given index.

- <code>int getWidth(int index)</code>
- <code>int getHeight(int index)</code>

  get the image width and height. Throw an <code>IndexOutOfBoundsException</code> if no such image is available.

- <code>ImageReaderSpi getOriginatingProvider()</code>

  gets the service provider that constructed this reader.

 javax.imageio.spi.IIOServiceProvider

- <code>String getVendorName()</code>
- <code>String getVersion()</code>

  get the vendor name and version of this service provider.

 javax.imageio.spi.ImageReaderWriterSpi

- <code>String[] getFormatNames()</code>
- <code>String[] getFileSuffixes()</code>
- <code>String[] getMIMETypes()</code>

  get the format names, file suffixes, and MIME types supported by the readers or writers that this service provider creates.

javax.imageio.ImageWriter

- void setOutput(Object output)

    Parameters: output   an ImageOutputStream object, or another object that this writer can accept

- void write(IIOImage image)
- void write(RenderedImage image)

    write a single image to the output.

- void writeInsert(int index, IIOImage image, ImageWriteParam param)

    write an image into a multi-image file.

    Parameters: index   the image index

                        image   the image to write

                        param   the write parameters, or null

- boolean canInsertImage(int index)

    returns true if it is possible to insert an image at the given index.

- ImageWriterSpi getOriginatingProvider()

    gets the service provider that constructed this writer.

javax.imageio.IIOImage

- IIOImage(RenderedImage image, List thumbnails, IIOMetadata metadata)

    constructs an IIOImage from an image, optional thumbnails and optional metadata.

    Parameters: image   an image

                        thumbnails a list of BufferedImage objects, or null

                        metadata   metadata, or null

Image Manipulation

Suppose you have an image and you would like to improve its appearance. You then need to access the individual pixels of the image and replace them with other pixels. Or perhaps you want to compute the pixels of an image from scratch, for example, to show the result of physical measurements or a mathematical computation. The BufferedImage class gives you control over the pixels in an image, and classes that implement the BufferedImageOp interface let you transform images.

This is a major change from the image support in JDK 1.0. At that time, the image classes were optimized to support *incremental rendering*. The original purpose of the classes was to render GIF and JPEG images that are down-loaded from the web, a scan line at a time, as soon as partial image data is available. In fact, scan lines can be *interlaced,* with all even scan lines coming first, followed by the odd scan lines. That mechanism lets a browser display an approximation of the image quickly while fetching the remainder of the image data. The `ImageProducer`, `ImageFilter`, and `ImageConsumer` interfaces in JDK 1.0 expose all the complexities of incremental rendering. Writing an image manipulation that fit well into that framework was quite complex.

Fortunately, the need for using these classes has completely gone away. The Java 2 platform replaces the "push model" of JDK 1.0 with a "direct" model that lets you access pixels directly and conveniently. We cover only the direct model in this chapter. The only disadvantage of the direct model is that it requires all image pixels to be in memory. (In practice, the "push model" had the same restriction. It would have required fiendish cunning to write image manipulation algorithms that processed pixels as they became available. Most users of the old model simply buffered the entire image before processing it.) Future versions of the Java platform may support a "pull" model where a processing pipeline can reduce memory consumption and increase speed by fetching and processing pixels only when they are actually needed.

Accessing Image Data

Most of the images that you manipulate are simply read in from an image file—they were either produced by a device such as a digital camera or scan-ner, or constructed by a drawing program. In this section, we will show you a different technique for constructing an image, namely, to build up an image a pixel at a time.

To create an image, construct a `BufferedImage` object in the usual way.

```
image = new BufferedImage(width, height,
   BufferedImage.TYPE_INT_ARGB);
```

Now, call the `getRaster` method to obtain an object of type `WritableRaster`. You use this object to access and modify the pixels of the image.

```
WritableRaster raster = image.getRaster();
```

The `setPixel` method lets you set an individual pixel. The complexity here is that you can't simply set the pixel to a `Color` value. You must know how the buffered image specifies color values. That depends on the *type* of the image. If your image has a type of `TYPE_INT_ARGB`, then each pixel is described by four values, for red, green, blue, and alpha, each of which is between 0 and 255. You need to supply them in an array of four integers.

```
int[] black = { 0, 0, 0, 255 };
raster.setPixel(i, j, black);
```

In the lingo of the Java 2D API, these values are called the *sample values* of the pixel.

CAUTION: There are also `setPixel` methods that take array parameters of types `float[]` and `double[]`. However, the values that you need to place into these arrays are *not* normalized color values between 0.0 and 1.0.

```
float[] red = { 1.0F, 0.0F, 0.0F, 1.0F };
raster.setPixel(i, j, red); // ERROR
```

You need to supply values between 0 and 255, no matter what the type of the array is.

You can supply batches of pixels with the `setPixels` method. Specify the starting pixel position and the width and height of the rectangle that you want to set. Then, supply an array that contains the sample values for all pixels. For example, if your buffered image has a type of `TYPE_INT_ARGB`, then you supply the red, green, blue, and alpha value of the first pixel, then the red, green, blue, and alpha value for the second pixel, and so on.

```
int[] pixels = new int[4 * width * height];
pixels[0] = . . . // red value for first pixel
pixels[1] = . . . // green value for first pixel
pixels[2] = . . . // blue value for first pixel
pixels[3] = . . . // alpha value for first pixel
. . .
raster.setPixels(x, y, width, height, pixels);
```

Conversely, to read a pixel, you use the `getPixel` method. Supply an array of four integers to hold the sample values.

```
int[] sample = new int[4];
raster.getPixel(x, y, sample);
Color c = new Color(sample[0], sample[1], sample[2], sample[3]);
```

You can read multiple pixels with the `getPixels` method.

```
raster.getPixels(x, y, width, height, samples);
```

If you use an image type other than `TYPE_INT_ARGB` and you know how that type represents pixel values, then you can still use the `getPixel`/`setPixel` methods. However, you have to know the encoding of the sample values in the particular image type.

If you need to manipulate an image with an arbitrary, unknown image type, then you have to work a bit harder. Every image type has a *color model* that can translate between sample value arrays and the standard RGB color model.

NOTE: The RGB color model isn't as standard as you might think. The exact look of a color value depends on the characteristics of the imaging device. Digital cameras, scanners, monitors, and LCD displays all have their own idiosyncrasies. As a result, the same RGB value can look quite different on different devices. The International Color Consortium (www.color.org) recommends that all color data be accompanied by an *ICC profile* that specifies how the colors map to a standard form such as the 1931 CIE XYZ color specification. That specification was designed by the Commission Internationale de l'Eclairage or CIE (www.cie.co.at/cie), the international organization in charge of providing technical guidance in all matters of illumination and color. The specification is a standard method for representing all colors that the human eye can perceive as a triple of coordinates called X, Y, Z. (See, for example, Foley, van Dam, Feiner, et al., Chapter 13, for more information on the 1931 CIE XYZ specification.) However, ICC profiles are complex. A simpler proposed standard, called sRGB (http://www.w3.org/Graphics/Color/sRGB.html), specifies an exact mapping between RGB values and the 1931 CIE XYZ values that was designed to work well with typical color monitors. The Java 2D API uses that mapping when converting between RGB and other color spaces.

The `getColorModel` method returns the color model.

```
ColorModel model = image.getColorModel();
```

To find the color value of a pixel, you call the `getDataElements` method of the `Raster` class. That call returns an `Object` that contains a color-model-specific description of the color value.

```
Object data = raster.getDataElements(x, y, null);
```

NOTE: The object that is returned by the `getDataElements` method is actually an array of sample values. You don't need to know this to process the object, but it explains why the method is called `getDataElements`.

The color model can translate the object to standard ARGB values. The `getRGB` method returns an `int` value that has the alpha, red, green, and blue values packed in four blocks of 8 bits each. You can construct a `Color` value out of that integer with the `Color(int argb, boolean hasAlpha)` constructor.

```
int argb = model.getRGB(data);
Color color = new Color(argb, true);
```

When you want to set a pixel to a particular color, you have to reverse these steps. The `getRGB` method of the `Color` class yields an `int` value with the alpha, red, green, and blue values. Supply that value to the `getDataElements` method of the `ColorModel` class. The return value is an `Object` that contains the color-model-specific description of the color value. Pass the object to the `setDataElements` method of the `WritableRaster` class.

```
int argb = color.getRGB();
Object data = model.getDataElements(argb, null);
raster.setDataElements(x, y, data);
```

To illustrate how to use these methods to build an image from individual pixels, we bow to tradition and draw a Mandelbrot set, as shown in Figure 7–30.

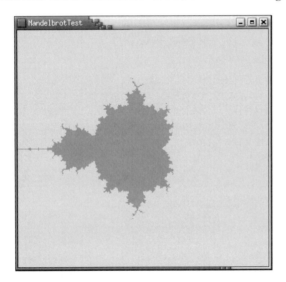

Figure 7–30: A Mandelbrot set

The idea of the Mandelbrot set is that you associate with each point in the plane a sequence of numbers. If that sequence stays bounded, you color the point. If it "escapes to infinity," you leave it transparent. The formulas for the number sequences come ultimately from the mathematics of complex numbers. We just take them for granted. For more on the mathematics of fractals, there are hundreds of books out there; one that is quite thick and comprehensive is *Chaos and Fractals: New Frontiers of Science* by Heinz-Otto Peitgen, Dietmar Saupe, and Hartmut Jurgens [Springer Verlag 1992].

Here is how you can construct the simplest Mandelbrot set. For each point (a,b), you look at sequences that start with $(x, y) = (0, 0)$ and iterate:

$$x_{new} = x^2 - y^2 + a$$
$$y_{new} = 2 \cdot x \cdot y + b$$

Check whether the sequence stays bounded or "escapes to infinity," that is, whether x and y keep getting larger. It turns out that if x or y ever get larger than

2, then the sequence escapes to infinity. Only the pixels that correspond to points (a,b) leading to a bounded sequence are colored.

Example 7–10 shows the code. In this program, we demonstrate how to use the ColorModel class for translating Color values into pixel data. That process is independent of the image type. Just for fun, change the color type of the buffered image to TYPE_BYTE_GRAY. You don't need to change any other code—the color model of the image automatically takes care of the conversion from colors to sample values.

Example 7–10: MandelbrotTest.java

```
1. import java.awt.*;
2. import java.awt.event.*;
3. import java.awt.image.*;
4. import javax.swing.*;
5.
6. /**
7.    This program demonstrates how to build up an image from
8.    individual pixels.
9. */
10. public class MandelbrotTest
11. {
12.    public static void main(String[] args)
13.    {
14.       JFrame frame = new MandelbrotFrame();
15.       frame.setDefaultCloseOperation(JFrame.EXIT_ON_CLOSE);
16.       frame.show();
17.    }
18. }
19.
20. /**
21.    This frame shows an image with a Mandelbrot set.
22. */
23. class MandelbrotFrame extends JFrame
24. {
25.    public MandelbrotFrame()
26.    {
27.       setTitle("MandelbrotTest");
28.       setSize(WIDTH, HEIGHT);
29.       BufferedImage image = makeMandelbrot(WIDTH, HEIGHT);
30.       getContentPane().add(new JLabel(new ImageIcon(image)),
31.          BorderLayout.CENTER);
32.    }
33.
34.    /**
35.       Makes the Mandelbrot image.
36.       @param width the width
37.       @parah height the height
```

```
38.        @return the image
39.     */
40.     public BufferedImage makeMandelbrot(int width, int height)
41.     {
42.        BufferedImage image = new BufferedImage(width, height,
43.           BufferedImage.TYPE_INT_ARGB);
44.        WritableRaster raster = image.getRaster();
45.        ColorModel model = image.getColorModel();
46.
47.        Color fractalColor = Color.red;
48.        int argb = fractalColor.getRGB();
49.        Object colorData = model.getDataElements(argb, null);
50.
51.        for (int i = 0; i < width; i++)
52.           for (int j = 0; j < height; j++)
53.           {
54.              double a = XMIN + i * (XMAX - XMIN) / width;
55.              double b = YMIN + j * (YMAX - YMIN) / height;
56.              if (!escapesToInfinity(a, b))
57.                 raster.setDataElements(i, j, colorData);
58.           }
59.        return image;
60.     }
61.
62.     private boolean escapesToInfinity(double a, double b)
63.     {
64.        double x = 0.0;
65.        double y = 0.0;
66.        int iterations = 0;
67.        do
68.        {
69.           double xnew = x * x - y * y + a;
70.           double ynew = 2 * x * y + b;
71.           x = xnew;
72.           y = ynew;
73.           iterations++;
74.           if (iterations == MAX_ITERATIONS) return false;
75.        }
76.        while (x <= 2 && y <= 2);
77.        return true;
78.     }
79.
80.     private static final double XMIN = -2;
81.     private static final double XMAX = 2;
82.     private static final double YMIN = -2;
83.     private static final double YMAX = 2;
84.     private static final int MAX_ITERATIONS = 16;
85.     private static final int WIDTH = 400;
86.     private static final int HEIGHT = 400;
87. }
```

java.awt.image.BufferedImage

- `BufferedImage(int width, int height, int imageType)`
  constructs a buffered image object.

  Parameters: width, height   the image dimensions

  imageType   a type such as `TYPE_INT_RGB`, `TYPE_INT_ARGB`, `TYPE_BYTE_GRAY`, `TYPE_BYTE_INDEXED`, `TYPE_USHORT_555_RGB`, and so on

- `ColorModel getColorModel()`
  returns the color model of this buffered image.

- `WritableRaster getRaster()`
  gets the raster for accessing and modifying pixels of this buffered image.

java.awt.image.Raster

- `Object getDataElements(int x, int y, Object data)`
  returns the sample data for a raster point, in an array whose element type and length depends on the color model. If `data` is not `null`, it is assumed to be an array that is appropriate for holding sample data, and it is filled. If `data` is `null`, a new array is allocated.

  Parameters: x, y   the pixel location

  data   `null` or an array that is suitable for being filled with the sample data for a pixel. Its element type and length depend on the color model.

- `int[] getPixel(int x, int y, int w, int h, int[] sampleValues)`
- `float[] getPixel(int x, int y, int w, int h, float[] sampleValues)`
- `double[] getPixel(int x, int y, int w, int h, double[] sampleValues)`
- `int[] getPixels(int x, int y, int w, int h, int[] sampleValues)`
- `float[] getPixels(int x, int y, int w, int h, float[] sampleValues)`
- `double[] getPixels(int x, int y, int w, int h, double[] sampleValues)`

  return the sample values for a raster point, or a rectangle of raster points, in an array whose length depends on the color model. If `sampleValues` is not `null`, it is assumed to be sufficiently long for holding the sample values and it is filled. If `sampleValues` is `null`, a new array is allocated. These methods are only useful if you know the meaning of the sample values for a color model.

  Parameters: x, y   the raster point location, or the top-left corner of the rectangle

  w, h   the width and height of the rectangle of raster points

  sampleValues   `null` or an array that is sufficiently long to be filled with the sample values

`java.awt.image.WritableRaster`

- void setDataElements(int x, int y, Object data)
  sets the sample data for a raster point.

  Parameters: x, y   the pixel location.

                 data   an array filled with the sample data for a pixel. Its element type and length depend on the color model.

- void setPixel(int x, int y, int w, int h, int[] sampleValues)
- void setPixel(int x, int y, int w, int h, float[] sampleValues)
- void setPixel(int x, int y, int w, int h, double[] sampleValues)
- void setPixels(int x, int y, int w, int h, int[] sampleValues)
- void setPixels(int x, int y, int w, int h, float[] sampleValues)
- void setPixels(int x, int y, int w, int h, double[] sampleValues)
  set the sample values for a raster point or a rectangle of raster points. These methods are only useful if you know the encoding of the sample values for a color model.

  Parameters: x, y   the raster point location, or the top-left corner of the rectangle.

                 w, h   the width and height of the rectangle of raster points.

                 sampleValues   an array filled with the sample data. Its element type and length depend on the color model.

`java.awt.image.ColorModel`

- int getRGB(Object data)
  returns the ARGB value that corresponds to the sample data passed in data.

  Parameters: data   an array filled with the sample data for a pixel. Its element type and length depend on the color model.

- Object getDataElements(int argb, Object data);
  returns the sample data for a color value. If data is not null, it is assumed to be an array that is appropriate for holding sample data, and it is filled. If data is null, a new array is allocated.

  Parameters: argb   the color value.

                 data   null or an array that is suitable for being filled with the sample data for a color value. Its element type and length depend on the color model.

java.awt.Color

- Color(int argb, boolean hasAlpha)

  creates a color with the specified combined ARGB value if hasAlpha is true, or the specified RGB value if hasAlpha is false.

- int getRGB()

  returns the ARGB color value corresponding to this color.

Filtering Images

In the preceding section, you saw how to build up an image from scratch. However, often you want to access image data for a different reason: you already have an image and you want to improve it in some way.

Of course, you can use the getPixel/getDataElements methods that you saw in the preceding section to read the image data, manipulate them, and then write them back. But fortunately, Java 2 technology already supplies a number of *filters* that carry out common image processing operations for you.

The image manipulations all implement the BufferedImageOp interface. After you construct the operation, you simply call the filter method to transform an image into another.

```
BufferedImageOp op = . . .;
BufferedImage filteredImage
   = new BufferedImage(image.getWidth(), image.getHeight(),
       image.getType());
op.filter(image, filteredImage);
```

Some operations can transform an image in place (op.filter(image, image)), but most can't.

There are five classes that implement the BufferedImageOp interface:

```
AffineTransformOp
RescaleOp
LookupOp
ColorConvertOp
ConvolveOp
```

The AffineTransformOp carries out an affine transformation on the pixels. For example, here is how you can rotate an image about its center.

```
AffineTransform transform
   = AffineTransform.getRotateInstance(Math.toRadians(angle),
       image.getWidth() / 2, image.getHeight() / 2);
AffineTransformOp op
   = new AffineTransformOp(transform, interpolation);
op.filter(image, filteredImage);
```

The `AffineTransformOp` constructor requires an affine transform and an *interpolation* strategy. Interpolation is necessary to determine pixels in the target image if the source pixels are transformed somewhere between target pixels. For example, if you rotate source pixels, then they will generally not fall exactly onto target pixels. There are two interpolation strategies: `AffineTransformOp.TYPE_BILINEAR` and `AffineTransformOp.TYPE_NEAREST_NEIGHBOR`. Bilinear interpolation takes a bit longer but looks better.

The program in Example 7–11 lets you rotate an image by 5 degrees (see Figure 7–31).

Figure 7–31: A rotated image

The `RescaleOp` carries out a rescaling operation

$$x_{\text{new}} = a \cdot x + b$$

for all sample values x in the image. Sample values that are too large or small after the rescaling are set to the largest or smallest legal value. If the image is in ARGB format, the scaling is carried out separately for the red, green, and blue values, but not for the alpha values. The effect of rescaling with $a > 1$ is to brighten the image. You construct the `RescaleOp` by specifying the scaling parameters and optional rendering hints. In Example 7–11, we use

```
float a = 1.5f;
float b = -20.0f;
RescaleOp op = new RescaleOp(a, b, null);
```

The `LookupOp` operation lets you specify an arbitrary mapping of sample values. You supply a table that specifies how each value should be mapped. In the example program, we compute the *negative* of all colors, changing the color c to $255 - c$.

The `LookupOp` constructor requires an object of type `LookupTable` and a map
of optional hints. The `LookupTable` class is abstract. There are two concrete subclasses: `ByteLookupTable` and `ShortLookupTable`. Since RGB color values are bytes, we use the `ByteLookupTable`. You construct such a table

from an array of bytes and an integer offset into that array. Here is how we construct the LookupOp for the example program.

```
byte negative[] = new byte[256];
for (int i = 0; i < 256; i++)
   negative[i] = (byte)(255 - i);
ByteLookupTable table = new ByteLookupTable(0, negative);
LookupOp op = new LookupOp(table, null);
```

The lookup is applied to each color value separately, but not to the alpha value.

> NOTE: You cannot apply a LookupOp to an image with an indexed color model. (In those images, each sample value is an offset into a color palette).

The ColorConvertOp is useful for color space conversions. We do not discuss it here.

The most powerful of the transformations is the ConvolveOp, which carries out a mathematical *convolution*. We do not want to get too deeply into the mathematical details of convolution, but the basic idea is simple. Consider, for example, the *blur filter* (see Figure 7–32).

Figure 7–32: Blurring an image

The blurring is achieved by replacing each pixel with the *average* value from the pixel and its eight neighbors. Intuitively, it makes sense why this operation would blur out the picture. Mathematically, the averaging can be expressed as a convolution operation with the following *kernel:*

$$\begin{bmatrix} \frac{1}{9} & \frac{1}{9} & \frac{1}{9} \\ \frac{1}{9} & \frac{1}{9} & \frac{1}{9} \\ \frac{1}{9} & \frac{1}{9} & \frac{1}{9} \end{bmatrix}$$

The kernel of a convolution is a matrix that tells what weights should be applied to the neighboring values. The kernel above leads to a blurred image. A different kernel

$$\begin{bmatrix} 0 & -1 & 0 \\ -1 & 4 & -1 \\ 0 & -1 & 0 \end{bmatrix}$$

carries out *edge detection,* locating areas of color changes (see Figure 7–33). Edge detection is an important technique for analyzing photographic images.

Figure 7–33: Edge detection

To construct a convolution operation, you first set up an array of the values for the kernel and construct a `Kernel` object. Then, construct a `ConvolveOp` object from the kernel and use it for filtering.

```
float[] elements =
    {
        0.0f, -1.0f, 0.0f,
        -1.0f,  4.f, -1.0f,
        0.0f, -1.0f, 0.0f
    };
Kernel kernel = new Kernel(3, 3, elements);
ConvolveOp op = new ConvolveOp(kernel);
op.filter(image, filteredImage);
```

The program in Example 7–11 allows a user to load in a GIF or JPEG image and to carry out the image manipulations that we discussed. Thanks to the power of the image operations that the Java 2D API provides, the program is very simple.

Example 7–11: ImageProcessingTest.java

```
1. import java.awt.*;
2. import java.awt.event.*;
3. import java.awt.geom.*;
4. import java.awt.image.*;
5. import java.io.*;
6. import javax.imageio.*;
7. import javax.swing.*;
8.
9. /**
```

```
10.     This program demonstrates various image processing operations.
11. */
12. public class ImageProcessingTest
13. {
14.     public static void main(String[] args)
15.     {
16.         JFrame frame = new ImageProcessingFrame();
17.         frame.setDefaultCloseOperation(JFrame.EXIT_ON_CLOSE);
18.         frame.show();
19.     }
20. }
21.
22. /**
23.     This frame has a menu to load an image and to specify
24.     various transformations, and a panel to show the resulting
25.     image.
26. */
27. class ImageProcessingFrame extends JFrame
28. {
29.     public ImageProcessingFrame()
30.     {
31.         setTitle("ImageProcessingTest");
32.         setSize(WIDTH, HEIGHT);
33.
34.         JPanel panel = new
35.             JPanel()
36.             {
37.                 public void paintComponent(Graphics g)
38.                 {
39.                     super.paintComponent(g);
40.                     if (image != null)
41.                         g.drawImage(image, 0, 0, null);
42.                 }
43.             };
44.
45.         getContentPane().add(panel, BorderLayout.CENTER);
46.
47.         JMenu fileMenu = new JMenu("File");
48.         JMenuItem openItem = new JMenuItem("Open");
49.         openItem.addActionListener(new
50.             ActionListener()
51.             {
52.                 public void actionPerformed(ActionEvent event)
53.                 {
54.                     openFile();
55.                 }
56.             });
57.         fileMenu.add(openItem);
58.
59.         JMenuItem exitItem = new JMenuItem("Exit");
```

```
60.    exitItem.addActionListener(new
61.        ActionListener()
62.        {
63.            public void actionPerformed(ActionEvent event)
64.            {
65.                System.exit(0);
66.            }
67.        });
68.    fileMenu.add(exitItem);
69.
70.    JMenu editMenu = new JMenu("Edit");
71.    JMenuItem blurItem = new JMenuItem("Blur");
72.    blurItem.addActionListener(new
73.        ActionListener()
74.        {
75.            public void actionPerformed(ActionEvent event)
76.            {
77.                float weight = 1.0f/9.0f;
78.                float[] elements = new float[9];
79.                for (int i = 0; i < 9; i++)
80.                    elements[i] = weight;
81.                convolve(elements);
82.            }
83.        });
84.    editMenu.add(blurItem);
85.
86.    JMenuItem sharpenItem = new JMenuItem("Sharpen");
87.    sharpenItem.addActionListener(new
88.        ActionListener()
89.        {
90.            public void actionPerformed(ActionEvent event)
91.            {
92.                float[] elements =
93.                {   0.0f, -1.0f,  0.0f,
94.                   -1.0f,   5.f, -1.0f,
95.                    0.0f, -1.0f,  0.0f
96.                };
97.                convolve(elements);
98.            }
99.        });
100.   editMenu.add(sharpenItem);
101.
102.   JMenuItem brightenItem = new JMenuItem("Brighten");
103.   brightenItem.addActionListener(new
104.       ActionListener()
105.       {
106.           public void actionPerformed(ActionEvent event)
107.           {
108.               float a = 1.5f;
109.               float b = -20.0f;
110.               RescaleOp op = new RescaleOp(a, b, null);
111.               filter(op);
```

```
112.              }
113.          });
114.      editMenu.add(brightenItem);
115.
116.      JMenuItem edgeDetectItem = new JMenuItem("Edge detect");
117.      edgeDetectItem.addActionListener(new
118.          ActionListener()
119.          {
120.              public void actionPerformed(ActionEvent event)
121.              {
122.                  float[] elements =
123.                  {   0.0f, -1.0f, 0.0f,
124.                     -1.0f,  4.f, -1.0f,
125.                      0.0f, -1.0f, 0.0f
126.                  };
127.                  convolve(elements);
128.              }
129.          });
130.      editMenu.add(edgeDetectItem);
131.
132.      JMenuItem negativeItem = new JMenuItem("Negative");
133.      negativeItem.addActionListener(new
134.          ActionListener()
135.          {
136.              public void actionPerformed(ActionEvent event)
137.              {
138.                  byte negative[] = new byte[256];
139.                  for (int i = 0; i < 256; i++)
140.                      negative[i] = (byte)(255 - i);
141.                  ByteLookupTable table
142.                      = new ByteLookupTable(0, negative);
143.                  LookupOp op = new LookupOp(table, null);
144.                  filter(op);
145.              }
146.          });
147.      editMenu.add(negativeItem);
148.
149.      JMenuItem rotateItem = new JMenuItem("Rotate");
150.      rotateItem.addActionListener(new
151.          ActionListener()
152.          {
153.              public void actionPerformed(ActionEvent event)
154.              {
155.                  AffineTransform transform
156.                      = AffineTransform.getRotateInstance(
157.                          Math.toRadians(5),
158.                          image.getWidth() / 2,
159.                          image.getHeight() / 2);
160.                  AffineTransformOp op
161.                      = new AffineTransformOp(transform,
```

```
162.                           AffineTransformOp.TYPE_BILINEAR);
163.                    filter(op);
164.                }
165.            });
166.        editMenu.add(rotateItem);
167.
168.        JMenuBar menuBar = new JMenuBar();
169.        menuBar.add(fileMenu);
170.        menuBar.add(editMenu);
171.        setJMenuBar(menuBar);
172.    }
173.
174.    /**
175.        Open a file and load the image.
176.    */
177.    public void openFile()
178.    {
179.        JFileChooser chooser = new JFileChooser();
180.        chooser.setCurrentDirectory(new File("."));
181.
182.        chooser.setFileFilter(new
183.            javax.swing.filechooser.FileFilter()
184.            {
185.                public boolean accept(File f)
186.                {
187.                    String name = f.getName().toLowerCase();
188.                    return name.endsWith(".gif")
189.                        || name.endsWith(".jpg")
190.                        || name.endsWith(".jpeg")
191.                        || f.isDirectory();
192.                }
193.                public String getDescription()
194.                {
195.                    return "Image files";
196.                }
197.            });
198.
199.        int r = chooser.showOpenDialog(this);
200.        if(r != JFileChooser.APPROVE_OPTION) return;
201.
202.        try
203.        {
204.            image = ImageIO.read(chooser.getSelectedFile());
205.        }
206.        catch (IOException exception)
207.        {
208.            JOptionPane.showMessageDialog(this, exception);
209.        }
```

```
210.          repaint();
211.      }
212.
213.      /**
214.          Apply a filter and repaint.
215.          @param op the image operation to apply
216.      */
217.      private void filter(BufferedImageOp op)
218.      {
219.          BufferedImage filteredImage
220.              = new BufferedImage(image.getWidth(), image.getHeight(),
221.                  image.getType());
222.          op.filter(image, filteredImage);
223.          image = filteredImage;
224.          repaint();
225.      }
226.
227.      /**
228.          Apply a convolution and repaint.
229.          @param elements the convolution kernel (an array of
230.          9 matrix elements)
231.      */
232.      private void convolve(float[] elements)
233.      {
234.          Kernel kernel = new Kernel(3, 3, elements);
235.          ConvolveOp op = new ConvolveOp(kernel);
236.          filter(op);
237.      }
238.
239.      private BufferedImage image;
240.      private static final int WIDTH = 400;
241.      private static final int HEIGHT = 400;
242. }
```

 java.awt.image.BufferedImageOp

- BufferedImage filter(BufferedImage source, BufferedImage dest)
  applies the image operation to the source image and stores the result in the
  destination image. If dest is null, a new destination image is created. The
  destination image is returned.

 java.awt.image.AffineTransformOp

- AffineTransformOp(AffineTransform t, int interpolationType)
  constructs an affine transform operator.

Parameters:	t	an affine transform
	interpolationType	one of TYPE_BILINEAR or TYPE_NEAREST_NEIGHBOR

`java.awt.image.RescaleOp`

- RescaleOp(float a, float b, RenderingHints hints)

  constructs a rescale operator.

Parameters:	a, b	coefficients of the transformation $x_{new} = a \cdot x + b$ that is applied to the sample values
	hints	rendering hints for color matching; can be null

`java.awt.image.LookupOp`

- LookupOp(LookupTable table, RenderingHints hints)

  constructs a lookup operator.

Parameters:	table	the table for mapping the sample values
	hints	rendering hints for color matching; can be null

`java.awt.image.ByteLookupTable`

- ByteLookupTable(int offset, byte[] data)

  constructs a byte lookup table.

Parameters:	offset	position of first data value to be used
	data	the table data

`java.awt.image.ConvolveOp`

- ConvolveOp(Kernel kernel)
- ConvolveOp(Kernel kernel, int edgeCondition, RenderingHints hints)

  construct a convolution operator.

Parameters:	kernel	the kernel matrix for the convolution.
	edgeCondition	specifies how edge values should be treated: one of EDGE_NO_OP and EDGE_ZERO_FILL. Edge values need to be treated specially because they don't have sufficient neighboring values to compute the convolution. The default is EDGE_ZERO_FILL.
	hints	rendering hints for color matching; can be null.

`java.awt.image.Kernel`

- `Kernel(int width, int height, float[] data)`
  constructs a kernel.

Parameters:	`width, height`	dimensions of the kernel matrix
	`data`	entries of the kernel matrix

Printing

The original Java Development Kit had no support for printing at all. It was not possible to print from applets, and you had to get a third-party library if you wanted to print in an application. SDK 1.1 introduced very lightweight printing support, just enough to produce simple printouts, as long as you were not too particular about the print quality. The 1.1 printing model was designed to allow browser vendors to print the surface of an applet as it appears on a web page (which, however, the browser vendors have not embraced). Apart from that, it is best if the 1.1 printing model sinks into the obscurity it so richly deserves.

SDK 1.2 introduced the beginnings of a robust printing model that is fully integrated with 2D graphics, and SDK 1.3 provided minor improvements. SDK 1.4 adds important enhancements, such as discovery of printer features and streaming print jobs for server-side print management.

In this section, we show you how you can easily print a drawing on a single sheet of paper, how you can manage a multipage printout, and how you can benefit from the elegance of the Java 2D imaging model and easily generate a print preview dialog.

NOTE: The Java platform also has support for printing user interface components. We do not cover this topic because it is mostly of interest to implementors of browsers, screen grabbers, and so on. For more information on printing components, see `http://java.sun.com/products/jdk/1.1/docs/guide/awt/designspec/printing.html`.

Printing Graphics

In this section, we will tackle what is probably the most common printing situation: to print a 2D graphic. Of course, the graphic can contain text in various fonts, or even consist entirely of text.

To generate a printout, you need to take care of these two items:

- You need to supply an object that implements the `Printable` interface.
- You need to start a print job.

The `Printable` interface has a single method:

```
int print(Graphics g, PageFormat format, int page)
```

That method is called whenever the print engine needs to have a page formatted for printing. Your code draws the text and image that need to be printed onto the graphics context. The page format tells you the paper size and the print margins. The page number tells you which page you need to render.

To start a print job, you use the `PrinterJob` class. First, you call the static `getPrinterJob` method to get a print job object. Then set the `Printable` object that you want to print.

```
Printable canvas = . . .;
PrinterJob job = PrinterJob.getPrinterJob();
job.setPrintable(canvas);
```

CAUTION: There is a class `PrintJob` that handles JDK 1.1 style printing. That class is now obsolete. Do not confuse it with the `PrinterJob` class.

Before starting the print job, you should call the `printDialog` method to display a print dialog (see Figure 7–34). That dialog gives the user a chance to select the printer to be used (in case there are multiple printers available), the page range that should be printed, and various printer settings.

NOTE: At the time of this writing, the Java printing dialogs do not yet work properly on Linux. To print on Linux, you need to generate a PostScript file with the stream print service that is described later in this chapter, and then spool the resulting file.

You collect printer settings in an object of a class that implements the `PrintRequestAttributeSet` interface to the `printDialog` method. The SDK provides a `HashPrintRequestAttributeSet` class for that purpose.

```
HashPrintRequestAttributeSet attributes
    = new HashPrintRequestAttributeSet();
. . .
```

Pass the `attributes` object to the `printDialog` method.

The `printDialog` method returns `true` if the user clicked OK and `false` if the user canceled the dialog. If the user accepted, call the `print` method of the `PrinterJob` class to start the printing process. The `print` method may throw a `PrinterException`. Here is the outline of the printing code.

```
if (job.printDialog(attributes))
{
   try
```

```
    {
        job.print();
    }
    catch (PrinterException exception)
    {
        . . .
    }
}
```

Figure 7–34: A Cross-Platform Print Dialog

NOTE: If you need to support SDK 1.2 or 1.3, you must modify your program to display the native print dialog instead of the cross-platform dialog that was added in SDK 1.4. See the sidebar at the end of this section for details.

During printing, the print method of the PrinterJob class makes repeated calls to the print method of the Printable object associated with the job.

Since the job does not know how many pages you want to print, it simply keeps calling the print method. As long as the print method returns the value Printable.PAGE_EXISTS, the print job keeps producing pages. When the print method returns Printable.NO_SUCH_PAGE, the print job stops.

CAUTION: The page numbers that the print job passes to the print method start with page 0.

Therefore, the print job doesn't have an accurate page count until after the printout is complete. For that reason, the print dialog can't display the correct page range and instead displays a page range of "Pages 1 to 1." You will see in the next section how to avoid this blemish by supplying a `Book` object to the print job.

During the printing process, the print job repeatedly calls the `print` method of the `Printable` object. The print job is allowed to make multiple calls *for the same page.* You should therefore not count pages inside the `print` method, but always rely on the page number parameter. There is a good reason why the print job may call the `print` method repeatedly for the same page. Some printers, in particular dot-matrix and inkjet printers, use *banding.* They print one band at a time, advance the paper, and then print the next band. The print job may use banding even for laser printers that print a full page at a time—it gives the print job a way of managing the size of the spool file.

If the print job needs the `Printable` object to print a band, then it sets the clip area of the graphics context to the requested band and calls the `print` method. Its drawing operations will be clipped against the band rectangle, and only those drawing elements that show up in the band will be rendered. Your `print` method does not need to be aware of that process, with one caveat: it should *not* interfere with the clip area.

CAUTION: The `Graphics` object that your `print` method gets is also clipped against the page margins. If you replace the clip area, you can draw outside the margins. Especially in a printer graphics context, you need to respect the clipping area. Call `clip`, not `setClip`, to further restrict the clipping area. If you must remove a clip area, then make sure to call `getClip` at the beginning of your `print` method, and restore that clip area.

The `PageFormat` parameter of the `print` method contains information about the printed page. The methods

```
getWidth
getHeight
```

return the paper size, measured in *points*. One point is 1/72 of an inch. (An inch equals 25.4 millimeters.) For example, A4 paper is approximately 595 by 842 points, and US letter-size paper is 612 by 792 points.

Points are a common measurement in the printing trade in the United States. Much to the chagrin of the rest of the world, the printing package uses point units for two purposes. Paper sizes and paper margins are measured in points. And the default unit for all print graphics contexts is one point. You can verify that in the example program at the end of this section. The program prints two lines of text that are 72 units apart from another. Run the example program and measure the distance between the baselines. They are exactly 1 inch or 25.4 millimeters apart.

The `getWidth` and `getHeight` methods of the `PageFormat` class give you the complete paper size. Not all of the paper area is printable. Users typically select margins, and even if they don't, printers need to somehow grip the sheets of paper on which they print and therefore have a small unprintable area around the edges. The methods

```
getImageableWidth
getImageableHeight
```

tell you the dimensions of the area that you can actually fill. However, the margins need not be symmetrical, so you also need to know the top-left corner of the imageable area (see Figure 7–35), which is obtained by the methods

```
getImageableX
getImageableY
```

 TIP: The graphics context that you receive in the `print` method is clipped to exclude the margins. But the origin of the coordinate system is nevertheless the top-left corner of the paper. It makes sense to translate the coordinate system to start at the top-left corner of the imageable area. Simply start your `print` method with

```
g.translate(pageFormat.getImageableX(),
    pageFormat.getImageableY());
```

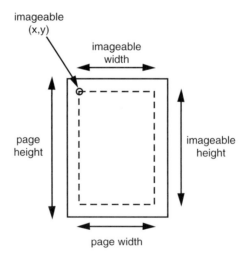

Figure 7–35: Page format measurements

If you want to have your users choose the settings for the page margins or have them switch between portrait and landscape orientation without setting other printing attributes, then you can call the `pageDialog` method of the `PrinterJob` class:

```
PageFormat format = job.pageDialog(attributes);
```

> **NOTE:** One of the tabs of the print dialog contains the page setup dialog (see Figure 7–36). You may still want to give users an option to set the page format before printing, especially if your program presents a "what you see is what you get" display of the pages to be printed. The `pageDialog` method returns a `PageFormat` object with the user settings.

Figure 7–36: A Cross-Platform Page Setup Dialog

Example 7–12 shows you how to render the same set of shapes on the screen and on the printed page. A subclass of `JPanel` implements the `Printable` interface. Both the `paintComponent` and the `print` methods call the same method to carry out the actual drawing.

```
class PrintPanel extends JPanel implements Printable
{
    public void paintComponent(Graphics g)
    {
        super.paintComponent(g);
        Graphics2D g2 = (Graphics2D)g;
        drawPage(g2);
    }

    public int print(Graphics g, PageFormat pf, int page)
        throws PrinterException
```

```
{
    if (page >= 1) return Printable.NO_SUCH_PAGE;
    Graphics2D g2 = (Graphics2D)g;
    g2.translate(pf.getImageableX(), pf.getImageableY());
    drawPage(g2);
    return Printable.PAGE_EXISTS;
}

public void drawPage(Graphics2D g2)
{
    // shared drawing code goes here
    . . .
}
. . .
}
```

CAUTION: SDK 1.2 does not set the paint to black when setting up a printer graphics context. If your pages come out all white, add a line `g2.setPaint(Color.black)` at the top of the `print` method. This problem has been fixed in SDK 1.3.

This example displays and prints the same image as Example 7–6 on page 611, namely the outline of the message "Hello, World" that is used as a clipping area for a pattern of lines (see Figure 7–22 on page 610).

Click on the Print button to start printing, or on the Page setup button to bring up the page setup dialog. Example 7–12 shows the code.

Using Native Print Dialogs

Prior to SDK 1.4, the printing system used the native print and page setup dialogs of the host platform. To show a native print dialog, call the `printDialog` method with no parameters. (There is no way to collect user settings in an attribute set.) Figure 7–37 shows a Windows print dialog.

One potential advantage of using the native print dialog is that some printer drivers have special features that are not accessible through the cross-platform dialog. At any rate, if you want to support SDK 1.2 and 1.3, you need to show the native dialogs.

To show a native page setup dialog, you pass a default `PageFormat` object to the `pageDialog` method. The method clones that object, modifies it according to the user selections in the dialog, and returns the cloned object.

```
PageFormat defaultFormat = printJob.defaultPage();
PageFormat selectedFormat = printJob.pageDialog(defaultFormat);
```

Figure 7–38 shows a page setup dialog for the Windows operating system.

Figure 7–37: A Windows print dialog

Figure 7–38: A Windows page setup dialog

Example 7–12: PrintTest.java

```
1. import java.awt.*;
2. import java.awt.event.*;
3. import java.awt.font.*;
4. import java.awt.geom.*;
5. import java.awt.print.*;
6. import java.util.*;
7. import javax.print.*;
8. import javax.print.attribute.*;
9. import javax.swing.*;
```

```
10.
11. /**
12.    This program demonstrates how to print 2D graphics
13. */
14. public class PrintTest
15. {
16.    public static void main(String[] args)
17.    {
18.       JFrame frame = new PrintTestFrame();
19.       frame.setDefaultCloseOperation(JFrame.EXIT_ON_CLOSE);
20.       frame.show();
21.    }
22. }
23.
24. /**
25.    This frame shows a panel with 2D graphics and buttons
26.    to print the graphics and to set up the page format.
27. */
28. class PrintTestFrame extends JFrame
29. {
30.    public PrintTestFrame()
31.    {
32.       setTitle("PrintTest");
33.       setSize(WIDTH, HEIGHT);
34.
35.       Container contentPane = getContentPane();
36.       canvas = new PrintPanel();
37.       contentPane.add(canvas, BorderLayout.CENTER);
38.
39.       attributes = new HashPrintRequestAttributeSet();
40.
41.       JPanel buttonPanel = new JPanel();
42.       JButton printButton = new JButton("Print");
43.       buttonPanel.add(printButton);
44.       printButton.addActionListener(new
45.          ActionListener()
46.          {
47.             public void actionPerformed(ActionEvent event)
48.             {
49.                try
50.                {
51.                   PrinterJob job = PrinterJob.getPrinterJob();
52.                   job.setPrintable(canvas);
53.                   if (job.printDialog(attributes))
54.                   {
55.                      job.print(attributes);
56.                   }
57.                }
58.                catch (PrinterException exception)
59.                {
60.                   JOptionPane.showMessageDialog(
```

```
61.                        PrintTestFrame.this, exception);
62.                }
63.             }
64.          });
65.
66.       JButton pageSetupButton = new JButton("Page setup");
67.       buttonPanel.add(pageSetupButton);
68.       pageSetupButton.addActionListener(new
69.          ActionListener()
70.          {
71.             public void actionPerformed(ActionEvent event)
72.             {
73.                PrinterJob job = PrinterJob.getPrinterJob();
74.                job.pageDialog(attributes);
75.             }
76.          });
77.
78.       contentPane.add(buttonPanel, BorderLayout.NORTH);
79.    }
80.
81.    private PrintPanel canvas;
82.    private PrintRequestAttributeSet attributes;
83.
84.    private static final int WIDTH = 300;
85.    private static final int HEIGHT = 300;
86. }
87.
88. /**
89.    This panel generates a 2D graphics image for screen display
90.    and printing.
91. */
92. class PrintPanel extends JPanel implements Printable
93. {
94.    public void paintComponent(Graphics g)
95.    {
96.       super.paintComponent(g);
97.       Graphics2D g2 = (Graphics2D)g;
98.       drawPage(g2);
99.    }
100.
101.   public int print(Graphics g, PageFormat pf, int page)
102.      throws PrinterException
103.   {
104.      if (page >= 1) return Printable.NO_SUCH_PAGE;
105.      Graphics2D g2 = (Graphics2D)g;
106.      g2.translate(pf.getImageableX(), pf.getImageableY());
107.      g2.draw(new Rectangle2D.Double(0, 0,
108.         pf.getImageableWidth(), pf.getImageableHeight()));
109.
110.      drawPage(g2);
```

```
111.        return Printable.PAGE_EXISTS;
112.    }
113.
114.    /**
115.        This method draws the page both on the screen and the
116.        printer graphics context.
117.        @param g2 the graphics context
118.    */
119.    public void drawPage(Graphics2D g2)
120.    {
121.        FontRenderContext context = g2.getFontRenderContext();
122.        Font f = new Font("Serif", Font.PLAIN, 72);
123.        GeneralPath clipShape = new GeneralPath();
124.
125.        TextLayout layout = new TextLayout("Hello", f, context);
126.        AffineTransform transform
127.            = AffineTransform.getTranslateInstance(0, 72);
128.        Shape outline = layout.getOutline(transform);
129.        clipShape.append(outline, false);
130.
131.        layout = new TextLayout("World", f, context);
132.        transform
133.            = AffineTransform.getTranslateInstance(0, 144);
134.        outline = layout.getOutline(transform);
135.        clipShape.append(outline, false);
136.
137.        g2.draw(clipShape);
138.        g2.clip(clipShape);
139.
140.        final int NLINES =50;
141.        Point2D p = new Point2D.Double(0, 0);
142.        for (int i = 0; i < NLINES; i++)
143.        {
144.            double x = (2 * getWidth() * i) / NLINES;
145.            double y = (2 * getHeight() * (NLINES - 1 - i))
146.                / NLINES;
147.            Point2D q = new Point2D.Double(x, y);
148.            g2.draw(new Line2D.Double(p, q));
149.        }
150.    }
151. }
```

java.awt.print.Printable

- `int print(Graphics g, PageFormat format, int pageNumber)`
  renders a page and returns PAGE_EXISTS, or returns NO_SUCH_PAGE.

  Parameters: g   the graphics context onto which the page is rendered

                            format   the format of the page to draw on

                            pageNumber   the number of the requested page

java.awt.print.PrinterJob

- `static PrinterJob getPrinterJob()`

  returns a printer job object.

- `PageFormat defaultPage()`

  returns the default page format for this printer.

- `boolean printDialog(PrintRequestAttributeSet attributes)`
- `boolean printDialog()`

  bring up print dialogs to give the user an opportunity to select the pages to be printed and to change print settings. The first method displays a cross-platform dialog, the second a native dialog. The first method modifies the `attributes` object to reflect the user settings. Both methods return `true` if the user accepts the dialog.

- `PageFormat pageDialog(PrintRequestAttributeSet attributes)`
- `PageFormat pageDialog(PageFormat defaults)`

  display page setup dialogs. The first method displays a cross-platform dialog, the second a native dialog. Both methods return a `PageFormat` object with the format that the user requested in the dialog. The first method modifies the `attributes` object to reflect the user settings. The second method does not modify the `defaults` object.

- `void setPrintable(Printable p)`
- `void setPrintable(Printable p, PageFormat format)`

  set the `Printable` of this print job and an optional page format.

- `void print()`

  prints the current `Printable` by repeatedly calling its `print` method and sending the rendered pages to the printer, until no more pages are available.

java.awt.print.PageFormat

- `double getWidth()`
- `double getHeight()`

  return the width and height of the page.

- `double getImageableWidth()`
- `double getImageableHeight()`

  return the width and height of the imageable area of the page.

- `double getImageableX()`
- `double getImageableY()`

  return the position of the top-left corner of the imageable area.

- `int getOrientation()`

    returns one of PORTRAIT, LANDSCAPE, REVERSE_LANDSCAPE. Page orientation is transparent to programmers since the page format and graphics context settings automatically reflect the page orientation.

Printing Multiple Pages

In practice, you don't usually want to pass a raw `Printable` object to a print job. Instead, you should obtain an object of a class that implements the `Pageable` interface. The Java platform supplies one such class, called `Book`. A book is made up of sections, each of which is a `Printable`. You make a book by adding `Printable` objects and their page counts.

```
Book book = new Book();
Printable coverPage = . . .;
Printable bodyPages = . . .;
book.append(coverPage, pageFormat); // append 1 page
book.append(bodyPages, pageFormat, pageCount);
```

Then, you use the `setPageable` method to pass the `Book` object to the print job.

```
printJob.setPageable(book);
```

Now the print job knows exactly how many pages to print. Then, the print dialog displays an accurate page range, and the user can select the entire range or subranges.

> CAUTION: When the print job calls the `print` methods of the `Printable` sections, it passes the current page number of the *book*, and not of each *section*, as the current page number. That is a huge pain—each section must know the page counts of the preceding sections to make sense of the page number parameter.

From a programmer's perspective, the biggest challenge about using the `Book` class is that you need to know how many pages each section will have when you print it. Your `Printable` class needs a *layout algorithm* that computes the layout of the material on the printed pages. Before printing starts, invoke that algorithm to compute the page breaks and the page count. You can retain the layout information so you have it handy during the printing process.

You must guard against the possibility that the user has changed the page format. If that happens, you must recompute the layout, even if the information that you want to print has not changed.

Example 7–13 shows how to produce a multipage printout. This program prints a message in very large characters on a number of pages (see Figure 7–39). You can then trim the margins and tape the pages together to form a banner.

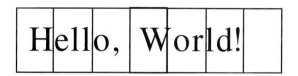

Figure 7–39: A banner

The layoutPages method of the Banner class computes the layout. We first lay out the message string in a 72-point font. Then, we compute the height of the resulting string and compare it against the imageable height of the page. We derive a scale factor from these two measurements. When printing the string, we will magnify it by that scale factor.

> CAUTION: To lay out your information precisely, you usually need access to the printer graphics context. Unfortunately, there is no way to obtain that graphics context until printing actually starts. In our example program, we make do with the screen graphics context and hope that the font metrics of the screen and printer match.

The getPageCount method of the Banner class first calls the layout method. Then it scales up the width of the string and divides it by the imageable width of each page. The quotient, rounded up to the next integer, is the page count.

It sounds like it might be difficult to print the banner since characters can be broken across multiple pages. However, thanks to the power of the Java 2D API, this turns out not to be a problem at all. When a particular page is requested, we simply use the translate method of the Graphics2D class to shift the top-left corner of the string to the left. Then, we set a clip rectangle that equals the current page (see Figure 7–40). Finally, we scale the graphics context with the scale factor that the layout method computed.

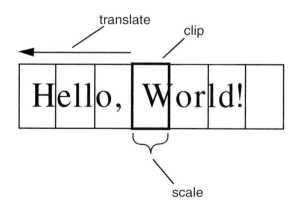

Figure 7–40: Printing a page of a banner

This example shows the power of transformations. The drawing code is kept simple, and the transformation does all the work of placing the drawing at the appropriate place. Finally, the clip cuts away the part of the image that falls outside the page. In the next section, you will see another compelling use of transformations, to display a print preview.

Print Preview

Most professional programs have a print preview mechanism that lets you look at your pages on the screen so that you won't waste paper on a printout that you don't like. The printing classes of the Java platform do not supply a standard "print preview" dialog. But it is easy to design your own (see Figure 7–41). In this section, we show you how. The PrintPreviewDialog class in Example 7–13 is completely generic—you can reuse it to preview any kind of printout.

To construct a PrintPreviewDialog, you supply either a Printable or a Book, together with a PageFormat object. The surface of the dialog contains a PrintPreviewCanvas. As you use the Next and Previous buttons to flip through the pages, the paintComponent method calls the print method of the Printable object for the requested page.

Normally, the print method draws the page context on a printer graphics context. However, we supply the screen graphics context, suitably scaled so that the entire printed page fits inside a small screen rectangle.

```
float xoff = . . .; // left of page
float yoff = . . .; // top of page
float scale = . . .; // to fit printed page onto screen
g2.translate(xoff, yoff);
g2.scale(scale, scale);
Printable printable = book.getPrintable(currentPage);
printable.print(g2, pageFormat, currentPage);
```

The print method never knows that it doesn't actually produce printed pages. It simply draws onto the graphics context, thereby producing a microscopic print preview on the screen. This is a very compelling demonstration of the power of the Java 2D imaging model.

Figure 7–41: A print preview dialog

Example 7–13 contains the code for the banner printing program and the print preview dialog. Type "Hello, World!" into the text field and look at the print preview, then print out the banner.

Example 7–13: BookTest.java

```
1. import java.awt.*;
2. import java.awt.event.*;
3. import java.awt.font.*;
4. import java.awt.geom.*;
5. import java.awt.print.*;
6. import java.util.*;
7. import javax.print.*;
8. import javax.print.attribute.*;
9. import javax.swing.*;
10.
11. /**
12.    This program demonstrates the printing of a multi-page
13.    book. It prints a "banner", by blowing up a text string
14.    to fill the entire page vertically. The program also
15.    contains a generic print preview dialog.
16. */
17. public class BookTest
18. {
19.    public static void main(String[] args)
20.    {
21.       JFrame frame = new BookTestFrame();
22.       frame.setDefaultCloseOperation(JFrame.EXIT_ON_CLOSE);
23.       frame.show();
24.    }
25. }
26.
27. /**
28.    This frame has a text field for the banner text and
29.    buttons for printing, page setup, and print preview.
30. */
31. class BookTestFrame extends JFrame
32. {
33.    public BookTestFrame()
34.    {
35.       setTitle("BookTest");
36.       setSize(WIDTH, HEIGHT);
37.
38.       Container contentPane = getContentPane();
39.       text = new JTextField();
40.       contentPane.add(text, BorderLayout.NORTH);
41.
42.       attributes = new HashPrintRequestAttributeSet();
```

```
43.
44.         JPanel buttonPanel = new JPanel();
45.
46.         JButton printButton = new JButton("Print");
47.         buttonPanel.add(printButton);
48.         printButton.addActionListener(new
49.            ActionListener()
50.            {
51.               public void actionPerformed(ActionEvent event)
52.               {
53.                  try
54.                  {
55.                     PrinterJob job = PrinterJob.getPrinterJob();
56.                     job.setPageable(makeBook());
57.                     if (job.printDialog(attributes))
58.                     {
59.                        job.print(attributes);
60.                     }
61.                  }
62.                  catch (PrinterException exception)
63.                  {
64.                     JOptionPane.showMessageDialog(
65.                        BookTestFrame.this, exception);
66.                  }
67.               }
68.            });
69.
70.         JButton pageSetupButton = new JButton("Page setup");
71.         buttonPanel.add(pageSetupButton);
72.         pageSetupButton.addActionListener(new
73.            ActionListener()
74.            {
75.               public void actionPerformed(ActionEvent event)
76.               {
77.                  PrinterJob job = PrinterJob.getPrinterJob();
78.                  pageFormat = job.pageDialog(attributes);
79.               }
80.            });
81.
82.         JButton printPreviewButton = new JButton("Print preview");
83.         buttonPanel.add(printPreviewButton);
84.         printPreviewButton.addActionListener(new
85.            ActionListener()
86.            {
87.               public void actionPerformed(ActionEvent event)
88.               {
89.                  PrintPreviewDialog dialog
90.                     = new PrintPreviewDialog(makeBook());
```

```
91.                    dialog.show();
92.                }
93.            });
94.
95.        contentPane.add(buttonPanel, BorderLayout.SOUTH);
96.    }
97.
98.    /**
99.        Makes a book that contains a cover page and the
100.       pages for the banner.
101.    */
102.    public Book makeBook()
103.    {
104.        if (pageFormat == null)
105.        {
106.            PrinterJob job = PrinterJob.getPrinterJob();
107.            pageFormat = job.defaultPage();
108.        }
109.        Book book = new Book();
110.        String message = text.getText();
111.        Banner banner = new Banner(message);
112.        int pageCount
113.            = banner.getPageCount((Graphics2D)getGraphics(),
114.                pageFormat);
115.        book.append(new CoverPage(message + " (" + pageCount
116.            + " pages)"), pageFormat);
117.        book.append(banner, pageFormat, pageCount);
118.        return book;
119.    }
120.
121.    private JTextField text;
122.    private PageFormat pageFormat;
123.    private PrintRequestAttributeSet attributes;
124.
125.    private static final int WIDTH = 300;
126.    private static final int HEIGHT = 100;
127. }
128.
129. /**
130.    A banner that prints a text string on multiple pages.
131. */
132. class Banner implements Printable
133. {
134.    /**
135.        Constructs a banner
136.        @param m the message string
137.    */
138.    public Banner(String m)
```

```
139.    {
140.        message = m;
141.    }
142.
143.    /**
144.        Gets the page count of this section.
145.        @param g2 the graphics context
146.        @param pf the page format
147.        @return the number of pages needed
148.    */
149.    public int getPageCount(Graphics2D g2, PageFormat pf)
150.    {
151.        if (message.equals("")) return 0;
152.        FontRenderContext context = g2.getFontRenderContext();
153.        Font f = new Font("Serif", Font.PLAIN, 72);
154.        Rectangle2D bounds = f.getStringBounds(message, context);
155.        scale = pf.getImageableHeight() / bounds.getHeight();
156.        double width = scale * bounds.getWidth();
157.        int pages = (int)Math.ceil(width / pf.getImageableWidth());
158.        return pages;
159.    }
160.
161.    public int print(Graphics g, PageFormat pf, int page)
162.        throws PrinterException
163.    {
164.        Graphics2D g2 = (Graphics2D)g;
165.        if (page > getPageCount(g2, pf))
166.            return Printable.NO_SUCH_PAGE;
167.        g2.translate(pf.getImageableX(), pf.getImageableY());
168.
169.        drawPage(g2, pf, page);
170.        return Printable.PAGE_EXISTS;
171.    }
172.
173.    public void drawPage(Graphics2D g2, PageFormat pf, int page)
174.    {
175.        if (message.equals("")) return;
176.        page--; // account for cover page
177.
178.        drawCropMarks(g2, pf);
179.        g2.clip(new Rectangle2D.Double(0, 0,
180.            pf.getImageableWidth(), pf.getImageableHeight()));
181.        g2.translate(-page * pf.getImageableWidth(), 0);
182.        g2.scale(scale, scale);
183.        FontRenderContext context = g2.getFontRenderContext();
184.        Font f = new Font("Serif", Font.PLAIN, 72);
185.        TextLayout layout = new TextLayout(message, f, context);
186.        AffineTransform transform
```

```
187.              = AffineTransform.getTranslateInstance(0,
188.                  layout.getAscent());
189.          Shape outline = layout.getOutline(transform);
190.          g2.draw(outline);
191.      }
192.
193.      /**
194.          Draws 1/2" crop marks in the corners of the page.
195.          @param g2 the graphics context
196.          @param pf the page format
197.      */
198.      public void drawCropMarks(Graphics2D g2, PageFormat pf)
199.      {
200.          final double C = 36; // crop mark length = 1/2 inch
201.          double w = pf.getImageableWidth();
202.          double h = pf.getImageableHeight();
203.          g2.draw(new Line2D.Double(0, 0, 0, C));
204.          g2.draw(new Line2D.Double(0, 0, C, 0));
205.          g2.draw(new Line2D.Double(w, 0, w, C));
206.          g2.draw(new Line2D.Double(w, 0, w - C, 0));
207.          g2.draw(new Line2D.Double(0, h, 0, h - C));
208.          g2.draw(new Line2D.Double(0, h, C, h));
209.          g2.draw(new Line2D.Double(w, h, w, h - C));
210.          g2.draw(new Line2D.Double(w, h, w - C, h));
211.      }
212.
213.      private String message;
214.      private double scale;
215. }
216.
217. /**
218.     This class prints a cover page with a title.
219. */
220. class CoverPage implements Printable
221. {
222.     /**
223.         Constructs a cover page.
224.         @param t the title
225.     */
226.     public CoverPage(String t)
227.     {
228.         title = t;
229.     }
230.
231.     public int print(Graphics g, PageFormat pf, int page)
232.         throws PrinterException
233.     {
234.         if (page >= 1) return Printable.NO_SUCH_PAGE;
235.         Graphics2D g2 = (Graphics2D)g;
```

```
236.          g2.setPaint(Color.black);
237.          g2.translate(pf.getImageableX(), pf.getImageableY());
238.          FontRenderContext context = g2.getFontRenderContext();
239.          Font f = g2.getFont();
240.          TextLayout layout = new TextLayout(title, f, context);
241.          float ascent = layout.getAscent();
242.          g2.drawString(title, 0, ascent);
243.          return Printable.PAGE_EXISTS;
244.       }
245.
246.    private String title;
247. }
248.
249. /**
250.    This class implements a generic print preview dialog.
251. */
252. class PrintPreviewDialog extends JDialog
253. {
254.    /**
255.       Constructs a print preview dialog.
256.       @param p a Printable
257.       @param pf the page format
258.       @param pages the number of pages in p
259.    */
260.    public PrintPreviewDialog(Printable p, PageFormat pf,
261.       int pages)
262.    {
263.       Book book = new Book();
264.       book.append(p, pf, pages);
265.       layoutUI(book);
266.    }
267.
268.    /**
269.       Constructs a print preview dialog.
270.       @param b a Book
271.    */
272.    public PrintPreviewDialog(Book b)
273.    {
274.       layoutUI(b);
275.    }
276.
277.    /**
278.       Lays out the UI of the dialog.
279.       @param book the book to be previewed
280.    */
281.    public void layoutUI(Book book)
282.    {
283.       setSize(WIDTH, HEIGHT);
284.
```

```
285.        Container contentPane = getContentPane();
286.        canvas = new PrintPreviewCanvas(book);
287.        contentPane.add(canvas, BorderLayout.CENTER);
288.
289.        JPanel buttonPanel = new JPanel();
290.
291.        JButton nextButton = new JButton("Next");
292.        buttonPanel.add(nextButton);
293.        nextButton.addActionListener(new
294.           ActionListener()
295.           {
296.              public void actionPerformed(ActionEvent event)
297.              {
298.                 canvas.flipPage(1);
299.              }
300.           });
301.
302.        JButton previousButton = new JButton("Previous");
303.        buttonPanel.add(previousButton);
304.        previousButton.addActionListener(new
305.           ActionListener()
306.           {
307.              public void actionPerformed(ActionEvent event)
308.              {
309.                 canvas.flipPage(-1);
310.              }
311.           });
312.
313.        JButton closeButton = new JButton("Close");
314.        buttonPanel.add(closeButton);
315.        closeButton.addActionListener(new
316.           ActionListener()
317.           {
318.              public void actionPerformed(ActionEvent event)
319.              {
320.                 setVisible(false);
321.              }
322.           });
323.
324.        contentPane.add(buttonPanel, BorderLayout.SOUTH);
325.     }
326.
327.     private PrintPreviewCanvas canvas;
328.
329.     private static final int WIDTH = 300;
330.     private static final int HEIGHT = 300;
331. }
332.
333. /**
```

```
334.    The canvas for displaying the print preview.
335. */
336. class PrintPreviewCanvas extends JPanel
337. {
338.    /**
339.       Constructs a print preview canvas.
340.       @param b the book to be previewed
341.    */
342.    public PrintPreviewCanvas(Book b)
343.    {
344.       book = b;
345.       currentPage = 0;
346.    }
347.
348.    public void paintComponent(Graphics g)
349.    {
350.       super.paintComponent(g);
351.       Graphics2D g2 = (Graphics2D)g;
352.       PageFormat pageFormat = book.getPageFormat(currentPage);
353.
354.       double xoff; // x offset of page start in window
355.       double yoff; // y offset of page start in window
356.       double scale; // scale factor to fit page in window
357.       double px = pageFormat.getWidth();
358.       double py = pageFormat.getHeight();
359.       double sx = getWidth() - 1;
360.       double sy = getHeight() - 1;
361.       if (px / py < sx / sy) // center horizontally
362.       {
363.          scale = sy / py;
364.          xoff = 0.5 * (sx - scale * px);
365.          yoff = 0;
366.       }
367.       else // center vertically
368.       {
369.          scale = sx / px;
370.          xoff = 0;
371.          yoff = 0.5 * (sy - scale * py);
372.       }
373.       g2.translate((float)xoff, (float)yoff);
374.       g2.scale((float)scale, (float)scale);
375.
376.       // draw page outline (ignoring margins)
377.       Rectangle2D page = new Rectangle2D.Double(0, 0, px, py);
378.       g2.setPaint(Color.white);
379.       g2.fill(page);
380.       g2.setPaint(Color.black);
381.       g2.draw(page);
```

```
382.
383.         Printable printable = book.getPrintable(currentPage);
384.         try
385.         {
386.             printable.print(g2, pageFormat, currentPage);
387.         }
388.         catch (PrinterException exception)
389.         {
390.             g2.draw(new Line2D.Double(0, 0, px, py));
391.             g2.draw(new Line2D.Double(0, px, 0, py));
392.         }
393.      }
394.
395.      /**
396.         Flip the book by the given number of pages.
397.         @param by the number of pages to flip by. Negative
398.         values flip backwards.
399.      */
400.      public void flipPage(int by)
401.      {
402.         int newPage = currentPage + by;
403.         if (0 <= newPage && newPage < book.getNumberOfPages())
404.         {
405.             currentPage = newPage;
406.             repaint();
407.         }
408.      }
409.
410.      private Book book;
411.      private int currentPage;
412. }
```

java.awt.print.PrinterJob

- void setPageable(Pageable p)

  sets a Pageable (such as a Book) to be printed.

java.awt.print.Book

- void append(Printable p, PageFormat format)
- void append(Printable p, PageFormat format, int pageCount)

  append a section to this book. If the page count is not specified, the first page is added.

- Printable getPrintable(int page)

  gets the printable for the specified page.

Print Services

So far, you have seen how to print 2D graphics. However, the printing API introduced in SDK 1.4 allows for far greater flexibility. The API defines a number of data types and lets you find print services that are able to print them. Among the data types are:

- Images in GIF, JPEG, or PNG format
- Documents in text, HTML, PostScript, or PDF format
- Raw printer code data
- Objects of a class that implements `Printable`, `Pageable`, or `RenderableImage`

The data themselves can be stored in a source of bytes or characters such as an input stream, a URL, or an array. A *document flavor* describes the combination of a data source and a data type. The `DocFlavor` class defines a number of inner classes for the various data sources. Each of the inner classes defines constants to specify the flavors. For example, the constant

```
DocFlavor.INPUT_STREAM.GIF
```

describes a GIF image that is read from an input stream. Table 7–3 lists the combinations.

Suppose you want to print a GIF image that is located in a file. You need to find out whether there is a *print service* that is capable of handling the task. The static `lookupPrintServices` method of the `PrintServiceLookup` class returns an array of `PrintService` objects that can handle the given document flavor.

```
DocFlavor flavor = DocFlavor.INPUT_STREAM.GIF;
PrintService[] services
    = PrintServiceLookup.lookupPrintServices(flavor, null);
```

The second parameter of the `lookupPrintServices` method is `null` to indicate that we don't want to constrain the search by specifying printer attributes. We will cover attributes in the next section.

NOTE: The SDK 1.4 supplies print services for basic document flavors such as images and 2D graphics. But if you try to print text or HTML documents, the lookup will return an empty array.

If the lookup yields an array with more than one element, you need to pick among the listed print services. You can call the `getName` method of the `PrintService` class to get the printer names, and then let the user choose.

Next, get a document print job from the service:

```
DocPrintJob job = services[i].createPrintJob();
```

Table 7–3: Document Flavors for Print Services

Data Source	Data Type	MIME Type
INPUT_STREAM	GIF	image/gif
URL	JPEG	image/jpeg
BYTE_ARRAY	PNG	image/png
	POSTSCRIPT	application/postscript
	PDF	application/pdf
	TEXT_HTML_HOST	text/html (using host encoding)
	TEXT_HTML_US_ASCII	text/html; charset=us-ascii
	TEXT_HTML_UTF_8	text/html; charset=utf-8
	TEXT_HTML_UTF_16	text/html; charset=utf-16
	TEXT_HTML_UTF_16LE	text/html; charset=utf-16le (little-endian)
	TEXT_HTML_UTF_16BE	text/html; charset=utf-16le (big-endian)
	TEXT_PLAIN_HOST	text/plain (using host encoding)
	TEXT_PLAIN_US_ASCII	text/plain; charset=us-ascii
	TEXT_PLAIN_UTF_8	text/plain; charset=utf-8
	TEXT_PLAIN_UTF_16	text/plain; charset=utf-16
	TEXT_PLAIN_UTF_16LE	text/plain; charset=utf-16le (little-endian)
	TEXT_PLAIN_UTF_16BE	text/plain; charset=utf-16be (big-endian)
	PCL	application/vnd.hp-PCL (Hewlett Packard Printer Control Language)
	AUTOSENSE	application/octet-stream (raw printer data)
READER	TEXT_HTML	text/html; charset=utf-16
STRING	TEXT_PLAIN	text/plain; charset=utf-16
CHAR_ARRAY		
SERVICE_FORMATTED	PRINTABLE	N/A
	PAGEABLE	N/A
	RENDERABLE_IMAGE	N/A

For printing, you need an object that implements the `Doc` interface. The SDK supplies a class `SimpleDoc` for that purpose. The `SimpleDoc` constructor requires the data source object, the document flavor, and an optional attribute set. For example,

```
InputStream in = new FileInputStream(fileName);
Doc doc = new SimpleDoc(in, flavor, null);
```

Finally, you are ready to print:

```
job.print(doc, null);
```

As before, the `null` parameter can be replaced by an attribute set.

Note that this printing process is quite different from that of the preceding section. There isn't any user interaction through print dialogs. For example, you can implement a server-side printing mechanism in which users submit print jobs through a web form.

The program in Example 7–14 demonstrates how to use a print service to print an image file.

Example 7–14: PrintServiceTest.java

```
 1. import java.awt.*;
 2. import java.awt.event.*;
 3. import java.awt.image.*;
 4. import java.io.*;
 5. import java.util.*;
 6. import javax.print.*;
 7. import javax.swing.*;
 8.
 9. /**
10.    This program demonstrates the use of print services.
11.    The program lets you print a GIF image to any of the print
12.    services that support the GIF document flavor.
13. */
14. public class PrintServiceTest
15. {
16.    public static void main(String[] args)
17.    {
18.       JFrame frame = new PrintServiceFrame();
19.       frame.setDefaultCloseOperation(JFrame.EXIT_ON_CLOSE);
20.       frame.show();
21.    }
22. }
23.
24. /**
25.    This frame displays the image to be printed. It contains
26.    menus for opening an image file, printing, and selecting
27.    a print service.
```

```
28. */
29. class PrintServiceFrame extends JFrame
30. {
31.     public PrintServiceFrame()
32.     {
33.         setTitle("PrintServiceTest");
34.         setSize(WIDTH, HEIGHT);
35.
36.         // set up menu bar
37.         JMenuBar menuBar = new JMenuBar();
38.         setJMenuBar(menuBar);
39.
40.         JMenu menu = new JMenu("File");
41.         menuBar.add(menu);
42.
43.         JMenuItem openItem = new JMenuItem("Open");
44.         menu.add(openItem);
45.         openItem.addActionListener(new
46.             ActionListener()
47.             {
48.                 public void actionPerformed(ActionEvent event)
49.                 {
50.                     openFile();
51.                 }
52.             });
53.
54.         JMenuItem printItem = new JMenuItem("Print");
55.         menu.add(printItem);
56.         printItem.addActionListener(new
57.             ActionListener()
58.             {
59.                 public void actionPerformed(ActionEvent event)
60.                 {
61.                     printFile();
62.                 }
63.             });
64.
65.         JMenuItem exitItem = new JMenuItem("Exit");
66.         menu.add(exitItem);
67.         exitItem.addActionListener(new
68.             ActionListener()
69.             {
70.                 public void actionPerformed(ActionEvent event)
71.                 {
72.                     System.exit(0);
73.                 }
74.             });
75.
```

```
76.        menu = new JMenu("Printer");
77.        menuBar.add(menu);
78.        DocFlavor flavor = DocFlavor.INPUT_STREAM.GIF;
79.        addPrintServices(menu, flavor);
80.
81.        // use a label to display the images
82.        label = new JLabel();
83.        Container contentPane = getContentPane();
84.        contentPane.add(label);
85.     }
86.
87.     /**
88.        Adds print services to a menu
89.        @param menu the menu to which to add the services
90.        @param flavor the flavor that the services need to support
91.     */
92.     public void addPrintServices(JMenu menu, DocFlavor flavor)
93.     {
94.        PrintService[] services
95.           = PrintServiceLookup.lookupPrintServices(flavor, null);
96.        ButtonGroup group = new ButtonGroup();
97.        for (int i = 0; i < services.length; i++)
98.        {
99.           final PrintService service = services[i];
100.          JRadioButtonMenuItem item
101.             = new JRadioButtonMenuItem(service.getName());
102.          menu.add(item);
103.          if (i == 0)
104.          {
105.             item.setSelected(true);
106.             currentService = service;
107.          }
108.          group.add(item);
109.          item.addActionListener(new
110.             ActionListener()
111.             {
112.                public void actionPerformed(ActionEvent event)
113.                {
114.                   currentService = service;
115.                }
116.             });
117.       }
118.    }
119.
120.    /**
121.       Open a GIF file and display the image.
122.    */
```

```
123.    public void openFile()
124.    {
125.        // set up file chooser
126.        JFileChooser chooser = new JFileChooser();
127.        chooser.setCurrentDirectory(new File("."));
128.
129.        // accept all files ending with .gif
130.        chooser.setFileFilter(new
131.            javax.swing.filechooser.FileFilter()
132.            {
133.                public boolean accept(File f)
134.                {
135.                    return f.getName().toLowerCase()
136.                        .endsWith(".gif")
137.                        || f.isDirectory();
138.                }
139.                public String getDescription()
140.                {
141.                    return "GIF Images";
142.                }
143.            });
144.
145.        // show file chooser dialog
146.        int r = chooser.showOpenDialog(PrintServiceFrame.this);
147.
148.        // if image file accepted, set it as icon of the label
149.        if(r == JFileChooser.APPROVE_OPTION)
150.        {
151.            fileName = chooser.getSelectedFile().getPath();
152.            label.setIcon(new ImageIcon(fileName));
153.        }
154.    }
155.
156.    /**
157.        Print the current file using the current print service.
158.    */
159.    public void printFile()
160.    {
161.        try
162.        {
163.            if (fileName == null) return;
164.            if (currentService == null) return;
165.            FileInputStream in = new FileInputStream(fileName);
166.            DocFlavor flavor = DocFlavor.INPUT_STREAM.GIF;
167.            Doc doc = new SimpleDoc(in, flavor, null);
168.            DocPrintJob job = currentService.createPrintJob();
169.            job.print(doc, null);
170.        }
```

```
171.        catch (FileNotFoundException exception)
172.        {
173.            JOptionPane.showMessageDialog(this, exception);
174.        }
175.        catch (PrintException exception)
176.        {
177.            JOptionPane.showMessageDialog(this, exception);
178.        }
179.    }
180.
181.    private JLabel label;
182.    private String fileName;
183.    private PrintService currentService;
184.    private static final int WIDTH = 300;
185.    private static final int HEIGHT = 400;
186. }
```

javax.print.PrintServiceLookup

- PrintService[] lookupPrintServices(DocFlavor flavor, Attribute-Set attributes)

  looks up the print services that can handle the given document flavor and attributes.

Parameters:	flavor	the document flavor
	attributes	the required printing attributes, or null if attributes should not be taken into consideration

javax.print.PrintService

- DocPrintJob createPrintJob()

  creates a print job for printing an object of a class that implements the Doc interface, such as a SimpleDoc.

javax.print.DocPrintJob

- void print(Doc doc, PrintRequestAttributeSet attributes)

  prints the given document with the given attributes.

Parameters:	doc	the Doc to be printed
	attributes	the required printing attributes, or null if no printing attributes are required

---

`javax.print.SimpleDoc`

- `SimpleDoc(Object data, DocFlavor flavor, DocAttributeSet attributes)`

  constructs a `SimpleDoc` that can be printed with a `DocPrintJob`

Parameters:	`data`	the object with the print data, such as an input stream or a `Printable`
	`flavor`	the document flavor of the print data
	`attributes`	document attributes, or `null` if attributes are not required

Stream Print Services

A print service sends print data to a printer. A stream print service generates the same print data but instead sends them to a stream, perhaps for delayed printing or because the print data format can be interpreted by other programs. In particular, if the print data format is PostScript, then it is useful to save the print data to a file since there are many programs that can process PostScript files.

SDK 1.4 includes a stream print service that can produce PostScript output from images and 2D graphics. You can use that service on all systems, even if there are no local printers.

Enumerating stream print services is a bit more tedious than locating regular print services. You need both the `DocFlavor` of the object to be printed and the MIME type of the stream output. You then get a `StreamPrintService-Factory` array of factories.

```
DocFlavor flavor = DocFlavor.SERVICE_FORMATTED.PRINTABLE;
String mimeType = "application/postscript";
StreamPrintServiceFactory[] factories
    = StreamPrintServiceFactory.lookupStreamPrintServiceFactories
        (flavor, mimeType);
```

The `StreamPrintServiceFactory` class doesn't have any methods that would help you distinguish any one factory from another, so we'll just take `factories[0]`. Call the `getPrintService` method with an output stream parameter to get a `StreamPrintService` object.

```
OutputStream out = new FileOutputStream(fileName);
StreamPrintService service = factories[0].getPrintService(out);
```

The `StreamPrintService` class is a subclass of `PrintService`. To produce a printout, simply follow the steps of the preceding section.

Example 7–15 prints the "Hello, World" graphic from the preceding examples to a PostScript file.

NOTE: Unlike the other printing programs, this program works fine on Linux. You can use GhostScript (`http://www.cs.wisc.edu/~ghost/`) to view or print the resulting output (see Figure 7–42).

Figure 7–42: Viewing a PostScript File

Example 7–15: StreamPrintServiceTest.java

```
1. import java.awt.*;
2. import java.awt.event.*;
3. import java.awt.font.*;
4. import java.awt.geom.*;
5. import java.awt.print.*;
6. import java.io.*;
7. import java.util.*;
8. import javax.print.*;
9. import javax.print.attribute.*;
10. import javax.swing.*;
11.
12.
13. /**
14.    This program demonstrates the use of a stream print service.
15.    It prints a 2D graphic to a PostScript file.
16. */
```

```
17. public class StreamPrintServiceTest
18. {
19.    public static void main(String[] args)
20.    {
21.       JFrame frame = new StreamPrintServiceFrame();
22.       frame.setDefaultCloseOperation(JFrame.EXIT_ON_CLOSE);
23.       frame.show();
24.    }
25. }
26.
27. /**
28.    This frame shows a panel with 2D graphics and buttons
29.    to print the graphics to a PostScript file and to set up
30.    the page format.
31. */
32. class StreamPrintServiceFrame extends JFrame
33. {
34.    public StreamPrintServiceFrame()
35.    {
36.       setTitle("StreamPrintServiceTest");
37.       setSize(WIDTH, HEIGHT);
38.
39.       Container contentPane = getContentPane();
40.       canvas = new PrintPanel();
41.       contentPane.add(canvas, BorderLayout.CENTER);
42.
43.       attributes = new HashPrintRequestAttributeSet();
44.
45.       JPanel buttonPanel = new JPanel();
46.       JButton printButton = new JButton("Print");
47.       buttonPanel.add(printButton);
48.       printButton.addActionListener(new
49.          ActionListener()
50.          {
51.             public void actionPerformed(ActionEvent event)
52.             {
53.                String fileName = getFile();
54.                if (fileName != null)
55.                   printPostScript(fileName);
56.             }
57.          });
58.
59.       JButton pageSetupButton = new JButton("Page setup");
60.       buttonPanel.add(pageSetupButton);
61.       pageSetupButton.addActionListener(new
62.          ActionListener()
63.          {
64.             public void actionPerformed(ActionEvent event)
65.             {
```

```
66.            PrinterJob job = PrinterJob.getPrinterJob();
67.            job.pageDialog(attributes);
68.         }
69.      });
70.
71.      contentPane.add(buttonPanel, BorderLayout.NORTH);
72.   }
73.
74.   /**
75.      Allows the user to select a PostScript file.
76.      @return the file name, or null if the user didn't
77.      select a file.
78.   */
79.   public String getFile()
80.   {
81.      // set up file chooser
82.      JFileChooser chooser = new JFileChooser();
83.      chooser.setCurrentDirectory(new File("."));
84.
85.      // accept all files ending with .ps
86.      chooser.setFileFilter(new
87.         javax.swing.filechooser.FileFilter()
88.         {
89.            public boolean accept(File f)
90.            {
91.               return f.getName().toLowerCase()
92.                  .endsWith(".ps")
93.                  || f.isDirectory();
94.            }
95.            public String getDescription()
96.            {
97.               return "PostScript Files";
98.            }
99.         });
100.
101.      // show file chooser dialog
102.      int r = chooser.showSaveDialog(this);
103.
104.      // if file accepted, return path
105.      if(r == JFileChooser.APPROVE_OPTION)
106.         return chooser.getSelectedFile().getPath();
107.      else
108.         return null;
109.   }
110.
111.   /**
112.      Prints the 2D graphic to a PostScript file.
113.      @param fileName the name of the PostScript file
114.   */
```

```
115.    public void printPostScript(String fileName)
116.    {
117.       try
118.       {
119.          DocFlavor flavor
120.             = DocFlavor.SERVICE_FORMATTED.PRINTABLE;
121.          String mimeType = "application/postscript";
122.          StreamPrintServiceFactory[] factories =
123.             StreamPrintServiceFactory
124.            .lookupStreamPrintServiceFactories(flavor, mimeType);
125.
126.          FileOutputStream out = new FileOutputStream(fileName);
127.          if (factories.length == 0) return;
128.          StreamPrintService service
129.             = factories[0].getPrintService(out);
130.
131.          Doc doc = new SimpleDoc(canvas, flavor, null);
132.          DocPrintJob job = service.createPrintJob();
133.          job.print(doc, attributes);
134.       }
135.       catch (FileNotFoundException exception)
136.       {
137.          JOptionPane.showMessageDialog(this, exception);
138.       }
139.       catch (PrintException exception)
140.       {
141.          JOptionPane.showMessageDialog(this, exception);
142.       }
143.
144.    }
145.
146.    private PrintPanel canvas;
147.    private PrintRequestAttributeSet attributes;
148.
149.    private static final int WIDTH = 300;
150.    private static final int HEIGHT = 300;
151. }
152.
153. /**
154.    This panel generates a 2D graphics image for screen display
155.    and printing.
156. */
157. class PrintPanel extends JPanel implements Printable
158. {
159.    public void paintComponent(Graphics g)
160.    {
161.       super.paintComponent(g);
162.       Graphics2D g2 = (Graphics2D)g;
163.       drawPage(g2);
```

```
164.     }
165.
166.     public int print(Graphics g, PageFormat pf, int page)
167.         throws PrinterException
168.     {
169.         if (page >= 1) return Printable.NO_SUCH_PAGE;
170.         Graphics2D g2 = (Graphics2D)g;
171.         g2.translate(pf.getImageableX(), pf.getImageableY());
172.         g2.draw(new Rectangle2D.Double(0, 0,
173.             pf.getImageableWidth(), pf.getImageableHeight()));
174.
175.         drawPage(g2);
176.         return Printable.PAGE_EXISTS;
177.     }
178.
179.     /**
180.         This method draws the page both on the screen and the
181.         printer graphics context.
182.         @param g2 the graphics context
183.     */
184.     public void drawPage(Graphics2D g2)
185.     {
186.         FontRenderContext context = g2.getFontRenderContext();
187.         Font f = new Font("Serif", Font.PLAIN, 72);
188.         GeneralPath clipShape = new GeneralPath();
189.
190.         TextLayout layout = new TextLayout("Hello", f, context);
191.         AffineTransform transform
192.             = AffineTransform.getTranslateInstance(0, 72);
193.         Shape outline = layout.getOutline(transform);
194.         clipShape.append(outline, false);
195.
196.         layout = new TextLayout("World", f, context);
197.         transform
198.             = AffineTransform.getTranslateInstance(0, 144);
199.         outline = layout.getOutline(transform);
200.         clipShape.append(outline, false);
201.
202.         g2.draw(clipShape);
203.         g2.clip(clipShape);
204.
205.         final int NLINES =50;
206.         Point2D p = new Point2D.Double(0, 0);
207.         for (int i = 0; i < NLINES; i++)
208.         {
209.             double x = (2 * getWidth() * i) / NLINES;
210.             double y = (2 * getHeight() * (NLINES - 1 - i))
211.                 / NLINES;
```

```
212.            Point2D q = new Point2D.Double(x, y);
213.            g2.draw(new Line2D.Double(p, q));
214.        }
215.    }
216. }
```

javax.print.StreamPrintServiceFactory

- `StreamPrintServiceFactory[] lookupStreamPrintServiceFactories (DocFlavor flavor, String mimeType)`

  looks up the stream print service factories that can print the given document flavor and produce an output stream of the given MIME type.

- `StreamPrintService getPrintService(OutputStream out)`

  gets a print service that sends the printing output to the given output stream.

Printing Attributes

The print service API contains a complex set of interfaces and classes to specify various kinds of attributes. There are four important groups of attributes. The first two specify requests to the printer.

- *Print request attributes* are used to request particular features for all doc objects in a print job, such as two-sided printing or the paper size.
- *Doc attributes* are request attributes that apply only to a single doc object.

The other two contain information about the printer and job status.

- *Print service attributes* give information about the print service, such as the printer make and model, or whether the printer is currently accepting jobs.
- *Print job attributes* give information about the status of a particular print job, such as whether the job is already completed.

To describe the various attributes, there is an interface `Attribute` with subinterfaces:

```
PrintRequestAttribute
DocAttribute
PrintServiceAttribute
PrintJobAttribute
SupportedValuesAttribute
```

Individual attribute classes implement one or more of these interfaces. For example, objects of the `Copies` class are used to describe the number of copies of a printout. That class implements both the `PrintRequestAttribute` and the `PrintJobAttribute` interfaces. Clearly, a print request may contain a request for multiple copies. Conversely, an attribute of the print job may be how many of these copies were actually printed. That number might be lower, perhaps because of printer limitations or because the printer ran out of paper.

The `SupportedValuesAttribute` interface indicates that an attribute value does not reflect actual request or status data but the capability of a service. For example, there is a `CopiesSupported` class implementing the `SupportedValuesAttribute` interface. An object of that class might describe that a printer supports 1 through 99 copies of a printout.

Figure 7–43 shows a class diagram of the attribute hierarchy:

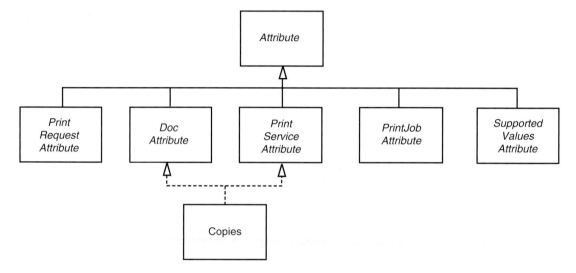

Figure 7–43: The Attribute Hierarchy

In addition to the interfaces and classes for individual attributes, the print service API defines interfaces and classes for attribute sets. There is a superinterface `AttributeSet` with four subinterfaces

```
PrintRequestAttributeSet
DocAttributeSet
PrintServiceAttributeSet
PrintJobAttributeSet
```

For each of these interfaces, there is an implementing class, yielding the five classes:

```
HashAttributeSet
HashPrintRequestAttributeSet
HashDocAttributeSet
HashPrintServiceAttributeSet
HashPrintJobAttributeSet
```

(See Figure 7–44.) For example, you construct a print request attribute set like this:

```
PrintRequestAttributeSet attributes
    = new HashPrintRequestAttributeSet();
```

After constructing the set, you no longer need to worry about the Hash prefix.

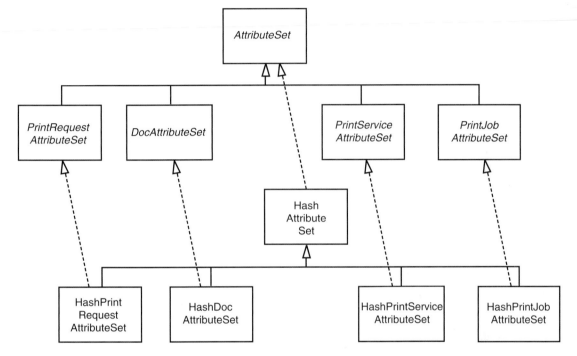

Figure 7–44: The Attribute Set Hierarchy

Why have all these interfaces? They make it possible to check for correct attribute usage. For example, a DocAttributeSet only accepts objects that implement the DocAttribute interface. Any attempt to add another attribute results in a runtime error.

An attribute set is a very specialized kind of map, where the keys are of type Class and the values belong to a class that implements the Attribute interface. For example, if you insert an object

```
new Copies(10)
```

into an attribute set, then its key is the Class object Copies.class. That key is called the *category* of the attribute. The Attribute interface declares a method

```
Class getCategory()
```

that returns the category of an attribute. The Copies class defines the method to return the object Copies.class, but it isn't a requirement that the category is the same as the class of the attribute.

When adding an attribute to an attribute set, the category is extracted automatically. You just add the attribute value:

```
attributes.add(new Copies(10));
```

If you subsequently add another attribute with the same category, it overwrites the first one.

To retrieve an attribute, you need to use the category as the key, for example

```
AttributeSet attributes = job.getAttributes();
Copies copies = (Copies)attribute.get(Copies.class);
```

Finally, attributes are organized by the values they can have. The `Copies` attribute can have any integer value. The `Copies` class extends the `IntegerSyntax` class which takes care of all integer-valued attributes. The `getValue` method returns the integer value of the attribute, for example

```
int n = copies.getValue();
```

There are also classes

```
TextSyntax
DateTimeSyntax
URISyntax
```

that encapsulate a string, date and time, or a URI (Uniform Resource Identifier).

Finally, there are many attributes that can take a finite number of values. For example, the `PrintQuality` attribute has three settings: draft, normal, and high. They are represented by three constants:

```
PrintQuality.DRAFT
PrintQuality.NORMAL
PrintQuality.HIGH
```

Attribute classes with a finite number of values extend the `EnumSyntax` class which provides a number of convenience methods to set up these enumerations in a typesafe manner. You don't need to worry about the mechanism when using such an attribute. Simply add the named values to attribute sets:

```
attributes.add(PrintQuality.HIGH);
```

Here is how you check the value of an attribute.

```
if (attributes.get(PrintQuality.class) == PrintQuality.HIGH)
    . . .
```

Table 7–4 lists the printing attributes. The second column lists the superclass of the attribute class (for example, `IntegerSyntax` for the `Copies` attribute), or the set of enumeration values for the attributes with a finite set of values. The last four columns indicate whether the attribute class implements the `DocAttribute` (DA), `PrintJobAttribute` (PJA), `PrintRequestAttribute` (PRA), and `PrintServiceAttribute` (PSA) interfaces.

NOTE: As you can see, there are lots of attributes, many of which are quite specialized. The source for most of the attributes is the Internet Printing Protocol 1.1 (RFC 2911).

This concludes our discussion on printing. You now know how to print 2D graphics and other document types, how to enumerate printers and stream print services, and how to set and retrieve attributes. Next, we will turn to two important user interface issues, the clipboard and support for the drag-and-drop mechanism.

NOTE: SDK 1.3 introduced the `JobAttributes` and `PageAttributes` classes, whose purpose is similar to the printing attributes covered in this section. Unless you need to specifically support SDK 1.3, you should instead use the more robust SDK 1.4 print service mechanism.

Table 7–4: Printing Attributes

Attribute	Superclass or enumeration constants	DA	PJA	PRA	PSA
Chromaticity	MONOCHROME, COLOR	x	x	x	
ColorSupported	SUPPORTED, NOT_SUPPORTED				x
Compression	COMPRESS, DEFLATE, GZIP, NONE	x			
Copies	IntegerSyntax		x	x	
DateTimeAtCompleted	DateTimeSyntax		x		
DateTimeAtCreation	DateTimeSyntax		x		
DateTimeAtProcessing	DateTimeSyntax		x		
Destination	URISyntax		x	x	
DocumentName	TextSyntax	x			
Fidelity	FIDELITY_TRUE, FIDELITY_FALSE		x	x	
Finishings	NONE, STAPLE, EDGE_STITCH, BIND, SADDLE_STITCH, COVER, . . .	x	x	x	

Table 7–4: Printing Attributes (continued)

Attribute	Superclass or enumeration constants	DA	PJA	PRA	PSA
JobHoldUntil	`DateTimeSyntax`		x	x	
JobImpressions	`IntegerSyntax`		x	x	
JobImpressionsCompleted	`IntegerSyntax`		x		
JobKOctets	`IntegerSyntax`		x	x	
JobKOctetsProcessed	`IntegerSyntax`		x		
JobMediaSheets	`IntegerSyntax`		x	x	
JobMediaSheetsCompleted	`IntegerSyntax`		x		
JobMessageFromOperator	`TextSyntax`		x		
JobName	`TextSyntax`		x	x	
JobOriginatingUserName	`TextSyntax`		x		
JobPriority	`IntegerSyntax`		x	x	
JobSheets	`STANDARD, NONE`		x	x	

JobState	`ABORTED, CANCELED,`
	`COMPLETED, PEND-`
	`ING, PENDING_HELD,`
	`PROCESSING,`
	`PROCESSING_STOPPED`
			x		

JobStateReason	`ABORTED_BY_SYSTEM,`
	`DOCUMENT_FORMAT_ERR`
	`OR,` many others				

JobStateReasons	`HashSet`		x		

MediaName	`ISO_A4_WHITE,`
	`ISO_A4_TRANSPARENT,`
	`NA_LETTER_WHITE,`
	`NA_LETTER_TRANSPARE`
	`NT`
		x	x	x	

MediaSize	`ISO.A0 - ISO.A10,`
	`ISO.B0 - ISO.B10,`
	`ISO.C0 - ISO.C10,`
	`NA.LETTER,`
	`NA.LEGAL,` various
	other paper and
	envelope sizes				

MediaSizeName	`ISO_A0 - ISO_A10,`
	`ISO_B0 - ISO_B10,`
	`ISO_C0 - ISO_C10,`
	`NA_LETTER,`
	`NA_LEGAL,` various
	other paper and
	envelope size names
		x	x	x	

Table 7–4: Printing Attributes (continued)

Attribute	Superclass or enumeration constants	DA	PJA	PRA	PSA
MediaTray	`TOP, MIDDLE, BOTTOM, SIDE, ENVELOPE, LARGE_CAPACITY, MAIN, MANUAL,`	X	X	X	
MultipleDocument-Handling	`SINGLE_DOCUMENT, SINGLE_DOCUMENT_NEW _SHEET, SEPARATE_DOCUMENTS_ COLLATED_COPIES, SEPARATE_DOCUMENTS_ UNCOLLATED_COPIES`		X	X	
NumberOfDocuments	`IntegerSyntax`		X		
NumberOfInterveningJobs	`IntegerSyntax`		X		
NumberUp	`IntegerSyntax`	X	X	X	
OrientationRequested	`PORTRAIT, LAND-SCAPE, REVERSE_PORTRAIT, REVERSE_LANDSCAPE`	X	X	X	
OutputDeviceAssigned	`TextSyntax`		X		
PageRanges	`SetOfInteger`	X	X	X	
PagesPerMinute	`IntegerSyntax`				X
PagesPerMinuteColor	`IntegerSyntax`				X
PDLOverrideSupported	`ATTEMPTED, NOT_ATTEMPTED`				X
PresentationDirection	`TORIGHT_TOBOTTOM, TORIGHT_TOTOP, TOBOTTOM_TORIGHT, TOBOTTOM_TOLEFT, TOLEFT_TOBOTTOM, TOLEFT_TOTOP, TOTOP_TORIGHT, TOTOP_TOLEFT`		X	X	
PrinterInfo	`TextSyntax`				X
PrinterIsAcceptingJobs	`ACCEPTING_JOBS, NOT_ACCEPTING_JOBS`				X
PrinterLocation	`TextSyntax`				X
PrinterMakeAndModel	`TextSyntax`				X
PrinterMessageFrom-Operator	`TextSyntax`				X

Table 7–4: Printing Attributes (continued)

Attribute	Superclass or enumeration constants	DA	PJA	PRA	PSA
PrinterMoreInfo	`URISyntax`				x
PrinterMoreInfoManufacturer	`URISyntax`				x
PrinterName	`TextSyntax`				x
PrinterResolution	`ResolutionSyntax`	x	x	x	
PrinterState	`PROCESSING, IDLE, STOPPED, UNKNOWN`				x
PrinterStateReason	`COVER_OPEN, FUSER_OVER_TEMP, MEDIA_JAM,` and many others				
PrinterStateReasons	`HashMap`				
PrinterURI	`URISyntax`				x
PrintQuality	`DRAFT, NORMAL, HIGH`	x	x	x	
QueuedJobCount	`IntegerSyntax`				x
ReferenceUriSchemesSupported	`FILE, FTP, GOPHER, HTTP, HTTPS, NEWS, NNTP, WAIS`				
RequestingUserName	`TextSyntax`			x	
Severity	`ERROR, REPORT, WARNING`				
SheetCollate	`COLLATED, UNCOLLATED`	x	x	x	
Sides	`ONE_SIDED, DUPLEX (=TWO_SIDED_LONG_EDGE), TUMBLE (=TWO_SIDED_SHORT_EDGE)`	x	x	x	

javax.print.attribute.Attribute

- `Class getCategory()`

  gets the category of this attribute.

- `String getName()`

  gets the name of this attribute.

`javax.print.attribute.AttributeSet`

- `boolean add(Attribute attr)`
  adds an attribute to this set. If the set has another attribute with the same category, that attribute is replaced by the given attribute. Returns `true` if the set changed as a result of this operation.

- `Attribute get(Class category)`
  retrieves the attribute with the given category key, or `null` if no such attribute exists.

- `boolean remove(Attribute attr)`
- `boolean remove(Class category)`
  remove the given attribute, or the attribute with the given category, from the set. Return `true` if the set changed as a result of this operation.

- `Attribute[] toArray()`
  returns an array with all attributes in this set.

`javax.print.PrintService`

- `PrintServiceAttributeSet getAttributes()`
  gets the attributes of this print service.

`javax.print.DocPrintJob`

- `PrintJobAttributeSet getAttributes()`
  gets the attributes of this print job.

The Clipboard

One of the most useful and convenient user interface mechanisms of graphical user interface environments (such as Windows and the X Window System) *is cut and paste.* You select some data in one program and cut or copy it to the clipboard. Then, you select another program and paste the clipboard contents into that application. Using the clipboard, you can transfer text, images, or other data from one document to another, or, of course, from one place in a document to another place in the same document. Cut and paste is so natural that most computer users never think about it.

However, in SDK 1.0, there was no support for cut and paste. You could not cut and paste between Java applications. For example, if you have a browser written in the Java programming language, then you could not copy text and images from a web page and transfer them into a word processor based on Java technology. SDK 1.1 implemented a rudimentary clipboard mechanism.

That mechanism has been gradually improved and is now quite usable on a number of platforms.

Even though the clipboard is conceptually simple, implementing clipboard services is actually harder than you might think. Suppose you copy text from a word processor into the clipboard. If you paste that text into another word processor, then you expect that the fonts and formatting will stay intact. That is, the text in the clipboard needs to retain the formatting information. But if you paste the text into a plain text field, then you expect that just the characters are pasted in, without additional formatting codes. To support this flexibility, the data provider can offer the clipboard data in multiple formats, and the data consumer can pick one of them.

The system clipboard implementations of Microsoft Windows, OS/2, and the Macintosh are similar, but, of course, there are slight differences. However, the X Window System clipboard mechanism is much more limited—cutting and pasting of anything but plain text is only sporadically supported. You should consider these limitations when trying out the programs in this section.

NOTE: Check out the file `jre/lib/flavormap.properties` on your platform to get an idea what kinds of objects can be transferred between Java programs and the system clipboard.

Often, programs need to support cut and paste of data types that the system clipboard cannot handle. The data transfer API supports the transfer of arbitrary local object references in the same virtual machine. Between different virtual machines, you can transfer serialized objects and references to remote objects.

Table 7–5 summarizes the data transfer capabilities of the clipboard mechanism.

Table 7–5: Capabilities of the Java data transfer mechanism

Transfer	Format
Between a program in Java programming language and a native program	Text, images, file lists, . . . (depending on the host platform)
Between two cooperating programs in the Java programming language	Serialized and remote objects
Within one program in the Java programming language	Any object

Classes and Interfaces for Data Transfer

Data transfer in the Java technology is implemented in a package called `java.awt.datatransfer`. Here is an overview of the most important classes and interfaces of that package.

- Objects that can be transferred via a clipboard must implement the `Transferable` interface.

- The `Clipboard` class describes a clipboard. Transferable objects are the only items that can be put on or taken off a clipboard. The system clipboard is a concrete example of a `Clipboard`.

- The `DataFlavor` class describes data flavors that can be placed on the clipboard.

- The `StringSelection` class is a concrete class that implements the `Transferable` interface. It is used to transfer text strings.

- A class must implement the `ClipboardOwner` interface if it wants to be notified when the clipboard contents have been overwritten by someone else. Clipboard ownership enables "delayed formatting" of complex data. If a program transfers simple data (such as a string), then it simply sets the clipboard contents and moves on to do the next thing. However, if a program wants to place complex data that can be formatted in multiple flavors onto the clipboard, then it may not actually want to prepare all the flavors, since there is a good chance that most of them are never needed. However, then it needs to hang on to the clipboard data so that it can create the flavors later when they are requested. The clipboard owner is notified (by calling its `lostOwnership` method) when the contents of the clipboard change. That tells it that the information is no longer needed. In our sample programs, we don't need to worry about clipboard ownership.

Transferring Text

The best way to get comfortable with the data transfer classes is to start with the simplest situation: transferring text to and from the system clipboard. The idea of the following program is simple. First, get a reference to the system clipboard.

```
Clipboard clipboard =
    Toolkit.getDefaultToolkit().getSystemClipboard();
```

For strings to be transferred to the clipboard, they need to be wrapped into `StringSelection` objects. The constructor takes the text you want to transfer.

```
String text = . . .
StringSelection selection = new StringSelection(text);
```

The actual transfer is done by a call to `setContents`, which takes a `String-Selection` object and a `ClipBoardOwner` as parameters. If you are not interested in designating a clipboard owner, set the second parameter to `null`.

```
clipboard.setContents(selection, null);
```

Let us look at the reverse operation, reading a string from the clipboard. Call the getContents method of the clipboard to get a Transferable object.

```
Transferable contents = clipBoard.getContents(null);
```

According to the API documentation, the parameter of the getContents call is an Object reference of the requesting object. It is not clear why the clipboard collects this information.

The return value of getContents may be null. That indicates that the clipboard is either empty or that it has no data that the Java platform knows how to retrieve.

The Transferable object can tell you in which flavors the clipboard information is available. We will discuss the details of flavor discovery later. For now, we want only the standard flavor called DataFlavor.stringFlavor. Use the isDataFlavorSupported method to find out whether the flavor that you want is actually available.

Finally, you pass the desired flavor to the getTransferData method. The method call must be enclosed in a try block because the method threatens to throw an UnsupportedFlavorException if the requested flavor is not available, or an IOException if it cannot read the data.

```
DataFlavor flavor = DataFlavor.stringFlavor;
if (contents.isDataFlavorSupported(flavor))
{
    try
    {
        String text = (String)(contents.getTransferData(flavor);
        do something with text;
    }
    catch(UnsupportedFlavorException exception)
    {
        . . .
    }
    catch(IOException exception)
    {
        . . .
    }
}
```

Example 7–16 is a program that demonstrates cutting and pasting between a Java application and the system clipboard. Figure 7–45 shows a screen shot. If you select an area of text in the text area and click on Copy, then the selected text is copied to the system clipboard. As Figure 7–46 shows, the copied text does indeed get stored on the system clipboard. When you subsequently click on the Paste button, the contents of the clipboard (which may come from a native program) are pasted at the cursor position.

Figure 7–45: The TextTransferTest program

Figure 7–46: The Windows clipboard viewer after a copy

Example 7–16: TextTransferTest.java

```
1. import java.awt.*;
2. import java.awt.datatransfer.*;
3. import java.awt.event.*;
4. import java.io.*;
5. import javax.swing.*;
6.
7. /**
8.    This program demonstrates the transfer of text
9.    between a Java application and the system clipboard.
10. */
```

```
11. public class TextTransferTest
12. {
13.    public static void main(String[] args)
14.    {
15.       JFrame frame = new TextTransferFrame();
16.       frame.setDefaultCloseOperation(JFrame.EXIT_ON_CLOSE);
17.       frame.show();
18.    }
19. }
20.
21. /**
22.    This frame has a text area and buttons for copying and
23.    pasting text.
24. */
25. class TextTransferFrame extends JFrame
26. {
27.    public TextTransferFrame()
28.    {
29.       setTitle("TextTransferTest");
30.       setSize(WIDTH, HEIGHT);
31.
32.       Container contentPane = getContentPane();
33.
34.       textArea = new JTextArea();
35.       contentPane.add(new JScrollPane(textArea),
36.          BorderLayout.CENTER);
37.       JPanel panel = new JPanel();
38.
39.       JButton copyButton = new JButton("Copy");
40.       panel.add(copyButton);
41.       copyButton.addActionListener(new
42.          ActionListener()
43.          {
44.             public void actionPerformed(ActionEvent event)
45.             {
46.                copy();
47.             }
48.          });
49.
50.       JButton pasteButton = new JButton("Paste");
51.       panel.add(pasteButton);
52.       pasteButton.addActionListener(new
53.          ActionListener()
54.          {
55.             public void actionPerformed(ActionEvent event)
56.             {
57.                paste();
58.             }
59.          });
60.
61.       contentPane.add(panel, BorderLayout.SOUTH);
62.    }
```

```
63.
64.     /**
65.        Copies the selected text to the system clipboard.
66.     */
67.     private void copy()
68.     {
69.        Clipboard clipboard
70.           = Toolkit.getDefaultToolkit().getSystemClipboard();
71.        String text = textArea.getSelectedText();
72.        if (text == null) text = textArea.getText();
73.        StringSelection selection = new StringSelection(text);
74.        clipboard.setContents(selection, null);
75.     }
76.
77.     /**
78.        Pastes the text from the system clipboard into the
79.        text area.
80.     */
81.     private void paste()
82.     {
83.        Clipboard clipboard
84.           = Toolkit.getDefaultToolkit().getSystemClipboard();
85.        Transferable contents = clipboard.getContents(this);
86.        if (contents == null) return;
87.        DataFlavor flavor = DataFlavor.stringFlavor;
88.        if (contents.isDataFlavorSupported(flavor))
89.        {
90.           try
91.           {
92.              String text
93.                 = (String)(contents.getTransferData(flavor));
94.              textArea.replaceSelection(text);
95.           }
96.           catch(UnsupportedFlavorException exception)
97.           {
98.              JOptionPane.showMessageDialog(this, exception);
99.           }
100.          catch(IOException exception)
101.          {
102.             JOptionPane.showMessageDialog(this, exception);
103.          }
104.       }
105.    }
106.
107.    private JTextArea textArea;
108.
109.    private static final int WIDTH = 300;
110.    private static final int HEIGHT = 300;
111. }
```

java.awt.Toolkit

- Clipboard getSystemClipboard()
  gets the system clipboard.

java.awt.datatransfer.Clipboard

- Transferable getContents(Object requester)
  gets the clipboard contents.

  Parameters: requester the object requesting the clipboard contents. This
                            value is not actually used.

- void setContents(Transferable contents, ClipboardOwner owner)
  puts contents on the clipboard.

  Parameters: contents the Transferable encapsulating the contents

                owner   the object to be notified (via its lostOwnership
                          method) when new information is placed on the
                          clipboard, or null if no notification is desired

java.awt.datatransfer.ClipboardOwner

- void lostOwnership(Clipboard clipboard, Transferable contents)
  notifies this object that it is no longer the owner of the contents of the clipboard.

  Parameters: clipboard the clipboard onto which the contents
                            were placed

                contents   the item that this owner had placed onto
                           the clipboard

java.awt.datatransfer.Transferable

- boolean isDataFlavorSupported(DataFlavor flavor)
  returns true if the specified flavor is one of the supported data flavors;
  false otherwise.

- Object getTransferData(DataFlavor flavor)
  returns the data, formatted in the requested flavor. Throws an
  UnsupportedFlavorException if the flavor requested is not supported.

The Transferable Interface and Data Flavors

The clipboard holds an object that implements the Transferable interface. You
can find out all data flavors that a transferable object supports:

```
DataFlavor[] flavors = transferable.getTransferDataFlavors()
```

A `DataFlavor` is defined by two characteristics:

- A MIME type name (such as `"image/gif"`)
- A representation class for accessing the data (such as `java.awt.Image`)

In addition, every data flavor has a human-readable name (such as `"GIF Image"`).

The representation class can be specified with a `class` parameter in the MIME type, for example,

```
image/gif;class=java.awt.Image
```

NOTE: This is just an example to show the syntax. There is no standard data flavor for transferring GIF image data.

If no `class` parameter is given, then the representation class is `InputStream`.

Sun Microsystems defines three MIME types:

```
application/x-java-jvm-local-objectref
application/x-java-serialized-object
application/x-java-remote-object
```

for transferring local, serialized, and remote Java objects.

NOTE: The `x-` prefix indicates that this is an experimental name, not one that is sanctioned by IANA, the organization that assigns standard MIME type names.

For example, the standard `stringFlavor` data flavor is described by the MIME type

```
application/x-java-serialized-object;class=java.lang.String
```

java.awt.datatransfer.DataFlavor

- `DataFlavor(String mimeType, String humanPresentableName)`
  creates a data flavor that describes stream data in a format described by a MIME type.

  Parameters: `mimeType`   a MIME type string

            `humanPresentableName`   a more readable version of the name

- `DataFlavor(Class class, String humanPresentableName)`
  creates a data flavor that describes a Java platform class. Its MIME type is `application/x-java-serialized-object;class=`*className*.

  Parameters: `class`   the class that is retrieved from the `Transferable`

            `humanPresentableName`   a readable version of the name

- `String getMimeType()`
  returns the MIME type string for this data flavor.

- `boolean isMimeTypeEqual(String mimeType)`
  tests whether this data flavor has the given MIME type.

- `String getHumanPresentableName()`
  returns the human-presentable name for the data format of this data flavor.

- `Class getRepresentationClass()`
  returns a `Class` object that represents the class of the object that a `Transferable` will return when called with this data flavor. This is either the `class` parameter of the MIME type or `InputStream`.

java.awt.datatransfer.Transferable

- `DataFlavor[] getTransferDataFlavors()`
  returns an array of the supported flavors.

Building an Image Transferable

Objects that you want to transfer via the clipboard must implement the `Transferable` interface. The `StringSelection` class is currently the only public class in the Java standard library that implements the `Transferable` interface. In this section, you will see how to transfer images into the clipboard. Since the SDK does not supply a class for image transfer, you must implement it yourself.

The class is completely trivial. It simply reports that the only available data format is `DataFlavor.imageFlavor`, and it holds an `image` object.

```
class ImageSelection implements Transferable
{
   public ImageSelection(Image image)
   {
      theImage = image;
   }

   public DataFlavor[] getTransferDataFlavors()
   {
      return new DataFlavor[] { DataFlavor.imageFlavor };
   }

   public boolean isDataFlavorSupported(DataFlavor flavor)
   {
      return flavor.equals(DataFlavor.imageFlavor);
   }

   public Object getTransferData(DataFlavor flavor)
      throws UnsupportedFlavorException
```

```
    {
        if(flavor.equals(DataFlavor.imageFlavor))
        {
            return theImage;
        }
        else
        {
            throw new UnsupportedFlavorException(flavor);
        }
    }

    private Image theImage;
}
```

NOTE: The SDK supplies the `DataFlavor.imageFlavor` constant and does all the heavy lifting to convert between Java images and native clipboard images. But, curiously, it does not supply the wrapper class that is necessary to place images into the clipboard.

The program of Example 7–17 demonstrates the transfer of images between a Java application and the system clipboard. When the program starts, it generates a Mandelbrot image. Click the Copy button to copy the image to the clipboard and then paste it into another application. (See Figure 7–47). From another application, copy an image into the system clipboard. Then click the Paste button and see the image being pasted into the example program. (See Figure 7–48).

Figure 7–47: Copying from a Java program to a native program

Figure 7–48: Copying from a native program to a Java program

The program is a straightforward modification of the text transfer program. The data flavor is now `DataFlavor.imageFlavor`, and we use the `ImageSelection` class to transfer an image to the system clipboard.

Example 7–17: ImageTransferTest.java

```
1. import java.io.*;
2. import java.awt.*;
3. import java.awt.datatransfer.*;
4. import java.awt.event.*;
5. import java.awt.image.*;
6. import javax.swing.*;
7.
8. /**
9.    This program demonstrates the transfer of images
10.   between a Java application and the system clipboard.
11. */
12. public class ImageTransferTest
13. {
14.    public static void main(String[] args)
15.    {
16.       JFrame frame = new ImageTransferFrame();
17.       frame.setDefaultCloseOperation(JFrame.EXIT_ON_CLOSE);
18.       frame.show();
19.    }
20. }
21.
22. /**
```

```
23.    This frame has an image label and buttons for copying and
24.    pasting text.
25. */
26. class ImageTransferFrame extends JFrame
27. {
28.    public ImageTransferFrame()
29.    {
30.       setTitle("ImageTransferTest");
31.       setSize(WIDTH, HEIGHT);
32.
33.       Container contentPane = getContentPane();
34.
35.       label = new JLabel();
36.       image = makeMandelbrot(WIDTH, HEIGHT);
37.       label.setIcon(new ImageIcon(image));
38.       contentPane.add(new JScrollPane(label),
39.          BorderLayout.CENTER);
40.       JPanel panel = new JPanel();
41.
42.       JButton copyButton = new JButton("Copy");
43.       panel.add(copyButton);
44.       copyButton.addActionListener(new
45.          ActionListener()
46.          {
47.             public void actionPerformed(ActionEvent event)
48.             {
49.                copy();
50.             }
51.          });
52.
53.       JButton pasteButton = new JButton("Paste");
54.       panel.add(pasteButton);
55.       pasteButton.addActionListener(new
56.          ActionListener()
57.          {
58.             public void actionPerformed(ActionEvent event)
59.             {
60.                paste();
61.             }
62.          });
63.
64.       contentPane.add(panel, BorderLayout.SOUTH);
65.    }
66.
67.    /**
68.       Copies the current image to the system clipboard.
69.    */
70.    private void copy()
71.    {
```

```
72.      Clipboard clipboard
73.         = Toolkit.getDefaultToolkit().getSystemClipboard();
74.      ImageSelection selection = new ImageSelection(image);
75.      clipboard.setContents(selection, null);
76.   }
77.
78.   /**
79.      Pastes the image from the system clipboard into the
80.      image label.
81.   */
82.   private void paste()
83.   {
84.      Clipboard clipboard
85.         = Toolkit.getDefaultToolkit().getSystemClipboard();
86.      Transferable contents = clipboard.getContents(null);
87.      if (contents == null) return;
88.      DataFlavor flavor = DataFlavor.imageFlavor;
89.      if (contents.isDataFlavorSupported(flavor))
90.      {
91.         try
92.         {
93.            image = (Image)(contents.getTransferData(flavor));
94.            label.setIcon(new ImageIcon(image));
95.         }
96.         catch(UnsupportedFlavorException exception)
97.         {
98.            JOptionPane.showMessageDialog(this, exception);
99.         }
100.        catch(IOException exception)
101.        {
102.           JOptionPane.showMessageDialog(this, exception);
103.        }
104.     }
105.  }
106.
107.  /**
108.     Makes the Mandelbrot image.
109.     @param width the width
110.     @parah height the height
111.     @return the image
112.  */
113.  public BufferedImage makeMandelbrot(int width, int height)
114.  {
115.     BufferedImage image = new BufferedImage(width, height,
116.        BufferedImage.TYPE_INT_ARGB);
117.     WritableRaster raster = image.getRaster();
118.     ColorModel model = image.getColorModel();
119.
120.     Color fractalColor = Color.red;
```

```
121.        int argb = fractalColor.getRGB();
122.        Object colorData = model.getDataElements(argb, null);
123.
124.        for (int i = 0; i < width; i++)
125.           for (int j = 0; j < height; j++)
126.           {
127.              double a = XMIN + i * (XMAX - XMIN) / width;
128.              double b = YMIN + j * (YMAX - YMIN) / height;
129.              if (!escapesToInfinity(a, b))
130.                 raster.setDataElements(i, j, colorData);
131.           }
132.        return image;
133.     }
134.
135.     private boolean escapesToInfinity(double a, double b)
136.     {
137.        double x = 0.0;
138.        double y = 0.0;
139.        int iterations = 0;
140.        do
141.        {
142.           double xnew = x * x - y * y + a;
143.           double ynew = 2 * x * y + b;
144.           x = xnew;
145.           y = ynew;
146.           iterations++;
147.           if (iterations == MAX_ITERATIONS) return false;
148.        }
149.        while (x <= 2 && y <= 2);
150.        return true;
151.     }
152.
153.     private JLabel label;
154.     private Image image;
155.
156.     private static final double XMIN = -2;
157.     private static final double XMAX = 2;
158.     private static final double YMIN = -2;
159.     private static final double YMAX = 2;
160.     private static final int MAX_ITERATIONS = 16;
161.
162.     private static final int WIDTH = 300;
163.     private static final int HEIGHT = 300;
164. }
165.
166. /**
167.    This class is a wrapper for the data transfer of image
168.    objects.
```

```
169. */
170. class ImageSelection implements Transferable
171. {
172.    /**
173.        Constructs the selection.
174.        @param image an image
175.    */
176.    public ImageSelection(Image image)
177.    {
178.        theImage = image;
179.    }
180.
181.    public DataFlavor[] getTransferDataFlavors()
182.    {
183.        return new DataFlavor[] { DataFlavor.imageFlavor };
184.    }
185.
186.    public boolean isDataFlavorSupported(DataFlavor flavor)
187.    {
188.        return flavor.equals(DataFlavor.imageFlavor);
189.    }
190.
191.    public Object getTransferData(DataFlavor flavor)
192.        throws UnsupportedFlavorException
193.    {
194.        if(flavor.equals(DataFlavor.imageFlavor))
195.        {
196.            return theImage;
197.        }
198.        else
199.        {
200.            throw new UnsupportedFlavorException(flavor);
201.        }
202.    }
203.
204.    private Image theImage;
205. }
```

Using a Local Clipboard to Transfer Object References

Suppose you want to copy and paste a data type that isn't one of the data types supported by the system clipboard. For example, in a drawing program, you may want to allow your users to copy and paste arbitrary shapes.

The program in Example 7–18 demonstrates this capability. As you can see in Figure 7–49, the program displays two panels. By moving the rectangle "grabbers" in the left panel, you can change the shape of a cubic curve. The panel on the right side can display an arbitrary shape.

When you click on the Copy button, the current cubic curve shape is copied. Click on Paste, and the `Shape` object in the clipboard is displayed in the panel on the right hand side. You can see that the shape is held in a clipboard by copying a curve and then modifying the curve before pasting. The copied shape, and not the current shape of the curve, is pasted into the right side panel.

To transfer an arbitrary Java object reference within the same JVM, you use the MIME type

```
application/x-java-jvm-local-objectref;class=className
```

However, the SDK doesn't include a `Transferable` wrapper for this type. You can find the code for the wrapper in the example program. It is entirely analogous to the `ImageSelection` wrapper of the preceding section.

An object reference is only meaningful within a single virtual machine. For that reason, you cannot copy the shape object to the system clipboard. Instead, this program uses a local clipboard:

```
Clipboard clipboard = new Clipboard("local");
```

The construction parameter is the clipboard name.

However, using a local clipboard has one major disadvantage. You need to synchronize the local and the system clipboard, so that users don't get confused between the two. Currently, the Java platform doesn't do that synchronization for you.

Figure 7–49: Transferring Local Objects

Example 7–18: LocalTransferTest.java

```
1. import java.awt.*;
2. import java.awt.datatransfer.*;
3. import java.awt.event.*;
4. import java.awt.geom.*;
```

```
 5. import java.io.*;
 6. import java.util.*;
 7. import javax.swing.*;
 8.
 9. /**
10.    This program demonstrates the transfer of object references
11.    within the same virtual machine.
12. */
13. public class LocalTransferTest
14. {
15.    public static void main(String[] args)
16.    {
17.       JFrame frame = new LocalTransferFrame();
18.       frame.setDefaultCloseOperation(JFrame.EXIT_ON_CLOSE);
19.       frame.show();
20.    }
21. }
22.
23. /**
24.    This frame contains a panel to edit a cubic curve, a
25.    panel that can display an arbitrary shape, and copy and
26.    paste buttons.
27. */
28. class LocalTransferFrame extends JFrame
29. {
30.    public LocalTransferFrame()
31.    {
32.       setTitle("LocalTransferTest");
33.       setSize(WIDTH, HEIGHT);
34.
35.       Container contentPane = getContentPane();
36.
37.       curvePanel = new CubicCurvePanel();
38.       curvePanel.setPreferredSize(new Dimension(WIDTH / 2,
39.          HEIGHT));
40.       shapePanel = new ShapePanel();
41.
42.       contentPane.add(new JSplitPane(JSplitPane.HORIZONTAL_SPLIT,
43.          curvePanel, shapePanel), BorderLayout.CENTER);
44.       JPanel panel = new JPanel();
45.
46.       JButton copyButton = new JButton("Copy");
47.       panel.add(copyButton);
48.       copyButton.addActionListener(new
49.          ActionListener()
50.          {
51.             public void actionPerformed(ActionEvent event)
52.             {
53.                copy();
54.             }
55.          });
```

```
56.
57.        JButton pasteButton = new JButton("Paste");
58.        panel.add(pasteButton);
59.        pasteButton.addActionListener(new
60.           ActionListener()
61.           {
62.              public void actionPerformed(ActionEvent event)
63.              {
64.                 paste();
65.              }
66.           });
67.
68.        contentPane.add(panel, BorderLayout.SOUTH);
69.     }
70.
71.     /**
72.        Copies the current cubic curve to the local clipboard.
73.     */
74.     private void copy()
75.     {
76.        LocalSelection selection = new LocalSelection(
77.           curvePanel.getShape());
78.        clipboard.setContents(selection, null);
79.     }
80.
81.     /**
82.        Pastes the shape from the local clipboard into the
83.        shape panel.
84.     */
85.     private void paste()
86.     {
87.        Transferable contents = clipboard.getContents(null);
88.        if (contents == null) return;
89.        try
90.        {
91.           DataFlavor flavor = new DataFlavor(
92. "application/x-java-jvm-local-objectref;class=java.awt.Shape");
93.           if (contents.isDataFlavorSupported(flavor))
94.              shapePanel.setShape(
95.                 (Shape)contents.getTransferData(flavor));
96.        }
97.        catch(ClassNotFoundException exception)
98.        {
99.           JOptionPane.showMessageDialog(this, exception);
100.       }
101.       catch(UnsupportedFlavorException exception)
102.       {
103.          JOptionPane.showMessageDialog(this, exception);
104.       }
105.       catch(IOException exception)
106.       {
```

```
107.                 JOptionPane.showMessageDialog(this, exception);
108.         }
109.     }
110.
111.     private CubicCurvePanel curvePanel;
112.     private ShapePanel shapePanel;
113.     private Clipboard clipboard = new Clipboard("local");
114.
115.     private static final int WIDTH = 300;
116.     private static final int HEIGHT = 300;
117. }
118.
119.
120. /**
121.     This panel draws a shape and allows the user to
122.     move the points that define it.
123. */
124. class CubicCurvePanel extends JPanel
125. {
126.     public CubicCurvePanel()
127.     {
128.         addMouseListener(new
129.             MouseAdapter()
130.             {
131.                 public void mousePressed(MouseEvent event)
132.                 {
133.                     for (int i = 0; i < p.length; i++)
134.                     {
135.                         double x = p[i].getX() - SIZE / 2;
136.                         double y = p[i].getY() - SIZE / 2;
137.                         Rectangle2D r
138.                             = new Rectangle2D.Double(x, y, SIZE, SIZE);
139.                         if (r.contains(event.getPoint()))
140.                         {
141.                             current = i;
142.                             return;
143.                         }
144.                     }
145.                 }
146.
147.                 public void mouseReleased(MouseEvent event)
148.                 {
149.                     current = -1;
150.                 }
151.             });
152.
153.         addMouseMotionListener(new
154.             MouseMotionAdapter()
155.             {
156.                 public void mouseDragged(MouseEvent event)
157.                 {
```

```
158.                    if (current == -1) return;
159.                    p[current] = event.getPoint();
160.                    repaint();
161.                }
162.            });
163.
164.        current = -1;
165.    }
166.
167.    public void paintComponent(Graphics g)
168.    {
169.        super.paintComponent(g);
170.        Graphics2D g2 = (Graphics2D)g;
171.        for (int i = 0; i < p.length; i++)
172.        {
173.            double x = p[i].getX() - SIZE / 2;
174.            double y = p[i].getY() - SIZE / 2;
175.            g2.fill(new Rectangle2D.Double(x, y, SIZE, SIZE));
176.        }
177.
178.        g2.draw(getShape());
179.    }
180.
181.    /**
182.        Gets the current cubic curve.
183.        @return the curve shape
184.    */
185.    public Shape getShape()
186.    {
187.        return new CubicCurve2D.Double(p[0].getX(), p[0].getY(),
188.            p[1].getX(), p[1].getY(), p[2].getX(), p[2].getY(),
189.            p[3].getX(), p[3].getY());
190.    }
191.
192.    private Point2D[] p =
193.    {
194.        new Point2D.Double(10, 10),
195.        new Point2D.Double(10, 100),
196.        new Point2D.Double(100, 10),
197.        new Point2D.Double(100, 200)
198.    };
199.    private static int SIZE = 10;
200.    private int current;
201. }
202.
203. /**
204.    This panel displays an arbitrary shape.
205. */
206. class ShapePanel extends JPanel
207. {
208.    /**
```

```
209.         Set the shape to be displayed in this panel.
210.         @param aShape any shape
211.      */
212.      public void setShape(Shape aShape)
213.      {
214.         shape = aShape;
215.         repaint();
216.      }
217.
218.      public void paintComponent(Graphics g)
219.      {
220.         super.paintComponent(g);
221.         Graphics2D g2 = (Graphics2D)g;
222.         if (shape != null) g2.draw(shape);
223.      }
224.
225.      private Shape shape;
226. }
227.
228. /**
229.    This class is a wrapper for the data transfer of
230.    object references that are transferred within the same
231.    virtual machine.
232. */
233. class LocalSelection implements Transferable
234. {
235.    /**
236.       Constructs the selection.
237.       @param o any object
238.    */
239.    LocalSelection(Object o)
240.    {
241.       obj = o;
242.    }
243.
244.    public DataFlavor[] getTransferDataFlavors()
245.    {
246.       DataFlavor[] flavors = new DataFlavor[1];
247.       Class type = obj.getClass();
248.       String mimeType
249.          = "application/x-java-jvm-local-objectref;class="
250.          + type.getName();
251.       try
252.       {
253.          flavors[0] = new DataFlavor(mimeType);
254.          return flavors;
255.       }
256.       catch (ClassNotFoundException exception)
257.       {
258.          return new DataFlavor[0];
259.       }
```

```
260.      }
261.
262.      public boolean isDataFlavorSupported(DataFlavor flavor)
263.      {
264.          return "application".equals(flavor.getPrimaryType())
265.              && "x-java-jvm-local-objectref".equals(
266.                  flavor.getSubType())
267.              && flavor.getRepresentationClass().isAssignableFrom(
268.                  obj.getClass());
269.      }
270.
271.      public Object getTransferData(DataFlavor flavor)
272.          throws UnsupportedFlavorException
273.      {
274.          if (! isDataFlavorSupported(flavor))
275.              throw new UnsupportedFlavorException(flavor);
276.
277.          return obj;
278.      }
279.
280.      private Object obj;
281. }
```

java.awt.datatransfer.Clipboard

- `Clipboard(String name)`
  constructs a local clipboard with the given name.

Transferring Java Objects via the System Clipboard

Suppose you want to copy and paste objects from one Java application to another. Then you cannot use local clipboards. Fortunately, you can place *serialized* Java objects onto the system clipboard.

The program in Example 7–19 demonstrates this capability. The program shows a color chooser. The Copy button copies the current color to the system clipboard as a serialized `Color` object. The Paste button checks whether the system clipboard contains a serialized `Color` object. If so, it fetches the color and sets it as the current choice of the color chooser.

You can transfer the serialized object between two Java applications (see Figure 7–50). Run two copies of the `SerialTransferTest` program. Click on "Copy" in the first program, then on "Paste" in the second program. The `Color` object is transferred from one virtual machine to the other.

To enable the data transfer, the Java platform places binary data on the system clipboard that contain the serialized object. Another Java program—not necessarily of the same type as the one that generated the clipboard data—can retrieve the clipboard data and deserialize the object.

Of course, a non-Java application will not know what to do with the clipboard data. For that reason, the example program offers the clipboard data in a second flavor, as text. The text is simply the result of the `toString` method, applied to the transferred object. To see the second flavor, run the program, click on a color, and then select the "Paste" command in your text editor. A string such as

```
java.awt.Color[r=255,g=51,b=51]
```

will be inserted into your document.

Essentially no additional programming is required to transfer a serializable object. You use the MIME type

```
application/x-java-serialized-object;class=className
```

As before, you have to build your own transfer wrapper—see the example code for details.

Figure 7–50: Data is copied between two instances of a Java application

Example 7–19: SerialTransferTest.java

```
1. import java.io.*;
2. import java.awt.*;
3. import java.awt.datatransfer.*;
4. import java.awt.event.*;
5. import java.awt.image.*;
6. import javax.swing.*;
7.
8. /**
9.    This program demonstrates the transfer of serialized objects
```

```
10.    between virtual machines.
11. */
12. public class SerialTransferTest
13. {
14.    public static void main(String[] args)
15.    {
16.       JFrame frame = new SerialTransferFrame();
17.       frame.setDefaultCloseOperation(JFrame.EXIT_ON_CLOSE);
18.       frame.show();
19.    }
20. }
21.
22. /**
23.    This frame contains a color chooser, and copy and
24.    paste buttons.
25. */
26. class SerialTransferFrame extends JFrame
27. {
28.    public SerialTransferFrame()
29.    {
30.       setTitle("SerialTransferTest");
31.
32.       Container contentPane = getContentPane();
33.
34.       chooser = new JColorChooser();
35.       contentPane.add(chooser, BorderLayout.CENTER);
36.       JPanel panel = new JPanel();
37.
38.       JButton copyButton = new JButton("Copy");
39.       panel.add(copyButton);
40.       copyButton.addActionListener(new
41.          ActionListener()
42.          {
43.             public void actionPerformed(ActionEvent event)
44.             {
45.                copy();
46.             }
47.          });
48.
49.       JButton pasteButton = new JButton("Paste");
50.       panel.add(pasteButton);
51.       pasteButton.addActionListener(new
52.          ActionListener()
53.          {
54.             public void actionPerformed(ActionEvent event)
55.             {
56.                paste();
57.             }
58.          });
59.
60.       contentPane.add(panel, BorderLayout.SOUTH);
```

```
61.          pack();
62.      }
63.
64.      /**
65.          Copies the chooser's color into the system clipboard.
66.      */
67.      private void copy()
68.      {
69.          Clipboard clipboard
70.              = Toolkit.getDefaultToolkit().getSystemClipboard();
71.          Color color = chooser.getColor();
72.          SerialSelection selection = new SerialSelection(color);
73.          clipboard.setContents(selection, null);
74.      }
75.
76.      /**
77.          Pastes the color from the system clipboard into the
78.          chooser.
79.      */
80.      private void paste()
81.      {
82.          Clipboard clipboard
83.              = Toolkit.getDefaultToolkit().getSystemClipboard();
84.          Transferable contents = clipboard.getContents(null);
85.          if (contents == null) return;
86.          try
87.          {
88.              DataFlavor flavor = new DataFlavor(
89. "application/x-java-serialized-object;class=java.awt.Color");
90.              if (contents.isDataFlavorSupported(flavor))
91.              {
92.                  Color color
93.                      = (Color)contents.getTransferData(flavor);
94.                  chooser.setColor(color);
95.              }
96.          }
97.          catch(ClassNotFoundException exception)
98.          {
99.              JOptionPane.showMessageDialog(this, exception);
100.         }
101.         catch(UnsupportedFlavorException exception)
102.         {
103.             JOptionPane.showMessageDialog(this, exception);
104.         }
105.         catch(IOException exception)
106.         {
107.             JOptionPane.showMessageDialog(this, exception);
108.         }
109.     }
110.
111.     private JColorChooser chooser;
```

```
112. }
113.
114. /**
115.    This class is a wrapper for the data transfer of
116.    serialized objects.
117. */
118. class SerialSelection implements Transferable
119. {
120.    /**
121.       Constructs the selection.
122.       @param o any serializable object
123.    */
124.    SerialSelection(Serializable o)
125.    {
126.       obj = o;
127.    }
128.
129.    public DataFlavor[] getTransferDataFlavors()
130.    {
131.       DataFlavor[] flavors = new DataFlavor[2];
132.       Class type = obj.getClass();
133.       String mimeType
134.          = "application/x-java-serialized-object;class="
135.          + type.getName();
136.       try
137.       {
138.          flavors[0] = new DataFlavor(mimeType);
139.          flavors[1] = DataFlavor.stringFlavor;
140.          return flavors;
141.       }
142.       catch (ClassNotFoundException exception)
143.       {
144.          return new DataFlavor[0];
145.       }
146.    }
147.
148.    public boolean isDataFlavorSupported(DataFlavor flavor)
149.    {
150.       return
151.          DataFlavor.stringFlavor.equals(flavor)
152.          || "application".equals(flavor.getPrimaryType())
153.          && "x-java-serialized-object".equals(
154.             flavor.getSubType())
155.          && flavor.getRepresentationClass().isAssignableFrom(
156.             obj.getClass());
157.    }
158.
159.    public Object getTransferData(DataFlavor flavor)
160.       throws UnsupportedFlavorException
161.    {
162.       if (!isDataFlavorSupported(flavor))
```

```
163.          throw new UnsupportedFlavorException(flavor);
164.
165.      if (DataFlavor.stringFlavor.equals(flavor))
166.          return obj.toString();
167.
168.      return obj;
169.   }
170.
171.   private Serializable obj;
172. }
```

Drag and Drop

When you use cut and paste to transmit information between two programs, the clipboard acts as an intermediary. The *drag and drop* metaphor cuts out the middleman and lets two programs communicate directly. The Java 2 platform offers basic support for drag and drop. You can carry out drag and drop operations between Java applications and native applications. This section shows you how to write a Java application that is a drop target, and an application that is a drag source.

Before going deeper into the Java platform support for drag and drop, let us have a quick look at the drag and drop user interface. We'll use the Windows Explorer and WordPad programs as examples—on another platform, you can experiment with locally available programs with drag and drop capabilities.

You initiate a *drag operation* with a *gesture* inside a *drag source*—usually, by first selecting one or more elements and then dragging the selection away from its initial location (see Figure 7–51).

todo.txt	6KB	Text Document
todo.txt.bak	7KB	BAK File
v2ch1.fm	2,350KB	Adobe FrameMaker ...
v2ch1-2.fm	2,357KB	Adobe FrameMaker ...
v2ch1-3.fm	3,445KB	Adobe FrameMaker ...
v2ch1-4.fm	3,392KB	Adobe FrameMaker ...
v2ch2.fm	1,571KB	Adobe FrameMaker ...
v2ch2.fm.lck	1KB	LCK File
v2ch2-2.fm	1,605KB	Adobe FrameMaker ...
v2ch2-3.fm	4,839KB	Adobe FrameMaker ...
v2ch2-4.fm	998KB	Adobe FrameMaker ...
v2ch3.fm	4,197KB	Adobe FrameMaker ...
v2ch3-2.fm	4,283KB	Adobe FrameMaker ...
v2ch4.fm	2,401KB	Adobe FrameMaker ...
v2ch4-2.fm	2,559KB	Adobe FrameMaker ...
v2ch5.fm	2,117KB	Adobe FrameMaker ...

Figure 7–51: Initiating a drag operation

When you release the mouse button over a drop target that accepts the drop operation, then the drop target queries the drag source for information about the dropped elements, and it initiates some operation. For example, if you drop a file icon from Windows Explorer to WordPad, then WordPad opens the file. However, if you drag a file icon on top of a directory icon in Windows Explorer, then it moves the file into that directory.

If you hold down the SHIFT or CTRL key while dragging, then the type of the drop action changes from a *move action* to a *copy action,* and a copy of the file is placed into the directory. If you hold down *both* SHIFT and CTRL keys, then a *link* to the file is placed into the directory. (Other platforms may use other keyboard combinations for these operations.)

Thus, there are three types of drop actions with different gestures:

- Move
- Copy
- Link

The intention of the link action is to establish a reference to the dropped element. Such links typically require support from the host operating system (such as symbolic links for files, or object linking for document components) and don't usually make a lot of sense in cross-platform programs. In this section, we'll focus on using drag and drop for copying and moving.

Not all programs are sensitive to the drop action types. For example, if you drop a file onto WordPad, it ignores the action type and always opens the file.

There is usually some visual feedback for the drag operation. Minimally, the cursor shape will change. As the cursor moves over possible *drop targets,* the cursor shape indicates whether the drop is possible or not. If a drop is possible, the cursor shape also indicates the type of the drop action. Figure 7–52 shows several cursor shapes over drop targets.

| Drop not allowed | Move | Copy | Link |

Figure 7–52: Cursor shapes over drop targets

You can also drag other elements besides file icons. For example, you can select text in WordPad and drag it. Try dropping text fragments into willing drop targets and see how they react.

NOTE: This experiment shows a disadvantage of drag and drop as a user interface mechanism. It can be difficult for users to anticipate what you can drag, where you can drop it, and what happens when you do. Because the default "move" action can remove the original, many users are understandably cautious about experimenting with drag and drop.

Drop Targets

In this section, we will construct a simple Java application that is a drop target. The example program does nothing useful; it simply demonstrates how you can detect that a user would like to initiate a drop, how to accept the drop, and how to analyze the data that is being dropped.

You can designate any AWT component to be a drop target. To do so, you need to construct a `DropTarget` object and pass the component and a drop target listener to the constructor. The constructor registers the object with the drag and drop system.

```
DropTarget target = new DropTarget(component, listener);
```

You can activate or deactivate the target with the `setActive` method. By default, the target is active.

```
target.setActive(b);
```

You can call the `setDefaultActions` method to set the drop operations that you want to accept by default. The operations are:

```
DndConstants.ACTION_COPY
DndConstants.ACTION_MOVE
DndConstants.ACTION_COPY_OR_MOVE
DndConstants.ACTION_LINK
```

By default, all operations are allowed.

Now you need to implement a drop target listener. The `DropTargetListener` interface has five methods:

```
void dragEnter(DropTargetDragEvent event)
void dragExit(DropTargetEvent event)
void dragOver(DropTargetDragEvent event)
void dropActionChanged(DropTargetDragEvent event)
void drop(DropTargetDropEvent event)
```

The `dragEnter` and `dragExit` methods are called when the cursor enters or exits the drop target component. In the `dragEnter` method, you have the chance to set the cursor shape to indicate whether the drop target is willing to accept the drop.

You don't usually worry about the `dragExit` method. However, if you built up some elaborate mechanism for visual feedback, then you can dispose of it in this method.

The `dragOver` method is called continuously as the user moves the mouse over the drop target component. You can use it to give detailed visual feedback about the effect of a drop. For example, if the drop target is a tree component, you can highlight the node under the cursor or even open up a subtree if the cursor hovers over a node.

The `dropActionChanged` method is called if the user changes the action gesture. For example, if the user presses or lifts the SHIFT or CTRL keys while moving the mouse over the drop target component, then this method is called. That gives you a chance to modify the visual feedback and match it to the changed action.

The most important method is the `drop` method. It is called when the user has committed to a drop by finishing the drop gesture, usually by releasing the mouse button. Note that this method is called whether or not you previously indicated that you would accept the drop.

Look carefully at the parameters of the `DropTargetListener` methods. Three of them are a `DropTarget`**Drag**`Event`. However, the `drop` method receives a `DropTarget`**Drop**`Event`, and the `dragExit` method receives a `DropTargetEvent`. The `DropTargetEvent` class is the superclass of the other two event classes. It has only one method, `getDropTargetContext`, which returns a class with no interesting public methods. Since the purpose of a `dragExit` method is to do cleanup, you probably won't even look at the parameter.

The `DropTargetDragEvent` and `DropTargetDropEvent` classes each have the following methods:

```
int getDropAction()
Point getLocation()
DataFlavor[] getCurrentDataFlavors()
boolean isDataFlavorSupported(DataFlavor flavor)
```

You need these methods to test whether to encourage a drag or allow a drop, and how to give visual feedback.

Unfortunately, since the methods are not available in the common superclass, you'll have to implement the test logic twice, once for the drag and then again for the drop.

If you don't want to encourage a drag, you should call the `rejectDrag` method of the `DropTargetDragEvent` class in the `dragEnter` or `dropAction-Changed` method. As a result, the cursor changes to a warning icon. If the user drops an item despite the warning, then you should call the `rejectDrop` method of the `DropTargetDropEvent` class.

The `getDropAction` method returns the drop action that the user intends to carry out. In many drag and drop operations, you don't want the action taken literally. For example, if you move a file icon into WordPad, then you don't want the drag source to delete the file. But you also don't want the drop target to insist that the user hold down a key when dragging. In this situation, the drop target should accept either copy or move actions. In the `drop` method, call the `acceptDrop` method of the `DropTargetDropEvent` with the *actual* action. If you call

```
event.acceptDrop(DnDConstants.ACTION_MOVE);
    // drag source deletes dragged items!
```

then the drag source will *delete* the dragged items.

TIP: Are you certain that your users understand the distinction between move and copy operations and the role of the SHIFT and CTRL modifiers? Do they realize that the default drag gesture (without a modifier) deletes the dragged items from the source? If not, you should accept a drop as

```
event.acceptDrop(DnDConstants.ACTION_COPY);
```

On the other hand, if you really want to make a distinction between move and copy, simply call

```
event.acceptDrop(event.getDropEvent()).
```

Here is an overview of a typical drop target listener:

```
class ADropTargetListener implements DropTargetListener
{
    // convenience methods
    public boolean isDragAcceptable(DropTargetDragEvent event)
    {
        look at drop action and available data flavors
    }

    public boolean isDropAcceptable(DropTargetDropEvent event)
    {
        carry out the same test as in isDragAcceptable
    }

    // listener methods
    public void dragEnter(DropTargetDragEvent event)
    {
        if (!isDragAcceptable(event))
        {
            event.rejectDrag();
            return;
        }
    }

    public void dragExit(DropTargetEvent event)
    {
    }

    public void dragOver(DropTargetDragEvent event)
    {
```

```
         // you can provide visual feedback here
      }

      public void dropActionChanged(DropTargetDragEvent event)
      {
         if (!isDragAcceptable(event))
         {
            event.rejectDrag();
            return;
         }
      }

      public void drop(DropTargetDropEvent event)
      {
         if (!isDropAcceptable(event))
         {
            event.rejectDrop();
            return;
         }
         event.acceptDrop(actual action);
         process data from drag source
         event.dropComplete(true);
      }
      . . .
   }
```

Once you accept a drop, you need to analyze the data from the drag source.
The getTransferable method of the DropTargetDropEvent class returns
a reference to a Transferable object. This is the same interface that is used
for copy and paste.

One data type that is more commonly used for drag and drop than for copy and
paste is the DataFlavor.javaFileListFlavor. A file list describes a set of
file icons that was dropped onto the target. The Transferable object yields an
object of type java.util.List whose items are File objects. Here is the
code for retrieving the files:

```
DataFlavor[] flavors = transferable.getTransferDataFlavors();
DataFlavor flavor = flavors[i];
if (flavor.equals(DataFlavor.javaFileListFlavor))
{
   java.util.List fileList
      = (java.util.List)transferable.getTransferData(flavor);
   Iterator iterator = fileList.iterator();
   while (iterator.hasNext())
   {
      File f = (File)iterator.next();
      do something with f;
   }
}
```

Another flavor that can be dropped is text. You can retrieve the text in various flavors. The most convenient is `DataFlavor.stringFlavor`. The other flavors have a MIME type of `text/plain` and a variety of representation classes, including `InputStream` and `[B` (byte array).

> CAUTION: Earlier versions of the Java platform did not go through the effort of converting dragged text to Unicode and giving you a `stringFlavor`. Instead, you had to retrieve the text through an `InputStream`. The `text/plain` MIME type contains a `charset` parameter that indicates the character encoding. To compound the inconvenience, those Java platform versions also used character encoding names that were different from the names that the `InputStreamReader` constructor expects. In particular, you had to convert `ascii` to `ISO-8859-1` and `unicode` to `Unicode`.
>
> Under Windows, you ran into additional problems. The end of input was indicated by a null character, and you should not read past it. The Unicode data didn't start with a Unicode byte order marker that the `InputStreamReader` expects, resulting in a `sun.io.MalformedInputException`. Thus, programmers had to bypass the `InputStreamReader` and construct the Unicode characters from pairs of bytes.
>
> Fortunately, these growing pains have been overcome in SDK 1.4.

Depending on the drag source, you may also find data in other formats such as

```
text/html
text/rtf
```

If you want to read the data in that format, pick a convenient flavor, for example an input stream, and obtain the data like this:

```
if (flavor.isMimeTypeEqual("text/html")
   && flavor.getRepresentationClass() == InputStream.class)
{
   String charset = flavor.getParameter("charset");
   InputStreamReader in = new InputStreamReader(
      transferable.getTransferData(flavor), charset);
   read data from in
}
```

Our sample program does not attempt to do anything useful. It simply lets you drop items onto a text area. When you start dragging over the text area, the drop action is displayed. Once you initiate a drop, the dropped data is displayed. If the data is in text format, the program reads both `ascii` and `unicode` encodings.

In our sample program, we will not give any visual feedback of the dragging process beyond the change to a warning cursor that automatically happens when calling the `rejectDrag` method.

The purpose of this program is simply to give you a drop target for experimentation. Try dropping a selection of file names from Windows Explorer, or a text fragment from WordPad (see Figure 7–53). Also see how a link attempt is rejected. If you press both the SHIFT and CTRL keys, then a warning icon appears when you drag an item over the text area.

Example 7–20 shows the complete program.

Figure 7–53: The DropTargetTest program

Example 7–20: DropTargetTest.java

```
1. import java.awt.*;
2. import java.awt.datatransfer.*;
3. import java.awt.event.*;
4. import java.awt.dnd.*;
5. import java.io.*;
6. import java.util.*;
7. import javax.swing.*;
8.
9. /**
10.    This is a test class to test drag and drop behavior. Drop
11.    items into the text area to see the MIME types of the
12.    drop target.
13. */
14. public class DropTargetTest
15. {
16.    public static void main(String[] args)
17.    {
18.       JFrame frame = new DropTargetFrame();
19.       frame.setDefaultCloseOperation(JFrame.EXIT_ON_CLOSE);
20.       frame.show();
21.    }
22. }
23.
```

```
24. /**
25.    This frame contains a text area that is a simple drop target.
26. */
27. class DropTargetFrame extends JFrame
28. {
29.    public DropTargetFrame()
30.    {
31.       setTitle("DropTarget");
32.       setSize(WIDTH, HEIGHT);
33.
34.       Container contentPane = getContentPane();
35.       JTextArea textArea
36.          = new JTextArea("Drop items into this text area.\n");
37.
38.       new DropTarget(textArea,
39.          new TextDropTargetListener(textArea));
40.       contentPane.add(new JScrollPane(textArea), "Center");
41.    }
42.
43.    private static final int WIDTH = 300;
44.    private static final int HEIGHT = 300;
45. }
46.
47. /**
48.    This listener displays the properties of a dropped object.
49. */
50. class TextDropTargetListener implements DropTargetListener
51. {
52.    /**
53.       Constructs a listener.
54.       @param aTextArea the text area in which to display the
55.       properties of the dropped object.
56.    */
57.    public TextDropTargetListener(JTextArea aTextArea)
58.    {
59.       textArea = aTextArea;
60.    }
61.
62.    public void dragEnter(DropTargetDragEvent event)
63.    {
64.       int a = event.getDropAction();
65.       if ((a & DnDConstants.ACTION_COPY) != 0)
66.          textArea.append("ACTION_COPY\n");
67.       if ((a & DnDConstants.ACTION_MOVE) != 0)
68.          textArea.append("ACTION_MOVE\n");
69.       if ((a & DnDConstants.ACTION_LINK) != 0)
70.          textArea.append("ACTION_LINK\n");
71.
72.       if (!isDragAcceptable(event))
```

```
73.        {
74.            event.rejectDrag();
75.            return;
76.        }
77.    }
78.
79.    public void dragExit(DropTargetEvent event)
80.    {
81.    }
82.
83.    public void dragOver(DropTargetDragEvent event)
84.    {
85.        // you can provide visual feedback here
86.    }
87.
88.    public void dropActionChanged(DropTargetDragEvent event)
89.    {
90.        if (!isDragAcceptable(event))
91.        {
92.            event.rejectDrag();
93.            return;
94.        }
95.    }
96.
97.    public void drop(DropTargetDropEvent event)
98.    {
99.        if (!isDropAcceptable(event))
100.       {
101.           event.rejectDrop();
102.           return;
103.       }
104.
105.       event.acceptDrop(DnDConstants.ACTION_COPY);
106.
107.       Transferable transferable = event.getTransferable();
108.
109.       DataFlavor[] flavors
110.           = transferable.getTransferDataFlavors();
111.       for (int i = 0; i < flavors.length; i++)
112.       {
113.           DataFlavor d = flavors[i];
114.           textArea.append("MIME type=" + d.getMimeType() + "\n");
115.
116.           try
117.           {
118.               if (d.equals(DataFlavor.javaFileListFlavor))
119.               {
120.                   java.util.List fileList = (java.util.List)
121.                       transferable.getTransferData(d);
```

```
122.              Iterator iterator = fileList.iterator();
123.              while (iterator.hasNext())
124.              {
125.                  File f = (File)iterator.next();
126.                  textArea.append(f + "\n");
127.              }
128.          }
129.          else if (d.equals(DataFlavor.stringFlavor))
130.          {
131.              String s = (String)
132.                  transferable.getTransferData(d);
133.              textArea.append(s + "\n");
134.          }
135.      }
136.      catch(Exception e)
137.      {
138.          textArea.append(e + "\n");
139.      }
140.  }
141.  textArea.append("\n");
142.  event.dropComplete(true);
143.  }
144.
145.  public boolean isDragAcceptable(DropTargetDragEvent event)
146.  {
147.      // usually, you check the available data flavors here
148.      // in this program, we accept all flavors
149.      return (event.getDropAction()
150.          & DnDConstants.ACTION_COPY_OR_MOVE) != 0;
151.  }
152.
153.  public boolean isDropAcceptable(DropTargetDropEvent event)
154.  {
155.      // usually, you check the available data flavors here
156.      // in this program, we accept all flavors
157.      return (event.getDropAction()
158.          & DnDConstants.ACTION_COPY_OR_MOVE) != 0;
159.  }
160.
161.  private JTextArea textArea;
162. }
```

java.awt.dnd.DropTarget

* DropTarget(Component c, DropTargetListener listener)

constructs a drop target that coordinates the drag and drop action onto a component.

Parameters: c   the drop target

               listener   the listener to be notified in the drop process

- `void setActive(boolean b)`
  activates or deactivates this drop target.

- `void setDefaultActions(int actions)`
  sets the actions that are permissible by default for this drop target. `actions` is a bit mask composed of constants defined in the `DnDConstants` class such as `ACTION_COPY`, `ACTION_MOVE`, `ACTION_COPY_OR_MOVE`, or `ACTION_LINK`.

java.awt.dnd.DropTargetListener

- `void dragEnter(DropTargetDragEvent event)`
  is called when the cursor enters the drop target.

- `void dragExit(DropTargetEvent event)`
  is called when the cursor exits the drop target.

- `void dragOver(DropTargetDragEvent event)`
  is called when the cursor moves over the drop target.

- `void dropActionChanged(DropTargetDragEvent event)`
  is called when the user changes the drop action while the cursor is over the drop target.

- `void drop(DropTargetDropEvent event)`
  is called when the user drops items into the drop target.

java.awt.dnd.DropTargetDragEvent

- `int getDropAction()`
  gets the currently selected drop action. Possible values are defined in the `DnDConstants` class.

- `void acceptDrag(int action)`
  should be called if the drop target wants to accept a drop action that is different from the currently selected action.

- `void rejectDrag()`
  notifies the drag and drop mechanism that this component rejects the current drop attempt.

- `Point getLocation()`
  returns the current location of the mouse over the drop target.

- `DataFlavor[] getCurrentDataFlavors()`
  returns the data flavors that the drag source can deliver.

- `boolean isDataFlavorSupported(DataFlavor flavor)`
  tests whether drag source supports the given flavor.

java.awt.dnd.DropTargetDropEvent

- `int getDropAction()`

  gets the currently selected drop action. Possible values are defined in the `DnDConstants` class.

- `void acceptDrop(int action)`

  should be called if the drop target has carried out a drop action that is different from the currently selected action.

- `void rejectDrop()`

  notifies the drag and drop mechanism that this component rejects the drop.

- `void dropComplete(boolean success)`

  notifies the drag source that the drop is complete and whether it was successful.

- `Point getLocation()`

  returns the current location of the mouse over the drop target.

- `DataFlavor[] getCurrentDataFlavors()`

  returns the data flavors that the drag source can deliver.

- `boolean isDataFlavorSupported(DataFlavor flavor)`

  tests whether the drag source supports the given flavor.

Drag Sources

Now that you saw how to implement a program that contains a drop target, we want to show you how to implement a drag source.

The program in Example 7–21 fills a `JList` with all files in the current directory (see Figure 7–54.) The list component is a drag source. You can drag file items from the list component to any drop target that is willing to accept a list of files.

To turn a component into a drag source, you need to obtain a `DragSource` object—you can simply call the static `DragSource.getDefaultDragSource` method. Then, call the `createDefaultDragGestureRecognizer` method and supply it with:

- The component that you want to turn into a drag source
- The drop actions that you want to allow
- An object that implements the `DragGestureListener` interface

For example,

```
DragSource dragSource = DragSource.getDefaultDragSource();
dragSource.createDefaultDragGestureRecognizer(component,
    DnDConstants.ACTION_COPY_OR_MOVE, dragGestureListener);
```

The `DragGestureListener` interface has a single method, `dragGesture-Recognized`. The gesture recognizer calls that method as soon as it has noticed that the user wants to initiate a drag operation. In that method, you need to build the `Transferable` that the drop target will ultimately read in its `drop` method. Once you have assembled the `Transferable`, you call the `startDrag` method of the `DragGestureEvent` class. You supply an optional cursor, or `null` if you want to use the default drag cursor, followed by the `Transferable` and an object that implements the `DragSourceListener` interface. For example,

```
event.startDrag(null, transferable, dragSourceListener);
```

You need to do the usual busywork of defining a `Transferable` wrapper—see the code in the example program for details.

The drag source listener is notified repeatedly as the drag operation progresses. The interface has five methods:

```
void dragEnter(DragSourceDragEvent event)
void dragOver(DragSourceDragEvent event)
void dragExit(DragSourceEvent event)
void dropActionChanged(DragSourceDragEvent event)
void dragDropEnd(DragSourceDropEvent event)
```

You can use the first four methods to give the user visual feedback of the drag operation. However, generally, such feedback should be the role of the drop target. Only the last method, `dragDropEnd`, is very important. This method is called when the `drop` method has finished. For a move operation, you need to check whether the drop has succeeded. In that case, you need to update the drag source. (For a copy operation, you probably don't have to do anything.)

NOTE: SDK 1.4 introduces a `DragSourceAdapter` helper class that implements all methods of the `DragSourceListener` interface as do-nothing methods. The sample program at the end of this section uses that class. If you use an earlier version of the SDK, you need to define the do-nothing methods yourself.

Here is the `dragDropEnd` method for our example program. When a move has succeeded, we remove the moved items from the list model.

```
public void dragDropEnd(DragSourceDropEvent event)
{
    if (event.getDropSuccess())
    {
        int action = event.getDropAction();
        if (action == DnDConstants.ACTION_MOVE)
        {
            for (int i = 0; i < draggedValues.length; i++)
                model.removeElement(draggedValues[i]);
        }
    }
}
```

In this method, we rely on the `drop` method to tell us what drop was actually carried out. Recall that the `drop` method can change a move action to a copy action if the source allowed both actions. The `event.getDropAction` of the `DragSourceDropEvent` class returns the action that the drop target reported when calling the `acceptDrop` method of the `DropTargetDropEvent`.

Try out the program in Example 7–21 and drag file items to various drop targets, such as the program in Example 7–20 or a native program such as Windows Explorer or WordPad.

NOTE: When you try the dragging, you have to be careful that the drag gesture doesn't interfere with the normal mouse effects of the list control. Select one or more items. Press the mouse button on a selected item and move the mouse *sideways,* until it leaves the list component. Now the drag gesture is recognized. *After* the mouse has left the list component, press the SHIFT or CTRL key to modify the drop action.

CAUTION: The default drop action is a *move.* If you drag a file item from the list component and drop it into Windows Explorer, then Explorer moves the file into the target folder.

As you have seen, support for the system clipboard and the drag and drop mechanism are still very much a work in progress. The basics work, but, hopefully, future versions of the Java platform will offer more robust and comprehensive support.

In this section, we have covered the basic mechanics of the drag and drop mechanism. For more information, particularly about programming visual feedback, we recommend *Core Swing: Advanced Programming* by Kim Topley [Prentice Hall 1999].

Figure 7–54: The DragSourceTest program

Example 7–21: DragSourceTest.java

```
1. import java.awt.*;
2. import java.awt.datatransfer.*;
```

```
3. import java.awt.dnd.*;
4. import java.awt.event.*;
5. import java.io.*;
6. import java.util.*;
7. import javax.swing.*;
8.
9. /**
10.    This is a sample drag source for testing purposes. It consists
11.    of a list of files in the current directory.
12. */
13. public class DragSourceTest
14. {
15.    public static void main(String[] args)
16.    {
17.       JFrame frame = new DragSourceFrame();
18.       frame.setDefaultCloseOperation(JFrame.EXIT_ON_CLOSE);
19.       frame.show();
20.    }
21. }
22.
23. /**
24.    This frame contains a list of files in the current
25.    directory with support for dragging files to a drop target.
26.    Moved files are removed from the list.
27. */
28. class DragSourceFrame extends JFrame
29. {
30.    public DragSourceFrame()
31.    {
32.       setTitle("DragSourceTest");
33.       setSize(WIDTH, HEIGHT);
34.
35.       Container contentPane = getContentPane();
36.       File f = new File(".").getAbsoluteFile();
37.       File[] files = f.listFiles();
38.       model = new DefaultListModel();
39.       for (int i = 0; i < files.length; i++)
40.          try
41.          {
42.             model.addElement(files[i].getCanonicalFile());
43.          }
44.          catch (IOException exception)
45.          {
46.             JOptionPane.showMessageDialog(this, exception);
47.          }
48.       fileList = new JList(model);
49.       contentPane.add(new JScrollPane(fileList),
50.          BorderLayout.CENTER);
51.       contentPane.add(new JLabel("Drag files from this list"),
52.          BorderLayout.NORTH);
53.
54.       DragSource dragSource = DragSource.getDefaultDragSource();
```

```
55.        dragSource.createDefaultDragGestureRecognizer(fileList,
56.           DnDConstants.ACTION_COPY_OR_MOVE, new
57.              DragGestureListener()
58.              {
59.                 public void dragGestureRecognized(
60.                    DragGestureEvent event)
61.                 {
62.                    draggedValues = fileList.getSelectedValues();
63.                    Transferable transferable
64.                       = new FileListTransferable(draggedValues);
65.                    event.startDrag(null, transferable,
66.                       new FileListDragSourceListener());
67.                 }
68.              });
69.        }
70.
71.     /**
72.        A drag source listener that removes moved
73.        files from the file list.
74.     */
75.     private class FileListDragSourceListener
76.        extends DragSourceAdapter
77.     {
78.        public void dragDropEnd(DragSourceDropEvent event)
79.        {
80.           if (event.getDropSuccess())
81.           {
82.              int action = event.getDropAction();
83.              if (action == DnDConstants.ACTION_MOVE)
84.              {
85.                 for (int i = 0; i < draggedValues.length; i++)
86.                    model.removeElement(draggedValues[i]);
87.              }
88.           }
89.        }
90.     }
91.
92.     private JList fileList;
93.     private DefaultListModel model;
94.     private Object[] draggedValues;
95.     private static final int WIDTH = 300;
96.     private static final int HEIGHT = 200;
97. }
98.
99. class FileListTransferable implements Transferable
100. {
101.    public FileListTransferable(Object[] files)
102.    {
103.       fileList = new ArrayList(Arrays.asList(files));
104.    }
105.
106.    public DataFlavor[] getTransferDataFlavors()
```

```
107.    {
108.        return flavors;
109.    }
110.
111.    public boolean isDataFlavorSupported(DataFlavor flavor)
112.    {
113.        return Arrays.asList(flavors).contains(flavor);
114.    }
115.
116.    public Object getTransferData(DataFlavor flavor)
117.        throws UnsupportedFlavorException
118.    {
119.        if(flavor.equals(DataFlavor.javaFileListFlavor))
120.            return fileList;
121.        else if(flavor.equals(DataFlavor.stringFlavor))
122.            return fileList.toString();
123.        else
124.            throw new UnsupportedFlavorException(flavor);
125.    }
126.
127.    private static DataFlavor[] flavors =
128.    {
129.        DataFlavor.javaFileListFlavor,
130.        DataFlavor.stringFlavor
131.    };
132.
133.    private java.util.List fileList;
134. }
```

java.awt.dnd.DragSource

- `static DragSource getDefaultDragSource()`
  gets a `DragSource` object to coordinate drag actions on components.

- `DragGestureRecognizer createDefaultDragGestureRecognizer(Component component, int actions, DragGestureListener listener)`
  creates a drag gesture recognizer.

Parameters:	component	the drag source
	actions	the permissible drop actions
	listener	the listener to be notified when a drag gesture has been recognized

java.awt.dnd.DragGestureListener

- `void dragGestureRecognized(DragGestureEvent event)`
  is called when the drag gesture recognizer has recognized a gesture.

java.awt.dnd.DragGestureEvent

- void startDrag(Cursor dragCursor, Transferable transferable, DragSourceListener listener)

  starts the drag action.

  Parameters: dragCursor   an optional cursor to use for the drag. May be null, in which case a default cursor is used.

                 transferable the data to be transferred to the drop target.

                 listener   the listener to be notified of the drag process.

java.awt.dnd.DragSourceListener

- void dragEnter(DragSourceDragEvent event)

  is called when the drag cursor enters the drag source.

- void dragExit(DragSourceEvent event)

  is called when the drag cursor exits the drag source.

- void dragOver(DragSourceDragEvent event)

  is called when the drag cursor moves over the drag source.

- void dropActionChanged(DragSourceDragEvent event)

  is called when the user changed the drop action.

- void dragDropEnd(DragSourceDropEvent event)

  is called after the drag and drop operation was completed or canceled.

java.awt.dnd.DragSourceDropEvent

- boolean getDropSuccess()

  returns true if the drop target reported a successful drop.

- int getDropAction()

  returns the action that the drop target actually carried out.

Data Transfer Support in Swing

Starting with SDK 1.4, Swing components have built-in support for data transfer that frees programmers from much of the burden of implementing copy and paste or drag and drop.

For example, start the TableSelectionTest program from Chapter 6 and highlight a range of cells. Then press CTRL+C and paste the clipboard contents into a text editor. The result is HTML-formatted text like this:

```
<html>
<table>
```

```
<tr>
   <th id=2>C
   <th id=3>D
   <th id=4>E
   <th id=5>F
<tr id=3>
   <td>12
   <td>16
   <td>20
   <td>24
   . . .
</table>
</html>
```

If you add the line

```
table.setDragEnabled(true);
```

after the table constructor and recompile the program, then you can drag the selection area to drop targets. The drop target receives the table selection as HTML formatted data.

Table 7–6 summarizes the Swing components that are sources and targets for data transfer. The standard "Cut," "Copy," and "Paste" keyboard shortcuts are enabled for all components except the JColorChooser. Dragging is not enabled by default. You must call the setDragEnabled method to activate it.

Table 7–6: Data Transfer Support in Swing Components

Component	Transfer source	Transfer target
JFileChooser	Exports file list	N/A
JColorChooser	Exports local reference to dolor object	Accepts any color object
JTextField JFormattedText-Field	Exports selected text	Accepts text
JPasswordField	N/A (for security reasons)	Accepts text
JTextArea JTextPane JEditorPane	Exports selected text	Accepts text and file lists. Text is inserted. Files are opened.
JList JLabel JTree	Exports HTML descrip-tion of selection	N/A

The Swing package provides a potentially useful mechanism to quickly turn a component into a drop target. If the component has a method

```
void setName(Type t)
```

then you turn it into a drop target for data flavors with representation class *Type* simply by calling

```
component.setTransferHandler("name");
```

When a drop occurs, then the transfer handler checks whether one of the data flavors has representation class *Type*. If so, it invokes the set*Name* method.

 NOTE: In JavaBeans terminology, the transfer handler sets the value of the *name* property. JavaBean properties are covered in Chapter 8.

For example, suppose you want to use drag and drop to change the background color of a text field. You need a transfer handler that invokes the

```
void setBackground(Color c)
```

method when a `Color` object is dragged onto the text field. Simply call

```
textField.setTransferHandler(new TransferHandler("background"));
```

Example 7–22 demonstrates this behavior. As you can see in Figure 7–55, the top of the frame contains a color chooser, and the bottom, a text field with the text "Drag color here." You need to drag the color from the inside of the "Preview" panel, not from one of the color swatches. When you drag it onto the text field, its background color changes.

 CAUTION: By installing this transfer handler into the text field, you disable the standard transfer handler. You can no longer cut, copy, paste, drag, or drop text in the text field. A Swing component can only have one transfer handler.

Figure 7–55: The Swing Drag and Drop Test Program

Example 7–22: SwingDnDTest.java

```
1. import java.awt.*;
2. import javax.swing.*;
3.
4. /**
5.    This program demonstrates how to easily add data transfer
6.    capabilities to Swing components. Drag a color from the
7.    "Preview" panel of the color chooser into the text field.
8. */
9. public class SwingDnDTest
10. {
11.    public static void main(String[] args)
12.    {
13.       JFrame frame = new SwingDnDFrame();
14.       frame.setDefaultCloseOperation(JFrame.EXIT_ON_CLOSE);
15.       frame.show();
16.    }
17. }
18.
19. /**
20.    This frame contains a color chooser and a text field. Dragging
21.    a color into the text field changes its background color.
22. */
23. class SwingDnDFrame extends JFrame
24. {
25.    public SwingDnDFrame()
26.    {
27.       setTitle("SwingDnDTest");
28.
29.       Container contentPane = getContentPane();
30.       JColorChooser chooser = new JColorChooser();
31.       chooser.setDragEnabled(true);
32.       contentPane.add(chooser, BorderLayout.CENTER);
33.       JTextField textField = new JTextField("Drag color here");
34.       textField.setDragEnabled(true);
35.       textField.setTransferHandler(
36.          new TransferHandler("background"));
37.       contentPane.add(textField, BorderLayout.SOUTH);
38.       pack();
39.    }
40. }
```

`javax.swing.JComponent`

● void setTransferHandler(TransferHandler handler)
  sets a transfer handler to handle data transfer operations (cut, copy, paste, drag, drop).

javax.swing.TransferHandler

- TransferHandler(String propertyName)

  constructs a transfer handler that reads or writes the JavaBean property with the given name when a data transfer operation is executed.

javx.swing.JFileChooser

javax.swing.JColorChooser

javax.swing.JTextComponent

javax.swing.JList

javax.swing.JTable

javax.swing.JTree

- void setDragEnabled(boolean b)

  enables or disables dragging of data out of this component.

Chapter **8**

JavaBeans™

The official definition of a bean, as given in the JavaBeans specification, is: "A bean is a reusable software component based on Sun's JavaBeans specification that can be manipulated visually in a builder tool."

Once you implement a bean, others can use it in a builder environment such as Forte, JBuilder, VisualAge, or Visual Café to produce applications or applets more efficiently.

We will not tell you in detail how to use those environments—you should refer to the documentation that the vendors provide. This chapter explains what you need to know about beans in order to *implement* them so that other programmers can use your beans easily.

Why Beans?

Programmers coming from a Windows background (specifically, Visual Basic or Delphi) will immediately know why beans are so important. Programmers coming from an environment where the tradition is to "roll your own" for

757

everything may not understand at once. In our experience, programmers who do not come from a Visual Basic background often find it hard to believe that Visual Basic is one of the most successful examples of reusable object technology. One reason for the popularity of Visual Basic becomes clear if you consider how you build a Visual Basic application. For those who have never worked with Visual Basic, here, in a nutshell, is how you do it:

1. You build the interface by dropping components (called *controls* in Visual Basic) onto a form window.

2. Through *property sheets*, you set properties of the components such as height, color, or other behavior.

3. The property sheets also list the events to which components can react. For some of those events, you write short snippets of event handling code.

For example, in Chapter 2 of Volume 1, we wrote a program that displays an image in a frame. It took a over a page of code. Here's what you would do in Visual Basic to create a program with pretty much the same functionality.

1. Add two controls to a window: an *Image* control for displaying graphics and a *Common Dialog* control for selecting a file.

2. Set the *Filter* properties of the CommonDialog control so that only files that the Image control can handle will show up. This is done in what Visual Basic calls the Properties window, as shown in Figure 8–1.

Figure 8–1: The Properties window in Visual Basic for an image application

Now, we need to write the five lines of Visual Basic code that will be activated when the project first starts running. This corresponds to an event called the `Form_Load`, so the code goes in the `Form_Load` event procedure. The following code pops up the file dialog box—but only files with the right extension are shown because of how we set the filter property. After the user selects an image file, the code then tells the Image control to display it. All the code you need for this sequence looks like this:

```
Private Sub Form_Load()
  On Error Resume Next
  CommonDialog1.ShowOpen
  Image1.Picture = LoadPicture(CommonDialog1.FileName)
End Sub
```

That's it. The layout activity, combined with these five lines of code, give essentially the same functionality as a page of Java programming language code. Clearly, it is a lot easier to learn how to drop down components and set properties than it is to write a page of code.

The point is that right now the Java programming language is still a tool used mostly by top-notch, object-oriented programmers. And, realistically, even such programmers are unlikely to be as productive as a good Visual Basic programmer for designing the user interface of a client application. The JavaBeans technology enables vendors to create environments that make it dramatically easier to develop user interfaces for Java applications.

Note that we do not want to imply that Visual Basic is a good solution for every problem. It is clearly optimized for a particular kind of problems—UI-intensive Windows programs. In contrast, Java technology will always have a much wider range of uses. And the good news is that with the advent of JavaBeans technology, some of the benefits of Visual Basic-style application building are on the horizon for programmers. In particular:

1. Beans with the same functionality as the most common Visual Basic controls are readily available.
2. Java technology builder tools have come much closer to the ease of use of the Visual Basic environment.

NOTE: Once you have built a bean, users of *any* environment enabled for JavaBeans technology can readily use it. Developers can even, through the magic of the ActiveX bridge technology, deploy JavaBeans in Visual Basic applications and Microsoft Office (see `http://java.sun.com/products/javabeans/software`).

The Bean-Writing Process

Most of the rest of this chapter shows you the techniques that you will use to write beans. Before we go into details, we give an overview of the process. First, we want to stress that writing a bean is not technically difficult—there are only a few new classes and interfaces for you to master.

In particular, the simplest kind of bean is really nothing more than a Java platform class that follows some fairly strict naming conventions for its event listeners and its methods. Example 8–1 at the end of this section shows the code for an Image Viewer Bean that could give a builder environment based on Java technology the same functionality as the Visual Basic image control that we mentioned in the previous section.

When you look at this code, notice that the `ImageViewerBean` class really doesn't look any different from any other class. For example, all accessor methods begin with `get`, all mutator methods begin with `set`. As you will soon see, builder tools use this standard naming convention to discover *properties*. For example, `fileName` is a property of this bean because it has `get` and `set` methods.

Note that a property is not the same as an instance variable. In this particular example, the `fileName` property is computed from the `file` instance variable. Properties are conceptually at a higher level than instance variables—they are features of the interface, whereas instance variables belong to the implementation of the class.

NOTE: For full support in a bean environment, beans should have a default constructor (or no constructor at all, in which case a default constructor is automatically provided), and they should be serializable. This allows the environment to instantiate new beans and to save beans between sessions. However, these are just practical recommendations, not requirements. The `ImageViewerBean` is serializable because it extends the serializable `JLabel` class.

One point that you need to keep in mind when you read through the examples in this chapter is that real-world beans are much more elaborate and tedious to code than our brief examples, for two reasons.

1. Beans need to be usable by less-than-expert programmers. Such people will access most of the functionality of your bean with a visual design tool that uses essentially no programming. You need to expose *lots of properties* to make it easy to customize the bean behavior.

2. The same bean needs to be usable in a wide *variety of contexts*. A bean that is too simplistic to be usable in the real world won't get much respect. Of course, that is why people can charge hundreds of dollars for a professional component, such as a full-featured chart control. For example, at the time of this writing, a popular chart control has

- 60 properties
- 14 methods

- 47 events
- 178 pages of documentation

Another good example of a bean with rich behavior is the `CalendarBean` by Kai Tödter (see Figure 8–2). The bean and its source code are freely available from `http://www.toedter.com/en/jcalendar.html`. This bean gives users a convenient way of entering dates, simply by locating them in a calendar display. This is obviously pretty complex and not something one would want to program from scratch. By using JavaBeans such as this one, you can take advantage of the work of others, simply by dropping the bean into a builder tool.

August	▼	2001	▲▼

Sun	Mon	Tue	Wed	Thu	Fri	Sat
			1	2	3	4
5	6	7	8	9	10	11
12	13	14	15	16	17	18
19	20		22	23	24	25
26	27	28	29	30	31	

Figure 8–2: A Calendar Bean

Obviously, a chart or calendar control is about as full-featured a control as one can imagine, but even a bean as simple as a text field for entering numbers turns out to be not quite so simple to code as one might first imagine.

Consider, for example, what should happen as the user types digits into the text field. Should the new numbers be *immediately* reported to the listeners? On the one hand, this approach is attractive because it gives instant feedback to the user of your bean. But many applications restrict the range for valid entries, and partial entries that can go into an eventual valid entry might not themselves be valid.

For example, suppose a listener wanted to receive only even numbers from the input field. If a user tried to enter 256, the listener would receive an invalid input 25. So, in this case, incremental update is a bad idea because the incremental value could be inappropriate. In cases like this, your bean should report the value to listeners only when the user has finished entering the number, that is, when the user presses ENTER or if the text field loses focus.

If you are writing a program for a single application, then you will simply choose one behavior or the other. But if you are building a bean, you aren't programming for yourself but for a wide audience of users with different needs. Therefore, it would be best to add a property called something like `incrementalUpdate` and implement both behaviors, depending on the value of that property. Add a few more options like this, and even a simple `IntTextBean` will end up with a dozen properties.

Fortunately, you need to master only a small number of concepts to write beans with a rich set of behaviors. The example beans in this chapter, while not trivial, are kept simple enough to illustrate the necessary concepts.

> TIP: You will find full-featured beans available for sale from many programming product stores, bundled with Java development environments, or for free at sites such as `http://www.gamelan.com` and the IBM alphaWorks site `http://alphaworks.ibm.com`.

Example 8–1: ImageViewerBean.java

```
1. import java.awt.*;
2. import java.io.*;
3. import javax.imageio.*;
4. import javax.swing.*;
5.
6. /**
7.    A bean for viewing an image.
8. */
9. public class ImageViewerBean extends JLabel
10. {
11.
12.    public ImageViewerBean()
13.    {
14.        setBorder(BorderFactory.createEtchedBorder());
15.    }
16.
17.    /**
18.        Sets the fileName property.
19.        @param fileName the image file name
20.    */
21.    public void setFileName(String fileName)
22.    {
23.        try
24.        {
25.            file = new File(fileName);
26.            setIcon(new ImageIcon(ImageIO.read(file)));
27.        }
28.        catch (IOException exception)
29.        {
30.            file = null;
31.            setIcon(null);
32.        }
33.    }
34.
35.    // Use this version for SDK1.3
36.    /*
37.    public void setFileName(String fileName)
38.    {
```

```
39.        file = new File(fileName);
40.        Image image
41.           = Toolkit.getDefaultToolkit().getImage(fileName);
42.        MediaTracker tracker = new MediaTracker(this);
43.        tracker.addImage(image, 0);
44.        try { tracker.waitForID(0); } catch (Exception e) {}
45.        setIcon(new ImageIcon(image));
46.        repaint();
47.     }
48.     */
49.
50.     /**
51.        Gets the fileName property.
52.        @return the image file name
53.     */
54.     public String getFileName()
55.     {
56.        if (file == null) return null;
57.        else return file.getPath();
58.     }
59.
60.     public Dimension getPreferredSize()
61.     {
62.        return new Dimension(XPREFSIZE, YPREFSIZE);
63.     }
64.
65.     private File file = null;
66.     private static final int XPREFSIZE = 200;
67.     private static final int YPREFSIZE = 200;
68. }
```

Using Beans to Build an Application

Before we get into the mechanics of writing beans, we want you to see how you might use or test them. The `ImageViewerBean` is a perfectly usable bean, but outside a builder environment it can't show off its special features. In particular, the only way to use it in an ordinary program in the Java programming language would be to write code that constructs an object of the bean class, places the object into a container, and calls the `setFileName` method. That's not rocket science, but it is more code than an overworked programmer may want to write. Builder environments aim to reduce the amount of drudgery that is involved in wiring together components into an application.

Each builder environment uses its own set of strategies to ease the programmer's life. We will cover one environment, the Forte Community Edition. We don't want to claim that Forte is better than other products—in fact, as you will see, it has its share of idiosyncrasies. We simply use Forte because it is a fairly typical programming environment, and because it is freely available.

If you prefer another builder environment, you can still follow the steps of the next sections. The basic principles are the same for most environments. Of course, the details differ.

If you don't want to download a large environment, you can use the BeanBox from Sun Microsystems. The BeanBox is a demonstration of bean capabilities that was designed as a showcase for tool developers. It has advanced features for bean composition, but it doesn't offer any facilities for laying out components nicely. At this point, the BeanBox is somewhat dated—it hasn't been updated since SDK 1.1.

> NOTE: You can download the Forte Community Edition at no charge from
> `http://www.sun.com/forte/ffj/buy.html`. The BeanBox is at
> `http://java.sun.com/products/javabeans/software`.

In this example, we will use two beans, `ImageViewerBean` and `FileNameBean`. You have already seen the code for the `ImageViewerBean`. The code for the `FileNameBean` is a bit more sophisticated. We'll analyze it in depth later in this chapter. For now, all you have to know is that clicking on the button with the "..." label will open a standard File Open dialog box where you can select a file.

Before we can go any further with showing you how to use these beans, we need to explain how to package the bean for import into a builder tool.

Packaging Beans in JAR files

To make any bean usable in a builder tool, package all class files that are used by the bean code into a JAR file. Unlike the JAR files for an applet that you saw previously, a JAR file for a bean needs a manifest file that specifies which class files in the archive are beans and should be included in the Toolbox. For example, here is the manifest file `ImageViewerBean.mf` for the ImageViewerBean.

```
Manifest-Version: 1.0

Name: ImageViewerBean.class
Java-Bean: True
```

Note the blank line between the manifest version and bean name.

If your class is in a package, use slashes to indicate the package, like this:

```
Name: com/horstmann/beans/ImageViewerBean.class
```

If your bean contains multiple class files, you only mention in the manifest those class files that are beans and that you want to have displayed in the toolbox. For example, you could place a `ImageViewerBean` and a `FileNameBean` into the same JAR file and use the manifest

```
Manifest-Version: 1.0

Name: ImageViewerBean.class
```

```
Java-Bean: True

Name: FileNameBean.class
Java-Bean: True
```

CAUTION: Some builder tools are extremely fussy about manifests. Make sure that there are no spaces after the ends of each line, that there are blank lines after the version and between bean entries, and that the last line ends in a newline.

To make the JAR file, follow these steps:

1. Edit the manifest file.
2. Gather all needed class files in a directory.
3. Run the `jar` tool as follows:

   ```
   jar cfm JarFile ManifestFile *.class
   ```

   For example,

   ```
   jar cfm ImageViewerBean.jar ImageViewerBean.mf *.class
   ```

You can also add other items, such as GIF files for icons, to the JAR file. We will discuss bean icons later in this chapter.

CAUTION: Make sure to include all files that your bean needs in the JAR file. In particular, pay attention to inner class files such as `ImageViewerBean$1.class`.

Builder environments have a mechanism for adding new beans, typically by loading JAR files. Here is what you need to do to import beans into Forte.

Compile the `ImageViewerBean` and `FileNameBean` classes and package them into JAR files. Then start Forte and follow these steps.

1. Select Tools -> Install new Java Bean from the menu.
2. In the file dialog, move to the `ImageViewerBean` directory and select `ImageViewerBean.jar`
3. Now a dialog pops up that lists all the beans that were found in the JAR file. Select `ImageViewerBean`.
4. Finally, you are asked into which palette you want to place the beans. Select "Beans." (There are other palettes for Swing components, AWT components, and so on.)
5. Have a look at the "Beans" palette. It now contains an icon representing the new bean (see Figure 8–3). However, the icon is just a default icon—you will see later how to add icons to a bean.

Figure 8–3: Adding a Bean to a Palette in Forte

Repeat this step with the `FileNameBean`. Now you are ready to compose these beans into an application.

Composing Beans in a Builder Environment

In Forte, select File -> New from the menu. A dialog pops up. Open the "Swing Forms" node of the tree on the left and select JFrame. On the right, specify the name of the frame as `ImageViewer` (see Figure 8–4).

Figure 8–4: Building a New Form

Now you get two windows: a form editor (Figure 8–5) and the familiar code editor (Figure 8–6). The form editor shows the outlines of a border layout, and the code editor contains a few lines of routine code.

Figure 8–5: The Form Editor Window

Figure 8–7: Adding a Bean to a Form

Figure 8–6: The Code Editor Window

To add a bean to the form, select the bean in the palette and click on one of the border layout regions.

NOTE: Other builders have different user interfaces. For example, you may need to drag the bean to the right place on the form.

Figure 8–7 shows the result of adding an image viewer bean to the center region of the frame.

Figure 8–7: Adding a Bean to a Form

If you look into the code editor window, you will find that the source code now contains the Java instructions to add an `ImageViewerBean` object to the content pane of the frame. The source code is bracketed by dire warnings that you should not edit it. Any edits would be lost when the builder environment updates the code as you modify the form.

NOTE: Not all builder environments update source code as you build an application. A builder environment may generate source code when you are done editing, serialize the beans you customized, or perhaps produce an entirely different description of your building activity.

In particular, SDK1.4 has methods for saving and loading XML descriptions of collections of JavaBeans. This technology is still somewhat experimental and mostly of interest to builder tool manufacturers. See `http://java.sun.com/products/jfc/tsc/articles/persistence2/index.html` for more information on this topic.

Now click on the `ImageViewerBean` in the form and select View->Properties from the menu. You get a property inspector that lists the bean property names and their current values (see Figure 8–8). This is a vital part of component-based development tools since setting properties at design time is how you set the initial state of a component.

Figure 8–8: A Property Inspector

For example, you can modify the `text` property of the label used for the image bean by simply typing in a new name into the property inspector. Changing the `text` property is simple—you just edit a string in a text field. Try it out—set the label text to `"Hello"`. The form is immediately updated to reflect your change. When you are done, set the text to the empty string since we don't want text to appear next to the image icon.

NOTE: When you change the setting of a property, the Forte environment updates the source code to reflect your action. For example, if you set the `text` field to `Hello`, the instruction

```
imageViewerBean.setText("Hello");
```

is added to the `initComponents` method. As already mentioned, other builder tools may have different strategies for recording property settings.

Properties don't have to be strings; they can be values of any Java platform type. To make it possible for users to set values for properties of any type, builder tools access specialized *property editors*. (Property editors either come with the builder or are supplied by the bean developer. You'll see how to write your own property editors later in this chapter.)

To see a simple property editor at work, look at the `background` property. The property type is `Color`. You can see the color editor, with a combo box containing standard color names, and a button labeled "..." that brings up a color dialog (see Figure 8–9).

Figure 8–9: Using a property editor to set properties

Go ahead and change the background to orange. Notice that you'll immediately see the change to the background color—the border changes color.

More interestingly, choose a file name for an image file in the property inspector. Once you do so, the `ImageViewerBean` automatically displays the image (see Figure 8–10).

Figure 8–10: The `ImageViewerBean` at work

NOTE: If you look at the property inspector in Figure 8–10, you will find a large number of mysterious properties such as `focusCycleRoot` and `iconTextGap`. These are inherited from the `JLabel` superclass. You will see later in this chapter how you can suppress them from the property inspector.

To complete our application, place a `FileNameBean` at the south end of the frame. Now we want the image to be loaded when the `fileName` property of the `FileNameBean` is changed. This happens through a `PropertyChange` event; we discuss these kinds of events a little later in this chapter.

To react to the event, select the `FileNameBean` and select the Events tab from its property inspector (see Figure 8–11). Then click on the <none> entry. A dialog appears that shows that there are currently no handlers associated with this event. Click on the Add button of the dialog. You will be prompted for a method name. Type in `loadImage`.

Figure 8–11: The Events Tab of the Property Inspector

Now have a look at the edit window (see Figure 8–12). It now contains additional event handling code and a new method

```
private void loadImage(java.beans.PropertyChange evt)
{
    // Add your handling code here
}
```

Add the following line of code:

```
imageViewerBean1.setFileName(fileNameBean1.getFileName());
```

Then compile and execute the application. Click on the button with the "..." label and select an image file. The image is displayed in the image viewer.

This process demonstrates that you can create a Java application from Java beans, by setting properties and providing a small amount of code for event handlers.

```
Source Editor [ImageViewer *]                           _ □ ×
40          ImageViewerBean1.setToolTipText( An Image );
41
42          getContentPane().add(imageViewerBean1, java.awt.BorderLay
43
44
45          java.awt.GridBagConstraints gridBagConstraints1;
46          fileNameBean1.addPropertyChangeListener(new java.beans.Pr
47              public void propertyChange(java.beans.PropertyChangeE
48                  loadImage(evt);
49              }
50          }
51          );
52
53          getContentPane().add(fileNameBean1, java.awt.BorderLayout
54
55      }
56  |
57    private void loadImage(java.beans.PropertyChangeEvent evt) {
58  // Add your handling code here:
59    }
60
61    /** Exit the Application */
62    private void exitForm(java.awt.event.WindowEvent evt) {
63        System.exit(0);
64    }
65
56:1    INS
```

Figure 8–12: Event Handling Code in The Edit Window

Some builder environments, such as the BeanBox, go even further, eliminating the need for writing any code at all. The BeanBox has built-in mechanisms for various common situations, among them:

- Calling a method when an event is triggered
- Setting a property when another property changes

With the BeanBox, you can build simple applications entirely without programming, just by dragging components onto a form, setting properties, and wiring events to methods or property setters.

By themselves, the mechanisms of the BeanBox are not sufficient to implement sophisticated applications. In contrast, the Forte mechanism allows the programmer to write applications with a mixture of visual manipulation and coding.

The JavaBeans mechanism doesn't attempt to force an implementation strategy on a builder tool. Instead, it aims to supply information about beans to builder tools that can choose to take advantage of the information in one way or another. You will see in the following sections how to program beans so that tools accurately discover that information.

Naming Patterns for Bean Properties and Events

First, we want to stress there is *no* cosmic beans class that you extend to build your beans. Visual beans directly or indirectly extend the Component class, but nonvisual beans don't have to extend any particular superclass. Remember, a bean is simply *any* class that can be manipulated in a builder tool. The builder tool does not look at the superclass to determine the bean nature of a class, but it analyzes the names of its methods. To enable this analysis, the method names for beans must follow certain patterns.

> NOTE: There is a `java.beans.Beans` class, but all methods in it are static. Extending it would, therefore, be rather pointless, even though you will see it done occasionally, supposedly for greater "clarity." Clearly, since a bean can't extend both `Beans` and `Component`, this approach can't work for visual beans. In fact, the `Beans` class contains methods that are designed to be called by builder tools, for example, to check whether the tool is operating at design time or run time.

Other languages for visual design environments, such as Visual Basic and Delphi, have special keywords such as "Property" and "Event" to express these concepts directly. The designers of the Java specification decided not to add keywords to the language to support visual programming. Therefore, they needed an alternative so that a builder tool could analyze a bean to learn its properties or events. Actually, there are two alternate mechanisms. If the bean writer uses standard naming patterns for properties and events, then the builder tool can use the reflection mechanism to understand what properties and events the bean is supposed to expose. Alternatively, the bean writer can supply a *bean information* class that tells the builder tool about the properties and events of the bean. We'll start out using the naming patterns because they are easy to use. You'll see later in this chapter how to supply a bean information class.

> NOTE: Although the documentation calls these standard naming patterns "design patterns," these are really only naming conventions and have nothing to do with the design patterns that are used in object-oriented programming.

The naming pattern for properties is simple: Any pair of methods

```
public X getPropertyName()
public void setPropertyName(X x)
```

corresponds to a read/write property of type *X*.

For example, in our `ImageViewerBean`, there is only one read/write property (for the file name to be viewed), with the following methods:

```
public String getFileName()
public void setFileName(String f)
```

If you have a `get` method but not an associated `set` method, you define a read-only property.

Be careful with the capitalization pattern you use for your method names. The designers of the JavaBeans specification decided that the name of the property in our example would be `fileName`, with a lowercase f, even though the `get` and `set` methods contain an uppercase F (`getFileName`, `setFileName`). The bean analyzer performs a process called *decapitalization* to derive the property name. (That is, the first character after `get` or `set` is converted to lower case.) The rationale is that this process results in method and property names that are more natural to programmers.

NOTE: The `get` and `set` methods you create can do more than simply get and set a private data field. Like any Java method, they can carry out arbitrary actions. For example, the `setFileName` method of the `ImageViewerBean` class not only sets the value of the `fileName` data field, but also opens the file and loads the image.

NOTE: In Visual Basic, properties also come from `get` and `set` methods. (Delphi uses `read` and `write`.) But, in both these languages there is a `Property` keyword so that the compiler doesn't have to second-guess the programmer's intentions by analyzing method names. And using a keyword in those languages has another advantage: Using a property name on the left side of an assignment automatically calls the `set` method. Using a property name in an expression automatically calls the `get` method. For example, in Visual Basic you can write

```
imageBean.fileName = "corejava.gif"
```
instead of
```
imageBean.setFileName("corejava.gif");
```

There is one exception to the `get`/`set` naming pattern. Properties that have Boolean values should use an `is`/`set` naming pattern, as in the following examples:

```
public boolean isPropertyName()
public void setPropertyName(boolean b)
```

For example, an animation might have a property `running`, with two methods

```
public boolean isRunning()
public void setRunning(boolean b)
```

The `setRunning` method would start and stop the animation. The `isRunning` method would report its current status.

For events, the naming pattern is even simpler. A bean builder environment will infer that your bean generates events when you supply methods to add and remove event listeners. Suppose your bean generates events of type `EventNameEvent`. (All events must end in `Event`.) Then, the listener interface must be called `EventNameListener`, and the methods to add and remove a listener must be called.

```
public void addEventNameListener(EventNameListener e)
public void removeEventNameListener(EventNameListener e)
```

If you look at the code for the `ImageViewerBean`, you'll see that it has no events to expose. Later, we will see a timer bean that generates `TimerEvent` objects and has the following methods to manage event listeners:

```
public void addTimerListener(TimerListener e)
public void removeTimerListener(TimerListener e)
```

> NOTE: What do you do if your class has a pair of `get` and `set` methods that don't correspond to a property that you want users to manipulate in a property inspector? In your own classes, you can of course avoid that situation by renaming your methods. But if you extend another class, then you inherit the method names from the superclass. This happens, for example, when your bean extends `JPanel` or `JLabel`—a large number of uninteresting properties show up in the property inspector. This shows that naming patterns are really a lousy way for designating properties. You will see later in this chapter how you can override the automatic property discovery process by supplying *bean information* that specifies exactly which methods correspond to properties.

Bean Property Types

A sophisticated bean will have lots of different kinds of properties that it should expose in a builder tool for a user to set at design time or get at run time. It can also trigger both standard and custom events. Properties can be as simple as the `fileName` property that you saw in the `ImageViewerBean` and the `FileNameBean` or as sophisticated as a color value or even an array of data points—we encounter both of these cases later in this chapter. Furthermore, properties can fire events, as you will see in this section.

Getting the properties of your beans right is probably the most complex part of building a bean because the model is quite rich. The JavaBeans specification allows four types of properties, which we illustrate by various examples.

Simple Properties

A simple property is one that takes a single value such as a string or a number. The `fileName` property of the ImageViewer is an example of a simple property. Simple properties are easy to program: just use the `set`/`get` naming convention we indicated earlier. For example, if you look at the code in Example 8–1, you can see that all it took to implement a simple string property is:

```
public void setFileName(String f)
{
    fileName = f;
    image = . . .
    repaint();
}
```

```
public String getFileName()
{
    if (file == null) return null;
    else return file.getPath();
}
```

Notice that, as far as the JavaBeans specification is concerned, we also have a read-only property of this bean because we have a method with this signature inside the class

```
public Dimension getPreferredSize()
```

without a corresponding `setPreferredSize` method. You would not normally be able to see read-only properties at design time in a property inspector.

Indexed Properties

An indexed property is one that gets or sets an array. A chart bean (see below) would use an indexed property for the data points. With an indexed property, you supply two pairs of `get` and `set` methods: one for the array and one for individual entries. They must follow the pattern:

```
X[] getPropertyName()
void setPropertyName(X[] x)
X getPropertyName(int i)
void setPropertyName(int i, X x)
```

Here's an example of the indexed property we use in the chart bean that you will see later in this chapter.

```
public double[] getValues() { return values; }
public void setValues(double[] v) { values = v; }
public double getValues(int i) { return values[i]; }
public void setValues(int i, double v) { values[i] = v; }
    . . .
private double[] values;
```

The `get`/`set` functions that set individual array entries can assume that `i` is within the legal range. Builder tools will not call them with an index that is less than 0 or larger than the length of the array. In particular, the

```
setPropertyName(int i, X[] x)
```

method cannot be used to *grow* the array. To grow the array, you must manually build a new array and then pass it to this method:

```
setPropertyName(X[] x)
```

As a practical matter, however, the `get` and `set` methods can still be called programmatically, not just by the builder environment. Therefore, it is best to add some error checking, after all. For example, here is the code that we really use in the `ChartBean` class.

```
public double getValues(int i)
{
    if (0 <= i && i < values.length) return values[i];
    return 0;
}

public void setValues(int i, double value)
{
    if (0 <= i && i < values.length) values[i] = value;
}
```

> NOTE: As we write this, neither Forte nor the BeanBox support indexed properties in the property inspector. You will see later in this chapter how to overcome this limitation by supplying a custom property editor for arrays.

Bound Properties

Bound properties tell interested listeners that their value has changed. For example, the `fileName` property in the `FileNameBean` is a bound property. When the file name changes, then the `ImageViewerBean` is automatically notified and it loads the new file.

To implement a bound property, you must implement two mechanisms.

1. Whenever the value of the property changes, the bean must send a `PropertyChange` event to all registered listeners. This change can occur when the `set` method is called or when the program user carries out an action, such as editing text or selecting a file.

2. To enable interested listeners to register themselves, the bean has to implement the following two methods:

   ```
   void addPropertyChangeListener(PropertyChangeListener
      listener)
   void removePropertyChangeListener(PropertyChangeListener
      listener)
   ```

The `java.beans` package has a convenience class, called `PropertyChange-Support`, that manages the listeners for you. To use this convenience class, your bean must have a data field of this class that looks like this:

```
private PropertyChangeSupport changeSupport
   = new PropertyChangeSupport(this);
```

You delegate the task of adding and removing property change listeners to that object.

```
public void addPropertyChangeListener(PropertyChangeListener
   listener)
{
    changeSupport.addPropertyChangeListener(listener);
}
```

```
public void removePropertyChangeListener(PropertyChangeListener
    listener)
{
    changeSupport.removePropertyChangeListener(listener);
}
```

Whenever the value of the property changes, use the `firePropertyChange` method of the `PropertyChangeSupport` object to deliver an event to all the registered listeners. That method has three parameters: the name of the property, the old value, and the new value. For example,

```
changeSupport.firePropertyChange("fileName",
    oldValue, newValue);
```

The values must be objects. If the property type is not an object, then you must use an object wrapper. For example,

```
changeSupport.firePropertyChange("running",
    new Boolean(false), new Boolean(true));
```

TIP: If your bean extends any Swing class that ultimately extends the `JComponent` class, then you do *not* need to implement the `addPropertyChangeListener` and `removePropertyChangeListener` methods. These methods are already implemented in the `JComponent` superclass.

To notify the listeners of a property change, simply call the `firePropertyChange` method of the `JComponent` superclass:

```
firePropertyChange("propertyName", oldValue, newValue);
```

For your convenience, that method is overloaded for the types `boolean`, `byte`, `char`, `double`, `float`, `int`, `long`, and `short`. If `oldValue` and `newValue` belong to these types, you do not need to use object wrappers.

Other beans that want to be notified when the property value changes must implement the `PropertyChangeListener` interface. That interface contains only one method:

```
void propertyChange(PropertyChangeEvent event)
```

The code in the `propertyChange` method is triggered whenever the property value changes, provided, of course, that you have added the recipient to the property change listeners of the bean that generates the event. The `PropertyChange-Event` object encapsulates the old and new value of the property, obtainable with

```
Object oldValue = event.getOldValue();
Object newValue = event.getNewValue();
```

If the property type is not a class type, then the returned objects are the usual wrapper types. For example, if a `boolean` property is changed, then a `Boolean` is returned and you need to retrieve the Boolean value with the `booleanValue` method.

Thus, a listening object must follow this model:

```
class Listener
{
    public Listener()
    {
        bean.addPropertyChangeListener(new
            PropertyChangeListener()
            {
                void propertyChange(PropertyChangeEvent event)
                {
                    Object newValue = event.getNewValue();
                    . . .
                }
            });
    }
    . . .
}
```

Example 8–2 is the full code for the `FileNameBean`. Since the `FileNameBean` extends the `JPanel` class, we did not have to explicitly use a `PropertyChange-Support` object. Instead, we rely on the ability of the `JPanel` class to manage property change listeners.

Example 8–2: FileNameBean.java

```
1. import java.awt.*;
2. import java.awt.event.*;
3. import java.beans.*;
4. import java.io.*;
5. import javax.swing.*;
6.
7. /**
8.    A bean for specifying file names.
9. */
10. public class FileNameBean extends JPanel
11. {
12.     public FileNameBean()
13.     {
14.         dialogButton = new JButton("...");
15.         nameField = new JTextField(30);
16.
17.         chooser = new JFileChooser();
18.         chooser.setCurrentDirectory(new File("."));
19.
20.         chooser.setFileFilter(new
21.             javax.swing.filechooser.FileFilter()
22.             {
23.                 public boolean accept(File f)
24.                 {
25.                     String name = f.getName().toLowerCase();
26.                     return name.endsWith("." + defaultExtension)
27.                         || f.isDirectory();
```

```
28.                }
29.            public String getDescription()
30.            {
31.                return defaultExtension + " files";
32.            }
33.        });
34.
35.    setLayout(new GridBagLayout());
36.    GridBagConstraints gbc = new GridBagConstraints();
37.    gbc.weightx = 100;
38.    gbc.weighty = 100;
39.    gbc.anchor = GridBagConstraints.WEST;
40.    gbc.fill = GridBagConstraints.BOTH;
41.    add(nameField, gbc, 0, 0, 1, 1);
42.
43.    dialogButton.addActionListener(
44.        new ActionListener()
45.        {
46.            public void actionPerformed(ActionEvent evt)
47.            {
48.                int r = chooser.showOpenDialog(null);
49.                if(r == JFileChooser.APPROVE_OPTION)
50.                {
51.                    File f = chooser.getSelectedFile();
52.                    try
53.                    {
54.                        String name = f.getCanonicalPath();
55.                        setFileName(name);
56.                    }
57.                    catch (IOException exception)
58.                    {
59.                    }
60.                }
61.            }
62.        });
63.    nameField.setEditable(false);
64.
65.    gbc.weightx = 0;
66.    gbc.anchor = GridBagConstraints.EAST;
67.    gbc.fill = GridBagConstraints.NONE;
68.    add(dialogButton, gbc, 1, 0, 1, 1);
69.    }
70.
71.    /**
72.       A convenience method to add a component to given grid bag
73.       layout locations.
74.       @param c the component to add
75.       @param gbc the grid bag constraints to use
76.       @param x the x grid position
77.       @param y the y grid position
78.       @param w the grid width
79.       @param h the grid height
80.    */
```

```
81.    public void add(Component c, GridBagConstraints gbc,
82.       int x, int y, int w, int h)
83.    {
84.       gbc.gridx = x;
85.       gbc.gridy = y;
86.       gbc.gridwidth = w;
87.       gbc.gridheight = h;
88.       add(c, gbc);
89.    }
90.
91.    /**
92.       Sets the fileName property.
93.       @param newValue the new file name
94.    */
95.    public void setFileName(String newValue)
96.    {
97.       String oldValue = nameField.getText();
98.       nameField.setText(newValue);
99.       firePropertyChange("fileName", oldValue, newValue);
100.   }
101.
102.   /**
103.      Gets the fileName property.
104.      @return the name of the selected file
105.   */
106.   public String getFileName()
107.   {
108.      return nameField.getText();
109.   }
110.
111.   /**
112.      Sets the defaultExtension property.
113.      @param s the new default extension
114.   */
115.   public void setDefaultExtension(String s)
116.   {
117.      defaultExtension = s;
118.   }
119.
120.   /**
121.      Gets the defaultExtension property.
122.      @return the default extension in the file chooser
123.   */
124.   public String getDefaultExtension()
125.   {
126.      return defaultExtension;
127.   }
128.
129.   public Dimension getPreferredSize()
130.   {
131.      return new Dimension(XPREFSIZE, YPREFSIZE);
132.   }
```

```
133.
134.     private static final int XPREFSIZE = 200;
135.     private static final int YPREFSIZE = 20;
136.     private JButton dialogButton;
137.     private JTextField nameField;
138.     private JFileChooser chooser;
139.     private String defaultExtension = "gif";
140. }
```

java.beans.PropertyChangeListener

- `void propertyChange(PropertyChangeEvent event)`
  is called when a property change event is fired.

  Parameters: event   the property change event

java.beans.PropertyChangeSupport

- `PropertyChangeSupport(Object sourceBean)`
  constructs the (convenience) `PropertyChangeSupport` object.

  Parameters: sourceBean   the bean that is the source of the property
  change (usually `this`)

- `void addPropertyChangeListener(PropertyChangeListener listener)`
  registers an interested listener for the bound property.

  Parameters: listener   the object that wants to be notified of a change
  in the bound property

- `void removePropertyChangeListener(PropertyChangeListener listener)`
  removes a previously registered interested listener for the bound property.

  Parameters: listener   the object to be removed from the list
  of listeners

- `void firePropertyChange(String propertyName, Object oldValue, Object newValue)`
  sends a `PropertyChangeEvent` to registered listeners.

  Parameters: propertyName   the name of the property

  oldValue   the old value

  newValue   the new value

java.beans.PropertyChangeEvent

- `PropertyChangeEvent(Object source, String propertyName, Object oldValue, Object newValue)`
  constructs a new `PropertyChangeEvent` object.

Parameters:	source	the bean source for the property
	propertyName	the name of the property
	oldValue	the old value
	newValue	the new value

- `Object getNewValue()`
  returns the new value of the property.

- `Object getOldValue();`
  returns the previous value of the property.

- `String getPropertyName()`
  returns the name of the property.

`javax.swing.JComponent`

- `void addPropertyChangeListener(String propertyName, Property-ChangeListener listener)`
  registers an interested listener for the bound property.

| *Parameters:* | propertyName | the name of the property to listen to |
| | listener | the object that wants to be notified of a change in the bound property |

- `void addPropertyChangeListener(PropertyChangeListener listener)`
  registers an interested listener for all bound properties of this component.

| *Parameters:* | listener | the object that wants to be notified of a change in the bound property |

- `void removePropertyChangeListener(String propertyName, Property-ChangeListener listener)`
  removes a previously registered interested listener for the bound property.

| *Parameters:* | propertyName | the name of the property to listen to |
| | listener | the object to be removed from the list of listeners |

- `void removePropertyChangeListener(PropertyChangeListener listener)`
  removes a previously registered interested listener for the bound properties of this component.

| *Parameters:* | listener | the object to be removed from the list of listeners |

- `void firePropertyChange(String propertyName, Xxx oldValue, Xxx newValue)`
  sends a `PropertyChangeEvent` to registered listeners.

Parameters:	`propertyName`	the name of the property
	`oldValue`	the old value
	`newValue`	the new value

Constrained Properties

A constrained property is the most interesting of the properties, and also the most complex to implement. Such a property is constrained by the fact that *any* listener can "veto" proposed changes, forcing it to revert to the old setting.

For example, consider a text field to enter a number, implemented as a bean `IntTextBean`. A consumer of that number may have restrictions on the value; for example, perhaps the number must be between 0 and 255. Such a restriction would be easy to implement: add a `minValue` and `maxValue` to the `IntTextBean`. However, the restriction may be more complex than that. Perhaps the number should be even. Or, it may depend on another number that also changes. In that case, no simple property of the `IntTextBean` is able to distinguish good user inputs from bad ones. Instead, the bean should notify its consumers of the new value and give the consumers the chance to *veto* the change. A property that can be vetoed is called a *constrained* property.

We will put this concept to use with a *range bean* (see Figure 8–13). This bean contains two `IntTextBean` fields to specify the lower and the upper bound of a range. (You might use such a bean in a print dialog where the user can specify the range of pages to be printed.) If the user enters a `to` value that is less than the current `from` value (or a `from` value that is greater than the current `to` value), then the `RangeBean` vetoes the change.

Figure 8–13: The range bean

In this example, the `IntTextBean` is the producer of the vetoable event, and the `RangeBean` is the consumer that may issue a veto.

To build a constrained property, your bean must have the following two methods to let it register `VetoableChangeListener` objects:

```
public void addVetoableChangeListener(VetoableChangeListener
    listener);
public void removeVetoableChangeListener(VetoableChangeListener
    listener);
```

Just as there is a convenience class to manage property change listeners, there is a convenience class, called `VetoableChangeSupport`, that manages vetoable change listeners. Your bean should contain an object of this class.

```
private VetoableChangeSupport vetoSupport
    = new VetoableChangeSupport(this);
```

Adding and removing listeners should be delegated to this object. For example:

```
public void addVetoableChangeListener(VetoableChangeListener
    listener)
{
    vetoSupport.addVetoableChangeListener(listener);
}
public void removeVetoableChangeListener(VetoableChangeListener
    listener)
{
    vetoSupport.removeVetoableChangeListener(listener);
}
```

> TIP: The JComponent class has some support for constrained properties, but it is not as extensive as that for bound properties. The JComponent class keeps a single listener list for vetoable change listeners, not a separate list for each property. And the fireVetoableChange method is not overloaded for basic types. If your bean extends JComponent and has a single constrained property (as is often the case), then the listener support of the JComponent superclass is entirely adequate, and you do not need a separate VetoableChangeSupport object.

An object that is able to veto changes needs to implement the VetoableChange-Listener interface. That interface contains one method:

```
void vetoableChange(PropertyChangeEvent event)
    throws PropertyVetoException
```

This method receives a PropertyChangeEvent object, from which it can retrieve the current value and the proposed new value with the getOldValue and getNewValue methods.

Notice that the vetoableChange method throws an exception. A listener indicates its disapproval with the proposed change by throwing a Property-VetoException. This exception forces the bean that produced the event to abandon the new value.

To see how to implement the VetoableChangeListener interface, look at the code for the RangeBean class. It attaches listeners to the from and to bean. Here is the code for the from listener:

```
public void vetoableChange(PropertyChangeEvent event)
    throws PropertyVetoException
{
    int v = ((Integer)event.getNewValue()).intValue();
    if (v > to.getValue())
        throw new PropertyVetoException("from > to", event);
}
```

It is highly recommended that constrained properties also be bound properties. That is, your bean should have methods to add `PropertyChangeListener` objects in addition to `VetoableChangeListener` objects. You saw how to implement those methods in the preceding section.

To update a constrained property value, a bean uses the following two-phase approach:

1. Notify all vetoable change listeners of the *intent* to change the property value. (Use the `fireVetoableChange` method of the `VetoableChange-Support` class.)

2. If none of the vetoable change listeners has thrown a `PropertyVetoException`, then update the value of the property.

3. Notify all property change listeners to *confirm* that a change has occurred.

Here is a typical example from the `IntTextBean` code.

```
public void setValue(int v) throws PropertyVetoException
{
    Integer oldValue = new Integer(getValue());
    Integer newValue = new Integer(v);
    vetoSupport.fireVetoableChange("value", oldValue, newValue);
    // survived, therefore no veto
    value = v;
    setText("" + v);
    changeSupport.firePropertyChange("value", oldValue,
        newValue);
}
```

It is important that you don't change the property value until all the registered vetoable change listeners have agreed with the proposed change. Conversely, a vetoable change listener should never assume that a change that it agrees with is actually happening. The only reliable way to get notified when a change is actually happening is through a property change listener.

Example 8–3 shows the code for the integer text bean that allows its values to be vetoed—it is based on the `IntTextField` class from Volume 1. Example 8–4 shows the code for the `RangeBean`. A range bean contains two `IntTextBean` objects and vetoes the change if it would result in an invalid range.

Note that the integer text field sets a *focus listener* that tracks focus events. When the text field gains focus, the original value is saved. When it gives up the focus, then the `editComplete` method is called.

```
public IntTextBean(int defval, int size)
{
    super("" + defval, size);
    addFocusListener(new
        FocusListener()
```

```
    {
        public void focusGained(FocusEvent event)
        {
            if (!event.isTemporary())
                lastValue = getValue();
        }
        public void focusLost(FocusEvent event)
        {
            if (!event.isTemporary())
                editComplete();
        }
    });
}
```

The editComplete method is similar to the setValue method; however, if a property change was vetoed, it restores the original value and resets the focus to the text field.

```
public void editComplete()
{
    Integer oldValue = new Integer(lastValue);
    Integer newValue = new Integer(getValue());
    try
    {
        fireVetoableChange("value", oldValue, newValue);
        // survived, therefore no veto
        firePropertyChange("value", oldValue, newValue);
    }
    catch(PropertyVetoException e)
    {
        // someone didn't like it
        JOptionPane.showMessageDialog(this, "" + e,
            "Input Error", JOptionPane.WARNING_MESSAGE);
        setText("" + lastValue);
        requestFocus();
    }
}
```

CAUTION: The requestFocus method does not work for Swing components in JDK 1.2—see bug #4128659 in the "bug parade" at http://developer.java.sun.com for details.

To see the veto mechanism at work, add the range bean to a form. Type a value into the from field that is larger than the value in the to field. Then, click inside the to field. You will see that the contents of the from field instantly revert to the old value.

Here is what happens:

1. You type a value into the `from` field.
2. You click on the `to` field.
3. The `from` field loses focus, and the focus listener of the `from` field calls the `editComplete` method.
4. That method fires a vetoable change.
5. The `to` field vetoes the change.
6. The `catch` clause in the `editComplete` method displays a warning dialog (see Figure 8–14), restores the original value, and requests focus.

Figure 8–14: A Veto Message

Here is another interesting experiment. Rather than editing the values of the text fields, use a property inspector to set the value of the `from` property to a value that is higher than the `to` property. You will find that the property inspector won't let you do that. The `setFrom` method throws a veto exception, and the value is never set. In some builder environments (but not Forte 2.0), the property inspector attaches itself as a veto listener, so that it can give you an error message and restore the old value in the inspector.

Whenever you build a constrained property into your bean, keep in mind that the bean may have multiple listeners, any of which can veto the change. Therefore, a constrained property that isn't bound doesn't make much sense. Listeners need to be notified when a proposed property change has actually been accepted by all listeners. For this reason, we strongly suggest that all your constrained properties be bound.

Example 8–3: **IntTextBean.java**

```
1. import java.awt.*;
2. import java.awt.event.*;
3. import java.beans.*;
4. import java.io.*;
5. import javax.swing.*;
6. import javax.swing.text.*;
7.
8. /**
9.    A bean for editing integer values
10. */
```

```
11. public class IntTextBean extends JTextField
12. {
13.    public IntTextBean()
14.    {
15.       super("0", TEXTSIZE);
16.       setInputVerifier(new IntTextFieldVerifier());
17.       addActionListener(new
18.          ActionListener()
19.          {
20.             public void actionPerformed(ActionEvent event)
21.             {
22.                editComplete();
23.             }
24.          });
25.       addFocusListener(new
26.          FocusListener()
27.          {
28.             public void focusGained(FocusEvent event)
29.             {
30.                if (!event.isTemporary())
31.                   lastValue = getValue();
32.
33.             }
34.             public void focusLost(FocusEvent event)
35.             {
36.                if (!event.isTemporary())
37.                   editComplete();
38.             }
39.          });
40.    }
41.
42.    protected Document createDefaultModel()
43.    {
44.       return new IntTextDocument();
45.    }
46.
47.    /**
48.       This method is called when the text field loses
49.       focus or the user hits Enter.
50.    */
51.    public void editComplete()
52.    {
53.       Integer oldValue = new Integer(lastValue);
54.       Integer newValue = new Integer(getValue());
55.       try
56.       {
57.          fireVetoableChange("value", oldValue, newValue);
58.          // survived, therefore no veto
59.          firePropertyChange("value", oldValue, newValue);
60.       }
61.       catch(PropertyVetoException e)
62.       {
63.          // someone didn't like it
```

```
64.        JOptionPane.showMessageDialog(this, "" + e,
65.           "Input Error", JOptionPane.WARNING_MESSAGE);
66.        setText("" + lastValue);
67.        requestFocus();
68.           // doesn't work in all JDK versions--see bug #4128659
69.     }
70.  }
71.
72.  /**
73.     Checks if the contents of this field is a valid integer.
74.     @return true of the field contents is valid
75.  */
76.  public boolean isValid()
77.  {
78.     return IntTextDocument.isValid(getText());
79.  }
80.
81.  /**
82.     Gets the numeric value of the field contents.
83.     @param the number that the user typed into the field, or
84.     0 if the field contents is not valid.
85.  */
86.  public int getValue()
87.  {
88.     try
89.     {
90.        return Integer.parseInt(getText());
91.     }
92.     catch(NumberFormatException e)
93.     {
94.        return 0;
95.     }
96.  }
97.
98.  /**
99.     Sets the constrained value property.
100.    @param v the new value
101. */
102. public void setValue(int v) throws PropertyVetoException
103. {
104.    Integer oldValue = new Integer(getValue());
105.    Integer newValue = new Integer(v);
106.    fireVetoableChange("value", oldValue, newValue);
107.    // survived, therefore no veto
108.    setText("" + v);
109.    firePropertyChange("value", oldValue, newValue);
110. }
111.
112. public Dimension getPreferredSize()
113. {
114.    return new Dimension(XPREFSIZE, YPREFSIZE);
115. }
116.
```

```
117.    private int lastValue;
118.    private static final int XPREFSIZE = 50;
119.    private static final int YPREFSIZE = 20;
120.    private static final int TEXTSIZE = 10;
121. }
122.
123. /**
124.    A document that can only hold valid integers or their
125.    substrings
126. */
127. class IntTextDocument extends PlainDocument
128. {
129.    public void insertString(int offs, String str,
130.       AttributeSet a)
131.       throws BadLocationException
132.    {
133.       if (str == null) return;
134.
135.       String oldString = getText(0, getLength());
136.       String newString = oldString.substring(0, offs)
137.          + str + oldString.substring(offs);
138.
139.       if (canBecomeValid(newString))
140.          super.insertString(offs, str, a);
141.    }
142.
143.    /**
144.       A helper function that tests whether a string is a valid
145.       integer
146.       @param s a string
147.       @return true if s is a valid integer
148.    */
149.    public static boolean isValid(String s)
150.    {
151.       try
152.       {
153.          Integer.parseInt(s);
154.          return true;
155.       }
156.       catch(NumberFormatException e)
157.       {
158.          return false;
159.       }
160.    }
161.
162.    /**
163.       A helper function that tests whether a string is a
164.       substring of a valid integer
165.       @param s a string
166.       @return true if s can be extended to a valid integer
167.    */
168.    public static boolean canBecomeValid(String s)
169.    {
```

```
170.        return s.equals("") || s.equals("-") || isValid(s);
171.    }
172. }
173.
174. /**
175.    A verifier that checks if the contents of a text component
176.    is a valid integer.
177. */
178. class IntTextFieldVerifier extends InputVerifier
179. {
180.    public boolean verify(JComponent component)
181.    {
182.        String text = ((JTextComponent)component).getText();
183.        return IntTextDocument.isValid(text);
184.    }
185. }
```

Example 8–4: RangeBean.java

```
1. import java.awt.*;
2. import java.beans.*;
3. import java.io.*;
4. import javax.swing.*;
5.
6. /**
7.    A bean with two integer text fields to specify a range
8.    of values.
9. */
10. public class RangeBean extends JPanel
11. {
12.    public RangeBean()
13.    {
14.        add(new JLabel("From"));
15.        add(from);
16.        add(new JLabel("To"));
17.        add(to);
18.
19.        from.addVetoableChangeListener(new
20.            VetoableChangeListener()
21.            {
22.                public void vetoableChange(PropertyChangeEvent event)
23.                    throws PropertyVetoException
24.                {
25.                    int v = ((Integer)event.getNewValue()).intValue();
26.                    if (v > to.getValue())
27.                        throw new PropertyVetoException("from > to",
28.                            event);
29.                }
30.            });
31.
32.        to.addVetoableChangeListener(new
33.            VetoableChangeListener()
34.            {
```

```
35.          public void vetoableChange(PropertyChangeEvent event)
36.             throws PropertyVetoException
37.             {
38.                int v = ((Integer)event.getNewValue()).intValue();
39.                if (v < from.getValue())
40.                   throw new PropertyVetoException("to < from",
41.                      event);
42.             }
43.          });
44.    }
45.
46.    /**
47.       Sets the from property.
48.       @param v the new lower bound of the range
49.    */
50.    public void setFrom(int v) throws PropertyVetoException
51.    {
52.       from.setValue(v);
53.    }
54.
55.    /**
56.       Gets the from property.
57.       @return the lower bound of the range
58.    */
59.    public int getFrom() { return from.getValue(); }
60.
61.    /**
62.       Sets the to property.
63.       @param v the new upper bound of the range.
64.    */
65.    public void setTo(int v) throws PropertyVetoException
66.    {
67.       to.setValue(v);
68.    }
69.
70.    /**
71.       Gets the to property.
72.       @return the upper bound of the range
73.    */
74.    public int getTo() { return to.getValue(); }
75.
76.    private IntTextBean from = new IntTextBean();
77.    private IntTextBean to = new IntTextBean();
78. }
```

 java.beans.VetoableChangeListener

- void vetoableChange(PropertyChangeEvent event)
  is called when a property is about to be changed. It should throw a
  PropertyVetoException if the change is not acceptable.

  Parameters: event   the event object describing the property change

java.beans.VetoableChangeSupport

- VetoableChangeSupport(Object sourceBean)
  constructs the (convenience) VetoableChangeSupport object.

  Parameters: sourceBean   the bean that is the source of the vetoable change (usually this)

- void addVetoableChangeListener(VetoableChangeListener listener)
  registers an interested listener for the constrained property.

  Parameters: listener   the bean that wants to have a chance to veto the constrained property

- void removeVetoableChangeListener(VetoableChangeListener listener)
  removes a previously registered interested listener for the constrained property.

  Parameters: listener   the bean to be removed from the list of listeners

- void fireVetoableChange(String propertyName, Object oldValue, Object newValue)
  sends a (convenience) PropertyChangeEvent to registered listeners prior to updating the property value.

  Parameters: propertyName   the name of the property

  oldValue   the current value

  newValue   the proposed new value

javax.swing.JComponent

- void addVetoableChangeListener(VetoableChangeListener listener)
  registers an interested listener for all constrained properties of this component.

  Parameters: listener   the object that wants to be notified of a change in the bound property

- void removeVetoableChangeListener(VetoableChangeListener listener)
  removes a previously registered interested listener for the constrained properties of this component.

  Parameters: listener   the object to be removed from the list of listeners

- void fireVetoableChange(String propertyName, Object oldValue, Object newValue)
  sends a PropertyChangeEvent to registered listeners.

  Parameters: propertyName   the name of the property

  oldValue   the old value

  newValue   the new value

java.beans.PropertyVetoException

- PropertyVetoException(String reason, PropertyChangeEvent event)
  creates a new PropertyVetoException.

  Parameters: reason   a string that describes the reason for the veto

                   event   the PropertyChangeEvent for the constrained property you want to veto

- PropertyChangeEvent getPropertyChangeEvent()
  returns the PropertyChangeEvent used to construct the exception.

Adding Custom Bean Events

When you add a bound or constrained property to a bean, you also enable the bean to fire events whenever the value of that property changes. However, there are other events that a bean can send out, for example,

- When the program user has clicked on a control within the bean;
- When new information is available;
- Or, simply when some amount of time has elapsed.

Unlike the PropertyChangeEvent events, these events belong to custom classes and need to be captured by custom listeners.

Here is how to write a bean that generates custom events. (Please consult Chapter 8 of Volume 1 for more details on event-handling in the Java platform.) Be sure to follow the first two steps precisely or the introspection mechanism will not recognize that you are trying to define a custom event.

1. Write a class *Custom*Event that extends EventObject. (The event name must end in Event in order for a builder to use the naming patterns to find it.)
2. Write an interface *Custom*Listener with one or more notification methods. Those methods can have any name, but they must have a single parameter of type *Custom*Event and return type void.
3. Supply the following two methods in the bean:
   ```
   public void addCustomListener(CustomListener e)
   public void removeCustomListener(CustomListener e)
   ```

 CAUTION: If your event class doesn't extend EventObject, chances are that your code will compile just fine because none of the methods of the EventObject class are actually needed, and none of the various other methods ever try to cast the event objects to the EventObject class. However, your bean will mysteriously fail—the introspection mechanism will not recognize the events.

To implement the methods needed for adding, removing, and delivering custom events, you can no longer rely on convenience classes that automatically manage the event listeners. Instead, you need to collect and manage all the event listeners. As we discussed in Chapter 8 of Volume 1, the EventListenerList is a convenience class that is designed for this purpose. Because it is possible for a listener object to implement multiple event listener interfaces, an event listener list entry is specified by the class object of the listener interface and the listener object.

Implementing the methods for adding and removing listeners is straightforward:

```
public void addCustomListener(CustomListener listener)
{
    listenerList.add(CustomListener.class, listener);
}

public void removeCustomListener(CustomListener listener)
{
    listenerList.remove(CustomListener.class, listener);
}
```

For each method in the listener interface, you should provide a convenience method for event firing.

```
public void fireMethodName(CustomEvent event)
{
    EventListener[] listeners = listenerList.getListeners(
        CustomListener.class);

    for (int i = 0; i < listeners.length; i++)
    {
        CustomListener listener = (CustomListener)listeners[i];
        listener.methodName(event);
    }
}
```

That method is not required by the JavaBeans specification—it just makes it easier to send events to all interested listeners.

Now, let's apply this technique to implementing a TimerBean. This bean should send TimerEvent objects to its listeners. (This is a modification of the Timer class from chapter 8 of Volume 1.) Timer events are generated at regular intervals, measured in milliseconds, provided that the running property is set to true. The interval length is determined by the interval property. Examples 8–5 through 8–7 show the code for the following:

- The TimerEvent class, the custom event that is generated by this bean;
- The TimerListener class with a notification method that we called timeElapsed;
- The TimerBean with methods addTimerListener and removeTimerListener.

Here is how you can test the bean in Forte.

1. Start a new application based on a JFrame, as previously described. Drop a timer bean into the frame. This is a *nonvisual bean*—it does not extend the Component class. It shows up in the frame's inspector under the heading "Non-visual Components" (see Figure 8–15).

2. Set its running property to true.

Figure 8–15: A Non-visual Bean

3. Add a scroll pane to the center of the frame. (Look inside the "Swing" tab in the component panel.)

4. Add a text area inside the scroll pane.

5. Hook up the timeElapsed event to a method with name update-TextArea and body

```
jTextArea1.append(evt + "\n");
```

6. Compile and run.

   You will see messages filling the text area (see Figure 8–16). If the messages don't show up, double-check that you set the running property to true.

Figure 8–16: Listening to a Custom Event

In the bean box, you can have a slightly more fun display by hooking up a `TimerBean` with an `EventMonitor` bean. You can then start and stop the timer by toggling the `running` property in the property editor.

Here's the complete code for the `TimerBean`.

Example 8–5: TimerBean.java

```
1. import java.io.*;
2. import java.util.*;
3. import javax.swing.event.*;
4.
5. /**
6.    A nonvisual bean that sends timer events.
7. */
8. public class TimerBean implements Serializable
9. {
10.    public TimerBean()
11.    {
12.       listenerList = new EventListenerList();
13.    }
14.
15.    /**
16.       Sets the interval property.
17.       @param i the interval between timer ticks (in milliseconds)
18.    */
19.    public void setInterval(int i) { interval = i; }
20.
21.    /**
22.       Gets the interval property.
23.       @return the interval between timer ticks (in milliseconds)
24.    */
25.    public int getInterval() { return interval; }
26.
27.    /**
28.       Sets the running property.
29.       @param b true if the timer is running
30.    */
31.    public void setRunning(boolean b)
32.    {
33.       if (b && runner == null)
34.       {
35.          if (interval <= 0) return;
36.          runner = new
37.             Thread()
38.             {
39.                public void run()
40.                {
41.                   try
42.                   {
43.                      while (!Thread.interrupted())
44.                      {
45.                         Thread.sleep(interval);
```

```
46.                        fireTimeElapsed(new TimerEvent(this));
47.                     }
48.                  }
49.               catch(InterruptedException e)
50.                  {
51.                  }
52.               }
53.            };
54.         runner.start();
55.      }
56.      else if (!b && runner != null)
57.      {
58.         runner.interrupt();
59.         runner = null;
60.      }
61.   }
62.
63.   /**
64.      Gets the running property.
65.      @return true if the timer is running
66.   */
67.   public boolean isRunning() { return runner != null; }
68.
69.   /**
70.      Adds a timer listener.
71.      @param listener the listener to add
72.   */
73.   public void addTimerListener(TimerListener listener)
74.   {
75.      listenerList.add(TimerListener.class, listener);
76.   }
77.
78.   /**
79.      Removes a timer listener.
80.      @param listener the listener to remove
81.   */
82.   public void removeTimerListener(TimerListener listener)
83.   {
84.      listenerList.add(TimerListener.class, listener);
85.   }
86.
87.   /**
88.      Sends a timer event to all listeners.
89.      @param event the event to send
90.   */
91.   public void fireTimeElapsed(TimerEvent event)
92.   {
93.      EventListener[] listeners = listenerList.getListeners(
94.         TimerListener.class);
95.
96.      for (int i = 0; i < listeners.length; i++)
97.         {
```

```
98.            TimerListener listener = (TimerListener)listeners[i];
99.            listener.timeElapsed(event);
100.        }
101.    }
102.
103.    private int interval = 1000;
104.    private EventListenerList listenerList;
105.    private Thread runner;
106. }
```

Example 8–6: TimerListener.java

```
1. import java.util.*;
2.
3. /**
4.    An interface for being notified when a timer tick occurs.
5. */
6. public interface TimerListener extends EventListener
7. {
8.    /**
9.        This method is called whenever the time between
10.       notifications has elapsed.
11.       @param evt the timer event that contains
12.       the time of notification
13.    */
14.    public void timeElapsed(TimerEvent evt);
15. }
```

Example 8–7: TimerEvent.java

```
1. import java.util.*;
2.
3. /**
4.    A class to describe timer events.
5. */
6. public class TimerEvent extends EventObject
7. {
8.    /**
9.        Constructs a timer event.
10.       @param source the event source
11.    */
12.    public TimerEvent(Object source)
13.    {
14.       super(source);
15.       now = new Date();
16.    }
17.
18.    /**
19.       Reports when the event was constructed.
20.       @return the construction date and time
21.    */
22.    public Date getDate()
23.    {
24.       return now;
```

```
25.    }
26.
27.    public String toString()
28.    {
29.        return now + ":" + super.toString();
30.    }
31.
32.    private Date now;
33. }
```

Property Editors

If you add an integer or string property to a bean, then that property is automatically displayed in the bean's property inspector. But what happens if you add a property whose values cannot easily be edited in a text field, for example, a date or a `Color`? Then, you need to provide a separate component that the user can use to specify the property value. Such components are called *property editors.* For example, a property editor for a date object might be a calendar that lets the user scroll through the months and pick a date. A property editor for a `Color` object would let the user select the red, green, and blue components of the color.

Actually, Forte already has a property editor for colors—you saw it in Figure 8–9. Also, of course, there are property editors for basic types such as `String` (a text field) and `boolean` (a choice list with values `true` and `false`). These property editors are registered with the *property editor manager.*

The process for supplying a new property editor is slightly involved. First, you create a bean info class to accompany your bean. The bean info is a collection of miscellaneous information about your bean. For example, if you have a property whose type is `int` or `String` but whose legal values are restricted in some way, you may not want to use the general-purpose property editor that is supplied by the builder tool. Instead, you can supply a specific editor for a particular property by naming it in the bean info.

The name of the bean info class must be the name of the bean, followed by the word `BeanInfo`. That class must implement the `BeanInfo` interface, an interface with eight methods. It is simpler to extend the `SimpleBeanInfo` class instead. This convenience class has do-nothing implementations for the eight methods. For example,

```
// bean info class for ChartBean
class ChartBeanBeanInfo
    extends SimpleBeanInfo
{
    . . .
}
```

To request a specific editor for a particular bean, you override the `getProperty-Descriptors` method. That method returns an array of `PropertyDescriptor` objects. You create one object for each property that should be displayed on a property editor, *even those for which you just want the default editor.*

You construct a `PropertyDescriptor` by supplying the name of the property and the class of the bean that contains it.

```
PropertyDescriptor descriptor
    = new PropertyDescriptor("titlePosition", ChartBean.class);
```

To request a specific editor for the property, you call the `setPropertyEditorClass` method of the `PropertyDescriptor` class.

```
descriptor.setPropertyEditorClass(TitlePositionEditor.class);
```

Next, you build an array of descriptors for properties of your bean. For example, the chart bean that we discuss in this section has four properties:

- A `String` property, `title`
- An `int` property, `titlePosition`
- A `double[]` property, `values`
- A `boolean` property, `inverse`

Figure 8–17 shows the chart bean. You can see the title on the top. Its position can be set to left, center, or right. The `values` property specifies the graph values. If the `inverse` property is true, then the background is colored and the bars of the chart are white. Example 8–8 lists the code for the chart bean; the bean is simply a modification of the chart applet in Volume 1, Chapter 10.

Figure 8–17: The chart bean

The code in Example 8–9 shows the `ChartBeanBeanInfo` class that specifies the property editors for these properties. It achieves the following:

1. In the `static` block, the `DoubleArrayEditor` is registered as an editor for any `double[]` array.

2. The `getPropertyDescriptors` method returns a descriptor for each property. The `title` and `graphColor` properties are used with the default editors, that is, the string and color editors that come with the builder tool.

3. The `titlePosition`, `values`, and `inverse` properties use special editors of type `TitlePositionEditor`, `DoubleArrayEditor` and `Inverse-Editor`, respectively.

Figure 8–18 shows the resulting property inspector. You'll see in the following sections how to implement these kinds of editors.

Figure 8–18: The property inspector for the chart bean

It is also possible to add property editors with the static `registerEditor` method of the `PropertyEditorManager` class, setting a property editor for all properties of a given type. Here is an example:

```
PropertyEditorManager.registerEditor(Date.class,
    CalendarSelector.class);
```

NOTE: You should not call the `registerEditor` method in your beans—the default editor for a type is a global setting that is properly the responsibility of the builder environment.

You can use the `findEditor` method in the `PropertyEditorManager` class to check whether a property editor exists for a given type in your builder tool. That method does the following:

1. It looks first to see which property editors are already registered with it. (These will be the editors supplied by the builder tool and by calls to the `registerEditor` method.)

2. Then, it looks for a class whose name consists of the name of the type plus the word `Editor`.

3. If neither lookup succeeds, then `findEditor` returns `null`.

For example, if a `CalendarSelector` class is registered for `java.util.Date` objects, then it would be used to edit a `Date` property. Otherwise, a `java.util.DateEditor` would be searched.

Example 8–8: ChartBean.java

```
1. import java.awt.*;
2. import java.awt.font.*;
3. import java.awt.geom.*;
4. import java.util.*;
5. import java.beans.*;
6. import java.io.*;
7. import javax.swing.*;
8.
9. /**
10.    A bean to draw a bar chart.
11. */
12. public class ChartBean extends JPanel
13. {
14.    public void paint(Graphics g)
15.    {
16.       Graphics2D g2 = (Graphics2D)g;
17.
18.       if (values == null || values.length == 0) return;
19.       double minValue = 0;
20.       double maxValue = 0;
21.       for (int i = 0; i < values.length; i++)
22.       {
23.          if (minValue > getValues(i)) minValue = getValues(i);
24.          if (maxValue < getValues(i)) maxValue = getValues(i);
25.       }
26.       if (maxValue == minValue) return;
27.
28.       Dimension d = getSize();
29.       Rectangle2D bounds = getBounds();
30.       double clientWidth = bounds.getWidth();
31.       double clientHeight = bounds.getHeight();
32.       double barWidth = clientWidth / values.length;
33.
34.       g2.setColor(inverse ? color : Color.white);
35.       g2.fill(bounds);
36.       g2.setColor(Color.black);
37.
38.       Font titleFont = new Font("SansSerif", Font.BOLD, 20);
39.       FontRenderContext context = g2.getFontRenderContext();
40.       Rectangle2D titleBounds
41.          = titleFont.getStringBounds(title, context);
42.
43.       double titleWidth = titleBounds.getWidth();
44.       double y = -titleBounds.getY();
45.       double x;
46.       if (titlePosition == LEFT)
47.          x = 0;
48.       else if (titlePosition == CENTER)
49.          x = (clientWidth - titleWidth) / 2;
50.       else
51.          x = clientWidth - titleWidth;
```

```
52.
53.          g2.setFont(titleFont);
54.          g2.drawString(title, (float)x, (float)y);
55.
56.          double top = titleBounds.getHeight();
57.          double scale = (clientHeight - top)
58.             / (maxValue - minValue);
59.          y = clientHeight;
60.
61.          for (int i = 0; i < values.length; i++)
62.          {
63.             double x1 = i * barWidth + 1;
64.             double y1 = top;
65.             double value = getValues(i);
66.             double height =  value * scale;
67.             if (value >= 0)
68.                y1 += (maxValue - value) * scale;
69.             else
70.             {
71.                y1 += (int)(maxValue * scale);
72.                height = -height;
73.             }
74.
75.             g2.setColor(inverse ? Color.white : color);
76.             Rectangle2D bar = new Rectangle2D.Double(x1, y1,
77.                barWidth - 2, height);
78.             g2.fill(bar);
79.             g2.setColor(Color.black);
80.             g2.draw(bar);
81.          }
82.       }
83.
84.       /**
85.          Sets the title property.
86.          @param t the new chart title.
87.       */
88.       public void setTitle(String t) { title = t; }
89.
90.       /**
91.          Gets the title property.
92.          @return the chart title.
93.       */
94.       public String getTitle() { return title; }
95.
96.       /**
97.          Sets the indexed values property.
98.          @param v the values to display in the chart.
99.       */
100.      public void setValues(double[] v) { values = v; }
101.
102.      /**
103.          Gets the indexed values property.
```

```
104.          @return the values to display in the chart.
105.      */
106.      public double[] getValues() { return values; }
107.
108.      /**
109.          Sets the indexed values property.
110.          @param i the index of the value to set
111.          @param value the new value for that index
112.      */
113.      public void setValues(int i, double value)
114.      {
115.          if (0 <= i && i < values.length) values[i] = value;
116.      }
117.
118.      /**
119.          Gets the indexed values property.
120.          @param i the index of the value to get
121.          @return the value for that index
122.      */
123.      public double getValues(int i)
124.      {
125.          if (0 <= i && i < values.length) return values[i];
126.          return 0;
127.      }
128.
129.      /**
130.          Sets the inverse property.
131.          @param b true if the display is inverted (white bars
132.          on colored background)
133.      */
134.      public void setInverse(boolean b) { inverse = b; }
135.
136.      /**
137.          Gets the inverse property.
138.          @return true if the display is inverted
139.      */
140.      public boolean isInverse() { return inverse; }
141.
142.      /**
143.          Sets the titlePosition property.
144.          @param p LEFT, CENTER, or RIGHT
145.      */
146.      public void setTitlePosition(int p) { titlePosition = p; }
147.
148.      /**
149.          Gets the titlePosition property.
150.          @return LEFT, CENTER, or RIGHT
151.      */
152.      public int getTitlePosition() { return titlePosition; }
153.
154.      /**
155.          Sets the graphColor property.
```

```
156.        @param c the color to use for the graph
157.     */
158.     public void setGraphColor(Color c) { color = c; }
159.
160.     /**
161.        Gets the graphColor property.
162.        @param c the color to use for the graph
163.     */
164.     public Color getGraphColor() { return color; }
165.
166.     public Dimension getPreferredSize()
167.     {
168.        return new Dimension(XPREFSIZE, YPREFSIZE);
169.     }
170.
171.     private static final int LEFT = 0;
172.     private static final int CENTER = 1;
173.     private static final int RIGHT = 2;
174.
175.     private static final int XPREFSIZE = 300;
176.     private static final int YPREFSIZE = 300;
177.     private double[] values = { 1, 2, 3 };
178.     private String title = "Title";
179.     private int titlePosition = CENTER;
180.     private boolean inverse;
181.     private Color color = Color.red;
182. }
```

Example 8–9: ChartBeanBeanInfo.java

```
1. import java.beans.*;
2.
3. /**
4.    The bean info for the chart bean, specifying the
5.    property editors.
6. */
7. public class ChartBeanBeanInfo extends SimpleBeanInfo
8. {
9.    public PropertyDescriptor[] getPropertyDescriptors()
10.    {
11.       try
12.       {
13.          PropertyDescriptor titlePositionDescriptor
14.             = new PropertyDescriptor("titlePosition",
15.                ChartBean.class);
16.          titlePositionDescriptor.setPropertyEditorClass(
17.             TitlePositionEditor.class);
18.          PropertyDescriptor inverseDescriptor
19.             = new PropertyDescriptor("inverse",
20.                ChartBean.class);
21.          inverseDescriptor.setPropertyEditorClass(
22.             InverseEditor.class);
23.          PropertyDescriptor valuesDescriptor
```

```
24.              = new PropertyDescriptor("values",
25.                  ChartBean.class);
26.           valuesDescriptor.setPropertyEditorClass(
27.              DoubleArrayEditor.class);
28.
29.           return new PropertyDescriptor[]
30.           {
31.              new PropertyDescriptor("title",
32.                  ChartBean.class),
33.              titlePositionDescriptor,
34.              valuesDescriptor,
35.              new PropertyDescriptor("graphColor",
36.                  ChartBean.class),
37.              inverseDescriptor
38.           };
39.        }
40.        catch(IntrospectionException e)
41.        {
42.           e.printStackTrace();
43.           return null;
44.        }
45.     }
46. }
```

java.beans.PropertyEditorManager

• `static PropertyEditor findEditor(Class targetType)`
  returns a property editor for the given type, or `null` if none is registered.

  Parameters: `targetType`   the `Class` object for the type to be edited,
                                 such as `Class.Color`

• `static void registerEditor(Class targetType, Class editorClass)`
  registers an editor class to edit values of the given type.

  Parameters: `targetType`   the `Class` object for the type to be edited

                 `editorClass`   the `Class` object for the editor class (`null`
                                 will unregister the current editor)

java.beans.PropertyDescriptor

• `PropertyDescriptor(String name, Class beanClass)`
  constructs a `PropertyDescriptor` object.

  Parameters: `name`   the name of the property

                 `beanClass`   the class of the bean to which the property
                                 belongs

• `void setPropertyEditorClass(Class editorClass)`
  sets the class of the property editor to be used with this property.

`java.beans.BeanInfo`

• `PropertyDescriptor[] getPropertyDescriptors()`

returns a descriptor for each property that should be displayed in the property inspector for the bean.

Writing a Property Editor

Before we begin showing you how to write a property editor, we want to point out that while each property editor works with a value of one specific type, it can nonetheless be quite elaborate. For example, a font property editor (which edits an object of type `Font`) could show font samples to allow the user to pick a font in a more congenial way.

Next, any property editor you write must implement the `PropertyEditor` interface, an interface with 12 methods. As with the `BeanInfo` interface, you will not want to do this directly. Instead, it is far more convenient to extend the convenience `PropertyEditorSupport` class that is supplied with the standard library. This support class comes with methods to add and remove property change listeners, and with default versions of all other methods of the `PropertyEditor` interface. For example, our editor for editing the title position of a chart in our chart bean starts out like this:

```
// property editor class for title position
class TitlePositionEditor
    extends PropertyEditorSupport
{
    . . .
}
```

Note that if a property editor class has a constructor, it must also supply a default constructor, that is, one without arguments.

Finally, before we get into the mechanics of actually writing a property editor, we want to point out that the editor is under the control of the builder, not the bean. The builder adheres to the following procedure to display the current value of the property:

1. It instantiates property editors for each property of the bean.
2. It asks the *bean* to tell it the current value of the property.
3. It then asks the *property editor* to display the value.

The property editor can use either text-based or graphically-based methods to actually display the value. We discuss these methods next.

Simple Property Editors

Simple property editors work with text strings. You override the `setAsText` and `getAsText` methods. For example, our chart bean has a property that lets you set where the title should be displayed: Left, Center, or Right. These choices are implemented as integer constants.

```
private static final int LEFT = 0;
private static final int CENTER = 1;
private static final int RIGHT = 2;
```

But of course, we don't want them to appear as numbers 0, 1, 2 in the text field—unless we are competing for inclusion in the User Interface Hall of Horrors. Instead, we define a property editor whose getAsText method returns the value as a string. The method calls the getValue method of the PropertyEditor to find the value of the property. Since this is a generic method, the value is returned as an Object. If the property type is a basic type, we need to return a wrapper object. In our case, the property type is int, and the call to getValue returns an Integer.

```
class TitlePositionEditor
    extends PropertyEditorSupport
{
    public String getAsText()
    {
        int i = ((Integer)getValue()).intValue();
        if (0 <= i && i < options.length) return options[i];
        return "";
    }
    . . .
    private String[] options = { "Left", "Center", "Right" };
}
```

Now, the text field displays one of these fields. When the user edits the text field, this triggers a call to the setAsText method to update the property value by invoking the setValue method. It, too, is a generic method whose parameter is of type Object. To set the value of a numeric type, we need to pass a wrapper object.

```
public void setAsText(String s)
{
    for (int i = 0; i < options.length; i++)
    {
        if (options[i].equals(s))
        {
            setValue(new Integer(i));
            return;
        }
    }
}
```

Actually, this property editor is not a good choice for the titlePosition property, unless, of course, we are also competing for entry into the User

Interface Hall of Shame. The user may not know what the legal choices are. It would be better to display all valid settings (see Figure 8–19). The `PropertyEditorSupport` class gives a simple method to display the selections in a property editor. We simply write a `getTags` method that returns an array of strings.

```
public String[] getTags() { return options; }
```

The default `getTags` method returns `null`. By returning a non-`null` value, we indicate a choice field instead of a text field.

We still need to supply the `getAsText` and `setAsText` methods. The `getTags` method simply specifies the values to be displayed in a combo box. The `getAsText`/ `setAsText` methods translate between the strings and the data type of the property (which may be a string, an integer, or a completely different type).

Figure 8–19: The TitlePositionEditor at work

Example 8–10 lists the complete code for this property editor.

Example 8–10: TitlePositionEditor.java

```
1. import java.beans.*;
2.
3. /**
4.    A custom editor for the titlePosition property of the
5.    ChartBean. The editor lets the user choose between
6.    Left, Center, and Right
7. */
8. public class TitlePositionEditor
9.    extends PropertyEditorSupport
10. {
11.    public String getAsText()
12.    {
13.       int value = ((Integer)getValue()).intValue();
14.       return options[value];
15.    }
16.
17.    public void setAsText(String s)
18.    {
19.       for (int i = 0; i < options.length; i++)
20.       {
21.          if (options[i].equals(s))
22.          {
23.             setValue(new Integer(i));
```

```
24.              return;
25.            }
26.         }
27.    }
28.
29.    public String[] getTags() { return options; }
30.
31.    private String[] options = { "Left", "Center", "Right" };
32. }
```

java.beans.PropertyEditorSupport

- `Object getValue()`

  returns the current value of the property. Basic types are wrapped into object wrappers.

- `void setValue(Object newValue)`

  sets the property to a new value. Basic types must be wrapped into object wrappers.

  Parameters: newValue the new value of the object; should be a newly created object that the property can own

- `String getAsText()`

  Override this method to return a string representation of the current value of the property. The default returns `null` to indicate that the property cannot be represented as a string.

- `void setAsText(String text)`

  Override this method to set the property to a new value that is obtained by parsing the text. May throw an `IllegalArgumentException` if the text does not represent a legal value or if this property cannot be represented as a string.

- `String[] getTags()`

  Override this method to return an array of all possible string representations of the property values so they can be displayed in a Choice box. The default returns `null` to indicate that there is not a finite set of string values.

GUI-Based Property Editors

More sophisticated property types can't be edited as text. Instead, they are represented in two ways. The property inspector contains a small area (which otherwise would hold a text box or combo box) onto which the property editor will draw a graphical representation of the current value. When the user clicks on that area, a custom editor dialog box pops up (see Figure 8–20). The dialog box contains a component to edit the property values, supplied by the property editor, and various buttons, supplied by the builder environment.

Figure 8–20: A custom editor dialog

To build a GUI-based property editor:

1. Tell the builder tool that you will paint the value and not use a string.
2. "Paint" the value the user enters onto the GUI.
3. Tell the builder tool that you will be using a GUI-based property editor.
4. Build the GUI.
5. Write the code to validate what the user tries to enter as the value.

For the first step, you override the getAsText method in the PropertyEditor interface to return null and the isPaintable method to return true.

```
public String getAsText()
{
   return null;
}

public boolean isPaintable()
{
   return true;
}
```

Then, you implement the paintValue method. It receives a Graphics context and the coordinates of the rectangle inside which you can paint. Note that this rectangle is typically small, so you can't have a very elaborate representation. To graphically represent the inverse property, we draw the string "Inverse" in white letters with a black background, or the string "Normal" in black letters with a white background (see Figure 8–18).

```
public void paintValue(Graphics g, Rectangle box)
{
   Graphics2D g2 = (Graphics2D)g;
   boolean isInverse = ((Boolean)getValue()).booleanValue();
   String s = isInverse ? "Inverse" : "Normal";
   g2.setColor(isInverse ? Color.black : Color.white);
   g2.fill(box);
   g2.setColor(isInverse ? Color.white : Color.black);
   // compute string position to center string
      . . .
   g2.drawString(s, (float)x, (float)y);
}
```

Of course, this graphical representation is not editable. The user must click on it to pop up a custom editor.

You indicate that you will have a custom editor by overriding the supports-CustomEditor in the PropertyEditor interface to return true.

```
public boolean supportsCustomEditor()
{
   return true;
}
```

Now, you write the code that builds up the component that will hold the custom editor. You will need to build a separate custom editor class for every property. For example, associated to our InverseEditor class is an InverseEditorPanel class (see Example 8–9) that describes a GUI with two radio buttons to toggle between normal and inverse mode. That code is straightforward. However, the GUI actions must update the property values. We did this as follows:

1. Have the custom editor constructor receive a reference to the property editor object and store it in a variable editor.
2. To read the property value, we have the custom editor call editor.getValue().
3. To set the object value, we have the custom editor call editor.setValue(newValue) followed by editor.firePropertyChange().

Next, the getCustomEditor method of the PropertyEditor interface constructs and returns an object of the custom editor class.

```
public Component getCustomEditor()
{
   return new InverseEditorPanel(this);
}
```

Example 8–11 shows the complete code for the InverseEditor that displays the current setting in the property inspector. Example 8–12 lists the code implementing the pop-up editor panel.

The other custom editor that we built for the chart bean class lets you edit a `double[]` array. Recall that neither Forte nor the BeanBox can edit array properties. We developed this custom editor to fill this obvious gap. Figure 8–21 shows the custom editor in action. All array values are shown in the list box, prefixed by their array index. Clicking on an array value places it into the text field above it, and you can edit it. You can also resize the array. The code for the `DoubleArray-Panel` class that implements the GUI is listed in Example 8–14.

The code for the property editor class (shown in Example 8–13) is almost identical to that of the `InverseEditor`, except that we simply paint a string consisting of the first few array values, followed by . . . in the `paintValue` method. And, of course, we return a different custom editor in the `getCustomEditor` method. These examples complete the code for the chart bean.

 NOTE: Unfortunately, we have to *paint* the array values. It would be more convenient to return a string with the `getAsText` method. However, some builder environments use a text field whenever the `getAsText` method returns a non-`null` string. Those environments won't pop up a custom editor if you click on the text, even if the `get-CustomEditor` method returns an editor component.

Figure 8–21: The custom editor dialog for editing an array

Example 8–11: InverseEditor.java

```
1. import java.awt.*;
2. import java.awt.font.*;
3. import java.awt.geom.*;
```

```
4. import java.beans.*;
5.
6. /**
7.    The property editor for the inverse property of the ChartBean.
8.    The inverse property toggles between colored graph bars
9.    and colored background.
10. */
11. public class InverseEditor extends PropertyEditorSupport
12. {
13.    public Component getCustomEditor()
14.    {
15.       return new InverseEditorPanel(this);
16.    }
17.
18.    public boolean supportsCustomEditor()
19.    {
20.       return true;
21.    }
22.
23.    public boolean isPaintable()
24.    {
25.       return true;
26.    }
27.
28.    public void paintValue(Graphics g, Rectangle box)
29.    {
30.       Graphics2D g2 = (Graphics2D)g;
31.       boolean isInverse = ((Boolean)getValue()).booleanValue();
32.       String s = isInverse ? "Inverse" : "Normal";
33.       g2.setColor(isInverse ? Color.black : Color.white);
34.       g2.fill(box);
35.       g2.setColor(isInverse ? Color.white : Color.black);
36.       FontRenderContext context = g2.getFontRenderContext();
37.       Rectangle2D stringBounds = g2.getFont().getStringBounds(
38.          s, context);
39.       double w = stringBounds.getWidth();
40.       double x = box.x;
41.       if (w < box.width) x += (box.width - w) / 2;
42.       double ascent = -stringBounds.getY();
43.       double y = box.y
44.          + (box.height - stringBounds.getHeight()) / 2 + ascent;
45.       g2.drawString(s, (float)x, (float)y);
46.    }
47.
48.    public String getAsText()
49.    {
50.       return null;
51.    }
52. }
```

Example 8–12: InverseEditorPanel.java

```
1. import java.awt.*;
2. import java.awt.event.*;
3. import java.text.*;
4. import java.lang.reflect.*;
5. import java.beans.*;
6. import javax.swing.*;
7.
8. /**
9.    The panel for setting the inverse property. It contains
10.   radio buttons to toggle between normal and inverse coloring.
11. */
12. public class InverseEditorPanel extends JPanel
13. {
14.    public InverseEditorPanel(PropertyEditorSupport ed)
15.    {
16.       editor = ed;
17.       ButtonGroup g = new ButtonGroup();
18.       boolean isInverse
19.          = ((Boolean)editor.getValue()).booleanValue();
20.       normal = new JRadioButton("Normal", !isInverse);
21.       inverse = new JRadioButton("Inverse", isInverse);
22.
23.       g.add(normal);
24.       g.add(inverse);
25.       add(normal);
26.       add(inverse);
27.
28.       ActionListener buttonListener =
29.          new ActionListener()
30.          {
31.             public void actionPerformed(ActionEvent event)
32.             {
33.                editor.setValue(
34.                   new Boolean(inverse.isSelected()));
35.                editor.firePropertyChange();
36.             }
37.          };
38.
39.       normal.addActionListener(buttonListener);
40.       inverse.addActionListener(buttonListener);
41.    }
42.
43.    private JRadioButton normal;
44.    private JRadioButton inverse;
45.    private PropertyEditorSupport editor;
46. }
```

Example 8–13: DoubleArrayEditor.java

```
1. import java.awt.*;
2. import java.awt.font.*;
3. import java.awt.geom.*;
```

```
 4.  import java.beans.*;
 5.
 6.  /**
 7.     A custom editor for an array of floating point numbers.
 8.  */
 9.  public class DoubleArrayEditor extends PropertyEditorSupport
10.  {
11.     public Component getCustomEditor()
12.     {
13.        return new DoubleArrayEditorPanel(this);
14.     }
15.
16.     public boolean supportsCustomEditor()
17.     {
18.        return true;
19.     }
20.
21.     public boolean isPaintable()
22.     {
23.        return true;
24.     }
25.
26.     public void paintValue(Graphics g, Rectangle box)
27.     {
28.        Graphics2D g2 = (Graphics2D)g;
29.        double[] values = (double[]) getValue();
30.        StringBuffer s = new StringBuffer();
31.        for (int i = 0; i < 3; i++)
32.        {
33.           if (values.length > i) s.append(values[i]);
34.           if (values.length > i + 1) s.append(", ");
35.        }
36.        if (values.length > 3) s.append("...");
37.
38.        g2.setColor(Color.white);
39.        g2.fill(box);
40.        g2.setColor(Color.black);
41.        FontRenderContext context = g2.getFontRenderContext();
42.        Rectangle2D stringBounds = g2.getFont().getStringBounds(
43.           s.toString(), context);
44.        double w = stringBounds.getWidth();
45.        double x = box.x;
46.        if (w < box.width) x += (box.width - w) / 2;
47.        double ascent = -stringBounds.getY();
48.        double y = box.y
49.           + (box.height - stringBounds.getHeight()) / 2 + ascent;
50.        g2.drawString(s.toString(), (float)x, (float)y);
51.     }
52.
53.     public String getAsText()
54.     {
55.        return null;
56.     }
57.  }
```

Example 8–14: DoubleArrayEditorPanel.java

```java
1. import java.awt.*;
2. import java.awt.event.*;
3. import java.text.*;
4. import java.lang.reflect.*;
5. import java.beans.*;
6. import javax.swing.*;
7. import javax.swing.event.*;
8.
9. /**
10.    The panel inside the DoubleArrayEditor. It contains
11.    a list of the array values, together with buttons to
12.    resize the array and change the currently selected list value.
13. */
14. public class DoubleArrayEditorPanel extends JPanel
15. {
16.    public DoubleArrayEditorPanel(PropertyEditorSupport ed)
17.    {
18.       editor = ed;
19.       setArray((double[])ed.getValue());
20.
21.       setLayout(new GridBagLayout());
22.       GridBagConstraints gbc = new GridBagConstraints();
23.
24.       gbc.weightx = 100;
25.       gbc.weighty = 0;
26.       gbc.fill = GridBagConstraints.HORIZONTAL;
27.
28.       add(sizeField, gbc, 0, 0, 1, 1);
29.       add(valueField, gbc, 0, 1, 1, 1);
30.
31.       gbc.fill = GridBagConstraints.NONE;
32.
33.       add(sizeButton, gbc, 1, 0, 1, 1);
34.       add(valueButton, gbc, 1, 1, 1, 1);
35.
36.       sizeButton.addActionListener(new
37.          ActionListener()
38.          {
39.             public void actionPerformed(ActionEvent event)
40.             {
41.                changeSize();
42.             }
43.          });
44.
45.       valueButton.addActionListener(new
46.          ActionListener()
47.          {
48.             public void actionPerformed(ActionEvent event)
49.             {
50.                changeValue();
51.             }
52.          });
```

```
53.
54.        gbc.weighty = 100;
55.        gbc.fill = GridBagConstraints.BOTH;
56.
57.        add(new JScrollPane(elementList), gbc, 0, 2, 2, 1);
58.
59.        elementList.setSelectionMode(
60.           ListSelectionModel.SINGLE_SELECTION);
61.
62.        elementList.addListSelectionListener(new
63.           ListSelectionListener()
64.           {
65.              public void valueChanged(ListSelectionEvent event)
66.              {
67.                 int i = elementList.getSelectedIndex();
68.                 if (i < 0) return;
69.                 valueField.setText("" + array[i]);
70.              }
71.           });
72.
73.        elementList.setModel(model);
74.        elementList.setSelectedIndex(0);
75.     }
76.
77.     /**
78.        A convenience method to add a component to given grid bag
79.        layout locations.
80.        @param c the component to add
81.        @param gbc the grid bag constraints to use
82.        @param x the x grid position
83.        @param y the y grid position
84.        @param w the grid width
85.        @param h the grid height
86.     */
87.     public void add(Component c, GridBagConstraints gbc,
88.        int x, int y, int w, int h)
89.     {
90.        gbc.gridx = x;
91.        gbc.gridy = y;
92.        gbc.gridwidth = w;
93.        gbc.gridheight = h;
94.        add(c, gbc);
95.     }
96.
97.     /**
98.        This method is called when the user wants to change
99.        the size of the array.
100.    */
101.    public void changeSize()
102.    {
103.       fmt.setParseIntegerOnly(true);
104.       int s = 0;
105.       try
```

```
106.          {
107.             s = fmt.parse(sizeField.getText()).intValue();
108.             if (s < 0)
109.                throw new ParseException("Out of bounds", 0);
110.          }
111.          catch(ParseException e)
112.          {
113.             JOptionPane.showMessageDialog(this, "" + e,
114.                "Input Error", JOptionPane.WARNING_MESSAGE);
115.             sizeField.requestFocus();
116.             return;
117.          }
118.          if (s == array.length) return;
119.          setArray((double[])arrayGrow(array, s));
120.          editor.setValue(array);
121.          editor.firePropertyChange();
122.       }
123.
124.       /**
125.          This method is called when the user wants to change
126.          the currently selected array value.
127.       */
128.       public void changeValue()
129.       {
130.          double v = 0;
131.          fmt.setParseIntegerOnly(false);
132.          try
133.          {
134.             v = fmt.parse(valueField.getText()).doubleValue();
135.          }
136.          catch(ParseException e)
137.          {
138.             JOptionPane.showMessageDialog(this, "" + e,
139.                "Input Error", JOptionPane.WARNING_MESSAGE);
140.             valueField.requestFocus();
141.             return;
142.          }
143.          int currentIndex = elementList.getSelectedIndex();
144.          setArray(currentIndex, v);
145.          editor.firePropertyChange();
146.       }
147.
148.       /**
149.          Sets the indexed array property.
150.          @param v the array to edit
151.       */
152.       public void setArray(double[] v)
153.       {
154.          if (v == null) array = new double[0];
155.          else array = v;
156.          model.setArray(array);
157.          sizeField.setText("" + array.length);
158.          if (array.length > 0)
```

```
159.          {
160.             valueField.setText("" + array[0]);
161.             elementList.setSelectedIndex(0);
162.          }
163.          else
164.             valueField.setText("");
165.       }
166.
167.       /**
168.          Gets the indexed array property.
169.          @return the array being edited
170.       */
171.       public double[] getArray()
172.       {
173.          return (double[])array.clone();
174.       }
175.
176.       /**
177.          Sets the indexed array property.
178.          @param i the index whose value to set
179.          @param value the new value for the given index
180.       */
181.       public void setArray(int i, double value)
182.       {
183.          if (0 <= i && i < array.length)
184.          {
185.             model.setValue(i, value);
186.             elementList.setSelectedIndex(i);
187.             valueField.setText("" + value);
188.          }
189.       }
190.
191.       /**
192.          Gets the indexed array property.
193.          @param i the index whose value to get
194.          @return the value at the given index
195.       */
196.       public double getArray(int i)
197.       {
198.          if (0 <= i && i < array.length) return array[i];
199.          return 0;
200.       }
201.
202.       /**
203.          Resizes an array
204.          @param a the array to grow
205.          @param newLength the new length
206.          @return an array with the given length and the same
207.          elements as a in the common positions
208.       */
209.       private static Object arrayGrow(Object a, int newLength)
210.       {
211.          Class cl = a.getClass();
```

```
212.        if (!cl.isArray()) return null;
213.        Class componentType = a.getClass().getComponentType();
214.        int length = Array.getLength(a);
215.
216.        Object newArray = Array.newInstance(componentType,
217.           newLength);
218.        System.arraycopy(a, 0, newArray, 0,
219.           Math.min(length, newLength));
220.        return newArray;
221.     }
222.
223.     private PropertyEditorSupport editor;
224.     private double[] array;
225.     private NumberFormat fmt = NumberFormat.getNumberInstance();
226.     private JTextField sizeField = new JTextField(4);
227.     private JTextField valueField = new JTextField(12);
228.     private JButton sizeButton = new JButton("Resize");
229.     private JButton valueButton = new JButton("Change");
230.     private JList elementList = new JList();
231.     private DoubleArrayListModel model = new DoubleArrayListModel();
232. }
233.
234. /**
235.    The list model for the element list in the editor.
236. */
237. class DoubleArrayListModel extends AbstractListModel
238. {
239.    public int getSize()
240.    {
241.       return array.length;
242.    }
243.
244.    public Object getElementAt(int i)
245.    {
246.       return "[" + i + "] " + array[i];
247.    }
248.
249.    /**
250.       Sets a new array to be displayed in the list.
251.       @param a the new array
252.    */
253.    public void setArray(double[] a)
254.    {
255.       int oldLength = array == null ? 0 : array.length;
256.       array = a;
257.       int newLength = array == null ? 0 : array.length;
258.       if (oldLength > 0) fireIntervalRemoved(this, 0, oldLength);
259.       if (newLength > 0) fireIntervalAdded(this, 0, newLength);
260.    }
261.
262.    /**
263.       Changes a value in the array to be displayed in the list.
264.       @param i the index whose value to change
265.       @param value the new value for the given index
```

```
266.     */
267.    public void setValue(int i, double value)
268.    {
269.        array[i] = value;
270.        fireContentsChanged(this, i, i);
271.    }
272.
273.    private double[] array;
274. }
```

Summing Up

For every property editor you write, you have to choose one of three ways to display and edit the property value:

- As a text string (define `getAsText` and `setAsText`)
- As a choice field (define `getAsText`, `setAsText`, and `getTags`)
- Graphically, by painting it (define `isPaintable`, `paintValue`, `supportsCustomEditor`, and `getCustomEditor`)

You saw examples of all three cases in the chart bean.

Finally, some property editors might want to support a method called `getJava-InitializationString`. With this method, you can give the builder tool the Java programming language code that sets a property to allow automatic code generation. We did not show you an example for this method.

`java.beans.PropertyEditorSupport`

- `boolean isPaintable()`
  Override this method to return `true` if the class uses the `paintValue` method to display the property.

- `void paintValue(Graphics g, Rectangle box)`
  Override this method to represent the value by drawing into a graphics context in the specified place on the component used for the property inspector.

  Parameters: g   the graphics object to draw onto

  box   a rectangle object that represents where on the property inspector component to draw the value

- `boolean supportsCustomEditor()`
  Override this method to return `true` if the property editor has a custom editor.

- `Component getCustomEditor()`
  Override this method to return the component that contains a customized GUI for editing the property value.

- `String getJavaInitializationString()`
  Override this method to return a Java programming language code string that can be used to generate code that initializes the property value. Examples are "0", "new Color(64, 64, 64)".

Going Beyond Naming Patterns

You have already seen that if you use the standard naming conventions for the members of your bean, then a builder tool can use reflection to determine the properties, events, and methods of your bean. This process makes it simple to get started with bean programming but is rather limiting in the end. As your beans become in any way complex, there *will* be features of your bean that naming patterns and reflection will simply not reveal. (Not to mention that using English naming patterns as the basis for all GUI builders in all languages for all times seems to be rather against the spirit of providing support for your international customers.) Moreover, as we already mentioned, there may well be get/set pairs that you do *not* want to expose as bean properties.

Luckily, the JavaBeans specification allows a far more flexible and powerful mechanism for storing information about your bean for use by a builder. As with many features of beans, the mechanism is simple in theory but can be tedious to carry out in practice. The idea is that you again use an object that implements the BeanInfo interface. (Recall that we used one feature of the BeanInfo class when we supplied property editors for the chart bean class.)

When you implement this interface to describe your bean, a builder tool will look to the methods from the BeanInfo interface to tell it (potentially quite detailed) information about the properties, events, and methods your bean supports. The BeanInfo is supposed to free you from the tyranny of naming patterns. Somewhat ironically, the JavaBeans specification does require that you use a naming pattern to associate a BeanInfo object to the bean. You specify the name of the bean info class by adding BeanInfo to the name of the bean. For example, the bean info class associated to the class ChartBean *must* be named ChartBeanBeanInfo. The bean info class must be part of the same package as the bean itself.

NOTE: Any descriptions you supply in the bean info associated to your bean override any information that the builder might obtain by reflecting on the member names. Moreover, if you supply information about a feature set (such as the properties that your bean supports), you must then provide information about all the properties in the associated bean info.

As you already saw, you won't normally write from scratch a class that implements the BeanInfo interface. Instead, you will probably turn again to the SimpleBeanInfo convenience class that has empty implementations (returning null) for all the methods in the BeanInfo interface. This practice is certainly convenient—just override the methods you really want to change. Moreover, this convenience class includes a useful method called loadImage that you can use to load an image (such as an icon—see below) for your bean. We use the `SimpleBeanInfo` class for all our examples of `BeanInfo` classes. For example, our `ChartBeanBeanInfo` class starts out:

```
public class ChartBeanBeanInfo extends SimpleBeanInfo
```

NOTE: That the methods in the `SimpleBeanInfo` class return `null` is actually quite important. This is exactly how the builder tool knows how to use naming patterns to find out the members of that feature set. A non-`null` return value turns off the reflective search.

For a taste of what you can do with the bean info mechanism, let's start with an easy-to-use, but most useful, method in the `BeanInfo` interface: the `getIcon` method that lets you give your bean a custom icon. This is useful since builder tools will usually want to have an icon for the bean for some sort of palette. Builder environments show the icons next to the bean name in the bean toolbox. Actually, you can specify separate icon bitmaps. The `BeanInfo` interface has four constants that cover the standard sizes.

```
ICON_COLOR_16x16
ICON_COLOR_32x32
ICON_MONO_16x16
ICON_MONO_32x32
```

Here is an example of how you might use the `loadImage` convenience method in the `SimpleBeanInfo` class to add an icon to a class:

```java
public Image getIcon(int iconType)
{
    String name = "";
    if (iconType == BeanInfo.ICON_COLOR_16x16)
        name = "COLOR_16x16";
    else if (iconType == BeanInfo.ICON_COLOR_32x32)
        name = "COLOR_32x32";
    else if (iconType == BeanInfo.ICON_MONO_16x16)
        name = "MONO_16x16";
    else if (iconType == BeanInfo.ICON_MONO_32x32)
        name = "MONO_32x32";
    else return null;
    return loadImage("ChartBean_" + name + ".gif");
}
```

where we have cleverly named the image files to be

```
ChartBean_COLOR_16x16.gif
ChartBean_COLOR_32x32.gif
```

and so on.

FeatureDescriptor *Objects*

The key to using any of the more advanced features of the `BeanInfo` class is the `FeatureDescriptor` class and its various subclasses. As its name suggests, a `FeatureDescriptor` object provides information about a feature. Examples of features are properties, events, methods, and so on. More precisely, the `FeatureDescriptor` class is the superclass for all descriptors, and it factors out the common operations that you need to deal with when trying to describe any feature. For example, the name of the feature is obtained through the `getName` method. Since this method is in the superclass, it works for all feature descriptors, no matter what they describe. Here are the subclasses of the `FeatureDescriptor` class:

- `BeanDescriptor`
- `EventSetDescriptor`
- `MethodDescriptor`
- `ParameterDescriptor`
- `PropertyDescriptor` (with a further subclass— `IndexedPropertyDescriptor`)

These classes all work basically the same. You create a descriptor object for each member you are trying to describe, and you collect all descriptors of a feature set in an array and return it as the return value of one of the `BeanInfo` methods.

For example, to turn off reflection for event sets, you'll return an array of `EventSetDescriptor` objects in your bean info class.

```
class MyBeanBeanInfo extends SimpleBeanInfo
{   public EventSetDescriptor[] getEventSetDescriptors()

    {   . . .

    }

    . . .
}
```

Next, you'll construct all the various `EventSetDescriptor` objects that will go into this array. Generally, all the constructors for the various kinds of `FeatureDescriptor` objects work in the same way. In particular, for events, the most common constructor takes:

- The class of the bean that has the event;
- The base name of the event;
- The class of the `EventListener` interface that corresponds to the event;
- The methods in the specified `EventListener` interface that are triggered by the event.

Other constructors let you specify the methods of the bean that should be used to add and remove `EventListener` objects.

A good example of all this can be found in the `BeanInfo` class associated with the `ExplicitButtonBean` that ships with the BDK. Let's analyze the code that creates the needed event descriptors for this bean. The `ExplicitButtonBean` fires two events: when the button is pushed and when the state of the button has changed. Here's how you build these two `EventSetDescriptor` objects associated to these two events:

```
EventSetDescriptor push = new EventSetDescriptor(beanClass,
    "actionPerformed",
    java.awt.event.ActionListener.class,
    "actionPerformed");

EventSetDescriptor changed = new EventSetDescriptor(beanClass,
    "propertyChange",
    java.beans.PropertyChangeListener.class,
    "propertyChange");
```

The next step is to set the various display names for the events for the `EventSetDescriptor`. In the code for the `ExplicitButton` in the `BeanInfo` class, this is done by

```
push.setDisplayName("button push");
changed.setDisplayName("bound property change");
```

Actually, it is a little messier to code the creation of the needed `EventSetDescriptor` objects than the above fragments indicate because all constructors for feature descriptor objects can throw an `IntrospectionException`. So, you actually have to build the array of descriptors in a try/catch block, as the following code indicates.

```
public EventSetDescriptor[] getEventSetDescriptors()
{
    try
    {
        EventSetDescriptor push = new
            EventSetDescriptor(beanClass,
                "actionPerformed",
                java.awt.event.ActionListener.class,
                "actionPerformed");

        EventSetDescriptor changed = new
            EventSetDescriptor(beanClass,
                "propertyChange",
                java.beans.PropertyChangeListener.class,
                "propertyChange");

        push.setDisplayName("button push");
        changed.setDisplayName("bound property change");
```

```
        return new EventSetDescriptor[] { push, changed };
    }
    catch (IntrospectionException e)
    {
        throw new RuntimeException(e.toString());
    }
}
```

This particular event set descriptor is needed because the event descriptors differ from the standard naming pattern. Specifically, there are two differences:

- The listener classes are not the name of the bean + `Listener`.
- The display names are not the same as the event names.

To summarize: When any feature of your bean differs from the standard naming pattern, you must do the following:

- Create feature descriptors for *all* features in that set (events, properties, methods).
- Return an array of the descriptors in the appropriate `BeanInfo` method.

java.beans.BeanInfo

- `EventSetDescriptor[] getEventSetDescriptors()`
- `MethodDescriptor[] getMethodDescriptors()`
- `PropertyDescriptor[] getPropertyDescriptors()`

    return an array of the specified descriptor objects. A return of `null` signals the builder to use the naming conventions and reflection to find the member. The `getPropertyDescriptors` method returns a mixture of plain and indexed property descriptors. Use `instanceof` to check if a specific `PropertyDescriptor` is an `IndexedPropertyDescriptor`.

- `Image getIcon(int iconType)`

    returns an image object that can be used to represent the bean in toolboxes, tool bars, and the like. There are four constants, as described earlier, for the standard types of icons.

    Parameters: `iconType`   the type of icon to use (16 x 16 color, 32 x 32 color, etc.)

- `int getDefaultEventIndex()`
- `int getDefaultPropertyIndex()`

    A bean can have a default event or property. Both of these methods return the array index that specifies which element of the descriptor array to use as that default member, or -1 if no default exists. A bean builder environment can visually enhance the default feature, for example, by placing it first in a list of features or by displaying its name in boldface.

- `BeanInfo[] getAdditionalBeanInfo()`

    returns an array of `BeanInfo` objects or `null`. Use this method when you want some information about your bean to come from `BeanInfo` classes for other beans. For example, you might use this method if your bean aggregated lots of other beans. The current `BeanInfo` class rules in case of conflict.

java.beans.SimpleBeanInfo

- `Image loadImage(String resourceName)`
  returns an image object file associated to the resource. Currently only GIFs are supported.

  Parameters: `resourceName` a path name (taken relative to the directory containing the current class)

java.beans.FeatureDescriptor

- `String getName()`
  returns the name used in the bean's code for the member.

- `void setName(String name)`
  sets the programmatic name for the feature.

  Parameters: `name` the name of the feature

- `String getDisplayName()`
  returns a localized display name for the feature. The default value is the value returned by `getName`. However, currently there is no explicit support for supplying feature names in multiple locales.

- `void setDisplayName(String displayName)`
  sets the localized display name for the feature.

  Parameters: `displayName` the name to use

- `String getShortDescription()`
  returns a localized string that a builder tool can use to provide a short description for this feature. The default value is the return value of `getDisplayName`.

- `void setShortDescription(String text)`
  sets the descriptive string (short—usually less than 40 characters) that describes the feature.

  Parameters: `text` the localized short description to associate with this feature

- `void setValue(String attributeName, Object value)`
  associates a named attribute to this feature.

  Parameters: `attributeName` the name of the attribute whose value you are setting

- `Object getValue(String attributeName)`
  gets the value of the feature with the given name.

  Parameters: `attributeName`   the name for the attribute to be retrieved

- `Enumeration attributeNames()`
  returns an enumeration object that contains names of any attributes registered with `setValue`.

- `void setExpert(boolean b)`
  lets you supply an expert flag that a builder can use to determine whether to hide the feature from a naive user. (Not every builder is likely to support this feature.)

  Parameters: `b`   `true` if you intend that this feature be used only by experts

- `boolean isExpert()`
  returns `true` if this feature is marked for use by experts.

- `void setHidden(boolean b)`
  marks a feature for use only by the builder tool.

  Parameters: `b`   `true` if you want to hide this feature

- `boolean isHidden()`
  returns `true` if the user of the builder shouldn't see this feature but the builder tool needs to be aware of it.

`java.beans.EventSetDescriptor`

- `EventSetDescriptor(Class sourceClass, String eventSetName, Class listener, String listenerMethod)`
  constructs an `EventSetDescriptor`. This constructor assumes that you follow the standard pattern for the names of the event class and the names of the methods to add and remove event listeners. Throws an `Introspection-Exception` if an error occurred during introspection.

  Parameters: `sourceClass`   the class firing the event

  `eventSetName`   the name of the event

  `listener`   the listener interface to which these events get delivered

  `listenerMethod`   the method triggered when the event gets delivered to a listener

- `EventSetDescriptor(Class sourceClass, String eventSetName, Class listener, String[] listenerMethods, String addListener-Method, String removeListenerMethod)` constructs an `EventSetDescriptor` with multiple listener methods and custom methods for adding and removing listeners . Throws an `IntrospectionException` if an error occurred during introspection.

Parameters:		
	`sourceClass`	the class firing the event
	`eventSetName`	the name of the event
	`listener`	the listener interface to which these events get delivered
	`listenerMethods`	the methods of the listener interface triggered when the event gets delivered to a listener
	`addListener-Method`	the method to add a listener to the bean
	`removeListener-Method`	the method to remove a listener from the bean

- `Method getAddListenerMethod()`
  returns the method used to register the listener.

- `Method getRemoveListenerMethod()`
  returns the method used to remove a registered listener for the event.

- `Method[] getListenerMethods()`
- `MethodDescriptor[] getListenerMethodDescriptors()`
  return an array of `Method` or `MethodDescriptor` objects for the methods triggered in the listener interface.

- `Class getListenerType()`
  returns a `Class` object for the target listener interface associated with the event.

- `void setUnicast(boolean b)`
  is set to `true` if this event can be propagated to only one listener.

- `boolean isUnicast()`
  is set to `true` if the event set is unicast (default is `false`).

`java.beans.PropertyDescriptor`

- `PropertyDescriptor(String propertyName, Class beanClass)`
- `PropertyDescriptor(String propertyName, Class beanClass, String getMethod, String setMethod)`
  construct a `PropertyDescriptor` object. The methods throw an `IntrospectionException` if an error occurred during introspection. The first constructor assumes that you follow the standard convention for the names of the `get` and `set` methods.

Parameters:	propertyName	the name of the property
	beanClass	the Class object for the bean being described
	getMethod	the name of the get method
	setMethod	the name of the set method

- `Class getPropertyType()`
  returns a Class object for the property type.
- `Method getReadMethod()`
  returns the get method.
- `Method getWriteMethod()`
  returns the set method.
- `void setBound(boolean b)`
  is set to true if this property fires a PropertyChangeEvent when its value is changed.
- `boolean isBound()`
  returns true if this is a bound property.
- `void setConstrained(boolean b)`
  is set to true if this property fires a VetoableChangeEvent before its value is changed.
- `boolean isConstrained()`
  returns true if this is a constrained property.

 java.beans.IndexedPropertyDescriptor

- `IndexedPropertyDescriptor(String propertyName, Class beanClass)`
- `IndexedPropertyDescriptor(String propertyName, Class bean-Class, String getMethod, String setMethod, String indexedGet-Method, String indexedSetMethod)`
  construct an IndexedPropertyDescriptor for the index property. The methods throw an IntrospectionException if an error occurred during introspection. The first constructor assumes that you follow the standard convention for the names of the get and set methods.

Parameters:	propertyName	the name of the property
	beanClass	the Class object for the bean being described
	getMethod	the name of the get method
	setMethod	the name of the set method

indexedGetMethod	the name of the indexed `get` method
indexedSetMethod	the name of the indexed `set` method

- `Class getIndexedPropertyType()`
  returns the Java platform class that describes the type of the indexed values of the property, that is, the return type of the indexed `get` method.
- `Method getIndexedReadMethod()`
  returns the indexed `get` method.
- `Method getIndexedWriteMethod()`
  returns the indexed `set` method.

java.beans.MethodDescriptor

- `MethodDescriptor(Method method)`
- `MethodDescriptor(Method method, ParameterDescriptor[] parameterDescriptors)`
  construct a method descriptor for the given method with the associated parameters; throw an `IntrospectionException` if an error occurred during introspection.

Parameters:	method	method object
	parameterDescriptors	an array of parameter descriptors that describe the parameters for the method

- `Method getMethod()`
  returns the method object for that method.
- `ParameterDescriptor[] getParameterDescriptors()`
  returns an array of parameter descriptor objects for the methods parameters.

java.beans.ParameterDescriptor

- `ParameterDescriptor()`
  creates a new parameter descriptor object. Parameter descriptors carry no information beyond that stored in the `FeatureDescriptor` superclass.

Customizers

A property editor, no matter how sophisticated, is responsible for allowing the user to set one property at a time. Especially if certain properties of a bean relate to each other, it may be more user friendly to give users a way to edit multiple properties at the same time. To enable this feature, you supply a *customizer* instead of (or in addition to) multiple property editors.

In the example program for this section, we develop a customizer for the chart bean. The customizer lets you set several properties of the chart bean at once, and it lets you specify a file from which to read the data points for the chart. Figure 8–22 shows you one pane of the customizer for the ChartBean.

Figure 8–22: The customizer for the ChartBean

To add a customizer to your bean, you must supply a BeanInfo class and override the getBeanDescriptor method, as shown in the following example.

```
public BeanDescriptor getBeanDescriptor()
{
    return new BeanDescriptor(ChartBean.class,
        ChartBeanCustomizer.class);
}
```

The general procedure for your customizers follows the same model.

1. Override the getBeanDescriptor method by returning a new BeanDescriptor object for your bean.
2. Specify the customizer class as the second parameter of the constructor for the BeanDescriptor object.

Note that you need not follow any naming pattern for the customizer class. The builder can locate it by

1. Finding the associated BeanInfo class;
2. Invoking its getBeanDescriptor method;
3. Calling the getCustomizerClass method.

(Nevertheless, it is customary to name the customizer as *BeanName*Customizer.)

Example 8–15 has the code for the ChartBeanBeanInfo class that references the ChartBeanCustomizer. You will see in the next section how that customizer is implemented.

Example 8–15: ChartBeanBeanInfo.java

```
1. import java.awt.*;
2. import java.beans.*;
3.
4. /**
5.    The bean info for the chart bean, specifying the
6.    icons and the customizer.
```

```
 7. */
 8. public class ChartBeanBeanInfo extends SimpleBeanInfo
 9. {
10.     public BeanDescriptor getBeanDescriptor()
11.     {
12.         return new BeanDescriptor(ChartBean.class,
13.             ChartBeanCustomizer.class);
14.     }
15.
16.     public Image getIcon(int iconType)
17.     {
18.         String name = "";
19.         if (iconType == BeanInfo.ICON_COLOR_16x16)
20.             name = "COLOR_16x16";
21.         else if (iconType == BeanInfo.ICON_COLOR_32x32)
22.             name = "COLOR_32x32";
23.         else if (iconType == BeanInfo.ICON_MONO_16x16)
24.             name = "MONO_16x16";
25.         else if (iconType == BeanInfo.ICON_MONO_32x32)
26.             name = "MONO_32x32";
27.         else return null;
28.         return loadImage("ChartBean_" + name + ".gif");
29.     }
30. }
```

`java.beans.BeanInfo`

- BeanDescriptor getBeanDescriptor()

  returns a `BeanDescriptor` object that describes features of the bean.

`java.beans.BeanDescriptor`

- BeanDescriptor(Class beanClass, Class customizerClass)

  constructs a `BeanDescriptor` object for a bean that has a customizer.

  Parameters: beanClass   the `Class` object for the bean

  customizerClass the `Class` object for the bean's
  customizer

- Class getBeanClass()

  returns the `Class` object that defines the bean.

- Class getCustomizerClass()

  returns the `Class` object that defines the bean's customizer.

Writing a Customizer Class

Any customizer class you write must implement the `Customizer` interface.
There are only three methods in this interface:

- The `setObject` method, which takes a parameter that specifies the bean
  being customized;

- The `addPropertyChangeListener` and `removePropertyChange-Listener` methods, which manage the collection of listeners that are notified when a property is changed in the customizer.

It is a good idea to update the visual appearance of the target bean by broadcasting a `PropertyChangeEvent` whenever the user changes any of the property values, not just when the user is at the end of the customization process.

Unlike property editors, customizers are not automatically displayed. In the BeanBox, you must select Edit -> Customize to pop up the customizer of a bean. At that point, the BeanBox will call the `setObject` method of the customizer that takes the bean being customized as a parameter. Notice that your customizer is thus created before it is actually linked to an instance of your bean. Therefore, you cannot assume any information about the state of a bean in the customizer, and you must provide a default constructor, that is, one without arguments.

There are three parts to writing a customizer class:

1. Building the visual interface;
2. Initializing the customizer in the `setObject` method;
3. Updating the bean by firing property change events when the user changes properties in the interface.

By definition, a customizer class is visual. It must, therefore, extend `Component` or a subclass of `Component`, such as `JPanel`. Since customizers typically present the user with many options, it is often handy to use the tabbed pane interface. We use this approach and have the customizer extend the `JTabbedPane` interface.

CAUTION: We had quite a bit of grief with placing a `JTabbedPane` inside the customizer dialog of the BeanBox. The BeanBox uses the old AWT components. Somehow the events became entangled between the AWT and Swing components and clicking on the tabs did not flip the panes. By trial and error, we found that trapping the tab clicks and calling `validate` fixed this problem. Presumably, in the long run, this issue will go away when all bean environments use Swing.

The customizer gathers the information in three panes:

- Graph color and inverse mode
- Title and title position
- Data points

Of course, developing this kind of user interface can be tedious to code—our example devotes over 100 lines just to set it up in the constructor. However, this task requires only the usual Swing programming skills, and we won't dwell on the details here.

There is one trick that is worth keeping in mind. You often need to edit property values in a customizer. Rather than implementing a new interface for setting the property value of a particular class, you can simply locate an existing property editor and add it to your user interface! For example, in our `ChartBean` customizer, we need to set the graph color. Since we know that the BeanBox has a perfectly good property editor for colors, we locate it as follows:

```
PropertyEditor colorEditor
    = PropertEditorManager.findEditor(Color.Class);
```

We then call `getCustomEditor` to get the component that contains the user interface for setting the colors.

```
Component colorEditorComponent = colorEditor.getCustomEditor();
// now add this component to the UI
```

Once we have all components laid out, we initialize their values in the `setObject` method. The `setObject` method is called when the customizer is displayed. Its parameter is the bean that is being customized. To proceed, we store that bean reference—we'll need it later to notify the bean of property changes. Then, we initialize each user interface component. Here is a part of the `setObject` method of the chart bean customizer that does this initialization.

```
public void setObject(Object obj)
{
    bean = (ChartBean)obj;
    titleField.setText(bean.getTitle());
    colorEditor.setValue(bean.getGraphColor());
    . . .
}
```

Finally, we hook up event handlers to track the user's activities. Whenever the user changes the value of a component, the component fires an event that our customizer must handle. The event handler must update the value of the property in the bean and must also fire a `PropertyChangeEvent` so that other listeners (such as the property inspector) can be updated. Let us follow that process with a couple of user interface elements in the chart bean customizer.

When the user types a new title, we want to update the title property. We attach a `DocumentListener` to the text field into which the user types the title.

```
titleField.getDocument().addDocumentListener(new
    DocumentListener()
    {
        public void changedUpdate(DocumentEvent event)
        {
            setTitle(titleField.getText());
        }
        public void insertUpdate(DocumentEvent event)
```

```
      {
         setTitle(titleField.getText());
      }
      public void removeUpdate(DocumentEvent event)
      {
         setTitle(titleField.getText());
      }
   });
```

The three listener methods call the `setTitle` method of the customizer. That method calls the bean to update the property value and then fires a property change event. (This update is necessary only for properties that are not bound.) Here is the code for the `setTitle` method.

```
public void setTitle(String newValue)
{
   if (bean == null) return;
   String oldValue = bean.getTitle();
   bean.setTitle(newValue);
   firePropertyChange("title", oldValue, newValue);
}
```

When the color value changes in the color property editor, we want to update the graph color of the bean. We track the color changes by attaching a listener to the property editor. Perhaps confusingly, that editor also sends out property change events.

```
colorEditor.addPropertyChangeListener(new
   PropertyChangeListener()
   {
      public void propertyChange(PropertyChangeEvent
         event)
      {
         setGraphColor((Color)colorEditor.getValue());
      }
   });
```

Whenever the color value of the color property editor changes, we call the `setGraphColor` method of the customizer. That method updates the `graphColor` property of the bean and fires a different property change event that is associated with the `graphColor` property.

```
public void setGraphColor(Color newValue)
{
   if (bean == null) return;
   Color oldValue = bean.getGraphColor();
   bean.setGraphColor(newValue);
   firePropertyChange("graphColor", oldValue, newValue);
}
```

Example 8–16 provides the full code of the chart bean customizer.

This particular customizer just sets properties of the bean. In general, customizers can call any methods of the bean, whether or not they are property setters. That is, customizers are more general than property editors. (Some beans may have features that are not exposed as properties and that can be edited only through the customizer.)

Example 8–16: ChartBeanCustomizer.java

```
1. import java.awt.*;
2. import java.awt.event.*;
3. import java.beans.*;
4. import java.io.*;
5. import java.text.*;
6. import java.util.*;
7. import javax.swing.*;
8. import javax.swing.event.*;
9.
10. /**
11.    A customizer for the chart bean that allows the user to
12.    edit all chart properties in a single tabbed dialog.
13. */
14. public class ChartBeanCustomizer extends JTabbedPane
15.    implements Customizer
16. {
17.    public ChartBeanCustomizer()
18.    {
19.       data = new JTextArea();
20.       JPanel dataPane = new JPanel();
21.       dataPane.setLayout(new BorderLayout());
22.       dataPane.add(new JScrollPane(data), BorderLayout.CENTER);
23.       JButton dataButton = new JButton("Set data");
24.       dataButton.addActionListener(new
25.          ActionListener()
26.          {
27.             public void actionPerformed(ActionEvent event)
28.             {
29.                setData(data.getText());
30.             }
31.          });
32.       JPanel p = new JPanel();
33.       p.add(dataButton);
34.       dataPane.add(p, BorderLayout.SOUTH);
35.
36.       JPanel colorPane = new JPanel();
37.       colorPane.setLayout(new BorderLayout());
38.
39.       normal = new JCheckBox("Normal", true);
40.       inverse = new JCheckBox("Inverse", false);
41.       p = new JPanel();
```

```
42.        p.add(normal);
43.        p.add(inverse);
44.        ButtonGroup g = new ButtonGroup();
45.        g.add(normal);
46.        g.add(inverse);
47.        normal.addActionListener(new
48.           ActionListener()
49.           {
50.              public void actionPerformed(ActionEvent event)
51.              {
52.                 setInverse(false);
53.              }
54.           });
55.
56.        inverse.addActionListener(
57.           new ActionListener()
58.           {
59.              public void actionPerformed(ActionEvent event)
60.              {
61.                 setInverse(true);
62.              }
63.           });
64.
65.        colorEditor
66.           = PropertyEditorManager.findEditor(Color.class);
67.        colorEditor.addPropertyChangeListener(
68.           new PropertyChangeListener()
69.           {
70.              public void propertyChange(PropertyChangeEvent
71.                 evt)
72.              {
73.                 setGraphColor((Color)colorEditor.getValue());
74.              }
75.           });
76.
77.        colorPane.add(p, BorderLayout.NORTH);
78.        colorPane.add(colorEditor.getCustomEditor(),
79.           BorderLayout.CENTER);
80.
81.        JPanel titlePane = new JPanel();
82.        titlePane.setLayout(new BorderLayout());
83.
84.        g = new ButtonGroup();
85.        position = new JCheckBox[3];
86.        position[0] = new JCheckBox("Left", false);
87.        position[1] = new JCheckBox("Center", true);
88.        position[2] = new JCheckBox("Right", false);
89.
90.        p = new JPanel();
```

```
91.      for (int i = 0; i < position.length; i++)
92.      {
93.         final int value = i;
94.         p.add(position[i]);
95.         g.add(position[i]);
96.         position[i].addActionListener(new
97.            ActionListener()
98.            {
99.               public void actionPerformed(ActionEvent event)
100.              {
101.                 setTitlePosition(value);
102.              }
103.           });
104.     }
105.
106.     titleField = new JTextField();
107.     titleField.getDocument().addDocumentListener(
108.        new DocumentListener()
109.        {
110.           public void changedUpdate(DocumentEvent evt)
111.           {
112.              setTitle(titleField.getText());
113.           }
114.           public void insertUpdate(DocumentEvent evt)
115.           {
116.              setTitle(titleField.getText());
117.           }
118.           public void removeUpdate(DocumentEvent evt)
119.           {
120.              setTitle(titleField.getText());
121.           }
122.        });
123.
124.     titlePane.add(titleField, BorderLayout.NORTH);
125.     titlePane.add(p, BorderLayout.SOUTH);
126.     addTab("Color", colorPane);
127.     addTab("Title", titlePane);
128.     addTab("Data", dataPane);
129.
130.     // workaround for a JTabbedPane bug in JDK 1.2
131.     addChangeListener(new
132.        ChangeListener()
133.        {
134.           public void stateChanged(ChangeEvent event)
135.           {
136.              validate();
137.           }
138.        });
139.  }
```

```
140.
141.     /**
142.         Sets the data to be shown in the chart.
143.         @param s a string containing the numbers to be displayed,
144.         separated by white space
145.     */
146.     public void setData(String s)
147.     {
148.         StringTokenizer tokenizer = new StringTokenizer(s);
149.
150.         int i = 0;
151.         double[] values = new double[tokenizer.countTokens()];
152.         while (tokenizer.hasMoreTokens())
153.         {
154.             String token = tokenizer.nextToken();
155.             try
156.             {
157.                 values[i] = Double.parseDouble(token);
158.                 i++;
159.             }
160.             catch (NumberFormatException exception)
161.             {
162.             }
163.         }
164.         setValues(values);
165.     }
166.
167.     /**
168.         Sets the title of the chart.
169.         @param newValue the new title
170.     */
171.     public void setTitle(String newValue)
172.     {
173.         if (bean == null) return;
174.         String oldValue = bean.getTitle();
175.         bean.setTitle(newValue);
176.         firePropertyChange("title", oldValue, newValue);
177.     }
178.
179.     /**
180.         Sets the title position of the chart.
181.         @param i the new title position (ChartBean.LEFT,
182.         ChartBean.CENTER, or ChartBean.RIGHT)
183.     */
184.     public void setTitlePosition(int i)
185.     {
186.         if (bean == null) return;
187.         Integer oldValue = new Integer(bean.getTitlePosition());
188.         Integer newValue = new Integer(i);
```

```
189.         bean.setTitlePosition(i);
190.         firePropertyChange("titlePosition", oldValue, newValue);
191.     }
192.
193.     /**
194.        Sets the inverse setting of the chart.
195.        @param b true if graph and background color are inverted
196.     */
197.     public void setInverse(boolean b)
198.     {
199.         if (bean == null) return;
200.         Boolean oldValue = new Boolean(bean.isInverse());
201.         Boolean newValue = new Boolean(b);
202.         bean.setInverse(b);
203.         firePropertyChange("inverse", oldValue, newValue);
204.     }
205.
206.     /**
207.        Sets the values to be shown in the chart.
208.        @param newValue the new value array
209.     */
210.     public void setValues(double[] newValue)
211.     {
212.         if (bean == null) return;
213.         double[] oldValue = bean.getValues();
214.         bean.setValues(newValue);
215.         firePropertyChange("values", oldValue, newValue);
216.     }
217.
218.     /**
219.        Sets the color of the chart
220.        @param newValue the new color
221.     */
222.     public void setGraphColor(Color newValue)
223.     {
224.         if (bean == null) return;
225.         Color oldValue = bean.getGraphColor();
226.         bean.setGraphColor(newValue);
227.         firePropertyChange("graphColor", oldValue, newValue);
228.     }
229.
230.     public void setObject(Object obj)
231.     {
232.         bean = (ChartBean)obj;
233.
234.         data.setText("");
235.         double[] values = bean.getValues();
236.         for (int i = 0; i < values.length; i++)
237.             data.append(values[i] + "\n");
```

```
238.
239.        normal.setSelected(!bean.isInverse());
240.        inverse.setSelected(bean.isInverse());
241.
242.        titleField.setText(bean.getTitle());
243.
244.        for (int i = 0; i < position.length; i++)
245.            position[i].setSelected(i == bean.getTitlePosition());
246.
247.        colorEditor.setValue(bean.getGraphColor());
248.     }
249.
250.     public Dimension getPreferredSize()
251.     {
252.        return new Dimension(XPREFSIZE, YPREFSIZE);
253.     }
254.
255.     private static final int XPREFSIZE = 200;
256.     private static final int YPREFSIZE = 120;
257.     private ChartBean bean;
258.     private PropertyEditor colorEditor;
259.
260.     private JTextArea data;
261.     private JCheckBox normal;
262.     private JCheckBox inverse;
263.     private JCheckBox[] position;
264.     private JTextField titleField;
265. }
```

java.beans.Customizer

- void setObject(Object bean)
  specifies the bean to customize.

The Bean Context

In this section, we show how you can write beans that take advantage of their environment. This is useful to implement beans that interact with other beans or with services that the bean context provides. In particular, you will see how to implement a bean that can change the value of an arbitrary integer property of another bean, and how a bean can use a bean context service.

CAUTION: Somewhat unhappily, the most commonly available builder environments on the market today (including Forte) do *not* implement bean contexts. The examples in this section work in the BeanBox, but they probably won't work at all in your favorite builder tool.

Advanced Uses of Introspection

From the point of view of the JavaBeans specification, introspection is simply the process by which a builder tool finds out which properties, methods, and events a bean supports. Introspection is carried out in two ways:

*   By searching for classes and methods that follow certain naming patterns;
*   By querying the `BeanInfo` of a class.

Normally, introspection is an activity that is reserved for bean environments. The bean environment uses introspection to learn about beans, but the beans themselves don't need to carry out introspection. However, there are some cases when one bean needs to use introspection to analyze other beans. A good example is when you want to tightly couple two beans on a form in a builder tool. Consider, for example, a spin bean, a small control element with two buttons, to increase or decrease a value (see Figure 8–23).

Figure 8–23: The spin bean

A spin bean by itself is not useful. It needs to be coupled with another bean. For example, a spin bean can be coupled to an integer text bean. Each time the user clicks on one of the buttons of the spin bean, the integer value is incremented or decremented. We will call the coupled bean the *buddy* of the spin bean. The buddy does not have to be an `IntTextBean`. It can be any other bean with an integer property.

You use the customizer of the spin bean to attach the buddy (see Figure 8–24).

Figure 8–24: The customizer of the `SpinBean`

Here is how you can try it out.

1. Compile the `SpinBean` and `IntTextBean` and create the JAR files.
2. Start the BeanBox.
3. Load the `SpinBean.jar` and `IntTextBean.jar` file.
4. Add the `SpinBean` and an `IntTextBean` on the form.
5. Pop up the customizer of the spin bean by selecting it and selecting Edit -> Customize from the menu.
6. Select the `IntTextBean` in the Buddy list.
7. Watch how all the `int` properties in the Property list are automatically filled in (see Figure 8–24).
8. Select `value` and click on Set Buddy.
9. Click on Done.
10. Then, click on + and – and watch the integer text field value increase and decrease (see Figure 8–25).

Figure 8–25: The SpinBean coupled with an IntTextBean buddy

It looks easy, but there were two challenges to implementing this customization.

- How do you find all properties of a bean whose values are of type `int`?
- How do you program the getting and setting of a property if you know it only at run time?

We use introspection (that is, the reflection API) to solve both of these problems. To analyze the properties of a bean, first get the bean info by calling the static `getBeanInfo` method of the `Introspector` class.

```
BeanInfo info
    = Introspector.getBeanInfo(buddy.getClass());
```

Once we have the bean info, we can obtain an array of property descriptors:

```
PropertyDescriptor[] props = info.getPropertyDescriptors();
```

In the spin bean customizer, the next step is to loop through this array, picking out all properties of type `int` and adding their names to a list component.

```
for (int i = 0; i < props.length; i++)
{
    Class propertyType = props[i].getPropertyType();
    if (int.class.equals(propertyType))
    {
        String name = props[i].getName();
        propModel.addElement(name);
```

```
      }
   }
```

This code shows how you can find out about the properties of a bean.

Next, we need to be able to get and set the property that the user selected. We obtain the `get` and `set` methods by calls to `getReadMethod` and `getWriteMethod`:

```
Method getMethod = prop.getReadMethod();
Method setMethod = prop.getWriteMethod();
```

(Why is it called `getReadMethod`? Probably because `getGetMethod` sounds too silly.)

Now, we invoke the methods to get a value, increment it, and set it. This process again uses the reflection API—see, for example, Chapter 5 of Volume 1. Note that we must use an `Integer` wrapper around the `int` value.

```
int value = ((Integer)getMethod.invoke(buddy,
    null)).intValue();
value += increment;
setMethod.invoke(buddy,
    new Object[] { new Integer(value) });
```

Could we have avoided reflection if we had demanded that the buddy have methods `getValue` and `setValue`? No. You can only call

```
int value = buddy.getValue();
```

when the compiler knows that `buddy` is an object of a type that has a `getValue` method. But `buddy` can be of any type—there is no type hierarchy for beans. Whenever one bean is coupled with another arbitrary bean, then you need to use introspection.

Finding Sibling Beans

In the preceding section, you saw how the spin bean buttons were able to change the value of the buddy component. However, there is another unrelated issue—how can the spin bean customizer present all possible buddies to the user?

It is a bit more difficult to enumerate all beans on a form than you might think. In the BeanBox, for example, you can't simply call

```
Component[] siblings = getParent().getComponents()
```

to get all the siblings of a bean. The reason you can't do this is that the Bean-Box surrounds every bean by a panel within a panel. (We suspect that is done to detect mouse clicks that select the bean, and to draw the outline around a selected bean.) So, in the BeanBox, we'd have to write

```
Component[] siblings
    = getParent().getParent().getParent().getComponents()
```

However, there is no guarantee that this solution would work in another builder environment—since those environments might be smart enough not to need all these extra panels.

In the Java 2 platform, we can solve this problem. The JavaBeans architecture now supports the concept of a *bean context*. Bean contexts express the *logical* containment between beans and bean containers, which, as you just saw, can be quite different from the physical containment.

A bean context can hold beans, services, and other bean contexts, just like an AWT container can hold components and other containers (see Figure 8–26).

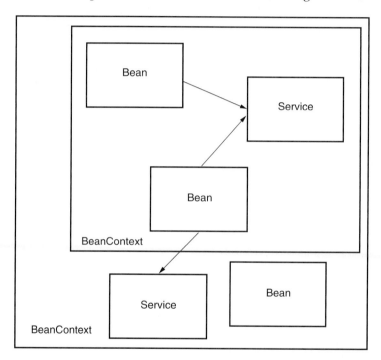

Figure 8–26: Bean Contexts

Currently, nested bean contexts aren't common. At best, you can expect that your beans live in a single bean context, the builder environment. For example, the BeanBox in BDK 1.1 is a bean context. The BeanBox provides a *message tracing service* that beans can use to display logging messages. Other bean contexts may provide different services. In the next section, we show you how your beans can use the message tracing service.

To communicate with its surrounding bean context, a bean can implement the BeanContextChild interface. That interface has six methods:

```
void setBeanContext(BeanContext bc)
BeanContext getBeanContext()
void addPropertyChangeListener(String name,
    PropertyChangeListener listener)
```

```
void removePropertyChangeListener(String name,
    PropertyChangeListener listener)
void addVetoableChangeListener(String name,
    VetoableChangeListener listener)
void removeVetoableChangeListener(String name,
    VetoableChangeListener listener)
```

A bean context calls the setBeanContext method when it begins managing your bean. You can hold on to the BeanContext parameter value and use it whenever you need to access the ambient bean context.

Since it is tedious to implement the change listeners, a convenience class BeanContextChildSupport implements these methods for you. However, there is a technical issue if you want to use this convenience class. Since your bean can't simultaneously extend a component class and the BeanContextChildSupport class, you use a proxy mechanism. Follow these steps:

1. Implement the BeanContextProxy interface.

2. Construct an instance variable of type BeanContextChildSupport.

    ```
    private BeanContextChildSupport childSupport
        = new BeanContextChildSupport();
    ```

3. Return that instance variable in the getBeanContextProxy method of the BeanContextProxy interface.

    ```
    public BeanContextChild getBeanContextProxy()
    {
        return childSupport;
    }
    ```

    The bean context calls this method to retrieve the proxy object. Then, it invokes the BeanContextChild methods on the returned object rather than on the bean itself.

4. Call the getBeanContext method of the childSupport object whenever you want to know the current bean context.

    ```
    BeanContext context = childSupport.getBeanContext();
    ```

Figure 8–27 shows the relationships between these classes.

Once you have the bean context, you can enumerate all beans that it contains. The BeanContext class implements the Collection interface. Therefore, you can simply enumerate the beans as follows:

```
Iterator iter = beanContext.iterator();
while (iter.hasNext())
{
    Object buddy = iter.next();
    do something with buddy
}
```

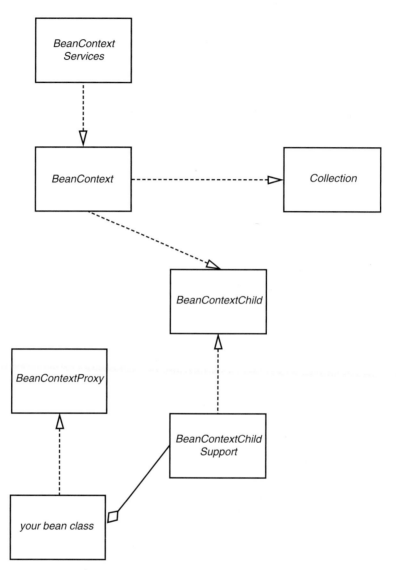

Figure 8–27: Relationships between the bean context classes

From a user interface perspective, our approach—to list the types of the potential buddies—is still not satisfactory. If there is more than one sibling of the same class in the form, then the user cannot tell them apart. It would be nice if we could physically move the spin bean next to its buddy or draw a box around the selected buddy, but the BeanContext does not expose position information. (It is useless to ask the buddy about its location. It only knows its location with respect to its enclosing panel.) Perhaps a future version of the JavaBeans specification will allow such manipulations.

Using Bean Context Services

In this section, we want to show you how your beans can access services that a bean context provides. You have to know the class that provides the service that you want. For example, the message tracer service that the BeanBox provides is implemented by the class `sunw.demo.methodtracer.MethodTracer`. First, you need to make sure that the bean context implements the `BeanContextSer-vices` interface—not all bean contexts do.

```
if (beanContext implements BeanContextServices)
{
    BeanContextServices services
      = (BeanContextServices)beanContext;
    . . .
}
```

Then, you ask the bean context if it supports the desired service.

```
tracerClass = Class.forName
    ("sunw.demo.methodtracer.MethodTracer");
if (services.hasService(tracerClass))
{
    . . .
}
```

If you run this bean in an environment other than the BeanBox, the `hasService` call may simply return `false`.

Finally, you need to get the object that carries out the service. You call the `getService` method with five parameters:

- The object that implements the `ChildBeanContext` interface; usually the proxy `BeanContextChildSupport` object;

- The requesting object;

- The class of the service that you want to obtain;

- An auxiliary object to select the right service, if the service requires it, or `null` otherwise;

- A `BeanContextServiceRevokedListener` object that is called when the service ceases to be available.

Here is a typical call.

```
BeanContextServiceRevokedListener revokedListener =
  new BeanContextServiceRevokedListener()
  {
      public void serviceRevoked
          (BeanContextServiceRevokedEvent event)
      {
          tracer = null;
```

```
        }
    };
    tracer = services.getService(childSupport, this, tracerClass,
        null, revokedListener);
```

Note that you typically do not have the service class available when you compile your program. For example, the class file for the `MethodTracer` class is not part of the standard runtime library, and the compiler will not find it even if you try to import the `sunw.demo.methodtracer` package.

For that reason, we use reflection to call service methods. The following statements call the `logText` method of the `MethodTracer` class to display a message in the method tracer window.

```
if (tracer != null)
{
    String text = "spin: value=" + value
        + " increment=" + increment;
    Method logText = tracerClass.getMethod("logText",
        new Class[] { String.class });
    logText.invoke(tracer, new Object[] { text });
}
```

Of course, we don't call the method if the bean context doesn't support the service. If it does, we use the `invoke` method to call it through the reflection mechanism.

When you try out this example, watch the Message Tracer window. It contains a message for each click on one of the spin buttons (see Figure 8–28).

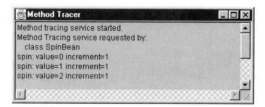

Figure 8–28: The Message Tracer window

Examples 8–17 through 8–19 contain the full code for the SpinBean, including the needed bean info class to hook in the customizer.

Example 8–17: SpinBean.java

```
1. import java.awt.*;
2. import java.awt.event.*;
3. import java.beans.*;
4. import java.beans.beancontext.*;
5. import java.lang.reflect.*;
6. import java.io.*;
```

```
7. import java.util.*;
8. import javax.swing.*;
9.
10. /**
11.    A bean with + and - buttons that can increment or decrement
12.    the value of a buddy bean.
13. */
14. public class SpinBean extends JPanel
15.    implements BeanContextProxy
16. {
17.    public SpinBean()
18.    {
19.       setLayout(new GridLayout(2, 1));
20.       JButton plusButton = new JButton("+");
21.       JButton minusButton = new JButton("-");
22.       add(plusButton);
23.       add(minusButton);
24.       plusButton.addActionListener(new
25.          ActionListener()
26.          {  public void actionPerformed(ActionEvent evt)
27.             {
28.                spin(1);
29.             }
30.          });
31.       minusButton.addActionListener(new
32.          ActionListener()
33.          {  public void actionPerformed(ActionEvent evt)
34.             {
35.                spin(-1);
36.             }
37.          });
38.
39.       childSupport = new
40.          BeanContextChildSupport()
41.          {
42.             public void setBeanContext(BeanContext context)
43.                throws PropertyVetoException
44.             {
45.                super.setBeanContext(context);
46.                setTracer(context);
47.             }
48.          };
49.    }
50.
51.    public BeanContextChild getBeanContextProxy()
52.    {
53.       return childSupport;
54.    }
55.
```

```
56.    /**
57.       Sets the buddy of this spin bean.
58.       @param b the buddy component
59.       @param p the descriptor of the integer property to
60.       increment or decrement
61.    */
62.    public void setBuddy(Component b, PropertyDescriptor p)
63.    {
64.       buddy = b;
65.       prop = p;
66.    }
67.
68.    /**
69.       Increments or decrements the value of the buddy.
70.       @param increment the amount by which to change the buddy's
71.       value
72.    */
73.    public void spin(int increment)
74.    {
75.       if (buddy == null) return;
76.       if (prop == null) return;
77.       Method readMethod = prop.getReadMethod();
78.       Method writeMethod = prop.getWriteMethod();
79.       try
80.       {  int value = ((Integer)readMethod.invoke(buddy,
81.             null)).intValue();
82.
83.          if (tracer != null)
84.          {  String text = "spin: value=" + value
85.                + " increment=" + increment;
86.             Method logText = tracerClass.getMethod("logText",
87.                new Class[] { String.class });
88.             logText.invoke(tracer, new Object[] { text });
89.          }
90.
91.          value += increment;
92.          writeMethod.invoke(buddy,
93.             new Object[] { new Integer(value) });
94.       }
95.       catch(Exception e)
96.       {
97.       }
98.    }
99.
100.   /**
101.      Attempts to set the message tracing service.
102.      @param context the bean context that may provide the
103.      service.
104.   */
```

```
105.    public void setTracer(BeanContext context)
106.    {
107.        try
108.        {
109.            BeanContextServices services
110.                = (BeanContextServices)context;
111.            tracerClass = Class.forName
112.                ("sunw.demo.methodtracer.MethodTracer");
113.            if (services.hasService(tracerClass))
114.            {   BeanContextServiceRevokedListener revokedListener =
115.                    new BeanContextServiceRevokedListener()
116.                {   public void serviceRevoked
117.                        (BeanContextServiceRevokedEvent event)
118.                    {   tracer = null;
119.                    }
120.                };
121.                tracer = services.getService(childSupport, this,
122.                    tracerClass, null, revokedListener);
123.            }
124.        }
125.        catch (Exception exception)
126.        {
127.            tracer = null;
128.        }
129.    }
130.
131.    public Dimension getPreferredSize()
132.    {
133.        return new Dimension(MINSIZE, MINSIZE);
134.    }
135.
136.    private static final int MINSIZE = 20;
137.    private Component buddy;
138.    private PropertyDescriptor prop;
139.    private Object tracer;
140.    private Class tracerClass;
141.    private BeanContextChildSupport childSupport;
142. }
```

Example 8–18: SpinBeanCustomizer.java

```
1. import java.awt.*;
2. import java.awt.event.*;
3. import java.beans.*;
4. import java.beans.beancontext.*;
5. import java.io.*;
6. import java.text.*;
7. import java.util.*;
8. import javax.swing.*;
9. import javax.swing.event.*;
```

```
10.
11. /**
12.    A customizer for the spin bean to pick its buddy.
13. */
14. public class SpinBeanCustomizer extends JPanel
15.    implements Customizer
16. {
17.    public SpinBeanCustomizer()
18.    {
19.       setLayout(new GridBagLayout());
20.       GridBagConstraints gbc = new GridBagConstraints();
21.       gbc.weightx = 0;
22.       gbc.weighty = 100;
23.       gbc.fill = GridBagConstraints.NONE;
24.       gbc.anchor = GridBagConstraints.EAST;
25.       add(new JLabel("Buddy"), gbc, 0, 0, 1, 1);
26.       add(new JLabel("Property"), gbc, 0, 1, 1, 1);
27.       gbc.weightx = 100;
28.       gbc.anchor = GridBagConstraints.WEST;
29.       gbc.fill = GridBagConstraints.BOTH;
30.       buddyModel = new DefaultListModel();
31.       propModel = new DefaultListModel();
32.       buddyList = new JList(buddyModel);
33.       propList = new JList(propModel);
34.       add(new JScrollPane(buddyList), gbc, 1, 0, 1, 1);
35.       add(new JScrollPane(propList), gbc, 1, 1, 1, 1);
36.       JButton setButton = new JButton("Set Buddy");
37.       JPanel p = new JPanel();
38.       p.add(setButton);
39.       add(p, gbc, 0, 2, 2, 1);
40.
41.       buddyList.addListSelectionListener(
42.          new ListSelectionListener()
43.          {
44.             public void valueChanged(ListSelectionEvent event)
45.             {
46.                findBuddyMethods();
47.             }
48.          });
49.
50.       setButton.addActionListener(
51.          new ActionListener()
52.          {
53.             public void actionPerformed(ActionEvent event)
54.             {  int buddyIndex = buddyList.getSelectedIndex();
55.                if (buddyIndex < 0) return;
56.                int propIndex = propList.getSelectedIndex();
57.                if (propIndex < 0) return;
```

```
58.                 bean.setBuddy(buddies[buddyIndex],
59.                    props[propIndex]);
60.                 }
61.             });
62.     }
63.
64.     /**
65.        A convenience method to add a component to given grid bag
66.        layout locations.
67.        @param c the component to add
68.        @param gbc the grid bag constraints to use
69.        @param x the x grid position
70.        @param y the y grid position
71.        @param w the grid width
72.        @param h the grid height
73.     */
74.     public void add(Component c, GridBagConstraints gbc,
75.         int x, int y, int w, int h)
76.     {
77.         gbc.gridx = x;
78.         gbc.gridy = y;
79.         gbc.gridwidth = w;
80.         gbc.gridheight = h;
81.         add(c, gbc);
82.     }
83.
84.     /**
85.        Finds the methods of the selected buddy.
86.     */
87.     public void findBuddyMethods()
88.     {
89.         int buddyIndex = buddyList.getSelectedIndex();
90.         if (buddyIndex < 0) return;
91.         Component buddy = buddies[buddyIndex];
92.         propModel.removeAllElements();
93.         try
94.         {
95.             BeanInfo info
96.                 = Introspector.getBeanInfo(buddy.getClass());
97.             props = info.getPropertyDescriptors();
98.             int j = 0;
99.             for (int i = 0; i < props.length; i++)
100.            {
101.                Class propertyType = props[i].getPropertyType();
102.                if (int.class.equals(propertyType))
103.                {
104.                    String name = props[i].getName();
105.                    propModel.addElement(name);
106.                    props[j++] = props[i];
```

```
107.                   }
108.               }
109.           }
110.         catch(IntrospectionException e){}
111.     }
112.
113.     public Dimension getPreferredSize()
114.     {
115.         return new Dimension(300, 200);
116.     }
117.
118.     public void setObject(Object obj)
119.     {
120.         bean = (SpinBean)obj;
121.         BeanContext context
122.             = bean.getBeanContextProxy().getBeanContext();
123.         buddies = new Component[context.size()];
124.         buddyModel.removeAllElements();
125.         Iterator iter = context.iterator();
126.         int i = 0;
127.         while (iter.hasNext())
128.         {   Object buddy = iter.next();
129.             if (buddy instanceof Component)
130.             {   buddies[i] = (Component)buddy;
131.                 String className = buddies[i].getClass().getName();
132.                 buddyModel.addElement(className);
133.                 i++;
134.             }
135.         }
136.     }
137.
138.     private SpinBean bean;
139.     private JList buddyList;
140.     private JList propList;
141.     private DefaultListModel buddyModel;
142.     private DefaultListModel propModel;
143.     private PropertyDescriptor[] props;
144.     private Component[] buddies;
145. }
```

Example 8–19: SpinBeanBeanInfo.java

```
1. import java.awt.*;
2. import java.beans.*;
3.
4. /**
5.    The bean info for the chart bean, specifying the
6.    customizer.
7. */
```

```
 8. public class SpinBeanBeanInfo extends SimpleBeanInfo
 9. {
10.    public BeanDescriptor getBeanDescriptor()
11.    {
12.       return new BeanDescriptor(SpinBean.class,
13.          SpinBeanCustomizer.class);
14.    }
15. }
```

java.beans.Introspector

- String decapitalize(String name)

  converts a string to the Java platform naming convention. SillyMethod becomes sillyMethod, for example. (When there are two consecutive capitals, nothing happens.)

- BeanInfo getBeanInfo(Class beanClass)

  gets the BeanInfo class associated to the bean or creates one on the fly, using the naming convention discussed earlier in this chapter; throws an IntrospectionException if the introspection fails.

java.beans.beancontext.BeanContextChild

- void setBeanContext(BeanContext bc)

  is called when a bean context adds this bean as a child. Must fire a property change event with property name "beanContext" to all vetoable listeners, then to all property change listeners.

- BeanContext getBeanContext()

  returns the current bean context for this bean.

- void addPropertyChangeListener(String name, PropertyChange-Listener listener)

  adds a listener for the named property.

- void removePropertyChangeListener(String name, PropertyChange-Listener listener)

  removes a listener for the named property.

- void addVetoableChangeListener(String name, VetoableChangeListener listener)

  adds a vetoable listener for the named property.

- void removeVetoableChangeListener(String name, VetoableChangeListener listener)

  removes a vetoable listener for the named property.

java.beans.beancontext.BeanContextChildSupport

- BeanContext getBeanContext()
  returns the current bean context for this bean.

javax.beans.beancontext.BeanContextProxy

- BeanContextChild getBeanContextProxy()
  returns the proxy object that handles the BeanContextChild methods.

javax.beans.beancontext.BeanContextServices

- boolean hasService(Class cl)
  tests whether this bean context supports the service carried out by the given class.

- Object getService(BeanContextChild child, Object requestor, Class cl, Object selector, BeanContextServiceRevokedListener listener)
  gets the object that carries out a bean context service.

Parameters:	child	the bean context child object that is linked as the child of the bean context
	requestor	the object requesting the service
	cl	the service class
	selector	an optional object to locate or instantiate the service
	listener	the listener to be notified when the service is no longer available

javax.beans.beancontext.BeanContextServiceRevokedListener

- void serviceRevoked(BeanContextServiceRevokedEvent event)
  is called when a service is revoked. You need to make sure the service is no longer called after this notification.

javax.beans.beancontext.BeanContextServiceRevokedEvent

- Class getServiceClass()
  gets the class that carries out the revoked service.

- boolean isServiceClass(Class cl)
  tests whether the given class object describes the class that carries out the revoked service.

Chapter 9

Security

▼ CLASS LOADERS

▼ BYTECODE VERIFICATION

▼ SECURITY MANAGERS AND PERMISSIONS

▼ DIGITAL SIGNATURES

▼ CODE SIGNING

▼ ENCRYPTION

When Java technology first appeared on the scene, the excitement was not about a well-crafted programming language but about the possibility of safely executing applets that are delivered over the Internet (see Chapter 10 of Volume 1 for more information about applets). Obviously, delivering executable applets is practical only when the recipients are sure that the code can't wreak havoc on their machines. For this reason, security was and is a major concern of both the designers and the users of Java technology. This means that unlike the case with other languages and systems where security was implemented as an afterthought or a reaction to break-ins, security mechanisms are an integral part of Java technology.

Three mechanisms in Java technology help ensure safety:

- Language design features (bounds checking on arrays, legal type conversions only, no pointer arithmetic, and so on);

- An access control mechanism that controls what the code can do (such as file access, network access, and so on);

861

- Code signing, whereby code authors can use standard cryptographic algorithms to authenticate Java programming language code. Then, the users of the code can determine exactly who created the code and whether the code has been altered after it was signed.

The Java virtual machine checks for bad pointers, invalid array offsets, and so on. The other steps require controlling what goes to the Java virtual machine.

When class files are loaded into the virtual machine, they are checked for integrity. We show you in detail how that process works. More importantly, we show you how to control what goes to the virtual machine by building your own *class loader*.

For maximum security, both the default mechanism for loading a class and a custom class loader need to work with a *security manager* class that controls what actions code can perform. You'll see how to write your own security manager class.

Finally, you'll see the cryptographic algorithms supplied in the `java.security` package, which allow for code signing and user authentication.

As always, we focus on those topics that are of greatest interest to application programmers. For an in-depth view, we recommend the book *Inside Java 2 Platform Security* by Li Gong [Addison-Wesley 1999].

Class Loaders

A Java programming language compiler converts source into the machine language of a hypothetical machine, called the *virtual machine*. The virtual machine code is stored in a class file with a `.class` extension. Class files contain the code for all the methods of one class. These class files need to be interpreted by a program that can translate the instruction set of the virtual machine into the machine language of the target machine.

Note that the virtual machine interpreter loads only those class files that are needed for the execution of a program. For example, suppose program execution starts with `MyProgram.class`. Here are the steps that the virtual machine carries out.

1. The virtual machine has a mechanism for loading class files, for example, by reading the files from disk or by requesting them from the Web; it uses this mechanism to load the contents of the `MyProgram` class file.

2. If the `MyProgram` class has instance variables or superclasses of another class type, these class files are loaded as well. (The process of loading all the classes that a given class depends on is called *resolving* the class.)

3. The virtual machine then executes the `main` method in `MyProgram` (which is static, so no instance of a class needs to be created).

4. If the `main` method or a method that `main` calls requires additional classes, these are loaded next.

The class loading mechanism doesn't just use a single class loader, however. Every Java program has at least three class loaders:

- The bootstrap class loader;
- The extension class loader;
- The system class loader (also sometimes called the application class loader).

The bootstrap class loader loads the system classes (typically, from the JAR file `rt.jar`). It is an integral part of the virtual machine, and is usually implemented in C. There is no `ClassLoader` object corresponding to the bootstrap class loader. For example,

```
String.class.getClassLoader()
```

returns `null`.

The extension class loader loads a standard extension from the `jre/lib/ext` directory. You can drop JAR files into that directory, and the extension class loader will find the classes in them, even without any class path. (Some people recommend this mechanism to avoid the "class path from hell," but see the pitfall later in this section.) The extension class loader is implemented in Java.

The system class loader loads the application classes. It locates classes in the directories and JAR/ZIP files on the class path, as set by the `CLASSPATH` environment variable or the `-classpath` command-line option. This class loader is also implemented in Java.

Class loaders have a *parent/child* relationship. Every class loader except for the bootstrap class loader has a parent class loader. A class loader is supposed to give its parent a chance to load any given class and only load it if the parent has failed. For example, when the system class loader is asked to load a system class (say, `java.util.ArrayList`), then it first asks the extension class loader. That class loader first asks the bootstrap class loader. The bootstrap class loader finds and loads the class in `rt.jar`, and neither of the other class loaders searches any further.

NOTE: It is entirely possible to implement a class loader that doesn't delegate class loading to its parent first. Such a class loader can even load its own version of system classes. However, there seems no benefit to such an arrangement. There is no security risk either—a class can load new code with a class loader, but it can't change its own class loader.

Applets, servlets, and RMI stubs are loaded with custom class loaders. You can even write your own class loader for specialized purposes. That lets you carry out specialized security checks before you pass the bytecodes to the virtual machine.

For example, you can write a class loader that can refuse to load a class that has not been marked as "paid for." The next section shows you how.

Given a class loader, you load a new class as follows:

```
ClassLoader loader = new MyClassLoader();
String className = ". . .";
Class cl = loader.loadClass(className);
```

Then that class loads other classes on which it depends.

With all these class loaders, you may wonder which one is in charge. Recall again when classes are loaded:

1. Implicitly, when a class is resolved, that is, when the classes on which it depends are loaded;

2. Explicitly, but without a named class loader, by calling `Class.forName(className);`

3. Through a class loader, by calling `loader.loadClass(className)`.

In the first case, the resolution process uses the same class loader as the one that is loading the original class. In the second case, the class loader of the class whose method contains the `Class.forName` instruction is used. In the third case, the specified class loader is in charge. This is the only way to switch to a new class loader.

CAUTION: You can run into grief if you drop a JAR file into the `jre/lib/ext` directory and one of its classes calls `Class.forName`. That call will *only* use the extension class loader, and not the system class loader, to find the class. In particular, the class path is never used. Keep that in mind before you use the extension directory as a way to minimize your class file hassles.

NOTE: That pitfall begs the question of what you should do if you must dynamically load classes in an extension library. You can call the static `ClassLoader.getSystemClassLoader` method to get the system class loader. However, that may not be the appropriate class loader to use in all circumstances. After all, the extension code may have been called from a class that was loaded with another class loader. To overcome this problem, every thread has a "context class loader," the class loader that is most reasonable to use when executing code in the thread. Call `loadClass` with that class loader instead of calling `Class.forName`:

```
Thread t = Thread.currentThread();
ClassLoader loader = t.getContextClassLoader();
Class cl = loader.loadClass(className);
```

Conversely, before starting a new thread, you can set the context class loader:

```
Thread t = new Thread(. . .);
t.setContextClassLoader(myClassLoader);
```

```
t.start();
```
If no context class loader is set, the thread takes the context class loader of the parent thread. The main thread of an application has the system class loader as its context class loader.

CAUTION: There is a second pitfall with dropping JAR files into the `jre/lib/ext` directory. Sometimes, programmers forget about the files they placed there months ago. Then they scratch their heads when the class loader seems to ignore the class path, when it is actually loading long-forgotten classes from the extension directory.

Every Java programmer knows that package names are used to eliminate name conflicts. There are two classes called `Date` in the standard library, but of course their real names are `java.util.Date` and `java.sql.Date`. The simple name is only a programmer convenience and requires the inclusion of appropriate `import` statements. In a running program, all class names contain their package name.

It may surprise you, however, that you can have two classes in the same virtual machine that have the same class *and package* name. A class is determined by its full name *and* the class loader. This technique is useful when loading code from multiple sources. For example, a browser uses separate instances of the applet class loader class for each web page. This allows the virtual machine to separate classes from different web pages, no matter what they are named.

NOTE: This technique has other uses as well, such as "hot deployment" of servlets and Enterprise Java Beans. See `http://developer.java.sun.com/developer/TechTips/2000/tt1027.html` for more information.

Writing Your Own Class Loader

To write your own class loader, you simply extend the `ClassLoader` class and override the method.

```
findClass(String className)
```
The `loadClass` method of the `ClassLoader` superclass takes care of the delegation to the parent and only calls `findClass` if the class hasn't already been loaded and if the parent class loader was unable to load the class.

NOTE: In earlier versions of the SDK, programmers had to override the `loadClass` method. That is no longer recommended.

Your implementation of this method must:

1. Load the bytecodes for the class from the local file system or from some other source.

2. Call the `defineClass` method of the `ClassLoader` superclass to present the bytecodes to the virtual machine.

In the program of Example 9–1, we implement a class loader that loads encrypted class files. The program asks the user for the name of the first class to load (that is, the class containing `main`) and the decryption key. It then uses a special class loader to load the specified class and calls the `main` method. The class loader decrypts the specified class and all nonsystem classes that are referenced by it. Finally, the program calls the `main` method of the loaded class (see Figure 9–1).

Figure 9–1: The `ClassLoaderTest` program

For simplicity, we ignore 2,000 years of progress in the field of cryptography and use the venerable Caesar cipher for encrypting the class files.

NOTE: David Kahn's wonderful book *The Codebreakers* [Macmillan, NY, 1967, p. 84] refers to Suetonius as a historical source for the Caesar cipher. Caesar shifted the 24 letters of the Roman alphabet by 3 letters. At the time of this writing, the U.S. government restricts the export of strong encryption methods. Therefore, we use Caesar's method for our example since it is so weak that it is presumably legal for export.

Our version of the Caesar cipher has as a key a number between 1 and 255. To decrypt, simply add that key to every byte and reduce modulo 256. The `Caesar.java` program of Example 9–2 carries out the encryption.

In order not to confuse the regular class loader, we use a different extension, `.caesar`, for the encrypted class files.

To decrypt, the class loader simply subtracts the key from every byte. On the CD-ROM for this book, you will find four class files, encrypted with a key value of 3—the traditional choice. You cannot load these classes via the regular byte-code interpreter, but you can run the encrypted program by using the custom class loader defined in our `ClassLoaderTest` program.

Encrypting class files has a number of practical uses (provided, of course, that you use a cipher stronger than the Caesar cipher). Without the decryption key, the class files are useless. They can neither be executed by a standard bytecode interpreter nor readily disassembled.

This means that you can use a custom class loader to authenticate the user of the class or to ensure that a program has been paid for before it will be allowed to run. Of course, encryption is only one application of a custom class loader. You can use other types of class loaders to solve other problems, for example, storing class files in a database.

Example 9–1: ClassLoaderTest.java

```
1. import java.util.*;
2. import java.io.*;
3. import java.lang.reflect.*;
4. import java.awt.*;
5. import java.awt.event.*;
6. import javax.swing.*;
7.
8. /**
9.    This program demonstrates a custom class loader that decrypts
10.   class files.
11. */
12. public class ClassLoaderTest
13. {
14.    public static void main(String[] args)
15.    {
16.       JFrame frame = new ClassLoaderFrame();
17.       frame.setDefaultCloseOperation(JFrame.EXIT_ON_CLOSE);
18.       frame.show();
19.    }
20. }
21.
22. /**
23.    This frame contains two text fields for the name of the class
24.    to load and the decryption key.
25. */
26. class ClassLoaderFrame extends JFrame
27. {
28.    public ClassLoaderFrame()
```

```
29.    {
30.       setTitle("ClassLoaderTest");
31.       setSize(WIDTH, HEIGHT);
32.       getContentPane().setLayout(new GridBagLayout());
33.       GridBagConstraints gbc = new GridBagConstraints();
34.       gbc.weightx = 0;
35.       gbc.weighty = 100;
36.       gbc.fill = GridBagConstraints.NONE;
37.       gbc.anchor = GridBagConstraints.EAST;
38.       add(new JLabel("Class"), gbc, 0, 0, 1, 1);
39.       add(new JLabel("Key"), gbc, 0, 1, 1, 1);
40.       gbc.weightx = 100;
41.       gbc.fill = GridBagConstraints.HORIZONTAL;
42.       gbc.anchor = GridBagConstraints.WEST;
43.       add(nameField, gbc, 1, 0, 1, 1);
44.       add(keyField, gbc, 1, 1, 1, 1);
45.       gbc.fill = GridBagConstraints.NONE;
46.       gbc.anchor = GridBagConstraints.CENTER;
47.       JButton loadButton = new JButton("Load");
48.       add(loadButton, gbc, 0, 2, 2, 1);
49.       loadButton.addActionListener(new
50.          ActionListener()
51.          {
52.             public void actionPerformed(ActionEvent event)
53.             {
54.                runClass(nameField.getText(), keyField.getText());
55.             }
56.          });
57.    }
58.
59.    /**
60.       A convenience method to add a component to given grid bag
61.       layout locations.
62.       @param c the component to add
63.       @param gbc the grid bag constraints to use
64.       @param x the x grid position
65.       @param y the y grid position
66.       @param w the grid width
67.       @param h the grid height
68.    */
69.    public void add(Component c, GridBagConstraints gbc,
70.       int x, int y, int w, int h)
71.    {
72.       gbc.gridx = x;
73.       gbc.gridy = y;
74.       gbc.gridwidth = w;
75.       gbc.gridheight = h;
76.       getContentPane().add(c, gbc);
77.    }
78.
79.    /**
80.       Runs the main method of a given class.
81.       @param name the class name
```

```
82.         @param key the decryption key for the class files
83.     */
84.     public void runClass(String name, String key)
85.     {
86.         try
87.         {
88.             ClassLoader loader
89.                 = new CryptoClassLoader(Integer.parseInt(key));
90.             Class c = loader.loadClass(name);
91.             String[] args = new String[] {};
92.
93.             Method m = c.getMethod("main",
94.                 new Class[] { args.getClass() });
95.             m.invoke(null, new Object[] { args });
96.         }
97.         catch (Throwable e)
98.         {
99.             JOptionPane.showMessageDialog(this, e);
100.        }
101.    }
102.
103.    private JTextField keyField = new JTextField("3", 4);
104.    private JTextField nameField = new JTextField(30);
105.    private static final int WIDTH = 300;
106.    private static final int HEIGHT = 200;
107. }
108.
109. /**
110.    This class loader loads encrypted class files.
111. */
112. class CryptoClassLoader extends ClassLoader
113. {
114.    /**
115.       Constructs a crypto class loader.
116.       @param k the decryption key
117.    */
118.    public CryptoClassLoader(int k)
119.    {
120.       key = k;
121.    }
122.
123.    protected Class findClass(String name)
124.       throws ClassNotFoundException
125.    {
126.       byte[] classBytes = null;
127.       try
128.       {
129.           classBytes = loadClassBytes(name);
130.       }
131.       catch (IOException exception)
132.       {
133.           throw new ClassNotFoundException(name);
134.       }
```

```
135.
136.        Class cl = defineClass(name, classBytes,
137.            0, classBytes.length);
138.        if (cl == null)
139.                throw new ClassNotFoundException(name);
140.        return cl;
141.    }
142.
143.    /**
144.        Loads and decrypt the class file bytes.
145.        @param name the class name
146.        @return an array with the class file bytes
147.    */
148.    private byte[] loadClassBytes(String name)
149.        throws IOException
150.    {
151.        String cname = name.replace('.', '/') + ".caesar";
152.        FileInputStream in = null;
153.        try
154.        {
155.            in = new FileInputStream(cname);
156.            ByteArrayOutputStream buffer
157.                = new ByteArrayOutputStream();
158.            int ch;
159.            while ((ch = in.read()) != -1)
160.            {
161.                byte b = (byte)(ch - key);
162.                buffer.write(b);
163.            }
164.            in.close();
165.            return buffer.toByteArray();
166.        }
167.        finally
168.        {
169.            if (in != null)
170.                in.close();
171.        }
172.    }
173.
174.    private Map classes = new HashMap();
175.    private int key;
176. }
```

Example 9–2: Caesar.java

```
1. import java.io.*;
2.
3. /**
4.    Encrypts a file using the Caesar cipher.
5. */
6. public class Caesar
7. {
```

```
8.    public static void main(String[] args)
9.    {
10.       if (args.length != 3)
11.       {
12.          System.out.println("USAGE: java Caesar in out key");
13.          return;
14.       }
15.
16.       try
17.       {
18.          FileInputStream in = new FileInputStream(args[0]);
19.          FileOutputStream out = new FileOutputStream(args[1]);
20.          int key = Integer.parseInt(args[2]);
21.          int ch;
22.          while ((ch = in.read()) != -1)
23.          {
24.             byte c = (byte)(ch + key);
25.             out.write(c);
26.          }
27.          in.close();
28.          out.close();
29.       }
30.       catch(IOException exception)
31.       {
32.          exception.printStackTrace();
33.       }
34.    }
35. }
```

java.lang.Class

- ClassLoader getClassLoader()
  gets the class loader that loaded this class.

java.lang.ClassLoader

- ClassLoader getParent()
  returns the parent class loader, or null if the parent class loader is the boot-strap class loader.

- static ClassLoader getSystemClassLoader()
  gets the system class loader, that is, the class loader that was used to load the first application class.

- protected Class findClass(String name)
  A class loader should override this method to find the bytecodes for a class and present them to the virtual machine by calling the defineClass method.

Parameters: `name` the name of the class. Use `.` as package name separator, and don't use a `.class` suffix

- `Class defineClass(String name, byte[] data, int offset, int length)`
adds a new class to the virtual machine.

Parameters: `name` the name of the class. Use `.` as package name separator, and don't use a `.class` suffix

`data` an array holding the bytecodes of the class

`offset` the start of the bytecodes in the array

`length` the length of the bytecodes in the array

`java.lang.Thread`

- `ClassLoader getContextClassLoader()`
gets the class loader that the creator of this thread has designated as the most reasonable class loader to use when executing this thread.

- `void setContextClassLoader(ClassLoader loader)`
sets a class loader for code in this thread to retrieve for loading classes. If no context class loader is set explicitly when starting a thread, the parent's context class loader is used.

Bytecode Verification

When a class loader presents the bytecodes of a newly loaded Java platform class to the virtual machine, these bytecodes are first inspected by a *verifier*. The verifier checks that the instructions cannot perform actions that are obviously damaging. All classes except for system classes are verified. However, you can deactivate verification with the undocumented `-noverify` option.

For example,

```
java -noverify Hello
```

Here are some of the checks that the verifier carries out:

- That variables are initialized before they are used;
- That method calls match the types of object references;
- That rules for accessing private data and methods are not violated;
- That local variable accesses fall within the runtime stack;
- That the runtime stack does not overflow.

If any of these checks fail, then the class is considered corrupted and will not be loaded.

> **NOTE:** If you are familiar with Gödel's theorem, you may wonder how the verifier can prove that a class file is free from type mismatches, uninitialized variables, and stack overflows. Gödel's theorem states that it is impossible to design algorithms whose inputs are program files and whose output is a Boolean value that states whether the input program has a particular property (such as being free from stack overflows). Is this a conflict between the public relations department at Sun Microsystems and the laws of logic? No—in fact, the verifier is *not* a decision algorithm in the sense of Gödel. If the verifier accepts a program, it is indeed safe. However, there may be many programs that the verifier rejects even though they would actually be safe.

This strict verification is an important security consideration. Accidental errors, such as uninitialized variables, can easily wreak havoc if they are not caught. More importantly, in the wide open world of the Internet, you must be protected against malicious programmers who create evil effects on purpose. For example, by modifying values on the runtime stack or by writing to the private data fields of system objects, a program can break through the security system of a browser.

However, you may wonder why there is a special verifier to check all these features. After all, the compiler would never allow you to generate a class file in which an uninitialized variable is used or in which a private data field is accessed from another class. Indeed, a class file generated by a compiler for the Java programming language always passes verification. However, the bytecode format used in the class files is well documented, and it is an easy matter for someone with some experience in assembly programming and a hex editor to manually produce a class file that contains valid but unsafe instructions for the Java virtual machine. Once again, keep in mind that the verifier is always guarding against maliciously altered class files, not just checking the class files produced by a compiler.

Here's an example of how to construct such an altered class file. We start with the program VerifierTest.java of Example 9–3. This is a simple program that calls a method and displays the method result. The program can be run both as a console program and as an applet. The fun method itself just computes 1 + 2.

```
static int fun()
{
    int m;
    int n;
    m = 1;
    n = 2;
    int r = m + n;
    return r;
}
```

As an experiment, try to compile the following modification of this program:

```
static int fun()
{
    int m = 1;
    int n;
    m = 1;
    m = 2;
    int r = m + n;
    return r;
}
```

In this case, n is not initialized, and it could have any random value. Of course, the compiler detects that problem and refuses to compile the program. To create a bad class file, we have to work a little harder. First, run the javap program to find out how the compiler translates the fun method. The command

```
javap -c VerifierTest
```

shows the bytecodes in the class file in mnemonic form.

```
Method int fun()
   0 iconst_1
   1 istore_0
   2 iconst_2
   3 istore_1
   4 iload_0
   5 iload_1
   6 iadd
   7 istore_2
   8 iload_2
   9 ireturn
```

We will use a hex editor to change instruction 3 from istore_1 to istore_0. That is, local variable 0 (which is m) is initialized twice, and local variable 1 (which is n) is not initialized at all. We need to know the hexadecimal values for these instructions. These values are readily available from *The Java Virtual Machine Specification* by Tim Lindholm and Frank Yellin [Addison-Wesley, 1999].

```
   0 iconst_1 04
   1 istore_0 3B
   2 iconst_2 05
   3 istore_1 3C
   4 iload_0  1A
   5 iload_1  1B
   6 iadd     60
   7 istore_2 3D
   8 iload_2  1C
   9 ireturn  AC
```

You can use a hex editor (such as Hex Workshop, which you can download from http://www.bpsoft.com) to carry out the modification. Or, of

course, you can use emacs in `hexl-mode`. In Figure 9–2, you see the class file
`VerifierTest.class` loaded into Hex Workshop, with the bytecodes of the
`fun` method highlighted.

```
H Hex Workshop - [VerifierTest.class]                                          _ □ ×
□ File  Edit  Disk  Options  Tools  Window  Help              Unregistered Version  _ ₧ ×
⌐ ⊒ ⌂ │ ╳ ╠ ╬ │ ⌐ │ ⌐ ⌐ │ ⌐ │ H  D │ B │ S │ L │ F │ D │ S │ U │ ← │ → │
00000250  74 01 00 07 70 72 69 6E 74 6C 6E 01 00 08 74 6F  t...println...to  ▲
00000260  53 74 72 69 6E 67 00 21 00 02 00 03 00 00 00 00  String.!........
00000270  00 04 00 09 00 33 00 1F 00 01 00 21 00 00 00 35  .....3.....!...5
00000280  00 04 00 01 00 00 00 19 B2 00 0D BB 00 06 59 12  .............Y.
00000290  01 B7 00 09 B8 00 0C B6 00 0A B6 00 0F B6 00 0E  ................
000002A0  B1 00 00 00 01 00 25 00 00 00 0A 00 02 00 00 00  ......%.........
000002B0  06 00 18 00 05 00 08 00 2D 00 18 00 01 00 21 00  ........-.....!.
000002C0  00 00 2E 00 02 00 03 00 00 00 0A 04 3B 05 3B 1A  ............`;.;.
000002D0  1B 60 3D 1C AC 00 00 00 01 00 25 00 00 00 12 00  .`=......%......
000002E0  04 00 00 00 0C 00 02 00 0D 00 04 00 0E 00 08 00  ................
000002F0  0F 00 01 00 35 00 1C 00 01 00 21 00 00 00 37 00  ....5.....!...7.
00000300  04 00 02 00 00 00 1B 2B BB 00 06 59 12 01 B7 00  .......+...Y....
00000310  09 B8 00 0C B6 00 0A B6 00 0F 10 14 10 14 B6 00  ................
00000320  0B B1 00 00 00 01 00 25 00 00 00 0A 00 02 00 00  .......%........
00000330  00 13 00 1A 00 12 00 01 00 20 00 1A 00 01 00 21  ......... .....!
00000340  00 00 00 1D 00 01 00 01 00 00 00 05 2A B7 00 08  ............*...
00000350  B1 00 00 00 01 00 25 00 00 00 06 00 01 00 00 00  ......%.........
00000360  04 00 01 00 28 00 00 00 02 00 2A              ....(.....*  ▼
Ready                      Offset: 000002CB │ Sel: 0xa bytes │ 875 bytes    OVR
```

Figure 9–2: Modifying bytecodes with a hex editor

Change 3C to 3B and save the class file. Then try running the `VerifierTest`
program. You get an error message:

```
Exception in thread "main" java.lang.VerifyError: (class: Verifi-
erTest, method:fun signature: ()I) Accessing value from unini-
tialized register 1
```

That is good—the virtual machine detected our modification.

Now run the program with the `-noverify` (or `-Xverify:none`) option.

```
java -noverify VerifierTest
```

The `fun` method returns a seemingly random value. This is actually 2 plus the
value that happened to be stored in the variable n, which never was initialized.
Here is a typical printout:

```
1 + 2 = 15102330
```

To see how browsers handle verification, we wrote this program to run either as
an application or an applet. Load the applet into a browser, using a file URL
such as

```
file:///C:/CoreJavaBook/v2ch9/VerifierTest/VerifierTest.html
```

Then, you see an error message displayed indicating that verification has failed
(see Figure 9–3).

NOTE: There is a curious hole in the verifier in the Java interpreter that has been known by many people for a long time but that persists for compatibility reasons. Suppose you have two class files A.java and B.java like this:

```
public class A { public int field; }

public class B
{
    public static void main(String[] args)
    {
        System.out.println(new A().field);
    }
}
```

This program compiles and runs, of course. Now edit *only* the file A.java to make field private. Recompile only that file. The resulting program should fail verification since B now attempts to access a private field of A. However, up to SDK 1.4, the program will run and merrily access the private field. Only if you run the Java interpreter with the -Xverify:all option will the error be caught.

The reason is backwards compatibility with an obscure and ill-considered optimization in JDK 1.0—see http://developer.java.sun.com/developer/bugParade/bugs/4030988.html. This is not considered a security risk because only classes loaded from the local file system are exempt from verification.

Example 9–3: VerifierTest.java

```
1. import java.awt.*;
2. import java.applet.*;
3.
4. /**
5.    This application demonstrates the bytecode verifier of
6.    the virtual machine. If you use a hex editor to modify the
7.    class file, then the virtual machine should detect the
8.    tampering.
9. */
10. public class VerifierTest extends Applet
11. {
12.    public static void main(String[] args)
13.    {
14.        System.out.println("1 + 2 == " + fun());
15.    }
16.
17.    /**
18.        A function that computes 1 + 2
19.        @return 3, if the code has not been corrupted
20.    */
21.    public static int fun()
22.    {
```

```
23.        int m;
24.        int n;
25.        m = 1;
26.        n = 2;
27.        // use hex editor to change to "m = 2" in class file
28.        int r = m + n;
29.        return r;
30.     }
31.
32.     public void paint(Graphics g)
33.     {
34.        g.drawString("1 + 2 == " + fun(), 20, 20);
35.     }
36. }
```

Figure 9–3: Loading a corrupted class file raises a method verification error

Security Managers and Permissions

Once a class has been loaded into the virtual machine by a class loader or by the default class loading mechanism and checked by the verifier, the third security mechanism of the Java platform springs into action: the *security manager*. A security manager is a class that controls whether a specific operation is permitted. Operations checked by a security manager include:

- Whether the current thread can create a new class loader;
- Whether the current thread can create a subprocess;

- Whether the current thread can halt the virtual machine;
- Whether the current thread can load a dynamic link library;
- Whether a class can access a member of another class;
- Whether the current thread can access a specified package;
- Whether the current thread can define classes in a specified package;
- Whether the current thread can access or modify system properties;
- Whether the current thread can read from or write to a specified file;
- Whether the current thread can delete a specified file;
- Whether the current thread can accept a socket connection from a specified host and port number;
- Whether the current thread can open a socket connection to the specified host and port number;
- Whether the current thread can wait for a connection request on a specified local port number;
- Whether the current thread can use IP multicast;
- Whether the current thread can invoke a `stop`, `suspend`, `resume`, `destroy`, `setPriority`/`setMaxPriority`, `setName`, or `setDaemon` method of a given thread or thread group;
- Whether the current thread can set a socket or stream handler factory;
- Whether a class can start a print job;
- Whether a class can access the system clipboard;
- Whether a class can access the AWT event queue;
- Whether the current thread is trusted to bring up a top-level window.

The default behavior when running Java applications is that *no* security manager is installed, so all these operations are permitted. The appletviewer, on the other hand, immediately installs a security manager (called `AppletSecurity`) that is quite restrictive.

For example, applets are not allowed to exit the virtual machine. If they try calling the `exit` method, then a security exception is thrown. Here is what happens in detail. The `exit` method of the `Runtime` class calls the `checkExit` method of the security manager. Here is the entire code of the `exit` method.

```
public void exit(int status)
{
   SecurityManager security = System.getSecurityManager();
   if (security != null)
       security.checkExit(status);
   exitInternal(status);
}
```

The security manager now checks if the exit request came from the browser or an individual applet. If the security manager agrees with the exit request, then the `checkExit` method simply returns, and normal processing continues. However, if the security manager doesn't want to grant the request, the `checkExit` method throws a `SecurityException`.

The `exit` method continues only if no exception occurred. It then calls the *private native* `exitInternal` method that actually terminates the virtual machine. There is no other way of terminating the virtual machine, and since the `exitInternal` method is private, it cannot be called from any other class. Thus, any code that attempts to exit the virtual machine must go through the `exit` method and thus through the `checkExit` security check without triggering a security exception.

Clearly, the integrity of the security policy depends on careful coding. The providers of system services in the standard library must be careful to always consult the security manager before attempting any sensitive operation.

When you run a Java application, the default is that no security manager is running. Your program can install a specific security manager by a call to the static `setSecurityManager` method in the `System` class. Once your program installs a security manager, any attempt to install a second security manager only succeeds if the first security manager agrees to be replaced. This is clearly essential; otherwise, a bad applet could install its own security manager. Thus, while it is possible to have multiple class loaders, a program in the Java programming language can be governed by only one security manager. It is up to the implementor of that security manager to decide whether to grant all classes the same access or whether to take the origins of the classes into account before deciding what to do.

The default security manager of the Java 2 platform allows both programmers and system administrators fine-grained control over individual security permissions. We describe these features in the following section. First, we give you an overview of the Java 2 platform security model. Then, we show how you can control permissions with *policy files*. Finally, you will see how you can define your own permission types and how you can extend the default security manager class.

Java 2 Platform Security

JDK 1.0 had a very simple security model: local classes had full permissions, and remote classes were confined to the *sandbox:* the applet security manager denied all access to local resources. JDK 1.1 implemented a slight modification: remote code that was signed by a trusted entity was granted the same permissions as local classes. However, both versions of the JDK provided an all-or-nothing approach. Programs either had full access or they had to play in the sandbox.

The Java 2 platform has a much more flexible mechanism. A *security policy* maps *code sources to permission sets* (see Figure 9–4).

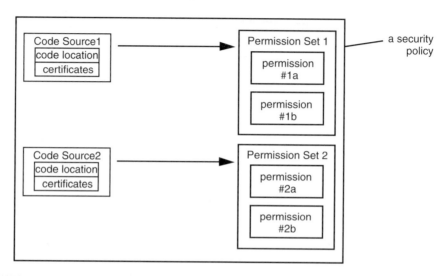

Figure 9–4: A security policy

A *code source* has two properties: the *code location* (for example, a code base URL or a JAR file) and *certificates*. You will see later in this chapter how code can be certified by trusted parties.

A *permission* is any property that is checked by a security manager. SDK 1.2 implementation supports a number of permission classes, each of which encapsulates the details of a particular permission. For example, the following instance of the `FilePermission` class states that it is ok to read and write any file in the `/tmp` directory.

```
FilePermission p = new FilePermission("/tmp/*", "read,write");
```

More importantly, the default implementation of the `Policy` class in SDK 1.2 reads permissions from a *permission file*. Inside a permission file, the same read permission is expressed as

```
permission java.io.FilePermission "/tmp/*", "read,write";
```

We discuss permission files in the next section.

Figure 9–5 shows the hierarchy of permission classes in SDK 1.2.

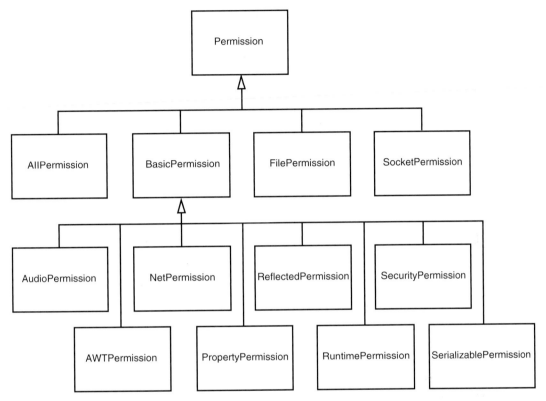

Figure 9–5: Permission hierarchy in JDK 1.2

In the preceding section, you saw that the `SecurityManager` class has security check methods such as `checkExit`. These methods exist only for the convenience of the programmer and for backward compatibility. All of them call one of the two following methods:

```
void checkPermission(Permission p)
void checkPermission(Permission p, Object context)
```

The second method is used if one thread carries out a security check for another thread. The `context` encapsulates the call stack at the time of the check. (See Gong's book for details on how to generate and use these context objects.)

For example, here is the source code for the `checkExit` method.

```
public void checkExit()
{
    checkPermission(new RuntimePermission("exitVM"));
}
```

Each security manager is free to provide its own implementation of the `checkPermission` method. However, the JDK provides a "standard model" of how to carry out permission checks. For the remainder of this section, we describe this standard model. The standard model relies on two classes:

```
java.security.SecureClassLoader
java.lang.SecurityManager
```

These are the superclasses of the class loader and security manager that are used in all practical settings (such as applets and remote method invocation). In principle, you can install your own class loader and security manager. However, that is a complex undertaking that few programmers will want to attempt. It is much more common to extend the standard classes.

The standard model relies on a `Policy` object to map code sources to permissions. There can be only one `Policy` object in effect at any given time. The static `getPolicy` method of the `Policy` class gets the current policy.

```
Policy currentPolicy = Policy.getPolicy();
```

The principal method of the `Policy` class is the `getPermissions` method that returns the permission collection for a particular code source.

```
PermissionCollection permissions
    = currentPolicy.getPermissions(codeBase);
```

Each class has a *protection domain,* an object that encapsulates both the code source and the collection of permissions of the class. The `getProtection-Domain` method of the `Class` class returns that domain.

```
ProtectionDomain domain
    = anObject.getClass().getProtectionDomain();
```

The `getCodeSource` and `getPermissions` methods of the `ProtectionDomain` method return the code source and permission collection.

In the standard model, the permission collection is entirely dependent on the code source. The protection domain is set when the `SecureClassLoader` loads the class. The `SecureClassLoader` queries the current policy for the permissions that match the code source. It then creates a `ProtectionDomain` object with the given code source and permissions. Finally, it passes that object to the `defineClass` method. Figure 9–6 shows the relationships between these security classes.

When the `SecurityManager` needs to check a permission, it looks at the classes of all methods currently on the call stack. It then gets the protection domains of all classes and asks each protection domain if its permission collection allows the operation that is currently being checked. If all domains agree, then the check passes. Otherwise, a `SecurityException` is thrown.

Why do all methods on the call stack need to allow a particular operation? Let us work through an example. Suppose the `init` method of an applet wants to open a file. It might call

```
Reader in = new FileReader(name);
```

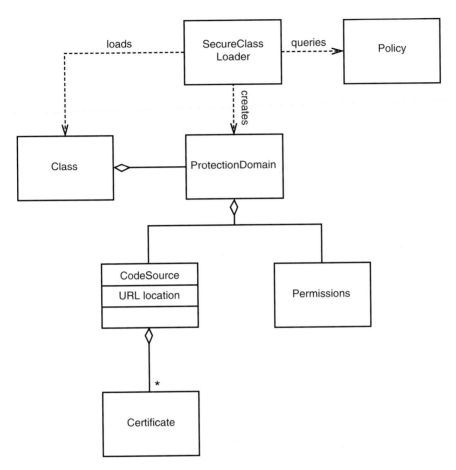

Figure 9–6: Relationship between security classes

The `FileReader` constructor calls the `FileInputStream` constructor, which calls the `checkRead` method of the security manager, which finally calls `checkPermission` with a `FilePermission(name, "read"` object. Table 9–1 shows the call stack.

Table 9–1: Call stack during permission checking

Class	Method	Code Source	Permissions
SecurityManager	SecurityManager	null	AllPermission
SecurityManager	checkRead	null	AllPermission
FileInputStream	constructor	null	AllPermission
FileReader	constructor	null	AllPermission
applet	init	applet code source	applet permissions

. . .

The `FileInputStream` and `SecurityManager` classes are *system classes* whose `CodeSource` is `null` and whose permissions consist of an instance of the `AllPermission` class, which allows all operations. Clearly, their permissions alone can't determine the outcome of the check. As you can see, the `checkPermission` method must take into account the restricted permissions of the applet class. By checking the entire call stack, the security mechanism ensures that one class can never ask another class to carry out a sensitive operation on its behalf.

> NOTE: This brief discussion of permission checking shows you the basic concepts. However, there are a number of technical details that we omit here. With security, the devil lies in the details, and we encourage you to read the book by Li Gong for more information. For a more critical view of the Java platform security model, see the book *Securing Java* by Gary McGraw and Ed Felten [John Wiley & Sons 1999]. You can find an online version of that book at `http://www.securingjava.com`.

java.lang.SecurityManager

- void checkPermission(Permission p)
- void checkPermission(Permission p, Object context)

  check whether the current security policy permits the given permission. The second method receives an object that encapsulates the call stack. That method is used if one thread asks another thread to carry out a permission check on its behalf.

java.security.Policy

- static Policy getPolicy()

  gets the current policy object, or `null` if no security policy is in effect.

- PermissionCollection getPermissions(CodeSource source)

  gets the permissions associated with the given code source.

java.lang.Class

- ProtectionDomain getProtectionDomain()

  gets the protection domain for this class, or `null` if this class was loaded without a protection domain.

- Class defineClass(String name, byte[] data, int offset, int

java.lang.ClassLoader

length, ProtectionDomain domain)
adds a new class to the virtual machine.

Parameters:	name	the name of the class. Use . as package name separator, and don't use a .class suffix.
	data	an array holding the bytecodes of the class.
	offset	the start of the bytecodes in the array.
	length	the length of the bytecodes in the array.
	domain	the protection domain for this class.

java.security.ProtectionDomain

• ProtectionDomain(CodeSource source, PermissionCollection collections)
constructs a protection domain with the given code source and permissions.

• CodeSource getCodeSource()
gets the code source of this protection domain.

• PermissionCollection getPermissions()
gets the permissions of this protection domain.

java.security.PermissionCollection

• void add(Permission p)
adds a permission to this permission collection.

• Enumeration elements()
returns an enumeration to iterate through all permissions in this collection.

java.security.CodeSource

• Certificate[] getCertificates()
gets the certificates for class file signature associated with this code source.

• URL getLocation()
gets the location of class files associated with this code source.

Security Policy Files

In the preceding section, you saw how the SecureClassLoader assigns permissions when loading classes, by asking a Policy object to look up the permissions for the code source of each class. In principle, you can install your own Policy class to carry out the mapping from code sources to permissions.

However, in this section, you will learn about the standard policy class that the JDK 1.2 interpreter uses.

NOTE: The policy class is set in the file `java.security` in the `jre/lib` subdirectory of the JDK home directory. By default, this file contains the line

```
policy.provider=sun.security.provider.PolicyFile
```

You can supply your own policy class and install it by changing this file.

The standard policy reads *policy files* that contain instructions for mapping code sources to permissions. You have seen these policy files in Chapter 5, where they were required to grant network access to programs that use the `RMISecurity-Manager`. Here is a typical policy file:

```
grant codeBase "www.horstmann.com/classes"
{
    permission java.io.FilePermission "/tmp/*", "read,write";
}
```

This file grants permission to read and write files in the `/tmp` directory to all code that was downloaded from `www.horstmann.com/classes`.

You can install policy files in standard locations. By default, there are two locations:

- The file `java.policy` in the Java platform home directory;
- The file `.java.policy` (notice the period at the beginning of the file name) in the user home directory.

NOTE: You can change the locations of these files in the `java.security` configuration file. The defaults are specified as

```
policy.url.1=file:${java.home}/lib/security/java.policy
policy.url.2=file:${user.home}/.java.policy
```

A system administrator can modify the `java.security` file and specify policy URLs that reside on another server and that cannot be edited by users. There can be any number of policy URLs (with consecutive numbers) in the policy file. The permissions of all files are combined.

During testing, we don't like to constantly modify these standard files. Therefore, we prefer to explicitly name the policy file that is required for each application. Simply place the permissions into a separate file, say, `MyApp.policy`, and start the interpreter as

```
java -Djava.security.policy=MyApp.policy MyApp
```

For applets, you use instead

```
appletviewer -J-Djava.security.policy=MyApplet.policy MyApplet.html
```

(You can use the `-J` option of the `appletviewer` to pass any command-line argument to the interpreter.)

In these examples, the `MyApp.policy` file is added to the other policies in effect. If you add a second equals sign, such as

```
java -Djava.security.policy==MyApp.policy MyApp
```

then your application uses *only* the specified policy file, and the standard policy files are ignored.

CAUTION: An easy mistake during testing is to accidentally leave a `.java.policy` file that grants a lot of permissions, perhaps even `AllPermission`, in the current directory. If you find that your application doesn't seem to pay attention to the restrictions in your policy file, check for a left-behind `.java.policy` file in your current directory. If you use a UNIX system, this is a particularly easy mistake to make because files whose names start with a period are not displayed by default.

As you saw previously, by default, Java applications do not install a security manager. Therefore, you won't see the effect of policy files until you install one. You can, of course, add a line

```
System.setSecurityManager(new SecurityManager());
```

into your `main` method. Or you can add the command-line option `-Djava.security.manager` when starting the interpreter.

```
java -Djava.security.manager
    -Djava.security.policy=MyApp.policy MyApp
```

In the remainder of this section, you will see in detail how to describe permissions in the policy file. We will describe the entire policy file format, except for code certificates, which we cover later in this chapter.

A policy file contains a sequence of `grant` entries. Each entry has the following form:

```
grant codesource
{
    permission_1;
    permission_2;
    . . .
}
```

The code source contains a code base (which can be omitted if the entry applies to code from all sources) and the names of trusted certificate signers (which can be omitted if signatures are not required for this entry).

The code base is specified as

```
codeBase "url"
```

If the URL ends in a /, then it refers to a directory. Otherwise, it is taken to be the name of a JAR file. For example

```
grant codeBase "www.horstmann.com/classes/" { . . . }
grant codeBase "www.horstmann.com/classes/MyApp.jar" { . . . }
```

The code base is an URL and should always contain forward slashes as file separators, even for file URLs in Windows. For example,

```
grant codeBase "file:C:/myapps/classes/"
```

NOTE: Everyone knows that http URLs start with two slashes (http://). But there seems sufficient confusion about file URLs that the policy file reader accepts two forms of file URLs, namely, file://localFile and file:localFile. Furthermore, a slash before a Windows drive letter is optional. That is, all of the following are acceptable:

```
file:C:/dir/filename.ext
file:/C:/dir/filename.ext
file://C:/dir/filename.ext
file:///C:/dir/filename.ext
```

Actually, we tested that file:////C:/dir/filename.ext is acceptable as well, and we have no explanation for that. In UNIX/Linux, you should use the form

```
file:/dir/filename.ext
```

The permissions have the following structure:

```
permission className targetName, actionList;
```

The class name is the fully qualified class name of the permission class (such as java.io.FilePermission). The *target name* is a permission-specific value, for example, a file or directory name for the file permission, or a host and port for a socket permission. The *action list* is also permission-specific. It is a list of actions, such as read or connect, separated by commas. Some permission classes don't need target names and action lists. Table 9–2 lists the standard permissions and their actions.

As you can see from Table 9–2, most permissions simply permit a particular operation. You can think of the operation as the target with an implied action "permit". These permission classes all extend the BasicPermission class (see Figure 9–5 on page 881). However, the targets for the file, socket, and property permissions are more complex, and we need to investigate them in detail.

Table 9–2 : Permissions and their associated targets and actions

Permission	Target	Action
`java.io.FilePermission`	file target (see text)	read, write, execute, delete
`java.net.SocketPermission`	socket target (see text)	accept, connect, listen, resolve
`java.util.PropertyPermission`	property target (see text)	read, write

`java.lang.RuntimePermission`	`createClassLoader`
	`getClassLoader`
	`setContextClassLoader`
	`createSecurityManager`
	`setSecurityManager`
	`exitVM`
	`setFactory`
	`setIO`
	`modifyThread`
	`modifyThreadGroup`
	`getProtectionDomain`
	`readFileDescriptor`
	`writeFileDescriptor`
	`loadLibrary.`*`libraryName`*
	`accessClassInPackage.`*`packageName`*
	`defineClassInPackage.`*`packageName`*
	`accessDeclaredMembers.`*`className`*
	`queuePrintJob`
	`stopThread`	

`java.awt.AWTPermission`	`showWindowWithoutWarningBanner`
	`accessClipboard`
	`accessEventQueue`
	`listenToAllAWTEvents`
	`readDisplayPixels`	

`java.net.NetPermission`	`setDefaultAuthenticator`
	`specifyStreamHandler`
	`requestPasswordAuthentication`	

`java.lang.reflect.Reflect-Permission`	`suppressAccessChecks`	
`java.io.SerializablePermission`	`enableSubclassImplementation` `enableSubstitution`	

`java.security.SecurityPermission`	`getPolicy`
	`setPolicy`
	`getProperty.key`
	`setProperty.key`
	`insertProvider.`*`providerName`*
	`removeProvider.`*`providerName`*
	`setSystemScope`
	`setIdentityPublicKey`
	`setIdentityInfo`
	`setIdentityCertificate`
	`removeIdentityCertificate`
	`printIdentity`
	`clearProviderProperties.`*`provider-Name`*
	`putProviderProperty.`*`providerName`*
	`removeProviderProperty.`*`provider-Name`*
	`getSignerPrivateKey`
	`setSignerKeyPair`	

`java.security.AllPermission`		

File permission targets can have the following form:

file	a file
directory/	a directory
directory/*	all files in the directory
*	all files in the current directory
directory/–	all files in the directory or one of its subdirectories
–	all files in the current directory or one of its subdirectories
`<<ALL FILES>>`	all files in the file system

For example, the following permission entry gives access to all files in the directory `/myapp` and any of its subdirectories.

```
permission java.io.FilePermission "/myapp/-",
    "read,write,delete";
```

You must use the \\ escape sequence to denote a backslash in a Windows file name.

```
permission java.io.FilePermission "c:\\myapp\\-",
    "read,write,delete";
```

Socket permission targets consist of a host and a port range. Host specifications have the following form:

hostname or *IPaddress*	a single host
`localhost` or the empty string	the local host
*.domainSuffix	any host whose domain ends with the given suffix
*	all hosts

Port ranges are optional and have the form:

`:`n	a single port
`:`n–	all ports numbered n and above
`:`–n	all ports numbered n and below
`:`$n1$–$n2$	all ports in the given range

Here is an example:

```
permission java.net.SocketPermission
    "*.horstmann.com:8000-8999", "connect";
```

Finally, property permission targets can have one of two forms:

property	a specific property
propertyPrefix.*	all properties with the given prefix

Examples are `"java.home"` and `"java.vm.*"`.

For example, the following permission entry allows a program to read all properties that start with `java.vm`.

```
permission java.util.PropertyPermission "java.vm.*", "read";
```

You can use system properties in policy files. The token `${property}` is replaced by the property value. For example, `${user.home}` is replaced by the home directory of the user. Here is a typical use of this system property in a permission entry.

```
permission java.io.FilePermission "${user.home}" "read,write";
```

To create platform-independent policy files, it is a good idea to use the `file.separator` property instead of explicit `/` or `\\` separators. To make this simpler, the special notation `${/}` is a shortcut for `${file.separator}`. For example,

```
permission java.io.FilePermission "${user.home}${/}-"
    "read,write";
```

is a portable entry for granting permission to read and write in the user's home directory and any of its subdirectories.

The SDK comes with a rudimentary tool, called `policytool`, that you can use to edit policy files. When you start the tool, you can read in a policy file. The tool then displays all code sources that have permissions assigned to them (see Figure 9–7). When you click the "Edit Policy Entry" button, then all permissions for that code source are displayed (see Figure 9–8). If you select a permission and click the "Edit Permission" button, you get a dialog that lets you edit the properties of a permission entry (see Figure 9–9). As you can see, the dialog displays the valid choices for targets and actions, which can be a convenience.

Of course, this tool is not suitable for end users who would be completely mystified by most of the settings. We view it as a proof of concept for an administration tool that might be used by system administrators who don't want to worry about the exact file format of the policy files. Still, what's missing is a sensible set of categories (such as low, medium, or high security) that is meaningful to nonexperts. As a general observation, we believe that the Java 2 platform certainly contains all the pieces for a fine-grained security model, but that it could benefit from some polish in delivering these pieces to end users and system administrators.

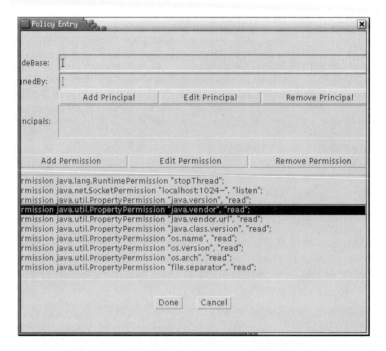

Figure 9–7: The policy tool displaying code sources

Figure 9–8: The policy tool displaying the permissions for a code source

Figure 9–9: Editing a permission with the policy tool

Custom Permissions

In this section, you will see how you can supply your own permission class that users can refer to in their policy files.

To implement your permission class, you extend the `Permission` class and supply the following methods:

- A constructor with two `String` parameters, for the target and the action list
- `String getActions()`
- `boolean equals()`
- `int hashCode()`
- `boolean implies(Permission other)`

The last method is the most important. Permissions have an *ordering*, in which more general permissions *imply* more specific ones. Consider the file permission

```
p1 = new FilePermission("/tmp/-", "read, write");
```

This permission allows reading and writing of any file in the /tmp directory and any of its subdirectories.

Here are some more-specific permissions that this permission implies:

```
p2 = new FilePermission("/tmp/-", "read");
p3 = new FilePermission("/tmp/aFile", "read, write");
p4 = new FilePermission("/tmp/aDirectory/-", "write");
```

In other words, a file permission p1 implies another file permission p2 if

1. The target file set of p1 contains the target file set of p2 ;
2. The action set of p1 contains the action set of p2 .

Here is an example of the use of the `implies` method. When the `FileInput-Stream` constructor wants to open a file for reading, it checks whether it has permission to do so. To carry out that check, a *specific* file permission object is passed to the the `checkPermission` method:

```
checkPermission(new FilePermission(fileName, "read"));
```

The security manager now asks all applicable permissions whether they imply this permission. If any one of them implies it, then the check passes.

In particular, the `AllPermission` implies all other permissions.

If you define your own permission classes, then you need to define a suitable notion of implication for your permission objects. Suppose, for example, that you define a `TVPermission` for a set-top box powered by Java technology. A permission

```
new TVPermission("Tommy:2-12:1900-2200", "watch,record")
```

might allow Tommy to watch and record television channels 2–12 between 19:00 and 22:00. You need to implement the `implies` method so that this permission implies a more specific one, such as

```
new TVPermission("Tommy:4:2000-2100", "watch")
```

Implementing a Permission Class

In the next sample program, we implement a new permission for monitoring the insertion of text into a text area. The program ensures that you cannot add "bad words" such as *sex, drugs,* and *C++* into a text area. We use a custom permission class so that the list of bad words can be supplied in a policy file.

The following subclass of `JTextArea` asks the security manager whether it is ok to add new text.

```
class WordCheckTextArea extends JTextArea
{
   public void append(String text)
   {
      WordCheckPermission p
         = new WordCheckPermission(text, "insert");
      SecurityManager manager = System.getSecurityManager();
      if (manager != null) manager.checkPermission(p);
      super.append(text);
   }
}
```

If the security manager grants the `WordCheckPermission`, then the text is appended. Otherwise, the `checkPermission` method throws an exception.

Word check permissions have two possible actions: `insert` (the permission to insert a specific text) and `avoid` (the permission to add any text that avoids certain bad words). You should run this program with the following policy file:

```
grant
{
    permission WordCheckPermission "sex,drugs,C++", "avoid";
};
```

This policy file grants the permission to insert any text that avoids the bad words *sex, drugs,* and *C++.*

When designing the WordCheckPermission class, we must pay particular attention to the implies method. Here are the rules that control whether permission p1 implies permission p2.

1. If p1 has action avoid and p2 has action insert, then the target of p2 must avoid all words in p1. For example, the permission

    ```
    WordCheckPermission "sex,drugs,C++", "avoid"
    ```

    implies the permission

    ```
    WordCheckPermission "Mary had a little lamb", "insert"
    ```

2. If p1 and p2 both have action avoid, then the word set of p2 must contain all words in the word set of p1. For example, the permission

    ```
    WordCheckPermission "sex,drugs,C++", "avoid"
    ```

    implies the permission

    ```
    WordCheckPermission "sex,drugs", "avoid"
    ```

3. If p1 and p2 both have action insert, then the text of p1 must contain the text of p2. For example, the permission

    ```
    WordCheckPermission "Mary had a little lamb", "insert"
    ```

    implies the permission

    ```
    WordCheckPermission "a little lamb", "insert"
    ```

You can find the implementation of this class in Example 9–5.

Note that you retrieve the permission target with the confusingly named getName method of the Permission class.

Since permissions are described by a pair of strings in policy files, permission classes need to be prepared to parse these strings. In particular, we use the following method to transform the comma-separated list of bad words of an avoid permission into a genuine Set.

```
public Set badWordSet()
{
    StringTokenizer tokenizer
        = new StringTokenizer(getName(), ",");
    Set set = new HashSet();
    while (tokenizer.hasMoreTokens())
        set.add(tokenizer.nextToken());
    return set;
}
```

This code allows us to use the `equals` and `containsAll` methods to compare sets. As you saw in Chapter 2, the `equals` method of a set class finds two sets to be equal if they contain the same elements in any order. For example, the sets resulting from `"sex,drugs,C++"` and `"C++,drugs,sex"` are equal.

> CAUTION: Make sure that your permission class is a public class. The policy file loader cannot load classes with package visibility outside the boot class path, and it silently ignores any classes that it cannot find.

The program in Example 9–5 shows how the `WordCheckPermission` class works. Type any text into the text field and press the "Insert" button. If the security check passes, the text is appended to the text area. If not, an error message appears (see Figure 9–10).

Make sure to start the program with the appropriate policy file.

```
java -Djava.security.policy=PermissionTest.policy
    PermissionTest
```

Otherwise, all attempts to insert text will fail.

Figure 9–10: The `PermissionTest` program

> CAUTION: If you carefully look at Figure 9–10, you will see that the frame window has a warning border with the misleading caption `"Java Applet Window."` The window caption is determined by the `showWindowWithoutWarningBanner` target of the `java.awt.AWTPermission`. If you like, you can edit the policy file to grant that permission.

Example 9–4: PermissionTest.java

```
1. import java.awt.*;
2. import java.awt.event.*;
```

```
3. import java.io.*;
4. import java.net.*;
5. import java.security.*;
6. import java.util.*;
7. import javax.swing.*;
8.
9. /**
10.    This class demonstrates the custom WordCheckPermission.
11. */
12. public class PermissionTest
13. {
14.    public static void main(String[] args)
15.    {
16.       System.setSecurityManager(new SecurityManager());
17.       JFrame frame = new PermissionTestFrame();
18.       frame.setDefaultCloseOperation(JFrame.EXIT_ON_CLOSE);
19.       frame.show();
20.    }
21. }
22.
23. /**
24.    This frame contains a text field for inserting words into
25.    a text area that is protected from "bad words".
26. */
27. class PermissionTestFrame extends JFrame
28. {
29.    public PermissionTestFrame()
30.    {
31.       setTitle("PermissionTest");
32.       setSize(WIDTH, HEIGHT);
33.
34.       textField = new JTextField(20);
35.       JPanel panel = new JPanel();
36.       panel.add(textField);
37.       JButton openButton = new JButton("Insert");
38.       panel.add(openButton);
39.       openButton.addActionListener(new
40.          ActionListener()
41.          {
42.             public void actionPerformed(ActionEvent event)
43.             {
44.                insertWords(textField.getText());
45.             }
46.          });
47.
48.       Container contentPane = getContentPane();
49.       contentPane.add(panel, BorderLayout.NORTH);
50.
51.       textArea = new WordCheckTextArea();
```

```
52.         contentPane.add(new JScrollPane(textArea),
53.             BorderLayout.CENTER);
54.      }
55.
56.      /**
57.         Tries to insert words into the text area.
58.         Displays a dialog if the attempt fails.
59.         @param words the words to insert
60.      */
61.      public void insertWords(String words)
62.      {
63.         try
64.         {
65.             textArea.append(words + "\n");
66.         }
67.         catch (SecurityException e)
68.         {
69.             JOptionPane.showMessageDialog(this,
70.                 "I am sorry, but I cannot do that.");
71.         }
72.      }
73.
74.      private JTextField textField;
75.      private WordCheckTextArea textArea;
76.      private static final int WIDTH = 400;
77.      private static final int HEIGHT = 300;
78. }
79.
80. /**
81.     A text area whose append method makes a security check
82.     to see that no bad words are added.
83. */
84. class WordCheckTextArea extends JTextArea
85. {
86.     public void append(String text)
87.     {
88.         WordCheckPermission p
89.             = new WordCheckPermission(text, "insert");
90.         SecurityManager manager = System.getSecurityManager();
91.         if (manager != null) manager.checkPermission(p);
92.         super.append(text);
93.     }
94. }
```

Example 9–5: WordCheckPermission.java

```
1. import java.security.*;
2. import java.util.*;
3.
4. /**
```

```
5.    A permission that checks for bad words.
6. */
7. public class WordCheckPermission extends Permission
8. {
9.    /**
10.       Constructs a word check permission
11.       @param target a comma separated word list
12.       @param anAction "insert" or "avoid"
13.    */
14.    public WordCheckPermission(String target, String anAction)
15.    {
16.       super(target);
17.       action = anAction;
18.    }
19.
20.    public String getActions() { return action; }
21.
22.    public boolean equals(Object other)
23.    {
24.       if (other == null) return false;
25.       if (!getClass().equals(other.getClass())) return false;
26.       WordCheckPermission b = (WordCheckPermission)other;
27.       if (!action.equals(b.action)) return false;
28.       if (action.equals("insert"))
29.          return getName().equals(b.getName());
30.       else if (action.equals("avoid"))
31.          return badWordSet().equals(b.badWordSet());
32.       else return false;
33.    }
34.
35.    public int hashCode()
36.    {
37.       return getName().hashCode() + action.hashCode();
38.    }
39.
40.    public boolean implies(Permission other)
41.    {
42.       if (!(other instanceof WordCheckPermission)) return false;
43.       WordCheckPermission b = (WordCheckPermission)other;
44.       if (action.equals("insert"))
45.       {
46.          return b.action.equals("insert") &&
47.             getName().indexOf(b.getName()) >= 0;
48.       }
49.       else if (action.equals("avoid"))
50.       {
51.          if (b.action.equals("avoid"))
52.             return b.badWordSet().containsAll(badWordSet());
53.          else if (b.action.equals("insert"))
```

```
54.              {
55.                  Iterator iter = badWordSet().iterator();
56.                  while (iter.hasNext())
57.                  {
58.                      String badWord = (String)iter.next();
59.                      if (b.getName().indexOf(badWord) >= 0)
60.                          return false;
61.                  }
62.                  return true;
63.              }
64.              else return false;
65.          }
66.          else return false;
67.      }
68.
69.      /**
70.          Gets the bad words that this permission rule describes.
71.          @return a set of the bad words
72.      */
73.      public Set badWordSet()
74.      {
75.          StringTokenizer tokenizer
76.              = new StringTokenizer(getName(), ",");
77.          Set set = new HashSet();
78.          while (tokenizer.hasMoreTokens())
79.              set.add(tokenizer.nextToken());
80.          return set;
81.      }
82.
83.      private String action;
84. }
```

 java.security.Permission

- `Permission(String name)`
  constructs a permission with the given target name.

- `String getName()`
  returns the target name of this permission.

- `boolean implies(Permission other)`
  checks whether this permission implies the other permission. That is the case
  if the other permission describes a more specific condition that is a consequence of the condition described by this permission.

A Custom Security Manager

In this section, we show you how to build a simple yet complete security manager. We call it the `WordCheckSecurityManager`. It monitors all file access and

ensures that you can't open a text file if it contains forbidden words such as *sex, drugs,* and *C++.*

We monitor file access by overriding the `checkPermission` method of the standard security manager class. If the permission isn't a file read permission, then we simply call `super.checkPermission`. To check that it is permissible to read from a file, we open the file and scan its contents. We grant access to the file only when it doesn't contain any of the forbidden words. (We only monitor files with extension `.txt` since we don't want to block access to system and property files.)

```
public class WordCheckSecurityManager extends SecurityManager
{
   public void checkPermission(Permission p)
   {
      if (p instanceof FilePermission
         && p.getActions().equals("read"))
      {
         String fileName = p.getName();
         if (containsBadWords(fileName))
            throw new SecurityException("Bad words in "
               + fileName);
      }
      else super.checkPermission(p);
   }
   . . .
}
```

NOTE: Another way of being notified of file read requests is to override the `checkRead` method. The `SecurityManager` class implements this method to call the `checkPermission` method with a `FilePermission` object. There are close to 30 methods for other security checks that all call the `checkPermission` method—see the API note at the end of this section. These methods exist for historical reasons. The permission system has been introduced in the Java 2 platform. We recommend that you do not override these methods but instead carry out all permission checks in the `checkPermission` method.

There is just one catch in our file check scenario. Consider one possible flow of events.

- A method of some class opens a file.
- Then, the security manager springs into action and uses its `checkPermission` method.
- The `checkPermission` method calls the `containsBadWords` method.

But the `containsBadWords` method must itself read the file to check its contents, which calls the security manager again! This would result in an infinite regression unless the security manager has a way of finding out in which context it was called. The `getClassContext` method is the way to find out how the method was called. This method returns an array of class objects that gives all the classes whose calls are currently pending. For example, when the security manager is called for the first time, that array is

```
class WordCheckSecurityManager
class SecurityManager
class java.io.FileInputStream
class java.io.FileReader
class SecurityManagerFrame
. . .
class java.awt.EventDispatchThread
```

The class at index 0 gives the currently executing call. Unfortunately, you only get to see the classes, not the names of the pending methods. When the security manager itself attempts to open the file, it is called again and the `getClassContext` method returns the following array.

```
class WordCheckSecurityManager
class SecurityManager
class java.io.FileInputStream
class java.io.FileReader
class WordCheckSecurityManager
class WordCheckSecurityManager
class SecurityManager
class java.io.FileInputStream
class java.io.FileReader
class SecurityManagerFrame
. . .
class java.awt.EventDispatchThread
```

In this case, the security manager should permit the file access. How can we do this? We could test whether

```
getClassContext()[0] == getClassContext()[4]
```

but this approach is fragile. Here's an obvious case of where it can go wrong: Imagine that if the implementation changed, for example, so the `FileReader` constructor calls the security manager directly, then the test would be meaningless because the positions would not be the same in the array. It is far more robust to test whether *any* of the pending calls came from the same security manager.

Here is a method that carries out this test. Since this method is called from `checkPermission`, there are at least two copies of the security manager class on the call stack. We skip these first and then look for another instance of the same security manager.

```
boolean inSameManager()
{
    Class[] cc = getClassContext();

    // skip past current set of calls to this manager
    int i = 0;
    while (i < cc.length && cc[0] == cc[i])
        i++;

    // check if there is another call to this manager
    while (i < cc.length)
    {
        if (cc[0] == cc[i]) return true;
        i++;
    }
    return false;
}
```

We call this method in the `checkPermission` method. If we find that the security manager is invoked recursively, then we do not call the `containsBadWords` method again.

```
if (p instanceof FilePermission
    && p.getActions().equals("read"))
{
    if (inSameManager())
        return;
    String fileName = p.getName();
    if (containsBadWords(fileName))
        throw new SecurityException("Bad words in "
            + fileName);
}
```

Example 9–6 shows a program that puts this security manager to work. The security manager is installed in the `main` method. When running the program, you can specify a file. The program will load its contents into the text area. However, if the file fails the security check, the program catches the security exception and displays a message instead (see Figure 9–11). For example, you can display "Alice in Wonderland," but the program refuses to load "The Count of Monte Cristo."

NOTE: You may wonder why we don't use a `JFileChooser` to select a file name. The `JFileChooser` class tries to read the files that it displays, probably to find out which of them are files and which are directories.

Figure 9–11: The SecurityManagerTest program

You need to be careful how you invoke this program. The WordCheckSecurity-
Manager class itself needs to be given AllPermission. The reason for this is subtle.
The WordCheckSecurityManager class calls the SecurityManager superclass for
all permissions other than file read permissions. When the SecurityManager class
evaluates a permission, it looks whether *all methods on the call stack* should be granted
that particular permission. The WordCheckSecurityManager is one of those classes.
But it is not a system class, so you must explicitly grant it all permissions without also
granting all permissions to the other classes of the program.

To separate the WordCheckSecurityManager class files from the other class
files, make a JAR file containing just that class file.

```
jar cvf WordCheck.jar WordCheckSecurityManager.class
```

Then delete the WordCheckSecurityManager.class file.

Next, create a policy file, WordCheck.policy, with the following contents:

```
grant codeBase "file:WordCheck.jar"
{
    permission java.security.AllPermission;
};
```

This policy grants all permissions to the classes in the WordCheck.jar file.
Finally, start the application as follows:

```
java -Djava.security.policy=WordCheck.policy
    -classpath WordCheck.jar:. SecurityManagerTest
```

TIP: If you are thinking of changing the security manager in your own programs, you
should first investigate whether you can instead use the standard security manager
and a custom permission, as described in the preceding section. Writing a security
manager is error prone and can cause subtle security flaws. It is much better to use
the standard security manager and augment the permission system instead.

Example 9–6: SecurityManagerTest.java

```
1. import java.awt.*;
2. import java.awt.event.*;
3. import java.io.*;
4. import java.net.*;
5. import java.util.*;
6. import javax.swing.*;
7.
8. /**
9.    This class demonstrates the use of a custom security manager
10.    that prohibits the reading of text files containing bad words.
11. */
12. public class SecurityManagerTest
13. {
14.    public static void main(String[] args)
15.    {
16.       System.setSecurityManager(new WordCheckSecurityManager());
17.       JFrame frame = new SecurityManagerFrame();
18.       frame.setDefaultCloseOperation(JFrame.EXIT_ON_CLOSE);
19.       frame.show();
20.    }
21. }
22.
23. /**
24.    This frame contains a text field to enter a file name and
25.    a text area to show the contents of the loaded file.
26. */
27. class SecurityManagerFrame extends JFrame
28. {
29.    public SecurityManagerFrame()
30.    {
31.       setTitle("SecurityManagerTest");
32.       setSize(WIDTH, HEIGHT);
33.
34.       fileNameField = new JTextField(20);
35.       JPanel panel = new JPanel();
36.       panel.add(new JLabel("Text file:"));
37.       panel.add(fileNameField);
38.       JButton openButton = new JButton("Open");
39.       panel.add(openButton);
40.       openButton.addActionListener(new
41.          ActionListener()
42.          {
43.             public void actionPerformed(ActionEvent event)
44.             {
45.                loadFile(fileNameField.getText());
46.             }
47.          });
```

```
48.
49.         Container contentPane = getContentPane();
50.         contentPane.add(panel, "North");
51.
52.         fileText = new JTextArea();
53.         contentPane.add(new JScrollPane(fileText), "Center");
54.      }
55.
56.      /**
57.         Attempt to load a file into the text area. If a security
58.         exception is caught, a message is inserted into the text
59.         area instead.
60.         @param filename the file name
61.      */
62.      public void loadFile(String filename)
63.      {
64.         try
65.         {
66.            fileText.setText("");
67.            BufferedReader in
68.               = new BufferedReader(new FileReader(filename));
69.            String s;
70.            while ((s = in.readLine()) != null)
71.            fileText.append(s + "\n");
72.            in.close();
73.         }
74.         catch (IOException e)
75.         {
76.            fileText.append(e + "\n");
77.         }
78.         catch (SecurityException e)
79.         {
80.            fileText.append("I am sorry, but I cannot do that.");
81.         }
82.      }
83.
84.      private JTextField fileNameField;
85.      private JTextArea fileText;
86.      private static final int WIDTH = 400;
87.      private static final int HEIGHT = 300;
88. }
```

Example 9–7: WordCheckSecurityManager.java

```
1. import java.io.*;
2. import java.security.*;
3.
4. /**
5.    This security manager checks whether bad words are
```

```
6.     encountered when reading a file.
7. */
8. public class WordCheckSecurityManager extends SecurityManager
9. {
10.    public void checkPermission(Permission p)
11.    {
12.       if (p instanceof FilePermission
13.          && p.getActions().equals("read"))
14.       {
15.          if (inSameManager())
16.             return;
17.          String fileName = p.getName();
18.          if (containsBadWords(fileName))
19.             throw new SecurityException("Bad words in "
20.                + fileName);
21.       }
22.       else super.checkPermission(p);
23.    }
24.
25.    /**
26.       Returns true if this manager is called while there
27.       is another call to itself pending.
28.       @return true if there are multiple calls to this manager
29.    */
30.    public boolean inSameManager()
31.    {
32.       Class[] cc = getClassContext();
33.
34.       // skip past current set of calls to this manager
35.       int i = 0;
36.       while (i < cc.length && cc[0] == cc[i])
37.          i++;
38.
39.       // check if there is another call to this manager
40.       while (i < cc.length)
41.       {
42.          if (cc[0] == cc[i]) return true;
43.          i++;
44.       }
45.       return false;
46.    }
47.
48.    /**
49.       Checks if a file contains bad words.
50.       @param fileName the name of the file
51.       @return true if the file name ends with .txt and it
52.       contains at least one bad word.
53.    */
```

```
54.    boolean containsBadWords(String fileName)
55.    {
56.       if (!fileName.toLowerCase().endsWith(".txt")) return false;
57.           // only check text files
58.       BufferedReader in = null;
59.       try
60.       {
61.           in = new BufferedReader(new FileReader(fileName));
62.           String s;
63.           while ((s = in.readLine()) != null)
64.           {
65.               for (int i = 0; i < badWords.length; i++)
66.               if (s.toLowerCase().indexOf(badWords[i]) != -1)
67.                   return true;
68.           }
69.           in.close();
70.           return false;
71.       }
72.       catch(IOException e)
73.       {
74.           return true;
75.       }
76.       finally
77.       {
78.           if (in != null)
79.               try { in.close(); } catch (IOException e) {}
80.       }
81.    }
82.
83.    private String[] badWords = { "sex", "drugs", "c++" };
84. }
```

java.lang.System

- void setSecurityManager(SecurityManager s)

  sets the security manager for the remainder of this application. If s is null, no action is taken. This method throws a security exception if the current security manager does not permit the installation of a new security manager.

- SecurityManager getSecurityManager()

  gets the system security manager; returns null if none is installed.

java.lang.SecurityManager

- Class[] getClassContext()

  returns an array of the classes for the currently executing methods. The element at position 0 is the class of the currently running method, the element at position 1 is the class of the caller of the current method, and so on. Only the class names, not the method names, are available.

- `void checkCreateClassLoader()`
  checks whether the current thread can create a class loader.

- `void checkAccess(Thread g)`
  checks whether the current thread can invoke the `stop`, `suspend`, `resume`, `setPriority`, `setName`, and `setDaemon` methods on the thread `g`.

- `void checkAccess(ThreadGroup g)`
  checks whether the current thread can invoke the `stop`, `suspend`, `resume`, `destroy`, and `setMaxPriority` methods on the thread group `g`.

- `void checkExit(int status)`
  checks whether the current thread can exit the virtual machine with status code `status`.

- `void checkExec(String cmd)`
  checks whether the current thread can execute the system command `cmd`.

- `void checkLink(String lib)`
  checks whether the current thread can dynamically load the library `lib`.

- `void checkRead(FileDescriptor fd)`
- `void checkRead(String file)`
- `void checkWrite(FileDescriptor fd)`
- `void checkWrite(String file)`
- `void checkDelete(String file)`
  check whether the current thread can read, write, or delete the given file.

- `void checkRead(String file, Object context)`
  checks whether another thread can read the given file. The other thread must have called `getSecurityContext`, and the return value of that call is passed as the value of the `context` parameter.

- `void checkConnect(String host, int port)`
  checks whether the current thread can connect to the given host at the given port.

- `void checkConnect(String host, int port, Object context)`
  checks whether another thread can connect to the given host at the given port. The other thread must have called `getSecurityContext`, and the return value of that call is passed as the `context` parameter.

- `void checkListen(int port)`
  checks whether the current thread can listen for a connection to the given local port.

- `void checkAccept(String host, int port)`
  checks whether the current thread can accept a socket connection from the given host and port.

- `void checkSetFactory()`
  checks whether the current thread can set the socket or stream handler factory.

- `void checkPropertiesAccess()`
- `void checkPropertyAccess(String key)`
  check whether the current thread can access the system properties or the system property with the given key.

- `void checkSecurityAccess(String key)`
  checks whether the current thread can access the security property with the given key.

- `boolean checkTopLevelWindow(Object window)`
  returns `true` if the given window can be displayed without a security warning.

- `void checkPrintJobAccess()`
  checks whether the current thread can access print jobs.

- `void checkSystemClipboardAccess()`
  checks whether the current thread can access the system clipboard.

- `void checkAwtEventQueueAccess()`
  checks whether the current thread can access the AWT event queue.

- `void checkPackageAccess(String pkg)`
  checks whether the current thread can load classes from the given package. This method is called from the `loadClass` method of some class loaders.

- `void checkPackageDefinition(String pkg)`
  checks whether the current thread can define new classes that are in the given package. This method is often called from the `loadClass` method of a custom class loader.

- `void checkMemberAccess(Class cl, int member_id)`
  checks whether the current thread can access a member of a class. (See Chapter 11 for information on how to obtain member IDs.)

User Authentication

Starting with SDK 1.4, it is possible to attach permissions to users, so that you can specify, for example, that Harry has a particular `FilePermission` but other users do not. The syntax is like this:

```
grant principal com.sun.security.auth.UnixPrincipal "harry"
{
    permission java.io.FilePermission "<<ALL FILES>>";
};
```

Here, `com.sun.security.auth.UnixPrincipal` is a class whose `getName` method returns the UNIX login name.

The Java Authentication and Authorization Service (JAAS) also supports NT logins, Kerberos authentication, and certificate-based authentication.

You must program a user login to allow the security manager to check such a grant statement. Here is the basic outline of the login code:

```
try
{
    System.setSecurityManager(new SecurityManager());
    LoginContext context = new LoginContext("Login1");
    context.login();
    System.out.println("Authentication successful.");
    // get the authenticated Subject
    Subject subject = context.getSubject();
    . . .
    context.logout();
}
catch (LoginException exception)
{
    exception.printStackTrace();
}
```

Now the `subject` denotes the individual who has been authenticated.

The string parameter `"Login1"` in the `LoginContext` constructor refers to an entry with the same name in the JAAS configuration file. Here is a sample configuration file:

```
Login1
{
    com.sun.security.auth.module.UnixLoginModule required;
};

Login2
{
    com.whizzbang.auth.module.SmartCardModule sufficient;
    com.whizzbang.auth.module.RetinaScanModule sufficient;
}
```

This configuration file requires that the user have a UNIX login for the first login policy. It is also possible to list other authentication modules, and label them `sufficient`, `requisite`, or `optional`. The authentication modules are executed in turn, until a `sufficient` module succeeds, a `requisite` module fails, or the end of the module list is reached.

Of course, there are no biometric login modules contained in the SDK. The SDK contains the following modules in the `com.sun.security.auth.module` package:

```
UnixLoginModule
NTLoginModule
```

```
Krb5LoginModule
JndiLoginModule
KeyStoreLoginModule
```

A login authenticates a *subject*, which can have multiple *principals*. As you have seen in the `grant` statement, principals govern permissions. Some permissions may be tied to a user name, but more likely, permissions are tied to group membership. The `UnixNumericGroupPrincipal` class can be used to test for membership in a UNIX group.

When a user has logged in, then you need to run the code that requires checking of principals in a separate access control context. Use the static `doAs` method to start a new `PrivilegedAction` whose `run` method executes the code:

```
Subject.doAs(subject, new
    PrivilegedAction()
    {
        public Object run()
        {
          // actions here are checked against subject principals
            . . .
            return null;
        }
    });
```

If the actions can throw checked exceptions, then you need to implement the `PrivilegedExceptionAction` interface instead.

The program in Example 9–8 demonstrates how to restrict permissions to certain users. The `AuthTest` program runs another Java program after performing a login. The name of the other program and its command line arguments are given on the command line, such as

```
java options AuthTest LineCount ../../gutenberg/alice30.txt
```

Here, `LineCount` is another program that simply counts the lines of all files specified on the command line (see Example 9–9).

To make this example work, you need to package the code for the login classes and the program classes into two separate JAR files:

```
javac AuthTest.java
jar cvf login.jar AuthTest*.class
javac LineCount.java
jar cvf prog.jar LineCount.class
```

If you look at the policy file in Example 9–10, you will see that the UNIX user with the name `harry` has the permission to read all files. Change `harry` to your login name. (If you run this test on Windows NT, change UNIX to NT in both `AuthTest.policy` and `jaas.config`—see Example 9–11). Then run the command

```
java -classpath "login.jar:prog.jar"
    -Djava.security.policy=AuthTest.policy
    -Djava.security.auth.login.config=jaas.config
    AuthTest LineCount ../../gutenberg/alice30.txt
```

On Windows, use

```
java -classpath "login.jar;prog.jar"
    -Djava.security.policy=AuthTest.policy
    -Djava.security.auth.login.config=jaas.config
    AuthTest LineCount ..\..\gutenberg\alice30.txt
```

The `LineCount` program should now display a line count. However, if you change the login name in the `AuthTest.policy` file, then a security exception should be thrown because you no longer have the required permission.

> CAUTION: Be careful to follow these instructions *exactly.* It is very easy to get the setup wrong by making seemingly innocuous changes. In particular, note that the permissions must be added *both* to the grant clause of the `login.jar` file and the grant clause of the principal. (Only the intersection of the rights is granted when the `doAs` method executes.) Also, you must add the program files to a JAR file. If you use the class path `"login.jar:."`, then the permissions are not applied to the classes loaded from the file system. That may well be a bug.

In this section, we have only scratched the surface of the JAAS capabilities. For more information, read the JAAS Reference Guide that is a part of the SDK documentation.

Example 9–8: AuthTest.java

```
1. import java.lang.reflect.*;
2. import java.security.*;
3. import javax.security.auth.*;
4. import javax.security.auth.login.*;
5.
6. /**
7.    This program authenticates a user via the Unix login
8.    and then executes the program specified by the command line
9.    with the user's principals.
10. */
11. public class AuthTest
12. {
13.     public static void main(final String[] args)
14.     {
15.         try
16.         {
17.             System.setSecurityManager(new SecurityManager());
18.
```

```
19.          LoginContext context = new LoginContext("Login1");
20.          context.login();
21.          System.out.println("Authentication successful.");
22.          Subject subject = context.getSubject();
23.          Subject.doAs(subject, new
24.             PrivilegedExceptionAction()
25.             {
26.                public Object run() throws Exception
27.                {
28.                   // invoke the main method of the class
29.                   // specified in args[0], with command line
30.                   // arguments args[1] args[2] . . .
31.                   Class cl = Class.forName(args[0]);
32.                   Method mainMethod = cl.getMethod("main",
33.                      new Class[] { String[].class });
34.                   String[] args1 = new String[args.length - 1];
35.                   System.arraycopy(args, 1,
36.                      args1, 0, args1.length);
37.                   mainMethod.invoke(null,
38.                      new Object[] { args1 });
39.                   return null;
40.                }
41.             });
42.
43.          context.logout();
44.       }
45.       catch (LoginException exception)
46.       {
47.          exception.printStackTrace();
48.       }
49.       catch (PrivilegedActionException exception)
50.       {
51.          exception.printStackTrace();
52.       }
53.    }
54. }
```

Example 9–9: LineCount.java

```
1. import java.io.*;
2.
3. /**
4.    This is a demonstration program that can be launched from
5.    the AuthTest program. It simply counts the lines in all
6.    files whose names are specified as command-line arguments.
7. */
8. public class LineCount
9. {
10.    public static void main(String[] args) throws Exception
11.    {
```

```
12.        for (int i = 0; i < args.length; i++)
13.        {
14.           int count = 0;
15.           String line;
16.           BufferedReader reader
17.              = new BufferedReader(new FileReader(args[i]));
18.           while ((line = reader.readLine()) != null) count++;
19.           System.out.println(args[i] + ": " + count);
20.        }
21.     }
22. }
```

Example 9-10: AuthTest.policy

```
1. grant codebase "file:login.jar"
2. {
3.    permission javax.security.auth.AuthPermission
4.       "createLoginContext.Login1";
5.    permission javax.security.auth.AuthPermission "doAs";
6.    permission java.io.FilePermission "<<ALL FILES>>", "read";
7. };
8.
9. grant principal com.sun.security.auth.UnixPrincipal "harry"
10. {
11.    permission java.io.FilePermission "<<ALL FILES>>", "read";
12. };
```

Example 9-11: jaas.config

```
1. Login1
2. {
3.    com.sun.security.auth.module.UnixLoginModule required;
4. };
```

`javax.security.auth.login.LoginContext`

- `LoginContext(String name)`
  constructs a login context. The name corresponds to the login descriptor in the JAAS configuration file.

- `void login()`
  establishes a login or throws a `LoginException` if the login failed. Invokes the `login` method on the managers in the JAAS configuration file.

- `void logout()`
  logs out the subject. Invokes the `logout` method on the managers in the JAAS configuration file.

- `Subject getSubject()`
  returns the authenticated subject.

`javax.security.auth.Subject`

- `Set getPrincipals()`
  gets the principals of this subject.

- `static Object doAs(Subject subject, PrivilegedAction action)`
- `static Object doAs(Subject subject, PrivilegedActionException action)`
  execute the privileged action on behalf of the subject. Returns the return value of the `run` method.

`java.security.PrivilegedAction`

- `Object run()`
  You must define this method to execute the code that you want to have executed on behalf of a subject.

`java.security.PrivilegedExceptionAction`

- `Object run()`
  You must define this method to execute the code that you want to have executed on behalf of a subject. This method may throw any checked exceptions.

`java.security.Principal`

- `String getName()`
  returns the identifying name of this principal.

Digital Signatures

As we said earlier, applets were what started the craze over the Java platform. In practice, people discovered that although they could write animated applets like the famous "nervous text" applet, applets could not do a whole lot of useful stuff in the JDK 1.0 security model. For example, because applets under JDK 1.0 were so closely supervised, they couldn't do much good on a corporate intranet, even though relatively little risk attaches to executing an applet from your company's secure intranet. It quickly became clear to Sun that for applets to become truly useful, it was important for users to be able to assign *different* levels of security, depending on where the applet originated. If an applet comes from a trusted supplier and it has not been tampered with, the user of that applet can then decide whether to give the applet more privileges.

This added control is now possible because of the applet-signing mechanism in Java 1.1. To give more trust to an applet, we need to know two things:

1. Where did the applet come from?

2. Was the code corrupted in transit?

In the past 50 years, mathematicians and computer scientists have developed sophisticated algorithms for ensuring the integrity of data and for electronic signatures. The `java.security` package contains implementations of many of these algorithms. Fortunately, you don't need to understand the underlying mathematics to use the algorithms in the `java.security` package. In the next sections, you will see how message digests can detect changes in data files and how digital signatures can prove the identity of the signer.

Message Digests

A message digest is a digital fingerprint of a block of data. For example, the so-called SHA1 (secure hash algorithm #1) condenses any data block, no matter how long, into a sequence of 160 bits (20 bytes). As with real fingerprints, one hopes that no two messages have the same SHA1 fingerprint. Of course, that cannot be true—there are only 2^{160} SHA1 fingerprints, so there must be some messages with the same fingerprint. But 2^{160} is so large that the probability of duplication occurring is negligible. How negligible? According to James Walsh in *True Odds: How Risks Affect Your Everyday Life* [Merritt Publishing 1996], the chance that you will die from being struck by lightning is about one in 30,000. Now, think of 9 other people, for example, your 9 least favorite managers or professors. The chance that you and *all of them* will die from lightning strikes is higher than that of a forged message having the same SHA1 fingerprint as the original. (Of course, more than 10 people, none of whom you are likely to know, will die from lightning. But we are talking about the far slimmer chance that *your particular choice* of people will be wiped out.)

A message digest has two essential properties.

1. If one bit or several bits of the data are changed, then the message digest also changes.

2. A forger who is in possession of a given message cannot construct a fake message that has the same message digest as the original.

The second property is again a matter of probabilities, of course. Consider the following message by the billionaire father:

> *"Upon my death, my property shall be divided equally among my children; however, my son George shall receive nothing."*

That message has an SHA1 fingerprint of

```
2D 8B 35 F3 BF 49 CD B1 94 04 E0 66 21 2B 5E 57 70 49 E1 7E
```

The distrustful father has deposited the message with one attorney and the fingerprint with another. Now, suppose George can bribe the lawyer holding the message. He wants to change the message so that Bill gets nothing. Of course, that changes the fingerprint to a completely different bit pattern:

```
2A 33 0B 4B B3 FE CC 1C 9D 5C 01 A7 09 51 0B 49 AC 8F 98 92
```

Can George find some other wording that matches the fingerprint? If he had been the proud owner of a billion computers from the time the Earth was formed, each computing a million messages a second, he would not yet have found a message he could substitute.

A number of algorithms have been designed to compute these message digests. The two best-known are SHA1, the secure hash algorithm developed by the National Institute of Standards and Technology, and MD5, an algorithm invented by Ronald Rivest of MIT. Both algorithms scramble the bits of a message in ingenious ways. For details about these algorithms, see, for example, *Cryptography and Network Security* by William Stallings [Prentice Hall 1998]. Note that recently, subtle regularities have been discovered in MD5, and some cryptographers recommend avoiding it and using SHA1 for that reason. (Both algorithms are easy to compute.)

The Java programming language implements both SHA1 and MD5. The MessageDigest class is a *factory* for creating objects that encapsulate the fingerprinting algorithms. It has a static method, called getInstance, that returns an object of a class that extends the MessageDigest class. This means the MessageDigest class serves double duty:

- As a factory class;
- As the superclass for all message digest algorithms.

For example, here is how you obtain an object that can compute SHA fingerprints.

```
MessageDigest alg = MessageDigest.getInstance("SHA-1");
```

(To get an object that can compute MD5, use the string "MD5" as the argument to getInstance.)

After you have obtained a MessageDigest object, you feed it all the bytes in the message by repeatedly calling the update method. For example, the following code passes all bytes in a file to the alg object created above to do the fingerprinting:

```
FileInputStream in = new FileInputStream(f);
int ch;

while ((ch = in.read()) != -1)
    alg.update((byte)ch);
```

Alternatively, if you have the bytes in an array, you can update the entire array at once:

```
byte[] bytes = . . .;
alg.update(bytes);
```

When you are done, call the `digest` method. This method pads the input—as required by the fingerprinting algorithm—does the computation, and returns the digest as an array of bytes.

```
byte[] hash = alg.digest();
```

The program in Example 9–12 computes a message digest, using either SHA or MD5. You can load the data to be digested from a file, or you can type a message in the text area. Figure 9–12 shows the application.

Figure 9–12: Computing a message digest

Example 9–12: MessageDigestTest.java

```
1. import java.io.*;
2. import java.security.*;
3. import java.awt.*;
4. import java.awt.event.*;
5. import javax.swing.*;
6.
7. /**
8.    This program computes the message digest of a file
9.    or the contents of a text area.
10. */
11. public class MessageDigestTest
12. {
13.    public static void main(String[] args)
14.    {
15.       JFrame frame = new MessageDigestFrame();
16.       frame.setDefaultCloseOperation(JFrame.EXIT_ON_CLOSE);
17.       frame.show();
18.    }
19. }
20.
21. /**
22.    This frame contains a menu for computing the message
23.    digest of a file or text area, radio buttons to toggle between
```

```
24.    SHA-1 and MD5, a text area, and a text field to show the
25.    message digest.
26. */
27. class MessageDigestFrame extends JFrame
28. {
29.    public MessageDigestFrame()
30.    {
31.       setTitle("MessageDigestTest");
32.       setSize(WIDTH, HEIGHT);
33.
34.       JPanel panel = new JPanel();
35.       ButtonGroup group = new ButtonGroup();
36.       addRadioButton(panel, "SHA-1", group);
37.       addRadioButton(panel, "MD5", group);
38.
39.       Container contentPane = getContentPane();
40.
41.       contentPane.add(panel, BorderLayout.NORTH);
42.       contentPane.add(new JScrollPane(message),
43.          BorderLayout.CENTER);
44.       contentPane.add(digest, BorderLayout.SOUTH);
45.       digest.setFont(new Font("Monospaced", Font.PLAIN, 12));
46.
47.       setAlgorithm("SHA-1");
48.
49.       JMenuBar menuBar = new JMenuBar();
50.       JMenu menu = new JMenu("File");
51.       JMenuItem fileDigestItem = new JMenuItem("File digest");
52.       fileDigestItem.addActionListener(new
53.          ActionListener()
54.          {
55.             public void actionPerformed(ActionEvent event)
56.             {
57.                loadFile();
58.             }
59.          });
60.       menu.add(fileDigestItem);
61.       JMenuItem textDigestItem
62.          = new JMenuItem("Text area digest");
63.       textDigestItem.addActionListener(new
64.          ActionListener()
65.          {
66.             public void actionPerformed(ActionEvent event)
67.             {
68.                String m = message.getText();
69.                computeDigest(m.getBytes());
70.             }
71.          });
72.       menu.add(textDigestItem);
```

```
73.        menuBar.add(menu);
74.        setJMenuBar(menuBar);
75.    }
76.
77.    /**
78.        Adds a radio button to select an algorithm.
79.        @param c the container into which to place the button
80.        @param name the algorithm name
81.        @param g the button group
82.    */
83.    public void addRadioButton(Container c, final String name,
84.        ButtonGroup g)
85.    {
86.        ActionListener listener = new
87.            ActionListener()
88.            {  public void actionPerformed(ActionEvent event)
89.                {
90.                    setAlgorithm(name);
91.                }
92.            };
93.        JRadioButton b
94.            = new JRadioButton(name, g.getButtonCount() == 0);
95.        c.add(b);
96.        g.add(b);
97.        b.addActionListener(listener);
98.    }
99.
100.    /**
101.        Sets the algorithm used for computing the digest.
102.        @param alg the algorithm name
103.    */
104.    public void setAlgorithm(String alg)
105.    {
106.        try
107.        {
108.            currentAlgorithm = MessageDigest.getInstance(alg);
109.            digest.setText("");
110.        }
111.        catch(NoSuchAlgorithmException e)
112.        {
113.            digest.setText("" + e);
114.        }
115.    }
116.
117.    /**
118.        Loads a file and computes its message digest.
119.    */
120.    public void loadFile()
121.    {
```

```
122.        JFileChooser chooser = new JFileChooser();
123.        chooser.setCurrentDirectory(new File("."));
124.
125.        int r = chooser.showOpenDialog(this);
126.        if (r == JFileChooser.APPROVE_OPTION)
127.        {
128.            String name
129.                = chooser.getSelectedFile().getAbsolutePath();
130.            computeDigest(loadBytes(name));
131.        }
132.    }
133.
134.    /**
135.        Loads the bytes in a file.
136.        @param name the file name
137.        @return an array with the bytes in the file
138.    */
139.    public byte[] loadBytes(String name)
140.    {
141.        FileInputStream in = null;
142.
143.        try
144.        {   in = new FileInputStream(name);
145.            ByteArrayOutputStream buffer
146.                = new ByteArrayOutputStream();
147.            int ch;
148.            while ((ch = in.read()) != -1)
149.                buffer.write(ch);
150.            return buffer.toByteArray();
151.        }
152.        catch (IOException e)
153.        {
154.            if (in != null)
155.            {
156.                try { in.close(); } catch (IOException e2) {}
157.            }
158.            return null;
159.        }
160.    }
161.
162.    /**
163.        Computes the message digest of an array of bytes
164.        and displays it in the text field.
165.        @param b the bytes for which the message digest should
166.        be computed.
167.    */
168.    public void computeDigest(byte[] b)
169.    {
```

```
170.        currentAlgorithm.reset();
171.        currentAlgorithm.update(b);
172.        byte[] hash = currentAlgorithm.digest();
173.        String d = "";
174.        for (int i = 0; i < hash.length; i++)
175.        {
176.           int v = hash[i] & 0xFF;
177.           if (v < 16) d += "0";
178.           d += Integer.toString(v, 16).toUpperCase() + " ";
179.        }
180.        digest.setText(d);
181.     }
182.
183.     private JTextArea message = new JTextArea();
184.     private JTextField digest = new JTextField();
185.     private MessageDigest currentAlgorithm;
186.     private static final int WIDTH = 400;
187.     private static final int HEIGHT = 300;
188. }
```

`java.security.MessageDigest`

- `static MessageDigest getInstance(String algorithm)`
  returns a `MessageDigest` object that implements the specified algorithm.
  Throws a `NoSuchAlgorithmException` if the algorithm is not provided.

  Parameters: algorithm   the name of the algorithm, such as `"SHA-1"` or `"MD5"`

- `void update(byte input)`
- `void update(byte[] input)`
- `void update(byte[] input, int offset, int len)`
  update the digest, using the specified bytes.

- `byte[] digest()`
  completes the hash computation, returns the computed digest, and resets the algorithm object.

- `void reset()`
  resets the digest.

Message Signing

In the last section, you saw how to compute a message digest, a fingerprint for the original message. If the message is altered, then the fingerprint of the altered message will not match the fingerprint of the original. If the message and its fingerprint are delivered separately, then the recipient can check whether the message has been tampered with. However, if both the message and the fingerprint were intercepted, it is an easy matter to modify the message and then recompute the fingerprint. After all, the message digest algorithms are publicly known, and they don't require any secret keys. In that case, the recipient of the forged message and the recomputed fingerprint would never know that the message has been altered. In this section, you will see how *digital signatures can authenticate* a message. When a message is authenticated, you *know*

- The message was not altered.
- The message came from the claimed sender.

To understand how digital signatures work, we need to explain a few concepts from the field called *public key cryptography.* Public key cryptography is based on the notion of a *public* key and *private* key. The idea is that you tell everyone in the world your public key. However, only you hold the private key, and it is important that you safeguard it and don't release it to anyone else. The keys are matched by mathematical relationships, but it is believed to be practically impossible to compute one from the other. That is, even though everyone knows your public key, they can't compute your private key in your lifetime, no matter how many computing resources they have available.

It may seem difficult to believe that nobody can compute the private key from the public keys, but nobody has ever found an algorithm to do this for the encryption algorithms that are in common use today. If the keys are sufficiently long, brute force—simply trying all possible keys—would require more computers than can be built from all the atoms in the solar system, crunching away for thousands of years. Of course, it is possible that someone could come up with algorithms for computing keys that are much more clever than brute force. For example, the RSA algorithm (the encryption algorithm invented by Rivest, Shamir, and Adleman) depends on the difficulty of factoring large numbers. For the last 20 years, many of the best mathematicians have tried to come up with good factoring algorithms, but so far with no success. For that reason, most cryptographers believe that keys with a "modulus" of 2,000 bits or more are currently completely safe from any attack.

There are two kinds of public/private key pairs: for *encryption* and for *authentication.* If anyone sends you a message that was encrypted with your public encryption key, then you can decrypt it with your private decryption key, but nobody else can. Conversely, if you sign a message with your private authentication key, then anyone else can verify the signature by checking with your public key. The verification passes only for messages that you signed, and it fails if anyone else used his key to sign the message. (Kahn remarks in the new edition of his book *The Codebreakers* that this was the first *new* idea in cryptography in hundreds of years.)

Many cryptographic algorithms, such as RSA and DSA (the Digital Signature Algorithm), use this idea. The exact structure of the keys and what it means for them to match depend on the algorithm. For example, here is a matching pair of public and private DSA keys.

Public key:

```
p: fca682ce8e12caba26efccf7110e526db078b05edecbcd1eb4a208f3ae16
17ae01f35b91a47e6df63413c5e12ed0899bcd132acd50d99151bdc43ee7375
92e17

q: 962eddcc369cba8ebb260ee6b6a126d9346e38c5

g: 678471b27a9cf44ee91a49c5147db1a9aaf244f05a434d6486931d2d1427
1b9e35030b71fd73da179069b32e2935630e1c2062354d0da20a6c416e50be79
4ca4

y: c0b6e67b4ac098eb1a32c5f8c4c1f0e7e6fb9d832532e27d0bdab9ca2d2a
8123ce5a8018b8161a760480fadd040b927281ddb22cb9bc4df596d7de4d1b97
7d50
```

Private key:

```
p: fca682ce8e12caba26efccf7110e526db078b05edecbcd1eb4a208f3ae16
17ae01f35b91a47e6df63413c5e12ed0899bcd132acd50d99151bdc43ee73759
2e17

q: 962eddcc369cba8ebb260ee6b6a126d9346e38c5

g: 678471b27a9cf44ee91a49c5147db1a9aaf244f05a434d6486931d2d1427
1b9e35030b71fd73da179069b32e2935630e1c2062354d0da20a6c416e50be79
4ca4

x: 146c09f881656cc6c51f27ea6c3a91b85ed1d70a
```

There is a mathematical relationship between these keys, but the exact nature of the relationship is not interesting for practical programming. (If you are interested, you can look it up in *Cryptography & Network Security* or *The Handbook of Cryptography* mentioned earlier.)

The obvious question is how to generate the pair of keys. Usually, this is done by feeding the result of some random process in to a deterministic procedure that returns the key pair to you. Luckily, how to get a random key pair for public key cryptography is not a question anyone but cryptographers and mathematicians need to worry about.

Here is how it works in practice. Suppose Alice wants to send Bob a message, and Bob wants to know this message came from Alice and not an impostor. Alice writes the message and then *signs* the message digest with her private key. Bob gets a copy of her public key. Bob then applies the public key to *verify* the signature. If the verification passes, then Bob can be assured of two facts:

1.   The original message has not been altered

2. The message was signed by Alice, the holder of the private key that matches the public key that Bob used for verification

See Figure 9–13.

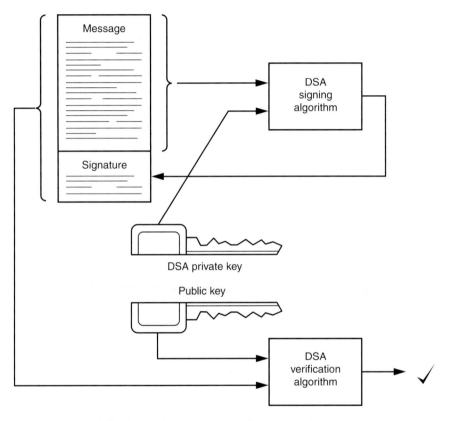

Figure 9–13: Public key signature exchange using DSA

You can see why security for private keys is all-important. If someone steals Alice's private key or if a government can require her to turn it over, then she is in trouble. The thief or a government agent can impersonate her by sending messages, money transfer instructions, and so on, that others will believe to have come from Alice.

The Java security package comes with DSA. If you want to use RSA, you'll need to buy the classes from RSA (www.rsa.com). Let us put the DSA algorithm to work. Actually, there are three algorithms:

1. To generate a key pair;

2. To sign a message;

3. To verify a signature.

Of course, you generate a key pair only once and then use it for signing and veri-fying many messages. To generate a new random key pair, make sure you use *truly random* numbers. For example, the regular random number generator in the Random class, seeded by the current date and time, is not random enough. (The jargon says the basic random number generator in `java.util` is not "crypto-graphically secure.") For example, supposing the computer clock is accurate to 1/10 of a second; then, there are at most 864,000 seeds per day. If an attacker knows the day a key was issued (as can often be deduced from the expiration date), then it is an easy matter to generate all possible seeds for that day.

The SecureRandom class generates random numbers that are far more secure than those produced by the Random class. You still need to provide a seed to start the number sequence at a random spot. The best method for doing this is to obtain random input from a hardware device such as a white-noise generator. Another reasonable source for random input is to ask the user to type away aim-lessly on the keyboard. But each keystroke should contribute only one or two bits to the random seed. Once you gather such random bits in an array of bytes, you pass it to the setSeed method.

```
SecureRandom secrand = new SecureRandom();
byte[] b = new byte[20];
// fill with truly random bits
secrand.setSeed(b);
```

If you don't seed the random number generator, then it will compute its own 20-byte seed by launching threads, putting them to sleep, and measuring the exact time when they are awakened.

> **NOTE:** This is an innovative algorithm that, at this point, is *not* known to be safe. And, in the past, algorithms that relied on timing other components of the computer, such as hard disk access time, were later shown not to be completely random.

Once you seed the generator, you can then draw random bytes with the nextBytes method.

```
byte[] randomBytes = new byte[64];
secrand.nextBytes(randomBytes);
```

Actually, to compute a new DSA key, you don't compute the random numbers yourself. You just pass the random number generator object to the DSA key gen-eration algorithm.

To make a new key pair, you need a KeyPairGenerator object. Just as with the MessageDigest class of the preceding section, the KeyPairGenerator class is both a factory class and the superclass for actual key pair generation algorithms.

To get a DSA key pair generator, you call the `getInstance` method with the string `"DSA"`.

```
KeyPairGenerator keygen = KeyPairGenerator.getInstance("DSA");
```

The returned object is actually an object of the class `sun.security.provider.DSAKeyPairGenerator`, which is a subclass of `KeyPairGenerator`.

To generate keys, you must initialize the key generation algorithm object with the key strength and a secure random number generator. Note that the key strength is not the length of the generated keys but the size of one of the building blocks of the key. In the case of DSA, it is the number of bits in the modulus, one of the mathematical quantities that makes up the public and private keys. Suppose you want to generate a key with a modulus of 512 bits:

```
SecureRandom secrand = new SecureRandom();
secrand.setSeed(...);
keygen.initialize(512, secrand);
```

Now you are ready to generate key pairs.

```
KeyPair keys = keygen.generateKeyPair();
KeyPair morekeys = keygen.generateKeyPair();
```

Each key pair has a public and a private key.

```
PublicKey pubkey = keys.getPublic();
PrivateKey privkey = keys.getPrivate();
```

To sign a message, you need a signature algorithm object. You use the `Signature` factory class:

```
Signature signalg = Signature.getInstance("DSA");
```

Signature algorithm objects can be used both to sign and to verify a message. To prepare the object for message signing, use the `initSign` method and pass the private key to the signature algorithm.

```
signalg.initSign(privkey);
```

Now, you use the `update` method to add bytes to the algorithm objects, in the same way as with the message digest algorithm.

```
while ((ch = in.read()) != -1)
    signalg.update((byte)ch);
```

Finally, you can compute the signature with the `sign` method. The signature is returned as an array of bytes.

```
byte[] signature = signalg.sign();
```

The recipient of the message must obtain a DSA signature algorithm object and prepare it for signature verification by calling the `initVerify` method with the public key as parameter.

```
Signature verifyalg = Signature.getInstance("DSA");
verifyalg.initVerify(pubkey);
```

Then, the message must be sent to the algorithm object.

```
while ((ch = in.read()) != -1)
    verifyalg.update((byte)ch);
```

Finally, you can verify the signature.

```
boolean check = verifyalg.verify(signature);
```

If the `verify` method returns `true`, then the signature was a valid signature of the message that was signed with the matching private key. That is, both the sender and the contents of the message have been authenticated.

Example 9–13 demonstrates the key generation, signing, and verification processes.

Example 9–13: SignatureTest.java

```
1. import java.security.*;
2.
3. /**
4.    This program demonstrates how to sign a message with a
5.    private DSA key and verify it with the matching public key.
6. */
7. public class SignatureTest
8. {
9.    public static void main(String[] args)
10.    {
11.       try
12.       {
13.          KeyPairGenerator keygen
14.             = KeyPairGenerator.getInstance("DSA");
15.          SecureRandom secrand = new SecureRandom();
16.          keygen.initialize(512, secrand);
17.
18.          KeyPair keys1 = keygen.generateKeyPair();
19.          PublicKey pubkey1 = keys1.getPublic();
20.          PrivateKey privkey1 = keys1.getPrivate();
21.
22.          KeyPair keys2 = keygen.generateKeyPair();
23.          PublicKey pubkey2 = keys2.getPublic();
24.          PrivateKey privkey2 = keys2.getPrivate();
25.
26.          Signature signalg = Signature.getInstance("DSA");
27.          signalg.initSign(privkey1);
28.          String message
29.             = "Pay authors a bonus of $20,000.";
30.          signalg.update(message.getBytes());
```

```
31.         byte[] signature = signalg.sign();
32.
33.         Signature verifyalg = Signature.getInstance("DSA");
34.         verifyalg.initVerify(pubkey1);
35.         verifyalg.update(message.getBytes());
36.         if (!verifyalg.verify(signature))
37.             System.out.print("not ");
38.         System.out.println("signed with private key 1");
39.
40.         verifyalg.initVerify(pubkey2);
41.         verifyalg.update(message.getBytes());
42.         if (!verifyalg.verify(signature))
43.             System.out.print("not ");
44.         System.out.println("signed with private key 2");
45.      }
46.      catch(Exception e)
47.      {
48.         e.printStackTrace();
49.      }
50.   }
51. }
```

java.security.KeyPairGenerator

- `static KeyPairGenerator getInstance(String algorithm)`
  returns a `KeyPairGenerator` object that implements the specified
  algorithm. Throws a `NoSuchAlgorithmException` if the algorithm is
  not provided.

  Parameters: `algorithm`   the name of the algorithm, such as `"DSA"`

- `void initialize(int strength, SecureRandom random)`

  Parameters: `strength`   an algorithm-specific measurement, typically,
  the number of bits of one of the algorithm
  parameters

  `random`   the source of random bits for generating keys

- `KeyPair generateKeyPair()`
  generate a new key pair.

java.security.KeyPair

- `PrivateKey getPrivate()`
  returns the private key from the key pair.

- `PublicKey getPublic()`
  returns the public key from the key pair.

java.security.Signature

- static Signature getInstance(String algorithm)

    returns a Signature object that implements the specified algorithm. Throws a NoSuchAlgorithmException if the algorithm is not provided.

    Parameters: algorithm   the name of the algorithm, such as "DSA"

- void initSign(PrivateKey privateKey)

    initializes this object for signing. Throws an InvalidKeyException if the key type does not match the algorithm type.

    Parameters: privateKey   the private key of the identity whose signature is being computed

- void update(byte input)
- void update(byte[] input)
- void update(byte[] input, int offset, int len)

    update the message buffer, using the specified bytes.

- byte[] sign()

    completes the signature computation and returns the computed signature.

- void initVerify(PublicKey publicKey)

    initializes this object for verification. Throws an InvalidKeyException if the key type does not match the algorithm type.

    Parameters: publicKey   the public key of the identity to be verified

- boolean verify(byte[] signature)

    checks whether the signature is valid.

Message Authentication

Suppose you get a message from your friend, signed by your friend with his private key, using the method we just showed you. You may already have his public key, or you can easily get it by asking him for a copy or by getting it from your friend's web page. Then, you can verify that the message was in fact authored by your friend and has not been tampered with. Now, suppose you get a message from a stranger who claims to represent a famous software company, urging you to run the program that is attached to the message. The stranger even sends you a copy of his public key so you can verify that he authored the message. You check that the signature is valid. This proves that the message was signed with the matching private key and that it has not been corrupted.

Be careful: *you still have no idea who wrote the message.* Anyone could have generated a pair of public and private keys, signed the message with the private key, and sent the signed message and the public key to you. The problem of determining the identity of the sender is called the *authentication problem.*

The usual way to solve the authentication problem is simple. Suppose the stranger and you have a common acquaintance whom you both trust. Suppose the stranger meets your acquaintance in person and hands over a disk with the public key. Your acquaintance later meets you, assures you that he met the stranger and that the stranger indeed works for the famous software company, and then gives you the disk (see Figure 9–14). That way, your acquaintance vouches for the authenticity of the stranger.

Figure 9–14 : Authentication through a trusted intermediary

In fact, your acquaintance does not actually need to meet you. Instead, he can apply his private signature to the stranger's public key file (see Figure 9–15).

When you get the public key file, you verify the signature of your acquaintance, and because you trust him, you are confident that he did check the stranger's credentials before applying his signature.

However, you may not have a common acquaintance. Some trust models assume that there is always a "chain of trust"—a chain of mutual acquaintances—so that you trust every member of that chain. In practice, of course, that isn't always true. You may trust your acquaintance, Alice, and you know that Alice trusts Bob, but you don't know Bob and aren't sure that you trust him. Other trust models assume that there is a benevolent big brother in whom we all trust. Some companies are working to become such big brothers, such as Verisign, Inc. (www.verisign.com), and, yes, the United States Postal Service.

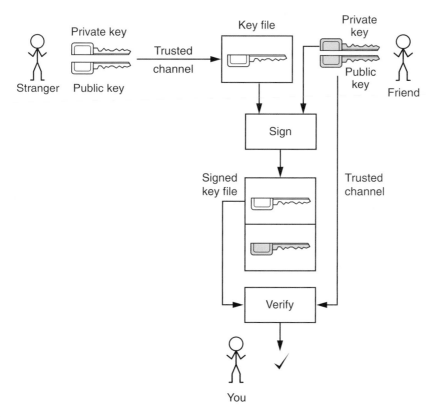

Figure 9–15: Authentication through a trusted intermediary's signature

You will often encounter digital signatures that are signed by one or more entities who will vouch for the authenticity, and you will need to evaluate to what degree you trust the authenticators. You might place a great deal of trust in Verisign, perhaps because you read their ponderous certification practice statements, or because you heard that they require multiple people with black attache cases to come together into a secure chamber whenever new master keys are to be minted.

However, you should have realistic expectations about what is actually being authenticated. Stratton Sclavos, the CEO of Verisign, does not personally meet every individual who has a public key that is authenticated by Verisign. More likely, that individual just filled out a form on a web page (see Figure 9–16).

Such a form asks the requestor to specify the name, organization, country, and e-mail address. Typically, the key (or instructions on how to fetch the key) is mailed to that e-mail address. Thus, you can be reasonably assured that the e-mail address is genuine, but the requestor could have filled in *any* name and organization. With a "class 1" ID from Verisign, that information is not verified. There are more stringent classes of IDs. For example, with a "class 3" ID, Verisign will require an individual requestor to appear before a notary public, and it will check the financial rating of a corporate requestor. Other authenticators will have different procedures. Thus, when you receive an authenticated message, it is important that you understand what, in fact, is being authenticated.

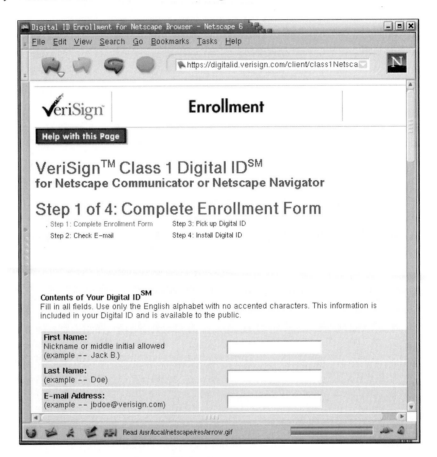

Figure 9–16: Request for a digital ID

The X.509 Certificate Format

One of the most common formats for signed certificates is the X.509 format. X.509 certificates are widely used by Verisign, Microsoft, Netscape, and many other companies, for signing e-mail messages, authenticating program code, and certifying many other kinds of data. The X.509 standard is part of the X.500 series of recommendations for a directory service by the international telephone standards body, the CCITT. In its simplest form, an X.509 certificate contains the following data:

- Version of certificate format;

- Serial number of certificate;

- Signature algorithm identifier (algorithm ID + parameters of the algorithm used to sign the certificate);

- Name of the signer of the certificate;

- Period of validity (begin/end date);

- Name of the identity being certified;

- Public key of identity being certified (algorithm ID + parameters of the algorithm + public key value);

- Signature (hash code of all preceding fields, encoded with private key of signer).

Thus, the signer guarantees that a certain identity has a particular public key.

Extensions to the basic X.509 format make it possible for the certificates to contain additional information. For more information on the structure of X.509 certificates, see `http://www.ietf.cnri.reston.va.us/ids.by.wg/X.509.html`. Peter Gutmann's web site (`http://www.cs.auckland.ac.nz/~pgut001/pubs/x509guide.txt`) contains an entertaining and informative description of the many discrepancies in the X.509 format, as it is implemented by different vendors.

The precise structure of X.509 certificates is described in a formal notation, called "abstract syntax notation #1" or ASN.1. Figure 9–17 shows the ASN.1 definition of version 3 of the X.509 format. The exact syntax is not important for us, but, as you can see, ASN.1 gives a precise definition of the structure of a certificate file. The *basic encoding rules*, or BER, describe precisely how to save this structure in a binary file. That is, BER describes how to encode integers, character strings, bit strings, and constructs such as SEQUENCE, CHOICE, and OPTIONAL.

Actually, the BER rules are not unique; there are several ways of specifying some elements. The *distinguished encoding rules* (DER) remove these ambiguities. For a readable description of the BER encoding format, we recommend *A Layman's Guide to a Subset of ASN.1, BER, and DER* by Burton S. Kaliski, Jr., available from `http://www.rsasecurity.com/rsalabs/pkcs/`. You can find the source code for a useful program for dumping BER encoded files at `http://www.cs.auckland.ac.nz/~pgut001/dumpasn1.c`.

Generating Certificates

The JDK comes with the `keytool` program, which is a command-line tool to generate and manage a set of certificates. We expect that ultimately the functionality of this tool will be embedded in other, more user-friendly programs. But right now, we will use `keytool` to show how Alice can sign a document and send it to Bob, and how Bob can verify that the document really was signed by Alice and not an impostor. We do not discuss all of the `keytool` features—see the JDK documentation for complete information.

The `keytool` program manages *key stores,* databases of certificates, and private keys. Each entry in the key store has an *alias.* Here is how Alice creates a keystore `alice.store` and generates a key pair with alias `alice`.

```
keytool -genkey -keystore alice.store -alias alice
```

When creating or opening a keystore, you will be prompted for a keystore password. For this example, just use `password`. If you were to use the `keytool`-generated keystore for any serious purpose, you would need to choose a good password and safeguard this file—it contains private signature keys.

When generating a key, you will be prompted for the following information:

```
Enter keystore password:  password
What is your first and last name?
  [Unknown]:  Alice Lee
What is the name of your organizational unit?
  [Unknown]:  Engineering Department
What is the name of your organization?
  [Unknown]:  ACME Software
What is the name of your City or Locality?
  [Unknown]:  Cupertino
What is the name of your State or Province?
  [Unknown]:  California
What is the two-letter country code for this unit?
  [Unknown]:  US
Is <CN=Alice Lee, OU=Engineering Department, O=ACME Software,
L=Cupertino, ST=California, C=US> correct?
  [no]:  Y
```

NOTE: You can find more information on ASN.1 in *ASN.1—Communication Between Heterogeneous Systems* by Olivier Dubuisson [Academic Press 2000] (`http://www.oss.com/asn1/dubuisson.html`) and *ASN.1 Complete* by John Larmouth [Morgan Kaufmann Publishers 1999] (`http://www.nokalva.com/asn1/larmouth.html`).

The `keytool` uses X.500 distinguished names, with components Common Name (CN), Organizational Unit (OU), Organization (O), Location (L), State (ST), and Country (C) to identify key owners and certificate issuers.

```
[Certificate   ::=   SEQUENCE  {
        tbsCertificate        TBSCertificate,
        signatureAlgorithm    AlgorithmIdentifier,
        signature             BIT STRING  }

   TBSCertificate  ::=  SEQUENCE  {
        version            [0]  EXPLICIT Version DEFAULT v1,
        serialNumber            CertificateSerialNumber,
        signature               AlgorithmIdentifier,
        issuer                  Name,
        validity                Validity,
        subject                 Name,
        subjectPublicKeyInfo  SubjectPublicKeyInfo,
        issuerUniqueID  [1]  IMPLICIT UniqueIdentifier OPTIONAL,
                             -- If present, version must be v2
                                or v3
        subjectUniqueID [2]  IMPLICIT UniqueIdentifier OPTIONAL,
                             -- If present, version must be v2
                                or v3
        extensions      [3]  EXPLICIT Extensions OPTIONAL
                             -- If present, version must be v3
        }

   Version  ::=  INTEGER  {  v1(0), v2(1), v3(2)  }

   CertificateSerialNumber  ::=  INTEGER

   Validity ::= SEQUENCE {
        notBefore       CertificateValidityDate,
        notAfter        CertificateValidityDate }

   CertificateValidityDate ::= CHOICE {
        utcTime         UTCTime,
        generalTime     GeneralizedTime }

   UniqueIdentifier  ::=  BIT STRING

   SubjectPublicKeyInfo  ::=  SEQUENCE  {
        algorithm               AlgorithmIdentifier,
        subjectPublicKey      BIT STRING  }

   Extensions  ::=  SEQUENCE OF Extension

   Extension  ::=  SEQUENCE  {
        extnID      OBJECT IDENTIFIER,
        critical    BOOLEAN DEFAULT FALSE,
        extnValue   OCTET STRING  }
```

Figure 9–17: ASN.1 definition of X.509v3

Finally, you need to specify a key password, or press ENTER to use the key store password as the key password.

Suppose Alice wants to give her public key to Bob. She needs to export a certificate file:

```
keytool -export -keystore alice.store -alias alice -file alice.cert
```

Now Alice can send the certificate to Bob. When Bob receives the certificate, he can print it:

```
keytool -printcert -file alice.cert
```

The printout looks like this:

```
Owner: CN=Alice Lee, OU=Engineering Department, O=ACME Software,
L=Cupertino, ST=California, C=US

Issuer: CN=Alice Lee, OU=Engineering Department, O=ACME Software,
L=Cupertino, ST=California, C=US

Serial number: 38107867

Valid from: Fri Oct 22 07:44:55 PDT 1999 until: Thu Jan 20
06:44:55 PST 2000

Certificate fingerprints:

MD5: 5D:00:0F:95:01:30:B4:FE:18:CE:9A:35:0F:C9:90:DD

SHA1:F8:C2:7C:E2:0B:1F:69:E2:6C:31:9A:F6:35:FA:A3:4F:83:81:6A:6A
```

This certificate is *self-signed*. Therefore, Bob cannot use another trusted certificate to check that this certificate is valid. Instead, he can call up Alice and have her read the certificate fingerprint over the phone.

Some certificate issuers publish certificate fingerprints on their web sites. For example, the JRE includes a key store cacerts in the jre/lib/security directory. It contains certificates from Thawte and VeriSign. To list the contents of a keystore, use the -list option:

```
keytool -list -keystore jre/lib/security/cacerts
```

The password for this keystore is changeit. One of the certificates in this keystore is

```
thawtepremiumserverca, Fri Feb 12 12:15:26 PST 1999, trustedCertEntry,
Certificate fingerprint (MD5):
06:9F:69:79:16:66:90:02:1B:8C:8C:A2:C3:07:6F:3A
```

You can check that your certificate is valid by visiting the Thawte web site at http://www.thawte.com/certs/trustmap.html.

> NOTE: Of course, this check requires that you trust that your copy of `keytool` (and the JRE code in `rt.jar` that the `keytool` program calls) has not been tampered with. If you are paranoid, you may want to copy the file to another machine (using a trusted file copy program) and check it on that machine with a freshly downloaded copy of the SDK.

Once Bob trusts the certificate, he can import it into his keystore.

```
keytool -import -keystore bob.store -alias alice -file alice.cert
```

> CAUTION: Never import a certificate into a keystore that you don't fully trust. Once a certificate is added to the keystore, any program that uses the keystore assumes that the certificate can be used to verify signatures.

Now Alice can start sending signed documents to Bob. The `jarsigner` tool signs and verifies JAR files. Alice simply adds the document to be signed into a JAR file.

```
jar cvf document.jar document.txt
```

Then she uses the `jarsigner` tool to add the signature to the file. She needs to specify the keystore, the JAR file and the alias of the key to use.

```
jarsigner -keystore alice.store document.jar alice
```

When Bob receives the file, he uses the `-verify` option of the `jarsigner` program.

```
jarsigner -verify -keystore bob.store document.jar
```

Bob does not need to specify the key alias. The `jarsigner` program finds the X.500 name of the key owner in the digital signature and looks for matching certificates in the keystore.

If the JAR file is not corrupted and the signature matches, then the `jarsigner` program prints

```
jar verified.
```

Otherwise, the program displays an error message.

Signing Certificates

In the preceding section, you saw how to use a self-signed certificate to distribute a public key to another party. However, the recipient of the certificate needed to ensure that the certificate was valid by verifying the fingerprint with the issuer. More commonly, a certificate is signed by a trusted intermediary.

The SDK does not contain tools for certificate signing. In this section, you will see how to write a program that signs a certificate with a private key from a keystore. This program is useful in its own right, and it shows you how to write programs that access the contents of certificates and keystores.

Before looking inside the program code, let's see how to put it to use. Suppose Alice wants to send her colleague Cindy a signed message. But Cindy doesn't want to call up everyone who sends her a signature file to verify the signature fingerprint. There needs to be an entity that Cindy trusts to verify signatures. In this example, we will suppose that Cindy trusts the Information Resources Department at ACME Software to perform this service. To simulate this process, you'll need to create an added keystore `acmesoft.store`. Generate a key and export the self-signed certificate.

```
keytool -genkey -keystore acmesoft.store -alias acmeroot
keytool -export -alias acmeroot -keystore acmesoft.store
    -file acmeroot.cert
```

Then add it to Cindy's key store.

```
keytool -import -alias acmeroot -keystore cindy.store
    -file acmeroot.cert
```

Cindy still needs to verify the fingerprint of that *root certificate*, but from now on, she can simply accept all certificates that are signed by it.

For Alice to send messages to Cindy and to everyone else at ACME Software, she needs to bring her certificate to the Information Resources Department and have it signed. However, the `keytool` program in the JDK does not have this functionality. That is where the certificate signer program in Example 9–14 comes in. The program reads a certificate file and signs it with a private key in a key store. An authorized staff member at ACME Software would verify Alice's identity and generate a signed certificate as follows:

```
java CertificateSigner -keystore acmesoft.store -alias acmeroot
    -infile alice.cert -outfile alice_signedby_acmeroot.cert
```

The certificate signer program must have access to the ACME Software keystore, and the staff member must know the keystore password. Clearly this is a sensitive operation.

Now Alice gives the file `alice_signedby_acmeroot.cert` file to Cindy and to anyone else in ACME Software. Alternatively, ACME Software can simply store the file in a company directory. Remember, this file contains Alice's public key and an assertion by ACME Software that this key really belongs to Alice.

NOTE: The `keytool` program supports a different mechanism for key signing. The `-certreq` option produces a certificate request in a standard format that can be processed by certificate authorities such as Thawte and Verisign, or local authorities running software such as the Netscape certificate server.

When Cindy imports the signed certificate into her key store, the key store verifies that the key was signed by a trusted root key that is already present in the key store and she is not asked to verify the certificate fingerprint.

> CAUTION: This scenario is for illustrative purposes only. The `keytool` is really not suitable as a tool for end-users. The `keytool` silently accepts certificates that are signed by a party that it already trusts, and it asks the user to confirm those that it cannot verify. It never rejects a certificate. It is all too easy for a confused user to accept an invalid certificate.

Once Cindy has added the root certificate and the certificates of the people who regularly send her documents, she never has to worry about the keystore again.

Now let us look at the source code of Example 9–14. First, we load the keystore. The `getInstance` factory method of the `KeyStore` class creates a keystore instance of the appropriate type. The `keytool`-generated keystore has a type of `"JKS"`. The provider of this keystore type is `"SUN"`.

```
KeyStore store = KeyStore.getInstance("JKS", "SUN");
```

Now, we need to load the keystore data. The `load` method requires an input stream and a password. Note that the password is specified as a `char[]` array, not a string. The JVM can keep strings around for a long time before they are garbage collected. Hackers could potentially find these strings, for example, by examining the contents of swap files. But character arrays can be cleared immediately after they are used.

Here is the code for loading the keystore. Note that we fill the password with spaces immediately after use.

```
InputStream in = . . .;
char[] password = . . .;
store.load(in, password);
Arrays.fill(password, ' ');
in.close();
```

Next, we use the `getKey` method to retrieve the private key for signing. The `getKey` method requires the key alias and key password. Its return type is `Key`, and we cast it to `PrivateKey` since we know that the retrieved key is a private key.

```
char[] keyPassword = . . .;
PrivateKey issuerPrivateKey
    = (PrivateKey)store.getKey(alias, keyPassword);
Arrays.fill(keyPassword, ' ');
```

Now we are ready to read in the certificate that needs to be signed. The `CertificateFactory` class can read in certificates from an input stream. First, you need to get a factory of the appropriate type:

```
CertificateFactory factory
   = CertificateFactory.getInstance("X.509");
```

Then, call the `generateCertificate` method with an input stream:

```
in = new FileInputStream(inname);
X509Certificate inCert
   = (X509Certificate)factory.generateCertificate(in);
in.close();
```

The return type of the `generateCertificate` method is the abstract `Certificate` class that is the superclass of concrete classes such as `X509Certificate`. Since we know that the input file actually contains an `X509Certificate`, we use a cast.

> CAUTION: There are two types called `Certificate`: a deprecated interface in the `java.security` package, and an abstract class in the `java.security.cert` package, which is the class that you want to use. If you import both the `java.security` and the `java.security.cert` package into your program, you need to resolve the ambiguity and explicitly reference the `java.security.cert.Certificate` class.

The purpose of this program is to sign the bytes in the certificate. You retrieve the bytes with the `getTBSCertificate` method:

```
byte[] inCertBytes = inCert.getTBSCertificate();
```

Next, we need the distinguished name of the issuer, which we will need to insert into the signed certificate. The name is stored in the issuer certificate in the keystore. You fetch certificates from the keystore with the `getCertificate` method. Since certificates are public information, you only supply the alias, not a password.

```
X509Certificate issuerCert
   = (X509Certificate)store.getCertificate(alias);
```

The `getCertificate` method has return type `Certificate`, but once again we know that the returned value is actually an `X509Certificate`. We obtain the issuer identity from the certificate by calling the `getSubjectDN` method. That method returns an object of some type that implements the `Principal` interface. Conceptually, a *principal* is a real-world entity such as a person, organization, or company.

```
Principal issuer = issuerCert.getSubjectDN();
```

We also retrieve the name of the signing algorithm.

```
String issuerSigAlg = issuerCert.getSigAlgName()
```

Now we must leave the realm of the standard security library. The standard library contains no methods for generating new certificates. Libraries for certificate generation are available from third-party vendors such as RSA Inc. and the Legion of Bouncy Castle (http://www.bouncycastle.org). However, we will use the classes in the sun.security.x509 package. The usual caveats apply. This package might not be supplied by third-party vendors of Java technology, and Sun Microsystems might change the behavior at any time.

The following code segment carries out these steps:

- Generates a certificate information object from the bytes in the certificate that is to be signed;

- Sets the issuer name;

- Creates the certificate and signs it with the issuer's private key;

- Saves the signed certificate to a file.

```
X509CertInfo info = new X509CertInfo(inCertBytes);
info.set(X509CertInfo.ISSUER,
    new CertificateIssuerName((X500Name)issuer));
X509CertImpl outCert = new X509CertImpl(info);
outCert.sign(issuerPrivateKey, issuerSigAlg);
outCert.derEncode(out);
```

We will not discuss the use of these classes in detail since we do not recommend the use of Sun libraries for production code. A future version of the SDK may contain classes for certificate generation. In the meantime, you may want to rely on third-party libraries or simply use existing certificate generation software.

Example 9–14: CertificateSigner.java

```
1.  import java.io.*;
2.  import java.security.*;
3.  import java.security.cert.*;
4.  import java.util.*;
5.
6.  import sun.security.x509.X509CertInfo;
7.  import sun.security.x509.X509CertImpl;
8.  import sun.security.x509.X500Name;
9.  import sun.security.x509.CertificateIssuerName;
10.
11. /**
12.    This program signs a certificate, using the private key of
13.    another certificate in a keystore.
14. */
15. public class CertificateSigner
16. {
17.    public static void main(String[] args)
18.    {
```

```
19.        String ksname = null; // the keystore name
20.        String alias = null; // the private key alias
21.        String inname = null; // the input file name
22.        String outname = null; // the output file name
23.        for (int i = 0; i < args.length; i += 2)
24.        {
25.           if (args[i].equals("-keystore"))
26.              ksname = args[i + 1];
27.           else if (args[i].equals("-alias"))
28.              alias = args[i + 1];
29.           else if (args[i].equals("-infile"))
30.              inname = args[i + 1];
31.           else if (args[i].equals("-outfile"))
32.              outname = args[i + 1];
33.           else usage();
34.        }
35.
36.        if (ksname == null || alias == null ||
37.           inname == null || outname == null) usage();
38.
39.        try
40.        {
41.           PushbackReader console = new PushbackReader(new
42.              InputStreamReader(System.in));
43.
44.           KeyStore store = KeyStore.getInstance("JKS", "SUN");
45.           InputStream in = new FileInputStream(ksname);
46.           System.out.print("Keystore password: ");
47.           System.out.flush();
48.           char[] password = readPassword(console);
49.           store.load(in, password);
50.           Arrays.fill(password, ' ');
51.           in.close();
52.
53.           System.out.print("Key password for " + alias + ": ");
54.           System.out.flush();
55.           char[] keyPassword = readPassword(console);
56.           PrivateKey issuerPrivateKey
57.              = (PrivateKey)store.getKey(alias, keyPassword);
58.           Arrays.fill(keyPassword, ' ');
59.
60.           if (issuerPrivateKey == null)
61.              error("No such private key");
62.
63.           in = new FileInputStream(inname);
64.
65.           CertificateFactory factory
66.              = CertificateFactory.getInstance("X.509");
67.
68.           X509Certificate inCert
69.              = (X509Certificate)factory.generateCertificate(in);
```

```
70.        in.close();
71.        byte[] inCertBytes = inCert.getTBSCertificate();
72.
73.        X509Certificate issuerCert
74.           = (X509Certificate)store.getCertificate(alias);
75.        Principal issuer = issuerCert.getSubjectDN();
76.        String issuerSigAlg = issuerCert.getSigAlgName();
77.
78.        FileOutputStream out = new FileOutputStream(outname);
79.
80.        X509CertInfo info = new X509CertInfo(inCertBytes);
81.        info.set(X509CertInfo.ISSUER,
82.           new CertificateIssuerName((X500Name)issuer));
83.
84.        X509CertImpl outCert = new X509CertImpl(info);
85.        outCert.sign(issuerPrivateKey, issuerSigAlg);
86.        outCert.derEncode(out);
87.
88.        out.close();
89.     }
90.     catch (Exception exception)
91.     {
92.        exception.printStackTrace();
93.     }
94.  }
95.
96.  /**
97.     Reads a password.
98.     @param in the reader from which to read the password
99.     @return an array of characters containing the password
100.  */
101.  public static char[] readPassword(PushbackReader in)
102.     throws IOException
103.  {
104.     final int MAX_PASSWORD_LENGTH = 100;
105.     int length = 0;
106.     char[] buffer = new char[MAX_PASSWORD_LENGTH];
107.
108.     while (true)
109.     {
110.        int ch = in.read();
111.        if (ch == '\r' || ch == '\n' || ch == -1
112.           || length == MAX_PASSWORD_LENGTH)
113.        {
114.           if (ch == '\r') // handle DOS "\r\n" line ends
115.           {
116.              ch = in.read();
117.              if (ch != '\n' && ch != -1) in.unread(ch);
118.           }
119.           char[] password = new char[length];
120.           System.arraycopy(buffer, 0, password, 0, length);
```

```
121.              Arrays.fill(buffer, ' ');
122.              return password;
123.           }
124.        else
125.        {
126.           buffer[length] = (char)ch;
127.           length++;
128.        }
129.     }
130.  }
131.
132.  /**
133.     Prints an error message and exits.
134.     @param message
135.  */
136.  public static void error(String message)
137.  {
138.     System.out.println(message);
139.     System.exit(1);
140.  }
141.
142.  /**
143.     Prints a usage message and exits.
144.  */
145.  public static void usage()
146.  {
147.     System.out.println("Usage: java CertificateSigner"
148.        + " -keystore keyStore -alias issuerKeyAlias"
149.        + " -infile inputFile -outfile outputFile");
150.     System.exit(1);
151.  }
152. }
```

java.security.KeyStore

- static getInstance(String type)
- static getInstance(String type, String provider)

  These messages construct a keystore object of the given type. If no provider is specified, the default provider is used. To work with keystores generated by the keytool, specify "JKS" as the type and "SUN" as the provider.

- void load(InputStream in, char[] password)

  loads a keystore from a stream. The password is kept in a character array so that it does not become part of the JVM string pool.

- Key getKey(String alias, char[] password)

  returns a private key with the given alias that is stored in this keystore.

- Certificate getCertificate(String alias)

  returns a certificate for a public key with the given alias that is stored in this keystore.

java.security.cert.CertificateFactory

- `CertificateFactory getInstance(String type)`
  creates a certificate factory for the given type. The type is a certificate type such as `"X509"`.

- `Certificate generateCertificate(InputStream in)`
  loads a certificate from an input stream.

java.security.cert.Certificate

- `PublicKey getPublicKey()`
  returns the public key that is being guaranteed by this certificate.

- `byte[] getEncoded()`
  gets the encoded form of this certificate.

- `String getType()`
  returns the type of this certificate, such as `"X509"`.

java.security.cert.X509Certificate

- `Principal getSubjectDN()`
- `Principal getIssuerDN()`
  get the owner (or subject) and issuer distinguished names from the certificate.

- `Date getNotBefore()`
- `Date getNotAfter()`
  get the validity period start and end dates of the certificate.

- `BigInteger getSerialNumber()`
  gets the serial number value from the certificate.

- `String getSigAlgName()`
- `byte[] getSignature()`
  get the signature algorithm name and the owner signature from the certificate.

- `byte[] getTBSCertificate()`
  gets the DER-encoded certificate information that needs to be signed by the certificate issuer.

Code Signing

One of the most important uses of authentication technology is signing executable programs. If you download a program, you are naturally concerned about damage that a program can do. For example, the program could have been infected by a virus. If you know where the code comes from *and* that it has not been tampered with since it left its origin, then your comfort level will be a lot higher than without this knowledge. In fact, if the program was also written in the Java programming language, you can then use this information to make a rational decision about what privileges you will allow that program to have. You might just want it to run in a sandbox as a regular applet, or you might want to grant it a different set of rights and restrictions. For example, if you download a word processing program, you might want to grant it access to your printer and to files in a certain subdirectory. But you may not want to give it the right to make network connections, so that the program can't try to send your files to a third party without your knowledge.

You now know how to implement this sophisticated scheme.

1.   First, use authentication to verify where the code came from.

2.   Then, run the code with a security policy that enforces the permissions that you want to grant the program, depending on its origin.

Signing JAR Files

At this point, code signing is still somewhat platform dependent. If you use JDK 1.1 applets with Netscape or Internet Explorer, you need to use the Netscape or Microsoft tools to sign your applets. See `www.securing-java.com/appdx-c/` or `www.suitable.com/Doc_CodeSigning.shtml` for more information on this topic.

In this section, we show you how to sign applets for use with the Java Plug-In software. There are two scenarios:

1.   Signed intranet applets;

2.   Signed Internet applets.

In the first scenario, a system administrator installs certificates and policy files on local machines. Whenever the Java Plug-in loads a signed applet, it consults the keystore for signatures and the policy file for the applet permissions. Installing the certificates and policies is straightforward and can be done once per desktop. End users can then run signed corporate applets outside the sandbox. Whenever a new applet is created or an existing applet is updated, it must be signed and deployed on the web server. However, no desktops need to be touched as the applets evolve. We think this is a reasonable scenario that can be an attractive alternative over deploying corporate applications on every desktop.

In the second scenario, software vendors obtain certificates that are signed by certificate authorities such as Thawte and Verisign. When an end user visits a web site that contains a signed applet, a dialog pops up that identifies the software vendor and gives the end user two choices: to run the applet with full privileges, or to confine it to the sandbox. We discuss this scenario in detail later.

For the remainder of this section, we describe how you can build policy files that grant specific permissions to applets from known sources. Building and deploying these policy files is not for casual end users. However, system administrators can carry out these tasks in preparation for distributing intranet applets.

Suppose ACME Software wants its users to run certain applets that require local file access. Since these applets cannot run inside the sandbox, ACME Software needs to install policy files on employee machines. As you saw earlier in this chapter, ACME could identify the applets by their code base. But that means that ACME would need to update the policy files each time the applet code is moved to a different web server. Instead, ACME decides to *sign* the JAR files that contain the applet code.

To make a signed JAR file, first add your class files to a JAR file.

```
jar cvf MyApplet.jar *.class
```

Then run the `jarsigner` tool and specify the JAR file and the alias of the private key:

```
jarsigner -keystore acmesoft.store MyApplet.jar acmeroot
```

In this example, the JAR file is signed with the self-signed root key. In practice, it would be more likely that ACME issues its programmers individual keys that are themselves signed by the root key.

Of course, the keystore containing the root key must be kept at a safe place. Let's make a second keystore `certs.store` for certificates and add the `acmeroot` certificate into it.

```
keytool -export -keystore acmesoft.store -alias acmeroot -file
    acmeroot.cert
keytool -import -keystore certs.store -alias acmeroot -file
    acmeroot.cert
```

Next, you need to create a policy file that gives the permission for all applets that are signed with signatures in that keystore.

You need to include the location of your keystore in the policy file. Add a line

```
keystore "keystoreURL", "keystoreType";
```

to the top of the policy file. The type is JKS if the keystore was generated by `keytool`.

```
keystore "file:certs.store", "JKS";
```

Then add `signedBy "alias"` to one or more `grant` clauses in the policy file. For example,

```
grant signedBy "acmeroot"
{
    permission java.io.FilePermission "<<ALL FILES>>", "read";
    . . .
};
```

Any signed code that can be verified with the public key associated with the alias is now granted these permissions.

You can try this out with the applet in Example 9–15. The applet tries to read from a local file (see Figure 9–18). The default security policy lets the applet read files from its code base and any subdirectories. Use `appletviewer` to run the applet and verify that you can view files from the code base directory, but not from other directories.

Figure 9–18: The FileReadApplet program

Now place the applet in a JAR file and sign it with the `acmeroot` key. Then create a policy file `applets.policy` with the contents:

```
keystore "file:certs.store", "JKS";
grant signedBy "acmeroot"
{
    permission java.io.FilePermission "<<ALL FILES>>", "read";
};
```

> NOTE: You can also use the `policytool` to create the policy file.

For this test, make sure that the keystore, policy file, and JAR file are all in the same directory.

Finally, tell the appletviewer to use the policy file:

```
appletviewer -J-Djava.security.policy=applets.policy
    FileReadApplet.html
```

Now the applet can read all files.

This shows that the signing mechanism works. To actually deploy this mechanism, you need to find appropriate places for the security files. We take up that topic in the next section.

As a final test, you may want to test your applet inside the Java Plug-In tool. Then, you need to modify the file `java.security` in the `jre/lib/security` directory. Locate the section

```
# The default is to have a single system wide policy file,
# and a policy file in the user's home directory.
policy.url.1=file:${java.home}/lib/security/java.policy
policy.url.2=file:${user.home}/.java.policy
```

Add a line with a file URL for the policy file, such as

```
policy.url.3=file:///home/test/applet.policy
```

CAUTION: Be sure to modify the correct `java.security` file. The Java Plug-In software uses the virtual machine in the JRE, *not* the one belonging to the JDK. In particular, under Windows, the JRE files are located inside the `\Program Files\JavaSoft` directory.

If you use the Java Plug-In software in Netscape 4 or Internet Explorer, you also need to change the HTML file to load the plug-in with an `EMBED` or `OBJECT` tag. Opera and Netscape 6 automatically load the Java Plug-In software when you use the `APPLET` tag. (See Chapter 10 of Volume 1 for more information on how to load the Java Plug-In tool.)

CAUTION: If you test your applet with the Java Plug-In instead of the appletviewer, then you need to be aware that the plug-in only reads the policy file *once,* when it is loaded for the first time. If you made a mistake in your policy file or keystore, then you need to close down the browser, fix your mistake, and restart the browser. Simply reloading the web page containing the applet does *not* work.

Example 9–15: FileReadApplet.java

```
1. import java.awt.*;
2. import java.awt.event.*;
3. import java.io.*;
4. import java.util.*;
5. import javax.swing.*;
6.
7. /**
8.    This applet can run "outside the sandbox" and
9.    read local files when it is given the right permissions.
10. */
```

```
11. public class FileReadApplet extends JApplet
12. {
13.     public FileReadApplet()
14.     {
15.         fileNameField = new JTextField(20);
16.         JPanel panel = new JPanel();
17.         panel.add(new JLabel("File name:"));
18.         panel.add(fileNameField);
19.         JButton openButton = new JButton("Open");
20.         panel.add(openButton);
21.         openButton.addActionListener(new
22.             ActionListener()
23.             {
24.                 public void actionPerformed(ActionEvent event)
25.                 {
26.                     loadFile(fileNameField.getText());
27.                 }
28.             });
29.
30.         Container contentPane = getContentPane();
31.         contentPane.add(panel, "North");
32.
33.         fileText = new JTextArea();
34.         contentPane.add(new JScrollPane(fileText), "Center");
35.     }
36.
37.     /**
38.         Loads the contents of a file into the text area.
39.         @param filename the file name
40.     */
41.     public void loadFile(String filename)
42.     {
43.         try
44.         {   fileText.setText("");
45.             BufferedReader in
46.                 = new BufferedReader(new FileReader(filename));
47.             String s;
48.             while ((s = in.readLine()) != null)
49.             fileText.append(s + "\n");
50.             in.close();
51.         }
52.         catch (IOException e)
53.         {
54.             fileText.append(e + "\n");
55.         }
56.         catch (SecurityException e)
57.         {
58.             fileText.append("I am sorry, but I cannot do that.");
59.         }
```

```
60.     }
61.
62.     private JTextField fileNameField;
63.     private JTextArea fileText;
64. }
```

Deployment Tips

The first decision you need to make is where to deploy policy files. There are two default locations:

- `java.policy` in the `${java.home}/lib/security` directory
- `.java.policy` in the `${user.home}` directory

We don't think either is a good choice. Instead, we recommend that you edit the `java.security` file in the `${java.home}/jre/lib/security` directory and add a line to include a third policy file, such as:

```
policy.url.3=http://intranet.acmesoft.com/admin/applet.policy
```

Then, you can set up a policy file on an intranet server. That is an advantage since you only need to manage a file in a single location.

Similarly, inside the policy file, you can specify the keystore location with an URL:

```
keystore "http://intranet.acmesoft.com/admin/certs.store", "JKS";
```

Add the certificate for the public key for corporate intranet applications to that keystore.

NOTE: You could add certificates to the `cacerts` keystore in the JRE. But then you would need to keep updating the JRE on every desktop when you change the keystore. We recommend that you don't touch the `cacerts` file.

Finally, sign the JAR files that contain the code for your intranet applications with the matching private key.

We suggest that you don't simply grant `AllPermission` to intranet applets, but that you augment the "sandbox" rights by specific privileges, such as accessing all directories inside a particular subdirectory, printing, network access within the intranet, and so on.

The deployment sounds a bit complex, but it is actually quite manageable. You need to minimally customize the Java Plug-In configuration on each desktop. The rest can be managed remotely. There are two benefits. At no time do you place a burden on your users to make solitary security decisions. And you have fine-grained control over the privileges of the remote code that your users execute.

NOTE: Because Java platform security combines authentication and control over code permissions, it offers a far more comprehensive security model than does Microsoft's ActiveX technology. ActiveX code is authenticated, but once it gains permission to run, it cannot be controlled at all.

Software Developer Certificates

Up to now, we discussed scenarios where applets are delivered in an intranet and a system administrator configures a security policy that controls the privileges of the applets. However, that strategy only works with applets from known sources.

Suppose you surf the Internet and you encounter a web site that offers to run an applet from an unfamiliar vendor, provided you grant it the permission to do so (see Figure 9–19). Such an applet is signed with a *software developer* certificate that is issued by a certificate authority such as Verisign. The pop-up dialog identifies the software developer and the certificate issuer. You now have two choices:

* To run the applet with full privileges, or
* To confine the applet to the sandbox.

Figure 9–19: Launching a signed applet

What facts do you have at your disposal that might influence your decision? Here is what you know:

1. Thawte sold a certificate to the software developer.
2. The applet really was signed with that certificate, and it hasn't been modified in transit.
3. The certificate really was signed by Thawte—it was verified by the public key in the local `cacerts` file.

Does that tell you whether the code is safe to run? Do you trust the vendor if all you know is the vendor name (`*.netbizz.dk`) and the fact that Thawte sold them a software developer certificate? Presumably Thawte went to some degree of trouble to assure itself that `*.netbizz.dk` is not an outright cracker.

However, no certificate issuer carries out a comprehensive audit of the honesty and competence of software vendors.

In the situation of an unknown vendor, an end user is ill-equipped to make an intelligent decision whether to let this applet run outside the sandbox, with all permissions of a local application. If the vendor is a well-known company, then the user can at least take the past track record of the company into account.

We don't like situations where a program demands "give me all rights, or I won't run at all." Naïve users are too often cowed into granting access that can put them into danger. Would it help if the applet explained what rights it needs and seeks specific permission for those rights? Unfortunately, as you have seen, that can get pretty technical. It doesn't seem reasonable for an end user to have to ponder whether an applet should really have the right to inspect the AWT event queue. Perhaps, a future version of a plug-in can define permission sets that are meaningful to an end user. Until that time, we remain unenthusiastic about applets that are signed with software developer certificates.

If you want to deploy your applets to the world at large and you think that your users trust you enough that they will allow your applets to run with full permissions on their machine, then you may want to purchase a certificate from Thawte or Verisign and use it to sign your applets. See `http://java.sun.com/products/plugin/1.2/docs/nsobjsigning.html` for more information.

Encryption

So far, we have discussed one important cryptographic technique that is implemented in the Java security API, namely authentication through digital signatures. A second important aspect of security is *encryption*. When information is authenticated, the information itself is plainly visible. The digital signature merely verifies that the information has not been changed. In contrast, when information is encrypted, it is not visible. It can only be decrypted with a matching key.

Authentication is sufficient for code signing—there is no need for hiding the code. But encryption is necessary when applets or applications transfer confidential information, such as credit card numbers and other personal data.

Until recently, patents and export controls have prevented many companies, including Sun, from offering strong encryption. Fortunately, export controls are now much less stringent, and the patent for the RSA algorithm finally expired in October 2000. As of SDK 1.4, good encryption support is part of the standard library. Crypto support is also available as a separate extension (called JCE) for older versions of the SDK.

Symmetric Ciphers

The Java cryptographic extensions contain a class `Cipher` which is the superclass for all encryption algorithms. You get a cipher object by calling the `getInstance` method:

```
Cipher cipher = Cipher.getInstance(algorithmName);
```

or

```
Cipher cipher = Cipher.getInstance(algorithmName, providerName);
```

The SDK comes with ciphers by the provider named `"SunJCE"`. That is the default provider that is used if you don't specify another provider name. You will see in the next section how to add other providers.

The algorithm name is a string such as `"DES"` or `"DES/CBC/PKCS5Padding"`.

DES, the Data Encryption Standard, is a venerable block cipher with a key length of 56 bits. Nowadays, the DES algorithm is considered obsolete because it has become possible to crack it with brute force (see, for example, `http://` `www.eff.org/descracker/`). A far better alternative is its successor, the Advanced Encryption Standard (AES). See `http://csrc.nist.gov/` `encryption/aes/` for more information on AES. At the time of this writing, the SunJCE provider supports DES but not AES.

Once you have a cipher object, you initialize it by setting the mode and the key.

```
int mode = . . .;
Key key = . . .;
cipher.init(mode, key);
```

The mode is one of

```
Cipher.ENCRYPT_MODE
Cipher.DECRYPT_MODE
Cipher.WRAP_MODE
Cipher.UNWRAP_MODE
```

The wrap and unwrap modes are used to encrypt one key with another—see the next section for an example.

Now you can repeatedly call the `update` method to encrypt blocks of data:

```
int blockSize = cipher.blockSize();
byte[] inBytes = new byte[blockSize];
. . . // read inBytes
int outputSize = cipher.outputSize(inLength);
byte[] outBytes = new byte[outputSize];
int outLength = cipher.update(inBytes, 0, outputSize, outBytes);
. . . // write outBytes
```

When you are done, you must call the `doFinal` method once. If there is a final block of input data available (with fewer than `blockSize` bytes), then call

```
outBytes = cipher.doFinal(inBytes, 0, inLength);
```

If all input data have been encrypted, call

```
outBytes = cipher.doFinal();
```

instead.

The call to doFinal is necessary to carry out *padding* of the final block. Consider the DES cipher. It has a block size of 8 bytes. Suppose the last block of the input data has less than 8 bytes. Of course, we can fill the remaining bytes with 0, to obtain one final block of 8 bytes, and encrypt it. But when decrypting, the result will have several trailing 0 bytes appended to it, and therefore it will be slightly different from the original input file. That may well be a problem, and a *padding scheme* is needed to avoid it. A commonly used padding scheme is the one described in the Public Key Cryptography Standard (PKCS) #5 by RSA Security Inc. (http://www.rsasecurity.com/rsalabs/pkcs/pkcs-5). In this scheme, the last block is not padded with a pad value of zero, but with a pad value that equals the number of pad bytes. In other words, if L is the last (incomplete) block, then it is padded as follows:

```
L 01                     if length(L) = 7
L 02 02                  if length(L) = 6
L 03 03 03               if length(L) = 5
   . . .
L 07 07 07 07 07 07 07   if length(L) = 1
```

Finally, if the length of the input is actually divisible by 8, then one block

```
08 08 08 08 08 08 08 08
```

is appended to the input and decrypted. When decrypting, the very last byte of the plaintext is a count of the padding characters to discard.

Finally, we need to explain how to obtain a key. You can generate a completely random key by following these steps.

1. Get a KeyGenerator for your algorithm.
2. Initialize the generator with a source for randomness. If the block length of the cipher is variable, you also need to specify the desired block length.
3. Call the generateKey method.

For example, here is how you generate a DES key.

```
KeyGenerator keygen = KeyGenerator.getInstance("DES");
SecureRandom random = new SecureRandom();
keygen.init(random);
Key key = keygen.generateKey();
```

Alternatively, you may want to produce a key from a fixed set of raw data (perhaps derived from a password or the timing of keystrokes). Then use a SecretKeyFactory like this:

```
SecretKeyFactory keyFactory
    = SecretKeyFactory.getInstance("DES");
byte[] keyData = . . .; // 8 bytes for DES
SecretKeySpec keySpec = new SecretKeySpec(keyData, "DES");
Key key = keyFactory.generateSecret(keySpec);
```

The sample program at the end of this section puts the DES cipher to work
(see Example 9–16). To use the program, you first need to generate a secret
key. Run

```
java DESTest -genkey secret.key
```

The secret key is saved in the file `secret.key`

Now you can encrypt with the command

```
java DESTest -encrypt plaintextFile encryptedFile secret.key
```

Decrypt with the command

```
java DESTest -decrypt encryptedFile decryptedFile secret.key
```

The program is straightforward. The -genkey option produces a new secret key
and serializes it in the given file. That operation takes a long time because the initialization of the secure random generator is time consuming. The -encrypt and
-decrypt options both call into the same crypt method that calls the update
and doFinal methods of the cipher. Note how the update method is called as
long as the input blocks have the full length, and the doFinal method is either
called with a partial input block (which is then padded) or with no additional
data (to generate one pad byte).

Example 9–16: DESTest.java

```
1. import java.io.*;
2. import java.security.*;
3. import javax.crypto.*;
4. import javax.crypto.spec.*;
5.
6. /**
7.    This program tests the DES cipher. Usage:
8.    java DESTest -genkey keyfile
9.    java DESTest -encrypt plaintext encrypted keyfile
10.   java DESTest -decrypt encrypted decrypted keyfile
11. */
12. public class DESTest
13. {
14.    public static void main(String[] args)
15.    {
16.       try
17.       {
18.          if (args[0].equals("-genkey"))
19.          {
20.             KeyGenerator keygen
21.                = KeyGenerator.getInstance("DES");
```

```
22.              SecureRandom random = new SecureRandom();
23.              keygen.init(random);
24.              SecretKey key = keygen.generateKey();
25.              ObjectOutputStream out = new ObjectOutputStream(
26.                 new FileOutputStream(args[1]));
27.              out.writeObject(key);
28.              out.close();
29.           }
30.           else
31.           {
32.              int mode;
33.              if (args[0].equals("-encrypt"))
34.                 mode = Cipher.ENCRYPT_MODE;
35.              else
36.                 mode = Cipher.DECRYPT_MODE;
37.
38.              ObjectInputStream keyIn = new ObjectInputStream(
39.                 new FileInputStream(args[3]));
40.              Key key = (Key) keyIn.readObject();
41.              keyIn.close();
42.
43.              InputStream in = new FileInputStream(args[1]);
44.              OutputStream out = new FileOutputStream(args[2]);
45.              Cipher cipher = Cipher.getInstance("DES");
46.              cipher.init(mode, key);
47.
48.              crypt(in, out, cipher);
49.              in.close();
50.              out.close();
51.           }
52.        }
53.        catch (IOException exception)
54.        {
55.           exception.printStackTrace();
56.        }
57.        catch (GeneralSecurityException exception)
58.        {
59.           exception.printStackTrace();
60.        }
61.        catch (ClassNotFoundException exception)
62.        {
63.           exception.printStackTrace();
64.        }
65.     }
66.
67.     /**
68.        Uses a cipher to transform the bytes in an input stream
69.        and sends the transformed bytes to an output stream.
70.        @param in the input stream
71.        @param out the output stream
72.        @param cipher the cipher that transforms the bytes
73.     */
74.     public static void crypt(InputStream in, OutputStream out,
```

```
75.          Cipher cipher) throws IOException, GeneralSecurityException
76.    {
77.       int blockSize = cipher.getBlockSize();
78.       int outputSize = cipher.getOutputSize(blockSize);
79.       byte[] inBytes = new byte[blockSize];
80.       byte[] outBytes = new byte[outputSize];
81.
82.       int inLength = 0;;
83.       boolean more = true;
84.       while (more)
85.       {
86.          inLength = in.read(inBytes);
87.          if (inLength == blockSize)
88.          {
89.             int outLength
90.                = cipher.update(inBytes, 0, blockSize, outBytes);
91.             out.write(outBytes, 0, outLength);
92.             System.out.println(outLength);
93.          }
94.          else more = false;
95.       }
96.       if (inLength > 0)
97.          outBytes = cipher.doFinal(inBytes, 0, inLength);
98.       else
99.          outBytes = cipher.doFinal();
100.      System.out.println(outBytes.length);
101.      out.write(outBytes);
102.   }
103. }
```

 `java.security.Cipher`

- `static Cipher getInstance(String algorithm)`
- `static Cipher getInstance(String algorithm, String provider)`
  returns a `Cipher` object that implements the specified algorithm. Throws a `NoSuchAlgorithmException` if the algorithm is not provided.

  Parameters: `algorithm`   The algorithm name, such as `"DES"` or `"DES/CBC/PKCS5Padding"`. Contact your provider for information on valid algorithm names.

                  `provider`   The provider name, such as `"SunJCE"` or `"BC"`.

- `int getBlockSize()`
  returns the size (in bytes) of a cipher block, or 0 if the cipher is not a block cipher.

- `int getOutputSize(int inputLength)`
  returns the size of an output buffer that is needed if the next input has the given number of bytes. This method takes into account any buffered bytes in the cipher object.

- `void init(int mode, Key key)`
  initializes the cipher algorithm object.

Parameters	mode	ENCRYPT_MODE, DECRYPT_MODE, WRAP_MODE, or UNWRAP_MODE
	key	the key to use for the transformation

- `byte[] update(byte[] in)`
- `byte[] update(byte[] in, int offset, int length)`
- `int update(byte[] in, int offset, int length, byte[] out)`
  transform one block of input data. The first two methods return the output. The third method returns the number of bytes placed into `out`.

Parameters:	in	the new input bytes to process
	offset	the starting index of input bytes in the array `in`
	length	the number of input bytes
	out	the array into which to place the output bytes

- `byte[] doFinal()`
- `byte[] doFinal(byte[] in)`
- `byte[] doFinal(byte[] in, int offset, int length)`
- `int doFinal(byte[] in, int offset, int length, byte[] out)`
  transform the last block of input data and flush the buffer of this algorithm object. The first three methods return the output. The fourth method returns the number of bytes placed into `out`.

Parameters:	in	the new input bytes to process
	offset	the starting index of input bytes in the array `in`
	length	the number of input bytes
	out	the array into which to place the output bytes

`java.security.KeyGenerator`

- `static KeyGenerator getInstance(String algorithm)`
  returns a `KeyGenerator` object that implements the specified algorithm. Throws a `NoSuchAlgorithmException` if the algorithm is not provided.

Parameters:	algorithm	the name of the algorithm, such as `"DES"`

- `void initialize(SecureRandom random)`
- `void initialize(int keySize, SecureRandom random`
  initialize the key generator.

Parameters:	keySize	the desired key size
	random	the source of randomness for generating keys

- `Key generateKey()`
  generates a new key.

javax.crypto.SecretKeyFactory

- `static SecretKeyFactory getInstance(String algorithm)`
- `static SecretKeyFactory getInstance(String algorithm, String provider)`
  returns a `SecretKeyFactory` object for the specified algorithm.

  Parameters: `algorithm` the algorithm name, such as `"DES"`

                    `provider` the provider name, such as `"SunJCE"` or `"BC"`

- `SecretKey generateSecret(KeySpec spec)`
  generates a new secret key from the given specification.

javax.crypto.spec.SecretKeySpec

- `SecretKeySpec(byte[] key, String algorithm)`
  constructs a key specification.

  Parameters: `key`   the bytes to use to make the key

                   `algorithm` the algorithm name, such as `"DES"`

Public Key Ciphers

The DES cipher that you have seen in the preceding section is a *symmetric* cipher. The same key is used for encryption and for decryption. The Achilles heel of symmetric ciphers is key distribution. If Alice sends Bob an encrypted method, then Bob needs the same key that Alice used. If Alice changes the key, then she needs to send Bob both the message, and, through a secure channel, the new key. But perhaps she has no secure channel to Bob, which is why she encrypts her messages to him in the first place.

Public key cryptography solves that problem. In a public key cipher, Bob has a key pair consisting of a public key and a matching private key. Bob can publish the public key anywhere, but he must closely guard the private key. Alice simply uses the public key to encrypt her messages to Bob.

Actually, it's not quite that simple. All known public key algorithms are *much* slower than symmetric key algorithms such as DES or AES. It would not be practical to use a public key algorithm to encrypt large amounts of information. But that problem can be overcome easily by combining a public key cipher with a fast symmetric cipher, like this:

1. Alice generates a random symmetric encryption key. She uses it to encrypt her plaintext.

2.   Alice encrypts the symmetric key with Bob's public key.

3.   Alice sends Bob both the encrypted symmetric key and the encrypted plaintext.

4.   Bob uses his private key to decrypt the symmetric key.

5.   Bob uses the decrypted symmetric key to decrypt the message.

Nobody but Bob can decrypt the symmetric key because only Bob has the private key for decryption. Thus, the expensive public key encryption is only applied to a small amount of key data.

The most commonly used public key algorithm is the RSA algorithm invented by Rivest, Shamir, and Adleman. Until October 2000, the algorithm was protected by a patent assigned to RSA Security Inc. Licenses were not cheap—typically a 3% royalty, with a minimum payment of $50,000 per year. Now the algorithm is in the public domain. Unfortunately, the SunJCE provider does not expose an RSA algorithm object, even though there is an RSA implementation within the SDK.

We found another provider, the "Legion of Bouncy Castle," which supports RSA as well as a number of other features missing from the SunJCE provider. Most importantly, the JAR file with the provider code has been signed by Sun Microsystems so that you can combine it with the JCE implementation of the SDK. (If an algorithm provider's code is not signed by Sun, you need to use an alternate "cleanroom" implementation of the JCE, not the one that is part of the SDK.) To test out the next sample program, you need to download the provider JAR file from http://www.bouncycastle.org/index.html.

There are two ways for installing a new provider. You can add a line to the security description file, jre/lib/security/java.security. By default, there are already several providers. To add a new provider, add a line such as

```
security.provider.6=org.bouncycastle.jce.provider
    .BouncyCastleProvider
```

Or you can dynamically load another security provider with the addProvider method of the Security class:

```
Security.addProvider(new BouncyCastleProvider());
```

In either case, you must make sure that the provider code is accessible. You can just move the JAR file into the jre/lib/ext directory, or you can add it to the class path.

To use the RSA algorithm, you need a public/private key pair. You use a KeyPairGenerator like this:

```
KeyPairGenerator pairgen
    = KeyPairGenerator.getInstance("RSA", "BC");
SecureRandom random = new SecureRandom();
```

```
pairgen.initialize(KEYSIZE, random);
KeyPair keyPair = pairgen.generateKeyPair();
Key publicKey = keyPair.getPublic();
Key privateKey = keyPair.getPrivate();
```

The program in Example 9–17 has three options. The -genkey option produces a key pair. The -encrypt option generates a DES key and *wraps* it with the public key.

```
Key key = . . .; // a DES key
Key publicKey = . . .; // a public RSA key
Cipher cipher = Cipher.getInstance("RSA", "BC");
cipher.init(Cipher.WRAP_MODE, publicKey);
byte[] wrappedKey = cipher.wrap(key);
```

It then produces a file that contains

- the length of the wrapped key
- the wrapped key bytes
- the plaintext encrypted with the DES key

The -decrypt option decrypts such a file. To try out the program, first generate the RSA keys:

```
java RSATest -genkey public.key private.key
```

Then encrypt a file

```
java RSATest -encrypt plaintextFile encryptedFile public.key
```

Finally, decrypt it and verify that the decrypted file matches the plain text.

```
java RSATest -decrypt encryptedFile decryptedFile private.key
```

NOTE: Before running this program, make sure you follow the instructions at the beginning of this section for installing the "Bouncy Castle" provider. Either edit the java.security file or edit the program and add a call to load the provider. Place the provider JAR file into the extensions directory or add it to the class path.

Example 9–17: RSATest.java

```
1. import java.io.*;
2. import java.security.*;
3. import javax.crypto.*;
4. import javax.crypto.spec.*;
5.
6. /**
7.    This program tests the RSA cipher. Usage:
8.    java RSATest -genkey public private
9.    java RSATest -encrypt plaintext encrypted public
```

```
10.    java RSATest -decrypt encrypted decrypted private
11. */
12. public class RSATest
13. {
14.    public static void main(String[] args)
15.    {
16.       try
17.       {
18.          if (args[0].equals("-genkey"))
19.          {
20.             KeyPairGenerator pairgen
21.                = KeyPairGenerator.getInstance("RSA", "BC");
22.             SecureRandom random = new SecureRandom();
23.             pairgen.initialize(KEYSIZE, random);
24.             KeyPair keyPair = pairgen.generateKeyPair();
25.             ObjectOutputStream out = new ObjectOutputStream(
26.                new FileOutputStream(args[1]));
27.             out.writeObject(keyPair.getPublic());
28.             out.close();
29.             out = new ObjectOutputStream(
30.                new FileOutputStream(args[2]));
31.             out.writeObject(keyPair.getPrivate());
32.             out.close();
33.          }
34.          else if (args[0].equals("-encrypt"))
35.          {
36.             KeyGenerator keygen
37.                = KeyGenerator.getInstance("DES");
38.             SecureRandom random = new SecureRandom();
39.             keygen.init(random);
40.             SecretKey key = keygen.generateKey();
41.
42.             // wrap with RSA public key
43.             ObjectInputStream keyIn = new ObjectInputStream(
44.                new FileInputStream(args[3]));
45.             Key publicKey = (Key) keyIn.readObject();
46.             keyIn.close();
47.
48.             Cipher cipher = Cipher.getInstance("RSA", "BC");
49.             cipher.init(Cipher.WRAP_MODE, publicKey);
50.             byte[] wrappedKey = cipher.wrap(key);
51.             DataOutputStream out = new DataOutputStream(new
52.                FileOutputStream(args[2]));
53.             out.writeInt(wrappedKey.length);
54.             out.write(wrappedKey);
55.
56.             InputStream in = new FileInputStream(args[1]);
57.             cipher = Cipher.getInstance("DES", "BC");
```

```
58.                cipher.init(Cipher.ENCRYPT_MODE, key);
59.                crypt(in, out, cipher);
60.                in.close();
61.                out.close();
62.             }
63.          else
64.             {
65.                DataInputStream in = new DataInputStream(new
66.                   FileInputStream(args[1]));
67.                int length = in.readInt();
68.                byte[] wrappedKey = new byte[length];
69.                in.read(wrappedKey, 0, length);
70.
71.                // unwrap with RSA private key
72.                ObjectInputStream keyIn = new ObjectInputStream(
73.                   new FileInputStream(args[3]));
74.                Key privateKey = (Key) keyIn.readObject();
75.                keyIn.close();
76.
77.                Cipher cipher = Cipher.getInstance("RSA", "BC");
78.                cipher.init(Cipher.UNWRAP_MODE, privateKey);
79.                Key key = cipher.unwrap(wrappedKey, "DES",
80.                   Cipher.SECRET_KEY);
81.
82.                OutputStream out = new FileOutputStream(args[2]);
83.                cipher = Cipher.getInstance("DES", "BC");
84.                cipher.init(Cipher.DECRYPT_MODE, key);
85.
86.                crypt(in, out, cipher);
87.                in.close();
88.                out.close();
89.             }
90.          }
91.       catch (IOException exception)
92.          {
93.             exception.printStackTrace();
94.          }
95.       catch (GeneralSecurityException exception)
96.          {
97.             exception.printStackTrace();
98.          }
99.       catch (ClassNotFoundException exception)
100.          {
101.             exception.printStackTrace();
102.          }
103.    }
104.
105.    /**
```

```
106.         Uses a cipher to transform the bytes in an input stream
107.         and sends the transformed bytes to an output stream.
108.         @param in the input stream
109.         @param out the output stream
110.         @param cipher the cipher that transforms the bytes
111.      */
112.      public static void crypt(InputStream in, OutputStream out,
113.         Cipher cipher) throws IOException, GeneralSecurityException
114.      {
115.         int blockSize = cipher.getBlockSize();
116.         int outputSize = cipher.getOutputSize(blockSize);
117.         byte[] inBytes = new byte[blockSize];
118.         byte[] outBytes = new byte[outputSize];
119.
120.         int inLength = 0;;
121.         boolean more = true;
122.         while (more)
123.         {
124.            inLength = in.read(inBytes);
125.            if (inLength == blockSize)
126.            {
127.               int outLength
128.                  = cipher.update(inBytes, 0, blockSize, outBytes);
129.               out.write(outBytes, 0, outLength);
130.            }
131.            else more = false;
132.         }
133.         if (inLength > 0)
134.            outBytes = cipher.doFinal(inBytes, 0, inLength);
135.         else
136.            outBytes = cipher.doFinal();
137.         out.write(outBytes);
138.      }
139.
140.      public static final int KEYSIZE = 128;
141.   }
```

java.security.Security

- static int addProvider(Provider provider)
  adds a provider to the set of providers.

- static void removeProvider(String name)
  removes the provider with the specified name, or does nothing if no matching provider exists.

- static Provider[] getProviders()
  returns the currently installed providers

- `static Provider getProvider(String name)`

  returns the provider with the specified name, or `null` if no matching provider exists.

- `static String getProperty(String key)`

  gets a security property. By default, security properties are stored in the file `jre/lib/java.security`.

- `static void setProperty(String key, String value)`

  gets a security property.

Cipher Streams

The JCE library provides a convenient set of stream classes that automatically encrypt or decrypt stream data. For example, here is how you can encrypt data to a file:

```
Cipher cipher = . . .;
cipher.init(Cipher.ENCRYPT_MODE, key);
CipherOutputStream out = new CipherOutputStream(
   new FileOutputStream(outputFileName), cipher);
byte[] bytes = new byte[BLOCKSIZE];
int inLength = getData(bytes); // get data from data source
while (inLength != -1)
{
   out.write(bytes, 0, inLength);
   inLength = getData(bytes); // get more data from data source
}
out.flush();
```

Similarly, you can use a `CipherInputStream` to read and decrypt data from a file:

```
Cipher cipher = . . .;
cipher.init(Cipher.DECRYPT_MODE, key);
CipherInputStream in = new CipherInputStream(
   new FileInputStream(inputFileName), cipher);
byte[] bytes = new byte[BLOCKSIZE];
int inLength = in.read(bytes);
while (inLength != -1)
{
   putData(bytes, inLength); // put data to destination
   inLength = in.read(bytes);
}
```

The cipher stream classes transparently handle the calls to `update` and `doFinal`, which is clearly a convenience.

javax.security.CipherInputStream

- CipherInputStream(InputStream in, Cipher cipher)
  constructs an input stream that reads data from in and decrypts or encrypts them using the given cipher.

- int read()
- int read(byte[] b, int off, int len)
  read data from the input stream, which is automatically decrypted or encrypted.

javax.security.CipherOutputStream

- CipherOutputStream(OutputStream out, Cipher cipher)
  constructs an output stream that writes data to out and encrypts or decrypts them using the given cipher.

- void write(int ch)
- void write(byte[] b, int off, int len)
  write data to the output stream, which is automatically encrypted or decrypted.

- void flush()
  flushes the cipher buffer and carries out padding, if necessary.

Chapter 10

Internationalization

▼ LOCALES

▼ NUMBERS AND CURRENCIES

▼ DATE AND TIME

▼ TEXT

▼ RESOURCE BUNDLES

▼ GRAPHICAL USER INTERFACE LOCALIZATION

There's a big world out there; we hope that lots of its inhabitants will be interested in your application or applet. The Internet, after all, effortlessly spans the barriers between countries. On the other hand, when you write your applet in U.S. English, using the ASCII character set, *you* are putting up a barrier. For example, even within countries that can function using the ASCII character set, things as basic as dates and numbers are displayed differently. To a German speaker, the date 3/4/95 means something different than it does to an English speaker. Or, an applet like our calculator from Chapter 10 of Volume 1 could confuse people who do not use the "." to separate the integer and fractional parts of a number.

Now, it is true that many Internet users are able to read English, but they will certainly be more comfortable with applets or applications that are written in their own language and that present data in the format with which they are most familiar. Imagine, for example, that you could write a retirement calculator applet that would change how it displays its results *depending on the location of the machine that is downloading it*. This kind of applet is immediately more valuable—and smart companies will recognize its value.

The Java programming language was the first language designed from the ground up to support internationalization. From the beginning, it had the one essential feature needed for effective internationalization: it used Unicode for all strings. Unicode support makes it easy to write programs in the Java programming language that manipulate strings in any one of multiple languages.

NOTE: The best source for Unicode character tables is *The Unicode Standard, Version 3.0*, [Addison-Wesley, 2000]. You can also see many of the code charts at `http://www.unicode.org`.

Many programmers believe that all they need to do to internationalize their application is to support Unicode and to translate the messages in the user interface. However, as you will see in this chapter, there is a lot more to internationalizing programs than just Unicode support. Operating systems and even browsers may not necessarily be Unicode-ready. For example, it is almost always necessary to have a translation layer between the character sets and fonts of the host machine and the Unicode-centric Java virtual machine. Also, dates, times, currencies—even numbers—are formatted differently in different parts of the world. You need an easy way to configure menu and button names, message strings, and keyboard shortcuts for different languages. You need to trigger the changes in a way that is based on information the ambient machine can report to your program.

In this chapter, you'll see how to write internationalized Java applications and applets. You will see how to localize date and time, numbers and text, and graphical user interfaces, and you'll look at the tools that the SDK offers for writing internationalized programs. (And, by the way, you will see how to write a retirement calculator applet that can change how it displays its results *depending on the location of the machine that is downloading it.*)

Locales

When you look at an application that is adapted to an international market, the most obvious difference you notice is the language. This observation is actually a bit too limiting for true internationalization: Countries can share a common language, but you still may need to do some work to make computer users of both countries happy.[1]

In all cases, menus, button labels, and program messages will need to be translated to the local language; they may also need to be rendered in a different script. There are many more subtle differences; for example, numbers are formatted quite differently in English and in German. The number

```
123,456.78
```

---

1. "We have really everything in common with America nowadays, except, of course, language." Oscar Wilde.

should be displayed as

```
123.456,78
```

for a German user. That is, the role of the decimal point and the decimal comma separator are reversed! There are similar variations in the display of dates. In the United States, dates are somewhat irrationally displayed as month/day/year. Germany uses the more sensible order of day/month/year, whereas in China, the usage is year/month/day. Thus, the date

```
3/22/61
```

should be presented as

```
22.03.1961
```

to a German user. Of course, if the month names are written out explicitly, then the difference in languages becomes apparent. The English

```
March 22, 1961
```

should be presented as

```
22. März 1961
```

in German, or

```
1961年3月22日
```

in Chinese.

You saw in Volume 1 that the `java.text` class has methods that can format numbers, currencies, and dates. These methods can, in fact, do much more when you give them a parameter that describes the location. To invoke these methods in a non-country-specific way, you only have to supply objects of the `Locale` class. A *locale* describes

- A language;
- A location;
- Optionally, a variant.

For example, in the United States, you use a locale with

    language=English, location=United States.

In Germany, you use a locale with

    language=German, location=Germany.

Switzerland has four official languages (German, French, Italian, and Rhaeto-Romance). A German speaker in Switzerland would want to use a locale with

    language=German, location=Switzerland

This locale would make formatting work similarly to how it would work for the German locale; however, currency values would be expressed in Swiss francs, not German marks.

Variants are, fortunately, rare and are needed only for exceptional or system-dependent situations. For example, the Norwegians are having a hard time agreeing on the spelling of their language (a derivative of Danish). They use two spelling rule sets: a traditional one called Bokmål and a new one called Nynorsk. The traditional spelling would be expressed as a variant

language=Norwegian, location=Norway, variant=Bokmål

There are "Euro" variants for several European locales. For example, the locale

language=German, location=Germany, variant=Euro

uses the euro sign $ instead of DM for displaying currencies.

It is also possible to encode platform-dependent information in the variant.

To express the language and location in a concise and standardized manner, the Java programming language uses codes that were defined by the International Standards Organization. The local language is expressed as a lowercase two-letter code, following ISO-639, and the country code is expressed as an uppercase two-letter code, following ISO-3166. Tables 10–1 and 10–2 show some of the most common codes.

NOTE: For a full list of ISO-639 codes, see, for example,
`http://www.ics.uci.edu/pub/ietf/http/related/iso639.txt`.
You can find a full list of the ISO-3166 codes at a number of sites, including
`http://www.niso.org/3166.html`.

Table 10–1: Common ISO-639 language codes

Language	Code
Chinese	zh
Danish	da
Dutch	nl
English	en
French	fr
Finnish	fi
German	de
Greek	el
Italian	it
Japanese	ja
Korean	ko
Norwegian	no
Portuguese	pt
Spanish	sp

975

Table 10–1: Common ISO-639 language codes (continued)

Language	Code
Swedish	sv
Turkish	tr

Table 10–2: Common ISO-3166 country codes

Country	Code
Austria	AT
Belgium	BE
Canada	CA
China	CN
Denmark	DK
Finland	FI
Germany	DE
Great Britain	GB
Greece	GR
Ireland	IE
Italy	IT
Japan	JP
Korea	KR
The Netherlands	NL
Norway	NO
Portugal	PT
Spain	ES
Sweden	SE
Switzerland	CH
Taiwan	TW
Turkey	TR
United States	US

These codes do seem a bit random, especially since some of them are derived from local languages (German = Deutsch = de, Chinese = zhongwen = zh), but they are, at least, standardized.

To describe a locale, you concatenate the language, country code, and variant (if any) and pass this string to the constructor of the Locale class. The variant is optional.

```
Locale germanGermany = new Locale("de", "DE");
Locale germanSwitzerland = new Locale("de", "CH");
Locale norwegianNorwayBokmål = new Locale("no", "NO", "B");
```

If you want to specify a locale that describes a language only and not a location, use an empty string as the second argument of the constructor.

```
Locale german = new Locale("de", "");
```

These kinds of locales can be used only for language-dependent lookups. Since the locales do not specify the location where German is spoken, you cannot use them to determine local currency and date formatting preferences.

For your convenience, the SDK predefines a number of locale objects:

```
Locale.CANADA
Locale.CANADA_FRENCH
Locale.CHINA
Locale.FRANCE
Locale.GERMANY
Locale.ITALY
Locale.JAPAN
Locale.KOREA
Locale.PRC
Locale.TAIWAN
Locale.UK
Locale.US
```

The SDK also predefines a number of language locales that specify just a language without a location.

```
Locale.CHINESE
Locale.ENGLISH
Locale.FRENCH
Locale.GERMAN
Locale.ITALIAN
Locale.JAPANESE
Locale.KOREAN
Locale.SIMPLIFIED_CHINESE
Locale.TRADITIONAL_CHINESE
```

Besides constructing a locale or using a predefined one, you have two other methods for obtaining a locale object.

The static getDefault method of the Locale class gets the default locale as stored by the local operating system. Similarly, in an applet, the getLocale method returns the locale of the user viewing the applet. Finally, all locale-dependent utility classes can return an array of the locales they support. For example,

```
Locale[] supportedLocales = DateFormat.getAvailableLocales();
```

returns all locales that the DateFormat class can handle. For example, at the time of this writing, the DateFormat class knows how to format dates in

Chinese but not in Vietnamese. Therefore, the `getAvailableLocales()` returns the Chinese locales but no Vietnamese ones.

> NOTE: We do not discuss how to create new language-specific elements. If you need to build a Brooklyn- or Texas-centric locale, please consult the SDK documentation.

Once you have a locale, what can you do with it? Not much, as it turns out. The only useful methods in the `Locale` class are the ones for identifying the language and country codes. The most important one is `getDisplayName`. It returns a string describing the locale. This string does not contain the cryptic two-letter codes, but it is in a form that can be presented to a user, such as

```
German (Switzerland)
```

Actually, there is a problem here. The display name is issued in the default locale. That may not be appropriate. If your user already selected German as the preferred language, you probably want to present the string in German. You can do just that by giving the German locale as a parameter: The code

```
Locale loc = new Locale("de", "CH");
System.out.println(loc.getDisplayName(Locale.GERMAN));
```

prints out

```
Deutsch (Schweiz)
```

But the real reason you need a `Locale` object is to feed it to locale-aware methods. For example, the `toLowerCase` and `toUpperCase` methods of the `String` class can take an argument of type `Locale` because the rules for forming uppercase letters differ by locale. In France, accents are generally dropped for uppercase letters. But in French-speaking Canada, they are retained. For example, the upper case of "étoile" (star) in France would be "ETOILE," but in Canada it would be "ÉTOILE."

```
String star = "étoile";
String fr = star.toUpperCase(Locale.FRANCE);
// should return "ETOILE"
String ca = star.toUpperCase(Locale.CANADA_FRENCH);
// returns "ÉTOILE"
```

Well, not quite: actually, this is the way it is *supposed* to work, but at least up to SDK 1.4, the `toUpperCase` method does not pay attention to the French locale. Still, we hope we have given you an idea of what you *will* be able to do with a `Locale` object. (Actually, you can give a `Locale` object to many other methods that carry out locale-specific tasks. You will see many examples in the following sections.)

java.util.Locale

- `static Locale getDefault()`
  returns the default locale.

- `static void setDefault(Locale l)`
  sets the default locale.

- `String getDisplayName()`
  returns a name describing the locale, expressed in the current locale.

- `String getDisplayName(Locale l)`
  returns a name describing the locale, expressed in the given locale.

- `String getLanguage()`
  returns the language code, a lowercase two-letter ISO-639 code.

- `String getDisplayLanguage()`
  returns the name of the language, expressed in the current locale.

- `String getDisplayLanguage(Locale l)`
  returns the name of the language, expressed in the given locale.

- `String getCountry()`
  returns the country code as an uppercase two-letter ISO-3166 code.

- `String getDisplayCountry()`
  returns the name of the country, expressed in the current locale.

- `String getDisplayCountry(Locale l)`
  returns the name of the country, expressed in the given locale.

- `String getVariant()`
  returns the variant string.

- `String getDisplayVariant()`
  returns the name of the variant, expressed in the current locale.

- `String getDisplayVariant(Locale l)`
  returns the name of the variant, expressed in the given locale.

- `String toString()`
  returns a description of the locale, with the language, country, and variant separated by underscores (e.g., `"de_CH"`).

Numbers and Currencies

We already mentioned how number and currency formatting is highly locale dependent. The Java programming language supplies a collection of formatter objects that can format and parse numeric values in the `java.text` class. You go through the following steps to format a number for a particular locale.

1. Get the locale object, as described in the preceding section.

2.   Use a "factory method" to obtain a formatter object.

3.   Use the formatter object for formatting and parsing.

The factory methods are static methods of the `NumberFormat` class that take a `Locale` argument. There are three factory methods: `getNumberInstance`, `getCurrencyInstance`, and `getPercentInstance`. These methods return objects that can format and parse numbers, currency amounts, and percentages, respectively. For example, here is how you can format a currency value in German.

```
Locale loc = new Locale("de", "DE");
NumberFormat currFmt = NumberFormat.getCurrencyInstance(loc);
double amt = 123456.78;
System.out.println(currFmt.format(amt));
```

This code prints

```
123.456,78 DM
```

Note that the currency symbol is DM and that it is placed at the end of the string. Also, note the reversal of decimal points and decimal commas.

Conversely, if you want to read in a number that was entered or stored with the conventions of a certain locale, then you use the `parse` method, which automatically uses the default locale. For example, the following code parses the value that the user typed into a text field. The `parse` method can deal with decimal points and commas, as well as digits in other languages.

```
TextField inputField;
. . .
NumberFormat fmt = NumberFormat.getNumberInstance();
// get number formatter for default locale
Number input = fmt.parse(inputField.getText().trim());
double x = input.doubleValue();
```

The return type of `parse` is the abstract type `Number`. The returned object is either a `Double` or a `Long` wrapper object, depending on whether the parsed number was a floating-point number. If you don't care about the distinction, you can simply use the `doubleValue` method of the `Number` class to retrieve the wrapped number.

If the number is not in the correct form, the method throws a `ParseException`. For example, leading white space in the string is *not* allowed. (Call `trim` to remove it.) However, any characters that follow the number in the string are simply ignored, so no exception is thrown.

Note that the classes returned by the `getXxxInstance` factory methods are not actually of type `NumberFormat`. The `NumberFormat` type is an abstract class, and the actual formatters belong to one of its subclasses.

The factory methods merely know how to locate the object that belongs to a particular locale.

It is quite obvious that it takes effort to produce a formatter object for a particular locale. Although the SDK supports only a limited number of localized formatters, more should follow over time, and you can, of course, write your own.

You can get a list of the currently supported locales with the static `getAvailableLocales` method. That method returns an array of the locales for which number formatter objects can be obtained.

The sample program for this section lets you experiment with number formatters (see Figure 10–1). The combo box at the top of the figure contains all locales with number formatters. You can choose between number, currency, and percentage formatters. Each time you make another choice, the number in the text field is reformatted. If you go through a few locales, then you get a good impression of how many ways there are to format a number or currency value. You can also type a different number and click on the Parse button to call the `parse` method, which tries to parse what you entered. If your input is successfully parsed, then it is passed to `format` and the result is displayed. If parsing fails, then a "Parse error" message is displayed in the text field.

Figure 10–1: The `NumberFormatTest` program

The code, shown in Example 10–1, is fairly straightforward. In the constructor, we call `NumberFormat.getAvailableLocales`. For each locale, we call `getDisplayName`, and we fill a combo box with the strings that the `getDisplayName` method returns. Whenever the user selects another locale or clicks on one of the radio buttons, we create a new formatter object and update the text field. When the user clicks on the Parse button, we call the `parse` method to do the actual parsing, based on the locale selected.

Example 10–1: NumberFormatTest.java

```
1. import java.awt.*;
2. import java.awt.event.*;
3. import java.text.*;
4. import java.util.*;
5. import javax.swing.*;
6.
7. /**
```

```
8.    This program demonstrates formatting numbers under
9.    various locales.
10. */
11. public class NumberFormatTest
12. {
13.    public static void main(String[] args)
14.    {
15.       JFrame frame = new NumberFormatFrame();
16.       frame.setDefaultCloseOperation(JFrame.EXIT_ON_CLOSE);
17.       frame.show();
18.    }
19. }
20.
21. /**
22.    This frame contains radio buttons to select a number format,
23.    a combo box to pick a locale, a text field to display
24.    a formatted number, and a button to parse the text field
25.    contents.
26. */
27. class NumberFormatFrame extends JFrame
28. {
29.    public NumberFormatFrame()
30.    {
31.       setSize(WIDTH, HEIGHT);
32.       setTitle("NumberFormatTest");
33.
34.       getContentPane().setLayout(new GridBagLayout());
35.
36.       ActionListener listener = new
37.          ActionListener()
38.          {
39.             public void actionPerformed(ActionEvent event)
40.             {
41.                updateDisplay();
42.             }
43.          };
44.
45.       JPanel p = new JPanel();
46.       addRadioButton(p, numberRadioButton, rbGroup, listener);
47.       addRadioButton(p, currencyRadioButton, rbGroup, listener);
48.       addRadioButton(p, percentRadioButton, rbGroup, listener);
49.
50.       GridBagConstraints gbc = new GridBagConstraints();
51.       gbc.fill = GridBagConstraints.NONE;
52.       gbc.anchor = GridBagConstraints.EAST;
53.       add(new JLabel("Locale"), gbc, 0, 0, 1, 1);
54.       add(p, gbc, 1, 1, 1, 1);
55.       add(parseButton, gbc, 0, 2, 1, 1);
56.       gbc.anchor = GridBagConstraints.WEST;
57.       add(localeCombo, gbc, 1, 0, 1, 1);
```

```
58.          gbc.fill = GridBagConstraints.HORIZONTAL;
59.          add(numberText, gbc, 1, 2, 1, 1);
60.
61.          locales = NumberFormat.getAvailableLocales();
62.          for (int i = 0; i < locales.length; i++)
63.             localeCombo.addItem(locales[i].getDisplayName());
64.          localeCombo.setSelectedItem(
65.             Locale.getDefault().getDisplayName());
66.          currentNumber = 123456.78;
67.          updateDisplay();
68.
69.          localeCombo.addActionListener(listener);
70.
71.          parseButton.addActionListener(new
72.             ActionListener()
73.             {
74.                public void actionPerformed(ActionEvent event)
75.                {
76.                   String s = numberText.getText();
77.                   try
78.                   {
79.                      Number n = currentNumberFormat.parse(s);
80.                      if (n != null)
81.                      {
82.                         currentNumber = n.doubleValue();
83.                         updateDisplay();
84.                      }
85.                      else
86.                      {
87.                         numberText.setText("Parse error: " + s);
88.                      }
89.                   }
90.                   catch(ParseException e)
91.                   {
92.                      numberText.setText("Parse error: " + s);
93.                   }
94.                }
95.             });
96.       }
97.
98.       /**
99.          A convenience method to add a component to given grid bag
100.         layout locations.
101.         @param c the component to add
102.         @param gbc the grid bag constraints to use
103.         @param x the x grid position
104.         @param y the y grid position
105.         @param w the grid width
106.         @param h the grid height
107.      */
```

```
108.   public void add(Component c, GridBagConstraints gbc,
109.      int x, int y, int w, int h)
110.   {
111.      gbc.gridx = x;
112.      gbc.gridy = y;
113.      gbc.gridwidth = w;
114.      gbc.gridheight = h;
115.      getContentPane().add(c, gbc);
116.   }
117.
118.   /**
119.      Adds a radio button to a container.
120.      @param p the container into which to place the button
121.      @param b the button
122.      @param g the button group
123.      @param listener the button listener
124.   */
125.   public void addRadioButton(Container p, JRadioButton b,
126.      ButtonGroup g, ActionListener listener)
127.   {
128.      b.setSelected(g.getButtonCount() == 0);
129.      b.addActionListener(listener);
130.      g.add(b);
131.      p.add(b);
132.   }
133.
134.   /**
135.      Updates the display and formats the number according
136.      to the user settings.
137.   */
138.   public void updateDisplay()
139.   {
140.      Locale currentLocale = locales[
141.         localeCombo.getSelectedIndex()];
142.      currentNumberFormat = null;
143.      if (numberRadioButton.isSelected())
144.         currentNumberFormat
145.            = NumberFormat.getNumberInstance(currentLocale);
146.      else if (currencyRadioButton.isSelected())
147.         currentNumberFormat
148.            = NumberFormat.getCurrencyInstance(currentLocale);
149.      else if (percentRadioButton.isSelected())
150.         currentNumberFormat
151.            = NumberFormat.getPercentInstance(currentLocale);
152.      String n = currentNumberFormat.format(currentNumber);
153.      numberText.setText(n);
154.   }
155.
156.   private Locale[] locales;
157.
```

```
158.        private double currentNumber;
159.
160.        private JComboBox localeCombo = new JComboBox();
161.        private JButton parseButton = new JButton("Parse");
162.        private JTextField numberText = new JTextField(30);
163.        private JRadioButton numberRadioButton
164.            = new JRadioButton("Number");
165.        private JRadioButton currencyRadioButton
166.            = new JRadioButton("Currency");
167.        private JRadioButton percentRadioButton
168.            = new JRadioButton("Percent");
169.        private ButtonGroup rbGroup = new ButtonGroup();
170.        private NumberFormat currentNumberFormat;
171.        private static final int WIDTH = 400;
172.        private static final int HEIGHT = 200;
173. }
```

java.text.NumberFormat

- `static Locale[] getAvailableLocales()`
  returns an array of `Locale` objects for which `NumberFormat` formatters are available.

- `static NumberFormat getNumberInstance()`
- `static NumberFormat getNumberInstance(Locale l)`
- `static NumberFormat getCurrencyInstance()`
- `static NumberFormat getCurrencyInstance(Locale l)`
- `static NumberFormat getPercentInstance()`
- `static NumberFormat getPercentInstance(Locale l)`
  return a formatter for numbers, currency amounts, or percentage values for the current locale or for the given locale.

- `String format(double x)`
- `String format(long x)`
  return the string resulting from formatting the given floating-point number or integer.

- `Number parse(String s)`
  parses the given string and returns the number value, as a `Double` if the input string described a floating-point number, and as a `Long` otherwise. The beginning of the string must contain a number; no leading white space is allowed. The number can be followed by other characters, which are ignored. Throws a `ParseException` if parsing was not successful.

- `void setParseIntegerOnly(boolean b)`
- `boolean isParseIntegerOnly()`
  set or get a flag to indicate whether this formatter should parse only integer values.

- `void setGroupingUsed(boolean b)`
- `boolean isGroupingUsed()`

  set or get a flag to indicate whether this formatter emits and recognizes decimal separators (such as `100,000`).

- `void setMinimumIntegerDigits(int n)`
- `int getMinimumIntegerDigits()`
- `void setMaximumIntegerDigits(int n)`
- `int getMaximumIntegerDigits()`
- `void setMinimumFractionDigits(int n)`
- `int getMinimumFractionDigits()`
- `void setMaximumFractionDigits(int n)`
- `int getMaximumFractionDigits()`

  set or get the maximum or minimum number of digits allowed in the integer or fractional part of a number.

Date and Time

When you are formatting date and time, there are four locale-dependent issues you need to worry about:

- The names of months and weekdays should be presented in the local language.

- There will be local preferences for the order of year, month, and day.

- The Gregorian calendar may not be the local preference for expressing dates.

- The time zone of the location must be taken into account.

The Java `DateFormat` class handles these issues. It is easy to use and quite similar to the `NumberFormat` class. First, you get a locale. You can use the default locale or call the static `getAvailableLocales` method to obtain an array of locales that support date formatting. Then, you call one of the three factory methods:

```
fmt = DateFormat.getDateInstance(dateStyle, loc);
fmt = DateFormat.getTimeInstance(timeStyle, loc);
fmt = DateFormat.getDateTimeInstance(dateStyle, timeStyle, loc);
```

To specify the desired style, these factory methods have a parameter that is one of the following constants:

`DateFormat.DEFAULT`

`DateFormat.FULL` (e.g., Thursday, September 18, 1997 8:42:46 o'clock A.M. PDT for the U.S. locale)

`DateFormat.LONG` (e.g., September 18, 1997 8:42:46 A.M. PDT for the U.S. locale)

`DateFormat.MEDIUM` (e.g., Sep 18, 1997 8:42:46 A.M. for the U.S. locale)

`DateFormat.SHORT` (e.g., 9/18/97 8:42 A.M. for the U.S. locale)

The factory method returns a formatting object that you can then use to format dates.

```
Date now = new Date();
String s = fmt.format(now);
```

Just as with the `NumberFormat` class, you can use the `parse` method to parse a date that the user typed. For example, the following code parses the value that the user typed into a text field.

```
TextField inputField;
. . .
DateFormat fmt = DateFormat.getDateInstance(DateFormat.MEDIUM);
    // get date formatter for default locale
Date input = fmt.parse(inputField.getText().trim());
```

If the number was not typed correctly, this code throws a `ParseException`. Note that leading white space in the string is *not* allowed here, either. You should again call `trim` to remove it. However, any characters that follow the number in the string will again be ignored. Unfortunately, the user must type the date exactly in the expected format. For example, if the format is set to MEDIUM in the U.S. locale, then dates are expected to look like

```
Sep 18, 1997
```

If the user types

```
Sep 18 1997
```

(without the comma) or the short format

```
9/18/97
```

then a parse error results.

A `lenient` flag interprets dates leniently. For example, `February 30, 1999` will be automatically converted to `March 2, 1999`. This seems dangerous, but, unfortunately, it is the default. You should probably turn off this feature. The calendar object that is used to interpret the parsed date will throw an `IllegalArgumentException` when the user enters an invalid day/month/year combination.

Example 10–2 shows the `DateFormat` class in action. You can select a locale and see how the date and time are formatted in different places around the world. If you see question-mark characters in the output, then you don't have the fonts installed for displaying characters in the local language. For example, if you pick a Chinese locale, the date may be expressed as

```
1997?9?19?
```

Figure 10–2 shows the program running under Chinese Windows; as you can see, it correctly displays the output.

You can also experiment with parsing. Type in a date or time, click the Parse lenient checkbox if desired, and click on the Parse date or Parse time button.

The only mysterious feature about the code is probably the `EnumCombo` class. We used this class to solve the following technical problem. We wanted to fill a combo with values such as `Short`, `Medium`, and `Long` and then automatically convert the user's selection to integer values `DateFormat.SHORT`, `DateFormat.MEDIUM`, and `DateFormat.LONG`. To do this, we convert the user's choice to upper case, replace all spaces with underscores, and then use reflection to find the value of the static field with that name. (See Chapter 5 of Volume 1 for more details about reflection.)

Figure 10–2: The `DateFormatTest` program running under Chinese Windows

Example 10–2: DateFormatTest.java

```
1. import java.awt.*;
2. import java.awt.event.*;
3. import java.text.*;
4. import java.util.*;
5. import javax.swing.*;
6.
7. /**
8.    This program demonstrates formatting dates under
9.    various locales.
10. */
11. public class DateFormatTest
12. {
13.    public static void main(String[] args)
14.    {
15.       JFrame frame = new DateFormatFrame();
16.       frame.setDefaultCloseOperation(JFrame.EXIT_ON_CLOSE);
17.       frame.show();
18.    }
19. }
20.
21. /**
22.    This frame contains combo boxes to pick a locale, date and
```

```
23.    time formats, text fields to display formatted date and time,
24.    buttons to parse the text field contents, and a "lenient"
25.    check box.
26. */
27. class DateFormatFrame extends JFrame
28. {
29.    public DateFormatFrame()
30.    {
31.       setSize(WIDTH, HEIGHT);
32.       setTitle("DateFormatTest");
33.
34.       getContentPane().setLayout(new GridBagLayout());
35.       GridBagConstraints gbc = new GridBagConstraints();
36.       gbc.fill = GridBagConstraints.NONE;
37.       gbc.anchor = GridBagConstraints.EAST;
38.       add(new JLabel("Locale"), gbc, 0, 0, 1, 1);
39.       add(new JLabel("Date style"), gbc, 0, 1, 1, 1);
40.       add(new JLabel("Time style"), gbc, 2, 1, 1, 1);
41.       add(new JLabel("Date"), gbc, 0, 2, 1, 1);
42.       add(new JLabel("Time"), gbc, 0, 3, 1, 1);
43.       gbc.anchor = GridBagConstraints.WEST;
44.       add(localeCombo, gbc, 1, 0, 2, 1);
45.       add(dateStyleCombo, gbc, 1, 1, 1, 1);
46.       add(timeStyleCombo, gbc, 3, 1, 1, 1);
47.       add(dateParseButton, gbc, 3, 2, 1, 1);
48.       add(timeParseButton, gbc, 3, 3, 1, 1);
49.       add(lenientCheckbox, gbc, 0, 4, 2, 1);
50.       gbc.fill = GridBagConstraints.HORIZONTAL;
51.       add(dateText, gbc, 1, 2, 2, 1);
52.       add(timeText, gbc, 1, 3, 2, 1);
53.
54.       locales = DateFormat.getAvailableLocales();
55.       for (int i = 0; i < locales.length; i++)
56.          localeCombo.addItem(locales[i].getDisplayName());
57.       localeCombo.setSelectedItem(
58.          Locale.getDefault().getDisplayName());
59.       currentDate = new Date();
60.       currentTime = new Date();
61.       updateDisplay();
62.
63.       ActionListener listener = new
64.          ActionListener()
65.          {
66.             public void actionPerformed(ActionEvent event)
67.             {
68.                updateDisplay();
69.             }
70.          };
71.
72.       localeCombo.addActionListener(listener);
```

```
73.        dateStyleCombo.addActionListener(listener);
74.        timeStyleCombo.addActionListener(listener);
75.
76.        dateParseButton.addActionListener(new
77.           ActionListener()
78.           {
79.              public void actionPerformed(ActionEvent event)
80.              {
81.                 String d = dateText.getText();
82.                 try
83.                 {
84.                    currentDateFormat.setLenient
85.                       (lenientCheckbox.isSelected());
86.                    Date date = currentDateFormat.parse(d);
87.                    currentDate = date;
88.                    updateDisplay();
89.                 }
90.                 catch(ParseException e)
91.                 {
92.                    dateText.setText("Parse error: " + d);
93.                 }
94.                 catch(IllegalArgumentException e)
95.                 {
96.                    dateText.setText("Argument error: " + d);
97.                 }
98.              }
99.           });
100.
101.       timeParseButton.addActionListener(new
102.          ActionListener()
103.          {
104.             public void actionPerformed(ActionEvent event)
105.             {
106.                String t = timeText.getText();
107.                try
108.                {
109.                   currentDateFormat.setLenient
110.                      (lenientCheckbox.isSelected());
111.                   Date date = currentTimeFormat.parse(t);
112.                   currentTime = date;
113.                   updateDisplay();
114.                }
115.                catch(ParseException e)
116.                {
117.                   timeText.setText("Parse error: " + t);
118.                }
119.                catch(IllegalArgumentException e)
120.                {
121.                   timeText.setText("Argument error: " + t);
122.                }
```

```
123.                  }
124.              });
125.      }
126.
127.      /**
128.         A convenience method to add a component to given grid bag
129.         layout locations.
130.         @param c the component to add
131.         @param gbc the grid bag constraints to use
132.         @param x the x grid position
133.         @param y the y grid position
134.         @param w the grid width
135.         @param h the grid height
136.      */
137.      public void add(Component c, GridBagConstraints gbc,
138.         int x, int y, int w, int h)
139.      {
140.         gbc.gridx = x;
141.         gbc.gridy = y;
142.         gbc.gridwidth = w;
143.         gbc.gridheight = h;
144.         getContentPane().add(c, gbc);
145.      }
146.
147.      /**
148.         Updates the display and formats the date according
149.         to the user settings.
150.      */
151.      public void updateDisplay()
152.      {
153.         Locale currentLocale = locales[
154.            localeCombo.getSelectedIndex()];
155.         int dateStyle = dateStyleCombo.getValue();
156.         currentDateFormat
157.            = DateFormat.getDateInstance(dateStyle,
158.            currentLocale);
159.         String d = currentDateFormat.format(currentDate);
160.         dateText.setText(d);
161.         int timeStyle = timeStyleCombo.getValue();
162.         currentTimeFormat
163.            = DateFormat.getTimeInstance(timeStyle,
164.            currentLocale);
165.         String t = currentTimeFormat.format(currentTime);
166.         timeText.setText(t);
167.      }
168.
169.      private Locale[] locales;
170.
171.      private Date currentDate;
```

```
172.    private Date currentTime;
173.    private DateFormat currentDateFormat;
174.    private DateFormat currentTimeFormat;
175.
176.    private JComboBox localeCombo = new JComboBox();
177.    private EnumCombo dateStyleCombo
178.       = new EnumCombo(DateFormat.class,
179.          new String[] { "Default", "Full", "Long",
180.          "Medium", "Short" });
181.    private EnumCombo timeStyleCombo
182.       = new EnumCombo(DateFormat.class,
183.          new String[] { "Default", "Full", "Long",
184.          "Medium", "Short" });
185.    private JButton dateParseButton = new JButton("Parse date");
186.    private JButton timeParseButton = new JButton("Parse time");
187.    private JTextField dateText = new JTextField(30);
188.    private JTextField timeText = new JTextField(30);
189.    private JTextField parseText = new JTextField(30);
190.    private JCheckBox lenientCheckbox
191.       = new JCheckBox("Parse lenient", true);
192.    private static final int WIDTH = 400;
193.    private static final int HEIGHT = 200;
194. }
195.
196. /**
197.    A combo box that lets users choose from among static field
198.    values whose names are given in the constructor.
199. */
200. class EnumCombo extends JComboBox
201. {
202.    /**
203.       Constructs an EnumCombo.
204.       @param cl a class
205.       @param labels an array of static field names of cl
206.    */
207.    public EnumCombo(Class cl, String[] labels)
208.    {
209.       for (int i = 0; i < labels.length; i++)
210.       {
211.          String label = labels[i];
212.          String name = label.toUpperCase().replace(' ', '_');
213.          int value = 0;
214.          try
215.          {
216.             java.lang.reflect.Field f = cl.getField(name);
217.             value = f.getInt(cl);
218.          }
219.          catch(Exception e)
220.          {
```

```
221.              label = "(" + label + ")";
222.          }
223.          table.put(label, new Integer(value));
224.          addItem(label);
225.      }
226.      setSelectedItem(labels[0]);
227.  }
228.
229.  /**
230.      Returns the value of the field that the user selected.
231.      @return the static field value
232.  */
233.  public int getValue()
234.  {
235.      return ((Integer)table.get(getSelectedItem())).intValue();
236.  }
237.
238.  private Map table = new HashMap();
239. }
```

java.text.DateFormat

- `static Locale[] getAvailableLocales()`
  returns an array of `Locale` objects for which `DateFormat` formatters are available.

- `static DateFormat getDateInstance(int dateStyle)`
- `static DateFormat getDateInstance(int dateStyle, Locale l)`
- `static DateFormat getTimeInstance(int timeStyle)`
- `static DateFormat getTimeInstance(int timeStyle, Locale l)`
- `static DateFormat getDateTimeInstance(int dateStyle, int timeStyle)`
- `static DateFormat getDateTimeInstance(int dateStyle, int timeStyle, Locale l)`
  return a formatter for date, time, or date and time for the default locale or the given locale.

  Parameters: `dateStyle, timeStyle` one of DEFAULT, FULL, LONG, MEDIUM, SHORT

- `String format(Date d)`
  returns the string resulting from formatting the given date/time.

- `Date parse(String s)`
  parses the given string and returns the date/time described in it. The beginning of the string must contain a date or time; no leading white space is allowed. The date can be followed by other characters, which are ignored. Throws a `ParseException` if parsing was not successful.

- `void setLenient(boolean b)`
- `boolean isLenient()`

  set or get a flag to indicate whether parsing should be lenient or strict. In lenient mode, dates such as `February 30, 1999` will be automatically converted to `March 2, 1999`. The default is lenient mode.

- `void setCalendar(Calendar cal)`
- `Calendar getCalendar()`

  set or get the calendar object used for extracting year, month, day, hour, minute, and second from the `Date` object. Use this method if you do not want to use the default calendar for the locale (usually the Gregorian calendar).

- `void setTimeZone(TimeZone tz)`
- `TimeZone getTimeZone()`

  set or get the time zone object used for formatting the time. Use this method if you do not want to use the default time zone for the locale. The default time zone is the time zone of the default locale, as obtained from the operating system. For the other locales, it is the preferred time zone in the geographical location.

- `void setNumberFormat(NumberFormat f)`
- `NumberFormat getNumberFormat()`

  set or get the number format used for formatting the numbers used for representing year, month, day, hour, minute, and second.

Text

There are many localization issues to deal with when you display even the simplest text in an internationalized application. In this section, we work on the presentation and manipulation of text strings. For example, the sorting order for strings is clearly locale specific. Obviously, you also need to localize the text itself: directions, labels, and messages will all need to be translated. (Later in this chapter, you'll see how to build *resource bundles.* These let you collect a set of message strings that work for a particular language.)

Collation (Ordering)

Sorting strings in alphabetical order is easy when the strings are made up of only English ASCII characters. You just compare the strings with the `compareTo` method of the `String` class. The value of

```
a.compareTo(b)
```

is a negative number if a is lexicographically less than b, 0 if they are identical, and positive otherwise.

Unfortunately, unless all your words are in uppercase English ASCII characters, this method is useless. The problem is that the `compareTo` method in the Java programming language uses the values of the Unicode character to determine the ordering. For example, lowercase characters have a higher Unicode value than do uppercase characters, and accented characters have even higher values. This leads to absurd results; for example, the following five strings are ordered according to the compareTo method:

```
America
Zulu
ant
zebra
Ångstrom
```

For dictionary ordering, you want to consider upper case and lower case to be equivalent. To an English speaker, the sample list of words would be ordered as

```
America
Ångstrom
ant
zebra
Zulu
```

However, that order would not be acceptable to a Danish user. In Danish, the letter Å is a different letter than the letter A, and it is collated *after* the letter Z! That is, a Danish user would want the words to be sorted as

```
America
ant
zebra
Zulu
Ångstrom
```

Fortunately, once you are aware of the problem, collation is quite easy. As always, you start by obtaining a Locale object. Then, you call the getInstance factory method to obtain a Collator object. Finally, you use the compare method of the collator, *not* the compareTo method of the String class, whenever you want to sort strings.

```
Locale loc = . . .;
Collator coll = Collator.getInstance(loc);
if (coll.compare(a, b) < 0) // a comes before b . . .;
```

Most importantly, the Collator class implements the Comparator interface. Therefore, you can pass a collator object to the Collections.sort method to sort a list of strings:

```
Collections.sort(strings, coll);
```

You can set a collator's *strength* to select how selective it should be. Character differences are classified as *primary, secondary,* and *tertiary.* For example, in English, the difference between "A" and "Z" is considered primary, the difference between "A" and "Å" is secondary, and between "A" and "a" is tertiary.

By setting the collator's strength to `Collator.PRIMARY`, you tell it to pay attention only to primary differences. By setting the strength to `Collator.SECONDARY`, the collator will take secondary differences into account. That is, two strings will be more likely to be considered different when the strength is set to "secondary." For example,

```
// assuming English locale
String a = "Angstrom";
String b = "Ångstrom";
coll.setStrength(Collator.PRIMARY);
if (coll.compare(a, b) == 0) System.out.print("same");
else System.out.print("different");
// will print "same"
coll.setStrength(Collator.SECONDARY);
if (coll.compare(a, b) == 0) System.out.print("same");
else System.out.print("different");
// will print "different"
```

Table 10–3 shows how a sample set of strings is sorted with the three collation strengths. Note that the strength indicates only whether two strings are considered identical.

Table 10–3: Collations with different strengths

Input	PRIMARY	SECONDARY	TERTIARY
Ant,	Angstrom = Ångstrom,	Angstrom,	Angstrom,
ant,	Ant = ant,	Ångstrom,	Ångstrom,
Angstrom,		Ant = ant	Ant,
Ångstrom,			ant

Finally, there is one technical setting, the *decomposition mode*. The default, "canonical decomposition," is appropriate for most uses. If you choose "no decomposition," then accented characters are not decomposed into their base form + accent. This option is faster, but it gives correct results only when the input does not contain accented characters. (It never makes sense to sort accented characters by their Unicode values.) Finally, "full decomposition" analyzes Unicode variants, that is, Unicode characters that ought to be considered identical. For example, Japanese displays have two ways of showing English characters, called half-width and full-width. The half-width characters have normal character spacing, whereas the full-width characters are spaced in the same grid as the ideographs. (One could argue that this is a presentation issue and it should not have resulted in different Unicode characters, but we don't make the rules.) With full decomposition, half-width and full-width variants of the same letter are recognized as identical.

It is wasteful to have the collator decompose a string many times. If one string is compared many times against other strings, then you can save the decomposition in a *collation* key object. The `getCollationKey` method returns a `CollationKey` object that you can use for further, faster comparisons. Here is an example:

```
String a = . . .;
CollationKey aKey = coll.getCollationKey(a);
if (aKey.compareTo(coll.getCollationKey(b) == 0)
    // fast comparison
    . . .
```

The program in Example 10–3 lets you experiment with collation order. Type a word into the text field and click on Add to add it to the list of words. Each time you add another word, or change the locale, strength, or decomposition mode, the list of words is sorted again. An = sign indicates words that are considered identical (see Figure 10–3).

Figure 10–3: The CollationTest program

Example 10–3: CollationTest.java

```
1. import java.io.*;
2. import java.awt.*;
3. import java.awt.event.*;
4. import java.text.*;
5. import java.util.*;
6. import java.util.List;
7. import javax.swing.*;
8.
9. /**
```

```
10.     This program demonstrates collating strings under
11.     various locales.
12. */
13. public class CollationTest
14. {
15.     public static void main(String[] args)
16.     {
17.         JFrame frame = new CollationFrame();
18.         frame.setDefaultCloseOperation(JFrame.EXIT_ON_CLOSE);
19.         frame.show();
20.     }
21. }
22.
23. /**
24.     This frame contains combo boxes to pick a locale, collation
25.     strength and decomposition rules, a text field and button
26.     to add new strings, and a text area to list the collated
27.     strings.
28. */
29. class CollationFrame extends JFrame
30. {
31.     public CollationFrame()
32.     {
33.         setSize(WIDTH, HEIGHT);
34.         setTitle("CollationTest");
35.
36.         getContentPane().setLayout(new GridBagLayout());
37.         GridBagConstraints gbc = new GridBagConstraints();
38.         gbc.fill = GridBagConstraints.NONE;
39.         gbc.anchor = GridBagConstraints.EAST;
40.         add(new JLabel("Locale"), gbc, 0, 0, 1, 1);
41.         add(new JLabel("Strength"), gbc, 0, 1, 1, 1);
42.         add(new JLabel("Decomposition"), gbc, 0, 2, 1, 1);
43.         add(addButton, gbc, 0, 3, 1, 1);
44.         gbc.anchor = GridBagConstraints.WEST;
45.         add(localeCombo, gbc, 1, 0, 1, 1);
46.         add(strengthCombo, gbc, 1, 1, 1, 1);
47.         add(decompositionCombo, gbc, 1, 2, 1, 1);
48.         gbc.fill = GridBagConstraints.HORIZONTAL;
49.         add(newWord, gbc, 1, 3, 1, 1);
50.         gbc.fill = GridBagConstraints.BOTH;
51.         add(new JScrollPane(sortedWords), gbc, 1, 4, 1, 1);
52.
53.         locales = Collator.getAvailableLocales();
54.         for (int i = 0; i < locales.length; i++)
55.             localeCombo.addItem(locales[i].getDisplayName());
56.         localeCombo.setSelectedItem(
57.             Locale.getDefault().getDisplayName());
58.
```

```
59.        strings.add("America");
60.        strings.add("ant");
61.        strings.add("Zulu");
62.        strings.add("zebra");
63.        strings.add("≈ngstrom");
64.        strings.add("Angstrom");
65.        strings.add("Ant");
66.        updateDisplay();
67.
68.        addButton.addActionListener(new
69.           ActionListener()
70.           {
71.              public void actionPerformed(ActionEvent event)
72.              {
73.                 strings.add(newWord.getText());
74.                 updateDisplay();
75.              }
76.           });
77.
78.        ActionListener listener = new
79.           ActionListener()
80.           {
81.              public void actionPerformed(ActionEvent event)
82.              {
83.                 updateDisplay();
84.              }
85.           };
86.
87.        localeCombo.addActionListener(listener);
88.        strengthCombo.addActionListener(listener);
89.        decompositionCombo.addActionListener(listener);
90.     }
91.
92.     /**
93.        A convenience method to add a component to given grid bag
94.        layout locations.
95.        @param c the component to add
96.        @param gbc the grid bag constraints to use
97.        @param x the x grid position
98.        @param y the y grid position
99.        @param w the grid width
100.       @param h the grid height
101.     */
102.     public void add(Component c, GridBagConstraints gbc,
103.        int x, int y, int w, int h)
104.     {
105.        gbc.gridx = x;
106.        gbc.gridy = y;
107.        gbc.gridwidth = w;
```

```
108.        gbc.gridheight = h;
109.        getContentPane().add(c, gbc);
110.     }
111.
112.     /**
113.        Updates the display and collates the strings according
114.        to the user settings.
115.     */
116.     public void updateDisplay()
117.     {
118.        Locale currentLocale = locales[
119.           localeCombo.getSelectedIndex()];
120.
121.        currentCollator
122.           = Collator.getInstance(currentLocale);
123.        currentCollator.setStrength(strengthCombo.getValue());
124.        currentCollator.setDecomposition(
125.           decompositionCombo.getValue());
126.
127.        Collections.sort(strings, currentCollator);
128.
129.        sortedWords.setText("");
130.        for (int i = 0; i < strings.size(); i++)
131.        {
132.           String s = (String)strings.get(i);
133.           if (i > 0
134.              && currentCollator.compare(s, strings.get(i - 1)) ==
0)
135.           {
136.              sortedWords.append("= ");
137.           }
138.           sortedWords.append(s + "\n");
139.        }
140.     }
141.
142.     private Locale[] locales;
143.     private List strings = new ArrayList();
144.     private Collator currentCollator;
145.
146.     private JComboBox localeCombo = new JComboBox();
147.     private EnumCombo strengthCombo
148.        = new EnumCombo(Collator.class,
149.           new String[] { "Primary", "Secondary", "Tertiary" });
150.     private EnumCombo decompositionCombo
151.        = new EnumCombo(Collator.class,
152.           new String[] { "Canonical Decomposition",
153.           "Full Decomposition", "No Decomposition" });
154.     private JTextField newWord = new JTextField(20);
155.     private JTextArea sortedWords = new JTextArea(10, 20);
```

```
156.    private JButton addButton = new JButton("Add");
157.    private static final int WIDTH = 400;
158.    private static final int HEIGHT = 400;
159. }
160.
161. /**
162.    A combo box that lets users choose from among static field
163.    values whose names are given in the constructor.
164. */
165. class EnumCombo extends JComboBox
166. {
167.    /**
168.       Constructs an EnumCombo.
169.       @param cl a class
170.       @param labels an array of static field names of cl
171.    */
172.    public EnumCombo(Class cl, String[] labels)
173.    {
174.       for (int i = 0; i < labels.length; i++)
175.       {
176.          String label = labels[i];
177.          String name = label.toUpperCase().replace(' ', '_');
178.          int value = 0;
179.          try
180.          {
181.             java.lang.reflect.Field f = cl.getField(name);
182.             value = f.getInt(cl);
183.          }
184.          catch(Exception e)
185.          {
186.             label = "(" + label + ")";
187.          }
188.          table.put(label, new Integer(value));
189.          addItem(label);
190.       }
191.       setSelectedItem(labels[0]);
192.    }
193.
194.    /**
195.       Returns the value of the field that the user selected.
196.       @return the static field value
197.    */
198.    public int getValue()
199.    {
200.       return ((Integer)table.get(getSelectedItem())).intValue();
201.    }
202.
203.    private Map table = new HashMap();
204. }
```

`java.text.Collator`

- `static Locale[] getAvailableLocales()`
  returns an array of `Locale` objects for which `Collator` objects are available.
- `static Collator getInstance()`
- `static Collator getInstance(Locale l)`
  return a collator for the default locale or the given locale.
- `int compare(String a, String b)`
  returns a negative value if a comes before b, 0 if they are considered identical, a positive value otherwise.
- `boolean equals(String a, String b)`
  returns `true` if they are considered identical, `false` otherwise.
- `void setStrength(int strength)` / `int getStrength()`
  sets or gets the strength of the collator. Stronger collators tell more words apart. Strength values are `Collator.PRIMARY`, `Collator.SECONDARY`, and `Collator.TERTIARY`.
- `void setDecomposition(int decomp)` / `int getDecompositon()`
  sets or gets the decomposition mode of the collator. The more a collator decomposes a string, the more strict it will be in deciding whether two strings ought to be considered identical. Decomposition values are `Collator.NO_DECOMPOSITION`, `Collator.CANONICAL_DECOMPOSITION`, and `Collator.FULL_DECOMPOSITION`.
- `CollationKey getCollationKey(String a)`
  returns a collation key that contains a decomposition of the characters in a form that can be quickly compared against another collation key.

`java.text.CollationKey`

- `int compareTo(CollationKey b)`
  returns a negative value if this key comes before b, 0 if they are considered identical, a positive value otherwise.

Text Boundaries

Consider a "sentence" in an arbitrary language: Where are its "words"? Answering this question sounds trivial, but once you deal with multiple languages, then just as with collation, it isn't as simple as you might think. Actually, the situation is even worse than you might think—consider the problem of determining where a *character starts and ends*. If you have a string such as `"Hello"`, then it is trivial to break it up into five individual characters: H|e|l|l|o. But accents throw a monkey wrench into this simple model. There are two ways of describing an accented character such as ä, namely, the character ä itself (Unicode `\u00E4`), or the character a followed by a combining diaeresis ¨ (Unicode \u0308). That is, the string with four Unicode characters Ba¨r is a sequence of three logical characters: B|a¨|r. This situation is still relatively easy; it gets much more complex for Asian languages such as the Korean Hangul script.

What about word breaks? Word breaks, of course, are at the beginning and the end of a word. In English, this is simple: sequences of characters are words. For example, the word breaks in

```
The quick, brown fox jump-ed over the lazy dog.
```

are

```
The| |quick|,| |brown| |fox| |jump-ed| |over| |the| |lazy| |dog.|
```

(The hyphen in `jump-ed` indicates a soft hyphen.)

Line boundaries are positions where a line can be broken on the screen or in printed text. In English text, this decision is relatively easy. Lines can be broken before a word or after a hyphen. For example, the line breaks in our sample sentence are

```
The |quick, |brown |fox |jump-|ed |over |the |lazy |dog.|
```

Note that line breaks are the points where a line *can* be broken, not the points where the lines are actually broken.

Determining character, word, and line boundaries is simple for European and Asian ideographic scripts, but it is quite complex for others, such as Devanagari, the script used to write classical Sanskrit and modern Hindi.

Finally, you will want to know about breaks between sentences. In English, for example, sentence breaks occur after periods, exclamation marks, and question marks.

Use the `BreakIterator` class to find out where you can break up text into components such as characters, words, lines, and sentences. You would use these classes when writing code for editing, displaying, and printing text.

Luckily, the break iterator class does not blindly break sentences at every period. It knows about the rules for periods inside quotation marks, and about "…" ellipses. For example, the string

```
The quick, brown fox jumped over the lazy "dog." And then
    ... what happened?
```

is broken into two sentences.

```
The quick, brown fox jumped over the lazy "dog." |And then
    ... what happened?|
```

Here is an example of how to program with break iterators. As always, you first get a break iterator with a static factory method. You can request one of four iterators to iterate through characters, words, lines, or sentences. Note that once you have a particular iterator object, such as one for sentences, it can iterate only through sentences. More generally, a break iterator can iterate only through the construct for which it was created. For example, the following code lets you analyze individual words:

```
Locale loc = . . .;
BreakIterator wordIter = BreakIterator.getWordInstance(loc);
```

Once you have an iterator, you give it a string to iterate through.

```
String msg = " The quick, brown fox";
wordIter.setText(msg);
```

Then, call the `first` method to get the offset of the first boundary.

```
int f = wordIter.first(); // returns 3
```

In our example, this call to `first` returns a 3—which is the offset of the first space inside the string. You keep calling the `next` method to get the offsets for the next tokens. You know there are no more tokens when a call to `next` returns the constant `BreakIterator.DONE`. For example, here is how you can iterate through the remaining word breaks.

```
int to;
while ((to = currentBreakIterator.next()) !=
    BreakIterator.DONE)
{  // do something with to
}
```

The program in Example 10–4 lets you type text into the text area on the top of the frame. Then, select the way you want to break the text (character, word, line, or sentence). You then see the text boundaries in the text area on the bottom (see Figure 10–4).

Figure 10–4: The TextBoundaryTest program

Example 10–4: TextBoundaryTest.java

```
1. import java.awt.*;
2. import java.awt.event.*;
3. import java.text.*;
4. import java.util.*;
5. import javax.swing.*;
6.
7. /**
8.    This program demonstrates breaking text under
9.    various locales.
10. */
11. public class TextBoundaryTest
12. {
13.    public static void main(String[] args)
14.    {
15.       JFrame frame = new TextBoundaryFrame();
16.       frame.setDefaultCloseOperation(JFrame.EXIT_ON_CLOSE);
17.       frame.show();
18.    }
19. }
20.
21. /**
22.    This frame contains radio buttons to select where to break
23.    the text, a combo box to pick a locale, a text field area
24.    to enter text, and a text area to display the broken text.
25. */
26. class TextBoundaryFrame extends JFrame
27. {
28.    public TextBoundaryFrame()
29.    {
30.       setSize(WIDTH, HEIGHT);
31.       setTitle("TextBoundaryTest");
32.
33.       ActionListener listener = new
34.          ActionListener()
35.          {
36.             public void actionPerformed(ActionEvent event)
37.             {
38.                updateDisplay();
39.             }
40.          };
41.
42.       JPanel p = new JPanel();
43.       addRadioButton(p, characterRadioButton, rbGroup, listener);
44.       addRadioButton(p, wordRadioButton, rbGroup, listener);
45.       addRadioButton(p, lineRadioButton, rbGroup, listener);
46.       addRadioButton(p, sentenceRadioButton, rbGroup, listener);
47.
48.       getContentPane().setLayout(new GridBagLayout());
49.       GridBagConstraints gbc = new GridBagConstraints();
50.       gbc.fill = GridBagConstraints.NONE;
```

```
51.      gbc.anchor = GridBagConstraints.EAST;
52.      add(new JLabel("Locale"), gbc, 0, 0, 1, 1);
53.      gbc.anchor = GridBagConstraints.WEST;
54.      add(localeCombo, gbc, 1, 0, 1, 1);
55.      add(p, gbc, 0, 1, 2, 1);
56.      gbc.fill = GridBagConstraints.BOTH;
57.      gbc.weighty = 100;
58.      add(new JScrollPane(inputText), gbc, 0, 2, 2, 1);
59.      add(new JScrollPane(outputText), gbc, 0, 3, 2, 1);
60.
61.      locales = BreakIterator.getAvailableLocales();
62.      for (int i = 0; i < locales.length; i++)
63.         localeCombo.addItem(locales[i].getDisplayName());
64.      localeCombo.setSelectedItem(
65.         Locale.getDefault().getDisplayName());
66.
67.      localeCombo.addActionListener(listener);
68.
69.      inputText.setText("The quick, brown fox jump-ed\n"
70.         + "over the lazy \"dog.\" And then...what happened?");
71.      updateDisplay();
72.   }
73.
74.   /**
75.      Adds a radio button to a container.
76.      @param p the container into which to place the button
77.      @param b the button
78.      @param g the button group
79.      @param listener the button listener
80.   */
81.   public void addRadioButton(Container p, JRadioButton b,
82.      ButtonGroup g, ActionListener listener)
83.   {
84.      b.setSelected(g.getButtonCount() == 0);
85.      b.addActionListener(listener);
86.      g.add(b);
87.      p.add(b);
88.   }
89.
90.   /**
91.      A convenience method to add a component to given grid bag
92.      layout locations.
93.      @param c the component to add
94.      @param gbc the grid bag constraints to use
95.      @param x the x grid position
96.      @param y the y grid position
97.      @param w the grid width
98.      @param h the grid height
99.   */
100.  public void add(Component c, GridBagConstraints gbc,
101.     int x, int y, int w, int h)
102.  {
```

```
103.        gbc.gridx = x;
104.        gbc.gridy = y;
105.        gbc.gridwidth = w;
106.        gbc.gridheight = h;
107.        getContentPane().add(c, gbc);
108.    }
109.
110.    /**
111.        Updates the display and breaks the text according
112.        to the user settings.
113.    */
114.    public void updateDisplay()
115.    {
116.        Locale currentLocale = locales[
117.            localeCombo.getSelectedIndex()];
118.        BreakIterator currentBreakIterator = null;
119.        if (characterRadioButton.isSelected())
120.            currentBreakIterator
121.                = BreakIterator.getCharacterInstance(currentLocale);
122.        else if (wordRadioButton.isSelected())
123.            currentBreakIterator
124.                = BreakIterator.getWordInstance(currentLocale);
125.        else if (lineRadioButton.isSelected())
126.            currentBreakIterator
127.                = BreakIterator.getLineInstance(currentLocale);
128.        else if (sentenceRadioButton.isSelected())
129.            currentBreakIterator
130.                = BreakIterator.getSentenceInstance(currentLocale);
131.
132.        String text = inputText.getText();
133.        currentBreakIterator.setText(text);
134.        outputText.setText("");
135.
136.        int from = currentBreakIterator.first();
137.        int to;
138.        while ((to = currentBreakIterator.next()) !=
139.            BreakIterator.DONE)
140.        {
141.            outputText.append(text.substring(from, to) + "|");
142.            from = to;
143.        }
144.        outputText.append(text.substring(from));
145.    }
146.
147.    private Locale[] locales;
148.    private BreakIterator currentBreakIterator;
149.
150.    private JComboBox localeCombo = new JComboBox();
151.    private JTextArea inputText = new JTextArea(6, 40);
152.    private JTextArea outputText = new JTextArea(6, 40);
153.    private ButtonGroup rbGroup = new ButtonGroup();
154.    private JRadioButton characterRadioButton
```

```
155.          = new JRadioButton("Character");
156.    private JRadioButton wordRadioButton
157.          = new JRadioButton("Word");
158.    private JRadioButton lineRadioButton
159.          = new JRadioButton("Line");
160.    private JRadioButton sentenceRadioButton
161.          = new JRadioButton("Sentence");
162.    private static final int WIDTH = 400;
163.    private static final int HEIGHT = 400;
164. }
```

`java.text.BreakIterator`

- `static Locale[] getAvailableLocales()`
  returns an array of `Locale` objects for which `BreakIterator` objects
  are available.

- `static BreakIterator getCharacterInstance()`
- `static BreakIterator getCharacterInstance(Locale l)`
- `static BreakIterator getWordInstance()`
- `static BreakIterator getWordInstance(Locale l)`
- `static BreakIterator getLineInstance()`
- `static BreakIterator getLineInstance(Locale l)`
- `static BreakIterator getSentenceInstance()`
- `static BreakIterator getSentenceInstance(Locale l)`
  return a break iterator for characters, words, lines, and sentences for the
  default or the given locale.

- `void setText(String text)`
- `void setText(CharacterIterator text)`
- `CharacterIterator getText()`
  set or get the text to be scanned.

- `int first()`
  moves the current boundary to the first boundary position in the scanned
  string and returns the index.

- `int next()`
  moves the current boundary to the next boundary position and returns
  the index. Returns `BreakIterator.DONE` if the end of the string has
  been reached.

- `int previous()`
  moves the current boundary to the previous boundary position and returns
  the index. Returns `BreakIterator.DONE` if the beginning of the string has
  been reached.

- `int last()`

  moves the current boundary to the last boundary position in the scanned string and returns the index.

- `int current()`

  returns the index of the current boundary.

- `int next(int n)`

  moves the current boundary to the nth boundary position from the current one and returns the index. If n is negative, then the position is set closer to the beginning of the string. Returns `BreakIterator.DONE` if the end or beginning of the string has been reached.

- `int following(int pos)`

  moves the current boundary to the first boundary position after offset `pos` in the scanned string, and returns the index. The returned value is larger than `pos`, or it is equal to `BreakIterator.DONE`.

Message Formatting

In the early days of "mail-merge" programs, you had strings like:

```
"On {2}, a {0} destroyed {1} houses and caused {3} of
    damage."
```

where the numbers in braces were placeholders for actual names and values. This technique is actually very convenient for doing certain kinds of internationalization, and the Java programming language has a convenience `MessageFormat` class to allow formatting text that has a pattern. To use the class, follow these steps.

1. Write the pattern as a string. You can use up to 10 placeholders `{0}`...`{9}`. You can use each placeholder more than once.

2. Construct a `MessageFormat` object with the pattern string as the constructor parameter.

3. Build an array of objects to substitute for the placeholders. The number inside the braces refers to the index in the array of objects.

4. Call the `format` method with the array of objects as a parameter.

CAUTION: Steps 1 and 2 build a `MessageFormat` object that uses the *current locale* for formatting numbers and dates. If you need to specify a different locale, you must *first* construct a `MessageFormat` object with a dummy pattern, then call the `setLocale` method, and finally call the `applyPattern` method with the actual pattern that you want to use.

```
MessageFormat format = new MessageFormat("");
format.setLocale(locale);
format.applyPattern(pattern);
```

Here is an example of these steps. We first supply the array of objects for the placeholders.

```
String pattern =
    "On {2}, a {0} destroyed {1} houses and caused {3} of
        damage.";
MessageFormat msgFmt = new MessageFormat(pattern);

Object[] msgArgs = {
    "hurricane",
    new Integer(99),
    new GregorianCalendar(1999, 0, 1).getTime(),
    new Double(10E7)
};
String msg = msgFmt.format(msgArgs);
System.out.println(msg);
```

The number of the placeholder refers to the index in the object array. For example, the first placeholder {2} is replaced with `msgArgs[2]`. Since we need to supply objects, we have to remember to wrap integers and floating-point numbers in their `Integer` and `Double` wrappers before passing them. Notice the cumbersome construction of the date that we used. The `format` method expects an object of type `Date`, but the `Date(int, int, int)` constructor is deprecated in favor of the `Calendar` class. Therefore, we have to create a `Calendar` object and then call the `getTime` (sic) method to convert it to a `Date` object.

This code prints:

```
On 1/1/99 12:00 AM, a hurricane destroyed 99 houses
    and caused 100,000,000 of damage.
```

That is a start, but it is not perfect. We don't want to display the time "12:00 AM," and we want the damage amount printed as a currency value. The way we do this is by supplying an (optional) format for some or all of the placeholders. There are two ways to supply formats:

- By adding them to the pattern string;
- By calling the `setFormat` or `setFormats` method.

Let's do the easy one first. We can set a format for each individual *occurrence* of a placeholder. In our example, we want the first occurrence of a placeholder (which is placeholder {2}) to be formatted as a date, without a time field. And we want the fourth placeholder to be formatted as a currency. Actually, the placeholders are numbered starting at 0, so we actually want to set the formats of placeholders 0 and 3. We will use the formatters that you saw earlier in this chapter, namely, `DateFormat.getDateInstance(loc)` and `NumberFormat.getCurrency-Instance(loc)`, where `loc` is the locale we want to use. Conveniently, all formatters have a common base class `Format`. The `setFormat` method of the

`MessageText` class receives an integer, the 0-based count of the placeholder to which the format should be applied, and a `Format` reference.

To build the format we want, we simply set the formats of placeholders 0 and 3 and then call the `format` method.

```
msgFmt.setFormat(0,
    DateFormat.getDateInstance(DateFormat.LONG, loc));
msgFmt.setFormat(3, NumberFormat.getCurrencyInstance(loc));
String msg = msgFmt.format(msgArgs);
System.out.println(msg);
```

Now, the printout is

```
On January 1, 1999, a hurricane destroyed 99 houses
and caused $100,000,000.00 of damage.
```

Next, rather than setting the formats individually, we can pack them into an array. Use `null` if you don't need any special format.

```
Format argFormats[] =
{
    DateFormat.getDateInstance(DateFormat.LONG, loc),
    null,
    null,
    NumberFormat.getCurrencyInstance(loc)
};
```

```
msgFmt.setFormats(argFormats);
```

Note that the `msgArgs` and the `argFormats` array entries *do not correspond to one another*. The `msgArgs` indexes correspond to the number inside the `{ }` delimiters. The `argFormats` indexes correspond to the position of the `{ }` delimiters inside the message string. This arrangement sounds cumbersome, but there is a reason for it. It is possible for the placeholders to be repeated in the string, and each occurrence may require a different format. Therefore, the formats must be indexed by position. For example, if the exact time of the disaster was known, we might use the date object twice, once to extract the day and once to extract the time.

```
String pattern =
    "On {2}, a {0} touched down at {2} and destroyed {1}
        houses.";
MessageFormat msgFmt = new MessageFormat(pattern);

Format argFormats[] =
{   DateFormat.getDateInstance(DateFormat.LONG, loc),
    null,
    DateFormat.getTimeInstance(DateFormat.SHORT, loc),
    null
};
```

```
msg.setFormats(argFormats);

Object[] msgArgs = {
    "hurricane",
    new Integer(99),
    new GregorianCalendar(1999, 0, 1, 11, 45, 0).getTime(),
};
String msg = msgFmt.format(msgArgs);
System.out.println(msg);
```

This example code prints:

```
On January 1, 1999, a hurricane touched down
at 11:45 AM and destroyed 99 houses.
```

Note that the placeholder {2} was printed twice, with two different formats!

Rather than setting placeholders dynamically, we can also set them in the message string. For example, here we specify the date and currency formats directly in the message pattern.

```
"On {2,date,long}, a {0} destroyed {1} houses
and caused {3,number,currency} of damage."
```

If you specify formats directly, you don't need to make a call to setFormat or setFormats. In general, you can make the placeholder index be followed by a type and a style. Separate the index, *type,* and *style* by commas. The type can be any of:

```
number
time
date
choice
```

If the type is number, then the style can be:

```
integer
currency
percent
```

or it can be a number format pattern such as $,##0. (See Chapter 3 of Volume 1 for a discussion of number format patterns.)

If the type is either time or date, then the style can be:

```
short
medium
long
full
```

or a date format pattern. (See the documentation of the SimpleDateFormat class for more information about the possible formats.)

Choice formats are more complex, and we take them up in the next section.

java.text.MessageFormat

- MessageFormat(String pattern)

  constructs a message format object with the specified pattern.

- void applyPattern(String pattern)

  sets the pattern of a message format object to the specified pattern.

- void setLocale(Locale loc)
- Locale getLocale()

  set or get the locale to be used for the placeholders in the message. The locale is *only* used for subsequent patterns that you set by calling the applyPattern method.

- void setFormats(Format[] formats)
- Format[] getFormats()

  set or get the formats to be used for the placeholders in the message.

- void setFormat(int i, Format format)

  sets the formats to be used for the ith placeholder in the message.

- String format(String pattern, Object[] args)

  formats the objects by using args[i] as input for placeholder {i}.

Choice Formats

Let's look closer at the pattern of the preceding section:

```
"On {2}, a {0} destroyed {1} houses and caused {3} of damage."
```

If we replace the disaster placeholder {0} with "earthquake", then the sentence is not grammatically correct in English.

```
On January 1, 1999, a earthquake destroyed . . .
```

That means what we really want to do is integrate the article "a" into the placeholder:

```
"On {2}, {0} destroyed {1} houses and caused {3} of damage."
```

Then, the {0} would be replaced with "a hurricane" or "an earthquake". That is especially appropriate if this message needs to be translated into a language where the gender of a word affects the article. For example, in German, the pattern would be

```
"{0} zerstörte am {2} {1} Häuser und richtete einen Schaden von
    {3} an."
```

The placeholder would then be replaced with the grammatically correct combination of article and noun, such as "Ein Wirbelsturm", "Eine Naturkatastrophe".

Now let us turn to the {1} parameter. If the disaster isn't all that catastrophic, then {1} might be replaced with the number 1, and the message would read:

```
On January 1, 1999, a mudslide destroyed 1 houses and . . .
```

We would ideally like the message to vary according to the placeholder value, so that it can read

```
no houses
one house
2 houses
. . .
```

depending on the placeholder value. The ChoiceFormat class was designed to let you do this. A ChoiceFormat object is constructed with two arrays:

* An array of *limits*

* An array of *format strings*

```
double[] limits = . . .;
String[] formatStrings = . . .;
ChoiceFormat choiceFmt = new ChoiceFormat(limits,
    formatStrings);
double input = . . .;
String s = choiceFmt.format(input);
```

The limits and formatStrings arrays must have the same length. The numbers in the limits array must be in ascending order. Then, the format method checks between which limits the input falls. If

```
limits[i] <= input && input < limits[i + 1]
```

then formatStrings[i] is used to format the input. If the input is at least as large as the last limit, then the last format string is used. And, if the input is less than limits[0], then formatStrings[0] is used anyway.

For example, consider these limits and format strings:

```
double[] limits = {0, 1, 2};
String[] formatStrings = {"no houses", "one house", "many
    houses"};
```

Table 10–4 shows the return values of the call to

```
String selected = choiceFmt.format(input);
```

Table 10–4: String selected by ChoiceFormat

input	selected
input < 0	"no houses"
0 <= input && input < 1	"no houses"
1 <= input && input < 2	"one house"
2 <= input	"many houses"

> **NOTE:** This example shows that the designer of the `ChoiceFormat` class was a bit muddleheaded. If you have three strings, you need two limits to separate them. In general, you need *one fewer limit* than you have strings. Thus, the first limit is meaningless, and you can simply set the first and second limit to the same number. For example, the following code works fine:
>
> ```
> double[] limits = {1, 1, 2};
> String[] formatStrings = {"no houses", "one house", "many
>     houses"};
> ChoiceFormat choiceFmt = new ChoiceFormat(limits,
>     formatStrings);
> ```

Of course, in our case, we don't want to return `"many houses"` if the number of houses is 2 or greater. We still want the value to be formatted. Here is the code to format the value.

```
double[] limits = {0, 1, 2};
String[] formatStrings = {"no houses", "one house", "{1}
    houses"};
ChoiceFormat choiceFmt = new ChoiceFormat(limits,
    formatStrings);
msgFmt.setFormat(2, choiceFmt);
```

That is, we create the choice format object and set it as the format to use for the third placeholder (because the count is 0-based).

Why do we use `{1}` in the format string? The usage is a little mysterious. When the message format applies the choice format on the placeholder, the choice format returns `"{1} houses"`. That string is then formatted again by the message format, and the answer is spliced into the result. As a rule, you should always feed back the same placeholder that was used to make the choice. Otherwise, you can create weird effects.

You can add formatting information to the returned string, for example,

```
String[] formatStrings
  = {"no houses", "one house", "{1, number, integer} houses"};
```

As you saw in the preceding section, it is also possible to express the choice format directly in a format string. When the format type is `choice`, then the next parameter is a list of pairs, each pair consisting of a limit and a format string, separated by a #. The pairs themselves are separated by |. Here is how to express the house format:

```
{1,choice,0#no houses|1#one house|2#{1} houses}
```

Thus, there are three sets of choices:

```
0#no houses
1#one house
2#{1} houses
```

The first one is used if the placeholder value is < 1, the second is used if the value is at least 1 but < 2, and the third is used if the value is at least 2.

NOTE: As previously noted, the first limit is meaningless. But here you can't set the first and second limits to the same value; the format parser complains that

```
1#no houses|1#one house|2#{1} houses
```

is an invalid choice. In this case, you must set the first limit to any number that is strictly less than the second limit. You can safely use -∞ as the first bound—write it as `-\u221E`, using the Unicode character for the infinity symbol.

The syntax would have been a lot clearer if the designer of this class realized that the limits belong *between* the choices, such as

```
no houses|1|one house|2|{1} houses
// not the actual format
```

You can use the < symbol to denote that a choice should be selected if the left bound is strictly less than the right bound.

The < symbol is translated into a limit that is the next floating point number after the number specified in the choice string. There is even a static method `Choice-Format.nextDouble` to compute that number.

You can also use the ≤ symbol (expressed as the Unicode character code `\u2264`) as a synonym for #.

For example,

```
{0,choice,-\u221E<negative|0\u2264zero|0<positive}
```

or

```
{0,choice,-∞<negative|0≤zero|0<positive}
```

yields the following strings:

- `negative` if -∞ ≤ input and input < 0:
- `zero` if 0 ≤ input and input < `ChoiceFormat.nextDouble(0)`
- `positive` if `ChoiceFormat.nextDouble(0)` ≤ input

Let's return to our natural disaster scenario. If we put the choice string inside the original message string, then we get the rather monstrous format instruction:

```
String pattern =
"On {2,date,long}, {0} destroyed {1,choice,0#no houses|1#one
    house|2#{1} houses}
and caused {3,number,currency} of damage.";
```

Or, in German,

```
String pattern =
"{0} zerstörte am {2,date,long} {1,choice,0#kein Haus|1#ein
```

```
        Haus|2#{1} Häuser}
    und richtete einen Schaden von {3,number,currency} an.";
```

Note that the ordering of the words is different in German, but the array of objects you pass to the format method is the *same*. The order of the placeholders in the format string takes care of the changes in the word ordering.

java.text.ChoiceFormat

- ChoiceFormat(String pattern)

  constructs a choice format from a pattern string containing a | delimited set of pairs, each of which is of the form limit#formatString.

- ChoiceFormat(double limits[], String formatStrings[])

  constructs a choice format with the given limits and formats. The limits must be increasing. If input is the value to be formatted, then it is formatted with the formatString[i], where i is the smallest index such that limits[i] <= input. However, all inputs that are less than limits[1] are formatted with formatString[0].

- static double nextDouble(double x)

  returns the smallest double-precision floating-point number that is strictly greater than x. For example, nextDouble(0) is 4.9E-324.

Character Set Conversion

As you know, the Java programming language itself is fully Unicode-based. However, operating systems typically have their own, homegrown, often incompatible character encoding, such as ISO 8859-1 (an 8-bit code sometimes called the "ANSI" code) in the United States, or BIG5 in Taiwan. So, the input that you receive from a user might be in a different encoding system, and the strings that you show to the user must eventually be encoded in a way that the local operating system understands.

Of course, *inside* your program, you should always use Unicode characters. You have to hope that the implementation of the Java virtual machine on that platform successfully converts input and output between Unicode and the local character set. For example, if you set a button label, you specify the string in Unicode, and it is up to the Java virtual machine to get the button to display your string correctly. Similarly, when you call getText to get user input from a text box, you get the string in Unicode, no matter how the user entered it.

However, you need to be careful with text files. Never read a text file one byte at a time! Always use the InputStreamReader or FileReader classes that were described in Volume 1, Chapter 12. These classes automatically convert from a particular character encoding to Unicode. By default, they use the local encoding scheme, but as you saw in Volume 1, Chapter 12, you can specify the encoding in the constructor of the `InputStreamReader` class, for example,

```
InputStreamReader in = new InputStreamReader(in, "8859_1");
```

Unfortunately, there is currently no connection between locales and character encodings. For example, if your user has selected the Chinese Traditional locale `zh_TW`, there is no method in the Java programming language that tells you that the BIG5 character encoding would be the most appropriate.

When writing text files, you need to decide:

* Is the output of the text file intended for humans to read or for use with other programs on their local machines?
* Is the output simply going to be fed into the same or another program?

If the output is intended for human consumption or a non-Unicode-enabled program, you'll need to convert it to the local character encoding by using a `PrintWriter`, as you saw in Volume 1, Chapter 12. Otherwise, just use the `writeUTF` method of the `DataOutputStream` to write the string in Unicode Text Format. Then, of course, the program reading the file must open it as a `DataInputStream`, and must read the string with the `readUTF` method.

TIP: In the case of input to a program in the Java programming language, an even better choice is to use serialization. Then, you never have to worry at all how strings are saved and loaded.

Of course, with both data streams and object streams, the output will not be in human-readable form.

International Issues and Source Files

It is worth keeping in mind that you, the programmer, will need to communicate with the Java compiler. And *you do that with tools on your local system.* For example, you can use the Chinese version of Notepad to write your Java source code files. The resulting source code files are *not portable* because they use the local character encoding (GB or BIG5, depending on which Chinese operating system you use). Only the compiled class files are portable—they will automatically use the UTF encoding for identifiers and strings. That means that even when a program is compiling and running, three character encodings are involved:

* Source files: local encoding
* Class files: UTF
* Virtual machine: Unicode

To make your source files portable, restrict yourself to using the plain ASCII encoding. That is, you should change all non-ASCII characters to their equivalent Unicode encodings. For example, rather than using the string `"Häuser"`, use `"H\u0084user"`. The SDK contains a utility, `native2ascii`, that you can use to convert the native character encoding to plain ASCII. This utility simply replaces every non-ASCII character in the input with a `\u` followed by the four hex digits of the Unicode value. To use the `native2ascii` program, simply provide the input and output file names.

```
native2ascii Myfile.java Myfile.temp
```

You can convert the other way with the `-reverse` option:

```
native2ascii -reverse Myfile.java Myfile.temp
```

And you can specify another encoding with the `-encoding` option. The encoding name must be one of those listed in the encodings table in Chapter 12 of volume 1.

```
native2ascii -encoding Cp437 Myfile.java Myfile.temp
```

Finally, we strongly recommend that you restrict yourself to plain ASCII class names. Since the name of the class also turns into the name of the *class file*, you are at the mercy of the local file system to handle any non-ASCII coded names—and it will almost certainly not do it right. For example, depressingly enough, Windows 95 uses yet another character encoding, the so-called *Code Page 437* or *original PC* encoding, for its file names. Windows 95 makes a valiant attempt to translate between ANSI and original names, but the JVM class loader does not. (NT is much better this way.) For example, if you make a class Bär, then the JDK class loader will complain that it "cannot find class BΣr." There is a reason for this behavior, but you don't want to know. Simply stick to ASCII for your class names until all computers around the world offer consistent support for Unicode.

Resource Bundles

When localizing an application, you'll probably have a dauntingly large number of message strings, button labels, and so on, that all need to be translated. To make this task feasible, you'll want to define the message strings in an external location, usually called a *resource*. The person carrying out the translation can then simply edit the resource files without having to touch the source code of the program.

NOTE: Java technology resources are not the same as Windows or Macintosh resources. A Windows executable program stores resources such as menus, dialog boxes, icons, and messages in a section separate from the program code. A resource editor can be used to inspect and update these resources without affecting the program code.

Java technology, unfortunately, does not have a mechanism for storing external resources in text files. Instead, all resource data must be put in a *class*, either as static variables or as return values of method calls. You create a different class for each locale, and then the `getBundle` method of the `ResourceBundle` class automatically locates the correct class for your locale.

NOTE: Chapter 10 of Volume 1 describes a concept of file resources, where data files, sounds, and images can be placed in a JAR file. The `getResource` method of the class `Class` finds the file, opens it, and returns a URL to the resource. Why? When you write a program that needs access to files, it needs to *find* the files. By placing the files into the JAR file, you leave the job of finding the files to the class loader, which already knows how to locate the class files. While this mechanism does not directly support internationalization, it is useful for locating localized property files, and we take advantage of it in the next section.

Locating Resources

When localizing an application, you need to make a set of classes that describe the locale-specific items (such as messages, labels, and so on) for each locale that you want to support. Each of these classes must extend the class `ResourceBundle`. (You'll see a little later the details involved in designing these kinds of classes.) You also need to use a naming convention for these classes, where the name of the class corresponds to the locale. For example, resources specific for Germany go to the class `ProgramResources_de_DE`, while those that are shared by all German-speaking countries go into `ProgramResources_de`. Taiwan-specific resources go into `ProgramResources_zh_TW`, and any Chinese language strings go into `ProgramResources_zh`. In general, use

```
ProgramResources_language_country
```

for all country-specific resources, and use

```
ProgramResources_language
```

for all language-specific resources. Finally, as a fallback, you can put the U.S. English strings and messages into the class `ProgramResources`, without any suffix. Then, compile all these classes and store them with the other application classes for the project.

Once you have a class for the resource bundle, you load it with the command

```
ResourceBundle currentResources =
    ResourceBundle.getBundle("ProgramResources", currentLocale);
```

The `getBundle` method attempts to load the class that matches the current locale by language, country, and variant. If it is not successful, then the variant, country, and language are dropped in turn. That is, the getBundle method tries to load one of the following classes until it is successful.

```
ProgramResources_language_country_variant
ProgramResources_language_country
ProgramResources_language
ProgramResources
```

If all these attempts are unsuccessful, then the getBundle method tries all over again, only this time it uses the default locale instead of the current locale. If even these attempts fail, the method throws a MissingResourceException.

Once the getBundle method has located a class, say, ProgramResources_de_DE, it will still keep looking for ProgramResources_de and ProgramResources. If these classes exist, they become the *parents* of the ProgramResources_de_DE class in a *resource hierarchy.* Later, when looking up a resource, the getObject method will search the parents if the lookup was not successful in the current class. That is, if a particular resource was not found in ProgramResources_de_DE, then the ProgramResources_de and ProgramResources will be queried as well.

This is clearly a very useful service and one that would be tedious to program by hand. A resource mechanism of the Java programming language lets you locate the class that is the best match for localization information. It is very easy to add more and more localizations to an existing program: all you have to do is add additional resource classes.

Now that you know how a program can locate the correct resource, we show you how to place the language-dependent information into the resource class. Ultimately, it would be nice if you could get tools that even a nonprogrammer could use to define and modify resources. We hope and expect that developers of integrated Java programming environments will eventually provide such tools. But right now, creating resources still involves some programming. We take that up next.

Placing Resources into Bundles

In the Java programming language, you place resources inside classes that extend the ResourceBundle class. Each resource bundle implements a lookup table. When you design a program, you provide a key string for each setting you want to localize, and you use that key string to retrieve the setting. Use getString to retrieve a string resource.

```
String computeButtonLabel
    = resources.getString("computeButton");
```

However, a resource bundle can store objects of *any* kind. Not all localized settings are strings! You use the getObject method to retrieve arbitrary objects from the bundle.

```
Color backgroundColor
    = (Color)resources.getObject("backgroundColor");
double[] paperSize
    = (double[])resources.getObject("defaultPaperSize");
```

TIP: You do not need to place all resources for your application into a single bundle. You could have one bundle for button labels, one for error messages, and so on.

To implement your own resource bundle class, you need to implement two methods:

```
Enumeration getKeys()
Object handleGetObject(String key)
```

The `getObject` and `getString` methods call the `handleGetObject` method that you supply. For example, you can write the following classes to provide German and U.S. English resources.

```
public class ProgramResources extends ResourceBundle
    // place getKeys method in common superclass
{
    public Enumeration getKeys()
    {
        return Collections.enumeration(Arrays.asList(keys));
    }

    private String[] keys = { "computeButton", "backgroundColor",
        "defaultPaperSize" };
}

public class ProgramResources_de extends ProgramResources
{
    public Object handleGetObject(String key)
    {
        if (key.equals("computeButton"))
            return "Rechnen";
        else if (key.equals("backgroundColor")
            return Color.black;
        else if (key.equals("defaultPaperSize")
            return new double[] { 210, 297 };
    }
}

public class ProgramResources_en_US extends ProgramResources
{
    public Object handleGetObject(String key)
    {
        if (key.equals("computeButton"))
            return "Compute";
        else if (key.equals("backgroundColor")
```

```
            return Color.blue;
         else if (key.equals("defaultPaperSize")
            return new double[] { 216, 279 };
      }
   }
```

Of course, it is extremely tedious to write this kind of code for every resource bundle. The Java standard library provides two convenience classes, `ListResourceBundle` and `PropertyResourceBundle`, to make the job easier.

The `ListResourceBundle` lets you place all your resources into an object array, and then it does the lookup for you. You need to supply the following skeleton:

```
public class ProgramResources_language_country
   extends ListResourceBundle
{
   public Object[][] getContents() { return contents;  }
   private static final Object[][] contents =
   {
      // localization information goes here
   }
}
```

For example,

```
public class ProgramResources_de
   extends ListResourceBundle
{
   public Object[][] getContents() { return contents;  }
   private static final Object[][] contents =
   {
      { "computeButton", "Rechnen" },
      { "backgroundColor", Color.black },
      { "defaultPaperSize", new double[] { 210, 297 } }
   }
}

public class ProgramResources_en_US
   extends ListResourceBundle
{
```

```
public Object[][] getContents() { return contents;   }
private static final Object[][] contents =
{
    { "computeButton", "Compute" },
    { "backgroundColor", Color.blue },
    { "defaultPaperSize", new double[] { 216, 279 } }
}
}
```

Note that you need not supply the getObject lookup method. The Java library provides it in the superclass ListResourceBundle.

As an alternative, if all your settings are strings, you can use the more convenient PropertyResourceBundle mechanism. You place all your strings into a property file, as described in Chapter 2. This is simply a text file with one key/value pair per line. A typical file would look like this:

```
computeButton=Rechnen
backgroundColor=black
defaultPaperSize=210x297
```

Then you name your property files according to the following pattern:

```
ProgramStrings.properties
ProgramStrings_en.properties
ProgramStrings_de_DE.properties
```

You can load the resources simply as

```
ResourceBundle bundle
    = ResourceBundle.getBundle("ProgramStrings", locale);
```

The getBundle locates the appropriate property file and turns it into a PropertyResourceBundle. You never work with the PropertyResourceBundle class directly.

Placing all resources into a text file is enormously attractive. It is much easier for the person performing the localization, especially if he or she is not familiar with the Java programming language, to understand a text file than a file with code. The downside is that your program must parse strings (such as the paper size "210x297" in the example above.) The best solution is, therefore, to put the string resources into property files and use a ListResourceBundle for those resource objects that are not strings.

CAUTION: Files for storing properties are always 7-bit ASCII files. If you need to place Unicode characters into a properties file, you need to encode them by using the \uxxxx encoding. For example, to specify "colorName=Grün", use

```
colorName=Gr\u00FCn
```

You can use the native2ascii tool to generate these files.

NOTE: In this section, you saw how to create resource bundles programmatically. Of course, a lot of the code is completely routine. The Java Internationalization and Localization Toolkit (`http://java.sun.com/products/jilkit`) is a tool that can help you manage the creation and maintenance of resource bundles.

`java.util.ResourceBundle`

- `static ResourceBundle getBundle(String baseName, Locale loc)`
- `static ResourceBundle getBundle(String baseName)`

  load the resource bundle class with the given name, for the given locale or the default locale, and its parent classes. If the resource bundle classes are located in a package, then the base name must contain the full package name, such as `"intl.ProgramResources"`. The resource bundle classes must be `public` so that the `getBundle` method can access them.

- `Object getObject(String name)`

  looks up an object from the resource bundle or its parents.

- `String getString(String name)`

  looks up an object from the resource bundle or its parents and casts it as a string.

- `String[] getStringArray(String name)`

  looks up an object from the resource bundle or its parents and casts it as a string array.

- `Enumeration getKeys()`

  returns an enumeration object to enumerate the keys of this resource bundle. It enumerates the keys in the parent bundles as well.

Graphical User Interface Localization

We have spent a lot of time showing you how to localize your applications. Now, we explain how localization requires you to change the kind of code you write. For example, you have to be much more careful how you code your event handlers for user interface events. Consider the following common style of programming:

```
public class MyApplet extends JApplet
   implements ActionListener
{
   public void init()
   {
      JButton cancelButton = new JButton("Cancel");
      cancelButton.addActionListener(this);
      . . .
```

```
    }

    public void actionPerformed(ActionEvent evt)
    {
        String arg = evt.getActionCommand();
        if (arg.equals("Cancel"))
            doCancel();
        else . . .
    }
    . . .
}
```

Many programmers write this kind of code, and it works fine as long as you never internationalize the interface. However, when the button name is translated to German, "Cancel" turns into "Abbrechen." Then, the name needs to be updated automatically in both the `init` method and the `actionPerformed` method. This is clearly error prone—it is a well-known corollary to Murphy's law in computer science that two entities that are supposed to stay in sync, won't. In this case, if you forget to update one of the occurrences of the string, then the button won't work. There are three ways you can eliminate this potential problem.

1.   Use inner classes instead of separate `actionPerformed` procedures.

2.   Identify components by their reference, not their label.

3.   Use the `name` attribute to identify components.

Let us look at these three strategies one by one.

Rather than having one handler that handles many actions, you can easily define a separate handler for every component. For example,

```
public class MyApplet extends JApplet implements ActionListener
{
    public void init()
    {
        JButton cancelButton = new JButton("Cancel");
        cancelButton.addActionListener(new
            ActionListener()
                {
                    public void actionPerformed(ActionEvent e)
                    {
                        doCancel();
                    }
                });
        . . .
    }
    . . .
}
```

This code creates an inner class that listens just to the Cancel button. Since the button and its listener are now tightly joined, there is no more code to parse the button label. Hence, there is only one occurrence of the label string to localize.

We think this is the best solution to the problem of joining a user interface component and its associated handler code. You may not like inner classes, either because they are confusing to read or because each inner class results in an additional class file. The next choice, therefore, is to make the button into an instance variable and compare its reference against the source of the command.

```
public class MyApplet extends JApplet implements ActionListener
{
    public void init()
    {
        cancelButton = new JButton("Cancel");
        cancelButton.addActionListener(this);
        . . .
    }

    public void actionPerformed(ActionEvent evt)
    {
        Object source = evt.getSource();
        if (source == cancelButton)
            doCancel();
        else . . .
    }
    . . .
    private JButton cancelButton;
}
```

This approach works fine too. Note that now every user interface element must be stored in an instance variable, and the `actionPerformed` method must have access to the variables.

Finally, you can give any class that inherits from `Component` (such as the `Button` class) a *name* property. This name may or may not be distinct from its label in a specific locale, but this is irrelevant; the name property stays constant *regardless* of locale changes. For example, if you give a cancel button the name `"cancel1"`, this is not a visual attribute of the button, it is simply a text string associated with the button. (Think of it as a property of the button—see Chapter 8 for more on properties.) When an action event is triggered, you first get the source and then you can find the name attribute of the source.

```
public class MyApplet extends JApplet implements ActionListener
{
```

```
    public void init()
    {
        JButton cancelButton = new JButton("Cancel");
        cancelButton.setName("cancel1");
        cancelButton.addActionListener(this);
        . . .
    }

    public void actionPerformed(ActionEvent evt)
    {
        Component source = (Component)evt.getSource();
        if (source.getName().equals("cancel1"))
            doCancel();
        . . .
    }
    . . .
}
```

`java.awt.Component`

- void setName(String s)
- String getName()

  set or get a component name, an arbitrary tag associated with the component.

Localizing an Applet

In this section, we apply the material from this chapter to localize a retirement calculator applet.

The applet calculates whether or not you are saving enough money for your retirement. You enter your age, how much money you save every month, and so on (see Figure 10–5).

The text area and the graph show the balance of the retirement account for every year. If the numbers turn negative toward the later part of your life and the bars in the graph show up below the x-axis, you need to do something; for example, save more money, postpone your retirement, die earlier, or be younger.

The retirement calculator now works in three locales (English, German, and Chinese). Here are some of the highlights of the internationalization.

- The labels, buttons, and messages are translated into German and Chinese. You can find them in the classes RetireResources_de, RetireResources_zh. English is used as the fallback—see the RetireResources file. To generate the Chinese messages, we first typed the file, using Notepad running in Chinese Windows, and then we used the native2ascii utility to convert the characters to Unicode.

Figure 10–5: The retirement calculator in English

- Whenever the locale changes, we reset the labels and reformat the contents of the text fields.

- The text fields handle numbers, currency amounts, and percentages in the local format.

- The computation field uses a `MessageFormat`. The format string is stored in the resource bundle of each language.

- Just to show that it can be done, we use different colors for the bar graph, depending on the language chosen by the user.

Examples 10–5 through 10–8 show the code. Examples 10–9 through 10–11 are the property files for the localized strings. Figures 10–6 and 10–7 show the outputs in German and Chinese. To see Chinese characters, you need to run the applet under Chinese Windows or manually install the Chinese fonts. Otherwise, all Chinese characters show up as "missing character" icons.

NOTE: This applet was harder to write than a typical localized application because the user can change the locale on-the-fly. The applet, therefore, had to be prepared to redraw itself whenever the user selects another locale. If you simply want to display your applet in the user's default locale, you will not need to work so hard. You can simply call `getLocale()` to find the locale of your user's system, and then use it for the entire duration of the applet.

In sum, while the localization mechanism of the Java programming language still has some rough edges, it does have one major virtue. Once you have organized your application for localization, it is extremely easy to add more localized versions. You simply provide more resource files, and they will be automatically loaded when a user wants them.

Figure 10–6: The retirement calculator in German

Figure 10–7: The retirement calculator in Chinese

Example 10–5: Retire.java

```
1. import java.awt.*;
2. import java.awt.event.*;
3. import java.awt.geom.*;
4. import java.applet.*;
5. import java.util.*;
6. import java.text.*;
7. import java.io.*;
8. import javax.swing.*;
9.
10. /**
11.    This applet shows a retirement calculator. The UI is displayed
12.    in English, German, and Chinese.
13. */
14. public class Retire extends JApplet
15. {
16.    public void init()
17.    {
18.       GridBagLayout gbl = new GridBagLayout();
19.       getContentPane().setLayout(gbl);
20.
21.       GridBagConstraints gbc = new GridBagConstraints();
22.       gbc.weightx = 100;
23.       gbc.weighty = 0;
24.
25.       gbc.fill = GridBagConstraints.NONE;
26.       gbc.anchor = GridBagConstraints.EAST;
27.       add(languageLabel, gbc, 0, 0, 1, 1);
28.       add(savingsLabel, gbc, 0, 1, 1, 1);
29.       add(contribLabel, gbc, 2, 1, 1, 1);
30.       add(incomeLabel, gbc, 4, 1, 1, 1);
31.       add(currentAgeLabel, gbc, 0, 2, 1, 1);
32.       add(retireAgeLabel, gbc, 2, 2, 1, 1);
33.       add(deathAgeLabel, gbc, 4, 2, 1, 1);
34.       add(inflationPercentLabel, gbc, 0, 3, 1, 1);
35.       add(investPercentLabel, gbc, 2, 3, 1, 1);
36.
37.       gbc.fill = GridBagConstraints.HORIZONTAL;
38.       gbc.anchor = GridBagConstraints.WEST;
39.       add(localeCombo, gbc, 1, 0, 2, 1);
40.       add(savingsField, gbc, 1, 1, 1, 1);
41.       add(contribField, gbc, 3, 1, 1, 1);
42.       add(incomeField, gbc, 5, 1, 1, 1);
43.       add(currentAgeField, gbc, 1, 2, 1, 1);
44.       add(retireAgeField, gbc, 3, 2, 1, 1);
45.       add(deathAgeField, gbc, 5, 2, 1, 1);
46.       add(inflationPercentField, gbc, 1, 3, 1, 1);
47.       add(investPercentField, gbc, 3, 3, 1, 1);
48.
```

```
49.        computeButton.setName("computeButton");
50.        computeButton.addActionListener(new
51.            ActionListener()
52.            {
53.                public void actionPerformed(ActionEvent event)
54.                {
55.                    getInfo();
56.                    updateData();
57.                    updateGraph();
58.                }
59.            });
60.        add(computeButton, gbc, 5, 3, 1, 1);
61.
62.        gbc.weighty = 100;
63.        gbc.fill = GridBagConstraints.BOTH;
64.        add(retireCanvas, gbc, 0, 4, 4, 1);
65.        add(new JScrollPane(retireText), gbc, 4, 4, 2, 1);
66.        retireText.setEditable(false);
67.        retireText.setFont(new Font("Monospaced", Font.PLAIN, 10));
68.
69.        info.setSavings(0);
70.        info.setContrib(9000);
71.        info.setIncome(60000);
72.        info.setCurrentAge(35);
73.        info.setRetireAge(65);
74.        info.setDeathAge(85);
75.        info.setInvestPercent(0.1);
76.        info.setInflationPercent(0.05);
77.
78.        localeCombo.addActionListener(new
79.            ActionListener()
80.            {
81.                public void actionPerformed(ActionEvent event)
82.                {
83.                    setCurrentLocale(
84.                        locales[localeCombo.getSelectedIndex()]);
85.                }
86.            });
87.
88.        locales = new Locale[]
89.            { Locale.US, Locale.CHINA, Locale.GERMANY };
90.
91.        int localeIndex = 0; // US locale is default selection
92.
93.        for (int i = 0; i < locales.length; i++)
94.            // if current locale one of the choices, we'll select it
95.            if (getLocale().equals(locales[i])) localeIndex = i;
96.
97.        setCurrentLocale(locales[localeIndex]);
```

```
98.      }
99.
100.     /**
101.        A convenience method to add a component to given grid bag
102.        layout locations.
103.        @param c the component to add
104.        @param gbc the grid bag constraints to use
105.        @param x the x grid position
106.        @param y the y grid position
107.        @param w the grid width
108.        @param h the grid height
109.     */
110.     public void add(Component c, GridBagConstraints gbc,
111.        int x, int y, int w, int h)
112.     {
113.        gbc.gridx = x;
114.        gbc.gridy = y;
115.        gbc.gridwidth = w;
116.        gbc.gridheight = h;
117.        getContentPane().add(c, gbc);
118.     }
119.
120.     /**
121.        Sets the current locale.
122.        @param locale the desired locale
123.     */
124.     public void setCurrentLocale(Locale locale)
125.     {
126.        currentLocale = locale;
127.
128.        int localeIndex = localeCombo.getSelectedIndex();
129.        localeCombo.removeAllItems();
130.        for (int i = 0; i < locales.length; i++)
131.        {
132.           String language
133.              = locales[i].getDisplayLanguage(currentLocale);
134.           localeCombo.addItem(language);
135.        }
136.        if (localeIndex >= 0)
137.           localeCombo.setSelectedIndex(localeIndex);
138.
139.        res = ResourceBundle.getBundle("RetireResources",
140.           currentLocale);
141.        resStrings = ResourceBundle.getBundle("RetireStrings",
142.           currentLocale);
143.        currencyFmt
144.           = NumberFormat.getCurrencyInstance(currentLocale);
145.        numberFmt
146.           = NumberFormat.getNumberInstance(currentLocale);
```

```
147.      percentFmt
148.         = NumberFormat.getPercentInstance(currentLocale);
149.
150.      updateDisplay();
151.      updateInfo();
152.      updateData();
153.      updateGraph();
154.   }
155.
156.   /**
157.      Updates all labels in the display.
158.   */
159.   public void updateDisplay()
160.   {
161.      languageLabel.setText(resStrings.getString("language"));
162.      savingsLabel.setText(resStrings.getString("savings"));
163.      contribLabel.setText(resStrings.getString("contrib"));
164.      incomeLabel.setText(resStrings.getString("income"));
165.      currentAgeLabel.setText(
166.         resStrings.getString("currentAge"));
167.      retireAgeLabel.setText(resStrings.getString("retireAge"));
168.      deathAgeLabel.setText(resStrings.getString("deathAge"));
169.      inflationPercentLabel.setText(
170.         resStrings.getString("inflationPercent"));
171.      investPercentLabel.setText(
172.         resStrings.getString("investPercent"));
173.      computeButton.setText(
174.         resStrings.getString("computeButton"));
175.
176.      validate();
177.   }
178.
179.   /**
180.      Updates the information in the text fields.
181.   */
182.   public void updateInfo()
183.   {
184.      savingsField.setText(
185.         currencyFmt.format(info.getSavings()));
186.      contribField.setText(
187.         currencyFmt.format(info.getContrib()));
188.      incomeField.setText(currencyFmt.format(info.getIncome()));
189.      currentAgeField.setText(
190.         numberFmt.format(info.getCurrentAge()));
191.      retireAgeField.setText(
192.         numberFmt.format(info.getRetireAge()));
193.      deathAgeField.setText(
194.         numberFmt.format(info.getDeathAge()));
195.      investPercentField.setText(
```

```
196.            percentFmt.format(info.getInvestPercent()));
197.        inflationPercentField.setText(
198.            percentFmt.format(info.getInflationPercent()));
199.     }
200.
201.     /**
202.        Updates the data displayed in the text area.
203.     */
204.     public void updateData()
205.     {
206.        retireText.setText("");
207.        MessageFormat retireMsg = new MessageFormat("");
208.        retireMsg.setLocale(currentLocale);
209.        retireMsg.applyPattern(resStrings.getString("retire"));
210.
211.        for (int i = info.getCurrentAge();
212.             i <= info.getDeathAge(); i++)
213.        {
214.            Object[] args = { new Integer(i),
215.                new Double(info.getBalance(i)) };
216.            retireText.append(retireMsg.format(args) + "\n");
217.        }
218.     }
219.
220.     /**
221.        Updates the graph.
222.     */
223.     public void updateGraph()
224.     {
225.        retireCanvas.setColorPre(
226.            (Color)res.getObject("colorPre"));
227.        retireCanvas.setColorGain(
228.            (Color)res.getObject("colorGain"));
229.        retireCanvas.setColorLoss(
230.            (Color)res.getObject("colorLoss"));
231.        retireCanvas.setInfo(info);
232.        repaint();
233.     }
234.
235.     /**
236.        Reads the user input from the text fields.
237.     */
238.     public void getInfo()
239.     {
240.        try
241.        {
242.            info.setSavings(currencyFmt.parse(
243.                savingsField.getText()).doubleValue());
244.            info.setContrib(currencyFmt.parse(
```

```
245.              contribField.getText()).doubleValue());
246.          info.setIncome(currencyFmt.parse(
247.              incomeField.getText()).doubleValue());
248.          info.setCurrentAge(numberFmt.parse(
249.              currentAgeField.getText()).intValue());
250.          info.setRetireAge(numberFmt.parse(
251.              retireAgeField.getText()).intValue());
252.          info.setDeathAge(numberFmt.parse(
253.              deathAgeField.getText()).intValue());
254.          info.setInvestPercent(percentFmt.parse(
255.              investPercentField.getText()).doubleValue());
256.          info.setInflationPercent(percentFmt.parse(
257.              inflationPercentField.getText()).doubleValue());
258.       }
259.       catch (ParseException exception)
260.       {
261.       }
262.    }
263.
264.    private JTextField savingsField = new JTextField(10);
265.    private JTextField contribField = new JTextField(10);
266.    private JTextField incomeField = new JTextField(10);
267.    private JTextField currentAgeField = new JTextField(4);
268.    private JTextField retireAgeField = new JTextField(4);
269.    private JTextField deathAgeField = new JTextField(4);
270.    private JTextField inflationPercentField = new JTextField(6);
271.    private JTextField investPercentField = new JTextField(6);
272.    private JTextArea retireText = new JTextArea(10, 25);
273.    private RetireCanvas retireCanvas = new RetireCanvas();
274.    private JButton computeButton = new JButton();
275.    private JLabel languageLabel = new JLabel();
276.    private JLabel savingsLabel = new JLabel();
277.    private JLabel contribLabel = new JLabel();
278.    private JLabel incomeLabel = new JLabel();
279.    private JLabel currentAgeLabel = new JLabel();
280.    private JLabel retireAgeLabel = new JLabel();
281.    private JLabel deathAgeLabel = new JLabel();
282.    private JLabel inflationPercentLabel = new JLabel();
283.    private JLabel investPercentLabel = new JLabel();
284.
285.    private RetireInfo info = new RetireInfo();
286.
287.    private Locale[] locales;
288.    private Locale currentLocale;
289.    private JComboBox localeCombo = new JComboBox();
290.    private ResourceBundle res;
291.    private ResourceBundle resStrings;
292.    private NumberFormat currencyFmt;
293.    private NumberFormat numberFmt;
```

```
294.    private NumberFormat percentFmt;
295. }
296.
297. /**
298.    The information required to compute retirement income data.
299. */
300. class RetireInfo
301. {
302.    /**
303.        Gets the available balance for a given year.
304.        @param year the year for which to compute the balance
305.        @return the amount of money available (or required) in
306.        that year
307.    */
308.    public double getBalance(int year)
309.    {
310.        if (year < currentAge) return 0;
311.        else if (year == currentAge)
312.        {
313.            age = year;
314.            balance = savings;
315.            return balance;
316.        }
317.        else if (year == age)
318.            return balance;
319.        if (year != age + 1)
320.            getBalance(year - 1);
321.        age = year;
322.        if (age < retireAge)
323.            balance += contrib;
324.        else
325.            balance -= income;
326.        balance = balance
327.            * (1 + (investPercent - inflationPercent));
328.        return balance;
329.    }
330.
331.    /**
332.        Gets the amount of prior savings.
333.        @return the savings amount
334.    */
335.    public double getSavings()
336.    {
337.        return savings;
338.    }
339.
340.    /**
341.        Sets the amount of prior savings.
342.        @param x the savings amount
```

```
343.     */
344.     public void setSavings(double x)
345.     {
346.        savings = x;
347.     }
348.
349.     /**
350.        Gets the annual contribution to the retirement account.
351.        @return the contribution amount
352.     */
353.     public double getContrib()
354.     {
355.        return contrib;
356.     }
357.
358.     /**
359.        Sets the annual contribution to the retirement account.
360.        @param x the contribution amount
361.     */
362.     public void setContrib(double x)
363.     {
364.        contrib = x;
365.     }
366.
367.     /**
368.        Gets the annual income.
369.        @return the income amount
370.     */
371.     public double getIncome()
372.     {
373.        return income;
374.     }
375.
376.     /**
377.        Sets the annual income.
378.        @param x the income amount
379.     */
380.     public void setIncome(double x)
381.     {
382.        income = x;
383.     }
384.
385.     /**
386.        Gets the current age.
387.        @return the age
388.     */
389.     public int getCurrentAge()
390.     {
391.        return currentAge;
```

```
392.    }
393.
394.    /**
395.       Sets the current age.
396.       @param x the age
397.    */
398.    public void setCurrentAge(int x)
399.    {
400.       currentAge = x;
401.    }
402.
403.    /**
404.       Gets the desired retirement age.
405.       @return the age
406.    */
407.    public int getRetireAge()
408.    {
409.       return retireAge;
410.    }
411.
412.    /**
413.       Sets the desired retirement age.
414.       @param x the age
415.    */
416.    public void setRetireAge(int x)
417.    {
418.       retireAge = x;
419.    }
420.
421.    /**
422.       Gets the expected age of death.
423.       @return the age
424.    */
425.    public int getDeathAge()
426.    {
427.       return deathAge;
428.    }
429.
430.    /**
431.       Sets the expected age of death.
432.       @param x the age
433.    */
434.    public void setDeathAge(int x)
435.    {
436.       deathAge = x;
437.    }
438.
439.    /**
440.       Gets the estimated percentage of inflation.
```

```
441.        @return the percentage
442.     */
443.    public double getInflationPercent()
444.    {
445.        return inflationPercent;
446.    }
447.
448.    /**
449.        Sets the estimated percentage of inflation.
450.        @param x the percentage
451.     */
452.    public void setInflationPercent(double x)
453.    {
454.        inflationPercent = x;
455.    }
456.
457.    /**
458.        Gets the estimated yield of the investment.
459.        @return the percentage
460.     */
461.    public double getInvestPercent()
462.    {
463.        return investPercent;
464.    }
465.
466.    /**
467.        Sets the estimated yield of the investment.
468.        @param x the percentage
469.     */
470.    public void setInvestPercent(double x)
471.    {
472.        investPercent = x;
473.    }
474.
475.    private double savings;
476.    private double contrib;
477.    private double income;
478.    private int currentAge;
479.    private int retireAge;
480.    private int deathAge;
481.    private double inflationPercent;
482.    private double investPercent;
483.
484.    private int age;
485.    private double balance;
486. }
487.
488. /**
489.    This panel draws a graph of the investment result.
```

```
490. */
491. class RetireCanvas extends JPanel
492. {
493.    public RetireCanvas()
494.    {
495.       setSize(WIDTH, HEIGHT);
496.    }
497.
498.    /**
499.       Sets the retirement information to be plotted.
500.       @param newInfo the new retirement info.
501.    */
502.    public void setInfo(RetireInfo newInfo)
503.    {
504.       info = newInfo;
505.       repaint();
506.    }
507.
508.    public void paintComponent(Graphics g)
509.    {
510.       Graphics2D g2 = (Graphics2D)g;
511.       if (info == null) return;
512.
513.       double minValue = 0;
514.       double maxValue = 0;
515.       int i;
516.       for (i = info.getCurrentAge();
517.            i <= info.getDeathAge(); i++)
518.       {
519.          double v = info.getBalance(i);
520.          if (minValue > v) minValue = v;
521.          if (maxValue < v) maxValue = v;
522.       }
523.       if (maxValue == minValue) return;
524.
525.       int barWidth = getWidth() / (info.getDeathAge()
526.          - info.getCurrentAge() + 1);
527.       double scale = getHeight() / (maxValue - minValue);
528.
529.       for (i = info.getCurrentAge();
530.            i <= info.getDeathAge(); i++)
531.       {
532.          int x1 = (i - info.getCurrentAge()) * barWidth + 1;
533.          int y1;
534.          double v = info.getBalance(i);
535.          int height;
536.          int yOrigin = (int)(maxValue * scale);
537.
538.          if (v >= 0)
```

```
539.            {
540.                y1 = (int)((maxValue - v) * scale);
541.                height = yOrigin - y1;
542.            }
543.            else
544.            {
545.                y1 = yOrigin;
546.                height = (int)(-v * scale);
547.            }
548.
549.            if (i < info.getRetireAge())
550.                g2.setColor(colorPre);
551.            else if (v >= 0)
552.                g2.setColor(colorGain);
553.            else
554.                g2.setColor(colorLoss);
555.            Rectangle2D bar = new Rectangle2D.Double(x1, y1,
556.                barWidth - 2, height);
557.            g2.fill(bar);
558.            g2.setColor(Color.black);
559.            g2.draw(bar);
560.        }
561.    }
562.
563.    /**
564.        Sets the color to be used before retirement.
565.        @param color the desired color
566.    */
567.    public void setColorPre(Color color)
568.    {
569.        colorPre = color;
570.        repaint();
571.    }
572.
573.    /**
574.        Sets the color to be used after retirement while
575.        the account balance is positive.
576.        @param color the desired color
577.    */
578.    public void setColorGain(Color color)
579.    {
580.        colorGain = color;
581.        repaint();
582.    }
583.
584.    /**
585.        Sets the color to be used after retirement when
586.        the account balance is negative.
587.        @param color the desired color
```

```
588.     */
589.     public void setColorLoss(Color color)
590.     {
591.        colorLoss = color;
592.        repaint();
593.     }
594.
595.     private RetireInfo info = null;
596.
597.     private Color colorPre;
598.     private Color colorGain;
599.     private Color colorLoss;
600.     private static final int WIDTH = 400;
601.     private static final int HEIGHT = 200;
602. }
```

Example 10–6: RetireResources.java

```
1. import java.util.*;
2. import java.awt.*;
3.
4. /**
5.    These are the English non-string resources for the retirement
6.    calculator.
7. */
8. public class RetireResources
9.     extends java.util.ListResourceBundle
10. {
11.    public Object[][] getContents() { return contents; }
12.    static final Object[][] contents =
13.    {
14.       // BEGIN LOCALIZE
15.       { "colorPre", Color.blue },
16.       { "colorGain", Color.white },
17.       { "colorLoss", Color.red }
18.       // END LOCALIZE
19.    };
20. }
```

Example 10–7: RetireResources_de.java

```
1. import java.util.*;
2. import java.awt.*;
3.
4. /**
5.    These are the German non-string resources for the retirement
6.    calculator.
7. */
8. public class RetireResources_de
9.     extends java.util.ListResourceBundle
```

```
10. {
11.    public Object[][] getContents() { return contents; }
12.    static final Object[][] contents =
13.    {
14.       // BEGIN LOCALIZE
15.       { "colorPre", Color.yellow },
16.       { "colorGain", Color.black },
17.       { "colorLoss", Color.red }
18.       // END LOCALIZE
19.    };
20. }
```

Example 10–8:   RetireResources_zh.java

```
1. import java.util.*;
2. import java.awt.*;
3.
4. /**
5.    These are the Chinese non-string resources for the retirement
6.    calculator.
7. */
8. public class RetireResources_zh
9.    extends java.util.ListResourceBundle
10. {
11.    public Object[][] getContents() { return contents; }
12.    static final Object[][] contents =
13.    {
14.       // BEGIN LOCALIZE
15.       { "colorPre", Color.red },
16.       { "colorGain", Color.blue },
17.       { "colorLoss", Color.yellow }
18.       // END LOCALIZE
19.    };
20. }
```

Example 10–9: RetireStrings.properties

```
1. language=Language
2. computeButton=Compute
3. savings=Prior Savings
4. contrib=Annual Contribution
5. income=Retirement Income
6. currentAge=Current Age
7. retireAge=Retirement Age
8. deathAge=Life Expectancy
9. inflationPercent=Inflation
10. investPercent=Investment Return
11. retire=Age: {0,number} Balance: {1,number,currency}
```

Example 10–10: RetireStrings_de.properties

1. language=Sprache
2. computeButton=Rechnen
3. savings=Vorherige Ersparnisse
4. contrib=J&hrliche Einzahlung
5. income=Einkommen nach Ruhestand
6. currentAge=Jetziges Alter
7. retireAge=Ruhestandsalter
8. deathAge=Lebenserwartung
9. inflationPercent=Inflation
10. investPercent=Investitionsgewinn
11. retire=Alter: {0,number} Guthaben: {1,number,currency}

Example 10–11: RetireStrings_zh.properties

1. language=\u8bed\u8a00
2. computeButton=\u8ba1\u7b97
3. savings=\u65e2\u5b58
4. contrib=\u6bcf\u5e74\u5b58\u91d1
5. income=\u9000\u4f11\u6536\u5165
6. currentAge=\u73b0\u5cad
7. retireAge=\u9000\u4f11\u5e74\u9f84
8. deathAge=\u9884\u671f\u5bff\u547d
9. inflationPercent=\u901a\u8d27\u81a8\u6da8
10. investPercent=\u6295\u8d44\u62a5\u916c
11. retire=\u5e74\u9f84: {0,number} \u603b\u7ed3: {1,number,currency}

java.applet.Applet

- Locale getLocale()

   gets the current locale of the applet. The current locale is determined from the client computer that executes the applet.

Chapter **11**

Native Methods

▼ CALLING A C FUNCTION FROM THE JAVA PROGRAMMING LANGUAGE

▼ NUMERIC PARAMETERS AND RETURN VALUES

▼ STRING PARAMETERS

▼ ACCESSING OBJECT FIELDS

▼ ACCESSING STATIC FIELDS

▼ SIGNATURES

▼ CALLING JAVA METHODS

▼ ARRAYS

▼ ERROR HANDLING

▼ THE INVOCATION API

▼ A COMPLETE EXAMPLE: ACCESSING THE WINDOWS REGISTRY

We hope that you are convinced that code written in the Java programming language has a number of advantages over code written in languages like C or C++—even for platform-specific applications. Here, of course, it is not portability that is the issue but rather features like these:

- You are more likely to produce bug-free code with the Java programming language than with C or C++.

- Multithreading is probably easier to code in the Java programming language than in most other languages.

- Networking code is a breeze.

Portability is simply a bonus that you may or may not want to take advantage of down the line.

While a "100% Pure Java" solution is nice in principle, realistically, for an application, there are situations where you will want to write (or use) code written in another language. (Such code is usually called *native* code.) There are three obvious reasons why this may be the right choice:

1. You have substantial amounts of tested and debugged code available in that language. Porting the code to the Java programming language would be time consuming, and the resulting code would need to be tested and debugged again.

2. Your application requires access to system features or devices, and using Java technology would be cumbersome, at best, or impossible, at worst.

3. Maximizing the speed of the code is essential. For example, the task may be time-critical, or it may be code that is used so often that optimizing it has a big payoff. This is actually the least plausible reason. With just-in-time (JIT) compilation, intensive computations coded in the Java programming language are not that much slower than compiled C code.

If you are in one of these three situations, it *might* make sense to call the native code from programs written in the Java programming language. Of course, with the usual security manager in place, once you start using native code, you are restricted to applications rather than applets. In particular, the native code library you are calling must exist on the client machine, and it must work with the client machine architecture.

To make calling native methods possible, Java technology comes with hooks for working with system libraries, and the JDK has a few tools to relieve some (but not all) of the programming tedium.

NOTE: The language you use for your native code doesn't have to be C or C++; you could use code compiled with a FORTRAN compiler, if you have access to a binding between the Java and FORTRAN programming languages.

Still, keep in mind: If you use native methods, you lose portability. Even when you distribute your program as an application, you must supply a separate native method library for every platform you wish to support. This means you must also educate your users on how to install these libraries! Also, while users may trust that applets can neither damage data nor steal confidential information, they may not want to extend the same trust to code that uses native method libraries. For that reason, many potential users will be reluctant to use programs in the Java programming language that require native code. Aside from the security issue, native libraries are unlikely to be as safe as code written in the Java programming language, especially if they are written in a language like C or C++ that offers no protection against overwriting memory through invalid pointer usage. It is easy to write native methods that corrupt the Java virtual machine, compromise its security, or trash the operating system.

Thus, we suggest using native code only as a last resort. If you must gain access to a device, such as a serial port, in a program, then you may need to write native code. If you need to access an existing body of code, why not consider native methods as a stopgap measure and eventually port the code to the Java programming language? If you are concerned about efficiency, benchmark a Java platform implementation. In most cases, the speed using a just-in-time compiler will be sufficient. A talk at the 1996 JavaOne conference showed this clearly. The implementors of the cryptography library at Sun Microsystems reported that a pure Java platform implementation of their cryptographic functions was more than adequate. It was true that the code was not as fast as a C implementation would have been, but it turned out not to matter. The Java platform implementation was far faster than the network I/O. And this turns out to be the real bottleneck.

In summary, there is no point in sacrificing portability for a meaningless speed improvement; don't go native until you determine that you have no other choice.

NOTE: In this chapter, we describe the so-called Java Native Interface (JNI) binding. An earlier language binding (sometimes called the raw native interface) was used with Java 1.0, and a variation of that earlier binding was used by the Microsoft Virtual Machine. Sun Microsystems has assured developers that the JNI binding described here is a permanent part of the Java platform, and that it needs to be supported by all Java virtual machines.

Finally, we use C as our language for native methods in this chapter because C is probably the language most often used for native methods. In particular, you'll see how to make the correspondence between Java data types, feature names, and function calls and those of C. (This correspondence is usually called the C *binding*.)

C++ NOTE: You can also use C++ instead of C to write native methods. There are a few advantages—type checking is slightly stricter, and accessing the JNI functions is a bit more convenient. However, JNI does not support any direct correspondence between Java platform classes and those in C++.

Calling a C Function from the Java Programming Language

Suppose you have a C function that does something you like and, for one reason or another, you don't want to bother reimplementing it in the Java programming language. For the sake of illustration, we'll assume it is the useful and venerable `printf` function. You want to be able to call `printf` from your programs. The Java programming language uses the keyword native for a native method, and you will obviously need to encapsulate the `printf` function in a class. So, you might write something like:

```
public class Printf
{
    public native String printf(String s);
}
```

You actually can compile this class, but when you go to use it in a program, then the virtual machine will tell you it doesn't know how to find `printf`—reporting an `UnsatisfiedLinkError`. So the trick is to give the run time enough information so that it can link in this class. As you will soon see, under the JDK this requires a three-step process:

1. Generate a C stub for a function that translates between the Java platform call and the actual C function. The stub does this translation by taking parameter information off the virtual machine stack and passing it to the compiled C function.

2. Create a special shared library and export the stub from it.

3. Use a special method, called `System.loadLibrary`, to tell the Java run-time environment to load the library from Step 2.

We now show you how to carry out these steps for various kinds of examples, starting from a trivial special-case use of `printf` and ending with a realistic example involving the registry function for Windows—platform-dependent functions that are obviously not available directly from the Java platform.

Working with the `printf` Function

Let's start with just about the simplest possible situation using `printf`: calling a native method that prints the message, "Hello, Native World." Obviously we are not even tapping into the useful formatting features of `printf`! Still, this is a good way for you to test that your C compiler works as expected before you try implementing more ambitious native methods.

As we mentioned earlier, you first need to declare the native method in a class. The native keyword alerts the compiler that the method will be defined externally. Of course, native methods will contain no code in the Java programming language, and the method header is followed immediately by a terminating semicolon. This means, as you saw in the example above, native method declarations look similar to abstract method declarations.

```
class HelloNative
{
```

```
        public native static void greeting();
        . . .
   }
```

In this particular example, note that we also declare the native method
as `static`. Native methods can be both static and nonstatic. This method
takes no parameters; we do not yet want to deal with parameter passing,
not even implicit parameters.

Next, write a corresponding C function. You must name that function *exactly* the
way the Java runtime environment expects. Here are the rules:

1.   Use the full Java method name, such as `HelloNative.greeting`.
     If the class is in a package, then prepend the package name, such as
     `com.horstmann.HelloNative.greeting`.

2.   Replace every period with an underscore, and append the prefix `Java_`.
     For example, `Java_HelloNative_greeting` or
     `Java_com_horstmann_HelloNative_greeting`.

3.   If the class name contains characters that are not ASCII letters or digits—
     that is, `'_'`, `'$'`, or Unicode characters with code > `'\u007F'`—replace
     them with `_0xxxx`, where *xxxx* is the sequence of four hexadecimal
     digits of the character's Unicode value.

NOTE: If you *overload* native methods, that is, if you provide multiple native
methods with the same name, then you must append a double underscore
followed by the encoded argument types. We describe the encoding of the
argument types later in this chapter. For example, if you have a native method,
`greeting`, and another native method `greeting(int repeat)`, then the
first one is called `Java_HelloNative_greeting__`, and the second,
`Java_HelloNative_greeting__I`.

Actually, nobody does this by hand; instead, you should run the `javah` utility,
which automatically generates the function names. To use `javah`, first, compile
the source file (given in Example 11–3).

```
javac HelloNative.java
```

Next, call the `javah` utility to produce a C header file. The `javah` executable can
be found in the `jdk/bin` directory.

```
javah HelloNative
```

NOTE: If you are still using JDK1.1, be sure to use the `-jni` flag when running
`javah`. Without that flag, the `javah` tool in JDK 1.1 generates the header file for
the Java 1.0 binding. Starting with JDK 1.2, the JNI binding is the default.

Using `javah` creates a header file, `HelloNative.h`, as in Example 11–1.

Example 11–1: HelloNative.h

```
1. /* DO NOT EDIT THIS FILE - it is machine generated */
2. #include <jni.h>
3. /* Header for class HelloNative */
4.
5. #ifndef _Included_HelloNative
6. #define _Included_HelloNative
7. #ifdef __cplusplus
8. extern "C" {
9. #endif
10. /*
11.  * Class:      HelloNative
12.  * Method:     greeting
13.  * Signature: ()V
14.  */
15. JNIEXPORT void JNICALL Java_HelloNative_greeting
16.   (JNIEnv *, jclass);
17.
18. ifdef __cplusplus
19. }
20. #endif
21. #endif
```

As you can see, this file contains the declaration of a function `Java_HelloNative_greeting`. (The strings `JNIEXPORT` and `JNICALL` are defined in the header file `jni.h`. They denote compiler-dependent specifiers for exported functions that come from a dynamically loaded library.)

Now, you simply have to copy the function prototype from the header file into the source file and give the implementation code for the function, as shown in Example 11–2.

Example 11–2: HelloNative.c

```
1. #include "HelloNative.h"
2. #include <stdio.h>
3.
4. JNIEXPORT void JNICALL Java_HelloNative_greeting(JNIEnv* env,
5.   jclass cl)
6. {
7.   printf("Hello world!\n");
8. }
```

In this simple function, we ignore the `env` and `cl` arguments. You'll see their use later.

C++ NOTE: You can use C++ to implement native methods. However, you must then declare the functions that implement the native methods as `extern "C"`. For example,

```
#include "HelloNative.h"
#include <stdio.h>

extern "C"
JNIEXPORT void JNICALL Java_HelloNative_greeting
    (JNIEnv* env, jclass cl)
{
    printf("Hello, Native World!\n");
}
```

Next, compile the C code into a dynamically loaded library. The details depend on your compiler.

For example, with the Gnu C compiler on Linux, use these commands:

```
gcc -c -fPIC -I/usr/local/jdk/include/
    -I/jdk/include/linux HelloNative.c
gcc -shared -o libHelloNative.so HelloNative.o
```

With the Sun compiler under the Solaris operating environment, the command to use is

```
cc -G -I/usr/local/jdk/include
    -I/usr/local/jdk/include/solaris
    HelloNative.c -o libHelloNative.so
```

With the Microsoft C++ compiler under Windows, the command you use is

```
cl -Ic:\jdk\include -Ic:\jdk\include\win32 -LD HelloNative.c
    -FeHelloNative.dll
```

You can also use the freely available Cygwin programming environment from `http://www.cygwin.com`. It contains the Gnu C compiler and libraries for UNIX-style programming on Windows. With Cygwin, use the commands

```
gcc -c -D__int64="long long"
    -Ic:/jdk/include/ -Ic:/jdk/include/win32 HelloNative.c
dllwrap --add-stdcall-alias -o HelloNative.dll HelloNative.o
```

You may need to use different paths to specify the locations of the header files, depending on which directory contains the SDK.

TIP: If you use the Microsoft C++ compiler to compile DLLs from a DOS shell, first run the batch file

```
c:\devstudio\vc\bin\vcvars32.bat
```

That batch file properly configures the command-line compiler by setting up the path and the environment variables needed by the compiler.

> NOTE: The Windows version of the header file `jni_md.h` contains the type declaration
>
> ```
> typedef __int64 jlong;
> ```
>
> which is specific to the Microsoft compiler. If you use the Gnu compiler, you may want to edit that file, for example
>
> ```
> #ifdef __GNUC__
>     typedef long long jlong;
> #else
>     typedef __int64 jlong;
> #endif
> ```
>
> Alternatively, compile with `-D__int64="long long"`, as shown in the sample compiler invocation.

Finally, we need to add the call to the `System.loadLibrary` method that ensures that the virtual machine will load the library prior to the first use of the class. The easiest way to do this is to use a static initialization block in the class that contains the native method, as in Example 11–3:

Example 11–3: HelloNative.java

```
1. class HelloNative
2. {
3.    public static native void greeting();
4.
5.    static
6.    {
7.        System.loadLibrary("HelloNative");
8.    }
9. }
```

Assuming you have followed all the steps given above, you are now ready to run the `HelloNativeTest` application shown in Example 11–4.

Example 11–4: HelloNativeTest.java

```
1. class HelloNativeTest
2. {
3.    public static void main(String[] args)
4.    {
5.        HelloNative.greeting();
6.    }
7. }
```

If you compile and run this program, the message "Hello, Native World!" is displayed in a terminal window.

Of course, this is not particularly impressive by itself. However, if you keep in mind that this message is generated by the C `printf` command and not by any Java programming language code, you will see that we have taken the first steps toward bridging the gap between the two languages!

> NOTE: Some shared libraries for native code need to run initialization code. You can place any initialization code into a `JNI_OnLoad` method. Similarly, when the VM shuts down, it will call the `JNI_OnUnload` method if you provide it. The prototypes are
>
> ```
> jint JNI_OnLoad(JavaVM* vm, void* reserved);
> void JNI_OnUnload(JavaVM* vm, void* reserved);
> ```
>
> The `JNI_OnLoad` method needs to return the minimum version of the VM that it requires, such as `JNI_VERSION_1_1`.

`java.lang.System`

- `void loadLibrary(String libname)`
  loads the library with the given name. The library is located in the library search path. The exact method for locating the library is operating-system dependent. Under Windows, this method searches first the current directory, then the directories listed in the `PATH` environment variable.

- `void load(String filename)`
  loads the library with the given file name. If the library is not found, then an `UnsatisfiedLinkError` is thrown.

Numeric Parameters and Return Values

When passing numbers between C and the Java programming language, you need to understand which types correspond to each other. For example, while C does have data types called `int` and `long`, their implementation is platform dependent. On some platforms, `int`s are 16-bit quantities, and on others they are 32-bit quantities. In the Java platform, of course, an `int` is *always* a 32-bit integer. For that reason, the Java Native Interface defines types `jint`, `jlong`, and so on.

Table 11–1 shows the correspondence between Java types and C types.

Table 11–1: Java types and C types

Java Programming Language	C Programming Language	Bytes
boolean	jboolean	1
byte	jbyte	1
char	jchar	2
short	jshort	2
int	jint	4
long	jlong	8
float	jfloat	4
double	jdouble	8

In the header file `jni.h`, these types are declared with `typedef` statements as the equivalent types on the target platform. That header file also defines the constants `JNI_FALSE = 0` and `JNI_TRUE = 1`.

Using `printf` for Formatting Numbers

Recall that the Java library has no elegant way for formatted printing of floating-point numbers. Of course, you can use the `DecimalFormat` class (see Volume 1, Chapter 3) and build custom formats—we just don't think this is as easy as a simple call to `printf`. Since `printf` is quick, easy, and well known, let's suppose you decide to implement the same functionality via a call to the `printf` function in a native method.

We don't actually recommend this approach: the native code needs to be compiled for every target platform. We are using it because it shows off the techniques of passing parameters to a native method and obtaining a return value.

Example 11–5 shows a class called `Printf1` that uses a native method to print a floating-point number with a given field width and precision.

Example 11–5: Printf1.java

```
1. class Printf1
2. {
3.     public static native int print(int width, int precision,
4.         double x);
5.
6.     static
7.     {
8.         System.loadLibrary("Printf1");
9.     }
10. }
```

Notice that when implementing the method in C, all `int` and `double` parameters are changed to `jint` and `jdouble`, as shown in Example 11–6.

Example 11–6: Printf1.c

```
1. #include "Printf1.h"
2. #include <stdio.h>
3.
4. JNIEXPORT jint JNICALL Java_Printf1_print
5.     (JNIEnv* env, jclass cl, jint width, jint precision, jdouble x)
6. {
7.     char fmt[30];
8.     jint ret;
9.     sprintf(fmt, "%%%d.%df", width, precision);
10.    ret = printf(fmt, x);
11.    fflush(stdout);
12.    return ret;
```

13. }

The function simply assembles a format string `"%w.pf"` in the variable `fmt`, then calls `printf`. It then returns the number of characters printed.

Example 11–7 shows the test program that demonstrates the `Printf1` class.

Example 11–7: Printf1Test.java

```
1. class Printf1Test
2. {
3.    public static void main(String[] args)
4.    {
5.       int count = Printf1.print(8, 4, 3.14);
6.       count += Printf1.print(8, 4, (double)count);
7.       System.out.println();
8.       for (int i = 0; i < count; i++)
9.          System.out.print("-");
10.      System.out.println();
11.   }
12. }
```

String Parameters

Next, we want to consider how to transfer strings to and from native methods. As you know, strings in the Java programming language are sequences of 16-bit Unicode characters; C strings are null-terminated strings of 8-bit characters, so strings are quite different in the two languages. The Java Native Interface has two sets of functions, one that converts Java strings to UTF (Unicode Text Format) and one that converts them to arrays of Unicode characters, that is, to `jchar` arrays. The UTF format was discussed in Chapter 1—recall that ASCII characters are encoded "as is," but all other Unicode characters are encoded as 2-byte or 3-byte sequences.

If your C code already uses Unicode, you'll want to use the second set of conversion functions. On the other hand, if all your Java strings are restricted to ASCII characters, you can use the UTF conversion functions.

A native method with a `String` parameter actually receives a value of an opaque type called `jstring`. A native method with a return value of type `String` must return a value of type `jstring`. JNI functions are used to read and construct these `jstring` objects. For example, the `NewStringUTF` function makes a new `jstring` object out of a `char` array that contains UTF-encoded characters. Unfortunately, JNI functions have a somewhat odd calling convention. Here is a call to the `NewStringUTF` function.

```
JNIEXPORT jstring JNICALL Java_HelloNative_getGreeting
    (JNIEnv* env, jclass cl)
{
    jstring jstr;
```

```
    char greeting[] = "Hello, Native World\n";
    jstr = (*env)->NewStringUTF(env, greeting);
    return jstr;
}
```

All calls to JNI functions use the `env` pointer that is the first argument of every native method. The `env` pointer is a pointer to a table of function pointers (see Figure 11–1). Therefore, you must prefix every JNI call with `(*env)->` to actually dereference the function pointer. Furthermore, `env` is the first parameter of every JNI function. This setup is somewhat cumbersome, and it could have easily been made more transparent to C programmers. We suggest that you simply supply the `(*env)->` prefix without worrying about the table of function pointers.

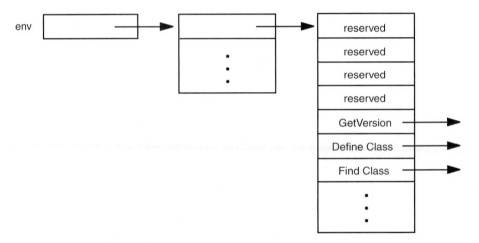

Figure 11–1: The env pointer

C++ NOTE: It is simpler to access JNI functions in C++. The C++ version of the `JNIEnv` class has inline member functions that take care of the function pointer lookup for you. For example, you can call the `NewStringUTF` function as

```
    jstr = env->NewStringUTF(greeting);
```

Note that you omit the `JNIEnv` pointer from the parameter list of the call.

The `NewStringUTF` function lets you construct a new `jstring`. To read the contents of an existing `jstring` object, use the `GetStringUTFChars` function. This function returns a `const jbyte*` pointer to the UTF characters that describe the character string. Note that a specific virtual machine is free to use UTF for its internal string representation, so you may get a character pointer into the actual Java string. Since Java strings are meant to be immutable, it is *very* important that you treat the `const` seriously and do not try to write into this character array. On the other hand, if the virtual machine uses Unicode characters for its internal string representation, then this function call allocates a new memory block that will be filled with the UTF equivalents.

The virtual machine must know when you are finished using the UTF string, so that it can garbage-collect it. (The garbage collector runs in a separate thread, and it can interrupt the execution of native methods.) For that reason, you must call the `ReleaseStringUTFChars` function.

Alternatively, you can supply your own buffer to hold the string characters by calling the `GetStringRegion` or `GetStringUTFRegion` methods.

Finally, the `GetStringUTFLength` function returns the number of characters needed for the UTF encoding of the string.

Accessing Java strings from C code

- `jstring NewStringUTF(JNIEnv* env, const char bytes[])`
  returns a new Java string object from an UTF string, or `NULL` if the string cannot be constructed.

Parameters:	env	the JNI interface pointer
	bytes	the null-terminated UTF string

- `jsize GetStringUTFLength(JNIEnv* env, jstring string)`
  returns the number of characters required for the UTF encoding.

Parameters:	env	the JNI interface pointer
	string	a Java string object

- `const jbyte* GetStringUTFChars(JNIEnv* env, jstring string, jboolean* isCopy)`
  returns a pointer to the UTF encoding of a string, or `NULL` if the character array cannot be constructed. The pointer is valid until `ReleaseString-UTFChars` is called.

Parameters:	env	the JNI interface pointer
	string	a Java string object
	isCopy	points to a `jboolean` that is filled with `JNI_TRUE` if a copy is made; with `JNI_FALSE` otherwise

- `void ReleaseStringUTFChars(JNIEnv* env, jstring string, const jbyte bytes[])`
  informs the virtual machine that the native code no longer needs access to the Java string through `bytes`.

Parameters:	env	the JNI interface pointer
	string	a Java string object
	bytes	a pointer returned by `GetStringUTFChars`

- `void GetStringRegion(JNIEnv *env, jstring string, jsize start, jsize length, jchar *buffer)`
  copies a sequence of Unicode characters from a string to a user-supplied buffer.

Parameters:	env	the JNI interface pointer
	string	a Java string object
	start	the starting index
	length	the number of characters to copy
	buffer	the user-supplied buffer

- `void GetStringUTFRegion(JNIEnv *env, jstring string, jsize start, jsize length, jbyte *buffer)`
  copies a sequence of UTF8 characters from a string to a user-supplied buffer. The buffer must be long enough to hold the bytes. In the worst case, $3 \times$ `length` bytes are copied.

- `jstring NewString(JNIEnv* env, const jchar chars[], jsize length)`
  returns a new Java string object from a Unicode string, or NULL if the string cannot be constructed.

Parameters:	env	the JNI interface pointer
	chars	the null-terminated UTF string
	length	the number of characters in the string

- `jsize GetStringLength(JNIEnv* env, jstring string)`
  returns the number of characters in the string.

Parameters:	env	the JNI interface pointer
	string	a Java string object

- `const jchar* GetStringChars(JNIEnv* env, jstring string, jboolean* isCopy)`
  returns a pointer to the Unicode encoding of a string, or NULL if the character array cannot be constructed. The pointer is valid until `ReleaseStringChars` is called.

Parameters:	env	the JNI interface pointer
	string	a Java string object
	isCopy	is either NULL or points to a `jboolean` that is filled with JNI_TRUE if a copy is made; with JNI_FALSE otherwise

- void ReleaseStringChars(JNIEnv* env, jstring string, const jchar chars[])

  informs the virtual machine that the native code no longer needs access to the Java string through chars.

Parameters:	env	the JNI interface pointer
	string	a Java string object
	chars	a pointer returned by GetStringChars

Calling sprintf in a Native Method

Let us put these functions we just described to work and write a class that calls the C function sprintf. We would like to call the function as shown in Example 11–8.

Example 11–8: Printf2Test.java

```
1. class Printf2Test
2. {
3.    public static void main(String[] args)
4.    {
5.       double price = 44.95;
6.       double tax = 7.75;
7.       double amountDue = price * (1 + tax / 100);
8.
9.       String s = Printf2.sprint("Amount due = %8.2f", amountDue);
10.      System.out.println(s);
11.   }
12. }
```

Example 11–9 shows the class with the native sprintf method.

Example 11–9: Printf2.java

```
1. class Printf2
2. {
3.    public static native String sprint(String format, double x);
4.
5.    static
6.    {
7.       System.loadLibrary("Printf2");
8.    }
9. }
```

Therefore, the C function that formats a floating-point number has the prototype

```
JNIEXPORT jstring JNICALL Java_Printf2_sprint
   (JNIEnv* env, jclass cl, jstring format, jdouble x)
```

Example 11–10 shows the code for the C implementation. Note the calls to GetStringUTFChars to read the format argument, NewStringUTF to generate the return value, and ReleaseStringUTFChars to inform the virtual machine that access to the string is no longer required.

Example 11–10: Printf2.c

```
1. #include "Printf2.h"
2. #include <string.h>
3. #include <stdlib.h>
4. #include <float.h>
5.
6. /**
7.    @param format a string containing a printf format specifier
8.    (such as "%8.2f"). Substrings "%%" are skipped.
9.    @return a pointer to the format specifier (skipping the '%')
10.   or NULL if there wasn't a unique format specifier
11. */
12. char* find_format(const char format[])
13. {
14.    char* p;
15.    char* q;
16.
17.    p = strchr(format, '%');
18.    while (p != NULL && *(p + 1) == '%') /* skip %% */
19.       p = strchr(p + 2, '%');
20.    if (p == NULL) return NULL;
21.    /* now check that % is unique */
22.    p++;
23.    q = strchr(p, '%');
24.    while (q != NULL && *(q + 1) == '%') /* skip %% */
25.       q = strchr(q + 2, '%');
26.    if (q != NULL) return NULL; /* % not unique */
27.    q = p + strspn(p, " -0+#"); /* skip past flags */
28.    q += strspn(q, "0123456789"); /* skip past field width */
29.    if (*q == '.') { q++; q += strspn(q, "0123456789"); }
30.       /* skip past precision */
31.    if (strchr("eEfFgG", *q) == NULL) return NULL;
32.       /* not a floating point format */
33.    return p;
34. }
35.
36. JNIEXPORT jstring JNICALL Java_Printf2_sprint(JNIEnv* env,
37.    jclass cl, jstring format, jdouble x)
38. {
39.    const char* cformat;
40.    char* fmt;
41.    jstring ret;
42.
```

```
43.   cformat = (*env)->GetStringUTFChars(env, format, NULL);
44.   fmt = find_format(cformat);
45.   if (fmt == NULL)
46.       ret = format;
47.   else
48.   {
49.       char* cret;
50.       int width = atoi(fmt);
51.       if (width == 0) width = DBL_DIG + 10;
52.       cret = (char*)malloc(strlen(cformat) + width);
53.       sprintf(cret, cformat, x);
54.       ret = (*env)->NewStringUTF(env, cret);
55.       free(cret);
56.   }
57.   (*env)->ReleaseStringUTFChars(env, format, cformat);
58.   return ret;
59. }
```

In this function, we chose to keep the error handling simple. If the format code to print a floating-point number is not of the form %w.pc, where c is one of the characters e, E, f, g, or G, then what we simply do is *not* format the number. You will see later how to make a native method throw an exception.

Accessing Object Fields

All the native methods that you saw so far were static methods with number and string parameters. We next consider native methods that operate on objects. As an exercise, we will implement a method of the Employee class that was introduced in Chapter 4 of Volume 1, using a native method. Again, this is not something you would normally want to do, but it does illustrate how to access object fields from a native method when you need to do so.

Consider the raiseSalary method. In the Java programming language, the code was simple.

```
public void raiseSalary(double byPercent)
{
    salary *= 1 + byPercent / 100;
}
```

Let us rewrite this as a native method. Unlike the previous examples of native methods, this is not a static method. Running javah gives the following prototype.

```
JNIEXPORT void JNICALL Java_Employee_raiseSalary
    (JNIEnv *, jobject, jdouble);
```

Note the second argument. It is no longer of type jclass but of type jobject. In fact, it is the equivalent of the this reference. Static methods obtain a reference to the class, whereas nonstatic methods obtain a reference to the implicit `this` argument object.

Now we access the `salary` field of the implicit argument. In the "raw" Java-to-C binding of Java 1.0, this was easy—a programmer could directly access object data fields. However, direct access requires all virtual machines to expose their internal data layout. For that reason, the JNI requires programmers to get and set the values of data fields by calling special JNI functions.

In our case, we need to use the `GetDoubleField` and `SetDoubleField` functions because the type of `salary` is a `double`. There are other functions— `GetIntField`/`SetIntField`, `GetObjectField`/`SetObjectField`, and so on—for other field types. The general syntax is:

```
x = (*env)->GetXxxField(env, class, fieldID);
(*env)->GetXxxField(env, class, fieldID, x);
```

Here, `class` is a value that represents a Java object of type `Class`, and `fieldID` is a value of a special type, `jfieldID`, that identifies a field in a structure and *Xxx* represents a Java data type (`Object`, `Boolean`, `Byte`, and so on). There are two ways for obtaining the `class` object. The `GetObjectClass` function returns the class of any object. For example:

```
jclass class_Employee = (*env)->GetObjectClass(env, obj_this);
```

The `FindClass` function lets you specify the class name as a string (curiously, with / instead of periods as package name separators).

```
jclass class_String
    = (*env)->FindClass(env, "java/lang/String");
```

Use the `GetFieldID` function to obtain the `fieldID`. You must supply the name of the field and its *signature*, an encoding of its type. For example, here is the code to obtain the field ID of the `salary` field.

```
jfieldID id_salary
    = (*env)->GetFieldID(env, class_Employee, "salary", "D");
```

The string `"D"` denotes the type `double`. You will learn the complete rules for encoding signatures in the next section.

You may be thinking that accessing a data field seems quite convoluted. However, since the designers of the JNI did not want to expose the data fields directly, they had to supply functions for getting and setting field values. To minimize the cost of these functions, computing the field ID from the field name—which is the most expensive step—is factored out into a separate step. That is, if you repeatedly get and set the value of a particular field, you incur only once the cost of computing the field identifier.

Let us put all the pieces together. The following code reimplements the `raiseSalary` method as a native method.

```
JNIEXPORT void JNICALL Java_Employee_raiseSalary
   (JNIEnv* env, jobject obj_this, jdouble byPercent)
{
   /* get the class */
   jclass class_Employee = (*env)->GetObjectClass(env,
      obj_this);

   /* get the field ID */
   jfieldID id_salary = (*env)->GetFieldID(env, class_Employee,
      "salary", "D");

   /* get the field value */
   jdouble salary = (*env)->GetDoubleField(env, obj_this,
      id_salary);

   salary *= 1 + byPercent / 100;

   /* set the field value */
   (*env)->SetDoubleField(env, obj_this, id_salary, salary);
}
```

CAUTION: Class references are only valid until the native method returns. Thus, you cannot cache the return values of `GetObjectClass` in your code. Do *not* store away a class reference for reuse in a later method call. You need to call `GetObjectClass` every time the native method executes. If this is intolerable, you can lock the reference with a call to `NewGlobalRef`:

```
static jclass class_X = 0;
static jfieldID id_a;
. . .
if (class_X == 0)
{
    jclass cx = (*env)->GetObjectClass(env, obj);
    class_X = (*env)->NewGlobalRef(env, cx);
    id_a = (*env)->GetFieldID(env, cls, "a", ". . .");
}
```

Now you can use the class reference and field IDs in subsequent calls. When you are done using the class, make sure to call

```
(*env)->DeleteGlobalRef(env, class_X);
```

Examples 11–11 and 11–12 show the Java code for a test program and the `Employee` class. Example 11–13 contains the C code for the native `raiseSalary` method.

Accessing Static Fields

Accessing static fields is similar to accessing nonstatic fields. You use the `GetStaticFieldID` and `GetStaticXxxField/SetStaticXxxField` functions. They work almost identically to their nonstatic counterpart. There are only two differences.

- Since you have no object, you must use `FindClass` instead of `GetObjectClass` to obtain the class reference.

- You supply the class, not the instance object, when accessing the field.

For example, here is how you can get a reference to `System.out`.

```
/* get the class */
jclass class_System = (*env)->FindClass(env,
    "java/lang/System");

/* get the field ID */
jfieldID id_out = (*env)->GetStaticFieldID(env,
    class_System, "out", "Ljava/io/PrintStream;");

/* get the field value */
jobject obj_out = (*env)->GetStaticObjectField(env,
    class_System, id_out);
```

Example 11–11: EmployeeTest.java

```
1. public class EmployeeTest
2. {
3.    public static void main(String[] args)
4.    {
5.       Employee[] staff = new Employee[3];
6.
7.       staff[0] = new Employee("Harry Hacker", 35000);
8.       staff[1] = new Employee("Carl Cracker", 75000);
9.       staff[2] = new Employee("Tony Tester", 38000);
10.
11.      int i;
12.      for (i = 0; i < 3; i++) staff[i].raiseSalary(5);
13.      for (i = 0; i < 3; i++) staff[i].print();
14.   }
15. }
```

Example 11–12: Employee.java

```
1. public class Employee
2. {
3.    public Employee(String n, double s)
4.    {
5.       name = n;
6.       salary = s;
7.    }
8.
9.    public native void raiseSalary(double byPercent);
10.
11.   public void print()
```

```
12.    {
13.        System.out.println(name + " " + salary);
14.    }
15.
16.    private String name;
17.    private double salary;
18.
19.    static
20.    {
21.        System.loadLibrary("Employee");
22.    }
23. }
```

Example 11–13: Employee.c

```
1. #include "Employee.h"
2.
3. #include <stdio.h>
4.
5. JNIEXPORT void JNICALL Java_Employee_raiseSalary(JNIEnv* env,
6.    jobject obj_this, jdouble byPercent)
7. {
8.    /* get the class */
9.    jclass class_Employee = (*env)->GetObjectClass(env,
10.        obj_this);
11.
12.    /* get the field ID */
13.    jfieldID id_salary = (*env)->GetFieldID(env,
14.        class_Employee, "salary", "D");
15.
16.    /* get the field value */
17.    jdouble salary = (*env)->GetDoubleField(env, obj_this,
18.        id_salary);
19.
20.    salary *= 1 + byPercent / 100;
21.
22.    /* set the field value */
23.    (*env)->SetDoubleField(env, obj_this, id_salary, salary);
24. }
```

Accessing object fields

- `jfieldID GetFieldID(JNIEnv *env, jclass cl, const char name[], const char sig[])`

  returns the identifier of a field in a class.

Parameters:	env	the JNI interface pointer
	cl	the class object
	name	the field name
	sig	the encoded field signature

- *Xxx* Get*Xxx*Field(JNIEnv *env, jobject obj, jfieldID id)
  returns the value of a field. The field type *Xxx* is one of Object, Boolean, Byte, Char, Short, Int, Long, Float, or Double.

Parameters:	env	the JNI interface pointer
	obj	the object whose field is being returned
	id	the field identifier

- void Set*Xxx*Field(JNIEnv *env, jobject obj, jfieldID id, *Xxx* value)
  sets a field to a new value. The field type *Xxx* is one of Object, Boolean, Byte, Char, Short, Int, Long, Float, or Double.

Parameters:	env	the JNI interface pointer
	obj	the object whose field is being set
	id	the field identifier
	value	the new field value

- jfieldID GetStaticFieldID(JNIEnv *env, jclass cl, const char name[], const char sig[])
  returns the identifier of a static field in a class.

Parameters:	env	the JNI interface pointer
	cl	the class object
	name	the field name
	sig	the encoded field signature

- *Xxx* GetStatic*Xxx*Field(JNIEnv *env, jclass cl, jfieldID id)
  returns the value of a static field. The field type *Xxx* is one of Object, Boolean, Byte, Char, Short, Int, Long, Float, or Double.

Parameters:	env	the JNI interface pointer
	cl	the class object whose static field is being set
	id	the field identifier

- void SetStatic*Xxx*Field(JNIEnv *env, jclass cl, jfieldID id, *Xxx* value)
  sets a static field to a new value. The field type *Xxx* is one of Object, Boolean, Byte, Char, Short, Int, Long, Float, or Double.

Parameters:	env	the JNI interface pointer
	cl	the class object whose static field is being set
	id	the field identifier
	value	the new field value

Signatures

To access object fields and call methods that are defined in the Java programming language, you need to learn the rules for "mangling" the names of data types and method signatures. (A method signature describes the parameters and return type of the method.) Here is the encoding scheme:

B	`byte`
C	`char`
D	`double`
F	`float`
I	`int`
J	`long`
L*classname*;	a class type
S	`short`
V	`void`
Z	`boolean`

Note that the semicolon at the end of the L expression is the terminator of the type expression, not a separator between parameters. For example, the constructor

```
Employee(java.lang.String, double, java.util.Date)
```

has a signature

```
"(Ljava/lang/String;DLjava/util/Date;)V"
```

As you can see, there is no separator between the D and `Ljava/util/Date;`.

Also note that in this encoding scheme, you must use / instead of . to separate the package and class names.

To describe an array type, use a `[`. For example, an array of strings is

```
[Ljava/lang/String;
```

A `float[][]` is mangled into

```
[[F
```

For the complete signature of a method, you list the parameter types inside a pair of parentheses and then list the return type. For example, a method receiving two integers and returning an integer is encoded as

```
(II)I
```

The print method that we used in the preceding example has a mangled signature of

```
(Ljava/lang/String;)V
```

That is, the method receives a string and returns `void`.

TIP: You can use the `javap` command with option `-s` to generate the field signatures from class files. For example, run:

```
javap -s -private Classname
```

You get the following output, displaying the signatures of all fields and methods.

```
public synchronized class Employee extends java.lang.Object
    /* ACC_SUPER bit set */
{
    private java.lang.String name;
        /*    Ljava/lang/String;    */
    private double salary;
        /*    D    */
    private java.util.Date hireDay;
        /*    Ljava/util/Date;    */
    public Employee(java.lang.String,double,java.util.Date);
        /*    (Ljava/lang/String;DLjava/util/Date;)V    */
    public void print();
        /*    ()V    */
    public void raiseSalary(double);
        /*    (D)V    */
    public int hireYear();
        /*    ()I    */

}
```

NOTE: There is no rational reason why programmers are forced to use this mangling scheme for describing signatures. The designers of the native calling mechanism could have just as easily written a function that reads signatures in the Java programming language style, such as `void(int,java.lang.String)`, and encodes them into whatever internal representation they prefer. Then again, using the mangled signatures lets you partake in the mystique of programming close to the virtual machine.

Calling Java Methods

Of course, Java programming language functions can call C functions—that is what native methods are for. Can we go the other way? Why would we want to do this anyway? The answer is that it often happens that a native method needs to request a service from an object that was passed to it. We first show you how to do it for nonstatic methods, and then we show you how to do it for static methods.

Nonstatic Methods

As an example of calling a Java method from native code, let's enhance the `Printf` class and add a member function that works similarly to the C function `fprintf`. That is, it should be able to print a string on an arbitrary `PrintWriter` object.

```
class Printf3
{
    public native static void fprint(PrintWriter out,
        String s, double x);
    . . .
}
```

We first assemble the string to be printed into a `String` object `str`, as in the `sprint` method that we already implemented. Then, we call the `print` method of the `PrintWriter` class from the C function that implements the native method.

You can call any Java method from C by using the function call

```
(*env)->CallXxxMethod(env, implicit parameter, methodID,
    explicit parameters)
```

Replace *Xxx* with `Void`, `Int`, `Object`, etc., depending on the return type of the method. Just as you need a `fieldID` to access a field of an object, you need a method ID to call a method. You obtain a method ID by calling the JNI function `GetMethodID` and supplying the class, the name of the method, and the method signature.

In our example, we want to obtain the ID of the `print` method of the `PrintWriter` class. As you saw in Chapter 1, the `PrintWriter` class has nine different methods, all called `print`. For that reason, you must also supply a string describing the parameters and return value of the specific function that you want to use. For example, we want to use `void print(java.lang.String)`. As described in the preceding section, we must now "mangle" the signature into the string `"(Ljava/lang/String;)V"`.

Here is the complete code to make the method call, by:

1. Obtaining the class of the implicit parameter;

2. Obtaining the method ID;

3. Making the call.

```
/* get the class */
class_PrintWriter = (*env)->GetObjectClass(env, out);

/* get the method ID */
id_print = (*env)->GetMethodID(env, class_PrintWriter,
    "print", "(Ljava/lang/String;)V");

/* call the method */
(*env)->CallVoidMethod(env, out, id_print, str);
```

Examples 11–14 and 11–15 show the Java code for a test program and the `Printf3` class. Example 11–16 contains the C code for the native `fprint` method.

NOTE: The numerical method IDs and field IDs are conceptually similar to `Method` and `Field` objects in the reflection API. You can convert between them with the following functions:

```
jobject ToReflectedMethod(JNIEnv* env, jclass class,
    jmethodID methodID); // returns Method object
methodID FromReflectedMethod(JNIEnv* env, jobject method);
jobject ToReflectedField(JNIEnv* env, jclass class,
    jfieldID fieldID); // returns Field object
fieldID FromReflectedField(JNIEnv* env, jobject field);
```

Static Methods

Calling static methods from native methods is similar to calling nonstatic methods. There are two differences.

- You use the `GetStaticMethodID` and `CallStatic`*Xxx*`Method` functions.

- You supply a class object, not an implicit parameter object, when invoking the method.

As an example of this, let's make the call to the static method

```
System.getProperty("java.class.path")
```

from a native method. The return value of this call is a string that gives the current class path.

First, we need to find the class to use. Since we have no object of the class `System` readily available, we use `FindClass` rather than `GetObjectClass`.

```
jclass class_System = (*env)->FindClass(env, "java/lang/System");
```

Next, we need the ID of the static `getProperty` method. The encoded signature of that method is

```
"(Ljava/lang/String;)Ljava/lang/String;"
```

since both the parameter and the return value are a string. Hence, we obtain the method ID as follows:

```
jmethodID id_getProperty = (*env)->GetStaticMethodID(env,
    class_System, "getProperty",
    "(Ljava/lang/String;)Ljava/lang/String;");
```

Finally, we can make the call. Note that the class object is passed to the `CallStaticObjectMethod` function.

```
jobject obj_ret = (*env)->CallStaticObjectMethod(env,
    class_System, id_getProperty,
    (*env)->NewStringUTF(env, "java.class.path"));
```

The return value of this method is of type `jobject`. If we want to manipulate it as a string, we must cast it to `jstring`:

```
jstring str_ret = (jstring)obj_ret;
```

> C++ NOTE: In C, the types `jstring`, `jclass`, as well as the array types that will be introduced later, are all type equivalent to `jobject`. The cast of the preceding example is therefore not strictly necessary in C. But in C++, these types are defined as pointers to "dummy classes" that have the correct inheritance hierarchy. For example, the assignment of a `jstring` to a `jobject` is legal without a cast in C++, but the assignment from a `jobject` to a `jstring` requires a cast.

Constructors

A native method can create a new Java object by invoking its constructor. You invoke the constructor by calling the `NewObject` function.

```
jobject obj_new = (*env)->NewObject(env, class, methodID,
    construction parameters);
```

You obtain the method ID needed for this call from the `GetMethodID` function by specifying the method name as `"<init>"` and the encoded signature of the constructor (with return type `void`). For example, here is how a native method can create a `FileOutputStream` object.

```
const char[] fileName = ". . .";
jstring str_fileName = (*env)->NewStringUTF(env, fileName);
jclass class_FileOutputStream = (*env)->FindClass(env,
    "java/io/FileOutputStream");
jmethodID id_FileOutputStream = (*env)->GetMethodID(env,
    class_FileOutputStream, "<init>", "(Ljava/lang/String;)V");
jobject obj_stream = (*env)->NewObject(env,
    class_FileOutputStream, id_FileOutputStream, str_fileName);
```

Note that the signature of the constructor takes a parameter of type `java.lang.String` and has a return type of `void`.

Alternative Method Invocations

There are several variants of the JNI functions for calling a Java method from native code. These are not as important as the functions that we already discussed, but they are occasionally useful.

The `CallNonvirtualXxxMethod` functions receive an implicit argument, a method ID, a class object (which must correspond to a superclass of the implicit argument), and explicit arguments. The function calls the version of the method in the specified class, bypassing the normal dynamic dispatch mechanism.

All call functions have versions with suffixes "A" and "V" that receive the explicit parameters in an array or a `va_list` (as defined in the C header `stdarg.h`).

Example 11–14: Printf3Test.java

```
1. import java.io.*;
2.
3. class Printf3Test
4. {
5.    public static void main(String[] args)
6.    {
7.       double price = 44.95;
8.       double tax = 7.75;
9.       double amountDue = price * (1 + tax / 100);
10.      PrintWriter out = new PrintWriter(System.out);
11.      Printf3.fprint(out, "Amount due = %8.2f\n", amountDue);
12.      out.flush();
13.   }
14. }
```

Example 11–15: Printf3.java

```
1. import java.io.*;
2.
3. class Printf3
4. {
5.    public static native void fprint(PrintWriter out,
6.       String format, double x);
7.
8.    static
9.    {
10.      System.loadLibrary("Printf3");
11.   }
12. }
```

Example 11–16: Printf3.c

```
1. #include "Printf3.h"
2. #include <string.h>
3. #include <stdlib.h>
4. #include <float.h>
5.
6. /**
7.    @param format a string containing a printf format specifier
8.    (such as "%8.2f"). Substrings "%%" are skipped.
9.    @return a pointer to the format specifier (skipping the '%')
10.   or NULL if there wasn't a unique format specifier
11. */
12. char* find_format(const char format[])
13. {
14.    char* p;
15.    char* q;
16.
17.    p = strchr(format, '%');
18.    while (p != NULL && *(p + 1) == '%') /* skip %% */
19.       p = strchr(p + 2, '%');
20.    if (p == NULL) return NULL;
```

```
21.    /* now check that % is unique */
22.    p++;
23.    q = strchr(p, '%');
24.    while (q != NULL && *(q + 1) == '%') /* skip %% */
25.       q = strchr(q + 2, '%');
26.    if (q != NULL) return NULL; /* % not unique */
27.    q = p + strspn(p, " -0+#"); /* skip past flags */
28.    q += strspn(q, "0123456789"); /* skip past field width */
29.    if (*q == '.') { q++; q += strspn(q, "0123456789"); }
30.       /* skip past precision */
31.    if (strchr("eEfFgG", *q) == NULL) return NULL;
32.       /* not a floating point format */
33.    return p;
34. }
35.
36. JNIEXPORT void JNICALL Java_Printf3_fprint(JNIEnv* env,
37.    jclass cl, jobject out, jstring format, jdouble x)
38. {
39.    const char* cformat;
40.    char* fmt;
41.    jstring str;
42.    jclass class_PrintWriter;
43.    jmethodID id_print;
44.
45.    cformat = (*env)->GetStringUTFChars(env, format, NULL);
46.    fmt = find_format(cformat);
47.    if (fmt == NULL)
48.       str = format;
49.    else
50.    {
51.       char* cstr;
52.       int width = atoi(fmt);
53.       if (width == 0) width = DBL_DIG + 10;
54.       cstr = (char*)malloc(strlen(cformat) + width);
55.       sprintf(cstr, cformat, x);
56.       str = (*env)->NewStringUTF(env, cstr);
57.       free(cstr);
58.    }
59.    (*env)->ReleaseStringUTFChars(env, format, cformat);
60.
61.    /* now call ps.print(str) */
62.
63.    /* get the class */
64.    class_PrintWriter = (*env)->GetObjectClass(env, out);
65.
66.    /* get the method ID */
67.    id_print = (*env)->GetMethodID(env, class_PrintWriter,
68.       "print", "(Ljava/lang/String;)V");
69.
70.    /* call the method */
71.    (*env)->CallVoidMethod(env, out, id_print, str);
72. }
```

Executing Java methods from C code

- jmethodID GetMethodID(JNIEnv *env, jclass cl, const char name[], const char sig[])

returns the identifier of a method in a class.

Parameters: env   the JNI interface pointer

cl   the class object

name   the method name

sig   the encoded method signature

- void Call*Xxx*Method(JNIEnv *env, jobject obj, jmethodID id, args)
- void Call*Xxx*MethodA(JNIEnv *env, jobject obj, jmethodID id, jvalue args[])
- void Call*Xxx*MethodV(JNIEnv *env, jobject obj, jmethodID id, va_list args)

These functions call a method. The return type *Xxx* is one of Object, Boolean, Byte, Char, Short, Int, Long, Float, or Double. The first function has a variable number of arguments—simply append the method parameters after the method ID. The second function receives the method arguments in an array of jvalue, where jvalue is a union defined as

```
typedef union jvalue
{
  jboolean z;
  jbyte b;
  jchar c;
  jshort s;
  jint i;
  jlong j;
  jfloat f;
  jdouble d;
  jobject l;
} jvalue;
```

The third function receives the method parameters in a va_list, as defined in the C header stdarg.h.

Parameters: env   the JNI interface pointer

obj   the implicit argument of the method

id   the method identifier

args   the method arguments

- void CallNonvirtual*Xxx*Method(JNIEnv *env, jobject obj, jclass cl, jmethodID id, args)
- void CallNonvirtual*Xxx*MethodA(JNIEnv *env, jobject obj, jclass cl, jmethodID id, jvalue args[])

- void CallNonvirtual*Xxx*MethodV(JNIEnv *env, jobject obj, jclass cl, jmethodID id, va_list args)

  These functions call a method, bypassing dynamic dispatch. The return type *Xxx* is one of Object, Boolean, Byte, Char, Short, Int, Long, Float, or Double. The first function has a variable number of arguments—simply append the method parameters after the method ID. The second function receives the method arguments in an array of jvalue. The third function receives the method parameters in a va_list, as defined in the C header stdarg.h.

Parameters:	env	the JNI interface pointer
	obj	the implicit argument of the method
	cl	the class whose implementation of the method is to be called
	id	the method identifier
	args	the method arguments

- jmethodID GetStaticMethodID(JNIEnv *env, jclass cl, const char name[], const char sig[])

  returns the identifier of a static method in a class.

Parameters:	env	the JNI interface pointer
	cl	the class object
	name	the method name
	sig	the encoded method signature

- void CallStatic*Xxx*Method(JNIEnv *env, jclass cl, jmethodID id, args)
- void CallStatic*Xxx*MethodA(JNIEnv *env, jclass cl, jmethodID id, jvalue args[])
- void CallStatic*Xxx*MethodV(JNIEnv *env, jclass cl, jmethodID id, va_list args)

  These functions call a static method. The return type *Xxx* is one of Object, Boolean, Byte, Char, Short, Int, Long, Float, or Double. The first function has a variable number of arguments—simply append the method parameters after the method ID. The second function receives the method arguments in an array of jvalue. The third function receives the method parameters in a va_list, as defined in the C header stdarg.h.

Parameters:	env	the JNI interface pointer
	cl	the class of the static method
	id	the method identifier
	args	the method arguments

- `jobject NewObject(JNIEnv *env, jclass cl, jmethodID id, args)`
- `jobject NewObjectA(JNIEnv *env, jclass cl, jmethodID id, jvalue args[])`
- `jobject NewObjectV(JNIEnv *env, jclass cl, jmethodID id, va_list args)`

These functions call a constructor. The method ID is obtained from `Get-MethodID` with a method name of `"<init>"` and a return type of `void`. The first function has a variable number of arguments—simply append the method parameters after the method ID. The second function receives the method arguments in an array of `jvalue`. The third function receives the method parameters in a `va_list`, as defined in the C header `stdarg.h`.

Parameters: env   the JNI interface pointer

cl   the class to be instantiated

id   the constructor method identifier

args   the constructor arguments

Arrays

All array types of the Java programming language have corresponding C types, as shown in Table 11–2.

Table 11–2: Correspondence between Java array types and C types

Java type	C type
boolean[]	jbooleanArray
byte[]	jbyteArray
char[]	jcharArray
int[]	jintArray
short[]	jshortArray
long[]	jlongArray
float[]	jfloatArray
double[]	jdoubleArray
Object[]	jobjectArray

The type `jarray` denotes a generic array.

C++ NOTE: In C, all these array types are actually type synonyms of `jobject`. In C++, however, they are arranged in the inheritance hierarchy shown in Figure 11–2.

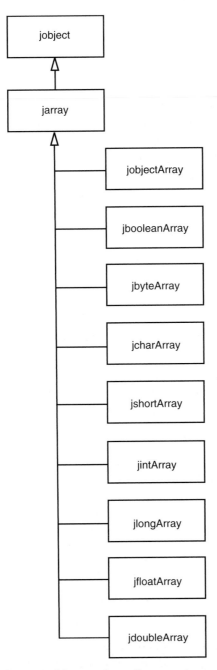

Figure 11–2: Inheritance hierarchy of array types

The GetArrayLength function returns the length of an array.

```
jarray array = ...;
jsize length = (*env)->GetArrayLength(env, array);
```

How you access elements in the array depends on whether the array stores objects or a primitive type (`bool`, `char`, or a numeric type). You access elements in an object array with the `GetObjectArrayElement` and `SetObjectArrayElement` methods.

```
jobjectArray array = ...;
int i, j;
jobject x = (*env)->GetObjectArrayElement(env, array, i);
(*env)->SetObjectArrayElement(env, array, j, x);
```

While simple, this approach is also clearly inefficient; you want to be able to access array elements directly, especially when doing vector and matrix computations.

The `GetXxxArrayElements` function returns a C pointer to the starting element of the array. As with ordinary strings, you must remember to call the corresponding `ReleaseXxxArrayElements` function to tell the virtual machine when you no longer need that pointer. Here, the type *Xxx* must be a primitive type, that is, not `Object`. You can then read and write the array elements directly. However, since the pointer *may point to a copy,* any changes that you make are guaranteed to be reflected in the original array only when you call the corresponding `ReleaseXxxArrayElements` function!

> NOTE: You can find out if an array is a copy by passing a pointer to a `jboolean` variable as the third parameter to a `GetXxxArrayElements` method. The variable is filled with `JNI_TRUE` if the array is a copy. If you aren't interested in that information, just pass a `NULL` pointer.

Here is a code sample that multiplies all elements in an array of `double` values by a constant. We obtain a C pointer `a` into the Java array and then access individual elements as `a[i]`.

```
jdoubleArray array_a = ...;
double scaleFactor = ...;
double* a = (*env)->GetDoubleArrayElements(env, array_a, NULL);
for (i = 0; i < (*env)->GetArrayLength(env, array_a); i++)
   a[i] = a[i] * scaleFactor;
(*env)->ReleaseDoubleArrayElements(env, array_a, 0);
```

Whether the virtual machine actually copies the array depends on how it allocates arrays and does its garbage collection. Some "copying" garbage collectors routinely move objects around and update object references. That strategy is not compatible with "pinning" an array to a particular location because the collector cannot update the pointer values in native code. However, the garbage collector in the current virtual machine supplied with the SDK is not a copying collector, which means that arrays are pinned.

NOTE: In the Sun JVM implementation, `boolean` arrays are represented as packed arrays, and the `GetBooleanArrayElements` method copies them into unpacked arrays of `jboolean` values.

If you want to access a few elements of a large array, use the `GetXxx-ArrayRegion` and `SetXxxArrayRegion` methods that copy a range of elements from the Java array into a C array and back.

You can create new Java arrays in native methods with the `NewXxxArray` function. To create a new array of objects, you specify the length, the type of the array elements, and an initial element for all entries (typically, `NULL`). Here is an example.

```
jclass class_Employee = (*env)->FindClass(env, "Employee");
jobjectArray array_e = (*env)->NewObjectArray(env, 100,
   class_Employee, NULL);
```

Arrays of primitive types are simpler. You just supply the length of the array.

```
jdoubleArray array_d = (*env)->NewDoubleArray(env, 100);
```

The array is then filled with zeroes.

NOTE: SDK 1.4 adds three methods to the JNI API

```
jobject NewDirectByteBuffer(JNIEnv* env, void* address, jlong
   capacity)
void* GetDirectBufferAddress(JNIEnv* env, jobject buf)
jlong GetDirectBufferCapacity(JNIEnv* env, jobject buf)
```

Direct buffers are used in the `java.nio` package to support more efficient input/output operations and to minimize the copying of data between native and Java arrays.

Manipulating Java Arrays in C code

- `jsize GetArrayLength(JNIEnv *env, jarray array)`
  returns the number of elements in the array.

  Parameters: env   the JNI interface pointer

                 array   the array object

- `jobject GetObjectArrayElement(JNIEnv *env, jobjectArray array, jsize index)`
  returns the value of an array element.

  Parameters: env   the JNI interface pointer

                 array   the array object

                 index   the array offset

- `void SetObjectArrayElement(JNIEnv *env, jobjectArray array, jsize index, jobject value)`

  sets an array element to a new value.

Parameters:	env	the JNI interface pointer
	array	the array object
	index	the array offset
	value	the new value

- `Xxx* GetXxxArrayElements(JNIEnv *env, jarray array, jboolean* isCopy)`

  yields a C pointer to the elements of a Java array. The field type *Xxx* is one of `Boolean`, `Byte`, `Char`, `Short`, `Int`, `Long`, `Float`, or `Double`. The pointer must be passed to `ReleaseXxxArrayElements` when it is no longer needed.

Parameters:	env	the JNI interface pointer
	array	the array object
	isCopy	is either `NULL` or points to a `jboolean` that is filled with `JNI_TRUE` if a copy is made; with `JNI_FALSE` otherwise

- `void ReleaseXxxArrayElements(JNIEnv *env, jarray array, Xxx elems[], jint mode)`

  notifies the virtual machine that a pointer obtained by `GetXxxArrayElements` is no longer needed.

Parameters:	env	the JNI interface pointer
	array	the array object
	elems	the pointer to the array elements that is no longer needed
	mode	`0` = free the `elems` buffer after updating the array elements
		`JNI_COMMIT` = do not free the `elems` buffer after updating the array elements
		`JNI_ABORT` = free the `elems` buffer without updating the array elements

- `void GetXxxArrayRegion(JNIEnv *env, jarray array, jint start, jint length, Xxx elems[])`

  copies elements from a Java array to a C array. The field type *Xxx* is one of `Boolean`, `Byte`, `Char`, `Short`, `Int`, `Long`, `Float`, or `Double`.

Parameters:	env	the JNI interface pointer
	array	the array object
	start	the starting index
	length	the number of elements to copy
	elems	the C array that holds the elements

- void Set*Xxx*ArrayRegion(JNIEnv *env, jarray array, jint start, jint length, *Xxx* elems[])

  copies elements from a C array to a Java array. The field type *Xxx* is one of Boolean, Byte, Char, Short, Int, Long, Float, or Double.

Parameters:	env	the JNI interface pointer
	array	the array object
	start	the starting index
	length	the number of elements to copy
	elems	the C array that holds the elements

Error Handling

Native methods are a significant security risk to programs in the Java programming language. The C runtime system has no protection against array bounds errors, indirection through bad pointers, and so on. It is particularly important that programmers of native methods handle all error conditions to preserve the integrity of the Java platform. In particular, when your native method diagnoses a problem that it cannot handle, then it should report this problem to the Java virtual machine. Then, you would naturally throw an exception in this situation. However, C has no exceptions. Instead, you must call the Throw or ThrowNew function to create a new exception object. When the native method exits, the Java virtual machine will throw that exception.

To use the Throw function, call NewObject to create an object of a subtype of Throwable. For example, here we allocate an EOFException object and throw it.

```
jclass class_EOFException = (*env)->FindClass(env,
   "java/io/EOFException");
jmethodID id_EOFException = (*env)->GetMethodID(env,
   class_EOFException,
   "<init>", "()V"); /* ID of default constructor */
jthrowable obj_exc = (*env)->NewObject(env, class_EOFException,
   id_EOFException);
(*env)->Throw(env, obj_exc);
```

It is usually more convenient to call ThrowNew, which constructs an exception object, given a class and a UTF string.

```
(*env)->ThrowNew(env, (*env)->FindClass(env,
   "java/io/EOFException"),
   "Unexpected end of file");
```

Both `Throw` and `ThrowNew` merely *post* the exception; they do not interrupt the control flow of the native method. Only when the method returns does the Java virtual machine throw the exception. Therefore, every call to `Throw` and `ThrowNew` should always immediately be followed by a `return` statement.

C++ NOTE: If you implement native methods in C++, you cannot currently throw a Java exception object in your C++ code. In a C++ binding, it would be possible to implement a translation between exceptions in the C++ and Java programming languages—however, this is not currently implemented. You need to use `Throw` or `ThrowNew` to throw a Java exception in a native C++ method, and you need to make sure that your native methods throw no C++ exceptions.

Normally, native code need not be concerned with catching Java exceptions. However, when a native method calls a Java method, that method might throw an exception. Moreover, a number of the JNI functions throw exceptions as well. For example, `SetObjectArrayElement` throws an `ArrayIndexOutOfBoundsException` if the index is out of bounds, and an `ArrayStoreException` if the class of the stored object is not a subclass of the element class of the array. In situations like these, a native method should call the `ExceptionOccurred` method to determine whether an exception has been thrown. The call

```
jthrowable obj_exc = (*env)->ExceptionOccurred(env);
```

returns `NULL` if no exception is pending, or it returns a reference to the current exception object. If you just want to check whether an exception has been thrown, without obtaining a reference to the exception object, use

```
jbool occurred = (*env)->ExceptionCheck(env);
```

Normally, a native method should simply return when an exception has occurred so that the virtual machine can propagate it to the Java code. However, a native method *may* analyze the exception object to determine if it can handle the exception. If it can, then the function

```
(*env)->ExceptionClear(env);
```

must be called to turn off the exception.

In our next example, we implement the `fprint` native method with the paranoia that is appropriate for a native method. Here are the exceptions that we throw:

- A `NullPointerException` if the format string is `NULL`;

- An `IllegalArgumentException` if the format string doesn't contain a `%` specifier that is appropriate for printing a `double`;

- An `OutOfMemoryError` if the call to `malloc` fails.

Finally, to demonstrate how to check for an exception when calling a Java method from a native method, we send the string to the stream, a character at a time, and call `ExceptionOccurred` after each call. Example 11–17 shows the code for the native method, and Example 11–18 contains the definition of the class containing the native method. Notice that the native method does not immediately terminate when an exception occurs in the call to `PrintWriter.print`—it first frees the `cstr` buffer. When the native method returns, the virtual machine again raises the exception. The test program in Example 11–19 demonstrates how the native method throws an exception when the formatting string is not valid.

Example 11–17: Printf4.c

```
1. #include "Printf4.h"
2. #include <string.h>
3. #include <stdlib.h>
4. #include <float.h>
5.
6. /**
7.    @param format a string containing a printf format specifier
8.    (such as "%8.2f"). Substrings "%%" are skipped.
9.    @return a pointer to the format specifier (skipping the '%')
10.   or NULL if there wasn't a unique format specifier
11. */
12. char* find_format(const char format[])
13. {
14.     char* p;
15.     char* q;
16.
17.     p = strchr(format, '%');
18.     while (p != NULL && *(p + 1) == '%') /* skip %% */
19.         p = strchr(p + 2, '%');
20.     if (p == NULL) return NULL;
21.     /* now check that % is unique */
22.     p++;
23.     q = strchr(p, '%');
24.     while (q != NULL && *(q + 1) == '%') /* skip %% */
25.         q = strchr(q + 2, '%');
26.     if (q != NULL) return NULL; /* % not unique */
27.     q = p + strspn(p, " -0+#"); /* skip past flags */
28.     q += strspn(q, "0123456789"); /* skip past field width */
29.     if (*q == '.') { q++; q += strspn(q, "0123456789"); }
30.         /* skip past precision */
31.     if (strchr("eEfFgG", *q) == NULL) return NULL;
```

```
32.        /* not a floating point format */
33.     return p;
34. }
35.
36. JNIEXPORT void JNICALL Java_Printf4_fprint(JNIEnv* env,
37.     jclass cl, jobject out, jstring format, jdouble x)
38. {
39.     const char* cformat;
40.     char* fmt;
41.     jclass class_PrintWriter;
42.     jmethodID id_print;
43.     char* cstr;
44.     int width;
45.     int i;
46.
47.     if (format == NULL)
48.     {
49.         (*env)->ThrowNew(env,
50.             (*env)->FindClass(env,
51.             "java/lang/NullPointerException"),
52.             "Printf4.fprint: format is null");
53.         return;
54.     }
55.
56.     cformat = (*env)->GetStringUTFChars(env, format, NULL);
57.     fmt = find_format(cformat);
58.
59.     if (fmt == NULL)
60.     {
61.         (*env)->ThrowNew(env,
62.             (*env)->FindClass(env,
63.             "java/lang/IllegalArgumentException"),
64.             "Printf4.fprint: format is invalid");
65.         return;
66.     }
67.
68.     width = atoi(fmt);
69.     if (width == 0) width = DBL_DIG + 10;
70.     cstr = (char*)malloc(strlen(cformat) + width);
71.
72.     if (cstr == NULL)
73.     {
74.         (*env)->ThrowNew(env,
75.             (*env)->FindClass(env, "java/lang/OutOfMemoryError"),
76.             "Printf4.fprint: malloc failed");
77.         return;
78.     }
79.
80.     sprintf(cstr, cformat, x);
81.
82.     (*env)->ReleaseStringUTFChars(env, format, cformat);
```

```
83.
84.    /* now call ps.print(str) */
85.
86.    /* get the class */
87.    class_PrintWriter = (*env)->GetObjectClass(env, out);
88.
89.    /* get the method ID */
90.    id_print = (*env)->GetMethodID(env, class_PrintWriter,
91.      "print", "(C)V");
92.
93.    /* call the method */
94.    for (i = 0; cstr[i] != 0 && !(*env)->ExceptionOccurred(env);
95.          i++)
96.      (*env)->CallVoidMethod(env, out, id_print, cstr[i]);
97.
98.    free(cstr);
99. }
```

Example 11–18: Printf4.java

```
1. import java.io.*;
2.
3. class Printf4
4. {
5.    public static native void fprint(PrintWriter ps,
6.        String format, double x);
7.
8.    static
9.    {
10.       System.loadLibrary("Printf4");
11.    }
12. }
```

Example 11–19: Printf4Test.java

```
1. import java.io.*;
2.
3. class Printf4Test
4. {
5.    public static void main(String[] args)
6.    {
7.       double price = 44.95;
8.       double tax = 7.75;
9.       double amountDue = price * (1 + tax / 100);
10.       PrintWriter out = new PrintWriter(System.out);
11.       /* This call will throw an exception--note the %% */
12.       Printf4.fprint(out, "Amount due = %%8.2f\n", amountDue);
13.       out.flush();
14.    }
15. }
```

Error handling in C code

- `jint Throw(JNIEnv *env, jthrowable obj)`

  prepares an exception to be thrown upon exiting from the native code. Returns 0 on success, a negative value on failure.

  Parameters: env   the JNI interface pointer

                  obj   the exception object to throw

- `jint ThrowNew(JNIEnv *env, jclass clazz, const char msg[])`

  prepares an exception to be thrown upon exiting from the native code. Returns 0 on success, a negative value on failure.

  Parameters: env   the JNI interface pointer

                  cl   the class of the exception object to throw

                  msg   a UTF string denoting the `String` construction argument of the exception object

- `jthrowable ExceptionOccurred(JNIEnv *env)`

  returns the exception object if an exception is pending, or NULL otherwise.

  Parameters: env   the JNI interface pointer

- `jboolean ExceptionCheck(JNIEnv *env)`

  returns `true` if an exception is pending.

  Parameters: env   the JNI interface pointer

- `void ExceptionClear(JNIEnv *env)`

  clears any pending exceptions.

  Parameters: env   the JNI interface pointer

The Invocation API

Up to now, we have considered programs in the Java programming language that made a few C calls, presumably because C was faster or allowed access to functionality that was inaccessible from the Java platform. Suppose you are in the opposite situation. You have a C or C++ program and would like to make a few calls to Java code, perhaps because the Java code is easier to program. Of course, you know how to call the Java methods. But you still need to add the Java virtual machine to your program so that the Java code can be interpreted. The so-called *invocation API* is used to embed the Java virtual machine into a C or C++ program. Here is the minimal code that you need to initialize a virtual machine.

```
JavaVMOption options[1];
JavaVMInitArgs vm_args;
JavaVM *jvm;
JNIEnv *env;
```

```
options[0].optionString = "-Djava.class.path=.";

memset(&vm_args, 0, sizeof(vm_args));
vm_args.version = JNI_VERSION_1_2;
vm_args.nOptions = 1;
vm_args.options = options;

JNI_CreateJavaVM(&jvm, (void**)&env, &vm_args);
```

The call to `JNI_CreateJavaVM` creates the virtual machine, and fills in a pointer `jvm` to the virtual machine and a pointer `env` to the execution environment.

You can supply any number of options to the virtual machine. Simply increase the size of the `options` array and the value of `vm_args.nOptions`. For example,

```
options[i].optionString = "-Djava.compiler=NONE";
```

deactivates the just-in-time compiler.

TIP: When you run into trouble and your program crashes, refuses to initialize the JVM, or can't load your classes, then turn on the JNI debugging mode. Set an option to

```
options[i].optionString = "-verbose:jni";
```

You will see a flurry of messages that indicate the progress in initializing the JVM. If you don't see your classes loaded, check both your path and your class path settings.

Once you have set up the virtual machine, you can call Java methods in the way described in the preceding sections: simply use the `env` pointer in the usual way. You need the `jvm` pointer only to call other functions in the invocation API. Currently, there are only four such functions. The most important one is the function to terminate the virtual machine:

```
(*jvm)->DestroyJavaVM(jvm);
```

The C program in Example 11–20 sets up a virtual machine and then calls the `main` method of the `Welcome` class, which was discussed in Chapter 2 of Volume 1. (Make sure to compile the `Welcome.java` file before starting the invocation test program.)

Example 11–20: InvocationTest.c

```
1. #include <jni.h>
2. #include <stdlib.h>
3.
4. int main()
5. {
6.    JavaVMOption options[2];
```

```
7.    JavaVMInitArgs vm_args;
8.    JavaVM *jvm;
9.    JNIEnv *env;
10.   long status;
11.
12.   jclass class_Welcome;
13.   jclass class_String;
14.   jobjectArray args;
15.   jmethodID id_main;
16.
17.   options[0].optionString = "-Djava.class.path=.";
18.
19.   memset(&vm_args, 0, sizeof(vm_args));
20.   vm_args.version = JNI_VERSION_1_2;
21.   vm_args.nOptions = 1;
22.   vm_args.options = options;
23.
24.   status = JNI_CreateJavaVM(&jvm, (void**)&env, &vm_args);
25.   if (status == JNI_ERR)
26.   {
27.      printf("Error creating VM\n");
28.      return 1;
29.   }
30.
31.   class_Welcome = (*env)->FindClass(env, "Welcome");
32.   id_main = (*env)->GetStaticMethodID(env, class_Welcome,
33.      "main", "([Ljava/lang/String;)V");
34.
35.   class_String = (*env)->FindClass(env, "java/lang/String");
36.   args = (*env)->NewObjectArray(env, 0, class_String, NULL);
37.   (*env)->CallStaticVoidMethod(env, class_Welcome,
38.      id_main, args);
39.
40.   (*jvm)->DestroyJavaVM(jvm);
41.
42.   return 0;
43. }
```

To compile this program under Linux, use:

```
gcc -I/usr/local/jdk/include -I/usr/local/jdk/include/linux
   -o InvocationTest
   -L/usr/local/jdk/jre/lib/i386/client
   -ljvm
   InvocationTest.c
```

Under Solaris, use:

```
cc -I/usr/local/jdk/include -I/usr/local/jdk/include/solaris
   -o InvocationTest
   -L/usr/local/jdk/jre/lib/sparc
```

```
-ljvm
InvocationTest.c
```

When compiling in Windows with the Microsoft C compiler, you use the command line:

```
cl -Ic:\jdk\include -Ic:\jdk\include\win32
    InvocationTest.c c:\jdk\lib\jvm.lib
```

With Cygwin, you have to work a little harder. First make a file `jvm.def` that contains the statement:

```
EXPORTS
    JNI_CreateJavaVM@12
```

Run the command:

```
dlltool -k --input-def jvm.def
    --dll c:\\jdk\\jre\\bin\\hotspot\\jvm.dll
    --output-lib jvm.a
```

Then compile with:

```
gcc -Ic:\jdk\include -Ic:\jdk\include\win32
    -D__int64="long long"
    -o InvocationTest
    InvocationTest.c jvm.a
```

Before you run the program under Linux/UNIX, you must make sure that the `LD_LIBRARY_PATH` contains the directories for the shared libraries. For example, if you use the `bash` shell on Linux, issue the command:

```
export LD_LIBRARY_PATH=/usr/local/jdk/jre/lib/i386/client
    :/usr/local/jdk/jre/lib/i386
```

On Windows, make sure the directory

```
c:\jdk\jre\bin\hotspot
```

is on the `PATH`.

CAUTION: The exact locations of the various library files varies somewhat from one release of the SDK to the next. You may need to search for files called `libjvm.so`, `jvm.dll`, or (with older SDK versions) `libjava.so`, in the `jdk/bin`, `jdk/lib`, and `jdk/jre/lib` directories, and adjust the instructions accordingly.

TIP: If you develop an application that invokes the virtual machine by using a Windows launcher, then you may not trust your users to set the library path. You can help your users and load the shared library or DLL manually. The `javac` and `java` programs do just that. For sample code, see the file `launcher/java_md.c` in the `src.jar` file that is a part of the SDK.

Invocation API functions

- `jint JNI_CreateJavaVM(JavaVM** p_jvm, void** p_env, JavaVM-InitArgs* vm_args)`

  initializes the Java virtual machine. The function returns 0 if successful, `JNI_ERR` on failure.

Parameters:	`p_jvm`	filled with a pointer to the invocation API function table
	`p_env`	filled with a pointer to the JNI function table
	`vm_args`	the virtual machine arguments

- `jint DestroyJavaVM(JavaVM* jvm)`

  destroys the virtual machine. Returns 0 on success, a negative number on failure. This function must be called through a virtual machine pointer, i.e., `(*jvm)->DestroyJavaVM(jvm)`.

Parameters:	`jvm`	the virtual machine pointer

A Complete Example: Accessing the Windows Registry

In this section, we describe a full, working example that covers everything we discussed in this chapter: using native methods with strings, arrays, objects, constructor calls, and error handling. What we show you is how to put a Java platform wrapper around a subset of the ordinary C-based API used to work with the Windows registry. Of course, being a Windows-specific feature, a program using the Windows registry is inherently nonportable. For that reason, the standard Java library has no support for the registry, and it makes sense to use native methods to gain access to it.

An Overview of the Windows Registry

For those who are not familiar with the Windows registry: It is a data depository that is accessed by the Windows operating system, and that is available as a storage area for application programs. (A good book is *Inside the Windows 95 Registry* by Ron Petrusha [O'Reilly 1996].) In older versions of Windows, the operating system as well as applications used so-called INI files to store configuration parameters. Windows programs are supposed to use the registry instead. The registry has a number of advantages.

- INI files store data as strings; the registry supports other data types such as integers and byte arrays.
- INI file sections cannot have subsections; the registry supports a complete tree structure.
- Configuration parameters were distributed over many INI files; placing them into the registry provides a single point for administration and backup.

On the downside, the registry is also a single point of failure—if you mess up the registry, your computer may malfunction or even fail to boot! The sample program that we present in this section is safe, but if you plan to make any modifications to it, you should learn how to back up the registry before proceeding. See the book by Petrusha for information on how to back up the Windows registry.

We don't suggest that you use the registry to store configuration parameters for your Java programs. XML files are a better solution—see chapter 12 for more information. We simply use the registry to demonstrate how to wrap a nontrivial native API into a Java class.

The principal tool for inspecting the registry is the *registry editor*. Because of the potential for error by naïve but enthusiastic users, there is no icon for launching the registry editor. Instead, start a DOS shell (or open the Start->Run dialog) and type `regedit`. Figure 11–3 shows the registry editor in action.

Figure 11–3: The registry editor

The left side shows the keys, which are arranged in a tree structure. Note that each key starts with one of the HKEY nodes like

```
HKEY_CLASSES_ROOT
HKEY_CURRENT_USER
HKEY_LOCAL_MACHINE
. . .
```

The right side shows the name/value pairs that are associated with a particular key. For example, the key

```
HKEY_LOCAL_MACHINE\SOFTWARE\JavaSoft\Java Development Kit\1.4
```

has two name/value pairs, such as,

```
JavaHome="c:\jdk1.4"
MicroVersion="0"
```

In this case, the values are strings. The values can also be integers or arrays of bytes.

A Java Platform Interface for Accessing the Registry

We will implement a simple interface to access the registry from Java code, and then implement this interface with native code. Our interface allows only a few registry operations; to keep the code size down, we omitted other important operations such as adding, deleting, and enumerating keys. (Following our model and the information supplied in Petrusha's book, it would be easy to add the remaining registry API functions.)

Even with the limited subset that we supply, you can

- Enumerate all names stored in a key;

- Read the value stored with a name;

- Set the value stored with a name.

Here is the Java platform class that encapsulates a registry key.

```
public class Win32RegKey
{
    public Win32RegKey(int theRoot, String thePath) { . . . }
    public Enumeration names() { . . . }
    public native Object getValue(String name);
    public native void setValue(String name, Object value);

    public static final int HKEY_CLASSES_ROOT = 0x80000000;
    public static final int HKEY_CURRENT_USER = 0x80000001;
    public static final int HKEY_LOCAL_MACHINE = 0x80000002;
    . . .
}
```

The names method returns an enumeration that holds all the names stored with the key. You can get at them with the familiar hasMoreElements/nextElement methods. The getValue method returns an object that is either a string, an Integer object, or a byte array. The value parameter of the setValue method must also be of one of these three types.

Here is a simple function that lists the strings that are stored with the key

```
HKEY_LOCAL_MACHINE\SOFTWARE\JavaSoft\Java Development Kit\1.4
```

(You should change the key to the version of the SDK that is installed on your system.)

```
public static void main(String[] args)
{
    Win32RegKey key = new Win32RegKey(
        Win32RegKey.HKEY_LOCAL_MACHINE,
        "SOFTWARE\JavaSoft\Java Development Kit\1.4");

    Enumeration enum = key.names();

    while (enum.hasMoreElements())
    {
        String name = (String)enum.nextElement();
        System.out.println(name + "=" + key.getValue(name));
    }
}
```

A typical output of this program is as follows:

```
JavaHome=c:\jdk1.4
MicroVersion=0
```

Implementing the Registry Access Functions as Native Methods

We need to implement three actions:

- Get the value of a key;
- Set the value of a key;
- Iterate through the names of a key.

Fortunately, you have seen essentially all the tools that are required, such as the conversion between Java strings and arrays and those of C. And you saw how to raise a Java exception in case something goes wrong.

Two issues make these native methods more complex than the preceding examples. The getValue and setValue methods deal with the type Object, which can be one of String, Integer, or byte[]. And the enumeration object needs to *store* the *state* between successive calls to hasMoreElements/nextElement.

Let us first look at the getValue method. The code (which is shown in Example 11–22) goes through the following steps.

1. Open the registry key. To read their values, the registry API requires that keys be open.

2. Query the type and size of the value that is associated with the name.

3. Read the data into a buffer.

4. If the type is REG_SZ (a string), then call NewStringUTF to create a new string with the value data.

5. If the type is REG_DWORD (a 32-bit integer), then invoke the Integer constructor.

6. If the type is REG_BINARY, then call NewByteArray to create a new byte array, and SetByteArrayRegion to copy the value data into the byte array.

7. If the type is none of these or if there was an error when calling an API function, throw an exception and carefully release all resources that had been acquired up to that point.

8. Close the key and return the object (String, Integer, or byte[]) that had been created.

As you can see, this example illustrates quite nicely how to generate Java objects of different types.

In this native method, coping with the generic return type is not difficult. The jstring, jobject, or jarray reference was simply returned as a jobject. However, the setValue method receives a reference to an Object, and it must determine its exact type so it can save it as either a string, integer, or byte array. We can make this determination by querying the class of the value object, finding the class references for java.lang.String, java.lang.Integer, and byte[], and comparing them with the IsAssignableFrom function.

If class1 and class2 are two class references, then the call

```
(*env)->IsAssignableFrom(env, class1, class2)
```

returns JNI_TRUE when class1 and class2 are the same class or class1 is a subclass of class2. In either case, references to objects of class1 can be cast to class2. For example, when

```
(*env)->IsAssignableFrom(env,
    (*env)->GetObjectClass(env, value)
    (*env)->FindClass(env, "[B"))
```

is true, then we know that value is a byte array.

Here is an overview of the code of the setValue method.

1. Open the registry key for writing.

2. Find the type of the value to write.

3. If the type is String, call GetStringUTFChars to get a pointer to the characters. Also, obtain the string length.

4. If the type is Integer, call the intValue method to get the integer stored in the wrapper object.

5. If the type is byte[], call GetByteArrayElements to get a pointer to the bytes. Also, obtain the string length.

6. Pass the data and length to the registry.

7. Close the key. If the type is String or byte[], then also release the pointer to the characters or bytes.

Finally, let us turn to the native methods that enumerate keys. These are methods of the `Win32RegKeyNameEnumeration` class (see Example 11–21). When the enumeration process starts, we must open the key. For the duration of the enumeration, we must retain the key handle. That is, the key handle must be stored with the enumeration object. The key handle is of type `DWORD`, a 32-bit quantity, and, hence, can be stored in a Java integer. It is stored in the `hkey` field of the enumeration class. When the enumeration starts, the field is initialized with `SetIntField`. Subsequent calls read the value with `GetIntField`.

TIP: As this example shows, using a Java object field to store native-state data is very useful for implementing native methods.

In this example, we store three other data items with the enumeration object. When the enumeration first starts, we can query the registry for the count of name/value pairs and the length of the longest name, which we need so we can allocate C character arrays to hold the names. These values are stored in the `count` and `maxsize` fields of the enumeration object. Finally, the `index` field is initialized with −1 to indicate the start of the enumeration, is set to 0 once the other object fields are initialized, and is incremented after every enumeration step.

Here, we walk through the native methods that support the enumeration. The `hasMoreElements` method is simple.

1. Retrieve the `index` and `count` fields.
2. If the index is −1, call the `startNameEnumeration` function, which opens the key, queries the count and maximum length, and initializes the `hkey`, `count`, `maxsize`, and `index` fields.
3. Return `JNI_TRUE` if `index` is less than `count`; `JNI_FALSE` otherwise.

The `nextElement` method needs to work a little harder.

1. Retrieve the `index` and `count` fields.
2. If the index is −1, call the `startNameEnumeration` function, which opens the key, queries the count and maximum length, and initializes the `hkey`, `count`, `maxsize`, and `index` fields.
3. If `index` equals `count`, throw a `NoSuchElementException`.
4. Read the next name from the registry.
5. Increment `index`.
6. If `index` equals `count`, close the key.

To compile the program, you must link in the `advapi32.lib` library.

Before compiling, remember to run `javah` on both `Win32RegKey` and `Win32RegKeyNameEnumeration`. The complete command line is

```
cl -Ic:\jdk\include -Ic:\jdk\include\win32 -LD
   Win32RegKey.c advapi32.lib -FeWin32RegKey.dll
```

With Cygwin, use

```
gcc -c -Ic:\jdk\include
    -Ic:\jdk\include\win32 -Ic:\cygwin\usr\include\w32api
    -D__int64="long long"
    Win32RegKey.c
dllwrap --add-stdcall-alias -o Win32RegKey.dll Win32RegKey.o
```

Example 11–23 shows a program to test our new registry functions. We add three name/value pairs, a string, an integer, and a byte array to the key.

```
HKEY_LOCAL_MACHINE\SOFTWARE\JavaSoft\Java Development Kit\1.4
```

You should edit the version number to match your SDK installation (or simply use some other existing registry key).

We then enumerate all names of that key and retrieve their values. The program should print out

```
JavaHome=c:\jdk1.4
MicroVersion=0
Default user=Harry Hacker
Lucky number=13
Small primes=2 3 5 7 11 13
```

Although adding these name/value pairs to that key probably does no harm, you may want to use the registry editor to remove them after running this program.

Example 11–21: Win32RegKey.java

```
1. import java.util.*;
2.
3. /**
4.    A Win32RegKey object can be used to get and set values of
5.    a registry key in the Windows registry.
6. */
7. public class Win32RegKey
8. {
9.    /**
10.      Construct a registry key object.
11.      @param theRoot one of HKEY_CLASSES_ROOT, HKEY_CURRENT_USER,
12.      HKEY_LOCAL_MACHINE, HKEY_USERS, HKEY_CURRENT_CONFIG,
13.      HKEY_DYN_DATA
14.      @param thePath the registry key path
15.    */
16.    public Win32RegKey(int theRoot, String thePath)
17.    {
```

```
18.        root = theRoot;
19.        path = thePath;
20.     }
21.
22.     /**
23.        Enumerates all names of registry entries under the path
24.        that this object describes.
25.        @return an enumeration listing all entry names
26.     */
27.     public Enumeration names()
28.     {
29.        return new Win32RegKeyNameEnumeration(root, path);
30.     }
31.
32.     /**
33.        Gets the value of a registry entry.
34.        @param name the entry name
35.        @return the associated value
36.     */
37.     public native Object getValue(String name);
38.
39.     /**
40.        Sets the value of a registry entry.
41.        @param name the entry name
42.        @param value the new value
43.     */
44.     public native void setValue(String name, Object value);
45.
46.     public static final int HKEY_CLASSES_ROOT = 0x80000000;
47.     public static final int HKEY_CURRENT_USER = 0x80000001;
48.     public static final int HKEY_LOCAL_MACHINE = 0x80000002;
49.     public static final int HKEY_USERS = 0x80000003;
50.     public static final int HKEY_CURRENT_CONFIG = 0x80000005;
51.     public static final int HKEY_DYN_DATA = 0x80000006;
52.
53.     private int root;
54.     private String path;
55.
56.     static
57.     {
58.        System.loadLibrary("Win32RegKey");
59.     }
60. }
61.
62. class Win32RegKeyNameEnumeration implements Enumeration
63. {
64.     Win32RegKeyNameEnumeration(int theRoot, String thePath)
65.     {
```

```java
66.        root = theRoot;
67.        path = thePath;
68.    }
69.
70.    public native Object nextElement();
71.    public native boolean hasMoreElements();
72.
73.    private int root;
74.    private String path;
75.    private int index = -1;
76.    private int hkey = 0;
77.    private int maxsize;
78.    private int count;
79. }
80.
81. class Win32RegKeyException extends RuntimeException
82. {
83.    public Win32RegKeyException() {}
84.    public Win32RegKeyException(String why)
85.    {
86.        super(why);
87.    }
88. }
```

Example 11–22: Win32RegKey.c

```c
1. #include "Win32RegKey.h"
2. #include "Win32RegKeyNameEnumeration.h"
3. #include <string.h>
4. #include <stdlib.h>
5. #include <windows.h>
6.
7. JNIEXPORT jobject JNICALL Java_Win32RegKey_getValue(JNIEnv* env,
8.    jobject this_obj, jstring name)
9. {
10.    const char* cname;
11.    jstring path;
12.    const char* cpath;
13.    HKEY hkey;
14.    DWORD type;
15.    DWORD size;
16.    jclass this_class;
17.    jfieldID id_root;
18.    jfieldID id_path;
19.    HKEY root;
20.    jobject ret;
21.    char* cret;
22.
23.    /* get the class */
24.    this_class = (*env)->GetObjectClass(env, this_obj);
25.
```

```
26.    /* get the field IDs */
27.    id_root = (*env)->GetFieldID(env, this_class, "root", "I");
28.    id_path = (*env)->GetFieldID(env, this_class, "path",
29.       "Ljava/lang/String;");
30.
31.    /* get the fields */
32.    root = (HKEY)(*env)->GetIntField(env, this_obj, id_root);
33.    path = (jstring)(*env)->GetObjectField(env, this_obj,
34.       id_path);
35.    cpath = (*env)->GetStringUTFChars(env, path, NULL);
36.
37.    /* open the registry key */
38.    if (RegOpenKeyEx(root, cpath, 0, KEY_READ, &hkey)
39.       != ERROR_SUCCESS)
40.    {
41.       (*env)->ThrowNew(env,
42.          (*env)->FindClass(env, "Win32RegKeyException"),
43.          "Open key failed");
44.       (*env)->ReleaseStringUTFChars(env, path, cpath);
45.       return NULL;
46.    }
47.
48.    (*env)->ReleaseStringUTFChars(env, path, cpath);
49.    cname = (*env)->GetStringUTFChars(env, name, NULL);
50.
51.    /* find the type and size of the value */
52.    if (RegQueryValueEx(hkey, cname, NULL, &type, NULL, &size)
53.       != ERROR_SUCCESS)
54.    {
55.       (*env)->ThrowNew(env,
56.          (*env)->FindClass(env, "Win32RegKeyException"),
57.          "Query value key failed");
58.       RegCloseKey(hkey);
59.       (*env)->ReleaseStringUTFChars(env, name, cname);
60.       return NULL;
61.    }
62.
63.    /* get memory to hold the value */
64.    cret = (char*)malloc(size);
65.
66.    /* read the value */
67.    if (RegQueryValueEx(hkey, cname, NULL, &type, cret, &size)
68.       != ERROR_SUCCESS)
69.    {
70.       (*env)->ThrowNew(env,
71.          (*env)->FindClass(env, "Win32RegKeyException"),
72.          "Query value key failed");
73.       free(cret);
74.       RegCloseKey(hkey);
75.       (*env)->ReleaseStringUTFChars(env, name, cname);
76.       return NULL;
77.    }
```

```
78.
79.    /* depending on the type, store the value in a string,
80.       integer or byte array */
81.    if (type == REG_SZ)
82.    {
83.       ret = (*env)->NewStringUTF(env, cret);
84.    }
85.    else if (type == REG_DWORD)
86.    {
87.       jclass class_Integer = (*env)->FindClass(env,
88.          "java/lang/Integer");
89.       /* get the method ID of the constructor */
90.       jmethodID id_Integer = (*env)->GetMethodID(env,
91.          class_Integer, "<init>", "(I)V");
92.       int value = *(int*)cret;
93.       /* invoke the constructor */
94.       ret = (*env)->NewObject(env, class_Integer, id_Integer,
95.          value);
96.    }
97.    else if (type == REG_BINARY)
98.    {
99.       ret = (*env)->NewByteArray(env, size);
100.      (*env)->SetByteArrayRegion(env, (jarray)ret, 0, size,
101.         cret);
102.   }
103.   else
104.   {
105.      (*env)->ThrowNew(env,
106.         (*env)->FindClass(env, "Win32RegKeyException"),
107.         "Unsupported value type");
108.      ret = NULL;
109.   }
110.
111.   free(cret);
112.   RegCloseKey(hkey);
113.   (*env)->ReleaseStringUTFChars(env, name, cname);
114.
115.   return ret;
116. }
117.
118. JNIEXPORT void JNICALL Java_Win32RegKey_setValue(JNIEnv* env,
119.    jobject this_obj, jstring name, jobject value)
120. {
121.    const char* cname;
122.    jstring path;
123.    const char* cpath;
124.    HKEY hkey;
125.    DWORD type;
126.    DWORD size;
127.    jclass this_class;
128.    jclass class_value;
129.    jclass class_Integer;
```

```
130.   jfieldID id_root;
131.   jfieldID id_path;
132.   HKEY root;
133.   const char* cvalue;
134.   int ivalue;
135.
136.   /* get the class */
137.   this_class = (*env)->GetObjectClass(env, this_obj);
138.
139.   /* get the field IDs */
140.   id_root = (*env)->GetFieldID(env, this_class, "root", "I");
141.   id_path = (*env)->GetFieldID(env, this_class, "path",
142.      "Ljava/lang/String;");
143.
144.   /* get the fields */
145.   root = (HKEY)(*env)->GetIntField(env, this_obj, id_root);
146.   path = (jstring)(*env)->GetObjectField(env, this_obj,
147.      id_path);
148.   cpath = (*env)->GetStringUTFChars(env, path, NULL);
149.
150.   /* open the registry key */
151.   if (RegOpenKeyEx(root, cpath, 0, KEY_WRITE, &hkey)
152.      != ERROR_SUCCESS)
153.   {
154.      (*env)->ThrowNew(env,
155.         (*env)->FindClass(env, "Win32RegKeyException"),
156.         "Open key failed");
157.      (*env)->ReleaseStringUTFChars(env, path, cpath);
158.      return;
159.   }
160.
161.   (*env)->ReleaseStringUTFChars(env, path, cpath);
162.   cname = (*env)->GetStringUTFChars(env, name, NULL);
163.
164.   class_value = (*env)->GetObjectClass(env, value);
165.   class_Integer = (*env)->FindClass(env, "java/lang/Integer");
166.   /* determine the type of the value object */
167.   if ((*env)->IsAssignableFrom(env, class_value,
168.      (*env)->FindClass(env, "java/lang/String")))
169.   {
170.      /* it is a string--get a pointer to the characters */
171.      cvalue = (*env)->GetStringUTFChars(env, (jstring)value,
172.         NULL);
173.      type = REG_SZ;
174.      size = (*env)->GetStringLength(env, (jstring)value) + 1;
175.   }
176.   else if ((*env)->IsAssignableFrom(env, class_value,
177.      class_Integer))
178.   {
179.      /* it is an integer--call intValue to get the value */
180.      jmethodID id_intValue = (*env)->GetMethodID(env,
181.         class_Integer, "intValue", "()I");
```

```
182.        ivalue = (*env)->CallIntMethod(env, value, id_intValue);
183.        type = REG_DWORD;
184.        cvalue = (char*)&ivalue;
185.        size = 4;
186.     }
187.     else if ((*env)->IsAssignableFrom(env, class_value,
188.        (*env)->FindClass(env, "[B")))
189.     {
190.        /* it is a byte array--get a pointer to the bytes */
191.        type = REG_BINARY;
192.        cvalue = (char*)(*env)->GetByteArrayElements(env,
193.           (jarray)value, NULL);
194.        size = (*env)->GetArrayLength(env, (jarray)value);
195.     }
196.     else
197.     {
198.        /* we don't know how to handle this type */
199.        (*env)->ThrowNew(env,
200.           (*env)->FindClass(env, "Win32RegKeyException"),
201.           "Unsupported value type");
202.        RegCloseKey(hkey);
203.        (*env)->ReleaseStringUTFChars(env, name, cname);
204.        return;
205.     }
206.
207.     /* set the value */
208.     if (RegSetValueEx(hkey, cname, 0, type, cvalue, size)
209.        != ERROR_SUCCESS)
210.     {  (*env)->ThrowNew(env,
211.           (*env)->FindClass(env, "Win32RegKeyException"),
212.           "Query value key failed");
213.     }
214.
215.     RegCloseKey(hkey);
216.     (*env)->ReleaseStringUTFChars(env, name, cname);
217.
218.     /* if the value was a string or byte array, release the
219.        pointer */
220.     if (type == REG_SZ)
221.     {
222.        (*env)->ReleaseStringUTFChars(env, (jstring)value,
223.           cvalue);
224.     }
225.     else if (type == REG_BINARY)
226.     {
227.        (*env)->ReleaseByteArrayElements(env, (jarray)value,
228.           cvalue, 0);
229.     }
230. }
231.
232. /* helper function to start enumeration of names */
233. static int startNameEnumeration(JNIEnv* env, jobject this_obj,
```

```
234.     jclass this_class)
235.  {
236.     jfieldID id_index;
237.     jfieldID id_count;
238.     jfieldID id_root;
239.     jfieldID id_path;
240.     jfieldID id_hkey;
241.     jfieldID id_maxsize;
242.
243.     HKEY root;
244.     jstring path;
245.     const char* cpath;
246.     HKEY hkey;
247.     int maxsize = 0;
248.     int count = 0;
249.
250.     /* get the field IDs */
251.     id_root = (*env)->GetFieldID(env, this_class, "root", "I");
252.     id_path = (*env)->GetFieldID(env, this_class, "path",
253.        "Ljava/lang/String;");
254.     id_hkey = (*env)->GetFieldID(env, this_class, "hkey", "I");
255.     id_maxsize = (*env)->GetFieldID(env, this_class, "maxsize",
256.        "I");
257.     id_index = (*env)->GetFieldID(env, this_class, "index",
258.        "I");
259.     id_count = (*env)->GetFieldID(env, this_class, "count",
260.        "I");
261.
262.     /* get the field values */
263.     root = (HKEY)(*env)->GetIntField(env, this_obj, id_root);
264.     path = (jstring)(*env)->GetObjectField(env, this_obj,
265.        id_path);
266.     cpath = (*env)->GetStringUTFChars(env, path, NULL);
267.
268.     /* open the registry key */
269.     if (RegOpenKeyEx(root, cpath, 0, KEY_READ, &hkey)
270.        != ERROR_SUCCESS)
271.     {
272.        (*env)->ThrowNew(env,
273.          (*env)->FindClass(env, "Win32RegKeyException"),
274.          "Open key failed");
275.        (*env)->ReleaseStringUTFChars(env, path, cpath);
276.        return -1;
277.     }
278.     (*env)->ReleaseStringUTFChars(env, path, cpath);
279.
280.     /* query count and max length of names */
281.     if (RegQueryInfoKey(hkey, NULL, NULL, NULL, NULL,
282.        NULL, NULL, &count, &maxsize, NULL, NULL, NULL)
283.        != ERROR_SUCCESS)
284.     {
285.        (*env)->ThrowNew(env,
```

```
286.         (*env)->FindClass(env, "Win32RegKeyException"),
287.            "Query info key failed");
288.         return -1;
289.      }
290.
291.      /* set the field values */
292.      (*env)->SetIntField(env, this_obj, id_hkey, (DWORD)hkey);
293.      (*env)->SetIntField(env, this_obj, id_maxsize, maxsize + 1);
294.      (*env)->SetIntField(env, this_obj, id_index, 0);
295.      (*env)->SetIntField(env, this_obj, id_count, count);
296.      return count;
297. }
298.
299. JNIEXPORT jboolean JNICALL
300. Java_Win32RegKeyNameEnumeration_hasMoreElements(JNIEnv* env,
301.      jobject this_obj)
302. {   jclass this_class;
303.     jfieldID id_index;
304.     jfieldID id_count;
305.     int index;
306.     int count;
307.     /* get the class */
308.     this_class = (*env)->GetObjectClass(env, this_obj);
309.
310.     /* get the field IDs */
311.     id_index = (*env)->GetFieldID(env, this_class, "index",
312.         "I");
313.     id_count = (*env)->GetFieldID(env, this_class, "count",
314.         "I");
315.
316.     index = (*env)->GetIntField(env, this_obj, id_index);
317.     if (index == -1) /* first time */
318.     {
319.         count = startNameEnumeration(env, this_obj, this_class);
320.         index = 0;
321.     }
322.     else
323.         count = (*env)->GetIntField(env, this_obj, id_count);
324.     return index < count;
325. }
326.
327. JNIEXPORT jobject JNICALL
328. Java_Win32RegKeyNameEnumeration_nextElement(JNIEnv* env,
329.      jobject this_obj)
330. {
331.     jclass this_class;
332.     jfieldID id_index;
333.     jfieldID id_hkey;
334.     jfieldID id_count;
335.     jfieldID id_maxsize;
336.
337.     HKEY hkey;
```

```
338.    int index;
339.    int count;
340.    int maxsize;
341.
342.    char* cret;
343.    jstring ret;
344.
345.    /* get the class */
346.    this_class = (*env)->GetObjectClass(env, this_obj);
347.
348.    /* get the field IDs */
349.    id_index = (*env)->GetFieldID(env, this_class, "index",
350.        "I");
351.    id_count = (*env)->GetFieldID(env, this_class, "count",
352.        "I");
353.    id_hkey = (*env)->GetFieldID(env, this_class, "hkey", "I");
354.    id_maxsize = (*env)->GetFieldID(env, this_class, "maxsize",
355.        "I");
356.
357.    index = (*env)->GetIntField(env, this_obj, id_index);
358.    if (index == -1) /* first time */
359.    {
360.        count = startNameEnumeration(env, this_obj, this_class);
361.        index = 0;
362.    }
363.    else
364.        count = (*env)->GetIntField(env, this_obj, id_count);
365.
366.    if (index >= count) /* already at end */
367.    {
368.        (*env)->ThrowNew(env,
369.            (*env)->FindClass(env,
370.            "java/util/NoSuchElementException"),
371.            "past end of enumeration");
372.        return NULL;
373.    }
374.
375.    maxsize = (*env)->GetIntField(env, this_obj, id_maxsize);
376.    hkey = (HKEY)(*env)->GetIntField(env, this_obj, id_hkey);
377.    cret = (char*)malloc(maxsize);
378.
379.    /* find the next name */
380.    if (RegEnumValue(hkey, index, cret, &maxsize, NULL, NULL,
381.        NULL, NULL) != ERROR_SUCCESS)
382.    {
383.        (*env)->ThrowNew(env,
384.            (*env)->FindClass(env, "Win32RegKeyException"),
385.            "Enum value failed");
386.        free(cret);
387.        RegCloseKey(hkey);
388.        (*env)->SetIntField(env, this_obj, id_index, count);
389.        return NULL;
```

```
390.      }
391.
392.      ret = (*env)->NewStringUTF(env, cret);
393.      free(cret);
394.
395.      /* increment index */
396.      index++;
397.      (*env)->SetIntField(env, this_obj, id_index, index);
398.
399.      if (index == count) /* at end */
400.      {
401.         RegCloseKey(hkey);
402.      }
403.
404.      return ret;
405. }
```

Example 11–23: Win32RegKeyTest.java

```
1. import java.util.*;
2.
3. public class Win32RegKeyTest
4. {
5.    public static void main(String[] args)
6.    {
7.       Win32RegKey key = new Win32RegKey(
8.          Win32RegKey.HKEY_LOCAL_MACHINE,
9.          "SOFTWARE\\JavaSoft\\Java Development Kit\\1.4");
10.
11.       key.setValue("Default user", "Harry Hacker");
12.       key.setValue("Lucky number", new Integer(13));
13.       key.setValue("Small primes", new byte[]
14.          { 2, 3, 5, 7, 11 });
15.
16.       Enumeration enum = key.names();
17.
18.       while (enum.hasMoreElements())
19.       {
20.          String name = (String)enum.nextElement();
21.          System.out.print(name + "=");
22.
23.          Object value = key.getValue(name);
24.
25.          if (value instanceof byte[])
26.          {
27.             byte[] bvalue = (byte[])value;
28.             for (int i = 0; i < bvalue.length; i++)
29.                System.out.print((bvalue[i] & 0xFF) + " ");
30.          }
31.          else System.out.print(value);
```

```
32.
33.          System.out.println();
34.      }
35.  }
36. }
```

Type inquiry functions

- `jboolean IsAssignableFrom(JNIEnv *env, jclass cl1, jclass cl2)`
  returns `JNI_TRUE` if objects of the first class can be assigned to objects of
  the second class; `JNI_FALSE` otherwise. This is the case when the classes
  are the same, `cl1` is a subclass of `cl2`, or `cl2` represents an interface that
  is implemented by `cl1` or one of its superclasses.

  Parameters: env   the JNI interface pointer

                       cl1, cl2   class references

- `jclass GetSuperClass(JNIEnv *env, jclass cl)`
  returns the superclass of a class. If `cl` represents the class `Object` or an
  interface, returns `NULL`.

  Parameters: env   the JNI interface pointer

                       cl   a class reference

Chapter **12**

XML

The preface of the book *Essential XML* by Don Box, et al. [Addison-Wesley 2000] states only half-jokingly: "The Extensible Markup Language (XML) has replaced Java, Design Patterns, and Object Technology as the software industry's solution to world hunger." Indeed, as you will see in this chapter, XML is a very useful technology for describing structured information. XML tools make it easy to process and transform that information. But XML is not a silver bullet. You need domain-specific standards and code libraries to use it effectively. Moreover, far from making Java obsolete, XML and Java work very well together. Essentially all important XML libraries have been implemented first in Java, and many of them are unavailable in any other programming language. Since the late 1990s, IBM, Apache, and others have been instrumental in producing high-quality Java libraries for XML processing. Starting with SDK 1.4, Sun has integrated the most important libraries into the Java 2 Platform, Standard Edition.

> NOTE: You can download the Java API for XML Processing (JAXP) library from `http://java.sun.com/xml` to add the same XML processing capabilities to older Java installations.

This chapter gives an introduction into XML and covers the XML features of SDK 1.4. As always, we will point out along the way when the hype surrounding XML is justified, and when you have to take it with a grain of salt and solve your problems the old-fashioned way, through good design and code.

An Introduction to XML

You have seen several examples of *property files* to describe the configuration of a program, for example in Chapters 2 and 4. A property file contains a set of name/value pairs, such as

```
fontname=Times Roman
fontsize=12
windowsize=400 200
color=0 50 100
```

You can use the `Properties` class to read in such a file with a single method call. That's a nice feature, but it doesn't really go far enough. In many cases, the information that you want to describe has more structure than the property file format can comfortably handle. For example, consider the `fontname`/`fontsize` entries in the example. It would be more object-oriented to have a single entry:

```
font=Times Roman 12
```

But then parsing the font description gets ugly—you have to figure out when the font name ends and when the font size starts.

Property files have a single flat hierarchy. You can often see programmers work around that limitation with key names such as

```
title.fontname=Helvetica
title.fontsize=36
body.fontname=Times Roman
body.fontsize=12
```

Another shortcoming of the property file format is caused by the fact that keys have to be unique. To store a sequence of values, you need another workaround, such as

```
menu.item.1=Times Roman
menu.item.2=Helvetica
menu.item.3=Goudy Old Style
```

The XML format solves these problems because it can express hierarchical structures, which is more flexible than the flat table structure of a property file.

An XML file for describing a program configuration might look like this:

```
<configuration>
    <title>
        <font>
            <name>Helvetica</name>
            <size>36</size>
        </font>
    </title>
    <body>
            <name>Times Roman</name>
            <size>12</size>
    </body>
    <window>
        <width>400</width>
        <height>200</height>
    </window>
    <color>
        <red>0</red>
        <green>50</green>
        <blue>100</blue>
    </color>
    <menu>
        <item>Times Roman</item>
        <item>Helvetica</item>
        <item>Goudy Old Style</item>
    </menu>
</configuration>
```

The XML format allows you to express the structure hierarchy and repeated elements without contortions.

As you can see, the format of an XML file is very straightforward. It looks very similar to an HTML file. There is a good reason—both the XML and HTML formats are descendants of the venerable Standard Generalized Markup Language (SGML).

SGML has been around since the 1970s for describing the structure of complex documents. It has been used with good success in some industries that require ongoing maintenance of massive documentation, in particular the aircraft industry. But SGML is quite complex, so it has never caught on in a big way. Much of that complexity arises from the fact that SGML has two conflicting goals. SGML wants to make sure that documents are formed according to the rules for their document type. But it also wants to make data entry easy by allowing shortcuts that reduce typing. XML was designed as a simplified version of SGML for use on the Internet. As is often true, simpler is better, and XML has enjoyed the immediate and enthusiastic reception that has eluded SGML for so long.

> NOTE: You can find a very nice version of the XML standard, with annotations by Tim Bray, at `http://www.xml.com/axml/axml.html`.

Even though XML and HTML have common roots, there are important differences between the two.

- Unlike HTML, XML is case sensitive. For example, `<H1>` and `<h1>` are different XML tags.

- In HTML, you can omit end tags such as `</p>` or `</li>` tags if it is clear from the context where a paragraph or list item ends. In XML, you can never omit an end tag.

- In XML, elements that have a single tag without a matching end tag must end in a /, such as `<img src="coffeecup.png" />`. That way, the parser knows not to look for a `</img>` tag.

- In XML, attribute values must be enclosed in quotation marks. In HTML, quotation marks are optional. For example, `<applet code="MyApplet.class" width=`**300**` height=`**300**`>` is legal HTML but not legal XML. In XML, you would have to use quotation marks: `width="300"`.

- In HTML, you can have attribute names without values, such as `<input type="radio" name="language" value="Java"` **checked**`>`. In XML, all attributes must have values, such as `checked="true"` or (ugh) `checked="checked"`.

> NOTE: The current recommendation for web documents by the World Wide Web Consortium (W3C) is the XHTML standard, which tightens up the HTML standard to be XML compliant. You can find a copy of the XHTML standard at `http://www.w3.org/TR/xhtml1/`. XHTML is backwards-compatible with current browsers, but unfortunately many current HTML authoring tools do not yet support it. Once XHTML becomes more widespread, you can use the XML tools that are described in this chapter to analyze web documents.

The Structure of an XML Document

An XML document should start with a header such as

```
<?xml version="1.0"?>
```

or

```
<?xml version="1.0" encoding="UTF-8"?>
```

Strictly speaking, a header is optional, but it is highly recommended.

NOTE: Because SGML was created for processing of real documents, XML files are called *documents*, even though most XML files describe data sets that one would not normally call documents.

The header is normally followed by a *document type declaration*, such as

```
<!DOCTYPE web-app PUBLIC
    "-//Sun Microsystems, Inc.//DTD Web Application 2.2//EN"
    "http://java.sun.com/j2ee/dtds/web-app_2_2.dtd">
```

Document type declarations are an important mechanism to ensure the correctness of a document, but they are not required. We will discuss them later in this chapter.

Finally, the body of the XML document contains the *root element*, which can contain other elements. For example,

```
<?xml version="1.0"?>
<!DOCTYPE configuration . . .>
<configuration>
    <title>
        <font>
            <name>Helvetica</name>
            <size>36</size>
        </font>
    </title>
    . . .
</configuration>
```

An element can contain *child elements*, text, or both. In the example above, the font element has two child elements, name and size. The name element contains the text "Helvetica".

TIP: It is best if you structure your XML documents such that an element contains *either* child elements *or* text. In other words, you should avoid situations such as

```
<font>
    Helvetica
    <size>36</size>
</font>
```

This is called *mixed contents* in the XML specification. As you will see later in this chapter, you can design much cleaner document type definitions if you avoid mixed contents.

XML elements can contain attributes, such as

```
<size unit="pt">36</size>
```

There is some disagreement among XML designers about when to use elements and when to use attributes. For example, it would seem easier to describe a font as

```
<font name="Helvetica" size="36"/>
```

than

```
<font>
    <name>Helvetica</name>
    <size>36</size>
</font>
```

However, attributes are much less flexible. Suppose you want to add units to the size value. If you use attributes, then you have to add the unit to the attribute value:

```
<font name="Helvetica" size="36 pt"/>
```

Ugh! Now you have to parse the string `"36 pt"`, just the kind of hassle that XML was designed to avoid. Adding an attribute to the `size` element is much cleaner:

```
<font>
    <name>Helvetica</name>
    <size unit="pt">36</size>
</font>
```

A commonly used rule of thumb is that attributes should only be used when they modify the interpretation of a value, not to specify values. If you find yourself engaged in metaphysical discussions about whether a particular setting is a modification of the interpretation of a value or not, then just say "no" to attributes and use elements throughout. Many useful DTDs don't use attributes at all.

NOTE: In HTML, the rule for attribute usage is simple: If it isn't displayed on the web page, it's an attribute. For example, consider a hyperlink

```
<a href="http://java.sun.com">Java Technology</a>
```

The string `Java Technology` is displayed on the web page, but the URL of the link is not a part of the displayed page. However, that rule isn't all that helpful for most XML files since the data in an XML file isn't normally meant to be viewed by humans.

Elements and text are the "bread and butter" of XML documents. There are a few other markup instructions that you may encounter.

- *Character references* have the form `&#d;` or `&#xh;`. Here d is a decimal Unicode value and h is a hexadecimal Unicode value. Examples are

  ```
  &#233;
  &#x2122;
  ```

  which denote the characters é and ™.

- *Entity references* have the form &*name*;. The entity references

  ```
  &lt;
  &gt;
  &amp;
  &quot;
  &apos;
  ```

  have predefined meanings: the less than, greater than, ampersand, quotation mark, and apostrophe characters. You can define other entity references in a Document Type Definition (DTD).

- *CDATA sections* are delimited by <![CDATA[and]]>. They are a special form of character data. You can use them to include strings that contain characters such as < > & without having them interpreted as markup, for example

  ```
  <![CDATA[< & > are my favorite delimiters]]>
  ```

  CDATA sections cannot contain the string]]>. Use this feature with caution! It is too often used as a backdoor for smuggling legacy data into XML documents.

- *Processing instructions* are delimited by <? and ?>, for example

  ```
  <?xml-stylesheet href="mystyle.css" type="text/css"?>
  ```

  These instructions are for the benefit of the application that processes the XML document. Every XML document starts with a processing instruction

  ```
  <?xml version="1.0"?>
  ```

- *Comments* are delimited by <!-- and -->, for example

  ```
  <!-- This is a comment. -->
  ```

  Comments should not contain the string --. Comments should only be information for human readers. They should never contain hidden commands. Use processing instructions for commands.

Parsing an XML Document

To process an XML document, you need to *parse* it. A parser is a program that reads a file, confirms that the file has the correct format, breaks it up into the constituent elements, and lets a programmer access those elements. There are two kinds of XML parsers:

- The Document Object Model (DOM) parser reads an XML document into a tree structure.

- The Simple API for XML (SAX) parser generates events as it reads an XML document.

The DOM parser is easier to use for most purposes, and we will explain it first.

You would want to consider the SAX parser if you process very long documents whose tree structures would use up a lot of memory, or if you are just interested in a few elements and you don't care about their context.

The DOM parser interface is standardized by the World Wide Web Consortium (W3C). The `org.w3c.dom` package contains the definitions of interface types such as `Document` and `Element`. Different suppliers, such as the Apache Organization and IBM, have written DOM parsers whose classes implement these interfaces. The Sun Java API for XML Processing (JAXP) library actually makes it possible to plug in any of these parsers. But Sun also includes its own DOM parser in the Java SDK. We'll use the Sun parser in this chapter.

To read an XML document, you need a `DocumentBuilder` object which you get from a `DocumentBuilderFactory`, like this:

```
DocumentBuilderFactory factory
    = DocumentBuilderFactory.newInstance();
DocumentBuilder builder
    = factory.newDocumentBuilder();
```

You can now read a document from a file:

```
File f = . . .
Document doc = builder.parse(f);
```

Alternatively, you can use an URL:

```
URL u = . . .
Document doc = builder.parse(u);
```

You can even specify an arbitrary input stream:

```
InputStream in = . . .
Document doc = builder.parse(in);
```

NOTE: If you use an input stream as an input source, then the parser will not be able to locate other files that are referenced relative to the location of the document, such as a DTD in the same directory. You can install an "entity resolver" to overcome that problem. But it is usually easier to just use a file or URL than an input stream.

The `Document` object is an in-memory representation of the tree structure of the XML document. It is composed of objects whose classes implement the `Node` interface and its various subinterfaces. Figure 12–1 shows the inheritance hierarchy of the subinterfaces.

You start analyzing the contents of a document by calling the `getDocument-Element` method. It returns the root element.

```
Element root = doc.getDocumentElement();
```

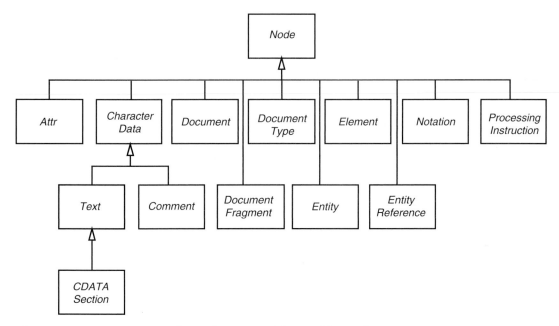

Figure 12–1: The Node interfaces and its subinterfaces

For example, if you are processing a document

```
<?xml version="1.0"?>
<font>
   . . .
</font>
```

then calling `getDocumentElement` returns the `font` element.

The `getTagName` method returns the tag name of an element. For example, in the preceding example, `root.getTagName()` returns the string `"font"`.

To get the element's children (which may be subelements, text, comments, or other nodes), use the `getChildNodes` method. That method returns a collection of type `NodeList`. That type was invented before the standard Java collections, and it has a different access protocol. The `item` method gets the item with a given index, and the `getLength` method gives the total count of the items. Therefore, you can enumerate all children like this:

```
NodeList children = root.getChildNodes();
for (int i = 0; i < children.getLength(); i++)
{
    Node child = children.item(i);
    . . .
}
```

You have to be careful when analyzing the children. Suppose for example that you are processing the document

```
<font>
    <name>Helvetica</name>
    <size>36</size>
</font>
```

You would expect the `font` element to have two children, but the parser reports five:

- The whitespace between `<font>` and `<name>`
- The `name` element
- The whitespace between `</name>` and `<size>`
- The `size` element
- The whitespace between `</size>` and `</font>`

Figure 12–2 shows the DOM tree.

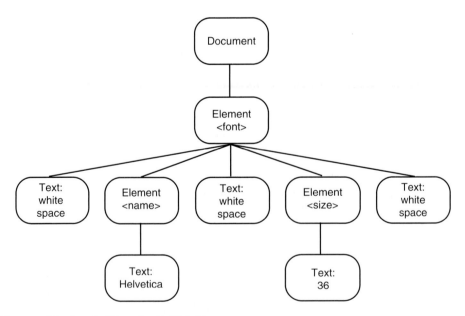

Figure 12–2: A Simple DOM Tree

If you only expect subelements, then you can ignore the whitespace:

```
for (int i = 0; i < children.getLength(); i++)
{
    Node child = children.item(i);
    if (child instanceof Element)
    {
        Element childElement = (Element)child;
```

```
      }
   }
```

Now you only look at two elements, with tag names `name` and `size`.

As you will see in the next section, you can do even better if your document has a document type declaration. Then the parser knows which elements don't have text nodes as children, and it can suppress the whitespace for you.

When analyzing the `name` and `size` elements, you want to retrieve the text strings that they contain. Those text strings are themselves contained in child nodes of type `Text`. Since you know that these `Text` nodes are the only children, you can use the `getFirstChild` method without having to traverse another `NodeList`. Then use the `getData` method to retrieve the string stored in the `Text` node.

```
for (int i = 0; i < children.getLength(); i++)
{
   Node child = children.item(i);
   if (child instanceof Element)
   {
      Element childElement = (Element)child;
      Text textNode = childElement.getFirstChild();
      String text = textNode.getData().trim();
      if (childElement.getTagName().equals("name"))
         name = text;
      else if (childElement.getTagName().equals("size"))
         size = Integer.parseInt(text);
   }
}
```

TIP: It is a good idea to call `trim` on the return value of the `getData` method. If the author of an XML file puts the beginning and the ending tag on separate lines, such as

```
<size>
   36
</size>
```

then the parser includes all line breaks and spaces in the text node data. Calling the `trim` method removes the whitespace surrounding the actual data.

You can also get the last child with the `getLastChild`, and the next sibling of a node with `getNextSibling`. Therefore, another way of traversing a set of child nodes is

```
for (Node childNode = element.getFirstChild();
   childNode != null;
   childNode = childNode.getNextSibling())
```

```
{
    . . .
}
```

> **NOTE:** It is rather tedious to search for nodes in an XML tree by looking at the root, its children, grandchildren, and so on. The XPath technology simplifies searches. For example, you can locate the node with the path `/configuration/title/font/name` with a single method call. However, XPath is not yet a part of the XML library in the Java platform. You can find out the XPath specification at `http://www.w3.org/TR/xpath`. The Xalan library from the Apache group contains an implementation of XPath; see `http://xml.apache.org/xalan-j/overview.html`.

To enumerate the attributes of a node, call the `getAttributes` method. It returns a `NamedNodeMap` object which contains `Node` objects that describe the attributes. You can traverse the nodes in a `NamedNodeMap` in the same way as a `NodeList`. Then call the `getNodeName` and `getNodeValue` methods to get the attribute names and values.

```
NamedNodeMap attributes = element.getAttributes();
for (int i = 0; i < attributes.getLength(); i++)
{
    Node attribute = attributes.item(i);
    String name = attribute.getNodeName();
    String value = attribute.getNodeValue();
    . . .
}
```

Alternatively, if you know the name of an attribute, you can retrieve the corresponding value directly:

```
String unit = element.getAttribute("unit");
```

You have now seen how to analyze a DOM tree. The program in Example 12–1 puts these techniques to work. You can use the File -> Open menu option to read in an XML file. A `DocumentBuilder` object parses the XML file and produces a `Document` object. The program displays the `Document` object as a `JTree` (see Figure 12–3).

The tree display shows clearly how child elements are surrounded by text containing whitespace and comments. For greater clarity, the program displays newline and return characters as \n and \r. (Otherwise, they would show up as hollow boxes, the default symbol for a character that Swing cannot draw in a string.)

If you followed the section on trees in Chapter 6, you will recognize the techniques that this program uses to display the tree. The `DOMTreeModel` class implements the `TreeModel` interface. The `getRoot` method returns the root element of the document. The `getChild` method gets the node list of children and returns the item with the requested index. However, the tree model returns DOM `Node` objects whose `toString` methods aren't necessarily descriptive. Therefore, the program installs a tree cell renderer that extends the default cell renderer and sets the label text to a more descriptive form. The cell renderer displays the following:

- For elements, the element tag name and all attributes;
- For character data, the interface (Text, Comment, or CDATASection), followed by the data, with new lines and returns replaced by \n and \r;
- For all other node types, the class name followed by the result of `toString`.

If you need to analyze XML documents that contain other node types (such as processing instructions), then you can enhance the program accordingly. The purpose of the program is not to be a polished XML viewer—there are many slicker programs available—but to show you how to analyze and enumerate the children and attributes of DOM tree nodes.

NOTE: You can get a very nice free XML viewer from IBM AlphaWorks at `http://www.alphaworks.ibm.com/tech/xmlviewer`.

Figure 12–3: A parse tree of an XML document

Example 12–1: DOMTreeTest.java

```
1. import java.awt.*;
2. import java.awt.event.*;
3. import java.io.*;
```

```
 4. import javax.swing.*;
 5. import javax.swing.event.*;
 6. import javax.swing.tree.*;
 7. import javax.xml.parsers.*;
 8. import org.w3c.dom.*;
 9. import org.xml.sax.*;
10.
11. /**
12.    This program displays an XML document as a tree.
13. */
14. public class DOMTreeTest
15. {
16.    public static void main(String[] args)
17.    {
18.       JFrame frame = new DOMTreeFrame();
19.       frame.setDefaultCloseOperation(JFrame.EXIT_ON_CLOSE);
20.       frame.show();
21.    }
22. }
23.
24. /**
25.    This frame contains a tree that displays the contents of
26.    an XML document.
27. */
28. class DOMTreeFrame extends JFrame
29. {
30.    public DOMTreeFrame()
31.    {
32.       setTitle("DOMTreeTest");
33.       setSize(WIDTH, HEIGHT);
34.
35.       JMenu fileMenu = new JMenu("File");
36.       JMenuItem openItem = new JMenuItem("Open");
37.       openItem.addActionListener(new
38.          ActionListener()
39.          {
40.             public void actionPerformed(ActionEvent event)
41.             {
42.                openFile();
43.             }
44.          });
45.       fileMenu.add(openItem);
46.
47.       JMenuItem exitItem = new JMenuItem("Exit");
48.       exitItem.addActionListener(new
49.          ActionListener()
50.          {
51.             public void actionPerformed(ActionEvent event)
52.             {
53.                System.exit(0);
```

```
54.                 }
55.             });
56.         fileMenu.add(exitItem);
57.
58.         JMenuBar menuBar = new JMenuBar();
59.         menuBar.add(fileMenu);
60.         setJMenuBar(menuBar);
61.     }
62.
63.     /**
64.         Open a file and load the document.
65.     */
66.     public void openFile()
67.     {
68.         JFileChooser chooser = new JFileChooser();
69.         chooser.setCurrentDirectory(new File("."));
70.
71.         chooser.setFileFilter(new
72.             javax.swing.filechooser.FileFilter()
73.             {
74.                 public boolean accept(File f)
75.                 {
76.                     return f.isDirectory()
77.                         || f.getName().toLowerCase().endsWith(".xml");
78.                 }
79.                 public String getDescription()
80.                 {
81.                     return "XML files";
82.                 }
83.             });
84.         int r = chooser.showOpenDialog(this);
85.         if (r != JFileChooser.APPROVE_OPTION) return;
86.         File f = chooser.getSelectedFile();
87.         try
88.         {
89.             if (builder == null)
90.             {
91.                 DocumentBuilderFactory factory
92.                     = DocumentBuilderFactory.newInstance();
93.                 builder = factory.newDocumentBuilder();
94.             }
95.
96.             Document doc = builder.parse(f);
97.             JTree tree = new JTree(new DOMTreeModel(doc));
98.             tree.setCellRenderer(new DOMTreeCellRenderer());
99.
100.            setContentPane(new JScrollPane(tree));
101.            validate();
102.        }
103.        catch (IOException exception)
```

```
104.        {
105.            JOptionPane.showMessageDialog(this, exception);
106.        }
107.        catch (ParserConfigurationException exception)
108.        {
109.            JOptionPane.showMessageDialog(this, exception);
110.        }
111.        catch (SAXException exception)
112.        {
113.            JOptionPane.showMessageDialog(this, exception);
114.        }
115.    }
116.
117.    private DocumentBuilder builder;
118.    private static final int WIDTH = 400;
119.    private static final int HEIGHT = 400;
120. }
121.
122. /**
123.    This tree model describes the tree structure of a Java
124.    object. Children are the objects that are stored in instance
125.    variables.
126. */
127. class DOMTreeModel implements TreeModel
128. {
129.    /**
130.       Constructs an empty tree.
131.    */
132.    public DOMTreeModel(Document aDoc)
133.    {
134.        doc = aDoc;
135.    }
136.
137.    public Object getRoot()
138.    {
139.        return doc.getDocumentElement();
140.    }
141.
142.    public int getChildCount(Object parent)
143.    {
144.        Node node = (Node)parent;
145.        NodeList list = node.getChildNodes();
146.        return list.getLength();
147.    }
148.
149.    public Object getChild(Object parent, int index)
150.    {
151.        Node node = (Node)parent;
152.        NodeList list = node.getChildNodes();
153.        return list.item(index);
```

```
154.      }
155.
156.      public int getIndexOfChild(Object parent, Object child)
157.      {
158.         Node node = (Node)parent;
159.         NodeList list = node.getChildNodes();
160.         for (int i = 0; i < list.getLength(); i++)
161.            if (getChild(node, i) == child)
162.               return i;
163.         return -1;
164.      }
165.
166.      public boolean isLeaf(Object node)
167.      {
168.         return getChildCount(node) == 0;
169.      }
170.
171.      public void valueForPathChanged(TreePath path,
172.         Object newValue) {}
173.
174.      public void addTreeModelListener(TreeModelListener l) {}
175.
176.      public void removeTreeModelListener(TreeModelListener l) {}
177.
178.      private Document doc;
179. }
180.
181. /**
182.    This class renders a class name either in plain or italic.
183.    Abstract classes are italic.
184. */
185. class DOMTreeCellRenderer extends DefaultTreeCellRenderer
186. {
187.      public Component getTreeCellRendererComponent(JTree tree,
188.         Object value, boolean selected, boolean expanded,
189.         boolean leaf, int row, boolean hasFocus)
190.      {
191.         super.getTreeCellRendererComponent(tree, value,
192.            selected, expanded, leaf, row, hasFocus);
193.         Node node = (Node)value;
194.         if (node instanceof Element)
195.            setText(elementString((Element)node));
196.         else if (node instanceof CharacterData)
197.            setText(characterString((CharacterData)node));
198.         else
199.            setText(node.getClass() + ": " + node.toString());
200.         return this;
201.      }
202.
203.      public static String elementString(Element e)
```

```
204.    {
205.        StringBuffer buffer = new StringBuffer();
206.        buffer.append("Element: <");
207.        buffer.append(e.getTagName());
208.        NamedNodeMap attributes = e.getAttributes();
209.        for (int i = 0; i < attributes.getLength(); i++)
210.        {
211.            buffer.append(' ');
212.            Node attributeNode = attributes.item(i);
213.            buffer.append(attributeNode.getNodeName());
214.            buffer.append('=');
215.            buffer.append('"');
216.            buffer.append(attributeNode.getNodeValue());
217.            buffer.append('"');
218.        }
219.        buffer.append('>');
220.        return buffer.toString();
221.    }
222.
223.    public static String characterString(CharacterData node)
224.    {
225.        StringBuffer buffer = new StringBuffer(node.getData());
226.        for (int i = 0; i < buffer.length(); i++)
227.        {
228.            if (buffer.charAt(i) == '\r')
229.            {
230.                buffer.replace(i, i + 1, "\\r");
231.                i++;
232.            }
233.            else if (buffer.charAt(i) == '\n')
234.            {
235.                buffer.replace(i, i + 1, "\\n");
236.                i++;
237.            }
238.            else if (buffer.charAt(i) == '\t')
239.            {
240.                buffer.replace(i, i + 1, "\\t");
241.                i++;
242.            }
243.        }
244.        if (node instanceof Text)
245.            buffer.insert(0, "Text: ");
246.        else if (node instanceof Comment)
247.            buffer.insert(0, "Comment: ");
248.        else if (node instanceof CDATASection)
249.            buffer.insert(0, "CDATASection: ");
250.
251.        return buffer.toString();
252.    }
253. }
```

javax.xml.parsers.DocumentBuilderFactory

- `static DocumentBuilderFactory newInstance()`
  returns an instance of the DocumentBuilderFactory class.

- `DocumentBuilder newDocumentBuilder()`
  returns an instance of the DocumentBuilder class.

javax.xml.parsers.DocumentBuilder

- `Document parse(File f)`
- `Document parse(String url)`
- `Document parse(InputStream in)`
  parse an XML document from the given file, URL, or input stream and
  returns the parsed document.

org.w3c.dom.Document

- `Element getDocumentElement()`
  returns the root element of the document.

org.w3c.dom.Element

- `String getTagName()`
  returns the name of the element.

- `String getAttribute(String name)`
  returns the attribute value of the attribute with the given name, or the empty
  string if there is no such attribute.

org.w3c.dom.Node

- `NodeList getChildNodes()`
  returns a node list that contains all children of this node.

- `Node getFirstChild()`
- `Node getLastChild()`
  get the first or last child node of this node, or `null` if this node has no children.

- `Node getNextSibling()`
- `Node getPreviousSibling()`
  get the next or previous sibling of this node, or `null` if this node has no siblings.

- `Node getParentNode()`
  gets the parent of this node, or `null` if this node is the document node.

- NamedNodeMap getAttributes()

  returns a node map that contains Attr nodes that describe all attributes of this node.

- String getNodeName()

  returns the name of this node. If the node is an Attr node, then the name is the attribute name.

- String getNodeValue()

  returns the value of this node. If the node is an Attr node, then the value is the attribute value.

org.w3c.dom.CharacterData

- String getData()

  returns the text stored in this node.

org.w3c.dom.NodeList

- int getLength()

  returns the number of nodes in this list.

- Node item(int index)

  returns the node with the given index. The index is between 0 and getLength() - 1.

org.w3c.dom.NamedNodeMap

- int getLength()

  returns the number of nodes in this map.

- Node item(int index)

  returns the node with the given index. The index is between 0 and getLength() - 1.

Document Type Definitions

In the preceding section, you saw how to traverse the tree structure of a DOM document. However, if you simply follow that approach, you'll find that you are going to have quite a bit of tedious programming and error checking. Not only do you have to deal with whitespace between elements, but you also need to check whether the document contains the nodes that you expect. For example, suppose you are reading an element:

```
<font>
    <name>Helvetica</name>
    <size>36</size>
</font>
```

You get the first non-whitespace child. Then you need to check that its tag name is `"name"`. You need to check that it has one child node of type `Text`. You move on to the next non-whitespace child and make the same check. What if the author of the document switched the order of the children, or added another child element? It is tedious to code all the error checking, and reckless to skip the checks.

Fortunately, one of the major benefits of an XML parser is that it can automatically verify that a document has the correct structure. Then the parsing becomes much simpler. For example, if you know that the `font` fragment has passed validation, then you can simply get the two grandchildren, cast them as `Text` nodes and get the text data, without any further checking.

To specify the document structure, you supply a document type definition (DTD). A DTD contains rules that explain how a document should be formed, by specifying the legal child elements and attributes for each element. For example, a DTD might contain a rule:

```
<!ELEMENT font (name,size)>
```

This rule expresses that a `font` element must always have two children, which are `name` and `size` elements.

It is not strictly a requirement for an XML document to use a DTD, but most serious uses of XML involve DTDs.

There are several methods for supplying a DTD. You can include a DTD in an XML document like this:

```
<?xml version="1.0"?>
<!DOCTYPE configuration [
   <!ELEMENT configuration . . .>
   more rules
   . . .
]>
<configuration>
  . . .
</configuration>
```

As you can see, the rules are included inside a `DOCTYPE` declaration, in a block delimited by `[. . .]`. The document type must match the name of the root element, such as `configuration` in our example.

Supplying a DTD inside an XML document is somewhat uncommon because DTDs can get lengthy. It makes more sense to store the DTD externally. The `SYSTEM` declaration can be used for that purpose. You specify a URL that contains the DTD, for example:

```
<!DOCTYPE configuration SYSTEM "config.dtd">
```

or

```
<!DOCTYPE configuration SYSTEM "http://myserver.com/config.dtd">
```

 CAUTION: If you use a relative URL for the DTD (such as `"config.dtd"`), then you need to give the parser a `File` or `URL` object, not an `InputStream`. If you must parse from an input stream, supply an entity resolver—see the following note.

Finally, there is a mechanism for identifying "well-known" DTDs that has its origin in SGML. Here is an example:

```
<!DOCTYPE web-app
    PUBLIC "-//Sun Microsystems, Inc.//DTD Web Application 2.2//EN"
    "http://java.sun.com/j2ee/dtds/web-app_2_2.dtd">
```

If an XML processor knows how to locate the DTD with the public identifier, then it need not go to the URL.

 NOTE: If you use a DOM parser, and would like to support a PUBLIC identifier, call the `setEntityResolver` method of the `DocumentBuilder` class to install an object of a class that implements the `EntityResolver` interface. That interface has a single method, `resolveEntity`. Here is the outline of a typical implementation:

```
class MyEntityResolver implements EntityResolver
{
    public InputSource resolveEntity(String publicID,
        String systemID)
    {
        if (publicID.equals(a known ID))
            return new InputSource(DTD data);
        else
            return null; // use default behavior
    }
}
```

You can construct the input source from an `InputStream`, a `Reader`, or a string.

Now that you have seen how the parser locates the DTD, let us consider the various kinds of rules.

The ELEMENT rule specifies what children an element can have. You specify a regular expression, made up of the components shown in Table 12–1.

Here are several simple but typical examples. The following rule states that a menu element contains 0 or more item elements.

Table 12–1: Rules for Element Content

Rule	Meaning
$E*$	0 or more occurrences of E
$E+$	1 or more occurrences of E
$E?$	0 or 1 occurrences of E
$E_1 \mid E_2 \mid \; \cdot \; \cdot \; \cdot \; \mid E_n$	One of $E_1, E_2, \ldots, E_n$
$E_1, E_2, \; \cdot \; \cdot \; \cdot \; , E_n$	E_1 followed by $E_2, \ldots, E_n$
`#PCDATA`	Text
`(#PCDATA`$\mid E_1 \mid E_2 \mid$ $\; \cdot \; \cdot \; \cdot$ $\mid E_n$`) *`	0 or more occurrences of text and $E_1, E_2, \ldots,$ E_n in any order (mixed content)
`ANY`	Any children allowed
`EMPTY`	No children allowed

```
<!ELEMENT menu (item)*>
```

This set of rules states that a font is described by a name followed by a size, each of which contain text.

```
<!ELEMENT font (name,size)>
<!ELEMENT name (#PCDATA)>
<!ELEMENT size (#PCDATA)>
```

The abbreviation PCDATA denotes parsed character data. The data is called "parsed" because the parser interprets the text string, looking for < characters that denote the start of a new tag, or & characters that denote the start of an entity.

NOTE: There is no way to express in a DTD that the text of the `size` element should be an integer. A newer specification, called XML Schema Definition (XSD), lets you specify the legal contents of a document with much greater precision. In XSD, the font specification can be expressed like this:

```
<xsd:complexType name="Font">
   <xsd:sequence>
      <xsd:element name="name" type="xsd:string"/>
      <xsd:element name="size" type="xsd:integer"/>
   </xsd:sequence>
</xsd:complexType>
<xsd:element name="font" type="Font"/>
```

You can find more information about the XML Schema specification at `http://www.w3.org/XML/Schema`. At this time, there is no support for the XML Schema technology in the Java SDK.

An element specification can contain regular expressions that are nested and complex. For example, here is a rule that describes the makeup of a chapter in this book:

```
<!ELEMENT chapter (intro,(heading,(para|image|table|note)+)+)
```

Each chapter starts with an introduction, which is followed by one or more sections consisting of a heading and one or more paragraphs, images, tables, or notes.

However, there is one common case when you can't define the rules to be as flexible as you might like. Whenever an element can contain text, then there are only two valid cases. Either the element contains nothing but text, such as

```
<!ELEMENT name (#PCDATA)>
```

Or the element contains *any combination of text and tags in any order*, such as

```
<!ELEMENT para (#PCDATA|em|strong|code)*>
```

It is not legal to specify other types of rules that contain #PCDATA. For example, the following rule is illegal:

```
<!ELEMENT captionedImage (image,#PCDATA)>
```

You have to rewrite such a rule, either by introducing another `caption` element, or by allowing any combination of `image` tags and text.

This restriction simplifies the job of the XML parser when parsing mixed content (a mixture of tags and text). Because you lose some control when allowing mixed content, it is best to design DTDs such that all elements contain either other elements or nothing but text.

> NOTE: Actually, it isn't quite true that you can specify arbitrary regular expressions of elements in a DTD rule. An XML parser may reject certain complex rule sets that lead to "non-deterministic" parsing. For example, a regular expression $((x,y)|(x,z))$ is non-deterministic. When the parser sees x, it doesn't know which of the two alternatives to take. This expression can be rewritten in a deterministic form, as $(x,(y|z))$. However, there are some expressions that can't be reformulated, such as $((x,y)*|x?)$. The Sun parser gives no warnings when presented with an ambiguous DTD. It simply picks the first matching alternative when parsing, which causes it to reject some correct inputs. Of course, the parser is well within its rights to do so, since the XML standard allows a parser to assume that the DTD is unambiguous.
>
> In practice, this isn't an issue over which you should lose sleep since most DTDs are so simple that you never run into ambiguity problems.

You also specify rules to describe the legal attributes of elements. The general syntax is

```
<!ATTLIST element attribute type default>
```

Table 12–2 shows the legal attribute types, and Table 12–3 shows the syntax for the defaults.

Table 12–2: Attribute types

Type	Meaning
CDATA	Any character string
$(A_1|A_2| \ldots |A_n)$	One of the string attributes A_1 A_2 $\ldots$ $|A_n$
NMTOKEN, NMTOKENS	One or more name tokens
ID	A unique ID
IDREF, IDREFS	One or more references to a unique ID
ENTITY, ENTITIES	One or more unparsed entities

Table 12–3: Attribute defaults

Default	Meaning
#REQUIRED	Attribute is required.
#IMPLIED	Attribute is optional.
A	Attribute is optional; the parser reports it to be A if it is not specified.
#FIXED A	The attribute must either be unspecified or A; in either case, the parser reports it to be A.

Here are two typical attribute specifications:

```
<!ATTLIST font style (plain|bold|italic|bold-italic) plain>
<!ATTLIST size unit CDATA #IMPLIED>
```

The first specification describes the `style` attribute of a `font` element. There are four legal attribute values, and the default value is `plain`. The second specification expresses that the `unit` attribute of the `size` element can contain any character data sequence.

NOTE: We generally recommend to use elements, not attributes, to describe data. Following that recommendation, the font style should be a separate element, such as `<font><style>plain</style>...</font>`. However, attributes have an undeniable advantage for enumerated types since the parser can verify that the values are legal. For example, if the font style is an attribute, the parser checks that it is one of the four allowed values, and it supplies a default if no value was given.

The handling of a CDATA attribute value is subtly different from the processing of #PCDATA that you have seen before, and quite unrelated to the `<![CDATA[...]]>` sections. The attribute value is first *normalized*, that is, the parser processes character and entity references (such as `&#233;` or `&lt;`) and replaces whitespace with spaces.

An `NMTOKEN` (or name token) is similar to `CDATA`, but most non-alphanumeric characters and internal whitespace are disallowed, and the parser removes leading and trailing whitespace. `NMTOKENS` is a whitespace-separated list of name tokens.

The `ID` construct is quite useful. An `ID` is a name token that must be unique in the document—the parser checks the uniqueness. You will see an application in the next sample program. An `IDREF` is a reference to an ID that exists in the same document—which the parser also checks. `IDREFS` is a whitespace-separated list of ID references.

An `ENTITY` attribute value refers to an "unparsed external entity." That is a hold-over from SGML that is rarely used in practice. The annotated XML specification at `http://www.xml.com/axml/axml.html` has an example.

A DTD can also define *entities*, or abbreviations that are replaced during parsing. You can find a good example for the use of entities in the user interface descriptions for the Mozilla/Netscape 6 browser. Those descriptions are formatted in XML and contain entity definitions such as

```
<!ENTITY back.label "Back">
```

Elsewhere, text can contain an entity reference, for example:

```
<menuitem label="&back.label;"/>
```

The parser replaces the entity reference with the replacement string. To internationalize the application, only the string in the entity definition needs to be changed. There are other uses of entities that are more complex and less commonly used. Look at the annotated XML specification for details.

This concludes the introduction to DTDs. Now that you have seen how to use DTDs, you can configure your parser to take advantage of them. First, tell the document builder factory to turn on validation.

```
factory.setValidating(true);
```

All builders produced by this factory will validate their input against a DTD. The most useful benefit of validation is to ignore whitespace in element content. For example, consider the XML fragment

```
<font>
   <name>Helvetica</name>
   <size>36</size>
</font>
```

A non-validating parser reports the whitespace between the `font`, `name`, and `size` elements because it has no way of knowing if the children of `font` are

```
(name,size)
(#PCDATA,name,size)*
```

or perhaps

```
ANY
```

Once the DTD specifies that the children are (name, size), the parser knows
that the whitespace between them is not text. Call

```
factory.setIgnoringElementContentWhitespace(true);
```

and the builder will stop reporting the whitespace in text nodes. That means, you
can now *rely upon* the fact that a font node has two children. You no longer need
to program a tedious loop:

```
for (int i = 0; i < children.getLength(); i++)
{
   Node child = children.item(i);
   if (child instanceof Element)
   {
      Element childElement = (Element)child;
      if (childElement.getTagName().equals("name")) . . .
      else if (childElement.getTagName().equals("size")) . . .
   }
}
```

Instead, you can simply access the first and second child:

```
Element nameElement = (Element)children.item(0);
Element sizeElement = (Element)children.item(1);
```

That is why DTDs are so useful. You don't overload your program with rule
checking code—the parser has already done that work by the time you get
the document.

TIP: Many programmers who start using XML are uncomfortable with DTDs and
end up analyzing the DOM tree on the fly. If you need to convince colleagues of
the benefit of using DTDs, show them the two coding alternatives—it should win
them over.

NOTE: There is a danger in accessing children by their position in the node list.
If the DTD evolves, the list positions may change. Using the XPath technology,
you can access tree elements in a more stable fashion by a path name, such as
`/configuration/title/font/name`. However, XPath is not currently a part of
the Java SDK.

When the parser reports an error, your application will want to do something
about it—log it, show it to the user, or throw an exception to abandon the parsing.

Therefore, you should install an error handler whenever you use validation. Supply an object that implements the `ErrorHandler` interface. That interface has three methods:

```
void warning(SAXParseException exception)
void error(SAXParseException exception)
void fatalError(SAXParseException exception)
```

You install the error handler with the `setErrorHandler` method of the `DocumentBuilder` class:

```
builder.setErrorHandler(handler);
```

 javax.xml.parsers.DocumentBuilder

- `void setEntityResolver(EntityResolver resolver)`

  sets the resolver to locate entities that are referenced in the XML documents to be parsed.

- `void setErrorHandler(ErrorHandler handler)`

  sets the handler to report errors and warnings that occur during parsing.

 org.xml.sax.EntityResolver

- `public InputSource resolveEntity(String publicID, String systemID)`

  returns an input source that contains the data referenced by the given ID(s), or `null` to indicate that this resolver doesn't know how to resolve the particular name. The `publicID` parameter may be `null` if no public ID was supplied.

 org.xml.sax.InputSource

- `InputSource(InputStream in)`
- `InputSource(Reader in)`
- `InputSource(String systemID)`

  construct an input source from a stream, reader, or system ID (usually a relative or absolute URL).

 org.xml.sax.ErrorHandler

- `void fatalError(SAXParseException exception)`
- `void error(SAXParseException exception)`
- `void warning(SAXParseException exception)`

  override these methods to provide handlers for fatal errors, nonfatal errors, and warnings.

org.xml.sax.SAXParseException

- int getLineNumber()
- int getColumnNumber()

  return the line and column number of the end of the processed input that caused the exception.

javax.xml.parsers.DocumentBuilderFactory

- boolean isValidating()
- void setValidating(boolean value)

  The "validating" property of the factory. If set to true, the parsers that this factory generate validate their input.

- boolean isIgnoringElementContentWhitespace()
- void setIgnoringElementContentWhitespace(boolean value)

  The "ignoringElementContentWhitespace" property of the factory. If set to true, the parsers that this factory generate ignore whitespace text between element nodes that don't have mixed content (i.e., a mixture of elements and #PCDATA).

A Practical Example

In this section, we will work through a practical example that shows the use of XML in a realistic setting. Recall from Volume 1 Chapter 9 that the GridBagLayout is the most useful layout manager for Swing components. However, it is feared not just for its complexity but also for the programming tedium. It would be much more convenient to put the layout instructions into a text file instead of producing large amounts of repetitive code. In this section, you will see how to use XML to describe a grid bag layout, and how to parse the layout files.

A grid bag is made up of rows and columns, very similar to an HTML table. Similar to an HTML table, we'll describe it as a sequence of rows, each of which contains cells:

```
<gridbag>
   <row>
      <cell>...</cell>
      <cell>...</cell>
      . . .
   </row>
   <row>
      <cell>...</cell>
      <cell>...</cell>
      . . .
   </row>
   . . .
</gridbag>
```

The `gridbag.dtd` specifies these rules:

```
<!ELEMENT gridbag (row)*>
<!ELEMENT row (cell)*>
```

Some cells can span multiple rows and columns. In the grid bag layout, that is achieved by setting the `gridwidth` and `gridheight` constraints to values larger than 1. We will use attributes of the same name:

```
<cell gridwidth="2" gridheight="2">
```

Similarly, we will use attributes for the other grid bag constraints `fill`, `anchor`, `gridx`, `gridy`, `weightx`, `weighty`, `ipadx`, and `ipady`. (We don't handle the `insets` constraint because its value is not a simple type, but it would be straightforward to support it.) For example,

```
<cell fill="HORIZONTAL" anchor="NORTH">
```

For most of these attributes, we provide the same defaults as the `GridBag-Constraints` default constructor:

```
<!ATTLIST cell gridwidth CDATA "1">
<!ATTLIST cell gridheight CDATA "1">
<!ATTLIST cell fill (NONE|BOTH|HORIZONTAL|VERTICAL) "NONE">
<!ATTLIST cell anchor (CENTER|NORTH|NORTHEAST|EAST
    |SOUTHEAST|SOUTH|SOUTHWEST|WEST|NORTHWEST) "CENTER">
<!ATTLIST cell ipadx CDATA "0">
<!ATTLIST cell ipady CDATA "0">
```

However, we use default weights of 100, which is more useful than the `GridBagConstraints` default of 0:

```
<!ATTLIST cell weightx CDATA "100">
<!ATTLIST cell weighty CDATA "100">
```

The `gridx` and `gridy` values get special treatment because it would be tedious and somewhat error-prone to specify them by hand. Supplying them is optional:

```
<!ATTLIST cell gridx CDATA #IMPLIED>
<!ATTLIST cell gridy CDATA #IMPLIED>
```

If they are not supplied, the program determines them according to the following heuristic: in column 0, the default `gridx` is 0. Otherwise, it is the preceding `gridx` plus the preceding `gridwidth`. The default `gridy` is always the same as the row number. Thus, you don't have to specify `gridx` and `gridy` in the most common cases, where a component spans multiple rows. But if a component spans multiple columns, then you need to specify `gridx` whenever you skip over that component.

> NOTE: Grid bag experts may wonder why we don't use the RELATIVE and REMAINDER mechanism to let the grid bag layout automatically determine the gridx and gridy positions. We tried, but no amount of fussing would produce the layout of the font dialog example of Volume 1. Reading through the Grid-BagLayout source code, it is apparent that the algorithm just won't do the heavy lifting that would be required to reliably find the appropriate positions.

The program parses the attributes and sets the grid bag constraints. For example, to read the grid width, the program contains a single statement:

```
constraints.gridwidth
   = Integer.parseInt(e.getAttribute("gridwidth"));
```

The program need not worry about a missing attribute since the parser automatically supplies the default value if no other value was specified in the document.

To test whether a gridx or gridy attribute was specified, we call the getAttribute method and check if it returns the empty string:

```
String value = e.getAttribute("gridy");
if (value.length() == 0) // use default
   constraints.gridy = r;
else
   constraints.gridx = Integer.parseInt(value);
```

A cell can contain any component, but we found it convenient to allow the user to specify more general Java beans. That lets us specify non-component types such as borders. A bean is defined by a class name and zero or more properties:

```
<!ELEMENT bean (class, property*)>
<!ELEMENT class (#PCDATA)>
```

As always when using beans, the class must have a default constructor.

A property contains a name and a value.

```
<!ELEMENT property (name, value)>
<!ELEMENT name (#PCDATA)>
```

The value is an integer, Boolean, string, or another bean:

```
<!ELEMENT value (int|string|boolean|bean)>
<!ELEMENT int (#PCDATA)>
<!ELEMENT string (#PCDATA)>
<!ELEMENT boolean (#PCDATA)>
```

Here is a typical example, a JLabel whose text property is set to the string "Face: ".

```
<bean>
  <class>javax.swing.JLabel</class>
  <property>
    <name>text</name>
    <value><string>Face: </string></value>
  </property>
</bean>
```

It seems like a bother to surround a string with the `<string>` tag. Why not just use #PCDATA for strings and leave the tags for the other types? Then we would need to use mixed content and weaken the rule for the value element to

```
<!ELEMENT value (#PCDATA|int|boolean|bean)*>
```

However, that rule would allow an arbitrary mixture of text and tags.

The program sets a property by using the `BeanInfo` class. The `BeanInfo` enumerates the property descriptors of the bean. We search for the property with the matching name, and then call its setter method with the supplied value.

When our program reads in a user interface description, it has enough information to construct and arrange the user interface components. But, of course, the interface is not alive—no event listeners have been attached. To add event listeners, it is necessary to locate the components. For that reason, we support an optional attribute of type ID for each bean:

```
<!ATTLIST bean id ID #IMPLIED>
```

For example, here is a combo box with an ID:

```
<bean id="face">
  <class>javax.swing.JComboBox</class>
</bean>
```

Recall that the parser checks that IDs are unique.

A programmer can attach event handlers like this:

```
gridbag = new GridBagPane("fontdialog.xml");
setContentPane(gridbag);
JComboBox face = (JComboBox)gridbag.get("face");
face.addListener(listener);
```

NOTE: In this example, we only use XML to describe the component layout and leave it to programmers to attach the event handlers in the Java code. You could go a step further and add the code to the XML description. The most promising approach is to use a scripting language such as BeanShell (`http://www.beanshell.org`) for the code.

The program in Example 12–2 shows how to use the `GridBagPane` class to do all the boring work of setting up the grid bag layout. The layout is defined in

Example 12–3. Figure 12–4 shows the result. The program only initializes the combo boxes (which are too complex for the bean property setting mechanism that the `GridBagPane` supports), and attaches event listeners. The `GridBag-Pane` class in Example 12–4 parses the XML file, constructs the components, and lays them out. Example 12–5 shows the DTD.

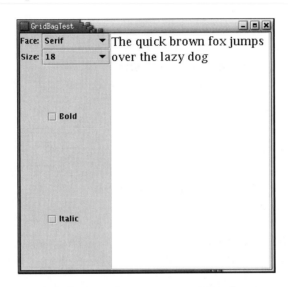

Figure 12–4: A font dialog defined by an XML layout

This example is a typical use of XML. The XML format is robust enough to express complex relationships. The XML parser adds real value by taking over the routine job of validity checking and supplying defaults. That reduces the effort for both the utility provider—the implementor of the `GridBagPane` class—and the user of this utility—the programmer who can now express user interface layouts in a file rather than lengthy code. Of course, authoring the XML file is still a bit tedious, even with an XML editor. The next step would be to provide a drag-and-drop authoring tool that automatically emits the XML code. With such an environment, the Java user interface programmer can enjoy the same productivity and convenience as a Windows or Mac programmer, while retaining the benefits of layout management.

NOTE: The JSR-057 working group is proposing a more ambitious XML-based standard to describe and archive Java beans. See `http://java.sun.com/products/jfc/tsc/articles/persistence/index.html` for more information.

Example 12–2: GridBagTest.java

```
1. import java.awt.*;
2. import java.awt.event.*;
```

```
 3. import javax.swing.*;
 4.
 5. /**
 6.    This program shows how to use an XML file to describe
 7.    a gridbag layout
 8. */
 9. public class GridBagTest
10. {
11.    public static void main(String[] args)
12.    {
13.       JFrame frame = new FontFrame();
14.       frame.setDefaultCloseOperation(JFrame.EXIT_ON_CLOSE);
15.       frame.show();
16.    }
17. }
18.
19. /**
20.    This frame contains a font selection dialog that
21.    is described by an XML file.
22. */
23. class FontFrame extends JFrame
24. {
25.    public FontFrame()
26.    {
27.       setSize(WIDTH, HEIGHT);
28.       setTitle("GridBagTest");
29.
30.       gridbag = new GridBagPane("fontdialog.xml");
31.       setContentPane(gridbag);
32.
33.       face = (JComboBox)gridbag.get("face");
34.       size = (JComboBox)gridbag.get("size");
35.       bold = (JCheckBox)gridbag.get("bold");
36.       italic = (JCheckBox)gridbag.get("italic");
37.
38.       face.setModel(new DefaultComboBoxModel(new Object[]
39.          {
40.             "Serif", "SansSerif", "Monospaced",
41.             "Dialog", "DialogInput"
42.          }));
43.
44.       size.setModel(new DefaultComboBoxModel(new Object[]
45.          {
46.             "8", "10", "12", "15", "18", "24", "36", "48"
47.          }));
48.
49.       ActionListener listener = new
50.          ActionListener()
```

```
51.          {
52.              public void actionPerformed(ActionEvent event)
53.              {
54.                  setSample();
55.              }
56.          };
57.
58.       face.addActionListener(listener);
59.       size.addActionListener(listener);
60.       bold.addActionListener(listener);
61.       italic.addActionListener(listener);
62.
63.       setSample();
64.    }
65.
66.    /**
67.       This method sets the text sample to the selected font.
68.    */
69.    public void setSample()
70.    {
71.       String fontFace = (String)face.getSelectedItem();
72.       int fontSize = Integer.parseInt(
73.          (String)size.getSelectedItem());
74.       JTextArea sample = (JTextArea)gridbag.get("sample");
75.       int fontStyle
76.          = (bold.isSelected() ? Font.BOLD : 0)
77.          + (italic.isSelected() ? Font.ITALIC : 0);
78.
79.       sample.setFont(new Font(fontFace, fontStyle, fontSize));
80.       sample.repaint();
81.    }
82.
83.    private GridBagPane gridbag;
84.    private JComboBox face;
85.    private JComboBox size;
86.    private JCheckBox bold;
87.    private JCheckBox italic;
88.    private static final int WIDTH = 400;
89.    private static final int HEIGHT = 400;
90. }
```

Example 12–3: fontdialog.xml

```
1. <?xml version="1.0"?>
2. <!DOCTYPE gridbag SYSTEM "gridbag.dtd">
3. <gridbag>
4.   <row>
5.     <cell anchor="EAST" weightx="0" weighty="0">
6.       <bean>
```

```
  7.          <class>javax.swing.JLabel</class>
  8.          <property>
  9.            <name>text</name>
 10.            <value><string>Face: </string></value>
 11.          </property>
 12.        </bean>
 13.      </cell>
 14.      <cell fill="HORIZONTAL" weighty="0">
 15.        <bean id="face">
 16.          <class>javax.swing.JComboBox</class>
 17.        </bean>
 18.      </cell>
 19.      <cell gridheight="4" fill="BOTH">
 20.        <bean id="sample">
 21.          <class>javax.swing.JTextArea</class>
 22.          <property>
 23.            <name>text</name>
 24.            <value><string>The quick brown fox jumps over the lazy
     dog</string></value>
 25.          </property>
 26.          <property>
 27.            <name>editable</name>
 28.            <value><boolean>false</boolean></value>
 29.          </property>
 30.          <property>
 31.            <name>lineWrap</name>
 32.            <value><boolean>true</boolean></value>
 33.          </property>
 34.          <property>
 35.            <name>border</name>
 36.            <value>
 37.              <bean>
 38.                <class>javax.swing.border.EtchedBorder</class>
 39.              </bean>
 40.            </value>
 41.          </property>
 42.        </bean>
 43.      </cell>
 44.    </row>
 45.    <row>
 46.      <cell anchor="EAST" weightx="0" weighty="0">
 47.        <bean>
 48.          <class>javax.swing.JLabel</class>
 49.          <property>
 50.            <name>text</name>
 51.            <value><string>Size: </string></value>
 52.          </property>
 53.        </bean>
```

```
54.    </cell>
55.    <cell fill="HORIZONTAL" weighty="0">
56.      <bean id="size">
57.        <class>javax.swing.JComboBox</class>
58.      </bean>
59.    </cell>
60.  </row>
61.  <row>
62.    <cell gridwidth="2" weightx="0" fill="NONE">
63.      <bean id="bold">
64.        <class>javax.swing.JCheckBox</class>
65.        <property>
66.          <name>text</name>
67.          <value><string>Bold</string></value>
68.        </property>
69.      </bean>
70.    </cell>
71.  </row>
72.  <row>
73.    <cell gridwidth="2" weightx="0" fill="NONE">
74.      <bean id="italic">
75.        <class>javax.swing.JCheckBox</class>
76.        <property>
77.          <name>text</name>
78.          <value><string>Italic</string></value>
79.        </property>
80.      </bean>
81.    </cell>
82.  </row>
83. </gridbag>
```

Example 12–4: GridBagPane.java

```
 1. import java.awt.*;
 2. import java.beans.*;
 3. import java.io.*;
 4. import java.lang.reflect.*;
 5. import javax.swing.*;
 6. import javax.xml.parsers.*;
 7. import org.w3c.dom.*;
 8. import org.xml.sax.*;
 9.
10. /**
11.    This panel uses an XML file to describe its
12.    components and their grid bag layout positions.
13. */
14. public class GridBagPane extends JPanel
15. {
16.    /**
17.       Constructs a grid bag pane.
```

```
18.         @param filename the name of the XML file that
19.         describes the pane's components and their positions
20.      */
21.     public GridBagPane(String filename)
22.     {
23.        setLayout(new GridBagLayout());
24.        constraints = new GridBagConstraints();
25.
26.        try
27.        {
28.           DocumentBuilderFactory factory
29.              = DocumentBuilderFactory.newInstance();
30.           factory.setValidating(true);
31.           factory.setIgnoringElementContentWhitespace(true);
32.           DocumentBuilder builder = factory.newDocumentBuilder();
33.           Document doc = builder.parse(new File(filename));
34.           parseGridbag(doc.getDocumentElement());
35.        }
36.        catch (ParserConfigurationException exception)
37.        {
38.           exception.printStackTrace();
39.        }
40.        catch (SAXException exception)
41.        {
42.           exception.printStackTrace();
43.        }
44.        catch (IOException exception)
45.        {
46.           exception.printStackTrace();
47.        }
48.     }
49.
50.     /**
51.        Gets a component with a given name
52.        @param name a component name
53.        @return the component with the given name, or null if
54.        no component in this grid bag pane has the given name
55.     */
56.     public Component get(String name)
57.     {
58.        Component[] components = getComponents();
59.        for (int i = 0; i < components.length; i++)
60.        {
61.           if (components[i].getName().equals(name))
62.              return components[i];
63.        }
64.        return null;
65.     }
66.
67.     /**
68.        Parses a gridbag element.
69.        @param e a gridbag element
```

```
70.      */
71.     private void parseGridbag(Element e)
72.     {
73.        NodeList rows = e.getChildNodes();
74.        for (int i = 0; i < rows.getLength(); i++)
75.        {
76.           Element row = (Element)rows.item(i);
77.           NodeList cells = row.getChildNodes();
78.           for (int j = 0; j < cells.getLength(); j++)
79.           {
80.              Element cell = (Element)cells.item(j);
81.              parseCell(cell, i, j);
82.           }
83.        }
84.     }
85.
86.     /**
87.        Parses a cell element.
88.        @param e a cell element
89.        @param r the row of the cell
90.        @param c the column of the cell
91.     */
92.     private void parseCell(Element e, int r, int c)
93.     {
94.        // get attributes
95.
96.        String value = e.getAttribute("gridx");
97.        if (value.length() == 0) // use default
98.        {
99.           if (c == 0) constraints.gridx = 0;
100.          else constraints.gridx += constraints.gridwidth;
101.       }
102.       else
103.          constraints.gridx = Integer.parseInt(value);
104.
105.       value = e.getAttribute("gridy");
106.       if (value.length() == 0) // use default
107.          constraints.gridy = r;
108.       else
109.          constraints.gridx = Integer.parseInt(value);
110.
111.       constraints.gridwidth
112.          = Integer.parseInt(e.getAttribute("gridwidth"));
113.       constraints.gridheight
114.          = Integer.parseInt(e.getAttribute("gridheight"));
115.       constraints.weightx
116.          = Integer.parseInt(e.getAttribute("weightx"));
117.       constraints.weighty
118.          = Integer.parseInt(e.getAttribute("weighty"));
119.       constraints.ipadx
120.          = Integer.parseInt(e.getAttribute("ipadx"));
121.       constraints.ipady
```

```
122.          = Integer.parseInt(e.getAttribute("ipady"));
123.
124.       // use reflection to get integer values of static fields
125.       Class cl = GridBagConstraints.class;
126.
127.       try
128.       {
129.          String name = e.getAttribute("fill");
130.          Field f = cl.getField(name);
131.          constraints.fill = f.getInt(cl);
132.       }
133.       catch(Exception ex)
134.       {
135.       }
136.
137.       try
138.       {
139.          String name = e.getAttribute("anchor");
140.          Field f = cl.getField(name);
141.          constraints.anchor = f.getInt(cl);
142.       }
143.       catch(Exception ex)
144.       {
145.       }
146.
147.       Component comp = (Component)parseBean(
148.          (Element)e.getFirstChild());
149.       add(comp, constraints);
150.    }
151.
152.    /**
153.       Parses a bean element.
154.       @param e a bean element
155.    */
156.    private Object parseBean(Element e)
157.    {
158.       try
159.       {
160.          NodeList children = e.getChildNodes();
161.          Element classElement = (Element)children.item(0);
162.          String className
163.             = ((Text)classElement.getFirstChild()).getData();
164.
165.          Class cl = Class.forName(className);
166.
167.          Object obj = cl.newInstance();
168.
169.          if (obj instanceof Component)
170.             ((Component)obj).setName(e.getAttribute("id"));
171.
172.          for (int i = 1; i < children.getLength(); i++)
173.          {
```

```
174.              Node propertyElement = children.item(i);
175.              Element nameElement
176.                 = (Element)propertyElement.getFirstChild();
177.              String propertyName
178.                 = ((Text)nameElement.getFirstChild()).getData();
179.
180.              Element valueElement
181.                 = (Element)propertyElement.getLastChild();
182.              Object value = parseValue(valueElement);
183.              BeanInfo beanInfo = Introspector.getBeanInfo(cl);
184.              PropertyDescriptor[] descriptors
185.                 = beanInfo.getPropertyDescriptors();
186.              boolean done = false;
187.              for (int j = 0; !done && j < descriptors.length; j++)
188.              {
189.                 if (descriptors[j].getName().equals(propertyName))
190.                 {
191.                    descriptors[j].getWriteMethod().invoke(obj,
192.                       new Object[] { value });
193.                    done = true;
194.                 }
195.              }
196.
197.           }
198.           return obj;
199.        }
200.        catch (Exception ex)
201.        {
202.           // the reflection methods can throw various exceptions
203.           ex.printStackTrace();
204.           return null;
205.        }
206.     }
207.
208.     /**
209.        Parses a value element.
210.        @param e a value element
211.     */
212.     private Object parseValue(Element e)
213.     {
214.        Element child = (Element)e.getFirstChild();
215.        if (child.getTagName().equals("bean"))
216.           return parseBean(child);
217.        String text = ((Text)child.getFirstChild()).getData();
218.        if (child.getTagName().equals("int"))
219.           return new Integer(text);
220.        else if (child.getTagName().equals("boolean"))
221.           return new Boolean(text);
222.        else if (child.getTagName().equals("string"))
223.           return text;
224.        else
225.           return null;
```

```
226.    }
227.
228.    private GridBagConstraints constraints;
229. }
```

Example 12–5: gridbag.dtd

```
 1. <!ELEMENT gridbag (row)*>
 2. <!ELEMENT row (cell)*>
 3. <!ELEMENT cell (bean)>
 4. <!ATTLIST cell gridx CDATA #IMPLIED>
 5. <!ATTLIST cell gridy CDATA #IMPLIED>
 6. <!ATTLIST cell gridwidth CDATA "1">
 7. <!ATTLIST cell gridheight CDATA "1">
 8. <!ATTLIST cell weightx CDATA "100">
 9. <!ATTLIST cell weighty CDATA "100">
10. <!ATTLIST cell fill (NONE|BOTH|HORIZONTAL|VERTICAL) "NONE">
11. <!ATTLIST cell anchor (CENTER|NORTH|NORTHEAST|EAST|SOUTH
      EAST|SOUTH|SOUTHWEST|WEST|NORTHWEST) "CENTER">
12. <!ATTLIST cell ipadx CDATA "0">
13. <!ATTLIST cell ipady CDATA "0">
14.
15. <!ELEMENT bean (class, property*)>
16. <!ATTLIST bean id ID #IMPLIED>
17. <!ELEMENT class (#PCDATA)>
18. <!ELEMENT property (name, value)>
19. <!ELEMENT name (#PCDATA)>
20. <!ELEMENT value (int|string|boolean|bean)>
21. <!ELEMENT int (#PCDATA)>
22. <!ELEMENT string (#PCDATA)>
23. <!ELEMENT boolean (#PCDATA)>
```

Namespaces

Java uses packages to avoid name clashes. Programmers can use the same name for different classes as long as they aren't in the same package. XML has a similar *namespace* mechanism for element and attribute names.

A namespace is identified by a Uniform Resource Identifier (URI), such as

```
http://www.w3.org/2001/XMLSchema
uuid:1c759aed-b748-475c-ab68-10679700c4f2
urn:com:books-r-us
```

The HTTP URL form is the most common. Note that the URL is just used as an identifier string, not to locate a document. For example, the namespace identifiers

```
http://www.horstmann.com/corejava
http://www.horstmann.com/corejava/index.html
```

denote *different* namespaces, even though a web server would serve the same document for both URLs.

There doesn't have to be any document at a namespace URL—the XML parser doesn't attempt to find anything at that location. However, as a help to programmers who encounter a possibly unfamiliar namespace, it is customary to place a document explaining the purpose of the namespace at the URL location. For example, if you point your browser to the namespace URL for the XML Schema namespace (`http://www.w3.org/2001/XMLSchema`), you will find a document describing the XML Schema standard.

Why use HTTP URLs for namespace identifiers? It is easy to ensure that they are unique. If you choose a real URL, then the host part's uniqueness is guaranteed by the domain name system. Your organization can then arrange for the uniqueness of the remainder of the URL. This is the same rationale that underlies the use of reversed domain names in Java package names.

Of course, while you want long namespace identifiers for uniqueness, you don't want to deal with long identifiers any more than you have to. In Java, you use the `import` mechanism to specify the long names of packages, and then use just the short class names. In XML, there is a similar mechanism, like this:

```
<element xmlns="namespace URI">
   children
</element>
```

The element and its children are now part of the given namespace.

A child can provide its own namespace, for example:

```
<element xmlns="namespace URI">
   <child xmlns="namespace URI #2">
      grandchildren
   </child>
   more children
</element>
```

Then the first child and the grandchildren are part of the second namespace.

That simple mechanism works well if you only need a single namespace, or if the namespaces are naturally nested. Otherwise, you will want to use a second mechanism that has no analog in Java. You can have an *alias* for a namespace—a short identifier that you choose for a particular document. Here is a typical example:

```
<xsl:stylesheet
      xmlns:xsl="http://www.w3.org/1999/XSL/Transform">
   <xsl:output method="html"/>
   . . .
</xsl:stylesheet>
```

The attribute

```
xmlns:alias="namespace URI"
```

defines a namespace and an alias. In our example, the alias is the string `xsl`. Thus, `xsl:stylesheet` really means "`stylesheet` in the namespace `http://www.w3.org/1999/XSL/Transform`".

NOTE: Only child elements inherit the namespace of their parent. Attributes without an explicit alias prefix are never part of a namespace. Consider this contrived example:

```
<configuration xmlns="http://www.horstmann.com/corejava"
    xmlns:si="http://www.bipm.fr/enus/3_SI/si.html"
>
    <size value="210" si:unit="mm"/>
    . . .
</configuration>
```

The elements `configuration` and `size` are part of the namespace with URI `http://www.horstmann.com/corejava`. The attribute `si:unit` is part of the namespace with URI `http://www.bipm.fr/enus/3_SI/si.html`. But the attribute `value` is not part of any namespace.

You can control how the parser deals with namespaces. By default, the Sun DOM parser is not "namespace aware."

To turn on namespace handling, call the `setNamespaceAware` method of the `DocumentBuilderFactory`:

```
factory.setNamespaceAware(true);
```

Then all builders that the factory produces support namespaces. Each node has three properties:

- The *qualified name*, with an alias prefix, returned by `getNodeName`, `getTagName`, and so on;
- The *local name*, without a prefix or a namespace, returned by the `getLocalName` method;
- The namespace URI, returned by the `getNamespaceURI` method.

Here is an example. Suppose the parser sees the following element:

```
<xsl:stylesheet
        xmlns:xsl="http://www.w3.org/1999/XSL/Transform">
```

Then it reports the following:

- Qualified name = `xsl:stylesheet`
- Local name = `stylesheet`
- Namespace URI = `http://www.w3.org/1999/XSL/Transform`

> NOTE: If namespace awareness is turned off, then `getLocalName` and
> `getNamespaceURI` return `null`.

`org.w3c.dom.Node`

- `String getLocalName()`

  returns the local name (without alias prefix), or `null` if the parser is not namespace aware.

- `String getNameSpaceURI()`

  returns the namespace URI, or `null` if the node is not part of a namespace, or if the parser is not namespace aware.

`javax.xml.parsers.DocumentBuilderFactory`

- `boolean isNamespaceAware()`
- `void setNamespaceAware(boolean value)`

  The "namespaceAware" property of the factory. If set to `true`, the parsers that this factory generates are namespace aware.

Using the SAX Parser

The DOM parser reads an XML document in its entirety into a tree data structure. For most practical applications, DOM works fine. But it can be inefficient if the document is large and if your processing algorithm is simple enough that you can analyze nodes "on the fly," without having to see all of the tree structure. In these cases, you want to use the SAX parser instead. The SAX parser reports events as it parses the components of the XML input. But it does not store the document in any way—it is up to the event handlers whether they want to build a data structure. In fact, the DOM parser is built on top of the SAX parser. It builds the DOM tree as it receives the parser events.

Whenever you use a SAX parser, you need a handler that defines the event actions for the various parse events. The `ContentHandler` interface defines several callback methods that the parser executes as it parses the document. Here are the most important ones:

- `startElement`/`endElement` are called when a start tag or end tag is encountered.
- `characters` is called whenever character data is encountered.
- `startDocument`/`endDocument` are called once each, at the start and the end of the document.

For example, when parsing the fragment

```
<font>
   <name>Helvetica</name>
   <size units="pt">36</size>
</font>
```

the parser makes sure the following calls are generated:

1. `startElement`, element name: `font`

2. `startElement`, element name: `name`

3. `characters`, content: `Helvetica`

4. `endElement`, element name: `name`

5. `startElement`, element name: `size`, attributes: `units="pt"`

6. `characters`, content: `36`

7. `endElement`, element name: `size`

8. `endElement`, element name: `font`

Your handler needs to override these methods and have them carry out whatever action you want to carry out as you parse the file. The program at the end of this section prints out all links `<a href="...">` in an HTML file. It simply overrides the `startElement` method of the handler to check for links with name `a` and an attribute with name `href`. This is potentially useful for implementing a "web crawler," a program that reaches more and more web pages by following links.

NOTE: Unfortunately, most HTML pages deviate so much from proper XML that the example program will not be able to parse them. As already mentioned, the World Wide Web Consortium (W3C) recommends that web designers use XHTML, an HTML dialect that can be displayed by current web browsers and that is also proper XML. See `http://www.w3.org/TR/xhtml1/` for more information on XHTML. Since the W3C "eats its own dog food," their web pages are written in XHTML. You can use those pages to test the example program. For example, if you run

```
java SAXTest http://www.w3c.org/MarkUp
```

then you will see a list of the URLs of all links on that page.

The sample program is a good example for the use of SAX. We don't care at all in which context the a elements occur, and there is no need to store a tree structure.

Here is how you get a SAX parser:

```
SAXParserFactory factory = SAXParserFactory.newInstance();
SAXParser parser = factory.newSAXParser();
```

You can now process a document:

```
parser.parse(source, handler);
```

Here, `source` can be a file, URL string, or input stream. The `handler` belongs to a subclass of `DefaultHandler`. The `DefaultHandler` class defines do-nothing methods for the four interfaces:

```
ContentHandler
DTDHandler
EntityResolver
ErrorHandler
```

The example program defines a handler that overrides the `startElement` method of the `ContentHandler` interface to watch out for a elements with an `href` attribute:

```
DefaultHandler handler = new
   DefaultHandler()
   {
      public void startElement(String namespaceURI,
         String lname, String qname, Attributes attrs)
      throws SAXException
      {
         if (lname.equalsIgnoreCase("a") && attrs != null)
         {
            for (int i = 0; i < attrs.getLength(); i++)
            {
               String aname = attrs.getLocalName(i);
               if (aname.equalsIgnoreCase("href"))
                  System.out.println(attrs.getValue(i));
            }
         }
      }
   };
```

The `startElement` method has three parameters that describe the element name. The `qname` parameter reports the qualified name of the form `alias:localname`. If namespace processing is turned on, then the `namespaceURI` and `lname` parameters describe the namespace and local (unqualified) name.

As with the DOM parser, namespace processing is turned off by default. You activate namespace processing by calling the `setNamespaceAware` method of the factory class:

```
SAXParserFactory factory = SAXParserFactory.newInstance();
factory.setNamespaceAware(true);
SAXParser saxParser = factory.newSAXParser();
```

Example 12–6 contains the code for the web crawler program. Later in this chapter, you will see another interesting use of SAX. An easy way of turning a non-XML data source into XML is to report the SAX events that an XML parser would report. See the section on XSL transformations for details.

Example 12–6: SAXTest.java

```
1. import java.io.*;
2. import java.net.*;
3. import javax.xml.parsers.*;
4. import org.xml.sax.*;
5. import org.xml.sax.helpers.*;
6.
7. /**
8.    This program demonstrates how to use a SAX parser. The
9.    program prints all hyperlinks links of an XHTML web page.
10.    Usage: java SAXTest url
11. */
12. public class SAXTest
13. {
14.    public static void main(String[] args) throws Exception
15.    {
16.       String url;
17.       if (args.length == 0)
18.       {
19.          url = "http://www.w3c.org";
20.          System.out.println("Using " + url);
21.       }
22.       else
23.          url = args[0];
24.
25.       DefaultHandler handler = new
26.          DefaultHandler()
27.          {
28.             public void startElement(String namespaceURI,
29.                String lname, String qname, Attributes attrs)
30.             {
31.                if (lname.equalsIgnoreCase("a") && attrs != null)
32.                {
33.                   for (int i = 0; i < attrs.getLength(); i++)
34.                   {
35.                      String aname = attrs.getLocalName(i);
36.                      if (aname.equalsIgnoreCase("href"))
37.                         System.out.println(attrs.getValue(i));
38.                   }
39.                }
40.             }
41.          };
42.
43.       SAXParserFactory factory = SAXParserFactory.newInstance();
44.       factory.setNamespaceAware(true);
```

```
45.        SAXParser saxParser = factory.newSAXParser();
46.        InputStream in = new URL(url).openStream();
47.        saxParser.parse(in, handler);
48.    }
49. }
```

javax.xml.parsers.SAXParserFactory

- `static SAXParserFactory newInstance()`
  returns an instance of the SAXParserFactory class.

- `SAXParser newSAXParser()`
  returns an instance of the SAXParser class.

- `boolean isNamespaceAware()`
- `void setNamespaceAware(boolean value)`
  The "namespaceAware" property of the factory. If set to true, the parsers that this factory generates are namespace aware.

- `boolean isValidating()`
- `void setValidating(boolean value)`
  The "validating" property of the factory. If set to true, the parsers that this factory generates validate their input.

javax.xml.parsers.SAXParser

- `void parse(File f, DefaultHandler handler)`
- `void parse(String url, DefaultHandler handler)`
- `void parse(InputStream in, DefaultHandler handler)`
  parse an XML document from the given file, URL, or input stream and reports parse events to the given handler.

org.xml.sax.ContentHandler

- `void startDocument()`
- `void endDocument()`
  These methods are called at the start and the end of the document.

- `void startElement(String uri, String lname, String qname, Attributes attr)`
- `void endElement(String uri, String lname, String qname)`
  These methods are called at the start and the end of an element.

  Parameters: uri   the URI of the namespace (if the parser is namespace aware)

  lname   the local name without alias prefix (if the parser is namespace aware)

> qname the element name (if the parser is not namespace aware), or the qualified name with alias prefix (if the parser reports qualified names in addition to local names)

- void characters(char[] data, int start, int length)

This method is called when the parser reports character data.

> *Parameters:* data an array of character data
>
> start the index of the first character in the data array that is a part of the reported characters
>
> length the length of the reported character string

org.xml.sax.Attributes

- int getLength()

returns the number of attributes stored in this attribute collection.

- String getLocalName(int index)

returns the local name (without alias prefix) of the attribute with the given index, or the empty string if the parser is not namespace aware.

- String getURI(int index)

returns the namespace URI of the attribute with the given index, or the empty string if the node is not part of a namespace, or if the parser is not namespace aware.

- String getQName(int index)

returns the qualified name (with alias prefix) of the attribute with the given index, or the empty string if the qualified name is not reported by the parser.

- String getValue(int index)
- String getValue(String qname)
- String getValue(String uri, String lname)

return the attribute value from a given index, qualified name, or namespace URI + local name. Returns null if the value doesn't exist.

Generating XML Documents

You now know how to write Java programs that read XML. Let us now turn to the opposite process, producing XML output. Of course, you could write an XML file simply by making a sequence of print calls, printing the elements, attributes, and text content. But that would not be a good idea. The code is rather tedious, and you can easily make mistakes if you don't pay attention to special symbols (such as " or <) in the attribute values and text content.

A better approach is to build up a DOM tree with the contents of the document, and then write out the tree contents. To build a DOM tree, you start out with an empty document. You can get an empty document by calling the `newDocument` method of the `DocumentBuilder` class.

```
Document doc = builder.newDocument();
```

Use the `createElement` method of the `Document` class to construct the elements of your document.

```
Element rootElement = doc.createElement(rootName);
Element childElement = doc.createElement(childName);
```

Use the `createTextNode` method to construct text nodes:

```
Text textNode = doc.createTextNode(textContents);
```

Add the root element to the document, and add the child nodes to their parents:

```
doc.appendChild(rootElement);
rootElement.appendChild(childElement);
childElement.appendChild(textNode);
```

As you build up the DOM tree, you may also need to set element attributes. Simply call the `setAttribute` method of the `Element` class:

```
rootElement.setAttribute(name, value);
```

Somewhat curiously, the DOM API currently has no support for writing a DOM tree to an output stream. To overcome this limitation, we will use the XML Style Sheet Transformations (XSLT) API. We will apply the "do nothing" transformation to the document and capture its output. To include a DOCTYPE node in the output, you also need to set the SYSTEM and PUBLIC identifiers as output properties.

```
// construct the "do nothing" transformation
Transformer t = TransformerFactory
    .newInstance().newTransformer();
// set output properties to get a DOCTYPE node
t.setOutputProperty("doctype-system", systemIdentifier);
t.setOutputProperty("doctype-public", publicIdentifier);
// apply the "do nothing" transformation
// and send the output to a file
t.transform(new DOMSource(doc),
    new StreamResult(new FileOutputStream(file)));
```

For more information about XSLT, turn to the next section. Right now, consider this code a "magic incantation" to produce XML output.

NOTE: The resulting XML file contains no whitespace (that is, no line breaks or indentations). If you like whitespace, set the `"indent"` output property to `"yes"`.

Example 12–7 is a typical program that produces XML output. The program draws a modernist painting—a random set of colored rectangles (see Figure 12–5). To save a masterpiece, we use the Scalable Vector Graphics (SVG) format. SVG is an XML format to describe complex graphics in a device-independent fashion. You can find more information about SVG at http://www.w3c.org/Graphics/SVG. To view SVG files, download the Apache Batik viewer (http://xml.apache.org/batik) or the Adobe browser plug-in (http://www.adobe.com/svg/main.html). Figure 12–6 shows the Apache Batik viewer.

Figure 12–5: Generating Modern Art

Figure 12–6: The Apache Batik SVG Viewer

We don't want to go into details about SVG. If you are interested in SVG, we suggest you start with the tutorial on the Adobe site. For our purposes, we just need to know how to express a set of colored rectangles. Here is a sample:

```
<?xml version="1.0" encoding="UTF-8"?>
<!DOCTYPE svg PUBLIC "-//W3C//DTD SVG 20000802//EN"
"http://www.w3.org/TR/2000/CR-SVG-20000802/DTD/svg-
20000802.dtd">
<svg width="300" height="150">
<rect x="231" y="61" width="9" height="12" fill="#6e4a13"/>
```

```
<rect x="107" y="106" width="56" height="5" fill="#c406be"/>
. . .
</svg>
```

As you can see, each rectangle is described as a `rect` node. The position, width, height, and fill color are attributes. The fill color is an RGB value in hexadecimal.

NOTE: As you can see, SVG uses attributes heavily. In fact, some attributes are quite complex. For example, here is a path element:

```
<path d="M 100 100 L 300 100 L 200 300 z">
```

The `M` denotes a "moveto" command, `L` is "lineto," and `z` is "closepath" (!). Apparently, the designers of this data format didn't have much confidence in using XML for structured data. In your own XML formats, you may want to use elements instead of complex attributes.

Here is the source code for the program. You can use the same technique whenever you need to generate XML output.

Example 12–7: XMLWriteTest.java

```
1. import java.awt.*;
2. import java.awt.geom.*;
3. import java.io.*;
4. import java.util.*;
5. import java.awt.event.*;
6. import javax.swing.*;
7. import javax.xml.parsers.*;
8. import javax.xml.transform.*;
9. import javax.xml.transform.dom.*;
10. import javax.xml.transform.stream.*;
11. import org.w3c.dom.*;
12.
13.
14. /**
15.    This program shows how to write an XML file. It saves
16.    a file describing a modern drawing in SVG format.
17. */
18. public class XMLWriteTest
19. {
20.    public static void main(String[] args)
21.    {
22.       XMLWriteFrame frame = new XMLWriteFrame();
23.       frame.setDefaultCloseOperation(JFrame.EXIT_ON_CLOSE);
24.       frame.show();
25.    }
26. }
27.
28. /**
```

```
29.    A frame with a panel for showing a modern drawing.
30. */
31. class XMLWriteFrame extends JFrame
32. {
33.    public XMLWriteFrame()
34.    {
35.       setTitle("XMLWriteTest");
36.       setSize(WIDTH, HEIGHT);
37.
38.       // add panel to frame
39.
40.       panel = new RectanglePanel();
41.       Container contentPane = getContentPane();
42.       contentPane.add(panel);
43.
44.       // set up menu bar
45.
46.       JMenuBar menuBar = new JMenuBar();
47.       setJMenuBar(menuBar);
48.
49.       JMenu menu = new JMenu("File");
50.       menuBar.add(menu);
51.
52.       JMenuItem newItem = new JMenuItem("New");
53.       menu.add(newItem);
54.       newItem.addActionListener(new
55.          ActionListener()
56.          {
57.             public void actionPerformed(ActionEvent event)
58.             {
59.                panel.newDrawing();
60.             }
61.          });
62.
63.       JMenuItem saveItem = new JMenuItem("Save");
64.       menu.add(saveItem);
65.       saveItem.addActionListener(new
66.          ActionListener()
67.          {
68.             public void actionPerformed(ActionEvent event)
69.             {
70.                try
71.                {
72.                   saveDocument();
73.                }
74.                catch (TransformerException exception)
75.                {
76.                   JOptionPane.showMessageDialog(
77.                      XMLWriteFrame.this, exception.toString());
78.                }
79.                catch (IOException exception)
80.                {
```

```
81.                    JOptionPane.showMessageDialog(
82.                       XMLWriteFrame.this, exception.toString());
83.                 }
84.              }
85.           });
86.
87.        JMenuItem exitItem = new JMenuItem("Exit");
88.        menu.add(exitItem);
89.        exitItem.addActionListener(new
90.           ActionListener()
91.           {
92.              public void actionPerformed(ActionEvent event)
93.              {
94.                 System.exit(0);
95.              }
96.           });
97.
98.     }
99.
100.    /**
101.       Saves the drawing in SVG format.
102.    */
103.    public void saveDocument()
104.       throws TransformerException, IOException
105.    {
106.       JFileChooser chooser = new JFileChooser();
107.       if (chooser.showSaveDialog(this) != JFileChooser.APPROVE_OPTION)
108.          return;
109.       File f = chooser.getSelectedFile();
110.       Document doc = panel.buildDocument();
111.       Transformer t = TransformerFactory
112.          .newInstance().newTransformer();
113.
114.       t.setOutputProperty("doctype-system",
115. "http://www.w3.org/TR/2000/CR-SVG-20000802/DTD/svg-20000802.dtd"
116.          );
117.       t.setOutputProperty("doctype-public",
118.          "-//W3C//DTD SVG 20000802//EN");
119.
120.       t.transform(new DOMSource(doc),
121.          new StreamResult(new FileOutputStream(f)));
122.    }
123.
124.    public static final int WIDTH = 300;
125.    public static final int HEIGHT = 200;
126.
127.    private RectanglePanel panel;
128. }
129.
130. /**
131.    A panel that shows a set of colored rectangles
132. */
```

```
133. class RectanglePanel extends JPanel
134. {
135.     public RectanglePanel()
136.     {
137.         rects = new ArrayList();
138.         colors = new ArrayList();
139.         generator = new Random();
140.
141.         DocumentBuilderFactory factory
142.             = DocumentBuilderFactory.newInstance();
143.         try
144.         {
145.             builder = factory.newDocumentBuilder();
146.         }
147.         catch (ParserConfigurationException exception)
148.         {
149.             exception.printStackTrace();
150.         }
151.     }
152.
153.     /**
154.         Create a new random drawing.
155.     */
156.     public void newDrawing()
157.     {
158.         int n = 10 + generator.nextInt(20);
159.         rects.clear();
160.         for (int i = 1; i <= n; i++)
161.         {
162.             int x = generator.nextInt(getWidth());
163.             int y = generator.nextInt(getHeight());
164.             int width = generator.nextInt(getWidth() - x);
165.             int height = generator.nextInt(getHeight() - y);
166.             rects.add(new Rectangle(x, y, width, height));
167.             int r = generator.nextInt(256);
168.             int g = generator.nextInt(256);
169.             int b = generator.nextInt(256);
170.             colors.add(new Color(r, g, b));
171.         }
172.         repaint();
173.     }
174.
175.     public void paintComponent(Graphics g)
176.     {
177.         if (rects.size() == 0) newDrawing();
178.         super.paintComponent(g);
179.         Graphics2D g2 = (Graphics2D)g;
180.
181.         // draw all rectangles
182.         for (int i = 0; i < rects.size(); i++)
183.         {
184.             g2.setColor((Color)colors.get(i));
```

```
185.        g2.fill((Rectangle2D)rects.get(i));
186.      }
187.   }
188.
189.   /**
190.      Creates an SVG document of the current drawing.
191.      @return the DOM tree of the SVG document
192.   */
193.   public Document buildDocument()
194.   {
195.
196.      Document doc = builder.newDocument();
197.      Element svgElement = doc.createElement("svg");
198.      doc.appendChild(svgElement);
199.      svgElement.setAttribute("width", "" + getWidth());
200.      svgElement.setAttribute("height", "" + getHeight());
201.
202.      for (int i = 0; i < rects.size(); i++)
203.      {
204.         Color c = (Color)colors.get(i);
205.         Rectangle2D r = (Rectangle2D)rects.get(i);
206.         Element rectElement = doc.createElement("rect");
207.         rectElement.setAttribute("x", "" + r.getX());
208.         rectElement.setAttribute("y", "" + r.getY());
209.         rectElement.setAttribute("width", "" + r.getWidth());
210.         rectElement.setAttribute("height", "" + r.getHeight());
211.         rectElement.setAttribute("fill", colorToString(c));
212.         svgElement.appendChild(rectElement);
213.      }
214.
215.      return doc;
216.   }
217.
218.   /**
219.      Converts a color to a hex value.
220.      @param c a color
221.      @return a string of the form #rrggbb
222.   */
223.   private static String colorToString(Color c)
224.   {
225.      StringBuffer buffer = new StringBuffer();
226.      buffer.append(Integer.toHexString(
227.         c.getRGB() & 0xFFFFFF));
228.      while(buffer.length() < 6) buffer.insert(0, '0');
229.      buffer.insert(0, '#');
230.      return buffer.toString();
231.   }
232.
233.   private ArrayList rects;
234.   private ArrayList colors;
235.   private Random generator;
236.   private DocumentBuilder builder;
237. }
```

1166

`javax.xml.parsers.DocumentBuilder`

- `Document newDocument()`
  returns an empty document.

`org.w3c.dom.Document`

- `Element createElement(String name)`
  returns an element with the given name.

- `Text createTextNode(String data)`
  returns a text node with the given data.

`org.w3c.dom.Node`

- `void appendChild(Node child)`
  appends a node to the list of children of this node.

`org.w3c.dom.Element`

- `void setAttribute(String name, String value)`
  sets the attribute with the given name to the given value.

- `void setAttributeNS(String uri, String qname, String value)`
  sets the attribute with the given namespace URI and qualified name to the given value.

Parameters:	uri	The URI of the namespace, or `null`.
	qname	The qualified name. If it has an alias prefix, then `uri` must not be `null`.
	value	The attribute value.

`javax.xml.transform.TransformerFactory`

- `static Transformer newInstance()`
  returns an instance of the `TransformerFactory` class.

- `Transformer newTransformer()`
  returns an instance of the `Transformer` class that carries out an identity or "do nothing" transformation.

`javax.xml.transform.Transformer`

- `void setOutputProperty(String name, String value)`
  sets an output property. See `http://www.w3.org/TR/xslt#output` for a listing of the standard output properties. The most useful ones are:

Parameter: `doctype-public` the public ID to be used in the DOCTYPE declaration

`doctype-system` the system ID to be used in the DOCTYPE declaration

`indent` yes or no

- `void transform(Source from, Result to)`
  transforms an XML document.

`javax.xml.transform.dom.DOMSource`

- `DOMSource(Node n)`
  constructs a source from the given node. Usually, n is a document node.

`javax.xml.transform.stream.StreamResult`

- `StreamResult(File f)`
- `StreamResult(OutputStream out)`
- `StreamResult(Writer out)`
- `StreamResult(String systemID)`
  construct a stream result from a file, stream, writer, or system ID (usually a relative or absolute URL).

XSL Transformations

As you have seen, the XML format is a very useful interchange format for structured data. However, most XML data is not intended for viewing by end-users. In this section, you will see how to transform XML data into presentation formats such as HTML or plain text.

NOTE: In this section, you will see how to transform XML data into HTML for presentation in a browser. An alternate approach is to display XML files directly in a browser. For example, Internet Explorer shows XML documents as trees. More importantly, the latest versions of Netscape, Internet Explorer, and Opera let you specify a cascading style sheet (CSS) with an XML document. With a style sheet, you can control how you want the browser to display the contents of XML elements. You can find the style sheet specification at `http://www.w3c.org/TR/REC-CSS2`. The article "XML and CSS: Structured Markup with Display Semantics" by Pankaj Kamthan (`http://tech.irt.org/articles/js198`) contains a nice discussion of the pros and cons of using CSS with XML.

The purpose of a style sheet with transformation templates is to describe the conversion of XML documents into some other format (see Figure 12–7).

Here is a typical example. We want to transform XML files with employee records into HTML documents. Consider this input file.

```
<staff>
   <employee>
      <name>Carl Cracker</name>
      <salary>75000</salary>
      <hiredate year="1987" month="12" day="15"/>
   </employee>
   <employee>
      <name>Harry Hacker</name>
      <salary>50000</salary>
      <hiredate year="1989" month="10" day="1"/>
   </employee>
   <employee>
      <name>Tony Tester</name>
      <salary>40000</salary>
      <hiredate year="1990" month="3" day="15"/>
   </employee>
</staff>
```

The desired output is an HTML table:

```
<table border="1">
<tr>
<td>Carl Cracker</td><td>$75000.0</td><td>1987-12-15</td>
</tr>
<tr>
<td>Harry Hacker</td><td>$50000.0</td><td>1989-10-1</td>
</tr>
<tr>
<td>Tony Tester</td><td>$40000.0</td><td>1990-3-15</td>
</tr>
</table>
```

This table can be included in a larger HTML document, for example a Java Server Page.

Figure 12–7: Applying XSL Transformations

The XSLT specification is quite complex, and entire books have been written on the subject. We can't possibly discuss all the features of XSLT, so we will only work through a representative example. You can find more information in the book *Essential XML* by Don Box, et al. The XSL specification is available at `http://www.w3.org/TR/xslt`.

A style sheet with transformation templates has this form:

```
<?xml version="1.0" encoding="ISO-8859-1"?>
<xsl:stylesheet
    xmlns:xsl="http://www.w3.org/1999/XSL/Transform"
    version="1.0">
    <xsl:output method="html"/>
    . . .
    templates
    . . .
</xsl:stylesheet>
```

In our example, the `xsl:output` element specifies the method as HTML. Other valid method settings are `xml` and `text`.

Here is a typical template:

```
<xsl:template match="/staff/employee">
    <tr><xsl:apply-templates/></tr>
</xsl:template>
```

The value of the `match` attribute is an *XPath* expression. XPath is yet another XML standard. An XPath describes a set of nodes in an XML document. For example, the XPath

```
/staff/employee
```

describes all `employee` elements that are children of the `staff` root element. The XPath

```
/staff/employee/hiredate/@year
```

describes all `year` attribute nodes of `hiredate` elements within `employee` elements that are children of the `staff` root node. The @ sign denotes an attribute.

The XPath

```
/staff/employee/name/text()
```

describes all text nodes that are children of `name` elements within `employee` elements that are children of the `staff` root node. The `()` denote a function—besides `text()`, there are a number of other functions that can be used inside XPath expressions.

There are many more elaborate XPath expressions—see *Essential XML* by Don Box or the specification at `http://www.w3c.org/TR/xpath`.

Let us now return to the example template. It states: Whenever you see a node in the XPath set `/staff/employee`, do the following:

- Emit the string `<tr>`.
- Keep applying templates as you process its children.
- Emit the string `</tr>` after you are done with all children.

In other words, this template generates the HTML table row markers around every employee record.

The XSLT processor starts processing by examining the root element. Whenever a node matches one of the templates, then it applies the template. (If multiple templates match, the best-matching one is used—see the specification for the gory details.) If no template matches, the processor carries out a default action. For text nodes, the default is to include the contents in the output. For elements, the default action is to create no output but to keep processing the children.

Here is a template for transforming `name` nodes in an employee file:

```
<xsl:template match="/staff/employee/name">
   <td><xsl:apply-templates/></td>
</xsl:template>
```

As you can see, the template produces the `<td>...</td>` delimiters, and it asks the processor to recursively visit the children of the `name` element. There is just one child, the text node. When the processor visits that node, it emits the text contents (provided, of course, that there is no other matching template).

You have to work a little harder if you want to copy attribute values into the output. Here is an example:

```
<xsl:template match="/staff/employee/hiredate">
   <td><xsl:value-of select="@year"/>-<xsl:value-of
   select="@month"/>-<xsl:value-of select="@day"/></td>
</xsl:template>
```

When processing a `hiredate` node, this template emits

- The string `<td>`
- The value of the `year` attribute
- A hyphen
- The value of the `month` attribute
- A hyphen
- The value of the `day` attribute
- A hyphen
- The string `</td>`

The `xsl:value-of` statement computes the string value of a node set. The node set is specified by the XPath value of the `select` attribute. In this case, the path is relative to the currently processed node. The node set is converted to a string by concatenating the string values of all nodes. The string value of an attribute node is its value. The string value of a text node is its contents. The string value of an element node is the concatenation of the string values of its child nodes (but not its attributes).

Example 12–9 contains all transformation templates to turn an XML file with employee records into an XML table.

Example 12–10 shows a different set of transformations. The input is the same XML file, and the output is plain text in the familiar property file format:

```
employee.1.name=Carl Cracker
employee.1.salary=75000.0
employee.1.hiredate=1987-12-15
employee.2.name=Harry Hacker
employee.2.salary=50000.0
employee.2.hiredate=1989-10-1
employee.3.name=Tony Tester
employee.3.salary=40000.0
employee.3.hiredate=1990-3-15
```

That example uses the position() function which yields the position of the current node, as seen from its parent. We get an entirely different output, simply by switching the style sheet. Thus, you can safely use XML to describe your data, even if some applications need the data in another format. Just use XSLT to generate the alternative format.

It is extremely simple to generate XSL transformations in Java. Set up a transformer factory for each style sheet. Then get a transformer object, and tell it to transform a source to a result.

```
File styleSheet = new File(filename);
StreamSource styleSource = new StreamSource(styleSheet);
Transformer t = TransformerFactory
    .newInstance().newTransformer(styleSource);
t.transform(source, result);
```

The parameters of the transform method are objects of classes that implement the Source and Result interfaces. There are three implementations of the Source interface:

```
DOMSource
SAXSource
StreamSource
```

You can construct a StreamSource from a file, stream, reader, or URL, and a DOMSource from the node of a DOM tree. For example, in the preceding section, we invoked the identity transformation as

```
t.transform(new DOMSource(doc), result);
```

In our example program, we will do something slightly more interesting. Rather than starting out with an existing XML file, we will produce a SAX XML reader that gives the illusion of parsing an XML file, by emitting appropriate SAX events. Actually, the XML reader reads a flat file, as described in Chapter 12 of Volume 1. The input file looks like this:

```
Carl Cracker|75000.0|1987|12|15
Harry Hacker|50000.0|1989|10|1
Tony Tester|40000.0|1990|3|15
```

The XML reader generates SAX events as it processes the input. Here is a part of the `parse` method of the `EmployeeReader` class that implements the `XMLReader` interface.

```
AttributesImpl attributes = new AttributesImpl();
handler.startDocument();
handler.startElement("", "staff", "staff", attributes);
while ((line = in.readLine()) != null)
{
    handler.startElement("", "employee", "employee", attributes);
    StringTokenizer t = new StringTokenizer(line, "|");
    handler.startElement("", "name", "name", attributes);
    String s = t.nextToken();
    handler.characters(s.toCharArray(), 0, s.length());
    handler.endElement("", "name", "name");
    . . .
    handler.endElement("", "employee", "employee");
}
handler.endElement("", rootElement, rootElement);
handler.endDocument();
```

The `SAXSource` for the transformer is constructed from the XML reader:

```
t.transform(new SAXSource(new EmployeeReader(),
    new InputSource(new FileInputStream(filename))), result);
```

This is an ingenious trick to convert non-XML legacy data into XML. Of course, most XSLT applications will already have XML input data, and you can simply invoke the `transform` method on a `StreamSource`, like this:

```
t.transform(new StreamSource(file), result);
```

The transformation result is an object of a class that implements the `Result` interface. The Java library supplies three classes:

```
DOMResult
SAXResult
StreamResult
```

To store the result in a DOM tree, use a `DocumentBuilder` to generate a new document node and wrap it into a `DOMResult`:

```
Document doc = builder.newDocument();
t.transform(source, new DOMResult(doc));
```

To save the output in a file, use a `StreamResult`:

```
t.transform(source, new StreamResult(file));
```

Example 12–8 contains the complete source code. Examples 12–9 and 12–10 contain two style sheets. This example concludes our discussion of the XML support in the Java library. We hope you now have a good perspective of the major strengths of XML, in particular automated parsing and validation, and a powerful transformation mechanism. Of course, all this technology is only going to work for you if you design your XML formats well. You need to make sure that the formats are rich enough to express all your business needs, that they are stable over time, and that your business partners are willing to accept your XML documents. Those issues can be far more challenging than dealing with parsers, DTDs or transformations.

Example 12–8: TransformTest.java

```
1. import java.io.*;
2. import java.util.*;
3. import javax.xml.parsers.*;
4. import javax.xml.transform.*;
5. import javax.xml.transform.dom.*;
6. import javax.xml.transform.sax.*;
7. import javax.xml.transform.stream.*;
8. import org.xml.sax.*;
9. import org.xml.sax.helpers.*;
10.
11. /**
12.    This program demonstrates XSL transformations. It applies
13.    a transformation to a set of employee records. The records
14.    are stored in the file employee.dat and turned into XML
15.    format. Specify the stylesheet on the command line, e.g.
16.    java TransformTest makeprop.xsl
17. */
18. public class TransformTest
19. {
20.    public static void main(String[] args) throws Exception
21.    {
22.       String filename;
23.       if (args.length > 0) filename = args[0];
24.       else filename = "makehtml.xsl";
25.       File styleSheet = new File(filename);
26.       StreamSource styleSource = new StreamSource(styleSheet);
27.
28.       Transformer t = TransformerFactory
29.          .newInstance().newTransformer(styleSource);
30.       t.transform(new SAXSource(new EmployeeReader(),
31.          new InputSource(new FileInputStream("employee.dat"))),
32.          new StreamResult(System.out));
33.    }
```

```
34. }
35.
36. /**
37.    This class reads the flat file employee.dat and reports SAX
38.    parser events to act as if it was parsing an XML file.
39. */
40. class EmployeeReader implements XMLReader
41. {
42.    public void parse(InputSource source)
43.       throws IOException, SAXException
44.    {
45.       InputStream stream = source.getByteStream();1
46.       BufferedReader in = new BufferedReader(
47.          new InputStreamReader(stream));
48.       String rootElement = "staff";
49.       AttributesImpl atts = new AttributesImpl();
50.
51.       if (handler == null)
52.          throw new SAXException("No content handler");
53.
54.       handler.startDocument();
55.     handler.startElement("", rootElement, rootElement, atts);
56.       String line;
57.       while ((line = in.readLine()) != null)
58.       {
59.       handler.startElement("", "employee", "employee", atts);
60.          StringTokenizer t = new StringTokenizer(line, "|");
61.
62.          handler.startElement("", "name", "name", atts);
63.          String s = t.nextToken();
64.          handler.characters(s.toCharArray(), 0, s.length());
65.          handler.endElement("", "name", "name");
66.
67.          handler.startElement("", "salary", "salary", atts);
68.          s = t.nextToken();
69.          handler.characters(s.toCharArray(), 0, s.length());
70.          handler.endElement("", "salary", "salary");
71.
72.          atts.addAttribute("", "year", "year", "CDATA",
73.             t.nextToken());
74.          atts.addAttribute("", "month", "month", "CDATA",
75.             t.nextToken());
76.          atts.addAttribute("", "day", "day", "CDATA",
77.             t.nextToken());
78.          handler.startElement("", "hiredate", "hiredate", atts);
79.          handler.endElement("", "hiredate", "hiredate");
80.          atts.clear();
81.
82.          handler.endElement("", "employee", "employee");
83.       }
84.
85.       handler.endElement("", rootElement, rootElement);
```

```
86.       handler.endDocument();
87.   }
88.
89.   public void setContentHandler(ContentHandler aHandler)
90.   {
91.       handler = aHandler;
92.   }
93.
94.   public ContentHandler getContentHandler()
95.   {
96.       return handler;
97.   }
98.
99.   // the following methods are just do-nothing implementations
100.   public void parse(String systemId)
101.       throws IOException, SAXException {}
102.   public void setErrorHandler(ErrorHandler handler) {}
103.   public ErrorHandler getErrorHandler() { return null; }
104.   public void setDTDHandler(DTDHandler handler) {}
105.   public DTDHandler getDTDHandler() { return null; }
106.   public void setEntityResolver(EntityResolver resolver) {}
107.   public EntityResolver getEntityResolver() { return null; }
108.   public void setProperty(String name, Object value) {}
109.   public Object getProperty(String name) { return null; }
110.   public void setFeature(String name, boolean value) {}
111.   public boolean getFeature(String name) { return false; }
112.
113.   private ContentHandler handler;
114. }
```

Example 12–9: makehtml.xsl

```
1. <?xml version="1.0" encoding="ISO-8859-1"?>
2.
3. <xsl:stylesheet
4.   xmlns:xsl="http://www.w3.org/1999/XSL/Transform"
5.   version="1.0">
6.
7.   <xsl:output method="html"/>
8.
9.   <xsl:template match="/staff">
10.       <table border="1"><xsl:apply-templates/></table>
11.   </xsl:template>
12.
13.   <xsl:template match="/staff/employee">
14.       <tr><xsl:apply-templates/></tr>
15.   </xsl:template>
16.
17.   <xsl:template match="/staff/employee/name">
18.       <td><xsl:apply-templates/></td>
19.   </xsl:template>
```

```
20.
21.    <xsl:template match="/staff/employee/salary">
22.        <td>$<xsl:apply-templates/></td>
23.    </xsl:template>
24.
25.    <xsl:template match="/staff/employee/hiredate">
26.        <td><xsl:value-of select="@year"/>-<xsl:value-of
27.        select="@month"/>-<xsl:value-of select="@day"/></td>
28.    </xsl:template>
29.
30. </xsl:stylesheet>
```

Example 12–10: makeprop.xsl

```
1. <?xml version="1.0"?>
2.
3. <xsl:stylesheet
4.    xmlns:xsl="http://www.w3.org/1999/XSL/Transform"
5.    version="1.0">
6.
7.    <xsl:output method="text"/>
8.
9.    <xsl:template match="/staff/employee">
10. employee.<xsl:value-of select="position()"/>.name=<xsl:value-of
    select="name/text()"/>
11. employee.<xsl:value-of select="position()"/>.salary=<xsl:value-
    of select="salary/text()"/>
12. employee.<xsl:value-of select="position()"/>.hire
    date=<xsl:value-of select="hiredate/@year"/>-<xsl:value-of
    select="hiredate/@month"/>-<xsl:value-of select="hiredate/@day"/>
13.    </xsl:template>
14.
15. </xsl:stylesheet>
```

javax.xml.transform.TransformerFactory

- Transformer newTransformer(Source from)
  returns an instance of the Transformer class that reads a style sheet from
  the given source.

javax.xml.transform.stream.StreamSource

- StreamSource(File f)
- StreamSource(InputStream in)
- StreamSource(Reader in)
- StreamSource(String systemID)
  construct a stream source from a file, stream, reader, or system ID (usually a
  relative or absolute URL).

`javax.xml.transform.sax.SAXSource`

- SAXSource(XMLReader reader, InputSource source)

  constructs a SAX source that obtains data from the given input source and uses the given reader to parse the input.

`org.xml.sax.XMLReader`

- void setContentHandler(ContentHandler handler)

  sets the handler that is notified of parse events as the input is parsed.

- void parse(InputSource source)

  parses the input from the given input source and sends parse events to the content handler.

`javax.xml.transform.dom.DOMResult`

- DOMResult(Node n)

  constructs a source from the given node. Usually, n is a new document node.

`org.xml.sax.helpers.AttributesImpl`

- void addAttribute(String uri, String lname, String qname, String type, String value)

  adds an attribute to this attribute collection.

Parameters:	uri	the URI of the namespace
	lname	the local name without alias prefix
	qname	the qualified name with alias prefix
	type	the type, one of "CDATA", "ID", "IDREF", "IDREFS", "NMTOKEN", "NMTOKENS", "ENTITY", "ENTITIES", or "NOTATION"
	value	the attribute value

- void clear()

  removes all attributes from this attribute collection.

Index

Sun Microsystems, Inc.
Binary Code License Agreement

READ THE TERMS OF THIS AGREEMENT AND ANY PROVIDED SUPPLEMENTAL LICENSE TERMS (COLLECTIVELY "AGREEMENT") CAREFULLY BEFORE OPENING THE SOFTWARE MEDIA PACKAGE. BY OPENING THE SOFTWARE MEDIA PACKAGE, YOU AGREE TO THE TERMS OF THIS AGREEMENT. IF YOU ARE ACCESSING THE SOFTWARE ELECTRONICALLY, INDICATE YOUR ACCEPTANCE OF THESE TERMS BY SELECTING THE "ACCEPT" BUTTON AT THE END OF THIS AGREEMENT. IF YOU DO NOT AGREE TO ALL THESE TERMS, PROMPTLY RETURN THE UNUSED SOFTWARE TO YOUR PLACE OF PURCHASE FOR A REFUND OR, IF THE SOFTWARE IS ACCESSED ELECTRONICALLY, SELECT THE "DECLINE" BUTTON AT THE END OF THIS AGREEMENT.

1. **LICENSE TO USE.** Sun grants you a non-exclusive and non-transferable license for the internal use only of the accompanying software and documentation and any error corrections provided by Sun (collectively "Software"), by the number of users and the class of computer hardware for which the corresponding fee has been paid.

2. **RESTRICTIONS** Software is confidential and copyrighted. Title to Software and all associated intellectual property rights is retained by Sun and/or its licensors. Except as specifically authorized in any Supplemental License Terms, you may not make copies of Software, other than a single copy of Software for archival purposes. Unless enforcement is prohibited by applicable law, you may not modify, decompile, or reverse engineer Software. You acknowledge that Software is not designed, licensed or intended for use in the design, construction, operation or maintenance of any nuclear facility. Sun disclaims any express or implied warranty of fitness for such uses. No right, title or interest in or to any trademark, service mark, logo or trade name of Sun or its licensors is granted under this Agreement.

3. **LIMITED WARRANTY.** Sun warrants to you that for a period of ninety (90) days from the date of purchase, as evidenced by a copy of the receipt, the media on which Software is furnished (if any and if provided by Sun) will be free of defects in materials and workmanship under normal use. Except for the foregoing, Software is provided "AS IS". Your exclusive remedy and Sun's entire liability under this limited warranty will be at Sun's option to replace Software media or refund the fee paid for Software, if any.

4. **DISCLAIMER OF WARRANTY.** UNLESS SPECIFIED IN THIS AGREEMENT, ALL EXPRESS OR IMPLIED CONDITIONS, REPRESENTATIONS AND WARRANTIES, INCLUDING ANY IMPLIED WARRANTY OF MERCHANTABILITY, FITNESS FOR A PARTICULAR PURPOSE OR NON-INFRINGEMENT ARE DISCLAIMED, EXCEPT TO THE EXTENT THAT THESE DISCLAIMERS ARE HELD TO BE LEGALLY INVALID.

5. **LIMITATION OF LIABILITY.** TO THE EXTENT NOT PROHIBITED BY LAW, IN NO EVENT WILL SUN OR ITS LICENSORS BE LIABLE FOR ANY LOST REVENUE, PROFIT OR DATA, OR FOR SPECIAL, INDIRECT, CONSEQUENTIAL, INCIDENTAL OR PUNITIVE DAMAGES, HOWEVER CAUSED REGARDLESS OF THE THEORY OF LIABILITY, ARISING OUT OF OR RELATED TO THE USE OF OR INABILITY TO USE SOFTWARE, EVEN IF SUN HAS BEEN ADVISED OF THE POSSIBILITY OF SUCH DAMAGES. In no event will Sun's liability to you, whether in contract, tort (including negligence), or otherwise, exceed the amount paid by you for Software under this Agreement. The foregoing limitations will apply even if the above stated warranty fails of its essential purpose.

6. **Termination.** This Agreement is effective until terminated. You may terminate this Agreement at any time by destroying all copies of Software. This Agreement will terminate immediately without notice from Sun if you fail to comply with any provision of this Agreement. Upon Termination, you must destroy all copies of Software.

7. **Export Regulations.** All Software and technical data delivered under this Agreement are subject to US export control laws and may be subject to export or import regulations in other countries. You agree to comply strictly with all such laws and regulations and acknowledge that you have the responsibility to obtain such licenses to export, re-export, or import as may be required after delivery to you.

8. **U.S. Government Restricted Rights.** If Software is being acquired by or on behalf of the U.S. Government or by a U.S. Government prime contractor or subcontractor (at any tier), then the Govern-

ment's rights in Software and accompanying documentation will be only as set forth in this Agreement; this is in accordance with 48 CFR 227.7201 through 227.7202-4 (for Department of Defense (DOD) acquisitions) and with 48 CFR 2.101 and 12.212 (for non-DOD acquisitions).

9. **Governing Law.** Any action related to this Agreement will be governed by California law and controlling U.S. federal law. No choice of law rules of any jurisdiction will apply.

10. **Severability.** If any provision of this Agreement is held to be unenforceable, this Agreement will remain in effect with the provision omitted, unless omission would frustrate the intent of the parties, in which case this Agreement will immediately terminate.

11. **Integration.** This Agreement is the entire agreement between you and Sun relating to its subject matter. It supersedes all prior or contemporaneous oral or written communications, proposals, representations and warranties and prevails over any conflicting or additional terms of any quote, order, acknowledgment, or other communication between the parties relating to its subject matter during the term of this Agreement. No modification of this Agreement will be binding, unless in writing and signed by an authorized representative of each party.

For inquiries please contact: Sun Microsystems, Inc. 901 San Antonio Road, Palo Alto, California 94303

JAVA™ 2 SOFTWARE DEVELOPMENT KIT STANDARD EDITION VERSION 1.3 SUPPLEMENTAL LICENSE TERMS

These supplemental license terms ("Supplemental Terms") add to or modify the terms of the Binary Code License Agreement (collectively, the "Agreement"). Capitalized terms not defined in these Supplemental Terms shall have the same meanings ascribed to them in the Agreement. These Supplemental Terms shall supersede any inconsistent or conflicting terms in the Agreement, or in any license contained within the Software.

1 **Internal Use and Development License Grant.** Subject to the terms and conditions of this Agreement, including, but not limited to, Section 2 (Redistributables) and Section 4 (Java Technology Restrictions) of these Supplemental Terms, Sun grants you a non-exclusive, non-transferable, limited license to reproduce the Software for internal use only for the sole purpose of development of your Java™ applet and application ("Program"), provided that you do not redistribute the Software in whole or in part, either separately or included with any Program.

2. **Redistributables.** In addition to the license granted in Paragraph 1 above, Sun grants you a non-exclusive, non-transferable, limited license to reproduce and distribute, only as part of your separate copy of JAVA^(TM) 2 RUNTIME ENVIRONMENT STANDARD EDITION VERSION 1.3 software, those files specifically identified as redistributable in the JAVA^(TM) 2 RUNTIME ENVIRONMENT STANDARD EDITION VERSION 1.3 "README" file (the "Redistributables") provided that: (a) you distribute the Redistributables complete and unmodified (unless otherwise specified in the applicable README file), and only bundled as part of the Java™ applets and applications that you develop (the "Programs:"); (b) you do not distribute additional software intended to supersede any component(s) of the Redistributables; (c) you do not remove or alter any proprietary legends or notices contained in or on the Redistributables; (d) you only distribute the Redistributables pursuant to a license agreement that protects Sun's interests consistent with the terms contained in the Agreement, and (e) you agree to defend and indemnify Sun and its licensors from and against any damages, costs, liabilities, settlement amounts and/or expenses (including attorneys' fees) incurred in connection with any claim, lawsuit or action by any third party that arises or results from the use or distribution of any and all Programs and/or Software.

3. **Separate Distribution License Required.** You understand and agree that you must first obtain a separate license from Sun prior to reproducing or modifying any portion of the Software other than as provided with respect to Redistributables in Paragraph 2 above.

4. **Java Technology Restrictions.** You may not modify the Java Platform Interface ("JPI", identified as classes contained within the "java" package or any subpackages of the "java" package), by creating additional classes within the JPI or otherwise causing the addition to or modification of the classes in the JPI. In the event that you create an additional class and associated API(s) which (i) extends the func-

tionality of a Java environment, and (ii) is exposed to third party software developers for the purpose of developing additional software which invokes such additional API, you must promptly publish broadly an accurate specification for such API for free use by all developers. You may not create, or authorize your licensees to create additional classes, interfaces, or subpackages that are in any way identified as "java", "javax", "sun" or similar convention as specified by Sun in any class file naming convention. Refer to the appropriate version of the Java Runtime Environment binary code license (currently located at `http://www.java.sun.com/jdk/index.html`) for the availability of runtime code which may be distributed with Java applets and applications.

5. **Trademarks and Logos.** You acknowledge and agree as between you and Sun that Sun owns the Java trademark and all Java-related trademarks, service marks, logos and other
brand designations including the Coffee Cup logo and Duke logo ("Java Marks"), and you agree to comply with the Sun Trademark and Logo Usage Requirements currently located at `http://www.sun.com/policies/trademarks`. Any use you make of the Java Marks inures to Sun's benefit.

6. **Source Code.** Software may contain source code that is provided solely for reference purposes pursuant to the terms of this Agreement.

7. **Termination.** Sun may terminate this Agreement immediately should any Software become, or in Sun's opinion be likely to become, the subject of a claim of infringement of a patent, trade secret, copyright or other intellectual property right.

LICENSE AGREEMENT: FORTE FOR JAVA, RELEASE 2.0, COMMUNITY EDITION FOR ALL PLATFORMS

To obtain Forte for Java, release 2.0, Community Edition for All Platforms, you must agree to the software license below.

Sun Microsystems Inc., Binary Code License Agreement
READ THE TERMS OF THIS AGREEMENT AND ANY PROVIDED SUPPLEMENTAL LICENSE TERMS (COLLECTIVELY "AGREEMENT") CAREFULLY BEFORE OPENING THE SOFTWARE MEDIA PACKAGE. BY OPENING THE SOFTWARE MEDIA PACKAGE, YOU AGREE TO THE TERMS OF THIS AGREEMENT. IF YOU ARE ACCESSING THE SOFTWARE ELECTRONICALLY, INDICATE YOUR ACCEPTANCE OF THESE TERMS BY SELECTING THE "ACCEPT"" BUTTON AT THE END OF THIS AGREEMENT. IF YOU DO NOT AGREE TO ALL THESE TERMS, PROMPTLY RETURN THE UNUSED SOFTWARE TO YOUR PLACE OF PURCHASE FOR A REFUND OR, IF THE SOFTWARE IS ACCESSED ELECTRONICALLY, SELECT THE "DECLINE" BUTTON AT THE END OF THIS AGREEMENT.

1. **LICENSE TO USE.** Sun grants you a non-exclusive and non-transferable license for the internal use only of the accompanying software and documentation and any error corrections provided by Sun (collectively "Software"), by the number of users and the class of computer hardware for which the corresponding fee has been paid.

2. **RESTRICTIONS.** Software is confidential and copyrighted. Title to Software and all associated intellectual property rights is retained by Sun and/or its licensors. Except as specifically authorized in any Supplemental License Terms, you may not make copies of Software, other than a single copy of Software for archival purposes. Unless enforcement is prohibited by applicable law, you may not modify, decompile, or reverse engineer Software. You acknowledge that Software is not designed, licensed or intended for use in the design, construction, operation or maintenance of any nuclear facility. Sun disclaims any express or implied warranty of fitness for such uses. No right, title or interest in or to any trademark, service mark, logo or trade name of Sun or its licensors is granted under this Agreement.

3. **LIMITED WARRANTY.** Sun warrants to you that for a period of ninety (90) days from the date of purchase, as evidenced by a copy of the receipt, the media on which Software is furnished (if any) will be free of defects in materials and workmanship under normal use. Except for the foregoing, Software is provided "AS IS". Your exclusive remedy and Sun's entire liability under this limited warranty will be at Sun's option to replace Software media or refund the fee paid for Software.

4.   **DISCLAIMER OF WARRANTY.** UNLESS SPECIFIED IN THIS AGREEMENT, ALL EXPRESS OR IMPLIED CONDITIONS, REPRESENTATIONS AND WARRANTIES, INCLUDING ANY IMPLIED WARRANTY OF MERCHANTABILITY, FITNESS FOR A PARTICULAR PURPOSE OR NON-INFRINGEMENT ARE DISCLAIMED, EXCEPT TO THE EXTENT THAT THESE DISCLAIMERS ARE HELD TO BE LEGALLY INVALID.

5.   **LIMITATION OF LIABILITY.** TO THE EXTENT NOT PROHIBITED BY LAW, IN NO EVENT WILL SUN OR ITS LICENSORS BE LIABLE FOR ANY LOST REVENUE, PROFIT OR DATA, OR FOR SPECIAL, INDIRECT, CONSEQUENTIAL, INCIDENTAL OR PUNITIVE DAMAGES, HOWEVER CAUSED REGARDLESS OF THE THEORY OF LIABILITY, ARISING OUT OF OR RELATED TO THE USE OF OR INABILITY TO USE SOFTWARE, EVEN IF SUN HAS BEEN ADVISED OF THE POSSIBILITY OF SUCH DAMAGES. In no event will Sun's liability to you, whether in contract, tort (including negligence), or otherwise, exceed the amount paid by you for Software under this Agreement. The foregoing limitations will apply even if the above stated warranty fails of its essential purpose.

6.   **Termination.** This Agreement is effective until terminated. You may terminate this Agreement at any time by destroying all copies of Software. This Agreement will terminate immediately without notice from Sun if you fail to comply with any provision of this Agreement. Upon Termination, you must destroy all copies of Software.

7.   **Export Regulations.** All Software and technical data delivered under this Agreement are subject to US export control laws and may be subject to export or import regulations in other countries. You agree to comply strictly with all such laws and regulations and acknowledge that you have the responsibility to obtain such licenses to export, re-export, or import as may be required after delivery to you.

8.   **U.S. Government Restricted Rights.** If Software is being acquired by or on behalf of the U.S. Government or by a U.S. Government prime contractor or subcontractor (at any tier), then the Government's rights in Software and accompanying documentation will be only as set forth in this Agreement; this is in accordance with 48 CFR 227.7201 through 227.7202-4 (for Department of Defense (DOD) acquisitions) and with 48 CFR 2.101 and 12.212 (for non-DOD acquisitions).

9.   **Governing Law.** Any action related to this Agreement will be governed by California law and controlling U.S. federal law. No choice of law rules of any jurisdiction will apply.

10. Severability. If any provision of this Agreement is held to be unenforceable, this Agreement will remain in effect with the provision omitted, unless omission would frustrate the intent of the parties, in which case this Agreement will immediately terminate.

11. Integration. This Agreement is the entire agreement between you and Sun relating to its subject matter. It supersedes all prior or contemporaneous oral or written communications, proposals, representations and warranties and prevails over any conflicting or additional terms of any quote, order, acknowledgment, or other communication between the parties relating to its subject matter during the term of this Agreement. No modification of this Agreement will be binding, unless in writing and signed by an authorized representative of each party.

JAVA(TM) DEVELOPMENT TOOLS FORTE(TM) FOR JAVA(TM), RELEASE 2.0, COMMUNITY EDITION SUPPLEMENTAL LICENSE TERMS

These supplemental license terms ("Supplemental Terms") add to or modify the terms of the Binary Code License Agreement (collectively, the "Agreement"). Capitalized terms not defined in these Supplemental Terms shall have the same meanings ascribed to them in the Agreement. These Supplemental Terms shall supersede any inconsistent or conflicting terms in the Agreement, or in any license contained within the Software.

1.   **Software Internal Use and Development License Grant.** Subject to the terms and conditions of this Agreement, including, but not limited to Section 3 (Java(TM) Technology Restrictions) of these Supplemental Terms, Sun grants you a non-exclusive, non-transferable, limited license to reproduce internally and use internally the binary form of the Software complete and unmodified for the sole purpose of designing, developing and testing your [Java applets and] applications intended to run on the Java platform ("Programs").

2.   **License to Distribute Redistributables.** In addition to the license granted in Section 1 (Redistributables Internal Use and Development License Grant) of these Supplemental Terms, subject to the terms and conditions of this Agreement, including but not limited to Section 3 (Java Technology Restrictions) of these Supplemental Terms, Sun grants you a non-exclusive, non-transferable, limited license to reproduce and distribute those files specifically identified as redistributable in the Software "README" file ("Redistributables") provided that: (i) you distribute the Redistributables complete and unmodified (unless otherwise specified in the applicable README file), and only bundled as part of your Programs, (ii) you do not distribute additional software intended to supersede any component(s) of the Redistributables, (iii) you do not remove or alter any proprietary legends or notices contained in or on the Redistributables, (iv) for a particular version of the Java platform, any executable output generated by a compiler that is contained in the Software must (a) only be compiled from source code that conforms to the corresponding version of the OEM Java Language Specification; (b) be in the class file format defined by the corresponding version of the OEM Java Virtual Machine Specification; and (c) execute properly on a reference runtime, as specified by Sun, associated with such version of the Java platform, (v) you only distribute the Redistributables pursuant to a license agreement that protects Sun's interests consistent with the terms contained in the Agreement, and (vi) you agree to defend and indemnify Sun and its licensors from and against any damages, costs, liabilities, settlement amounts and/or expenses (including attorneys' fees) incurred in connection with any claim, lawsuit or action by any third party that arises or results from the use or distribution of any and all Programs and/or Software.

3.   **Java Technology Restrictions.** You may not modify the Java Platform Interface ("JPI", identified as classes contained within the "java" package or any subpackages of the "java" package), by creating additional classes within the JPI or otherwise causing the addition to or modification of the classes in the JPI. In the event that you create an additional class and associated API(s) which (i) extends the functionality of the Java platform, and (ii) is exposed to third party software developers for the purpose of developing additional software which invokes such additional API, you must promptly publish broadly an accurate specification for such API for free use by all developers. You may not create, or authorize your licensees to create, additional classes, interfaces, or subpackages that are in any way identified as "java", "javax", "sun" or similar convention as specified by Sun in any naming convention designation.

4.   **Java Runtime Availability.** Refer to the appropriate version of the Java Runtime Environment binary code license (currently located at `http://www.java.sun.com/jdk/index.html`) for the availability of runtime code which may be distributed with Java applets and applications.

5.   **Trademarks and Logos.** You acknowledge and agree as between you and Sun that Sun owns the SUN, SOLARIS, JAVA, JINI, FORTE, STAROFFICE, STARPORTAL and iPLANET trademarks and all SUN, SOLARIS, JAVA, JINI, FORTE, STAROFFICE, STARPORTAL and iPLANET-related trademarks, service marks, logos and other brand designations ("Sun Marks"), and you agree to comply with the Sun Trademark and Logo Usage Requirements currently located at `http://www.sun.com/policies/trademarks`. Any use you make of the Sun Marks inures to Sun's benefit.

6.   **Source Code.** Software may contain source code that is provided solely for reference purposes pursuant to the terms of this Agreement. Source code may not be redistributed unless expressly provided for in this Agreement.

7.   **Termination for Infringement.** Either party may terminate this Agreement immediately should any Software become, or in either party's opinion be likely to become, the subject of a claim of infringement of any intellectual property right.

For inquiries please contact: Sun Microsystems, Inc. 901 San Antonio Road, Palo Alto, California 94303

- Change to that directory.
- Execute the command
  ```
  jar xvf corejava.zip
  ```

Updates and Bug Fixes

The CD-ROM contains well over a hundred sample programs, and some of them are bound to have minor glitches and inconsistencies. We keep a list of frequently asked questions, a list of typographical errors, and bug fixes on the Core Java Web page at `http://www.horstmann.com/corejava.html`. We very much welcome any reports of typographical errors, example program bugs, and suggestions for improvement.

Before contacting us, please consider the following:

1. Please check the FAQ and list of bug reports on the Core Java Web page before mailing us. We get many duplicate queries and bug reports.

2. Please, no requests for handholding. Many readers have successfully compiled and executed the programs on the CD-ROM. If you have problems, there is an overwhelming likelihood that the problem is on your end, not because of a flaw with the CD-ROM contents. On the other hand, if we goofed and there is a serious problem with the CD-ROM, then there is an overwhelming chance that hundreds of readers complained to us already and that you will find a resolution on the FAQ.

3. We want to support and improve the Core Java book and example files, but we cannot help you with problems with your development environment or the free programs on the CD-ROM. Please contact the product vendor for assistance in those cases.

4. Finally, when contacting us, please use e-mail only. Please don't be disappointed if we don't answer every query or if we don't get back to you immediately. We do read all e-mail and consider your input to make future editions of this book clearer and more informative.

About the CD-ROM

Use of this software is subject to the Sun Microsystems, Inc. Binary Code License Agreement contained on page 1200 of the accompanying book. Read this agreement carefully. By opening this package, you are agreeing to be bound by the terms and conditions of this agreement.

Contents of the CD-ROM

The `corejava` directory contains the example files for this volume of Core Java. The `forte` directory contains Forte™ for Java Community Edition (Release 2.0) for Windows, Solaris, and Linux. The `jdk` directory contains the Java™2 SDK Standard Edition, v. 1.3, for Windows, Solaris, and Linux.

NOTE: If you do not have a CD-ROM drive, you can download these files from:

```
Core Java files      www.phptr.com/corejava
Java 2 SDK           java.sun.com/j2se/1.3/
Forte for Java       www.sun.com/forte/ffj/ce/
```

TIP: Sun Microsystems frequently releases updates to the Java 2 SDK. You should check the Java Web site `http://java.sun.com/j2se/` to see whether a newer version is available. In that case, we recommend that you download and install the SDK from the Web instead of the CD.

Installing the Core Java Example Files

The CD-ROM contains the source code for all example programs in the book. All files are packed inside a single ZIP archive, `corejava.zip`.

If you have a ZIP utility such as WinZip, you can use it to unzip the files. Otherwise, you need to first install the Java 2 SDK. Then use the `jar` program to unzip the file:

- Make sure the SDK is installed.
- Make a directory `CoreJavaBook`.
- Copy the `corejava.zip` file to that directory.

(continued on previous page)